THE
WORLD CRISIS
1911–1918

BY THE RIGHT HON.

WINSTON S.
CHURCHILL

C.H., M.P.

With an Introduction by Martin Gilbert

ABRIDGED AND REVISED EDITION
With an Additional Chapter on The Battle of the Marne

FREE PRESS
NEW YORK   LONDON   TORONTO   SYDNEY

FREE PRESS
A Division of Simon & Schuster Inc.
1230 Avenue of the Americas
New York, NY 10020

First Free Press trade paperback edition 2005

FREE PRESS and colophon are trademarks of Simon & Schuster, Inc.

For information about special discounts for bulk purchases,
please contact Simon & Schuster Special Sales:
1-800-456-6798 or business@simonandschuster.com

Manufactured in the United States of America

5   7   9   10   8   6   4

Library of Congress Cataloging-in-Publication Data

Churchill, Winston, Sir, 1874–1965.
The world crisis / by Winston S. Churchill; with an introduction by Martin Gilbert.—
Abridged and rev. ed., with an additional chapter on the Battle of the Marne.
p.   cm.
The unabridged edition was issued in five volumes.
1. World War, 1914–1918.   2. World War, 1914–1918—Great Britain.
I. Title
D521 .C5 2005
941.3—dc22   2005051869

ISBN 13: 978-0-7432-8343-4
ISBN 10:   0-7432-8343-0

On the idle hill of summer,
    Sleepy with the sound of streams,
Far I hear the steady drummer
    Drumming like a noise in dreams.

Far and near and low and louder,
    On the roads of earth go by,
Dear to friends and food for powder,
    Soldiers marching, all to die.

THE SHROPSHIRE LAD, XXXV

CONTENTS

TABLE OF MAPS AND PLANS

INTRODUCTION

Churchill's five-volume history *The World Crisis* is arguably one of his most important works. A detailed study of the First World War, it has considerable resonance in today's world. John Maynard Keynes called one of its volumes "a tractate against war," and in the substantial array of books published in the decade after the Armistice, it is certainly one of the strongest criticisms of the war of attrition: the pitting of equally matched armies against each other along a 430-mile line of fortified and impenetrable trenches.

The genesis of these volumes was the failure of the Dardanelles and Gallipoli campaigns of 1915, with both of which Churchill was closely associated. The soldiers who were sent there, he argued at the time, "have the right to a plan as well as to a cause." Based on the evidence that he assembled for the Dardanelles Commission of Enquiry a year after the disaster, the Dardanelles and Gallipoli chapters combine the raw material of history—the orders, telegrams, and secret War Cabinet discussions—with a deep sense of the futility of ill-prepared offensives and poorly thought-out strategies.

The first volume was published in 1923; the fifth volume appeared eight years later, simultaneously with the abridgment of the first four. Every facet of the war was covered in its pages: the Western and Eastern fronts, the Turkish fronts, the wars at sea and in the air, and the politics and diplomacy of the belligerents. Volume One contains a graphic and moving account of how the war came. It is a catalog of failures and hesitations, lack of vision and national extremisms. Churchill's own two attempts to secure a calming down of Anglo-German naval rivalry before the outbreak of the war reveal his frustration at the determination of the leading industrial nations of Europe not to compromise. As war loomed, he proposed to the British Cabinet that the rulers of the Great Powers, the "Kings and Emperors," as he called them, should get together and save their peoples from war. His suggestion was brushed aside.

As Churchill pressed ahead with the writing, he wrote to his wife Clementine of how the book was "a great chance to put my whole case in agreeable form to an attentive audience." It would also, he pointed out to her, earn enough money "to make us feel very comfortable." His pace of writing was formidable: in one six-day period he wrote more than twenty thousand words, a high rate for any author.

Churchill intended his book to be limited to his own years in charge of the Royal Navy, from October 1911 to May 1915, and to deal primarily with Anglo-German naval rivalry and the war at sea. For this reason he chose the title "The Great Amphibian," which had been suggested to him by the editor of *The Times*. The American publishers felt that this was too restrictive and asked him to choose between "Sea Power in the World Crisis," or, even less specialist, "The World Crisis." He deferred to the American pressure, and as he worked expanded his focus far beyond the war at sea. One complete volume is about the fighting on the Eastern Front, the narrative derived from the published sources available to Churchill as he was writing.

The more Churchill wrote, the wider became his interest and his reading. He devoured each new book on the war as it was published. Whole sections of his work derived, with acknowledgment, from the work of others, including British naval and war historians, and senior German and French and Russian participants.

In the preface to Volume One, Churchill expresses the hope that his readers "will feel that perhaps after all Britain and her Empire have not been so ill-guided through the great convulsions as it is customary to declare."

Volume Two is dominated by the Dardanelles and Gallipoli. This was the geographic region, the narrow waterway that, together with the Bosporus, links the Mediterranean and the Black Sea. This was the battleground in which Churchill felt the terrible stalemate of trench warfare could be broken. Attack Turkey at its most vulnerable point, and advance into Central Europe by way of the Black Sea and the Danube River. Churchill's successor as Prime Minister in 1945, the Labour leader Clement Attlee, who had fought at Gallipoli, praised Churchill's conception, but, like Churchill, was deeply critical of the execution. Volume Two is Churchill's pugnacious defense of his actions. It is as if Margaret Thatcher had written a 557-page book about the Falklands War, or as if George W. Bush were to write a similar, sustained narrative and defense about the war in Iraq.

Volume Three, which was published in two parts, is about the prolonged and bloody fighting on the Western Front, dominated by the battles on the Somme and at Passchendaele. It is the volume most critical of the generals and trench warfare, of which Churchill had five months' personal experience, as a colonel of a Scottish battalion at the beginning of 1916. The criticisms in this volume reflect his opinions and advice at the time, including several parliamentary speeches so critical of the higher conduct of the war on the Western Front that they were published in pamphlet form as *The Fighting Line*.

Volume Four, *The Eastern Front*, is devoted to the fighting between Russia and the combined forces of the German, Austro-Hungarian, and Turkish empires, a vast battleground about which little had been written in English then, and not a great deal more since.

The final volume, *The Aftermath,* which is not included here as the abridgment focuses solely on the conflict itself, is dominated by the Bolshevik Revolution, the Treaty of Versailles, the struggles in the East between Russia and Poland, and the emergence of postwar Turkey. As Secretary of State for War between 1919 and 1921, Churchill had wanted the former Allies to continue to work together to ensure the defeat of Soviet power. This theme is reflected in the documents and narrative that he chose for the volume.

Churchill's vivid descriptions of the interaction between politicians and generals, the fate of the ordinary soldier, sailor, and airman, and the suffering of whole nations as the war became more and more total—including the bombing of London and Paris and foreshadowing the Second World War—are of intense interest in the current era, when we can see how the hope that the First World War would be "the war to end war" has been mocked in each successive generation. Churchill asks in this book, "Is this the end of the story?" The answer he gives shows that he is fearful that it was not.

The last word I will leave with Churchill. "How strange it is," he wrote to a friend when the fifth and final volume was published, "that the past is so little understood and so quickly forgotten. We live in the most thoughtless of ages. Every day headlines and short views. I have tried to drag history up a little nearer to our own times in case it should be helpful in the present difficulties."

MARTIN GILBERT
March 31, 2005

PREFACE

During the ten years after the war I wrote the four volumes which are concentrated in this book. I have long wished to bring them together in a form acceptable to a wider public. Naturally volumes published at intervals of two years contain overlappings and differ from one another in scope and proportion. Moreover, much has been published which adds to our knowledge. I have therefore recast the whole account so as to present a continuous narrative in a more compendious form. I have not found it necessary to alter in any material way the facts and foundations of the story, nor the conclusions which I drew from them. The key documents are reprinted in their integrity. I have however pruned a mass of technical detail and some personal justifications which do not seem to me so important now as they did ten years ago. I have allowed the main theme of the narrative to predominate over special discussions in which I was involved.

I have however profited by the new knowledge wherever possible. I have had to record a somewhat different account of Lord Fisher's resignation from that which appeared in the original edition. Mr. Asquith's disclosures in his 'Memoirs' and Lord Fisher's own biographers have cast a less charitable light upon the conduct of the old Admiral than that in which I had viewed it. I have given a much fuller account of the great opening battles in France based upon a study of the latest trustworthy information. In the main however I have found myself unable to alter the critical judgments which I formed upon the many aspects of the naval, military and political conduct of the war.

This book in its combined edition strives to follow throughout the methods and balance of Defoe's *Memoirs of a Cavalier*. It is a contribution to history strung upon a fairly strong thread of personal reminiscence. It does not pretend to be a comprehensive record; but it aims at helping to disentangle from an immense mass of material the crucial issues and cardinal decisions. Throughout I have set myself to explain faithfully and to the best of my ability what happened and why. For the ten or twelve years of the Great War period I was in a position to follow with the fullest knowledge available the march of supreme events; and for the greater part of that time I held offices of high responsibility as First Lord of the Admiralty and Minister of Munitions.

I rest myself with confidence upon the facts, figures and conclusions which these pages set forth. The individual volumes have been reprinted in at least seven languages and have been the subject of criticism and comments in thousands of articles. Upon no important point of substance or broad deduction therefrom do I desire to alter what I wrote; and in presenting the complete story to the reader I have a sure conviction that it will not in essentials be overturned by the historians of the future.

WINSTON S. CHURCHILL
CHARTWELL, KENT,
July 1, 1930

PART I

To My Wife

CHAPTER I

THE VIALS OF WRATH

1870–1904

It was the custom in the palmy days of Queen Victoria for statesmen to expatiate upon the glories of the British Empire, and to rejoice in that protecting Providence which had preserved us through so many dangers and brought us at length into a secure and prosperous age. Little did they know that the worst perils had still to be encountered and that the greatest triumphs were yet to be won.

Children were taught of the Great War against Napoleon as the culminating effort in the history of the British peoples, and they looked on Waterloo and Trafalgar as the supreme achievements of British arms by land and sea. These prodigious victories, eclipsing all that had gone before, seemed the fit and predestined ending to the long drama of our island race, which had advanced over a thousand years from small and weak beginnings to a foremost position in the world. Three separate times in three different centuries had the British people rescued Europe from a military domination. Thrice had the Low Countries been assailed: by Spain, by the French Monarchy, by the French Empire. Thrice had British war and policy, often maintained single-handed, overthrown the aggressor. Always at the outset the strength of the enemy had seemed overwhelming, always the struggle had been prolonged through many years and across awful hazards, always the victory had at last been won; and the last of all the victories had been the greatest of all, gained after the most ruinous struggle and over the most formidable foe.

Surely that was the end of the tale, as it was so often the end of the book. History showed the rise, culmination, splendour, transition and decline of States and Empires. It seemed inconceivable that the same series of tremendous events through which since the days of Queen Elizabeth we had three times made our way successfully, should be repeated a fourth time and on an immeasurably larger scale. Yet that is what has happened, and what we have lived to see.

The Great War differed from all ancient wars in the immense power of the combatants and their fearful agencies of destruction, and from all modern wars in the utter ruthlessness with which it was fought. All the horrors of all the ages were brought together, and not only armies but whole populations were thrust into the midst of them. The mighty educated States involved conceived with reason that their very existence was at stake. Germany having let Hell loose kept well in the van of terror; but she was followed step by step by the desperate and ultimately avenging nations she had assailed. Every outrage against humanity or international law was repaid by reprisals often on a greater scale and of longer duration. No truce or parley mitigated the strife of the armies. The wounded died between the lines: the dead mouldered into the soil. Merchant ships and neutral ships and hospital ships were sunk on the seas and all on board left to their fate, or killed as they swam. Every effort was made to starve whole nations into submission without regard to age or sex. Cities and monuments were smashed by artillery. Bombs from the air were cast down indiscriminately. Poison gas in many forms stifled or seared the soldiers. Liquid fire was projected upon their bodies. Men fell from the air in flames, or were smothered, often slowly, in the dark recesses of the sea. The fighting strength of armies was limited only by the manhood of their countries. Europe and large parts of Asia and Africa became one vast battlefield on which after years of struggle not armies but nations broke and ran. When all was over, Torture and Cannibalism were the only two expedients that the civilized, scientific, Christian States had been able to deny themselves: and these were of doubtful utility.

But nothing daunted the valiant heart of man. Son of the Stone Age, vanquisher of nature with all her trials and monsters, he met the awful and self-inflicted agony with new reserves of fortitude. Freed in the main by his intelligence from mediæval fears, he marched to death with inherent dignity. His nervous system was found in the twentieth century capable of enduring physical and moral stresses before which the simpler natures of primeval times would have collapsed. Again and again to the hideous bombardment, again and again from the hospital to the front, again and again to the hungry submarines, he strode unflinching. And withal, as an individual, preserved through these torments the glories of a reasonable and compassionate mind.

In the beginning of the twentieth century men were everywhere unconscious of the rate at which the world was growing. It required the convulsion of the war to awaken the nations to the knowledge of their strength. For a year after the war had begun hardly anyone understood how terrific, how almost inexhaustible were the resources in force, in substance, in virtue, behind every one of the combatants. The vials of wrath were full: but so were the reservoirs of power. From the end of the Napoleonic Wars, and still more after 1870, the accumulation of wealth and health by every civilized community had been practically unchecked. Here and there a retarding episode had occurred. The waves had recoiled after advancing: but the mounting tides still flowed. And when the dread signal of Armageddon was made, mankind was found to be many times stronger in valour, in endurance, in brains, in science, in apparatus, in organization, not only than it had ever been before, but than even its most audacious optimists had dared to dream.

The Victorian Age was the age of accumulation; not of a mere piling up of material wealth, but of the growth and gathering in every land of all those elements and factors which go to make up the power of States. Education spread itself over the broad surface of the millions. Science had opened the limitless treasure-house of nature. Door after door had been unlocked. One dim mysterious gallery after another had been lighted up, explored, made free for all: and every gallery entered gave access to at least two more. Every morning when the world woke up, some new machinery had started running. Every night while the world had supper, it was running still. It ran on while all men slept.

And the advance of the collective mind was at a similar pace. Disraeli said of the early years of the nineteenth century, "In those days England was for the few—and for the very few." Every year of Queen Victoria's reign saw those limits broken and extended. Every year brought in new thousands of people in private stations who thought about their own country and its story and its duties towards other countries, to the world and to the future, and understood the greatness of the responsibilities of which they were the heirs. Every year diffused a wider measure of material comfort among the higher ranks of labour. Substantial progress was made in mitigating the hard lot of the mass. Their health improved, their lives and the lives of their children were brightened, their stature grew, their securities against some of their gravest misfortunes were multiplied, their numbers greatly increased.

Thus when all the trumpets sounded, every class and rank had something to give to the need of the State. Some gave their science and some their wealth, some gave their business energy and drive, and some their wonderful personal prowess, and some their patient strength or patient weakness. But none gave more, or gave more readily, than the common man or woman who had nothing but a precarious week's wages between them and poverty, and owned little more than the slender equipment of a cottage, and the garments in which they stood upright. Their love and pride of country, their loyalty to the symbols with which they were familiar, their keen sense of right and wrong as they saw it, led them to outface and endure perils and ordeals the like of which men had not known on earth.

But these developments were no monopoly of any one nation. In every free country, great or small, the spirit of patriotism and nationality grew steadily; and in every country, bond or free, the organization and structure into which men were fitted by the laws, gathered and armed this sentiment. Far more than their vices, the virtues of nations ill-directed or mis-directed by their rulers, became the cause of their own undoing and of the general catastrophe. And these rulers, in Germany, Austria, and Italy; in France, Russia or Britain, how far were they to blame? Was there any man of real eminence and responsibility whose devil heart conceived and willed this awful thing? One rises from the study of the causes of the Great War with a prevailing sense of the defective control of individuals upon world fortunes. It has been well said, 'there is always more error than design in human affairs.' The limited minds even of the ablest men, their disputed authority, the climate of opinion in which they dwell, their transient and partial contributions to the mighty problem, that problem itself so far beyond their compass, so vast in scale and detail, so changing in its aspect—all this must surely be considered before the complete condemnation of the vanquished or the complete acquittal of the victors can be pronounced. Events also got on to certain lines, and no one could get them off again. Germany clanked obstinately, recklessly, awkwardly towards the crater and dragged us all in with her. But fierce resentments dwelt in France, and in Russia there were wheels within wheels. Could we in England perhaps by some effort, by some sacrifice of our material interests, by some compulsive gesture, at once of friendship and command, have reconciled France and Germany in time and formed that grand association on which alone the peace and glory of Europe would be safe? I cannot tell. I only know that we tried our best to steer our country through the gathering dangers of the armed peace without bringing her to war or others to war, and when these efforts failed, we drove through the tempest without bringing her to destruction.

There is no need here to trace the ancient causes of quarrel between the Germans and the French, to catalogue the conflicts with which they have scarred the centuries, nor to appraise the balance of injury or of provocation on one side or the other. When on the 18th of January, 1871, the triumph of the Germans was consolidated by the Proclamation of the German Empire in the Palace of Versailles, a new volume of European history was opened. 'Europe,' it was said, 'has lost a mistress and has gained a master.' A new and mighty State had come into being, sustained by an overflowing population, equipped with science and learning, organized for war and crowned with victory. France, stripped of Alsace and Lorraine, beaten, impoverished, divided and alone, condemned to a decisive and increasing numerical inferiority, fell back to ponder in shade and isolation on her departed glories.

But the chiefs of the German Empire were under no illusions as to the formidable character and implacable resolves of their prostrate antagonist. "What we gained by arms in half a year," said Moltke, "we must protect by arms for half a century, if it is not to be torn from us again." Bismarck, more prudent still, would never have taken Lorraine. Forced by military pressure to assume the double burden against his better judgment, he exhibited from the outset and in every act of his policy an extreme apprehension. Restrained by the opinion of the world, and the decided attitude of Great Britain, from striking down a reviving France in 1875, he devoted his whole power and genius to the construction of an elaborate system of alliances designed to secure the continued ascendancy of Germany and the maintenance of her conquests. He knew the quarrel with France was irreconcilable except at a price which Germany would never consent to pay. He understood that the abiding enmity of a terrific people would be fixed on his new-built Empire. Everything else must be subordinated to that central fact. Germany could afford no other antagonisms. In 1879 he formed an alliance with Austria. Four years later this was expanded into the Triple Alliance between Germany, Austria and Italy. Roumania was brought into the system by a secret alliance in 1883. Not only must there be Insurance; there must be Reinsurance. What he feared most was a counter-alliance between France and Russia; and none of these extending arrangements met this danger. His alliance with Austria indeed, if left by itself, would naturally tend to draw France and Russia together. Could he not make a league of the three Emperors—Germany, Austria, and Russia united? There at last was overwhelming strength and enduring safety. When in 1887, after six years, this supreme ideal of Bismarck was ruptured by the clash of Russian and Austrian interests in the Balkans, he turned—as the best means still open to him—to his Reinsurance Treaty with Russia. Germany, by this arrangement, secured herself against becoming the object of an aggressive combination by France and Russia. Russia on the other hand was reassured that the Austro-German alliance would not be used to undermine her position in the Balkans.

All these cautious and sapient measures were designed with the object of enabling Germany to enjoy her victory in peace. The Bismarckian system, further, always included the principle of good relations with Great Britain. This was necessary, for it was well known that Italy would never willingly commit herself to anything that would bring her into war with Great Britain, and had, as the world now knows, required this fact to be specifically stated in the original and secret text of the Triple Alliance. To this Alliance in its early years Great Britain had been wholly favourable. Thus France was left to nurse her scars alone, and Germany, assured in her predominance on the Continent, was able to take the fullest advantage of the immense industrial developments which characterized the close of the nineteenth century. The policy of Germany further encouraged France as a consolation to develop her colonial possessions in order to take her thoughts off Europe, and incidentally to promote a convenient rivalry and friction with Great Britain.

This arrangement, under which Europe lived rigidly but peacefully for twenty years, and Germany waxed in power and splendour, was ended in 1890 with the fall of Bismarck. The Iron Chancellor was gone, and new forces began to assail the system he had maintained with consummate ability so long. There was a constant danger of conflagration in the Balkans and in the Near East through Turkish misgovernment. The rising tides of pan-Slavism and the strong anti-German currents in Russia began to wash against the structure of the Reinsurance Treaty. Lastly, German ambitions grew with German prosperity. Not content with the hegemony of Europe, she sought a colonial domain. Already the greatest of military Empires, she began increasingly to turn her thoughts to the sea. The young Emperor, freed from Bismarck and finding in Count Caprivi, and the lesser men who succeeded him, complacent coadjutors, began gaily to dispense with the safeguards and precautions by which the safety of Germany had been buttressed. While the quarrel with France remained open and undying, the Reinsurance Treaty with Russia was dropped, and later on the naval rivalry with Britain was begun. These two sombre decisions rolled forward slowly as the years unfolded. Their consequences became apparent in due season.

In 1892 the event against which the whole policy of Bismarck had been directed came to pass. The Dual Alliance was signed between Russia and France. Although the effects were not immediately visible, the European situation was in fact transformed. Henceforward for the undisputed but soberly exercised predominance of Germany, there was substituted a balance of power. Two vast combinations, each disposing of enormous military resources, dwelt together at first side by side, but gradually face to face.

Although the groupings of the great Powers had thus been altered sensibly to the disadvantage of Germany, there was in this alteration nothing that threatened her with war. The abiding spirit of France had never abandoned the dream of recovering the lost provinces, but the prevailing temper of the French nation was pacific, and all classes remained under the impression of the might of Germany and of the terrible consequences likely to result from war.

Moreover, the French were never sure of Russia in a purely Franco-German quarrel. True, there was the Treaty; but the Treaty to become operative required aggression on the part of Germany. What constitutes aggression? At what point in a dispute between two heavily armed parties, does one side or the other become the aggressor? At any rate there was a wide field for discretionary action on the part of Russia. Of all these matters she would be the judge, and she would be the judge at a moment when it might be said that the Russian people would be sent to die in millions over a quarrel between France and Germany in which they had no direct interest. The word of the Tsar was indeed a great assurance. But Tsars who tried to lead their nations, however honourably, into unpopular wars might disappear. The policy of a great people, if hung too directly upon the person of a single individual, was liable to be changed by his disappearance. France, therefore, could never feel certain that if on any occasion she resisted German pressure and war resulted, Russia would march.

Such was the ponderous balance which had succeeded the unquestioned ascendancy of Germany. Outside both systems rested England, secure in an overwhelming, and as yet unchallenged, naval supremacy. It was evident that the position of the British Empire received added importance from the fact that its adhesion to either Alliance would decide the predominance of strength. But Lord Salisbury showed no wish to exploit this favourable situation. He maintained steadily the traditional friendly attitude towards Germany combined with a cool detachment from Continental entanglements.

It had been easy for Germany to lose touch with Russia; but the alienation of England was a far longer process. So many props and ties had successively to be demolished. British suspicions of Russia in Asia, the historic antagonism to France, memories of Blenheim, of Minden and of Waterloo, the continued disputes with France in Egypt and in the Colonial sphere, the intimate business connexions between Germany and England, the relationship of the Royal Families—all these constituted a profound association between the British Empire and the leading State in the Triple Alliance. It was no part of British policy to obstruct the new-born Colonial aspirations of Germany, and in more than one instance, as at Samoa, we actively assisted them. With a complete detachment from strategic considerations, Lord Salisbury exchanged Heligoland for Zanzibar. Still even before the fall of Bismarck the Germans did not seem pleasant diplomatic comrades. They appeared always to be seeking to enlist our aid and reminding us that they were our only friend. To emphasize this they went even farther. They sought in minor ways to embroil us with France and Russia. Each year the Wilhelmstrasse looked inquiringly to the Court of St. James's for some new service or concession which should keep Germany's diplomatic goodwill alive for a further period. Each year they made mischief for us with France and Russia, and pointed the moral of how unpopular Great Britain was, what powerful enemies she had, and how lucky she was to find a friend in Germany. Where would she be in the councils of Europe if German assistance were withdrawn, or if Germany threw her influence into the opposing combination? These manifestations, prolonged for nearly twenty years, produced very definite sensations of estrangement in the minds of the rising generation at the British Foreign Office.

But none of these woes of diplomatists deflected the steady course of British policy. The Colonial expansion of Germany was viewed with easy indifference by the British Empire. In spite of their rivalry in trade, there grew up a far more important commercial connexion between Britain and Germany. In

Europe we were each other's best customers. Even the German Emperor's telegram to President Kruger on the Jameson Raid in 1896, which we now know to have been no personal act but a decision of the German Government, produced only a temporary ebullition of anger. All the German outburst of rage against England during the Boer War, and such attempts as were made to form a European coalition against us, did not prevent Mr. Chamberlain in 1901 from advocating an alliance with Germany, or the British Foreign Office from proposing in the same year to make the alliance between Britain and Japan into a Triple Alliance including Germany. During this period we had at least as serious differences with France as with Germany, and sufficient naval superiority not to be seriously disquieted by either. We stood equally clear of the Triple and of the Dual Alliance. We had no intention of being drawn into a Continental quarrel. No effort by France to regain her lost provinces appealed to the British public or to any political party. The idea of a British Army fighting in Europe amid the mighty hosts of the Continent was by all dismissed as utterly absurd. Only a menace to the very life of the British nation would stir the British Empire from its placid and tolerant detachment from Continental affairs. But that menace Germany was destined to supply.

"Among the Great Powers," said Moltke in his Military Testament, "England necessarily requires a strong ally on the Continent. She would not find one which corresponds better to all her interests than a United Germany, that can never make claim to the command of the sea."

From 1873 to 1900 the German Navy was avowedly not intended to provide for the possibility of "a naval war against great naval Powers." Now in 1900 came a Fleet Law of a very different kind.

"In order to protect German trade and commerce under existing conditions," declared the preamble of this document, "only one thing will suffice, namely, Germany must possess a battle fleet of such a strength that, even for the most powerful naval adversary, a war would involve such risks as to make that Power's own supremacy doubtful."

The determination of the greatest military Power on the Continent to become at the same time at least the second naval Power was an event of first magnitude in world affairs. It would, if carried into full effect, undoubtedly reproduce those situations which at previous periods in history had proved of such awful significance to the Islanders of Britain.

Hitherto all British naval arrangements had proceeded on the basis of the two-Power standard, namely, an adequate superiority over the next two strongest Powers, in those days France and Russia. The possible addition of a third European Fleet more powerful than either of these two would profoundly affect the life of Britain. If Germany was going to create a Navy avowedly measured against our own, we could not afford to remain "in splendid isolation" from the European systems. We must in these circumstances find a trustworthy friend. We found one in another island Empire situated on the other side of the globe and also in danger. In 1901 the Alliance was signed between Great Britain and Japan. Even less could we afford to have dangerous causes of quarrel open both with France and Russia. In 1902 the British Government, under Mr. Balfour and Lord Lansdowne, definitely embarked upon the policy of settling up our differences with France. Still, before either of these steps was taken the hand was held out to Germany. She was invited to join with us in the alliance with Japan. She was invited to make a joint effort to solve the Moroccan problem. Both offers were declined.

In 1903, the war between Russia and Japan broke out. Germany sympathized mainly with Russia; England stood ready to fulfil her Treaty engagements with Japan, while at the same time cultivating good relations with France. In this posture the Powers awaited the result of the Far Eastern struggle. It brought a surprise to all but one. The military and naval overthrow of Russia by Japan and the internal convulsions of the Russian State produced profound changes in the European situation. Although German influence had leaned against Japan, she felt herself enormously strengthened by the Russian collapse. Her Continental predominance was restored. Her self-assertion in every sphere became sensibly and immediately pronounced. France, on the other hand, weakened and once again, for the time being, isolated and in real danger, became increasingly anxious for an *Entente* with England. England, whose statesmen with penetrating eye alone in Europe had truly measured the martial power of Japan, gained remarkably in strength and security. Japan, her new ally, was triumphant: France, her ancient enemy, sought her friendship: the German Fleet was still only a-building, and meanwhile all the British battleships in China seas could now be safely brought home.

The settlement of outstanding differences between England and France proceeded, and at last in 1904 the Anglo-French Agreement was signed. There were various clauses; but the essence of the compact was that the French desisted from opposition to British interests in Egypt, and Britain gave a general support to the French views about Morocco. This agreement was acclaimed by the Conservative forces in England, among whom the idea of the German menace had already taken root. It was also hailed somewhat short-sightedly by Liberal statesmen as a step to secure general peace by clearing away misunderstandings and differences with our traditional enemy. It was therefore almost universally welcomed. Only one profound observer raised his voice against it. "My mournful and supreme conviction," said Lord Rosebery, "is that this agreement is much more likely to lead to complications than to peace." This unwelcome comment was indignantly spurned from widely different standpoints by both British parties, and general censure fell upon its author.

Still, England and all that she stood for had left her isolation, and had re-appeared in Europe on the opposite side to Germany. For the first time since 1870, Germany had to take into consideration a Power outside her system which was in no way amenable to threats, and was not unable if need be to en-counter her single-handed. The gesture which was to sweep Delcassé from power in 1905, the apparition "in shining armour" which was to quell Russia in 1908, could procure no such compliance from the independent Island girt with her Fleet and mistress of the seas.

Up to this moment the Triple Alliance had on the whole been stronger than France and Russia. Although war against these two Powers would have been a formidable undertaking for Germany, Austria and Italy, its ultimate issue did not seem doubtful. But if the weight of Britain were thrown into the ad-verse scale and that of Italy withdrawn from the other, then for the first time since 1870 Germany could not feel certain that she was on the stronger side. Would she submit to it? Would the growing, bounding ambitions and asser-tions of the new German Empire consent to a situation in which, very politely no doubt, very gradually perhaps, but still very surely, the impression would be conveyed that her will was no longer the final law of Europe? If Germany and her Emperor would accept the same sort of restraint that France, Russia and England had long been accustomed to, and would live within her rights as an equal in a freer and easier world, all would be well. But would she? Would she tolerate the gathering under an independent standard of nations outside her system, strong enough to examine her claims only as the merits appealed to them, and to resist aggression without fear? The history of the next ten years was to supply the answer.

Side by side with these slowly marshalling and steadily arming antagonisms between the greatest Powers, processes of degeneration were at work in weaker Empires almost equally dangerous to peace. Forces were alive in Turkey which threatened with destruction the old regime and its abuses on which Germany had chosen to lean. The Christian States of the Balkans, growing stronger year by year, awaited an opportunity to liberate their compatriots still writhing under Turkish misrule. The growth of national sentiment in every country cre-ated fierce strains and stresses in the uneasily knit and crumbling Austro-Hungarian Empire. The Balkan States saw also in this direction kinsmen to rescue, territory to recover, and unities to achieve. Italy watched with ardent eyes the decay of Turkey and the unrest of Austria. It was certain that from all these regions of the South and of the East there would come a succession of events deeply agitating both to Russia and to Germany.

To create the unfavourable conditions for herself in which Germany afterwards brought about the war, many acts of supreme unwisdom on the part of her rulers were nevertheless still necessary. France must be kept in a state of continued apprehension. The Russian nation, not the Russian Court alone, must be stung by some violent affront inflicted in their hour of weakness. The slow, deep, restrained antagonism of the British Empire must be roused by the continuous and repeated challenge to the sea power by which it lived. Then and then only could those conditions be created under which Germany by an act of aggression would bring into being against her, a combination strong enough to resist and ultimately to overcome her might. There was still a long road to travel before the Vials of Wrath were full. For ten years we were to journey anxiously along that road.

It was for a time the fashion to write as if the British Government during these ten years were either entirely unconscious of the approaching danger or had a load of secret matters and deep forebodings on their minds hidden altogether from the thoughtless nation. In fact, however, neither of these alternatives, taken separately, was true; and there is a measure of truth in both of them taken together.

The British Government and the Parliaments out of which it sprang, did not believe in the approach of a great war, and were determined to prevent it; but at the same time the sinister hypothesis was continually present in their thoughts, and was repeatedly brought to the attention of Ministers by disquieting incidents and tendencies.

During the whole of those ten years this duality and discordance were the keynote of British politics; and those whose duty it was to watch over the safety of the country lived simultaneously in two different worlds of thought. There was the actual visible world with its peaceful activities and cosmopolitan aims; and there was a hypothetical world, a world "beneath the threshold," as it were, a world at one moment utterly fantastic, at the next seeming about to leap into reality—a world of monstrous shadows moving in convulsive combinations through vistas of fathomless catastrophe.

CHAPTER II

MILESTONES TO ARMAGEDDON

1905–1910

If the reader is to understand this tale and the point of view from which it is told, he should follow the author's mind in each principal sphere of causation. He must not only be acquainted with the military and naval situations as they existed at the outbreak of war, but with the events which led up to them. He must be introduced to the Admirals and to the Generals; he must study the organization of the Fleets and Armies and the outlines of their strategy by sea and land; he must not shrink even from the design of ships and cannon; he must extend his view to the groupings and slow-growing antagonisms of modern States; he must contract it to the humbler but unavoidable warfare of parties and the interplay of political forces and personalities.

The *dramatis personæ* of the previous chapter have been great States and Empires and its theme their world-wide balance and combinations. Now the stage must for a while be narrowed to the limits of these islands and occupied by the political personages and factions of the time and of the hour.

In the year 1895 I had the privilege, as a young officer, of being invited to lunch with Sir William Harcourt. In the course of a conversation in which I took, I fear, none too modest a share, I asked the question, "What will happen then?" "My dear Winston," replied the old Victorian statesman, "the experiences of a long life have convinced me that nothing ever happens." Since that moment, as it seems to me, nothing has ever ceased happening. The growth of the great antagonisms abroad was accompanied by the progressive aggravation of party strife at home. The scale on which events have shaped themselves, has dwarfed the episodes of the Victorian Era. Its small wars between great nations, its earnest disputes about superficial issues, the high, keen intellectualism of its personages, the sober, frugal, narrow limitations of their action, belong to a vanished period. The smooth river with its eddies and ripples along which we then sailed, seems inconceivably remote from the cataract down which we have been hurled and the rapids in whose turbulence we are now struggling.

I date the beginning of these violent times in our country from the Jameson Raid, in 1896. This was the herald, if not indeed the progenitor, of the South African War. From the South African War was born the Khaki Election, the Protectionist Movement, the Chinese Labour cry and the consequent furious reaction and Liberal triumph of 1906. From this sprang the violent inroads of the House of Lords upon popular Government, which by the end of 1908 had reduced the immense Liberal majority to virtual impotence, from which condition they were rescued by the Lloyd George Budget in 1909. This measure became, in its turn, on both sides, the cause of still greater provocations, and its rejection by the Lords was a constitutional outrage and political blunder almost beyond compare. It led directly to the two General Elections of 1910, to the Parliament Act, and to the Irish struggle, in which our country was brought to the very threshold of civil war. Thus we see a succession of partisan actions continuing without intermission for nearly twenty years, each injury repeated with interest, each oscillation more violent, each risk more grave, until at last it seemed that the sabre itself must be invoked to cool the blood and the passions that were rife.

In July, 1902, Lord Salisbury retired. With what seems now to have been only a brief interlude, he had been Prime Minister and Foreign Secretary since 1885. In all those seventeen years the Liberal Party had never exercised any effective control upon affairs. Their brief spell in office had only been obtained by a majority of forty Irish Nationalist votes. During thirteen years the Conservatives had enjoyed homogeneous majorities of 100 to 150, and in addition there was the House of Lords. This long reign of power had now come to an end. The desire for change, the feeling that change was impending, was widespread. It was the end of an epoch.

Lord Salisbury was followed by Mr. Balfour. The new Prime Minister never had a fair chance. He succeeded only to an exhausted inheritance. Indeed, his wisest course would have been to get out of office as decently, as quietly, and, above all, as quickly as possible. He could with great propriety have declared that the 1900 Parliament had been elected on war conditions and on a war issue; that the war was now finished successfully; that the mandate was exhausted and that he must recur to the sense of the electors before proceeding farther with his task. No doubt the Liberals would have come into power, but not by a large majority; and they would have been faced by a strong, united Conservative Opposition, which in four or five years, about 1907, would have resumed effective control of the State. The solid ranks of Conservative members who acclaimed Mr. Balfour's accession as First Minister were however in no mood to be dismissed to their constituencies when the Parliament was only two years old and had still four or five years more to run. Mr. Balfour therefore addressed himself to the duties of Government with a serene indifference to the vast alienation of public opinion and the consolidation of hostile forces which were proceeding all around him.

Mr. Chamberlain, his almost all-powerful lieutenant, was under no illusions. He felt, with an acute political sensitiveness, the evergrowing strength of the tide setting against the ruling combination. But instead of pursuing courses of moderation and prudence, he was impelled by the ardour of his nature to a desperate remedy. The Government was reproached with being reactionary. The moderate Conservatives and the younger Conservatives were all urging Liberal and conciliatory processes. The Opposition was advancing hopefully towards power, heralded by a storm of angry outcry. He would show them, and show doubting or weary friends as well, how it was possible to quell indignation by violence, and from the very heart of reaction to draw the means of popular victory. He unfurled the flag of Protection.

Time, adversity and the recent Education Act had united the Liberals; Protection, or Tariff Reform as it was called, split the Conservatives. Ultimately, six Ministers resigned and fifty Conservative or Unionist members definitely withdrew their support from the Government. Among them were a number of those younger men from whom a Party should derive new force and driving power, and who are specially necessary to it during a period of opposition. The action of the Free Trade Unionists was endorsed indirectly by Lord Salisbury himself from his retirement, and was actively sustained by such pillars of the Unionist Party as Sir Michael Hicks-Beach and the Duke of Devonshire. No such formidable loss had been sustained by the Conservative Party since the expulsion of the Peelites.

But if Mr. Balfour had not felt inclined to begin his reign by an act of abdication, he was still less disposed to have power wrested from his grasp. Moreover, he regarded a Party split as the worst of domestic catastrophes, and responsibility for it as the unforgivable sin. He therefore laboured with amazing patience and coolness to preserve a semblance of unity, to calm the tempest, and to hold on as long as possible in the hope of its subsiding. With the highest subtlety and ingenuity he devised a succession of formulas designed to enable people who differed profoundly to persuade themselves they were in agreement. When it came to the resignation of Ministers, he was careful to shed Free Trade and Protectionist blood as far as possible in equal quantities. Like Henry VIII, he decapitated Papists and burned hot Gospellers on the same day for their respective divergencies in opposite directions from his central, personal and artificial compromise.

In this unpleasant situation Mr. Balfour maintained himself for two whole years. Vain the clamour for a General Election, vain the taunts of clinging to office, vain the solicitations of friends and the attempts of foes to force a crucial issue. The Prime Minister remained immovable, inexhaustible, imperturbable; and he remained Prime Minister. His clear, just mind, detached from small things, stood indifferent to the clamour about him. He pursued, as has been related, through the critical period of the Russo-Japanese War, a policy in support of Japan of the utmost firmness. He resisted all temptations, on the other hand, to make the sinking of our trawlers on the Dogger Bank by the Russian Fleet an occasion of war with Russia. He formed the Committee of Imperial Defence—the instrument of our preparedness. He carried through the agreement with France of 1904, the momentous significance of which the preceding chapter has explained. But in 1905 political Britain cared for none of these things. The credit of the Government fell steadily. The process of degeneration in the Conservative Party was continuous. The storm of opposition grew unceasingly, and so did the unification of all the forces opposed to the dying regime.

Late in November, 1905, Mr. Balfour tendered his resignation as Prime Minister to the King. The Government of Sir Henry Campbell-Bannerman was formed, and proceeded in January to appeal to the constituencies. This Government represented both the wings into which the Liberal Party had been divided by the Boer War. The Liberal Imperialists, so distinguished by their talents, filled some of the greatest offices. Mr. Asquith went to the Exchequer; Sir Edward Grey to the Foreign Office; Mr. Haldane became Secretary of State for War. On the other hand, the Prime Minister, who himself represented the main stream of Liberal opinion, appointed Sir Robert Reid Lord Chancellor, and Mr. John Morley, Secretary of State for India. Both these statesmen, while not opposing actual war measures in South Africa, had unceasingly condemned the war; and in Mr. Lloyd George and Mr. John Burns, both of whom entered the Cabinet, were found democratic politicians who had gone even farther. The dignity of the Administration was enhanced by the venerable figures of Lord Ripon, Sir Henry Fowler, and the newly returned Viceroy of India, Lord Elgin.

The result of the polls in January, 1906, was a Conservative landslide. Never since the election following the great Reform Bill, had anything comparable occurred in British parliamentary history. In Manchester, for instance, which was one of the principal battlegrounds, Mr. Balfour and eight Conservative colleagues were dismissed and replaced by nine Liberals or Labour men. The Conservatives, after nearly twenty years of power, crept back to the House of Commons barely a hundred and fifty strong. The Liberals had gained a majority of more than one hundred over all other parties combined. Both great parties harboured deep grievances against the other; and against the wrong of the Khaki Election and its misuse, was set the counterclaim of an unfair Chinese Labour cry.

Sir Henry Campbell-Bannerman was still receiving the resounding acclamations of Liberals, peace-lovers, anti-jingoes, and anti-militarists, in every part of the country, when he was summoned by Sir Edward Grey to attend to business of a very different character. The Algeciras Conference was in its throes. When the Anglo-French Agreement on Egypt and Morocco had first been made known, the German Government accepted the situation without protest or complaint. The German Chancellor, Prince Bülow, had even declared in 1904 that there was nothing in the Agreement to which Germany could take exception. "What appears to be before us is the attempt by the method of friendly understanding to eliminate a number of points of difference which exist between England and France. We have no objection to make against this from the standpoint of German interest." A serious agitation most embarrassing to the German Government was, however, set on foot by the Pan-German and Colonial parties. Under this pressure the attitude of the Government changed, and a year later Germany openly challenged the Agreement and looked about for an opportunity to assert her claims in Morocco. This opportunity was not long delayed.

Early in 1905 a French mission arrived in Fez. Their language and actions seemed to show an intention of treating Morocco as a French Protectorate, thereby ignoring the international obligations of the Treaty of Madrid. The Sultan of Morocco appealed to Germany, asking if France was authorized to speak in the name of Europe. Germany was now enabled to advance as the champion of an international agreement, which she suggested France was violating. Behind this lay the clear intention to show France that she could not afford, in consequence of her agreement with Britain, to offend Germany. The action taken was of the most drastic character. The German Emperor was persuaded to go to Tangiers, and there, against his better judgment, on March 31, 1905, he delivered, in very uncompromising language chosen by his ministers, an open challenge to France. To this speech the widest circulation was given by the German Foreign Office. Hot-foot upon it (April 11 and 12) two very threatening despatches were sent to Paris and London, demanding a conference of all the Signatory Powers to the Treaty of Madrid. Every means was used by Germany to make France understand that if she refused the conference there would be war; and to make assurance doubly sure a special envoy[1] was sent from Berlin to Paris for that express purpose.

France was quite unprepared for war; the army was in a bad state; Russia was incapacitated; moreover, France had not a good case. The French Foreign Minister, Monsieur Delcassé, was, however, unwilling to give way. The German attitude became still more threatening; and on June 6 the French Cabinet of Monsieur Rouvier unanimously, almost at the cannon's mouth, accepted the principle of a conference, and Monsieur Delcassé at once resigned.

So far Germany had been very successful. Under a direct threat of war she had compelled France to bow to her will, and to sacrifice the Minister who had negotiated the Agreement with Great Britain. The Rouvier Cabinet sought

---

[1] Prince Henckel von Donnesmarck.

earnestly for some friendly solution which, while sparing France the humiliation of a conference dictated in such circumstances, would secure substantial concessions to Germany. The German Government were, however, determined to exploit their victory to the full, and not to make the situation easier for France either before or during the conference. The conference accordingly assembled at Algeciras in January, 1906.

Great Britain now appeared on the scene, apparently quite unchanged and unperturbed by her domestic convulsions. She had in no way encouraged France to refuse the conference. But if a war was to be fastened on France by Germany as the direct result of an agreement made recently in the full light of day between France and Great Britain, it was held that Great Britain could not remain indifferent. Sir Henry Campbell-Bannerman therefore authorized Sir Edward Grey to support France strongly at Algeciras. He also authorized, almost as the first act of what was to be an era of Peace, Retrenchment, and Reform, the beginning of military conversations between the British and French General Staffs with a view to concerted action in the event of war. This was a step of profound significance and of far-reaching reactions. Henceforward the relations of the two Staffs became increasingly intimate and confidential. The minds of our military men were definitely turned into a particular channel. Mutual trust grew continually in one set of military relationships, mutual precautions in the other. However explicitly the two Governments might agree and affirm to each other that no national or political engagement was involved in these technical discussions, the fact remained that they constituted an exceedingly potent tie.

The attitude of Great Britain at Algeciras turned the scale against Germany. Russia, Spain and other signatory Powers associated themselves with France and England. Austria revealed to Germany the limits beyond which she would not go. Thus Germany found herself isolated, and what she had gained by her threats of war evaporated at the Council Board. In the end a compromise suggested by Austria, enabled Germany to withdraw without open loss of dignity. From these events, however, serious consequences flowed. Both the two systems into which Europe was divided, were crystallized and consolidated. Germany felt the need of binding Austria more closely to her. Her open attempt to terrorize France had produced a deep impression upon French public opinion. An immediate and thorough reform of the French Army was carried out, and the *Entente* with England was strengthened and confirmed. Algeciras was a milestone on the road to Armageddon.

The illness and death of Sir Henry Campbell-Bannerman at the beginning of 1908 opened the way for Mr. Asquith. The Chancellor of the Exchequer had been the First Lieutenant of the late Prime Minister, and, as his chief's strength

failed, had more and more assumed the burden. He had charged himself with
the conduct of the new Licensing Bill which was to be the staple of the Session
of 1908, and in virtue of this task he could command the allegiance of an extreme and doctrinaire section of his Party from whom his Imperialism had previously alienated him. He resolved to ally to himself the democratic gifts and
rising reputation of Mr. Lloyd George. Thus the succession passed smoothly
from hand to hand. Mr. Asquith became Prime Minister; Mr. Lloyd George became Chancellor of the Exchequer and the second man in the Government.
The new Cabinet, like the old, was a veiled coalition. A very distinct line of
cleavage was maintained between the Radical-Pacifist elements who had followed Sir Henry Campbell-Bannerman and constituted the bulk both of the
Cabinet and the Party on the one hand, and the Liberal Imperialist wing on the
other. Mr. Asquith, as Prime Minister, had now to take an impartial position;
but his heart and sympathies were always with Sir Edward Grey, the War Office
and the Admiralty, and on every important occasion when he was forced to reveal himself, he definitely sided with them. He was not, however, able to give
Sir Edward Grey the same effectual countenance, much as he might wish to do
so, that Sir Henry Campbell-Bannerman had done. The old chief's word was
law to the extremists of his Party. They would accept almost anything from
him. They were quite sure he would do nothing more in matters of foreign policy and defence than was absolutely necessary, and that he would do it in the
manner least calculated to give satisfaction to jingo sentiments. Mr. Asquith,
however, had been far from "sound" about the Boer War, and was the lifelong
friend of the Foreign Secretary, who had wandered even farther from the strait
path into patriotic pastures. He was therefore in a certain sense suspect, and
every step he took in external affairs was watched with prim vigilance by the El-
ders. If the military conversations with France had not been authorized by Sir
Henry Campbell-Bannerman, and if his political virtue could not be cited in
their justification, I doubt whether they could have been begun or continued
by Mr. Asquith.

   Since I had crossed the Floor of the House in 1904 on the Free Trade issue,
I had worked in close political association with Mr. Lloyd George. He was the
first to welcome me. We sat and acted together in the period of opposition preceding Mr. Balfour's fall, and we had been in close accord during Sir Henry
Campbell-Bannerman's administration, in which I had served as Under-
Secretary of State for the Colonies. This association continued when I entered
the new Cabinet as President of the Board of Trade, and in general, though
from different angles, we leaned to the side of those who would restrain the
froward both in foreign policy and in armaments. It must be understood that
these differences of attitude and complexion, which in varying forms reproduce
themselves in every great and powerful British Administration, in no way pre-

vented harmonious and agreeable relations between the principal personages, and our affairs proceeded amid many amenities in an atmosphere of courtesy, friendliness and goodwill.

It was not long before the next European crisis arrived. On October 5, 1908, Austria, without warning or parley, proclaimed the annexation of Bosnia and Herzegovina. These provinces of the Turkish Empire had been administered by her under the Treaty of Berlin, 1878; and the annexation only declared in form what already existed in fact. The Young Turk Revolution which had occurred in the summer, seemed to Austria likely to lead to a reassertion of Turkish sovereignty over Bosnia and Herzegovina, and this she was concerned to forestall. A reasonable and patient diplomacy would probably have secured for Austria the easements which she needed. Indeed, negotiations with Russia, the Great Power most interested, had made favourable progress. But suddenly and abruptly Count Aerenthal, the Austrian Foreign Minister, interrupted the discussions by the announcement of the annexation, before the arrangements for a suitable concession to Russia had been concluded. By this essentially violent act a public affront was put upon Russia, and a personal slight upon the Russian negotiator, Monsieur Isvolsky.

A storm of anger and protest arose on all sides. England, basing herself on the words of the London Conference in 1871, "That it is an essential principle of the law of nations that no Power can free itself from the engagements of a Treaty, nor modify its stipulations except by consent of the contracting parties," refused to recognize either the annexation of Bosnia and Herzegovina or the declaration of Bulgarian independence which had synchronized with it. Turkey protested loudly against a lawless act. An effective boycott of Austrian merchandise was organized by the Turkish Government. The Serbians mobilized their army. But it was the effect on Russia which was most serious. The bitter animosity excited against Austria throughout Russia became a penultimate cause of the Great War. In this national quarrel the personal differences of Aerenthal and Isvolsky played also their part.

Great Britain and Russia now demanded a conference, declining meanwhile to countenance what had been done. Austria, supported by Germany, refused. The danger of some violent action on the part of Serbia became acute. Sir Edward Grey, after making it clear that Great Britain would not be drawn into a war on a Balkan quarrel, laboured to restrain Serbia, to pacify Turkey, and to give full diplomatic support to Russia. The controversy dragged on till April, 1909, when it was ended in the following remarkable manner. The Austrians had determined, unless Serbia recognized the annexation of Bosnia and Herzegovina, to send an ultimatum and to declare war upon her. At this point the German Chancellor, Prince von Bülow, intervened. Russia, he insisted, should herself advíse Serbia to give way. The Powers should officially recognize the annexation without a conference being summoned and without any kind of compensation to Serbia. Russia was to give her consent to this action, without previously informing the British or French Governments. If Russia did not consent, Austria would declare war on Serbia *with the full and complete support of Germany.* Russia, thus nakedly confronted by war both with Austria and Germany, collapsed under the threat, as France had done three years before. England was left an isolated defender of the sanctity of Treaties and the law of nations. The Teutonic triumph was complete. But it was a victory gained at a perilous cost. France, after her treatment in 1905, had begun a thorough military reorganization. Now Russia, in 1910, made an enormous increase in her already vast army; and both Russia and France, smarting under similar experiences, closed their ranks, cemented their alliance, and set to work to construct with Russian labour and French money the new strategic railway systems of which Russia's western frontier stood in need.

It was next the turn of Great Britain to feel the pressure of the German power.

In the spring of 1909, the First Lord of the Admiralty, Mr. McKenna, suddenly demanded the construction of no less than six Dreadnought battleships. He based this claim on the rapid growth of the German Fleet and its expansion and acceleration under the new naval law of 1908, which was causing the Admiralty the greatest anxiety. I was still a sceptic about the danger of the European situation, and not convinced by the Admiralty case. In conjunction with the Chancellor of the Exchequer, I proceeded at once to canvass this scheme and to examine the reasons by which it was supported. The conclusions which we both reached were that a programme of four ships would sufficiently meet our needs. In this process I was led to analyse minutely the character and composition of the British and German Navies, actual and prospective. I could not agree with the Admiralty contention that a dangerous situation would be reached in the year 1912. I found the Admiralty figures on this subject were exaggerated. I did not believe that the Germans were building Dreadnoughts secretly in excess of their published Fleet Laws. I held that our margin in pre-Dreadnought ships would, added to a new programme of four Dreadnoughts, assure us an adequate superiority in 1912, "the danger year" as it was then called. In any case, as the Admiralty only claimed to lay down the fifth and sixth ships in the last month of the financial year, i.e. March, 1910, these could not affect the calculations. The Chancellor of the Exchequer and I therefore proposed that four ships should be sanctioned for 1909, and that the additional two should be considered in relation to the programme of 1910.

Looking back on the voluminous papers of this controversy in the light of what actually happened, there can be no doubt whatever that, so far as facts and figures were concerned, we were strictly right. The gloomy Admiralty anticipations were in no respect fulfilled in the year 1912. The British margin was found to be ample in that year. There were no secret German Dreadnoughts, nor had Admiral von Tirpitz made any untrue statement in respect of major construction.

The dispute in the Cabinet gave rise to a fierce agitation outside. The process of the controversy led to a sharp rise of temperature. The actual points in dispute never came to an issue. Genuine alarm was excited throughout the country by what was for the first time widely recognized as a German menace. In the end a curious and characteristic solution was reached. The Admiralty had demanded six ships: the economists offered four: and we finally compromised on eight. However, five out of the eight were not ready before 'the danger year' of 1912 had passed peacefully away.

But although the Chancellor of the Exchequer and I were right in the narrow sense, we were absolutely wrong in relation to the deep tides of destiny. The greatest credit is due to the First Lord of the Admiralty, Mr. McKenna, for the resolute and courageous manner in which he fought his case and withstood his Party on this occasion. Little did I think, as this dispute proceeded, that when the next Cabinet crisis about the Navy arose our rôles would be reversed; and little did he think that the ships for which he contended so stoutly would eventually, when they arrived, be welcomed with open arms by me.

Whatever differences might be entertained about the exact number of ships required in a particular year, the British nation in general became conscious of the undoubted fact that Germany proposed to reinforce her unequalled army by a navy which in 1920 would be far stronger than anything up to the present possessed by Great Britain. To the Navy Law of 1900 had succeeded the amending measure of 1906; and upon the increases of 1906 had followed those of 1908. In a flamboyant speech at Reval in 1904 the German Emperor had already styled himself "The Admiral of the Atlantic." All sorts of sober-minded people in England began to be profoundly disquieted. What did Germany want this great navy for? Against whom, except us, could she measure it, match it, or use it? There was a deep and growing feeling, no longer confined to political and diplomatic circles, that the Prussians meant mischief, that they envied the splendour of the British Empire, and that if they saw a good chance at our expense, they would take full advantage of it. Moreover, it began to be realized that it was no use trying to turn Germany from her course by abstaining from counter-measures. Reluctance on our part to build ships was attributed in Germany to want of national spirit, and as another proof that the virile race should advance to replace the effete over-civilized and pacifist society which was no longer capable of sustaining its great place in the world's affairs. No one could run his eyes down the series of figures of British and German construction for the first three years of the Liberal Administration, without feeling in presence of a dangerous, if not a malignant, design.

In 1905 Britain built 4 ships, and Germany 2.

In 1906 Britain *decreased* her programme to 3 ships, and Germany *increased* her programme to 3 ships.

In 1907 Britain *further decreased* her programme to 2 ships, and Germany *further increased* her programme to 4 ships.

These figures are monumental.

It was impossible to resist the conclusion, gradually forced on nearly everyone, that if the British Navy lagged behind, the gap would be very speedily filled.

We have now seen how within the space of five years Germany's policy and the growth of her armaments led her to arouse and alarm most profoundly three of the greatest Powers in the world. Two of them, France and Russia, had been forced to bow to the German will by the plain threat of war. Each had been quelled by the open intention of a neighbour to use force against them to the utmost limit without compunction. Both felt they had escaped a bloody ordeal and probable disaster only by submission. The sense of past humiliation was aggravated by the fear of future affronts. The third Power—unorganized for war, but inaccessible and not to be neglected in the world's affairs—Britain, had also been made to feel that hands were being laid upon the very foundation of her existence. Swiftly, surely, methodically, a German Navy was coming into being at our doors which must expose us to dangers only to be warded off by strenuous exertions, and by a vigilance almost as tense as that of actual war. As France and Russia increased their armies, so Britain under the same pressure increased her fleet. Henceforward the three disquieted nations will act more closely together and will not be taken by their adversary one by one. Henceforward their military arrangements will be gradually concerted. Henceforward they will consciously be facing a common danger.

Ah! foolish-diligent Germans, working so hard, thinking so deeply, marching and counter-marching on the parade grounds of the Fatherland, poring over long calculations, fuming in new-found prosperity, discontended amid the splendour of mundane success, how many bulwarks to your peace and glory did you not, with your own hands, successively tear down!

"In the year 1909," writes von Bethmann-Hollweg, then the successor of Prince von Bülow, "the situation was based on the fact that England had firmly taken its stand on the side of France and Russia in pursuit of its traditional policy of opposing whatever Continental Power for the time being was the strongest; and that Germany held fast to its naval programme, had given a definite direction to its Eastern policy, and had moreover to guard against a French antagonism that had in no wise been mitigated by its policy in later years. And if Germany saw a formidable aggravation of all the aggressive tendencies of Franco-Russian policy in England's pronounced friendship with this Dual Alliance, England on its side had grown to see a menace in the strengthening of the German Fleet and a violation of its ancient rights in our Eastern policy. Words had already passed on both sides. The atmosphere was chilly and clouded with distrust." Such, in his own words, was the inheritance of the new German Chancellor.

He was now to make his own contribution to the anxieties of the world.

CHAPTER III

THE CRISIS OF AGADIR

In the spring of 1911 a French expedition occupied Fez. This action, added to the growing discontent in Germany over the Moroccan question, tempted the German Government at the beginning of July to an abrupt act. The Brothers Mannesmann, a German firm at that time very active in European financial circles, claimed that they had large interests in a harbour on the Atlantic seaboard of the Moroccan Coast and in the hinterland behind it. This harbour bore the name of Agadir. Herr von Kiderlen-Wächter, the German Foreign Minister, raised this point with the French. The French Government fully realized that the advantages they were gaining in Morocco, justified Germany in seeking certain colonial compensations in the Congo area. The German press, on the other hand, was indignant at exchanging German interests in the moderate climate of Morocco for unhealthy tropical regions of which they had already more than enough. The questions involved were complicated and intrinsically extremely unimportant. The French prepared themselves for a prolonged negotiation. So far as the harbour and hinterland of Agadir were concerned, there seemed to be no difficulty. They denied altogether the existence of any German interests there. They said there was only a sandy bay untouched by the hand of man; there was no German property on the shore, not a trading establishment, not a house; there were no German interests in the interior. But these facts could easily be ascertained by a visit of accredited representatives of both countries. Such a visit to ascertain the facts they professed themselves quite ready to arrange. They also courted a discussion of the frontier of the Congo territories.

Suddenly and unexpectedly, on the morning of July 1, without more ado, it was announced that His Imperial Majesty the German Emperor had sent his gunboat the *Panther* to Agadir to maintain and protect German interests. This small ship was already on its way. All the alarm bells throughout Europe began immediately to quiver. France found herself in the presence of an act which could not be explained, the purpose behind which could not be measured. Great Britain, having consulted the atlas, began to wonder what bearing a German naval base on the Atlantic coast of Africa would have upon her maritime security, "observing," as the sailors say when they have to write official letters to each other, that such a fact must be taken in conjunction with German activities at Madeira and in the Canaries and with the food routes and trade routes from South America and South Africa which converged and passed through these waters. Europe was uneasy. France was genuinely alarmed. When Count Metternich apprised Sir Edward Grey of the German action, he was informed that the situation was so important that it must be considered by the Cabinet. On July 5, after the Cabinet, he was told that the British Government could not disinterest themselves in Morocco, and that until Germany's intentions were made known their attitude must remain one of reserve. From that date until July 21 not one word was spoken by the German Government. There is no doubt that the decided posture of Great Britain was a great surprise to the German Foreign Office. There ensued between the Governments what was called at the time "the period of silence." Meanwhile the French and German newspapers carried on a lively controversy, and the British press wore a very sombre air.

It was difficult to divine from the long strings of telegrams which day after day flowed in from all the European Chancelleries, what was the real purpose behind the German action. I followed attentively the repeated discussions on the subject in the British Cabinet. Was Germany looking for a pretext of war with France, or was she merely trying by pressure and uncertainty to improve her colonial position? In the latter case the dispute would no doubt be adjusted after a period of tension, as so many had been before. The great Powers marshalled on either side, preceded and protected by an elaborate cushion of diplomatic courtesies and formalities, would display to each other their respective arrays. In the forefront would be the two principal disputants, Germany and France, and echeloned back on either side at varying distances and under veils of reserves and qualifications of different density, would be drawn up the other parties to the Triple Alliance and to what was already now beginning to be called the Triple Entente. At the proper moment these seconds or supporters would utter certain cryptic words indicative of their state of mind, as a consequence of which France or Germany would step back or forward a very small distance or perhaps move slightly to the right or to the left. When these delicate rectifications in the great balance of Europe, and indeed of the world, had been made, the formidable assembly would withdraw to their own apartments with ceremony and salutations and congratulate or condole with each other in whispers on the result. We had seen it several times before.

But even this process was not free from danger. One must think of the intercourse of the nations in those days not as if they were chessmen on the board, or puppets dressed in finery and frillings grimacing at each other in a quadrille, but as prodigious organizations of forces active or latent which, like planetary bodies, could not approach each other in space without giving rise to profound magnetic reactions. If they got too near, the lightnings would begin to flash, and beyond a certain point they might be attracted altogether from the orbits in which they were restrained and draw each other into dire collision. The task of diplomacy was to prevent such disasters; and as long as there was no conscious or subconscious purpose of war in the mind of any Power or race, diplomacy would probably succeed. But in such grave and delicate conjunctions one violent move by any party, would rupture and derange the restraints upon all, and plunge Cosmos into Chaos.

I thought myself that the Germans had a certain grievance about the original Anglo-French agreement. We had received many conveniences in Egypt. France had gained great advantages in Morocco. If Germany felt her relative position prejudiced by these arrangements, there was no reason why patiently and amicably she should not advance and press her own point of view. And it seemed to me that Britain, the most withdrawn, the least committed of the Great Powers, might exercise a mitigating and a modifying influence and procure an accommodation; and that of course was what we tried to do. But if Germany's intention were malignant, no such process would be of the slightest use. In that event a very decided word would have to be spoken, and spoken before it was too late. Nor would our withdrawing altogether from the scene have helped matters. Had we done so all our restraining influence would have vanished, and an intenser aggravation of the antagonistic forces must have occurred. Therefore I read all the papers and telegrams which began to pass with a suspicion, and I could see beneath the calm of Sir Edward Grey a growing and at some moments a grave anxiety.

The sultry obscurity of the European situation was complicated by the uncertain play of forces within our own council chamber. There again in miniature were reproduced the balances and reserves of the external diplomatic situation. The Ministers who were conducting the foreign policy of Britain, with the ponderous trident of sea power towering up behind them, were drawn entirely from the Liberal Imperialist section of the Government. They were narrowly watched and kept in equipoise by the Radical element, which included the venerable figures of Lord Morley and Lord Loreburn, on whose side the Chancellor of the Exchequer and I had usually leaned. It was clear that this equipoise might easily make it impossible for Great Britain to speak with a decided voice either on one side or the other if certain dangerous conditions supervened. We should not, therefore, either keep clear ourselves by withdrawing from the danger nor be able by resolute action to ward it off in time. In these circumstances the attitude of the Chancellor of the Exchequer became of peculiar importance.

For some weeks he offered no indication of what his line would be, and in our numerous conversations he gave me the impression of being sometimes on one side and sometimes on the other. But on the morning of July 21, when I visited him before the Cabinet, I found a different man. His mind was made up. He saw quite clearly the course to take. He knew what to do and how and when to do it. The tenor of his statement to me was that we were drifting into war. He dwelt on the oppressive silence of Germany so far as we were concerned. He pointed out that Germany was acting as if England did not count in the matter in any way; that she had completely ignored our strong representation; that she was proceeding to put the most severe pressure on France; that a catastrophe might ensue; and that if it was to be averted we must speak with great decision, and we must speak at once. He told me that he was to address the Bankers at their Annual Dinner that evening, and that he intended to make it clear that if Germany meant war, she would find Britain against her. He showed me what he had prepared, and told me that he would show it to the Prime Minister and Sir Edward Grey after the Cabinet. What would they say? I said that of course they would be very much relieved; and so they were, and so was I.

The accession of Mr. Lloyd George in foreign policy to the opposite wing of the Government was decisive. We were able immediately to pursue a firm and coherent policy. That night at the Bankers' Association the Chancellor of the Exchequer used the following words:

> If a situation were to be forced upon us in which peace could only be preserved by the surrender of the great and beneficent position Britain has won by centuries of heroism and achievement, by allowing Britain to be treated where her interests were vitally affected as if she were of no account in the Cabinet of nations, then I say emphatically that peace at that price would be a humiliation intolerable for a great country like ours to endure.

His City audience, whose minds were obsessed with the iniquities of the Lloyd George Budget and the fearful hardships it had inflicted upon property and wealth—little did they dream of the future—did not comprehend in any way the significance or the importance of what they heard. They took it as if it had been one of the ordinary platitudes of ministerial pronouncements upon foreign affairs. But the Chancelleries of Europe bounded together.

Four days later, at about 5:30 in the afternoon, the Chancellor of the Exchequer and I were walking by the fountains of Buckingham Palace. Hot-foot on our track came a messenger. Will the Chancellor of the Exchequer go at once to Sir Edward Grey? Mr. Lloyd George stopped abruptly and turning to me said, "That's my speech. The Germans may demand my resignation as they did Delcassé's." I said, "That will make you the most popular man in England" (he was not actually the most popular at that time). We returned as fast as we could and found Sir Edward Grey in his room at the House of Commons. His first words were: "I have just received a communication from the German Ambassador so stiff that the Fleet might be attacked at any moment. I have sent for McKenna to warn him!" He then told us briefly of the conversation he had just had with Count Metternich. The Ambassador had said that after the speech of the Chancellor of the Exchequer no explanation could be made by Germany. In acrid terms he had stated that if France should repel the hand offered her by the Emperor's Government, the dignity of Germany would compel her to secure by all means full respect by France for German treaty rights. He had then read a long complaint about Mr. Lloyd George's speech, "which to say the least could have been interpreted as a warning to Germany's address and which as a matter of fact had been interpreted by the presses of Great Britain and France as a warning bordering on menace." Sir Edward Grey had thought it right to reply that the tone of the communication which had just been read to him, rendered it inconsistent with the dignity of His Majesty's Government to give explanations with regard to the speech of the Chancellor of the Exchequer. The First Lord arrived while we were talking, and a few minutes later hurried off to send the warning orders.

They sound so very cautious and correct, these deadly words. Soft, quiet voices purring, courteous, grave, exactly-measured phrases in large peaceful rooms. But with less warning cannons had opened fire and nations had been struck down by this same Germany. So now the Admiralty wireless whispers through the ether to the tall masts of ships, and captains pace their decks absorbed in thought. It is nothing. It is less than nothing. It is too foolish, too fantastic to be thought of in the twentieth century. Or is it fire and murder leaping out of the darkness at our throats, torpedoes ripping the bellies of half-awakened ships, a sunrise on a vanished naval supremacy, and an island well-guarded hitherto, at last defenceless? No, it is nothing. No one would do such things. Civilization has climbed above such perils. The interdependence of nations in trade and traffic, the sense of public law, the Hague Convention, Liberal principles, the Labour Party, high finance, Christian charity, common sense have rendered such nightmares impossible. Are you quite sure? It would be a pity to be wrong. Such a mistake could only be made once—once for all.

The Mansion House speech was a surprise to all countries: it was a thunderclap to the German Government. All their information had led them to believe that Mr. Lloyd George would head the peace party and that British action would be neutralized. Jumping from one extreme to another, they now assumed that the British Cabinet was absolutely united, and that the Chancellor of the Exchequer of all others had been deliberately selected as the most Radical Minister by the British Government to make this pronouncement:[1] They could not understand how their representatives and agents in Great Britain could have been so profoundly misled. Their vexation proved fatal to Count Metternich, and at the first convenient opportunity he was recalled. Here was an Ambassador who, after ten years' residence in London, could not even forecast the action of one of the most powerful Ministers on a question of this character. It will be seen from what has been written that this view was hard on Count Metternich. How could he know what Mr. Lloyd George was going to do? Until a few hours before, his colleagues did not know. Working with him in close association, I did not know. No one knew. Until his mind was definitely made up, he did not know himself.

It seems probable now that the Germans did not mean war on this occasion. But they meant to test the ground; and in so doing they were prepared to go to the very edge of the precipice. It is so easy to lose one's balance there: a touch, a gust of wind, a momentary dizziness, and all is precipitated into the abyss. But whether in the heart of the German State there was or was not a war purpose before England's part had been publicly declared, there was no such intention afterwards.

After the speech of the Chancellor of the Exchequer and its sequel the German Government could not doubt that Great Britain would be against them if a war was forced upon France at this juncture. They did not immediately recede from their position, but they were most careful to avoid any fresh act of provocation; and all their further conduct of the negotiations with France tended to open in one direction or another paths of accommodation and of retreat. It remained extremely difficult for us to gauge the exact significance of the various points at issue, and throughout the months of July, August and September the situation continued obscure and oppressive. The slight yet decisive change which came over the character of German diplomacy, was scarcely perceptible, and at the same time certain precautionary military measures which were taken behind the German frontiers, so far as they were known to us, had the effect of greatly increasing our anxiety. In consequence the atmosphere in England became constantly more heavily charged with electricity as one hot summer's day succeeded another.

Hitherto as Home Secretary I had not had any special part to play in this affair, though I had followed it with the utmost attention as a Member of the

[1] Von Tirpitz's account is quite correct. "At his [von Kiderlen-Wächter's] suggestion the Chancellor dispatched the gunboat *Panther* to the Moroccan port Agadir on July 1, 1911, and left the British Government, when it asked the reason, completely in the dark and without a reply for many weeks. The result was that on July 21 Lloyd George delivered a speech which had been drawn up in the British Cabinet, in which he warned Germany that she would find British power on the side of France in the event of a challenge."

Cabinet. I was now to receive a rude shock. On the afternoon of July 27, I attended a garden party at 10, Downing Street. There I met the Chief Commissioner of Police, Sir Edward Henry. We talked about the European situation, and I told him that it was serious. He then remarked that by an odd arrangement the Home Office was responsible, through the Metropolitan Police, for guarding the magazines at Chattenden and Lodge Hill, in which all the reserves of naval cordite were stored. For many years these magazines had been protected without misadventure by a few constables. I asked what would happen if twenty determined Germans in two or three motor cars arrived well armed upon the scene one night. He said they would be able to do what they liked. I quitted the garden party.

A few minutes later I was telephoning from my room in the Home Office to the Admiralty. Who was in charge? The First Lord was with the Fleet at Cromarty; the First Sea Lord was inspecting. Both were, of course, quickly accessible by wireless or wire. In the meantime an Admiral (he shall be nameless) was in control. I demanded Marines at once to guard these magazines, vital to the Royal Navy. I knew there were plenty of Marines in the depôts at Chatham and Portsmouth. The Admiral replied over the telephone that the Admiralty had no responsibility and had no intention of assuming any; and it was clear from his manner that he resented the intrusion of an alarmist civilian Minister. "You refuse then to send the Marines?" After some hesitation he replied, "I refuse." I replaced the receiver and rang up the War Office. Mr. Haldane was there. I told him that I was reinforcing and arming the police that night, and asked for a company of infantry for each magazine in addition. In a few minutes the orders were given: in a few hours the troops had moved. By the next day the cordite reserves of the Navy were safe.

The incident was a small one, and perhaps my fears were unfounded. But once one had begun to view the situation in this light, it became impossible to think of anything else. All around flowed the busy life of peaceful, unsuspecting, easy-going Britain. The streets were thronged with men and women utterly devoid of any sense of danger from abroad. For nearly a thousand years no foreign army had landed on British soil. For a hundred years the safety of the homeland had never been threatened. They went about their business, their sport, their class and party fights year after year, generation after generation, in perfect confidence and considerable ignorance. All their ideas were derived from conditions of peace. All their arrangements were the result of long peace. Most of them would have been incredulous, many would have been very angry if they had been told that we might be near a tremendous war, and that perhaps within this City of London, which harboured confidingly visitors from every land, resolute foreigners might be aiming a deadly blow at the strength of the one great weapon and shield in which we trusted.

I began to make inquiries about vulnerable points. I found the far-seeing Captain Hankey, then Assistant Secretary to the Committee of Imperial Defence, already on the move classifying them for the War Book, which project had actually been launched.[1] I inquired further about sabotage and espionage and counter-espionage. I came in touch with other officers working very quietly and very earnestly, but in a small way and with small means. I was told about German spies and agents in the various British ports. Hitherto the Home Secretary had to sign a warrant when it was necessary to examine any particular letter passing through the Royal Mails. I now signed general warrants authorizing the examination of all the correspondence of particular people upon a list, to which additions were continually made. This soon disclosed a regular and extensive system of German-paid British agents. It was only in a very small part of the field of preparation that the Home Secretary had any official duty of interference, but once I got drawn in, it dominated all other interests in my mind. For seven years I was to think of little else. Liberal politics, the People's Budget, Free Trade, Peace, Retrenchment and Reform—all the war cries of our election struggles began to seem unreal in the presence of this new preoccupation. Only Ireland held her place among the grim realities which came one after another into view. No doubt other Ministers had similar mental experiences. I am telling my own tale.

I now began to make an intensive study of the military position in Europe. I read everything with which I was supplied. I spent many hours in argument and discussion. The Secretary of State for War told his officers to tell me everything I wanted to know. The Chief of the General Staff, Sir William Nicholson, was an old friend of mine. I had served with him as a young officer on Sir William Lockhart's staff at the end of the Tirah Expedition in 1898. He wrote fine broad appreciations and preached a clear and steady doctrine. But the man from whom I learned most was the Director of Military Operations, General Wilson (afterwards Field-Marshal Sir Henry Wilson). This officer had extraordinary vision and faith. He had acquired an immense and, I expect, an unequalled volume of knowledge about the Continent. He knew the French Army thoroughly. He was deeply in the secrets of the French General Staff. He had been Head of the British Staff College. For years he had been labouring with one object, that if war came we should act immediately on the side of France. He was sure that war would come sooner or later. All the threads of military information were in his hands. The whole wall of his small room was covered by a gigantic map of Belgium, across which every practicable road by which the German armies could march for the invasion of France, was painted

---

[1] The work had been begun by Lieutenant-Colonel Adrian Grant-Duff, afterwards killed on the Aisne.

clearly. All his holidays he spent examining these roads and the surrounding country. He could not do much in Germany: the Germans knew him too well.

One night the German ambassador, still Count Metternich, whom I had known for ten years, asked me to dine with him. We were alone, and a famous hock from the Emperor's cellars was produced. We had a long talk about Germany and how she had grown great; about Napoleon and the part he had played in uniting her; about the Franco-German War and how it began and how it ended. I said what a pity it was that Bismarck had allowed himself to be forced by the soldiers into taking Lorraine, and how Alsace-Lorraine lay at the root of all the European armaments and rival combinations. He said these had been German provinces from remote antiquity until one day in profound peace Louis XIV had pranced over the frontier and seized them. I said their sympathies were French: he said they were mixed. I said that anyhow it kept the whole thing alive. France could never forget her lost provinces, and they never ceased to call to her. The conversation passed to a kindred but more critical subject. Was he anxious about the present situation? He said people were trying to ring Germany round and put her in a net, and that she was a strong animal to put in a net. I said, how could she be netted when she had an alliance with two other first-class Powers, Austria-Hungary and Italy? *We* had often stood quite alone for years at a time without getting flustered. He said it was a very different business for an island. But when you had been marched through and pillaged and oppressed so often and had only the breasts of your soldiers to stand between you and invasion, it ate into your soul. I said that Germany was frightened of nobody, and that everybody was frightened of her.

Then we came to the Navy. Surely, I said, it was a great mistake for Germany to try to rival Britain on the seas. She would never catch us up. We should build two to one or more if necessary, and at every stage antagonism would grow between the countries. Radicals and Tories, whatever they might say about each other, were all agreed on that. No British Government which jeopardized our naval supremacy could live. He said Mr. Lloyd George had told him very much the same thing, but the Germans had no thought of naval supremacy. All they wanted was a Fleet to protect their commerce and their colonies. I asked what was the use of having a weaker Fleet? It was only another hostage to fortune. He said that the Emperor was profoundly attached to his Fleet, and that it was his own creation. I could not resist saying that Moltke had pronounced a very different opinion of Germany's true interest.

I have recorded these notes of a pleasant though careful conversation, not because they are of any importance, but because they help to show the different points of view. I learned afterwards that the Chancellor of the Exchequer in similar circumstances had spoken more explicitly, saying that he would raise a hundred millions in a single year for the British Navy if its supremacy were really challenged.

Count Metternich was a very honourable man, serving his master faithfully but labouring to preserve peace, especially peace between England and Germany. I have heard that on one occasion at Berlin in a throng of generals and princes, someone had said that the British Fleet would one day make a surprise and unprovoked attack upon Germany. Whereupon the Ambassador had replied that he had lived in England for nearly ten years, and he knew that such a thing was absolutely impossible. On this remark being received with obvious incredulity, he had drawn himself up and observed that he made it on the honour of a German officer and that he would answer for its truth with his honour. This for a moment had quelled the company.

It is customary for thoughtless people to jeer at the old diplomacy and to pretend that wars arise out of its secret machinations. When one looks at the petty subjects which have led to wars between great countries and to so many disputes, it is easy to be misled in this way. Of course such small matters are only the symptoms of the dangerous disease, and are only important for that reason. Behind them lie the interests, the passions and the destiny of mighty races of men; and long antagonisms express themselves in trifles. "Great commotions," it was said of old, "arise out of small things, but not concerning small things." The old diplomacy did its best to render harmless the small things: it could not do more. Nevertheless, a war postponed may be a war averted. Circumstances change, combinations change, new groupings arise, old interests are superseded by new. Many quarrels that might have led to war have been adjusted by the old diplomacy of Europe and have, in Lord Melbourne's phrase, "blown over." If the nations of the world, while the sense of their awful experiences is still fresh upon them, are able to devise broader and deeper guarantees of peace and build their houses on a surer foundation of brotherhood and interdependence, they will still require the courtly manners, the polite and measured phrases, the imperturbable demeanour, the secrecy and discretion of the old diplomatists of Europe. This is, however, a digression.

On August 23, after Parliament had risen and Ministers had dispersed, the Prime Minister convened very secretly a special meeting of the Committee of Imperial Defence. He summoned the Ministers specially concerned with the foreign situation and with the fighting services, including of course the Chancellor of the Exchequer. There were also the principal officers of the Army and the Navy. I was invited to attend, though the Home Office was not directly concerned. We sat all day. In the morning the Army told its tale: in the afternoon, the Navy.

General Wilson, as Director of Military Operations, stated the views of the

General Staff. Standing by his enormous map, specially transported for the purpose, he unfolded, with what proved afterwards to be extreme accuracy, the German plan for attacking France in the event of a war between Germany and Austria on the one hand and France and Russia on the other. It was briefly as follows:

In the first place, the Germans would turn nearly four-fifths of their strength against France and leave only one-fifth to contain Russia. The German armies would draw up on a line from the Swiss frontier to Aix-la-Chapelle. They would then swing their right wing through Belgium, thus turning the line of fortresses by which the eastern frontiers of France were protected. This enormous swinging movement of the German right arm would require every road which led through Belgium from Luxembourg to the Belgian Meuse. There were fifteen of these roads, and three divisions would probably march along each. The Belgian Meuse flowed parallel to the march of these divisions and protected their right flank. Along this river were three important fortified passages or bridgeheads. First, nearest Germany, Liège; the last, nearest France, Namur; and midway between the two, the fort of Huy. Now arose the question, Would the Germans after seizing these bridgeheads confine themselves to the eastern side of the Belgian Meuse and use the river for their protection, or would they be able to spare and bring a large body of troops to prolong their turning movement west of the Belgian Meuse and thus advance beyond it instead of inside it? This was the only part of their plan which could not be foreseen. Would they avoid the west side of the Belgian Meuse altogether? Would they skim along it with a cavalry force only, or would they march infantry divisions or even army corps west of that river? When the time came, as we now know, they marched two whole armies. At that date, however, the most sombre apprehension did not exceed one, or at the outside two, army corps.

Overwhelming detailed evidence was adduced to show that the Germans had made every preparation for marching through Belgium. The great military camps in close proximity to the frontier, the enormous depôts, the reticulation of railways, the endless sidings, revealed with the utmost clearness and beyond all doubt their design. Liège would be taken within a few hours of the declaration of war, possibly even before it, by a rush of motor cars and cyclists from the camp at Elsenborn. That camp was now (August, 1911) crowded with troops, and inquisitive persons and ordinary countryfolk were already being roughly turned back and prevented from approaching it.

What would Belgium do in the face of such an onslaught? Nothing could save Liège, but French troops might reach Namur in time to aid in its defence. For the rest the Belgian Army, assuming that Belgium resisted the invader, would withdraw into the great entrenched camp and fortress of Antwerp. This extensive area, intersected by a tangle of rivers and canals and defended by three circles of forts, would become the last refuge of the Belgian monarchy and people.

The position of Holland was also examined. It was not thought that the Germans would overrun Holland as they would Belgium, but they might find it very convenient to march across the curiously shaped projection of Holland which lay between Germany and Belgium, and which in the British General Staff parlance of that time was called "the Maestricht Appendix." They would certainly do this if any considerable body of their troops was thrown west of the Belgian Meuse.

The French plans for meeting this formidable situation were not told in detail to us; but it was clear that they hoped to forestall and rupture the German enveloping movement by a counter-offensive of their own on the greatest scale.

The numbers of divisions available on both sides and on all fronts when mobilization was completed were estimated as follows:

French   85
German   110

It was asserted that if the six British divisions were sent to take position on the extreme French left, immediately war was declared, the chances of repulsing the Germans in the first great shock of battle were favourable. Every French soldier would fight with double confidence if he knew he was not fighting alone. Upon the strength of Russia General Wilson spoke with great foresight, and the account which he gave of the slow mobilization of the Russian Army swept away many illusions. It seemed incredible that Germany should be content to leave scarcely a score of divisions to make head against the might of Russia. But the British General Staff considered that such a decision would be well-founded. We shall see presently how the loyalty of Russia and of the Tsar found the means by prodigious sacrifices to call back to the East vital portions of the German Army at the supreme moment. Such action could not be foreseen then, and most people have forgotten it now.

There was of course a considerable discussion and much questioning before we adjourned at 2 o'clock. When we began again at three, it was the turn of the Admiralty, and the First Sea Lord, Sir Arthur Wilson, with another map expounded his views of the policy we should pursue in the event of our being involved in such a war. He did not reveal the Admiralty war plans. Those he kept locked away in his own brain, but he indicated that they embodied the principle of a close blockade of the enemy's ports. It was very soon apparent that a profound difference existed between the War Office and the Admiralty view. In the main the Admiralty thought that we should confine our efforts to the sea; that if our small Army were sent to the Continent it would be swallowed up among the immense hosts conflicting there, whereas if kept in ships or ready to embark for counter-strokes upon the German coast, it would draw off more than its own weight of numbers from the German fighting line. This view, which was violently combatted by the Generals, did not commend itself to the bulk of those present, and on many points of detail connected with the landings of these troops the military and naval authorities were found in complete discord. The serious disagreement between the military and naval staffs in such critical times upon fundamental issues was the immediate cause of my going to the Admiralty. After the Council had separated, Mr. Haldane intimated to the Prime Minister that he would not continue to be responsible for the War Office unless a Board of Admiralty was called into being which would work in full harmony with the War Office plans, and would begin the organization of a proper Naval War Staff. Of course I knew nothing of this, but it was destined soon to affect my fortunes in a definite manner.

I thought that the General Staff took too sanguine a view of the French Army. Knowing their partisanship for France, I feared the wish was father to the thought. It was inevitable that British military men, ardently desirous of seeing their country intervene on the side of France, and convinced that the destruction of France by Germany would imperil the whole future of Great Britain, should be inclined to overrate the relative power of the French Army and accord it brighter prospects than were actually justified. The bulk of their information was derived from French sources. The French General Staff were resolute and hopeful. The principle of the offensive was the foundation of their military art and the mainspring of the French soldier. Although according to the best information, the French pre-war Army when fully mobilized was only three-fourths as strong as the German pre-war Army, the French mobilization from the ninth to the thirteenth day yielded a superior strength on the fighting front. High hopes were entertained by the French Generals that a daring seizure of the initiative and a vigorous offensive into Alsace-Lorraine would have the effect of rupturing the carefully thought out German plans of marching through Belgium on to Paris. These hopes were reflected in the British General Staff appreciations.

I could not share them. I had therefore prepared a memorandum for the Committee of Imperial Defence which embodied my own conclusions upon all I had learned from the General Staff. It was dated August 13, 1911. It was, of course, only an attempt to pierce the veil of the future; to conjure up in the mind a vast imaginary situation; to balance the incalculable; to weigh the imponderable. I named the *twentieth* day of mobilization as the date by which 'the French armies will have been driven from the line of the Meuse and will be falling back on Paris and the South,' and the *fortieth* day as that by which "Germany should be extended at full strain both internally and on her war fronts," and that "opportunities for the decisive trial of strength may then occur." I am quite free to admit that these were not intended to be precise dates, but as guides to show what would probably happen. In fact, however, both these forecasts were almost literally verified three years later by the event.

I reprinted this memorandum on the 2nd of September, 1914, in order to encourage my colleagues with the hope that if the unfavourable prediction about the twentieth day had been borne out, so also would be the favourable prediction about the fortieth day. And so indeed it was.

MILITARY ASPECTS OF THE CONTINENTAL PROBLEM
Memorandum by Mr. Churchill

August 13, 1911.

The following notes have been written on the assumption . . . that a decision has been arrived at to employ a British military force on the Continent of Europe. It does not prejudge that decision in any way.

It is assumed that an alliance exists between Great Britain, France, and Russia, and that these Powers are attacked by Germany and Austria.

1. The decisive military operations will be those between France and Germany. The German army is at least equal in quality to the French, and mobilizes 2,200,000 against 1,700,000. The French must therefore seek for a situation of more equality. This can be found either before the full strength of the Germans has been brought to bear or after the German army has become extended. The first might be reached between the ninth and thirteenth days; the latter about the fortieth.

2. The fact that during a few days in the mobilization period the French are equal or temporarily superior on the frontiers is of no significance, except on the assumption that France contemplates adopting a strategic offensive. The Germans will not choose the days when they themselves have least superiority for a general advance; and if the French advance, they lose at once all the advantages of their own internal communications, and by moving towards the advancing German reinforcements annul any numerical advantage they may for the moment possess. The French have therefore, at the beginning of the war, no option but to remain on the defensive, both upon their own fortress line and behind the Belgian frontier; and the choice of the day when the first main collision will commence rests with the Germans, who must be credited with the wisdom of choosing the best possible day, and cannot be forced into decisive action against their will, except by some reckless and unjustifiable movement on the part of the French.

3. A prudent survey of chances from the British point of view ought to contemplate that, when the German advance decisively begins, it will be backed by sufficient preponderance of force, and developed on a sufficiently wide front to compel the French armies to retreat from their positions behind the Belgian frontier, even though they may hold the gaps between the fortresses on the Verdun-Belfort front. No doubt a series of great battles will have been fought with varying local fortunes, and there is always a possibility of a heavy German check. But, even if the Germans were brought to a standstill, the French would not be strong enough to advance in their turn; and in any case we ought not to count on this. The balance of probability is that by the twentieth day the French armies will have been driven from the line of the Meuse and will be falling back on Paris and the south. All plans based upon the opposite assumption ask too much of fortune.

4. This is not to exclude the plan of using four or six British divisions in these great initial operations. Such a force is a material factor of significance. Its value to the French would be out of all proportion to its numerical strength. It would encourage every French soldier and make the task of the Germans in forcing the frontier much more costly. But the question which is of most practical consequence to us, is what is to happen after the frontier has been forced and the invasion of France has begun. France will not be able to end the war successfully by any action on the frontiers. She will not be strong enough to invade Germany. Her only chance is to conquer Germany in France. It is this problem which should be studied before any final decision is taken.

5. The German armies in advancing through Belgium and onwards into France will be relatively weakened by all or any of the following causes:

By the greater losses incidental to the offensive (especially if they have tested unsuccessfully the French fortress lines);

By the greater employment of soldiers necessitated by acting on exterior lines;

By having to guard their communications through Belgium and France (especially from the sea flank);

By having to invest Paris (requiring at least 500,000 men against 100,000) and to besiege or mask other places, especially along the seaboard;

By the arrival of the British army;

By the growing pressure of Russia from the thirtieth day;

And generally by the bad strategic situation to which their right-handed advance will commit them as it becomes pronounced.

All these factors will operate increasingly in proportion as the German advance continues and every day that passes.

6. Time is also required for the naval blockade to make itself felt on German commerce, industry, and food prices, as described in the Admiralty Memorandum, and for these again to react on German credit and finances already burdened with the prodigious daily cost of the war. All these pressures will develop simultaneously and progressively. [The Chancellor of the Exchequer has drawn special attention to this and to the very light structure of German industry and economic organizations.]

7. By the fortieth day Germany should be extended at full strain both internally and on her war fronts, and this strain will become daily more severe and ultimately overwhelming, unless it is relieved by decisive victories in France. If the French army has not been squandered by precipitate or desperate action, the balance of forces should be favourable after the fortieth day, and will improve steadily as time passes. For the German armies will be confronted with a situation which combines an ever-growing need for a successful offensive, with a battle-front which tends continually towards numerical equality. Opportunities for the decisive trial of strength may then occur.

W. S. C.

The Conference separated. Apprehension lay heavy on the minds of all who had participated in it.

The War Office hummed with secrets in those days. Not the slightest overt action could be taken. But every preparation by forethought was made and every detail was worked out on paper. The railway time-tables, or graphics as they were called, of the movement of every battalion—even where they were to drink their coffee—were prepared and settled. Thousands of maps of Northern France and Belgium were printed. The cavalry manoeuvres were postponed "on account of the scarcity of water in Wiltshire and the neighbouring counties." The press, fiercely divided on party lines, overwhelmingly pacific in tendency, without censorship, without compulsion, observed a steady universal reticence. Not a word broke the long-drawn oppressive silence. The great railway strike came to an end with mysterious suddenness. Mutual concessions were made by masters and men after hearing a confidential statement from the Chancellor of the Exchequer.

In the middle of August I went to the country for a few days. I could not think of anything else but the peril of war. I did my other work as it came along, but there was only one field of interest fiercely illuminated in my mind.

From the smiling country which stretches around Mells I wrote the following letter to Sir Edward Grey. It speaks for itself.

30 August, 1911.

Perhaps the time is coming when decisive action will be necessary. Please consider the following policy for use if and when the Morocco negotiations fail.

Propose to France and Russia a triple alliance to safeguard *(inter alia)* the independence of Belgium, Holland, and Denmark.

Tell Belgium that, if her neutrality is violated, we are prepared to come to her aid and to make an alliance with France and Russia to guarantee her independence. Tell her that we will take whatever military steps will be most effective for that purpose. But the Belgian Army must take the field in concert with the British and French Armies, and Belgium must immediately garrison properly Liège and Namur. Otherwise we cannot be responsible for her fate.

Offer the same guarantee both to Holland and to Denmark contingent upon their making their utmost exertions.

We should, if necessary, aid Belgium to defend Antwerp and to feed that fortress and any army based on it. We should be prepared at the proper moment to put extreme pressure on the Dutch to keep the Scheldt open for *all* purposes. If the Dutch close the Scheldt, we should retaliate by a blockade of the Rhine.

It is very important to us to be able to blockade the Rhine, and it gets more important as the war goes on. On the other hand, if the Germans do not use the "Maestricht Appendix" in the first days of the war, they will not want it at all.

Let me add that I am not at all convinced about the wisdom of a close blockade, and I did not like the Admiralty statement. If the French send cruisers to Mogador and Saffi, I am of opinion that we should (for our part) move our main fleet to the north of Scotland into its war station. Our interests are European, and not Moroccan. The significance of the movement would be just as great as if we sent our two ships with the French.

Please let me know when you will be in London; and will you kindly send this letter on to the Prime Minister.

My views underwent no change in the three years of peace that followed. On the contrary they were confirmed and amplified by everything I learned. In some respects, as in the abolition of the plan of close blockade and the sending of the Fleet to its war station, I was able to carry them out. In other cases, such as the defence of Antwerp, I had not the power to do in time what I believed to be equally necessary. But I tried my best, not, as has frequently been proclaimed, upon a foolish impulse, but in pursuance of convictions reached by pondering and study. I could not help feeling a strong confidence in the truth of these convictions, when I saw how several of them were justified one after the other in that terrible and unparalleled period of convulsion. I had no doubts whatever what ought to be done in certain matters, and my only difficulty was to persuade or induce others.

The Agadir crisis came however peacefully to an end. It terminated in the diplomatic rebuff of Germany. Once more she had disturbed all Europe by a sudden and menacing gesture. Once more she had used the harshest threats towards France. For the first time she had made British statesmen feel that sense of direct contact with the war peril which was never absent from Continental minds. The French, however, offered concessions and compensations. An intricate negotiation about the frontiers of French and German territory in West Africa, in which the "Bec de Canard" played an important part, had resulted in an agreement between the two principals. To us it seemed that France had won a considerable advantage. She was not, however, particularly pleased. Her Prime Minister, Monsieur Caillaux, who had presided during those anxious days, was dismissed from office on grounds which at the time it was very difficult to appreciate here, but which viewed in the light of subsequent events can more easily be understood. The tension in German governing circles must have been very great. The German Colonial Secretary, von Lindequist, resigned rather than sign the agreement. There is no doubt that deep and violent passions of humiliation and resentment were coursing beneath the glittering uniforms which thronged the palaces through which the Kaiser moved. And of those passions the Crown Prince made himself the exponent. The world has heaped unbounded execrations upon this unlucky being. He was probably in fact no better and no worse than the average young cavalry subaltern who had not been through the ordinary mill at a public school nor had to think about earning his living. He had a considerable personal charm, which he lavished principally upon the fair sex, but which in darker days has captivated the juvenile population of Wieringen. His flattered head was turned by the burning eyes and guttural words of great captains and statesmen and party leaders. He therefore threw himself forward into this strong favouring current, and became a power, or rather the focus of a power, with which the Kaiser was forced to reckon. Germany once more proceeded to increase her armaments by land and sea.

"It was a question," writes von Tirpitz (page 191), "of our keeping our nerve, *continuing to arm on a grand scale,* avoiding all provocation, and waiting without anxiety *until our sea power was established*[1] and forced the English to let

---

[1] The italics are mine.

us breathe in peace." Only to breathe in peace! What fearful apparatus was required to secure this simple act of respiration!

We must now trace the reaction of these events in France.

Early in 1911 General Michel, Vice-President of the Superior Council of War and Commander-in-Chief designate of the French Army in the event of war, had drawn up a report upon the plan of campaign. He declared that Germany would certainly attack France through Belgium; that her turning movement would not be limited to the southern side of the Belgian Meuse but would extend far beyond it, comprising Brussels and Antwerp in its scope. He affirmed that the German General Staff would use immediately not only their twenty-one active army corps but in addition the greater part of the twenty-one reserve corps which it was known they intended to form on general mobilization. France should therefore be prepared to meet an immense turning movement through Belgium and a hostile army which would comprise *at the outset* the greater part of forty-two army corps. To confront this invasion he proposed that the French should organize and use a large proportion of their own reserves from the very beginning. For this purpose he desired to create a reserve formation at the side of each active formation, and to make both units take the field together under the officer commanding the active unit. By this means the strength of the French Army on mobilization would be raised from 1,300,000 to 2,000,000, and the German invading army would be confronted with at least equal numbers. Many of the French corps would be raised to 70,000 men and most of the regiments would become brigades of six battalions.

These forces General Michel next proceeded to distribute. He proposed to place his greatest mass, nearly 500,000 strong, between Lille and Avesnes to counter the main strength of the German turning movement. He placed a second mass of 300,000 men on the right of the first between Hirson and Rethel; he assigned 220,000 men for the garrison of Paris, which was also to act as the general reserve. His remaining troops were disposed along the Eastern frontier. Such was the plan in 1911 of the leading soldier of France.

These ideas ran directly counter to the main stream of French military thought. The General Staff did not believe that Germany would make a turning movement through Belgium, certainly not through Northern Belgium. They did not believe that the Germans would use their reserve formations in the opening battles. They did not believe that reserve formations could possibly be made capable of taking part in the struggle until after a prolonged period of training. They held, on the contrary, that the Germans, using only their active army, would attack with extreme rapidity and must be met and forestalled by a French counter-thrust across the Eastern frontier. For this purpose the French should be organized with as large a proportion of soldiers actually serving and as few reservists as possible, and with this end in view they demanded the institution of the Three Years' Service Law which would ensure the presence of at least two complete contingents of young soldiers. The dominant spirits in the French Staff, apart from their Chief, belonged to the Offensive school, of whom the most active apostle was Colonel de Grandmaison, and believed ardently that victory could be compelled from the first moment by a vehement and furious rush upon the foe.

This collision of opinion was fatal to General Michel. It may be that his personality and temperament were not equal to the profound and penetrating justice of his ideas. Such discrepancies have often marred true policies. An overwhelming combination was formed against him by his colleagues on the Council of War. During the tension of Agadir the issue reached a head. The new Minister of War, Colonel Messimy, insisted upon a discussion of the Michel scheme in full Council. The Vice-President found himself alone; almost every other General declared his direct disagreement. In consequence of this he was a few days later informed by the War Minister that he did not possess the confidence of the French Army, and on July 23 he resigned the position of Vice-President of the War Council.

It had been intended by the Government that Michel should be succeeded either by Galliéni or Pau; but Pau made claims to the appointing of General Officers which the Minister would not accept. His nomination was not proceeded with, ostensibly on the score of his age, and this pretext once given was still more valid against Galliéni, who was older. It was in these circumstances that the choice fell upon General Joffre.

Joffre was an engineer officer who, after various employments in Madagascar under Galliéni and in Morocco, had gained a reputation as a well-balanced, silent, solid man, and who in 1911 occupied a seat on the Superior Council of War. It would have been difficult to find any figure more unlike the British idea of a Frenchman than this bull-headed, broad-shouldered, slow-thinking, phlegmatic, bucolic personage. Nor would it have been easy to find a type which at the first view would have seemed less suited to weave or unravel the profound and gigantic webs of modern war. He was the junior member of the War Council. He had never commanded an army nor directed great manœuvres even in a War Game. In such exercises he had played the part of Inspector-General of the Lines of Communication, and to this post he was at that time assigned on mobilization.

Joffre received the proposal for his tremendous appointment with misgiving and embarrassment which were both natural and creditable. His reluctances were overcome by the assurance that General de Castelnau, who was deeply versed in the plans and theories of the French Staff and in the great operations of war, would be at his special disposal. Joffre therefore assumed power as the nominee of the dominant elements in the French Staff and as the exponent of their doctrines. To this conception he remained constantly loyal, and the immense disasters which France was destined to suffer three years later became from that moment almost inevitable.

General Joffre's qualities however fitted him to render most useful service to the various fleeting French Administrations which preceded the conflict. He represented and embodied "Stability" in a world of change, and "Impartiality" in a world of faction. He was a 'good Republican' with a definite political view, without being a political soldier, or one who dealt in intrigue. No one could suspect him of religion, but neither on the other hand could anyone accuse him of favouring Atheist generals at the expense of Catholics. Here at any rate was something for France, with her politicians chattering, fuming and frothing along to Armageddon, to rest her hand upon. For nearly three years and under successive Governments Joffre continued to hold his post, and we are assured that his advice on technical matters was almost always taken by the various Ministers who flitted across the darkening scene. He served under Caillaux and Messimy; he served under Poincaré and Millerand; he served under Briand and Étienne; he was still serving under Viviani and Messimy again when the explosion came.

Lastly let us return to Great Britain.

In October Mr. Asquith invited me to stay with him in Scotland. The day after I had arrived there, on our way home from the links, he asked me quite abruptly whether I would like to go to the Admiralty. He had put the same question to me when he first became Prime Minister. This time I had no doubt what to answer. All my mind was full of the dangers of war. I accepted with alacrity. I said, "Indeed I would." He said that Mr. Haldane was coming to see him the next day and we would talk it over together. But I saw that his mind was made up. The fading light of evening disclosed in the far distance the silhouettes of two battleships steaming slowly out of the Firth of Forth. They seemed invested with a new significance to me.

That night when I went to bed, I saw a large Bible lying on a table in my bedroom. My mind was dominated by the news I had received of the complete change in my station and of the task entrusted to me. I thought of the peril of Britain, peace-loving, unthinking, little prepared, of her power and virtue, and of her mission of good sense and fair-play. I thought of mighty Germany, towering up in the splendour of her Imperial State and delving down in her profound, cold, patient, ruthless calculations. I thought of the army corps I had watched tramp past, wave after wave of valiant manhood, at the Breslau manœuvres in 1907; of the thousands of strong horses dragging cannon and great howitzers up the ridges and along the roads around Wurzburg in 1910. I thought of German education and thoroughness and all that their triumphs in science and philosophy implied. I thought of the sudden and successful wars by which her power had been set up. I opened the Book at random, and in the 9th Chapter of Deuteronomy I read:

> *Hear, O Israel: Thou art to pass over Jordan this day, to go in to possess nations greater and mightier than thyself, cities great and fenced up to heaven,*
>
> *2. A people great and tall, the children of the Anakims, whom thou knowest, and of whom thou hast heard say, Who can stand before the children of Anak!*
>
> *3. Understand therefore this day, that the Lord thy God is he which goeth over before thee; as a consuming fire he shall destroy them, and he shall bring them down before thy face: so shalt thou drive them out, and destroy them quickly, as the Lord hath said unto thee.*
>
> *4. Speak not thou in thine heart, after that the Lord thy God hath cast them out from before thee, saying, For my righteousness the Lord hath brought me in to possess this land: but for the wickedness of these nations the Lord doth drive them out from before thee.*
>
> *5. Not for thy righteousness, or for the uprightness of thine heart, dost thou go to possess their land: but for the wickedness of these nations the Lord thy God doth drive them out from before thee, and that he may perform the word which the Lord sware unto thy fathers, Abraham, Isaac, and Jacob.*

It seemed a message full of reassurance.

CHAPTER IV

AT THE ADMIRALTY

Mr. McKenna and I changed guard with strict punctilio. In the morning he came over to the Home Office and I introduced him to the officials there. In the afternoon I went over to the Admiralty; he presented his Board and principal officers and departmental heads to me, and then took his leave. I knew he felt greatly his change of office, but no one would have divined it from his manner. As soon as he had gone, I convened a formal meeting of the Board, at which the Secretary read the new Letters Patent constituting me its head, and I thereupon in the words of the Order-in-Council became "responsible to Crown and Parliament for all the business of the Admiralty." I was to endeavour to discharge this responsibility for the four most memorable years of my life.

I forthwith addressed myself to those naval questions of prime importance which I conceived required new treatment. First, the War Plans of the Fleet, which up to that moment had been based upon the principle of close blockade. Second, the organization of the fleets with a view to increasing their instantly ready strength. Third, measures to guard against all aspects of surprise in the event of a sudden attack. Fourth, the formation of a Naval War Staff. Fifth, the concerting of the War Plans of the Navy and the Army by close co-operation of the two departments. Sixth, further developments in design to increase the gun power of our new ships in all classes. Seventh, changes in the high commands of the Fleet and in the composition of the Board of Admiralty.

I gave, moreover, certain personal directions to enable me "to sleep quietly in my bed." The naval magazines were to be effectively guarded under the direct charge of the Admiralty. The continuous attendance of naval officers, additional to that of the resident clerks, was provided at the Admiralty, so that at any hour of the day or night, weekdays, Sundays, or holidays, there would never be a moment lost in giving the alarm; and one of the Sea Lords was always to be on duty in or near the Admiralty building to receive it. Upon the wall behind my chair I had an open case fitted, within whose folding doors spread a large chart of the North Sea. On this chart every day a Staff Officer marked with flags the position of the German Fleet. Never once was this ceremony omitted until the war broke out, and the great maps, covering the whole of one side of the War Room, began to function. I made a rule to look at my chart once every day when I first entered my room. I did this less to keep my-self informed, for there were many other channels of information, than in order to inculcate in myself and those working with me a sense of ever-present dan-ger. In this spirit we all worked.

I must now introduce the reader to the two great Admirals-of-the-Fleet, Lord Fisher and Sir Arthur Wilson, whose outstanding qualities and life's work, afloat and at the Admiralty, added to and reacted upon by the energies and pa-triotism of Lord Charles Beresford, had largely made the Royal Navy what it was at this time. The names of both Fisher and Wilson must often recur in these pages, for they played decisive parts in the tale I have to tell.

For at least ten years all the most important steps taken to enlarge, improve or modernize the Navy had been due to Fisher. The water-tube boiler, the "all big gun ship," the introduction of the submarine ("Fisher's toys," as Lord Charles Beresford called them), the common education scheme, the system of nucleus crews for ships in reserve, and latterly—to meet the German rivalry—the concentration of the Fleets in Home waters, the scrapping of great quan-tities of ships of little fighting power, the great naval programmes of 1908 and 1909, the advance from the 12-inch to the 13.5-inch gun—all in the main were his.

In carrying through these far-reaching changes he had created violent op-positions to himself in the Navy, and his own methods, in which he gloried, were of a kind to excite bitter animosities, which he returned and was eager to repay. He made it known, indeed he proclaimed, that officers of whatever rank who opposed his policies would have their professional careers ruined. As for traitors, i.e. those who struck at him openly or secretly, "their wives should be widows, their children fatherless, their homes a dunghill." This he repeated again and again. "Ruthless, relentless and remorseless" were words always on his lips, and many grisly examples of Admirals and Captains eating out their hearts "on the beach" showed that he meant what he said. He did not hesitate to ex-press his policy in the most unfavourable terms, as if to challenge and defy his enemies and critics. "Favouritism," he wrote in the log of Dartmouth College, "is the secret of efficiency." What he meant by "favouritism" was selection with-out regard to seniority by a discerning genius in the interests of the public; but the word "favouritism" stuck. Officers were said to be "in the fish-pond"—unlucky for them if they were not. He poured contempt upon the opinions and arguments of those who did not agree with his schemes, and abused them roundly at all times both by word and letter.

In the Royal Navy, however, there were a considerable number of officers of social influence and independent means, many of whom became hostile to Fisher. They had access to Parliament and to the Press. In sympathy with them, though not with all their methods, was a much larger body of good and proved sea officers. At the head of the whole opposition stood Lord Charles Beresford, at that time Commander-in-Chief of the Channel or principal Fleet. A deplorable schism was introduced into the Royal Navy, which spread to every squadron and to every ship. There were Fisher's men and Beresford's men. Whatever the First Sea Lord proposed the Commander-in-Chief opposed, and through the whole of the Service Captains and Lieutenants were encouraged to take one side or the other. The argument was conducted with technicalities and with personalities. Neither side was strong enough to crush the other. The Admiralty had its backers in the Fleet, and the Fleet had its friends in the Admiralty: both sides therefore had good information as to what was passing in the other camp. The lamentable situation thus created might easily have ruined the discipline of the Navy but for the fact that a third large body of officers resolutely refused, at whatever cost to themselves, to participate in the struggle. Silently and steadfastly they went about their work till the storms of partisanship were past. To these officers a debt is due.

There is no doubt whatever that Fisher was right in nine-tenths of what he fought for. His great reforms sustained the power of the Royal Navy at the most critical period in its history. He gave the Navy the kind of shock which the British Army received at the time of the South African War. After a long period of serene and unchallenged complacency, the mutter of distant thunder could be heard. It was Fisher who hoisted the storm-signal and beat all hands to quarters. He forced every department of the Naval Service to review its position and question its own existence. He shook them and beat them and cajoled them out of slumber into intense activity. But the Navy was not a pleasant place while this was going on. The "Band of Brothers" tradition which Nelson had handed down, was for the time, but only for the time, discarded; and behind the open hostility of chieftains flourished the venomous intrigues of their followers.

I have asked myself whether all this could not have been avoided; whether we could not have had the Fisher reforms without the Fisher methods. My conviction is that Fisher was maddened by the difficulties and obstructions which he encountered, and became violent in the process of fighting so hard at every step. In the government of a great fighting service there must always be the combination of the political and professional authorities. A strong First Sea Lord, to carry out a vigorous policy, needs the assistance of a Minister, who alone can support him and defend him. The authority of both is more than doubled by their union. Each can render the other services of supreme importance when they are both effective factors. Working in harmony, they multiply each other. By the resultant concentration of combined power, no room or chance is given to faction. For good or for ill what they decide together in the interests of the Service must be loyally accepted. Unhappily, the later years of

Fisher's efforts were years in which the Admiralty was ruled by two Ministers, both of whom were desperately and even mortally ill. Although most able and most upright public men, both Lord Cawdor and Lord Tweedmouth, First Lords from 1904 to 1908, were afflicted with extreme ill-health. Moreover, neither was in the House of Commons and able himself, by exposition in the responsible Chamber, to proclaim in unquestioned accents the policy which the Admiralty would follow and which the House of Commons should ratify. When in 1908 Mr. McKenna became First Lord, there was a change. Gifted with remarkable clearness of mind and resolute courage, enjoying in the prime of life the fullest vigour of his faculties, and having acquired a strong political position in the House of Commons, he was able to supply an immediate steadying influence. But it was too late for Fisher. The Furies were upon his track. The opposition and hatreds had already grown too strong. The schism in the Navy continued, fierce and open.

The incident which is most commonly associated with the end of this part of his career is that of the "Bacon letters." Captain Bacon was one of the ablest officers in the Navy and a strong Fisherite. In 1906 he had been serving in the Mediterranean under Lord Charles Beresford. Fisher had asked him to write to him from time to time and keep him informed of all that passed. This he did in letters in themselves of much force and value, but open to the reproach of containing criticisms of his immediate commander. This in itself might have escaped unnoticed; but the First Sea Lord used to print in beautiful and carefully considered type, letters, notes and memoranda on technical subjects for the instruction and encouragement of the faithful. Delighted at the cogency of the arguments in the Bacon letters, he had them printed in 1909 and circulated fairly widely throughout the Admiralty. A copy fell at length into hostile hands and was swiftly conveyed to a London evening newspaper. The First Sea Lord was accused of encouraging subordinates in disloyalty to their immediate commanders. The episode was fatal, and at the beginning of 1910 Sir John Fisher quitted the Admiralty and passed, as everyone believed, finally into retirement and the House of Lords, crowned with achievements, loaded with honours, but pursued by much obloquy, amid the triumph of his foes.

As soon as I knew for certain that I was to go to the Admiralty I sent for Fisher: he was abroad in sunshine. We had not seen each other since the dispute about the Naval Estimates of 1909. He conceived himself bound in loyalty to Mr. McKenna, but as soon as he learned that I had had nothing to do with the decision which had led to our changing offices, he hastened home. We passed three days together in the comfort of Reigate Priory.

I found Fisher a veritable volcano of knowledge and of inspiration; and as soon as he learnt what my main purpose was, he passed into a state of vehement eruption. It must indeed have been an agony to him to wait and idly watch from the calm Lake of Lucerne through the anxious weeks of the long-drawn Agadir crisis, with his life's work, his beloved Navy, liable at any moment to be put to the supreme test. Once he began, he could hardly stop. I plied him with questions, and he poured out ideas. It was always a joy to me to talk to him on these great matters, but most of all was he stimulating in all that related to the design of ships. He also talked brilliantly about Admirals, but here one had to make a heavy discount on account of the feuds. My intention was to hold the balance even, and while adopting in the main the Fisher policy, to insist upon an absolute cessation of the vendetta.

Knowing pretty well all that has been written in the preceding pages, I began our conversations with no thought of Fisher's recall. But by the Sunday night the power of the man was deeply borne in upon me, and I had almost made up my mind to do what I did three years later, and place him again at the head of the Naval Service. It was not the outcry that I feared; that I felt strong enough at this time to face. But it was the revival and continuance of the feuds; and it was clear from his temper that this would be inevitable. Then, too, I was apprehensive of his age. I could not feel complete confidence in the poise of the mind at 71. All the way up to London the next morning I was on the brink of saying "Come and help me," and had he by a word seemed to wish to return, I would surely have spoken. But he maintained a proper dignity, and in an hour we were in London. Other reflections supervened, adverse counsels were not lacking, and in a few days I had definitely made up my mind to look elsewhere for a First Sea Lord.

I wonder whether I was right or wrong.

For a man who for so many years filled great official positions and was charged with so much secret and deadly business, Lord Fisher appeared amazingly voluminous and reckless in correspondence. When for the purpose of this work and for the satisfaction of his biographers I collected all the letters I had received from the Admiral in his own hand, they amounted when copied to upwards of 300 closely typewritten pages. In the main they repeat again and again the principal naval conceptions and doctrines with which his life had been associated. Although it would be easy to show many inconsistencies and apparent contradictions, the general message is unchanging. The letters are also presented in an entertaining guise, interspersed with felicitous and sometimes recondite quotations, with flashing phrases and images, with mordant jokes and corrosive personalities. All were dashed off red-hot as they left his mind, his strong pen galloping along in the wake of the imperious thought. He would often audaciously fling out on paper thoughts which other people would hardly admit to their own minds. It is small wonder that his turbulent passage left so many foes foaming in his wake. The wonder is that he did not shipwreck himself a score of times. The buoyancy of his genius alone supported the burden.

Indeed, in the process of years the profuse and imprudent violence of his letters became, in a sense, its own protection. People came to believe that this was the breezy style appropriate to our guardians of the deep, and the old Admiral swept forward on his stormy course.

To me, in this period of preparation, the arrival of his letters was always a source of lively interest and pleasure. I was regaled with eight or ten closely-written double pages, fastened together with a little pearl pin or a scrap of silken ribbon, containing every kind of news and counsel, varying from blistering reproach to the highest forms of inspiration and encouragement. From the very beginning his letters were couched in an affectionate and paternal style. "My beloved Winston," they began, ending usually with a variation of "Yours to a cinder," "Yours till Hell freezes," or "Till charcoal sprouts," followed by a P.S. and two or three more pages of pregnant and brilliant matter. I have found it impossible to re-read these letters without sentiments of strong regard for him, his fiery soul, his volcanic energy, his deep creative mind, his fierce outspoken hatreds, his love of England. Alas, there was a day when Hell froze and charcoal sprouted and friendship was reduced to cinders; when "My beloved Winston" had given place to "First Lord: I can no longer be your colleague." I am glad to be able to chronicle that this was not the end of our long and intimate relationship.

Sir Arthur Wilson, the First Sea Lord, received me with his customary dignified simplicity. He could not, of course, be wholly unaware of the main causes which had brought me to the Admiralty. In conversation with the other Sea Lords when the well-kept secret of my appointment first reached the Admiralty, he said: "We are to have new masters: if they wish us to serve them, we will do so, and if not, they will find others to carry on the work." I had only met him hitherto at the conferences of the Committee of Imperial Defence, and my opinions were divided between an admiration for all I heard of his character and a total disagreement with what I understood to be his strategic views. He considered the creation of a War Staff quite unnecessary: I had come to set one up. He did not approve of the War Office plans for sending an army to France in the event of war: I considered it my duty to perfect these arrangements to the smallest detail. He was, as I believed, still an advocate of a close blockade of the German ports, which to my lay or military mind the torpedo seemed already to have rendered impossible.[1] These were large and vital differences. He on his side probably thought we had got into an unnecessary panic over the

---

[1] The close blockade of the German ports was prescribed in the war orders of 1909, during Lord Fisher's term of office. Sir Arthur Wilson did not reveal any modification which he had made in consequence of new conditions to anyone.

Agadir crisis, and that we did not properly understand the strength and mobility of the British Fleet nor the true character of British strategic power. He was due to retire for age from the Service in three or four months, unless his tenure had been extended, while I, for my part, came to the Admiralty with a very clear intention to have an entirely new Board of my own choosing. In these circumstances our association was bound to be bleak.

This is, however, the moment for me to give an impression of this striking naval personality. He was, without any exception, the most selfless man I have ever met or even read of. He wanted nothing, and he feared nothing—absolutely nothing. Whether he was commanding the British Fleet or repairing an old motor car, he was equally keen, equally interested, equally content. To step from a great office into absolute retirement, to return from retirement to the pinnacle of naval power, were transitions which produced no change in the beat of that constant heart. Everything was duty. It was not merely that nothing else mattered. There was nothing else. One did one's duty as well as one possibly could, be it great or small, and naturally one deserved no reward. This had been the spirit in which he had lived his long life afloat, and which by his example he had spread far and wide through the ranks of the Navy. It made him seem very unsympathetic on many occasions, both to officers and men. Orders were orders, whether they terminated an officer's professional career or led him on to fame, whether they involved the most pleasant or the most disagreeable work; and he would snap his teeth, and smile his wintry smile to all complaints and to sentiment and emotion in every form. Never once did I see his composure disturbed. He never opened up, never unbent. Never once, until a very dark day for me, did I learn that my work had met with favour in his eyes.

All the same, for all his unsympathetic methods, "Tug," as he was generally called (because he was always working, i.e. pulling, hauling, tugging), or alternatively "old 'Ard 'Art," was greatly loved in the Fleet. Men would do hard and unpleasant work even when they doubted its necessity, because he had ordered it and it was "his way." He had served as a midshipman in the Crimean War. Everyone knew the story of his V.C., when the square broke at Tamai in the Soudan, and when he was seen, with the ammunition of his Gatling exhausted, knocking the Dervish spearmen over one after another with his fists, using the broken hilt of his sword as a sort of knuckle-duster. Stories were told of his apparent insensibility to weather and climate. He would wear a thin monkey-jacket in mid-winter in the North Sea with apparent comfort while everyone else was shivering in great-coats. He would stand bareheaded under a tropical sun without ill-effects. He had a strong inventive turn of mind, and considerable mechanical knowledge. The system of counter-mining in use for forty years in the Navy, and the masthead semaphore which continued till displaced by wireless telegraphy, were both products of his ingenuity. He was an experienced and masterly commander of a Fleet at sea. In addition to this, he expressed himself with great clearness and thoroughness on paper, many of his documents being extended arguments of exact detail and widely comprehensive scope. He impressed me from the first as a man of the highest quality and stature, but, as I thought, dwelling too much in the past of naval science, not sufficiently receptive of new ideas when conditions were changing so rapidly, and, of course, tenacious and unyielding in the last degree.

After we had had several preliminary talks and I found we were not likely to reach an agreement, I sent him a minute about the creation of a Naval War Staff, which raised an unmistakable issue. He met it by a powerfully reasoned and unqualified refusal, and I then determined to form a new Board of Admiralty without delay. The Lords of the Admiralty hold quasi-ministerial appointments, and it was of course necessary to put my proposals before the Prime Minister and obtain his assent. After informing him on November 5 that, in view of Sir Arthur Wilson's opposition to the whole principle of a War Staff for the Navy, I considered it imperative that a new Board of Admiralty be installed no later than January, I was able on November 16 to send him my full proposals: Sir Francis Bridgeman as First Sea Lord, Prince Louis of Battenberg as Second Sea Lord, Captain Pakenham as Fourth Sea Lord; Rear-Admiral Briggs was to be retained in his post as Controller and Third Sea Lord. Vice-Admiral Sir George Callaghan, second in command, was proposed to replace Sir Francis Bridgeman in command of the Home Fleet. The decisive appointment afloat, however, was that of Sir John Jellicoe as second in command. He thus in effect passed over the heads of four or five of the most important senior Admirals on the active list and became virtually designated for the supreme command in the near future.

The announcement of these changes (November 28) created a considerable sensation in the House of Commons when, late at night, they became known. All the Sea Lords, except one, had been replaced by new men. I was immediately interrogated, "Had they resigned, or been told to go?" and so on. I gave briefly such explanations as were necessary. At this time I was very strong, because most of those who knew the inner history of the Agadir crisis were troubled about the Fleet, and it was well known that I had been sent to the Admiralty to make a new and a vehement effort.

Sir Arthur Wilson and I parted on friendly, civil, but at the same time cool terms. He showed not the least resentment at the short curtailment of his tenure. He was as good-tempered and as distant as ever. Only once did he show the slightest sign of vehemence. That was when I told him that the Prime Minister was willing to submit his name to the King for a Peerage. He disengaged himself from this with much vigour. What would he do with such a thing? It would be ridiculous. However, His Majesty resolved to confer upon him the

Order of Merit, and this he was finally persuaded to accept. On his last night in office he gave a dinner to the new Sea Lords in the true "Band of Brothers" style, and then retired to Norfolk. I could not help thinking uncomfortably of the famous Tenniel cartoon, "Dropping the Pilot," where the inexperienced and impulsive German Emperor is depicted carelessly watching the venerable figure of Bismarck descending the ladder. Nevertheless I had acted on high public grounds and on those alone, and I fortified myself with them.

As will be seen in its proper place, I was to work with Sir Arthur Wilson again later on.

A few weeks after my arrival at the Admiralty I was told that among several officers of Flag rank who wished to see me was Rear-Admiral Beatty. I had never met him before, but I had the following impressions about him. First, that he was the youngest Flag Officer in the Fleet. Second, that he had commanded the white gunboat which had come up the Nile as close as possible to support the 21st Lancers when we made the charge at Omdurman. Third, that he had seen a lot of fighting on land with the army, and that consequently he had military as well as naval experience. Fourth, that he came of a hard-riding stock; his father had been in my own regiment, the 4th Hussars, and I had often heard him talked of when I first joined. The Admiral, I knew, was a very fine horseman, with what is called "an eye for country." Fifth, that there was much talk in naval circles of his having been pushed on too fast. Such were the impressions aroused in my mind by the name of this officer, and I record them with minuteness because the decisions which I had the honour of taking in regard to him were most serviceable to the Royal Navy and to the British arms.

I was, however, advised about him at the Admiralty in a decisively adverse sense. He had got on too fast, he had many interests ashore. His heart it was said was not wholly in the Service. He had been offered an appointment in the Atlantic Fleet suited to his rank as Rear-Admiral. He had declined this appointment—a very serious step for a Naval Officer to take when appointments were few in proportion to candidates—and he should in consequence not be offered any further employment. It would be contrary to precedent to make a further offer. He had already been unemployed for eighteen months, and would probably be retired in the ordinary course at the expiration of the full three years' unemployment.

But my first meeting with the Admiral induced me immediately to disregard this unfortunate advice. He became at once my Naval Secretary (or Private Secretary, as the appointment was then styled). Working thus side by side in rooms which communicated, we perpetually discussed during the next fifteen months the problems of a naval war with Germany. It became increasingly clear to me that he viewed questions of naval strategy and tactics in a different light from the average naval officer: he approached them, as it seemed to me, much more as a soldier would. His war experiences on land had illuminated the facts he had acquired in his naval training. He was no mere instrumentalist. He did not think of *matériel* as an end in itself but only as a means. He thought of war problems in their unity by land, sea and air. His mind had been rendered quick and supple by the situations of polo and the hunting-field, and enriched by varied experiences against the enemy on Nile gunboats, and ashore. It was with equal pleasure and profit that I discussed with him our naval problem, now from this angle, now from that; and I was increasingly struck with the shrewd and profound sagacity of his comments expressed in language singularly free from technical jargon.

I had no doubts whatever when the command of the Battle-Cruiser Squadron fell vacant in the spring of 1913, in appointing him over the heads of all to this incomparable command, the nucleus as it proved to be of the famous Battle-Cruiser Fleet—the strategic cavalry of the Royal Navy, that supreme combination of speed and power to which the thoughts of the Admiralty were continuously directed. And when two years later (February 3, 1915) I visited him on board the *Lion,* with the scars of victorious battle fresh upon her from the action of the Dogger Bank, I heard from his Captains and his Admirals the expression of their respectful but intense enthusiasm for their leader. Well do I remember how, as I was leaving the ship, the usually imperturbable Admiral Pakenham caught me by the sleeve, "First Lord, I wish to speak to you in private," and the intense conviction in his voice as he said, "Nelson has come again." Those words often recurred to my mind.

So much of my work in endeavouring to prepare the Fleet for war was dependent upon the guidance and help I received from Prince Louis of Battenberg, who, taking it as a whole, was my principal counsellor, as Second Sea Lord from January, 1912, to March, 1913 (when Sir Francis Bridgeman's health temporarily failed), and as First Sea Lord thenceforward to the end of October, 1914, that it is necessary to give some description of this remarkable Prince and British sailor. All the more is this necessary since the accident of his parentage struck him down in the opening months of the Great War and terminated his long professional career.

Prince Louis was a child of the Royal Navy. From his earliest years he had been bred to the sea. The deck of a British warship was his home. All his interest was centred in the British Fleet. So far from his exalted rank having helped him, it had hindered his career: up to a certain point no doubt it had been of assistance, but after that it had been a positive drawback. In consequence he had spent an exceptionally large proportion of his forty years' service afloat usually in the less agreeable commands. One had heard at Malta how he used to bring his Cruiser Squadron into that small, crowded harbour at speed and then in the nick of time, with scarcely a hundred yards to spare, by dropping his anchors, checking on his cables and going full speed astern, bring it safely into station. He had a far wider knowledge of war by land and sea and of the Continent of Europe than most of the other Admirals I have known. His brother, as King of Bulgaria, had shown military aptitudes of a very high order at the Battle of Slivnitza, and he himself was deeply versed in every detail, practical and theoretic, of the British Naval Service. It was not without good reason that he had been appointed under Lord Fisher to be Head of the British Naval Intelligence Department, that vital ganglion of our organization. He was a thoroughly trained and accomplished Staff Officer, with a gift of clear and lucid statement and all that thoroughness and patient industry which we have never underestimated in the German race.

It was recounted of him that on one occasion, when he visited Kiel with King Edward, a German Admiral in high command had reproached him with serving in the British Fleet, whereat Prince Louis, stiffening, had replied, "Sir, when I joined the Royal Navy in the year 1868, the German Empire did not exist."

The part which he played in the events with which I am dealing, will be recorded as the story unfolds.

Our first labour was the creation of the War Staff. All the details of this were worked out by Prince Louis and approved by the First Sea Lord. I also resorted to Sir Douglas Haig, at that time in command at Aldershot. The general furnished me with a masterly paper setting forth the military doctrine of Staff organization and constituting in many respects a formidable commentary on existing naval methods. Armed with these various opinions, I presented my conclusions to the public in January, 1912, in a document, designed so far as possible to disarm the prejudices of the naval service.

I never ceased to labour at the formation of a true General Staff for the Navy.

But such a task requires a generation. No wave of the wand can create those habits of mind in seniors on which the efficiency and even the reality of a Staff depends. Young officers can be trained, but thereafter they have to rise step by step in the passage of time to positions of authority in the Service. The dead weight of professional opinion was adverse. They had got on well enough without it before. They did not want a special class of officer professing to be more brainy than the rest. Sea-time should be the main qualification, and next to that technical aptitudes. Thus when I went to the Admiralty I found that there was no moment in the career and training of a naval officer, when he was obliged to read a single book about naval war, or pass even the most rudimentary examination in naval history. The Royal Navy had made no important contribution to Naval literature. The standard work on Sea Power was written by an American Admiral.[1] The best accounts of British sea fighting and naval strategy were compiled by an English civilian.[2] "The Silent Service" was not mute because it was absorbed in thought and study, but because it was weighted down by its daily routine and by its ever-complicating and diversifying technique. We had competent administrators, brilliant experts of every description, unequalled navigators, good disciplinarians, fine sea-officers, brave and devoted hearts: but at the outset of the conflict we had more captains of ships than captains of war. In this will be found the explanation of many untoward events. At least fifteen years of consistent policy were required to give the Royal Navy that widely extended outlook upon war problems and of war situations without which seamanship, gunnery, instrumentalisms of every kind, devotion of the highest order, could not achieve their due reward.

Fifteen years! And we were only to have thirty months!

I have shown how forward the Chancellor of the Exchequer was during the crisis of Agadir in every matter that could add to the strength of the British attitude. But as soon as the danger was passed he adopted a different demeanour. He felt that an effort should be made to heal any smart from which Germany might be suffering, and to arrive at a common understanding on naval strength. We knew that a formidable new Navy Law was in preparation and would shortly be declared. If Germany had definitely made up her mind to antagonize Great Britain, we must take up the challenge; but it might be possible by friendly, sincere and intimate conversation to avert this perilous development. We were no enemies to German Colonial expansion, and we would even have taken active steps to further her wishes in this respect. Surely something could be done to break the chain of blind causation. If aiding Germany in the Colonial sphere was a means of procuring a stable situation, it was a price we were well prepared to pay. I was in full accord with this view. Apart from wider reasons, I felt I should be all the stronger in asking the Cabinet and the House of Commons for the necessary monies, if I could go hand in hand with the Chancellor of the Exchequer and testify that we had tried our best to secure a mitigation of the naval rivalry and failed. We therefore jointly consulted Sir Edward Grey, and then with the Prime Minister's concurrence we invited Sir Ernest Cassel to go to Berlin and get into direct touch with the Emperor. Sir Ernest was qualified for this task, as he knew the Emperor well and was at the same time devoted to British interests. We armed him with a brief but pregnant memorandum, which cannot be more tersely summarized than in von Bethmann-Hollweg's own words[3]: "Acceptance of English superiority at sea—no

---

[1] Admiral Mahan.
[2] Sir Julian Corbett.
[3] *Reflections on the World War,* v. Bethmann-Hollweg, p. 48.

augmentation of the German naval programme—a reduction as far as possible of that programme—and on the part of England, no impediment to our Colonial expansion—discussion and promotion of our Colonial ambitions—proposals for mutual declarations that the two Powers would not take part in aggressive plans or combinations against one another." Cassel accepted the charge and started at once. He remained only two days in Berlin and came at once to me on his return. He brought with him a cordial letter from the Emperor and a fairly full statement by von Bethmann-Hollweg of the new German Navy Law. We devoured this invaluable document all night long in the Admiralty. It made it plain that our contemplated six-year programme of 4, 3, 4, 3, 4, 3, as against their 2, 2, 2, 2, 2, 2, must be increased to 5, 4, 5, 4, 5, 4, to meet their prospective 3, 2, 3, 2, 3, 2. This would maintain a 60 per cent superiority in Dreadnoughts and Dreadnought Cruisers over Germany only, and would lay down two keels to their one on their additional three ships. The creation of a third German squadron would compel us to bring home the Mediterranean battleships and rely on France in the Mediterranean. To meet their increase in personnel we should have to double our intended increase, and add 4,000 men in that year and 4,000 in the next.

We laid these matters before the Cabinet, who decided that a British Cabinet Minister should go to Berlin and selected Mr. Haldane for that purpose. After preliminary exchanges between the Governments, the Secretary of State for War accompanied by Sir Ernest Cassel, started on February 6 for Berlin.

I had undertaken some weeks earlier to make a speech in support of the Home Rule Bill in Belfast. Violent hostility to this project developed in the inflammable capital of Ulster. Being publicly committed, I had no choice but to fulfil my engagement, though to avoid unnecessary provocation the meeting-place was changed from the Ulster Hall to a large tent which was erected in the outskirts of the city. Threats of violence and riot were loudly proclaimed on every side and nearly 10,000 troops were concentrated in the area to keep the peace. I had planned, if all went well at Belfast, to go on the next day to Glasgow to inspect some of the shipbuilding works along the Clyde, and to make a speech on the Naval position, which should state very plainly our root intentions and be the necessary counterpart of the Haldane mission. As I was waiting for the train for Ireland to leave the London railway station, I read in the late edition of the evening papers the German Emperor's speech on the opening of the Reichstag announcing Bills for the increase both of the Army and the Navy. The new Navy Law was still a secret to the British and German nations alike, but knowing as I did its scope and character and viewing it in conjunction with the Army Bill, I sustained a strong impression at this moment of the approaching danger. One sentence, full of German self-revelation, stood out vividly. "It is my constant duty and care to maintain and to strengthen on land

and water, the power of defence of the German people, *which has no lack of young men fit to bear arms.*" It was indeed true. One thought of France with her declining birth-rate peering out across her fortresses into the wide German lands and silently reflecting on these "young men fit to bear arms" of whom there was indeed "no lack." My mind, skipping over the day of Irish turmoil and the worry of the speech that lay before me, fixed upon Glasgow as the place where some answer to this threat of continental domination might perhaps be provided. Once again Europe might find a safeguard against military overlordship in an island which had never been and never would be "lacking in trained and hardy mariners bred from their boyhood up to the service of the sea."

Accordingly, after the Irish ordeal was over, I said at Glasgow:

The purposes of British naval power are essentially defensive. We have no thoughts, and we have never had any thoughts of aggression, and we attribute no such thoughts to other great Powers. There is, however, this difference between the British naval power and the naval power of the great and friendly Empire—and I trust it may long remain the great and friendly Empire—of Germany. The British Navy is to us a necessity and, from some points of view, the German Navy is to them more in the nature of a luxury. Our naval power involves British existence. It is existence to us; it is expansion to them . . .

We have great reserves of seamen in this country. There are measures which may be taken to make a greater use of our reserves than has hitherto been found possible, and I have given directions for that part of the subject to be carefully studied by the naval experts upon whom I rely. Our reserves, both from the Royal Navy and from the Mercantile Marine, are a great resource, *and this island has never been, and never will be, lacking in trained and hardy mariners bred from their boyhood up to the service of the sea.*

Whatever may happen abroad there will be no whining here, no signals of distress will be hoisted, no cries for help or succour will go up. We will face the future as our ancestors would have faced it, without disquiet, without arrogance, but in stolid and inflexible determination. We should be the first Power to welcome any retardation or slackening of naval rivalry. We should meet any such slackening not by words but by deeds. . . .

If there are to be increases upon the Continent of Europe, we shall have no difficulty in meeting them to the satisfaction of the country. *As naval competition becomes more acute, we shall have not only to increase the number of the ships we build, but the ratio which our naval strength will have to bear to other great naval Powers,* so that our margin of superiority will become larger and not smaller as the strain grows greater. Thus we shall make it clear that other naval Powers, instead of overtaking us by additional efforts, will only be more outdistanced in consequence of the measures which we ourselves shall take.

This speech created a considerable outcry in Germany, which was immediately re-echoed by a very large proportion of our own Liberal press. It appeared that the word "luxury" had a bad significance when translated into German. The *"Luxus Flotte"* became an expression passed angrily from lip to lip in Germany. As I expected, on my return to London I found my colleagues offended. Their congratulations upon Belfast were silenced by their reproaches about Glasgow. Mr. Haldane returned two days later from Berlin, and the Cabinet was summoned to receive an account of his mission. Contrary to general expectation, however, the Secretary of State for War declared that so far from being a hindrance to him in his negotiations, the Glasgow speech had been the greatest possible help. He had in fact used almost identical arguments to von Bethmann-Hollweg the day before. He had told the Chancellor that if Germany added a third squadron we should have "to maintain five or even six squadrons in Home waters, perhaps bringing ships from the Mediterranean to strengthen them"; that if ships were added to the existing programme we should "proceed at once to lay down two keels to each of the new German additions"; and that for the sake of the Navy "people would not complain of the addition of another shilling to the income tax." He described how he had read the operative passages in my speech himself to the Emperor and von Tirpitz in proof and confirmation of what he had himself been saying during their previous discussions. This settled the matter so far as I was concerned. It was only another instance of the very manly and loyal part which Mr. Haldane took at all times and on every question connected with the preparedness of this country for war with Germany.

Mr. Haldane brought back with him the actual text of the new German Navy Law, or "Novelle" as it was called. This had been handed to him by the Emperor during the course of the discussion. It was an elaborate technical document. Mr. Haldane had had the prudence to refuse to express any opinion upon it till it had been examined by the Admiralty experts. We now subjected this document to a rigorous scrutiny. The result more than confirmed first unfavourable impressions.

On March 9 I pointed out that the fundamental proposition of the negotiations from the Admiralty point of view had been that the existing German Navy Law should not be increased, but, if possible, reduced, whereas on the contrary a new law was certainly to be enacted providing for large and progressive increases not only in 1912 but in the five following years. Practically four-fifths of the German Navy were to be placed permanently upon a war footing. The German Government would be able to have available at all seasons of the year twenty-five, or perhaps twenty-nine, fully commissioned battleships, "whereas at the present time the British Government have in full commission in Home waters only twenty-two, even counting the Atlantic Fleet."

Thus on the fundamental proposition we encountered an unyielding attitude. Nevertheless we persevered and the discussion was transferred to the question of a mutual declaration against aggressive plans. Here Sir Edward Grey offered the following formula: "England will make no unprovoked attack upon Germany, and pursue no aggressive policy towards her. Aggression upon Germany is not the subject, and forms no part of any treaty, understanding, or combination to which England is now a party, nor will she become a party to anything that has such an object." The German Government considered this formula inadequate and suggested through their Ambassador the following additional clause: "England will therefore observe at least a benevolent neutrality should war be forced upon Germany"; or, "England will therefore, as a matter of course, remain neutral if a war is forced upon Germany."

This last condition would have carried us far beyond our original intention, and might well have been held to deprive us of the power to come to the aid of France in a war "forced," or alleged to be "forced," upon Germany as the result of a quarrel between Austria and Russia. It would certainly have been regarded as terminating the *Entente*. Moreover, even if we had taken this step the new German Navy Law was not to be withdrawn. At the most it was to be modified. Thus a complete deadlock was reached at an early stage. Still, so important did we think it to create at least a friendly spirit, and so desirous were we of placating Germany and gratifying her aspirations, that we still persisted in an endeavour to come to an arrangement beneficial to Germany in the colonial sphere. These negotiations were still progressing and had almost reached a conclusion definitely advantageous to Germany, when the war broke out.

Early in March, while the new German Navy Law was still unannounced, it was necessary to present our Estimates to the House of Commons. It would of course have been a breach of faith with the German Emperor to let any suggestion pass my lips that we already knew what the text of the Navy Law was. I was therefore obliged to make my first speech on naval matters on a purely hypothetical basis: "This is what we are going to do if no further increases are made in the German Fleet. Should unhappily the rumours which we hear prove true, I shall have to present a Supplementary Estimate to the House, etc."

In this speech I laid down clearly, with the assent of the Cabinet, the principles which should govern our naval construction in the next five years, and the standards of strength we should follow in capital ships. This standard was as follows: Sixty per cent in Dreadnoughts over Germany as long as she adhered to her present declared programme, and two keels to one for every additional ship laid down by her. Any ships provided by the Dominions were to be additional to anything we might build ourselves. Otherwise the efforts of the Dominions would not have resulted in any accession to our naval strength, and consequently these efforts might have been discouraged. Proceeding on these lines I set out the six years of British construction at 4, 3, 4, 3, 4, 3, against a uniform German construction of 2. These numbers were well received by the House of Commons. We were not sure whether the Germans would adhere to an offer made to Mr. Haldane to drop one of the three extra ships embodied in their new Navy Law. This, however, proved ultimately to be the case and was at any rate a tangible result of the Haldane mission. In Tirpitz's words: "He (Haldane) next came out with a proposal of a certain delay in the building of the three ships; could we not distribute them over twelve years? . . . He only wanted a token of our readiness to meet England, more for the sake of form. . . . Haldane himself proposed that we should retard the rate of our increase 'in order to lubricate the negotiations,' or that we should at least cancel the first of the three ships. He outlined in writing of his own accord the same principle which I had previously fixed upon in my own mind as a possible concession. I *therefore sacrificed the ship.*"

We therefore "sacrificed" two hypothetical ships, and our programmes, which would have been increased to 5, 4, 5, 4, 5, 4, were ultimately declared at 4, 5, 4, 4, 4, 4. The splendid gift of the *Malaya* by the Federated Malay States raised the figure of the first year from 4 to 5.

In announcing these decisions to Parliament later in the same month I made publicly and definitely those proposals for a Naval Holiday which were fruitless so far as Britain and Germany were concerned, but the principle of which has since been adopted by the English-speaking peoples of the world:

> Take, as an instance of this proposition I am putting forward for general consideration, the year 1913. In that year, as I apprehend, Germany will build three capital ships, and it will be necessary for us to build five in consequence.
>
> Supposing we were both to take a holiday for that year and introduce a blank page into the book of misunderstanding; supposing that Germany were to build no ships that year, she would save herself between six and seven millions sterling. But that is not all. In ordinary circumstances we should not begin our ships until Germany had started hers. The three ships that she did not build would therefore automatically wipe out no fewer than five British potential super-Dreadnoughts. That is more than I expect they could hope to do in a brilliant naval action.

By the beginning of April it became certain that no general arrangement for a naval holiday could be effected with Germany. The Emperor sent me a courteous message through Sir Ernest Cassel expressing his great regret, but adding that such arrangements would only be possible between allies.

The growth of the German Navy produced its inevitable consequences. The British Fleet for safety's sake had to be concentrated in Home waters. We saw ourselves compelled to withdraw the battleships from the Mediterranean. Only by this measure could the trained men be obtained to form the Third Battle Squadron in full commission in Home waters. It was decided by the Cabinet that we must still maintain a powerful force in the Mediterranean, and ultimately, four battle cruisers and an armoured cruiser squadron were accordingly based on Malta. It was further decided that a Dreadnought battle squadron should also be developed in the Mediterranean by the year 1916 equal in strength to that of the growing Austrian battle fleet. These decisions were taken with the deliberate object of regaining our complete independence. But the withdrawal—even if only for a few years—of the battleships from the Mediterranean was a noteworthy event. It made us appear to be dependent upon the French Fleet in those waters. The French also at the same time redisposed their forces. Under the growing pressure of German armaments Britain transferred her whole Battle Fleet to the North Sea, and France moved all her heavy ships into the Mediterranean. And the sense of mutual reliance grew swiftly between both navies.

It is astonishing that Admiral von Tirpitz should never have comprehended what the consequences of his policy must be. Even after the war he could write:

> In order to estimate the strength of the trump card which our fleet put in the hands of an energetic diplomacy at this time, one must remember that in consequence of the concentration of the English forces which we had caused in the North Sea, the English control of the Mediterranean and Far-Eastern waters had practically ceased.

The only "trump card" which Germany secured by this policy was the driving of Britain and France closer and closer together. From the moment that the Fleets of France and Britain were disposed in this new way our common naval interests became very important. And the moral claims which France could make upon Great Britain if attacked by Germany, whatever we had stipulated to the contrary, were enormously extended. Indeed, my anxiety was aroused to try to prevent this necessary recall of our ships from tying us up too tightly with France and depriving us of that liberty of choice on which our power to stop a war might well depend.

When in August, 1912, the Cabinet decided that naval conversations should take place between the French and British Admiralties, similar to those which had been held since 1906 between the General Staffs, I set forth this point as clearly as possible in a minute which I addressed to the Prime Minister and the Foreign Secretary, and we did our utmost to safeguard ourselves.

August 23, 1912.

Sir Edward Grey,
Prime Minister.

The point I am anxious to safeguard is our freedom of choice if the occasion arises, and consequent power to influence French policy beforehand. That freedom will be sensibly impaired if the French can say that they have denuded their Atlantic seaboard, and concentrated in the Mediterranean on the faith of naval arrangements made with us. This will not be true. If we did not exist, the French could not make better dispositions than at present. They are not strong enough to face Germany alone, still less to maintain themselves in two theatres. They therefore rightly concentrate their Navy in the Mediterranean where it can be safe and superior and can assure their African communications. Neither is it true that we are relying on France to maintain our position in the Mediterranean. . . . If France did not exist, we should make no other disposition of our forces.

Circumstances might arise which in my judgment would make it desirable and right for us to come to the aid of France with all our force by land and sea. But we ask nothing in return. If we were attacked by Germany, we should not make it a charge of bad faith against the French that they left us to fight it out alone; and nothing in naval and military arrangements ought to have the effect of exposing us to such a charge if, when the time comes, we decide to stand out.

This is my view, and I am sure I am in line with you on the principle. I am not at all particular how it is to be given effect to, and I make no point about what document it is set forth in. But [consider] how tremendous would be the weapon which France would possess to compel our intervention, if she could say, "On the advice of and by arrangement with your naval authorities we have left our Northern coasts defenceless. We cannot possibly come back in time." Indeed [I added somewhat inconsequently], it would probably be decisive whatever is written down now. Everyone must feel who knows the facts that we have the obligations of an alliance without its advantages, and above all without its precise definitions.

W. S. C.

The difficulty proved a real one. The technical naval discussions could only be conducted on the basis that the French Fleet should be concentrated in the Mediterranean, and that in case of a war in which both countries took part, it would fall to the British fleet to defend the Northern and Western coasts of France. The French, as I had foreseen, naturally raised the point that if Great Britain did not take part in the war, their Northern and Western coasts would be completely exposed. We however, while recognizing the difficulty, steadfastly declined to allow the naval arrangements to bind us in any political sense. It was eventually agreed that if there was a menace of war, the two Governments should consult together and concert beforehand what common action, if any, they should take. The French were obliged to accept this position and to affirm definitely that the naval conversations did not involve any obligation of common action. This was the best we could do for ourselves and for them. When the time came there was no doubt what England wished to do.

The organization of a Fleet differs throughout from that of an Army. Armies only keep a small proportion of their soldiers in regular service. These form the framework of the battalions, train the recruits and keep guard in times of peace. When the order is given to mobilize, all the men who have been already trained but are living at home in civil life are called up as they are wanted: and then and not till then the Army is ready to fight.

Navies on the other hand were in the main always ready. The British Navy had all its best ships fully and permanently manned with whole-time men (called active service ratings). Measured by quality nearly the whole of its power was therefore constantly available. Measured even by numbers nearly three-quarters of the ships could go into action without calling out the Reserves. Only the oldest and most obsolete ships were manned in time of war by the Naval Reserve, i.e. men who had left the Navy and had returned to civil life. These obsolete vessels were the only part of the Fleet which had to be 'mobilized' like the armies of Europe.

Thus mobilization, which is the foundation of all great armies, plays only a very small part in fleets. Every ship that really counted was always ready to steam and fight as soon as an order reached her.

The organization of the British Home Fleets when I came to the Admiralty seemed to a mind accustomed to military symmetry, to leave much to be desired. In consultation with Sir Francis Bridgeman, Prince Louis and Rear-Admiral Troubridge, the first Chief of the new War Staff, I designed a new and symmetrical organization for the Fleets.

All the ships available for Home Defence were divided into the First, Second and Third Fleets, comprising eight battle squadrons of eight battleships each, together with their attendant cruiser squadrons, flotillas and auxiliaries. The First Fleet comprised a Fleet Flagship and four battle squadrons of ships "in full commission" manned entirely with active service ratings, and therefore *always ready.* To form this Fleet it was necessary to base the former "Atlantic Fleet" on Home Ports instead of on Gibraltar, and to base the battleships hitherto in the Mediterranean on Gibraltar instead of Malta. By this concentration an additional battle squadron of strong ships *(King Edwards)* was *always ready* in Home waters. The Second Fleet consisted of two battle squadrons, also fully manned with active service ratings, but having about 40 per cent of these learning and requalifying in the gunnery, torpedo and other schools. This Fleet was termed "in active commission" because it could fight at any moment: but to realize its highest efficiency, it required to touch at its Home Ports, and march on board its balance crews from the schools. In all these six battle squadrons, containing with their cruiser squadrons every modern and middle-aged ship in the Navy, there was not to be found a single reservist. No mobilization was therefore necessary to bring the whole of this force into action. The Third Fleet also consisted of two battle squadrons and five cruiser squadrons of our oldest ships. These were only manned by care and maintenance parties and required the Reserves to be called out before they could put to sea. In order to accelerate the mobilization of the leading battle squadrons and certain cruisers of the Third Fleet, a special class of the Reserve was now formed called the "Immediate Reserve," who received higher pay and periodical training and were liable to be called up in advance of general mobilization.

Germany was adding a third squadron to the High Sea Fleet, thus increasing her *always ready* strength from 17 to 25. We in reply, by the measures set out above and various others too technical for description here, raised our *always ready* Fleet from 33 battleships to 49, and other forces in like proportion. On mobilization the German figures would rise to 38, and the British at first to 57, and ultimately, as the new organization was completed, to 65.

The reader will not be able to understand the issues involved in the completion and mobilization of the Fleets on the eve of the war unless this organization as explained above is mastered.

We made a great assembly of the Navy this spring of 1912 at Portland. The flags of a dozen admirals, the broad pennants of as many commodores and the pennants of a hundred and fifty ships were flying together. The King came in the Royal Yacht, the Admiralty flag at the fore, the Standard at the main, and the Jack at the mizzen, and bided among his sailors for four days. One day there is a long cruise out into the mist, dense, utterly baffling—the whole Fleet steaming together all invisible, keeping station by weird siren screamings and hootings. It seemed incredible that no harm would befall. And then suddenly the fog lifted and the distant targets could be distinguished and the whole long line of battleships, coming one after another into view, burst into tremendous flares of flame and hurled their shells with deafening detonations while the water rose in tall fountains. The Fleet returns—three battle squadrons abreast, cruisers and flotillas disposed ahead and astern. The speed is raised to twenty knots. Streaks of white foam appear at the bows of every vessel. The land draws near. The broad bay already embraces this swiftly moving gigantic armada. The ships in their formation already fill the bay. The foreign officers I have with me on the *Enchantress* bridge stare anxiously. We still steam fast. Five minutes more and the van of the Fleet will be aground. Four minutes, three minutes. There! At last. The signal! A string of bright flags is hauled down from the *Neptune's* halyards. Every anchor falls together; their cables roar through the hawser holes; every propeller whirls astern. In a hundred and fifty yards, it seems, every ship is stationary. Look along the lines, miles this way and miles that, they might have been drawn with a ruler. The foreign observers gasped.

These were great days. From dawn to midnight, day after day, one's whole mind was absorbed by the fascination and novelty of the problems which came crowding forward. And all the time there was a sense of power to act, to form, to organize: all the ablest officers in the Navy standing ready, loyal and eager, with argument, guidance, information; everyone feeling a sense that a great danger had passed very near us; that there was a breathing space before it would return; that we must be better prepared next time. Saturdays, Sundays and any other spare day I spent always with the Fleets at Portsmouth or at Portland or Devonport, or with the Flotillas at Harwich. Officers of every rank came on board to lunch or dine and discussion proceeded without ceasing on every aspect of naval war and administration.

The Admiralty yacht *Enchantress* was now to become largely my office, almost my home; and my work my sole occupation and amusement. In all, I spent eight months afloat in the three years before the war. I visited every dockyard, shipyard and naval establishment in the British Isles and in the Mediterranean and every important ship. I examined for myself every point of strategic consequence and every piece of Admiralty property. I got to know what everything looked like and where everything was, and how one thing fitted into another. In the end I could put my hand on anything that was wanted and knew thoroughly the current state of our naval affairs.

I recall vividly my first voyage from Portsmouth to Portland, where the Fleet lay. A grey afternoon was drawing to a close. As I saw the Fleet for the first time drawing out of the haze a friend reminded me of "that far-off line of storm-beaten ships on which the eyes of the grand Army had never looked," but which had in their day "stood between Napoleon and the dominion of the world." In Portland Harbour the yacht lay surrounded by the great ships; the whole harbour was alive with the goings and comings of launches and small craft of every kind, and as night fell ten thousand lights from sea and shore sprang into being and every masthead twinkled as the ships and squadrons conversed with one another. Who could fail to work for such a service? Who could fail when the very darkness seemed loaded with the menace of approaching war?

For consider these ships, so vast in themselves, yet so small, so easily lost to sight on the surface of the waters. Sufficient at the moment, we trusted, for their task, but yet only a score or so. They were all we had. On them, as we conceived, floated the might, majesty, dominion and power of the British Empire. All our long history built up century after century, all our great affairs in every part of the globe, all the means of livelihood and safety of our faithful, industrious, active population depended upon them. Open the sea-cocks and let them sink beneath the surface, as another Fleet was one day to do in another British harbour far to the North, and in a few minutes—half an hour at the most—the whole outlook of the world would be changed. The British Empire would dissolve like a dream; each isolated community struggling forward by itself; the central power of union broken; mighty provinces, whole Empires in themselves, drifting hopelessly out of control, and falling a prey to strangers; and Europe after one sudden convulsion passing into the iron grip and rule of the Teuton and of all that the Teutonic system meant. There would only be left far off across the Atlantic unarmed, unready, and as yet uninstructed America, to maintain, single-handed, law and freedom among men.

Guard them well, admirals and captains, hardy tars and tall marines; guard them well and guide them true.

CHAPTER V

THE NORTH SEA FRONT

Until I got to the Admiralty I had never properly appreciated the service which Mr. McKenna and Lord Fisher had rendered to the Fleet in 1909 by their big leap forward from the 12-inch to the 13.5-inch gun. The increase of 1½ inch in the calibre of the gun was enough to raise the British shell from 850 pounds to 1,400 pounds. No fewer than twelve ships were actually building on the slips for the Royal Navy armed with these splendid weapons, quite unsurpassed at that time in the world, and firing a projectile nearly half as heavy again as the biggest fired by the German Fleet.

I immediately sought to go one size better. I mentioned this to Lord Fisher at Reigate, and he hurled himself into its advocacy with tremendous passion. "Nothing less than the 15-inch gun could be looked at for all the battleships and battle-cruisers of the new programme. To achieve the supply of this gun was the equivalent of a great victory at sea; to shrink from the endeavour was treason to the Empire. What was it that enabled Jack Johnson to knock out his opponents? It was the big punch. And where were those miserable men with bevies of futile pop-guns crowding up their ships?" No one who has not experienced it has any idea of the passion and eloquence of this old lion when thoroughly roused on a technical question. I resolved to make a great effort to secure the prize, but the difficulties and the risks were very great, and looking back upon it, one feels that they were only justified by success. Enlarging the gun meant enlarging the ships, and enlarging the ships meant increasing the cost. Moreover, the redesign must cause no delay and the guns must be ready as soon as the turrets were ready. No such thing as a modern 15-inch gun existed. None had ever been made. The advance to the 13.5-inch had in itself been a great stride. Its power was greater; its accuracy was greater; its life was much longer. Could the British designers repeat this triumph on a still larger scale and in a still more intense form? The Ordnance Board were set to work and they rapidly produced a design. Armstrongs were consulted in deadly secrecy, and they undertook to execute it. I had anxious conferences with these experts, with whose science I was of course wholly unacquainted, to see what sort of men they were and how they really felt about it. They were all for it. One did not need to be an expert in ballistics to discern that. The Director of Naval Ordnance, Rear-Admiral Moore, was ready to stake his professional existence upon it. But after all there could not be absolute certainty. We knew the 13.5-inch well. All sorts of new stresses might develop in the 15-inch model. If only we could make a trial gun and test it thoroughly before giving the orders for the whole of the guns of all the five ships, there would be no risk; but then we should lose an entire year, and five great vessels would go into the line of battle carrying an inferior weapon to that which we had it in our power to give them. Several there were of the responsible authorities consulted who thought it would be more prudent to lose the year. For, after all, if the guns had failed, the ships would have been fearfully marred. I hardly remember ever to have had more anxiety about any administrative decision than this.

I went back to Lord Fisher. He was steadfast and even violent. So I hardened my heart and took the plunge. The whole outfit of guns was ordered forthwith. We arranged that one gun should be hurried on four months in front of the others by exceptional efforts so as to be able to test it for range and accuracy and to get out the range tables and other complex devices which depended upon actual firing results. From this moment we were irrevocably committed to the whole armament, and every detail in these vessels, extending to thousands of parts, was redesigned to fit them. Fancy if they failed. What a disaster. What an exposure. No excuse would be accepted. It would all be brought home to me—"rash, inexperienced," "before he had been there a month," "altering all the plans of his predecessors" and producing "this ghastly fiasco," "the mutilation of all the ships of the year." What could I have said? Moreover, although the decision, once taken, was irrevocable, a long period of suspense—fourteen or fifteen months at least—was unavoidable. However, I dissembled my misgivings. I wrote to the First Sea Lord that "Risks have to be run in peace as well as in war, and courage in design now may win a battle later on."

But everything turned out all right. British gunnery science proved exact and true, and British workmanship as sound as a bell and punctual to the day. The first gun was known in the Elswick shops as "the hush and push gun," and was invariably described in all official documents as "the 14-inch experimental." It proved a brilliant success. It hurled a 1,920-pound projectile 35,000 yards; it achieved remarkable accuracy at all ranges without shortening its existence by straining itself in any way. No doubt I was unduly anxious; but when I saw the gun fired for the first time a year later and knew that all was well, I felt as if I had been delivered from a great peril.

In one of those nightmare novels that used to appear from time to time before the war, I read in 1913 of a great battle in which, to the amazement of the defeated British Fleet, the German new vessels opened fire with a terrible, unheard-of 15-inch gun. There was a real satisfaction in feeling that anyhow this boot was on the other leg.

The gun dominated the ship, and was the decisive cause of all the changes we then made in design. From the beginning there appeared in our plans a ship carrying ten 15-inch guns, and therefore at least 600 feet long with room inside her for engines which would drive her 21 knots and capacity to carry armour which on the armoured belt, the turrets and the conning tower would reach the thickness unprecedented in the British Service of 13 inches. For less armour you could have more speed: for less speed you could have more armour, and so on within very considerable limits. But now a new idea began to dawn. Eight 15-inch guns would fire a simultaneous broadside of approximately 16,000 lb. Ten of the latest 13.5-inch would only fire 14,000 lb. Therefore, we could get for eight 15-inch guns a punch substantially greater than that of ten 13.5-inch. Nor did the superiority end there. With the increased size of the shell came a far greater increase in the capacity of the bursting charge. It was not quite a geometric progression, because other considerations intervened; but it was in that order of ideas. There was no doubt about the punch. On the other hand, look at the speed. Twenty-one knots was all very well in its way, but suppose we could get a much greater speed. Suppose we could cram into the hull a horse-power sufficient to drive these terrific vessels, already possessing guns and armour superior to that of the heaviest battleship, at speeds hitherto only obtained by the lightly armoured 12-inch gun battle-cruisers, should we not have introduced a new element into naval war?

And here we leave the region of material. I have built the process up stage by stage as it was argued out, but of course all the processes proceeded in simultaneous relation, and the result was to show a great possibility. Something like the ship described above could be made if it were wanted. Was it wanted? Was it the right thing to make? Was its tactical value sufficient to justify the increase in cost and all the changes in design? We must turn for the answer to the tactical sphere.

A squadron of ships possessing a definite superiority of speed could be so disposed in the approaching formation of your own Fleet as to enable you, whichever way the enemy might deploy, to double the fire after a certain interval upon the head of his line, and also to envelop it and across it and so force him into a circular movement and bring him to bay once and for all without hope of escape.

Hitherto in all our battle plans this role had been assigned to the battle-cruisers. Their speed would certainly enable them to get there. But we must imagine that they would also be met by the enemy's battle-cruisers, whereupon they might easily fight a separate action of their own without relation to the supreme conflict. Further, the battle-cruisers, our beautiful "Cats," as their squadron was irreverently called,[1] had thin skins compared to the enemy's

---

[1] *Lion, Tiger, Queen Mary, Princess Royal.*

strongest battleships, which presumably would head his line. It is a rough game to pit battle-cruisers against battleships with only seven or nine inches of armour against twelve or thirteen, and probably with a weaker gun-power as well.

Suppose, however, we could make a division of ships fast enough to seize the advantageous position and yet as strong in gun-power and armour as any battleship afloat. Should we not have scored almost with certainty an inestimable and decisive advantage? The First Sea Lord, Sir Francis Bridgeman, fresh from the command of the Home Fleet, and most of his principal officers, certainly thought so. The Fast Division was the dream of their battle plans. But could we get such ships? Could they be designed and constructed?

At this stage the War College were asked to work out on the tactical board the number of knots superiority in speed required in a Fast Division in order to ensure this Division being able to manœuvre around the German Fleet as it would be in the years 1914 and 1915.

The answer was that if the Fast Division could steam in company 25 knots or better, they could do all that was necessary. We therefore wanted 4 or 5 knots additional speed. How were we to get it? With every knot the amount of horse-power required is progressively greater. Our new ship would steam 21 knots, but to steam 25 to 26 she wanted 50,000 horse-power. Fifty thousand horse-power meant more boilers, and where could they be put? Why, obviously they could be put where the fifth turret would go, and having regard to the increased punch of the 15-inch gun we could spare the fifth turret.

But even this would not suffice. We could not get the power required to drive these ships at 25 knots except by the use of oil fuel.

The advantages conferred by liquid fuel were inestimable. First, speed. In equal ships oil gave a large excess of speed over coal. It enabled that speed to be attained with far greater rapidity. It gave forty per cent greater radius of action for the same weight of coal. It enabled a fleet to re-fuel at sea with great facility. An oil-burning fleet can, if need be and in calm weather, keep its station at sea, nourishing itself from tankers without having to send a quarter of its strength continually into harbour to coal, wasting fuel on the homeward and outward journey. The ordeal of coaling ship exhausted the whole ship's company. In wartime it robbed them of their brief period of rest; it subjected everyone to extreme discomfort. With oil, a few pipes were connected with the shore or with a tanker and the ship sucked in its fuel with hardly a man having to lift a finger. Less than half the number of stokers was needed to tend and clean the oil furnaces. Oil could be stowed in spare places in a ship from which it would be impossible to bring coal. As a coal ship used up her coal, increasingly large numbers of men had to be taken, if necessary from the guns, to shovel the coal from remote and inconvenient bunkers to bunkers nearer to the furnaces or to the furnaces themselves, thus weakening the fighting efficiency of the ship perhaps at the most critical moment in the battle. For instance, nearly a hundred men were continually occupied in the *Lion* shovelling coal from one steel chamber to another without ever seeing the light either of day or of the furnace fires. The use of oil made it possible in every type of vessel to have more gun-power and more speed for less size or less cost. It alone made it possible to realize the high speeds in certain types which were vital to their tactical purpose. All these advantages were obtained simply by burning oil instead of coal under the boilers. Should it at any time become possible to abolish boilers altogether and explode the oil in the cylinders of internal combustion engines, every advantage would be multiplied tenfold.

On my arrival at the Admiralty we had already built or were building 56 destroyers solely dependent on oil and 74 submarines which could only be driven by oil; and a proportion of oil was used to spray the coal furnaces of nearly all ships. We were not, however, dependent upon oil to such an extent as to make its supply a serious naval problem. To build any large additional number of oil-burning ships meant basing our naval supremacy upon oil. But oil was not found in appreciable quantities in our islands. If we required it, we must carry it by sea in peace or war from distant countries. We had, on the other hand, the finest supply of best steam coal in the world, safe in our mines under our own hand.

To change the foundation of the Navy from British coal to foreign oil was a formidable decision in itself. If it were taken it must raise a whole series of intricate problems all requiring heavy initial expense. First there must be accumulated in Great Britain an enormous oil reserve large enough to enable us to fight for many months if necessary, without bringing in a single cargo of oil. To contain this reserve enormous installations of tanks must be erected near the various naval ports. Would they not be very vulnerable? Could they be protected? Could they be concealed or disguised? The word *"Camouflage"* was not then known. Fleets of tankers had to be built to convey the oil from the distant oilfields across the oceans to the British Isles, and others of a different pattern to take it from our naval harbours to the fleets at sea.

Owing to the systems of finance by which we had bound ourselves, we were not allowed to borrow even for capital or "once for all" expenditure. Every penny must be won from Parliament year by year, and constituted a definite addition to the inevitably rising and already fiercely challenged Naval Estimates. And beyond these difficulties loomed up the more intangible problems of markets and monopolies. The oil supplies of the world were in the hands of vast oil trusts under foreign control. To commit the Navy irrevocably to oil was indeed "to take arms against a sea of troubles." Wave after wave, dark with storm, crested with foam, surged towards the harbour in which we still sheltered. Should we drive out into the teeth of the gale, or should we bide contented where we were? Yet beyond the breakers was a great hope. If we overcame the difficulties and surmounted the risks, we should be able to raise the whole power and efficiency of the Navy to a definitely higher level; better ships, better crews, higher economies, more intense forms of war-power—in a word, mastery itself was the prize of the venture. A year gained over a rival might make the difference. Forward, then!

The three programmes of 1912, 1913 and 1914 comprised the greatest additions in power and cost ever made to the Royal Navy. With the lamentable exception of the battleships of 1913—and these were afterwards corrected—they did not contain a coal-burning ship. Submarines, destroyers, light cruisers, fast battleships—all were based irrevocably on oil. The fateful plunge was taken when it was decided to create the Fast Division. Then, for the first time, the supreme ships of the Navy, on which our life depended, were fed by oil and could only be fed by oil. The decision to drive the smaller craft by oil followed naturally upon this. The camel once swallowed, the gnats went down easily enough.

I shall show presently the difficulties into which these decisions to create a fast division of battleships and to rely upon oil led me into during the years 1913 and 1914. Nor can I deny that colleagues who could not foresee the extra expense which they involved had grounds of complaint. Battleships were at that time assumed to cost 2¼ millions each. The *Queen Elizabeth* class of fast battleships cost over three millions each. The expenditure of upwards of 10 millions was required to create the oil reserve, with its tanks and its tankers, though a proportion of this would have been needed in any case. On more than one occasion I feared I should succumb. I had, however, the unfailing support of the Prime Minister. The Chancellor of the Exchequer whose duty it was to be my most severe critic, was also my most friendly colleague. And so it all went through. Fortune rewarded the continuous and steadfast facing of these difficulties by the Board of Admiralty and brought us a prize from fairyland far beyond our brightest hopes.

An unbroken series of consequences conducted us to the Anglo-Persian Oil Convention. The first step was to set up a Royal Commission on Oil Supply. Lord Fisher was invited and induced to preside over it. Simultaneously with the setting up of this Commission we pursued our own Admiralty search for oil. On the advice of Sir Francis Hopwood and Sir Frederick Black,[1] I sent Admiral Slade with an expert Committee to the Persian Gulf to examine the oil fields on the spot. These gentlemen were also the Admiralty representatives on the Royal Commission. To them the principal credit for the achievement is due. At the later financial stage the Governor of the Bank of England,

---

[1] Director of Admiralty contracts.

afterwards Lord Cunliffe, and the directors of the Anglo-Persian and Royal Burmah Oil Companies were most serviceable. All through 1912 and 1913 our efforts were unceasing.

Thus each link forged the next. From the original desire to enlarge the gun we were led on step by step to the Fast Division, and in order to get the Fast Division we were forced to rely for vital units of the Fleet upon oil fuel. This led to the general adoption of oil fuel and to all the provisions which were needed to build up a great oil reserve. This led to enormous expense and to tremendous opposition on the Naval Estimates. Yet it was absolutely impossible to turn back. We could only fight our way forward, and finally we found our way to the Anglo-Persian Oil agreement and contract, which for an initial investment of two millions of public money (subsequently increased to five millions) has not only secured to the Navy a very substantial proportion of its oil supply, but has led to the acquisition by the Government of a controlling share in oil properties and interests which are at present valued at scores of millions sterling, and also to very considerable economies, which are still continuing, in the purchase price of Admiralty oil.

On this basis it may be said that the aggregate profits, realized and potential, of this investment may be estimated at a sum not merely sufficient to pay for all the programme of ships, great and small of that year and for the whole pre-war oil fuel installation, but are such that we may not unreasonably expect that one day we shall be entitled also to claim that the mighty fleets laid down in 1912, 1913 and 1914, the greatest ever built by any Power in an equal period, were added to the British Navy without costing a single penny to the taxpayer.

Such is the story of the creation of a Fast Division of five famous battleships, the *Queen Elizabeth, Warspite, Barham, Valiant* and *Malaya,* all oil-driven, each capable of steaming a minimum of 25 knots, mounting eight 15-inch guns and protected by 13 inches of armour. These ships survive to-day among the fifteen capital units of the Fleet. We shall see later on what part they played at Jutland.

Space does not allow me to recount here, as I should like to do, the designs of the light armoured cruisers—the *Arethusas*—of which in peace and war no fewer than forty were eventually built for the Navy.

The traditional war policy of the Admiralty grew up during the prolonged wars and antagonisms with France. It consisted in establishing immediately upon the outbreak of war a close blockade of the enemy's ports and naval bases by means of flotillas of strong small craft supported by cruisers with superior battle fleets in reserve. The experience of 200 years had led all naval strategists to agree on this fundamental principle, "Our first line of defence is the enemy's ports."

When the torpedo was invented, the French tried to frustrate this well-known British policy by building large numbers of torpedo-boats, and the Admiralty, after some years, retorted by building torpedo-boat destroyers. These destroyers fulfilled two conditions: first, they were large enough to keep the seas in most weathers and to operate across the Channel for sufficient periods; secondly, their guns were heavy enough to destroy or dominate the French torpedo-boats. Thus, in spite of the advent of the torpedo, we preserved our power to maintain stronger flotillas in close proximity to the enemy's naval bases. Meanwhile, all along the South Coast of England a series of fortified torpedo-proof harbours in the neighborhood of our great naval establishments afforded safe, close, and convenient stations for our battle fleets and other supporting vessels when not actually at sea.

When early in the present century our potential enemy for the first time became not France, but Germany, our naval strategic front shifted from the South to the East Coast and from the Channel to the North Sea.[1] But although the enemy, the front, and the theatre had changed, the sound principle of British naval strategy still held good. Our first line of defence was considered to be the enemy's ports. The Admiralty policy was still a close blockade of those ports by means of stronger flotillas properly supported by cruisers and ultimately by the battle fleets.

It was not to be expected that our arrangements on this new front could rapidly reach the same degree of perfection as the conflicts of so many generations had evolved in the Channel; and so far as our naval bases were concerned, we were still in the process of transition when the Great War began. More serious, however, was the effect of the change on the utility of our destroyers. Instead of operating at distances of from 20 or 60 miles across the Channel with their supporting ships close at hand in safe harbours, they were now called upon to operate in the Heligoland Bight, across 240 miles of sea, and with no suitable bases for their supporting battle fleet nearer than the Thames or the Forth. Nevertheless, the Admiralty continued to adhere to their traditional strategic principle, and their war plans up till 1911 contemplated the close blockade of the enemy's ports immediately upon the declaration of war. Our destroyers were constructed with ever-increasing sea-keeping qualities and with a great superiority of gun-power. The Germans, on the other hand, adhered rather to the French conception of the torpedo-boat as a means of attack upon our large ships. While we relied in our destroyer construction principally on gun-power and sea-keeping qualities, they relied upon the torpedo and high speed in fair weather opportunities. But the much greater distances over which our destroyers had now to operate across the North Sea immensely reduced their effectiveness. Whereas across the Channel they could work in two reliefs,

[1] See general map of the North Sea on pp. 190–91.

they required three across the North Sea. Therefore only one-third instead of one-half of our fighting flotillas could be available at any given moment. Against this third the enemy could at any moment bring his whole force. In order to carry out our old strategic policy from our Home bases we should have required flotillas at least three and probably four times as numerous as those of Germany. This superiority we had not got and were not likely to get.

Therefore from shortly before 1905 when the French agreement was signed, down to the Agadir crisis in 1911, the Admiralty made plans to capture one or other of the German islands. On this it was intended to establish an oversea base at which from the beginning of the war our blockade flotillas could be re-plenished and could rest, and which as war progressed would have developed into an advanced citadel of our sea-power. In this way, therefore, the Admiralty would still have carried out their traditional war policy of beating the enemy's flotillas and light craft into his ports and maintaining a constant close blockade.

These considerations were not lost upon the Germans. They greatly in-creased the fortifications of Heligoland, and they proceeded to fortify one after another such of the Frisian Islands as were in any way suitable for our purposes. At the same time a new and potent factor appeared upon the scene—the sub-marine. The submarine not only rendered the capture and maintenance of an oversea base or bases far more difficult and, as some authorities have steadfastly held, impossible, but it threatened with destruction our cruisers and battleships without whose constant support our flotillas would easily have been destroyed by the enemy's cruisers.

This was the situation in October, 1911, when immediately after the Agadir crisis I became First Lord and proceeded to form a new Board of Admiralty. Seeing that we had not for the time being the numerical force of destroyers able to master the destroyers of the potential enemy in his home waters, nor the power to support our flotillas with heavy ships, and having regard also to the difficulty and hazard in all the circumstances of storming and capturing one of his now fortified islands, we proceeded forthwith to revise altogether the War Plans and substitute, with the full concurrence of our principal commanders afloat, the policy of distant blockade set out in the Admiralty War Orders of 1912.

The policy of distant blockade was not adopted from choice, but from necessity. It implied no repudiation on the part of the Admiralty of their fun-damental principle of aggressive naval strategy, but only a temporary abandon-ment of it in the face of unsolved practical difficulties; and it was intended that every effort should be made, both before and after a declaration of war, to over-come those difficulties. It was rightly foreseen that by closing the exits from the North Sea into the Atlantic Ocean, German commerce would be almost com-pletely cut off from the world. It was expected that the economic and financial pressure resulting from such a blockade would fatally injure the German power to carry on a war. It was hoped that this pressure would compel the German fleet to come out and fight, not in his own defended waters, but at a great numerical disadvantage in the open sea. It was believed that we could continue meanwhile to enjoy the full command of the seas without danger to our sea communications or to the movement of our armies, and that the British Isles could be kept safe from invasion. There was at that time no reason to suppose that these conditions would not continue indefinitely with undiminished advantage to ourselves and increasing pressure upon the enemy. So far as all surface vessels are concerned, and certainly for the first three years of the war, these expectations were confirmed by experience.

Under these orders the Fleet was disposed strategically so as to block the exits from the North Sea by placing the Grand Fleet at Scapa Flow and drawing a cordon of destroyers across the Straits of Dover supported by the older battleships and protected by certain minefields. These conclusions stood the test of the war. They were never departed from in any important respect by any of the Boards of Admiralty which held office. By this means the British Navy seized and kept the effective control of all the oceans of the world.

Of all the dangers that menaced the British Empire, none was comparable to a surprise of the Fleet. If the Fleet or any vital part of it were caught unawares or unready and our naval preponderance destroyed, we had lost the war, and there was no limit to the evils which might have been inflicted upon us, except the mercy of an all-powerful conqueror. We have seen in recent years how little completely victorious nations can be trusted to restrain their passions against a prostrate foe. Great Britain, deprived of its naval defence, could be speedily starved into utter submission to the will of the conqueror. Her Empire would be dismembered: the Dominions, India, and her immense African and island possessions would be shorn off or transferred to the victors. Ireland would be erected into a hostile well-armed republic on the flank of Great Britain; and the British people, reduced to a helpless condition, would be loaded with overwhelming indemnities calculated to shatter their social system, if, indeed, they were not actually reduced, in Sir Edward Grey's mordant phrase, to the position of "the conscript appendage of a stronger Power." Less severe conditions than have since been meted out to Germany would certainly have sufficed to destroy the British Empire at a stroke for ever. The stakes were very high. If our naval defence were maintained we were safe and sure beyond the lot of any other European nation; if it failed, our doom was certain and final.

To what lengths, therefore, would the Germans go to compass the destruction of the British Fleet? Taking the demonic view of their character which it was necessary to assume for the purposes of considering a war problem, what forms of attack ought we to reckon with? Of course, if Germany had no will to war, all these speculations were mere nightmares. But if she had the will and intention of making war, it was evident that there would be no difficulty in finding a pretext arising out of a dispute with France or Russia, to create a situation in which war was inevitable, and create it at the most opportune moment for herself. The wars of Frederick and of Bismarck had shown with what extraordinary rapidity and suddenness the Prussian nation was accustomed to fall upon its enemy. The Continent was a powder magazine from end to end. One single hellish spark and the vast explosion might ensue. We had seen what had happened to France in 1870. We had seen what neglect to take precautions had brought upon the Russian fleet off Port Arthur in 1904. We know now what happened to Belgium in 1914, and, not less remarkable, the demand Germany decided to make upon France on August 1, 1914, that if she wished to remain neutral while Germany attacked Russia, she must as a guarantee hand over to German garrisons her fortresses of Verdun and Toul.

Obviously, therefore, the danger of a "bolt from the blue" was by no means fantastic. Still, might one not reasonably expect certain warnings? There would probably be some kind of dispute in progress between the great Powers enjoining particular vigilance upon the Admiralty. We might hope to get information of military and naval movements. It was almost certain that there would be financial perturbations in the Exchanges of the world indicating a rise of temperature. Could we therefore rely upon a week's notice, or three days' notice, or at least twenty-fours hours' notice before any blow actually fell?

In Europe, where great nations faced each other with enormous armies, there was an automatic safeguard against surprise. Decisive events could not occur till the armies were mobilized, and that took at least a fortnight. The supreme defence of France, for instance, could not therefore be overcome without a great battle in which the main strength of the French nation could be brought to bear. But no such assurance was enjoyed by the British Fleet. No naval mobilization was necessary on either side to enable all the modern ships to attack one another. They had only to raise steam and bring the ammunition to the guns. But beyond this grim fact grew the torpedo menace. So far as gunfire alone was concerned, our principal danger was for our Fleet to be caught divided and to have one vital part destroyed without inflicting proportionate damage on the enemy. This danger was greatly reduced by wireless, which enabled the divided portions to be instantly directed to a common rendezvous and to avoid action till concentration was effected. Besides, gunfire was a game that two could play at. One could not contemplate that the main strength of the fleets would ever be allowed to come within range of each other without taking proper precautions. But the torpedo was essentially a weapon of surprise, or even treachery; and all that was true of the torpedo in a surface vessel applied with tenfold force to the torpedo of a submarine.

Obviously there were limits beyond which it was impossible to safeguard oneself. It was not simply a case of a few weeks of special precautions. The British Navy had to live its ordinary life in time of peace. It had to have its cruises and its exercises, its periods of leave and refit. Our harbours were open to the commerce of the world. Absolute security against the worst conceivable treachery was physically impossible. On the other hand, even treachery, which required the co-operation of very large numbers of people in different stations and the setting in motion of an immense and complicated apparatus, is not easy to bring about. It was ruled by the Committee of Imperial Defence, after grave debate, that the Admiralty must not assume that if it made the difference between victory and defeat, Germany would stop short of an attack on the Fleet in full peace without warning or pretext. We had to do our best to live up to this standard, and in the main I believe we succeeded. Certainly the position and condition of the British Fleet was every day considered in relation to that of Germany. I was accustomed to check our dispositions by asking the Staff from time to time, unexpectedly, "What happens if war with Germany begins to-day?" I never found them without an answer which showed that we had the power to effect our main concentration before any portion of the Fleet could be brought to battle. Our Fleet did not go for its cruises to the coast of Spain until we knew that the German High Seas Fleet was having its winter refits. When we held Grand Manœuvres we were very careful to arrange the coaling and leave which followed in such a way as to secure us the power of meeting any blow which could possibly reach us in a given time. I know of no moment in the period of which I am writing up to the declaration of war in which it was physically possible for the main British Fleet to have been surprised or caught dispersed and divided by any serious German force of surface vessels. An attempt in full peace to make a submarine attack upon a British squadron in harbour or exercising, or to lay mines in an area in which they might be expected to exercise, could not wholly be provided against; but in all human probability its success would only have been partial. Further, I do not believe that such treachery was ever contemplated by the German Admiralty, Government or Emperor. While trying as far as possible to guard against even the worst possibilities, my own conviction was that there would be a cause of quarrel accompanied by a crisis and a fall in markets, and followed very rapidly by a declaration of war, or by acts of war intended to be simultaneous with the declaration, but possibly occurring slightly before. What actually did happen was not unlike what I thought would happen.

In time of war there is great uncertainty as to what the enemy will do and what will happen next. But still, once you are at war the task is definite and all-dominating. Whatever may be your surmises about the enemy or the future, your own action is circumscribed within practical limits. There are only a certain number of alternatives open. Also, you live in a world of reality where theories are constantly being corrected and curbed by experiment. Resultant facts accumulate and govern to a very large extent the next decision.

But suppose the whole process of war is transported out of the region of reality into that of imagination. Suppose you have to assume to begin with that there will be a war at all: secondly, that your country will be in it when it comes: thirdly, that you will go in as a united nation and that the nation will be united and convinced *in time,* and that the necessary measures will be taken before it is *too late,*—then the processes of thought become speculative indeed. Every set of assumptions which it is necessary to make, draws new veils of varying density in front of the dark curtain of the future. The life of the thoughtful soldier or sailor in time of peace is made up of these experiences—intense effort, amid every conceivable distraction, to pick out across and among a swarm of confusing hypotheses what actually will happen on a given day and what actually must be done to meet it before that day is ended. Meanwhile all around people, greatly superior in authority and often in intelligence, regard him as a plotting knave, or at the best an overgrown child playing with toys, and dangerous toys at that.

Therefore the most we could do in the days before the war was to attempt to measure and forecast what would happen to England on the outbreak and in the first few weeks of a war with Germany. To look farther was beyond the power of man. To try to do so was to complicate the task beyond mental endurance. The paths of thought bifurcated too rapidly. Would there be a great sea battle or not? What would happen then? Who would win the great land battle? No one could tell. Obviously the first thing was to be ready; not to be taken unawares: to be concentrated; not to be caught divided: to have the strongest Fleet possible in the best stations under the best conditions, and in good time, and then if the battle came one could await its result with a steady heart. Everything, therefore, to guard against surprise; everything, therefore, to guard against division; everything, therefore, to increase the strength of the forces available for the supreme sea battle.

But suppose the enemy did not fight a battle at sea. And suppose the battle on land was indeterminate in its results. And suppose the war went on not for weeks or months, but for years. Well, then it would be far easier to judge those matters at the time, and far easier then, when everybody was alarmed and awake and active, to secure the taking of the necessary steps; and there would be time to take them. No stage would be so difficult or so dangerous as the first stage. The problems of the second year of war must be dealt with by the experience of the first year of war. The problems of the third year of war must be met by results observed and understood in the second, and so on.

I repulse, therefore, on behalf of the Boards of Admiralty over which I presided down to the end of May, 1915, all reproaches directed to what occurred in 1917 and 1918. I cannot be stultified by any lessons arising out of those years. It is vain to tell me that if the Germans had built in the three years before the war, the submarines they built in the three years after it had begun, Britain would have been undone; or that if England had had in August, 1914, the army which we possessed a year later, there would have been no war. Every set of circumstances involved every other set of circumstances. Would Germany in profound peace have been allowed by Great Britain to build an enormous fleet of submarines which could have no other object than the starvation and ruin of this island through the sinking of unarmed merchant ships? Would Germany have waited to attack France while England raised a powerful conscript army to go to her aid?

Every event must be judged in fair relation to the circumstances of the time, and only in such relation.

CHAPTER VI

IRELAND AND THE
EUROPEAN BALANCE

During the whole of 1913 I was subjected to an ever-growing difficulty about the oil supply. We were now fully committed to oil as the sole motive power for a large proportion of the Fleet, including all the newest and most vital units. There was great anxiety on the Board of Admiralty and in the War Staff about our oil-fuel reserves. The Second Sea Lord, Sir John Jellicoe, vehemently pressed for very large increases in the scales contemplated. The Chief of the War Staff was concerned not only about the amount of the reserves, but about the alleged danger of using so explosive a fuel in ships of war. Lastly, Lord Fisher's Royal Commission, actuated by Admiralty disquietude, showed themselves inclined to press for a reserve equal to four years' expected war consumption. The war consumption itself had been estimated on the most liberal scale by the Naval Staff. The expense of creating the oil reserve was however enormous. Not only had the oil to be bought in a monopoly-ridden market, but large installations of oil tanks had to be erected and land purchased for the purpose. Although this oil-fuel reserve when created was clearly, whether for peace or war, as much an asset of the State as the gold reserve in the Bank of England, we were not allowed to treat it as capital expenditure: all must be found out of the current Estimates. At the same time, the Treasury and my colleagues in the Cabinet were becoming increasingly indignant at the naval expense, which it might be contended was largely due to my precipitancy in embarking on oil-burning battleships and also in wantonly increasing the size of the guns and the speed and armour of these vessels. On the one hand, therefore, I was subjected to this ever-growing naval pressure, and on the other to a solid wall of resistance to expense. In the midst of all lay the existence of our naval power.

I had thus to fight all the year on two fronts: on one to repulse the excessive and, as I thought, extravagant demands of the Royal Commission and of my naval advisers, and on the other to wrest the necessary supplies from the Treasury and the Cabinet. I had to be very careful that arguments intended for one front did not become known to my antagonists on the other.

All our financial commitments, fomented by rising prices and the ever-increasing complexity and refinement of naval appliances, came remorselessly to a head at the end of 1913 when the Estimates for the new year had to be presented first to the Treasury and then to the Cabinet.

We failed to reach any agreement with the Treasury in the preliminary discussions, and the whole issue was remitted to the Cabinet at the end of November. There followed nearly five months of extreme dispute and tension, during which Naval Estimates formed the main and often the sole topic of conversation at no less than fourteen full and prolonged meetings of the Cabinet. At the outset I found myself almost in a minority of one. I was not in a position to give way on any of the essentials, especially in regard to the Battleship programme, without departing from the calculated and declared standards of strength on which the whole of our policy towards Germany depended. The Cabinet had decided in 1912 to maintain equality in the Mediterranean with the Austrian Fleet, four Dreadnoughts of which were steadily building. Moreover, the issue was complicated by the promised three Canadian Dreadnoughts. The Canadian Government had stipulated that these should be additional to the 60 per cent standard. We had formally declared that they were indispensable, and on this assurance Sir Robert Borden was committed to a fierce party fight in Canada. As it was now clear, owing to the action of the Canadian Senate, that these "additional" "indispensable" ships would not be laid down in the ensuing year, I was forced to demand the earlier laying down of three at least of the battleships of the 1914–15 programme. This was a very hard matter for the Cabinet to sanction. By the middle of December it seemed to me certain that I should have to resign. The very foundations of naval policy were challenged, and the controversy was maintained by Ministerial critics specially acquainted with Admiralty business, versed in every detail of the problem and entitled to be exactly informed on every point. The Prime Minister, however, while appearing to remain impartial, so handled matters that no actual breach occurred. On several occasions when it seemed that disagreement was total and final, he prevented a decision adverse to the Admiralty by terminating the discussion; and in the middle of December, when this process could go on no longer, he adjourned the whole matter till the middle of January.

The interval for reflection produced a certain change in the situation, and on my return to England in the middle of January, I was informed by several of my most important colleagues that they considered the Admiralty case on main essentials had been made good. The conflict, however, renewed itself with the utmost vigour. We continued to pump out documents and arguments from the Admiralty in a ceaseless stream, dealing with each new point as it was challenged.

Meanwhile, echoes of the controversy had found their way into the newspapers. As early as January 3, the Chancellor of the Exchequer, in an interview with the *Daily Chronicle,* had deplored the folly of expenditure upon armaments, had pointedly referred to the resignation of Lord Randolph Churchill on the subject of economy, and had expressed the opinion that the state and prospects of the world were never more peaceful. The Liberal and Radical press were loud in their economy chorus, and a very strong movement against the Admiralty developed among our most influential supporters in the House of Commons. However, Parliament soon reassembled. The Irish question began to dominate attention. Eager partisans of the Home Rule cause were by no means anxious to see the Government weakened by the resignation of the entire Board of Admiralty. We were already so hard pressed in the party struggle that the defection even of a single Minister might have produced a serious effect. No one expected me to pass away in sweet silence. The prospect of a formidable naval agitation added to the Irish tension was recognized as uninviting. In order to strengthen myself with my party, I mingled actively in the Irish controversy; and in this precarious situation the whole of February and part of March passed without any ground given or taken on either side.

At last, thanks to the unwearying patience of the Prime Minister, and to his solid, silent support, the Naval Estimates were accepted practically as they stood. In all these months of bickering we had only lost three small cruisers and twelve torpedo-boats for harbour defence. Estimates were presented to Parliament for 52½ millions. We had not secured this victory without being compelled to give certain general assurances with regard to the future. I agreed, under proper reserves, to promise a substantial reduction on the Estimates of the following year.

But when the time came, I was not pressed to redeem this undertaking.

The spring and summer of 1914 were marked in Europe by an exceptional tranquility. Ever since Agadir the policy of Germany towards Great Britain had not only been correct, but considerate. All through the tangle of the Balkan Conferences British and German diplomacy laboured in harmony. The long distrust which had grown up in the Foreign Office, though not removed, was sensibly modified. Some at least of those who were accustomed to utter warnings began to feel the need of revising their judgment. The personalities who expressed the foreign policy of Germany, seemed for the first time to be men to whom we could talk and with whom common action was possible. The peaceful solution of the Balkan difficulties afforded justification for the feeling of confidence. For months we had negotiated upon the most delicate questions on the brink of local rupture, and no rupture had come. There had been a score of opportunities had any Power wished to make war. Germany seemed, with us, to be set on peace. Although abroad the increase of armaments was proceeding with constant acceleration, although the fifty million capital tax had been levied in Germany, and that alarm bell was ringing for those that had ears to hear, a distinct feeling of optimism passed over the mind of the British Government and the House of Commons. There seemed also to be a prospect that the personal goodwill and mutual respect which had grown up between the principal people on both sides might play a useful part in the future; and some there were who looked forward to a wider combination in which Great Britain and Germany, without prejudice to their respective friendships or alliances, might together bring the two opposing European systems into harmony and give to all the anxious nations solid assurances of safety and fair-play. Naval rivalry had at the moment ceased to be a cause of friction. We were proceeding inflexibly for the third year in succession with our series of programmes according to scale and declaration. Germany had made no further increases since the beginning of 1912. It was certain that we could not be overtaken as far as capital ships were concerned.

The strange calm of the European situation contrasted with the rising fury of party conflict at home. The quarrel between Liberals and Conservatives had taken on much of that tense bitterness and hatred belonging to Irish affairs. As it became certain that the Home Rule Bill would pass into law under the machinery of the Parliament Act, the Protestant counties of Ulster openly developed their preparations for armed resistance. In this they were supported and encouraged by the whole Conservative Party. The Irish Nationalist leaders— Mr. Redmond, Mr. Dillon, Mr. Devlin and others—watched the increasing gravity of the situation in Ulster with apprehension. But there were elements behind them whose fierceness and whose violence were indescribable; and every step or gesture of moderation on the part of the Irish Parliamentary Party excited passionate anger. Between these difficulties Mr. Asquith's Government sought to thread their way.

From the earliest discussions on the Home Rule Bill in 1909 the Chancellor of the Exchequer and I had always advocated the exclusion of Ulster on a basis of county option or some similar process. We had been met by the baffling argument that such a concession might well be made as the final means of securing a settlement, but would be fruitless till then. The time had now arrived when the Home Rule issue had reached its supreme climax, and the Cabinet was generally agreed that we could not go farther without providing effectually for the exclusion of Ulster. In March, therefore, the Irish leaders were informed that the Government had so resolved. They resisted vehemently. They had it in their power at any time to turn out the Government, and they would have been powerfully reinforced from within the Liberal Party itself. There is no doubt that the Irish leaders feared, and even expected, that any weakening of the Bill would lead to its and their repudiation by the Irish people. Confronted, however, with the undoubted fact that the Government would not shrink from being defeated and broken up on the point, they yielded. Amendments were framed which secured to any Ulster county the right to vote itself out of the Home Rule Bill until after two successive General Elections had taken place in the United Kingdom. There could be no greater practical safeguard than this. It preserved the principle of Irish unity, but it made certain that unity could never be achieved except by the free consent of the Protestant North after seeing a Dublin Parliament actually on trial for a period of at least five years.

These proposals were no sooner announced to Parliament than they were rejected with contumely by the Conservative opposition. We, however, embodied them in the text of the Bill and compelled the Irish Party to vote for their inclusion. We now felt that we could go forward with a clear conscience and enforce the law against all who challenged it. My own personal view had always been that I would never coerce Ulster to make her come under a Dublin Parliament, but I would do all that was necessary to prevent her stopping the rest of Ireland having the Parliament they desired. I believe this was sound and right, and in support of it I was certainly prepared to maintain the authority of Crown and Parliament under the Constitution by whatever means were necessary. I spoke in this sense at Bradford on March 14.

It is greatly to be hoped that British political leaders will never again allow themselves to be goaded and spurred and driven by each other or by their followers into the excesses of partisanship which on both sides disgraced the year 1914, and which were themselves only the culmination of that long succession of biddings and counter-biddings for mastery to which a previous chapter has alluded. No one who has not been involved in such contentions can understand the intensity of the pressures to which public men are subjected, or the way in which every motive in their nature, good, bad and indifferent, is marshalled in the direction of further effort to secure victory. The vehemence with which great masses of men yield themselves to partisanship and follow the struggle as if it were a prize fight, their ardent enthusiasm, their glistening eyes, their swift anger, their distrust and contempt if they think they are to be baulked of their prey; the sense of wrongs mutually interchanged, the extortion and enforcement of pledges, the infectious loyalties, the praise that waits on violence; the chilling disdain, the honest disappointment, the cries of "treachery" with which every proposal of compromise is hailed; the desire to keep good faith with those who follow, the sense of right being on one's side, the harsh unreasonable actions of opponents—all these acting and reacting reciprocally upon one another tend towards the perilous climax. To fall behind is to be a laggard or a weakling, not sincere, not courageous; to get in front of the crowd, if only to command them and to deflect them, prompts often very violent action. And at a certain stage it is hardly possible to keep the contention within the limits of words or laws. Force, that final arbiter, that last soberer, may break upon the scene.

The preparations of the Ulstermen continued. They declared their intention of setting up a provisional Government. They continued to develop and train their forces. They imported arms unlawfully and even by violence. It need scarcely be said that the same kind of symptoms began to manifest themselves among the Nationalists. Volunteers were enrolled by thousands, and efforts were made to procure arms.

As all this peril grew, the small military posts in the North of Ireland, particularly those containing stores of arms, became a source of preoccupation to the War Office. So also did the position of the troops in Belfast. The Orangemen would never have harmed the Royal forces. It was more than probable that the troops would fraternize with them. But the Government saw themselves confronted with a complete overturn of their authority throughout North-East Ulster. In these circumstances, military and naval precautions were indispensable. On 14th March it was determined to protect the military stores at Carrickfergus and certain other places by small reinforcements, and as it was expected that the Great Northern Railway of Ireland would refuse to carry the troops, preparations were made to send them by sea. It was also decided to move a battle squadron and a flotilla from Arosa Bay, where they were cruising, to Lamlash, whence they could rapidly reach Belfast. It was thought that the popularity and influence of the Royal Navy might produce a peaceable solution, even if the Army had failed. Beyond this nothing was authorized; but the Military Commanders, seeing themselves confronted with what might well be the opening movements in a civil war, began to study plans of a much more serious character on what was the inherently improbable assumption that the British troops would be forcibly resisted and fired upon by the Orange army.

These military measures, limited though they were, and the possible consequences that might follow them, produced the greatest distress among the officers of the Army, and when on 20th March the Commander-in-Chief in Ireland and other Generals made sensational appeals to gatherings of officers at the Curragh to discharge their constitutional duty in all circumstances, they encountered very general refusals.

These shocking events caused an explosion of unparalleled fury in Parliament and shook the State to its foundations. The Conservatives accused the Government of having plotted the massacre of the loyalists of Ulster, in which design they had been frustrated only by their patriotism of the Army. The Liberals replied that the Opposition were seeking to subvert the Constitution by openly committing themselves to preparations for rebellion, and had seduced not the Army but its officers from their allegiance by propaganda. We cannot read the debates that continued at intervals through April, May and June, without wondering that our Parliamentary institutions were strong enough to survive the passions by which they were convulsed. Was it astonishing that German agents reported and German statesmen believed, that England was paralysed by faction and drifting into civil war, and need not be taken into account as a factor in the European situation? How could they discern or measure the deep unspoken understandings which lay far beneath the froth and foam and fury of the storm?

During the whole of May and June the party warfare proceeded in its most strident form, but underneath the surface, negotiations for a settlement between the two great parties were steadily persisted in. These eventuated on the 20th July in a summons by the King to the leaders of the Conservative, Liberal and Irish parties to meet in conference at Buckingham Palace.

At the end of June the simultaneous British naval visits to Kronstadt and Kiel took place. For the first time for several years some of the finest ships of the British and German Navies lay at their moorings at Kiel side by side surrounded by liners, yachts and pleasure craft of every kind. Undue curiosity in technical matters was banned by mutual agreement. There were races, there were banquets, there were speeches. There was sunshine, there was the Emperor. Officers and men fraternized and entertained each other afloat and ashore. Together they strolled arm in arm through the hospitable town, or dined with all goodwill in mess and wardroom. Together they stood bareheaded at the funeral of a German officer killed in flying an English seaplane.

In the midst of these festivities, on the 28th June, arrived the news of the murder of the Archduke Charles at Sarajevo. The Emperor was out sailing when he received it. He came on shore in noticeable agitation, and that same evening, cancelling his other arrangements, quitted Kiel.

Like many others, I often summon up in my memory the impression of those July days. The world on the verge of its catastrophe was very brilliant. Nations and Empires crowned with princes and potentates rose majestically on every side, lapped in the accumulated treasures of the long peace. All were fitted and fastened—it seemed securely—into an immense cantilever. The two mighty European systems faced each other glittering and clanking in their panoply, but with a tranquil gaze. A polite, discreet, pacific, and on the whole sincere diplomacy spread its web of connections over both. A sentence in a despatch, an observation by an ambassador, a cryptic phrase in a Parliament seemed sufficient to adjust from day to day the balance of the prodigious structure. Words counted, and even whispers. A nod could be made to tell. Were we after all to achieve world security and universal peace by a marvellous system of combinations in equipoise and of armaments in equation, of checks and counter-checks on violent action ever more complex and more delicate? Would Europe thus marshalled, thus grouped, thus related, unite into one universal and glorious organism capable of receiving and enjoying in undreamed-of abundance the bounty which nature and science stood hand in hand to give? The old world in its sunset was fair to see.

But there was a strange temper in the air. Unsatisfied by material prosperity the nations turned restlessly towards strife internal or external. National passions, unduly exalted in the decline of religion, burned beneath the surface of nearly every land with fierce, if shrouded, fires. Almost one might think the world wished to suffer. Certainly men were everywhere eager to dare. On all sides the military preparations, precautions and counter precautions had reached their height. France had her Three Years' military service; Russia her growing strategic Railways. The Ancient Empire of the Hapsburgs, newly smitten by the bombs of Sarajevo, was a prey to intolerable racial stresses and profound processes of decay. Italy faced Turkey; Turkey confronted Greece; Greece, Serbia and Roumania stood against Bulgaria. Britain was rent by faction and seemed almost negligible. America was three thousand miles away. Germany, her fifty million capital tax expended on munitions, her army increases completed, the Kiel Canal open for Dreadnought battleships that very month, looked fixedly upon the scene and her gaze became suddenly a glare.

In the autumn of 1913, when I was revolving the next year's Admiralty policy in the light of the coming Estimates, I had sent the First Sea Lord a minute advising that for the purposes of economy we should omit the Grand Manœuvres in the year 1914–15, and substitute a mobilization of the Third Fleet. The entire Royal Fleet Reserve and all the Reserve officers were to be mobilized and trained together for a week or ten days on Third Fleet ships carrying the exact complements they would have in war, thereby subjecting the entire mobilization system to a real test. This was to be followed later in the year by a mobilization of the entire Royal Naval Volunteer Reserve on First Fleet ships for a week, additional to the regular complements.

Prince Louis agreed. The necessary measures were taken and the project was mentioned to Parliament on the 18th March, 1914. In pursuance of these orders and without connection of any kind with the European situation, the Test Mobilization began on 15th July. Although there was no legal authority to compel the reservists to come up, the response was general, upwards of 20,000 men presenting themselves at the naval depôts. The whole of our mobilization arrangements were thus subjected for the first time in naval history to a practical test and thorough overhaul. Officers specially detached from the Admiralty watched the process of mobilization at every port in order that every defect, shortage or hitch in the system might be reported and remedied. Prince Louis and I personally inspected the process at Chatham. All the reservists drew their kits and proceeded to their assigned ships. All the Third Fleet ships coaled and raised steam and sailed for the general concentration at Spithead. Here on the 17th and 18th of July was held the grand review of the Navy. It constituted incomparably the greatest assemblage of naval power ever witnessed in the history of the world. The King himself was present and inspected ships of every class. On the morning of the 19th the whole Fleet put to sea for exercises of various kinds. It took more than six hours for this armada, every ship decked with flags and crowded with bluejackets and marines, to pass, with bands playing and at 15 knots, before the Royal Yacht, while overhead the naval seaplanes and aeroplanes circled continuously. Yet it is probable that the uppermost thought in the minds both of the Sovereign and those of his Ministers there present, was not the imposing spectacle of British majesty and might defiling before their eyes, not the oppressive and even sultry atmosphere of continental politics, but the haggard, squalid, tragic Irish quarrel which threatened to divide the British nation into two hostile camps.

One after another the ships melted out of sight beyond the Nab. They were going on a longer voyage than any of us could know.

CHAPTER VII

THE CRISIS

July 24–July 30

The Cabinet on Friday afternoon sat long revolving the Irish problem. The Buckingham Palace Conference had broken down. The disagreements and antagonisms seemed as fierce and as hopeless as ever, yet the margin in dispute, upon which such fateful issues hung, was inconceivably petty. The discussion turned principally upon the boundaries of Fermanagh and Tyrone. To this pass had the Irish factions in their insensate warfare been able to drive their respective British champions. Upon the disposition of these clusters of humble parishes turned at that moment the political future of Great Britain. The North would not agree to this, and the South would not agree to that. Both the leaders wished to settle; both had dragged their followers forward to the utmost point they dared. Neither seemed able to give an inch. Meanwhile, the settlement of Ireland must carry with it an immediate and decisive abatement of party strife in Britain, and those schemes of unity and co-operation which had so intensely appealed to the leading men on both sides, ever since Mr. Lloyd George had mooted them in 1910, must necessarily have come forward into the light of day. Failure to settle on the other hand meant something very like civil war and the plunge into depths of which no one could make any measure. And so, turning this way and that in search of an exit from the deadlock, the Cabinet toiled around the muddy byways of Fermanagh and Tyrone. One had hoped that the events of April at the Curragh and in Belfast would have shocked British public opinion, and formed a unity sufficient to impose a settlement on the Irish factions. Apparently they had been insufficient. Apparently the conflict would be carried one stage further by both sides with incalculable consequences before there would be a recoil. Since the days of the Blues and the Greens in the Byzantine Empire, partisanship had rarely been carried to more absurd extremes. An all-sufficient shock was, however, at hand.

The discussion had reached its inconclusive end, and the Cabinet was about to separate, when the quiet grave tones of Sir Edward Grey's voice were heard reading a document which had just been brought to him from the Foreign Office. It was the Austrian note to Serbia. He had been reading or speaking for several minutes before I could disengage my mind from the tedious and bewildering debate which had just closed. We were all very tired, but gradually as the phrases and sentences followed one another, impressions of a wholly different character began to form in my mind. This note was clearly an ultimatum; but it was an ultimatum such as had never been penned in modern times. As the reading proceeded it seemed absolutely impossible that any State in the world could accept it, or that any acceptance, however abject, would satisfy the aggressor. The parishes of Fermanagh and Tyrone faded back into the mists and squalls of Ireland, and a strange light began immediately, but by perceptible gradations, to fall and grow upon the map of Europe.

I always take the greatest interest in reading accounts of how the war came upon different people; where they were, and what they were doing, when the first impression broke on their mind, and they first began to feel this overwhelming event laying its fingers on their lives. I never tire of the smallest detail, and I believe that so long as they are true and unstudied they will have a definite value and an enduring interest for posterity; so I shall briefly record exactly what happened to me.

I went back to the Admiralty at about 6 o'clock. I said to my friends who have helped me so many years in my work[1] that there was real danger and that it might be war.

I took stock of the position, and wrote out to focus them in my mind a series of points which would have to be attended to if matters did not mend. My friends kept these as a check during the days that followed and ticked them off one by one as they were settled.

1. First and Second Fleets. Leave and disposition.
2. Third Fleet. Replenish coal and stores.
3. Mediterranean movements.
4. China dispositions.
5. Shadowing cruisers abroad.
6. Ammunition for self-defensive merchantmen.
7. Patrol Flotillas. Disposition.
    Leave.
    Complete.
    35 ex-Coastals.
8. Immediate Reserve.
9. Old Battleships for Humber. Flotilla for Humber.
10. Ships at emergency dates.
    Ships building for Foreign Powers.
11. Coastal Watch.
12. Anti-aircraft guns at Oil Depôts.

---

[1] Mr. Marsh and Mr. (now Sir James) Masterton Smith.

13. Aircraft to Sheerness. Airships and Seaplanes.
14. K. Espionage.
15. Magazines and other vulnerable points.
16. Irish ships.
17. Submarine dispositions.

I discussed the situation at length the next morning (Saturday) with the First Sea Lord. For the moment, however, there was nothing to do. At no time in all these last three years were we more completely ready.

The test mobilization had been completed, and with the exception of the Immediate Reserve, all the reservists were already paid off and journeying to their homes. But the whole of the 1st and 2nd Fleets were complete in every way for battle and were concentrated at Portland, where they were to remain till Monday morning at 7 o'clock, when the 1st Fleet would disperse by squadrons for various exercises and when the ships of the 2nd Fleet would proceed to their Home Ports to discharge their balance crews. Up till Monday morning therefore, a word instantaneously transmitted from the wireless masts of the Admiralty to the *Iron Duke* would suffice to keep our main force together. If the word were not spoken before that hour, they would begin to separate. During the first twenty-four hours after their separation they could be reconcentrated in an equal period; but if no word were spoken for forty-eight hours (i.e. by Wednesday morning), then the ships of the 2nd Fleet would have begun dismissing their balance crews to the shore at Portsmouth, Plymouth and Chatham, and the various gunnery and torpedo schools would have recommenced their instruction. If another forty-eight hours had gone before the word was spoken, i.e. by Friday morning, a certain number of vessels would have gone into dock for refit, repairs or laying up. Thus on the Saturday morning we had the Fleet in hand for at least four days.

The night before (Friday), at dinner, I had met Herr Ballin. He had just arrived from Germany. We sat next to each other, and I asked him what he thought about the situation. With the first few words he spoke, it became clear that he had not come here on any mission of pleasure. He said the situation was grave. "I remember," he said, "old Bismarck telling me the year before he died that one day the great European War would come out of some damned foolish thing in the Balkans." These words, he said, might come true. It all depended on the Tsar. What would he do if Austria chastised Serbia? A few years before there would have been no danger, as the Tsar was too frightened for his throne, but now again he was feeling himself more secure upon his throne, and the Russian people besides would feel very hardly anything done against Serbia. Then he said, "If Russia marches against Austria, we must march; and if we march, France must march, and what would England do?" I was not in a position to say more than that it would be a great mistake to assume that England would necessarily do nothing, and I added that she would judge events as they arose. He replied, speaking with very great earnestness, "Suppose we had to go to war with Russia and France, and suppose we defeated France and yet took nothing from her in Europe, not an inch of her territory, only some colonies to indemnify us. Would that make a difference to England's attitude? Suppose we gave a guarantee beforehand." I stuck to my formula that England would judge events as they arose, and that it would be a mistake to assume that we should stand out of it whatever happened.

I reported this conversation to Sir Edward Grey in due course, and early in the following week I repeated it to the Cabinet. On the Wednesday following the exact proposal mooted to me by Herr Ballin, about Germany not taking any territorial conquests in France but seeking indemnities only in the colonies, was officially telegraphed to us from Berlin and immediately rejected. I have no doubt that Herr Ballin was directly charged by the Emperor with the mission to find out what England would do.

Herr Ballin has left on record his impression of his visit to England at this juncture. "Even a moderately skilled German diplomatist," he wrote, "could easily have come to an understanding with England and France, who could have made peace certain and prevented Russia from beginning war." The editor of his memoirs adds: "The people in London were certainly seriously concerned at the Austrian Note, but the extent to which the Cabinet desired the maintenance of peace may be seen (as an example) from the remark which Churchill, almost with tears in his eyes, made to Ballin as they parted: 'My dear friend, don't let us go to war.'"

I had planned to spend the Sunday with my family at Cromer, and I decided not to alter my plans. I arranged to have a special operator placed in the telegraph office so as to ensure a continuous night and day service. On Saturday afternoon the news came in that Serbia had accepted the ultimatum. I went to bed with a feeling things might blow over. We had had, as this account has shown, so many scares before. Time after time the clouds had loomed up vague, menacing, constantly changing; time after time they had dispersed. We were still a long way, as it seemed, from any danger of war. Serbia had accepted the ultimatum, could Austria demand more? And if war came, could it not be confined to the East of Europe? Could not France and Germany, for instance, stand aside and leave Russia and Austria to settle their quarrel? And then, one step further removed, was our own case. Clearly there would be a chance of a conference, there would be time for Sir Edward Grey to get to work with conciliatory processes such as had proved so effective in the Balkan difficulties the year before. Anyhow, whatever happened, the British Navy had never been in a better condition or in greater strength. Probably the call would not come, but if it did, it could not come in a better hour. Reassured by these reflections I slept peacefully, and no summons disturbed the silence of the night.

At 9 o'clock the next morning I called up the First Sea Lord by telephone. He told me that there was a rumour that Austria was not satisfied with the Serbian acceptance of the ultimatum, but otherwise there were no new developments. I asked him to call me up again at twelve. I went down to the beach and played with the children. We dammed the little rivulets which trickled down to the sea as the tide went out. It was a very beautiful day. The North Sea shone and sparkled to a far horizon. What was there beyond that line where sea and sky melted into one another? All along the East Coast, from Cromarty to Dover, in their various sally-ports, lay our patrol flotillas of destroyers and submarines. In the Channel behind the torpedo-proof moles of Portland Harbour waited all the great ships of the British Navy. Away to the north-east, across the sea that stretched before me, the German High Sea Fleet, squadron by squadron, was cruising off the Norwegian coast.

At 12 o'clock I spoke to the First Sea Lord again. He told me various items of news that had come in from different capitals, none however of decisive importance, but all tending to a rise of temperature. I asked him whether all the reservists had already been dismissed. He told me they had. I decided to return to London. I told him I would be with him at nine, and that meanwhile he should do whatever was necessary.

Prince Louis awaited me at the Admiralty. The situation was evidently degenerating. Special editions of the Sunday papers showed intense excitement in nearly every European capital. The First Sea Lord told me that in accordance with our conversation he had told the Fleet not to disperse. I took occasion to refer to this four months later in my letter accepting his resignation. I was very glad publicly to testify at that moment of great grief and pain for him that his loyal hand had sent the first order which began our vast naval mobilization.

I then went round to Sir Edward Grey, who had rented my house at 33 Eccleston Square. No one was with him except Sir William Tyrrell of the Foreign Office. I told him that we were holding the Fleet together. I learned from him that he viewed the situation very gravely. He said there was a great deal yet to be done before a really dangerous crisis was reached, but that he did not at all like the way in which this business had begun. I asked whether it would be helpful or the reverse if we stated in public that we were keeping the Fleet together. Both he and Tyrrell were most insistent that we should proclaim it at the earliest possible moment: it might have the effect of sobering the Central Powers and steadying Europe. I went back to the Admiralty, sent for the First Sea Lord, and drafted the necessary communiqué.

The next morning the following notice appeared in all the papers:

BRITISH NAVAL MEASURES
ORDERS TO FIRST AND SECOND FLEETS
No Manœuvre Leave

We received the following statement from the Secretary of the Admiralty at an early hour this morning:

Orders have been given to the First Fleet, which is concentrated at Portland, not to disperse for manœuvre leave for the present. All vessels of the Second Fleet are remaining at their home ports in proximity to their balance crews.

On Monday began the first of the Cabinets on the European situation, which thereafter continued daily or twice a day. It is to be hoped that sooner or later a detailed account of the movement of opinion in the Cabinet during this period will be compiled and given to the world. There is certainly no reason for anyone to be ashamed of honest and sincere counsel given either to preserve peace or to enter upon a just and necessary war. Meanwhile it is only possible, without breach of constitutional propriety, to deal in the most general terms with what took place.

The Cabinet was overwhelmingly pacific. At least three-quarters of its members were determined not to be drawn into a European quarrel, unless Great Britain were herself attacked, which was not likely. Those who were in this mood were inclined to believe first of all that Austria and Serbia would not come to blows; secondly, that if they did, Russia would not intervene; thirdly, if Russia intervened, that Germany would not strike; fourthly, they hoped that if Germany struck at Russia, it ought to be possible for France and Germany mutually to neutralize each other without fighting. They did not believe that if Germany attacked France, she would attack her through Belgium or that if she did the Belgians would forcibly resist; and it must be remembered, that during the whole course of this week Belgium not only never asked for assistance from the guaranteeing Powers but pointedly indicated that she wished to be left alone. So here were six or seven positions, all of which could be wrangled over and about none of which any final proof could be offered except the proof of events. It was not until Monday, August 3, that the direct appeal from the King of the Belgians for French and British aid raised an issue which united the overwhelming majority of Ministers and enabled Sir Edward Grey to make his speech on that afternoon to the House of Commons.

My own part in these events was a very simple one. It was first of all to make sure that the diplomatic situation did not get ahead of the naval situation, and that the Grand Fleet should be in its War Station before Germany could know whether or not we should be in the war, *and therefore if possible before we had decided ourselves.* Secondly, it was to point out that if Germany attacked

France, she would do so through Belgium, that all her preparations had been made to this end, and that she neither could nor would adopt any different strategy or go round any other way. To these two tasks I steadfastly adhered.

Every day there were long Cabinets from eleven onwards. Streams of telegrams poured in from every capital in Europe. Sir Edward Grey was plunged in his immense double struggle *(a)* to prevent war and *(b)* not to desert France should it come. I watched with admiration his activities at the Foreign Office and cool skill in Council. Both these tasks acted and reacted on one another from hour to hour. He had to try to make the Germans realize that we were to be reckoned with, without making the French or Russians feel they had us in their pockets. He had to carry the Cabinet with him in all he did. During the many years we acted together in the Cabinet, and the earlier years in which I read his Foreign Office telegrams, I thought I had learnt to understand his methods of discussion and controversy, and perhaps without offence I might describe them.

After what must have been profound reflection and study, the Foreign Secretary was accustomed to select one or two points in any important controversy which he defended with all his resources and tenacity. They were his fortified villages. All around in the open field the battle ebbed and flowed, but if at nightfall these points were still in his possession, his battle was won. All other arguments had expended themselves, and these key positions alone survived. The points which he selected over and over again proved to be inexpugnable. They were particularly adapted to defence. They commended themselves to sensible and fair-minded men. The sentiments of the patriotic Whig, the English gentleman, the public school boy all came into the line for their defence, and if they were held, the whole front was held, including much debatable ground.

As soon as the crisis had begun he had fastened upon the plan of a European conference, and to this end every conceivable endeavour was made by him. To get the Great Powers together round a table in any capital that was agreeable, with Britain there to struggle for peace, and if necessary to threaten war against those who broke it, was his plan. Had such a conference taken place, there could have been no war. Mere acceptance of the principle of a conference by the Central Powers would have instantly relieved the tension. A will to peace at Berlin and Vienna would have found no difficulties in escaping from the terrible net which was drawing in upon us all hour by hour. But underneath the diplomatic communications and manoeuvres, the baffling proposals and counter-proposals, the agitated interventions of Tsar and Kaiser, flowed a deep tide of calculated military purpose. As the ill-fated nations approached the verge, the sinister machines of war began to develop their own momentum and eventually to take control themselves.

The Foreign Secretary's second cardinal point was the English Channel. Whatever happened, if war came, we could not allow the German Fleet to come down the Channel to attack the French ports. Such a situation would be insupportable for Great Britain. Everyone who counted was agreed on that from a very early stage in our discussions. But in addition we were, in a sense, morally committed to France to that extent. No bargain had been entered into. All arrangements that had been concerted were, as has been explained, specifically preluded with a declaration that neither party was committed to anything further than consultation together if danger threatened. But still the fact remained that the whole French Fleet was in the Mediterranean. Only a few cruisers and flotillas remained to guard the Northern and Atlantic Coasts of France; and simultaneously with that redisposition of forces, though not contingent upon it or dependent upon it, we had concentrated all our battleships at home, and only cruisers and battle-cruisers maintained British interests in the Mediterranean. The French had taken their decision on their own responsibility without prompting from us, and we had profited by their action to strengthen our margin in the Line of Battle at home. Whatever disclaimers we had made about not being committed, could we, when it came to the point, honourably stand by and see the naked French coasts ravaged and bombarded by German Dreadnoughts under the eyes and within gunshot of our Main Fleet?

It seemed to me, however, very early in the discussion that the Germans would concede this point to keep us out of the war, at any rate till the first battles on land had been fought without us; and sure enough they did. Believing as I did and do, that we could not, for our own safety and independence, allow France to be crushed as the result of aggressive action by Germany, I always from the very earliest moment concentrated upon our obligations to Belgium, through which I was convinced the Germans must inevitably march to invade France. Belgium did not count so largely in my sentiments at this stage. I thought it very unlikely that she would resist. I thought, and Lord Kitchener, who lunched with me on the Tuesday (28th), agreed, that Belgium would make some formal protest and submit. A few shots might be fired outside Liège or Namur, and then this unfortunate State would bow its head before overwhelming might. Perhaps, even, there was a secret agreement allowing free passage to the Germans through Belgium. How otherwise would all these preparations of Germany, the great camps along the Belgian Frontier, the miles and miles of sidings, the intricate network of railways have been developed? Was it possible that German thoroughness could be astray on so important a factor as the attitude of Belgium?

Those wonderful events which took place in Belgium on Sunday and Monday and in the week that followed could not be foreseen by us. I saw in

Belgium a country with whom we had had many differences over the Congo and other subjects. I had not discerned in the Belgium of the late King Leopold the heroic nation of King Albert. But whatever happened to Belgium, there was France whose very life was at stake, whose armies in my judgment were definitely weaker than those by whom they would be assailed, whose ruin would leave us face to face alone with triumphant Germany: France, in those days schooled by adversity to peace and caution, thoroughly democratic, already stripped of two fair provinces, about to receive the final smashing blow from overwhelming brutal force. Only Britain could redress the balance, could defend the fair-play of the world. Whatever else failed, we must be there, and we must be there in time. A week later every British heart burned for little Belgium. From every cottage labouring men, untrained to war but with the blood of an unconquered people in their veins, were hurrying to the recruiting stations with intent to rescue Belgium. But at this time it was not Belgium one thought of, but France. Still, Belgium and the Treaties were indisputably an obligation of honour binding upon the British State such as British Governments have always accepted; and it was on that ground that I personally, with others, took my stand.

I will now examine the alternative question of whether more decided action by Sir Edward Grey at an early stage would have prevented the war. We must first ask, At what early stage? Suppose after Agadir or on the announcement of the new German Navy Law in 1912 the Foreign Secretary had, in cold blood, proposed a formal alliance with France and Russia, and in execution of military conventions consequential upon the alliance had begun to raise by compulsion an army adequate to our responsibilities and to the part we were playing in the world's affairs; and suppose we had taken this action as a united nation; who shall say whether that would have prevented or precipitated the war? But what chance was there of such action being unitedly taken? The Cabinet of the day would never have agreed to it. I doubt if our Ministers would have agreed to it. But if the Cabinet had been united upon it, the House of Commons would not have accepted their guidance. Therefore the Foreign Minister would have had to resign. The policy which he had advocated would have stood condemned and perhaps violently repudiated; and with that repudiation would have come an absolute veto upon all those informal preparations and non-committal discussions on which the defensive power of the Triple Entente was erected. Therefore, by taking such a course in 1912, Sir Edward Grey would only have paralysed Britain, isolated France, and increased the preponderant and growing power of Germany.

Suppose again, that now after the Austrian ultimatum to Serbia, the Foreign Secretary had proposed to the Cabinet that if matters were so handled that Germany attacked France or violated Belgian territory, Great Britain would declare war upon her. Would the Cabinet have assented to such a communication? I cannot believe it. If Sir Edward Grey could have said on Monday that if Germany attacked France or Belgium, England would declare war upon her, might there not still have been time to ward off the catastrophe? The question is certainly arguable. But the knowledge which we now have of events in Berlin tends to show that even then the German Government were too deeply committed by their previous action. They had before their eyes the deliberate British announcement that the Fleet was being held together. That at least was a serious if silent warning. Under its impression the German Emperor, as soon as he returned to Berlin, made on this same Monday and succeeding days strong efforts to bring Austria to reason and so to prevent war. But he could never overtake events or withstand the contagion of ideas. However this may be, I am certain that if Sir Edward Grey had sent the kind of ultimatum suggested, the Cabinet would have broken up, and it is also my belief that up till Wednesday or Thursday at least, the House of Commons would have repudiated his action. Nothing less than the deeds of Germany would have converted the British nation to war. To act in advance of those deeds would have led to an exposure of division worse than the guarded attitude which we maintained, which brought our country into the war united. After Wednesday or Thursday it was too late. By the time we could speak decisive words of warning, the hour of words had certainly passed for ever.

It is true to say that our *Entente* with France and the military and naval conversations that had taken place since 1906, had led us into a position where we had the obligations of an alliance without its advantages. An open alliance, if it could have been peacefully brought about at an earlier date, would have exercised a deterring effect upon the German mind, or at the least would have altered their military calculations. Whereas now we were morally bound to come to the aid of France and it was our interest to do so, and yet the fact that we should come in appeared so uncertain that it did not weigh as it should have done with the Germans. Moreover, as things were, if France had been in an aggressive mood, we should not have had the unquestioned right of an ally to influence her action in a pacific sense: and if as the result of her aggressive mood war had broken out and we had stood aside, we should have been accused of deserting her, and in any case would have been ourselves grievously endangered by her defeat.

However, in the event there was no need to moderate the French attitude. Justice to France requires the explicit statement that the conduct of her Government at this awful juncture was faultless. She assented instantly to every proposal that could make for peace. She abstained from every form of provocative action. She even compromised her own safety, holding back her covering troops at a considerable distance behind her frontier, and delaying her mobilization in the face of continually gathering German forces till the latest moment. Not until she was confronted with the direct demand of Germany to break her Treaty and abandon Russia, did France take up the challenge; and even had she acceded to the German demand, she would only, as we now know, have been faced with a further ultimatum to surrender to German military occupation as a guarantee for her neutrality the fortresses of Toul and Verdun. Thus there never was any chance of France being allowed to escape the ordeal. Even cowardice and dishonour would not have saved her. The Germans had resolved that if war came from any cause, they would take and break France forthwith as its first operation. The German military chiefs burned to give the signal, and were sure of the result. She would have begged for mercy in vain. She did not beg.

The more I reflect upon this situation, the more convinced I am that we took the only practical course that was open to us or to any British Cabinet; and that the objections which may be urged against it were less than those which would have attended any other sequence of action.

After hearing the discussions at Monday's Cabinet and studying the telegrams, I sent that night to all our Commanders-in-Chief the following very secret warning:

July 27, 1914.

This is not the Warning Telegram, but European political situation makes war between Triple Entente and Triple Alliance Powers by no means impossible. Be prepared to shadow possible hostile men-of-war and consider dispositions of H.M. ships under your command from this point of view. Measure is purely precautionary. No unnecessary person is to be informed. The utmost secrecy is to be observed.

On Tuesday morning I sent the following minute to the First Sea Lord, to which he replied marginally the same day:

July 28, 1914.

1. It would appear that the minesweepers should be quietly collected at some suitable point for attendance on the Battle Fleet, should it move.

Will go North with Fleet.

2. Let me have a short statement on the coal position and what measures you propose.

Done.

3. I presume *Firedrake* and *Lurcher* will now join their proper flotilla.

Yes.

4. All the vessels engaged on the coast of Ireland should be considered as available on mobilization, and on receipt of the warning telegram should move to their war stations without the slightest delay.

Have been ordered away.

5. It would certainly be desirable that *Triumph* should be quietly mobilized and that she should be ready to close [i.e. join] the China flagship with available destroyers. The position of the German heavy cruisers in China waters makes it clear that this can be done. Please examine and report what disadvantages this mobilization would entail. We can then discuss whether it is worth while taking them in the present circumstances. The China Squadron must be capable of concentrating as soon as the warning telegram is sent and before a main action is necessary. Without the *Triumph* the margin of superiority is small and any reinforcement from other stations would be slow.

Will be done as soon as F.O. concur.

Should concentrate at Hong-Kong at once.

6. You should consider whether the position of the *Goeben*[1] at Pola does not justify the detachment of the *New Zealand* to join the Mediterranean flag.

Decided "No" at Conference.

7. Yesterday, after consultation with the Prime Minister, I arranged personally with the Chief of the Imperial General Staff for the better guarding of magazines and oil tanks against evilly-disposed persons and attacks by aircraft. These measures have now been taken. See attached letter from the Chief of the Imperial General Staff and my reply. You should direct the Director of Operations Division to obtain full detailed information from the War Office of what has been done, and in the event of any place being overlooked, to make the necessary representations.

Settled personally with C. of I.G.S.

8. Director of the Air Division should be asked to report the exact positions of the aircraft

Done.

[1] I have adopted the familiar spelling of this ship's name instead of *Göben*.

which were concentrated yesterday in the neighbourhood of the Thames Estuary, and further to
state what is being done to reach a complete understanding between the aircraft and the military
authorities in charge of the aerial gun defences at
various points. This is of the utmost importance   L. B.
if accidents are to be avoided.

W. S. C.

The official "warning telegram" was dispatched from the Admiralty on
Wednesday, the 29th. On this same day I obtained from the Cabinet the authority to put into force the "Precautionary Period" regulations. The work of
Ottley and of Hankey and generally of the Committee of Imperial Defence,
was now put to the proof. It was found in every respect thorough and comprehensive, and all over the country emergency measures began to astonish the
public. Naval harbours were cleared, bridges were guarded, steamers were
boarded and examined, watchers lined the coasts.

Our war arrangements comprised an elaborate scheme for dealing with vessels under construction. In 1912 measures had been taken to keep it perpetually
up to date. The principle was that for the first three months of a war all efforts
should be concentrated on finishing ships that could be ready in the first six
months, other vessels whose dates of completion were more remote being
somewhat retarded. This ensured the greatest possible superiority in the early
months, and would give us time to see what kind of a war it was and how it
went, before dealing with more distant contingencies. The plan of course covered all ships building in Great Britain for foreign Powers. Of these there were
two battleships building for Turkey, three flotilla leaders for Chili, four destroyers for Greece, and three monitors for Brazil. There were also other important
ships, including a Chilian and a Brazilian battleship and a Dutch cruiser, which
would not be ready till much later. The Turkish battleships were vital to us.
With a margin of only seven Dreadnoughts we could not afford to do without
these two fine ships. Still less could we afford to see them fall into bad hands
and possibly be used against us. Had we delivered them to Turkey, they would,
as the event turned out, have formed with the *Goeben* a hostile force which
would have required a force of not less than four British Dreadnought battleships or battle-cruisers to watch them. Thus the British numbers would have
been reduced by two instead of being increased by two. One of the Turkish battleships (the *Reshadieh*)which Armstrongs were building on the Tyne when the
crisis began, was actually complete. The Turkish crew, over 500 strong, had already arrived to take her over and were lying in their steamer in the river. There
seemed to be a great danger of their coming on board, brushing aside Messrs.

Armstrongs' workmen and hoisting the Turkish flag, in which case a very difficult diplomatic situation would have been created. I determined to run no
risks, and on the 31st July I sent written instructions that adequate military
guards were to be placed on board this vessel and that in no circumstances was
she to be boarded by the Turks. The far-reaching consequences of this action
will be narrated in a later chapter.

It is interesting to read in the German Official History what they knew
about our preparations at this time.

At 6:30 p.m. on July 28 the following telegram was received in Berlin from
the German Naval Attaché:

> Admiralty are not publishing ships' movements. 2nd Fleet remains
> fully manned. Schools closed in naval bases; preliminary measures taken
> for recall from leave. According to unconfirmed news 1st Fleet still at
> Portland, one submarine flotilla left Portsmouth. It is to be assumed that
> Admiralty is preparing for mobilization on the quiet.

He telegraphed later on the same day as follows:

> As already reported by telegram, the British Fleet is preparing for
> all eventualities. In broad outline the present distribution is as follows: 1st
> Fleet is assembled at Portland. The battleship *Bellerophon* which was pro-
> ceeding to Gibraltar for refit has been recalled. The ships of the 2nd Fleet
> are at their bases: they are fully manned. The schools on shore have not
> reopened. Ships of the 2nd and 3rd Fleets have coaled, completed with
> ammunition and supplies, and are at their bases. In consequence of the
> training of reservists, just completed, latter can be manned more quickly
> than usual and with more or less practised personnel, the *Times* says,
> within 48 hours. The destroyer and patrol flotillas and the submarines are
> either at or *en route* for their stations. No leave is being granted, officers
> and men already on leave have been recalled.
>
> In the naval bases and dockyards great activity reigns; in addition spe-
> cial measures of precaution have been adopted, all dockyards, magazines,
> oil tanks, etc., being put under guard. Repairs of ships in dockyard hands
> are being speeded up. A great deal of night work is being done.
>
> The Press reports that the Mediterranean squadron had left Alexan-
> dria; it is said that it will remain at Malta.
>
> All ships and squadrons have orders to remain ready for sea.
>
> Outwardly complete calm is preserved, in order not to cause anxiety
> by alarming reports about the Fleet.
>
> Movements of ships, which are generally published daily by the Ad-
> miralty, have been withheld since yesterday. . . .

The above preparations have been made on the Admiralty's Independent initiative. The result is the same, whoever gave the orders.

The German Naval Attaché thus showed himself extremely well informed. As I have already mentioned in an earlier chapter, the general warrants to open the letters of certain persons which I had signed three years before as Home Secretary, had brought to light a regular network of minor agents, mostly British, in German pay in all our naval ports. Had we arrested them, others of whom we might not have known, would have taken their place. We therefore thought it better, having detected them, to leave them at large. In this way one saw regularly from their communications, which we carefully forwarded, what they were saying to their paymasters in Berlin during these years, and we knew exactly how to put our hands upon them at the proper moment. Up to this point we had no objection to the German Government knowing that exceptional precautions were being taken throughout the Navy. Indeed, apart from details, it was desirable that they should know how seriously we viewed the situation. But the moment had now come to draw down the curtain. We no longer forwarded the letters and a few days later, on a word from me to the Home Secretary, all these petty traitors, who for a few pounds a month were seeking to sell their country, were laid by the heels. Nor was it easy for the Germans to organize on the spur of the moment others in their places.

The most important step remains to be recounted. As early as Tuesday, July 28, I felt that the Fleet should go to its War Station. It must go there at once, and secretly; it must be steaming to the north while every German authority, naval or military, had the greatest possible interest in avoiding a collision with us. If it went thus early it need not go by the Irish Channel and north-about. It could go through the Straits of Dover and through the North Sea, and therefore the island would not be uncovered even for a single day. Moreover, it would arrive sooner and with less expenditure of fuel.

At about 10 o'clock, therefore, on the Tuesday morning I proposed this step to the First Sea Lord and the Chief of the Staff and found them wholeheartedly in favour of it. We decided that the Fleet should leave Portland at such an hour on the morning of the 29th as to pass the Straits of Dover during the hours of darkness, that it should traverse these waters at high speed and without lights, and with the utmost precaution proceed to Scapa Flow. I feared to bring this matter before the Cabinet, lest it should mistakenly be considered a provocative action likely to damage the chances of peace. It would be unusual to bring movements of the British Fleet in Home waters from one British port to another before the Cabinet. I only therefore informed the Prime Minister, who at once gave his approval. Orders were accordingly sent to Sir George Callaghan, who was told incidentally to send the Fleet up under his second-in-command and to travel himself by land through London in order that we might have an opportunity of consultation with him.

ADMIRALTY TO COMMANDER-IN-CHIEF HOME FLEETS.

July 28, 1914. Sent 5 p.m.

To-morrow, Wednesday, the First Fleet is to leave Portland for Scapa Flow. Destination is to be kept secret except to flag and commanding officers. As you are required at the Admiralty, Vice-Admiral 2nd Battle Squadron is to take command. Course from Portland is to be shaped to southward, then a middle Channel course to the Straits of Dover. The Squadrons are to pass through the Straits without lights during the night and to pass outside the shoals on their way north. *Agamemnon* is to remain at Portland, where the Second Fleet will assemble.

We may now picture this great Fleet, with its flotillas and cruisers, steaming slowly out of Portland Harbour, squadron by squadron, scores of gigantic castles of steel wending their way across the misty, shining sea, like giants bowed in anxious thought. We may picture them again as darkness fell, eighteen miles of warships running at high speed and in absolute blackness through the narrow Straits, bearing with them into the broad waters of the North the safeguard of considerable affairs.

Although there seemed to be no conceivable motive, chance or mischance, which could lead a rational German Admiralty to lay a trap of submarines or mines or have given them the knowledge and the time to do so, we looked at each other with much satisfaction when on Thursday morning (the 30th) at our daily Staff Meeting the Flagship reported herself and the whole Fleet well out in the centre of the North Sea.[1]

The German Ambassador lost no time in complaining of the movement of the Fleet to the Foreign Office. According to the German Official Naval History, he reported to his Government on the evening of the 30th that Sir Edward Grey had answered him in the following words:

The movements of the Fleet are free of all offensive character, and the Fleet will not approach German waters.

[1] Later in the morning I learnt that Lord Fisher was in the office and I invited him into my room. I told him what we had done and his delight was wonderful to see.

Foolish statements have been made from time to time that this sending of the Fleet to the North was done at Lord Fisher's suggestion. The interview with me which Lord Fisher records in his book is correctly given by him as having taken place on the 30th. The Fleet had actually passed the Straits of Dover the night before. I think it necessary to place on record the fact that my sole naval adviser on every measure taken prior to the declaration of war was the First Sea Lord.

"But," adds the German historian, "the strategic concentration of the Fleet had actually been accomplished with its transfer to Scottish ports." This was true. We were now in a position, whatever happened, to control events, and it was not easy to see how this advantage could be taken from us. A surprise torpedo attack before or simultaneous with the declaration of war was at any rate one nightmare gone for ever. We could at least see for ten days ahead. If war should come no one would know where to look for the British Fleet. Somewhere in that enormous waste of waters to the north of our islands, cruising now this way, now that, shrouded in storms and mists, dwelt this mighty organization. Yet from the Admiralty building we could speak to them at any moment if need arose. The king's ships were at sea.

CHAPTER VIII

THE MOBILIZATION OF THE NAVY

July 31–August 4

There was complete agreement in the Cabinet upon every telegram sent by Sir Edward Grey and in his handling of the crisis. But there was also an invincible refusal on the part of the majority to contemplate British intervention by force of arms should the Foreign Secretary's efforts fail and a European war begin. Thus, as the terrific week wore on and the explosion became inevitable, it seemed probable that a rupture of the political organism by which the country had so long been governed was also rapidly approaching. I lived this week entirely in the official circle, seeing scarcely anyone but my colleagues of the Cabinet or of the Admiralty, and moving only to and fro across the Horse Guards between Admiralty House and Downing Street. Each day as the telegrams arrived showing the darkening scene of Europe, and each Cabinet ended in growing tension, I pulled over the various levers which successively brought our naval organization into full preparedness. It was always necessary to remember that if Peace was preserved, every one of these measures, alarmist in their character and involving much expense, would have to be justified to a Liberal House of Commons. That assembly once delivered from the peril, would certainly proceed upon the assumption that British participation in a continental struggle would have been criminal madness. Yet it was not practicable often to divert the main discussions of the Cabinet into purely technical channels. It was therefore necessary for me to take a peculiar and invidious personal responsibility for many things that had to be done when their turn came. I had also to contemplate a break-up of the governing instrument. Judged by reports and letters from members, the attitude of the House of Commons appeared most uncertain.

On Thursday evening I entered into communication with the Unionist leaders through Mr. F. E. Smith.[1] I informed him of the increasing gravity of the European situation and of the military preparations which were everywhere in progress in Europe. I stated that no decision had been reached by the Cabinet, and that I had received letters from one or two Unionists of influence protesting vehemently against our being drawn into a Continental war. I asked

---

[1] Now Lord Birkenhead.

him to let me know where he and his friends stood on the supreme issue. He replied at once that he himself was unreservedly for standing by France and Belgium. After consulting with Mr. Bonar Law, Sir Edward Carson and others who were gathered at Sir Edward Goulding's house at Wargrave, he sent me a written assurance, which I showed to Mr. Asquith the next morning (Saturday).

At the Cabinet I demanded the immediate calling out of the Fleet Reserves and the completion of our naval preparations. I based this claim on the fact that the German Navy was mobilizing, and that we must do the same. The Cabinet, who were by no means ill-informed on matters of naval organization, took the view after a sharp discussion that this step was not necessary to our safety, as mobilization only affected the oldest ships in the Fleet, and that our main naval power was already in full preparedness for war and the Fleet in its war station. I replied that though this was true, we needed the Third Fleet ships, particularly the older cruisers, to fulfil the rôles assigned to them in our war plan. However, I did not succeed in procuring assent.

On Saturday evening I dined alone at the Admiralty. The foreign telegrams came in at short intervals in red boxes which already bore the special label "Sub-Committee," denoting the precautionary period. The flow was quite continuous, and the impression produced on my mind after reading for nearly an hour was that there was still a chance of peace. Austria had accepted the conference, and intimate personal appeals were passing between the Tsar and the Kaiser. It seemed to me, from the order in which I read the series of telegrams, that at the very last moment Sir Edward Grey might succeed in saving the situation. So far no shot had been fired between the Great Powers. I wondered whether armies and fleets could remain mobilized for a space without fighting and then demobilize.

I had hardly achieved this thought when another Foreign Office box came in. I opened it and read "Germany has declared war on Russia." There was no more to be said. I walked across the Horse Guards Parade and entered 10, Downing Street, by the garden gate. I found the Prime Minister upstairs in his drawing-room: with him were Sir Edward Grey, Lord Haldane and Lord Crewe; there may have been other Ministers. I said that I intended instantly to mobilize the Fleet notwithstanding the Cabinet decision, and that I would take full personal responsibility to the Cabinet the next morning. The Prime Minister, who felt himself bound to the Cabinet, said not a single word, but I was clear from his look that he was quite content. As I walked down the steps of Downing Street with Sir Edward Grey, he said to me, "You should know I have just done a very important thing. I have told Cambon that we shall not allow the German fleet to come into the Channel." I went back to the Admiralty and gave forthwith the order to mobilize. We had no legal authority for calling up the Naval Reserves, as no proclamation had been submitted to His

Majesty in view of the Cabinet decision, but we were quite sure that the Fleet men would unquestioningly obey the summons. This action was ratified by the Cabinet on Sunday morning, and the Royal Proclamation was issued some hours later.

Another decision and a painful one was required. Sir George Callaghan's command of the Home Fleets had been extended by a year, and was now due to end on the 1st October. It had been announced that he would then be succeeded by Sir John Jellicoe. Further, our arrangements prescribed that Sir John Jellicoe should act as second-in-command in the event of war. The First Sea Lord and I had a conference with Sir George Callaghan, on his way through London to the North on the 30th. As the result of this conference we decided that if war came, it would be necessary to appoint Sir John Jellicoe immediately to the chief command. We were doubtful as to Sir George Callaghan's health and physical strength being equal to the immense strain that would be cast upon him; and in the crash of Europe it was no time to consider individuals. Sir John Jellicoe left London for the Fleet with sealed instructions, directing him on the seals being broken to take over the command. On the night of August 2, when we considered war certain, we telegraphed to both Admirals apprising them of the Admiralty decision. It was naturally a cruel blow to Sir George Callaghan to have to lay down his charge at such a moment, and his protests were re-echoed by practically all the principal Admirals who had served under him and by Sir John Jellicoe himself. It was also a grave matter to make a change in the command of the Fleets at this juncture. However, we did what we thought right, and that without an hour's delay. To Sir John Jellicoe I telegraphed: "Your feelings do you credit, and we understand them. But the responsibility rests with us, and we have given our decision. Take up your great task in buoyancy and hope. We are sure that all will be well." Sir John Jellicoe assumed command on the evening of August 3, and received almost immediately an order from the Admiralty to proceed to sea at daylight on the 4th.

The Cabinet sat almost continuously throughout the Sunday, and up till luncheon-time it looked as if the majority would resign. The grief and horror of so many able colleagues were painful to witness. But what could anyone do? In the luncheon interval I saw Mr. Balfour, a veritable rock in times like these, and learned that the Unionist leaders had tendered formally in writing to the Prime Minister their unqualified assurances of support.

I returned to the Admiralty. We telegraphed to our Commanders-in-Chief:

> To-day, August 2, at 2:20 the following note was handed to the French and German Ambassadors. [*Begins*] The British Government would not allow the passage of German ships through the English

Channel or the North Sea in order to attack the coasts or shipping of France [*ends*].

Be prepared to meet surprise attacks.

Meanwhile events were influencing opinion hour by hour. When the Cabinet met on Sunday morning we were in presence of the violation of the Grand Duchy of Luxemburg by the German troops. In the evening the German ultimatum to Belgium was delivered. The next day arrived the appeal of the King of the Belgians that the guaranteeing Powers should uphold the sanctity of the Treaty regarding the neutrality of Belgium. This last was decisive. By Monday the majority of Mr. Asquith's colleagues regarded war as inevitable. Discussion was resumed on Monday morning in a different atmosphere, though it seemed certain that there would be numerous resignations.

Before the Cabinet separated on Monday morning, Sir Edward Grey had procured a predominant assent to the principal points and general tone of his statement to Parliament that afternoon. Formal sanction had been given to the already completed mobilization of the Fleet and to the immediate mobilization of the Army. No decision had been taken to send an ultimatum to Germany or to declare war upon Germany, still less to send an army to France. These supreme decisions were never taken at any Cabinet. They were compelled by the force of events, and rest on the authority of the Prime Minister. We repaired to the House of Commons to hear the statement of the Foreign Secretary. I did not know which of our colleagues had resigned or what the composition of a War Government would be. The aspect of the assembly was awed but resolute. No one could mistake its intention. Sir Edward Grey made his statement with the utmost moderation. In order that there should be no ground for future reproaches, he informed the House that the Germans were willing to comply with the British demand that no German warships should be sent into the English Channel. The sombre march of his argument carried this weighty admission forward in its stride. When he sat down he was possessed in an overwhelming measure of the support of the assembly. Neither he nor I could remain long in the House. Outside, I asked him, "What happens now?" "Now," he said, "we shall send them an ultimatum to stop the invasion of Belgium within 24 hours."

Some of the Ministers still clung to the hope that Germany would comply with the British ultimatum and would arrest the onrush of her armies upon Belgium. As well recall the avalanche, as easily suspend in mid-career the great ship that has been launched and is sliding down the ways. Germany was already at war with Russia and France. It was certain that in 24 hours she would be at war with the British Empire also.

All through the tense discussions of the Cabinet one had in mind another greater debate which must begin when these were concluded. Parliament, the nation, the Dominions, would have to be convinced. That the cause was good, that the argument was overwhelming, that the response would be worthy, I did not for a moment doubt. But it seemed that an enormous political task awaited us, and I saw in the mind's eye not only the crowded House of Commons, but formidable assemblies of the people throughout the land requiring full and swift justification of the flaming action taken in their name. But such cares were soon dispersed. When the Council doors had opened and ministers had come into the outer air, the British nation was already surging forward in its ancient valour, and the Empire had sprung to arms.

> Men met each other with erected look,
> The steps were higher that they took,
> Friends to congratulate their friends made haste,
> And long-inveterate foes saluted as they passed.[1]

Meanwhile in the Mediterranean a drama of intense interest, and as it ultimately proved of fateful consequence, was being enacted.

The event which would dominate all others, if war broke out, was the main shock of battle between the French and German armies. We knew that the French were counting on placing in the line a whole army corps of their best troops from North Africa, and that every man was needed. We were informed also that they intended to transport these troops across the Mediterranean as fast as ships could be loaded, under the general protection of the French Fleet, but without any individual escort or system of convoys. The French General Staff calculated that whatever happened most of the troops would get across. The French Fleet disposed between this stream of transports and the Austrian Fleet afforded a good guarantee. But there was one ship in the Mediterranean which far outstripped in speed every vessel in the French Navy. She was the *Goeben*. The only heavy ships in the Mediterranean that could attempt to compete with the *Goeben* in speed were the three British battle-cruisers. It seemed that the *Goeben*, being free to choose any point on a front of three or four hundred miles, would easily be able to avoid the French Battle Squadrons and, brushing aside or outstripping their cruisers, break in upon the transports and sink one after another of these vessels crammed with soldiers. It occurred to me at this time that perhaps that was the task she had been sent to the Mediterranean to perform. For this reason as a further precaution I had suggested to the First Sea Lord as early as July 28 that an additional battle-cruiser, the *New Zealand*, should be sent to reinforce our squadron. When it came to the pinch a

---

[1] Dryden, *Threnodia Augustalis*.

few days later, Admiral Boué de Lapeyrère, the French Commander-in-Chief, adopted a system of convoys; and on August 4 he prudently delayed the embarkation of the troops until he could organize adequate escorts. But of this change of plan the Admiralty was not advised.

On July 30 I called for the war orders of the Mediterranean command and discussed them fully with the First Sea Lord. These orders, issued in August, 1913, had had to take into consideration a variety of political contingencies, viz. Great Britain at war with Germany only, with Germany and Austria only, or with Germany, Austria and Italy; and Great Britain and France allied together against each or any of the three aforesaid opponents. The course to be followed differed somewhat in each case. Briefly, if Britain found herself single-handed against the whole Triple Alliance, we should temporarily have to abandon the Mediterranean and concentrate at Gibraltar. In all other cases the concentration would be at Malta, and if the French were allies our squadrons would join them for a general battle. It now seemed necessary to give the Commander-in-Chief in the Mediterranean some more specific information and directions.

ADMIRALTY TO COMMANDER-IN-CHIEF, MEDITERRANEAN.
July 30, 1914.

It now seems probable should war break out and England and France engage in it, that Italy will remain neutral and that Greece can be made an ally. Spain also will be friendly and possibly an ally. The attitude of Italy is however uncertain, and it is especially important that your Squadron should not be seriously engaged with Austrian ships before we know what Italy will do. Your first task should be to aid the French in the transportation of their African army by covering and if possible bringing to action individual fast German ships, particularly *Goeben,* which may interfere with that transportation. You will be notified by telegraph when you may consult with the French Admiral. Except in combination with the French as part of a general battle, do not at this stage be brought to action against superior forces. The speed of your Squadrons is sufficient to enable you to choose your moment. You must husband your force at the outset and we shall hope later to reinforce the Mediterranean.

These directions on which the First Sea Lord and I were completely in accord, gave the Commander-in-Chief guidance in the general conduct of the naval campaign; they warned him against fighting a premature single-handed battle with the Austrian Fleet in which our battle-cruisers and cruisers would be confronted with Austrian Dreadnought battleships; they told him to aid the French in transporting their African forces, and they told him how to do it, viz.

"by covering and, if possible, bringing to action individual fast German ships, particularly *Goeben.*" So far as the English language may serve as a vehicle of thought, the words employed appear to express the intentions we had formed.

Sir Berkeley Milne accordingly replied on July 31 that he would keep his forces concentrated in readiness to assist the French Fleet to protect the transports, and he rightly left our trade in the Eastern Mediterranean to shift for itself. In this posture he awaited permission to consult with the French Admiral. This permission could not be given him till August 2 at 7:06 p.m., when I telegraphed as follows to our Commanders-in-Chief all over the world:

> Situation very critical. Be prepared to meet surprise attacks. You can enter into communication with the French Senior Officer on your station for combined action in case Great Britain should decide to become ally of France against Germany.

Earlier that same day the following, initialled both by the First Sea Lord and myself, was also sent to Sir Berkeley Milne from the Admiralty.

> *Goeben* must be shadowed by two battle-cruisers. Approaches to Adriatic must be watched by cruisers and destroyers. Remain near Malta yourself. It is believed that Italy will remain neutral, but you cannot yet count absolutely on this.

At 12:50 a.m. on August 3, I emphasized the importance of the *Goeben* compared with all other objectives by a further telegram, which I drafted myself, to Sir Berkeley Milne:

> Watch on mouth of Adriatic should be maintained, but *Goeben* is your objective. Follow her and shadow her wherever she goes and be ready to act on declaration of war, which appears probable and imminent.

Early on the morning of August 4 we were delighted by the following news from the Commander-in-Chief, Mediterranean, to the Admiralty:

> *Indomitable, Indefatigable* shadowing *Goeben* and *Breslau* 37°44′ North 7°56′ East.

We replied:

> Very good. Hold her. War imminent.
> (This to go now.)

Goeben is to be prevented by force from interfering with French transports.   (This to await early confirmation.)

I then informed the Prime Minister and Sir Edward Grey of the situation and of my desire to send the additional instructions. Both agreed to it, but the Prime Minister asked that it should be mentioned to the Cabinet, which was meeting almost immediately, for their confirmation. On this I sent, before going to the Cabinet, the following:

If *Goeben* attacks French transports you should at once engage her. You should give her fair warning of this beforehand.

The Cabinet, however, adhered formally to the view that no act of war should be committed by us before the expiration of the ultimatum. The moral integrity of the British Empire must not be compromised at this solemn moment for the sake of sinking a single ship.

The *Goeben* of course did not attack the French transports. In fact, though this we did not know at the time, she was steaming away from the French transport routes when sighted by the *Indomitable* and *Indefatigable.* Even if, however, she had attacked transports, the decision of the British Cabinet would have prevented our battle-cruisers from interfering. This decision obviously carried with it the still more imperative veto against opening fire on the *Goeben,* if she did not attack French transports, during the hours when we had her in our power. I cannot impeach the decision. It is right that the world should know of it. But little did we imagine how much this spirit of honourable restraint was to cost us and all the world.

In consequence of the Cabinet decision, the First Sea Lord sent by my directions the following telegram from the Admiralty:

ADMIRALTY TO ALL SHIPS, AUGUST 4, 2:05 p.m.
The British ultimatum to Germany will expire at midnight Greenwich Mean Time, August 4. No act of war should be committed before that hour, at which time the telegram to commence hostilities against Germany will be dispatched from the Admiralty.
Special addition to Mediterranean, *Indomitable, Indefatigable.*
This cancels the authorization to *Indomitable* and *Indefatigable* to engage *Goeben* if she attacks French transports.

At about the same time I received the following minute from the First Sea Lord:

First Lord   August 4.
   In view of the Italian declaration of neutrality, propose to telegraph to
Commander-in-Chief, Mediterranean, acquainting him and enjoining
him to respect this rigidly and not to allow a ship to come within six miles
of the Italian coast.
                                                                    B.

Bearing in mind how disastrous it would be if any petty incident occurred
which could cause trouble at this fateful moment with Italy and approving of
the First Sea Lord's precaution, I replied in writing:

                                                              August 4.
   So proceed. Foreign Office should intimate this to Italian Government.
                                                              W. S. C.

Thereupon at 12:55 p.m. the following telegram was sent by the Admiralty
to the Commander-in-Chief in the Mediterranean:

   Italian Government have declared neutrality. You are to respect this
   neutrality rigidly and should not allow any of His Majesty's ships to come
   within six miles of Italian coast.

This certainly as it turned out, was destined to complicate the task of
catching the *Goeben;* but not, as it will appear, in a decisive manner.
   During the afternoon I sent the following minute to the Chief of the Staff
and the First Sea Lord:

                                                          August 4, 1914.
   I presume you have fully informed French Admiralty of our intentions and that the closest co-operation has been established at all points
with the French Fleet. If not, this should be done immediately.
                                                              W. S. C.

On this the Chief of the Staff sent the following telegram to all stations:
"You can enter into the closest co-operation with the French officers on your
station."

Throughout this long summer afternoon three great ships, hunted and
hunters, were cleaving the clear waters of the Mediterranean in tense and oppressive calm. At any moment the *Goeben* could have been smitten at under

10,000 yards range by sixteen 12-inch guns firing nearly treble her own weight of metal. At the Admiralty we suffered the tortures of Tantalus.

At about 5 o'clock Prince Louis observed that there was still time to sink the *Goeben* before dark. In the face of the Cabinet decision I was unable to utter a word. Nothing less than the vital safety of Great Britain could have justified so complete an overriding of the authority of the Cabinet. We hoped to sink her the next day. Where could she go? Pola seemed her only refuge throughout the Mediterranean. According to international law nothing but internment awaited her elsewhere. The Turks had kept their secret well. As the shadows of night fell over the Mediterranean the *Goeben* increased her speed to twenty-four knots, which was the utmost that our two battle-cruisers could steam. She increased her speed still further. We have since learned that she was capable for a very short time of an exceptional speed, rising even to twenty-six or twenty-seven knots. Aided by this, she shook off her unwelcome companions and vanished gradually in the gathering gloom.

We shall return to this story in due course.

At 5:50 p.m. we sent the following message:

ADMIRALTY TO ALL SHIPS.

General message. The war telegram will be issued at midnight authorizing you to commence hostilities against Germany, but in view of our ultimatum they may decide to open fire at any moment. You must be ready for this.

Now, after all the stress and convulsion of the preceding ten days, there came to us at the Admiralty a strange interlude of calm. All the decisions had been taken. The ultimatum to Germany had gone: it must certainly be rejected. War would be declared at midnight. As far as we had been able to foresee the event, all our preparations were made. Mobilization was complete. Every ship was in its station: every man at his post. All over the world, every British captain and admiral was on guard. It only remained to give the signal. What would happen then? It seemed that the next move lay with the enemy. What would he do? Had he some deadly surprise in store? Some awful design, long planned and perfected, ready to explode upon us at any moment **NOW?** Would our ships in foreign waters have been able to mark down their German antagonists? If so, morning would witness half a dozen cruiser actions in the outer seas. Telegrams flowed in from the different naval stations round our coasts reporting the movements of vessels and rumours of sighting of enemies. Telegrams still flowed in from the Chancelleries of Europe as the last futile appeals of reason were overtaken by the cannonade. In the War Room of the Admiralty, where I sat waiting, one could hear the clock tick. From Parliament Street came the murmurs of the crowd; but they sounded distant and the world seemed very still. The tumult of the struggle for life was over; it was succeeded by the silence of ruin and death. We were to awake in Pandemonium.

I had the odd sense that it was like waiting for an election result. The turmoil of the contest seemed finished: the votes were being counted, and in a few hours the announcement would be made. One could only wait; but for what a result! Although the special duties of my office made it imperative that I, of all others, should be vigilant and forward in all that related to preparation for war, I claim, as these pages show, that in my subordinate station I had in these years before the war done nothing wittingly or willingly to impair the chances of a peaceable solution, and had tried my best as opportunity offered to make good relations possible between England and Germany. I thank God I could feel also in that hour that our country was guiltless of all intended purpose of war. Even if we had made some mistakes in the handling of this awful crisis, though I do not know them, from the bottom of our hearts we could say that we had not willed it. Germany it seemed had rushed with head down and settled resolved to her own undoing. And if this were what she had meant all along, if this was the danger which had really menaced us hour by hour during the last ten years, and would have hung over us hour by hour until the crash eventually came, was it not better that it should happen now: now that she had put herself so hopelessly in the wrong, now that we were ready beyond the reach of surprise, now that France and Russia and Great Britain were all in the line together?

The First Sea Lord and the Chief of the Staff came in with French Admirals who had hurried over to concert in detail arrangements for the co-operation of the two Fleets in the Channel and in the Mediterranean. They were fine figures in uniform, and very grave. One felt in actual contact with these French officers how truly the crisis was life or death for France. They spoke of basing the French Fleet on Malta—that same Malta for which we had fought Napoleon for so many years, which was indeed the very pretext of the renewal of the war in 1803. *"Malte ou la guerre!"* Little did the Napoleon of St. Helena dream that in her most desperate need France would have at her disposal the great Mediterranean base which his strategic instinct had deemed vital. I said to the Admirals, "Use Malta as if it were Toulon."

The minutes passed slowly.

Once more now in the march of centuries Old England was to stand forth in battle against the mightiest thrones and dominations. Once more in defence of the liberties of Europe and the common right must she enter upon a voyage of great toil and hazard across waters uncharted, towards coasts unknown, guided only by the stars. Once more "the far-off line of storm-beaten ships" was to stand between the Continental Tyrant and the dominion of the world.

It was 11 o'clock at night—12 by German time—when the ultimatum expired. The windows of the Admiralty were thrown wide open in the warm night air. Under the roof from which Nelson had received his orders were gathered a small group of Admirals and Captains and a cluster of clerks, pencil in hand, waiting. Along the Mall from the direction of the Palace the sound of an immense concourse singing "God save the King" floated in. On this deep wave there broke the chimes of Big Ben; and, as the first stroke of the hour boomed out, a rustle of movement swept across the room. The war telegram, which meant "Commence hostilities against Germany," was flashed to the ships and establishments under the White Ensign all over the world.

I walked across the Horse Guards Parade to the Cabinet room and reported to the Prime Minister and the Ministers who were assembled there that the deed was done.

CHAPTER IX

WAR: THE PASSAGE OF THE ARMY

AUGUST 4–AUGUST 22, 1914

The entry of Great Britain into war with the most powerful military Empire which has ever existed was strategically impressive. Her large Fleets vanished into the mists at one end of the island. Her small Army hurried out of the country at the other. By this double gesture she might seem to uninstructed eyes to divest herself of all her means of defence, and to expose her coasts nakedly to the hostile thrust. Yet these two movements, dictated by the truest strategy, secured at once our own safety and the salvation of our Allies. The Grand Fleet gained the station whence the control of the seas could be irresistibly asserted. The Regular Army reached in the nick of time the vital post on the flank of the French line. Had all our action been upon this level, we should to-day be living in an easier world.

The differences which had prevailed about entering the war were aggravated by a strong cross-current of opinion, by no means operative only in the Cabinet, that if we participated it should be by naval action alone. Men of great power and influence, who throughout the struggle laboured tirelessly and rendered undoubted services, were found at this time resolutely opposed to the landing of a single soldier on the Continent. And, if everything had not been prepared, if the plan had not been perfected, if it had not been the only plan, and if all military opinion had not been industriously marshalled round it—who shall say what fatal hesitancy might not have intervened?

On the afternoon of August 5 the Prime Minister convened an extraordinary Council of War at Downing Street. I do not remember any gathering like it. It consisted of the Ministers most prominently associated with the policy of our entering the war, the chiefs of the Navy and the Army, all the high military commanders, and in addition Lord Kitchener and Lord Roberts. Decision was required upon the question, How should we wage the war that had just begun? Those who spoke for the War Office knew their own minds and were united. The whole British Army should be sent at once to France, according to what may justly be called the Haldane Plan. Everything in that Minister's eight years' tenure of the War Office had led up to this and had been sacrificed for this. To place an army of four or six divisions of infantry thoroughly equipped with their necessary cavalry on the left of the French line within twelve or fourteen days of the order to mobilize, and to guard the home island meanwhile by the fourteen Territorial Divisions he had organized, was the scheme upon which, aided by Field-Marshals Nicholson and French, he had concentrated all his efforts and his stinted resources. It was a simple plan, but it was a practical plan. It had been persistently pursued and laboriously and minutely studied. It represented approximately the maximum war effort that the voluntary system would yield applied in the most effective and daring manner to the decisive spot; and mobilization schemes, railway graphics, time-tables, the organization of bases, depôts, supply arrangements, etc., filling many volumes, regulated and ensured a thorough and concerted execution. A commander whose whole life led up to this point had been chosen. All that remained to be done was to take the decision and give the signal.

At this point I reported on behalf of the Admiralty that our mobilization being in every respect complete and all our ships in their war stations, we would waive the claim we had hitherto made in all the discussions of the Committee of Imperial Defence that two Regular Divisions should be retained in Great Britain as a safeguard against invasion, and that so far as the Admiralty was concerned, not four but the whole six divisions could go at once; that we would provide for their transportation and for the security of the island in their absence. This considerable undertaking was made good by the Royal Navy.

Discussion then turned upon the place to which they should be dispatched. Lord Roberts inquired whether it was not possible to base the British Army on Antwerp so as to strike, in conjunction with the Belgian armies, at the flank and rear of the invading German hosts. We were not able from an Admiralty point of view to guarantee the sea communications of so large a force on the enemy side of the Straits of Dover, but only inside the Anglo-French flotilla cordon which had already taken up its station. Moreover, no plans had been worked out by the War Office for such a contingency. They had concentrated all their thought upon integral co-operation with the French left wherever it might be. It was that or nothing.

Another discussion took place upon how far forward the British Expeditionary Force should be concentrated. Some high authorities, dwelling on the fact that the mobilization of the British army had begun three days later than the French, were for concentrating it around Amiens for intervention after the first shock of battle had been taken. But in the end Sir John French and the forward school had their way, and it was felt that we must help France in the way the French Staff thought would be most effective.

When I next went to the Cabinet after the declaration of war, I found myself with new companions. During the previous seven years Lord Morley had always sat on the left of the Prime Minister, and I had always sat next to Lord Morley. Many a wise and witty admonition had I received pencilled in scholarly phrase from my veteran neighbour, and many a charming courtesy such as he excelled in had graced the toilsome path of business. He had said to me on the Sunday of Resolve, "If it has to be, I am not the man to do it. I should only hamper those like you who have to bear the burden." Now he was gone. In his place sat Lord Kitchener. On my left also there was a fresh figure—the new Minister of Agriculture, Lord Lucas. I had known him since South African War days, when he lost his leg: and to know him was to delight in him. His open, gay, responsive nature, his witty, ironical, but never unchivalrous tongue, his pleasing presence, his compulsive smile, made him much courted by his friends, of whom he had many and of whom I was one. Young for the Cabinet, heir to splendid possessions, happy in all that surrounded him, he seemed to have captivated Fortune with the rest.

Both these two men were marked for death at the hands of the enemy, the young Minister grappling with his adversary in the high air, the old Field-Marshal choking in the icy sea. I wonder what the twenty politicians round the table would have felt if they had been told that the prosaic British Cabinet was itself to be decimated in the war they had just declared. I think they would have felt a sense of pride and of relief in sharing to some extent the perils to which they were to send their countrymen, their friends, their sons.

At the Council of War on August 5, Lord Kitchener had not yet become Secretary of State for War, but I knew that his appointment was impending. The Prime Minister, then also Secretary of State for War, could not possibly be burdened with the continuous flow of inter-departmental work proceeding between the War Office and the Admiralty and requiring to be transacted between Ministers. He therefore invited Lord Kitchener to undertake ministerial charge of the War Office, and the Field-Marshal, who had certainly not sought this post in any way, had no choice but to accept.

My relations with Lord Kitchener had been limited. Our first meeting had been on the field of Omdurman, when as a lieutenant in the 21st Lancers I had been sent back to report verbally to the Commander-in-Chief the position of the advancing Dervish Army. He had disapproved of me severely in my youth, had endeavoured to prevent me from coming to the Soudan Campaign, and was indignant that I had succeeded in getting there. It was a case of dislike before first sight. On my side, I had dealt with his character and campaigns in two bulky volumes conceived throughout in a faithful spirit of critical impartiality. It was twelve years before I saw him again, when we were formally introduced to each other and had a brief talk at the Army Manœuvres in 1910. I got to know him a little at the Malta Conference in 1912, and thenceforward we used to talk over Imperial Defence topics when from time to time we met. On these occasions I had found him much more affable than I had been led to expect from my early impressions or from all I had heard about him. In the week before the war we had lunched and dined together two or three times, and we had discussed all the possibilities so far as we could foresee them. I was glad when he was appointed Secretary of State for War, and in those early days we worked together on close and cordial terms. He consulted me constantly on the political aspects of his work, and increasingly gave me his confidence in military matters. Admiralty and War Office business were so interlaced that during the whole of the first ten months we were in almost daily personal consultation. I cannot forget that when I left the Admiralty in May, 1915, the first and, with one exception, the only one of my colleagues who paid me a visit of ceremony was the overburdened Titan whose disapprobation had been one of the disconcerting experiences of my youth.

As is well known, the British armies on mobilization consisted of a highly organized expeditionary force of six Regular Divisions of Infantry and a Cavalry Division. In addition there were two Regular Infantry Divisions, the 7th and 8th, which had to be collected from their garrisons all over the Empire or formed out of troops surplus to the Expeditionary Force at home; and it was decided also to employ two divisions, half British and half native, from India. Behind these trained forces, unquestionably of a very high order, stood fourteen Territorial Divisions and thirteen mounted Brigades to whom the defence of Britain must be confided. These were little trained, lightly equipped with artillery, but composed of far-sighted and intelligent men who had not waited for the hour of danger to make their country's cause their own. In six months or, as some thought, in a shorter period, such troops could be made to play their part.

Lord Kitchener now came forward to the Cabinet, on almost the first occasion after he joined us, and in soldierly sentences proclaimed a series of inspiring and prophetic truths. Everyone expected that the war would be short; but wars took unexpected courses, and we must now prepare for a long struggle. Such a conflict could not be ended on the sea or by sea-power alone. It could be ended only by great battles on the Continent. In these the British Empire must bear its part on a scale proportionate to its magnitude and power. We must be prepared to put armies of millions in the field and maintain them for several years. In no other way could we discharge our duty to our allies or to the world.

These words were received by the Cabinet in silent assent; and it is my belief that had Lord Kitchener proceeded to demand universal national service to be applied as it might be required, his request would have been acceded to. He, however, proposed to content himself with calling for volunteers, and in the first instance to form six new regular divisions. It would have been far better to have formed the new volunteers upon the cadres of the Territorial Army, each of which could have been duplicated or quadruplicated in successive stages. But the new Secretary of State had little knowledge of and no faith in the British territorial system. The name itself was to him a stumbling-block. In the war of 1870 he had been present at a battle on the Loire, probably Le Mans, in which the key of the position, confided to French Territorial troops, had been cast away, entailing the defeat of the whole army. He dwelt on this incident to me on several occasions, and I know it had created fixed impressions in his mind. Vain to explain how entirely different were the characters of the troops forming the French and British Territorial forces—the former aged conscripts in their last periods of service; the latter keen and ardent youths of strong military predilections. They were Territorials, and that was the end of it.

This at the very outset aggravated the difficulties of his already gigantic task. He set himself to create the cadres first of six, then of twelve, and ultimately of twenty-four "Kitchener Army" divisions, at the same time that the recruits were pouring in upon him by the hundred thousand. That this vast feat of improvisation was accomplished must certainly rank among the wonders of the time.

The arguments against compulsory service, cogent as they no doubt were, were soon reinforced by the double event of overwhelming numbers of volunteers and of a total lack of arms and equipment. Apart from the exiguous stores held by the Regular Army, there was literally nothing. The small scale of our military forces had led to equally small factories for war material. There were no spare rifles, there were no extra guns; and the modest supplies of shells and ammunition began immediately to flash away with what seemed appalling rapidity. Many months must elapse, even if the best measures were taken, before new sources of supply even on a moderate scale could be opened up. One was now to learn for the first time that it took longer to make a rifle than a gun; and rifles were the cruellest need of all. We had nothing but staves to put in the hands of the eager men who thronged the recruiting stations. I ransacked the Fleet and the Admiralty stores and scraped together another 30,000 rifles, which literally mean another 30,000 men in the field. Afloat only the Marines would have their rifles; Jack must, in the last resort, trust to his cutlass as of old.

At the moment when Lord Kitchener began the formation of his first six new army divisions and before the great rush of recruits had begun, I offered him the Royal Naval Division, which he gladly accepted. Before the war we had foreseen the fact that the Navy would on mobilization have many thousands of men in their depôts for whom there would be no room in any ship of war that we could send to sea. I had therefore proposed to the Committee of Imperial Defence in 1913 the formation of three brigades, one composed of Marines and the other two of men of the Royal Naval Volunteer Reserve and of the Royal

Fleet Reserve. These brigades it was intended to use to assist in home defence in the early stages of a war. The cadres were therefore easily formed from the available resources. The Marine Brigade was already virtually in existence, and it was clear that all three would be ready for action long before any of the new troops that were being raised. The Naval Volunteers, who longed to serve afloat, accepted the new task with many heartburnings but with boundless loyalty. Alas, for most of them it proved a fateful decision. Few there were of that gallant company that survived unscathed. As for their deeds, they will not be forgotten in the history even of these crowded times.

It fell to my lot to prescribe the arrangements for the departure of the German Ambassador and, eight days later, of his Austrian colleague. Accordingly on the morning of August 5, I sent my Naval Secretary Admiral Hood in uniform to the German Embassy desiring to know in what manner we might facilitate Prince Lichnowsky's wishes and convenience. While the German mob were insulting and even pelting the departing French and British Ambassadors, we set ourselves to work with meticulous care to secure the observance of every propriety and courtesy towards those for whom we were responsible. Prince Lichnowsky has given his own record of his ceremonious treatment, which appeared to make a marked impression upon his mind.

To Count Mensdorf, the Austrian Ambassador, I wrote as follows:

> August 13, 1914.
>
> My Naval Secretary Admiral Hood, who brings this letter, is instructed to put himself at your disposal in arranging for the comfort and convenience of your journey by sea. If there is any way in which I can be of service to you at this time, you will not I hope fail to command me.
>
> Although the terrible march of events has swept aside the ancient friendship between our countries, the respect and regard which spring from so many years of personal association cannot pass from the hearts of your English friends.

The Austrian Ambassador asked that a ship might be provided to take him direct to Trieste, and that consideration might be shown to a number of unhappy Austrian non-combatants long resident in London who now had to fly the country. I therefore arranged that upwards of 200 persons should embark in the Ambassador's ship. I felt sure that in taking these measures I was acting in accord with what British dignity required.

By the Letters Patent and Orders in Council constituting his office, the First Lord is responsible to Crown and Parliament for all the business of the Admiralty. In virtue of this he delegates to an eminent sailor the responsibility for its technical and professional conduct. But he cannot thus relieve himself either in theory or in fact. He is held strictly accountable for all that takes place; for every disaster he must bear the blame. The credit of victories rightly goes to the commanders who gain them; the burden of defeat or miscarriage must be shouldered by the Admiralty, and the censures of the nation fall primarily upon its Head.

How then is a civilian Minister appointed for political or parliamentary reasons and devoid of authoritative expert knowledge, to acquit himself of his duty? Clearly it depends upon the character, temperament and capacity both of the First Lord and the First Sea Lord. They must settle it between themselves, and if they cannot agree whole-heartedly on the momentous problems with which they are confronted in swift succession, another combination must be chosen by the Sovereign on the advice of the Prime Minister. I interpreted my duty in the following way: I accepted full responsibility for bringing about successful results, and in that spirit I exercised a close general supervision over everything that was done or proposed. Further, I claimed and exercised an unlimited power of suggestion and initiative over the whole field, subject only to the approval and agreement of the First Sea Lord on all operative orders. Right or wrong, that is what I did, and it is on that basis that I wish to be judged. In practice the difficulties were less than would be imagined. Indeed, over long periods of unending crisis and tension the machine worked very smoothly.

On the outbreak of war, the Naval Secretary of State von Tirpitz, himself an admiral, found himself cut off entirely from the strategical and quasi-tactical control of the fleets, to such an extent that he declares "he did not know the naval war plans." He was confined to purely administrative business, and thus charged, he was carried off as an adjunct to the Emperor's suite at Great Headquarters. The Naval Staff, headed in the first instance by von Pohl, alone had the ear of the Emperor and received from the lips of the All-Highest indications of his Imperial pleasure. The position of Admiral von Tirpitz was therefore most unhappy. The Naval Staff warded him off the Emperor as much as possible, and persuaded the Emperor to repulse his efforts to break in. The Emperor, oppressed with the whole burden of the State, gave to the Staff from time to time directions and uttered passing expressions which thereafter operated with irresistible authority. It is to this state of affairs that Admiral von Tirpitz ascribes the paralysis which gripped the German Fleet through the first critical months of the naval war. This it was, according to him, that lost the opportunity of fighting the supreme battle under the least unfavourable conditions, enabled the control of the seas to pass into our hands practically without a struggle, and secured the uninterrupted transport of our armies to the Continent. If our solution of the difficult problem of naval war direction was imperfect, so also was that of our enemy.

Our known margin of superiority in Home waters was smaller then than at any subsequent moment in the war. The Grand Fleet as concentrated in its Northern war station on August 1, 1914, comprised 24 vessels classified as "Dreadnoughts" or better. In addition the battle-cruiser *Invincible* was at Queenstown watching the Atlantic, the two *Lord Nelsons* were with the Channel Fleet, and three battle-cruisers were in the Mediterranean. The Germans actually mobilized 16 ships similarly classed.[1] We could not be absolutely certain, though we thought it unlikely, that they might not have ready two, or even three, more; and these of the greatest power. Happily, every British ship was ready and in perfect order. None was under repair. Our strength for an immediate fleet action was 24 to a certain 16 and a possible 19. These figures do not, as the tables in the Appendix reveal, do justice to the full material strength of the British Fleets as a whole, still less to the gun-power of the British Line of Battle, which after the Dreadnoughts comprised eight King Edwards markedly superior to the next eight Germans. But apart from all that may be said on this, and of the confidence which it inspired, the fact remains that from five to eight Dreadnoughts was all the certain numerical superiority we had. There was not much margin here for mischance, nor for the percentage of mechanical defects which in so large a Fleet has to be expected, and no margin whatever for a disaster occasioned by surprise had we been unready. To a superficial observer who from the cliffs of Dover or Portland had looked down upon a Battle Squadron of six or seven ships, lying in distant miniature below, the foundation upon which the British world floated would have presented itself in a painfully definite form. If the intelligence and courage of British seamen were not all that we believed them to be; if the workmanship which had built these great vessels were not honest and thorough; if our seamanship or our gunnery had turned out to be inferior; if some ghastly novelty or blunder supervened—the battle might be very even.

It is easy to understand how tense were the British naval expectations. If the German Navy was ever to fight a battle, now at the beginning was its best chance. The German Admiralty knew, of course, what ships we had available, and that we were mobilized, concentrated and at sea. Even if they assumed the extraordinary fact that every one of our Dreadnoughts was ready and that not one of them had developed a defect, they could fight to German eyes a battle 16 against a maximum 27—heavy odds from their point of view, still heavier when the survey was extended to the whole of the Fleets, but yet odds far less heavy

[1] Admiral Scheer, p. 13.

than they would have to face after six months, after twelve months or at any later period. For look at the reinforcements which were approaching these two opposing Fleets. They must assume that, in addition to completing our own vessels, we should requisition every battleship building for a foreign Power in our yards, and on this basis seven great ships must join the Grand Fleet within three months, and twelve great ships within six months, against which only three in three months and five in six months could be reckoned on their side, leaving the balance in three months at 34 to 19 and in six months at 39 to 21; and this took no account of three battle-cruisers in the Mediterranean and one (*Australia*) in the Pacific which obviously we could bring home if necessary.

Here, then, was the least unfavourable moment for Germany; here was the best chance they would ever see. Was it not also the strategic moment? Might they not assume that the transportation of the British Army to France would be a grave preoccupation for the Admiralty? Was it not clear that a victory, even a partial victory, would be more fruitful at this juncture than at any other? Forty-two fast German merchant cruisers needed only a breathing space to get loose and to arm upon the seas, requiring afterwards to be hunted down one by one. Might not above all the interruption and delay in the transportation of the Army be of real effect in the supreme trial of strength on land? The German Staff believed in a short war. They were staking everything upon a supreme trial of strength on land. Why should not the German Fleet be hurled in too and play its part for what it was worth in the supreme decision? To what other equal use could it ever be put?

We therefore looked for open battle on the sea. We expected it and we courted it. The news that the two Navies were approaching each other to take a decision in blue water would have been received in the Fleet with unaffected satisfaction, and at the Admiralty with composure. We could not send our Grand Fleet into the minefields and submarine-infested areas of the Heligoland Bight. But had battle been offered by the enemy under any conditions which did not put us at a serious disadvantage, it would have been at once accepted.

In fact, however, the sober confidence of the Admiralty was based upon calculations of relative naval strength, the soundness of which was not disputed by the German Naval Staff. Even von Tirpitz, the advocate of action, writes (p. 356): "Against an immediate fight was the fact that the whole English Fleet was ready for battle when the war broke out owing to the test mobilization, whereas only our active squadrons were ready." "Great Britain," says the Official German Naval History, ". . . had secured extensive military advantages by her test mobilization and her subsequent measures, regardless of the uneasiness necessarily provoked thereby . . . which advantage Germany could not counter or overtake." The German Staff felt that even if this was the best chance for a trial of strength, it was still a chance so hazardous and even so forlorn that it was not worth taking; and their Battle Fleet remained hoarded up in harbour for an ignominious day, imposing upon the British, no doubt, a continued and serious expenditure of our resources for naval purposes, gaining for Germany substantial advantages of a secondary character, but not exercising any decisive influence upon the whole course of the war.

So we waited; and nothing happened. No great event immediately occurred. No battle was fought. The Grand Fleet remained at sea: the German Fleet did not quit the shelter of its harbours. There were no cruiser actions. A German minelayer sowing a minefield off Harwich was chased and sunk by a flotilla of destroyers led by the *Amphion;* and the *Amphion* returning, was blown up on the German minefield. Otherwise silence unbroken by cannon brooded over the broad and narrow waters. But during that silence and from its first moment the sea-power of Great Britain ruled unchallenged throughout the world. Every German cruiser in foreign waters vanished into the immense spaces of the sea; every German merchant ship, from the earliest moment when the entry of Britain into the war became apparent, fled for neutral harbours. Seven out of eight potential commerce destroyers were bottled up without ever a shot being fired. German seaborne trade outside the Baltic ceased to exist from the night of August 4. On the other hand, after a few days of hesitation the swarming mercantile marine of Britain, encouraged by a Government insurance of no more than 6 per cent, began to put to sea; and even before the main armies had met in battle on the Continent, the whole vast ocean traffic of the British Empire was proceeding with the utmost activity. By the end of August the rate of insurance had already fallen to 3 per cent, and the Admiralty was able to announce that of the forty-two German liners from whom attacks on trade were to be apprehended, eleven were tied up unarmed in harbours of the United States watched outside territorial limits by British cruisers, six had taken refuge in other neutral harbours, where they were either dismantled or observed, fourteen were in German ports gripped by the blockade, six were held as prizes in British hands, and only five remained unaccounted for and unlocated. The fate of these five will be recounted later.

None of these gloomy prophecies which had formed the staple of so many debates and articles, that our merchant ships would be hunted from the seas by German raiders, that scores of additional British cruisers would be required for commerce protection, that British merchant ships once safe in harbour would not venture to sea, materialized; and they might be relegated to the limbo of exploded alarms. The three great naval dangers which had bulked most largely in our minds in the years before the war—first, the danger of surprise of the Fleet; second, the Mine danger; third, the paralysis of our seaborne trade—rolled away behind us like giant waves which a ship has finally surmounted.

More than a hundred years had passed since the British Navy had been called upon to face an emergency of the first magnitude. If a hundred years hence, in similar circumstances, it is found equally ready, we shall have no more reason to complain of our descendants than they will find in the history of this convulsion, reason to complain of us.

It is time to return to the Mediterranean.

Admiral Souchon, the German Commander, having outdistanced our shadowing cruisers in the darkness of the night, pursued his course to Messina, where he arrived with the *Goeben* and *Breslau* on the morning of August 5. He had already received, as we now know, a telegram sent from Nauen at 1:35 a.m. on the preceding day by the German Admiralty. This message gave him all-important information. It stated that an alliance had been concluded between Germany and Turkey, and directed him to proceed to Constantinople immediately. Of this treaty we knew nothing. All our reports were of an entirely different tenor; nor was it till long afterwards that we learnt the true attitude of Turkey at this hour.

On arrival at Messina the *Goeben* and *Breslau* began to coal from German colliers. This occupied the whole of the day, the whole of the night and the greater part of the next day, the 6th. Exactly thirty-six hours elapsed before the *Goeben* moved. Meanwhile the light cruiser *Gloucester*, watching off the Southern exit of the Straits of Messina, reported at 3:35 p.m. on August 5 to Sir Berkeley Milne that the strength of the wireless signals she was taking in indicated that the *Goeben* must be at Messina.

The British Commander-in-Chief had left the Malta Channel in his flagship the *Inflexible* after midnight of August 4, and at about 11 a.m. on August 5 he had assembled all his three battle-cruisers and two light cruisers off Pantellaria island, midway between Sicily and the African coast.[1] According to his own published account[2] he had learned on the 4th that the German mail steamer *General* was remaining at Messina at the disposition of the *Goeben*. He therefore believed throughout the whole of the 5th that "the *Goeben*, *Breslau* and *General* were all at Messina." His belief was correct.

One of his battle-cruisers, the *Indomitable*, had to coal. He sent her to Biserta. This was an important decision. Considering that he believed that the *Goeben* was at Messina, and that he intended himself to watch to the Northward with two battle-cruisers, some authorities have held that it would have been a sensible precaution to let this third ship coal at Malta, where facilities were certain and instant, and whence she could so easily move to close the Southern exit from Messina, or join Rear-Admiral Troubridge in the mouth of

---

[1] See map on p. 137.
[2] *The Flight of the Goeben,* Admiral Sir Berkeley Milne.

the Adriatic, as that officer had been led to expect.[1] By sending the *Indomitable* to coal at Malta, he could have placed two battle-cruisers watching the Northern exit and one at the Southern. But the Commander-in-Chief decided to keep all three battle-cruisers together in his own hand and to patrol off the Western end of Sicily between Sardinia and Biserta. The Southern exit was therefore left completely open to the *Goeben:* and a severe action was reserved for Rear-Admiral Troubridge if, as seemed likely, she ran up the Adriatic.

At 5 p.m. on the 5th, Sir Berkeley Milne received the signal sent by the *Gloucester* at 3:35 p.m. reporting the presence of the *Goeben* at Messina. Here was certain confirmation of his belief. He was at this moment about 100 miles West of Sicily. He continued however to cruise with his two ships between Sicily and Sardinia, and as late as the evening of August 6, his orders to the *Indomitable* were still to join him thereabouts. He did this because he considered that placing all three battle-cruisers in this position was his surest way of carrying out the instructions of the Admiralty telegram of July 30 about aiding the French in the transport of their African army. That it was one method of carrying out these orders cannot be disputed, and the Admiral has set out in his book the reasons which led him to adopt it. The superior speed of the *Goeben* made it necessary, he states, if he were to intercept her, that he should stand a long way off and have timely notice of her approach. To place his whole force in this way between her and the French transports was, he argues, the best chance of catching the *Goeben* if she tried to attack them. He reported his intended dispositions late on the 4th to the Admiralty, whose only comment upon them was, "Watch over the Adriatic should be maintained for the double purpose of preventing the Austrians from coming out or the Germans from entering." The exceedingly prompt manner in which the *Goeben* had been found, although in the open sea, on the 4th had given the Admiralty the feeling that the Admiral on the spot had a grip of the situation and needed no further directions.

Sir Berkeley Milne had not, however, succeeded in communicating with the French Admiral, although he had made repeated attempts by wireless and had sent the *Dublin* to Biserta with a letter. He did not know where the French Fleet or the French transports were. He did not tell the Admiralty this. The Admiralty for their part, after the general telegram of August 4 enjoining immediate consultation with the French, assumed that the two Commanders-in-Chief in the Mediterranean were acting in concert. They did not therefore ask the French for any information, nor was any volunteered by the French Admiralty. Any inquiry addressed to Paris would have elicited the fact that the French had changed their plans and that no transports were yet at sea. All parties were on this point to some extent in fault.

[1] See Official Naval History, pp. 60, 61.

Meanwhile the British Ambassador in Rome was endeavouring to tell the Admiralty as soon as the pressure on the wires allowed, that the *Goeben* was at Messina. The news did not reach London till 6 p.m. on August 5. The Admiralty passed it without comment, though with some delay, to Sir Berkeley Milne, who already knew from other sources. It is a fair criticism on the Admiralty that they did not immediately they knew the *Goeben* was at Messina authorize the British ships to follow her into the Straits. The point was not put to me either by the First Sea Lord or the Chief of the Staff, and as I had not myself been concerned in initiating or drafting the telegram about rigidly respecting Italian neutrality, it was not specially in my mind. Had it been put to me I should at once have consented. This was no petty incident and the prize was well worth the risk of vexing the Italians. In fact, permission to chase through the Straits was given by the Admiralty unasked to Sir Berkeley Milne, as soon as it was realized that the *Goeben* was escaping unblocked to the Southward. It was then too late.

In pursuance of the orders he had received from Germany, Admiral Souchon with the *Goeben* and *Breslau,* having at length completed coaling and made his will, steamed out of Messina harbour at 5 p.m. on August 6, cleared for action and with his bands playing. He no doubt expected to encounter at least one and possibly two of the British battle-cruisers as soon as he was outside territorial waters. In view of the fact that, as he was aware, his position must have been accurately known to the British Commander-in-Chief for many hours, this assumption was not unreasonable. Unhappily, as has been described, every one of the three British battle-cruisers was otherwise engaged. Thus when the German Admiral rounded the Southern point of Italy and turned Eastward, the only three antagonists whose combination of power and speed he had to dread were already far astern.

Still there was the British armoured cruiser squadron watching the Adriatic. This squadron consisted of four good ships, viz. *Defence, Warrior, Duke of Edinburgh* and *Black Prince.* It was commanded by Rear-Admiral Troubridge, who had also under his orders eight destroyers, and was being joined by the light cruiser *Dublin* and two more destroyers from Malta. It is necessary to re-state the facts of this officer's action.

On the assumption—which was dominant—that the *Goeben* would make for Pola, Admiral Troubridge was well placed for meeting her. It was not until he heard from the *Gloucester* that she had turned South and was persistently steering on a South-Easterly course that any new decision was required from him. He received no orders to quit his station from Sir Berkeley Milne. He was in constant hope of receiving a battle-cruiser. But Admiral Troubridge decided to act on his own responsibility. Eight minutes after midnight on August 6 (i.e. 0:08, August 7) he gave orders to his four cruisers and his eight destroyers to steam Southward at full speed for the purpose of intercepting the *Goeben*. He also signalled to the *Dublin* (Captain John Kelly), at that moment coming from Malta to join him with the two extra destroyers, to head her off. He reported his decision to the Commander-in-Chief. Thus at midnight August 6–7 sixteen British vessels were converging upon the *Goeben* and *Breslau* and were in positions from which they could hardly fail to intercept the enemy shortly after daylight. At 3:50 a.m., however, after further reflection and having received no orders or reply from Sir Berkeley Milne, Admiral Troubridge became convinced that he could not hope to engage the *Goeben* under the advantageous conditions of the half light of dawn, and that in an action fought in broad waters in full daylight, his four ships would be sunk one after another by the *Goeben*, who all the time would keep outside the range—16,000 yards—of the British 9.2-inch guns. This is thought by some naval officers to be an extreme view. The limited ammunition of the *Goeben* would have had to have been wonderfully employed to have sunk all four British armoured cruisers *seriatim* at this long range.[1] Moreover, if the *Goeben* and *Breslan* had become involved in an action, it is hard to believe that none of the sixteen British cruisers and destroyers which were available could have closed in upon them and attacked them with gun or torpedo. All the destroyers were capable of reaching the enemy and could have found their opportunity to attack. It would have been indeed a prodigious feat on the part of the Germans to dispose of so many antagonists at once. However, the Admiral came to the conclusion that the *Goeben* was "a superior force" which by his instructions, passed to him by the Commander-in-Chief, he was not to engage. And in this conclusion he has been sustained by a British naval court-martial.

He thereupon desisted from his attempt to intercept the *Goeben*, turned his ships and destroyers and entered the harbour of Zante about 10 a.m. preparatory to resuming his watch in the Adriatic. The *Dublin* and her two destroyers having asked and been refused permission to make a daylight attack, had attempted to intercept the *Goeben* before dawn, but did not succeed in finding her in the darkness.

By 6 o'clock therefore on the morning of August 7 the *Goeben*, already the fastest capital unit in the Mediterranean, was steaming on an unobstructed course for the Dardanelles, carrying with her for the peoples of the East and Middle East more slaughter, more misery and more ruin than has ever before been borne within the compass of a ship.

Thus of all the British vessels which were or could have been brought

---

[1] At the Falklands the two British battle-cruisers used up nearly three-quarters of their ammunition to sink only two weaker antagonists, using 12-inch guns against 8.8 inch. The *Goeben* single-handed would have had to have sunk four, using 11-inch guns against 9.2 inch.

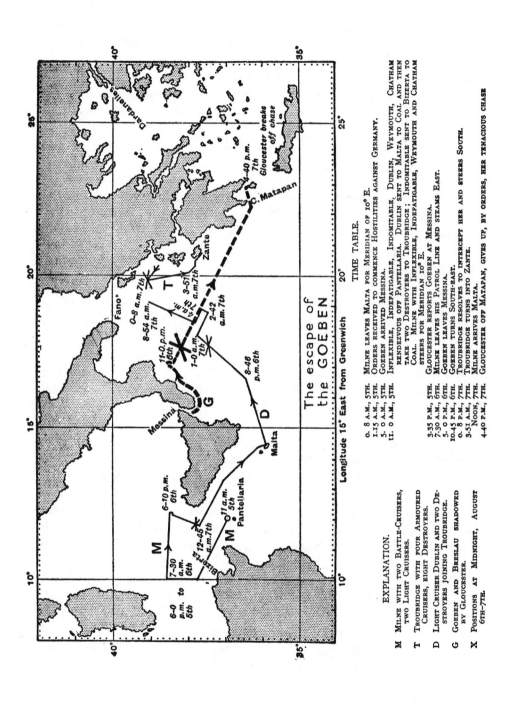

The escape of the GOEBEN

Longitude 15° East from Greenwich

EXPLANATION.

M MILNE WITH TWO BATTLE-CRUISERS, TWO LIGHT CRUISERS.

T TROUBRIDGE WITH FOUR ARMOURED CRUISERS, EIGHT DESTROYERS.

D LIGHT CRUISER DUBLIN AND TWO DESTROYERS JOINING TROUBRIDGE.

G GOEBEN AND BRESLAU SHADOWED BY GLOUCESTER.

X POSITIONS AT MIDNIGHT, AUGUST 6TH–7TH.

TIME TABLE.

0. 8 A.M., 5TH.   MILNE LEAVES MALTA FOR MERIDIAN OF 10° E.
1.15 A.M., 5TH.   ORDERS RECEIVED TO COMMENCE HOSTILITIES AGAINST GERMANY.
5. 0 A.M., 5TH.   GOEBEN ARRIVED MESSINA.
11. 0 A.M., 5TH. INFLEXIBLE, INDEFATIGABLE, INDOMITABLE, DUBLIN, WEYMOUTH, CHATHAM RENDEZVOUS OFF PANTELLARIA. DUBLIN SENT TO MALTA TO COAL, AND THEN TAKE TWO DESTROYERS TO TROUBRIDGE; INDOMITABLE SENT TO BIZERTA TO COAL. MILNE WITH INFLEXIBLE, INDEFATIGABLE, WEYMOUTH AND CHATHAM STEERS FOR MERIDIAN 10° E.

3.35 P.M., 5TH.   GLOUCESTER REPORTS GOEBEN AT MESSINA.
7.30 A.M., 6TH.   MILNE LEAVES WITH INFLEXIBLE, INDEFATIGABLE, WEYMOUTH AND CHATHAM AND STEAMS EAST.
5. 0 P.M., 6TH.   GOEBEN LEAVES MESSINA.
10.45 P.M., 6TH. GOEBEN TURNS SOUTH-EAST.
0. 8 P.M., 7TH.   TROUBRIDGE RESOLVES TO INTERCEPT HER AND STEERS SOUTH.
3.51 A.M., 7TH.   TROUBRIDGE TURNS INTO ZANTE.
NOON, 7TH.   MILNE ARRIVES MALTA.
4.40 P.M., 7TH.   GLOUCESTER OFF MATAPAN, GIVES UP, BY ORDERS, HER TENACIOUS CHASE

within effective distance, none did anything useful excepting only the two light cruisers *Dublin* and *Gloucester,* commanded, as it happened, by two brothers. The *Dublin* (Captain John Kelly) as we have seen did all in her power to place herself and her two destroyers athwart the enemy's course and to fight him by night or day; and the *Gloucester* (Captain W. A. Howard Kelly) hung on to the heels of the *Goeben* till late in the afternoon, in extreme danger and with the utmost tenacity, and only relinquished the chase under the direct orders of the Commander-in-Chief.

In all this story of the escape of the *Goeben* one seems to see the influence of that sinister fatality which at a later stage and on a far larger scale was to dog the enterprise against the Dardanelles. The terrible "If's" accumulate. If my first thoughts on July 27 of sending the *New Zealand* to the Mediterranean had materialized; if we could have opened fire on the *Goeben* during the afternoon of August 4; if we had been less solicitous for Italian neutrality; if Sir Berkeley Milne had sent the *Indomitable* to coal at Malta instead of Biserta; if the Admiralty had sent him direct instructions when on the night of the 5th they learned where the *Goeben* was; if Rear-Admiral Troubridge in the small hours of August 7 had not changed his mind; if the *Dublin* and her two destroyers had intercepted the enemy during the night of the 6th–7th—the story of the *Goeben* would have ended here. There was, however, as it turned out, one more chance of annulling the doom of which she was the bearer. That chance, remote though it was, the Fates were vigilant to destroy.

At 1 a.m. on August 8 Sir Berkeley Milne, having collected and coaled his three battle-cruisers at Malta, set out at a moderate speed on an Easterly course in pursuit of the *Goeben*. At this juncture the Fates moved a blameless and punctilious Admiralty clerk to declare war upon Austria. The code telegram ordering hostilities to be commenced against Austria was inadvertently released without any authority whatever. The mistake was repaired a few hours later; but the first message reached Sir Berkeley Milne at 2 p.m. on August 8 when he was half-way between Sicily and Greece. His original war orders had prescribed that in the event of a war with Austria he should in the first instance concentrate his fleet near Malta, and faithful to these instructions he turned his ships about and desisted from the pursuit of the *Goeben*. Twenty-four hours were thus lost before orders could reach him to resume it. But the *Goeben* herself had come to a standstill. Admiral Souchon was cruising irresolutely about the Greek islands endeavouring to make sure that he would be admitted by the Turks to the Dardanelles. He dallied thirty-six hours at Denusa and was forced to use his telltale wireless on several occasions. It was not till the evening of the 10th that he entered the Dardanelles and the Curse descended irrevocably upon Turkey and the East.

• • •

From the 9th to the 22nd of August the Army was crossing the Channel. This was a period of great anxiety to us. All the most fateful possibilities were open. We were bound to expect a military descent upon our coasts with the intention of arresting or recalling our Army, or a naval raid into the Channel to cut down the transports, or a concentrated submarine attack upon these vessels crowded with our troops. The great naval battle might begin at any moment, either independently or in connection with any of these operations. It was a period of extreme psychological tension.

The naval dispositions by which the passage of the Army was covered have been fully described in the Official History of the War and in other Service works. The northern approaches to the Straits of Dover were patrolled by cruiser squadrons and by flotillas from Harwich and the Thames. The Straits of Dover were minutely watched by the British and French Destroyer flotillas of the Dover cordon and by the Submarine flotillas of Commodore Keyes. Behind these there was constituted on August 7 the Channel Fleet, comprising nineteen battleships of the 5th, 7th and 8th Battle Squadrons, now all fully mobilized. This fleet, having assembled under the command of Admiral Burney at Portland, cruised in readiness for battle at the western end of the Channel at such distances from the Dover cordon as its commander might judge convenient. The western entrance to the Channel was guarded by other cruiser squadrons.

During the first few days of the transportation no great numbers of troops were crossing the Channel, but from the 12th to the 17th the bulk of the Army was in transit, and the strategic tension reached its climax. Until this period was reached the Grand Fleet was kept in its northern station and was even permitted to cruise northwards of the Orkneys, but on August 12 Admiral Jellicoe was directed to re-enter the North Sea and to cruise southward into a position of effective proximity.

During the three days of heaviest transportation, August 15, 16 and 17, the Heligoland Bight was closely blockaded by submarines and destroyers, supported between the Horn Reef and the Dogger Bank by the whole of the Grand Fleet. Thus battle in open water was offered to the German Navy during the three days when their inducements to fight were at their maximum. But except for an occasional submarine, no sign betrayed the existence of the enemy's naval power.

All went well. Not a ship was sunk, not a man was drowned: all arrangements worked with the utmost smoothness and punctuality. The Army concentration was completed three days in advance of Sir John French's original undertaking to General Lanrezac;[1] and with such secrecy was the whole of this

---

[1] General Lanrezac: *Le Plan de Campagne Française*, p. 110.

vast operation enshrouded, that on the evening of August 21, only a few hours before the British cavalry patrols were in contact with the Germans, General von Kluck, commanding the First German Army in Belgium, received from the Supreme Command no better information than the following:

> A landing of British troops at Boulogne and their advance from about Lille must be reckoned with. It is believed that no landing of British troops on a big scale has yet taken place.[1]

Three days later the whole British Army was fighting at Mons.

---

[1] General von Kluck: *The March on Paris*, p. 38.

CHAPTER X

THE INVASION OF FRANCE

Since August 1 the armies of Europe had been mobilizing. Millions of men pouring along the roads and railroads, flowing across the Rhine bridges, entraining from the farthest provinces of the Russian Empire, streaming northwards from Southern France and Northern Africa, were forming in immense masses of manœuvre or in the line of battle. Yet the silence at sea was accompanied by suspense on land. There was a long stifling pause before the breaking of the storm. The combatants were taking up their stations with every precaution and strictest secrecy; and apart from the splutters of cannon fire at Liège and Belgrade—in the little countries first to be attacked—and unrecorded frontier bickering, there reigned over Europe for the first fortnight of Armageddon a strange, dull hush.

The opening was not only the first, but incomparably the greatest, crisis of the war. From August 18 to the middle of September all the best-trained troops of the seven warring states were continuously hurled against one another in open warfare with ample ammunition and in all the ardour of warlike inexperience arising from what, for most, had been a generation of peace. In this awful month more divisions fought on more days, and more men were killed and wounded than in any whole year of the struggle. There were in fact two crises—one in the West and one in the East—each surpassing in scale and intensity anything subsequently endured, and each reacting reciprocally upon the other.

There had arisen for Germany the long foreseen and profoundly studied case of the War on Two Fronts. For this she had prepared the Schlieffen plan. The main German effort was directed against France. More than seven-eighths of the German armies was employed in the West. Out of 40 German Army Corps less than five were left to defend the eastern provinces of Germany against the onslaught of the Russian Empire. The Schlieffen plan staked everything upon the invasion of France and the destruction of the French armies by means of an enormous turning march through Belgium. In order to strengthen this movement by every means, General von Schlieffen was resolved to run all risks and make all sacrifices in every other quarter. He was prepared to let the Austrians bear the brunt of the Russian attack from the east, and to let all East

Prussia be overrun by the Russian armies, even if need be to the Vistula. He was ready to have Alsace and Lorraine successfully invaded by the French. The violation and trampling down of Belgium, even if it forced England to declare war, was to him only a corollary of his main theme. In his conception nothing could resist the advance of Germany from the north into the heart of France, and the consequent destruction of the French armies, together with the incidental capture of Paris and the final total defeat of France within six weeks. Nothing, as he saw it, would happen anywhere else in those six weeks to prevent this supreme event from dominating the problem and ending the war in victory.

To this day no one can say that the Schlieffen plan was wrong. However, Schlieffen was dead. His successors on the German General Staff applied his plan faithfully, resolutely, solidly—but with certain reservations enjoined by prudence. These reservations were fatal. Moltke, the nephew of the great Commander, assigned 20 per cent more troops to the defence of the German western frontier and 20 per cent less troops to the invasion of northern France than Schlieffen had prescribed. Confronted with the Russian invasion of East Prussia he still further weakened the Great Right Wheel into France. Thus as will be seen the Schlieffen plan applied at four-fifths of its intensity just failed, and we survive to this day.

We have seen how accurately General Wilson was able to forecast to the British Cabinet in August, 1911, the true German Schlieffen plan, and how he measured almost exactly the number of German divisions which would be used in the great turning movement. The accession of General Joffre to the chief command had led to a complete recasting of the French ideas. Under the Joffre regime the French General Staff had made a new plan of which they darkly nursed the secret. They called it "Plan XVII."

"Plan XVII" consisted in a general offensive in an easterly and northeasterly direction on both sides of Metz by four French armies, with the last remaining army in reserve behind their centre. It was based upon an ardent faith that the French right would penetrate deeply into Alsace and Lorraine and an obstinate disbelief that the French left would be turned by a German movement west of the Meuse through Belgium. Both these calculations were to be completely falsified by the first events of the war. From the very earliest days it was clear that the views which the British General Staff had consistently held since 1911, of a great German turning movement through Belgium, probably on both sides of the Belgian Meuse, were correct. Why should the Germans with their eyes open throw first Belgium and then the British Empire into the scales against them unless for an operation of supreme magnitude? Besides, there were the evidences of their long preparations—camps, railways and railway sidings—which the British Staff under Sir John French and Sir Henry Wilson had so minutely studied. Lastly, reported with much accuracy from day to day, there came the enormous troop movements on the German right, towards and into Belgium on both sides of the Meuse. Before the end of the first week in August, General Lanrezac, the Commander of the left French Army (the Fifth), was raising loud cries of warning and alarm about the menace to his left, and indeed his rear, if he carried out the rôle assigned to him and attacked as ordered in a north-easterly direction. By the end of the second week the presence of the accumulating masses of the German right could no longer be denied by the French High Command, and certain measures, tardy and inadequate, were taken to cope with it. Nevertheless, after the raid of a corps and a cavalry division into Alsace on the 13th August, General Joffre began his offensive into Lorraine with the two armies of the French right, the centre armies conforming a few days later; and up till the evening of the 18th General Lanrezac and the left or Fifth French Army were still under orders to advance north-east. Three days later this same army was defending itself in full battle from an attack from the north and north-west. It had been compelled to make a complete left wheel.

The Germans, as General Michel and Sir Henry Wilson had predicted three years before, made their vast turning movement through Belgium. They brought into action almost immediately 34 Army corps, of which 13 or their equivalent were reserve formations. Of the 2,000,000 men who marched to invade France and Belgium 700,000 only were serving conscripts and 1,300,000 were reservists. Against these General Joffre could muster only 1,300,000, of whom also 700,000 were serving conscripts but only 600,000 were reservists. 1,200,000 additional French reservists responded immediately to the national call, encumbering the depôts without equipment, without arms, without cadres, without officers. In consequence the Germans outnumbered the French at the outbreak by 3 to 2 along the whole line of battle, and as they economized the forces on their left they were able to deliver the turning movement on their right in overwhelming strength. At Charleroi they were 3 to 1.

It was for the tactical sphere that General Joffre and his school of "Young Turks," as they came to be called in France, had reserved their crowning mistakes. The French infantry marched to battle conspicuous on the landscape in blue breeches and red coats. Their artillery officers in black and gold were even more specially defined targets. Their cavalry gloried in ludicrous armour. The doctrine of the offensive raised to the height of a religious frenzy animated all ranks, and in no rank was restricted by the foreknowledge of the modern rifle and machine gun. A cruel surprise lay before them.

The battle began on the 20th when the two armies of the French right advanced to the south of Metz. They were resisted on the front by strongly prepared German defences and violently attacked upon their left by the Bavarian Army issuing from the radial roads and railways of the fortress. The Third

French Army marching north towards Arlon blundered into the Germans in the morning mist of August 22, four or five of its divisions having their heads shorn away while they were still close to their camping grounds. Everywhere along the battle front, whenever Germans were seen, the signal was given to charge. "Vive la France!" "A la balonnette," "En Avant"—and the brave troops, nobly led by their regimental officers, who sacrificed themselves in even greater proportion, responded in all the magnificent fighting fury for which the French nation has been traditionally renowned. Sometimes these hopeless onslaughts were delivered to the strains of the Marseillaise, six, seven or even eight hundred yards from the German positions. Though the Germans invaded, it was more often the French who attacked. Long swathes of red and blue corpses littered the stubble fields. The collision was general along the whole battle front, and there was a universal recoil. In the mighty battle of the Frontiers, the magnitude and terror of which is scarcely now known to British consciousness, more than 300,00 Frenchmen were killed, wounded or made prisoners.

These disasters heralded the enormous perils to which the French and British armies on the left or northern flank were now to be exposed. The Fifth French Army had no sooner completed with severe exertions its deployment on the Sambre, and the British Army advancing by forced marches had no sooner reached the neighbourhood of Mons, when the overwhelming force of the German turning movement through Belgium fell upon them. Both General Lanrezac and Sir John French were about to be launched in a vehement offensive which the French Headquarters believed would hurl back the wheeling German right. The British Command accepted this guidance with implicit faith. Lanrezac, sure that Joffre was utterly adrift from facts, watched with insolent distrust the impending disaster. But even he, never imagined the weight and sweep of the German enveloping swing. The two armies of the left only escaped disaster by the timely retreat which Lanrezac and Sir John French each executed independently and on his own initiative. And also by the most stubborn resistance and rifle fire of the highly trained professional British infantry. Many faults of temperament and indeed of loyalty to the British Army on his left are urged against General Lanrezac. Nevertheless his grasp of the situation and stern decision to retreat while the time remained has earned the gratitude of France. It was a pity he forgot to tell his British allies about it.

The utmost secrecy had naturally been maintained by the French about their general plan. The existence of their nation was at stake. Neither the British Cabinet nor what was left of the War Office were in a position to understand what was passing. I do not know how far Lord Kitchener was specially informed. I think it very improbable that he shared the secrets of the French Headquarters to the extent of being able to measure what was happening on the front as a whole. If he shared them, he did not show it by any remark which escaped him. He knew, of course, all there was to be known about the situation of our own army, and a good deal about the forces contiguous to it.

Late on the evening of August 23 I had a talk with Lord Kitchener. We knew the main battle had been joined and that our men had been fighting all day; but he had received no news. He was darkly hopeful. The map was produced. The dense massing of German divisions west of the Belgian Meuse and curling round the left flank of the Anglo-French line was visible as a broad effect. So was the pivot of Namur, in front of which this whole vast turning movement seemed precariously to be hinged. He had in his mind a great French counterstroke—a thrust at the shoulder, as it were, of the long, straining, encircling arm which should lop it off or cripple it fatally. He said of the Germans, "They are running a grave risk. No one can set limits to what a well-disciplined army can do; but if the French were able to cut in here," he made a vigorous arrow N.W. from Namur, "the Germans might easily have a Sedan of their own on a larger scale." I had a pleasing vision of the first phase of Austerlitz, with the Austrians stretching and spreading their left far out to the villages of Tellnitz and Sokolnitz, while Napoleon remained crouched for his spring at the Pratzen plateau. But had France a Napoleon? One had marched through Charleroi ninety-nine years before. Was there another? And were the Germans like the Austrians and Russians of Austerlitz? However, we went anxiously but hopefully to our slumbers.

At 7 o'clock the next morning I was sitting up in bed in Admiralty House working at my boxes, when the door of my bedroom opened and Lord Kitchener appeared. These were the days before he took to uniform, and my recollection is that he had a bowler hat on his head, which he took off with a hand which also held a slip of paper. He paused in the doorway and I knew in a flash and before ever he spoke that the event had gone wrong. Though his manner was quite calm, his face was different. I had the subconscious feeling that it was distorted and discoloured as if it had been punched with a fist. His eyes rolled more than ever. His voice, too, was hoarse. He looked gigantic. "Bad news," he said heavily and laid the slip of paper on my bed. I read the telegram. It was from Sir John French.

> My troops have been engaged all day with the enemy on a line roughly east and west through Mons. The attack was renewed after dark, but we held our ground tenaciously. I have just received a message from G.O.C. 5th French Army that his troops have been driven back, that Namur has fallen, and that he is taking up a line from Maubeuge to Rocroi. I have therefore ordered a retirement to the line Valenciennes-Longueville-Maubeuge, which is being carried out now. It will prove a

difficult operation, if the enemy remains in contact. I remember your precise instructions as to method and direction of retirement if necessity arises.

I think that immediate attention should be directed to the defence of Havre.

I did not mind it much till I got to Namur. Namur fallen! Namur taken in a single day—although a French brigade had joined the Belgians in its defence. We were evidently in the presence of new facts and of a new standard of values. If strong fortresses were to melt like wisps of vapour in a morning sun, many judgments would have to be revised. The foundations of thought were quaking. As for the strategic position, it was clear that the encircling arm was not going to be hacked off at the shoulder, but would close in a crushing grip. Where would it stop? What of the naked Channel ports? Dunkirk, Calais, Boulogne! "Fortify Havre," said Sir John French. One day's general battle and the sanguine advance and hoped-for counterstroke had been converted into "Fortify Havre." "It will be difficult to withdraw the troops if the enemy remains in contact"—a disquieting observation. I forget much of what passed between us. But the apparition of Kitchener *Agonistes* in my doorway will dwell with me as long as I live. It was like seeing old John Bull on the rack!

When I met the Admirals later, at ten, they were deeply perturbed about these Channel ports. They had never taken the War Office view of the superiority of the French Army. They saw in this first decisive shock the confirmation of their misgivings. Someone suggested we should at any rate make sure of the Cotentin peninsula, as an ample place of arms, girt on three sides by the sea, from which the British armies of the future might proceed to the rescue of France. Fortify Havre indeed! Already we looked to Cherbourg and St. Nazaire.

Then came the days of retreat. We saw that the French armies of the right were holding their own, but all the centre and left was marching southwards towards Paris as fast as possible, while our own five divisions[1] were for several days plainly in the very jaws of destruction. At the Admiralty we received requests to shift the base of the whole army from Havre to St. Nazaire; and with this complicated business we had to cope. The process of retreat continued day after day. A seemingly irresistible compulsion was pressing and forcing backwards the brave armies of France. Why should it stop? Would they ever be able to turn? If France could not save herself, nothing could save her.

Personally, I was hopeful that the wave of invasion would spend its fury, and as I had indicated in my memorandum of three years before, I believed that

---

[1] The Fourth Division (fifth in order of embarkation) arrived on the field at the beginning of the battle of Le Cateau.

unless the French forces had already been squandered by precipitate action on the frontiers an opportunity of striking the decisive blow would occur about the fortieth day. In order to encourage my colleagues I reprinted this memorandum and circulated it to the whole Cabinet on September 2, pointing out that I had never counted upon a victorious issue at the frontiers, had always expected that the French armies would be driven into retreat by the twentieth day, but that in spite of this, there were good hopes of success. But I had no means of measuring the forces by which this result would be achieved, except by the most general processes.

And at this culminating moment the Russian pressure began to produce substantial effects. Honour must ever be done to the Tsar and Russian nation for the noble ardour and loyalty with which they hurled themselves into the war. A purely Russian treatment of their military problem would have led the Russian armies into immediate withdrawals from their frontiers until the whole of their vast mobilization was completed. Instead of this, they added to a forward mobilization an impetuous advance not only against Austria but into Germany. The flower of the Russian Army was soon to be cut down in enormous and fearful battles in East Prussia. But the results of their invasion were gathered at the decisive point. The nerve of the German Headquarters failed. On August 25 two army corps and a cavalry division of the German right were withdrawn from France. On August 31 Lord Kitchener was able to telegraph to Sir John French: "Thirty-two trains of German troops were yesterday reported moving from the western field to meet the Russians."[1]

What had happened in the East? The Russians had invaded East Prussia with their two converging northern armies, one under Rennenkampf marching from Wilna along the Baltic shore, the other under Samsonov striking upwards from Warsaw. The defence of East Prussia had been confided to General von Prittwitz, who with an army of about 5½ corps had to meet a double attack of two armies each the equal of his own. Prittwitz had advanced to arrest Rennenkampf near the eastern frontier and on August 20 began to fight the battle of Gumbinnen. The day was indecisive although the superior qualities of the Germans were apparent. In the evening Prittwitz, alarmed by the advance of the Warsaw army, which threatened his line of retreat, broke off the battle of Gumbinnen and telephoned to Moltke at the German main headquarters at Luxemburg that in the face of the overpowering Russian masses he must retreat to the Vistula, and that in view of the low state of the river he could not even guarantee to hold this line. His agitated manner emphasized his grave tidings. Moltke when he hung up the receiver determined there and then to supersede him. Telegrams were dispatched to a Major-General named Ludendorff, a High

---

[1] Official History of the War, Appendix 22, p. 473.

Staff Officer who had distinguished himself in the capture of Liège, and to General von Hindenburg, a retired commander of massive qualities, to defend the German hearths and homes in East Prussia. Moltke further urged the Austrian Commander-in-Chief, Conrad von Hötzendorff, to hasten the offensive of the Austrian Army in order to relieve the perilous situation in East Prussia. Hötzendorff thereupon, with many misgivings and without his whole strength, advanced to meet the vast tide of Russian invasion and was defeated a week later in the 200-mile battle called Lemberg. Ludendorff and Hindenburg hastened to East Prussia, where they found the situation largely restored by the unerring decisions of Prittwitz's brilliant Staff Officer, General Hoffman. They arrived to find all the movements in progress which five days later were to result in the awful battle of Tannenberg.

The night of August 25 brought a solid assurance of victory to the German High Command. From every part of the immense battle front in the West the news was good. Everywhere the French had failed in their advances or were retreating. It was at this moment that Moltke felt able to cope with the anxieties which had oppressed him since; five days earlier, he had received Prittwitz's panic-stricken telephone message about Gumbinnen. Believing that the decision in France had been reached and that the supreme clash of arms was now bound speedily to end in favour of Germany, Moltke turned his eyes eastward. All Germany was in uproar about the invasion of East Prussia. The Emperor was indignant at this violation of "our lovely Masurian Lakes." Now is the time to send reinforcements to the east. Tappen, Head of the Operations Branch, is told to make plans for transferring thither *six army corps* from the west, two from each of the right, centre and left. However it is better not to promise more than you can give. Four of these corps are at the moment closely engaged in action or pursuit. There are only two which seem immediately available. These two are upon the wheeling German right. In the profound design of the German war plans these two corps had been reserved for the siege of Namur and they had crossed the Belgian frontier banked up behind Bülow's advancing army. But now there was no siege of Namur; it had fallen almost at the first salvos of the heavy howitzers. It was already in German hands, and the two corps which were to have made the siege were, so it seemed, free. Give *them* anyhow to Ludendorff at Marienburg: the others can go later.

So Tappen clears the line, and Ludendorff on the eve of Tannenberg, a prey to all its measureless uncertainties, is offered immediately two of the best German corps, including one regular Guards division. Such an offer was a temptation to any general. It was a peculiar temptation to a man of Ludendorff's temperament; but curiously enough a temptation against which his high intellectuality and commanding view afforded him adequate protection. Although he was fighting in East Prussia for everything he cared for, including (not negligible) his own power and importance, he still retained his trained view of the general situation. Of course, he said, he would like to have the corps, but they could not arrive in time for the impending battle in the East, and anyhow the situation in the West ought not to be endangered on his account. Several notable deeds have been inscribed upon Ludendorff's record which have faded or even been expunged: here is one which will endure a long time. However, the decision is Moltke's, and the two corps situated at the very thong of the German right-handed stroke, placed in the exact position where they could have followed so easily the marches of the armies and advanced to fill any gap which might open between them, are already being entrained with magnificent German efficiency for their 700-mile journey to the Vistula.

During the whole of the next week everything continued to go well with Germany. All her armies in France strode forward on the heels of the retreating French and British as fast as men could march; and from the East arrived the dazzling news of Tannenberg. The Emperor was in what the German Staff has described as a "shout hurrah mood." Sure that not only victory but escape from war was in his grasp, he urged on his commanders who in their turn halloaed their troops. But Moltke's outlook seems to have undergone a change. The stubborn and unexpected French resistance of Lanrezac's army at Guise, the bloody repulse which the Bavarians had received when they in their turn attacked the French fortress lines before Nancy, the fact that Kluck had found himself in contact with an unexpectedly substantial British army which, though retiring before his masses, had at Mons, Le Cateau, Néry and Villers-Cotterets not only inflicted much slaughter, but produced a formidable military impression on the German General Staff mind—all these added to the increasing distance of the German columns from their rail-heads, mingled a dark and broadening streak of misgivings with the general rejoicings. "Are these enemy armies really defeated?" asked the anxious Chief of the German General Staff. "Is the battle over?" "Where are the prisoners? Where are the captured guns? Where is the disorganization?" In fact, as August ticked out its last crimson minutes, the most anxious man in Germany was the man who knew the most.

Meanwhile what of Joffre? We have no record of the reactions produced in the minds of the so-called "Young Turks," who formed his *entourage,* and walled him in from the principal commanders, of the perfect failure and frustration of all their plans. But we do know that Joffre preserved a calm, impassive and resolute demeanour and rested for a while like George II at the battle of Dettingen, *"sans peur et sans avis."* Obviously something must be done to stem the enveloping German right wheel. Accordingly on the 25th when the results of the battles of the frontier were apparent, the following "Instruction No. 2" was issued from G.Q.G.[1]: "It having proved impossible to execute the offensive manœuvre projected, further operations will be arranged in such a manner as to constitute on our left by the junction of the Fourth and Fifth Armies, the British Army, and new forces drawn from the east, a mass capable of resuming the offensive, while the other armies restrain the efforts of the enemy for the present." In pursuance of this a new French army, the Sixth, under General Maunoury, an officer of high quality, soon afterwards to be blinded by a bullet, began during the last five days to form around Amiens. The troops composing it were transported swiftly by railway from the eastern fortress line where the armies of Dubail, Castelnau, and we must in justice add Sarrail, had begun for the first time to discover and reveal the power of modern weapons when used from trenches.

But now observe the intrusion of politics into the military sphere. Hitherto Joffre and his circle have had that unfettered discretion which great captains have only enjoyed when they were kings or emperors. But the crash on the frontiers has given a dismal stimulus to the civil power. On this same 25th August the French Minister of War, Messimy, himself a military man but turned politician, sent an officer to Joffre's headquarters with the following order: "If victory does not crown the success of our armies and if these armies are reduced to retreat, an army of at least three active corps should be directed upon the entrenched camp of Paris to secure its protection." M. Messimy gave in the war abundant proofs of courage and decision both as Deputy and soldier; but in this case he had behind him a far greater figure. In fact it is the purpose of this account to suggest that in General Galliéni, newly appointed Military Governor of Paris and holding commission as "contingent successor" (successeur éventuel) to General Joffre, will be found the saviour of France.

The "Young Turks" were disgusted at this intervention and we may suppose that they took care that the emergence of Galliéni, the potential successor, at the head of important forces in the capital city was not lost upon General Joffre. But the order was imperative. Messimy, about to be replaced almost in a few hours by a new minister, wielded a constitutional authority the traditions of which were founded by the Jacobin Committee of Public Safety in the ferocious days of 1793. So Joffre and his Staff had to find the troops, and where were they to be procured? No more can be taken from the eastern fortress lines. Assuredly none can be withdrawn from the line of armies retreating from the north. Well, there is this army of Maunoury's which we should have liked to assemble on the left flank, a mixed lot—some shattered regulars, some reserve divisions mauled in their first unsuccessful action! If we have to lock up an army

[1] Grand Quartier Général.

in Paris, if the Government insist upon it, theirs shall be the responsibility and these shall be the troops! However, no sooner had Maunoury's army begun to gather round Amiens than it was forced to conform to the general retirement. The blind force of events decreed that it should be directed on Paris, there to become the sword of Galliéni.

CHAPTER XI

THE MARNE

As the German armies rolled southwards Paris loomed before them like an enormous breakwater. The enemy capital was not only the heart of France, it was also the largest fortress in the world. It was the centre of an intricate spider's web of railways. Masses of troops could debouch in almost unlimited numbers in any direction upon passers-by. No one could count on entering it without a formal siege, the German cannon for which were at this moment deploying before Antwerp. To advance upon both sides of Paris, the Germans had not the troops; to enter Paris, they had not at this moment the guns. What then remained? They must march between Paris and Verdun—which exerted a similar influence—and guarding their flanks from both these fortresses push on to the destruction of the French field armies. Surely also this was the classical tradition? Had not Moltke—not this one but the great Moltke, now dead a quarter of a century—proclaimed "Direction: Paris! Objective: the enemy's field armies!"[1]

At noon on August 31 a Captain Lepic sent to reconnoitre with his squadron reported from Gournay-sur-Aronde that the interminable columns of Kluck's First Army were turning south-east towards Compiègne instead of continuing their march on Paris. This news was confirmed the next day both by British and French aviators. By nightfall on the 2nd General Maunoury's Sixth Army, which had now arrived in the northern environs of Paris, reported that there were no German troops west of the line Senlis-Paris. It was upon these indications, confirmed again by British aviators on the 3rd, that Galliéni acted.

Assuredly no human brain had conceived the design, nor had human hand set the pieces on the board. Several separate and discrepant series of events had flowed together. First, the man Galliéni is on the spot. Fixed in his fortress, he could not move towards the battle; so the mighty battle has been made to come to him. Second—the weapon has been placed in his hands—the army of Maunoury. It was given him for one purpose, the defence of Paris; he will use it for another—a decisive manœuvre in the field. It was given him against the wish of Joffre. It will prove the means of Joffre's salvation. Third, the Opportunity:

[1] See map on p. 158.

Kluck, swinging forward in hot pursuit of, as he believed, the routed British and demoralized French, will present his whole right flank and rear as he passes Paris to Galliéni with Maunoury in his hand. Observe, not one of these factors would have counted without the other two. All are interdependent; all are here, and all are here now.

Galliéni realized the position in a flash. "I dare not believe it," he exclaimed; "it is too good to be true." But it is true. Confirmation arrives hour by hour. He vibrates with enthusiasm. Instantly on the 3rd, he orders the army of Maunoury to positions on the northeast of Paris, which in 48 hours will enable them on the 5th to strike Kluck and with him the whole advancing line of German armies behind their right shoulder-blade. But this is not enough. What can one army—hastily improvised—do by itself amid events on such a scale? He must secure the British; he must animate Joffre. At half-past eight on the evening of the 3rd he wrote requesting Joffre's authority for the movement, which he has already ordered Maunoury's army to make, and urging a general offensive by all the French armies between Paris and Verdun simultaneously with his attack.

Joffre and Great Headquarters had arrived that day at Bar-sur-Aube. The numerous bureaux composing the elaborate staff machine had been on the move for two days and were now installing themselves at a new centre. We must not suppose that Joffre and his assistants have not been thinking about things. It was evident to any trained observer that if the fortresses of Verdun and Paris were strongly defended by mobile armies, the German invasion would bulge forward into a wide crescent between these two points; and that this would give an opportunity for a general French attack. Somehow, somewhere, sometime, Joffre and his Staff intended this. In principle they and Galliéni were agreed. From the beginning of the retreat he had said, "I will attack when my two wings have an enveloping position." But the How, the Where, and the When. These were the rubs; and on these vital matters it is certain that not only no resolve or design had been formed, but that important orders had been issued inconsistent with such a plan.

Galliéni's messenger reached Bar-sur-Aube on the night of the 3rd, and all the next morning while Maunoury's army was marching into its preparatory stations Galliéni waited in acute anxiety. In the afternoon of the 4th he set off by motor car to Melun to ask Sir John French for British co-operation. Remember that this man had had Joffre under his command in Madagascar and that he is his formally designated successor. He is not thinking only of the local situation around Paris. He thinks for France and he behaves with the spontaneous confidence of genius in action. But French is out with his troops. Murray, Chief of his Staff, receives the Governor of Paris. The interview is lengthy and somewhat bleak.

It was an unpropitious moment for a subordinate French General to propose a new and desperate battle to the British command. On September 2 Sir
John French had written to Joffre offering, if the French would turn and fight a
general battle on the Marne, to throw in the British Army and put all things to
the proof; and Joffre had written back, "I do not think it possible to contemplate at this moment *(actuellement)* a general operation on the Marne with the
whole of our forces." And the British leader who had braced himself for a
supreme ordeal with his small, weary and shot-torn army had been chilled. By a
swift reaction, remembering all that had passed since the battle of Mons began,
he had reached precipitately, but not inexcusably, the conclusion that the
French had lost heart and did not feel themselves capable of regaining the
offensive—at any rate for some time to come. So far, his allies had produced
nothing but repulse, defeat and retreat. All their plans, in so far as he was informed of them, seemed to have failed. He knew that the Government was
quitting Paris for Bordeaux. He saw that the rearmost lines of places mentioned
in Joffre's Instruction No. 2 as the limits of the retreat were far behind the positions he occupied at the moment. He could not exclude, from his mind, on the
morrow of his offer being declined, the possibility of a general collapse of
French resistance. Indeed it was evident that the Germans, by the very fact of
disdaining Paris, sought nothing less than the destruction of the French armies.
Had he been in the German Headquarters, he would have learned that at this
moment Moltke looked confidently forward to driving the French masses either into Switzerland or, if Rupprecht could break through between Nancy and
Toul, on to the back of their own eastern fortress line, thus swiftly compelling a
universal surrender. If he had been admitted to the secrets of the French Headquarters, he would have learned that Joffre had proposed to declare Paris an
open town and to surrender it to the first German troops who arrived; that he
had simultaneously sent orders to General Sarrail to abandon Verdun; and that
only Messimy's intrusion and Sarrail's stubbornness had prevented both these
catastrophes from being already accomplished facts. One really cannot blame
Sir Archibald Murray on the knowledge that he had, and in the absence of his
Chief, from viewing with scepticism the ardent and admittedly unauthorized
projects of the Governor of Paris. However he promised provisionally to stop
the southward movement of the British Army and to face about on a certain
rather rearward line.

Meanwhile, early on the 4th, Joffre at Bar-sur-Aube had received Galliéni's
letter of the night before. All the morning he pondered upon it. Then at noon
he authorized Galliéni by telegram to use the army of Maunoury as he had proposed, but with the express condition that it should not attack north, but south
of the Marne. A little later he telegraphed to Franchet d'Espérey, now commanding the Fifth French Army, asking him when he could be ready to take

part in a general offensive. Franchet replied at 4 p.m. on the 4th that he could attack on the morning of the 6th. This answer reached Joffre between 5 and 6 o'clock. But for the next three hours he did nothing. He took no decision; he sent no orders.

Galliéni arrived back in Paris from Melun shortly before 8 o'clock. He had been absent from his Headquarters for five hours, and meanwhile Joffre's reply to his letter had arrived. He was disturbed by the Commander-in-Chief's express condition that the army of Maunoury should not attack north but only south of the Marne. Other disconcerting news reached him. He heard by telegram from Sir Henry Wilson (Murray's assistant) that the British Army was continuing its retreat; and soon after he received from Colonel Huguet, the French *liaison* officer at the British Headquarters, Sir John French's reply to his proposals: "Prefer on account of continual changes of the situation to re-study it before deciding on further operations."

It was now 9 o'clock. Apparently nothing was happening. All the armies would before dawn resume their retreat. So far as he knew, he had received nothing but the permission to make an isolated flank attack with Maunoury's Army. Galliéni went to the telephone. He called up Joffre. The Commander-in-Chief came. The two men talked. As the Commander-in-Chief of the French armies circulating his orders through the official channels, Joffre towered above Galliéni; but now, almost in personal contact, Galliéni and his old subordinate spoke at least as equals; and Joffre, to his honour, rising above jealousies and formalities, felt the strong, clear guidance of his valiant comrade. He agreed that Galliéni should attack *north* of the Marne on the 5th, and returning to his circle of officers, ordered the general battle for the 6th. Unfortunately his hesitation and previous delays bred others. We can see from the times quoted how long these vital orders take to prepare and encipher for telegraph, and decipher on arrival. It was nearly midnight before they were dispatched. They were in fact outstripped by duplicates carried by officers in motor cars. Foch, being nearest, received his orders at 1:30 a.m. But neither Franchet nor Sir John French learned of the great decision until after 3 a.m., when their armies had already begun a further day's march to the south.

Nevertheless the die is now cast. The famous order of the day is sent out; and from Verdun to Paris the electrifying right-about-turn points a million bayonets and 1,000 cannon upon the invading hosts. The Battle of the Marne has begun.

One must suppose upon the whole that the Marne was the greatest battle ever fought in the world. The elemental forces which there met in grapple and collision of course far exceeded anything that has ever happened. It is also true that the Marne decided the World War. Half a dozen other cardinal crises have left their gaunt monuments along the road of tribulation which the nations trod; and it may well be argued that any of these might in part at least have reversed the decision of the Marne. The Allies might have been beaten on other occasions, and Germany might have emerged from the World War upon a victorious peace. If in 1917 the French Army had succumbed, if the British Navy had not strangled the submarine, if the United States had not entered the war, students of to-day and to-morrow would bend over different history books and different maps. But never after the Marne had Germany a chance of absolute triumph. Never again was there the possibility of all the claims of their proud militarism receiving complete vindication. Never again could the domination of scientific force have achieved its lasting establishment. Deep changes took place in the world and among warring powers in the terrible years that followed. The nations fought desperately, but they fought in a different atmosphere and on a lower plane. The carnage and the cannonade increased; but never were the moral or the military issues at the same pitch of intensity. By the end of 1915 England was a great warlike power, and the whole British Empire was roused and marshalling its strength. By the end of 1916 Germany was deeply conscious of her weakness. In 1917 the United States had been drawn into the conflict. It is obvious that the British Empire and the United States could in the long run have crushed Germany, even if France had been completely subjugated. But the battle of the Marne might have ended the war in six weeks; and the Kaiser and his twenty kinglets and their feudal aristocracy might have founded for many generations the legend of invincible military force.

We must remember that on September 3 the Emperor William II and the German General Staff knew that they were victorious in the East and had every reason to believe that within a week they would capture or destroy all the armies that withstood them in the West. On the 10th, according to wide report, Moltke informed his master with rugged truth that "Germany had lost the war." Evidently an immense transformation took place. Something of enormous and mysterious potency had worked its will, and the question which will puzzle posterity as much as it astonished those who lived through the deluge, is—what?

At the time nobody worried about the causes. Everyone facing the new perils of the hour or the week, was concerned only with the result. The German invasion of France was stopped. "The avalanche of fire and steel" was not only brought to a standstill, but hurled backwards. The obsession of German invincibility was dispersed. There would be time for all the world to go to war—time even for the most peaceful and unprepared countries to turn themselves into arsenals and barracks. Surely that was enough. All bent their backs or their heads to the toil of war; and in the instructed circles of the allies none, and in those of the Germans few, doubted which way the final issue would go. Never again need we contemplate the entire surrender of the French Army before any other armies were afoot to take its place. At the very worst there would be parley, negotiation, barter, compromise, and a haggled peace.

Since the war laborious studies have been set in train, and an enormous mass of publications, official, non-official and counter-official, has been produced. These have together assembled a multitudinous array of facts. But there are so many facts adduced and some few vitally important facts withheld, and such disputations over the one or the other, that half a dozen explanatory theories may well be championed; and the world, harassed with paying the bill, has been content to rest on the solid assurance that the French beat the Germans at the battle of the Marne.

The French official history carries its discreet narration down to midnight on September 5. According to this account, with little generosity to Galliéni, the battle of the Marne does not begin till the 6th, and in the presence of this event the French military historians are mute. From the evening of September 5 till January, 1915, their pages are blank. Obviously the controversies of rival schools of professional opinion, fierce disputes about facts and their valuations, respect for the feelings of illustrious men, have induced the chroniclers to leave this climax of their tale till time has wrought its smoothing work.

So far as we may judge from the French account of the preliminaries, they consider the battle as having reached from Paris to Verdun. The German account, on the other hand, in harmony with their own schemes, comprehends it as extending from Paris right round the corner of Verdun to the Vosges Mountains. The Germans consider that all their seven armies were engaged at the Marne; the French that only five of theirs and the British Army were comprised in the battle. We have to contemplate on either view the collision of thirteen or fourteen armies, each containing the adult male population of a very large city, and all consuming food, material, ammunition, treasure and life at a prodigious rate per hour. We have to remember also that the French and British are armies whose springs are compressed back on their reserves and supplies; and that the German armies have hurried on far beyond their rearward organization and their railheads. The French have perfect communications sideways and otherwise; the Germans have not yet restored the broken roads and bridges over which their rapid advance had been made. The French are upon interior lines; the Germans are stretched round the fortified Verdun corner. It was upon this basis that the battle began.

It was less like a battle than any other ever fought. Comparatively few were killed or wounded. No great recognizable feat of arms, no shock proportionate to the event can be discerned. Along a front of more than 200 miles weary, war-ravaged troops were in a loose-desperate contact; then all of a sudden one side sustained the impression that it was the weaker, and that it had had the worst

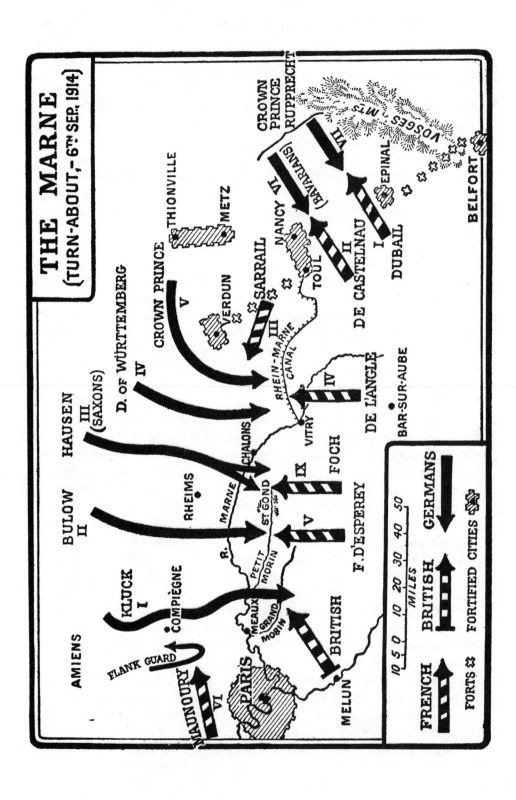

THE MARNE
(TURN-ABOUT, - 6TH SEP, 1914)

AMIENS

KLUCK I

COMPIÈGNE

FLANK GUARD

MAUNOURY VI

PARIS

MELUN

MEAUX

BRITISH

F. D'ESPEREY

R. MARNE

PETIT MORIN

GRAND MORIN

BULOW II

RHEIMS

ST GOND

V

IX

FOCH

CHALONS

HAUSEN III (SAXONS)

D. of WÜRTEMBERG IV

CROWN PRINCE V

VERDUN

SARRAIL

III

RHEIN-MARNE CANAL

VITRY

IV

DE L'ANGLE

BAR-SUR-AUBE

THIONVILLE

METZ

CROWN PRINCE RUPPRECHT

NANCY VI (BAVARIANS)

TOUL

DE CASTELNAU

II

DUBAIL I

EPINAL

VOSGES MTS.

BELFORT

10 5 0 10 20 30 40 50
MILES

FRENCH

BRITISH

GERMANS

FORTS ✪   FORTIFIED CITIES

of it. But what was the mechanical causation which induced this overpowering psychological reaction? I can only try to burnish a few links of a chain that is still partly buried.

The popular conception of the battle of the Marne as a wild counter-rush of France upon Germany, as a leopard spring at the throat of the invaders, as an onslaught carried forward on the wings of passion and ecstasy, is in singular contrast to the truth. It took some time to turn round the French armies retreating between Verdun and Paris. These ponderous bodies could only effectually reverse their motion after a substantial number of hours and even days. No sooner had the French turned about and begun to advance, than they met the pursuing Germans advancing towards them. Most prudently they stopped at once and fired upon the Germans, and the Germans withered before their fire. It is the Battle of the Frontiers fought the other way round. No longer the French advance madly to the strains of the Marseillaise while the German invaders stop and shoot them down with machine guns and artillery; the conditions are reversed. It is the Germans who try to advance and feel for the first time the frightful power of the French artillery. If only the French had done this at the frontiers; if only they had used modern firearms upon hostile flesh and blood at the outset, how different the picture of the world might look to-day!

The battle of the Marne was won when Joffre had finished his conversation with Galliéni on the night of September 4. Although the French armies had been defeated, had suffered grievous losses and had retreated day after day, they were still an enormous, unbeaten, fighting force of a very high order. Although the British had retreated with great rapidity and had lost 15,000 men, the soldiers knew they had fought double their numbers and had inflicted far heavier casualties upon the German masses. Drafts and reinforcements had reached them, and they were at the moment of the turn certainly stronger than they had ever been. Although the Germans had 78 divisions on their western front compared to 55 French and British, this superiority was not enough for the supreme objective which they had in view. The Schlieffen plan, the "receipt for victory," had prescribed 97 divisions against France alone, and of these 71 were to execute the great offensive wheel through Belgium. Moltke had 19 fewer divisions in the west and 16 fewer in the great offensive wheel. From these again he had withdrawn 2 army corps (4 divisions) to send to the eastern front. He had not thought it worth while to attempt to stop or delay the transport of the British Expeditionary Force across the Channel. According to the German naval history "the chief of the General Staff personally replied that the Navy should not allow the operations that it would have otherwise carried out to be interfered with on this account. It would even be of advantage if the armies in the west could settle with the 160,000 English at the same time as with the

French and Belgians." Thus when Joffre's decision was taken the balance had already turned strongly in favour of the allies.

Contrary to the French official narrative, the battle began on the 5th when Maunoury's Army came into action on the Ourcq. Let us hasten thither.

General von Kluck's army is marching south and passes Paris in sight of the Eiffel Tower. One of his five corps is acting as flank guard. Bright and cloudless skies! Suddenly about one o'clock the flank corps begins to brush against French troops advancing upon it from Paris. In order to test the strength of their assailants, the Germans attack. At once a violent action flares out and spreads. The French appear in ever-growing strength; the flank guard is beaten. The corps retreats seven miles with heavy losses. The attack from Paris grows and lengthens with more and more weight behind it. Night comes on. The defeated General, hoping to retrieve his fortunes with the morning, sends no word to Kluck. But a German aviator has noticed the conflict far below and the unexpected position of the fighting lines and his report goes to the Army Headquarters. It is not till nearly midnight that Kluck is informed that the shield on which he had counted has been shivered. Then, and not till then did he remember Moltke's orders, namely that in the main advance to drive the French into Switzerland, the armies of Kluck and Bülow should form a defensive flank against attacks from Paris. So far from giving protection to the line of German armies, he has had his own flank torn open; and in four hours another day will break!

So Kluck without more ado pulls back the two corps of his centre, and bids them recross the Marne and form to the north of his defeated flank guard; and as the pressure of Maunoury's attack continues during the 6th, he next takes the last of his army, the two corps of his left, marches them 60 miles in 48 hours, resolved whatever befall not to be out-flanked in the north, and have his communications cut. So here is Kluck who was pressing southward so fast to find the remains of the defeated English, now suddenly turned completely round and drawing up his whole army facing west to ward off Maunoury's continuing attack from Paris. But all this takes time and it is not till the morning of the 9th that Kluck has got himself into his new position and is ready to fall upon Maunoury in superior strength and drive him back upon the Paris fortifications. Meanwhile the war has been going on.

Next in the line to Kluck is Bülow. He too remembers his orders to form a flank guard against Paris. Moreover, the withdrawal of Kluck's army corps has left his right in the air. So Bülow pivots on his centre. His right arm goes back, his left arm comes forward, and in the course of the 6th, 7th, 8th and 9th he draws himself up in position facing Paris, and almost at right angles to his previous front. But anyone who looks at the diagram on page 162 can see that both Kluck and Bülow have now exposed their left hands to the attack of any allied forces who may he advancing upon them from the south. We know that the British Army and the Fifth French Army (Franchet d'Espérey) have turned about on the morning of the 5th and are advancing. This was only the beginning. Not only had Kluck and Bülow exposed their left flanks to the attack of powerful forces, but a hideous gap had opened between them. A gap of over 30 miles, and practically nothing to fill it with except cavalry! A great mass of cavalry indeed, two cavalry corps, the corps of Marwitz provided by Kluck and of Richthofen provided by Bülow—still only cavalry and without a common commander! An awful gap merely skinned over! We may imagine the feelings of the German Main Headquarters in Luxemburg as this apparition gradually but inexorably resolved itself upon the map. "If we only had a couple of corps marching forward behind the main front, here is their place and this is their hour." "What did we do with the two corps that were to have besieged Namur?" "Ah! yes, we sent them to the Vistula! So we did! How far have they got?" "They are now disembarking from 80 trains 700 miles away." Well might the Kaiser have exclaimed, "Moltke, Moltke, give me back my legions!"

If the immense organisms of modern armies standing in a row together find there is a wide gap in their ranks, and have no reserves to come up and fill it, they cannot edge towards one another sideways like companies or battalions. They can only close the gap by an advance or by a retreat. Which is it to be? To answer this question we must see what has been happening on the rest of the long battle line.

Beginning round the corner at the extreme left of the German invasion, Prince Rupprecht has found he cannot pierce the front between Toul and Epinal. The heavy guns of the French fortresses, the prepared positions and the obstinate armies of Dubail and Castelnau have, with much slaughter, stopped him and his Bavarians. He has been dragging the heavy cannon out of Metz; but it takes a long time to move them. Now they are called for elsewhere. Rupprecht therefore reports on September 8 that he cannot break through the Trouée des Charmes and that he is in fact at a standstill. Northeast of Verdun Sarrail faces the Army of the German Crown Prince. Here again the guns of the fortress strike heavy blows. The Crown Prince's columns skirting Verdun at a respectful distance are mauled and hampered. Next come the armies of the Duke of Württemberg and General von Hausen. These are confronted respectively by the army of de Langle de Cary and around the marshes of St. Gond by the army of General Foch.

Throughout the centre the fighting was confused, obscure, and to say the least, indecisive. On the left of Bülow's army (with which was now associated nearly half of Hausen's) an attempt was made to advance against Foch with a desperate, gigantic bayonet attack at dawn. The Germans claim that this assault was successful. The outposts and advance troops of one of Foch's army corps

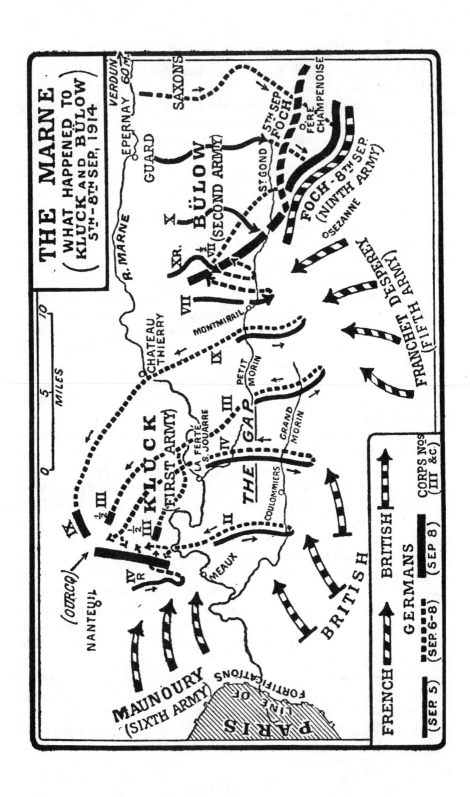

THE MARNE
(WHAT HAPPENED TO
KLUCK AND BÜLOW)
5TH–8TH SEP, 1914

MILES
0   5   10

VERDUN
SAXONS
EPERNAY 60M.
GUARD
5TH SEP.
FOCH
FÈRE
CHAMPENOISE
BÜLOW
(SECOND ARMY)
XR.
X
St GOND
FOCH–8TH SEP.
(NINTH ARMY)
OSEZANNE
VII
VII
R. MARNE
CHATEAU
THIERRY
MONTMIRAIL
IX
FRANCHET DESPEREY
(FIFTH ARMY)
KLÜCK
(FIRST ARMY)
½ III
¼
III
½
III
IX
LA FERTÉ
S. JOUARRE
IV
III
PETIT
MORIN
THE GAP
GRAND
MORIN
COULOMMIERS
II
(OURCQ)
NANTEUIL
IV
R
MEAUX
BRITISH
MAUNOURY
(SIXTH ARMY)
PARIS
LINE OF
FORTIFICATIONS

FRENCH ▰▰▰ GERMANS ▰▰▰ (SEP.6–8) BRITISH ▰▰▰
(SEP.5) ▰▰▰ (SEP.8) CORPS NOS ▰▰▰ (III &c.)

were certainly driven back; but the main line of the French field artillery intact continued its devastating fire. Everyone remembers Foch's staccato phrases: "My flanks are turned; my centre gives way; I attack!"

Three German armies had tried to advance directly against the French and had failed. The French wisely and though hardly with a conscious decision abstaining from their own onslaught, had been content to shoot them down. Broadly speaking, the armies of the German Crown Prince, the Duke of Würt-temberg and General von Hausen were by September 8 at a complete standstill in front of those of Sarrail, de L'Angle and Foch. The centres of the French and German fronts were leaning up against each other in complete equipoise. We are witnessing the birth throes of trench warfare.

But what meanwhile has been happening to the gap? We must not forget the gap. It is still open, thirty miles of it between the two armies of the German right. Into this gap are now marching steadily the British Army together with the left of the Fifth French Army (Franchet's). On they march, these 5 British divisions preceded by 5 brigades of their own cavalry and a French cavalry division. They go on marching. The German aeroplanes see five dark 15-mile-long caterpillars eating up the white roads. They report "heavy British masses advancing." And what was there to stop them? Only one corps of cavalry now, the other has been called away by Bülow; 6 battalions of Jäger, and—a long way back—one rather battered infantry division. There is no possibility of such forces stopping or indeed delaying the march of a professional army of 120,000 men. There are three rivers or streams to cross; four wooded ridges of ground to be cleared. But nothing can prevent this wedge from being driven into the gap. With every hour and every mile of its advance the strategic embarrassments of Bülow and Kluck increased. Nothing had happened so far. The German cavalry and Jäger were being driven back before aggressive British rifle-using cavalry, backed by swiftly gathering bayonets and cannon. But in the whole four days the British lost under 2,000 men. The effects were not tactical; they were strategic.

No human genius planned that the British Army should advance into this gap. A series of tumultuous events had cast them into this position in the line. When they advanced, there was the gap in front of them. On the whole front it was the line of least resistance. Along it they bored and punched, and it led into the strategic vitals of the German right wing. High destiny, blind fate regulated the none too vigorous, but nevertheless decisive movements of this British Army. It marches on, wondering what has happened to the monster which had pursued it with whip and yell since Mons. Bülow finds his right flank being rolled back by the Fifth French Army, and himself cut off continually from his right-hand comrade, Kluck, by the British advance. Kluck, just as he has got himself into a fine position to fight Maunoury, finds his left and all the rear of his left, hopelessly compromised and exposed.

All these developments present themselves in the first instance upon the maps at Bülow's and Kluck's headquarters, loaded with a hundred details concerning the supplies, the safety and even the escape of at least one-third of the whole of both their armies. And the sum of these disquietudes, unwillingly disclosed item by item, reveals its terrors to the highest centre of authority.

We must now transport ourselves, as is our privilege, to the Emperor's headquarters at Luxemburg. Time: the morning of September 8. The magnates there assembled were already alarmed at the lack of reports of the hourly victories to which they had become accustomed. Instead comes Rupprecht's tale that he is at a standstill. Next there is brought a captured copy of Joffre's battle orders of the 5th. The whole French Army is attacking! The Crown Prince says he is pinned down. "We can make only contemptible advances," he reports. "We are plagued with artillery fire. The infantry simply get under cover. There are no means of advancing. What are we to do?" The Duke of Württemberg and Hausen tell the same tale in similar terms, varied only by the bayonet attack episode. As for Bülow and Kluck, one has only got to look at the map. One does not need to read the tactical reports from these armies, when their strategic torture is disclosed, by aeroplane and other reports. Here at the summit in spacious rooms, in an atmosphere of order, salutes and heel-clicking, far from the cannonade and desperate, squalid, glorious confusion of the fighting lines, the resultants of the pressures upon the immense body of the German invasion of France are totalled and recorded, as if by a Wall Street ticker during a crash of the market. Values are changing from minute to minute. The highest authorities are reconciling themselves to new positions. The booming hopes of the 3rd are replaced by the paper collapse of the 8th. It is the same story in terms of blood instead of scrip.

Colonel Bauer, an accomplished Staff Officer of middle rank, has furnished us with a picture of the scene.

> Desperate panics seized severely the entire army, or to be more correct the greater part of the leaders. It looked at its worst at the supreme command. Moltke completely collapsed. He sat with a pallid face gazing at the map, dead to all feeling, a broken man. General von Stein (Moltke's deputy) certainly said "We must not lose our heads," but he did not take charge. He was himself without confidence and gave expression to his feelings by saying "We cannot tell how things will go." Tappen (head of the Operations Section of whom we have heard before) was as calm as ever and did not consider that the failure was altogether his fault; nor was it, for he did not lose his nerve. But he did nothing. "We younger people could not get a hearing."

Thus Bauer!

Everything now converged upon Moltke. Who was Moltke? He was the shadow of a great name; he was the nephew of the old Field Marshal and had been his aide-de-camp. He was an ordinary man, rather a courtier; a man about the Palace agreeable to the Emperor in the palmy days of peace. The sort of man who does not make too much trouble with a Sovereign, who knows how to suppress his own personality—what there is of it; a good, harmless, respectable, ordinary man. And on to this ill-fated being crashes the brutal, remorseless, centripetal impingement of tides and impulses under which the greatest captains of history might have blenched!

There is hardly any doubt what he should have done. A simple message to all the German armies to be imparted to every division, "If you cannot advance, hold on, dig in, yield not a scrap of conquered territory; *vestigia nulla retrorsum,*" might well have stabilized the situation. At this time, however, only the British Army knew (from the Boer War) the power of modern weapons on the defensive. The French were just enjoying their first exultant experience of it. None of the military men on the other side yet knew that as a matter of fact a 30-mile gap in a front of 200 is only a trap for the attackers who enter into it. Almost instantly it becomes not a victory but a dangerous salient, a bulge subject to crossfire and counter-attack from both flanks, the worst place in the world for a further offensive.

The officers of the German General Staff formed a close corporation and confraternity, and bore the same relation to the German Army and its leaders, as the Jesuits of the seventeenth and eighteenth centuries bore to the priests and cardinals of the Roman Catholic Church. They spoke their own language, they had their own special affiliations, they moved men and things with the higher intelligence which comes from knowledge and organization. To one of these officers, Colonel Hentsch, the head of the Intelligence, about midday September 8, Moltke imparted his views or mood. Both men are now dead. Neither has left a record of the conversation. We only know what followed from it. Colonel Hentsch got in his long grey car and went along the whole line of the Armies, stopping at each of their headquarters and finally reached Bülow's headquarters about dark. He saw his brother Staff Officer of that army. He wrestled with him long. It was agreed between them that if the British Army was actually found to be across the Marne in force and advancing into the gap between Bülow and Kluck, Bülow should retreat to the Aisne in conformity with all the other German armies of the right and centre. Hentsch spared a few moments for a civil chat with old Bülow. The conversation, we are told, was pessimistic. He slept the night at Bülow's headquarters. He started at 7 o'clock the next morning, and the old man not being called till 9, he talked again with

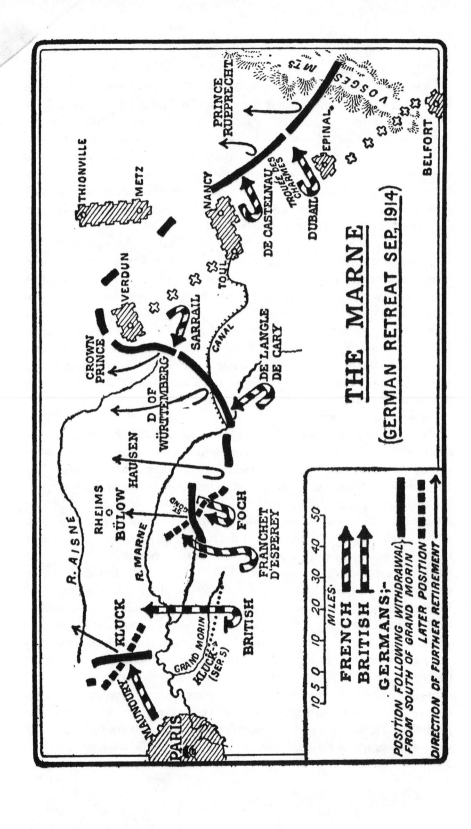

THE MARNE

(GERMAN RETREAT SEP, 1914)

MILES:
10 5 0   10   20   30   40   50

FRENCH ➤
BRITISH ➤
GERMANS:—
POSITION FOLLOWING WITHDRAWAL
FROM SOUTH OF GRAND MORIN
LATER POSITION
DIRECTION OF FURTHER RETIREMENT ➤

PARIS
MAUNOURY
KLUCK
KLUCK (SEP. 5)
GRAND MORIN
BRITISH
FRANCHET D'ESPEREY
R. AISNE
RHEIMS
BÜLOW
R. MARNE
HAUSEN
GRAND MORIN
FOCH
CROWN PRINCE
VERDUN
D OF WÜRTTEMBERG
SARRAIL
DE LANGLE DE CARY
CANAL
TOUL
THIONVILLE
METZ
NANCY
DE CASTELNAU
TROUÉE DES CHARMES
DUBAIL
ÉPINAL
PRINCE RUPPRECHT
VOSGES MTS
BELFORT

the General Staff Officer. It is clear that by this time—the reports of the previous day having been considered—there was no doubt about the heads of the British columns being across the Marne. Therefore the conditions established the night before had been fulfilled. Bülow "on his own initiative," as directed by his Staff Officer, ordered the retreat of the Second Army when in due course he entered his Headquarters' office.

Hentsch, knowing what the Second Army was doing, proceeded on his way. He had some difficulty in reaching Kluck. He had to cross the grisly gap and his car was blocked by masses of retreating German cavalry. He was involved in a "panic," as he describes it, following a British aeroplane raid. It was not till after noon that he reached Kluck's headquarters. Here again he dealt only with the Staff Officer. He never saw Kluck at all. He told von Kühl, Kluck's Chief of Staff, that as the English were now known to be advancing into the gap, Bülow's army would be retreating. But according to Hentsch, Kühl, some two hours before, had issued an order for retreat. Kühl, who is still alive and has written a massive book, admits that such an order had been telephoned by his subordinate (now dead), but that this subordinate had misconceived what he had intended. He declares that Hentsch gave him a positive order to withdraw Kluck's army to the Aisne, and seeks to lay the whole burden upon him.

At the inquiry into this celebrated episode ordered by Ludendorff in 1917 Colonel Hentsch was exonerated. It was found that his mission from Moltke was in short to see if a retreat was necessary, and if so to co-ordinate the retrograde movements of the five German armies. For this he had been given plenary authority in the name of the Supreme Command. And he had been given it only by word of mouth. But the duel between Kühl and Hentsch has been continued by Kühl over his adversary's grave. He declares the order to retreat was positive. It is however to be noted that he did not ask for this vital order in writing and that he did not tell Kluck about it till several hours had passed.

However it may be, Hentsch, a peripatetic focus of defeat, traversed and re-traversed the entire line of the German armies. On the outward journey he gathered evil tidings, and as he returned he issued fateful orders. He used the powers confided to him to order successively the First, Second, Third, Fourth and Fifth German armies to retreat upon the line of the Aisne or in general conformity with that line. Only at one point was any objection raised. The German Crown Prince, who has been so mocked at, received Moltke's emissary in person. Confronted with an order to retreat, he demanded it in writing, and refused otherwise to obey. All Hentsch's directions had been verbal as from one General Staff Officer to another. Here was the first Commander with whom he had come in contact. So he said "he would have a formal order sent from Luxemburg." And sent it was by telegraph the next day.

So ended the battle of the Marne. Until a retreat began, the only Ally army which had crossed the Marne was the British. In fact we may say that along the whole front from Verdun to Paris the French did not advance at all in the battle of the Marne. Some of them indeed on the left of Foch and the right of Franchet actually retreated. The only Ally army which advanced continually was the British. They advanced northwards in the four days September 5–8 more than 40 miles. But lest the reader should think this an assertion of national vainglory, let me hasten to repeat *first* that at the moment when the British Army was turned round, it had farther to go than the others before it came into contact; and *secondly* that when it met the enemy it found in the main only a cavalry screen covering the fatal gap. Nevertheless the fact remains that it probed its way into the German liver.

Thus, by a succession of unforeseeable and uncontrolled events was decided almost at its beginning the fate of the war on land, and little else was left but four years of senseless slaughter. Whether General von Moltke actually said to the Emperor, "Majesty, we have lost the war," we do not know. We know anyhow that with a prescience greater in political than in military affairs, he wrote to his wife on the night of the 9th, "Things have not gone well. The fighting east of Paris has not gone in our favour, *and we shall have to pay for the damage we have done.*"

CHAPTER XII

THE WAR AT SEA

I now have to chronicle a brilliant episode which came at a most timely moment and throughout which we enjoyed the best of good luck. My insistent desire to develop a minor offensive against the Germans in the Heligoland Bight led to conferences with Commodore Tyrwhitt, who commanded the light cruisers and destroyers of "The Harwich Striking Force," and Commodore Keyes, the head of the Submarine Service also stationed at Harwich. On August 23 Commodore Keyes called personally upon me at the Admiralty with a proposal for "a well-organized drive commencing before dawn from inshore close to the enemy's coast." On the 24th I presided at a meeting in my room between him and Commodore Tyrwhitt and the First Sea Lord and the Chief of the Staff.

The plan which the two Commodores then outlined was at once simple and daring. Since the first hours of the war our submarines had prowled about in the Heligoland Bight. They had now accumulated during a period of three weeks accurate information about the dispositions of the enemy. They knew that he was in the habit of keeping a flotilla of destroyers attended by a couple of small cruisers, cruising and patrolling each night to the North of Heligoland, and that these were accustomed to be relieved shortly after daylight by a second flotilla which worked on a much less extended beat. They proposed to take two flotillas of our best destroyers and two light cruisers from Harwich by night and reach just before dawn a point inside the Northern Coast of the Heligoland Bight not far from the island of Sylt. From this point they would make a left-handed scoop inshore, falling upon and chasing back the outcoming flotilla if they met it, and then would all turn together in a long line abreast Westward towards home to meet and if possible destroy the incoming German flotilla. Six British submarines in two divisions would take part in the operation so as to attack the German heavy ships should they come out, and two battle-cruisers (the *Invincible* and *New Zealand*) then stationed at the Humber would act as support.

Such was in short the plan proposed by these officers and approved by the First Sea Lord. Action was fixed for the 28th. As soon as Sir John Jellicoe was informed of these intentions, he offered to send in further support three battle-cruisers and six light cruisers. He did more. He sent Sir David Beatty. The result was a success which far exceeded the hopes of the Admiralty, and produced results of a far-reaching character upon the whole of the naval war.

At dawn on the 28th, Admiral Tyrwhitt's flotillas, led by the *Arethusa* and *Fearless,* reached their point of attack and, in the words of Admiral Scheer, "broke into the Heligoland Bight." The enemy was taken by surprise. The weather near the land was increasingly misty. The Heligoland batteries came into action, but without effect. The German battleships and battle-cruisers could not cross the bar of the outer Jade owing to the tide till 1 p.m. Only the German light cruisers on patrol or close at hand in the Elbe or the Ems could come to the aid of their flotillas. A confused, dispersed and prolonged series of combats ensued between the flotillas and light cruisers and continued until after four o'clock in the afternoon. During all this time the British light forces were rampaging about the enemy's most intimate and jealously guarded waters.

Very little, however, turned out as had been planned. Owing to a mischance, arising primarily from a fault in Admiralty staff work, the message apprising Commodores Keyes and Tyrwhitt of the presence of Admiral Beatty with his additional battle-cruisers and light cruisers, did not reach them in time; nor was Admiral Beatty aware of the areas in which the British submarines were working. Several awkward embarrassments followed from this and might easily have led to disastrous mistakes. However, fortune was steady, and the initial surprise together with the resolute offensive carried us safely through. The German light cruisers precipitately proceeding to the assistance of their flotillas and animated by the hopes of cutting off our own, ran into the British battle-cruisers. Admiral Beatty, in spite not only of the risk of mines and submarines, but also—for all he could know—of meeting superior forces, had with extraordinary audacity led his squadron far into the Bight. Two enemy cruisers (the *Ariadne* and the *Köln*) were smashed to pieces by the enormous shells of the *Lion* and the *Princess Royal;* a third (the *Mainz*) was sunk by the light cruisers and destroyers. Three others (the *Frauenlob, Strassburg* and the *Stettin*) limped home with many casualties. One German destroyer was sunk. The rest in the confusion and light mist escaped, though several were injured.

The good news trickled into the Admiralty during the day, but for some time we were very anxious about the *Arethusa.* A feed-pipe had been smashed by a shell and her steaming power was reduced to seven or eight knots. However, she returned unmolested to the Thames.

Not a single British ship was sunk or, indeed, seriously injured; and our casualties did not exceed thirty-five killed and about forty wounded, in spite of the fact that, in the words of the German Lieutenant Tholens, "The English ships made the greatest efforts to pick up the survivors."[1] Two hundred and twenty-four Germans, many desperately wounded, were rescued in circumstances of much danger by Commodore Keyes on the destroyer *Lurcher,* and brought to England. Considerably more than a thousand Germans, including the Flotilla Admiral and the Destroyer Commodore, perished. A son of Admiral von Tirpitz was among the prisoners. Much more important, however, than these material gains was the effect produced upon the morale of the enemy. The Germans knew nothing of our defective Staff work and of the risks we had run. All they saw was that the British did not hesitate to hazard their greatest vessels as well as their light craft in the most daring offensive action and had escaped apparently unscathed. They felt as we should have felt had German destroyers broken into the Solent and their battle-cruisers penetrated as far as the Nab. The results of this action were far reaching. Henceforward the weight of British naval prestige lay heavy across all German sea enterprise. Upon the Emperor the impression produced was decisive. Thus Scheer: "The restrictions imposed on the Battle Fleet were adhered to." And still more explicit, von Tirpitz: " . . . August 28th, a day fateful, both in its after-effects and incidental results, for the work of our navy. . . . The Emperor did not want losses of this sort. . . . Orders were issued by the Emperor . . . after an audience to Pohl, to which I as usual was not summoned, to restrict the initiative of the Commander-in-Chief of the North Sea Fleet: the loss of ships was to be avoided, fleet sallies and any greater undertakings must be approved by His Majesty in advance," etc. On von Tirpitz protesting against "this muzzling policy" . . . "there sprang up from that day forth an estrangement between the Emperor and myself, which steadily increased."

The German Navy was indeed "muzzled." Except for furtive movements by individual submarines and minelayers not a dog stirred from August till November. Meanwhile our strength, both offensive afloat and defensive in our harbours, was steadily and rapidly increasing.

The news of this naval action reached the French and British armies in the dark hour before the dawn of victory and was everywhere published to the retreating troops.

On an August morning, behold also the curious sight of a British Cabinet of respectable Liberal politicians sitting down deliberately and with malice aforethought to plan the seizure of the German colonies in every part of the world! A month before, with what horror and disgust would most of those present have averted their minds from such ideas! But our sea communications

---

[1] Admiral Scheer.

depended largely upon the prompt denial of these bases or refuges to the German cruisers; and further, with Belgium already largely overrun by the German armies, everyone felt that we must lose no time in taking hostages for her eventual liberation. Accordingly, with maps and pencils, the whole world was surveyed, six separate expeditions were approved in principle and remitted to the Staffs for study and execution. An enterprising Captain [1] had already on the outbreak of war invaded the German colony of Togoland. We now proposed, in conjunction with the French, to attack the Cameroons—a much more serious undertaking. General Botha had already declared his intention of invading German South-West Africa. The New Zealand and Australian Governments wished at once to seize Samoa and the German possessions in the Pacific. An Anglo-Indian expedition was authorized for the attack of German East Africa. The Staff work in preparation for the military side of this last expedition was by no means perfect, and resulted in a serious rebuff. The transportation of the expeditionary forces simultaneously in all these different directions while the seas were still scoured by the German cruisers threw another set of responsibilities upon the Admiralty.

From the middle of September onwards we began to be at our fullest strain. The great map of the world which covered one whole wall of the War Room now presented a remarkable appearance. As many as twenty separate enterprises and undertakings dependent entirely upon sea-power were proceeding simultaneously in different parts of the globe. Apart from the expeditions set forth above, the enormous business of convoying from all parts of the Empire the troops needed for France, and of replacing them in some cases with Territorials from home, lay heavy upon us. It was soon to be augmented.

It had been easy to set on foot the organization of the three Naval Brigades and other Divisional troops for the Royal Naval Division; but at a very early stage I found the creation of the artillery beyond any resources of which I could dispose. We could, and did, order a hundred field-guns in the United States, but the training, mounting and equipping of the artillerymen could not and ought not to be undertaken apart from the main preparation of the Army. My military staff officer, Major Ollivant, at this stage had a very good idea which provoked immediately far-reaching consequences. He advised me to ask Lord Kitchener for a dozen British batteries from India to form the artillery of the Royal Naval Division, letting India have Territorial batteries in exchange. I put this to Lord Kitchener the same afternoon. He seemed tremendously struck by the idea. What would the Cabinet say? he asked. If the Government of India refused, could the Cabinet overrule them? Would they? Would I support him in the matter? And so on. I had to leave that night for the North to visit the Fleet,

[1] Captain F. C. Bryant.

which was lying in Loch Ewe, on the west coast of Scotland. Forty-eight hours later, when I returned, I visited Lord Kitchener and asked him how matters were progressing. He beamed with delight. "Not only," he said, "am I going to take twelve batteries, but thirty-one; and not only am I going to take batteries, I am going to take battalions. I am going to take thirty-nine battalions: I am going to send them Territorial divisions instead—three Territorial divisions. You must get the transports ready at once." After we had gloated over this prospect of succouring our struggling front, I observed that I could now count on the twelve batteries for the Royal Naval Division. "Not one," he said. "I am going to take them all myself"; and he rubbed his hands together with every sign of glee. So the Naval Division was left again in the cold and had to go forward as infantry only.

This new development involved a heavy addition to our convoy work, and the situation in the Indian and Pacific Oceans must now be examined by the reader.

When war began the Germans had the following cruisers on foreign stations: *Scharnhorst, Gneisenau, Emden, Nürnberg, Leipzig* (China); *Königsberg* (East Africa and Indian Ocean); *Dresden, Karlsruhe* (West Indies). All these ships were fast and modern, and every one of them did us serious injury before they were destroyed. There were also several gunboats: *Geier, Planet, Komet, Nusa* and *Eber,* none of which could be ignored. In addition, we expected that the Germans would try to send to sea upwards of forty fast armed merchantmen to prey on commerce. Our arrangements were, however, as has been narrated, successful in preventing all but five from leaving harbour. Of these five the largest, the *Kaiser Wilhelm der Grosse,* was sunk by the *High-flyer* (Captain Buller) on August 26; the *Cap Trafalgar* was sunk on September 14 by the British armed merchant cruiser *Carmania* (Captain Noel Grant) after a brilliant action between these two naked ships; and the three others took refuge and were interned in neutral harbours some months later. Our dispositions for preventing a cruiser and commerce-raider attack upon our trade were from the outset very largely successful; and in the few months with which this volume deals, every one of the enemy ships was reduced to complete inactivity, sunk or pinned in port.

Nevertheless, it is a fair criticism that we ought to have had more fast cruisers in foreign waters, and in particular that we ought to have matched every one of the German cruisers with a faster ship as it was our intention to do. The *Karlsruhe* in the West Indies gave a chance to our hunting vessels at the outbreak of war, and the *Königsberg* in the Indian Ocean was sighted a few days earlier. But our ships were not fast enough to bring the former to action or keep in close contact with the latter till war was declared. As will be seen, nearly every one of these German cruisers took its prey before being caught, not only of merchant ships but of ships of war. The *Scharnhorst* and *Gneisenau* sank the *Monmouth* and *Good Hope,* the *Königsberg* surprised and destroyed the *Pegasus,* and the *Emden* sank the Russian crusier *Zemchug* and the French destroyer *Mousquet.* Certainly they did their duty well.

The keynote of all the Admiralty dispositions at the outbreak of war was to be as strong as possible in Home waters in order to fight a decisive battle with the whole German Navy. To this end the foreign stations were cut down to the absolute minimum necessary to face the individual ships abroad in each theatre. The Fleet was weak in fast light cruisers and the whole of my administration had been occupied in building as many of them as possible. None of the *Arethusas* had, however, yet reached the Fleet. We therefore grudged every light cruiser removed from Home waters, feeling that the Fleet would be tactically incomplete without its sea cavalry. The principle of first things first, and of concentrating in a decisive theatre against the enemy's main power, had governed everything, and had led to delay in meeting an important and well-recognized subsidiary requirement. The inconvenience in other parts of the globe had to be faced. It was serious.

Nowhere did this inconvenience show itself more than in the Indian Ocean. After being sighted and making off on the 31st of July, the *Königsberg* became a serious preoccupation in all movements of troops and trade. Another fast German cruiser, the *Emden,* which on the outbreak of war was on the China Station, also appeared in the middle of September in Indian waters, and being handled with enterprise and audacity began to inflict numerous and serious losses upon our mercantile marine. These events produced consequences.

By the end of August we had already collected the bulk of the 7th Division from all the fortresses and garrisons of the Empire. During September the two British Indian divisions with additional cavalry (in all nearly 50,000 men) were already crossing the Indian Ocean. On top of this came the plans for exchanging practically all the British infantry and artillery in India for Territorial batteries and battalions, and the formation of the 27th, 28th and 29th Divisions of regular troops. The New Zealand contingent must be escorted to Australia and there, with 25,000 Australians, await convoys to Europe. Meanwhile the leading troops of the Canadian Army, about 25,000 strong, had to be brought across the Atlantic. All this was of course additional to the main situation in the North Sea and to the continued flow of drafts, reinforcements and supplies across the Channel. Meanwhile the enemy's Fleet remained intact, waiting, as we might think, its moment to strike; and his cruisers continued to prey upon the seas. To strengthen our cruiser forces we had already armed and commissioned twenty-four liners as auxiliary cruisers, and had armed defensively fifty-four merchantmen. Another forty suitable vessels were in preparation. In order to lighten the strain in the Indian Ocean and to liberate our light cruisers for their proper work of hunting down the enemy, I proposed the employment of our old battleships (*Canopus* class) as escorts to convoys. In September I issued instructions that the whole convoy system in the Indian Ocean should be placed on a basis of regular fortnightly sailings, and that the *Dartmouth, Chatham* and *Black Prince* be released by the utilization of three old battleships.

Besides employing these old battleships on convoy, we had also at the end of August sent three others abroad as rallying points for our cruisers in case a German heavy cruiser should break out: thus the *Glory* was sent to Halifax, the *Albion* to Gibraltar and the *Canopus* to the Cape de Verde station. Naval history afforded numerous good examples of the use of a protective battleship to give security and defensive superiority to a cruiser force—to serve, in fact, as a floating fortress round which the faster vessels could manœuvre, and on which they could fall back. These battleships also gave protection to the colliers and supply ships at the various oceanic bases, without which all our cruiser system would have broken down. The reader will see the system further applied as the war advances.

The position in the Pacific was also complicated. Our squadron there consisted of the *Minotaur* and *Hampshire,* with the light cruiser *Yarmouth.* This was doubtfully a match for the two powerful German cruisers *Scharnhorst* and *Gneisenau.* We had however in 1913 devised a frugal scheme by which the *Triumph*—one of the two battleships which had been built for Chili and bought from her, to prevent their falling into Russian hands at the outbreak of the Russo-Japanese War—was made to serve as a depôt ship manned on mobilization from the crews of the river gunboats in the Yangtse. Once the *Triumph* was mobilized our superiority except in speed was overwhelming, and we could afford to see how greater matters went at home before deciding whether to reinforce the China station or not. As early as the 28th July I proposed to the First Sea Lord the discreet mobilization of the *Triumph* and the concentration of the China Squadron upon her; and this was accordingly effected in good time. Five thousand miles to the southward was the Australian squadron, consisting of the battle-cruiser *Australia,* and the two excellent modern light cruisers *Sydney* and *Melbourne.* The *Australia* by herself could, of course, defeat the *Scharnhorst* and *Gneisenau,* though by running different ways one of the pair could have escaped destruction. Our last look round the oceans before the fateful signal, left us therefore in no immediate anxiety about the Pacific.

On the outbreak of war the French armoured cruisers *Montcalm* and *Dupleix* and the Russian light cruisers *Askold* and *Zemchug,* in the Far East, were placed under British command, thus sensibly increasing our predominance. A few days later an event of the greatest importance occurred. The attitude of

Japan towards Germany suddenly became one of fierce menace. No clause in the Anglo-Japanese Treaty entitled us to invoke the assistance of Japan. But it became evident before the war had lasted a week that the Japanese nation had not forgotten the circumstances and influences under which they had been forced, at the end of the Chinese War, to quit Port Arthur. They now showed themselves resolved to extirpate all German authority and interests in the Far East. On the 15th, Japan addressed an ultimatum to Germany demanding within seven days the unconditional surrender of the German naval base Tsing Tau [Kiaochow], couching this demand in the very phrases in which nineteen years before they had been summoned to leave Port Arthur at the instance of Germany. In reply the German Emperor commanded his servants to resist to the end; and here, as almost in every other place where Germans found themselves isolated in the face of overwhelming force, he was obeyed with constancy.

The entry of Japan into the war enabled us to use our China squadron to better advantage in other theatres. The *Newcastle* was ordered across the Pacific, where our two old sloops (the *Algerine* and *Shearwater*) were in jeopardy from the German light cruiser *Leipzig*. The *Triumph* was sent to participate with a small British contingent in the Japanese attack upon the fortress of Tsing Tau. General arrangements were made by the British and Japanese Admiralties whereby responsibility for the whole of the Northern Pacific, except the Canadian Coast, was assumed by Japan.

The table on p. 178 sets forth the rival forces in the Western Pacific at the outbreak of war. Even without the ships employed by Japan or the great Japanese reserves which lay behind them, the superior strength of the Allies was overwhelming. But the game the two sides had to play was by no means as unequal as it looked. It was indeed the old game of Fox and Geese. The two powerful German cruisers *Scharnhorst* and *Gneisenau,* with their two light cruisers, formed a modern squadron fast and formidable in character. Our battle-cruiser *Australia* could catch them and could fight them single-handed. The *Minotaur* and the *Hampshire* could just catch them and, as we held, could fight them with good prospects of success; but it would be a hard-fought action. If the *Triumph* were added to *Minotaur* and *Hampshire,* there was no risk at all in the fight but almost insuperable difficulty in bringing the enemy to action. Among the light cruisers, the *Yarmouth, Melbourne, Sydney* and the Japanese *Chikuma* could both catch and kill *Emden* or *Nürnberg.* Of our older light cruisers, *Fox* and *Encounter* could have fought *Emden* or *Nürnberg* with a chance of killing or at least of crippling them before being killed: but neither was fast enough to catch them. Our remaining cruisers could only be used in combination with stronger vessels. With our forces aided by two French and two Russian ships and by the Japanese to the extent which will be described, the Admiralty had to protect all the expeditions, convoys and trade in the Pacific. To wit—

The New Zealand convoy to Australia.

The Australian and New Zealand convoy from Australia to Europe.

The convoy of the British Far Eastern garrisons to Europe.

The convoy of Indian troops to relieve our Far Eastern garrisons.

The expedition to Samoa.

The expedition to New Guinea.

All these were in addition to the general trade, which continued uninterruptedly.

Admiral von Spee, the German Commander in the Pacific, had therefore no lack of objectives. He had only to hide and to strike. The vastness of the Pacific and its multitude of islands offered him their shelter, and, once he had vanished, who should say where he would reappear? On the other hand, there were considerable checks on his action and a limit, certain though indefinite, to the life of his squadron. With the blockade of Tsing Tau he was cut from his only base on that side of the world. He had no means of docking his ships or executing any serious repairs, whether necessitated by battle or steaming. The wear and tear on modern ships is considerable, and difficulties multiply with every month out of dock. To steam at full speed or at high speed for any length of time on any quest was to use up his life rapidly. He was a cut flower in a vase; fair to see, yet bound to die, and to die very soon if the water was not constantly renewed. Moreover, the process of getting coal was one of extraordinary difficulty and peril. The extensive organization of the Admiralty kept the closest watch in every port on every ton of coal and every likely collier. The purchase of coal and the movement of a collier were tell-tale traces which might well lay the pursuers on his track. His own safety and his power to embarrass us alike depended upon the uncertainty of his movements. But this uncertainty might be betrayed at any moment by the movement of colliers or by the interception of wireless messages. Yet how could colliers be brought to the necessary rendezvous without wireless messages? There existed in the Pacific only five German wireless stations, Yap, Apia, Nauru, Rabaul, Anguar, all of which were destroyed by us within two months of the outbreak of war. After that there remained only the wireless on board the German ships, with which it was very dangerous to breathe a word into the ether. Such was the situation of Admiral von Spee.

The problem of the Admiralty was also delicate and complex. All our enterprises lay simultaneously under the shadow of a serious potential danger. You could make scare schemes which showed that von Spee might turn up with his whole squadron almost anywhere. On the other hand, we could not possibly be strong enough every day everywhere to meet him. We had, therefore, either to balance probabilities and run risks, or reduce our movements and affairs to very

WARSHIPS IN THE WESTERN PACIFIC.[1]

AUGUST TO OCTOBER, 1914.

	German.	British.	Japanese.[2]	French.	Russian.
Battle-cruisers		*Australia*	*Ibuki*		
Battleships		*Triumph*			
Armoured Cruisers	*Scharnhorst* *Gneisenau*	*Minotaur* *Hampshire*		*Montcalm* *Dupleix*	
Fast Light Cruisers	*Emden* *Nürnberg*	*Yarmouth* *Melbourne*	*Chikuma*		
Older Light Cruisers		*Sydney* *Encounter* *Pioneer* *Philomel* *Pyramus* *Psyche*			*Askold* *Zemchug*
Armed Merchant Cruisers	*Prince Eitel Friedrich* *Cormoran*	*Empress of Asia* *Empress of Japan* *Empress of Russia* *Himalaya*			
Gunboats	*Geier*	*Cadmus* *Clio*		*Kersaint* *Zélée*	

Ships on fixed patrolling beats not available for offensive action :—

[1] The underlining denotes approximately the comparative values of the units.

[2] Only those ships of the Japanese Navy who took part in the operations are included.

narrow limits. Absolute security meant something very like absolute paralysis; yet fierce would have been the outcry attendant either upon stagnation or disaster. We decided deliberately to carry on our affairs and to take the risk. After all, the oceans were as wide for us as for von Spee. The map of the world in the Admiralty War Room measured nearly 20 feet by 30. Being a seaman's map, its centre was filled by the greatest mass of water on the globe: the enormous areas of the Pacific filling upwards of 300 square feet. On this map the head of an ordinary veil-pin represented the full view to be obtained from the masts of a ship on a clear day. There was certainly plenty of room for ships to miss one another.

As has been stated, the British China Squadron mobilized and concentrated at Hong-Kong, and the Australian Navy at Sydney. Admiral von Spee was at Ponape in the Caroline Islands when Great Britain declared war upon Germany. From Hong-Kong and Sydney to Ponape the distances were each about 2,750 miles. Although Japan had not yet entered the war, the German Admiral did not attempt to return to Kiaochau, as this might have involved immediate battle with the British China Squadron. He proceeded only as far as the Ladrone Islands (German), where the *Emden* from Kiaochau, escorting his supply ships, met him on August 12. He sent the *Emden* into the Indian Ocean to prey on commerce and turned himself eastward towards the Marshall Islands. On August 22 he detached the *Nürnberg* to Honolulu to obtain information and send messages, to cut the cable between Canada and New Zealand, and to rejoin him at Christmas Island on September 8. Here he was in the very centre of the Pacific.

The Admiralty knew nothing of these movements beyond a report that he was coaling at the Caroline Islands on August 9. Thereafter he vanished completely from our view. We could know nothing for certain. The theory of the Admiralty Staff, however, endorsed by Admiral Sir Henry Jackson, who was making a special and profound study of this theatre, was that he would go to the Marshall Islands and thereafter would most probably work across to the west coast of South America, or double the Horn on his way back to Europe. This theory, and the intricate reasoning by which it was supported, proved to be correct. In the main, though we could by no means trust ourselves to it and always expected unpleasant surprises, it was our dominant hypothesis. It is on this basis that the operations in the Pacific should be studied.

As early as August 2 the New Zealand Government—ever in the van of the Empire—had convinced themselves that war was inevitable, and had already made proposals for raising forces and striking at the enemy. The Operations Division of the War Staff proposed in consequence the capture of Samoa and the destruction of the wireless station there; and this was recommended to me by the First Sea Lord and the Chief of the Staff as a feasible operation. By August 8 New Zealand telegraphed that if a naval escort could be furnished the expedition to attack Samoa could start on August 11. The Staff concurred in this, holding that the *Gneisenau* and *Scharnhorst* were adequately covered by the Australian squadron. I assented the same day. It was arranged that the expedition should meet the battle-cruiser *Australia* and the French cruiser *Montcalm* at or on the way to Noumea.

Another expedition from Australia to attack German New Guinea had also been organized by the Government of the Commonwealth. The uncertainty about the *Scharnhorst* and *Gneisenau* invested all movements in those waters with a certain hazardous delicacy. It was thought, however, that the light cruisers *Melbourne*[1] and *Sydney* could convoy the Commonwealth New Guinea expedition northward, keeping inside the Barrier Reef, and that before they came out into open waters the New Guinea convoy could be joined by *Australia* and *Montcalm,* who would by then have completed the escort of the New Zealand expedition to Samoa. We thought it above all things important that these expeditions, once they had landed and taken possession of the German colonies, should be self-sufficing, and that no weak warships should be left in the harbours to support them. Any such vessels, apart from the difficulty of sparing them, would be an easy prey for the two large German cruisers.

Samoa was occupied on the 30th August. The wireless station at Nauru was destroyed on the 10th September. The Australian contingent was picked up by the battle-cruiser *Australia* on September 9 and arrived at Rabaul safely two days later.

We had now to provide for the Australian convoy to Europe which was due to leave Sydney on September 27 for Port Adelaide, where they would be joined by the New Zealand contingent and its own escort as well as by the "Australian Fleet" (*Australia, Sydney* and *Melbourne*) as soon as they were free from the New Guinea expedition. Our original proposal for the escort of the Australian Army was, therefore, *Australia, Sydney* and *Melbourne,* with the small cruisers from New Zealand. To cover the Commonwealth during the absence of all her Fleet, it was arranged that the *Minotaur,* together with the Japanese *Ibuki* and *Chikuma,* should come south to New Britain Islands.

In the middle of September the New Zealand contingent was due to sail for Adelaide. The *Australia* and her consorts were still delayed in New Guinea, where some delay was caused by the German resistance. Great anxiety was felt in New Zealand at the prospect of throwing their contingent across to Australia with no better escort than the two P class cruisers. They pointed out the dangers from the *Scharnhorst* and *Gneisenau,* which on September 14 had been reported off Samoa. The Admiralty view was that it was most improbable the *Scharnhorst* and *Gneisenau* could know of the contemplated New Zealand

---

[1] *Encounter* went instead of *Melbourne.*

expedition, still less of the date of its sailing; that in order to deliver an attack in New Zealand waters they would have to steam far from their coaling bases north of the Equator, and would indeed have to be accompanied by their colliers, greatly reducing their speed and hampering their movements. In these circumstances the Admiralty foresaw but little danger to the New Zealand convoy in the first part of their voyage, were unable to provide further protection for this stage, and expressed the opinion that the risk should be accepted. To this decision the New Zealand Government bowed on September 21, and it was settled that the New Zealand convoy should sail on the 25th. Meanwhile, however, renewed exploits by the *Emden* in the Bay of Bengal created a natural feeling of alarm in the mind of the New Zealand and Australian public; and without prejudice to our original view, we decided to make arrangements to remove these apprehensions.

On the 24th news arrived that the New Guinea expedition had successfully overcome all opposition, and we then determined on the following change of plans, viz. *Minotaur* and *Ibuki* to go to Wellington and escort the New Zealanders to Adelaide, while *Australia* and *Montcalm,* after convoying the auxiliaries and weak warships back from New Guinea to within the shelter of the Barrier Reef, should hunt for the *Scharnhorst* and *Gneisenau* in the Marshall Islands, whither it seemed probable they were proceeding. This decision altered the composition of the escort of the Australian convoy, and their protection across the Pacific and Indian Oceans was to an important extent confided to a vessel which flew the war flag of Japan. This historic fact should be an additional bond of goodwill among the friendly and allied nations who dwell in the Pacific.

Meanwhile the depredations of the *Emden* in the Bay of Bengal continued. On the 22nd she appeared off Madras, bombarded the Burma Company's oil tanks, and threw a few shells into the town before she was driven off by the batteries. This episode, following on the disturbance of the Calcutta-Colombo trade route and the numerous and almost daily sinkings of merchant ships in the Bay of Bengal, created widespread alarm, and on October 1 I sent a minute to the First Sea Lord, proposing, *inter alia,* a concentration on a large scale in Indian waters against the *Emden.* This concentration would comprise *Hampshire, Yarmouth, Sydney, Melbourne, Chikuma* (Japan), *Zemchug* and *Askold* (Russian), *Psyche, Pyramus* and *Philomel*—a total of ten—and was capable of being fully effective in about a month.

I repeated on October 15:

Sydney should escort Australians and thereafter hunt *Emden.*

This shot as will presently be seen went home.

• • •

It remained to carry the Canadian Army across the Atlantic. Upwards of 25,000 volunteers of a very high individual quality, partially trained in Valcartier camp, were embarked in the St. Lawrence in a convoy of thirty-one ships, to which were added two ships carrying the Newfoundland contingent and a British battalion from Bermuda. Rear-Admiral Wemyss with a squadron of light cruisers was entrusted with the actual duties of escort, but the essential protection of the convoy was secured by far more distant and powerful agencies. All the Cruiser Squadrons of the Grand Fleet were spread in two lines between the coasts of Norway and Scotland to guard against a sortie by the German fast vessels, and the Grand Fleet itself remained at sea in their support to the northward. The North American Squadron under Rear-Admiral Hornby covered the German merchant cruisers which were lurking in New York Harbour. Two old battleships, the *Glory* and the *Majestic,* were ordered to meet the convoy at a rendezvous well off the beaten track, and Admiral Hornby himself in the *Lancaster* accompanied them the first portion of the route. Lastly, the *Princess Royal* was detached from the Grand Fleet to meet the convoy in mid-Atlantic and thus guard against any German battle-cruiser which might conceivably have slipped through the wide areas patrolled by Sir John Jellicoe. The movements of the *Princess Royal* were kept secret from everybody, and even the Canadian Government, in spite of their natural anxiety, were denied this reassurance.

The convoy sailed on October 3 and ten days later safely approached the mouth of the English Channel. The intention had been to disembark the Canadian troops at Portsmouth, where all arrangements had been made for them. But on the very day they were due to arrive, a German submarine was reported off Cherbourg and another was sighted off the Isle of Wight by the Portsmouth Defence Flotilla. On this we insisted, whatever the military inconvenience, on turning the whole convoy into Plymouth. During October 14 this armada bearing the first Army sent Eastward across the Atlantic was safely berthed in Plymouth Sound.

With this event all the initial movements in the Imperial concentration had been completed. They had comprised the transportation of the equivalent of 5 divisions from India to Europe and their replacement by 3 divisions of Territorials from England; the collection of the 7th and 8th divisions from all the garrisons and fortresses of the British Empire with consequential replacements from home and from India; the transportation of approximately 2 divisions from Canada to England; and lastly—though this was not finished till December—that of approximately 2 divisions from Australia and New Zealand to Egypt. The effect of this concentration was to add a reinforcement of 5 British regular divisions (7th, 8th, 27th, 28th and 29th) and 2 Anglo-Indian divisions to the regular forces immediately available to support the 6 regular divisions with which we had begun the war, raising our army in France by the end of November to approximately 13 divisions of highly trained long-serviced troops. In addition the 4 Canadian and Australian divisions were completing their training in England and Egypt and were held to be in a more advanced state of preparation than the 10 divisions of Territorials which remained in England, or the 24 divisions of the New Army which Lord Kitchener was raising. The whole business of transportation by sea while all the enemy's cruisers were still at large had been conducted without accident of any kind or without the loss of a single ship or a single life.

On September 16 Marshal Joffre had telegraphed to Lord Kitchener asking whether a Brigade of Marines could not be sent to Dunkirk to reinforce the garrison and to confuse the enemy with the idea of British as well as French forces being in this area. Lord Kitchener asked me whether the Admiralty would help in this matter. I agreed to send the brigade if he would also send some Yeomanry Cavalry for its local protection. He sent a regiment. I was thus led, though by no means unwillingly, into accepting a series of minor responsibilities of a very direct and personal kind, which made inroads both upon my time and thought and might well—though I claim they did not—have obscured my general view. I formed a small administration to handle the business, in which Colonel Ollivant was the moving spirit. On his suggestion we took fifty motor omnibuses from the London streets so as to make our Marines as mobile as possible, and very soon we had British detachments ostentatiously displaying themselves in Ypres, Lille, Tournal and Douai. Many risks were run by those engaged in these petty operations, first under General Aston and subsequently when his health had failed, under General Paris. No mishap occurred either to the Marines or to the Yeomanry. They played their part in the general scheme without loss or misadventure. It was, however, with sincere relief that a month later, on the arrival of the leading troops of Sir John French's Army in the neighbourhood, I transferred these detachments to the Commander-in-Chief, and divested myself of anxieties which though subsidiary were burdensome.

This chapter, which began with good luck and success, must end, however, with misfortune. The original War Orders had been devised to meet the situation on the outbreak of hostilities. They placed the pieces on the board in what we believed to be the best array, and left their future disposition to be modified by experience. Under these orders, the 7th Cruiser Squadron in the Third Fleet, consisting of the old cruisers of the *Bacchante* class (*Bacckante*, *Euryalus* (flagship), *Cressy, Aboukir, Hogue*), was based on the Nore "in order to ensure the presence of armoured ships in the southern approaches of the North

Sea and eastern entrance to the Channel, and to support the 1st and 3rd Flotillas operating in that area from Harwich." The object of these flotillas was "to keep the area south of the 54th parallel clear of enemy torpedo craft and minelayers." The Cruiser Force was "to support them in the execution of these duties and also, with the flotillas, to keep a close watch over enemy war vessels and transports in order that their movement may be reported at the earliest moment."

This very necessary patrol had accordingly been maintained day after day without incident of any kind happening, and we had now been six weeks at war. In war all repetitions are perilous. You can do many things with impunity if you do not keep on doing them over and over again.

It was no part of my duty to deal with the routine movements of the Fleet and its squadrons, but only to exercise a general supervision. I kept my eyes and ears open for every indication that would be useful, and I had many and various sources of information. On September 17, during my visit to the Grand Fleet, I heard an expression used by an officer which instantly arrested my attention. He spoke of "the live-bait squadron." I demanded what was meant, and was told that the expression referred to these old cruisers patrolling the narrow waters in apparently unbroken peace. I thereupon reviewed the whole position in this area. I discussed it with Commodore Tyrwhitt and with Commodore Keyes. The next morning I addressed the following minute to the First Sea Lord:

September 18, 1914.

Secretary,
First Sea Lord.

The force available for operations in the narrow seas should be capable of minor action without the need of bringing down the Grand Fleet. To this end it should have effective support either by two or three battle-cruisers or battleships of the Second Fleet working from Sheerness. This is the most efficiently air and destroyer patrolled anchorage we possess. They can lie behind the boom, and can always be at sea when we intend a raid. Battle-cruisers are much to be preferred.

The *Bacchantes* ought not to continue on this beat. The risk to such ships is not justified by any services they can render. The narrow seas, being the nearest point to the enemy, should be kept by a small number of good modern ships.

The *Bacchantes* should go to the western entrance of the Channel and set Bethell's battleships—and later Wemyss' cruisers—free for convoy and other duties.

The first four *Arethusas* should join the flotillas of the narrow seas.

I see no sufficient reason to exchange these flotillas now that they know their work, with the northern ones.

As the "M" boats are delivered they should be formed into a separate half-flotilla and go north to work with the Grand Fleet.

The *King Alfred* should pay off and be thoroughly repaired.

Prince Louis immediately agreed and gave directions to the Chief of the Staff to make the necessary redistribution of forces. With this I was content, and I dismissed the matter from my mind, being sure that the orders given would be complied with at the earliest moment. Before they could take effect, disaster occurred.

Pending the introduction of the new system, the Admiralty War Staff carried on with the old. The equinoctial weather was, however, so bad that the destroyer flotillas were ordered back to harbour by the Admiral commanding the *Bacchante* squadron. That officer, however, proposed to continue his patrol in the Dogger area with the cruisers alone. The Admiralty War Staff acquiesced in the principle of these arrangments, but on the 19th instructed him to watch instead the Broad Fourteens:

The Dogger Bank patrol need not be continued. Weather too bad for destroyers to go to sea. Arrange for cruisers to watch Broad Fourteens.

This routine message did not of course come before me. It was not sent, however, by the War Staff without proper consideration. In the short steep seas which are the features of gales in these narrow waters, a submarine would be at a serious disadvantage and could only observe with extreme difficulty and imperfection. The rough weather which drove in our destroyers was believed to be an important protection against enemy submarines.

Both Admiral and Admiralty, therefore, were in agreement to leave the cruisers at sea without their flotilla. If the weather moderated, it was intended that one of Commodore Tyrwhitt's flotillas should join them there on the morning of the 20th. The sea, however, continued so high on the 20th that the flotilla, led by the *Fearless,* had to turn back to Harwich. Thus all through the 19th, 20th and 21st the three cruisers, the *Aboukir, Cressy* and *Hogue,* were left to maintain the watch in the narrow waters without a flotilla screen. The Admiral in the *Euryalus* had to return to harbour on the 20th to coal his ship. He left the squadron in command of the senior captain after enjoining special precautions. There was no more reason to expect that they would be attacked at this time than at any other. On the contrary, rumours of German activity to the northward had brought the whole Grand Fleet out in a southerly sweep down to the line between Flamborough Head and the Horn Reef. Nor was there any connection between the orders to these cruisers and the movement of the Marine Brigade from Dover to Dunkirk which took place on the 20th. The cruisers were simply fulfilling their ordinary task, which from frequent repetition had already become dangerous and for which they were not in any case well suited.

As soon as the weather began to abate on the 21st, Commodore Tyrwhitt started off again for the Broad Fourteens with eight destroyers, and was already well on his way when the morning of the 22nd broke. As the sea subsided, the danger from submarines revived. The three cruisers however instead of going to meet their destroyers, steamed slowly northward without zigzagging and at under ten knots, as no doubt they had often done before. Meanwhile a single German submarine, becoming more venturesome every day, was prowling southward down the Dutch coast. At 6:30 a.m., shortly after daylight, the *Aboukir* was struck by a torpedo. In twenty-five minutes this old vessel capsized. Some of her boats were smashed by the explosion, and hundreds of men were swimming in the water or clinging to wreckage. Both her consorts had hurried with chivalrous simplicity to the aid of the sinking ship. Both came to a dead standstill within a few hundred yards of her and lowered all their boats to rescue the survivors. In this posture they in their turn were both sunk, first the *Hogue* and then the *Cressy,* by the same submarine. Out of over 2,200 men on board these three ships, only 800 were saved, and more than 1,400 perished. The ships themselves were of no great value: they were among the oldest cruisers of the Third Fleet and contributed in no appreciable way to our vital margins. But like all Third Fleet ships, they were almost entirely manned with reservists, most of whom were married men; and they carried also young cadets from Osborne posted for safety to ships which it was thought would not be engaged in the great battles. This cruel loss of life, although small compared to what the Army was enduring, constituted the first serious forfeit exacted from the Navy in the war. It greatly stimulated and encouraged the enterprise of the German submarines. The commander of the fatal boat (Lieutenant Weddigen) was exultantly proclaimed as a national hero. Certainly the destruction with his own fingers of fourteen hundred persons was an episode of a peculiar character in human history. But, as it happened, he did not live long to enjoy his sombre fame. A storm of criticism was directed at the Admiralty, and naturally it was focused on me. "Here was an instance of the disaster which followed from the interference of a civilian Minister in naval operations and the over-riding of the judgment of skilful and experienced Admirals." The writer[1] of a small but venomous brochure which was industriously circulated in influential circles in

---

[1] Mr. Thomas Gibson Bowles.

London did not hesitate to make this charge in the most direct form,[1] and it was repeated in countless innuendoes throughout the British Press. I did not, however, think it possible to make any explanation or reply.

I caused the most searching inquiries to be made in the Admiralty into the responsibility for this tragic event. The necessary Court of Inquiry was convened. The Court found that the responsibility for the position of the cruisers on that day, was attributable to the Admiralty War Staff telegram of the 19th which has been already quoted. The First Sea Lord held that this was a reflection upon the Admiralty by a subordinate Court; but it seemed to me that the criticism was just and that it should stand. It was, however, by no means exhaustive. One would expect senior officers in command of cruiser squadrons to judge for themselves the danger of their task, and especially of its constant repetition; and while obeying any orders they received, to represent an unsatisfactory situation plainly to the Admiralty instead of going on day after day, and week after week, until superior authority intervened or something lamentable happened. One would expect also that ordinary precautions would be observed in the tactical conduct of squadrons. Moreover, although the impulse which prompted the *Hogue* and *Cressy* to go to the rescue of their comrades in the sinking *Aboukir* was one of generous humanity, they could hardly have done anything more unwise or more likely to add to the loss of life. They should at once have steamed away in opposite directions, lowering boats at the first opportunity.

I remitted all these matters to Lord Fisher when two months later he arrived at the Admiralty; but he laconically replied that "most of the officers concerned were on half pay, that they had better remain there, and that no useful purpose would be served by further action."

---

[1] "The loss on September 22," wrote Mr. Gibson Bowles, "of the *Aboukir,* the *Cressy* and the *Hogue,* with 1,459 officers and men killed, occurred because, despite the warnings of admirals, commodores and captains, Mr. Churchill refused, until it was too late, to recall them from a patrol so carried on as to make them certain to fall victims to the torpedoes of an active enemy."

CHAPTER XIII

ANTWERP AND THE CHANNEL PORTS

From the moment when the German hopes of destroying the French armies by a general battle and thus of ending the war at a single stroke had definitely failed, all the secondary and incidental objectives which hitherto they had rightly discarded became of immense consequence. As passion declined, material things resumed their values. The struggle of *armies* and *nations* having failed to reach a decision, *places* recovered their significance, and geography rather than psychology began to rule the lines of war. Paris now unattainable, the Channel Ports—Dunkirk, Calais and Boulogne—still naked, and lastly Antwerp, all reappeared in the field of values like submerged rocks when the tidal wave recedes.

The second phase of the war now opened. The French, having heaved the Germans back from the Marne to the Aisne, and finding themselves unable to drive them farther by frontal attacks, continually reached out their left hand in the hopes of outflanking their opponents. The race for the sea began. The French began to pass their troops from right to left. Castelnau's army, marching behind the front from Nancy, crashed into battle in Picardy, striving to turn the German right, and was itself outreached on its left. Foch's army, corps after corps, hurried by road and rail to prolong the fighting front in Artois; but round the left of this again lapped the numerous German cavalry divisions of von der Marwitz—swoop and counter-swoop. On both sides every man and every gun were hurled as they arrived into the conflict, and the unceasing cannonade drew ever northwards and westwards—ever towards the sea.

Where would the grappling armies strike blue water? At what point on the coast? Which would turn the other's flank? Would it be north or south of Dunkirk? Or of Gravelines or Calais or Boulogne? Nay, southward still, was Abbeville even attainable? All was committed to the shock of an ever-moving battle. But as the highest goal, the one safe inexpugnable flank for the Allies, the most advanced, the most daring, the most precious—worth all the rest, guarding all the rest—gleamed Antwerp, could Antwerp but hold out.

Antwerp was not only the sole stronghold of the Belgian nation: it was also the true left flank of the Allied front in the west. It guarded the whole line of the Channel ports. It threatened the flanks and rear of the German armies in

ANTWERP AND THE CHANNEL PORTS

France. It was the gateway from which a British army might emerge at any moment upon their sensitive and even vital communications. No German advance to the sea-coast, upon Ostend, upon Dunkirk, upon Calais and Boulogne, seemed possible while Antwerp was unconquered.[1]

From the moment when German Main Headquarters had extricated and reformed their armies after the failure at the Marne, the capture of Antwerp became more urgently necessary to them. Accordingly on the afternoon of September 9, as is now known, the German Emperor was moved to order the capture of that city. Nothing was apparent to the Allies until the 28th. The Belgian and German troops remained in contact along the fortress line without any serious siege or assaulting operations developing. But on the 28th the Germans suddenly opened fire upon the forts of the Antwerp exterior lines with 17-inch howitzers hurling projectiles of over a ton.

Almost immediately the Belgian Government gave signs of justified alarm. British intelligence reports indicated that the Germans were seriously undertaking the siege of Antwerp, that their operations were not intended as a demonstration to keep the Belgian troops occupied or to protect the lines of communication. Information had come from Brussels that the Emperor had ordered the capture of the town, that this might cost thousands of lives, but that the order must be obeyed. Large bodies of German reserve troops were also reported assembling near Liège. In view of all these reports it was evident that the rôle of our small British force of marines, omnibuses, armoured cars, aeroplanes, etc., operating from Dunkirk was exhausted. They had no longer to deal with Uhlan patrols or raiding parties of the enemy. Large hostile forces were approaching the coastal area, and the imposture whereby we had remained in occupation of Lille and Tournai could be sustained no longer.

The Belgian Field Army was about 80,000 strong, in addition to which there were some 70,000 fortress troops. Four divisions of the Belgian Army were defending the southern portion of the outer perimeter of the Antwerp defences, with the 5th Division in reserve, and one weak division was at Termonde. A cavalry division of about 3,600 sabres was south-west of Termonde guarding communications between Antwerp and the coast. Ghent was held by some volunteers.

On the night of October 1 our Minister, Sir Francis Villiers, reported that the German attack had destroyed two of the main Antwerp forts and had occupied Belgian trenches between them: the Belgian troops were however still holding out on either side of the River Nethe. Lord Kitchener now showed himself strongly disposed to sustain the advance or effect the relief of Antwerp and to use the regular forces he still had in England for this purpose, provided

[1] See map on pp. 190–91.

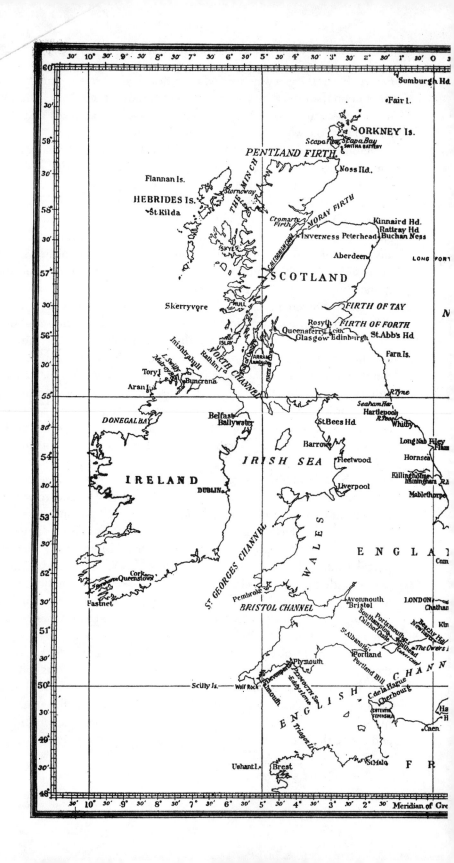

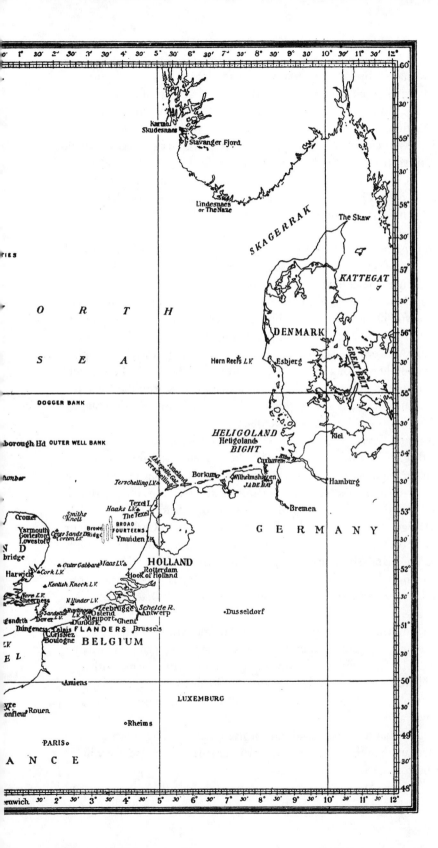

60°

30′

Karmö
Skudesnaes

59°

Stavanger Fjord

30′

Lindesnaes
or The Naze

58°

The Skaw

30′

SKAGERRAK

57°

KATTEGAT

30′

DENMARK

56°

Horn Reefs L.V.   Esbjerg

30′

GREAT BELT

55°

DOGGER BANK

30′

borough Hd   OUTER WELL BANK

Kiel

54°

HELIGOLAND
Heligoland
BIGHT

umber

Cuxhaven

30′

Terschelling L.V.   Borkum   Wilhelmshaven
JADE BAY

Hamburg

53°

Texel I.
Haaks L.V.   The Texel

Smiths
Knoll   BROAD
FOURTEENS

Cromer

30′

Yarmouth
Gorleston   Ridge
Lowestoft   Corton L.V.   Brown
Ymuiden L.V.

N D
bridge

Outer Gabbard   Maas L.V.

HOLLAND

52°

Harwich   Cork L.V.   Rotterdam
Hook of Holland

Kentish Knock L.V.

30′

G E R M A N Y

Nore L.V.
Sheerness   N.Hinder L.V.

Dusseldorf

Ruytingen
L.V.   Zeebrugge   Schelde R.
Sandettie   Ostend   Antwerp
L.V.   Dunkirk   Neuport   Ghent
Dover   Calais   FLANDERS   Brussels

51°

gsnorth
Dungeness   C.GrisNez

Bremen

Boulogne   BELGIUM

L.V.

30′

E L

50°

Amiens

LUXEMBURG

30′

yre
onfleur   Rouen

49°

Rheims

30′

PARIS

A N C E

45°

the French would co-operate eventually. He had already dispatched guns and Staff Officers to the beleaguered city. Early in the evening of October 2 he moved Sir Edward Grey to telegraph to the French Government urging their active intervention. The French Territorial division which they had promised was, he said, insufficient, the situation at Antwerp was very grave; he would only send British troops if the French did the same. He added that "if General Joffre can bring about a decisively favourable action in France in two or three days the relief of Antwerp may be made the outcome of that; but if not, unless he now sends some regular troops the loss of Antwerp must be contemplated."

Up to this point I had not been brought into the affair in any way. I read, of course, all the telegrams almost as soon as they were received or dispatched by Lord Kitchener, and followed the situation constantly. I warmly approved the efforts which he was making to provide or obtain succour for Antwerp, and I shared to the full his anxieties. I saw him every day. But I had no personal responsibility, nor was I directly concerned. My impression at this time was that the situation at Antwerp was serious but not immediately critical; that the place would certainly hold out for a fortnight more; and that meanwhile Lord Kitchener's exertions or the influence of the main battle in France would bring relief. So much was this the case that I proposed to be absent from the Admiralty for about eighteen hours on the 2nd–3rd October.

I had planned to visit Dunkirk on October 3 on business connected with the Marine Brigade and other details sent there at General Joffre's request. At 11 o'clock on the night of the 2nd I was some twenty miles out of London on my way to Dover when the special train in which I was travelling suddenly stopped, and without explanation returned to Victoria Station. I was told on arrival I was to go immediately to Lord Kitchener's house in Carlton Gardens. Here I found shortly before midnight besides Lord Kitchener, Sir Edward Grey, the First Sea Lord, and Sir William Tyrrell of the Foreign Office. They showed me the following telegram from our Minister, Sir Francis Villiers, sent from Antwerp at 8:20 p.m. and received in London at 10 p.m. on October 2:

> The Government have decided to leave to-morrow for Ostend, acting on advice unanimously given by Superior Council of War in presence of the King. The King with field army will withdraw, commencing with advanced guard to-morrow in the direction of Ghent to protect coast-line, and eventually, it is hoped, to co-operate with the Allied armies. The Queen will also leave.
>
> It is said that town will hold out for five or six days, but it seems most unlikely that when the Court and Government are gone resistance will be so much prolonged.

I saw that my colleagues had received this news, which they had already been discussing for half an hour, with consternation. The rapidity with which the situation had degenerated was utterly unexpected. That the great fortress and city of Antwerp with its triple line of forts and inundations, defended by the whole Belgian Field Army (a force certainly equal in numbers to all the German troops in that neighbourhood), should collapse in perhaps forty-eight hours seemed to all of us not only terrible but incomprehensible. That this should happen while preparations were in progress both in France and England for the relief or succour of the city, while considerable forces of fresh and good troops undoubtedly stood available on both sides of the Channel, and before General Joffre had even been able to reply to Lord Kitchener's telegram, was too hard to bear. We looked at each other in bewilderment and distress. What could have happened in the last few hours to make the Belgians despair? Our last telegram from Colonel Dallas, received that afternoon, had said: "Situation unchanged during night and Germans have not made further progress. Great slaughter of Germans reported and corresponding encouragement to Belgians, who are about to undertake counter-attack in neighbourhood of Fort Ste. Catherine." And now a message at 10 p.m. announced immediate evacuation and impending fall!

Those who in years to come look back upon the first convulsions of this frightful epoch will find it easy with after-knowledge and garnered experience to pass sagacious judgments on all that was done or left undone. There is always a strong case for doing nothing, especially for doing nothing yourself. But to the small group of Ministers who met that midnight in Lord Kitchener's house, the duty of making sure that Antwerp was not cast away without good cause while the means of saving it might well be at hand was clear. I urged strongly that we should not give in without a struggle: and we decided unitedly upon the following telegram to Sir F. Villiers:

October 3, 1914, 12:45 a.m.
The importance of Antwerp being held justifies a further effort till the course of the main battle in France is determined. We are trying to send you help from the main army, and, if this were possible, would add reinforcements from here. Meanwhile a brigade of Marines will reach you to-morrow to sustain the defence. We urge you to make one further struggle to hold out. Even a few days may make the difference. We hope Government will find it possible to remain and field army to continue operations.

On the other hand, the danger of urging the Belgian Government to hold out against their considered judgment without a full knowledge of the local situation was present in every mind, and even if the forces for the relieving army were to come into view, there was much to be arranged and decided before precise dates and definite assurances could be given. We were confronted with the hard choice of having either to take decisions of far-reaching importance in the utmost haste and with imperfect information, or on the other hand tamely to let Antwerp fall.

In these circumstances, it was a natural decision that someone in authority who knew the general situation should travel swiftly into the city and there ascertain what could be done on either side. As I was already due at Dunkirk the next morning, the task was confided to me: Lord Kitchener expressed a decided wish that I should go; the First Sea Lord consented to accept sole responsibility in my absence. It was then about half-past one in the morning. I went at once to Victoria Station, got into my train which was waiting and started again for Dover. A few minutes before I left, Lord Kitchener received the answer to his telegram of the 2nd. The French Foreign Minister promised that with the shortest delay two Territorial divisions complete with artillery and cavalry would be sent to Ostend for the relief of the fortress. This was in addition to the advance of the main French armies in the general battle. On this Lord Kitchener threw himself into the task of concentrating and organizing a relieving army.

Meanwhile a telegram was sent (1:15 a.m., October 3) by Sir Edward Grey to the Belgian Government saying that I was arriving on the morning of the 3rd and asking that their final decision should be postponed till then. On this the Belgian Council of War sitting at dawn on the 3rd suspended the order for the evacuation of the city.

I did not reach Antwerp till after 3 p.m., and was immediately visited by the Belgian Prime Minister. Monsieur de Broqueville was a man of exceptional vigour and clarity both of mind and speech. He had been called to the helm of the Belgian State at the moment of the decision not to submit to wrongful aggression. He explained to me the situation with precision. General Deguise, the Commander of the fortress, added his comments. The outer forts were falling one by one. Five or six shells from the enormous German howitzers were sufficient to smash them to their foundations, to destroy their defenders even in the deepest casemates, and to wreck the platforms of the guns. Now the forts of the inner line were being similarly attacked, and there was no conceivable means of preventing their destruction one after another at the rate of about a fort a day. The army was tired and dispirited through having been left so long entirely upon its own resources without ever a sign of the Allies for whom they had risked so much. Material of every kind—guns, ammunition, searchlights, telephones, entrenching materials—was scanty. The water supply of the city had been cut off. There were many rumours of German sympathizers in its large population of 400,000. At any moment the front might be broken in under the heavy artillery attack which was then in progress. But this was only half the danger. The life and honour of the Belgian nation did not depend on Antwerp, but on its army. To lose Antwerp was disastrous; to lose the army as well was fatal. The Scheldt was barred by a severe interpretation of neutrality. The only line of retreat was by a dangerous flank march parallel to the Dutch frontier and the sea-coast. Two Belgian divisions and the cavalry division were staving off the Germans from this only remaining line of retreat. But the pressure was increasing and the line of the Dendre was no longer intact. If Ghent fell before the Belgian Army made good its retreat, nothing would be saved from the ruin.

In these circumstances they had decided first to withdraw to what was called the entrenched camp on the left bank of the Scheldt, that is to say, towards their right; and, secondly, in the same direction through Ghent towards the left flank of the Allied armies. These orders had been suspended in consequence of the telegram from the British Government.

I then exposed Lord Kitchener's plan and stated the numbers of the French and British troops already available for the assistance of the Belgian Army. I emphasized the importance of holding the city and delaying the Germans as long as possible without compromising the retreat of the army. I pointed out that the issue of the battle for the seaward flank still hung in the balance, and that the main armies were drawing nearer to Belgium every day. I asked whether the relieving forces mentioned, if actually sent, would influence their decision. They replied that this was a new situation; that had this help been forthcoming earlier, events might have taken a different course. Even now, if their line of retreat were safeguarded by the arrival of Allied troops in the neighbourhood of Ghent, they were prepared to continue the resistance. I thereupon drew up, with their approval and agreement:

> Every preparation to be made by Belgian Government now for a resistance of at least ten days, and every step taken with utmost energy. Within three days we are to state definitely whether we can launch big field operation for their relief or not, and when it will probably take effect. If we cannot give them a satisfactory assurance of substantial assistance within three days, they are to be quite free to abandon defence if they think fit. In this case, should they wish to clear out with field army, we (although not able to launch the big operation) are to help their field army to get away by sending covering troops to Ghent or other points on line of retreat. Thus, anything they will have lost in time by going on defending Antwerp with all their strength will be made up to them as far as possible by help on their way out.
>
> Further, we will meanwhile help their local defence in all minor ways, such as guns, marines, naval brigades, etc.
>
> I have put the terms high to avoid at all costs our undertaking any-

thing we could not perform, and also to avoid hurry in our saying what troops we can spare for big operations. You will be able, as your telegram No. 7 (to Colonel Dallas) indicates, to do much better than this, and to give decided promise within three days, but the vital thing is that Belgian Government and army should forthwith hurl themselves with revived energy into the defence.

Attack is being harshly pressed at this moment, and half measures would be useless, but Prime Minister informs me that they are confident they can hold out for three days, pretty sure they can hold out for six, and will try ten.

This arrangement, if adopted, will give time necessary for problem to be solved calmly.

Two thousand marines are arriving this evening.

I am remaining here till to-morrow.

I have read this telegram to Belgian Prime Minister, who says that we are in full agreement, subject to ratification by Council of Ministers which is now being held.

If you clinch these propositions, pray give the following order to the Admiralty: Send at once both naval brigades, minus recruits, via Dunkirk, into Antwerp, with five days' rations and 2,000,000 rounds of ammunition, but without tents or much impedimenta.

When can they arrive?

While waiting for the reply from London that afternoon and also the next morning, I went out and examined the front: a leafy enclosed country, absolutely flat; a crescent of peering German kite balloons; a continuous bombardment; scarcely anything in the nature of an infantry attack; wearied and disheartened defenders. It was extremely difficult to get a clear view and so understand what kind of fighting was actually going on. We were, however, at length able to reach the actual inundations beyond which the enemy was posted. Entrenching here was impossible for either side, owing to the water met with at a foot's depth. The Belgian pickets crouched behind bushes. There was at that moment no rifle fire, but many shells traversed the air overhead on their way to the Belgian lines.

Although the artillery fire of the Germans at Antwerp was at no time comparable to the great bombardments afterwards endured on the Western Front, it was certainly severe. The Belgian trenches were broad and shallow, and gave hardly any protection to their worn-out and in many cases inexperienced troops. As we walked back from the edge of these inundations along a stone-paved high-road, it was a formidable sight to see on either hand the heavy shells bursting in salvos of threes and fours with dense black smoke near or actually inside these scanty shelters in which the supporting troops were kneeling in fairly close order. Every prominent building—château, tower or windmill—was constantly under fire; shrapnel burst along the roadway, and half a mile to the left a wooded enclosure was speckled with white puffs. Two or three days at least would be required to make sound breastworks or properly constructed and drained trenches or rifle pits. Till then it must be mainly an affair of hedges and of houses; and the ineffective trenches were merely shell traps.

Antwerp presented a case, till the Great War unknown, of an attacking force marching methodically without regular siege operations through a permanent fortress line behind advancing curtains of artillery fire. Fort after fort was wrecked by the two or three monster howitzers; and line after line of shallow trenches was cleared by the fire of field-guns. And following gingerly upon these iron foot-prints, German infantry, weak in numbers, raw in training, inferior in quality, wormed and waddled their way forward into "the second strongest fortress in Europe."

As the fire of the German guns drew ever nearer to the city, and the shells began to fall each day upon new areas, the streams of country folk escaping from their ruined homes trickled pitifully along the roads, interspersed with stragglers and wounded. Antwerp itself preserved a singular calm. The sunlit streets were filled with people listening moodily to the distant firing. The famous spires and galleries of this ancient seat of wealth and culture, the spacious warehouses along the Scheldt, the splendid hotels "with every modern convenience," the general air of life, prosperity and civilization created an impression of serene security wholly contradicted by the underlying facts. It was a city in a trance.

The Marines did not arrive until the morning of the 4th, and went immediately into the line. When I visited them the same evening they were already engaged with the Germans in the outskirts of Lierre. Here, for the first time, I saw German soldiers creeping forward from house to house or darting across the street. The Marines fired with machine-guns from a balcony. The flashes of the rifles and the streams of flame pulsating from the mouth of the machine-guns, lit up a warlike scene amid crashing reverberations and the whistle of bullets.

Twenty minutes in a motor car, and we were back in the warmth and light of one of the best hotels in Europe, with its perfectly appointed tables and attentive servants all proceeding as usual!

The reply of the British Government reached me on the morning of the 4th, and I sent it at once to Monsieur de Broqueville:

LORD KITCHENER TO FIRST LORD.

Am arranging Expeditionary Force for relief of Antwerp as follows:—
British Force.

7th Division, 18,000 men, 63 guns, under General Capper. Cavalry Division, 4,000 men, 12 guns, under General Byng, to arrive at Zeebrugge 6th and 7th October. Naval detachment, 8,000 men already there, under General Aston, also Naval and Military heavy guns and detachments already sent. Headquarter Staff will be subsequently notified.

French Force.

Territorial Division, 15,000 men, proper complement of guns and 2 squadrons, General Roy, to arrive Ostend 6th to 9th October. Fusiliers Marins Brigade, 8,000 men, under Rear-Admiral Ronarc'h. Grand total, 53,000 men. Numbers are approximately correct.

Also one from Prince Louis, 10:30 a.m.:

The Naval Brigades will embark at Dover at 4 p.m. for Dunkirk, where they should arrive between 7 or 8 o'clock. Provisions and ammunition as indicated in your telegram.

The matter had now passed into the region of pure action. Could Antwerp resist the enemy's attack long enough to enable the French and British relieving force to come to her aid? Secondly, if this succeeded, could nine or ten Allied divisions at Antwerp and Ghent hold the Germans in check until the left wing of the main armies, advancing daily from the south, could join hands with them? In that case the Allied lines in the west might be drawn through Antwerp, Ghent and Lille. All this turned on a few days, and even on a few hours.

Judged by the number of troops available on both sides, the chances of the Allies appeared good. On paper they were nearly twice as strong as the enemy. But the Belgian Army had been left without aid or comfort too long. The daily destruction of their trusted forts, the harsh and unceasing bombardment of a vastly superior artillery, their apprehensions for their line of retreat, the cruel losses and buffetings they had suffered since the beginning of the war, had destroyed their confidence and exhausted their strength.

The prime and vital need was to maintain the defence of Antwerp against the unceasing artillery attack to which its whole southern front was exposed. The position behind the river was capable of being made a strong one. It was, potentially, stronger in many respects than the line of the Yser, along which a fortnight later this same Belgian Army, in spite of further losses and discouragements, was to make a most stubborn and glorious defence. But despondency in the face of an apparently irresistible artillery, and the sense of isolation, struck a deadly chill.

Meanwhile, however, help was hurrying forward. The Marines were already in the line. Armoured trains with naval guns and British bluejackets came into action on the morning of the 4th. The two Naval Brigades reached Dunkirk that night, and were due to enter Antwerp on the evening of the 5th. At the special request of the Belgian Staff they were to be interspersed with Belgian divisions to impart the encouragement and assurance that succour was at hand.

The British 7th Division and 3rd Cavalry Division, carried daringly across the water upon personal orders from Prince Louis in the teeth of submarines, began to disembark at Ostend and Zeebrugge from the morning of the 6th onward. The French division was embarking at Havre. Admiral Ronarc'h and his 8,000 Fusiliers Marins[1] were already entrained for Dunkirk. If only Antwerp could hold out. . . .

Meanwhile, also, it must be remembered, Sir John French was secretly withdrawing the British Army from the Aisne and moving round behind the French front to the neighbourhood of St. Omer with the intention of striking at Lille and beating in the German right. Every day that large German forces were detained in front of Antwerp helped and covered the detrainment and deployment of his army and increased its chances of success. But every day became graver also the peril to the Belgian Army of being cut off if, after all, the Germans should be the victors in the main battle.

The anxieties and uncertainties of this tremendous situation had to be supported by the Belgian chiefs in addition to those of the actual German attack battering on the crumbling Antwerp front and its exhausted defenders. That they were borne with constancy and coolness, that the defence was prolonged for five momentous days, and that although the Antwerp front was broken in before effective help could arrive, the Belgian Field Army was safely extricated, was a memorable achievement.

The attitude of the King and Queen through these tense and tragic days was magnificent. The impression of the grave, calm soldier King presiding at Council, sustaining his troops and commanders, preserving an unconquerable majesty amid the ruin of his kingdom, will never pass from my mind.

Meanwhile Lord Kitchener and Prince Louis continued to give the necessary orders from London.

I now found myself suddenly, unexpectedly and deeply involved in a tremendous and hideously critical local situation which might well continue for some time. I had also assumed a very direct responsibility for exposing the city to bombardment and for bringing into it the inexperienced, partially equipped

---

[1] Sent instead of the Second Territorial Division.

and partially trained battalions of the Royal Naval Division. I felt it my duty to see the matter through. On the other hand, it was not right to leave the Admiralty without an occupant. I therefore telegraphed on the 4th to the Prime Minister offering to take formal military charge of the British forces in Antwerp and tendering my resignation of the office of First Lord of the Admiralty. This offer was not accepted. I have since learned that Lord Kitchener wrote proposing that it should be, and wished to give me the necessary military rank. But other views prevailed: and I certainly have no reason for regret that they did so. I was informed that Sir Henry Rawlinson was being sent to the city and was requested to do my best until he arrived.

October 5 was a day of continuous fighting. The situation fluctuated from hour to hour. In the evening I went to General Paris's Headquarters on the Lierre road for the purpose of putting him in command of the other two Naval Brigades about to arrive. The fire along this road was now heavier. Shrapnel burst overhead as I got out of the car and struck down a man at my feet. As we discussed around the cottage table, the whole house thudded and shook from minute to minute with the near explosions of shells whose flashes lit the window panes. In such circumstances was it that General Paris received from the representative of the Admiralty the command of the Royal Naval Division which he was destined to hold with so much honour until he fell grievously wounded in his trenches after three years' war. This was the most important military command exercised in the Great War by an officer of the Royal Marines.

The general result of the fighting on the 5th raised our hopes. The counter-attack by one British and nine Belgian battalions drove the enemy back. All the positions that had been lost were regained, and the line of the Nethe was almost re-established. At midnight at the Belgian Headquarters General Deguise received in my presence by telephone a favourable report from every single sector. The enemy had, however, succeeded in maintaining a foothold across the river, and it seemed certain they would throw bridges in the night. General Deguise therefore resolved to make a further counter-attack under the cover of darkness in the hope of driving the enemy altogether across the river.

It was 2 o'clock before I went to bed. I had been moving, thinking and acting with very brief intervals for nearly four days in Council and at the front in circumstances of undefined but very onerous responsibility. Certainly the situation seemed improved. The line of the Nethe was practically intact and the front unbroken. The Naval Brigades, already a day behind my hopes, were arriving in the morning. By land and sea troops were hastening forward. All the various personalities and powers were now looking the same way and working for the same object. France and Britain, the Admiralty and the War Office, the Belgian Government and the Belgian Command were all facing in the same direction. Rawlinson would arrive to-morrow, and my task would be concluded. But what would the morrow bring forth? I was now very tired, and slept soundly for some hours.

All through the night the fighting was continual, but no definite reports were available up till about 9 o'clock. At the Belgian Headquarters I was told that the Belgian night attack had miscarried, that the Germans were counter-attacking strongly, that the Belgian troops were very tired and the situation along the Nethe obscure. General Paris and the Marine Brigade were also heavily engaged. The Naval Brigades had arrived and detrained and were now marching to their assigned positions in the line. But where was the line? It was one thing to put these partially trained and ill-equipped troops into a trench line, and quite another to involve them in the manœuvres of a moving action. Solidly dug in with their rifles and plenty of ammunition, these ardent, determined men would not be easily dislodged. But they were not capable of manœuvre. It seemed to me that they should take up an intermediate position until we knew what was happening on the front. General Paris was involved in close fighting with his brigade, and had not been able to take over command of the whole force. It was necessary therefore for me to give personal directions. I motored to the Belgian Headquarters, told General Deguise that these new troops must have fixed positions to fight in, and would be wasted if flung in piecemeal. I proposed to stop them about four miles short of their original des-. tination as a support and rallying line for the Belgian troops who were falling back. He agreed that this was wise and right, and I went myself to see that the orders were carried out.

The moment one left the city gates the streams of wounded and of fugitives betokened heavy and adverse fighting. Shells from the enemy's field artillery were falling frequently on roads and villages which yesterday were beyond his range. We were by no means sure at what point the flow of refugees would end and the wave of pursuers begin. However, by about midday the three Naval and Marine Brigades were drawn up with the Belgian reserves astride of the Antwerp-Lierre road on the line Contich-Vremde.

In this position we awaited the next development and expected to be almost immediately attacked. The Germans to our relief did not molest the retirement of the three Belgian divisions. They waited to gather strength and to bring up and use again the remorseless artillery upon which they were mainly relying. As no German infantry appeared and no heavy bombardment began, the Naval Brigades moved forward in their turn and took up positions nearer to where the enemy had halted. I remained in the line on the Lierre road. Here at about 5 o'clock Sir Henry Rawlinson joined me.

The General took, as might be expected, a robust view of the situation, and was by no means disposed to give up the quarrel either on the Antwerp front or on the line of communications, which were already being more severely pressed. In fact I found in this officer, whom I had known for many years, that innate, instinctive revolt against acquiescing in the will of the enemy which is an invaluable quality in military men. These sentiments were also shared by Colonel Bridges, former British military attaché in Belgium, who had arrived from Sir John French. At 7 o'clock a Council of War was held in the Palace under the presidency of the King. We affirmed the readiness and ability of the British Government to execute punctually and fully the engagements into which we had entered two days earlier. But the Belgian chiefs were convinced that even if the Antwerp front along the line of the Nethe could be restored, the danger to their communications had become so great that they must without delay resume the movement of their army to the left bank of the Scheldt, which had been interrupted three days previously. Here they conceived themselves able to join hands with any Anglo-French relieving force while at the same time securing their own retreat on Ghent, which they had already on September 4 reinforced by a brigade. It was not for us to contest their view, and events have shown that they were right. General Rawlinson and I left the city together that night, and after an anxious drive over roads luckily infested by nothing worse than rumour, I boarded the *Attentive* at Ostend and returned to England.

After the departure of the Belgian Field Army the further defence of the remaining lines of Antwerp was left to the fortress troops, the 2nd Belgian Division, and the three British Naval Brigades, who held on their front the equivalent of more than five complete German divisions, to wit: the 5th Reserve, 6th Reserve, 4th Ersatz and Marine Division, and the 26th, 37th, and 1st Bavarian Landwehr Brigades.

At midnight on the 7th the Germans, having advanced their artillery, began to bombard the city and the forts of the inner line. The forts melted under the fire, and a great proportion of the civil population fled through the night, lighted by conflagrations, over the bridges of the Scheldt to the open country, along the roads towards Ghent or into Holland. The enemy's attack was pressed continuously, and the enceinte of the city was considered to be untenable by the evening of the 8th. The Belgian Division and the British Naval Brigades evacuated Antwerp that night, crossed the Scheldt safely, and began their retreat by road and rail on Ghent and Ostend. Two naval airmen,[1] as a Parthian shot, blew up after long flights a Zeppelin in its shed at Düsseldorf and bombed the railway station at Cologne. German patrols, after many precautions, entered Antwerp towards evening on the 9th, and on the 10th the stouthearted Governor, who had retired to one of the surviving forts, capitulated.

---

[1] Commanders Marix and Spenser-Grey.

• • •

The resistance of the city had been prolonged for five days. Would there then be time for the French and British Armies to rest their left upon that fortress and hold the Germans from the seaboard along a line Antwerp-Ghent-Lille? This depended not only upon the local operations but on the result of the series of outflanking battles which marked the race for the sea. A decisive victory gained by the French in the neighbourhood of Peronne, or by the British beyond Armentières and towards Lille, would have opened all this prospect. High French authorities have concluded that a more rapid and therefore no doubt more daring transference of force from the right and centre of the French front to its left, "looking sixty kilometers ahead instead of twenty-five," and generally a more vigorous attempt to outflank the Germans following immediately upon the victory of the Marne and the arrest of the armies at the Aisne, might well have shouldered the Germans not only away from the sea, but even out of a large part of occupied France. In the event, however, and with the forces employed, the French and British did not succeed in turning the enemy's flank. The battles at Albert, La Bassée and Armentières produced no decisive result; Peronne and Lille could not be reached and the fighting lines continued simply to prolong themselves to the north-west. The retention of Antwerp would have rewarded the victory of the main armies with a prize of the utmost value. Its extended resistance diminished the consequences of their failure. Everything at Antwerp had depended on a victory to the southward. And this victory had been denied. Nevertheless, as will now be shown, the effort was fruitful in a remarkable degree.

The fall of Antwerp released the besieging army. A marine division marched into the city on the 10th.[1] The rest of the German divisions were already streaming south and west in hot pursuit, and hoped for interception of the Belgian Army. But a surprise awaited them.

On the night of the 9th the German forces who had crossed the Dendre river had come in contact with French Fusiliers Marins at Melle and Meirelbeke, and during the 10th they found themselves in presence of British regular troops of unknown strength, whose patrols were feeling their way forward from Ghent to meet them. The 7th Division and the 3rd Cavalry Division had come upon the scene in accordance with the fourth condition of the Anglo-Belgian agreement of October 4. The British, French and Belgian forces from Ghent thus threatened the left flank of any serious German cutting-off movement northwards to the Dutch frontier.

---

[1] It was perhaps an unconsious recognition of the naval significance of Antwerp that all three great Powers—Germany, France and Britain—used in its attack and defence Naval Brigades formed since the outbreak of war.

Uncertain of the size of the army by which they were confronted, and mystified by the indefinite possibilities of landings from the sea, the Germans paused to collect their strength. They knew that the bulk of the British Army had already left the Aisne. Where was it? Where would it reappear? What were these British regulars, who stood so confidently in their path? On the 12th when they considered themselves strong enough to advance upon Ghent, the whole of the Belgian Field Army had passed the dangerous points in safety, only one single squadron being intercepted. Of this complicated operation the victorious Germans became spectators.

Only weak parties of Germans ventured beyond Lokeren during the night of the 9th–10th to molest the retreat of the Antwerp troops. The 2nd Belgian Division and two out of the three Naval Brigades came through intact. But the railway and other arrangements for the rear brigade were misunderstood, and about two and a half battalions of very tired troops, who through the miscarriage of an order had lost some hours, were led across the Dutch frontier in circumstances on which only those who know their difficulties are entitled to form a judgment.

At the time the British Government decided to send help to Antwerp the total German strength in Northern Belgium had been correctly estimated at four or five divisions. But before the city capitulated and while the British troops were still at Ghent, there began to manifest itself that tremendous unexpected development of German force which from the moment of Antwerp's fall was launched against the Allied left and aimed at Calais. Besides the liberated Siege Army and the troops which had threatened the Antwerp communications, no fewer than four fresh Army Corps (XXIInd, XXIIIrd, XXVIth and XXVIIth), newly formed in Germany and concentrating in Belgium, were already at hand. And in front of this formidable army there stood from October 10 to October 21 only the wearied Belgians, the Fusiliers Marins, and the British 3rd Cavalry and 7th Divisions. The caution of the German advance may perhaps have been induced by their uncertainty as to the whereabouts and intentions of the British Army, and their fear that it might be launched against their right from the sea flank. But, however explained, the fact remains, and to it we owe the victory of the Yser and Ever-Glorious Ypres.

A simple examination of dates will reveal the magnitude of the peril which the Allied cause escaped. Antwerp fell twenty-four hours after the last division of the Belgian Field Army left the city. Had this taken place on October 3rd or 4th, the city would have surrendered on the 4th or 5th. No British 4th Corps[1] or Fusiliers Marins would have been at Ghent to cover the Belgian retreat. But assuming that the Belgian Army had made this good unaided, the same

---

[1] Rawlinson's Force was so styled.

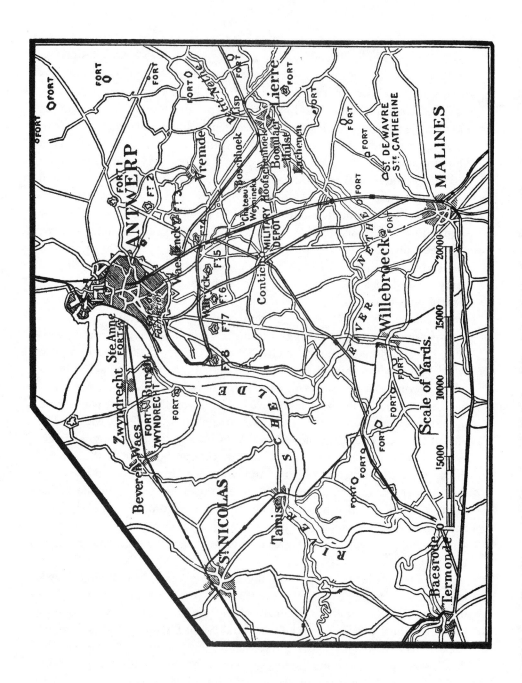

marches would have carried them *and their German pursuers* to the Yser by the 10th. There would have been nothing at all in front of Ypres. Sir John French could not come into action north of Armentières till the 15th. His detrainments at St. Omer, etc., were not completed till the 19th. Sir Douglas Haig with the 1st Corps could not come into line north of Ypres till about the 21st. Had the German Siege Army been released on the 5th, and, followed by their great reinforcements already available, advanced at once, nothing could have saved Dunkirk, and perhaps Calais and Boulogne. The loss of Dunkirk was certain and that of both Calais and Boulogne probable. Ten days were wanted, and ten days were won.

We had next without respite to meet the great German drive against the Channel ports. The six divisions released from the siege of Antwerp, and the eight new divisions, whose apparition had been so unexpected to the British and French Staffs, rolled southward in a double-banked wave. The Belgian Army trooped back in a melancholy procession along the sea-shore to the Yser. General Rawlinson, with the 7th Division and the 3rd Cavalry Division, extricating himself skilfully from large German forces—how great was not then known—and lingering at each point to the last minute without becoming seriously engaged, found himself by October 15 in the neighbourhood of a place called Ypres[1] Meanwhile Sir John French, detraining at St. Omer, and hopefully believing that he was turning the German right, struck through Armentières towards Lille, and sent imperative orders to Rawlinson, over whose head the storm was about to break, to advance in conformity and seize Menin. The French forces intended for the relief of Antwerp and the beginnings of larger French reinforcements endeavoured to close the gap between Rawlinson and the Belgians. The dykes were opened and large inundations began to appear. In this manner was formed a thin, new, loosely organized, yet continuous allied front from the neighbourhood of La Bassée to the sea at the mouth of the Yser; and upon this front, which grew up and fixed itself at every point in and by the actual collision of hostile forces, was now to be fought the third great battle in the West.

These events involved the Admiralty at many points. The position of Rawlinson's troops in the presence of vastly superior forces was precarious, and for some days we stood ready to re-embark them. We laboured to salve everything possible from the Belgian wreck. The Royal Naval Division must be brought back to refit, reorganize and resume its interrupted training. The Admiralty details—aeroplanes, armoured trains, armoured cars, motor omnibus transport, etc.—with which I had been endeavouring during the previous weeks to con-

---

[1] The heavy losses of the 7th Division have often been attributed to their attempt to relieve Antwerp. In fact, however, these losses did not begin until after they had joined the main army.

ceal our nakedness in the vital coastal area, could now be merged in the arriving British armies.

On October 16 General Joffre telegraphed to Lord Kitchener as follows:

> Now that the operations extend up to the coast of the North Sea between Ostend and the advanced defences of Dunkirk, it would be important for the two Allied Navies to participate in these operations by supporting our left wing and acting with long-range guns on the German right wing. The Commander of the Naval Forces would then act in concert with General Foch through the Governor of Dunkirk.

This duty we instantly accepted.

FIRST LORD TO SIR JOHN FRENCH.

October 17, 1914.

Monitors were delayed by weather, but will be in position from daylight 18th; meanwhile eight destroyers should have arrived on the flank between 4 and 5 p.m. 17th, and two scout cruisers an hour later. They have been told to communicate with Colonel Bridges on the quays of Nieuport.

We are sending two battleships mounting eight 12-inch guns to Dunkirk roadstead to-morrow to cover the fortress and its coast approaches.

We set to work forthwith to support the Allied left flank. I entrusted this operation, which required an officer of first quality, to Admiral Hood, till then my Naval Secretary. He was now appointed to the Dover Command, while I took in his stead Admiral Oliver. On the 18th the three ex-Brazilian monitors, renamed *Humber, Mersey* and *Severn,* escorted by four destroyers, arrived at Dunkirk and a series of naval operations on the Belgian Coast began.

There was no difficulty in finding plenty of ships of different classes to cover the flank of the army. Besides the three monitors, a large proportion of the destroyers from Dover were readily available. There were many old battleships, and these at certain states of the tide could get into suitable positions for bombarding. In addition there was the Scout class, seven of which were available, all happily newly rearmed with the very best 4-inch guns. But Admiralty reserves of ammunition had been based upon the needs of purely naval actions, which are few and far between, and not many of which all ships survive. Bombarding the German positions on the Belgian Coast week after week, and possibly for months, made demands upon our stores of a totally different character. We had to pick ships primarily for the class of ammunition they fired; ships that could use up old ammunition and ships whose value was so small that we could afford to spend all their ammunition. As October wore on we scoured the dockyards for every little vessel that carried a gun of any kind. Even the smallest gunnery tenders, 250-ton gunboats forty years old, were pressed into service, and in one way or another the fire was continuously maintained.

It was evident that these operations would have to be carried on under unceasing submarine attack. Moreover, we had to be prepared for a sudden dash by German cruisers and destroyers. We trusted to Commodore Tyrwhitt with the Harwich Striking Force either to protect us from this or to exact retribution on the return journey. On the 17th the Germans, torn between the will to wound and the fear to strike, broke all the commandments of the text-books by sending a feeble force of four small destroyers from the Ems down the Dutch Coast. They were almost immediately destroyed by the Commodore, the British ships engaged being the light cruiser *Undaunted* and the destroyers *Lance, Lennox, Legion* and *Loyal.*

From the middle of October onwards the German hosts could look upon salt water. First Zeebrugge was occupied, then Ostend, then mile by mile the sand-dunes and golf courses and gay villas of that pleasure coast were devoured by invading war. In his first contact with the new element the land monster committed several imprudences. Apparently contemptuous of the power of ships' guns, he deployed batteries of artillery on the open beach, and opened fire on our Scouts and destroyers. These experiments were not repeated. A Swedish writer, Dr. Sven Hedin, at that time with the German armies, belauding them and bowing obsequiously before what he had convinced himself was world-conquering power, has described a scene in the restaurant of the best Ostend hotel. The room was crowded with hungry officers of the invading army, just marched in, all sitting down to excellent fare.

A destroyer had just detached itself from the rest and was making at full speed for Ostend, parallel with the coast, as close as possible to the shore. Presently another destroyer appeared, following in the wake of the first. What could they want, these ruffians? Strong language was heard—it was a piece of consummate impudence to come steaming right under our noses like this. Evidently they were reconnoitring—but what insolence, they must have known that we had occupied Ostend! Aha! they suspect that there are submarines and destroyers in the inner harbour, and want to see whether they can detect anything from outside! . . . Astounding insolence. Two small German guns are hurried up. "Are they going to shoot?" I asked. "Oh yes, they are going to shoot all right." . . . The first shot rang out. . . . Directly the German shots had been fired, the two destroyers swung round to port and at the same moment opened fire. Their guns seemed to flash out straight at us. . . .

The results were instantaneous. The restaurant, which had been "one of the most elegant in Europe," was blasted into a smoking shambles of ruin and death.

In this manner the German Army and the British Navy first came into contact with one another.

Meanwhile the struggle along the Yser had begun.

Reading again the brief operative telegrams which flashed to and fro in those days, I feel once more the battle going on, the exhausted Belgians clinging desperately to the last few miles of soil left to their nation, their dauntless King and Queen amid the shells at Furnes; the French troops hastening up, but only in driblets; the heroic Fusiliers Marins holding Dixmude till not a fifth were left alive; our little ships barking away along the coast with the submarines stabbing at them from underneath and heavier metal opening on them every day from the shore; inundations slowly growing, a shield of merciful water rising inch by inch, hour by hour, between the fainting Belgian line and the cruel monster who had come upon them; and all the time our own men fighting against appalling odds, ten days, twenty days, thirty days, from Ypres to Armentières; nothing to send anyone, not a man, not a musket. Each night Colonel Bridges spoke to me on the telephone from the Belgian Headquarters at Furnes. Each night we felt it might be the last time he would speak from that address. It was only very gradually towards the end of October that one began to feel that the French and Belgian troops were getting a firm grip of the line of the Yser, and that Sir John French could write, "The Germans will never get further west." But three more weeks of agony ensued before the decision at Ypres finally declared itself in favour of the British Army.

We are, I feel, entitled to treat the Antwerp episode as an integral and vital part of this tremendous battle for the Channel Ports. If we had not made our belated effort to prolong its defence, the whole aftercourse of events would have been different, and could hardly have been better. But for the time gained at Antwerp and the arrival in such a forward situation of the British and French forces assigned so hurriedly for its relief, the impulsion of the Allied Armies towards the sea—already less than was required—must have been sensibly weakened. The great collision and battle with the German right would have taken place all the same. Perhaps the same result would have been achieved. But where? Where would the line have been drawn when the armies settled down into trenches from which they were not appreciably displaced for more than four years? At the very best the water defences, Gravelines-St. Omer-Aire, would have been secured. Dunkirk and its fine harbour would have become another nest of submarines to prey on our communications in the Channel; and Calais would have been exposed to a constant bombardment. The complications of these evils—the least that could be expected—must have reacted formidably upon the whole subsequent fortunes of the Allied Armies in France.

If this be true—and history must pronounce—the men who were responsible for the succour of Antwerp will have no reason to be ashamed of their effort. Hazard and uncertainty pervade all operations of war. It is idle to pretend that Lord Kitchener or anyone else foresaw all the consequences that flowed from the decisions of October 4. The event was very different from both hopes and expectations. But rarely in the Great War were more important results achieved by forces so limited and for losses so small, as those which rewarded this almost forlorn enterprise; nor is there in modern times, a more remarkable example of the flexibility, the celebrity, and the baffling nature of that amphibious power which Britain alone wields, but which she has so often neglected.

CHAPTER XIV

LORD FISHER

OCTOBER AND NOVEMBER, 1914

All the anxieties recorded in the last chapter faded before our preoccupations about the Fleet. Indeed, the alarums and excursions on the Belgian Coast were at times almost a relief compared to the stress of our prime responsibilities. Everything depended upon the Fleet, and during these same months of October and November the Fleet was disquieted about the very foundations of its being. There lay the mighty ships; every man, from stoker to Admiral, was ready to die at his duty at any moment; no personal or individual fear found foothold. Still, at the summit from which we watched, one could feel a new and heart-shaking sensation. The Grand Fleet was uneasy. She could not find a resting-place except at sea. Conceive it, the *ne plus ultra,* the one ultimate sanction of our existence, the supreme engine which no one had dared to brave, whose authority encircled the globe—no longer sure of itself. The idea had got round—*"the German submarines were coming after them into the harbours."*

On the South Coast no one would have minded. You could go inside the Portland breakwater and literally shut the door. On the East Coast no such absolutely sealed harbour existed. But Scapa was believed to be protected by its currents from submarine attack. Destroyers no doubt could attack it—if they cared to run the very serious risk of the long daylight passage, to and fro, across the North Sea: but no one, we had believed, could take a submarine *submerged* through the intricate and swirling channels. Now, all of a sudden, the Grand Fleet began to see submarines in Scapa Flow. Two or three times the alarm was raised. The climax came on October 17. Guns were fired, destroyers thrashed the waters, and the whole gigantic Armada put to sea in haste and dudgeon.

Of course there never was a German submarine in Scapa. None during the whole war achieved the terrors of the passage. One was destroyed in the outer approaches towards the end of November in circumstances which remained a mystery to the enemy. At the very end of the war in November, 1918, after the mutiny of the German fleet, a German submarine manned entirely by officers seeking to save their honour, perished in a final desperate effort. Thus none ever penetrated the lair of the Grand Fleet. But nevertheless the mere apprehension of submarines attacking the sleeping ships on which all else reposed, was sufficient in the winter of 1914 to destroy that sense of security which every Fleet demands when in its own war harbours.

Up till the end of September, 1914, no one seriously contemplated hostile submarines in time of war entering the war harbours of either side and attacking the ships at anchor. To achieve this the submarine would have to face all the immense difficulties of making its way up an estuary or inlet amid shoal water and intricate navigation, submerged all the time and with only an occasional glimpse through the periscope; secondly, while doing this, to avoid all the patrolling craft which for many miles kept watch and ward on the approaches; thirdly, to brave the unknown and unknowable terrors of mines and obstructions of all sorts, with which it must be assumed the channels would become increasingly infested. It was thought that these deterrents would prove effectual. Looking back on the events in the light of after-knowledge, we can see now that this assumption was correct. There is no recorded instance of a German submarine having penetrated into any British war harbour. The British submarine service was certainly not inferior in enterprise to the Germans, and from the very first hours of the war our boats were in the Heligoland Bight; but no British submarine officer attempted actually to penetrate a German war harbour or run actually into the mouths of the Elbe, the Jade, the Weser or the Ems. The nearest approaches to such an enterprise were the numerous passages of the Dardanelles made by the British submarines, beginning at the end of December with the heroic exploits of Commander Holbrook. For these feats the submarines were able to start only a few miles from the mouth of the Dardanelles and, diving along a very deep channel over two miles wide, succeeded again and again in entering the Sea of Marmora. This was not comparable to penetrating a British war harbour or river-mouth; and it did not occur until experience of the war capabilities of submarines had much increased.

During August and September the Admiralty made most strenuous efforts to increase the protection of our bases in Scotland and upon the East Coast by mounting guns, by posting guardships, by placing obstructions, by preparing booms, by laying torpedo nets. But the danger against which these defences were designed in those months, was primarily not the submarine, but a regular attack by enemy destroyers on the fleet or squadrons at anchor, or, secondly, a raid by cruisers upon bases in the temporary absence of the fleet. It was not until the middle or end of September that increasing knowledge and evidences of the power of the largest submarines under war conditions, fostered the idea that the German submarines might actually enter our northern war harbours at the Forth, at Cromarty, and at Scapa Flow. Once this idea took root, it became a grave preoccupation. Precautions taken against a rush of torpedo boats, were clearly insufficient to stop a vessel which might dive under booms and past protecting guns.

This submarine danger was one which did not in fact materialize at the outbreak of war. Six months later the position was different. The enterprise and the skill of submarine commanders had greatly grown, and all sorts of possibilities never previously envisaged came successively into view. But by that time the submarines had to face a very different set of obstructions. By the time they were convinced of the possibility, the possibility had disappeared.

It seemed real enough, however, in the month of October, 1914. The booms and obstructions which were everywhere being improvised were not complete or only partially in position, while the danger had begun to take full shape in the minds both of the Fleet and of the Admiralty. There was nothing to be done but to await the completion of the booms and obstructions, and meanwhile to keep the Fleet as far as possible out of harm's way. It really only felt safe when it was at sea. There, steaming in the broad waters, the Grand Fleet was herself again: but this involved a great strain on officers, men and machinery and a large consumption of fuel.

On September 30 Sir John Jellicoe wrote to me on the general Fleet position. He pointed out that Germany had got a lead over us in oversea submarines, that we always expected that the preliminary stages of a modern naval war would be a battle of the small craft, and that the question of keeping heavy ships out of the North Sea altogether, until the small craft menace had been reduced, had been frequently discussed. He thought it suicidal to forego our advantageous position in big ships by risking them in waters infested by submarines. He was of opinion that the submarine had a very limited sphere of action, could not hurt our oversea commerce (at that time this was in the main true), nor could they help their own ships to get in. He proposed therefore to use the Battle Fleet far to the North, spread to intercept trade. We had not nearly sufficient cruisers to form the double line that was really necessary to stop all ships during the short days and long nights. It was perfectly easy, he said, to run through the line at night, as its approximate positions soon got known and could not be much varied. But with the Battle Fleet helping in waters free from the submarine danger, one could make much more certain. This, however, entailed giving up the idea of southerly Battle Fleet movements. He suggested that the French submarines as well as our own should be employed on the probable paths of the German submarines. He emphasized the importance of fitting a number of our trawlers with wireless installations. He desired me to show this letter to the First Sea Lord and to know whether we were in agreement with his views, whether steps would be taken to establish a trawler patrol, and whether the idea of utilizing the Grand Fleet effectively to shut up the Northern entrance to the North Sea was approved. He concluded by urging the hastening of the submarine defences for Scapa.

On the day of my return from Antwerp, I wrote to him in full agreement:

In order to secure the greatest amount of rest and security for the Fleet, and the maintenance of the highest efficiency both of the steaming and fighting of its ships, you are justified in using occasional anchorages even more remote than Scapa and Loch Ewe; but on this you should make proposals officially. You need not fear that by these withdrawals you will miss a chance of bringing the German Battle Fleet to action. If that ever comes out it will be with some definite tactical object—for instance, to cover the landing of an invading force, to break the line of blockade to the northward in order to let loose battle-cruisers on to the trade routes, or simply for the purpose of obtaining a naval decision by fighting a battle. In the first two of these cases you would have the time to come round and meet or intercept them before their operation was completed; in the third instance, their wishes would be the same as yours. . . .

With regard to anchorages you have only to make your proposals and we will do our best to equip with anti-submarine nets, lights, and guns the places which you may wish to use. It is of importance that these should be varied, absolute safety lying much more in the uncertainty attending the movements of the Grand Fleet than in any passive or fixed defence of any particular place. We must not be led into frittering away resources by keeping half a dozen anchorages in a state of semi-defence, and so far as possible we must organize a movable defence of guardships, trawlers, patrolling yachts, mine-sweepers, destroyers with towing charges, and seaplanes, which can move while the Fleet is at sea and prepare the new resting-place for its reception.

The employment of a portion or occasionally of the whole of the Battle Fleet, to supplement the Northern Blockade from time to time is a matter on which you must be the judge. A large part of your time must necessarily be spent cruising at sea, and this being so the cruising should be made as useful as possible. Here, again, anything in the nature of routine or regular stations would be dangerous, and would, after a while, draw upon you, even in remote northern waters, the danger of submarine attack.

These general conclusions governed our policy during the next few months. But as October wore on our anxieties were steadily aggravated. The tension grew.

On October 17 Sir John Jellicoe telegraphed that a German submarine had been reported entering Scapa at 5 p.m. the previous day. Although he thought the report false, he took the whole Fleet to sea forthwith. He appealed urgently for submarine obstructions as he had "no safe base at present, and the only way to coal ships is to shift the coaling anchorages constantly which seriously dislocates the organization of supply." On the 18th he stated that Scapa Flow could not be used till the Submarine Defence was placed. On the 19th he asked the Admiralty whether he should risk the submarine menace at Scapa Flow or move the Fleet to remote bases on the west coast of Scotland or Ireland "more than 300 miles from the Pentland Firth." He added, "It cannot be stated with absolute certainty that submarines were inside Scapa Flow, although Captain D, 4th Destroyer Flotilla, is positive H.M.S. *Swift* was fired at inside. I am of opinion that it is not difficult to get inside at slack water."

Another very serious warning reached me almost simultaneously from Sir David Beatty:

> The feeling, he wrote, is gradually possessing the Fleet that all is not right somewhere. The menace of mines and submarines is proving larger every day, and adequate means to meet or combat them are not forthcoming, and we are gradually being pushed out of the North Sea, and off our own particular perch. How does this arise? By the very apparent fact that we have no Base where we can with *any* degree of safety lie for coaling, replenishing, and refitting and repairing, after two and a half months of war. This spells trouble. . . . The remedy is to fix upon a base and make it impervious to submarine attack; as I have pointed out I am firmly convinced this can be done. . . .
>
> I think you know me well enough to know that I do not shout without cause. The Fleet's tail is still well over the back. We hate running away from our base and the effect is appreciable. We are not enjoying ourselves. But the morale is high and confidence higher. I would not write thus if I did not know that you with your quick grasp of detail and imagination would make something out of it.

Meanwhile, however, the Admiralty, particularly the First and Fourth Sea Lords, had been labouring since the end of September to devise and make the necessary protective structures. By dint of extraordinary exertions the first instalment of these was already approaching completion, and on October 20 Prince Louis was in a position to telegraph to the Commander-in-Chief:

> The defences for Scapa will leave Dockyards on 24th October.

The Commander-in-Chief, in accordance with Admiralty authorization, withdrew at the end of October to the north coast of Ireland for a few days' rest and gunnery practice. By extraordinary ill-luck, the arrival of the Fleet off Loch Swilly coincided with the visit of a German minelayer to those waters. The minelayer had no idea of catching the Fleet or that British warships would be in those waters. Her objective was the Liverpool trade route, but the shot aimed at a crow brought down an eagle.

On October 27 Prince Louis hurried into my room with the grave news that the *Audacious* had been struck by mine or torpedo North of Loch Swilly, and that it was feared she was sinking. In the afternoon the Commander-in-Chief telegraphed urging that every endeavour should be made to keep the event from being published; and that night, in reporting that the *Audacious* had sunk, he repeated his hope that the loss could be kept secret. I saw great difficulties in this, but promised to bring the matter before the Cabinet. Meanwhile I telegraphed to the Commander-in-Chief, October 28, 12:30 a.m.:

> I am sure you will not be at all discouraged by *Audacious* episode. We have been very fortunate to come through three months of war without the loss of a capital ship. I expected three or four by this time, and it is due to your unfailing vigilance and skill that all has gone so well. The Army too has held its own along the whole line, though with at least 14,000 killed and wounded. Quite soon the harbours will be made comfortable for you. Mind you ask for all you want.

Measured by military standards, the *Audacious* was the first serious loss we had sustained. She was one of those vital units in which we never were at that time more than six or seven to the good, and upon which all strategic calculations were based both by friend and foe. When I brought the question of keeping her loss secret before the Cabinet, there was a considerable division of opinion. It was urged that public confidence would be destroyed if it were thought that we were concealing losses, that it was bound to leak out almost immediately, and that the Germans probably knew already. To this I replied that there was no reason why the Germans should not be left to collect their own information for themselves, that the moment they knew the *Audacious* was sunk they would proclaim it, and that then we could quite easily explain to the public why it was we had preserved secrecy. I cited the effective concealment by Japan of the loss of the battleship *Yashima* off Port Arthur in 1904. If Sir John French had lost an Army Corps, every effort would be made to conceal it from the enemy. Why then should the Navy be denied a similar freedom? Lord Kitchener strongly supported me; and our views were eventually accepted by the Cabinet.

The Press were asked by the Admiralty to abstain from making any reference to the event. Some newspapers complied with an ill grace. It was represented that hundreds of people knew already, including all the passengers of the liner *Olympic* which had passed the sinking vessel; that German spies in England would certainly convey the news to Germany in a few days, and that, anyhow, long accounts of the sinking with actual photographs would be dispatched by the next mail to the United States, whence the news would be immediately telegraphed to Germany. We, however, remained obdurate, watching the German Press very carefully for the slightest indication that they knew. Meanwhile it was thought clever by certain newspapers to write articles and paragraphs in which the word "audacious" was frequently introduced, while I was much blamed. I found it necessary to issue a secret appeal, which, aided by the loyal efforts of the Newspaper Press committee, certainly had some effect. In the upshot it took more than five weeks before the German Admiralty learned that the *Audacious* had been sunk, and even then they were by no means convinced that they were not the victims of rumour.

Says Admiral Scheer:

> The English succeeded in keeping secret for a considerable time the loss of this great battleship, a loss which was a substantial success for our efforts at equalization. . . . The behaviour of the English was inspired at all points by consideration for what would serve their military purpose. . . . In the case of the *Audacious* we can but approve the English attitude of not revealing a weakness to the enemy, because accurate information about the other side's strength has a decisive effect on the decisions taken.

I do not remember any period when the weight of the war seemed to press more heavily on me than these months of October and November, 1914. In August one was expecting the great sea battle and the first great battles on land; but our course was obvious, and, when taken, we had only to wait for decisions. All September was dominated by the victory of the Marne. But in October and November the beast was at us again. The sense of grappling with and being overpowered by a monster of appalling and apparently inexhaustible strength on land, and a whole array of constant, gnawing anxieties about the safety of the Fleet from submarine attack at sea and in its harbours, oppressed my mind. Not an hour passed without the possibility of some disaster or other in some part of the world. Not a day without the necessity of running risks.

My own position was already to some extent impaired. The loss of the three cruisers had been freely attributed to my personal interference. I was accused of having overridden the advice of the Sea Lords and of having wantonly sent the squadron to its doom. Antwerp became a cause of fierce reproach. One might almost have thought I had brought about the fall of the city by my meddling. The employment of such untrained men as the Naval Brigades was generally censured. The internment in Holland of three of their battalions was spoken of as a great disaster entirely due to my inexcusable folly. One unhappy phrase—true enough in thought, and indeed in the event—about "Digging rats out of holes," which had slipped from my tongue in a weary speech at Liverpool, was fastened upon and pilloried. These were the only subjects with which my name was connected in the newspapers. My work at the Admiralty—such as it was—was hidden from the public. No Parliamentary attack gave me an opportunity of defending myself. In spite of being accustomed to years of abuse, I could not but feel the adverse and hostile currents that flowed about me. One began to perceive that they might easily lead to a practical result. Luckily there was not much time for such reflections.

The Admiralty had entered upon the war with commanding claims on public confidence. The coincidence of the test mobilization with the European crisis, was generally attributed to profound design. The falsification one after another of the gloomy predictions that we should be taken unawares, that the German commerce destroyers would scour the seas, and that our own shipping, trade and food would be endangered, was recognized with widespread relief. The safe transportation of the Army to France and the successful action in the Heligoland Bight were acclaimed as fine achievements. But with the first few incidents of misfortune a different note prevailed in circles which were vocal. The loss of the three cruisers marked a turning-point in the attitude of those who in the evil times of war are able to monopolize the expression of public opinion. As the expectation of an imminent great sea battle faded, the complaint began to be heard, "What is the Navy doing?" It was perhaps inevitable that there should be a sense of disappointment as week succeeded week and the tremendous engine of British naval power seemed to be neither seen nor heard. There was a general opinion that we should have begun by attacking and destroying the German Fleet. Vain to point to the ceaseless stream of troops and supplies to France, or to the world-wide trade of Britain proceeding almost without hindrance. Impossible, in the hearing of the enemy, to explain the intricate movement of reinforcements or expeditions escorted across every ocean from every part of the Empire, or to unfold the reasons which rendered it impossible to bring the German Fleet to battle. There was our little Army fighting for its life, and playing to British eyes almost as large a part as all the armies of France; and meanwhile our great Navy—the strongest in the world—lay apparently in an inertia diversified only by occasional mishap.

Eaten bread is soon forgotten. Dangers which are warded off by effective precautions and foresight are never even remembered. Thus it happened that the Admiralty was inconsiderately judged in this opening phase. To me, who saw the perils against which we had prepared and over which we had triumphed, and who felt a sense of profound thankfulness for the past and absolute confidence for the future, these manifestations of discontent seemed due only to lack of understanding and to impatience pardonable in the general stress of the times. But they were none the less disquieting. Nor was it easy to deal with them. The questions could not be argued out in public or in Parliament. No formal indictment was ever preferred; nor could one have been fully answered without injury to national interests. We had to endure all this carping in silence. A certain proportion of losses at sea was inevitable month by month; and in each case it was easy to assert that someone had blundered. In most cases, indeed, this was true. With a thousand ships upon the sea and a thousand hazards, real or potential, every day to menace them, accidents and mistakes were bound to happen. How many were made for which no forfeit was claimed by Fortune! There was never an hour when risks against which no provision could be made were not being run by scores of vessels, or when problems of novelty and difficulty were not being set to sea captains, scarcely any of whom had ever been tried in war. Was it wonderful that we fell occasionally into error, or even into loss? "Another naval disaster. Five hundred men drowned. What are the Admiralty doing?" While all the time the armies reeled about in the confusion of the mighty battles, and scores of thousands were sent, often needlessly or mistakenly, to their deaths: while all the time every British operation of war and trade on the seas proceeded without appreciable hindrance.

This censorious mood produced a serious development in the case of Prince Louis. In the first flush of our successful mobilization and entry upon the war, no comment had been made upon his parentage. But now the gossip of the clubs and of the streets began to produce a stream of letters, signed and anonymous, protesting in every variety of method and often in violent terms against one of Teutonic birth filling the vital position of First Sea Lord. This was cruel; but it was not unnatural, and I saw with anxiety and distress the growth of very widespread misgiving. I gathered also from occasional remarks which he made that this atmosphere was becoming apparent to the First Sea Lord. He was thus coming to be placed in the invidious position of having to take great responsibilities and risks day by day without that support in public confidence to which he was absolutely entitled, and with the certainty that accidents would occur from time to time. I was therefore not surprised when, towards the end of October, Prince Louis asked to be relieved of his burden. The uncomplaining dignity with which he made this sacrifice and accepted self-effacement as a requital for the great and faithful service he had rendered to the British nation and to the Royal Navy was worthy of a sailor and a Prince. I had now to look for a successor, and my mind had already turned in one direction and in one direction alone.

Lord Fisher used to come occasionally to the Admiralty, and I watched him narrowly to judge his physical strength and mental alertness. There seemed no doubt about either. On one occasion, when inveighing against someone whom he thought obstructive, he became so convulsed with fury that it seemed that every nerve and blood-vessel in his body would be ruptured. However, they stood the strain magnificently, and he left me with the impression of a terrific engine of mental and physical power burning and throbbing in that aged frame. I was never in the least afraid of working with him, and I thought I knew him so well, and had held an equal relationship and superior constitutional authority so long, that we could come through any difficulty together. I therefore sounded him in conversation without committing myself, and soon saw that he was fiercely eager to lay his grasp on power, and was strongly inspired with the sense of a message to deliver and a mission to perform. I therefore determined to act without delay. I sought the Prime Minister and submitted to him the arguments which led me to the conclusion that Fisher should return, and that I could work with no one else. I also spoke of Sir Arthur Wilson as his principal coadjutor. I was well aware that there would be strong, natural and legitimate, opposition in many quarters to Fisher's appointment, but having formed my own conviction I was determined not to remain at the Admiralty unless I could do justice to it. So in the end, for good or for ill, I had my way.

The decision to recall Lord Fisher to the Admiralty was very important. He was, as has been here contended, the most distinguished British Naval officer since Nelson. The originality of his mind and the spontaneity of his nature freed him from conventionalities of all kinds. His genius was deep and true. Above all, he was in harmony with the vast size of events. Like them, he was built upon a titanic scale.

But he was seventy-four years of age. As in a great castle which has long contended with time, the mighty central mass of the donjon towered up intact and seemingly everlasting. But the outworks and the battlements had fallen away, and its imperious ruler dwelt only in the special apartments and corridors with which he had a lifelong familiarity. Had he and his comrade, Sir Arthur Wilson, been born ten years later, the British naval direction at the outbreak of the Great War would have reached its highest state of perfection, both at the Admiralty and afloat. The new figures which the struggle was producing—Beatty, Keyes, Tyrwhitt—had not yet attained the authority which would have made them acceptable to the Navy in the highest situations. Fisher and Wilson had outlived their contemporaries and towered above the naval generation which had followed them. It was to these two great old men and weather-beaten sea-dogs, who for more than half a century had braved the battle and the breeze, and were Captains afloat when I was in my cradle, that the professional conduct of the naval war was now to be confided.

It was clear, however, to me, who knew both these Admirals-of-the-Fleet quite well and had had many opportunities in the previous three years of hearing and reading their views, that the day-to-day organization of our Staff machinery would have to be altered. This necessitated a change in the Chief of the

War Staff. In Admiral Sturdee the Navy had a sea officer of keen intelligence and great practical ability—a man who could handle and fight his ship or his squadron with the utmost skill and resolution. But he was not a man with whom Lord Fisher could have worked satisfactorily at the supreme executive centre. Happily, there was no difficulty in agreeing upon his successor.

Since Antwerp, Admiral Oliver had been my Naval Secretary. During the year before the war he had been Director of Naval Intelligence. In this capacity I had had to rely continually upon him, as upon Captain Thomas Jackson before him, for all the facts and figures upon which the controversy about British and German naval strength depended. His accuracy in detail and power of continuous and tenacious mental toil were extraordinary. He combined with capacious knowledge an unusual precision of mind and clarity of statement. His credentials as a sea officer were unimpeachable. He had been Navigating Commander to Sir Arthur Wilson, and everyone in the Navy knew the story of how in the 1901 Naval manœuvres these two had taken the Channel Fleet from off Rathlin's Island at the North of Ireland through the Irish Channel to the Scillies in thick mist without sighting land or lights, and without being inclined to make a single remark to each other. On the third day the mist lifting suddenly revealed the Scilly Islands to the astonished Fleet, which had already dropped anchor in the roads.

I was very glad when Lord Fisher proposed to me that Admiral Oliver should be made Chief of the Staff, and when he offered also to give me in exchange, for my Private Office, his own personal assistant, Commodore De Bartolomé. Everything thus started fair. We reformed the War Group, which met at least once each day, as follows: First Lord, First Sea Lord, Sir Arthur Wilson, Admiral Oliver and Commodore De Bartolomé (the last named representing the younger school of sea officers), together with the invaluable Secretary, Sir Graham Greene. Sir Henry Jackson was also frequently summoned, but not so continuously as to impose an accountable responsibility upon him.

To add to the distractions of this hard month of November, 1914, an invasion scare took a firm hold of the military and naval authorities. It was argued by the War Office that the lull on the fighting fronts would enable the Germans to spare large numbers of good troops—250,000 if necessary—for the invasion of Great Britain. Lord Kitchener directed all defensive preparations to be made, and Lord Fisher threw himself into the task with gusto. Although I was sceptical on this subject, I felt that the precautions were justifiable, and would at any rate add interest to the life of our coast and Home defence forces. I therefore allowed myself to succumb to the suppressed excitement which grew throughout the highest circles, and did my utmost to aid and speed our preparations. We stationed as described the 3rd Battle Squadron at the Forth, brought the 2nd

Fleet to the Thames, disposed the old *Majestic* battleships in the various harbours along the East Coast, arranged block ships to be sunk, and laid mines to be exploded, at the proper time in the mouths of our undefended harbours; while the whole coastal watch, military, aerial and marine, throbbed with activity. The Army arrangements were complicated by the fact that some of the divisions which were sufficiently trained to be used to repel the invaders, had lent their rifles to those that were undergoing training, and these rifles had to be collected and redistributed as a part of the procedure prescribed for the supreme emergency. To such expedients were we reduced! However, the Germans remained absolutely quiescent; the tides and moon, which for some days before November 20 were exceptionally favourable to nocturnal landings, ceased to present these conditions, and the sense of some great impending event gradually faded from our minds.

Lord Fisher hurled himself into the business of new construction with explosive energy. He summoned around him all the naval constructors and shipbuilding firms in Britain, and in four or five glorious days, every minute of which was pure delight to him, he presented me with schemes for a far greater construction of submarines, destroyers and small craft than I or any of my advisers had ever deemed possible. Mr. Schwab was at that time passing through England on his return to the United States. We invited him to the Admiralty; and he undertook to build twenty-four submarines—twelve in Canada and twelve in the United States—the bulk of which were to be completed in the hitherto incredibly short period of six months. I arranged a system of heavy bonuses for early delivery. These large negotiations were completed and the subsequent work was carried out with wonderful thoroughness and punctuality by the immense organization of the Bethlehem Steel Company. One evening, as Lord Fisher, Mr. Schwab and I sat round the octagonal table in the Admiralty, after a long discussion on the submarine contracts, we asked Mr. Schwab, "Have you got anything else that will be of use to us?" He thereupon told us that he had four turrets carrying two 14-inch guns each which had almost been completed for the Greek battleship *Salamis* then building in Germany for Greece. We set our hearts on these; and I had an idea. The reader will remember the three small monitors building for Brazil, which although no one could see any use for them at the time, I had decided to take over at the outbreak of war. The operations on the Belgian Coast had shown their value. I suggested to Lord Fisher that we should buy these 14-inch turrets and build monitors to carry them. The Admiral was delighted with the plan, and in a few hours he was closeted with his constructors designing the vessels. We soon embarked on an extensive scheme of monitor building.

In the autumn of 1914, under various programmes culminating in the

Fisher impetus, we set on foot the following enormous Fleet, all due to complete by the end of 1915:

Battleships and Battle-cruisers of the greatest power	7
Light cruisers	12
Destroyers of the largest class and leaders	65
Oversea submarines	40
Coastal submarines	22
Monitors—	
Heavy	18
Medium	14
Light	5
Sloops and smaller anti-submarine vessels	107
Motor launches	60
Ex-lighters with internal combustion engines	240

This tremendous new Navy, for it was nothing less, was a providential aid to the Admiralty when more than two years later the real German submarine attack began. Its creation on such a scale is one of the greatest services which the nation has owed to the genius and energy of Lord Fisher. Probably Fisher in all his long life never had a more joyous experience than this great effort of new construction. No man knew better than he how to put war thought into a ship. Ship-building had been the greatest passion of his life. Here were all the yards of Britain at his disposal and every Treasury barrier broken down.

Of the battle-cruisers *Repulse* and *Renown,* and still more of the light battle-cruisers *Courageous, Furious* and *Glorious,* to which I consented four months later in circumstances which will be narrated in their place, it must be said that they were an old man's children. Although possessing marvellous qualities never hitherto combined in a ship of war, they were light in the bone; and the Navy always considered them wanting in the structural strength and armour which the new conditions of war more than ever required. None the less, their parent loved them dearly and always rallied with the utmost vehemence when any slur was cast upon their qualities.

I presided over all this process in November and December with the greatest admiration for the First Sea Lord, but with some misgivings on the score of expense. I was not yet satisfied that the war would be prolonged beyond 1915, and I did not wish to draw away from the armies men or material which might be needed in their service. Not until April, 1915, when the failure of Russia as a decisive factor became final, did I authorize a further extension of view to December 31, 1916, and agree to plans for additional new construction being made within that limit. Meanwhile I endeavoured to satisfy Lord Fisher as best I could. I pointed out to him repeatedly that from some points of view a ship finished twelve months before the end of the war was worth twelve times as much as a ship finished one month before its end, and urged continuously that vessels nearest completion must in no way suffer. He was, however, very difficult to feed. In a day he would sketch the design of a capital ship. In a week he would devour a programme and come back asking for more. A tit-bit like an 18-inch experimental gun which I suggested he should make, was snapped up the moment it was mentioned. "I will put it in a light cruiser and drive her 40-knots," he cried. "Hit how you like, when you like, where you like." This was his theme; but what about his doctrine "Armour is vision"? However, I backed him up all I could. He was far more often right than wrong, and his drive and life-force made the Admiralty quiver like one of his great ships at its highest speed.

Lord Fisher's age and the great strain to which he was now to be subjected made it necessary for him to lead a very careful life. He usually retired to rest shortly after 8 o'clock, awaking refreshed between four and five, or even earlier. In these morning hours he gave his greatest effort, transacting an immense quantity of business, writing innumerable letters and forming his resolutions for the day. Indeed, his methods corresponded closely to the maxims of the poet Blake: "Think in the morning; act in the noon; eat in the evening; sleep in the night." But I never heard him use this quotation. As the afternoon approached the formidable energy of the morning gradually declined, and with the shades of night the old Admiral's giant strength was often visibly exhausted. Still, judged from the point of view of physical and mental vigour alone, it was a wonderful effort, and one which filled me, who watched him so closely, with admiration and, I will add, reassurance.

I altered my routine somewhat to fit in with that of the First Sea Lord. I slept usually an hour later in the morning, being called at eight instead of seven, and I slept again, if possible, for an hour after luncheon. This enabled me to work continuously till one or two in the morning without feeling in any way fatigued. We thus constituted an almost unsleeping watch throughout the day and night. In fact, as Fisher put it, "very nearly a perpetual clock." Telegrams came in at the Admiralty at all hours of the day and night, and there was scarcely an hour when an immediate decision could not be given, if necessary, by one or the other of us always awake.

This arrangement was also convenient from the point of view of business. The First Lord completed everything with which he was concerned before going to bed, and three hours later the First Sea Lord addressed himself to the whole budget, and I, awaking at eight, received his dawn output. I had not previously seen the pulse of the Admiralty beat so strong and regular.

We made the agreement between ourselves that neither of us should take any important action without consulting the other, unless previous accord had been reached. To this agreement we both scrupulously adhered. We had thus formed, for the first time, an overwhelmingly strong control and central authority over the whole course of the naval war, and were in a position to make our will prevail throughout the fleets and all branches of the naval administration, as well as to hold our own against all outside interference. I had for a long time been accustomed to write my minutes in red ink. Fisher habitually used a green pencil. To quote his words, "it was the port and starboard lights." As long as the port and starboard lights shone together, all went well. We had established a combination which, while it remained unbroken, could not have been overthrown by intrigue at home or the foe on the sea.

CHAPTER XV

CORONEL AND THE FALKLANDS

OCTOBER, NOVEMBER AND DECEMBER, 1914

As has already been described, Admiral von Spee, the German Commander-in-Chief in the Far East, sailed from Tsingtau (Kiauchow),[1] in the last week of June, with the *Scharnhorst* and *Gneisenau,* and on August 5, immediately after the British declaration of war, these two powerful ships were reported as being near the Solomon Islands. They were subsequently reported at New Guinea on the 7th August, and coaling at the Caroline Islands on the 9th. After this they vanished into the immense Pacific with its innumerable islands, and no one could tell where they would reappear. As the days succeeded one another and grew into weeks, our concern on their account extended and multiplied. Taking the Caroline Islands as the centre, we could draw daily widening circles, touching ever more numerous points where they might suddenly spring into action. These circles were varied according as the Germans were credited with proceeding at most economical speed, at three-quarter speed, or at full speed; and the speed at which they would be likely to steam depended upon the nature of the potential objective which in each case might attract them.

We have seen how the mystery of their whereabouts affected the movements of the New Zealand and Australian convoys, and what very anxious decisions were forced upon us. We have seen how the uncertainty brooded over the little expedition from New Zealand to Samoa: how glad we were when it arrived safely and seized the island: how prompt we were—providentially prompt—to snatch every vessel away from the roadstead of Samoa the moment the troops and stores were landed. When at length more than five weeks had passed without any sign of their presence, we took a complete review of the whole situation. All probabilities now pointed to their going to the Magellan Straits or to the West Coast of South America. The Australian convoy was now provided with superior escort. Not a British vessel could be found in the anchorage at Samoa. The old battleships were already on their way to guard the convoys in the Indian Ocean. There was nowhere where they could do so much harm as in the Straits of Magellan. Moreover, we thought we had indications of

---

[1] Throughout this chapter the map on pp. 248–49 and the table of ships on p. 247 will be found useful.

German coaling arrangements on the Chilean Coast. There were rumours of a fuelling base in the Magellan Straits, for which diligent search was being made. There was certainly German trade still moving along the Western Coast of South America.

Accordingly, on the 14th September, the Admiralty sent the following telegram to Rear-Admiral Cradock, who commanded on the South American Station:

ADMIRALTY TO REAR-ADMIRAL CRADOCK, H.M.S. "GOOD HOPE."

September 14, 5:50 p.m.

The Germans are resuming trade on West Coast of South America, and *Scharnhorst* and *Gneisenau* may very probably arrive on that coast or in Magellan Straits.

Concentrate a squadron strong enough to meet *Scharnhorst* and *Gneisenau,* making Falkland Islands your coaling base, and leaving sufficient force to deal with *Dresden* and *Karlsruhe.*

Defence is joining you from Mediterranean, and *Canopus* is now *en route* to Abrolhos.[1] You should keep at least one County class and *Canopus* with your flagship until *Defence* joins.

When you have superior force, you should at once search Magellan Straits with squadron, keeping in readiness to return and cover the River Plate, or, according to information, search as far as Valparaiso northwards, destroy the German cruisers, and break up the German trade. . . .

Two days later all uncertainties, and with them our anxieties, vanished, and news was received that both *Scharnhorst* and *Gneisenau* had appeared off Samoa on the 14th September. There was nothing for them to hurt there. The empty roadstead mocked their power. The British flag flew on shore, and a New Zealand garrison far too strong for any landing party snarled at them from behind defences. Thus informed of the fate of their colony, the German cruisers put to sea after firing a few shells at the Government establishments.

A week later, the 22nd, they were at Papeete, which they bombarded, destroying half the town and sinking the little French gunboat *Zélé* which was in harbour. They left the same morning, steering on a Northerly course. We did not hear of this till the 30th. Then once again silence descended on the vast recesses of the Pacific.

We could now begin drawing our circles again from the beginning; and at any rate for several weeks we need not worry about these ships. Accordingly the Admiralty telegraphed to Admiral Cradock, on the 16th September, telling him

---

[1] The rocks of Abrolhos off the Brazilian Coast were our secret coaling base in these waters.

the new situation and that he need not now concentrate his cruisers, but could proceed at once to attack German trade in the Straits of Magellan and on the Chilean Coast.

Nothing more happened for a fortnight. On October 4, wireless signals from the *Scharnhorst* were heard by Suva wireless station, and also at Wellington, New Zealand. From this it appeared that the two vessels were on the way between the Marquesas Islands and Easter Island. Evidently the South American plan was in their mind. We passed our information to Admiral Cradock with the following telegram:

ADMIRALTY TO REAR-ADMIRAL CRADOCK. (OCTOBER 5.)
It appears from information received that *Gneisenau* and *Scharnhorst* are working across to South America. *Dresden* may be scouting for them. You must be prepared to meet them in company. *Canopus* should accompany *Glasgow, Monmouth* and *Otranto,* and should search and protect trade in combination.

On the 8th (received 12th) Admiral Cradock replied as follows:

Without alarming, respectfully suggest that, in event of the enemy's heavy cruisers and others concentrating West Coast of South America, it is necessary to have a British force on each coast strong enough to bring them to action.

For, otherwise, should the concentrated British force sent from South-East Coast be evaded in the Pacific, which is not impossible, (? and) thereby (? get) behind the enemy, the latter could destroy Falkland, English Bank, and Abrolhos coaling bases in turn with little to stop them, and with British ships unable to follow up owing to want of coal, enemy might possibly reach West Indies.

And on the same day (received 11th) he reported evidences of the presence of the *Dresden* in South American waters:

Following intelligence *re Scharnhorst* and *Gneisenau* has been received. Evidence found by *Good Hope* revisiting Orange Bay on 7th October that *Dresden* had been there 11th September, and there are indications that *Scharnhorst* and *Gneisenau* may be joined by *Nürnberg, Dresden,* and *Leipzig.* I intend to concentrate at Falkland Islands and avoid division of forces. I have ordered *Canopus* to proceed there, and *Monmouth, Glasgow,* and *Otranto* not to go farther north than Valparaiso until German cruisers are located again. . . .

With reference to Admiralty telegram No. 74, does *Defence* join my command?

This was an important telegram. It showed a strong probability that the enemy was concentrating with the intention to fight. In these circumstances we must clearly concentrate too. I now looked at the Staff telegram of 5th October, and thought it was not sufficiently explicit on the vital point, viz., concentration for battle. In order that there should be no mistake, I wrote across the back of Admiral Cradock's telegram received on the 12th October the following minute:

First Sea Lord.

In these circumstances it would be best for the British ships to keep within supporting distance of one another, whether in the Straits or near the Falklands, and to postpone the cruise along the West Coast until the present uncertainty about *Scharnhorst-Gneisenau* is cleared up.

They and not the trade are our quarry for the moment. Above all, we must not miss them.

W. S. C.

The First Sea Lord the same evening added the word "Settled."

On the 14th October, I discussed the whole situation which was developing with the First Sea Lord, and in accordance with my usual practice I sent him a minute after the conversation of what I understood was decided between us.

First Sea Lord.

I understood from our conversation that the dispositions you proposed for the South Pacific and South Atlantic were as follows:

(1) Cradock to concentrate at the Falklands *Canopus, Monmouth, Good Hope* and *Otranto.*

(2) To send *Glasgow* round to look for *Leipzig* and attack, and protect trade on the West Coast of South America as far north as Valparaiso.

(3) *Defence* to join *Carnarvon* in forming a new combat squadron on the great trade route from Rio.

(4) *Albion* to join the flag of C.-in-C. Cape for the protection of the Luderitz Bay expedition.

These arrangements have my full approval.

Will you direct the Chief of the Staff to have a statement prepared showing the dates by which these dispositions will be completed, and the earliest date at which *Scharnhorst* and *Gneisenau* could arrive in the respective spheres.

I presume Admiral Cradock is fully aware of the possibility of *Scharn-horst* and *Gneisenau* arriving on or after the 17th instant in his neighbour-hood; and that if not strong enough to attack, he will do his utmost to shadow them, pending the arrival of reinforcements.

The following telegram was sent to Admiral Cradock:

> ADMIRALTY TO REAR-ADMIRAL CRADOCK, OCTOBER 14.
> Concur in your concentration of *Canopus, Good Hope, Glasgow, Mon-mouth, Otranto,* for combined operation.
> We have ordered Stoddart in *Carnarvon* to Montevideo as Senior Naval Officer north of that place.
> Have ordered *Defence* to join *Carnarvon.*
> He will also have under his orders *Cornwall, Bristol, Orama* and *Macedonia.*
> *Essex* is to remain in West Indies.

On the 18th Admiral Cradock telegraphed:

> I consider it possible that *Karlsruhe* has been driven West, and is to join the other five. I trust circumstances will enable me to force an action, but fear that strategically, owing to *Canopus,* the speed of my squadron cannot exceed 12 knots.

Thus it is clear that up to this date the Admiral fully intended to keep con-centrated on the *Canopus,* even though his squadron speed should be reduced to 12 knots. Officially the *Canopus* could steam from 16 to 17 knots. Actually in the operations she steamed 15½.

Let us now examine the situation which was developing.[1] The *Scharnhorst* and the *Gneisenau* were drawing near the South Coast of America. On the way they might be met by the light cruisers *Leipzig, Dresden* and *Nürnberg.* The squadron which might thus be formed would be entirely composed of fast modern ships. The two large cruisers were powerful vessels. They carried each eight 8-inch guns arranged in pairs on the upper deck, six of which were capa-ble of firing on either beam. Both ships being on permanent foreign service were fully manned with the highest class of German crews; and they had in fact only recently distinguished themselves as among the best shooting ships of the whole German Navy. Against these two vessels and their attendant light cruis-ers, Admiral Cradock had the *Good Hope* and the *Monmouth.* The *Good Hope*

---

[1] The table of ships on p. 247 will be found useful.

was a fine old ship from the Third Fleet with a 9.2-inch gun at either end and a battery of sixteen 6-inch guns amidships. She had exceptionally good speed (23 knots) for a vessel of her date. Her crew consisted mainly of reservists, and though she had good gunlayers she could not be expected to compare in gunnery efficiency with the best manned ships either in the British or German Navies. The *Monmouth* was one of the numerous County class against which Fisher had so often inveighed—a large ship with good speed but light armour, and carrying nothing heavier than a battery of fourteen 6-inch guns, of which nine could fire on the beam. These two British armoured cruisers had little chance in an action against the *Scharnhorst* and *Gneisenau*. No gallantry or devotion could make amends for the disparity in strength, to say nothing of gunnery. If brought to battle only the greatest good fortune could save them from destruction. It was for this reason that the moment the Admiralty began to apprehend the possibility of the arrival of the *Scharnhorst* and *Gneisenau* on the South American station, we sent a capital ship to reinforce Admiral Cradock. Our first intention had been to send the *Indomitable* from the Dardanelles, and at one time she had already reached Gibraltar on her way to South America when increasing tension with Turkey forced her to return to the Dardanelles. As we did not conceive ourselves able to spare a single battle-cruiser from the Grand Fleet at that time, there was nothing for it but to send an old battleship and by the end of September the *Canopus* was already steaming from Abrolhos rocks through the South Atlantic.

With the *Canopus,* Admiral Cradock's squadron was safe. The *Scharnhorst* and *Gneisenau* would never have ventured to come within decisive range of her four 12-inch guns. To do so would have been to subject themselves to very serious damage without any prospect of success. The old battleship, with her heavy armour and artillery, was in fact a citadel around which all our cruisers in those waters could find absolute security. It was for this reason that the Admiralty had telegraphed on 14th September: "Keep at least *Canopus* and one County class with your flagship"; and again, on the 5th October: *"Canopus* should accompany *Glasgow, Monmouth* and *Otranto."* It was for this reason that I was glad to read Admiral Cradock's telegram. "Have ordered *Canopus* to Falkland Islands, where I intend to concentrate and avoid division of forces," on which I minuted: "In these circumstances it would be best for the British ships to keep within supporting distance of one another, whether in the Straits or near the Falklands"; and it was for this same reason that the Admiralty telegraphed on the 14th October: "Concur in your concentration of *Good Hope, Canopus, Monmouth, Glasgow, Otranto* for combined operation. . . ."

It was quite true that the speed of the *Canopus* was in fact only fifteen and a half knots, and that as long as our cruisers had to take her about with them they could not hope to catch the Germans. All the *Canopus* could do was to prevent the Germans catching and killing them. But that would not be the end of the story; it would only be its beginning. When the Germans reached the South American coast after their long voyage across the Pacific, they would have to coal and take in supplies: they were bound to try to find some place where colliers could meet them, and where they could refit and revictual. The moment they were located, either by one of our light cruisers or reported from the shore, the uncertainty of their whereabouts was at an end. We could instantly concentrate upon them from many quarters. The Japanese battleship *Hizen* and cruiser *Idzumo,* with the British light cruiser *Newcastle,* were moving southward across the Northern Pacific towards the coast of South America—a force also not capable of catching the *Scharnhorst* and *Gneisenau,* but too strong to be attacked by them. On the East Coast of South America was Rear-Admiral Stoddart's squadron with the powerful modern armoured cruiser *Defence,* with two more County class cruisers, *Carnarvon* (7.5-inch guns) and *Cornwall,* the light cruiser *Bristol,* and the armed merchant cruisers *Macedonia* and *Orama.* All these ships could be moved by a single order into a common concentration against the German squadron the moment we knew where they were; and meanwhile, so long as he kept within supporting distance of the *Canopus,* Admiral Cradock could have cruised safely up the Chilean coast, keeping the Germans on the move and always falling back on his battleship if they attempted to attack him. The *Good Hope* and *Monmouth* steaming together were scarcely inferior in designed speed to the *Scharnhorst* and *Gneisenau,* and these last had been long at sea. Admiral Cradock could, therefore, have kept on observing the Germans, disturbing them, provoking them and drawing them on to the *Canopus.* Moreover, in the *Glasgow* he had a light cruiser which was much superior in speed to the *Scharnhorst* and *Gneisenau,* and superior both in strength and speed to any one of the German light cruisers concerned.

I cannot therefore accept for the Admiralty any share in the responsibility for what followed. The first rule of war is to concentrate superior strength for decisive action and to avoid division of forces or engaging in detail. The Admiral showed by his telegrams that he clearly appreciated this. The Admiralty orders explicitly approved his assertion of these elementary principles. We were not, therefore, anxious about the safety of Admiral Cradock's squadron. A more important and critical situation would arise, if in cruising up the West Coast of South America with his concentrated force Admiral Cradock missed the Germans altogether, and if they passed to the southward of him through the Straits of Magellan or round the Horn, refuelling there in some secret bay, and so came on to the great trade route from Rio. Here they would find Admiral Stoddart, whose squadron when concentrated, though somewhat faster and stronger than the Germans, had not much to spare in either respect. It was for this reason that I had deprecated in my minute of the 12th October Admiral Cradock's movement up the West Coast and would have been glad to see him remaining near the Straits of Magellan, where he could either bar the path of the *Scharnhorst* and the *Gneisenau,* or manœuvre to join forces with Admiral Stoddart. However, I rested content with the decisions conveyed in the Admiralty telegram of the 14th October, and awaited events.

Suddenly, on the 27th October, there arrived a telegram from Admiral Cradock which threw me into perplexity:

REAR-ADMIRAL CRADOCK TO ADMIRALTY.

Good Hope. 26th October, 7 p.m. At sea.

Admiralty telegram received 7th October. With reference to orders to search for enemy and our great desire for early success, I consider that owing to slow speed of *Canopus* it is impossible to find and destroy enemy's squadron.

Have therefore ordered *Defence* to join me after calling for orders at Montevideo.

Shall employ *Canopus* on necessary work of convoying colliers.

We were then in the throes of the change in the office of First Sea Lord, and I was gravely preoccupied with the circumstances and oppositions attending the appointment of Lord Fisher. But for this fact I am sure I should have reacted much more violently against the ominous sentence: "Shall employ *Canopus* on necessary work of convoying colliers." As it was I minuted to the Naval Secretary (Admiral Oliver) as follows:

This telegram is very obscure, and I do not understand what Admiral Cradock intends and wishes.

I was reassured by his reply on the 29th October:

The situation on the West Coast seems safe. If *Gneisenau* and *Scharnhorst* have gone north they will meet eventually *Idzumo, Newcastle,* and *Hizen* moving south, and will be forced south on *Glasgow* and *Monmouth* who have good speed and can keep touch and draw them south on to *Good Hope* and *Canopus,* who should keep within supporting distance of each other.

The half fear which had begun to grow in my mind that perhaps the Admiral would go and fight without the *Canopus,* which I thought was so improbable that I did not put it on paper, was allayed. It would, of course, be possible for him to manœuvre forty or fifty miles ahead of the *Canopus* and still close her before fighting. To send the *Defence* to join Admiral Cradock would have left Admiral Stoddart in a hopeless inferiority. Indeed, in a few hours arrived Admiral Stoddart's protest of the 29th October. The Admiralty Staff had, however, already replied to Admiral Cradock in accordance with all our decisions that the *Defence* was to remain on the East Coast with Stoddart's command to ensure a sufficient force on each side of South America.

But neither this nor any further message reached Admiral Cradock. He had taken his own decision. Without waiting for the *Defence,* even if we had been able to send her, and leaving the *Canopus* behind to guard the colliers, he was already steaming up the Chilean coast. But though he left the inexpugnable *Canopus* behind because she was too slow, he took with him the helpless armed merchant cruiser *Otranto,* which was scarcely any faster. He was thus ill-fitted either to fight or run.

He telegraphed to us from off Vallenar at 4 p.m. on 27th October (received 1st November, 4:33 a.m.):

> Have received your telegram 105. Have seized German mails. *Monmouth, Good Hope* and *Otranto* coaling at Vallenar. *Glasgow* patrolling vicinity of Coronel to intercept German shipping rejoining flag later on. I intend to proceed northward secretly with squadron after coaling and to keep out of sight of land. Until further notice continue telegraphing to Montevideo.

And at noon on 29th October (received 1st November, 7:40 a.m.):

> Until further notice mails for Rear-Admiral Cradock, *Good Hope, Canopus, Monmouth, Glasgow, Otranto,* should be forwarded to Valparaiso.

The inclusion of the *Canopus* in the middle of the latter message seemed to indicate the Admiral's intention to work in combination with the *Canopus* even if not actually concentrated. These were the last messages received from him.

On the 30th October Lord Fisher became First Sea Lord. As soon as he entered the Admiralty I took him to the War Room and went over with him on the great map the positions and tasks of every vessel in our immense organization. It took more than two hours. The critical point was clearly in South American waters. Speaking of Admiral Cradock's position, I said, "You don't suppose he would try to fight them without the *Canopus*?" He did not give any decided reply.

Early on the 3rd November we got our first certain news of the Germans.

(Sent 5:20 p.m., 2nd November. Received 3:10 a.m., 3rd November.)
Master of Chilean merchant vessel reports that on 1st November
1 p.m. he was stopped by *Nürnberg* 5 miles off Cape Carranza about 62
miles north of Talcahuano. Officers remained on board 45 minutes. Two
other German cruisers lay west about 5 and 10 miles respectively. Master
believes one of these was *Scharnhorst.* On 26th October, 1 p.m. *Leipzig*
called at Mas-a-Fuera having crew 456 and 10 guns, 18 days out from
Galapagos. She was accompanied by another cruiser name unknown.
They bought oxen and left same day. On 29th October unknown warship
was seen in lat. 33 south, long. 74 west, steaming towards Coquimbo.

Here at last was the vital message for which the Admiralty Staff had waited
so long. Admiral von Spee's squadron was definitely located on the West Coast
of South America. He had not slipped past Admiral Cradock round the Horn
as had been possible. For the moment Admiral Stoddart was perfectly safe.
With the long Peninsula of South America between him and the *Scharnhorst*
and *Gneisenau,* there was no longer any need for him to keep the *Defence.* She
could join Cradock for what we must hope would be an early battle. After surveying the new situation we telegraphed to Admiral Stoddart as follows:

(Sent 6:20 p.m., 3rd November.)
Defence to proceed with all possible dispatch to join Admiral Cradock
on West Coast of America. Acknowledge.

This telegram was initialled by Admiral Sturdee and Lord Fisher.
We also telegraphed to Admiral Cradock once more reiterating the instructions about the *Canopus:*

(Sent 6:55 p.m., 3rd November.)
Defence has been ordered to join your flag with all dispatch. *Glasgow*
should find or keep in touch with the enemy. You should keep touch with
Glasgow concentrating the rest of your squadron including *Canopus.* It is
important you should effect your junction with *Defence* at earliest possible
moment subject to keeping touch with *Glasgow* and enemy. Enemy sup-
poses you at Corcovados Bay, Acknowledge.

But we were already talking to the void.

When I opened my boxes at 7 o'clock on the morning of November 4, I read
the following telegram:

MACLEAN, VALPARAISO, TO ADMIRALTY.
(Sent November 3, 1914, 6:10 p.m.)

Have just learnt from Chilean Admiral that German Admiral states that on Sunday at sunset, in thick and wicked weather, his ships met *Good Hope, Glasgow, Monmouth,* and *Otranto.* Action was joined, and *Monmouth* turned over and sank after about an hour's fighting.

Good Hope, Glasgow and *Otranto* drew off into darkness.

Good Hope was on fire, an explosion was heard, and she is believed to have sunk.

Gneisenau, Scharnhorst and *Nürnberg* were among the German ships engaged.

The story of what had happened, so far as it ever can be known, is now familiar; it is fully set out in the official history, and need only be summarized here. Arrived on the Chilean coast, having refuelled at a lonely island, and hearing that the British light cruiser *Glasgow* was at Coronel, Admiral von Spee determined to make an attempt to cut her off, and with this intention steamed southward on November 1 with his whole squadron. By good fortune the *Glasgow* left harbour before it was too late. Almost at the same moment, Admiral Cradock began his sweep northward, hoping to catch the *Leipzig,* whose wireless had been heard repeatedly by the *Glasgow.* He was rejoined by the *Glasgow* at half-past two, and the whole squadron proceeded northward abreast about fifteen miles apart. At about half-past four the smoke of several vessels was seen to the northward, and in another quarter of an hour the *Glasgow* was able to identify the *Scharnhorst, Gneisenau* and a German light cruiser. The *Canopus* was nearly 300 miles away. Was there still time to refuse action? Undoubtedly there was. The *Good Hope* and *Monmouth* had normal speeds of 23 knots and 22.4 respectively and could certainly steam 21 knots in company that day. The *Glasgow* could steam over 25. The *Scharnhorst* and *Gneisenau* had nominal speeds of 23.2 and 23.5; but they had been long in southern seas and out of dock. On the knowledge he possessed at that moment Admiral Cradock would have been liberal in allowing them 22 knots. Rough weather would reduce speeds equally on both sides. Had he turned at once and by standing out to sea offered a stern chase to the enemy, he could only be overhauled one knot each hour. When the enemy was sighted by the *Glasgow* at 4:45, the nearest armoured ships were about 20 miles apart. There were scarcely two hours to sundown and less than three to darkness.

But the *Otranto* was a possible complication. She could only steam 18 knots, and against the head sea during the action she did in fact only steam 15 knots. As this weak, slow ship had been for some unexplained reason sent on ahead with the *Glasgow,* she was at the moment of sighting the enemy only 17 miles distant. Assuming that Admiral von Spee could steam 22 knots, less 3 for the head sea, i.e. 19, he would overhaul the *Otranto* 4 knots an hour. On this he might have brought her under long-range fire as darkness closed in. To that extent she reduced the speed of the British squadron and diminished their chances of safety. This may have weighed with Admiral Cradock.

We now know, of course, that in spite of being cumbered with the *Otranto* he could, as it happened, easily and certainly have declined action had he attempted to do so. At the moment of being sighted, Admiral von Spee had only steam for 14 knots, and had to light two more boilers to realize his full speed. Further, his ships were dispersed. To concentrate and gain speed took an hour and a half off the brief daylight during which the British ships would actually have been increasing their distance. Moreover, in the chase and battle of the Falklands the greatest speed ever developed by the *Scharnhorst* and *Gneisenau* did not exceed 20 knots in favourable weather. There is therefore no doubt he could have got away untouched.

But nothing was farther from the mind of Admiral Cradock. He instantly decided to attack. As soon as the *Glasgow* had sighted the enemy, she had turned back towards the flagship, preceded by the *Monmouth* and the *Otranto* all returning at full speed. But Admiral Cradock at 5:10 ordered the squadron to concentrate, not on his flagship the *Good Hope,* the farthest ship from the enemy, but on the *Glasgow,* which though retreating rapidly was still the nearest. At 6:18 he signalled to the distant *Canopus:* "I am now going to attack enemy." The decision to fight sealed his fate, and more than that the fate of the squadron.

To quote the log of the *Glasgow,* "The British Squadron turned to port four points together towards the enemy with a view to closing them and forcing them to action before sunset, which if successful would have put them at a great disadvantage owing to the British Squadron being between the enemy and the sun." The German Admiral easily evaded this manœvre by turning away towards the land and keeping at a range of at least 18,000 yards. Both squadrons were now steaming southward on slightly converging courses—the British to seaward with the setting sun behind them, and the Germans nearer the land. And now began the saddest naval action in the war. Of the officers and men in both the squadrons that faced each other in these stormy seas so far from home, nine out of ten were doomed to perish. The British were to die that night: the Germans a month later. At 7 o'clock the sun sank beneath the horizon, and the German Admiral, no longer dazzled by its rays, opened fire. The British ships were silhouetted against the after-glow, while the Germans were hardly visible against the dark background of the Chilean coast. A complete reversal of advantage had taken place. The sea was high, and the main deck 6-inch guns both of the *Monmouth* and of the *Good Hope* must have been much affected by the dashing spray. The German batteries, all mounted in modern fashion on the upper deck, suffered no corresponding disadvantage from the rough weather. The unequal contest lasted less than an hour. One of the earliest German salvos probably disabled the *Good Hope's* forward 9.2-inch gun, which was not fired throughout the action. Both she and the *Monmouth* were soon on fire. Darkness came on and the sea increased in violence till the *Good Hope,* after a great explosion, became only a glowing speck which was presently extinguished; and the *Monmouth,* absolutely helpless but refusing to surrender, was destroyed by the *Nürnberg,* and foundered, like her consort, with her flag still flying. The *Otranto,* an unarmoured merchantman, quite incapable of taking part in the action, rightly held her distance and disappeared into the gloom. Only the little *Glasgow,* which miraculously escaped fatal damage among the heavy salvos, continued the action until she was left alone in darkness on the stormy seas. There were no survivors from the two British ships: all perished, from Admiral to seaman. The Germans had no loss of life.

Quoth the *Glasgow* in her subsequent report:

> . . . Throughout the engagement the conduct of officers and men was entirely admirable. Perfect discipline and coolness prevailed under trying circumstances of receiving considerable volume of fire without being able to make adequate return. The men behaved exactly as though at battle practice; there were no signs of wild fire, and when the target was invisible the gunlayers ceased firing of their own accord. Spirit of officers and ship's company of *Glasgow* is entirely unimpaired by serious reverse in which they took part, and that the ship may be quickly restored to a condition in which she can take part in further operations against the same enemy is the unanimous wish of us all.

This as it happened they were not to be denied.

We had now to meet the new situation. Our combinations, such as they were, were completely ruptured, and Admiral von Spee, now in temporary command of South American waters, possessed a wide choice of alternatives. He might turn back into the Pacific, and repeat the mystery tactics which had been so baffling to us. He might steam northward up the West Coast of South America and make for the Panama Canal. In this case he would run a chance of being brought to battle by the Anglo-Japanese Squadron which was moving southward. But of course he might not fall in with them, or, if he did, he could avoid battle owing to his superior speed. He might come round to the East Coast and interrupt the main trade route. If he did this he must be prepared to fight Admiral Stoddart; but this would be a very even and hazardous combat. Admiral

Stoddart had against the two armoured German ships three armoured ships, of which the *Defence,* a later and a better ship than either of the Germans, mounted four 9.2-inch and ten 7.5-inch guns, and was one of our most powerful armoured-cruiser class. Lastly, he might cross the Atlantic, possibly raiding the Falkland Islands on his way, and arrive unexpectedly on the South African coast. Here he would find the Union Government's expedition against the German colony in full progress and his arrival would have been most unwelcome. General Botha and General Smuts, having suppressed the rebellion, were about to resume in a critical atmosphere their attack upon German South-West Africa, and a stream of transports would soon be flowing with the expedition and its supplies from Cape Town to Luderitz Bay. Subsequently or alternatively to this intrusion, Admiral von Spee might steam up the African coast and strike at the whole of the shipping of the expedition to the Cameroons, which was quite without means of defending itself against him.

All these unpleasant possibilities had to be faced by us. We had to prepare again at each of many points against a sudden blow; and, great as were our resources, the strain upon them became enormous. The first step was to restore the situation in South American waters. This would certainly take a month. In this grave need my mind immediately turned to wrestling a battle-cruiser from the Grand Fleet which, joined with the *Defence, Carnarvon, Cornwall* and *Kent,* would give Admiral Stoddart an overwhelming superiority.

4/11/14.

Director of Operations Division.

1. How far is it, and how long would it take *Dartmouth* and *Weymouth* to reach Punta Arenas, Rio, or Abrolhos respectively, if they started this afternoon with all dispatch?

2. How long would it take—

(*a*) KENT to reach Rio and Abrolhos?

(*b*) *Australia* (1) without, and (2) with *Montcalm* to reach Galapagos via Makada Islands, and also *Idzumo* and *Newcastle* to reach them?

(*c*) The Japanese 2nd Southern Squadron to replace *Australia* at Fiji?

(*d*) *Defence,* CARNARVON and CORNWALL respectively to reach Punta Arenas?

(*e*) INVINCIBLE to reach Abrolhos, Rio, Punta Arenas?

(*f*) *Hizen* and *Asama* to reach Galapagos or Esquimalt? [1]

W. S. C.

[1] All the ships in small capitals fought eventually in the battle of the Falkland Islands.

But I found Lord Fisher in a bolder mood. He would take two battle-cruisers from the Grand Fleet for the South American station. More than that, and much more questionable, he would take a third—the *Princess Royal*—for Halifax and later for the West Indies in case von Spee came through the Panama Canal. There never was any doubt what ought to be sent. The question was what could be spared. We measured up our strength in Home waters anxiously, observing that the *Tiger* was about to join the 1st Battle-Cruiser Squadron, that the new battleships *Benbow*, *Emperor of India* and *Queen Elizabeth* were practically ready. We sent forthwith the following order to the Commander-in-Chief:

(November 4, 1914, 12:40 p.m.)
Order *Invincible* and *Inflexible* to fill up with coal at once and proceed to Berehaven with all dispatch. They are urgently needed for foreign service. Admiral and Flag-Captain *Invincible* to transfer to *New Zealand*. Captain *New Zealand* to *Invincible*. *Tiger* has been ordered to join you with all dispatch. Give her necessary orders.

Sir John Jellicoe rose to the occasion and parted with his two battle-cruisers without a word. They were ordered to steam by the West Coast to Devonport to fit themselves for their southern voyage. Our plans for the second clutch at von Spee were now conceived as follows[1]:

(1) Should he break across the Pacific, he would be dealt with by the very superior Japanese 1st Southern Squadron, based on Suva to cover Australia and New Zealand, and composed as follows:—*Kurama* (battleship), *Tsukuba* and *Ikoma* (battle-cruisers), *Chikuma* and *Yahagi* (light cruisers). At Suva also were the *Montcalm* and *Encounter*. Another strong Japanese squadron (four ships) was based on the Caroline Islands.

(2) To meet him, should he proceed up the West Coast of South America, an Anglo-Japanese Squadron, comprising *Australia* (from Fiji), *Hizen*, *Idzumo*, *Newcastle*, was to be formed off the North American Coast.

(3) Should he come round on to the East Coast, *Defence*, *Carnarvon*, *Cornwall*, *Kent* were ordered to concentrate off Montevideo, together with *Canopus*, *Glasgow* and *Bristol*, and not seek action till joined by *Invincible* and *Inflexible*, thereafter sending the *Defence* to South Africa.

(4) Should he approach the Cape station, he would be awaited by *Defence* and also *Minotaur* (released from the Australian convoy, after we knew of von Spee's arrival in South American waters), together with the old battleship

---

[1] Here the reader should certainly look at the map on pp. 248–49, which deals directly with this situation.

Albion, and *Weymouth, Dartmouth, Astræa* and *Hyacinth,* light cruisers: the Union Expedition being postponed for 14 days.

(5) Should he come through the Panama Canal, he would meet the *Princess Royal,* as well as the *Berwick* and *Lancaster,* of the West Indian Squadron, and the French *Condé.*

(6) Cameroons were warned to be ready to take their shipping up the river beyond his reach.

(7) Should he endeavour to work homewards across the South Atlantic, he would come into the area of a new squadron under Admiral de Robeck to be formed near the Cape de Verde Islands, comprising the old battleship *Vengeance,* the strong armoured cruisers *Warrior* and *Black Prince* and the *Donegal, Highflyer,* and later *Cumberland.*

Thus to compass the destruction of five warships, only two of which were armoured, it was necessary to employ nearly thirty, including twenty-one armoured ships, the most part of superior metal, and this took no account of the powerful Japanese squadrons, and of French ships or of armed merchant cruisers, the last-named effective for scouting.

I telegraphed to the Japanese Admiralty announcing our new concentration in the South Atlantic against the German Squadron, and proposing the concentration off the North American coast of the *Newcastle, Idzumo, Hizen* and *Australia,* to be joined by the *Asama* after the latter had effected the internment or the destruction of the *Geier.* I proposed that a Japanese squadron should go to Fiji to take the place of the *Australia* in guarding Australia and New Zealand in case the Germans should return. Against the *Emden,* I proposed that the Japanese squadrons not involved in the eastward movement should draw westward to the vicinity of Sumatra and the Dutch East Indies in order to block every exit and deny every place of shelter up to the 90th meridian of east longitude. The Japanese Admiralty's response was general agreement.

Meanwhile it had been necessary to provide, as far as possible, for the safety of the surviving ships of Admiral Cradock's squadron and to move the reinforcing ships. The *Canopus, Glasgow* and *Otranto* were ordered to join the *Defence* off Montevideo; Admiral Stoddart was ordered to take the *Carnarvon* and the *Cornwall* there to absorb this concentration under his flag; the *Kent* was ordered to proceed from Sierra Leone via Abrolhos to join Admiral Stoddart's squadron. The Governor of the Falkland Islands was told to prepare for a possible German cruiser raid. Learning that her continuous fast steaming had led to boiler troubles in the *Canopus,* we had to redirect her to the Falklands. She was instructed to obtain a good berth in Stanley Harbour so that her guns could command the entrance, prepare to defend herself against bombardment, and await orders.

The strain upon British naval resources in the outer seas, apart from the main theatre of naval operations, was now at its maximum and may be partially appreciated from the following approximate enumerations:

Combination against von Spee, 30 ships.

In search of the *Emden* and *Königsberg,* 8 ships.

General protection of trade by vessels other than the above, 40 ships.

Convoy duty in the Indian Ocean, 8 ships.

Blockade of the Turco-German Fleet at the Dardanelles, 3 ships.

Defence of Egypt, 2 ships.

Miscellaneous minor tasks, 11 ships.

Total, 102 ships of all classes.

We literally could not lay our hands on another vessel of any sort or kind which could be made to play any useful part. But we were soon to have relief.

Already on October 30 news had reached us that the *Königsberg* had been discovered hiding in the Rufigi River in German East Africa, and it was instantly possible to mark her down with two ships of equal value and liberate the others. On November 9 far finer news arrived. The reader will remember for what purposes the *Sydney* and *Melbourne* had been attached to the great Australian convoy which was now crossing the Indian Ocean. On the 8th, the *Sydney,* cruising ahead of the convoy, took in a message from the wireless station at Cocos Island that a strange ship was entering the Bay. Thereafter, silence from Cocos Island. Thereupon the large cruiser *Ibuki* increased her speed, displayed the war flag of Japan and demanded permission from the British Officer in command of the convoy to pursue and attack the enemy. But the convoy could not divest itself of this powerful protection, and the coveted task was accorded to the *Sydney.* At 9 o'clock she sighted the *Emden* and the first sea fight in the history of the Australian Navy began. It could have only one ending. In a hundred minutes the *Emden* was stranded, a flaming mass of twisted metal, and the whole of the Indian Ocean was absolutely safe and free.

In consideration of all the harm this ship had done us without offending against humanity or the laws of sea war as we conceived them we telegraphed:

ADMIRALTY TO COMMANDER-IN-CHIEF, CHINA.
November 11, 1914.

Captain, officers and crew of *Emden* appear to be entitled to all the honours of war. Unless you know of any reason to the contrary, Captain and officers should be permitted to retain swords.

These martial courtesies were, however, churlishly repaid.

The clearance of the Indian Ocean liberated all those vessels which had been searching for the *Emden* and the *Königsberg.* Nothing could now harm the

Australian convoy. Most of its escort vanished. The *Emden* and the *Königsberg* were accounted for, and von Spee was on the other side of the globe. The *Minotaur* had already been ordered with all speed to the Cape. All the other vessels went through the Red Sea into the Mediterranean, where their presence was very welcome in view of the impending Turkish invasion of Egypt.

Meanwhile the *Invincible* and *Inflexible* had reached Devonport. We had decided that Admiral Sturdee on vacating the position of Chief of the Staff should hoist his flag in the *Invincible,* should take command on the South American station, and should assume general control of all the operations against von Spee. We were in the highest impatience to get him and his ships away. Once vessels fall into dockyard hands, a hundred needs manifest themselves.

On November 9, when Lord Fisher was in my room, the following message was put on my table:

> The Admiral Superintendent, Devonport, reports that the earliest possible date for completion of *Invincible* and *Inflexible* is midnight 13th November.

I immediately expressed great discontent with the dockyard delays and asked, "Shall I give him a prog?" or words to that effect. Fisher took up the telegram. As soon as he saw it he exclaimed, "Friday the thirteenth. What a day to choose!" I then wrote and signed the following order, which was the direct cause of the Battle of the Falklands.

ADMIRALTY TO C.-IN-C., DEVONPORT

Ships are to sail Wednesday 11th. They are needed for war service and dockyard arrangements must be made to conform. If necessary dockyard men should be sent away in the ships to return as opportunity may offer. You are held responsible for the speedy despatch of these ships in a thoroughly efficient condition. Acknowledge.

W. S. C.

The ships sailed accordingly and in the nick of time. They coaled on November 26 at Abrolhos, where they joined and absorbed Admiral Stoddart's squadron *(Carnarvon, Cornwall, Kent, Glasgow, Bristol* and *Orama)* and dispatched *Defence* to the Cape, and without ever coming in sight of land or using their wireless they reached Port Stanley, Falkland Islands, on the night of December 7. Here they found the *Canopus* in the lagoon, prepared to defend herself and the colony in accordance with the Admiralty instructions. They immediately began to coal.

• • •

After his victory at Coronel, Admiral von Spee comported himself with the dignity of a brave gentleman. He put aside the fervent acclamations of the German colony of Valparaiso, and spoke no word of triumph over the dead. He was under no delusion as to his own danger. He said of the flowers which were presented to him, "They will do for my funeral." Generally, his behaviour would lead us to suppose that the inability of the Germans to pick up any British survivors was not due to want of humanity; and this view has been accepted by the British Navy.

After a few days at Valparaiso he and his ships vanished again into the blue. We do not know what were the reasons which led him to raid the Falkland Islands, nor what his further plans would have been in the event of success. Presumably he hoped to destroy this unfortified British coaling base and so make his own position in South American waters less precarious. At any rate, at noon on December 6 he set off to the eastward from the Straits of Magellan with his five ships; and about 8 o'clock on December 8 his leading ship (the *Gneisenau*) was in sight of the main harbour of the Falklands. A few minutes later a terrible apparition broke upon German eyes. Rising from behind the promontory, sharply visible in the clear air, were a pair of tripod masts. One glance was enough. They meant certain death.[1] The day was beautifully fine and from the tops the horizon extended thirty or forty miles in every direction. There was no hope for victory. There was no chance of escape. A month before, another Admiral and his sailors had suffered a similar experience.

At 5 o'clock that afternoon I was working in my room at the Admiralty when Admiral Oliver entered with the following telegram. It was from the Governor of the Falkland Islands and ran as follows:

Admiral Spee arrived at daylight this morning with all his ships and is now in action with Admiral Sturdee's whole fleet, *which was coaling*.

We had had so many unpleasant surprises that these last words sent a shiver up my spine. Had we been taken by surprise and, in spite of all our superiority, mauled, unready, at anchor? "Can it mean that?" I said to the Chief of the Staff. "I hope not," was all he said. I could see that my suggestion, though I hardly meant it seriously, had disquieted him. Two hours later, however, the door opened again, and this time the countenance of the stern and sombre Oliver

---

[1] Only Dreadnoughts had tripods.

Cypher A

435

Admiralty to C in C
Devonport.

Ships are to sail Wednesday 11th. They are needed for war service and dockyard arrangements must be made to conform. If necessary dockyard men should be sent away in the ships to return as opportunity may offer. You are held responsible for the speedy despatch of these ships in a thoroughly efficient condition.

Acknowledge.

WSC
9.11.

1L
1SL
DYB
DC (for DOD)

6 cables

COPIED.

(Sent ~~Devonport~~)
12 5 a.m. 10/11

wore something which closely resembled a grin. "It's all right, sir; they are all at the bottom." And with one exception so they were.

When the leading German ships were sighted far away on the distant horizon, Admiral Sturdee and his squadron were indeed coaling. From the intelligence he had received he had convinced himself that the Germans were at Valparaiso, and he intended to sail the next day in the hope of doubling the Horn before the enemy could do so. More than two hours passed after the enemy first came in sight before he could raise steam and get under way. The first shots were fired by the 12-inch guns of the *Canopus* from her stationary position on the mud-banks of the inner harbour. The *Gneisenau* had continued to approach until she saw the fatal tripods, whereupon she immediately turned round and, followed by one of her light cruisers, made off at full speed to join her main body. In a few moments the whole of the German Squadron was steaming off in a west-erly direction with all possible speed. At 10 o'clock, the *Kent, Carnarvon* and *Glasgow* having already sailed, Admiral Sturdee came out of the harbour in the *Invincible,* followed by the *Inflexible* and *Cornwall;* while the light cruisers, one of whom (the *Bristol*) had her engines actually opened up, hurried on after as fast as possible.

The whole five ships of the German Squadron were now visible, hull down on the horizon about fifteen miles away. The order was given for general chase, but later on, having the day before him, the Admiral regulated the speeds, the battle cruisers maintaining only about 20 knots. This, however, was quite suffi-cient to overhaul the Germans, who after their long sojourn in the Pacific with-out docking were not able to steam more than 18 knots in company. Even so, the *Leipzig* began to lag behind, and shortly before 1 o'clock, the *Inflexible* opened fire upon her at 16,000 yards. Confronted with having his ships de-voured one by one, von Spee took a decision which was certainly in accor-dance with the best traditions of the sea. Signalling to his light cruisers to make their escape to the South American coast, he turned with the *Scharnhorst* and *Gneisenau* to face his pursuers. The action which followed was on the British side uneventful. The German Admiral endeavoured more than once to close to ranges at which his powerful secondary armament of 5.9's could play their part. The British held off just far enough to make this fire ineffective, and pounded their enemy with their 12-inch guns. At this long range, however, it took a con-siderable time and much ammunition to achieve the destruction of the German cruisers. The *Scharnhorst,* with the Admiral and all hands, sank at 4:17 p.m., her last signal to her consort being to save herself. *Gneisenau* continued to fight against hopeless odds with the utmost fortitude until about 6 o'clock when, being in a completely disabled condition, she opened her sea-cocks and van-ished, with her flag still flying, beneath the icy waters of the ocean. The British

CORONEL AND THE FALKLANDS.

SHIPS DIRECTLY INVOLVED.

Approximate Figure of Comparative Power.	Name.	Effective Speed: Knots.	Guns.
BATTLE CRUISERS.			
5	INVINCIBLE	24	8 12-inch
5	INFLEXIBLE	24	8 12-inch
BATTLESHIP.			
4	CANOPUS...	15½	4 12-inch, 12 6-inch
CRUISERS.			
3	DEFENCE...	22	4 9·2-inch, 10 7·5-inch
2	GOOD HOPE	21½	2 9·2-inch, 16 6-inch
1½	CARNARVON	21	4 7·5-inch, 6 6-inch
1	MONMOUTH	21	14 6-inch
1	KENT	21½	14 6-inch
1	CORNWALL	21	14 6-inch
LIGHT CRUISERS.			
	GLASGOW	24	2 6-inch, 10 4-inch
	BRISTOL ...	24	2 6-inch, 10 4-inch
ARMED MERCHANT SHIPS.			
	MACEDONIA	17	
	OTRANTO ...	16	4 4·7-inch

Approximate Figure of Comparative Power.	Name.	Effective Speed: Knots.	Guns.
CRUISERS.			
2¼	SCHARNHORST	22	8 8·2-inch, 6 5·9-inch
2¼	GNEISENAU	22	8 8·2-inch, 6 5·9-inch
LIGHT CRUISERS.			
	LEIPZIG ...	21	10 4·1-inch
	NURNBERG	22	10 4·1-inch
	DRESDEN	22	10 4·1-inch

NOTE:—The figures of comparative value are only intended to enable the reader to follow the account. As broad classifications they are true, but they can only be taken as approximate.

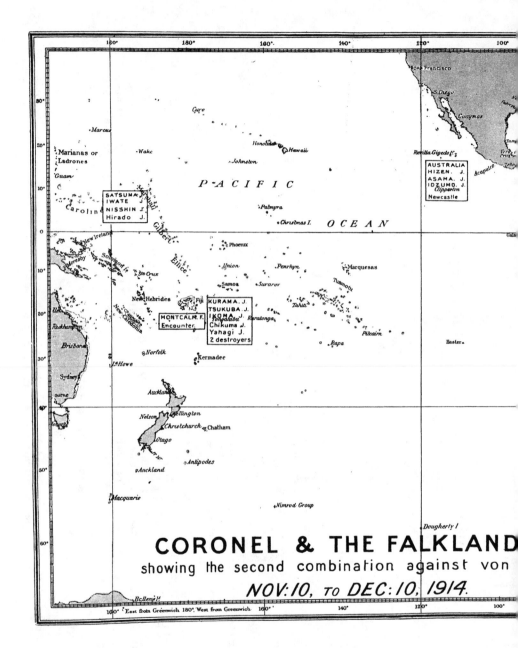

S.San Francisco

30°

S.Diego

Gure

Guaymas

20°   Marcus

Honolulu

Hawaii

Marianas or
Ladrones

Wake

Johnston

Revilla Gigedo I?

Vera
Cruz

Guam

Acapulco

10°

AUSTRALIA
HIZEN. J.
ASAMA. J.
IDZUMO. J.
Clipperton
Newcastle

SATSUMA
IWATE
NISSHIN
Hirado

P·ACIFIC

Carolin

Palmyra

0°

Christmas I.   OCEAN

Gala

New Ireland

Phoenix

Moresby

Solomon Is

10°   Sta Cruz

Union

Penrhyn

Marquesas

Samoa

Suvarov

Tuamotu

New Hebrides

Fiji

KURAMA. J.
TSUKUBA. J.
IKOMA. J.
Chikuma J.
Yahagi J.
2 destroyers

Tahiti

20°   New Caledonia

MONTCALM. F.
Encounter.

Rarotonga

Ua

Rockhampton

Rapa

Pitcairn

Brisbane

Norfolk

Kermadec

Easter

30°   Ld Howe

Sydney

ourne

Auckland

40°

Nelson   Wellington

Christchurch   Chatham

Otago

50°   Auckland

Antipodes

Macquarie

Nimrod Group

Dougherty I

60°

CORONEL & THE FALKLAND

showing the second combination against von

NOV: 10, TO DEC: 10, 1914.

Balleny I?

ships rushing to the spot and lowering every available boat were able only to save 200 Germans, many of whom died the next day from the shock of the cold water. When both the *Scharnhorst* and *Gneisenau* had sunk, the *Inflexible* had only thirty and the *Invincible* only twenty-two rounds left for each of their 12-inch guns.

Meanwhile, the other British cruisers had each selected one of the flying German light vessels, and a series of chases ensued. The *Kent* (Captain Allen) overtook and sunk the *Nürnberg* by an effort of steaming which surpassed all previous records and even, it is stated, her designed speed. The *Nürnberg* refused to surrender, and as she foundered by the head, the victors could see a group of men on her uplifted stern waving to the last the German flag. The *Leipzig* was finished off by the *Glasgow* and the *Cornwall.* The *Dresden* alone for the time made good her escape. She was hunted down and destroyed three months later in the roadstead of Mas-a-Fuera.

Thus came to an end the German cruiser warfare in the outer seas. With the exception of the *Karlsruhe,* of which nothing had been heard for some time and which we now know was sunk by an internal explosion on November 4, and the *Dresden* soon to be hunted down, no German ships of war remained on any of the oceans of the world. It had taken four months from the beginning of the war to achieve this result. Its consequences were far-reaching, and affected simultaneously our position in every part of the globe. The strain was everywhere relaxed. All our enterprises, whether of war or commerce, proceeded in every theatre without the slightest hindrance. Within twenty-four hours orders were sent to a score of British ships to return to Home waters. For the first time we saw ourselves possessed of immense surpluses of ships of certain classes, of trained men and of naval supplies of all kinds, and were in a position to use them to the best advantage. The public, though gratified by the annihilating character of the victory, was quite unconscious of its immense importance to the whole naval situation.

CHAPTER XVI

THE BOMBARDMENT OF SCARBOROUGH AND HARTLEPOOL

Our Intelligence service has won and deserved world-wide fame. More than perhaps any other Power, we were successful in the war in penetrating the intentions of the enemy. Again and again the forecasts both of the military and of the Naval Intelligence Staffs were vindicated to the wonder of friends and the chagrin of foes. The three successive chiefs of the Naval Intelligence Division, Captain Thomas Jackson, Rear-Admiral Oliver, and lastly, Captain Reginald Hall, were all men of mark in the service, and continuously built and extended an efficient and profound organization. There were others—a brilliant confederacy—whose names even now are better wrapt in mystery. Our information about German naval movements was principally obtained (1) from the reports of secret agents in neutral and enemy countries and particularly in Germany, (2) from the reports of our submarines, which lay far up in the Heligoland Bight in perilous vigilance, and (3) from a special study we had made of the German wireless. In this we were for a time aided by great good luck.

At the beginning of September, 1914, the German light cruiser *Magdeburg* was wrecked in the Baltic. The body of a drowned German under-officer was picked up by the Russians a few hours later, and clasped in his bosom by arms rigid in death, were the cypher and signal books of the German Navy and the minutely squared maps of the North Sea and Heligoland Bight. On September 6 the Russian Naval Attaché came to see me. He had received a message from Petrograd telling him what had happened, and that the Russian Admiralty with the aid of the cypher and signal books had been able to decode portions at least of the German naval messages. The Russians felt that as the leading naval Power, the British Admiralty ought to have these books and charts. If we would send a vessel to Alexandrov, the Russian officers in charge of the books would bring them to England. We lost no time in sending a ship, and late on an October afternoon Prince Louis and I received from the hands of our loyal allies these sea-stained priceless documents. We set on foot at once an organization for the study of the German wireless and for the translating of the messages when taken in. At the head of the organization was placed Sir Alfred Ewing, the Director of Naval Education, whose services to the Admiralty in this and other matters were of the first order. The work was of great complexity, as of course the cypher is only one element in the means of preserving the secrecy of a message. But gradually during the beginning of November our officers succeeded in translating intelligible portions of various German naval messages. They were mostly of a routine character. "One of our torpedo boats will be running out into square 7T at 8 p.m.," etc. But a careful collection of these scraps provided a body of information from which the enemy's arrangements in the Heligoland Bight could be understood with a fair degree of accuracy. The Germans, however, repeatedly changed their codes and keys and it was only occasionally and for fitful periods that we were able to penetrate them. As the war went on they became increasingly suspicious and devised measures which were completely baffling. While, however, this source of information lasted, it was obviously of the very greatest value.

The German official history shows itself at last well-informed upon this subject (p. 194): "Even if doubt were to exist that the British Admiralty were in possession of the whole secret cyphering system of the German Fleet, it has been cleared away by the reliable news from Petrograd, that after the stranding of the *Magdeburg* off Odensholm the secret papers of that ship, which had been thrown overboard, were picked up by the Russians and communicated to their Allies."

Lastly, largely through the foresight of Admiral Oliver, we had begun setting up directional stations in August, 1914. We thus carried to an unrivalled and indeed unapproached degree of perfection our means of fixing the position and, by successive positions, the course of any enemy ship that used its wireless installation.

"The English," says Scheer (p. 73), "received news through their 'directional stations' which they already had in use, but which were only introduced by us at a much later period. . . . In possessing them the English had a very great advantage in the conduct of the war, as they were thus able to obtain quite accurate information of the locality of the enemy as soon as any wireless signals were sent by him. In the case of a large fleet, whose separate units are stationed far apart and communication between them is essential, an absolute cessation of all wireless intercourse would be fatal to any enterprise."

But between collecting and weighing information, and drawing the true moral therefrom, there is very often an unbridged gap. Signals have been made, the wireless note of a particular ship is heard, lights are to be shown on certain channels at certain hours, ships are in movement, sweeping vessels are active, channels are buoyed, lock-gates are opened—what does it all mean? At first sight it all appears to be only ordinary routine. Yet taking the items together may lead to a tremendous revelation. Suffice it to say that all these indications, from whatever sources they emanated, were the subject of a special study by Sir

Arthur Wilson, and he had the solemn duty of advising our War Group upon them.

The silence of the North Sea remained unbroken until the afternoon of Monday, December 14. At about 7 o'clock Sir Arthur Wilson came to my room and asked for an immediate meeting with the First Sea Lord and the Chief of the Staff. It took only a few minutes to gather them. He then explained that his examination of the available intelligence about the enemy indicated the probability of an impending movement which would involve their battle-cruisers and perhaps—though of this there was no positive evidence—have an offensive character against our coasts. The German High Sea Fleet, he stated definitely, appeared not to be involved. The indications were obscure and uncertain. There were gaps in the argument. But the conclusion reached after hearing Sir Arthur Wilson was that we should act as if we knew that our assumptions and suppositions were true. It was decided not to move the whole Grand Fleet. A great deal of cruising had been imposed on the Fleet owing to the unprotected state of Scapa, and it was desirable to save wear and tear of machinery and condensers as much as possible. Moreover, the risks of accident, submarine and mine, which were incurred every time that immense organization was sent to sea, imposed a certain deterrent upon its use except when clearly necessary.

This decision, from which the Commander-in-Chief did not dissent, was, in the light of subsequent events, much to be regretted. But it must be remembered that the information on which the Admiralty was acting, had never yet been tested; that it seemed highly speculative in character, and that for whatever it was worth, it excluded the presence at sea of the German High Sea Fleet. Orders were therefore given immediately for the battle-cruisers and the 2nd Battle Squadron, with a light cruiser squadron and a flotilla of destroyers, to raise steam and to proceed to sea at such hours and at such speeds as to enable them to be in an intercepting position at daylight the next morning. Orders were sent to Commodore Tyrwhitt's Harwich Force to be at sea off Yarmouth, and to Commodore Keyes to place our eight available oversea submarines in a position off Terschelling to guard against a southward raid. The coastal forces were also put upon the alert.[1]

ADMIRALTY TO COMMANDER-IN-CHIEF.

December 14, 1914. Sent 9:30 p.m.

Good information just received shows German 1st Cruiser Squadron with Destroyers leave Jade River on Tuesday morning early and return on Wednesday night. It is apparent from the information that the Battleships are very unlikely to come out.

[1] See map on pp. 268–69.

The enemy force will have time to reach our coast.

Send at once leaving to-night the Battle Cruiser Squadron and Light Cruiser Squadron supported by a Battle Squadron preferably the Second.

At daylight on Wednesday morning they should be at some point where they can make sure of intercepting the enemy on his return.

Tyrwhitt with his Light Cruisers and Destroyers will try to get in touch with enemy off British coast and shadow him keeping Admiral informed.

From our information the German 1st Cruiser Squadron consists of 4 Battle-Cruisers and 5 Light Cruisers and there will possibly be three flotillas of Destroyers.

Acknowledge.

ADMIRALTY TO COMMODORE 'T' HARWICH.

December 15, 1914. Sent 2:5 p.m.

There is good probability of German Battle-Cruisers, Cruisers and Destroyers being off our coast to-morrow about daybreak.

One M Class Destroyer is to patrol vicinity of North Hinder Lightship from midnight until 9 a.m. A second M Class Destroyer is to patrol a line extending 15 miles south magnetic from a position lat. 53° 0′ N., long. 3° 5′ E. from midnight until 9 a.m.

The duty of these Destroyers is to look out for and report the enemy and trust to their speed to escape.

If the weather is too bad, they are to return to Harwich. Report their names.

The 1st and 3rd Flotillas with all available Light Cruisers are to be under way off Yarmouth before daylight to-morrow ready to move to any place where the enemy may be reported from, whether it is to the northward or southward.

Their duty is to get touch with the enemy, follow him and report his position to the Vice-Admiral 2nd Battle Squadron and Vice-Admiral 1st Battle Cruiser Squadron.

The 2nd Battle Squadron, 1st Battle Cruiser Squadron, 3rd Cruiser Squadron and Light Cruiser Squadron will be in a position in N. lat. 54° 10′ E. long. 3° 0′ at 7:30 a.m. ready to cut off retreat of enemy.

Should an engagement result your Flotillas and Light Cruisers must endeavour to join our Fleet and deal with enemy Destroyers.

If the weather is too bad for Destroyers use Light Cruisers only and send Destroyers back. Acknowledge.

All measures having been taken on the chance of their being necessary, we awaited during thirty-six hours the events of Wednesday morning with a doubting but expectant curiosity. On the morning of December 16 at about half-past eight I was in my bath, when the door opened and an officer came hurrying in from the War Room with a naval signal which I grasped with dripping hand. "German battle-cruisers bombarding Hartlepool." I jumped out of the bath with exclamations. Sympathy for Hartlepool was mingled with what Mr. George Wyndham once called "the anodyne of contemplated retaliation." Pulling on clothes over a damp body, I ran downstairs to the War Room. The First Sea Lord had just arrived from his house next door. Oliver, who invariably slept in the War Room and hardly ever left it by day, was marking the positions on the map. Telegrams from all the naval stations along the coast affected by the attack, and intercepts from our ships in the vicinity speaking to each other, came pouring in two and three to the minute. The Admiralty also spread the tidings and kept the Fleets and flotillas continuously informed of all we knew.

Everything was now sent to sea or set in motion. The 3rd Battle Squadron (*King Edwards*) from the Forth was ordered to prevent the enemy escaping to the Northward. As a further precaution (though, unless the Germans were driven far to the North, this could hardly be effective in time), the Grand Fleet itself was after all brought out. Commodore Tyrwhitt and his cruisers and destroyers of the Harwich Striking Force were directed to join Sir George Warrender, who commanded the Second Battle Squadron, and was the senior Admiral with the intercepting force. The weather was, however, too rough for the destroyers, and only the light cruisers could proceed. Lastly, later in the day Commodore Keyes, who was in the *Lurcher*—one of our latest destroyers and had also with him the destroyer *Firedrake*—was told to take his submarines from his preliminary station off Terschelling into the Heligoland Bight and try to catch the enemy returning.

The bombardment of open towns was still new to us at that time. But, after all, what did that matter now? (The war map showed the German battle-cruisers identified one by one within gunshot of the Yorkshire coast, while 150 miles to eastward *between them and Germany*, cutting mathematically their line of retreat, steamed in the exact positions intended, four British battle-cruisers and six of the most powerful battleships in the world forming the 2nd Battle Squadron. Attended and preceded by their cruiser squadrons and flotilla, this fleet of our newest and fastest ships all armed with the heaviest gun then afloat, could in fair weather cover and watch effectively a front of nearly 100 miles. In the positions in which dawn revealed the antagonists, only one thing could enable the Germans to escape annihilation at the hands of an overwhelmingly superior force. And while the great shells crashed into the little houses of Hartlepool and Scarborough, carrying their cruel message of pain and destruction to unsuspecting English homes, only one anxiety dominated the thoughts of the Admiralty War Room.

The word "Visibility" assumed a sinister significance. At present it was quite good enough. Both Warrender and Beatty had horizons of nearly ten miles: near the coast fighting was actually in progress at 7,000 yards. There was nothing untoward in the weather indications. At 9 a.m. the German bombardment ceased, and their ships were soon out of sight of land, no doubt on their home-ward voyage. We went on tenter-hooks to breakfast. To have this tremendous prize—the German battle-cruiser squadron whose loss would fatally mutilate the whole German Navy and could never be repaired—actually within our claws, and to have the event all turn upon a veil of mist, was a racking ordeal. Meanwhile telegraph and telephone were pouring the distress of Hartlepool and Scarborough to all parts of the Kingdom, and by half-past ten, when the War Committee of the Cabinet met, news magnified by rumour had produced excite-ment. I was immediately asked how such a thing was possible. "What was the Navy doing, and what were they going to do?" In reply I produced the chart which showed the respective positions at the moment of the British and Ger-man naval forces, and I explained that subject to moderate visibility we hoped that collision would take place about noon. These disclosures fell upon all with a sense of awe, and the Committee adjourned till the afternoon.

At 10:30 the Admiralty learned that the enemy was leaving our coasts and apprised Admiral Warrender accordingly.

> Enemy is probably returning towards Heligoland. You should keep
> him outside minefield and steer so as to cut him off.

But now already ominous telegrams began to arrive. Warrender soon had horizons of only 7,000 yards; Beatty of only 6,000; some of the light cruisers nearer to the coast already mentioned 5,000; and later on 4,000 was signalled. Meanwhile no contact. Noon passed, and then 1 o'clock. The weather got steadily worse. It was evident that the mist curtains were falling over the North Sea. 3,000 yards visibility, 2,000 yards visibility were reported by ships speaking to each other. The solemn faces of Fisher and Wilson betrayed no emotion, but one felt the fire burning within. I tried to do other work, but it was not much good. Obscure messages were heard from our Fleet. Evidently they were very close to the enemy, groping for him in a mist which allowed vessels to be dis-tinguished only within 2,000 yards. We heard Warrender order his priceless ships to steam through the located German minefield off the Yorkshire coast apparently in an endeavour to close with something just out of sight, just be-yond his finger-tips. Then all of a sudden we heard Rear-Admiral Goodenough with the light cruisers report that he had opened fire upon a German light cruiser at 3,000 yards. Hope flared up. Once contact was established, would it not drag all other events in its train? The prospect of a confused battle at close range had no terrors for the Admiralty. They had only one fear—lest the enemy should escape. Even the proposed movement of the 2nd Battle Squadron through the minefield was received in utter silence.

About half-past one Sir Arthur Wilson said, "They seem to be getting away from us." But now occurred a new development of a formidable kind. At 1:50 we learned that the High Sea Fleet was at sea. Up till noon this great Fleet had not spoken. Once she had spoken and the necessary calculations had been made, which took some time, we could both recognize and locate her. She had already in fact advanced far into the North Sea. The apparition of the German Fleet, which as we then supposed was advancing to the support of the German battle-cruisers, entirely altered the balance of strength. Our ten great ships steaming together with their light squadrons and flotillas, were not only the strongest but the fastest naval force in the world. No equal German force existed which could at once overtake and overcome them. On the other hand, they were not capable of meeting the High Sea Fleet. The German battle-cruisers were still separated from their fleet by 150 miles, but it seemed to us that a running action begun with the German battle-cruisers, might in the thick weather then prevailing conceivably lead to a surprise encounter with the main naval power of the enemy. This was certainly not the wish of the Admiralty. We instantly warned our squadrons.

ADMIRALTY TO 2ND BATTLE SQUADRON AND
1ST BATTLE CRUISER SQUADRON.

Sent 1:50 p.m.

(Urgent.)

High Sea Fleet is out and was in latitude 54° 38′ N. longitude 5° 55′ E.[1] at 0:30 p.m. to-day, so do not go too far to Eastward.

These sinister possibilities soon faded like our earlier hopes. The High Sea Fleet was not, as we imagined, coming out, but had long been out and was now retiring.

At 3 o'clock I went over and told the War Committee what was passing; but with what a heavy heart did I cross again that Horse Guards Parade. I returned to the Admiralty. The War Group had reassembled around the octagonal table in my room. The shades of a winter's evening had already fallen. Sir Arthur Wilson then said, in his most ordinary manner, "Well, there you are, they have got away. They must be about here by now," and he pointed to the

---

[1] i.e., about 80 miles West of Heligoland.

chart on which the Chief of the Staff was marking the positions every fifteen minutes. It was evident that the Germans had eluded our intercepting force, and that even their light cruisers with whom we had been in contact had also escaped in the mist. Said Admiral Warrender in his subsequent report, "They came out of one rainstorm and disappeared in another."

It was now nearly 8 o'clock.

Was it then all over? I inquired about our submarines. They had already been collected by Commodore Keyes from their first position and were now moving on to the German line of retreat. But whether the enemy's course would come within their limited range was a matter of luck. Sir Arthur Wilson then said, "There is only one chance now. Keyes with the *Lurcher* and *Firedrake,* is with the submarines. He could probably make certain of attacking the German battle-cruiser squadron as it enters the Bight to-night. He may torpedo one or even two." It seemed indeed a forlorn hope to send these two frail destroyers, with their brave Commodore and faithful crews, far from home, close to the enemy's coast, utterly unsupported, into the jaws of this powerful German force with its protecting vessels and flotillas. There was a long silence. We all knew Keyes well. Then someone said, "It is sending him to his death." Someone else said, "He would be the last man to wish us to consider that." There was another long pause. However, Sir Arthur Wilson had already written the following message:

8:12 p.m.

We think Heligoland and Amrun lights will be lit when ships are going in. Your destroyers might get a chance to attack about 2 a.m. or later on the line given you.

The First Sea Lord nodded assent. The Chief of the Staff took it, got up heavily and quitted the room. Then we turned to the ordinary business of the day and also to the decision of what could be told to the public about the event.

Two days later when I received Admiral Keyes in my room at the Admiralty, I said, "We sent you a terrible message the other night. I hardly expected to see you again." "It *was* terrible," he said, "not getting it till I was nearly home. I waited three hours in the hopes of such an order, and I very nearly did it on my own responsibility," and he proceeded to reproach himself without need.[1]

---

[1] It must be explained that in these days the wireless communication with destroyers and still more submarines was not as perfect as it became later on. The *Firedrake* had therefore been stationed in the morning midway between the submarines and Harwich to pass on messages. She had late in the afternoon, after the orders to take the submarines into the Bight had reached her, rejoined Commodore Keyes and the link was, for the time being, broken.

* * *

So far I have described this episode of December 16 exactly as it appeared from the War Room of the Admiralty, and as we understood it at the time. But let us now see in essentials what had happened.[1] No one could tell at what point on our shores the German attack would fall; and with 500 miles of coast studded with possible objectives to guard, there could be no certain solution. The orders issued by the Commander-in-Chief, however, and the dawn position selected, ably comprehended the design of the enemy. In pursuance of these orders the 2nd Battle Squadron (6 ships) and the Battle Cruiser Squadron (4 ships), together with the 3rd Cruiser Squadron, a Squadron of Light Cruisers and a flotilla, steaming down from Scapa, Cromarty and the Forth, arrived at about 5:30 in the morning of the 16th, two hours and a half before daybreak, at the Southern edge of the Dogger Bank. Here in the very centre of the North Sea, almost on a line drawn from Hartlepool to Heligoland, the advanced screen of British destroyers became engaged with German destroyers and light cruisers, and when daylight came they sighted a large German cruiser identified as the *Roon*. Fighting ensued, some of our destroyers were hit, and the Germans retreated to the Eastward. Thereupon Admiral Beatty with his battle-cruisers began to chase the *Roon*. From this pursuit he was recalled by the news which reached him and Admiral Warrender from the Admiralty about 9 a.m., that the German battle-cruisers were bombarding Hartlepool and later Scarborough. All the British ships at once turned to the Westward and steamed abreast in a long line towards the British coast and the German battle-cruisers, whose interception appeared highly probable.

During the war we were puzzled to understand what the *Roon* and the German light forces were doing on the edge of the Dogger Bank at this hour in the morning. It was an ill-assorted force to be in so exposed a position, and it was not a force, or in a position, which could be of any help to the German cruisers raiding the British coasts. Now we know the answer. The *Roon* and her cruisers and destroyers were part of the advanced screen of the German High Sea Fleet who were out in full force, three squadrons strong, with all their attendant vessels and numerous flotillas. Admiral von Ingenohl in command of the High Sea Fleet had sailed from Cuxhaven after darkness had fallen on the evening of the 15th (between 4 and 5 p.m.) and before dawn on the 16th was pushing boldly out towards the Dogger Bank in support of his battle-cruisers who, under Admiral von Hipper, were already approaching the British shores. Had von

---

[1] The whole of this operation is described in minute detail in the official British Naval History, and should be studied with the excellent charts by those who are interested in its technical aspect. So complicated is the full story that the lay reader cannot see the wood for the trees. I have endeavoured to render intelligible the broad effects.—W. S. C.

Ingenohl continued on his course, as was his intention, his scouts would be-tween 8 and 9 o'clock, in the clear weather of that morning in this part of the North Sea, have come in sight of the British battle-cruisers and the 2nd Battle Squadron coming down from the North. A meeting was almost certain. What would have happened? Admiral von Tirpitz proclaims that this was the one heaven-sent never-recurring opportunity for a battle with the odds enormously in German favour. "On December 16," he wrote a few weeks later, "Ingenohl had the fate of Germany in the palm of his hand. I boil with inward emotion whenever I think of it." We will examine this claim later. Let us first follow the event.

Admiral von Ingenohl had already strained his instructions by going so far to sea. An appeal by him against the "Muzzling Order," which the Emperor had issued after the action of the Heligoland Bight (August 28), had recently encountered a rebuff. "The Fleet must be held back and avoid actions which might lead to heavy losses." Such had been the latest *ukase*. And here was the Fleet right out in the middle of the North Sea in the darkness of a December dawn. Suddenly the flashes of guns, English destroyers reported in action with the cruisers of his screen, the screen retiring, the destroyers pursuing—and still two hours before daylight. Von Ingenohl conceived himself in danger of a tor-pedo attack in darkness. At about 5:30 therefore he turned his whole Fleet about and steamed off South-Eastward, and shortly after 6 o'clock, increasingly disquieted by his hampering instructions, but knowing no more of the presence of our squadrons than they of him, he, in the justly chosen words of the British official historian, "fairly turned tail and made for home, leaving his raiding force in the air." Even so, at 6 o'clock the two Fleets were only about 50 miles apart and their light forces in contact! Says Scheer, who was in command of the German Second Squadron (p. 71), "Our premature turning on to an East-South-East course had robbed us of the opportunity of meeting certain divi-sions of the enemy according to the prearranged plan, which is now seen to have been correct."

There was, however, no compulsion upon Admirals Warrender and Beatty to fight such an action. Their squadrons were moving properly protected by their screen of cruisers and destroyers. In this part of the sea and at this hour the weather was quite clear. They would have known what forces they were in presence of, before they could become seriously engaged. There would not have been any justification for trying to fight the High Sea Fleet of twenty battle-ships, with six battleships and four battle-cruisers, even though these comprised our most powerful vessels. Nor was there any need. The British 2nd Battle Squadron could steam in company at 20 knots, or could escape with Forced Draught at 21, and only six of von Ingenohl's ships could equal that speed. As for the battle-cruisers, nothing could catch them. The safety of this force acting detached from the main British Fleet was inherent in its speed. Admirals War-render and Beatty could therefore have refused battle with the German Fleet, and it would certainly have been their duty to do so. Still, having regard to the large numbers of destroyers at sea with the German Fleet and the chances of darkness and weather, the situation at this juncture, as we now know it to have been, gives cause for profound reflection. That it never materialized un-favourably was the reward of previous audacity. The sixteenth of December lay under the safe-guard of the twenty-eighth of August.

We now enter upon the second phase of this extraordinary day. All four British squadrons with their flotilla between 9 and 10 o'clock were steaming to-wards the British coasts. The German raiding cruisers, having finished their bombardments, were now seeking to return home with the utmost speed. There were two large minefields which had been laid earlier in the war by the Germans off the Yorkshire coast, and we, having located them and considering them as a protection against raiding, had improved them by laying additional mines. Between these minefields there was opposite Whitby and Scarborough a gap about fifteen miles wide. Sir John Jellicoe, reflecting upon the whole posi-tion from the *Iron Duke* from afar, formed the opinion that the enemy would either try to escape to the Northward by steaming up our coast inside the mine-field or, much more probably, would come straight out Eastward through the gap opposite Whitby and Scarborough. He had ordered the 3rd Battle Squadron from the Forth to close the gap to the Northward and this was rap-idly being effected. At 10:10 he signalled to Sir George Warrender telling him the position of the gap in the minefields opposite Whitby and adding, "Enemy will in all probability come out there." Admirals Warrender and Beatty were al-ready proceeding on this assumption, which in fact correctly divined what the Germans were doing.

At 11 o'clock, therefore, the four German battle-cruisers, with their light cruisers returning independently 60 miles ahead of them, were steaming due East for Heligoland at their highest speed. At the same time all our four squadrons were steaming due West in a broad sweep directly towards them. The distance between the fleets was about 100 miles, and they were approach-ing each other at an aggregate speed of over 40 miles an hour. Across the course of our fleet lay the South-West patch of the Dogger Bank on which there was not enough water for battle-cruisers, either British or German. The British sweeping line therefore divided—Beatty and the light cruisers going North of the patch, Warrender with the battleships and the 3rd Cruiser Squadron going South of it. This involved a certain detour and delay in our advance. The weather, moreover, became very bad. The mist descended and the sea ran high. The German light cruisers were now sighted by our Light Cruiser Squadron scouting ahead of Beatty through the driving mist and rainstorms. The

Southampton, the most Southerly light cruiser, opened fire and was answered by the enemy. Hopes on board the *Lion* rose. Just at the place and just at the moment when they might expect it, was the enemy's cruiser screen. Clearly the main body was behind them: probably it was not far behind. But now Mischance intervened.

The other three British light cruisers, seeing the *Southampton* engaged to the Southward, turned in that direction to join in the fight and the *Birmingham* opened fire. This was not in accordance with the wishes of Admiral Beatty, who wished to keep his scouts in front of him at the time when he must expect to be closely approaching the enemy's battle-cruisers, and when the danger of missing them was so great. He therefore ordered his light cruisers to return to their stations. The signal, instead of being directed by name to the two vessels who were not engaged, was made general to the Light Cruiser Squadron, and acting on this order the *Southampton* and *Birmingham* both broke off their action with the German cruiser and resumed their places in the line. The German light cruisers turned off to the Southward and vanished in the mist. Contact with them was thus lost.

Meanwhile, however, the battle-cruisers on both sides continued rapidly to approach each other. At 12:15 Admiral von Hipper warned by his light cruisers that an enemy force was immediately in front of him, also turned slightly and to the South-East. Admiral Beatty continued on his course till 12:30. At this moment the two battle-cruiser forces were only 25 miles apart and still rapidly closing.[1] But now again Mischance! The German light cruisers, deflected away to the Southward from Beatty, came into contact with the 3rd Cruiser Squadron in front of Warrender. Fire again was opened and returned, and again the enemy cruisers were lost in the thick mist. They reported to von Hipper that on this path also was a blocking force. Thereupon at 12:45 he made "a three-quarters left about turn" (if I may employ a cavalry term), and dodged off due North. This by itself would not have saved him. Had Admiral Beatty held on his original course for another quarter of an hour, an action at decisive ranges must have begun before 1 o'clock. But observe what had happened.

At 12:30 Admiral Beatty had received a signal from Sir George Warrender at the moment of the second contact with the German light cruisers, "Enemy cruisers and destroyers in sight." He therefore concluded that the German battle-cruisers had slipped past him to the Southward, and acting in addition on the sound principle of keeping between the enemy and the enemy's home at all costs, he too whipped round and steamed back on his course, i.e., Eastward, for three-quarters of an hour. At 1:15, hearing that the enemy battle-cruisers had turned North, he too turned North; but contact was never re-established. Von Hipper

---

[1] See map on pp. 268–69.

succeeded in escaping round the Northern flank of our squadrons. His light cruisers, so thick was the weather, made their way through the 3rd Cruiser Squadron, passing for a few moments actually in sight of Warrender's battleships.

Thus ended this heart-shaking game of Blind Man's Buff.

It remains only to mention the action of our British submarines. By 3:30 Commodore Keyes had collected four of his boats from their station submerged off Terschelling, and in accordance with Admiralty orders was making for the Heligoland Bight. Eventually he succeeded in placing three boats on the Southern side of Heligoland and one on the Northern. This solitary boat, under Commander Nasmith, on the morning of the 17th found itself in the middle of von Hipper's squadron and flotillas returning from their raid and fired two torpedoes at battle-cruisers under very difficult conditions and without effect.

Such was the episode of the Scarborough and Hartlepool raids. All that we could tell the public was contained in the following communiqué which was issued in the morning papers of December 17:

Admiralty, December 16, 9:20 p.m.

This morning a German cruiser force made a demonstration upon the Yorkshire coast, in the course of which they shelled Hartlepool, Whitby, and Scarborough.

A number of their fastest ships were employed for this purpose, and they remained about an hour on the coast. They were engaged by the patrol vessels on the spot.

As soon as the presence of the enemy was reported, a British patrolling squadron endeavoured to cut them off. On being sighted by British vessels the Germans retired at full speed, and, favoured by the mist, succeeded in making good their escape.

The losses on both sides are small, but full reports have not yet been received.

The Admiralty take the opportunity of pointing out that demonstrations of this character against unfortified towns or commercial ports, though not difficult to accomplish provided that a certain amount of risk is accepted, are devoid of military significance.

They may cause some loss of life among the civil population and some damage to private property, which is much to be regretted; but they must not in any circumstances be allowed to modify the general naval policy which is being pursued.

Naturally there was much indignation at the failure of the Navy to prevent, or at least to avenge, such an attack upon our shores. What was the Admiralty doing? Were they all asleep? Although the bombarded towns, in which nearly five hundred civilians had been killed and wounded, supported their ordeal with fortitude, dissatisfaction was widespread. However, we could not say a word in explanation. We had to bear in silence the censures of our countrymen. We could never admit for fear of compromising our secret information where our squadrons were, or how near the German raiding cruisers had been to their destruction. One comfort we had. The indications upon which we had acted had been confirmed by events. The sources of information upon which we relied were evidently trustworthy. Next time we might at least have average visibility. But would there be a next time? The German Admiral must have known that he was very near to powerful British ships, but which they were, or where they were, or how near he was, might be a mystery. Would it not also be a mystery how they came to be there? On the other hand, the exultation of Germany at the hated English towns being actually made to feel for the first time the real lash of war might encourage a second attempt. Even the indignation of our own newspapers had a value for this purpose. One could only hope for the best. Meanwhile British naval plans and secrets remained wrapped in impenetrable silence.

At this point it will be convenient to examine some of the wider strategic aspects presented by the naval situation in the North Sea.

German naval chroniclers are accustomed to dwell in biting terms upon the failure of the British Fleet to attack them at the beginning of the war. They describe the martial ardour which inspired the German Navy, and their constant and instant expectation of battle. Admiral Scheer relates how as early as August 2, 1914, his colleague commanding the 1st German Squadron urged him to come through the Kiel Canal that very night to join the rest of the Fleet at Wilhelmshaven lest if he waited till daylight he should be too late. He describes the feverish energy with which every scrap of woodwork and paint was stripped from the interiors of German ships the better to prepare them for action. He professes astonishment, not unmingled with derision, that the British disappointed his hope. Considering that the German Fleet remained for the first four months of the war absolutely motionless in its strongly fortified river mouths and harbours protected by its minefields and its submarines, this attitude of mind on the part of a skilful sailor appears to be somewhat forced.

If the Germans really believed that the Grand Fleet would be sent through their minefields to give them battle in their war harbours, they must have rated our intelligence very low. Such a course could only have cast away the British Fleet and achieved our ruin in a few hours. Nor would empty demonstrations off Heligoland, Sylt or Borkum have achieved any useful object. Both Scheer and Tirpitz write as if we had only to appear off these islands to compel the German High Sea Fleet to put to sea for the decisive battle. Yet at the same time we are told that the orders to the German Navy were not to fight a general battle until the British Fleet had been worn down by minor losses to a condition of equality. Why then should the Germans con out and fight a battle at heavy odds because British warships were exchanging shells with the batteries on the German islands? A much more sensible course for the Germans would be to send submarines by day and destroyers by night to torpedo the demonstrators and to sow the area with mines in case they should return. In this way the German equalization policy would have had a very good chance; and one can believe that such action by the British Fleet would have been very agreeable to German wishes. What more, indeed, could they want than that the British Fleet should be swiftly worn down in patrolling boastfully and idiotically outside the German harbours?

We also were anxious for a battle; but not a fool's battle, or even an equal battle. It was our duty to take the fullest advantage of our superiority, and to fight only under conditions which gave solid assurances of victory. Moreover, while the Germans lay in harbour we had secured and were enjoying the full command of the sea. On the outbreak of war the British Fleet, from its war station at Scapa Flow, cut Germany off from the rest of the world. This was in itself an offensive act of prime intensity. It was for the Germans to prevent it if they dared and if they could. We had to convoy our Army to France and collect our forces from all parts of the British Empire. These armies were being sent to the decisive battle front on land. To hinder this transportation was surely a highly important strategic object for Germany and her Navy. If the British Army could have been prevented from reaching its station on the French left, who shall say whether the war might not have ended at the Battle of the Marne? Yet the German Navy, with the formal and explicit assent of the German General Staff, remained inert, impassive behind its minefields and fortifications, while the whole business of the world and of the war proceeded under British authority on the high seas.

"If you are a great general," said Pompaedius Silo to Marius, "come down and fight." "If you are a great general," was the famous answer, "make me fight against my will." This was, in fact, the problem with which the Admiralty was nakedly confronted once the first phase of the naval war was over. The obvious forms of naval offensive open to the British Fleet were attempts and measures to draw the enemy's fleet out of their harbours and force them to accept battle. The distant blockade, apart from its own immense influence upon the war, was a provocation to the enemy of the highest order. Another constant provocation was the ceaseless flow of troops and supplies to France. So important indeed

were these functions of the Royal Navy, and so direct and insistent their challenge to the German Fleet, that the prevailing Admiralty view throughout the
war rested content with them and did not wish for anything more. Once the
first phase of the naval war was over and the outer seas were cleared, this strategy cannot be regarded as wholly sufficing. Without risking the Grand Fleet
otherwise than in a battle upon favourable conditions, every device and form of
pressure to make the enemy come out and bring on a naval crisis and climax
ought to have been perseveringly studied. If the enemy would not come out to
break the blockade, some other effective provocation should be sought for, and
sought for with ceaseless diligence and audacity of conception. The Admirals in
command and the prevailing authorities at the Admiralty, however, rested content with their distant blockade and their protection of the lines of communication. They endeavoured to gather as many ships as possible, adding squadron
to squadron and flotilla to flotilla, and then thought they had done all that
could be expected of them. When reproached from time to time for their inactivity, they replied by using all the perfectly correct arguments about not jeop-
ardizing the Grand Fleet.

But this was not for them the end of the story. It was their business to in-
vent or discover some offensive plan which without engaging the Grand Fleet
at a disadvantage either forced the Germans to give battle or helped the allied
armies in some notable way and took some of the pressure off them. A civilian
Minister could never compel them to such a course. He could suggest, encourage and sustain. But if they remained immovable, nothing could be done.

What then would draw the German Fleet from its harbours with the intention of battle? The blockade had not provoked them; the passage of the
Army did not tempt them; idle demonstrations off the German islands ought
not to have enticed them. Something must be discovered and done which when
done would immediately be insupportable to Germany, which she could by no
means sit still and endure; something so urgent, so clamant, so deadly that
whatever the odds her whole fleet must be at once engaged. Military history
shows many examples of Commanders marching swiftly into an enemy's country and seizing some key position of defensive strength against which the
enemy is afterwards forced to dash himself. Thus are combined the advantages
of a strategic offensive with those of a tactical defensive. This situation reproduced itself to a very large extent in France during the Great War, where the invading German stood on the defensive and the invaded Frenchman had to
expend his manhood assaulting wire and machine guns. How could such simple military conceptions be applied to a naval war? What was there that we
could do which would force the German Navy to fight us at our own selected
moment and on our own terms? Surely such a study should have commanded a
first place in British naval thought.

• • •

On August 19, 1914, I had, with the consent of the Prime Minister, entered into communication with the Russian Government with the object of directing attention continuously upon the strategic aspects of the Baltic. I pointed out that if the British Admiralty should gain the naval command of the Baltic—either by winning a decisive general battle at sea or by blocking the Kiel Canal—it would be possible to land a Russian army to turn the flank and rear of the Dantzig-Thorn line, or to attack Berlin from the north, or to attack Kiel and the Canal in force and drive the German fleet to sea; for any or all of these operations by the Russian Army, the British Admiralty could carry, convoy and land the necessary force. The Russian reply, returned on August 24, was an acceptance in principle: they considered the suggested landing operation feasible and expedient, provided the general military situation favoured its application.

These ideas received a powerful impetus from the arrival at the Admiralty, three months later, of Lord Fisher. The First Sea Lord was deeply convinced that the command of the Baltic, and the consequent letting loose of the Russian armies upon the whole of the unprotected Northern seaboard of Germany, would be a mortal blow. In a weighty memorandum, which has since been published, he stated his case with sure insight. It was undoubtedly the prime goal of a naval offensive. When I showed him my correspondence with the Russian Government on this subject, he rallied enthusiastically to the idea. I told the War Council in his presence during our December discussions, in words which he often afterwards referred to, that there were three phases in the naval war. "First, the clearance of the outer seas; second, the blocking in of the German Fleet; and third, the entry of the Baltic." But all this was a good deal easier said than done. The second stage stood in the way of the third, and until that was achieved the third could not begin. The second stage was in itself an operation of even greater consequence and hazard than the one that lay beyond. In order to close up the Heligoland Bight it was necessary to storm and hold one or more of the German islands, and this would in all probability have brought about the decisive sea battle between the British and German Fleets. It was really very difficult to see beyond such an event. Indeed, it was the biggest naval event that could possibly happen. The difficulties of this preliminary decisive stage were such that the Admiralty throughout the whole war, even when possessed of the most enormous superiority of strength, recoiled from facing it.

Let us see what exactly was this prime operation which stood in the path of all the rest.

In my earliest meetings with Lord Fisher in 1907 he had explained to me that the Admiralty plans at that date in the event of hostilities with Germany were for the seizure as early as possible in the war of the island of Borkum as an advanced base for all our flotillas and inshore squadrons blockading the Ger-

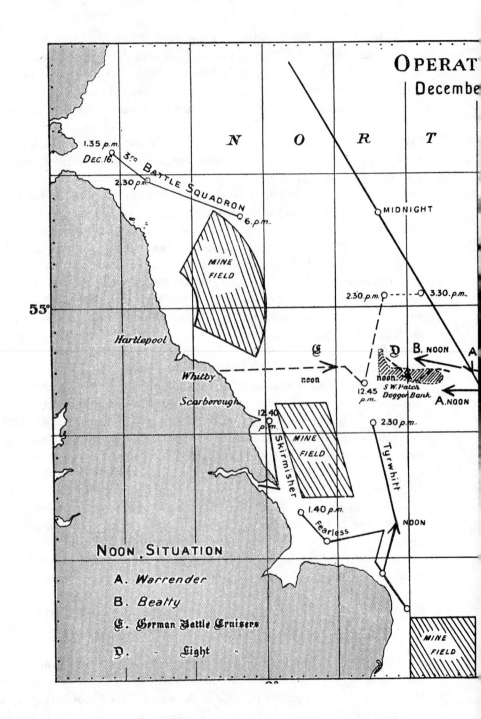

OPERAT

Decembe

N   O   R   T

1.35 p.m.
DEC.16.   3ʳᴰ BATTLE SQUADRON
2.30 p.m.
6.p.m.

MIDNIGHT

MINE
FIELD

55°

2.30.p.m. ----- 3.30.p.m.

Hartlepool

C   D   B. NOON
noon   A
12.45   noon   S.W.Patch
p.m.   Dogger Bank   A.NOON

Whitby

Scarborough   12.40
                 p.m.
                        MINE
                        FIELD   2.30 p.m.

Skirmisher

Tyrwhitt

NOON

1.40 p.m.
Fearless

NOON SITUATION

A. *Warrender*

B. *Beatty*

C. 𝔊erman 𝔅attle 𝔊ruisers

D.   "   𝔏ight

MINE
FIELD

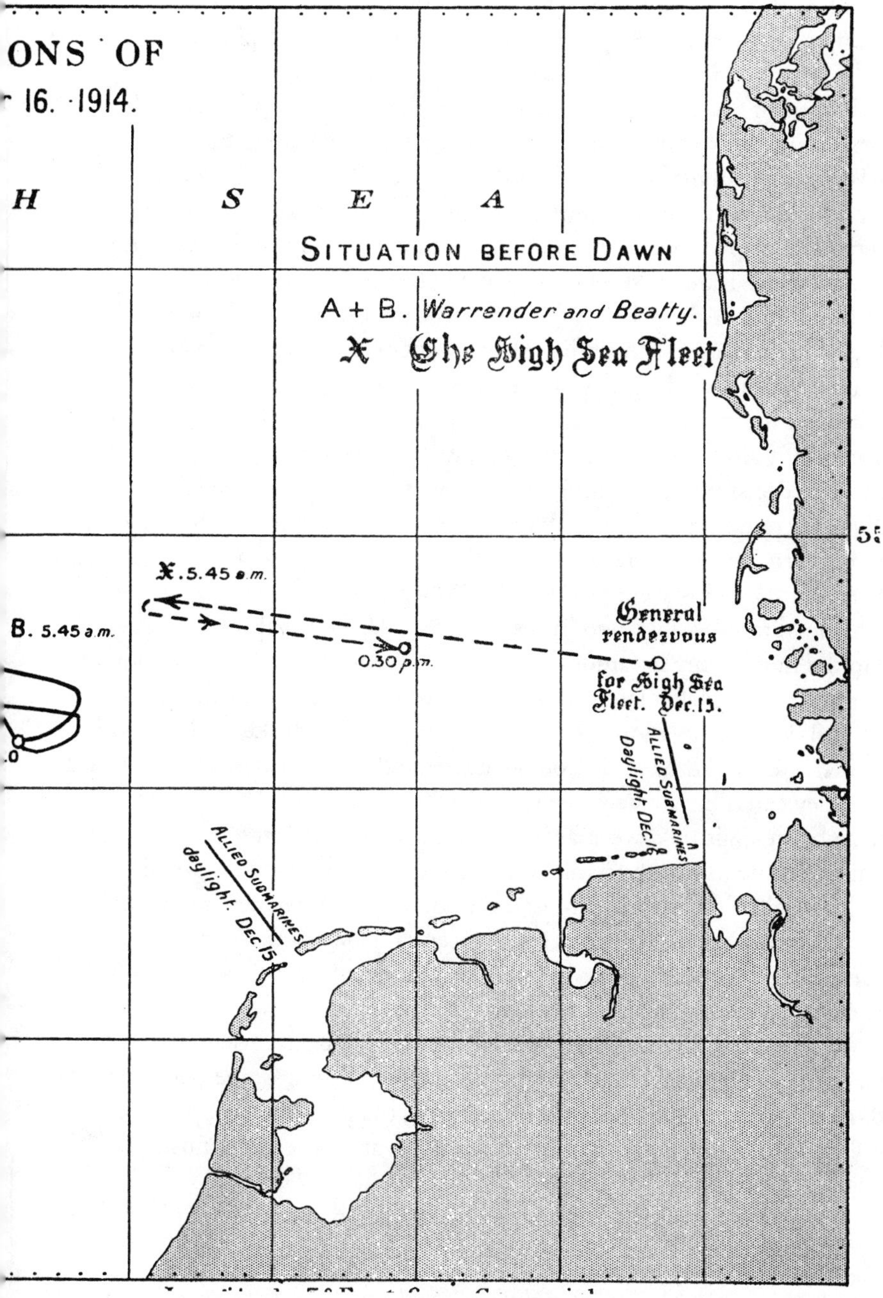

H S E A

SITUATION BEFORE DAWN

A + B. *Warrender and Beatty.*

X 𝕿𝖍𝖊 𝕳𝖎𝖌𝖍 𝕾𝖊𝖆 𝕱𝖑𝖊𝖊𝖙

X . 5.45 a.m.

B. 5.45 a.m.

0.30 p.m.

General
rendezvous
for High Sea
Fleet. Dec. 15.

ALLIED SUBMARINES
Daylight. Dec. 16

ALLIED SUBMARINES
daylight. Dec 15

55

man river mouths. I was always deeply interested in this view. I found it strongly held by Admiral Lewis Bayly. In 1913, this officer, who stood in the very first rank of the younger Admirals of the Navy, had been employed on examining the methods by which the capture and maintenance of this island could be effected in the event of a war, and how the problem had been influenced in the meanwhile by new conditions. The new elements were formidable: to wit, aviation, the submarine and the long-range gun. But they favoured or hindered both sides in various degrees at the different stages of the operation. As an alternative, or possibly as an accompaniment, the island of Sylt was also studied. Very careful models in relief were made of the German river mouths and of all the islands. Admiral Bayly's reports and plans were available in the staff archives. There was no possibility of using them at the beginning of the war. At least three or four brigades of the finest regular infantry we possessed were required for the storm of an island, though a smaller force would have sufficed to garrison it after it was taken. There was no possibility of sparing these troops from the decisive battle front in France. Moreover, as has been seen, the Navy had plenty to do on the outbreak of the war in securing the command of the sea and in ferrying the Army across.

In principle the plans were favoured by Prince Louis. Sir Arthur Wilson thought the operation feasible, and in his first views of the naval was was even disposed to the much more hazardous and much less fruitful enterprise of bombarding and storming Heligoland.[1] Lord Fisher, when he arrived at the Admiralty, was still favourable in principle to the attack on Borkum, but like everyone else he realized the momentous character and consequences of such an operation. They could hardly have been less than the immediate bringing on of the supreme battle. Within a week at the latest of the island being in our possession, much more probably while the operation of landing was still in progress, the whole German Navy must have come out to defend the Fatherland from this deadly strategic thrust. It was essentially one of those great projects to be prepared in absolute secrecy and in perfect detail, and to be used only when the circumstances warranted the taking of the great resolve. Lord Fisher and I in full agreement directed the War Staff in November to review Admiral Bayly's plans for the oversea offensive with a view to action at some period in 1915, and on January 7 I obtained, with his support, the provisional approval of the War Council to this operation in principle if and when circumstances should render it desirable.

But although the First Sea Lord's strategic conceptions were centred in the

---

[1] Sir John Jellicoe in his book, *The Grand Fleet,* erroneously attributes this idea to me. I was never its advocate, but merely placed Sir Arthur Wilson's opinions before the Commander-in-Chief and his officers, and invited their comments.

entry of the Baltic, and although he was in principle favourable to the seizure of Borkum as a preliminary, I did not find in him that practical, constructive and devising energy which in other periods of his career and at this period on other subjects he had so abundantly shown. I do not think he ever saw his way clearly through the great decisive and hazardous steps which were necessary for the success of the operation. He spoke a great deal about Borkum, its importance and its difficulties; but he did not give that strong professional impulsion to the staffs necessary to secure the thorough exploration of the plan. Instead, he talked in general terms about making the North Sea impassable by sowing mines broadcast and thus preventing the Germans from entering it while the main strength of the British Fleet was concentrated in the Baltic. I could not feel any conviction that this would give us the necessary security. First of all we had not got more than 5,000 mines—whereas many scores of thousands were needed, and could not be supplied for many months; and even had we got them, what was to prevent the Germans, unless we guarded the minefields with our Fleet, from sweeping their way through them at leisure?

Therefore, while the First Sea Lord continued to advocate in general terms the entry of the Baltic, I persistently endeavoured to concentrate attention upon the practical steps necessary to storm and seize the island of Borkum, and thus either block in the German Fleet or bring it out to battle. In this task I addressed myself not only to the First Sea Lord and to the Staff, but also to the Commander-in-Chief. Had I found, as the result, any solid response in naval opinion, I should have been enabled to advance the subject to the point where a decision could be taken. But so far from securing such a response, I found a steady and palpable reluctance, which grew as the details of the problem came into view, and which manifested itself by lethargy and a complete absence of positive effort. There is no doubt the naval instinct was against running such risks. But if that were so, it was idle to talk airily of entering the Baltic.

On December 21, 1914, as the result of long discussions and resistances on my part to various petty mining projects, I wrote to the First Sea Lord:

> The key to the naval situation is an oversea base, taken by force and held by force, from which our C class submarines and heavily gunned destroyers can blockade the Bight night and day; and around which and for which a series of desperate fights would take place by sea and land, to the utter ruin of the enemy.
>
> But I cannot find anyone to make such a plan alive and dominant, and till then our situation is as I have told you, and as you justly say, that of waiting to be kicked, and wondering when and where. . . .

And again, on the 22nd December:

> I am wholly with you about the Baltic. But you must close up this side first. You must take an island and block them in, *à la* Wilson; or you must break the canal or the locks, or you must cripple their Fleet in a general action.
>
> No scattering of mines will be any substitute for these alternatives.

The first practical step was to find a Commander who was favourable to the enterprise and who possessed the professional skill and personal resolution to carry it through. All these conditions were fulfilled by Admiral Lewis Bayly.

The monitors would not be ready for many months. In the meanwhile we had a number of older battleships that could be conveniently formed into a bombarding squadron. Sir Arthur Wilson had argued that effective bombardment from the sea required intensive gunnery training and exercises in order to direct and co-ordinate the fire of the ships in the highest state of perfection. We proposed, therefore, to form during the early months of 1915 a special squadron which ultimately, when the monitors arrived, would be available for the great operation, and which in the meantime could be used as required on Zeebrugge and Ostend in support of the Army. In December the First Sea Lord, Sir Arthur Wilson and I being in full agreement, Sir Lewis Bayly was transferred from his command of the 1st Battle Squadron in the Grand Fleet to command the 5th Battle Squadron ("Formidables") at the Nore, with the intention of making this squadron the nucleus of the future bombarding fleet and its new Commander the leader of the naval offensive of 1915. The reader will see how incontinently these hopes were frustrated.

CHAPTER XVII

TURKEY AND THE BALKANS[1]

N o State plunged into the World War so wilfully as Turkey.

The Ottoman Empire was in 1914 already moribund. Italy, using sea power, had invaded and annexed Tripoli in 1909, and a desultory warfare was still proceeding in the interior of this province, when the Balkan States in 1912 drew the sword upon their ancient conqueror and tyrant. Important provinces and many islands were ceded by the defeated Turkish Empire in the Treaty of London, and the division of the spoils became a new cause of bloodshed among the Balkan victors. Rich prizes still remained in European Turkey to tempt the ambition or satisfy the claims of Roumania, Bulgaria, Serbia and Greece; and through all Constantinople glittered as the supreme goal. But imminent as were the dangers of the Turkish Empire from the vengeance and ambition of the Balkan States, nothing could supplant in the Turkish mind the fear of Russia. Russia was in contact with Turkey by land and water along a thousand-mile frontier which stretched from the western shores of the Black Sea to the Caspian. England, France and Italy (Sardinia) in the Crimean War, the exceptional power of England under Disraeli in 1878, had preserved the Turkish Empire from ruin and Constantinople from conquest. Although before the Balkan Allies quarrelled among themselves, the Bulgarians had marched to the gates of Constantinople from the West, the sense of peril from the North still outweighed all else in Turkish thoughts.

To this was added the antagonism of the Arab race in the Yemen, the Hedjas, Palestine, Syria, Mosul, and Iraq. The population of Kurdistan and the widely distributed Armenian race were estranged. From every quarter the nations and races who for five or six hundred years had waged war against the Turkish Empire or had suffered the fate of Turkish captives, turned their gaze in a measureless hatred and hunger upon the dying Empire from which they had endured so much so long. The hour of retribution and restoration was at hand; and the only doubt was how long could the busily spun webs of European diplomacy, and particularly of English diplomacy, postpone the final reckoning. The imminent collapse of the Turkish Empire like the progressive decay and

---

[1] See map of the Balkan Peninsula on p. 523.

disruption of the Austrian Empire, arising from forces beyond human control, had loosened the whole foundations of Eastern and South-Eastern Europe. Change—violent, vast, incalculable, but irresistible and near, brooded over the hearths and institutions of 120 millions of people.

It was at this hour and on this scene that Germany had launched her army to the invasion of France through Belgium, and all other quarrels had re-aligned themselves in accordance with the supreme struggle. What was to happen to scandalous, crumbling, decrepit and penniless Turkey in this earthquake?

She received what seemed to British eyes the most favourable offer ever made to any government in history. She was guaranteed at the price merely of maintaining her neutrality the absolute integrity of all her dominions. She was guaranteed this upon the authority not only of her friends, France and Britain, but on that of her enemy, Russia. The guarantee of France and England would have protected Turkey from the Balkan States, and especially Greece; the guarantee of Russia suspended to indefinite periods the overhanging menace from the North. The influence of Britain could largely allay and certainly postpone the long rising movement of the Arabs. Never, thought the Allies, was a fairer proposition made to a weaker and more imperilled State.

But there was another side to the picture. Within the decaying fabric of the Turkish Empire and beneath the surface of its political affairs lay fierce, purposeful forces both in men and ideas. The disaster of the first Balkan War created from these elements a concealed, slow-burning fire of strange intensity unrealized by all the Embassies along the shores of the Bosphorus—all save one. "During this time" (the years before the Great War), wrote a profoundly informed Turk in 1915, "the whole future of the Turkish people was examined by Committees down to the smallest details."[1]

The Pan-Turk Committee accepted the Anglo-Russian Convention of 1907 as a definite alliance between the Power who had been Turkey's strongest and most disinterested supporter and friend with the Power who was her ancient and inexorable enemy. They therefore looked elsewhere for help in the general European war which they were convinced was approaching. Their plan, which seemed in 1913 merely visionary, was based upon the recreation of Turkey on a solely Turkish human foundation: to wit, the Turkish peasantry of Anatolia. It contemplated as a national ideal the uniting of the Moslem areas of Caucasia, the Persian province of Azerbaijan, and the Turkish Trans-Caspian provinces of Russia (the homeland of the Turkish race) with the Turks of the Anatolian peninsula; and the extension of Turkey into the Caspian Basin. It included the rejection of theocratic government; a radical change of relationship between

---

[1] *Turkish and Pan-Turkish Ideals,* by "Tekin Alp." First published in German, 1915.

Church and State; the diversion of the "Pious Foundations"; endowments to the secular needs of the State, and a rigorous disciplining of the professional religious classes. It included also the startling economic, social and literary changes which have recently been achieved in Turkey. Mustapha Kemal has in fact executed a plan decided upon, and to which he may well have been a party, fifteen years ago. The centre point of all the Pan-Turk schemes was the use of Germany to rid Turkey of the Russian danger. Marschall von Bieberstein, for so many years German Ambassador at Constantinople, nursed these hidden fires with skilful hands.

Pan-Turkish schemes might have remained in dreamland but for the fact that in a fateful hour there stood almost at the head of Turkey a man of action. A would-be Turkish Napoleon, in whose veins surged warrior blood, by his individual will, vanity and fraud was destined to launch the Turkish Empire upon its most audacious adventure. Enver, the German-trained but Turkish-hearted subaltern, had "thrown his cap over the fence" (to quote himself) as the signal for the Young Turk Revolution in 1909. Together with his handful of Young Turk friends forming the committee of Union and Progress, he had bravely faced all the gathering foes. When Italy had seized Tripoli, it was in the deserts of Tripoli that Enver had fought; when the armies of Balkan Allies were at the lines of Chatalja, it was Enver who had never despaired. "Adrianople," said Mr. Asquith, then Prime Minister in 1912, "will never be restored to Turkey." But Enver entered Adrianople within a month, and Adrianople is Turkish to-day. The outbreak of the Great War saw Enver with his associate, Talaat, and his skilful and incorruptible Finance Minister, Djavid, in control of Turkish affairs. Above them, an imposing façade, were the Sultan and the Grand Vizier: but these men and their adherents were the unquestioned governing power, and of them Enver in all action was the explosive force.[1]

The Turkish leaders rated the might of Russia for the rough and tumble of a general war far lower than did the Western allies of the Czar. They were convinced that the Germanic group would win the war on land, that Russia would be severely mauled and that a revolution would follow. Turkey would secure in the moment of a German victory gains in territory and population in the Caucasus which would at least ward off the Russian danger for several generations. In the long preliminary discussions Germany promised Turkey territorial satisfaction in the Caucasus in the event of a victory by the Central Powers. This promise was decisive upon Turkish policy.

The policy of the Pan-Turks in every sphere of Turkish life and their terri-

---

[1] I happened to know all these men personally. I had met Enver at the German manœuvres in 1910. Talaat and Djavid had been our hosts when, with Lord Birkenhead, I visited Constantinople in 1909.

torial ambitions were embodied in a definite war plan. This plan required as its foundation the Turkish command of the Black Sea. Whenever the Great War should come—as come they were sure it must—and Russia was at grips with Germany and Austria, the Pan-Turks intended to invade and conquer the Caucasus. The control of the sea route from Constantinople to Trebizond was indispensable to an advance from Trebizond to Erzerum. Hence Turkey must have a navy. Popular subscriptions opened in 1911 and 1912 throughout Anatolia, and even throughout Islam, provided the money for the building for Turkey in Great Britain of two dreadnoughts. The arrival of one at least of these battleships at Constantinople was the peg upon which the whole Turkish war plan hung. The supreme question in July, 1914, among the Turkish leaders was: Would the ships arrive in time? Obviously the margin was small. The first Turkish dreadnought, the *Reshadieh,* was due for completion in July; the second, a few weeks later. Already Turkish agents in Russian territory round Olti, Ardahan and Kars were busy arranging for the hoarding of corn crops by the Moslem Turkish peasantry who formed the bulk of the population, in order to make possible the advance of the Turkish columns down the valley of the Chorukh and against the Russian rear. On July 27 a secret defensive and offensive alliance between Germany and Turkey against Russia was proposed by Turkey, accepted forthwith by Germany, and signed on August 2. The mobilization of the Turkish Army was ordered on July 31.

But now came a surprise. England suddenly assumed an attitude of definite resistance to Germany. The British fleets had put to sea in battle order. On July 28 I requisitioned both the Turkish dreadnoughts for the Royal Navy. I took this action solely for British naval purposes. The addition of the two Turkish dreadnoughts to the British Fleet seemed vital to national safety. No one in the Admiralty, nor so far as I know in England, had any knowledge of the Turkish designs or of the part these ships were to play in them. We built better than we knew. I was later in the year criticized in some quarters for having requisitioned the Turkish ships. The rage and disappointment excited thereby throughout Turkey was said to have turned the scale and provoked Turkey into war against us. We now know the inner explanation of this disappointment. The requisitioning of these ships, so far from making Turkey an enemy, nearly made her an Ally.

But there still remained to the Turks one hope: the *Goeben.* This fast German battle-cruiser was as has been described in the western Mediterranean under peace time orders to refit at Pola in the Adriatic. She was in herself sufficient to dominate the Russian squadron in the Black Sea. Would the Germans send the *Goeben* back to Constantinople? Would she get there? It was at this moment that the news of the British ultimatum to Germany, carrying with it the certainty of the British declaration of war, reached Constantinople. The

Turkish realists had never counted on such an event. It transformed the naval situation in the Mediterranean. Could the *Goeben* escape the numerous British flotillas and cruiser squadrons and the three more powerful though less speedy British battle-cruisers which lay between her and the sea? When on the night of August 3 Enver learned that the *Goeben* was under orders to escape up the Adriatic to Pola, his anxiety knew no bounds. He immediately sought the Russian military attaché, General Leontev, and casting all previous schemes to the wind, including the agreement he had signed with Germany the day before, proposed to this astonished officer an alliance between Turkey and Russia on various conditions, including Turkish compensations in Western Thrace. Whether the Germans realized that they would never be forgiven by the Pan-Turks unless the *Goeben* made an effort to reach Constantinople, or whether it was already part of their war plan, fresh orders to go to Constantinople were at this moment (August 3) being sent by Admiral Tirpitz to the *Goeben* then about to coal at Messina; and after events which are well known she reached the Dardanelles on the 10th and was after some parley admitted to the Sea of Marmora.

Enver's confidence was now restored, for the command of the Black Sea rested potentially with the Turks. But the certain hostility of Great Britain was serious, in view of her naval supremacy and the undefended conditions of the Dardanelles. Moreover Italy had unexpectedly separated herself from the Triple Alliance. It might therefore perhaps be prudent for Turkey to see how the impending great battles on land, and especially those upon the Russian front, were decided. Meanwhile the mobilization of the Turkish Army could proceed unostentatiously and be justified as a precautionary measure. Thus there followed a period lasting for about three months of Turkish hesitation and delay, having the effect of consummate duplicity. I can recall no great sphere of policy about which the British Government was less completely informed than the Turkish. It is strange to read the telegrams we received through all channels from Constantinople during this period in the light of our present knowledge. But all the Allies, now encouraged by the friendly assurances of the Grand Vizier and the respectable-effete section of the Cabinet, now indignant at the refusal to intern and disarm the *Goeben* and generally mystified by many contradictory voices, believed that Turkey had no policy and might still be won or lost. This period was ended when Enver in November, acting as the agent of all the Pan-Turk forces, delivered the unprovoked attack by the *Goeben* and the Turkish Fleet upon the Russian Black Sea ports, and thus plunged Turkey brutally into the war.

The Turkish position could only be judged in relation to the general situation in the Balkans; and this could not be understood unless the dominant facts of pre-war Balkan history were continually borne in mind. The first Balkan war saw Bulgaria triumphantly bearing the brunt of the attack on Turkey. While her armies were advancing on Constantinople against the best troops of the Turkish Empire, the Greeks and Serbians were overrunning the comparatively weakly-held regions of Thrace and Macedonia. The Bulgarians, having fought the greatest battles and sustained by far the heaviest losses, found themselves finally checked before Constantinople, and, turning round, beheld almost the whole of the conquered territory in the hands of their Allies. The destination of this territory had been regulated before the war by treaty between the four belligerent minor States. Adrianople had not however surrendered, and in obedience to the treaty the Serbians came to the aid of the Bulgarian forces, and played a prominent part in the capture of that fortress. Both the Serbians and the Greeks utilized the argument that the war had been prolonged through the need of reducing Adrianople as a ground for claiming to repudiate in important particulars the pre-war treaty, and meanwhile they retained occupation of all the conquered districts in their possession. The Bulgarians were quick to repay this claim with violence. They attacked the Greeks and Serbians, were defeated by the more numerous armies of these two Powers, and in the moment of extreme weakness and defeat were invaded from the other side by Roumania, who, having taken no part in the conflict, had intact armies to strike with. At the same time the Turks advanced in Thrace, and led by Enver Pasha recaptured Adrianople. Thus the end of the second Balkan war saw Bulgaria stripped not only of almost all her share of the territory conquered from the Turks (and this entirely divided between Greece and Serbia), but even her native province of the Dobroudja had been wrested from her by Roumania. The terrible cruelties and atrocities which had been perpetrated on both sides in the internecine struggle that followed the expulsion of the Turks had left a river of blood between the Greeks and Serbians on the one hand and the Bulgarians on the other.

It is possible that no nation ever contemplated its fortunes with more profound and desperate resolve than the Bulgarians at this juncture. All their sacrifices had been useless and worse than useless. All the fruits of their conquests had gone to aggrandize their rivals. They had been, as they considered, stabbed in the back and blackmailed by Roumania, to whom they had given no provocation of any kind. They saw the great Powers, England in the van, forbid the return of the Turk to Adrianople without offering the slightest attempt to make their words good. They saw not only Salonika, but even Kavala, seized by the Greeks. They saw large districts inhabited largely by the Bulgarian race newly liberated from the Turks pass under the yoke—to them scarcely less odious—of Serbians and Greeks. It was in these circumstances that the Bulgarian Army, in the words of King Ferdinand, "furled its standards" and retired to wait for better days.

This warlike and powerful Bulgaria, with its scheming King and its valiant peasant armies brooding over what seemed to them intolerable wrongs, was the dominant factor in the Balkans in 1914 and 1915.

On August 19, 1914, Monsieur Venizelos, then Prime Minister of Greece, with the approval which he had, astonishing to relate, obtained of King Constantine, formally placed at the disposal of the *Entente* powers all the naval and military resources of Greece from the moment when they might be required. He added that this offer was made in a special sense to Great Britain with whose interests those of Greece were indissolubly bound. The resources of Greece, he said, were small, but she could dispose of 250,000 troops, and her navy and her ports might be of some use. This magnanimous offer, made as it was while all was so uncertain, and even before the main battle in France had been joined, greatly attracted me. No doubt on the one hand it was a serious thing to run the risk of adding Turkey to our enemies. On the other hand, the Greek Army and Navy were solid factors; and a combination of the Greek armies and fleet with the British Mediterranean squadron offered a means of settling the difficulties of the Dardanelles in a most prompt and effective manner. The Gallipoli Peninsula was then only weakly occupied by Turkish troops, and the Greek General Staff were known to be ready with well-thought-out plans for its seizure. Moreover, it seemed to me that anyhow Turkey was drifting into war with us. Her conduct in regard to the *Goeben* and *Breslau* continued openly fraudulent. The presence of these two vessels themselves in German hands in the Sea of Marmora offered a means of putting decisive pressure on the neutrality party in Constantinople. If we were not going to secure honest Turkish neutrality, then let us, in the alternative, get the Christian States of the Balkans on our side. Could we not get them on our side? Could we not make a Balkan confederation of Serbia, Greece, Bulgaria and Roumania? Whatever happened, we ought not to fall between two stools.

Sir Edward Grey, however, after very anxious consideration, moved the Cabinet to decline Monsieur Venizelos's proposal, as he feared, no doubt with weighty reasons, that an alliance with Greece meant immediate war with Turkey and possibly Bulgaria. He feared that it might jeopardize Greece without our being able to protect her. He was anxious above all things not to foster a Greek enterprise against Constantinople in such a way as to give offence to Russia. And, lastly, he hoped that Sir Louis Mallet, who was in close and intimate relations with the Grand Vizier and the leaders of the Turkish neutrality party in Constantinople, would after all be able to keep the peace. Certainly nothing could exceed the skill and perseverance with which the British Ambassador laboured. It followed from this that we should maintain the very handsome offer we had made in common with France and Russia at the outbreak of the war to guarantee the integrity of the Turkish Empire in return for her faithful neutrality. I naturally conformed to the Cabinet decision, but with increasing misgivings. I still continued to work and hope for a Balkan confederation.

In the early days of September it seemed highly probable that Turkey, under the influence of the German advance on Paris, would make war upon us and upon Greece whatever we did. I began immediately to prepare for the event by arranging for a conference between representatives of the Admiralty and the Military Operations Department of the War Office to work out a plan for the seizure of the Gallipoli Peninsula by a Greek army, with a view to admitting a British fleet to the Sea of Marmora. The resulting estimate of 60,000 men as the requisite force seemed well within the Greek resources, and conversations with the Greek Government ensued, through the medium of Rear-Admiral Mark Kerr, the head of our naval mission to Greece. The Greek General Staff regarded the joint operation with favour, but declared that Bulgaria must at the same time attack Turkey with all her force; they were unwilling to accept Bulgaria's guarantee to remain neutral.

On September 6 Monsieur Venizelos told our Minister in Athens that he was not afraid of a single-handed attack from Turkey by land as the Greek General Staff were confident of being able to deal with it. The Greek Government had received from Sofia positive assurances of definite neutrality, but did not trust them. They would, however, be satisfied with a formal protest by the Bulgarian Government against a violation of Bulgarian territory by Turkish troops proceeding to attack Greece. If, however, Bulgaria joined Turkey while Serbia was occupied with Austria, the situation would be critical. On this I pointed out to the Foreign Secretary on the same date that a Russian Army Corps could easily be brought from Archangel, from Vladivostok, or with Japanese consent from Port Arthur to attack the Gallipoli Peninsula. "The price to be paid in taking Gallipoli would no doubt be heavy, but there would be no more war with Turkey. A good army of 50,000 men and sea power—that is the end of the Turkish menace."

But it was easier to look for armies than to find them. Sir Edward Grey replied by sending me a telegram that had been received that very morning from Petrograd stating that in view of the very large number of German troops which were being transferred from the Western to the Eastern theatre, Russia was calling up every available man from Asia and the Caucasus, and was only leaving one Army Corps in the latter. Greece would therefore, according to the Petrograd telegram, have to bear the brunt of the war single-handed unless she could placate Bulgaria by territorial concessions. He added on the back of my note, "You will see from the telegram from St. Petersburg that Russia can give no help against Turkey. I do not like the prospect in the Mediterranean at all, unless there is some turn of the tide in France."

It is only by faithful study of this problem that its immense difficulties are portrayed. Lest it should be thought that I underrated the gravity of a war with Turkey, it must be remembered that I had convinced myself that Turkey would attack us sooner or later, and that I was also proceeding on the belief that the German invasion of France would be brought to a standstill. Both these assumptions proved true. I do not claim that my view was the wisest, but only to expose it to historical judgment. The policy emerging from such a view would of course at this juncture have offered Cyprus to Greece in compensation for her offering Kavala to Bulgaria. It would have put the most extreme pressure on Serbia to make concessions to Bulgaria in Monastir. Whether these measures would have succeeded at this time I do not pronounce.

By September 9 the behaviour of the Turks about the *Goeben* and the *Breslau* had become so openly defiant that it became necessary to withdraw the British Naval Mission, who were exposed to daily insolences at the hands of the Germans and of the Turkish war party. It was my intention to appoint the head of our naval mission to Turkey, Rear-Admiral Limpus, to command the squadron watching the Dardanelles, and orders were sent definitely to that effect. This project was not, however, pursued, it being thought that it would be indelicate to employ on this station the very officer who had just ceased to be the teacher of the Turkish Fleet. No doubt this was a weighty argument, but in bowing to it we lost the advantages of having at this fateful spot the Admiral who of all others knew the Turks, and knew the Dardanelles with all its possibilities. It was a small link in a long chain. Delay was caused and I had to make fresh arrangements.

On September 21, I telegraphed to Vice-Admiral Carden, who was in charge of the Malta Dockyard, to assume command of the squadron off the Dardanelles to be augmented by the *Indomitable* and two French battleships with the sole duty of sinking the *Goeben* and *Breslau,* no matter what flag they might be flying, if they should come out of the Dardanelles.

The victory of the Marne, although afterwards discounted by adverse events, checked the developments in the Near East. Turkey was steadied for the moment, and her attitude towards Greece became less menacing. This however produced a corresponding cooling at Athens about joining in the European war. From the middle of September the conditions throughout the Balkans had declined again from crisis into suspense. They remained however fundamentally vicious.

I continued increasingly to press as opportunity served for a policy of uniting the Balkan States without reference to what might happen in Turkey. I have never swerved from this view; but the reader should understand the other arguments by which the Cabinet was ruled. The loyal desire not to spread the war to regions still uncursed; the dangers in India of a British quarrel with Turkey; our awful military weakness in 1914; Lord Kitchener's expressed wish to keep the East as quiet as possible till the two Indian Divisions were safely through the Suez Canal; the difficulties of winning the support of Greece, and particularly of King Constantine, without exciting the suspicion and jealousies of Russia about Constantinople; and, lastly, the doubts—admittedly substantial— whether Bulgaria and King Ferdinand could ever, in the absence of substantial military successes in the main theatres or strong local intervention by Allied forces in the Balkans, be detached from the Teutonic system.

When I talked these questions over at the time with Sir Edward Grey it was upon this last argument that he was most inclined to dwell. "Until Bulgaria believes that Germany is not going to win the war, she will not be moved by any promises of other people's territory which we may make her." The swift overrunning of Northern France by the German armies, the withdrawal of the French Government to Bordeaux, the fall of Antwerp, the tremendous victories of Hindenburg over the Russians, were events all of which dominated the Bulgarian equally with the Turkish mind. England, without an army, with not a soldier to spare, without even a rifle to send, with only her Navy and her money, counted for little in the Near East. Russian claims to Constantinople directly crossed the ambitions both of King Ferdinand and of King Constantine. In all the Balkans only one *clairvoyant* eye, only the genius of Venizelos, discerned the fundamental moral issues of the struggle, measured justly the relative powers of the mighty combatants, and appraised at their true value both the victories of the German Army, and the Sea Power under which were slowly gathering the latent but inexhaustible resources of the British Empire.

So the Allies continued to wait and hope at Constantinople, and the days slipped swiftly by. By the middle of October we learnt that Turkish preparations to invade Egypt were actually being made. We learned also from a secret source, that the Austrian Ambassador at Constantinople had received solemn assurances from Enver that Turkey would enter the war against the *Entente* at an early date. At the end of October, our outposts beyond the Suez Canal had to be withdrawn in face of gathering Turkish forces; and finally, about October 27, the *Breslau,* with the Turkish cruiser *Hamidieh* and a division of destroyers, followed by the *Goeben,* steamed into the Black Sea, and on the 29th and 30th bombarded the Russian fortress of Sevastopol, sank a Russian transport, raided the harbour of Odessa, torpedoed a gunboat, and, lastly, practically destroyed Novorossisk, its oil tanks and all the shipping in the port.

On this the Russian Ambassador at Constantinople immediately demanded his passports; and the British Foreign Office at 8:15 p.m. on October 30, after reciting its many griefs against the Turks, especially their invasion of the Sinai Peninsula and their misconduct about the *Goeben,* sent an ultimatum requiring repudiation of these acts and the dismissal of the German Military and Naval Missions within 12 hours.

Russia declared war on Turkey at the expiry of the ultimatum; and the British and French Ambassadors, in company with their Russian colleague, left Constantinople on November 1—the same day on which at the other end of the world the battle of Coronel was being fought. Naval orders to commence hostilities were sent, in concert with the Foreign Office, in conformity with the expiry of the ultimatum.

On November 1 two of our destroyers, entering the Gulf of Smyrna, destroyed a large armed Turkish yacht which was lying by the jetty carrying mines; and late that same day Admiral Carden was instructed to bombard the outer Dardanelles forts at long range on the earliest suitable occasion. This bombardment was carried out on the morning of November 3. The two British battle-cruisers, firing from a range beyond that of the Turkish guns, shelled the batteries on the European side at Sedd-el-Bahr and Cape Helles. The French battleships fired at the Asiatic batteries at Kum Kali and Orkanieh. About eighty rounds were fired altogether, resulting in considerable damage to the Turkish forts, and in several hundred casualties to the Turks and Germans who manned them.

The reasons for this demonstration have been greatly canvassed. They were simple though not important. A British squadron had for months been waiting outside the Dardanelles. War had been declared with Turkey. It was natural that fire should be opened upon the enemy as it would be on the fronts of hostile armies. It was necessary to know accurately the effective ranges of the Turkish guns and the conditions under which the entrance to the blockaded port could be approached. It has been stated that this bombardment was an imprudent act, as it was bound to put the Turks on their guard and lead them to strengthen their defences. That the organization of the defences of the Straits should be improved steadily from the declaration of war was inevitable. To what extent this process was stimulated by the bombardment is a matter of conjecture. When, three and a half months later (February 19, 1915), Admiral Carden again bombarded these same forts, the Gallipoli Peninsula was however totally unprepared for defence, and was still weakly occupied; and small parties of Marines were able to make their way unopposed into the shattered forts and a considerable distance beyond them.

We had now to provide against the impending Turkish attack upon Egypt. The First Cruiser Squadron, comprising the *Black Prince, Duke of Edinburgh* and *Warrior,* had been either employed on escort duties at sea or on guard at Alexandria or Port Said. Even before the news of Coronel had reached us, the increasing strain upon our resources had made it necessary to replace these fine ships by older smaller vessels. They were now urgently required to form a combat squadron near the Cape de Verde Islands as part of the second general combination against von Spee. They were also promised to the Commander-in-

Chief for the Grand Fleet at the earliest possible moment thereafter. We should have been hard pressed in these circumstances to find a new and satisfactory naval force for the defence of the Canal against the now imminent Turkish attack. The discovery and blocking in of the *Königsberg* on 31st October liberated two out of the three vessels searching for her. But this was not enough. The destruction of the *Emden* on the 9th November was an event of a very different order. It afforded us immediate relief, and relief exactly where we required it. The Indian Ocean was now clear. The battleship *Swiftsure* from the East Indian station was at once ordered to the Canal. Of the fast cruisers that had been searching for the *Emden*, the *Gloucester, Melbourne, Sydney, Hampshire* and *Yarmouth* were immediately brought homewards through the Red Sea into the Mediterranean. I searched the oceans for every available ship. During the second and third weeks of November the *Swiftsure* and the squadron and flotilla mentioned above, together with the French *Requin* and the Russian *Askold*, entered the Canal for the defence of Egypt. The Turkish attack proved however to be only of a tentative character. Finding themselves confronted with troops and ships, they withdrew after feeble efforts into the Eastern deserts to gather further strength.

All this time the great Australasian convoy, carrying the Australian and New Zealand Army Corps, "A.N.Z.A.C.," had been steaming steadily towards France across the Pacific and Indian Oceans. Preparations had been made if necessary to divert them to Cape Town. But before the convoy reached Colombo, General Botha and General Smuts had suppressed the rebellion in South Africa. The Australians and New Zealanders therefore continued their voyage to Europe under the escort of the *Ibuki* and the *Hampshire*. By the end of November their transports were entering the Canal. As the Turkish invasion of Egypt was still threatening, the need of resolute and trustworthy troops in Egypt was great, and on the first day of December Lord Kitchener, in the fateful unfolding of events, began to disembark the whole Australian and New Zealand Force at Suez for the double purpose of completing their training and defending the line of the Canal.

At this point we may leave the Turkish situation for a time. The German grip was strengthening every day on Turkey. The distresses of her peoples and the improvement of her military organization were advancing together. Under the guns of the *Goeben* and *Breslau*, doubt, division and scarcity, dwelt in Constantinople. Outside the Straits the British Squadron maintained its silent watch. Greece, perplexed at the attitude of Britain, distracted by the quarrels of Venizelos and King Constantine, had fallen far from the high resolve of August. Serbia stoutly contended with the Austrian armies. Roumania and Bulgaria brooded on the past and watched each other with intent regard. In Egypt the training of the Australian and New Zealand Army Corps perfected itself week by week.

Thus, as this act in the stupendous world drama comes to its close, we see already the scene being set and the actors assembling for the next. From the uttermost ends of the earth ships and soldiers are approaching or gathering in the Eastern Mediterranean in fulfilment of a destiny as yet not understood by mortal man. The clearance of the Germans from the oceans liberated the Fleets, the arrival of the Anzacs in Egypt created the nucleus of the Army needed to attack the heart of the Turkish Empire. The deadlock on the Western Front, where all was now frozen into winter trenches, afforded at once a breathing space and large possibility of further troops. While Australian battalions trampled the crisp sand of the Egyptian desert in tireless evolutions, and Commander Holbrook in his valiant submarine dived under the minefields of Chanak and sank a Turkish transport in the throat of the Dardanelles, far away in the basins of Portsmouth the dockyard men were toiling night and day to mount the fifteen-inch guns and turrets of the *Queen Elizabeth.* As yet all was unconscious, inchoate, purposeless, uncombined. Any one of a score of chances might have given, might still give, an entirely different direction to the event. No plan has been made, no resolve taken. But new ideas are astir, new possibilities are coming into view, new forces are at hand, and with them there marches towards us a new peril of the first magnitude. Russia, mighty steam-roller, hope of suffering France and prostrate Belgium— Russia is failing. Her armies are grappling with Hindenburg and Ludendorff, and behind their brave battle fronts already the awful signs of weakness, of deficiency, of disorganization, are apparent to anxious Cabinets and Councils. Winter has come and locked all Russia in its grip. No contact with her Allies, no help from them, is possible. The ice blocks the White Sea. The Germans hold the Baltic. The Turks have barred the Dardanelles. It needs but a cry from Russia for help, to make vital what is now void, and to make purposeful what is now meaningless. But as yet no cry has come.

The reader has now followed the steady increase of strain upon Admiralty resources which marked in every theatre the months of September, October and November, 1914. He must understand that, although for the purposes of the narrative it is necessary to deal in separate chapters with each separate set of strains and crises, many of the events were proceeding simultaneously in all theatres at once, and the consequent strains were cumulative and reciprocally reacting on one another, with the result that during November an extraordinary pitch of intensity was reached which could not well be prolonged and could not possibly have been exceeded.

It is worth while to review the whole situation. First, the transport of troops and supplies to France was unceasing and vital to our Army. On the top of all this came the operations on the Belgian Coast, the approach of the enemy to the Channel ports, and the long-drawn crisis of the great battle of Ypres-Yser. Secondly, all the enemy's cruisers were still alive, and a number of hostile armed merchantmen were free in the outer seas, each threatening an indefinite number of points and areas and requiring from five to ten times their numbers to search for them and protect traffic while they were at large. At the same time the great convoys of troops from India, from Canada, from Australia, and the collection of the British regular garrisons from all parts of the world were proceeding; and no less than six separate expeditions, viz., Samoa, New Guinea, German East Africa, Togoland, the Cameroons and German South-West Africa, were in progress or at a critical stage. Upon this was thrust the outbreak of war with Turkey, the attack upon the Suez Canal, and the operations in the Persian Gulf.

To meet these fierce obligations we had to draw no less than three decisive units from the Grand Fleet. This Fleet, which at the outset of the war was in perfect order, was already requiring refits by rotation, with consequent reduction of available strength. Meanwhile, the submarine menace had declared itself in a serious form, and was moreover exaggerated in our minds. Although the most vehement efforts were being made to give security to our fleets in their Northern harbours, these measures took many weeks during which anxiety was continual. Behind all stood the German Fleet, aware, as we must suppose, of the strain to which we were being subjected, and potentially ready at any moment to challenge the supreme decision. With the long nights of winter, the absence of all regular troops from the country, the then inadequate training of the Territorial Force and the embryonic condition of the new Kitchener armies, the fear of invasion revived; and, although we rejected it in theory, nevertheless we were bound to take in practice a whole series of precautionary measures. It was a formidable time. More than once the thought occurred that the Admiralty would be forced to contract their responsibilities and abandon to their fate for a time some important interests, in order that those which were vital might be secured. In the event we just got through. It may be claimed that during these months we met every single call that was made upon us, guarded every sea, carried every expedition, brought every convoy safely in, discharged all our obligations both to the Army in France and to the Belgians, and all the time maintained such a disposition of our main forces that we should never have declined battle had the enemy ventured to offer it.

Then suddenly all over the world the tension was relaxed. One after another the German cruisers and commerce destroyers were blocked in or hunted down. The great convoys arrived. The Expeditions were safely landed. Ocean after ocean became clear. The boom defences of our harbours were completed.

A score of measures for coping with the submarine were set on foot. Large reinforcements of new ships of the highest quality and of every class began to join the Fleet. The attack on the Suez Canal was stemmed. The rebellion in South Africa was quelled. The dangers of invasion, if such there were, diminished every day with the increasing efficiency of the Territorials and the New Armies. The great battle for the Channel ports ended in decisive and ever glorious victory. And finally with the Battle of the Falkland Islands the clearance of the oceans was complete, and soon, except in the land-locked Baltic and Black Seas and in the defended area of the Heligoland Bight, the German flag had ceased to fly on any vessel in any quarter of the world.[1]

As December passed, a sense of indescribable relief stole over the Admiralty. We had made the great transition from peace to war without disaster, almost without mishap. All the perils which had haunted us before the war, and against which we had prepared, had been warded off or surmounted or had never come to pass. There had been no surprise. The Fleet was ready. The Army had reached the decisive battlefield in time and was satisfactorily maintained. The Mine danger had been overcome. We thought we had the measure of the submarine, and so indeed we had for nearly two years to come. All the enemy's plans for commerce destruction and all our alarms about them had come to nought. British and allied commerce proceeded without hesitation throughout the world; the trade and food of Britain were secured; the war insurance dropped to one per cent. A feeling of profound thankfulness filled our hearts as this first Christmas of the war approached; and of absolute confidence in final victory.

The mighty enemy, with all the advantages of preparation and design, had delivered his onslaught and had everywhere been brought to a standstill. It was our turn now. The initiative had passed to Britain—the Great Amphibian. The time and the means were at our command. It was for us to say where we would strike and when. The strength of the Grand Fleet was, as we believed, ample; and in addition the whole of those numerous squadrons which hitherto had been spread over the outer seas now formed a surplus fleet capable of intervening in the supreme struggle without in any way compromising the foundation of our naval power.

But these realizations were only permissible as the prelude to fresh and still more intense exertions. It would indeed be shameful, so it seemed at least to me, for the Admiralty to rest contented with the accomplishment of the first and most hazardous stage of its task and to relax into a supine contemplation of regained securities and dangers overcome. Now was the time to make our

---

[1] The *Dresden* and two armed merchant cruisers were alive for a few weeks more, but in complete inactivity.

weight tell, perhaps decisively, but certainly most heavily, in the struggle of the armies. Now was the time to fasten an offensive upon the Germans, unexpected and unforeseeable, to present them with a succession of surprising situations leading on from crisis to crisis and from blow to blow till their downfall was achieved.

Moreover, these same Germans were, of all the enemies in the world, the most to be dreaded when pursuing their own plans; the most easily disconcerted when forced to conform to the plans of their antagonist. To leave a German leisure to evolve his vast, patient, accurate designs, to make his slow, thorough, infinitely far-seeing preparations, was to court a terrible danger. To throw him out of his stride, to baffle his studious mind, to break his self-confidence, to cow his spirit, to rupture his schemes by unexpected action, was surely the path not only of glory but of prudence.

Here then ends the first phase of the naval war. The first part of the British task is done both by land and sea. Paris and the Channel ports are saved, and the oceans are cleared. It is certain that the whole strength of the British Empire can be turned into war power and brought to bear upon the enemy. There is no chance of France being struck down, before the British Empire is ready; there is no chance of the British Empire itself being paralysed, before its full force can be applied to the struggle. The supreme intiative passes from the Teutonic Powers to the Allies. Resources, almost measureless and of indescribable variety in ships, in men, in munitions and devices of war, will now flow month by month steadily into our hands. What shall we do with them? Strategic alternatives on the greatest scale and of the highest order present themselves to our choice. Which shall we choose? Shall we use our reinforced fleets and great new armies of 1915, either to turn the Teutonic right in the Baltic or their left in the Black Sea and the Balkans? Or shall we hurl our manhood against sandbags, wire and concrete in frontal attack upon the German fortified lines in France? Shall we by a supreme effort make direct contact with our Russian ally or leave her in a dangerous isolation? Shall we by decisive action, in hopes of shortening the conflict, marshal and draw in the small nations in the North and in the South who now stand outside it? Or shall we plod steadily forward at what lies immediately in our front? Shall our armies toil only in the mud of Flanders, or shall we break new ground? Shall our fleets remain contented with the grand and solid results they have won, or shall they ward off future perils by a new inexhaustible audacity?

The answers to these momentous questions will appear as this tale is carried forward to a further stage.

PART II

———————————

To All Who Tried

CHAPTER XVIII

THE DEADLOCK IN THE WEST

The year 1915 was fated to be disastrous to the cause of the Allies and to the whole world. By the mistakes of this year the opportunity was lost of confining the conflagration within limits which though enormous were not uncontrolled. Thereafter the fire roared on till it burnt itself out. Thereafter events passed very largely outside the scope of conscious choice. Governments and individuals conformed to the rhythm of the tragedy, and swayed and staggered forward in helpless violence, slaughtering and squandering on ever-increasing scales, till injuries were wrought to the structure of human society which a century will not efface, and which may conceivably prove fatal to the present civilization. But in January, 1915, the terrific affair was still not unmanageable. It could have been grasped in human hands and brought to rest in righteous and fruitful victory before the world was exhausted, before the nations were broken, before the empires were shattered to pieces, before Europe was ruined.

It was not to be. Mankind was not to escape so easily from the catastrophe in which it had involved itself. Pride was everywhere to be humbled, and nowhere to receive its satisfaction. No splendid harmony was to crown the wonderful achievements. No prize was to reward the sacrifices of the combatants. Victory was to be bought so dear as to be almost indistinguishable from defeat. It was not to give even security to the victors. There never was to be "The silence following great words of Peace."[1] To the convulsions of the struggle must succeed the impotent turmoil of the aftermath. Noble hopes, high comradeship and glorious daring were in every nation to lead only to disappointment, disillusion and prostration. The sufferings and impoverishment of peoples might arrest their warfare, the collapse of the defeated might still the cannonade, but their hatreds continue unappeased and their quarrels are still unsettled. The most complete victory ever gained in arms has failed to solve the European problem or remove the dangers which produced the war.

When the old year closed a complete deadlock existed between the great combatants in the West by land and by sea. The German fleet remained sheltered in

---

[1] Rupert Brooke—his last and most pregnant line.

its fortified harbours, and the British Admiralty had discovered no way of drawing it out. The trench lines ran continuously from the Alps to the sea, and there was no possibility of manœuvre. The Admirals pinned their faith to the blockade; the Generals turned to a war of exhaustion and to still more dire attempts to pierce the enemy's front. All the wars of the world could show nothing to compare with the continuous front which had now been established. Ramparts more than 350 miles long, ceaselessly guarded by millions of men, sustained by thousands of cannon, stretched from the Swiss frontier to the North Sea. The Germans had tried in October and November to break through while these lines were still weak and thin. They had failed with heavy losses. The French and British Headquarters had still to be instructed in the defensive power of barbed wire and entrenched machine guns.

For more than forty years frontal attacks had been abandoned on account of the severity of modern fire. In the Franco-German War the great German victories had been won by wide turning movements executed on one flank or the other by considerable forces. In the Russo-Japanese War this method was invariably pursued by the victors. Thus at Liao-yang it was General Kuroki's army which turned the Russian left; and at Mukden General Nogi's army brought specially from Port Arthur turned the Russian right. It was certain that frontal attacks unaccompanied by turning movements on the flank would be extremely costly and would probably fail. But now, in France and Flanders for the first time in recorded experience there were no flanks to turn. The turning movement, the oldest manœuvre in war, became impossible. Neutral territory or salt water barred all further extension of the Front, and the great armies lay glaring at each other at close quarters without any true idea of what to do next.

It was in these circumstances that the French High Command, carrying with them the British, turned again to the forlorn expedient of the frontal attack which had been discarded in the bitter experiences of the past. Meanwhile, the power of modern weapons had doubled and trebled since the Russo-Japanese War, and was increasing almost daily. Moreover, the use of barbed wire and the consequent need of prolonged bombardment to destroy it, effectually prevented any chance of surprise. There existed at this period no means of taking the offensive successfully in France: the centre could not be pierced, and there were no flanks to turn. Confronted with this deadlock, military art remained dumb; the Commanders and their General Staffs had no plan except the frontal attacks which all their experience and training had led them to reject; they had no policy except the policy of exhaustion.

No war is so sanguinary as the war of exhaustion. No plan could be more unpromising than the plan of frontal attack. Yet on these two brutal expedients the military authorities of France and Britain consumed, during three successive years, the flower of their national manhood. Moreover, the dull carnage of the policy of exhaustion did not even apply equally to the combatants. The Anglo-French offensives of 1915, 1916 and 1917 were in nearly every instance, and certainly in the aggregate, far more costly to the attack than to the German defence. It was not even a case of exchanging a life for a life. Two, and even three, British or French lives were repeatedly paid for the killing of one enemy, and grim calculations were made to prove that in the end the Allies would still have a balance of a few millions to spare. It will appear not only horrible but incredible to future generations that such doctrines should have been imposed by the military profession upon the ardent and heroic populations who yielded themselves to their orders.

It is a tale of the torture, mutilation or extinction of millions of men, and of the sacrifice of all that was best and noblest in an entire generation. The crippled, broken world in which we dwell to-day is the inheritor of these awful events. Yet all the time there were ways open by which this slaughter could have been avoided and the period of torment curtailed. There were regions where flanks could have been turned; there were devices by which fronts could have been pierced. And these could have been discovered and made mercifully effective, not by any departure from the principles of military art, but simply by the true comprehension of those principles and their application to the actual facts.

Battles are won by slaughter and manœuvre. The greater the general, the more he contributes in manœuvre, the less he demands in slaughter. The theory which has exalted the *"bataille d'usure"* or "battle of wearing down" into a foremost position, is contradicted by history and would be repulsed by the greatest captains of the past. Nearly all the battles which are regarded as masterpieces of the military art, from which have been derived the foundation of states and the fame of commanders, have been battles of manœuvre in which very often the enemy has found himself defeated by some novel expedient or device, some queer, swift, unexpected thrust or stratagem. In many such battles the losses of the victors have been small. There is required for the composition of a great commander not only massive common sense and reasoning power, not only imagination, but also an element of legerdemain, an original and sinister touch, which leaves the enemy puzzled as well as beaten. It is because military leaders are credited with gifts of this order which enable them to ensure victory and save slaughter that their profession is held in such high honour. For if their art were nothing more than a dreary process of exchanging lives, and counting heads at the end, they would rank much lower in the scale of human esteem.

There are many kinds of manœuvres in war, some only of which take place upon the battlefield. There are manœuvres far to the flank or rear. There are manœuvres in time, in diplomacy, in mechanics, in psychology; all of which are removed from the battlefield, but react often decisively upon it, and the object of all is to find easier ways, other than sheer slaughter, of achieving the main purpose. The distinction between politics and strategy diminishes as the point of view is raised. At the summit true politics and strategy are one. The manœuvre which brings an ally into the field is as serviceable as that which wins a great battle. The manœuvre which gains an important strategic point may be less valuable than that which placates or overawes a dangerous neutral. We suffered grievously at the beginning of the war from the want of a common clearing house where these different relative values could be established and exchanged. A single prolonged conference, between the allied chiefs, civil and martial, in January, 1915, might have saved us from inestimable misfortune. Nothing could ever be thrashed out by correspondence. Principals must be brought together, and plans concerted in common. Instead each allied state pursued in the main its own course, keeping the others more or less informed. The armies and navies dwelt in every country in separate compartments. The war problem, which was all one, was tugged at from many different and disconnected standpoints. War, which knows no rigid divisions between French, Russian and British Allies, between Land, Sea and Air, between gaining victories and alliances, between supplies and fighting men, between propaganda and machinery, which is, in fact, simply the sum of all forces and pressures operative at a given period, was dealt with piecemeal. And years of cruel teaching were necessary before even imperfect unifications of study, thought, command and action were achieved. The men of the Beginning must not be judged wholly by the light of the End. All had to learn and all had to suffer. But it was not those who learned the slowest who were made to suffer most.

But if a complete deadlock had been reached in the West, events were moving with imperious violence in the East. These events justify a brief retrogression in the narrative.

When, in August, 1914, it was seen that the Germans were concentrating practically four-fifths of their armies against France and leaving only a handful of Divisions to guard their eastern frontiers against Russia, high hopes were entertained that these slender forces would be overwhelmed or forced to retreat, and that Germany would be invaded continuously from the east. In the darkest moments before the Marne, when it was necessary to contemplate the loss of Paris and a resistance desperately maintained along the Loire, we had comforted ourselves with the belief that the Russian masses would be rolling forward upon Dantzig, upon Breslau, onwards into the heart of the German Empire. We counted on this increasing pressure from the East to retrieve the situation in the West, and to force the Germans to recall their invading armies to the defence of their own soil. We have seen how the loyal conduct of the

Czar and the ardour of the Russian armies and nation had precipitated a rapid offensive into East Prussia within a fortnight of the outbreak of war. We know that the effects of this offensive upon the nerves of the German Headquarters Staff had led to the withdrawal of two Army Corps from the German right in Belgium during the crisis before the Marne. It may well be argued that this event was decisive upon the fate of the battle. And if this be true, homage will be rendered to the Czar and his soldiers long after this ingrate generation has passed away.

But, for this supreme achievement Russia had paid a fearful price. No sooner were the armies in contact in the East than the bravery and superior numbers of the Russians were found quite unequal to the leadership, the science and the discipline of Germany. The twenty cavalry and infantry divisions which formed the Army of Rennenkampf, the fifteen divisions of Samsonoff, were confronted by fourteen German divisions, and at the head of this small but resolute and trustworthy army stood the rugged Hindenburg and a Major-General fresh from the capture of Liège whose name, till then unknown, will rank with the great Commanders of the past. In the frightful battles of Tannenberg (August 25–31) and of the Masurian Lakes (September 5–15) the Army of Samsonoff was cut to pieces with the slaughter or capture of 100,000 men, and the Army of Rennenkampf decisively defeated. The audacious combinations whereby Hindenburg and Ludendorff overwhelmed within little more than a fortnight two armies, each of which was stronger than their own, have appeared so astonishing that treachery has been invoked as the only possible explanation. History, however, will dwell upon the results, and it was with these that we were confronted.

The Russian armies, which even in their first vigour and when fully equipped were no match for the Germans, showed themselves on the whole superior to the variegated forces of the Austro-Hungarian Empire. While the defeats of Tannenberg and of the Masurian Lakes were endured by Russia in the North, her armies pressed forward into Galicia, and in a series of tumultuous struggles over a great expanse of ground gained a substantial victory in what has been called the Battle of Lemberg. This event covered, masked and partially counter-balanced the disasters in the North. In fact the victory in Galicia bulked so largely in the accounts published in France and Britain, that the catastrophe in East Prussia made little or no impression. Hindenburg and Ludendorff now laid hands upon the defeated Austrians and proceeded to reinforce and reorganize their front. There followed the winter war in the East. In the snow or mud of Poland and Galicia, over enormous fronts swaying backwards and forwards with varying fortunes, the Russians grappled manfully with their antagonists. The German situation in France after the Battle of the Marne, and the great drive in October and November against the Channel ports, forbade the withdrawal from the West of reinforcements for the East. Ludendorff's first combined movement against Warsaw, conceived with his usual hardihood, proved a task beyond his strength. The Grand Duke Nicholas stubbornly and skilfully withstood him, and the advancing German armies were forced to re-coil amid the indescribable conditions of a Polish winter. Yet here again the trustworthy qualities of the German troops and leadership were displayed, and more than once, nearly surrounded by superior numbers, they cut their way out and fought their way back with discipline and determination. Against Aus-tria, Russia continued to make headway. In November, 1914, the Grand Duke could still contemplate an advance through Silesia into the heart of Germany.

But thereafter came an awful change. Russia had entered the war with about 5,000 guns and 5,000,000 shells. During the first three months of fight-ing she fired on an average about *45,000 shells a day*. The output of her factories in Russia did not exceed *35,000 shells a month*. By the beginning of December, 1914, scarcely 300,000 shells, or barely a week's requirement, remained out of the initial reserve. At the moment when the Russian armies needed the greatest support from their artillery, they found their guns suddenly frozen into silence. No less grim was the shortage of rifles. In the fierce, confused, unceasing fight-ing of the first three months over 1,000,000 rifles out of five and a half millions had been lost, captured or destroyed. By the end of the year over 1,350,000 Rus-sians had been killed, wounded or made prisoners. The barracks of the Empire were full of lusty manhood. 800,000 trained drafts were ready for despatch to the front, but there were no weapons to place in their hands. Every Russian bat-tery was silenced; every Russian battalion was depleted to two-thirds its strength. Many months must elapse before the flow of shells could be resumed; many more months, before the supplies of rifles could overtake the daily wastage. Meanwhile, the Russian armies, hamstrung and paralysed, must await and endure the vengeance of their foes. Such was the prospect which opened upon Russia and her Allies before the first Christmas of the war was reached.

The British Government had at the Russian Headquarters an agent of sin-gular discernment in Colonel Knox. All the facts set out above were unearthed and reported by this officer during November and December. General Sukhomlinoff, the Minister of War, might persist in blind or guilty optimism; the General Staff in Petrograd might declare in answer to the anxious inquiries of General Joffre at the end of September that "the rate of expenditure of am-munition gave no cause for anxiety"; the Grand Duke himself, absorbed in the actual operations, might be unconscious that the ground was crumbling under his feet; but the terrifying secrets of the Russian administration were penetrated by the remorseless scrutiny of Knox. In a series of luminous and pitiless despatches he exposed the position to the British Government, and these grave forebodings lay upon us during the closing weeks of 1914.

It seemed at times that Russia might be torn in pieces before she could be re-armed. While the deadlock continued on the Western Front, while Joffre pursued the policy of "nibbling"—*"Je les grignote"*—and his staff elaborated schemes for a frontal attack on the German lines in the spring, Russia, with her inexhaustible resources in men and food, might collapse altogether or be forced into a separate peace. And then the whole weight of the Teutonic powers would fall after an interval upon the hard-pressed armies of France and the unready armies of Britain. At the best a long period of weakness, of quiescence and of retirement, must be expected from our great Ally.

No one could measure the disasters which this period must contain. Although in appearance the lines in the East presented a continuous front, they in no way reproduced the conditions of the West. The distances were much greater, the communications much worse. The lines were thinly held on both sides; they could be bulged or broken by any decided advance. How could the Russians maintain their front with hardly any artillery fire, with very few machine guns, and with an increasing scarcity of rifles? Moreover, the Turkish attack on Russia had compelled her in November, at the very moment when the worst facts of her position were becoming apparent and munitions of all kinds were failing, to create and to develop a new front in the Caucasus against the advancing Ottoman armies.

Russia had, however, one last supreme resource—territory. The enormous size of the country afforded almost unlimited possibilities of retirement; and judicious and timely retirement might secure the vital breathing space. Once again, as in 1812, the Russian armies might withdraw intact into the heart of their Empire, all the time holding on their front large numbers of the enemy. Once again the invaders might be lured into the vast expanses of Russia. And meanwhile the factories of the world could be set to work to supply and re-equip the Russian armies. The situation, though tragic, was not necessarily fatal. If only the will-power of Russia did not fail in the ordeal that lay before her, if she could be encouraged to dwell upon the prizes of victory, if intimate and continuous contact could be established between her and the Western Allies, there was no reason why her strength should not be restored before the end of 1915.

It is on this basis that the strategy and policy of 1915 can alone be studied.

The essence of the war problem was not changed by its enormous scale. The line of the Central Powers from the North Sea to the Ægean and stretching loosely beyond even to the Suez Canal was, after all, in principle not different from the line of a small army entrenched across an isthmus, with each flank resting upon water. As long as France was treated as a self-contained theatre, a complete deadlock existed, and the Front of the German invaders could neither be pierced nor turned. But once the view was extended to the whole scene of the war, and that vast war conceived as if it were a single battle, and once the sea power of Britain was brought into play, turning movements of a most far-reaching character were open to the Allies. These turning movements were so gigantic and complex that they amounted to whole wars in themselves. They required armies which in any other war would have been considered large. They rested on sea power, and they demanded a complete diplomacy of their own.

At the very moment when the French High Command was complaining that there were no flanks to turn, the Teutonic Empires were in fact vulnerable in an extreme degree on either flank. Thus the three salient facts of the war situation at the beginning of 1915 were: first, the deadlock in France, the main and central theatre; secondly, the urgent need of relieving that deadlock before Russia was overwhelmed; and thirdly, the possibility of relieving it by great amphibious and political-strategic operations on either flank.

Let us, at this point, cast a preliminary glance upon each of the flanks of the battle line.

On the Northern flank lay a group of small but virile and cultivated peoples. All were under the impression of the German power, and connected with Germany by many ties: but all were acutely conscious that the victory of Germany would reduce them to a state of subservience to the conqueror; and all trembled at the fate which had overtaken Belgium. Holland, mobilized and heavily armed, stood on anxious guard of her frontiers. Denmark, through whose territory passed the gateway of the Baltic, was practically defenceless. Norway and Sweden were under the apprehension of Russia not less than of Germany. It would have been wrong to embroil any of these Powers without being able to defend them by sea and land, and to combine their forces. Had it been possible to achieve this, the position of Germany would have become desperate. The Dutch Army was a substantial factor. The Dutch islands offered invaluable strategic advantages to the British Navy. Denmark could open the door of the Baltic to a British fleet; and the command of the Baltic by the Allies would have afforded a means of direct contact with Russia. This would have rendered the blockade absolute, and would have exposed all Northern Germany to the constant menace of Russian invasion by sea.

Even more remarkable was the aspect of the Southern Flank.[1] Here Serbia, by heroic exertions, had twice repelled the Austrian invaders. Here a weak, divided, and ill-organized Turkey had lately declared war upon the Allies. Three of the warlike States of the Balkan Peninsula, namely Greece, Serbia, and Rou-

[1] See map of the Balkan Peninsula on p. 523.

mania were divided from the fourth, Bulgaria, by the hatreds of their recent war; but all four were the natural enemies both of Turkey and of Austria and the traditional friends of Britain. Between them these four Powers disposed of organized armies which amounted to 1,100,000 men (Serbia 250,000, Greece 200,000, Bulgaria 300,000, Roumania, 350,000); and their total military manpower was of course greater still. They had freed themselves from the Turks after centuries of oppression. They could only expand at the expense of Austria and Turkey. Serbia was already fighting for her life against Austria; Roumania coveted Transylvania from Austria-Hungary. Bulgaria looked hungrily to Adrianople, to the Enos-Midia line, and, indeed, to Constantinople itself; while Greece saw great numbers of her citizens still held down under the Turkish yoke and several of the fairest provinces and islands of the Turkish Empire mainly inhabited by men of Greek blood. If these four States could be induced to lay aside their intestine quarrels and enter the war together under British guidance against Turkey and Austria, the speedy downfall of the Turk was certain. Turkey would be cut off completely from her allies and forced into a separate peace during 1915. The whole of the forces of the Balkan confederation could then have been directed against the underside of Austria in the following year. If we may consider the fighting forces of the Turkish Empire as the equivalent of 700,000 men, it will be seen that the striking out of this hostile factor, and the simultaneous accession to our strength of new Balkan armies of nearly 1,000,000 men, meant an improvement of our position as against Germany and Austria by one and three-quarter million soldiers. We should have 700,000 soldiers less against us and 1,000,000 more soldiers on our side. The possibility of effecting such a transference of fighting strength was surely a military object of first consequence.

But it was also certain that the rally of the Balkans and the attack upon Turkey could not leave Italy indifferent. Italy was known to be profoundly friendly to the Allied cause, and particularly to Great Britain. She was the hereditary enemy of Austria. She had immense interests in the Balkan Peninsula, in the Turkish Empire, and in the Turkish islands. It seemed highly probable that any decisive or successful action taken by Great Britain in this quarter of the world must draw Italy, with her army of about two millions, directly into the ambit of the Great War as a first-class Ally on our side.

The success of amphibious descents or invasions depends upon whether forces superior to the defender can be carried to the spot in time, and whether these can be continually reinforced more quickly than the enemy. In this the defenders are at a grave disadvantage. Even after the expedition has put to sea, no one can tell for certain where the descent will be made. Although the Central Powers were working on interior lines, this advantage did not countervail the superior mobility of sea power. Britain could at any time in 1915, for instance, have moved 250,000 men (if they had been available) to suitable points on the shores of the Eastern Mediterranean in a fraction of the time required to send an equal number of Germans or Austrians. Moreover, the selection of these points would remain a mystery to the enemy up to the last minute. He would no doubt learn that the expedition was preparing, and that transports had assembled. But whether they would go North or South could not be known till after they had put to sea. Against such uncertainties it was impossible to prepare with precision beforehand. The amphibious assailants could have plans prepared for either alternative, and need not decide till the last moment which to use. They might pretend to be going North, and then go South. They might change their minds at the last moment. They might practise every feint and deception known to war. If, therefore, the defenders had reinforced their Northern flank, that would be a reason for attacking the Southern, and conversely. Thus the defence must wait till it was actually struck before knowing what to do. Then and then only could the transportation of armies to the scene begin. Even if the road were open—on the Southern flank it was not—the movement of considerable armies and their supplies, and their organization in a new theatre, was a matter of months. What could not the sea invaders achieve in the interval? What territory could they overrun? What positions could they seize? What defences could they construct? What magazines could they accumulate? What local forces could they defeat or destroy? What allies could they gain? All this lay in our choice in the spring and summer of 1915.

As the war advanced the chances constantly diminished, and the difficulties constantly grew. In the later periods of the war the scale of the armies necessary to secure swift victory in the Southern theatre began to exceed the resources, strained in so many ways, of the British Mercantile Marine. There were limits even to the sea power of the Great Amphibian. Gradually under ever-increasing burdens and continual attack and injury these limits became apparent. But 1915 was her hour of overwhelming strength. There lay the supreme opportunity.

There were, in fact, at this juncture, two great plans of using sea power to relieve the murderous deadlock in the West. Both aimed at breaking into and dominating the land-locked waters which guarded the Teutonic flanks. Both would give direct contact with Russia and would rescue our Eastern Ally from her deadly isolation. Both would affect in a decisive manner a group of neutral States. Both in proportion, as they succeeded, would open up enormous new drains on the resources of the Teutonic Empires. Should we look to Holland, Denmark, Norway, and Sweden, or to Greece, Bulgaria, and Roumania? Should we strike through the Belts at the Baltic, or through the Dardanelles at Constantinople and the Black Sea?

• • •

No doubt all these schemes of action were attended by risk, not only to those who executed but to those who devised them. They required intense exertions on a great scale, and involved the certainty of cost. Against such risks, exertions, and costs of action, must be balanced the dangers and consequences of inaction. Before projects of penetrating the Baltic or forcing the Dardanelles by the British Fleet are dismissed as "unsafe" or impracticable, before an invasion of Schleswig-Holstein or the despatch of an army to the Balkan Peninsula or to Gallipoli are condemned as "unsound," the mind of the reader must also dwell upon the bloody slaughters of Loos-Champagne, of the Somme, of Passchendaele; upon the disasters, almost fatal, of Caporetto, 1917, and of the 21st of March, 1918; upon the Russian collapse, revolution and desertion; upon the awful peril of the submarine warfare in 1917. It is on such a background that all plans for finding, by sudden and complex manœuvres or devices, short cuts to victory can alone be effectually depicted.

But as a key to the complicated and debatable alternatives which these pages expose, certain practical propositions may be presented. If these are comprehended and assented to, the rest will follow naturally and each thought will fall into its proper place and just relation. I therefore set them down categorically forthwith.

On Land.

1. The Decisive theatre is the theatre where a vital decision may be obtained at any given time. The Main theatre is that in which the main armies or fleets are stationed. This is not at all times the Decisive theatre.

2. If the fronts or centres of armies cannot be broken, their flanks should be turned. If these flanks rest on the seas, the manœuvres to turn them must be amphibious and dependent on sea power.

3. The least-guarded strategic points should be selected for attack, not those most strongly guarded.

4. In any hostile combination, once it is certain that the strongest Power cannot be directly defeated itself, but cannot stand without the weakest, it is the weakest that should be attacked.

5. No offensive on land should be launched until an effective means—numbers, surprise, munitions, or mechanical devices—of carrying it through has been discovered.

On Sea.

1. The Grand Fleet should not be hazarded for any purpose less than that of a general sea battle.

2. A naval decision should be provoked at the earliest opportunity.

3. The Navy should actively aid the Army with its surplus forces.

These general principles remained my guides throughout the whole war. They run counter, of course, to the dominant military view, and diverge to some extent from the naval practice. How far they were justified by events, others must judge; but the history of the struggle will afford many illustrations of their adoption or repudiation by both the combatants and of the consequences which followed therefrom.

CHAPTER XIX

THE ORIGIN OF TANKS AND SMOKE

Mechanical not less than strategic conditions had combined to produce at this early period in the war a deadlock both on sea and land. The strongest fleet was paralysed in its offensive by the menace of the mine and the torpedo. The strongest army was arrested in its advance by the machine gun. On getting into certain positions necessary for offensive action, ships were sunk by underwater explosions, and soldiers were cut down by streams of bullets. This was the evil which lay at the root of all our perplexities. It was no use endeavouring to remedy this evil on sea by keeping the ships in harbour, or on land by squandering the lives and valour of endless masses of men. The mechanical danger must be overcome by a mechanical remedy. Once this was done, both the stronger fleet and the stronger armies would regain their normal offensive rights. Until this were done, both would be baffled and all would suffer. If we master the fact that this was the crux of the war problem, as it was plainly apparent from the end of 1914 onwards, the next steps in thought will be found equally simple. Something must be discovered which would render ships immune from the torpedo, and make it unnecessary for soldiers to bare their breasts to the machine gun hail. This very definite evil and ugly fact that a torpedo or mine would blow a hole in the bottom of a ship, and that any one bullet out of countless streams discharged by machinery would fatally pierce the body of a man, was not one which could be ignored. It must be conquered if the war was to progress and victory to be won. The remedy when stated appeared to be so simple that it was for months or even years scouted and disregarded by many of the leading men in both the great fighting professions.

Reduced to its rudiments, it consisted in interposing a thin plate of steel between the side of the ship and the approaching torpedo, or between the body of a man and the approaching bullet.

Here then was one of the great secrets of the war and of the world in 1915. But hardly anyone would believe it. This sovereign, priceless key to inestimable blessings lay there in the dust for everyone to see, and almost all the great responsible authorities stood gazing at it with vacant eyes. Those who perceived it, soldiers, sailors, airmen, civilians, were a class apart, outside the currents of orthodox opinion, and for them was reserved the long and thankless struggle to convert authority and to procure action. Eventually they succeeded. On sea authority intervened at an early stage: on land the process was more painful. The Monitor and the "bulged" or "blistered ship" were the beginning of the torpedo-proof fleet, the Tank was the beginning of the bullet-proof army. Both of these devices, when the difficulties of their application were surmounted, would have restored to the stronger fleet or army the offensive powers of which they had been deprived by new mechanical developments. But when at last Monitors, "Blisters" and Tanks had been devised and built and were placed under Naval and Military Commanders-in-Chief, the usefulness of both was largely thrown away. The Monitors—the original types of which were no doubt far from perfect—were not developed, and were never employed as a part of any great naval offensive, while the Tanks were improvidently exposed to the enemy long before they were numerous enough to produce decisive effects. Nevertheless the Tanks survived to play their part.

Closely allied to the problem of finding ways of attacking by sea and land lay the great subject of Smoke. To make an artificial fog which would blanket off a particular area so that men or ships could traverse it or occupy it without the enemy seeing where to shoot at them, was a second most simple and obvious expedient. Smoke was the ally and comrade of the Steel Plate. They went forward together each helping the other and multiplying their joint effect.

And behind smoke lay a more baleful development—Poisonous Smoke: smoke that would not only obstruct the vision but destroy the eye, smoke that would not only blindfold the machine gunner but strangle him.

All these ideas had already dawned before the year 1914 was over.

In the early weeks of the war the Admiralty had been asked to assume responsibility for the defence of Britain against aerial attack. This necessitated the posting on the Belgian and French coasts of Air Squadrons based on Dunkirk to attack any Zeppelin or aeroplane shed which the enemy might establish in the invaded territories. This led to the formation of armoured-car squadrons to protect the advanced bases which our naval aeroplanes might require to use. The enemy, harassed by the armoured cars, cut gaps in the roads, and I called immediately for means of bridging these gaps. Meanwhile the armoured cars began to multiply, but just as they became numerous and efficient, the trench lines on both sides reached the sea, and there was no longer any open ground for manoeuvre or any flanks to turn. As we could not go round the trenches, it was evidently necessary to go over them. Thus the Air was the first cause that took us to Dunkirk. The armoured car was the child of the air; and the Tank its grandchild. This was the point which the chain of causation had reached in the second week of October, 1914.

Since Admiral Bacon had retired from the Navy, he had become general manager of the Coventry Ordnance Works. In 1913 I had kept this firm, which comprised one-third of our heavy-gun-producing power, alive by assigning it some of the 15-inch guns and turrets for the fast battleships. A few days after the war had begun I received a letter from Admiral Bacon stating that he had designed a 15-inch howitzer that could be transported by road. Interested in this astonishing assertion, I sent for him. He then spoke with energy and conviction about the general artillery aspects of the war predicting in particular that existing fortresses would not be able to withstand the shells of great modern cannon or howitzers which were far more formidable than any contemplated at the date of their construction. I listened with interest, and when during the next fortnight the forts first of Liège and then of Namur were swiftly destroyed by the German siege guns, I sent for Admiral Bacon again. I told him his prediction had come true, and I asked whether he could make some big howitzers for the British Army, and how long it would take. He replied he could make a 15-inch howitzer in five months and thereafter deliver one every fortnight. I thereupon proposed to the War Office to order ten.

General von Donop, the Master General, was staggered at the idea of "this novel piece of ordnance," and expressed doubts whether it could be made or would be useful when made. But Lord Kitchener was much attracted by the idea, and the order went forward forthwith. I promised Admiral Bacon that if he completed his howitzers in the incredibly short time fixed, he should himself command them in France. The utmost expedition was therefore assured, and in fact the first of these monsters, though not ordered till after the fall of Namur, fired in the battle of Neuve Chapelle.

I was kept closely informed about their design and progress, and at the outset learned that each one with his ammunition and platform would be moved in the field in sections, by eight enormous caterpillar tractors. The pictures of these vehicles were extremely suggestive, and when Admiral Bacon showed them to me in October, I at once asked whether they would be able to cross trenches and carry guns and fighting men, or whether he could make any that would. As the result of the discussion that followed, Admiral Bacon produced a design for a caterpillar tractor which would cross a trench by means of a portable bridge which it laid down before itself and hauled up after passing over; and early in November, 1914, I directed him to make an experimental machine, and to lay the project before both Sir John French and Lord Kitchener meanwhile. On February 13, 1915, the model showing promise, I ordered thirty to be constructed. It was not until May, 1915, that the first of these engines with the bridging device was tested by the War Office. It was then rejected because it could not descend a four-foot bank and go through three feet of water (a feat not achieved by any tank up to the end of the war) or fulfil other extremely severe and indeed vexatious conditions. My order for the thirty had, however, been cancelled before their trial took place, as by that time we had achieved a better design through an altogether different agency. Thus ended the first and earliest effort to make a trench-crossing vehicle or so-called "Tank" during the Great War.

The sequence of events in the second attempt to make a tank and secure its adoption by the military authorities was as follows:

Quite independently of what has been narrated above, about the middle or end of October, Colonel E. D. Swinton, who was attached to General Head-quarters, France, as Eye-Witness or Official Correspondent, also realized and visualized the need of such a weapon. He accordingly broached the project to Colonel Hankey.[1] At the end of December, Colonel Hankey wrote a paper on the need of this and other mechanical devices, which he circulated to the various Members of the Cabinet directly concerned in the conduct of the war.

Reading this paper brought me back to the subject on which Admiral Bacon had already been given instructions, and on January 5 I wrote a letter to the Prime Minister from which I quote the significant paragraphs:

> It would be quite easy in a short time to fit up a number of steam tractors with small armoured shelters, in which men and machine guns could be placed, which would be bullet-proof. Used at night they would not be affected by artillery fire to any extent. The caterpillar system would enable trenches to be crossed quite easily, and the weight of the machine would destroy all wire entanglements. Forty or fifty of these engines prepared secretly and brought into position at nightfall could advance quite certainly into the enemy's trenches, smashing away all the obstructions and sweeping the trenches with their machine-gun fire and with grenades thrown out of the top. They would then make so many *points d'appui* for the British supporting infantry to rush forward and rally on them. They can then move forward to attack the second line of trenches. The cost would be small. If the experiment did not answer, what harm would be done? An obvious measure of prudence would have been to have started something like this two months ago. It should certainly be done now.
>
> The shield is another obvious experiment which should have been made on a considerable scale. What does it matter which is the best pattern? A large number should have been made of various patterns; some to carry, some to wear, some to wheel. If the mud now prevents the workings of shields or traction engines, the first frost would render them fully effective. With a view to this I ordered a month ago twenty shields on wheels

---

[1] Afterwards Sir Maurice Hankey, Secretary of the Committee of Imperial Defence and at this time of the War Council.

to be made on the best design the Naval Air Service could devise. These will be ready shortly, and can, if necessary, be used for experimental purposes.

A third device which should be used systematically and on a large scale is smoke artificially produced. It is possible to make small smoke barrels which on being lighted generate a great column of dense black smoke which could be turned off or on at will. There are other matters closely connected with this to which I have already drawn your attention, but which are of so secret a character that I do not put them down on paper.

One of the most serious dangers that we are exposed to is the possibility that the Germans are acting and [are] preparing all these surprises, and that we may at any time find ourselves exposed to some entirely new form of attack. A committee of engineer officers and other experts ought to be sitting continually at the War Office to formulate schemes and examine suggestions, and I would repeat that it is not possible in most cases to have lengthy experiments beforehand. If the devices are to be ready by the time they are required it is indispensable that manufacture should proceed simultaneously with experiment. The worst that can happen is that a comparatively small sum of money is wasted.

Mr. Asquith, two or three days after receiving my letter of January 5, laid it personally before Lord Kitchener, and urged him strongly to prosecute research into all these matters. Lord Kitchener, who was entirely favourable, thereupon remitted the project to the Department of the Master General of the Ordnance. This process was mortal to the second attempt to make a Tank, and the project was decently interred in the archives of the War Office.

I did not know what had happened as a result of my letter to the Prime Minister, or what the War Office were doing; but I formed the impression that no real progress was being made, and that the military authorities were quite unconvinced either of the practicability of making such engines or of their value when made. I, however, continued to think about the subject from time to time whenever the very great pressure of Admiralty and public business afforded an opportunity. Accordingly, on January 19, 1915, I sent a minute to the Director of the Air Division instructing him to make certain experiments with steam rollers with a view to smashing in the trenches of the enemy by the mere weight of the engine. I had of course no expert knowledge of mechanics, and could only give or foster ideas of a suggestive character and provide funds and give orders for experiments and action. This particular variant (which was mentioned in Colonel Hankey's paper of December 28) broke down through its mechanical defects, but there is no doubt that it played its part in forming opinions among the armoured-car officers and experts connected with the armoured-car squadrons and in setting imagination to work for other and more helpful solutions.

So here are three quite separate efforts to procure the manufacture and adoption of the kind of vehicles afterwards called "Tanks," all of which had been brought to failure either by mechanical defects or by official obstruction. This deadlock might well have continued for an indefinite period of time. No demand for such weapons had come, or for many months came, from the military authorities in France: every suggestion from civilian or other quarters had been turned down by the War Office. The Dardanelles operations were beginning, and almost every hour of my day was occupied with grave Admiralty business. However, the Duke of Westminster, who commanded a squadron of armoured cars and who was himself a focus of discussion on these subjects, invited me to dine on February 17 to meet several officers from the armoured-car squadrons. The conversation turned on cross-country armoured vehicles, and Major Hetherington, who also belonged to the armoured-car squadrons and knew of the various experiments which had been made, spoke with force and vision on the whole subject, advocating the creation of land battleships on a scale far larger than has ever been found practicable.

As a result of this conversation, I went home determined that I would give imperative orders without delay to secure the carrying forward in one form or another of the project in which I had so long believed. Accordingly I directed Major Hetherington to submit his plans, which were at that time for a platform mounted on enormous wheels 40 feet in diameter, and I forwarded these plans two days later to the First Sea Lord (Lord Fisher), urging him to devote his great energies and mechanical aptitudes to getting them carried through. In addition to this, the next day, the 20th, I sent for Mr. Tennyson-d'Eyncourt,[1] the Chief Constructor of the Navy, and convened a conference which, as I was ill at the time, was held in my bedroom at the Admiralty on the afternoon of that day. As the result of it the Landships Committee of the Admiralty was formed by my orders, under the Presidency of Mr. Tennyson-d'Eyncourt, reporting direct to me, and they were urged in the most strenuous manner to labour to the very utmost to secure a solution of the problem.

From the formation of this committee on February 20, 1915, till the appearance of tanks in action in August, 1916, during the Battle of the Somme, there is an unbroken chain of causation.

On March 20, Mr. Tennyson-d'Eyncourt reported to me that his committee had evolved two possible types, much smaller than Major Hetherington had

---

[1] Afterwards Sir Eustace Tennyson-d'Eyncourt.

imagined, one moved by large wheels and the other by caterpillar action. I immediately called by minute for estimates of time and money.

These were supplied, and on March 26 I took the responsibility for ordering eighteen of these vehicles, which at that time were called landships, six of which were to be of the wheel type and twelve of the caterpillar type.

I thus took personal responsibility for the expenditure of the public money involved, about £70,000. I did not invite the Board of Admiralty to share this responsibility with me. I did not inform the War Office, for I knew they would raise objections to my interference in this sphere, and I knew by this time that the Department of the Master General of the Ordnance was not very receptive of such ideas. Neither did I inform the Treasury.

It was a serious decision to spend this large sum of money on a project so speculative, about the merits of which no high expert military or naval authority had been convinced. The matter, moreover, was entirely outside the scope of my own Department or of any normal powers which I possessed. Had the tanks proved wholly abortive or never been accepted or never used in war by the military authorities, and had I been subsequently summoned before a Parliamentary Committee, I could have offered no effective defence to the charge that I had wasted public money on a matter which was not in any way my business and in regard to which I had not received expert advice in any responsible military quarter. The extremely grave situation of the war, and my conviction of the need of breaking down the deadlock which blocked the production of these engines, are my defence; but that defence is only valid in view of their enormous subsequent success.

A general observation may here be made. There was no novelty about the idea of an armoured vehicle to travel across country and pass over trenches and other natural obstacles while carrying guns and fighting men. Mr. H. G. Wells, in an article written in 1903, had practically exhausted the possibilities of imagination in this sphere. Moreover, from very early times the history of war is filled with devices of this character for use in the attack of fortresses and fortified positions. The general principles of applying the idea were also fairly obvious. Bullet-proof armour had been carried to a high point of perfection by various hardening processes. The internal-combustion engine supplied the motive power. The Pedrail and Caterpillar systems were both well known, and had been widely applied in many parts of the world. Thus the three elements out of which tanks have been principally constituted were at hand to give effect to the idea.

There are, however, two things to be kept distinct:

(*a*) The responsibility for initiating and sustaining the action which led to the tanks being produced, and (*b*) the credit for solving the extremely difficult problems connected with design apart from main principles.

These services were entirely separate. There never was a moment when it was possible to say that a tank had been "invented." There never was a person about whom it could be said "this man invented the tank." But there was a moment when the actual manufacture of the first tanks was definitely ordered, and there was a moment when an effective machine was designed as the direct outcome of this authorization.

I consider that the responsibility for the mechanical execution of the project was borne by Mr. Tennyson-d'Eyncourt. Without his high authority and immense expert knowledge the project could not have been carried to success. Under his guidance, invaluable services in the sphere of adaptation and manufacture were rendered by Sir William Tritton and Major Wilson. But I sanctioned the expenditure of public money in reliance upon Mr. Tennyson-d'Eyncourt's gifts and knowledge, and his assurances that the mechanical difficulties could be solved. I trusted him, as I would have trusted Admiral Bacon in the earlier project, to say whether the thing could be done or not and to find a way round and through the technical difficulties. And once he said it could be done, I was prepared to incur both risk and responsibility in providing the necessary funds and in issuing the necessary authority. It was with him alone that I dealt, and it was from me alone that he received his orders.

Others, such as Colonel Swinton and Captain T. G. Tulloch, had seized the idea and had even laid specific proposals before the War Office in January, 1915. These officers had not however the executive authority which alone could ensure progress and their efforts were brought to nothing by the obstruction of some of their superiors. They were unfortunate in not being able to command the resources necessary for action, or to convince those who had the power to act.

After I left the Admiralty at the end of May, 1915, another moment of extreme peril threatened the enterprise. The new Board of Admiralty included three out of the four naval members of the old Board. Reinforced by Sir Henry Jackson, the new First Sea Lord, they appear to have viewed the financial commitments which had already been incurred to an extent of about £45,000 as either undesirable or wholly beyond the sphere of Admiralty interests. They therefore, in the general disfavour in which my affairs were at this time involved, proposed to terminate the contracts and scrap the whole project. However, Mr. Tennyson-d'Eyncourt remained faithful to the charge I had laid upon him. He warned me of the decisions which were impending, or which had perhaps been taken, and I thereupon as a Member of the War Committee of the Cabinet appealed personally to Mr. Balfour, the new First Lord. After consideration, Mr. Balfour decided that the construction of one experimental machine should be proceeded with. One alone survived. But this proved to be the "Mother Tank" which, displayed in Hatfield Park in January, 1916, became the exact model of the tanks which fought on the Somme in August, 1916, and was the parent and in principle the prototype of all the heavy tanks that fought in the Great War.

The paragraph in my letter of January 5 to the Prime Minister upon the use of smoke and the reference to secrets which lay behind it, also requires a digression.

Early in September, 1914, Lieutenant-General Lord Dundonald, the grandson of the famous Admiral Cochrane, spoke to Lord Kitchener of various plans left by his ancestor for making smoke screens, and also for driving an enemy from his position by means of noxious though not necessarily deadly fumes. "Lord Kitchener," writes Lord Dundonald, "at once told me that he did not consider that the plans were of any use for land operations, and as they were invented by an Admiral, I had better see the Admiralty about them."[1] Lord Dundonald therefore obtained an introduction to the Second Sea Lord, Sir Frederick Hamilton, with whom he had an interview on September 28. The Second Sea Lord was generally favourable, and wrote (September 29), "I have talked the matter over with Prince Louis and he thinks you had better see Churchill and not mention us." I had served in Lord Dundonald's Brigade in South Africa during the Relief of Ladysmith, and I at once made an appointment to receive him. I was immediately interested in his ideas, and asked to see the plans of the illustrious Cochrane. Lord Dundonald replied after a few days' consideration that he felt that the national emergency at last justified him in revealing the secret which he had guarded all his life, and in the middle of October he brought me the historic papers which once before, in the Crimean War, had been placed at the disposal of the British Government. On the inner covering of the packet in the delicate writing of the old Admiral, were the words, "To the Imperial mind one sentence will suffice: All fortifications, especially marine fortifications, can under cover of dense smoke be irresistibly subdued by fumes of sulphur kindled in masses to windward of their ramparts." The reader, captivated by the compliment, will no doubt rise to the occasion and grasp at once the full significance of the idea. I sent for the First Sea Lord (Prince Louis of Battenberg) without delay and we had a prolonged discussion.

I now cast about for means of exploring the subject without endangering its secrecy. In the first instance I had recourse to Sir Arthur Wilson, whose practical and inventive turn of mind seemed specially adapted to the task. The results were, however, negative. During the weeks that followed Lord Dundonald

[1] Memorandum of the Earl of Dundonald. (Unpublished.)

continued to send me admirable suggestions, based on his grandfather's ideas, and, after giving decisive instructions to make experiments, I continued to endeavour to secure in secrecy powerful professional endorsement. He wrote me in October:

> The successful use of the plan above all depends on a favourable wind. . . . The wind statistics from the coast of Holland to Berlin show that the wind from [westerly directions] is far more prevalent than from the opposite or eastern section of the compass, especially is this so during November, December, January, and February. . . .
> . . . The vehicles with sulphur would be conducted and operated by men in Gas-proof helmets. . . .
> An attack against miles of entrenchment would be made on sectional fronts by sulphur and smoke, the intervening blocks where sulphur would not be employed being smoked only, in order to blind the hostile artillery.

There can be no question but that Lord Dundonald had grasped at this time the whole idea of gas and smoke warfare, and that he had derived it directly from the papers of his grandfather. To these conceptions modern chemistry offered terrible possibilities. The use of noxious or poisonous fumes was explicitly prohibited by International Law. We could not therefore employ it ourselves unless and until the enemy himself began. But when from time to time, amid the rush of the war, I turned my mind to this subject, and thought of German chemical science and German mentality, I became increasingly disquieted. As it was very difficult to obtain any high Military or Naval assistance, and I had not the life and strength to carry this additional load of thought myself, I turned to another quarter. In January I advised Lord Dundonald to lay his grandfather's scheme before Colonel Hankey, and on March 21 I ordered a strong technical Committee on the subject to be formed under the presidency of Lord Dundonald. I made it clear, however, that we could not depart from the accepted Laws of War.

I kept in close touch with the work of the Committee. Progress, even in the limited sphere to which we were confined by International Law and State Policy, was slow and fitful; but on April 10 I was able to write to Sir John French:

MR. CHURCHILL TO SIR JOHN FRENCH.
April 10, 1915.
I have seen some wonderful smoke-making experiments carried out by my directions. A light portable metal cone of the simplest construction 3 feet high and 6 feet wide at the base is fed by gravity at the base with

benzol. The oil spreads over the surface of the cone, causing a dense smoke which you can turn off instantaneously by a tap on the fuel supply.

I am developing this system for naval purposes, but my reflections lead me increasingly to believe in its importance in the kind of warfare you are now waging. If the wind were favourable, you could blanket off absolutely in a few minutes a whole sector of the enemy's artillery and rifle fire. You could use it to cut out a particular village or line of trenches till your men were actually upon them with the bayonet. Or again you could cover the bringing up to the decisive point of a large mass of cavalry at the critical moment.

On April 22, 1915, the Germans, violating the Laws of War, made their first poison-gas attack, and the second battle of Ypres began. This crime and folly was destined to expose them to severe retaliation from those who had the advantage of the prevailing winds, and in the end of the superior science; but who had hitherto been restrained by respect for international usage from turning their favourable position to account.

There is one further stage in the tale of the Tanks to be described, and for this I must considerably anticipate chronology. When I resigned from the Cabinet in November, 1915, in circumstances which will be presently related, and joined the Army in France, I conceived myself to be the bearer to them of a good gift. This gift was the conception of a battle and of a victory; and I knew that the Commander-in-Chief, Sir John French, would study the proposals I submitted with deep and friendly attention. Accordingly on arrival at General Headquarters I drew up a paper dated December 3 called "Variants of the Offensive," which was printed for the Commitee of Imperial Defence. I laid this before Sir John French, and later before his successor, Sir Douglas Haig. The first of these Variants may be quoted here.

CATERPILLARS.

The cutting of the enemy's wire and the general domination of his firing-line can be effected by engines of this character. About seventy are now nearing completion in England, and should be inspected. None should be used until all can be used at once. They should be disposed secretly along the whole attacking front two or three hundred yards apart. Ten or fifteen minutes before the assault these engines should move forward over the best line of advance open, passing through or across our trenches at prepared points. They are capable of traversing any ordinary obstacle, ditch, breastwork, or trench. They carry two or three Maxims each, and can be fitted with flame apparatus. Nothing but a direct hit from a field gun will stop them. On reaching the enemy's wire they turn to the left or right and run down parallel to the enemy's trench, sweeping his parapet with their fire, and crushing and cutting the barbed wire in lanes and in a slightly serpentine course. While doing this the Caterpillars will be so close to the enemy's line that they will be immune from his artillery. Through the gaps thus made the shield-bearing infantry will advance.

If artillery is used to cut wire, the direction and imminence of the attack is proclaimed days beforehand. But by this method the assault follows the wire-cutting almost immediately, i.e. before any reinforcements can be brought up by the enemy, or any special defensive measures taken.[1]

4. The Caterpillars are capable of actually crossing the enemy's trench and advancing to cut his communication trenches; but into this aspect it is not necessary to go now. One step at a time. It will be easy, when the enemy's front line is in our hands, to find the best places for the Caterpillars to cross by for any further advance which may be required. They can climb any slope. They are, in short, movable machine-gun cupolas as well as wire-smashers. The naval torpedo-net-cutter, fixed in front of them with guides to lead the gathered wires into it, has proved absolutely successful. The spectacle of such a machine cutting wire entanglements has only to be witnessed to carry conviction. It resembles the reaping operations of a self-binder. Three or four days' notice to the Trench Warfare Department should enable this demonstration to be made.

5. It is obvious that the above form of attack requires, at the present season, frost, darkness, and surprise. The parry to the Caterpillar is either protective mining galleries, fougasses, buried shells, etc., or field guns concealed in the parapet. But if this trick works once, a new one can be devised for next time. Until these machines are actually in France, it is not possible to measure the full limit of their powers. But it is believed that during the dark hours of a winter's night not one but several successive lines of trenches could be taken by their agency. As they moved forward into the enemy's positions, his artillery would be increasingly hampered in firing at them, and, with deepening confusion, the location of and laying the guns upon these moving structures will become almost impossible. Daylight would leave them an easy prey,[2] but if daylight witnessed an entirely new situation they would have done their part, even if they could not be withdrawn. They would, as they advanced, carry the infantry attack along with them and serve as movable *points d'appui*, guiding and defining the attack.

---

[1] The italics are new.
[2] I underrated their immunity.

The scheme of attack by caterpillar vehicles thus unfolded was not put into operation until the first Battle of Cambrai in November, 1917. In the light of years of experience many errors can be detected in this forecast; but it might well have served as a basis for intense military study. Three months later, in February, 1916, Colonel Swinton, who was then serving on the Secretariat of the Committee of Imperial Defence, and had witnessed the early trials of "Mother Tank," set forth and printed in careful and accurate detail the plan of a Tank battle on a great scale. In spite of this it took the High Command nearly two whole years more to learn to use tanks in the manner and conditions for which they were originally conceived. During the interval every conceivable mistake was committed, which lack of comprehension could suggest. The first twenty tanks, in spite of my protests and the far more potent objections of Mr. Asquith and Mr. Lloyd George, were improvidently exposed to the enemy at the Battle of the Somme. The immense advantage of novelty and surprise was thus squandered while the number of the tanks was small, while their condition was experimental and their crews almost untrained. This priceless conception, containing if used in its integrity and on a sufficient scale, the certainty of a great and brilliant victory, was revealed to the Germans for the mere petty purpose of taking a few ruined villages. Mercifully the high military authorities of all countries belonged to the same school of thought. The revelation passed unappreciated by the German Command. Though full of novelty and terror, the tank could no longer be an apparition, but at least we were not ourselves confronted with German tanks in large numbers in 1917.

That year was to witness the further misuse of the British tank. Instead of employing them all at once in dry weather on ground not torn by bombardment, in some new sector where they could operate very easily and by surprise, they were plunged in fours and fives as a mere minor adjunct of the infantry into the quagmires and craterfields of Passchendaele. The enemy was familiarized with them by their piecemeal use; and they themselves were brought wallowing to a standstill in the mud. Indeed at the end of 1917 many high authorities in the British Army had become almost convinced that they were useless, and gilded wiseacres were beginning to unearth again their original condemnations of such unprofessional expedients. Fortunately, the mishandling of the tanks and their consequent failure produced a similar impression on the German mind, and once again the enemy lost the opportunity of hoisting us "with our own petard."

In spite of the reasoning of two years before and the steady appeals and arguments of the officers of the Tank Corps, it was not until Passchendaele was over that the tanks were given their chance. They were at last to have their own battle. They were at last to be allowed to show that they could destroy wire without a bombardment which would warn the enemy, and consequently restore the element of surprise to a modern offensive. To General Byng fell the honour of organizing the Battle of Cambrai which began on November 20, 1917. Tardily and doubtingly as they were used, the results were decisive. In a few hours a victory was gained almost without loss. However, as no adequate preparations had been made to exploit it, the after consequences were disappointing, and even a few days later disastrous. It was not until 1918 that the combination of smoke with tanks, and the use of smoke to cover the advance of numbers of tanks, were actually adopted in the field. Had the war continued into 1919, every tank would have possessed the means of making its own smoke, and all tank operations would have been conducted under clouds of artificial fog. But after the Battle of Cambrai the fame of the tanks was secure, and henceforward throughout 1918 they became to the eyes of friend and foe alike, the great decisive weapon and distinctive feature of the British, French and American offensives.

CHAPTER XX

THE CHOICE

The New Year opened for the Admiralty under queer and stormy skies. We have seen how Vice-Admiral Bayly had been brought from the Grand Fleet to command the 5th Battle Squadron at the Nore, and how this squadron was to become the nucleus of a specially trained bombarding fleet, through which it was hoped to develop the means of a naval offensive. The Admiral came down from the North by no means enamoured of a change which gave him a squadron of "Formidables" in place of the "Dreadnoughts" which he had commanded. Like most sailors, his heart was with the Grand Fleet; but he addressed himself to his new work with his customary zeal. He sought permission from the Admiralty to take his squadron into the Channel for a cruise. He passed the Straits in daylight under flotilla escort arranged from the Admiralty and spent December 31 exercising off Portland. The flotilla, after seeing him through the Straits, left him at dusk to return to Dover, and no evil consequences had occurred during the daylight. The ships turned westward down channel after dark and by 2 a.m. were approaching the Start. The wind and sea were rising, but the moon shone brightly. The speed was 10 knots and the course direct, not zigzag. A German submarine, cruising on the surface of the Channel, unobserved in the moonlight amid the dancing waves, fired a torpedo with fatal effect against the *Formidable*, the last ship of the line. In two hours and a half the vessel sank with the loss of Captain Loxley and over 500 officers and men, the highest forms of discipline and devotion being observed by all ranks.

This melancholy news reached the Admiralty with the light of New Year's Day. Lord Fisher was indignant at the manner in which the squadron had been handled. The explanations which were demanded of the Admiral were not considered satisfactory by his naval chiefs. To my extreme regret, both on personal and on far wider grounds, it was decided to remove him from his command. I therefore appointed him to the control of Greenwich College, where he remained for some time.[1]

---

[1] Vice-Admiral Sir Lewis Bayly in the later years of the war, as is well known, fully vindicated the high qualities with which he had been credited.

Various attempts were now made to survey the general situation and make plans for the spring. On January 1 the Chancellor of the Exchequer, Mr. Lloyd George, circulated a paper of the highest importance, drawing attention to the unfounded optimism which prevailed about the war situation, to the increasing failure of Russia as a prime factor, and to the need for action in the Balkan Peninsula to rally Greece and Bulgaria to the cause of the Allies. There was also a pregnant and prescient Memorandum by Colonel Hankey, which is referred to in the Report of the Dardanelles Commission. Both these papers pointed to the Near East as the true field for our action and initiative in 1915. After reading advance copies of these documents I forwarded the latter on December 31 to the Prime Minister, saying:

> We are substantially in agreement, and our conclusions are not incompatible.
> I wanted Gallipoli attacked on the declaration of war. . . . Meanwhile the difficulties have increased. . . . I think the War Council ought to meet daily for a few days next week. No topic can be pursued to any fruitful result at weekly intervals.

On January 2 I received the following letter from Lord Kitchener:

> You have no doubt seen Buchanan's telegram about the Russians and Turks; if not Fitzgerald is taking it over.
> Do you think any naval action would be possible to prevent [the] Turks sending more men into the Caucasus and thus denuding Constantinople?

With this note, Colonel Fitzgerald brought the telegram from which the following extract is relevant:

> Early this week the position of Russians in the Caucasus gave cause for grave anxiety. Turks having commenced enveloping movement seriously threatening Russian forces. Commander-in-Chief of the Army in the Caucasus pressed most urgently for reinforcements, many Caucasian troops being now employed against Germans, but Grand Duke has told him he must manage to keep on as he is.
> *Grand Duke, however, asked if it would be possible for Lord Kitchener to arrange for a demonstration of some kind against Turks elsewhere, either naval or military, and to spread reports which would cause Turks, who he says*

are very liable to go off at a tangent, to withdraw some of the forces now act-ing against Russians in the Caucasus, and thus ease the position of Russians.[1]

Grand Duke added that, even if Lord Kitchener was unable to help, he should stick to his present plans.

Later in the day Lord Kitchener came over himself to see me at the Admiralty, and we had a full discussion on the Russian telegram and whether the Navy could do anything to help. All the possible alternatives in the Turkish theatre were mentioned. We both had in mind our discussions of November on the possibilities of a descent from Egypt upon Gallipoli. We both saw clearly the far-reaching consequences of a successful attack upon Constantinople. If there was any prospect of a serious attempt to force the Straits of the Dardanelles at a later stage, it would be in the highest degree improvident to stir them up for the sake of a mere demonstration. I put this point forward, and suggested alternative diversions to help the Russians. Lord Kitchener did not dissent from the argument, but he returned steadily and decidedly to the statement that he had no troops to spare, and could not face a large new expansion of our military commitments. I have no record of this conversation, but my recollection of it is confirmed by the second letter which I received from Lord Kitchener on this same day (January 2).

LORD KITCHENER TO MR. CHURCHILL.

January 2, 1915.

I do not see that we can do anything that will very seriously help the Russians in the Caucasus.

The Turks are evidently withdrawing most of their troops from Adrianople and using them to reinforce their army against Russia, probably sending them by the Black Sea.

In the Caucasus and Northern Persia the Russians are in a bad way.

We have no troops to land anywhere. A demonstration at Smyrna would do no good and probably cause the slaughter of Christians. Alexandretta has already been tried, and would have no great effect a second time. The coast of Syria would have no effect. The only place that a demonstration might have some effect in stopping reinforcements going East would be the Dardanelles. Particularly if, as the Grand Duke says, reports could be spread at the same time that Constantinople was threatened.

We shall not be ready for anything big for some months.

[1] The italics are mine.

On the same day Lord Kitchener, as the result no doubt of the conversation which he had had with me, sent through the Foreign Office the following telegram to Petrograd:

> Please assure the Grand Duke that steps will be taken to make a demonstration against the Turks. It is, however, feared that any action we can devise and carry out will be unlikely to seriously affect numbers of enemy in the Caucasus, or cause their withdrawal.

This telegram committed us to a demonstration against the Turks of some kind or another, but it did not commit us in respect of its direction, character or scope. It was the least that could have been said in answer to a request of a hard-pressed Ally.

The next morning (January 3) Lord Fisher entered the field. He had been considering all these matters, had read the various Cabinet papers and the Russian telegram, and had full knowledge of my conversation with Lord Kitchener. The letter which he now sent me is of great importance. It reveals Lord Fisher's position fully and clearly. The turbulence of its style in no way affects the shrewdness and profundity of its vision. I do not think that Lord Fisher ever took any action or expressed any opinions which were irreconcilable with the general principles of these first thoughts. He was always in favour of a great scheme against the Turks and to rally the Balkans. He always believed that Bulgaria was the key to the situation in this quarter. He was always prepared to risk the old battleships as part of a large naval, military and diplomatic combination. In all this we were, as his letter shows, in entire agreement. That these large schemes were not carried into effect was not his fault nor mine.

January 3, 1915.

Dear Winston,

I've been informed by Hankey that War Council assembles next Thursday, and I suppose it will be like a game of ninepins! Everyone will have a plan and one ninepin in falling will knock over its neighbour! I CONSIDER THE ATTACK ON TURKEY HOLDS THE FIELD!—but ONLY if it's IMMEDIATE! However, it won't be! Our Aulic Council will adjourn till the following Thursday fortnight! (N.B. *When did we meet last and what came of it???*)

We shall decide on a futile bombardment of the Dardanelles which wears out the irreplaceable guns of the *Indefatigable* which probably will require replacement. What good resulted from the last bombardment? Did it move a single Turk from the Caucasus? And so the war goes on! You want ONE man!

This is the Turkey plan:

I. Appoint Sir W. Roberston the present Quartermaster-General to command the Expeditionary Force.

II. Immediately replace all Indians and 75,000 seasoned troops from Sir John French's command with Territorials, etc., from England (as you yourself suggested) and embark this Turkish Expeditionary Force ostensibly for protection of Egypt! WITH ALL POSSIBLE DESPATCH at *Marseilles!* and land them at Besika Bay direct with previous feints before they arrive with troops now in Egypt against Haifa and Alexandretta, the latter to be a REAL occupation because of its inestimable value as regards the oil fields of the Garden of Eden, with which by rail it is in direct communication, and we shove out the Germans now established at Alexandretta with an immense Turkish concession—the last act of that arch-enemy of England, Marschall von Bieberstein!

III. The Greeks to go for Gallipoli at the same time as we go for Besika, and the Bulgarians for Constantinople, and the Russians, the Servians, and Roumanians for Austria *(all this you said yourself!).*

IV. Sturdee forces the Dardanelles at the same time with "Majestic" class and "Canopus" class! God bless him!

But as the great Napoleon said, "CELEBRITY"—without it—"FAILURE"!

In the history of the world—a Junta has never won! You want *one* man!

Yours,

F.

There never was the slightest chance of the whole of the Fisher plan being carried into effect. Sir William Robertson, to whom he proposed to entrust it, would presumably have advised strongly against it, his policy being, concentration in the main, or, as he would no doubt have described it, the decisive theatre. The withdrawal of the Indian Corps and 75,000 seasoned troops from Sir John French's command and their replacement by Territorial Divisions would have been resisted to the point of resignation by the Commander-in-Chief, supported by his whole staff. General Joffre and the French Government would have protested in a decisive manner. Lord Fisher's third paragraph about the Greeks, Bulgarians, Serbians and Roumanians expressed exactly what everybody wanted. It was the obvious supreme objective in this part of the world. The question was, How to procure it? This was the root of the matter. It was in connection with this that Lord Fisher's fourth paragraph made its impression upon me. Here for the first time was the suggestion of forcing the Dardanelles with the old battleships.

This series of weighty representations had the effect of making me move. I thought I saw a great convergence of opinion in the direction of that attack upon the Dardanelles which I had always so greatly desired. The arguments in its favour were overwhelming. And now the highest authorities, political, naval and military, were apparently ready to put their shoulders to the wheel. All Mr. Lloyd George's advocacy and influence seemed about to be cast in the direction of Turkey and the Balkans. Though his method was different, the ultimate object, namely, the rallying of the Balkan States against Austria and Turkey, was the same, and all his arguments applied equally to either method. I knew from my talks with Mr. Balfour that he too was profoundly impressed by the advantages which might be reaped by successful action in this South-Eastern theatre. Lastly, the Foreign Office and Sir Edward Grey were, of course, keenly interested. Here was a great consensus of opinion. Here it seemed at last was a sufficient impulse and unity for action. But was there a practicable scheme? This I determined to find out, and on January 3, with the active agreement of Lord Fisher and after a talk with Sir Henry Jackson who was specially studying this theatre and advising us thereupon, I telegraphed to Vice-Admiral Carden, commanding at the Dardanelles, as follows:

ADMIRALTY TO VICE-ADMIRAL CARDEN.

January 3, 1915.

From First Lord:

Do you consider the forcing of the Dardanelles by ships alone a practicable operation?

It is assumed older battleships fitted with mine-bumpers would be used, preceded by colliers or other merchant craft as mine-bumpers and sweepers.

Importance of results would justify severe loss.

Let me know your views.

All this was purely exploratory. I did not commit myself at this stage even to the general principle of an attack upon Turkey. I wanted to see the alternatives weighed and to see what support such projects would in fact command. All our affairs at this time were complicated with the plans which, as has been explained in the last chapter, were under discussion for the advance of the Army along the coast and for the closing up of Zeebrugge.

I was still thinking a great deal of the Northern theatre, of Borkum and of the Baltic. "We had better," I wrote on January 4 in a note to the First Sea Lord on various points that would come up for discussion at the War Council the next day, "hear what others have to say about the Turkish plans before taking a decided line. I would not grudge 100,000 men, because of the great political effects in the Balkan Peninsula. . . ."

"The naval advantages," he replied the same day, "of the possession of Constantinople and the getting of wheat from the Black Sea are so overwhelming that I consider Colonel Hankey's plan for Turkish operations vital and imperative and very pressing." [1]

There is no doubt we could have worked together unitedly and with the utmost enthusiasm for the Southern amphibious plan, if it had been pressed forward by the War Council on a great scale and with the necessary drive and decision.

On January 5 the answer from Admiral Carden arrived. It was remarkable.

VICE-ADMIRAL CARDEN TO FIRST LORD.

January 5, 1915.

With reference to your telegram of 3rd instant, I do not consider Dardanelles can be rushed.

They might be forced by extended operations with large number of ships.

At the War Council that afternoon the question of an attack on Turkey and a diversion in the Near East was one of the principal subjects discussed. Everyone seemed alive to all its advantages, and Admiral Carden's telegram; which I read out, was heard with extreme interest. Its significance lay in the fact that it offered a prospect of influencing the Eastern situation in a decisive manner without opening a new military commitment on a large scale; and further it afforded an effective means of helping the Grand Duke without wasting the Dardanelles possibilities upon nothing more than a demonstration. On my return to the Admiralty I found that the idea of a gradual forcing of the Straits by extended operations was reviewed with favour both by Admiral Oliver, the Chief of the Staff, and by Sir Henry Jackson. I had a conversation with Sir Henry Jackson, who had that day completed a memorandum upon the question (which I read some days later). Sir Henry Jackson deprecated any attempt to rush the Straits, but he spoke of the considerable effects of the brief bombardment of November 3, and he was attracted by the idea of a step-by-step reduction of the fortresses, though troops would be needed to follow up and complete the naval attack and especially to occupy Constantinople. So here we had the Chief of the Staff, the Admiral studying this particular theatre, and the Admiral in command, all apparently in general accord in principle. This coincidence of opinion in officers so widely separated and so differently circum-

---

[1] The word "plan" is hardly correct. Colonel Hankey had presented a general appreciation upon the importance of the Turkish theatre.

stanced impressed me very much, and I therefore telegraphed on January 6 to Vice-Admiral Carden as follows:

FIRST LORD TO ADMIRAL CARDEN.

January 6, 1915.

Your view is agreed with by high authorities here. Please telegraph in detail what you think could be done by extended operations, what force would be needed, and how you consider it should be used.

There was another meeting of the War Council on January 8 and prolonged discussion of the Eastern theatre. Dealing with the various alternatives, Lord Kitchener expressed an opinion in favour of an attack on the Dardanelles. He told the Council that the Dardanelles appeared to be the most suitable military objective, as an attack there could be made in co-operation with the Fleet. He estimated that 150,000 men would be sufficient for the capture of the Dardanelles, but reserved his final opinion until a close study had been made. He offered no troops and made it clear that none were available. His contribution was therefore, and was intended to be, purely theoretic.

On January 11 arrived the detailed Carden plan.[1] It was in its details largely the work of a very able officer of Marines—Captain Godfrey (who was one of the Vice-Admiral's Staff)—and of the gunnery experts of the *Inflexible.* I set it out in all essentials.

Possibility of operations:

(A.) Total reduction of defences at the entrance.

(B.) Clear defences inside of Straits up to and including Kephez Point Battery No. 8.

(C.) Reduction of defences at the Narrows, Chanak.

(D.) Clear passage through minefield, advancing through Narrows, reducing forts above Narrows, and final advance to Marmora.

Force required, 12 battleships, of which 4 fitted with mine-bumpers. Three battle-cruisers—2 should be available on entering Marmora—3 light cruisers, 1 flotilla leader, 16 destroyers, 1 depôt repairing ship, 6 submarines, 4 seaplanes and the *Foudre,* 12 mine-sweepers, including, perhaps, 4 fleet sweepers, 1 hospital ship, 6 colliers at Tenedos Island, 2 supply and ammunition ships. The above force allows for casualties.

Details of action:

---

[1] See map of Dardanelles on pp. 406–7.

Frequent reconnaissance by seaplanes indispensable.

(A.) Indirect bombardment of forts, reduction completed by direct bombardment at decisive range; torpedo tubes at the entrance and guns commanding minefield destroyed; minefield cleared.

(B.) Battleships, preceded by mine-sweepers, enter Straits, working way up till position reached from which battery No. 8 can be silenced.

(C.) Severe bombardment of forts by battle-cruisers from Gaba Tepe spotted from battleships; reduction completed by direct fire at decisive range.

(D.) Battleships, preceded by sweepers, making way up towards Narrows. Forts 22, 23, 24 first bombarded from Gaba Tepe, spotting for 22 by seaplanes, then direct fire. Sweep minefields in Narrows, the fort at Nagara reduced by direct fire, battle force proceeds to Marmora preceded by mine-sweepers.

Expenditure on ammunition for (C) would be large, but if supplies sufficient, result should be successful. Difficulty as to (B) greatly increased if *Goeben* assisting defence from Nagara. It would, unless submarine attacks successful, necessitate employment of battle-cruisers from Gaba Tepe or direct.

Time required for operations depends greatly on *moral* of enemy under bombardment; garrison largely stiffened by the Germans; also on the weather conditions. Gales now frequent. Might do it all in a month about.

Expenditure of ammunition would be large. Approximate estimate of quantity required being prepared.

Disposition of squadron on completion of operations: Marmora, 2 battle-cruisers, 4 battleships, 3 light cruisers, 1 flotilla leader, 12 torpedo-boat destroyers, 3 submarines, 1 supply and ammunition ship, 4 mine-sweepers, collier.

Remainder of force keeping Straits open and covering mine-sweepers completing clearing minefield.

This plan produced a great impression upon everyone who saw it. It was to me in its details an entirely novel proposition. My telegram had contemplated something in the nature of an organized "rush" in accordance with Lord Fisher's suggestion about Admiral Sturdee forcing the Straits with the "Canopus" class of battleships. I sent a copy of the plan at once to the Prime Minister and some others, and it was freely discussed among those who were informed. Both the First Sea Lord and the Chief of the Staff seemed favourable to it. No one at any time threw the slightest doubt upon its technical soundness. No one, for instance, of the four or five great naval authorities each with his technical staff who were privy said, "This is absurd. Ships cannot fight forts," or criticized its details. On the contrary, they all treated it as an extremely interesting and hopeful proposal; and there grew up in the secret circles of the Admiralty a perfectly clear opinion favourable to the operation. It was then that the War Staff made a suggestion which certainly greatly affected the issue.

The *Queen Elizabeth,* the first in order of the five fast battleships armed with 15-inch guns, was now ready. It had been decided to send her to fire her gunnery trials and calibration exercises in the safe, calm waters of the Mediterranean. She was actually under orders to proceed thither. The Staff now proposed that she should test her enormous guns against the Dardanelles and pointed out that she could fire at ranges far outside those of the Turkish forts. This had not occurred to me before. But the moment it was mentioned, its importance was apparent. We all felt ourselves in the presence of a new fact. Moreover, the *Queen Elizabeth* came into the argument with a cumulative effect. Vice-Admiral Carden had never dreamed of having her. Our previous discussions and his detailed plan had ignored any help that she might give.

I now called for definite plans and orders to be worked out by the Staff, and I outlined the fleet that was evidently available for the operation.

Secretary.
First Sea Lord
Chief of Staff.

January 12.

(1) The forcing of the Dardanelles as proposed, and the arrival of a squadron strong enough to defeat the Turkish Fleet in the Sea of Marmora, would be a victory of first importance, and change to our advantage the whole situation of the war in the East.

(2) It would appear possible to provide the force required by Admiral Carden without weakening the margins necessary in Home waters, as follows:

> *Ocean, Swiftsure* and *Triumph* (already in or assigned to this theatre).
> *Vengeance, Canopus* (from the Atlantic).
> *Albion* (from the Cape).
> *Cæsar* and *Prince George* (from Gibraltar).
> *Victorious, Mars, Magnificent, Hannibal* (already ordered to be dismantled at home).
> *Queen Elizabeth* (detailed for gunnery preparation at Gibraltar).
> *Inflexible* (ordered to Mediterranean to relieve *Indefatigable*).
> *Indefatigable* (already on the spot).

Thus no capital ship would be ordered from Home waters, except four already ordered to be dismantled.

(3) The above takes no account of four French battleships on the spot, and six others reported available. . . .

(4) Operations could begin on February 1, by long-range fire from *Queen Elizabeth* on forts at the entrance. It is not necessary to develop the full attack until the effect of the first stage of the operation has become apparent. All arrangements should be secretly concerted for carrying the plan through, the seaplanes and ancillary craft being provided. Admiral Carden to command. . . .

Definite plans should be worked out accordingly.

W. S. C.

Lord Fisher approved this minute, and himself at a later date (February 9) added to the proposed fleet the two quasi-Dreadnought battleships, the *Lord Nelson* and the *Agamemnon*. This was a great reinforcement, and involved a diminution to that extent in the margin of the Grand Fleet.

On January 13 I brought the project before the War Council. I circulated Admiral Carden's telegram twenty-four hours beforehand to its principal members, including, of course, the Prime Minister and Lord Kitchener. Lord Kitchener thought the plan was worth trying. "We could leave off the bombardment," he said, "if it did not prove effective." Lord Fisher and Sir Arthur Wilson were both present. Neither made any remark and I certainly thought that they agreed. The decision of the Council was unanimous, and was recorded in the following curious form:

That the Admiralty should consider promptly the possibility of effective action in the Adriatic at Cattaro or elsewhere—with a view *(inter alia)* of bringing pressure on Italy.

That the Admiralty should also prepare for a naval expedition in February to bombard and take the Gallipoli Peninsula with Constantinople as its objective.

After the Council I sent the following telegram on January 15 with Lord Fisher's concurrence to Admiral Carden.

Your scheme was laid by the First Sea Lord and myself before the Cabinet War Council yesterday, and was approved in principle.

We see no difficulty in providing the force you require, including the *Queen Elizabeth,* by February 15.

We entirely agree with your plan of methodical piecemeal reduction of forts as the Germans did at Antwerp.

We propose to entrust this operation to you.

Admiral de Robeck will probably be your second in command.

The sooner we can begin the better.

You will shortly receive the official instructions of the Board.

Continue to perfect your plan.

I now proceeded to open the matter to the French Government, with whom among other things the question of the command in the Mediterranean required readjustment.

I outlined our plan for forcing the Dardanelles and added:

The Admiralty do not wish, in view of this very important operation, that any change in the local command in that portion of the Mediterranean should be made at the present time. They hope, however, that the squadron of French battleships, together with the French submarines and destroyers and the seaplane ship *Foudre,* will co-operate under a French rear-admiral.

Before handing this note to the French naval attaché I took care to have the draft formally countersigned by the Prime Minister, Lord Kitchener, and Sir Edward Grey, as well as by the First Sea Lord and the Chief of the Staff. This precaution was appropriate to a matter of grave importance, about which it was essential there should be no subsequent misunderstanding.

I made a similar communication to the Grand Duke Nicholas.

It will be seen that the genesis of this plan and its elaboration were purely naval and professional in their character. It was Admiral Carden and his staff gunnery officers who proposed the gradual method of piecemeal reduction by long-range bombardment. It was Sir Henry Jackson and the Admiralty staff who embraced this idea and studied and approved its detail. Right or wrong, it was a Service plan. Similarly the Admiralty orders were prepared exclusively by the Chief of the Staff and his assistants. I outlined the resources at our disposal in the old battleships. But it was the staff who proposed the addition of the *Queen Elizabeth,* with all the possibilities that that ship opened out. It was the First Sea Lord who added the other two most powerful vessels, the *Lord Nelson* and the *Agamemnon,* to the Dardanelles Fleet. At no point did lay or civilian interference mingle with or mar the integrity of a professional conception.

I write this not in the slightest degree to minimize or shift my own responsibility. But this was not where it lay. I did not and I could not make the plan. But when it had been made by the naval authorities, and fashioned and endorsed by high technical authorities and approved by the First Sea Lord, I seized upon it and set it on the path of action; and thereafter espoused it with all my resources. When others weakened or changed their opinion without adducing new reasons, I held them strongly to their previous decisions; and so in view of the general interest of the Allies, thrust the business steadily forward into actual experiment.

Thus is completed the account of the first phase in the initiation of the enterprise against the Dardanelles. There can be very little dispute about the facts in the face of the documents. For twenty days the project has been under discussion among the leading naval authorities of the day, and among the members of the War Council. At the Admiralty it has been the question most debated in our secret circle. So far all opinions are favourable. So far no voice has been raised and no argument advanced against it. The writer of the Australian official history has thought it right to epitomize the story in the following concluding sentence:

"So through a Churchill's excess of imagination, a layman's ignorance of artillery, and the fatal power of a young enthusiasm to convince older and slower brains, the tragedy of Gallipoli was born."

It is my hope that the Australian people, towards whom I have always felt a solemn responsibility, will not rest content with so crude, so inaccurate, so incomplete and so prejudiced a judgment, but will study the facts for themselves.

CHAPTER XXI

THE ACTION OF THE DOGGER BANK, JANUARY 24

During the middle of January uneasiness about our naval situation manifested itself in the high and secret circles of the Government. Sir John Jellicoe has described in his book what he considered the exceptional weakness of the Grand Fleet at this juncture. His letters to the First Sea Lord were filled with disquieting computations of the relative strength of the British and German navies in the event of a great battle. Several of his Dreadnoughts were undergoing their normal refits, and two more, the *Monarch* and the *Conqueror*, were temporarily disabled by a collision. He returned to the theory which he had developed in the preceding November, that the Germans had secretly armed their latest battleships with much heavier guns. But whereas in November the suggestion had been that four ships were now armed with 14-inch guns, it had by this time grown to six ships and 15-inch guns. There was of course no possibility of such a transformation having taken place. Our Intelligence had secured us identifications of these vessels out of dock and in movement at various dates which made it unbelievable that such enormous reconstructions could have been accomplished. I was, however, forced to combat these arguments and others equally alarming in character, and in particular to set up a Committee under the Third Sea Lord to allay the apprehension that this great re-armament had taken place.

Another request of the Commander-in-Chief caused me much embarrassment. He showed himself extremely anxious that the battle-cruisers which had been stationed at the Forth should be withdrawn to Cromarty in order to be in closer relation with the main Fleet. This proposal, if acceded to, would have deprived us of the means of acting with any effect against a German raid upon our coasts, should the enemy repeat the experiment which he had tried on December 16 against Hartlepool and Scarborough. Cromarty was as far from Heligoland as Scapa, and the withdrawal of Admiral Beatty and the battle-cruisers to this remote station seemed to involve us in unnecessary helplessness. I would have preferred indeed that the whole Battle Fleet should come south to the Forth. But if this could not yet be achieved, I strongly objected to the battle-cruisers being withdrawn from strategic relation with the enemy's fast vessels. I therefore minuted to the First Sea Lord on January 20:

> The battle-cruisers ought to be kept together, as then we shall always have a force strong enough to beat the whole of the German fast vessels. They will be quite out of reach for any action to protect the coasts of England if they go to Cromarty, which is the same distance from Heligoland as Scapa. I therefore think they should not be divided or moved from the Forth, unless Admiral Beatty reports that he finds the navigational conditions dangerous.

I discussed this question and other matters connected with the strength of the Grand Fleet with Lord Fisher fully the next morning, and he agreed to the view which I took. I therefore minuted to the Chief of the Staff, on the afternoon of the 21st:

> The battle-cruisers should be kept together at the Forth as at present, unless Admiral Beatty reports that he finds the navigational conditions dangerous. . . . Action accordingly.

The repercussion of these misgivings manifested itself in the War Council; and on January 21 the Prime Minister wrote informing me that he was summoning a meeting of the War Council for the 28th and that he desired that Sir John Jellicoe should be invited to be present. I became conscious that adverse currents were once more flowing around the Admiralty. I did not think that it was right to bring Sir John Jellicoe away from his fleet to London in order to attend a War Council during a period admittedly one of stringency in our own strength, and during which from every indication enemy activity might well be expected. I therefore resisted the summoning of Sir John Jellicoe to London.

As the result of discussions which proceeded between the German naval staff and the Emperor at the beginning of the year, rigorous restrictions had been imposed upon the German Fleet. In consequence of these Imperial decisions, Admiral von Ingenohl arranged to send his most powerful battle squadron, the Third, consisting of the "Kaisers" and the "Königs," into the Baltic for training. He intended, however, that there should first be another enterprise of a limited character by the Fleet in the North Sea. Owing to bad weather this enterprise was postponed from day to day. Towards the middle of January he and the German naval staff led themselves to believe that a great British naval offensive was imminent. They had heard about the dummy warships which were being constructed in Belfast, and they connected these with a plan for running block ships into the river mouths of the Heligoland Bight. They passed some days in a fever heat of excitement and at a high pitch of readiness. On the morning of the 19th a German seaplane sixty miles out from Heligoland sighted "numerous

English ships bound upon an easterly course, among them several battle-cruisers and close upon a hundred small craft." This then they thought was the great blockading operation. It was, in fact, a reconnaissance in force by the Harwich destroyer and submarine flotillas supported by the battle-cruisers. When nothing happened and later reports showed the Germans that a large part of the British Fleet had approached their coast and had then retired, von Ingenohl concluded that the blocking operation had been abandoned or at any rate postponed. He proceeded forthwith on the 20th to relax his special precautions, and on the 21st sent the Third Squadron through the Kiel Canal for their exercises in the Baltic. The contradictory and inconsequent decisions which followed are sourly described in the German Official History.

After this general relaxation of the state of readiness it would have been quite natural if, in accordance with the guiding lines laid down in the Commander-in-Chief's report and in his war diary, he had now shown still less initiative than before as regards offensive operations in the North Sea. But the weather improved just at this time, and Vice-Admiral Eckerman, the Chief of Staff, wanted to take the opportunity of making up for inactivity during the bad weather. Accordingly on January 22 he submitted the following suggestions to the Commander-in-Chief in writing:

"If the weather to-morrow remains as it has been this afternoon and evening, a cruiser and destroyer advance to the Dogger Bank would in my opinion be very advisable. No special preparations are needed; an order issued to-morrow morning to the Senior Officer, Scouting Forces, would be sufficient.

"Proceed out at night, arrive in the forenoon, return in the evening."

Admiral von Ingenohl [says the German historian] at once realized that this proposal was in contradiction to the guiding lines just laid down, and he made the following marginal note:

"I should prefer it if such advances were made only when the Fleet can proceed in company. Unfortunately this is impossible at the moment."

Nevertheless he gave his consent. . . .

At 10:25 the next morning the following order was sent to Rear-Admiral von Hipper by Wireless Telegraphy:

"First and Second Scouting Groups, Senior Officer of Destroyers and two flotillas to be selected by the Senior Officer Scouting Forces are to reconnoitre the Dogger Bank. They are to leave harbour this evening after dark and to return to-morrow evening after dark."

On the 23rd Lord Fisher, who in spite of several divergences of view which will be dealt with later, had been very staunch and good to me over the Jellicoe incident, was laid up with a cold. I therefore visited him at Archway House, which adjoins the Admiralty buildings. We had a long and pleasant talk over our various problems. It was nearly noon when I regained my room in the Admiralty. I had hardly sat down when the door opened quickly and in marched Sir Arthur Wilson unannounced. He looked at me intently, and there was a glow in his eye. Behind him came Oliver with charts and compasses.

"First Lord, these fellows are coming out again."

"When?"

"To-night. We have just got time to get Beatty there."

We sent successively at brief intervals the following telegrams:

ADMIRALTY TO COMMODORE (T),[1] HARWICH.

Negative plan Z. All your destroyers and light cruisers will be wanted to-night. Negative sending destroyers to Sheerness for escort.

ADMIRALTY TO VICE-ADMIRAL 'LION,' ROSYTH.

Get ready to sail at once with all battle-cruisers and light cruisers and sea-going destroyers. Further orders follow.

ADMIRALTY TO COMMANDER-IN-CHIEF GRAND FLEET.

First, Second and Fourth Battle Squadrons, cruisers and light cruisers should be ready to sail after dark this evening.

This done, Sir Arthur explained briefly the conclusions which he had formed from the intercepted German message which our cryptographers had translated, and from other intelligence of which he was a master. All the German fast vessels were putting to sea at dark, and a raid upon the British coast was clearly to be expected. My companions then addressed themselves to fixing the rendezvous for the various British forces. The chart and the compass circles showed in a moment that only Beatty from the Forth and Tyrwhitt from Har-

---

[1] The officer commanding the Flotillas, Commodore Tyrwhitt, was styled in naval parlance Commodore of Torpedoes, or for short, "Commodore (T)." Similarly the Captain of Submarines was called "Captain (S)."

wich could intercept the Germans before they could strike and escape. The Grand Fleet could not reach the scene till the next afternoon, nor could any ships stationed at Cromarty. There was, however, just time for Beatty and Tyrwhitt to join forces at daylight near the Dogger Bank. Wilson and Oliver had already drawn on the chart, with what afterwards proved to be almost exact accuracy, the probable line of the enemy's course. They stepped it out with the compasses hour by hour, at what they guessed would be the German speed, till it reached our coasts. They then drew from the Forth and Harwich the intercepting lines of Beatty and of Tyrwhitt. The intention was that the British forces should meet and be united at daybreak at some point about ten miles, or half an hour behind the enemy after he had passed Westward, and consequently be *between* him and *his* home. We discussed whether we could run the risk of a more adventurous scoop, i.e. a rendezvous for our ships still farther to the eastward. This would give more certainty of being between the enemy and his home, but also more chance of missing him if the weather became thick; and remembering what had happened on December 16, this last possibility seemed a very serious one. Thus the rendezvous was fixed for 7 the next morning the 24th, in 55° 13′ North, 3° 12′ East, i.e. 180 miles from Heligoland and almost in a line drawn from Heligoland to the Firth of Forth.[1] The following telegram was sent to the Commander-in-Chief with the Grand Fleet at Scapa, to Admiral Bradford with the Third Battle Squadron, to Admiral Beatty with the battle-cruisers at Rosyth, and to Commodore Tyrwhitt with the light cruisers and destroyers at Harwich:[2]

> Four German battle-cruisers, six light cruisers and twenty-two destroyers will sail this evening to scout on Dogger Bank, probably returning to-morrow evening. All available battle-cruisers, light cruisers, and destroyers from Rosyth should proceed to a rendezvous in 55° 13′ N., 3° 12′ E., arriving at 7:0 a.m. to-morrow. Commodore (T) is to proceed with all available destroyers and light cruisers from Harwich to join Vice-Admiral *Lion,* at 7:0 a.m. at above rendezvous. If enemy is sighted by Commodore (T) while crossing their line of advance, they should be attacked. W[ireless] T[elegraphy] is not to be used unless absolutely necessary. Telegram has been sent to Commander-in-Chief Home Fleet; Vice-Admiral *Lion;* Vice-Admiral Third Battle Squadron; and Commodore (T).

Nearly an hour had passed in these calculations and discussions, and meanwhile the First Sea Lord was still unaware of what was taking place. I therefore

---

[1] The attention of the reader is directed to the map and plan on pp. 342–43.

[2] This telegram has already been published in Mr. Filson Young's account of this action, *With the Battle Cruisers,* p. 174.

asked Sir Arthur Wilson and the Chief of the Staff to take the charts and the draft telegram over to Archway House, and unless there was any difference of opinion, to dispatch it forthwith. Lord Fisher was quite content with the decisions which were proposed, and action was taken accordingly.

The reader may imagine the tense feelings with which the long hours of the afternoon and evening were loaded. We shared our secret with none. That night I attended a dinner which the French Ambassador was giving to Monsieur Millerand, then Minister of War and in London on a mission of consequence. One felt separated from the distinguished company who gathered there, by a film of isolated knowledge and overwhelming inward preoccupation. In December we had hardly credited our sources of information. All was uncertain. It had even seemed probable that nothing would occur. Now with that experience wrought into one's being, only one thought could reign—battle at dawn! Battle for the first time in history between mighty super-Dreadnought ships! And there was added a thrilling sense of a Beast of Prey moving stealthily forward hour by hour towards the Trap.

We were afoot the next morning while it was still dark, and Fisher, Wilson, Oliver and I were all in the War Room when daylight began to grow out of doors. The ordinary night staff of the various departments were still at their posts. Suddenly, with the sureness of destiny and the punctuality of a parade, a telegram intercepted from the Fleet was laid before us. It was from the 1st Light Cruiser Squadron to the *Lion* (Beatty) and the *Iron Duke* (Jellicoe):

(Sent 7:30 a.m. Received 8:10 a.m.)
Urgent. Enemy in sight. Lat. 54° 54′ N., Long. 3° 30′ E. Steering
East. Consisting of battle-cruisers and cruisers, number unknown.

And two minutes later:

Urgent. Lat. 55° 24′ N., Long. 4° 12′ E. Enemy in sight consisting of cruisers and destroyers, battle-cruisers, light cruisers, steering between South-east and South.

So once again it had all come true!

There can be few purely mental experiences more charged with cold excitement than to follow, almost from minute to minute, the phases of a great naval action from the silent rooms of the Admiralty. Out on blue water in the fighting ships amid the stunning detonations of the cannonade, fractions of the event unfold themselves to the corporeal eye. There is the sense of action at its highest; there is the wrath of battle; there is the intense, self-effacing, physical or mental toil. But in Whitehall only the clock ticks, and quiet men enter with quick steps laying slips of pencilled paper before other men equally silent who draw lines and scribble calculations, and point with the finger or make brief subdued comments. Telegram succeeds telegram at a few minutes' interval as they are picked up and decoded, often in the wrong sequence, frequently of dubious import; and out of these a picture always flickering and changing rises in the mind, and imagination strikes out around it at every stage flashes of hope or fear.

1ST LIGHT CRUISER SQUADRON TO COMMANDER-IN CHIEF.
(Sent 8 a.m. Received 8:20 a.m.)
Enemy's ships have altered course to N.E.

"LION" TO COMMANDER-IN-CHIEF.
(Sent 8:30 a.m. Received 8:37 a.m.)
Enemy sighted consisting four battle-cruisers, four light cruisers, destroyers number unknown, bearing S. 61 E. 11 miles. My position Lat. 54° 50′ N., Long. 3° 37′ E. Course S. 40 E. 26 knots.

COMMANDER-IN-CHIEF TO 3RD BATTLE SQUADRON.
(Sent 9 a.m. Received 9:18 a.m.)
Steer towards Heligoland.

COMMODORE TYRWHITT TO COMMANDER-IN-CHIEF.
(Sent 9:05 a.m. Received 9:27 a.m.)
1st Flotilla and 3rd Flotilla are astern of battle-cruisers. 2 miles.

COMMANDER-IN-CHIEF TO 3RD BATTLE SQUADRON.
(Sent 9:20 a.m. Received 9:28 a.m.)
Act to support 1st Battle Cruiser Squadron.

"LION" TO COMMANDER-IN CHIEF.
(Sent 9:30 a.m. Received 9:48 a.m.)
Am engaging enemy battle-cruisers. Range 16,000 yards.

1ST LIGHT CRUISER SQUADRON TO "LION."
(Sent 10:08 a.m. Received 10:18 a.m.)
Enemy detached one rearmost battle-cruiser. Am driven off.

1ST LIGHT CRUISER SQUADRON TO "LION."

(Sent 10:21 a.m. Received 10:27 a.m.)

Am keeping touch with enemy.

1ST LIGHT CRUISER SQUADRON TO COMMANDER-IN-CHIEF AND "LION."

(Sent 10:15 a.m. Received 10:59 a.m.)

Enemy's airships E.S.E.

We had not heard the *Lion* speak for nearly an hour and a half, during the whole of which period presumably she and the First Battle Cruiser Squadron were in full battle. Evidently Sir John Jellicoe also felt the weight of this oppressive silence.

COMMANDER-IN-CHIEF TO "LION."

(Sent 11:01 a.m. Received by Admiralty 11:09 a.m.)

Are you in action?

Another twenty minutes' silence, seeming much longer, ensued. Then at last at 11:37 came in the following message not from the *Lion* or the First Battle Cruiser Squadron, but from the Senior Officer commanding the *Second* Battle Cruiser Squadron to the Commander-in-Chief:

Heavy engagement with enemy battle-cruisers. Lat. 54° 19′ N., Long. 5° 05′ E.

Someone said, "Moore is reporting; evidently the *Lion* is knocked out."

Across my mind there rose a purely irrelevant picture. I thought of the Memorial Services I had so often attended in Westminster Abbey: the crowd and uniforms, the coffin with the Union Jack, the searching music, Beatty! That vision at least was not true; but alas, too true indeed, "The *Lion* knocked out."

It is time to escape from the tense atmosphere of the War Room and watch the squadrons on blue water.

When the first light of the clear winter's morning shone on a calm sea, Admiral Beatty with his five battle-cruisers (*Lion, Tiger, Princess Royal, New Zealand* and *Indomitable*) and four light cruisers reached the rendezvous. Ten minutes later he sighted Commodore Tyrwhitt in the *Arethusa* with seven of his fastest "M" class destroyers, constituting the van of the Harwich force, and almost simultaneously there came the flash of the first gun. The *Aurora*, following the Commodore as fast as possible at a few miles' distance, with the *Undaunted* and twenty-eight more destroyers of the First and Third Flotillas, came into contact with Admiral von Hipper who, with the *Seydlitz, Moltke, Derfflinger* and *Blücher,* accompanied by four light cruisers and twenty-two German destroyers, was steaming along the very course and almost at the very moment which Wilson and Oliver had forecast. The *Aurora* opened fire upon a German light cruiser, and signalled immediately that she was engaged "with the High Seas fleet." Thus all three lines of advance met almost at a single point.

We have seen the causes that led to Admiral von Hipper's excursion. As day broke his ships were spread in line abreast on a considerable front, searching no doubt for British fishing vessels and light patrol forces. What followed is extremely simple. The moment the German Commander discovered himself in the presence of numerous British warships, including the battle-cruisers, his decision was taken. He collected his ships, turned completely round, and ran for home with the utmost possible despatch. Meanwhile Admiral Beatty, working up his speed with equal zeal, had already passed somewhat to the southward of the Germans, and by 8 o'clock was steaming on a parallel course about 14 miles behind them. A tremendous race of all the fastest vessels in the two navies now began. Because of the danger of the retreating enemy dropping mines behind him, all the British vessels avoided his actual wake, Commodore Goodenough and his four light cruisers keeping slightly to the north, Tyrwhitt with his whole force of destroyers and cruisers slightly to the south, and the British battle-cruisers farther southward still.

In pursuit on land the battlefield is stationary and the troops move; in a stern chase at sea the ships alter their relative positions very gradually, while the battlefield rushes past as fast as a horse can gallop. In this posture, therefore, all parties to the event continued for a spell. Meanwhile the speed of the British battle-cruisers developed continually, and it soon became evident that they were gaining on the Germans. By 8:30 26 knots was realized, or one knot more than the designed speeds of the *Indomitable* and the *New Zealand.* Admiral Beatty signalled "Well done, *Indomitable,*" and demanded 27, 28 and 29 knots in succession at brief intervals. These immense speeds could only be approached by his three leading ships: the *Lion* in the van, the *Tiger* and the *Princess Royal.* It was his intention to overtake the enemy and bring him to battle in the first instance with his three ships against four.

The distance between the rearmost Germans and the leading British ships was now diminishing steadily. So great was the speed of the Super-Dreadnoughts that the destroyers could barely hold their own with them. As the event had fallen, at the moment of contact Tyrwhitt and his forty vessels were pursuing a course which led between the hostile battle-cruiser squadrons.

This was inconvenient, because by advancing and drawing abreast of the battle-cruisers—as did the fast "M" boats—they would obstruct their view with enormous clouds of smoke. On the other hand, at the pace at which all were going, it was not possible to shift them to the southern flank where they could have pressed ahead at a minimum of 27 knots. To fall back behind the British battle-cruisers and to turn off obliquely would have thrown them out of the hunt for good and all. They were therefore not able to overtake and head off the enemy, and remained some what shut in slightly astern and inside the British battle-cruiser line.

About 9 o'clock the *Lion* opened fire.[1] Up to 1914 the greatest range for battle practice had been 10,000 yards. In the spring of that year I had ordered an experimental firing at 14,000 yards, when to universal astonishment considerable accuracy was immediately attained. But this lesson had not been digested when the war broke out. Now in the first action between Super-Dreadnought ships, the pursuers spontaneously opened fire at the hitherto unprecedented range of 20,000 yards. The second shot passed over the *Blücher,* and the *Lion* now began a deliberate fire upon this ship. As the range gradually shortened, the *Tiger* and the *Princess Royal* joined in, and hits upon the *Blücher* were almost immediately observed. At a quarter-past nine the Germans replied. The *Lion* now reached out after the *Derfflinger,* while the *Tiger* and the *Princess Royal* continued firing upon the *Blücher.* The fire became effective on both these two German ships. The third salvo hit the *Blücher* on the water-line, reducing her speed; the fourth wrought tremendous damage, disabling two after-turrets and between 200 and 300 men. At 9:35, the *New Zealand* having come into range of the *Blücher,* Admiral Beatty signalled his ships to engage their opposite numbers, ship for ship, he himself firing at the German flagship, *Seydlitz,* which was leading the retreat. The first shell of the *Lion* that hit the *Seydlitz* at over 17,000 yards range inflicted fearful damage, shattering her stern and wrecking both her rear turrets. "The entire gun crews of both turrets," wrote Admiral Scheer, "perished very quickly; the flames rose above the turrets as high as a house."

Meanwhile, however, the enemy had also begun to hit. Owing to a misunderstanding of her orders, the *Tiger,* as well as the *Lion,* was firing upon the *Seydlitz* and missing her badly. The *Princess Royal* was rightly engaging the *Derfflinger;* the *New Zealand,* the *Blücher;* and the *Indomitable* was not within range. Thus the *Moltke* was free from all attack and able to fire undisturbed on

---

[1] I have followed in the main the account given by the official historian, modified by the narrative of Commander Filson Young, an eye-witness in the foretop of the *Lion,* and corrected and supplemented by other first-hand information.

the *Lion.*[1] All the three leading German ships concentrated their fire upon the *Lion,* and for the next hour and a half this noble vessel, hurled forward at her utmost speed, carried the dauntless flag of the Admiral into the teeth of the storm. The sea rose in mighty fountains all around her, which fell in hundreds of tons upon her deck. The splinters from shells bursting close alongside filled the air with fragments. From half-past nine onwards she was repeatedly struck. A little before ten her foremost turret was smashed in and one of its guns disabled. A few minutes later her armour was pierced by an 11-inch shell. At 10:18 two 12-inch shells from the *Derfflinger* struck her—one piercing the armour, bursting behind it and flooding several compartments; the other driving in an armoured plate below the water-line. The Admiral, disdaining the conning tower and standing with his staff upon the open bridge, continued to drive his flagship forward at her extreme speed, which was not yet impaired, zigzagging from time to time to spoil the accuracy of the enemy's fire. The situation was favourable. None of our battle-cruisers had been seriously damaged, and the *Indomitable* was available to deal with any wounded enemy ships. The critical period of the action was now approaching.

At 10:22 Admiral Beatty finding his ships greatly hampered by smoke interference, ordered the battle-cruisers to "Form on a Line of Bearing N.N.W.,"[2] and to proceed at their utmost speed. His intention was to avoid the smoke and splashes and bring the rear of his squadron into closer action with the enemy, who had formed on a Line of Bearing to Port of the *Seydlitz.* The German flotillas by altering their course to starboard threatened to draw him across their wake, i.e. into water where their mines and torpedoes might be encoun-

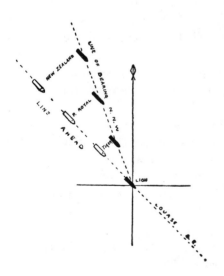

tered. This Parthian menace forced Admiral Beatty to desist from his closing movement, and to resume his parallel course under a tremendous fire. The *Blücher* was now burning and falling out of the German line; and at 10:45 Admiral Beatty ordered his rearmost ship, the *Indomitable,* which was some distance astern but rapidly over-

---

[1] The Official Naval History has by mistake interchanged the *Moltke* and the *Derfflinger.* According to the German accounts it is clear that the *Moltke* was the ship running free and that she alone had no antagonist and no casualties.

[2] "Line of Bearing" [see drawing at left] is an échelon formation.

hauling the *Blücher*, to "Attack the enemy breaking away to the Northward," meaning thereby the *Blücher*. He made further efforts to close, but at 10:52 while in the hottest action, with the *Seydlitz*, the *Moltke* and the *Derfflinger*, the *Lion*, which had already received fourteen hits, was suddenly struck in a spot vital to her speed and fatal, as it proved, to our complete victory. Her port engine failed, she listed 10 degrees and her speed sank in a few minutes to 15 knots.

At this moment (10:54) when the *Lion* was falling out of the line, and the *Tiger*, the *Princess Royal* and *New Zealand* were drawing swiftly past her, the wash of a periscope on the starboard bow was reported from the *Lion's* foretop to Admiral Beatty, and seen by both the Admiral and his staff. German submarines were, as we now know, actually in this area at the time. To avoid this new danger by a quick manœuvre, he ordered the whole squadron to turn 8 points to port together, i.e., across the rear of the enemy and at right angles to his own previous course. This movement was intended to be of the briefest duration, and four minutes later the Admiral modified it by the signal "Course North East." Matters now, however, passed completely beyond his control. The *Lion* was falling far astern of her consorts. Her wireless had been shot away, her searchlights were smashed, and only two signal halyards were left. Thus at this crisis when the great vessels, friend and foe, were shearing through the water at nearly 30 miles an hour and, once deflected, were altering their relationship in space every second, the *Lion*, carrying in Admiral Beatty the whole spirit and direction of the battle, was crippled and almost dumb. Her last two signals were "Attack the rear of the enemy," and then as a parting injunction, "'Keep closer to the enemy. Repeat the signal the Admiral is now making." But the signal flags blowing end on were difficult to read and none of the battle-cruisers took in the final order.

It was at this juncture and in these circumstances that Rear-Admiral Moore, whose flag was flying in the *New Zealand*, now third in the line, succeeded to the command. He was an officer whose distinguished abilities had made him invaluable as Third Sea Lord during the greater part of my tenure at the Admiralty. He had earnestly desired a sea command adequate to his rank and services. His wish had been accorded, and now almost at once Fortune presented herself to him in mocking and dubious guise. He was not certain at first that he had succeeded to the command. It was never formally transferred. He did not know why Admiral Beatty had suddenly turned so sharply to the north. No hostile submarines had been reported to him. The signal "Attack the rear of the enemy" was hoisted by the *Lion* before the compass signal "Course North East" had been hauled down. Both signals were therefore read by all the battle-cruisers as one, and this was interpreted by Rear-Admiral Moore as a direct order to attack the forlorn and isolated *Blücher*, which actually bore north-east

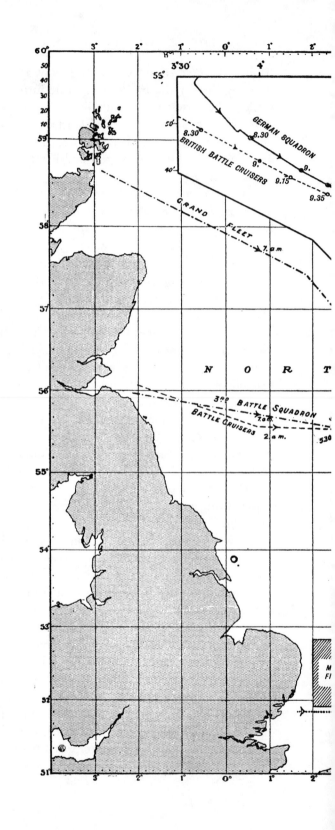

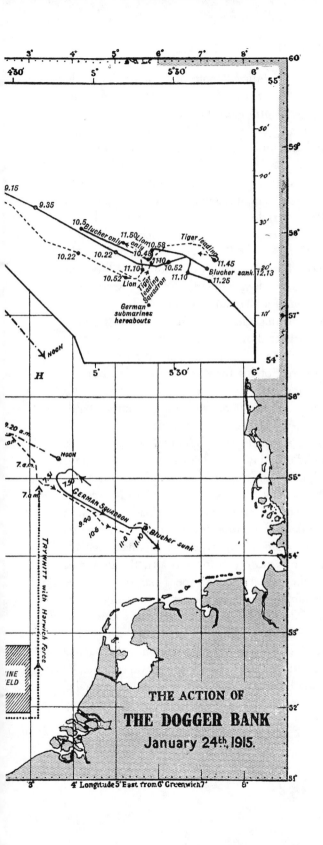

THE ACTION OF

THE DOGGER BANK

January 24th, 1915.

from him at that moment. Neither Admiral Moore nor any of the battle-cruisers ever received the signal "Keep closer to the enemy." He therefore suffered the *Tiger*, his leading ship, to continue on her course under the same misconstruction of Admiral Beatty's orders which she had independently sustained. He gave no order of any kind until 11:52, nearly an hour after the *Lion* had fallen out of the line.

The whole operation therefore went to pieces. All four of the British battle-cruisers ceased firing on the retreating Germans, and began to circle round the wretched *Blücher* which, already a terrible wreck, was being engaged by the light cruisers and the "M" destroyers. At ten minutes past twelve the *Blücher*, fighting with desperate courage to the last, rolled over and sank beneath the waves. Of her crew of nearly twelve hundred men, two hundred and fifty were picked up by the British destroyers and light cruisers; and more would have been saved, but for the intervention of a German seaplane which dropped its bombs indiscriminately on the drowning Germans and the British rescuers. Meanwhile Admiral von Hipper, delivered by a single fateful shot from almost certain destruction, continued to make off at his best speed towards Heligoland, then 80 miles away, two out of his three remaining ships burning fiercely, cumbered with wreckage and crowded with dead and wounded. Thus for the second time, when already in the jaws of destruction, the German Battle Cruiser Squadron escaped.

In the opinion of his professional superiors at the Admiralty Rear-Admiral Moore had warrant for what he did or did not do. He had not departed from a strict interpretation of the actual orders taken in by his ships. These orders, uncorrected by the receipt of the final signal, "Keep closer to the enemy," seemed to suggest that some reason unknown to Rear-Admiral Moore had led the most daring of our naval leaders to break off the action. It is not easy to fix the precise moment, while the *Lion* was dropping astern, when the command actually passed to him. The greater his confidence in Admiral Beatty, the slower he would be to assume control and the more impressive the signal to change the course across the enemy's rear would appear. A quarter of an hour might well have been accounted for in this way; and a quarter of an hour was a long time. Ships just holding their own in pursuit or in station on other ships, with only a small margin of speed to spare, lose distance very quickly once the parallel course is departed from. It was certainly open to him, once he was sure that he was in command and that Admiral Beatty was out of it, to resume the parallel course and reopen the action with von Hipper's disappearing vessels. But a long delay must have ensued before he could have come within range; and his squadron would all the time have been drawing nearer to Heligoland and the German High Seas Fleet.

• • •

The tests to which the Admirals in high command are subjected during a naval engagement are far more searching than those of Generals in a battle on land. The Admiral actually leads the Fleet in person and is probably under as severe fire and in as great danger as any man in it; a General, whatever his wishes, has no choice but to remain in his headquarters in complete tranquility, ten, fifteen or even twenty miles away. The General is forced to rely on the reports of others which flow upwards to him from Brigades, Divisions and Corps, and transmits his orders through the same channel after consultation with his staff; the Admiral sees with his own eyes, and with his own lips pronounces the orders which move the whole mighty event. The phases of a naval action succeed one another at intervals of two or three minutes; whereas in modern battles two or three hours, and sometimes even days, elapse before fresh decisions are required from an Army Commander. Once the sea battle is joined the whole event is in the hand of the Admiral or his successor as long as he can signal; whereas on land, after zero hour has struck, it escapes for the time being almost entirely from the control of the General.

There are a hundred ways of explaining a defeat on land and of obscuring the consequences of any mistake. Of these the simplest is to continue the attack next day in a different direction or under different conditions. But on the sea no chance returns. The enemy disappears for months and the battle is over. The Admiral's orders uttered from minute to minute are recorded for ever in the log-book of every vessel engaged. The great ships, unless their mechanism ceases to function, obey punctually and inexorably the directions they receive from the human will. The course and speed of every vessel at every moment are recorded. The value of every vessel sunk is known. Their names are published. The charts and compasses are produced, and with almost exact accuracy the position and movement of every ship can be fixed in relation to every other. The battlefield is flat and almost unvarying. Exact explanations can be required at every point, and the whole intense scene can be reconstructed and analyzed in the glare of history. This should always be borne in mind in forming judgments.

While these grave matters had so decided themselves, Admiral Beatty, far astern and believing the chase was being continued, had resolved to quit the wounded *Lion* and, hoisting his flag upon the destroyer *Attack*, hastened forward to overtake the battle. Instead, somewhat after noon, he met his ships coming back towards him. In the first bitterness at learning that the rest of the enemy had escaped he ordered the chase to be resumed, although there was now no chance of its succeeding. Twenty or thirty precious minutes had been lost, and with them twenty or thirty thousand yards. This was irretrievable. And realizing that further pursuit was useless, he turned back and steered towards the *Lion* to make provision for her safety and return to the Forth.

The condition of the *Lion* seemed for some time critical: her speed fell to 8 knots, her list increased, and serious anxiety arose. Her engines finally became incapable of steaming at all. She was taken in tow by the *Indomitable,* and in this fashion began her long, slow and dangerous return to the Forth. Sixty destroyers under Commodore Tyrwhitt surrounded her in ceaseless evolutions, protecting her from torpedo or submarine attack all through the night of the 24th and through the 25th. "If submarines are seen," ordered the Commodore, "shoot and ram them without regard to your neighbours." At daylight on the 26th the *Lion,* amid cheering crowds, was brought safely to anchor at Rosyth.

The victory of the Dogger Bank brought for the time being abruptly to an end the adverse movement against my administration of the Admiralty, which had begun to gather. Congratulations flowed in from every side, and we enjoyed once again an adequate measure of prestige. The sinking of the *Blücher* and the flight, after heavy injuries, of the other German ships was accepted as a solid and indisputable result. The German Emperor was confirmed in the gloomy impressions he had sustained after the action of August 28, 1914. All enterprise in the German Admiralty was again effectually quelled, and apart from submarine warfare a period of nearly fifteen months' halcyon calm reigned over the North Sea and throughout Home waters. The neutral world accepted the event as a decisive proof of British supremacy at sea: and even at home the Admiralty felt the benefit in a sensible increase of confidence and goodwill.

CHAPTER XXII

SECOND THOUGHTS AND
FINAL DECISION

U p to about January 20 there seemed to be unanimous agreement in favour
of the naval enterprise against the Dardanelles. War Office, Foreign Office, Admiralty seemed by their representatives to be equally in earnest. The
War Council had taken its decision. It is true it was not a final or irrevocable
decision. It authorized and encouraged the Admiralty to survey their resources
and develop their plans. If these plans broke down in preparation, it would be
quite easy for us to report the fact to the War Council and go no farther. But
the staff work continued to progress smoothly, and all the Admirals concerned
appeared in complete accord. It was not until the end of January, when negotiations with the French and Russian Governments were far advanced, when
many preparations had been made, when many orders had been given and
when many ships were moving with his full authority, that Lord Fisher began to
manifest an increasing dislike and opposition to the scheme.

Meanwhile the possibilities of a British naval offensive or of amphibious
action in Northern waters were becoming continually more remote. Correspondence with Sir John Jellicoe showed the Commander-in-Chief averse from
anything in the nature of an attack upon Borkum or an attempt to enter the
Baltic. To strengthen our naval forces by every conceivable means, to add every
new vessel to the Grand Fleet and to remain in an attitude of inactive expectancy was the sum and substance of the naval policy advocated from this
quarter. At the same time the opposition of General Joffre to Sir John French's
plans for an advance in force along the Belgian coast brought that project also
to an end. It was clear that no serious naval offensive would take place in the
Northern theatre for an indefinite period, and that any plans which might
gradually be perfected for such an offensive would derive no encouragement
from the Commander-in-Chief of the Grand Fleet.

All this made me only the more anxious to act in the Mediterranean. That
seemed to be the direction reserved for our surplus ships and ammunition, by
the failure or postponement of other alternatives. It was the only direction in
which we had a practical plan, properly worked out by the staff, and supported
by a powerful consensus of naval and political opinion.

As soon, however, as the Commander-in-Chief realized that the *Queen*

Elizabeth, a battle-cruiser, and other powerful ships were to be assigned to the Mediterranean theatre, he began to dwell again upon the weakness of his fleet and the insufficiency of his margins. And now for the first time he found a ready listener in the First Sea Lord. Lord Fisher's sudden dislike of the Dardanelles project seemed to arise at this time largely and even primarily from his reluctance to undertake the bombardment and blocking in of Zeebrugge. This operation appeared all the more necessary now that the Army had abandoned their intention of an advance along the Belgian coast. It was strongly urged by the War Council, by the Admiralty Staff and especially by Sir Arthur Wilson. "If we do not block the Zeebrugge canal," Sir Arthur had written on January 4, "I think we shall inevitably lose more ships and also many transports. If we had done it last time we bombarded, we should not have lost *Formidable.* We cannot keep ships entirely locked up in harbour without deterioration. So far very few of our losses have been incurred while the ships have been employed in any active operations." I was in cordial agreement with this doctrine. Ultimately, as everyone knows, the blocking of Zeebrugge had to be carried out under circumstances of infinitely greater difficulty and after we had suffered grievous injury. The First Sea Lord, finding himself entirely alone on the question, became very much disturbed. His dislike of the Zeebrugge operation was extended not only to the Dardanelles plan, but to all plans of naval attack on hostile coasts which were not combined with large land forces, and ultimately he expressed opinions which seemed opposed to any form of naval intervention in any quarter. This was a great change, at variance both with his earlier and later attitudes, and I was concerned to observe it.

Lord Fisher's arguments did not take the form of criticizing the details of either operation in question. He did not, for instance, deal with the gunnery aspects of the Dardanelles, or with any purely technical aspect, in regard to which any valid argument would have had to be met, or the plan abandoned. It was about the safety of the Grand Fleet and its margin of superiority that he now professed to be seriously perturbed. This was a subject with which I was extremely familiar. Had we not been two months before over the whole ground together in the discussions of November with the Commander-in-Chief? There was no real substance in the apprehensions with which I was now confronted. An important fact however lay behind them. Lord Fisher had on reflection, on second thoughts, on some prompting or other, turned against the operation which he had hitherto willingly supported. Nevertheless matters had moved forward to a point where mere vague misgivings could not be allowed to paralyse action. Good reasoning or new facts were required.

On January 20 in response to the First Sea Lord's real or affected misgivings I sent him a minute, observing:

You seem to have altered your views, since taking office, about the relative strengths of the British and German Grand and High Sea Fleets. In November you advised the removal of *Princess Royal, Inflexible,* and *Invincible,* together with 8 "King Edwards" and 5 "Duncans," a total of 16 capital ships, from the Grand Fleet, some for temporary duties of importance, but the battleships for permanent service in the south. The dispositions were carried out. Since then the Commander-in-Chief has received back the 8 "King Edwards" and the *Princess Royal;* he has gained the *Indomitable;* he has received the *Warrior, Duke of Edinburgh, Black Prince, Gloucester, Yarmouth, Caroline, Galatea, Donegal,* and *Leviathan,* together with 16 destroyers additional, and, I think, about 50 extra trawlers and yachts. These are immense additions to his strength, and I know of no new circumstances which have arisen or of reinforcements which have reached the enemy which ought to make us anxious now if we were not anxious before these great additions reached Sir John Jellicoe.

Lord Fisher did not dispute this general argument; but he returned to the charge on the question of destroyers, admittedly our weakest point, and demanded the return of a whole flotilla from the Dardanelles. I could not agree to this, as of course it would have paralysed the Dardanelles Fleet and destroyed the plans which the staff were maturing. At the same time Sir Arthur Wilson continued to press for action against Zeebrugge.

This double pressure brought matters to a head.

January 25, 1915.

First Lord,

I have no desire to continue a useless resistance in the War Council to plans I cannot concur in, but I would ask that the enclosed may be printed and circulated to its members before the next meeting.

The Memorandum has an argument for adherence to the Fleet's "policy of steady pressure" and for remaining passive except for efforts to force a general action. The following paragraphs may be quoted:

Of all strategical attitudes that of a naval defensive as adopted by Germany is the most difficult to meet and the most deeply fraught with danger for the opposing belligerent, if he is weak ashore as we are, and his enemy strong ashore as Germany is. Nevertheless, all through our history we have had to encounter similar situations. The policy of the French in nearly all our naval wars was the policy which Germany has now adopted.

Our reply to-day must be the same as our reply was then, namely, to be content to remain in possession of our command of the sea, husbanding our strength until the gradual pressure of sea power compels the enemy's fleet to make an effort to attack us at a disadvantage.

In the Seven Years' War the French preserved their fleet from a decision for five years. Nelson was off Toulon for two years. By comparison, the six months during which Sir John Jellicoe has had to wait are short, and they have been relieved by incidents which have considerably diminished the enemy's forces.

The pressure of sea power to-day is probably not less but greater and more rapid in action than in the past; but it is still a slow process and requires great patience. In time it will almost certainly compel the enemy to seek a decision at sea, particularly when he begins to realize that his offensive on land is broken. This is one reason for husbanding our resources. Another reason is that the prolongation of war at sea tends to raise up fresh enemies for the dominant naval power in a much higher degree than it does on land owing to the exasperation of neutrals. This tendency will only be checked by the conviction of an overwhelming naval supremacy behind the nation exercising sea power.

We play into Germany's hands if we risk fighting ships in any subsidiary operations such as coastal bombardments or the attack of fortified places without military co-operation, for we thereby increase the possibility that the Germans may be able to engage our fleet with some approach to equality of strength. The sole justification of coastal bombardments and attacks by the fleet on fortified places, such as the contemplated prolonged bombardment of the Dardanelles Forts by our fleet, is to force a decision at sea, and so far and no farther can they be justified.

So long as the German High Sea Fleet preserves its present great strength and splendid gunnery efficiency, so long is it imperative and indeed vital that no operation whatever should be undertaken by the British Fleet, calculated to impair its present superiority. . . . Even the older ships should not be risked, for they cannot be lost without losing men and they form our only reserve behind the Grand Fleet.

Ours is the supreme necessity and difficulty of remaining passive except in so far as we can force the enemy to abandon his defensive and to expose his fleet to a general action. . . .

It has been said that the first function of the British Army is to assist the fleet in obtaining command of the sea. This might be accomplished by military co-operation with the Navy in such operations as the attack of Zeebrugge or the forcing of the Dardanelles, which might bring out the German and Turkish fleets respectively. Apparently, however, this is not to be. The English Army is apparently to continue to provide a small sector of the allied front in France, where it no more helps the Navy than if it were at Timbuctoo.

Being already in possession of all that a powerful fleet can give a country we should continue quietly to enjoy the advantage without dissipating our strength in operations that cannot improve the position.

Fisher.

This paper was not, I think, except for the last few characteristic sentences, Lord Fisher's own composition. It had been prepared in accordance with his directions. It was, of course, absolutely counter to all my convictions. No one, certainly, wished to "dissipate our strength in operations that cannot improve the position." To write thus was to beg the question. But the naval policy emerging from its last sentence would have condemned us to complete inactivity. It was no doubt the policy pursued by the Commander-in-Chief and the Admiralty after I quitted office. It was the policy which led directly to the supreme submarine peril in 1917.

Meanwhile on the 26th arrived the Russian reply to my telegram informing the Grand Duke of the Dardanelles plans. It was of course favourable but not helpful. Sir Edward Grey forwarded it to me with the following remarks:

This is the Russian reply about Dardanelles. It shows that, though Russia cannot help, the operation has her entire goodwill and the Grand Duke attaches the greatest importance to its success.

This fact may be used with Augagneur[1] to show that we must go ahead with it and that failure to do so will disappoint Russia and react most unfavourably upon the military situation, about which France and we are specially concerned just now. . . .

I now addressed myself to the First Sea Lord's paper which I forwarded to the Prime Minister with the following reply, of which I sent Lord Fisher a copy.

MEMORANDUM BY THE FIRST LORD.

January 27, 1915.

The main principle of the First Sea Lord's paper is indisputable. The foundation of our naval policy is the maintenance in a secure position of a Battle Fleet with all ancillary vessels capable at any time of defeating the German High Sea Fleet in battle, and reserved for that purpose above and

[1] The French Minister of Marine.

before all other duties. This principle has been and will be fully and strictly observed.

The ships engaged in Sunday's action [the Dogger Bank] on both sides represented very fairly, so far as individual quality is concerned, the classes of vessels which would be opposed in a general fleet action. The event proved that a superiority of 5 to 4 in our favour is decisive. On these terms the German ships thought of nothing but retreat, and the British of attack. Very heavy loss was inflicted upon the Germans: one ship was sunk out of four, and 2 other ships most severely damaged. Had the action been fought out, the destruction of the others was certain.

We are now no longer in the region of mere speculation. The relative qualities of seamanship and gunnery of the two sides have been put to the test and reveal no inferiority on our part, while the superiority of the 13.5-inch gun and the effect of heavier metal generally has now been shown. There is therefore every reason to believe that the best 21 British battleships and battle-cruisers could defeat decisively at even numbers the 21 German Dreadnoughts. Any British ships additional to this number must be regarded as an insurance against unexpected losses by mine and torpedo.

On the declaration of war the maximum numbers available in Home Waters on both sides were: Great Britain, 24+2 "Lord Nelsons"; Germany, 21. Since then the following capital units have joined the Fleet: *Queen Elizabeth, Erin, Agincourt, Benbow, Emperor of India, Tiger, Indomitable;* and the following will join during the next month: *Inflexible, Invincible,* and perhaps *Australia;* against which we have lost *Audacious.* In addition to these the Grand Fleet and Harwich Striking Force have been strengthened by eighteen cruisers and thirty-six destroyers.[1]

Meanwhile the German Fleet in Home Waters has received no new accession of strength and has suffered the following losses in modern ships: *Blücher, Magdeburg, Köln, Mainz,* and 10 or 12 Destroyers.

It should be recognized that the progressive improvement in types has been so marked that ships over 12 years old can only play a secondary part in the war. Their speed would probably prevent them from participating in the main action, except against each other, and would expose them to almost certain destruction if overtaken by the latest types. However, in this pre-Dreadnought class we have also an immense superiority. The 8 "King Edwards" are already a part of the Grand Fleet, and it can be strengthened at any time by the addition of the 2 "Lord Nelsons"[2] and the

[1] Names omitted.

[2] The 2 Lord Nelsons (i.e. *Lord Nelson* and *Agamemnon*) had not yet been added by Lord Fisher to the Dardanelles Fleet.

6 remaining "Formidables." This fleet would easily and certainly destroy the whole of the German pre-Dreadnought battle fleet.

During the course of the present year 8 battleships, 5 of over 26-knots speed and the whole armed with 15-inch guns, constituting a squadron probably capable of fighting by itself the two best squadrons of the German Navy, will be available for reinforcement or replacement of casualties. Since the war commenced 8 light cruisers have already been commissioned for service in Home Waters; 8 more will be delivered in the next three months, and 4 more in the three months after that. All these cruisers are superior in speed and gun power to any of the German light cruisers afloat. There will also be available during the year 56 destroyers, between 50 and 75 submarines, 24 small gunboats for subsidiary duties, together with other miscellaneous auxiliary vessels. It is therefore certain that the strength of the Grand Fleet, which was originally sufficient, has now been greatly augmented and will continually increase. The first principle laid down by the First Sea Lord is thus most fully met.

The second vital function of the Navy is the protection of trade and the control of sea communications. All German cruisers and gunboats abroad have been sunk, blocked in, or interned, with the exception of the *Karlsruhe* and *Dresden,* which are hiding. There are great doubts as to the efficiency of the *Karlsruhe,* of whom nothing has been heard for nearly three months. There are believed to be 2 German armed merchantmen at large (the *Kronprinz Wilhelm* and *Prinz Eitel Friedrich*). All the rest of the 42 prepared for arming and which it has been intended to let loose on the trade routes have been blockaded, interned, sunk, or captured. . . .

Meanwhile the other functions of the Navy, viz., the control of the English Channel and its approaches, the patrol of the Straits of Dover, the patrol flotillas of the East Coast, and the special Harwich Striking Force, are all provided for.

Over and above all the foregoing, and after meeting all purely naval claims, we have available the following battleships completely manned and supplied with their own ammunition and its reserve:

5 "Duncans."
6 "Canopus."
9 "Majestics."
1 "Royal Sovereign."

Between the beginning of April and the end of July we shall also receive 14 heavily armoured, shallow-draft Monitors; 2 armed with two 15-inch guns, 4 armed with two 14-inch guns, and 8 armed with two 12-inch guns.

These last 8 will be armed by taking the turrets out of 4 of the "Majestics." It is this force which it is proposed to use for special services and for bombarding as may be necessary from time to time in furtherance of objects of great strategic and political importance, among which the following may be specifically mentioned:

1. The operations at the Dardanelles;
2. The support of the left flank of the Army;
3. The bombardment of Zeebrugge; and later on
4. The seizure of Borkum.

It is believed that with care and skill losses may be reduced to a minimum and certainly kept within limits fully justified by the importance and necessity of the operations. It cannot be said that this employment of ships which are (except the "Duncans") not needed and not suited to fight in the line of battle, conflicts with any of the sound principles of naval policy set forth by the First Sea Lord. Not to use them where necessary because of some fear that there will be an outcry if a ship is lost would be wrong, and, if certain proportion of loss of life among officers and men of the Royal Navy serving on these ships can achieve important objects of the war and save a very much greater loss of life among our comrades and allies on shore, we ought certainly not to shrink from it.

W. S. C.

The First Sea Lord could not in his heart feel at all anxious about the Grand Fleet margin. He knew that I knew his real convictions about it. He did not attempt to continue the discussion on a false basis: but he expressed an intention of not attending the War Council which was fixed for the next day—the 28th. This was, of course, impossible. I insisted that he should be present, and arranged for a private meeting for both of us with the Prime Minister before the Council. To this Lord Fisher consented.

We repaired accordingly to Mr. Asquith's room twenty minutes before the War Council was to meet. No written record of this discussion has been preserved, but there is no dispute about it. "Save in respect of some points of slight importance as regards the precise language used," say the Dardanelles Commissioners, "the accounts given us by Mr. Asquith and Lord Fisher, as regards what occurred at this private meeting, tally." Lord Fisher indicated very briefly his objections to both the Zeebrugge and Dardanelles schemes, and indicated his preference for a great operation in the Baltic or for a general advance of the Army along the Belgian coast with strong naval support. Lord Fisher, say the

Dardanelles Commissioners, "did not criticize the attack on the Gallipoli peninsula on its own merits. Neither did he mention to the Prime Minister that he had any thought of resigning if his opinions were overruled." This is quite true. I contended that both Zeebrugge and the Dardanelles scheme should be undertaken, but that if either were to be dropped it should be Zeebrugge, to which the First Sea Lord seemed more particularly opposed. The Prime Minister, after hearing both sides, expressed his concurrence with my views, and decided that Zeebrugge should be dropped but that the Dardanelles should go forward. Lord Fisher seemed on the whole content, and I went downstairs with him under the impression that all was well.

The Council was already waiting. Colonel Hankey's record of the discussion which followed has already been made public in the Report of the Dardanelles Commission.

> Mr. Churchill said that he had communicated to the Grand Duke Nicholas and to the French Admiralty the project for a naval attack on the Dardanelles. The Grand Duke had replied with enthusiasm, and believed that this [attack] might assist him. The French Admiralty had also sent a favourable reply, and had promised cooperation. Preparations were in hand for commencing about the middle of February. He asked if the War Council attached importance to this operation, which undoubtedly involved some risks?
>
> Lord Fisher said that he understood that this question would not be raised to-day. The Prime Minister was well aware of his own views in regard to it.
>
> The Prime Minister said that, in view of the steps which had already been taken, the question could not well be left in abeyance
>
> Lord Kitchener considered the naval attack to be vitally important. If successful, its effect would be equivalent to that of a successful campaign fought with the new armies. One merit of the scheme was that, if satisfactory progress was not made, the attack could be broken off.
>
> Mr. Balfour pointed out that a successful attack on the Dardanelles would achieve the following results:
>
> It would cut the Turkish Army in two;
>
> It would put Constantinople under our control;
>
> It would give us the advantage of having the Russian wheat, and enable Russia to resume exports;
>
> This would restore the Russian exchanges, which were falling owing to her inability to export, and causing great embarrassment;
>
> It would also open a passage to the Danube;
>
> It was difficult to imagine a more helpful operation.

Sir Edward Grey said it would also finally settle the attitude of Bulgaria and the whole of the Balkans.

Mr. Churchill said that the naval Commander-in-Chief in the Mediterranean had expressed his belief that it could be done. He required from three weeks to a month to accomplish it. The necessary ships were already on their way to the Dardanelles. In reply to Mr. Balfour, he said that, in response to his inquiries, the French had expressed their confidence that Austrian submarines would not get as far as the Dardanelles.

Lord Haldane asked if the Turks had any submarines.

Mr. Churchill said that, so far as could be ascertained, they had not. He did not anticipate that we should sustain much loss in the actual bombardment, but in sweeping for mines some losses must be expected. The real difficulties would begin after the outer forts had been silenced, and it became necessary to attack the Narrows. He explained the plan of attack on a map.

This record does not, however, complete the story. During the Council an incident occurred which has subsequently obtained much publicity. Here is Lord Fisher's own account[1]:

9TH MEETING OF WAR COUNCIL, JANUARY 28, 1915, 11:30 A.M.

(*Note.*—Before this meeting the Prime Minister discussed with Mr. Churchill and Lord Fisher the proposed Dardanelles operations and decided in favour of considering the project in opposition to Lord Fisher's opinion.)

THE DARDANELLES.

Mr. Churchill asked if the War Council attached importance to the proposed Dardanelles operations, which undoubtedly involved risks.

Lord Fisher said that he had understood that this question was not to be raised at this meeting. The Prime Minister knew his (Lord Fisher's) views on the subject.

The Prime Minister said that, in view of what had already been done, the question could not be left in abeyance.

(*Note.*—Thereupon Lord Fisher left the Council table. He was followed by Lord Kitchener, who asked him what he intended to do. Lord Fisher replied to Lord Kitchener that he would not return to the Council table, and would resign his office as First Sea Lord. Lord Kitchener then pointed out to Lord Fisher that he (Lord Fisher) was the only dissentient,

[1] *Memories,* by Lord Fisher, p. 80.

and that the Dardanelles operations had been decided upon by the Prime Minister; and he urged on Lord Fisher that his duty to his country was to go on carrying out the duties of First Sea Lord. After further talk Lord Fisher reluctantly gave in to Lord Kitchener and went back to the Council table.)

It must be emphasized here, as well as in regard to Lord Kitchener's statement to the War Council dated May 14, 1915, that Lord Fisher considered that it would be both improper and unseemly for him to enter into an altercation either at the War Council or elsewhere with his chief Mr. Churchill, the First Lord. Silence or resignation was the right course.

After the meeting was over, we adjourned for several hours. Although the War Council had come to a decision with which I heartily agreed, and no voice had been raised against the naval plan, I thought I must come to a clear understanding with the First Sea Lord. I had noticed the incident of his leaving the table and Lord Kitchener following him to the window and arguing with him, and I did not know what was the upshot in his mind. After luncheon I asked him to come and see me in my room and we had a long talk. I strongly urged him not to turn back from the Dardanelles operation; and in the end, after a long and very friendly discussion which covered the whole Admiralty and naval position, he definitely consented to undertake it. There never has been any dispute between us subsequently as to this. "When I finally decided to go in," said Lord Fisher to the Dardanelles Commissioners, "I went the whole hog, *totus porcus.*" We then repaired to the afternoon War Council Meeting, Admiral Oliver, Chief of the Staff, coming with us, and I announced on behalf of the Admiralty, and with the agreement of Lord Fisher, that we had decided to undertake the task with which the War Council had charged us so urgently. This I took as the point of final decision. After it, I never looked back. We had left the region of discussion and consultation, of balancings and misgivings. The matter had passed into the domain of action.

I am in no way concealing the great and continuous pressure which I put upon the old Admiral. This pressure was reinforced by Lord Kitchener's personal influence, by the collective opinion of the War Council, and by the authoritative decision of the Prime Minister. It was a pressure not only of opinion, which was overwhelming, but of arguments to which he could find no answer. Moreover, there was in addition on the technical side a very great weight of support at the Admiralty. "Naval opinion was unanimous," said Lord Fisher afterwards, "Mr. Churchill had them all on his side. I was the only rebel."

Was it wrong to put this pressure upon the First Sea Lord? I cannot think so. War is a business of terrible pressures, and persons who take part in it must fail if they are not strong enough to withstand them. As a mere politician and civilian, I would never have agreed to the Dardanelles project if I had not believed in it. I would have done my utmost to break it down in argument and to marshal opinion against it. Had I been in Lord Fisher's position and held his views, I would have refused point-blank. There was no need for him to resign. Only the First Sea Lord can order the ships to steam and the guns to fire. First Sea Lords have to stand up to facts and take their decisions resolutely at the moment of choice. To go back on a decision after an enterprise has been launched, risks run and sacrifices made, is quite a different matter. During the period of choice, a man must fight for his opinion with the utmost tenacity. But once the choice has been made, then the business must be carried through in loyal comradeship.

I have asked myself in these later years, What would have happened if I had taken Lord Fisher's advice and refused point-blank to take any action at the Dardanelles unless or until the War Office produced on their responsibility an adequate army to storm the Gallipoli Peninsula? Should we by holding out in this way have secured a sufficient army and a good plan? Should we have had all the advantages of the Dardanelles policy without the mistakes and misfortunes for which we had to pay so dearly? The Dardanelles Commissioners, studying the story from an entirely different angle, obviously felt that if there had been no naval plan in the field, there would later on have been a really well-conceived and well-concerted amphibious attack. No one can probe this imaginary situation very far, and it is impossible to pronounce. But I think myself that nothing less than the ocular demonstration and practical proof of the strategic meaning of the Dardanelles, and the effects of attacking it on every Balkan and Mediterranean Power, would have lighted up men's minds sufficiently to make a large abstraction of troops from the main theatre a possibility. I do not believe that anything less than those tremendous hopes, reinforced as they were by dire necessity, would have enabled Lord Kitchener to wrest an army from France and Flanders. In cold blood, it could never have been done. General Headquarters, and the French General Staff would have succeeded in shattering any plan put forward so long as it was a mere theoretical proposal for a large diversion of force to the Southern theatre. At one moment they would have told us that, owing to the Russian failure, great masses of Germans were returning to the West to deliver an overwhelming offensive: at another that they could not spare a round of ammunition and were in desperate straits for the want of it: at a third, that they had a wonderful plan for a great offensive which would shatter the German line and drive them out of a large portion of France. All these arguments were in fact used, and their effect was, as will be seen, to cripple the Dardanelles operations even after they had actually begun. How much more would they have overwhelmed any paper plan for an Eastern campaign. There would have been no Dardanelles with its hopes, its glories, its losses and its ultimate heart-breaking failure.

But who shall say what would have happened instead? A few weeks' more delay in the entry of Italy into the war, and the continuance of the great Russian defeats in Galicia, would have rendered that entry improbable in the extreme. A few more months' acceleration of the Bulgarian declaration of war against us, and the whole of the Balkans, except Serbia, might have been rallied to the Teutonic standards. The flower of the Turkish Army, which was largely destroyed on the Gallipoli Peninsula, would certainly have fought us or our Allies somewhere else. The destruction of the Russian Army of the Caucasus could not have been long averted. I do not believe that by adopting the negative attitude we should ever have got our good and well-conceived amphibious operation. We should have got no operation at all. We should have done nothing, and have been confronted with diplomatic and military reactions wholly unfavourable throughout the Southern and Eastern theatre. Searching my heart, I cannot regret the effort. It was good to go as far as we did.

Not to persevere—that was the crime.

CHAPTER XXIII

THE GENESIS OF THE
MILITARY ATTACK

Up to this point in the story of the Dardanelles the War Council and the Admiralty had accepted unquestioningly the basis that no troops were available for offensive operations against Turkey. In his first letter to me of January 2, Lord Kitchener had said: "We have no troops to land anywhere. . . . We shall not be ready for anything big for some months." The first telegram to Admiral Carden of January 3 had asked: "Are you of opinion that it is practicable to force the Dardanelles *using ships alone?*" At the evening meeting of the War Council on January 28 when the final decision was taken, Lord Kitchener repeated: "We have at present no troops to spare." It was on that foundation alone that all our decisions in favour of a purely naval attack had been taken. But henceforward a series of new facts and pressures came into play which gradually but unceasingly changed the character and enormously extended the scale of the enterprise. Under these influences in less than two months the naval attack, with its lack of certainty but with its limited costs and risks, became subsidiary, and in its place there arose a military development of great magnitude. Over this new plan the Admiralty had no responsible control. Our advice did not prevail; our criticisms were not welcomed; and even inquiries became a matter of delicacy and tact. Nevertheless, by the results of this military operation we had to stand or fall.

After all there was an Army. From the very moment when the purely naval attack had been finally resolved troops from many quarters began to come into view. From that moment the pressure to employ troops in one way or another grew steadily in every mind. The decision to abandon or postpone indefinitely an advance along the Belgian coast liberated portions of the reinforcements destined for Sir John French. The feeble character of the Turkish attack on Egypt and its repulse liberated the greater part of the Army concentrated there. The continued improvement in the training of the Australian and Territorial troops in this army increasingly fitted them for offensive operations. The suppression of the rebellion in South Africa had removed other anxieties. Meanwhile the First and Second of the New Armies (in all twelve divisions) were improving in training and progressing in equipment. A number of Territorial divisions fully equipped and in good order, whose training was now advanced, were also available at home. The large numbers of armed and organized soldiers in the United Kingdom should have removed all apprehension of oversea invasion.

At intervals during the next three months there were actually ordered to the Dardanelles:

From England.
The 29th Division.
Two first-line Territorial divisions.
The Royal Naval Division.
A Yeomanry mounted division.

From Egypt.
Two Australian divisions.
One extra Australian brigade.
The Lancashire Territorial Division.
One Indian Brigade.

From France.
Two French divisions.

All these troops were available for moving at this moment. The transport for their conveyance by sea could readily have been procured. All, or their equivalent, and more were subsequently sent. Together they comprised an army of at least 150,000 men. This army could have been concentrated in the Eastern Mediterranean in readiness to intervene at any point selected, some time before the end of March. If at any time in January it had been deliberately decided to use such an army, according to some good plan and with a resolute purpose, in a great combined operation to seize the Gallipoli Peninsula and thus open the passage for the Fleet, few will now doubt that a complete victory would have been gained. On the other hand, apart from the 29th Division, all these troops had been raised or permanently embodied only since the outbreak of the war. To open a new campaign on a large scale was a most serious decision, in view of their partially trained character and of the general shortage of munitions. This was the justification for the naval attack. It also within its limits presented a logical and consistent scheme of war. Either plan was defensible. But for what happened there can be no defence except human infirmity. To drift into a new campaign piecemeal and without any definite decision or careful plan, would have been scouted by everyone. Yet so obliquely were these issues presented, so baffling were the personal factors involved, that the War Council were drawn insensibly and irresistibly into the gulf.

• • •

The workings of Lord Kitchener's mind constituted at this period a feature almost as puzzling as the great war problem itself. His prestige and authority were immense. He was the sole mouthpiece of War Office opinion in the War Council. Everyone had the greatest admiration for his character, and everyone felt fortified, amid the terrible and incalculable events of the opening months of the war, by his commanding presence. When he gave a decision it was invariably accepted as final. He was never, to my belief, overruled by the War Council or the Cabinet in any military matter, great or small. No single unit was ever sent or withheld contrary, not merely to his agreement, but to his advice. Scarcely anyone ever ventured to argue with him in Council. Respect for the man, sympathy for him in his immense labours, confidence in his professional judgment, and the belief that he had plans deeper and wider than any we could see, silenced misgivings and disputes, whether in the Council or at the War Office. All-powerful, imperturbable, reserved, he dominated absolutely our counsels at this time in all that concerned the organization and employment of the armies.

Yet behind this imposing and splendid front lay many weaknesses, evidences of which became increasingly disquieting. The Secretary of State for War had burdens laid upon him which no man, no three men even of his great capacity, could properly discharge. He had absorbed the whole War Office into his spacious personality. The General Staff was completely in abeyance, save as a machine for supplying him with information. Even as such a machine it was woefully weak. All the ablest officers and leading and strongest minds in the General Staff and Army Council, with the exception of Sir John Cowans, the Quartermaster-General, had hurried eagerly out of the country with the Expeditionary Force and were now in France, feeling that they ought to control the whole conduct of the war from the highly localized point of view of the British General Headquarters at St. Omer. In their place, filling vitally important situations, were officers on the retired list or men whose opinions had never counted weightily in British military thought. These officers were petrified by Lord Kitchener's personality and position. They none of them showed the natural force and ability to argue questions out with him vigorously as man to man. He towered up in his uniform as a Field-Marshal and Cabinet Minister besides, and they saluted as subordinates on a drill-ground. They never presented him with well-considered general reasonings about the whole course of the war. They stood ready to execute his decisions to the best of their ability. It was left to the Members of the War Council to write papers upon the broad strategic view of the war. It was left to the Chancellor of the Exchequer, Mr. Lloyd George, to discern and proclaim to the Cabinet in unmistakable terms the impending military collapse of Russia. It was left to me to offer at any rate one method of influencing the political situation in the Near East in default of comprehensive military schemes. And Lord Kitchener himself was left to face the rushing, swirling torrent of events with no rock of clear, well-thought-out doctrine and calculation at his back.

In consequence he gave decisions now in this direction, now in that, which were markedly influenced by the daily impressions he sustained, which impressions were often of a fleeting nature. As a result his decisions were sometimes contradictory. He was torn between two perfectly clear-cut views of the war, both urged upon him with force and passion, with wealth of fact and argument. All the leading soldiers in the British Army, all the august authority of the French High Command, asserted that the sole path to victory lay in sending every single man and gun and shell to the French Front to "kill Germans" and break their lines in the West. All the opinion of the War Council, which certainly contained men who had established themselves as the leading figures of the public life of their generation, was focused upon the Southern and Eastern theatre as the scene for the campaign of 1915. Kitchener himself was strongly drawn in this direction by his own Eastern interest and knowledge. He saw to the full the vision of what success in this quarter would mean, but he also felt what we did not feel in the same degree—the fearful alternative pressure to which he was continually subjected from the French Front.

The problem was not insoluble. The task of reconciling these apparently opposed conceptions was not impossible. A well-conceived and elaborated plan and programme could have been devised in January for action in the Near East in March, April, May or even June, and for a subsequent great concentration and operation on the Western Front in the autumn of 1915, or better still under far more favourable conditions in the spring of 1916. The successive development of both policies in their proper sequence and each in its integrity was perfectly feasible if the great authorities concerned could have been won over. However, in the event Lord Kitchener succumbed to conflicting forces and competing policies.

Beside these trials and burdens, to which he was certainly not able to rise superior, stood the whole vast business of recruiting, organizing and equipping the New Armies; and behind this again there now marched steadily into view a series of problems connected with the manufacture and purchase of munitions upon a scale never dreamed of by any human being up till this period. These problems comprised the entire social and industrial life of the country and touched the whole economic and financial system of the world. Add to this the daily exposition of all military business in Cabinet and in Council—a process most trying and burdensome to Lord Kitchener, and one in which he felt himself at a disadvantage: add, further, the continuous series of decisions upon executive matters covering the vast field of the war, including important operations and expeditions which were campaigns in themselves, and it will be realized that the strain that descended upon the King's greatest subject was far more than mortal man could bear.

It must, however, be stated that Lord Kitchener in no way sought to lighten these terrific burdens. On the contrary, he resented promptly any attempt to interfere in and even scrutinize his vast domains of responsibility. He resisted tenaciously the efforts which were made from January onwards to remove the production of munitions of all kinds from his control as Secretary of State. He devolved on to subordinates as little as he could. He sought to manage the Great War by the same sort of personal control that he had used with so much success in the command of the tiny Nile Expedition. He kept the General Staff, or what was left of it, in a condition of complete subservience and practical abeyance. He even reached out, as his Cabinet Office justified, into political spheres in questions of Ireland, of Temperance, and of Industrial Organization.

It is idle at this date to affect to disregard or conceal these facts. Indeed, the greatness of Lord Kitchener and his lasting claims upon the respect and gratitude of succeeding generations of his fellow-countrymen, for whose cause and safety he fought with single-hearted purpose and a giant's strength, will only be fortified by the fullest comprehension of his character and of his difficulties. If this story and the facts and documents on which it rests constitute any reflection upon his military policy, I must also testify to the overwhelming weight of the burdens laid upon him, to his extraordinary patience and courage in all the difficulties and perplexities through which we were passing, and to his unvarying kindness and courtesy to me.

The War Council of January 28, besides deciding definitely and finally in favour of the naval attempt upon the Dardanelles, showed itself earnestly desirous of procuring some military force to influence the political situation in the Balkans. It was not thought at this time that any force which could be collected would be equal to the storming of the Gallipoli Peninsula, and this operation never received the slightest countenance at this juncture. All that was hoped for was to secure the subtraction from the forces in England, but destined for France, of one or two divisions, including the 29th Division (our remaining Regular Division), and the employment of this force as a lever to encourage M. Venizelos and the Greek King and Government to enter the war on our side in aid of Serbia.

After much discussion with Sir John French, the War Council of February 9 decided to offer the 29th Division (which was still in England) to Greece, together with a French division, if she would join the Allies. I thought that this offer, taken by itself and apart from any effects which might result from the naval attack on the Dardanelles, was wholly inadequate. I did not believe that

Greece, and still less Bulgaria, would be influenced by the prospects of such very limited aid. Indeed, the exiguous dimensions of the assistance were in themselves a confession of our weakness. This view was justified, and the offer was promptly declined by M. Venizelos.

Meanwhile the preparations for the naval attack had been steadily moving forward. All the ships assigned to the task were already on the spot or approaching it. By an informal arrangement with M. Venizelos the island of Lemnos, containing the spacious harbour of Mudros, had been placed at our disposal as a base for the assembling fleet, and two battalions of Marines from the Royal Naval Division had already been dispatched thither. The sole object of this small force was to provide landing parties for Admiral Carden's fleet, in case during his operations the opportunity should offer of destroying guns or forts already disabled in parts of the Gallipoli Peninsula where the enemy's resistance had virtually ceased. But once it began to be realized that troops in considerable numbers were becoming available, Sir Henry Jackson and Lord Fisher began to press for their employment in the Dardanelles operation. "The provision of the necessary military forces," wrote Sir Henry Jackson on February 15, "to enable the fruits of this heavy naval undertaking to be gathered must never be lost sight of; the transports carrying them should be in readiness to enter the Straits as soon as it is seen the forts at the Narrows will be silenced. . . . The naval bombardment is not recommended as a sound military operation, unless a strong military force is ready to assist in the operation, or, at least, follow it up immediately the forts are silenced." There was much mixed thinking in this. The difference between "assisting in the operation" and "following it up immediately the forts are silenced" was fundamental. Fisher on the other hand was perfectly clear. He wanted the Gallipoli Peninsula stormed and held by the Army. This idea neither Lord Kitchener nor the War Council would at this time have entertained.

"I hope you were successful with Kitchener," wrote the First Sea Lord to me on the evening of February 16, "in getting divisions sent to Lemnos *to-morrow!* Not a grain of wheat will come from the Black Sea unless there is military occupation of the Dardanelles, and it will be the wonder of the ages that no troops were sent to co-operate with the Fleet with half a million soldiers in England.

"*The war of lost opportunities!!! Why did Antwerp fall?*

"The Haslar boats might go *at once* to Lemnos, as somebody will land at Gallipoli some time or other."

I still adhered to the integrity of the naval plan. Knowing what I did of the military situation and of the state of our armies, I did not underrate the serious nature of a decision to commit British troops to severe and indefinite fighting with the Turks on the Gallipoli Peninsula. I had of course thought long and earnestly about what would follow if the naval attack succeeded and a British fleet entered the Marmora. I expected that if, and when, the Turkish forts began to fall, the Greeks would join us, and that the whole of their armies would be at our disposal thenceforward. I hoped that the apparition of a British fleet off Constantinople and the flight or destruction of the *Goeben* and the *Breslau* would be followed by political reactions of a far-reaching character, as the result of which the Turkish Government would negotiate or withdraw to Asia. I trusted that good diplomacy following hot-foot on a great war event, would induce Bulgaria to march on Adrianople. Lastly, I was sure that Russia, whatever her need elsewhere, would not remain indifferent to the fate of Constantinople and that further reinforcements would be forthcoming from her. It was on these quasi-political factors that I counted in our own military penury, for the means of exploiting and consolidating any success which might fall to the Fleet. The reader will see how far these speculations appear to have been well founded.

But of course, if after all Lord Kitchener and the War Council saw their way to form a substantial British army in the East, the prospects of a great and successful combination were vastly more hopeful. Such an army assembled in Egypt and the Greek islands might well be the motor muscle which would decide and animate all the rest. It could either seize the Isthmus of Bulair if the Turks evacuated the Peninsula after the Fleet had passed the Straits; or if a Convention was made with Turkey, it could occupy Constantinople promptly. Incidentally, if landing parties on a larger scale were needed during the passage of the Fleet, they could be supplied from this source. Thus a considerable unity was established on the immediate step of sending troops to the East between persons who on the further steps held very different views. Amid the conflicting opinions, competing plans and shifting exigencies of the situation, the desirability of concentrating the largest possible army in the Eastern Mediterranean with extreme promptitude, and placing at its head a supreme general, seemed to all of us at the Admiralty to be obvious. Therefore we at all times, in all discussions, supported everything that would promote and expedite this concentration.

February 16 was a Day of Resolve. At a meeting of the principal Ministers on the War Council, including the Prime Minister, Lord Kitchener and myself, the following decisions, eventually incorporated in the Decisions of the War Council, were taken:

(1) The 29th Division to be dispatched to Lemnos at the earliest possible date, preferably within nine or ten days.

(2) Arrangements to be made to send a force from Egypt, if required.

(3) The whole of the above forces, with the Royal Marine battalions already

dispatched, to be available in case of necessity to support the naval attack on the Dardanelles.

(4) Horse-boats to be taken out with the 29th Division, and the Admiralty to make arrangements to collect small craft, tugs and lighters in the Levant.

The decision of February 16 is the foundation of the military attack upon the Dardanelles. "It had not," say the Dardanelles Commissioners, "been definitely decided to use troops on a large scale, but they were to be massed so as to be in readiness should their assistance be required." On this day Admiral Carden was informed that Mudros harbour could be used by him as a base, and Rear-Admiral Wemyss was appointed as senior naval officer there. In the evening of the 16th in pursuance of the decisions which had been taken, I directed Admiral Oliver, Chief of the War Staff, to have transports collected with the utmost speed for the 29th Division, and he issued orders to this effect on the same day. The resolve to concentrate an army undoubtedly carried with it acceptance of the possibility of using it in certain eventualities. But these were not as yet defined.

During the 17th it appeared that great pressure was being put upon Lord Kitchener from General Headquarters not to divert the 29th Division from France. In fact, as has been justly observed by the Official Naval Historian, the use of the 29th Division became a cardinal issue between what were beginning to be called in our secret circles "The Western" and "The Eastern" policies. Lord Kitchener became the prey of these contending opinions and forces, and he was plunged into a state of most painful indecision between them.

So far, not a shot had been fired at the Dardanelles, but we were on the eve of the attack on the outer forts. When we met in Council again on the 19th, it became clear that Lord Kitchener had changed his mind. He informed us that he could not consent to the dispatch of the 29th Division to the East. He gave as his reason the dangerous weakness of Russia and his fear lest large masses of German troops should be brought back from the Russian Front to attack our troops in France. I cannot believe that this argument had really weighed with him. He must have known that, apart from all other improbabilities, it was physically impossible for the Germans to transport great armies from Russia to the French Front under two or three months at the very least, and that the 29th Division—one single division—could not affect the issue appreciably if they did so. He used the argument to fortify a decision which he had arrived at after a most painful heart-searching on other and general grounds.

The Council bowed to Lord Kitchener's will, though its wishes and opinions were unaltered. It was decided to postpone the departure of the 29th Division, but the Admiralty was instructed nevertheless to continue the preparation of transports for it and other troops. On the 20th I minuted to the Director of Transports: "All preparations are to be made to embark the 29th Division with the least possible delay. The dispatch of this division is not, however, finally decided."

The 20th was a day of Recoil. Lord Kitchener had refused to send the 29th Division. He even seemed opposed to any large concentration of troops in the East. "The French," he wrote to me (February 20), "are in a great way about so many troops being employed as you told them of. I have just seen Grey and hope we shall not be saddled with a French contingent for the Dardanelles." He deprecated my gathering transports at Alexandria for 40,000 men as a precautionary measure, to which he had previously assented. He went further. He sent his Aide-de-Camp, the brave and accomplished Colonel Fitzgerald, over to the First Sea Lord and the Admiralty Transport Department to say that the 29th Division was not to go. The First Sea Lord and the Director of Naval Transport thereupon assumed that the question had been finally settled by agreement between Lord Kitchener and me. The orders for the collection and fitting of the transports for this Division, which had been operative since the 16th, were accordingly cancelled, and the whole fleet of twenty-two vessels was released for other duties and dispersed without my being informed.

The discussion was resumed on February 24 and 26, but we now met under the impression of the actual attack on the Dardanelles. The bombardment of the Outer Forts had begun on February 19, and although the operations had been interrupted by bad weather a favourable impression had been sustained. Moreover, open action had now been taken. If the 16th had been a day of Resolve, and the 20th a day of Recoil, the 24th and 26th were days of Compromise and Half-measures. On the 24th Lord Kitchener said that he "felt that if the Fleet could not get through the Straits unaided the Army ought to see the business through. The effect of a defeat in the Orient would be very serious. There could be no going back." Thus, at a stroke, the idea of discarding the naval attack, if it proved too difficult, and turning to some other objective, was abandoned and the possibility of a great military enterprise seemed to be accepted. On this I again argued strenuously, both on the 24th and on the 26th, for the dispatch of the 29th Division, and I used to the full the hopes and interest which the naval attack was increasingly exciting.

Lord Kitchener notwithstanding his pronouncement adhered to his refusal. He had sent General Birdwood, an officer whom he knew well, and in whom he rightly had confidence, from Egypt (where he was commanding the Australasian Army Corps) to the Dardanelles to report on the prospects and possibilities of military action. On February 24 the War Office requested the Admiralty to send the following telegram, which was drafted by Sir Henry Jackson, to Admiral Carden:

"... The War Office consider the occupation of the Southern end of the peninsula to the line Suandere-Chana Ovasi as not an obligatory operation for ensuring success of the first main object which is to destroy the permanent batteries. Though troops should always be held in readiness to assist in minor operations on both sides of the Straits in order to destroy masked batteries and engage the enemy forces covering them, our main army can remain in camp at Lemnos till the passage of the Straits is in our hands, when holding Bulair lines may be necessary to stop all supplies reaching the peninsula. You should discuss this operation with General Birdwood on his arrival before deciding any major operations beyond covering range of ships' guns and report conclusions arrived at." Yet two days later, on February 26, Lord Kitchener authorized General Birdwood to draw upon the Australasian Army Corps "up to the total limit of its strength" for the purpose of aiding the Fleet.

All these half-measures, which nevertheless were assuming serious proportions and marked a change in the whole character of the operation, appeared so perilous to me that at the Council on the 26th I formally disclaimed responsibility for the consequences of any military operations that might arise. My disclaimer was entered in the records. Then the Prime Minister, making a marked intervention, appealed most strongly to Lord Kitchener not to allow the force available in the East to be deprived of the one Regular Division so necessary to its effective composition. It was useless. After the Council I waited behind. I knew the Prime Minister agreed with me, and indeed the whole Council, with the exception of Lord Kitchener, were of one mind. I urged the Prime Minister to make his authority effective and to insist upon the dispatch of the 29th Division to Lemnos or Alexandria. I felt at that moment in an intense way a foreboding of disaster. I knew it was a turning-point in the struggle, as surely as I know now that the consequences are graven on the monuments of history. The Prime Minister did not feel that anything more could be done. He had done his best to persuade Lord Kitchener. He could not overrule him or face his resignation upon a question like this, for the whole military opinion of the General Staff and of the French authorities would be upon his side.

On February 25 I had prepared an appreciation of the general situation and I had used this to argue from in the War Council of the 26th. It was now printed and circulated to the Prime Minister, the Chancellor of the Exchequer and Mr. Balfour. I reprint it here as it explains my position more clearly than any other document of this period.

APPRECIATION.

1. *Russia.*—We must not expect Russia to invade Germany successfully for many months to come. But though the Russian offensive is paralysed, we may count on her not only maintaining a successful defensive,

but effectively containing and retaining very large German forces on her front. There is no reason to believe that Germany will be able to transfer to the West anything like 1,000,000 men at any time; nor anyhow that German forces large enough to influence the situation can arrive in the West before the middle of April.

2. The Anglo-French lines in the West are very strong, and cannot be turned. Our position and forces in France are incomparably stronger than at the beginning of the war, when we had opposed to us nearly three-fourths of the first line of the German Army. We ought to welcome a German assault on the largest possible scale. The chances of repulsing it would be strong in our favour; and even if its success necessitated retirement to another line, the superior losses of the Germans would afford good compensation. The issue in the West in the next three months ought not to cause anxiety. But, anyhow, it is not an issue which could be decisively affected by four or five British divisions.

3. For us the decisive point, and the only point where the initiative can be seized and maintained, is in the Balkan Peninsula. With proper military and naval co-operation, and with forces which are available, we can make certain of taking Constantinople by the end of March, and capturing or destroying all Turkish forces in Europe (except those in Adrianople). This blow can be struck before the fate of Serbia is decided. Its effect on the whole of the Balkans will be decisive. It will eliminate Turkey as a military factor.

4. The following military forces (at least) are available immediately:

		Men.
In England { 29th Division / Another Territorial Division }		36,000
Under orders for Lemnos: R.N. Division · · · · · · · · · · · ·		12,000
From Egypt: 2 Australian Divisions · · · · · · · · · · · · · · ·		39,000
French Division ·	(say)	20,000
Russian Brigade ·	(say)	8,000
Total ·		115,000

5. All these troops are capable of being concentrated within striking distance of the Bulair Isthmus by March 21 if orders are given now. If the naval operations have not succeeded by then, they can be used to attack the Gallipoli Peninsula and make sure that the fleet gets through. As soon as the Dardanelles are open, they can either *(a)* operate from Constantinople to extirpate any Turkish forces in Europe; or *(b)* if Bulgaria comes in at our invitation to occupy up to the Enos-Midia line, they can proceed through Bulgaria to the aid of Serbia; or *(c)* if Bulgaria is merely con-

firmed in a friendly neutrality, but Greece comes in, they can proceed through Salonika to the aid of Serbia.

W. S. C.

February 25, 1915

And on the 27th:

I must now put on record my opinion that the military force provided, viz., two Australasian divisions supported by the nine naval battalions and the French division, is not large enough for the work it may have to do; and that the absence of any British regular troops will, if fighting occurs, expose the naval battalions and the Australians to undue risk.

Even if the Navy succeed unaided in forcing the passage, the weakness of the military force may compel us to forgo a large part of the advantages which would otherwise follow.

I still hoped after the meeting of the 26th that in a day or two Lord Kitchener's mood would change, that the Prime Minister would manage to bring him round to the general view, and that the 29th Division would be allowed to start. The War Council, while deferring to his decision, had decided that the transports were still to be held together in readiness for it. After the meeting of the 26th was over I inquired from the Transport Department as to what exact state of preparation the transports were in, expecting to find that they were ready. I then learned that on the 20th they had been countermanded and were now utterly dispersed. I was staggered at this, and wrote at once to Lord Kitchener in protest.

I immediately renewed the orders to the Transport Department, but it was not found possible to reassemble and fit the necessary vessels before March 16.

The actual opening of the bombardment and the success of the Navy at the outer forts, which will be described in the next chapter, induced a further change of view. "Another meeting of the War Council," to quote the report of the Dardanelles Commission, "was held on March 3. By this time Lord Kitchener's opposition to the despatch of the 29th Division had apparently weakened. On the question being raised by Mr. Churchill he said that he proposed to leave the question open until March 10, when he hoped to have heard from General Birdwood." General Birdwood, however, arrived at the Dardanelles before the 10th. On the 5th he telegraphed to Lord Kitchener: "I am very doubtful if the Navy can force the passage unassisted." . . .

This was followed on the 6th by a telegram to the following effect: "I have already informed you that I consider the Admiral's forecast is too sanguine, and though we may have a better estimate by March 12, I doubt his ability to force the passage unaided." On March 10, Lord Kitchener, being then somewhat reassured as regards the position in other theatres of war, and being also possibly impressed by General Birdwood's reports, announced to the War Council that "he felt that the situation was now sufficiently secure to justify the despatch of the 29th Division."

". . . The decision of February 16, the execution of which had been suspended on the 20th, again became operative on March 10. In the meanwhile, three weeks of valuable time had been lost. The transports, which might have left on February 22, did not get away till March 16."

We shall soon be forced to face the consequences of this delay. The repeated changes of plan were baffling in the last degree. But even after decision was at last taken to send an army including the 29th Division, the use to which that army was to be put remained a Secret of the Sphinx. When Lord Kitchener had decided in his heart that if the Navy failed to force the Dardanelles, he would storm the Gallipoli Peninsula, he ought to have declared it to his colleagues. Failing this he should at any rate have so moved and organized his troops as to leave the different alternatives of action open to him. Most of all should he have set his General Staff to work out plans for the various contingencies which were now plainly coming into view. It would have committed him to nothing to have had the military problem studied scientifically, or to choose a commander in good time.

"From the time the decision of February 16 was taken," say the Dardanelles Commissioners, "there were really only two alternatives which were thoroughly defensible. One was to accept the view that by reason of our existing commitments elsewhere an adequate force could not be made available for expeditionary action in the Eastern Mediterranean; to face the possible loss of prestige which would have been involved in an acknowledgment of partial failure, and to have fallen back on the original plan of abandoning the naval attack on the Dardanelles, when once it became apparent that military operations on a large scale would be necessary. The other was to have boldly faced the risks which would have been involved elsewhere and at once to have made a determined effort to force the passage of the Dardanelles by a rapid and well-organized combined attack in great strength. Unfortunately, the Government adopted neither of these courses. . . . We think that Mr. Churchill was quite justified in attaching the utmost importance to the delays which occurred in despatching the 29th Division and the Territorial Division from this country."

CHAPTER XXIV

FALL OF THE OUTER FORTS AND
THE SECOND GREEK OFFER

At nine minutes to ten on the morning of February 19 the British and French fleets concentrated at the Dardanelles began the bombardment of the outer forts.[1] These forts were four in number and mounted nineteen primary guns. Of these all but four were old pattern short guns with a maximum range of 6,000 to 8,000 yards. Only the two pairs of 9.4-inch guns in the two smaller forts could fire above 11,000 yards. The whole of these defences therefore were exposed to bombardment from the ships at ranges to which they could make no effective reply.

The attacking fleet was formed into three divisions:

1ST DIVISION.	2ND DIVISION.	3RD DIVISION.
Inflexible	*Vengeance*	*Suffren*
Agamemnon	*Albion*	*Bouvet*
Queen Elizabeth	*Cornwallis*	*Charlemagne*
	Irresistible	*Gaulois*
	Triumph	

These vessels mounted 178 guns of 5½-inch and upwards, for the most part more modern than those in the forts, heavier and capable of outranging them in every class of gun. The operations which ensued are minutely described in the Official Naval History, the manœuvres of every ship and the results of almost every shot being carefully set out. It is not intended to repeat this here.

The attack was to have been divided into two parts: first, a long-range bombardment, and, second, overwhelming the forts at short range and sweeping a channel towards the entrance of the Straits. Ammunition was sparingly used and at first the ships were kept under way. It soon became evident that the moving ships could not achieve sufficient accuracy of fire, and at 10:30 all were ordered to anchor in positions outside the enemy's range which enabled one ship to observe from a different angle the fire of another. By 2 o'clock it was considered that the effect of the slow long-range bombardment was sufficient

---

[1] The map on pp. 406–7 will be found relevant to this chapter.

to enable the closer attack to be made, and the bombarding vessels closed to about 6,000 yards. Up till this time no fort had replied to the fire. But at 4:45 p.m., on the *Suffren, Vengeance* and *Cornwallis* advancing to within 5,000 yards range, the two smaller forts with their modern guns came into action, showing that their guns had not been damaged by the long-range firing. The *Vengeance* and *Cornwallis,* reinforced by the *Agamemnon, Inflexible* and *Gaulois,* returned the fire, temporarily silencing one of the forts. Rear-Admiral de Robeck, the second in command, whose flag was flying in the *Vengeance,* wished to continue the action at close range, but as it was now nearly half-past five and the light was fading, the Commander-in-Chief signalled a "General Recall," and the day's operations came to a close. Only 139 12-inch shells had been fired by the fleet. The results of this inconclusive bombardment seemed to show, first, that it was necessary for ships to anchor before accurate shooting could be made; secondly, that direct fire was better than indirect fire; and, thirdly, that it was not sufficient to hit the forts with the naval shells—actual hits must be made on the guns or their mountings. This last fact was important.

The next day the weather broke and no operations were possible for five days. On the 25th the bombardment was resumed in the light of the experience gained. The *Agamemnon* fired at Fort Helles, the *Queen Elizabeth* at Sedd-el-Bahr and later at Fort Helles, the *Irresistible* at Orkanie and the *Gaulois* at Kum Kale. All these ships and others reciprocally observed and checked each other's fire. The forts replied, but without much success. The effect of the bombardment was remarkable. It proved conclusively the great accuracy of naval fire, provided good observation could be obtained. After eighteen rounds the *Queen Elizabeth* hit directly and disabled both the modern guns in Fort Helles. With an expenditure of thirty-five rounds the *Irresistible* destroyed both the modern guns in Orkanie, one early and one late in the day. Thus all four long-range guns defending the mouth of the Straits were individually disabled or destroyed for a very moderate expenditure of ammunition. In the afternoon the ships advanced to within close range of the forts and brought a heavy fire to bear on all of them. All the forts were silenced. The older forts with their short-range armament were considered by the Turks mere shell-traps and their garrisons were withdrawn from them. After the Armistice the Turks stated that the batteries and ammunition dumps were all destroyed, but none of the magazines touched. The forts were evacuated because the short-range fire of the fleet had destroyed them entirely. The loss of life on both sides was small. Practically no damage was done to the fleet, although the *Agamemnon* was hit six or seven times. In all only three men were killed and seven wounded.

It will be seen that this was a very important and satisfactory day. Only thirty-one 15-inch shells had been fired in all, besides eighty-one British 12-inch and fifty from the corresponding French guns. The bombardment clearly proved the power of the ships anchored at about 12,000 yards, if good observation at right angles to the range was available, to destroy the Turkish guns without undue expenditure of ammunition. It was now possible to sweep the approaches and the entrance to the Straits, which was done on the evenings of the 25th and the 26th. Three battleships entered the Straits and completed the ruin of the Outer Forts from inside. A still more remarkable and, as we thought at the time, more hopeful development followed. On the 26th and following days, covered by the guns of the fleet, demolition parties of 50 to 100 sailors and marines were landed, who blew to pieces with guncotton all the guns in Sedd-el-Bahr, as well as in the two forts on the Asiatic side. They were not seriously opposed by the Turks. In all forty-eight guns were destroyed or found in a disabled condition by the landing parties, only nine men being killed and wounded.[1]

Thus by March 2 the whole of the outer defences of the Dardanelles were destroyed, including nineteen primary guns, of which four were modern. These constituted approximately in number and in quality one-fifth of the whole of the gun defences of the Straits. The fleet was now able to sweep and enter the Straits for a distance of six miles up to the limit of the Kephez minefield. The first phase of the Dardanelles operations was thus completed.

The greatest satisfaction was expressed at the Admiralty, and I found myself in these days surrounded by smiling faces. Lord Kitchener told me that his officers who were in contact with the Admiralty reported a spirit of strong confidence. If the Dardanelles Commissioners could only have taken the expert evidence on the feasibility of ships attacking forts in the first week of March, 1915, instead of in the spring of 1917, they would have been impressed by the robust character of naval opinion on these questions. They would also have been struck by the number of persons who were in favour of the Dardanelles operations and claimed to have contributed to their initiation. In short, their task would have resembled the labours of the Royal Commission which inquired into the origin of the Tanks.

Each day at the meetings of the Admiralty War Group I invited Sir Henry Jackson to give his appreciation of the telegrams from the fleet. These appreciations were up to this point highly encouraging. I telegraphed to Admiral Carden at the end of February asking how many fine days he estimated he would require to get through. He replied on March 2: "Fourteen." It really looked as if we had found a way in which the Navy could help the allied cause in a new and

---

[1] Of the ten heavy guns in Sedd-el-Bahr only three had been destroyed by the bombardment. Of the ten guns in Kum Kale seven were apparently found undamaged. Fort Orkanie was also entered and both guns were found disabled. Six modern howitzers on the cliff to the east of Sedd-el-Bahr and a number of smaller guns were also destroyed.

most important direction. However, I observe that I informed the War Council on February 26 that "the Admiralty could not guarantee success and that the main difficulty would be encountered at the Narrows. All that could be said was that the reduction of the Outer Forts gave a good augury for success." I also pointed out repeatedly that a purely naval operation would not in itself make the Straits free for unarmoured merchant ships.

The Inner and Intermediate Defences of the Dardanelles were now exposed to the attack of the fleet. These defences consisted of ten forts and batteries of varying size and importance equally disposed on the European and Asiatic shores; of the minefields closing the Straits in successive lines; and of the mobile batteries and howitzers which protected both the forts and the minefields. To this problem the Fleet now addressed itself.

From February 24 onwards I could contemplate that Lord Kitchener would in certain circumstances be willing to use an army not merely to exploit a victory of the Fleet, but actually if need be to contribute to it on a large scale. All else was uncertain. What he would do, when and how he would do it, remained impenetrable. The increasing possibilities of extensive military action made me anxious about the conditions which prevailed in the War Office. I knew that practically no military staff work was being done. The various contingencies possible were not being studied in detail. Numbers, dates, supplies and the organization appropriate to the various forms of action which might be required, were in the most vague condition, in so far as they were not carried in the comprehensive mind of the Secretary of State for War himself. He was in constant communication with General Birdwood at the Dardanelles. But he did not allow the General Staff nor the Quartermaster-General to meddle in the business at all at this stage, nor give them any inkling of the grave decisions which in certain circumstances he might wish to take, and which were evidently forming in his mind. Seeing all this I became increasingly apprehensive in the first week of March lest a military breakdown should occur. I was determined not to be involved in responsibility for action far more momentous than any which the Admiralty was taking, but over which I had absolutely no control. I therefore early in March asked the Prime Minister to arrange an interview between me and Lord Kitchener in his presence. I then asked Lord Kitchener formally and pointedly whether he assumed responsibility for any military operations that might arise, and in particular for the measure of the forces required to achieve success. He replied at once that he certainly did so, and the Admiralty thereupon transferred on March 12 the Royal Naval Division to his command.

On March 10 the 29th Division was ordered to Lemnos, and on March 16 the earliest of its transports sailed. The War Office, however, did not embark it in the ships in any order or organization to fight on arrival at its destination.

The success of the naval attack upon the outer forts of the Dardanelles and the first penetration of the Straits produced reactions of high consequence throughout Europe, and their repercussion was apparent all over the world. "The Turkish Headquarters at the end of February," writes General Liman von Sanders, then the head of the German Military Mission, "expected the success of a break through by the hostile Fleet. Arrangements were made for the Sultan, the Court and Treasury to take refuge in the interior of Asia Minor." [1] Far away on the Chicago Stock Exchange wheat prices fell with suddenness.

In Europe, Russia asked for a public declaration about Constantinople. At the outset of the war the attitude of Russia had been perfectly correct. She had joined with England and France in assuring Turkey that the territorial integrity of the Ottoman Empire would be respected at the peace. But once Turkey, rejecting this fair offer, had taken sides against her, the Russian attitude changed. "The Turkish aggression," writes Monsieur Paléologue, the French Ambassador in Petrograd, November 9, 1914, "has resounded to the depths of the Russian conscience. . . . All the romantic Utopias of Slavism have suddenly awakened." [2] The supreme need of encouraging Russia in the midst of her disasters and defeats led Sir Edward Grey, as early as November 14, 1914, to instruct Sir George Buchanan to inform M. Sazonoff that the British Government recognized that "the question of the Straits and of Constantinople should be settled in conformity with Russian desires." At the time this had remained a complete secret. But now in 1915 that there seemed to be a prospect of Constantinople falling into the hands of the Allies, Russian opinion required public reassurance. Such an announcement was bound to cause unfavourable reactions in Greece, Bulgaria and Roumania. Could we, on the other hand, afford to quarrel with or even dishearten Russia at the moment when she was reeling under the German cannonade, but was nevertheless contending manfully and was all the time vital to our hopes of general victory? So important was the decision judged, that at the beginning of March the Prime Minister invited the leaders of the Conservative Party, Lord Lansdowne and Mr. Bonar Law, to attend our Council on the subject. I was glad of this development and strongly advised it. I had long wanted to see a National Coalition formed. I viewed with great disquiet the spectacle of this powerful Conservative Party—almost all-powerful it had become since Liberal politics were shattered for the time by the outbreak of the

---

[1] *Five Years in Turkey,* by Liman von Sanders, p. 72.
[2] *La Russie des Tsars,* by Maurice Paléologue, Vol. 1, p. 187.

struggle—brooding morosely outside, with excellent information from the Services and complete detachment from all responsibility for the terrible business which had to go forward from day to day. We needed their aid. The Empire needed their aid. We wanted all their able men in positions of high and active authority. I had frequently talked to Mr. Asquith in this sense in the early months of the war, and I now pointed out that this moment, when some fruition and promise of success had come to us in the East, was of all others the time when the necessary fusion and coalition could be effected on terms honourable to both great parties. The Prime Minister was far from being unconscious of this aspect, or of the political instability which the situation would present should the general state of the war take a turn for the worse, as seemed very likely. I hoped that this first meeting with the official chiefs of the Opposition—Mr. Balfour being already in our councils—might lead to rapid developments in the direction of our national unity and cohesion. The two Conservative leaders, however, showed plainly by their manner that they did not care to become responsible for a fraction only of the policy of the State and were chary of committing themselves in regard to a single incident. This was natural, but the results were unfortunate. The Council did not march satisfactorily, although a united decision was reached. And on the whole, as the result, a chilling impression of domestic politics was, I think, sustained by the Prime Minister.

In the early days of March both Great Britain and France apprised the Russian Government that they would agree to the annexation of Constantinople by Russia as a part of a victorious peace; and this momentous fact was accordingly made public on the 12th.

In the Balkans the effect of the naval operations was electrical. The attitude of Bulgaria changed with lightning swiftness. Within a fortnight our Intelligence Reports showed that the Turks were being forced to move back to Adrianople and develop their front against Bulgaria. General Paget, the head of a special Mission then at Sofia, telegraphed to Lord Kitchener on March 17 that after an audience with the King he was convinced that "the operations in the Dardanelles have made a deep impression, that all possibility of Bulgaria attacking any Balkan State that might side with the *Entente* is now over, and there is some reason to think that shortly the Bulgarian Army will move against Turkey to co-operate in the Dardanelles operations." The attitude of Roumania also became one of extreme and friendly vigilance. Russia, although she had not previously been able to spare more than 1,000 Cossacks for action in the Balkans, now offered the fullest naval co-operation and began to concentrate an army corps under General Istomine at Batoum to participate in what was believed to be the impending fall of Constantinople.

On March 2 our Minister at Bucharest telegraphed that the Roumanian

Prime Minister had said that his conviction that Italy "would move soon" had become stronger. "My Russian colleague has twice seen the Italian Minister and while the latter had often before spoken to him about . . . Italy . . . joining us in the war, his language on the last two occasions was more precise than ever before and was indeed almost pressing. He spoke of acquisitions on the Adriatic coast, *and a share in the eventual partition of Turkey. . . .* Italy would have in a month's time an army of 1,800,000 men ready to move. . . ." Other similar indications flowed in. On March 5 I minuted to Sir Edward Grey: "The attitude of Italy is remarkable. If she can be induced to join with us, the Austrian Fleet would be powerless and the Mediterranean as safe as an English lake. Surely some effort should be made to encourage Italy to come forward. From leaving an alliance to declaring war is only a step." The Foreign Secretary replied in writing, "I will neglect no opportunity."

Most important of all were the effects upon Greece. We have seen how on February 11 M. Venizelos, in spite of his friendship for the Allies and his deep desire to join them, had refused to be drawn into the war by the futile offer of a British and French division. But the attack on the Dardanelles produced an immediate change. On March 1 the British Minister in Athens telegraphed that M. Venizelos had put forward a proposal that a Greek army corps of three divisions should be sent to Gallipoli. Sir Edward Grey promptly replied that H.M. Government would gladly accept this aid, and added that the Admiralty were very anxious that the Greeks should assist with ships as well as troops in the Dardanelles. The British Minister replied on March 2: "M. Venizelos hopes to be in a position to make us a definite offer to-morrow. . . . He had already approached the King, who," added the Minister, "I learn from another source, is in favour of war."

On the 3rd the British Military Attaché at Athens telegraphed that "The view of the Greek General Staff was universally that the naval attack should be assisted by land operations. Their plan was to disembark four or five Greek divisions at the Southern extremity of the Peninsula and to advance against the heights East of Maidos. Three successive defended positions would have to be carried, but Turks could not develop large forces owing to lack of space for deployment. If simultaneously an attack by a separate and sufficient force was made against lines of Bulair, either by disembarking troops North of [the] lines or at head of Gulf of Xeros, the Turks would have to abandon the Maidos region or run risk of being cut off."

Thus at this moment we had within our reach or on the way not only the Australasian Army Corps and all the other troops in Egypt, the Royal Naval Division, and a French Division, we had also at least a Greek army corps of three divisions and possibly more, while a Russian army corps was assembling at Batoum. It would have been quite easy, in addition, to have sent the 29th Division and one or two Territorial divisions from England. There was surely a reasonable prospect that with all these forces playing their respective parts in a general scheme, the Gallipoli Peninsula could even now have been seized and Constantinople taken before the end of April. Behind all lay Bulgaria and Roumania, determined not to be left out of the fall of Constantinople and the collapse of the Turkish Empire. One step more, one effort more—and Constantinople was in our hands and all the Balkan States committed to irrevocable hostility to the Central Powers. One must pause, and with the tragic knowledge of after days dwell upon this astounding situation which had been produced swiftly, easily, surely, by a comparatively small naval enterprise directed at a vital nerve-centre of the world.

But now a terrible fatality intervened. Russia—failing, reeling backward under the German hammer, with her munitions running short, cut off from her allies—Russia was the Power which ruptured irretrievably this brilliant and decisive combination. On March 3 the Russian Foreign Minister informed our Ambassador that

> The Russian Government could not consent to Greece participating in operations in the Dardanelles, as it would be sure to lead to complications. . . .

"The Emperor," M. Sazonoff added, "had in an audience with him yesterday, declared he could not in any circumstances consent to Greek co-operation in the Dardanelles." This was a hard saying. Was there no finger to write upon the wall, was there no ancestral spirit to conjure up before this unfortunate Prince, the downfall of his House, the ruin of his people—the bloody cellar of Ekaterinburg?

In Athens the Russian Minister, under orders from his Government, was active to discourage and resist the Greek intervention. In particular, the King of Greece was made aware that in no circumstances would he be allowed to enter Constantinople with his troops. Other suggestions were made, that perhaps one Greek division might be allowed to participate, "this having the advantage that the King could not take the field in person." Can one wonder that, with his German consort and German leanings, with every appeal on the one hand and this violent rebuff upon the other, King Constantine was thrown back, and relapsed into his previous attitude of hostile reserve?

Further advices from the French Foreign Office on March 4 stated:

> The Russian Government would not at any price accept the co-operation of Greece in Constantinople expedition. . . . If the Greek Government offer co-operation in the Dardanelles expedition they

should be told that co-operation of Greece in the war must be entire and she must give active support to Serbia.

Our Minister at Athens, the well-informed and vigilant Elliot, left us in no doubt of the Greek position.

"To insist on Greek support of Serbia," he telegraphed on the 6th, "except in the event of a Bulgarian attack, would be to wreck the prospect of Greek co-operation with us. The Prime Minister himself had been convinced by the arguments of the General Staff as to the strategical danger of such an operation."

The British Military Attaché telegraphed on the 6th:

My Russian colleague told me to-day that he thought Russia would object to presence of King of Greece in Constantinople, and might make a stipulation that he did not come, a condition of acceptance of the present Greek offer. Any such restriction might lead to collapse of the whole proposal. I urged him to represent to Russian General Staff the strategic advantages of the proposal. Entry of Greece into the war would give best guarantee of succouring Serbia if again attacked by Austria, and maintenance of Greek forces intact would have initially a deterrent effect upon Bulgaria, which in turn might set Roumania free to co-operate with Russia in Bukovina. The French would benefit by securing Corfu as a naval base for the Adriatic, and a general movement in favour of the Triple Entente would be set going in the Balkans.

"The King," he added, "will not initially accompany force, but when Constantinople is approached he may alter his mind. If so, it is conceivable that the King of the Bulgarians might like to anticipate him by co-operating against the Turkish Army—which might have decisive results.

"Russia's objection to temporary presence of either King would be then most unfortunate.

"M. Venizelos," he concluded, "received a great ovation in procession to-day, but main reason for popularity of his proposal to join us, is the hope of Greek troops reaching Constantinople."

Feeling this situation, as I did, in every nerve of my body, I was acutely distressed. The time-honoured quotation one learnt as a schoolboy—"Quos Deus vult perdere prius dementat"—resounded in all its deep significance now that conditions as tragic and fate-laden as those of ancient Rome had again descended upon the world. This was, indeed, the kind of situation for which such terrible sentences had been framed—perhaps it was for this very situation that this sentence had been prophetically reserved.

In my distress I wrote, late on the night of the 6th, to Sir Edward Grey.

Mr. Churchill to Sir Edward Grey.

March 6, 1915.

I beseech you at this crisis not to make a mistake in falling below the level of events. Half-hearted measures will ruin all, and a million men will die through the prolongation of the war. You must be bold and violent. You have a right to be. Our fleet is forcing the Dardanelles. No armies can reach Constantinople but those which we invite, yet we seek nothing here but the victory of the common cause.

Tell the Russians that we will meet them in a generous and sympathetic spirit about Constantinople. But no impediment must be placed in the way of Greek co-operation. We must have Greece and Bulgaria, if they will come. I am so afraid of your losing Greece, and yet paying all the future into Russian hands. If Russia prevents Greece helping, I will do my utmost to oppose her having Constantinople. She is a broken power but for our aid, and has no resource open but to turn traitor—and this she cannot do.

If you don't back up *this* Greece—the Greece of Venizelos—you will have another which will cleave to Germany.

I put this letter aside till the next morning, and in the morning there arrived the following laconic telegram from Athens:

The King, having refused to agree to M. Venizelos' proposals, the Cabinet have resigned.

I put my letter away unsent, and print it now not in any reproach of Sir Edward Grey or the Foreign Office. They felt as we did. They did all in their power. But I print it because it registers a terrible moment in the long struggle to save Russia from her foes and from herself.

CHAPTER XXV

THE NEW RESOLVE

While the attention of so many States, great and small, was riveted upon the Dardanelles, and while so many profound and far-reaching reactions were occurring over the whole field of the war, the naval operations which had produced these great effects began to falter and to flag. From March 3 onwards the progress of Admiral Carden's attack became continually slower. The weather was frequently unsuitable to long-range firing, our seaplanes in those early days were neither numerous nor very efficient, the co-ordination of the gunnery and the observation, though based on sound principles, was in practice primitive through lack of experience. The mobile howitzers which began to fire in larger numbers each day from both sides of the Straits harassed the bombarding ships and forced them to keep on the move. Landing parties sent ashore on March 4 met with much stiffer resistance, and failed to reach the forts. The attempts to sweep up the minefields encountered considerable and increasing Turkish fire from field guns well directed by searchlights. The minesweeping trawlers which had been provided for this service proved inadequate for so severe a task. The ordeal was very trying to their erstwhile civilian personnel who, though familiar with mines, had never previously encountered artillery fire.

Three separate and successive bombardments were made between March 2 and March 8 upon the Turkish forts constituting the inner defences of the Dardanelles.

First, on the 2nd and 3rd the *Canopus, Swiftsure, Cornwallis, Albion, Triumph* and *Prince George* at different times bombarded various forts, Fort Dardanos (8) receiving the main fire. The forts were silenced, but as the ships were kept moving sometimes in circles by the howitzer fire, no guns were hit. Altogether 121 12-inch shells were fired. No definite conclusions could be formed as to the effect of the fire, but the expenditure of ammunition was considered serious.

The method was now changed. On March 5 the *Queen Elizabeth* began the indirect bombardment of the forts at the Narrows. She was stationed outside the Straits two miles from Gaba Tepe and fired across the peninsula. During the day thirty-three 15-inch shells were fired, twenty-eight at Fort 13 and five at

Fort 17. Everything depended upon the arrangements for spotting the fall of the shots. This was provided so far as possible by three seaplanes and by three battleships (*Irresistible, Canopus,* and *Cornwallis*) manœuvring inside the Straits at right angles to the line of fire. Spotting for elevation by the ships was comparatively easy, but they were from their position unable to spot for direction. This depended upon the seaplanes, and for this all-important purpose our seaplane force was found inadequate. The first machine sent up crashed owing to the propeller bursting at 3,000 feet. The second machine was forced to descend after being hit six times by rifle bullets and the pilot wounded. The third machine gave one correction only.

The indirect bombardment was continued on March 6. By this time the Turks had brought up small guns and howitzers on the Gallipoli Peninsula which fired upon the *Queen Elizabeth,* causing her to increase her range to 20,000 yards. The old Turkish battleship *Barbarossa* also opened fire upon her with her 11-inch guns from inside the Straits off Maidos. None of our ships was damaged, although all were hit on several occasions by the howitzers and field guns.

The results of the firing are now known to be as follows:—Fort 13 was hit eleven times and Fort 17 about seven times. The barracks in rear of both these forts were destroyed and one magazine was hit. No guns were damaged, but the firing, coming from an unprotected angle, had a disturbing effect on the Turkish guns' crews. Had aeroplane observation been possible, there is little doubt that great damage would have been done to the forts, and with a sufficient expenditure of ammunition every gun might have been smashed. The forts were quite unprotected from this direction, and each gun and mounting presented a maximum target. The instruction contained in the original Admiralty orders about the sparing use of ammunition and the inadequate arrangements for observation from the air led to a premature discontinuance of this form of attack. This was a great pity. The long-range bombardment by the *Queen Elizabeth* was one of the prime features in the naval plan. Good supplies of ammunition were available for the 15-inch guns, but the Admiralty did not give permission to draw upon these till after March 18. The rule about economy therefore stood. It would have been possible in a few weeks to reinforce and improve the aerial spotting, and this was, in fact, done. The principle underlying the use of the *Queen Elizabeth* against the forts, as embodied in the original Admiralty plan, was sound. The failure was due to the restriction on the expenditure of ammunition and to the inadequate aerial observation. Both these were subsequently remedied, but meanwhile the method had itself been precipitately condemned and was never resumed.

The attack by indirect fire being assumed to have failed, direct attacks upon the forts at the Narrows were resumed on March 17 by the *Agamemnon* and *Lord Nelson* at ranges of from 12,000 to 13,000 yards. The French squadron also engaged Forts 7 and 8. The day was inconclusive. On the 8th the *Queen Elizabeth*, aided by the *Canopus, Cornwallis* and *Irresistible,* renewed the attack. The light was bad owing to rain squalls, and low clouds prevented seaplane observation. All the ships came under the usual howitzer fire, which however did them no serious harm. The forts were apparently silenced, but the Turks claim that they were reserving their ammunition for shorter ranges, and that they ceased firing to clear the guns of grit and débris thrown up by the exploded shells in their vicinity.

The operations continued till the 12th with fitful bombardments and tentative attempts to sweep the minefields. During these days I began to doubt whether there was sufficient determination behind the attack. In one of his telegrams, for instance, the Admiral reported that the minesweepers had been driven back by heavy fire which, he added, had caused no casualties. Considering what was happening on the Western Front and the desperate tasks and fearful losses which were accepted almost daily by the allied troops, I could not but feel disquieted by an observation of this kind. In further telegrams the Admiral explained the difficulties, and that he was reorganizing his mine-sweeping service with regular naval personnel. This reorganization was not, however, complete until a much later period in the operations. Meanwhile, although several further determined attempts were made, happily not attended by heavy losses, the minefields remained substantially intact.

It was clear that a much more vehement effort must be made.

The appointment of a military Commander-in-Chief for the forces assembling in the Eastern Mediterranean and his dispatch to the scene of operations was long overdue. By the end of the first week in March Lord Kitchener had virtually decided to select Sir Ian Hamilton, who was at that time in command of the Central Force at home. He did not, however, reveal his purpose to this officer until the morning of the 12th, when he sent for him and observed laconically: "We are sending a military force to support the Fleet now at the Dardanelles, and you are to have command." [1]

Waiting for this decision, delayed without reason day after day, while troops and events were swiftly moving forward, had been very trying to me and to Lord Fisher. The concentration of transports had been timed for the 18th, and a host of intricate and imperious questions connected with the feeding, watering and organization of large numbers of men and animals were impending at Mudros. The French Division was also on the sea and looking to us for directions and arrangements. All questions of the use of the troops were addi-

---

[1] Sir Ian Hamilton: *Gallipoli Diary,* p. 2.

tional to these administrative problems. On the other hand, Lord Kitchener showed himself restive under repeated inquiries, and was prompt to resent anything that looked like pressure or forcing his hand. We were anxious to have whatever troops he would send on the spot as soon as possible, and great tact was necessary. It was not until the 11th that I was sure he had decided upon Sir Ian Hamilton. I immediately ordered a special train for the afternoon of the 12th in case it should be wanted.

The following were the salient points from Lord Kitchener's written instructions to Sir Ian Hamilton:

(1) The Fleet have undertaken to force the passage of the Dardanelles. The employment of military forces on any large scale for land operations at this juncture is only contemplated in the event of the Fleet failing to get through after every effort has been exhausted.

(2) Before any serious undertaking is carried out in the Gallipoli Peninsula, all the British military forces detailed for the expedition should be assembled so that their full weight can be thrown in.

(3) Having entered on the project of forcing the Straits, there can be no idea of abandoning the scheme. It will require time, patience and methodical plans of co-operation between the naval and military commanders. The essential point is to avoid a check which will jeopardize our chances of strategical and political success.

(4) This does not preclude the probability of minor operations being engaged upon to clear areas occupied by the Turks with guns annoying the Fleet or for demolition of forts already silenced by the Fleet. But such minor operations should be as much as possible restricted to the forces necessary to achieve the object in view, and should as far as practicable not entail permanent occupation of positions on the Gallipoli Peninsula.

Whatever military criticisms may be levelled at these instructions, they represented fairly all that had been settled by the War Council up to that moment. With these instructions in his pocket, and accompanied by a small group of Staff officers appointed during the preceding day, and now meeting for the first time, Sir Ian Hamilton left Charing Cross for the Dardanelles on the evening of March 13. The thirty-knot light cruiser, *Phaeton*, awaited him under steam at Marseilles and carried him at full speed to the Dardanelles by the morning of the 17th.

The increasing perplexities of the naval attack and the surprising case with which the small parties of Marines had been landed at the end of February upon the Peninsula made the immediate employment of troops very tempting both at the Admiralty and on the spot. It was difficult to judge the prospects of a military landing at this juncture. No one knew what troops the Turks had on the spot. Vice-Admiral Carden had stated in his telegram of February 23 that "the garrison of the Gallipoli Peninsula is about 40,000 men." This was also the working basis assumed by the War Office. We now know that the force actually in the Peninsula at this date was under 20,000, scattered along the coast in small parties without supports or reserves. It seems probable that if the 29th Division had been on the spot in fighting order, it could have been landed, with whatever troops were sent from Egypt, at this period without severe loss, and could have occupied very important and probably decisive positions. Thereafter the force landed would have had to sustain heavy and increasing Turkish attack. But there is no reason why they should not have held their ground, and they could have been continually reinforced from Egypt, and later from England, at a far greater rate than the enemy. The possession of the vital observation-point of Achi Baba would have enabled the indirect naval fire to be directed with the utmost accuracy upon the forts at the Narrows. Heavy guns and howitzers, including our new 15-inch howitzers, could also have been landed and brought into action against them at effective ranges. In these circumstances the destruction of the forts within a reasonable time was certain, and the passage of the fleet into the Marmora must have followed. The use of troops on this scale would however have involved a new and serious decision. It meant nothing less than beginning a new campaign, and this would have had to be balanced against further perseverance in the purely naval attack which had not yet been pressed to any conclusion.

I thought it right, without pronouncing an opinion myself, to ask Lord Kitchener for a formal statement of the War Office view. His reply was only what I expected.

First Lord.   March 13, 1915.
    In answer to your question, unless it is found that our estimate of the Ottoman strength on the Gallipoli Peninsula is exaggerated and the position on the Kilid Bahr Plateau less strong than anticipated, no operations on a large scale should be attempted until the 29th Division has arrived and is ready to take part in what is likely to prove a difficult undertaking, in which severe fighting must be anticipated.

                                                                      K.

I do not criticize this decision. It seemed the wisest open in the circumstances. The error lay earlier. Had the 29th Division been sent as originally decided from February 22 onwards, it would have reached the scene by the middle of March instead of three weeks later. Had it been packed on the transports in order of battle, it would have gone into action within a few days of its arrival. All the other troops allocated to this theatre were either conveyed to Lemnos from England or France or were waiting with transports alongside at Alexandria by March 17 or 18. From the 20th onwards they were all available (so far as sea transport was concerned) for an operation upon the Gallipoli Peninsula. The concentration of all troops allotted, including the French Division, was effected as promised by the Admiralty punctually to the date named, namely, March 17. The naval attack reached its culminating point on the 18th. No large Turkish reinforcements had yet reached the Peninsula. But without the 29th Division, the army could do nothing. This was the vital *key* division, the sole regular division, whose movements and arrival governed everything. Therefore four-fifths of the force assigned to this theatre were concentrated punctually as arranged, and the indispensable remaining fifth, without which they could not act, was three weeks behind them. Thus they were all rendered useless.

By the middle of March we had therefore reached a turning point not only in the naval operations but in the whole enterprise. Hitherto no serious risks have been run, no losses have been sustained, and no important forces deeply engaged. The original Carden plan of gradual piecemeal reduction has been pursued. It has not failed, but it has lagged, and it is now so feebly pressed as almost to be at a standstill. Meanwhile, time is passing. Nearly a month has gone since we opened fire. What are the Turks doing? Clearly they must be reinforcing, fortifying, laying new mines, erecting new torpedo-tubes, mounting new guns under the organizing energy of their German instructors. What have the Germans themselves been doing? It would probably take about a month to send submarines from the Elbe to the Ægean. Have they been sent? Are they on their way? How far off are they? *They may be very near.* This was a rapidly growing anxiety. It was also a spur. Surely now the moment has been reached to review the whole position and policy. Surely this is the very moment foreseen from the beginning when, "if matters did not go as we hoped, if the resistance of the forts proved too strong," we could, if we chose, break off the operation. Observe we could, in fact, do it in a moment. One gesture with the wand, and the whole armada assembled at the Dardanelles, or moving thither— battleships, cruisers, destroyers, trawlers, supply ships, transports—would melt and vanish away. Evening would close on a mighty Navy engaged in a world-arresting attack; and the sun might rise on empty seas and silent shores.

Further, was not this the moment to consider alternatives. The prolonged bombardment of the Dardanelles had assuredly drawn continually increasing Turkish forces to the Gallipoli Peninsula and the Asiatic shore. Guns, ammunition supplies of every kind, with which the Turks were so ill-provided, had been scraped and dragged from every other point, or were on the move. Moreover, the Russians had, by a brilliant effort, largely restored the situation in the Caucasus. The British and French troops now on the sea might not be strong enough to land and storm the plateaus and ridges of Gallipoli. But no one could doubt their ability to take and hold Alexandretta—thus cutting from the Turkish Empire one vast portion, severing the communications of their army threatening Egypt, and intercepting the stream of sorely needed supplies and food-stuffs from the East. For such a descent, the Dardanelles operations were the best of all preliminaries—a sincere feint.

On me these considerations made no impression. I knew them all and I rejected them all. I was unswervingly set upon the main enterprise. I believed that if we tried hard enough we could force the Dardanelles, and that if we succeeded in this a truly decisive victory would have been gained. But where were the admirals, generals and statesmen, who did not share these clear-cut conclusions, who had doubts—had always had doubts about the feasibility of the operation, about the margin of the Grand Fleet, about the utility of operations in the Eastern theatre! Here surely was the time for them. Here surely was the time for Lord Fisher. He could say with perfect propriety and consistency, "We have given the Carden plan a good trial. I never liked it much. It has not come off: but it has been a very good demonstration; it has fooled the Turks; it has helped the Russians; it has cost us practically nothing—now let us break off altogether or turn to something else." Later on in April, when we were far more deeply committed, had suffered palpable loss and rebuff, and could not withdraw without great injury to our war prestige, suggestions of this kind were indeed made. But now it was certainly an arguable policy to close the account, and in a naval sense it was the easiest thing in the world to do.

But what happened? So far from wishing to break off the operation, the First Sea Lord was never at any time so resolute in its support. He assented willingly and cordially to the new decision which was now taken to change the gradual tentative limited-liability advance into a hard, determined and necessarily hazardous attack. He approved the momentous Admiralty telegrams which I now drafted after full discussions in our War Group, and, of course, with continuous reference to the Prime Minister. He even offered to go out and hoist his flag and take command at the Dardanelles himself, saying that the responsibility was so great that it could only be borne by the highest authority. Subsequently, although it greatly complicated his position, Lord Fisher himself informed the Dardanelles Commissioners of this fact in a very frank and chivalrous manner.

So far as the other responsible authorities cited in these pages were concerned, no sign of disagreement was manifested. Sir Arthur Wilson, Sir Henry Jackson, Admiral Oliver, Commodore de Bartolomé all were united and agreed to press on and to press hard. The Ministers seemed equally decided. War Office and Foreign Office were eager and hopeful. The Prime Minister did not even think it necessary to summon a council and put the point to them. I have never concealed my opinion. I rejoiced to find so much agreement and force gathering behind the enterprise. My only complaint has been that this high resolve was not carried through by all parties to a definite conclusion.

What was the explanation of this unity and resolution? The vision of victory had lighted the mental scene. The immense significance of the Dardanelles and of the city which lay beyond had possessed all minds. The whole combination which had been dispersed by Russia on March 6 was still latent. The attitude of Italy, of Bulgaria, of Roumania, of Greece absorbed attention. Everyone's blood was up. There was a virile readiness to do and dare. All the will-power and cohesion necessary to mount and launch a great operation by sea and land were now forthcoming. But alas, a month too late!

On the Admiralty War Group all were agreed upon the following telegram to Admiral Carden.

March 11, 1915, 1:35 p.m.

101. Your original instructions laid stress on caution and deliberate methods, and we approve highly the skill and patience with which you have advanced hitherto without loss.

The results to be gained are, however, great enough to justify loss of ships and men if success cannot be obtained without. The turning of the corner at Chanak may decide the whole operation and produce consequences of a decisive character upon the war, and we suggest for your consideration that a point has now been reached when it is necessary, choosing favourable weather conditions, to overwhelm the forts at the Narrows at decisive range by the fire of the largest number of guns, great and small, that can be brought to bear upon them. . . .

We do not wish to hurry you or urge you beyond your judgment, but we recognize clearly that at a certain period in your operations you will have to press hard for a decision, and we desire to know whether you consider that point has now been reached. We shall support you in well-conceived action for forcing a decision, even if regrettable losses are entailed.

And on the 15th:

109. We understand that it is your intention to sweep a good clear passage through the minefields to enable the forts at the Narrows eventually to be attacked at close range, and to cover this operation whether against the forts or [against] the light and movable armament, by what-

ever fire is necessary from the Battle Fleet, and that this task will probably take several days. After this is completed we understand you intend to engage the forts at the Narrows at decisive range and put them effectually out of action. You will then proceed again at your convenience with the attack on the forts beyond, and any further sweeping operations which may be necessary. If this is your intention, we cordially approve it. We wish it to be pressed forward without hurry, but without loss of time.

The Admiral replied:

> March 15, 1915, 9:15 a.m.
>
> I fully appreciate the situation, and intend, as stated in my telegram of March 14, to vigorously attack fortresses at the Narrows, clearing minefields under cover of attack. Good visibility is essential, and I will take first favourable opportunity. . . .

These two Admiralty telegrams 101 and 109 were very serious messages to send to the fleet. They had the intention among other things of making the Admiral feel that if he made a determined effort to force the passage and suffered very heavy losses, or the whole operation miscarried, the responsibility would rest with his superiors at home. He had only to think of his task and of the enemy in his front.

Everything being settled for the attack, I took two days' holiday and went to Sir John French's Headquarters (where I was of course on the direct telephone) to await results. I had no sooner got there than I received a telegram from Vice-Admiral Carden to the Admiralty stating that he had been obliged to go on the sick list under decision of his Medical Officer. He recommended that the conduct of the operations should be entrusted to Vice-Admiral de Robeck who, he said, "was well in touch with all the arrangements present and future and has been of the greatest assistance in their preparation."

This was a disconcerting event. We had arrived at complete understanding with Vice-Admiral Carden. He was the responsible author of the gradual naval attack. He had declared himself in the fullest agreement with the adoption of a more vigorous method. He was deeply engaged in the business, and was bound to fight it through to a conclusion. Now on the eve of battle he had suddenly collapsed. We had to begin again with somebody else. I had become acquainted with Admiral de Robeck during the previous three years. He bore an exceptionally high reputation in the service. He was a good sea officer and a fine disciplinarian. Before the war he had served during my tenure for two years on the East Coast as Admiral of Patrols. I had not always agreed with the schemes which he made in this capacity for dealing with war problems. One could not feel that his training and experience up to this period had led him to think deeply on the larger aspects of strategy and tactics. His character, personality, and zeal inspired confidence in all. The course of events pointed to him as the proper successor of Admiral Carden. He was, it is true, junior in substantive rank to Rear-Admiral Wemyss, now commanding the base at Mudros; but he had been Second-in-Command throughout the operations and had all their threads in his hands. Wemyss also was deeply engaged in the administrative crisis caused by the hourly arrival of the transports containing the Army. To exchange these officers merely on grounds of seniority seemed clearly wrong.

Wemyss himself, with high public spirit spontaneously telegraphed: "I am quite prepared to act under the orders of de Robeck if you should think it desirable to promote him. De Robeck and I are in perfect accord and can loyally co-operate whichever way you decide." The decision was virtually inevitable. Thus carefully did Destiny pick her footsteps at the Dardanelles.

I deemed it indispensable to come to a complete understanding with Admiral de Robeck and to make sure once and for all that he was in full agreement with the Admiralty and ready to take up the operations from the point at which Vice-Admiral Carden had been forced to relinquish them. I therefore sent, after consulting Lord Fisher, the following telegram from Sir John French's Headquarters:—

ADMIRALTY TO VICE-ADMIRAL DE ROBECK.

March 17, 1915.

Personal and Secret from First Lord.

In entrusting to you with great confidence the command of the Mediterranean Detached Fleet I presume you are in full accord with Admiralty telegram 101 and Admiralty telegram 109 and Vice-Admiral Carden's answers thereto, and that you consider, after separate and independent judgment, that the immediate operations proposed are wise and practicable. If not, do not hesitate to say so. If so, execute them without delay and without further reference at the first favourable opportunity. Report fully from day to day. Work in closest harmony with General Hamilton. Make any proposals you think fit for the subordinate commands. Wemyss is your second in command. All good fortune attend you.

VICE-ADMIRAL DE ROBECK TO ADMIRALTY.

March 17, 1915, 10:20 a.m.

First Lord of Admiralty. Secret and Personal.

228. From Vice-Admiral de Robeck. Thank you for your telegram. I am in full agreement with telegrams mentioned. Operations will pro-

ceed to-morrow, weather permitting. My view is that everything depends on our ability to clear the minefields for forcing the Narrows, and this necessitates silencing the forts during the process of sweeping. Generals Hamilton and D'Amade and Admiral Wemyss have been on board to-day, and interview entirely satisfactory.

And the next day:

March 18, 1915.

Weather fine. Operations about to begin.

CHAPTER XXVI

THE EIGHTEENTH OF MARCH

On the morning of March 18 the whole Allied fleet advanced to the attack of the Narrows.

Admiral de Robeck's plan was to silence simultaneously the forts which guarded the Narrows and the batteries protecting the minefields. Ten battleships were assigned to the attack and six to their relief at four-hour intervals. The attack was to be opened at long range by the four modern ships. When the forts were partially subdued the four ships of the French squadron were to pass through the intervals of first line and engage the forts at 8,000 yards. As soon as the forts were dominated the mine-sweepers were to clear a 900-yards channel through the five lines of mines constituting the Kephez minefield. The sweeping was to be continued throughout the night, covered by two battleships, while the rest of the fleet withdrew. The next morning, if the channel had been cleared, the fleet would advance through it into Sari Siglar Bay, and batter the forts at the Narrows at short and decisive range. The sweeping of the minefields at the Narrows would follow the destruction or effective disablement of these forts.

The actual distribution of duties was as follows:—

Line A. *Queen Elizabeth*
Agamemnon — To fire at the forts at the Narrows at 14,000 yards.
Lord Nelson
Inflexible

Triumph — To fire at the intermediate defences.
Prince George

Line B. *Suffren*
Bouvet — To fire later at the forts at the Narrows at 8,000 yards.
Charlemagne
Gaulois

Cornwallis — To cover the mine-sweeping during the night.
Canopus

Vengeance
Irresistible
Albion — Relief.
Ocean
Swiftsure
Majestic

The foundation of the whole plan was that the battleships would only fight and manœuvre in waters which had been thoroughly swept and were known to be clear of mines. On March 7 the bombarding area had been found free and was, in fact, free from mines. Sweeping operations had been carried out almost every night up to 8,000 yards from the Narrows and a few sweeps had been made along the Asiatic shore. Eren Keui Bay had not, however, been swept to any large extent. An experiment carried out by the *Ark Royal* had led to the belief that a seaplane or aeroplane flying above a minefield could discern mines at 18-feet depth in the clear water below. The seaplanes frequently reported the presence of mines in the regular minefields, and their reports had come to be relied upon not only in the positive sense that mines were in a certain place, but in the much wider and more questionable negative sense that there were no mines where none were reported. We now know that the experiment of the *Ark Royal* was misleading. The seaplanes could not, in fact, locate the regular Turkish minefields, and what they saw and reported were only mines exceptionally near the surface or submerged net buoys. Every allowance must be made for the difficulty of the task and for the limited means available for discharging it. But the operation of sweeping the areas from which the ships were to bombard, which were fully under our control and not at all to be confused with the strongly guarded regular minefields, was the indispensable preliminary to any naval attack upon the forts. This, as we now know, was not achieved because the sweepers were inadequate both in numbers and efficiency, and this fact led directly to the losses in the attack of March 18, and indirectly to the abandonment of the whole naval enterprise.

For in the early and squally dawn of March 8, while the British night patrol of destroyers was withdrawing from the Straits, the little Turkish steamer *Nousret* had laid a new line of twenty mines in Eren Keui Bay parallel to the shore and moored about 100 to 150 yards apart. These mines were intended to catch ships attempting to renew the bombardment from the positions in which they had worked on March 6 and 7. In fact, however, they played a recognizable part in the history of the Great War. Three of them were found and destroyed by the sweepers on March 16, but as no more were encountered, it was not realized that they were part of a line of mines. There the rest lay during the ten days before the attack undetected and unsuspected. There they were now lying when in the brilliant sunshine of March 18 the tremendous armada assembled under Admiral de Robeck's command advanced majestically to the execution of a momentous plan.

At about half-past eleven the *Queen Elizabeth, Agamemnon, Lord Nelson* and *Inflexible* opened fire in succession on the forts at the Narrows at 14,400 yards range and a few minutes later the whole of Line A was in action. The ships were immediately subjected to a heavy fire from the movable howitzers and field guns of the Intermediate Defences. All ships were struck several times, but their armour effectually protected them from damage. The forts also began to fire, but the range was too great for them. At 11:50 a big explosion took place in Fort 20 on which the *Queen Elizabeth* was firing and both the *Agamemnon* and *Lord Nelson* were seen to be hitting Forts 13 and 17 repeatedly. A few minutes after midday the French Squadron advanced through the bombarding line and, gallantly led by Admiral Guépratte, began to engage the forts at closer range. All the forts replied vigorously and the firing on both sides became tremendous, the whole of Lines A and B firing simultaneously both at the forts and at the lighter batteries. The spectacle at this period is described as one of terrible magnificence. The mighty ships wheeling, manœuvring and firing their guns, great and small, amid fountains of water; the forts in clouds of dust and smoke pierced by enormous flashes; the roar of the cannonade reverberating back from the hills on each side of the Straits, both shores alive with the discharges of field guns; the attendant destroyers, the picket-boats darting hither and thither on their perilous service—all displayed under shining skies and upon calm blue water, combined to make an impression of inconceivable majesty and crisis. This period lasted for about an hour. A little before 1 o'clock a great explosion occurred in Fort 13. A quarter of an hour later Fort 8 ceased firing. The *Gaulois* and the *Charlemagne* were now hitting Forts 13 and 16 with regularity. At half-past one the fire of the forts slackened appreciably. By a quarter to two their fire had almost ceased. Their men had been driven, or withdrawn, from the guns, and the whole interior of the works was obstructed with debris.

The mine-sweepers were now ordered to advance. The French Squadron which had borne the brunt was recalled and the battleships of the relief moved forward to take their places. Scarcely any damage had been done to the British ships, though the *Inflexible* had her forebridge wrecked and on fire; and several of the French ships had been a good deal knocked about. In the whole fleet, however, not one vessel had been injured in its fighting or motive power. The crews, protected by the strong steel armour, had suffered scarcely any loss. Not forty men in all had been killed or wounded. So far the plan seemed to be working well. The general impression was that the forts were dominated and that, had there been no minefield, the ships could have steamed through the Straits, keeping the forts pinned down by their fire with little loss. It is certain, at any rate, that we had the measure of the forts. But now the first of the disasters occurred.

At 1:54, as the *Bouvet* was coming out of the Straits, following her flagship, the *Suffren,* she struck one of the mines in Eren Keui Bay. The explosion fired her magazine and in two minutes she vanished beneath the surface in a cloud of smoke and steam, only 66 men being saved. The cause of her destruction was attributed on the *Queen Elizabeth* to a heavy shell, and the operations continued without pause.[1]

At 2 o'clock the forts were completely silent and only the *Queen Elizabeth* and the *Lord Nelson* continued to fire at them. The minesweepers were now ordered to enter the Straits; and the relieving line of "B" battleships at the same time advanced to engage the forts at closer range. All the forts resumed a rapid but ineffective fire, and the *Queen Elizabeth* replied with salvos. This second phase also continued for over an hour, the forts firing spasmodically and without injuring the fleet. There is no doubt that at this time the Turkish fire control and communications were deranged. Meanwhile, the minesweepers were advancing slowly against the current towards the Kephez minefield. On their way they exploded three and fished up three more of the newly laid mines in Eren Keui Bay. It was of this moment in the action that Admiral de Robeck subsequently reported, "At 4 p.m. the forts of the Narrows were practically silenced; the batteries guarding the minefields were put to flight, and the situation appeared to be most favourable for clearing the minefields."

At 4:11 the *Inflexible,* which all day had been lying in or close to the unknown minefield, reported she had struck a mine. She took a serious list and her condition was evidently one of danger. Three minutes later it was seen that the *Irresistible* had also listed and was apparently unable to move. At 4:50 Admiral de Robeck learned for certain that this ship also had struck a mine. The appearance of these mines in water which it had been confidently believed was entirely free from them, and in which the fleet had been manœuvring all day, was profoundly disconcerting. It was not thought possible at this time that a line of moored mines could have been laid in our own waters, nor was this known till the end of the war. What then was the mysterious and terrific agency which had struck these deadly blows? Was it torpedoes fired from some concealed or submerged station on the shore? Was it a great shoal of floating mines thrown overboard by the Turks above the Narrows and only now carried by the current among the fleet? Several such mines were seen drifting down during the afternoon, and had been grappled with by the hardy picket-boats. Moreover, just before the beginning of the action four Turkish steamers had been seen waiting in the Narrows, presumably to discharge cargoes of mines at the proper moment.[2] This was therefore the more probable explanation. But anyhow, it was obvious that the area in which the ships were working was not free from mines, or that some other even more alarming cause was active.

On this, Admiral de Robeck determined to break off the action. No one

---

[1] There is still doubt whether the *Bouvet* struck a mine, or whether a shell exploded her magazine. She was over the new minefield, and the Turks think she was destroyed by it.

[2] There was in fact one ship for that purpose.

can accuse this decision. It was impossible to continue the attack on the forts in the face of such losses and uncertainty. The two battleships which were to have covered the sweeping operations during the night could not be left in the Straits. Moreover, the Intermediate Forts (7 and 8) were not yet controlled. The sweeping operations could not therefore proceed and the whole operation must be interrupted. About 5 o'clock orders were given for a general retirement, and all attention was concentrated on the wounded ships and the saving of their crews. While going to the aid of the *Irresistible* the *Ocean* ran into the same minefield and was also stricken. The rest of the story is soon told. The *Inflexible* reached Tenedos Island safely and was anchored in shallow water. The crews of the *Irresistible* and *Ocean* were taken off in destroyers which were most skilfully and courageously handled, and both these derelict battleships foundered during the night in the depths of the Straits.

This ended the action of March 18. For all the tremendous firing and prodigious aspect of the battle, the bloodshed on both sides was incredibly small. The Turkish lost less than 150 men in their batteries and forts, and in the whole British Fleet only 61 men were killed and wounded. The French, however, had to mourn the crew of the *Bouvet,* of whom nearly 600 perished. Of the ships, the *Inflexible* was put out of action for six weeks; the *Gaulois* had been severely injured by gunfire; and three of the old battleships had been sunk. We shall see later on what was the condition of the enemy and his defences.

I passed the day of the 18th in the French trenches among the sand-dunes of the Belgian coast. Here the snarling lines which stretched from Switzerland touched the sea, and the barbed wire ran down the beach into salt water. Corpses entangled in the wire were covered with seaweed and washed by the tides as they mouldered. Others in groups of ten or twelve lay at the foot of the sandhills blasted in their charge, but with the sense and aspect of attack still eloquent in their attitude and order. These dead had lain there for months, and the sand gradually gained upon them, softening their outlines. It was as if Nature was gathering them to herself. The lines were very close together, and in places only a few yards apart. A vigilant silence reigned, broken by occasional guns. The defences in the sand were complicated and novel. They presented features I had not seen on any other part of the front. It was fine weather, and I was thankful to keep my mind from dwelling on the events that I knew were taking place on the other sea flank of the hostile line. I returned to England during the night of the 18th in order to receive the account of the action.

It reached me in the morning, and at the first glance one could see that no good result had been achieved.

A later message added:

With the exception of ships lost and damaged, squadron is ready for immediate action, but the plan of attack must be reconsidered and means found to deal with floating mines.

I regarded this news only as the results of the first day's fighting. It never occurred to me for a moment that we should not go on within the limits of what we had decided to risk, until we reached a decision one way or the other. I found Lord Fisher and Sir Arthur Wilson in the same mood. Both met me together that morning with expressions of firm determination to fight it out. The First Sea Lord immediately ordered two battleships, the *London* and *Prince of Wales,* to reinforce Admiral de Robeck's fleet and to replace casualties, in addition to the *Queen* and *Implacable* which were already on their way. The French Minister of Marine telegraphed that he was sending the *Henri IV* to replace the *Bouvet.* We all repaired to the War Council which met at 11 o'clock. The War Council was also quite steady and determined, and after hearing our news authorized "The First Lord of the Admiralty to inform Vice-Admiral de Robeck that he could continue the naval operations against the Dardanelles if he thought fit."

On this we sent a telegram of encouragement to Admiral de Robeck, apprising him of the ships coming to reinforce him. We added:

> It appears important not to let the forts be repaired, or to encourage enemy by an apparent suspension of the operations. Ample supplies of 15-inch ammunition are available for indirect fire of *Queen Elizabeth* across the peninsula.

On the 20th Admiral de Robeck telegraphed to the Admiralty the details of the reorganization of the mine-sweeping which he was putting into effect. He hoped, he said, to be in a position to renew operations in three or four days; the necessity of some preliminary practice for the new mine-sweeper crews and for the destroyers had imposed an inevitable delay. No ship was to enter the Dardanelles unless everything was in readiness for a sustained attack.

Later in the day he telegraphed that the fighting efficiency of his surviving ships was unimpaired, the damage being confined to funnels, superstructure, and decks.

Thus everything was so far steady and resolved. The First Sea Lord and the Admiralty War Group, the Prime Minister and the War Council, the French Ministry of Marine, Admiral de Robeck and the French Admiral on the spot—all had no other idea but to persevere in accordance with the solemn decisions which had been taken.

But now suddenly on the 23rd came a telegram of a totally different character.

VICE-ADMIRAL DE ROBECK TO ADMIRALTY.

March 23, 1915. (Received 6:30 a.m.)

818. At meeting to-day with Generals Hamilton and Birdwood the former told me Army will not be in a position to undertake any military operations before 14th April. In order to maintain our communications when the fleet penetrates into the Sea of Marmora it is necessary to destroy all guns of position guarding the Straits. These are numerous, and only small percentage can be rendered useless by gunfire. The landing of demolishing party on the 26th February evidently surprised enemy. From our experience on the 4th March it seems in future destruction of guns will have to be carried out in face of strenuous and well-prepared opposition. I do not think it a practicable operation to land a force adequate to undertake this service inside Dardanelles. General Hamilton concurs in this opinion. If the guns are not destroyed, any success of fleet may be nullified by the Straits closing up after the ships have passed through, and as loss of *matériel* will possibly be heavy, ships may not be available to keep Dardanelles open. The mine menace will continue until the Sea of Marmora is reached, being much greater than was anticipated. It must be carefully and thoroughly dealt with, both as regards mines and floating mines. This will take time to accomplish, but our arrangements will be ready by the time Army can act. It appears better to prepare a decisive effort about the middle of April rather than risk a great deal for what may possibly be only a partial solution.

I read this telegram with consternation. I feared the perils of the long delay; I feared still more the immense and incalculable extension of the enterprise involved in making a military attack on a large scale. The mere process of landing an army after giving the enemy at least three weeks' additional notice seemed to me to be a most terrible and formidable hazard. It appeared to me at the time a far graver matter in every way than the naval attack. Moreover, what justification was there for abandoning the naval plan on which hitherto all our reasoning and conclusions had been based? The loss of life in the naval operations had been very small. In the whole operation only one ship of any importance (the *Inflexible*) had been damaged, and a month or six weeks in the dockyard at Malta would repair her thoroughly. As for the old battleships, they were doomed in any case to the scrap-heap. Every ship lost was being replaced. Only on the 20th the Admiral had telegraphed: "From experience gained on 18th I consider forts at the Narrows and the batteries guarding minefields can be dominated after a few days' engagement sufficient to enable mine-sweepers to clear Kephez minefields." But, if so, why not do this? It was what we had always meant to do. It was what we had decided to do. Why turn and change at this fateful hour and impose upon the Army an ordeal of incalculable severity? An attack by the Army if it failed would commit us irrevocably in a way no naval attack could have done. The risk was greater; the stakes were far higher. I had no doubt whatever what orders should be sent to Admiral de Robeck. I convened an immediate meeting of the Admiralty War Group, and placed the following telegram before them:

ADMIRALTY TO VICE-ADMIRAL DE ROBECK.

Your 818. In view of the dangers of delay through submarine attack and of heavy cost of army operation, and possibility that it will fail or be only partly effective in opening the Straits, and that the danger of mines will not be relieved by it, we consider that you ought to persevere methodically but resolutely with the plan contained in your instruction and in Admiralty telegram 109, and that you should make all preparations to renew the attack begun on 18th at the first favourable opportunity. You should dominate the forts at the Narrows and sweep the minefield and then batter the forts at close range, taking your time, using your aeroplanes, and all your improved methods of guarding against mines. The destruction of the forts at the Narrows may open the way for a further advance. The entry into the Marmora of a fleet strong enough to beat Turkish Fleet would produce decisive results on the whole situation, and you need not be anxious about your subsequent line of communications. We know the forts are short of ammunition and supply of mines is limited. We do not think the time has yet come to give up the plan of forcing Dardanelles by a purely naval operation.

Commodore de Bartolomé, who starts to-day, will give you our views on points of detail. Meanwhile all your preparations for renewing attack should go forward.

But now immediately I encountered insuperable resistance. The Chief of the Staff was quite ready to order the renewal of the attack; but the First Sea Lord would not agree to the proposed telegram, nor did Sir Arthur Wilson nor Sir Henry Jackson who was present. Lord Fisher took the line that hitherto he had been willing to carry the enterprise forward because it was supported and recommended by the Commander on the spot. But now that Admiral de Robeck and Sir Ian Hamilton had decided on a joint operation, we were bound to accept their views. In fact, he was immensely relieved that the operation was at last assuming the form which in the earliest days he and all of us would have

Admiralty to V.A. de Robeck

(42.) Not sent

Your 818

In view of dangers of ~~for~~ delay through
Submarine attack and of heavy
cost of Army operation and
possibility that it will fail or be
only partly effective in opening
the ~~way~~ Straits and that
the danger of mines will not
be relieved by it we consider
that you ought to persevere
~~methodically~~ but resolutely
with the plan contained in
your instructions and in
Admiralty telegram 109 and that
you should make all preparations
to renew the attack ~~if this~~
begun on 18th at the
first favourable opportunity.
You should dominate the
forts at the Narrows &
sweep the minefield and
then batter the forts at
close range taking your time

using your aeroplanes, &
all your improved methods
of guarding against mines.
The destruction of the forts
at the Narrows may open
the way for a further advance.
The entry into the Marmara of ~~the~~ a Fleet
strong ~~enough~~ to beat.
Turkish fleet would
~~produce~~ decisive results
on the whole situation
∟And you ~~need~~ not be
~~at this stage~~ anxious
about your subsequent line of
communications. We know
the forts are short of ammunition
and supply of mines is
limited. We do not ~~think~~
~~the time has of know~~
~~of any~~ think the time has
yet come to give up the
plan of forcing Dardanelles
by a purely naval operation.
Commodore de Bartolomé
who starts to day will give
you our views on points of detail.
Meanwhile all your preparations
for renewing attack shd go forward.

preferred. "What more could we want? The Army were going to do it. They ought to have done it all along." But I, seeing how woefully and fearfully the situation was changed to our disadvantage by the delay and exposure, could not stand this. I saw a vista of terrible consequences behind this infirm relaxation of purpose. For the first time since the war began, high words were used around the octagonal table. I pressed to the very utmost the duty and the need of renewing the naval attack. In this I was stoutly supported by Commodore de Bartolomé; but he was the youngest there, and I could make no headway. I closed the meeting without a decision. I took the draft of my telegram to the Prime Minister. I found him in hearty agreement with it, as was also Mr. Balfour, with whom I discussed it during the day.

Looking back, one can see now that this was the moment for the Prime Minister to intervene and make his view effective. As for me, what could I do? If by resigning I could have procured the decision, I would have done so without a moment's hesitation. It was clear, however, that this would only have made matters worse. Nothing that I could do could overcome the Admirals now they had definitely stuck their toes in. They had only to point to the losses of ships which had been incurred, and everyone would have sided with them. I was therefore compelled under extreme duress to abandon the intention of sending direct orders to Admiral de Robeck to renew the attack.

The First Sea Lord endeavoured to console me.

> It is the right thing [he wrote on the 24th], without any doubt whatever to send Bartolomé[1] *and the sooner the better. You are very wrong to worry and excite yourself.* Do try and remember that we are the lost ten tribes of Israel. We are sure to win!!! I know I am an optimist! *Always have been!! Thank God. . . . Hustle Bartolomé! Send no more telegrams! Let it alone!*

Was I, in the light of all that followed, "wrong to worry and excite myself"? Await the sequel. It is right to feel the things that matter: and to feel them while time remains.

---

[1] This project was not carried out.

CHAPTER XXVII

ADMIRAL DE ROBECK'S
CHANGE OF PLAN

What had happened at the Dardanelles? The Army had arrived. From the earliest moment permitted to them the Admiralty had carried all the troops to the point of concentration with punctuality. Sir Ian Hamilton had reached the Dardanelles on the eve of the naval attack on the Narrows, and had witnessed from the bridge of the *Phaeton* its closing scenes. The impression of the sinking of the battleships, the spectacle of the crippled *Inflexible* listed and slowly steaming out of the Straits, the destroyers crowded with the rescued crews, was strong in his mind. These appearances aroused, in a nature chivalrous to a fault, an intense desire to come to the aid and rescue of the sister Service. It was in this mood that he addressed himself to the problem with which he was immediately confronted.

That problem was indeed grave and perplexing in an extreme degree. If the Navy asked for help, Sir Ian Hamilton was resolved to give it to the utmost of his power. If a landing on the tip of the Peninsula and the capture of the Kilid Bahr Plateau would largely solve the naval difficulties, he would attempt it. But obviously then there was not a moment to lose. Every day, every hour, the Turkish defences and preparations would improve and their forces accumulate. A fortnight before, the disembarkation of 40,000 men on the Peninsula might have been effected without great difficulty. But now sharp fighting must be expected. Still, General Birdwood, who had been watching events on the spot since the beginning of March, was eager to land then and there, and confident that the opposition would be overcome by a prompt attack.

But now, for the first time in these military operations, the General Staff were allowed to have their say. They unfolded to their Commander a massive and overwhelming case. The preparations for the landing under fire required an intense degree of organization. No preparations had been made. To carry out such an enterprise required, above all, a proportion at least of most highly-trained troops. None was available. The Australians, however brave and ardent, were, like the Royal Naval Division, only partly trained. The 29th Division had just sailed from England, and would not arrive before the first week in April. But how would it then arrive? It had been embarked in twenty-two transports without any idea of having to fight immediately. The ammunition was in one

405

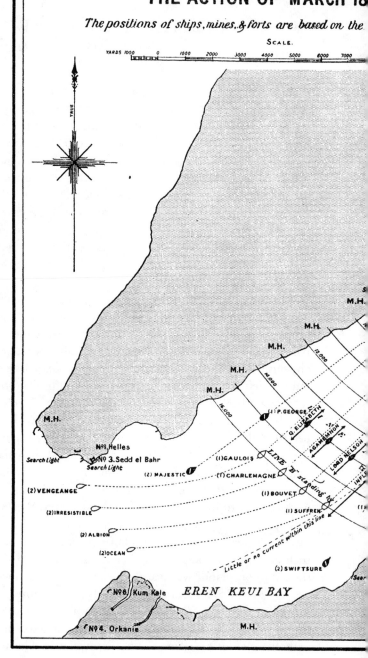

THE DARDANELL

THE ACTION OF MARCH 18

The positions of ships, mines, & forts are based on the

SCALE.

YARDS 1000   0   1000   2000   3000   4000   5000   6000   7000

TRUE

M.H.

M.H.

M.H.

M.H.

M.H.

M.H.

M.H.

12,000

14,000

16,000

(1) P.GEORGE

Q. ELIZABETH

AGAMEMNON

LORD NELSON

LINE "B" standing by

No 1. Helles

Search Light

No 3. Sedd el Bahr

Search Light

(1) GAULOIS

(2) MAJESTIC

(1) CHARLEMAGNE

(2) VENGEANGE

(1) BOUVET

(2) IRRESISTIBLE

(1) SUFFREN

(2) ALBION

(2) OCEAN

Little or no current within this line

(2) SWIFTSURE

No 6. Kum Kale

EREN KEUI BAY

No 4. Orkanie

M.H.

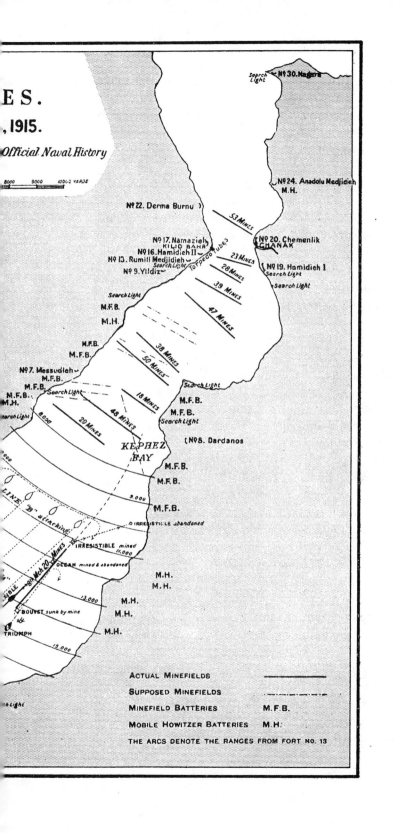

E S.

, 1915.

Official Naval History

8000   9000   10000 YARDS

Nº 30. Nagara

Search Light

Nº 24. Anadolu Medjidieh
M.H.

Nº 22. Derma Burnu)

53 MINES

Nº 17. Namazieh
KILID BAHR
Nº 16. Hamidieh II
Nº 13. Rumili Medjidieh
Search Light
Nº 9. Yildiz

Torpedo Tubes

Nº 20. Chemenlik
CHANAK

23 MINES

28 MINES

Nº 19. Hamidieh I
Search Light

Search Light

39 MINES

Search Light

M.F.B.

M.H.

47 MINES

M.F.B.

M.F.B.

38 MINES

50 MINES

Nº 7. Messudieh
M.F.B.

M.F.B.

Search Light

M.F.B.
M.H.

Search Light

8.000

18 MINES

M.F.B.

M.F.B.

Search Light

29 MINES

48 MINES

(Nº 8. Dardanos

KEPHEZ
BAY

M.F.B.

"B" attacking

M.F.B.

9.000

M.F.B.

IRRESISTIBLE abandoned

IRRESISTIBLE mined
11.000

8th Mch 20 MINES

OCEAN mined & abandoned

12.000

M.H.
M.H.

M.H.

BOUVET sunk by mine

M.H.

TRIUMPH

M.H.

15.000

ACTUAL MINEFIELDS

SUPPOSED MINEFIELDS

MINEFIELD BATTERIES   M.F.B.

MOBILE HOWITZER BATTERIES   M.H.

THE ARCS DENOTE THE RANGES FROM FORT NO. 13

Search Light

ship, the transport in another, the harness in a third, the machine guns at the bottom of the hold, and so on. Before these trained and excellent troops could go into action, they would have to be disembarked either by small boats in still water or upon a quay, and then completely re-sorted, and organized in fighting trim. Mudros harbour (in Lemnos) offered neither facility. Moreover, although nearly 60,000 men were now available within striking distance of the Gallipoli Peninsula, the supplies were scattered throughout the Mediterranean, the hospitals were not prepared, the staff had never come together.

In the choice of evils which now alone was open to Sir Ian Hamilton, his staff pronounced that whatever were the risks of delay, they were less than those of a precipitate and unorganized assault. The General therefore determined to transfer his base and his Army from Lemnos to Alexandria, leaving only sufficient troops at the Dardanelles for minor enterprises, and to organize from Egypt any large military operation which the Navy might require.

Admiral de Robeck had come out of action on March 18 with every intention of resuming the attack at the earliest opportunity. But now occurred the sudden and extraordinary change, the repercussion of which we have witnessed at the Admiralty. On the 22nd a Conference was held on board the *Queen Elizabeth*. There were present Admiral de Robeck, Admiral Wemyss, Sir Ian Hamilton, General Birdwood, General Braithwaite and Captain Pollen. Sir Ian Hamilton has recorded of this Conference:

> The moment we sat down de Robeck told us *he was now quite clear he could not get through without the help of all my troops.*
> Before ever we went aboard, Braithwaite, Birdwood and I had agreed that, whatever we landsmen might think, we must leave the seamen to settle their own job saying nothing for or against land operations or amphibious operations until the sailors themselves turned to us and said they had abandoned the idea of forcing the passage by naval operations alone.
> They have done so . . .
> So there was no discussion. At once we turned our faces to the land scheme.[1]

It is clear that Admiral de Robeck came to his decision during the afternoon or night of the 21st. It was a far-reaching decision. It put aside altogether the policy of the Government and of the Admiralty, with which, up to this, the Admiral had declared himself in full accord. The plans which had emanated from the Fleet, on which both Admiral and Admiralty had been agreed, were

---

[1] *Gallipoli Diary,* p. 41.

cast to the winds. It withdrew the Fleet from the struggle, and laid the responsibilities of the Navy upon the Army. It committed the Army in the most unfavourable conditions to an enterprise of extreme hazard and of first magnitude. It was a decision entirely contrary to the whole spirit, and indeed to the explicit terms, of the latest messages Admiral de Robeck had received from the Admiralty *after* the news of the action of March 18. It was outside the scope of the orders with which, on accepting the command, the Admiral had stated he was in full agreement. It is true that the Admiralty Telegram, No. 109, of March 15, had said: "You must concert any military operations on a large scale which you consider necessary with General Hamilton when he arrives." But this was not intended to cover, nor did it from its context cover, the total abandonment of the naval attack and the substitution of a purely military effort.

Thus at this Conference on the 22nd two grave decisions became operative: first, that the naval attack should be abandoned in favour of a general assault by the Army; and secondly, that the Army should go back to Alexandria to organize and prepare for this attack, although this process would involve at least three weeks' delay. The Army had in fact arrived too late and too ill-organized to deliver its own surprise attack, but in plenty of time by its very presence to tempt the Navy to desist from theirs.

One must, however, make great allowances for the Admiral and for the naval point of view which he represented. To statesmen or soldiers, ships in time of war possess no sentimental value. They are engines of war to be used, risked, and if necessary expended in the common cause and for the general policy of the State. To such minds the life of a soldier was every whit as precious as that of a sailor, and an old battleship marked for the scrap-heap was an instrument of war to be expended in a good cause as readily as artillery ammunition is fired to shelter and support a struggling infantry attack. But to an Admiral of this standing and upbringing, these old ships were sacred. They had been the finest ships afloat in the days when he as a young officer had first set foot upon their decks. The discredit and even disgrace of casting away a ship was ingrained deeply by years of mental training and outlook. The spectacle of this noble structure on which so many loyalties centred, which was the floating foothold of daily life, foundering miserably beneath the waves, appeared as an event shocking and unnatural in its character. Whereas a layman or soldier might have rejoiced that so important an action as that of March 18 could have been fought with a loss of less than thirty British lives and two or three old worthless ships, and that so many valuable conclusions had been attained at such a slender cost, Admiral de Robeck was saddened and consternated to the foundations of his being. These emotions were also present around the Admiralty table in Whitehall.

There is a distinct discrepancy between the statements of Admiral de

Robeck and Sir Ian Hamilton. The Admiral represents that his change of mind was the result of "proposals" made to him by the General, whereas the General states explicitly, "The moment we sat down de Robeck told us he was now quite clear he could not get through without the help of all my troops." The probable explanation is as follows: Until the evening of the 21st the Admiral thought that the Army were not authorized to storm any part of the Peninsula, but only to occupy the Bulair lines after the Fleet had forced the passage. As soon as he learned that the Army were free to act in any direction, and that Sir Ian Hamilton was ready, if called on by him, to descend in full force upon the Southern end of the Peninsula, he immediately abandoned the naval attack, and invited the Army to open the passage.

Whatever may be the explanation, the arguments of Admiral de Robeck's telegram were decisive. At the Admiralty they consolidated all the oppositions to action. At the front they paralysed the Fleet.

On the 24th Sir Ian Hamilton and his staff sailed for Alexandria, whither all the transports carrying troops through the Mediterranean were directed. On this day also on the enemy's side an important step was taken. General Liman von Sanders had hitherto been the head of the German military mission to Turkey, but had not exercised any executive command. The distress and the apprehensions of the Turks, and the crisis of the operations, induced Enver Pasha on March 24 to summon General Liman von Sanders to Constantinople and to place in his hands the entire control of the Turkish forces available for the defence of the Peninsula. General von Sanders assumed the command on the 26th. "The distribution," he writes, "of the available five divisions for both sides of the Marmora which had obtained until the 26th March had to be completely altered. They had stood until this according to quite other principles, scattered along the whole coast like the frontier guards of the good old times. The enemy on landing would have found resistance everywhere, but no forces or reserves to make a strong and energetic counter-attack." [1]

It was with grief that I announced to the Cabinet on the 23rd the refusal of the Admiral and the Admiralty to continue the naval attack, and that it must, at any rate for the time being, be abandoned. Since the crisis of August, 1914, many undertakings had been given on behalf of the Royal Navy, and hitherto all had been made good. It was now again open to the Prime Minister, to Lord Kitchener, to the Cabinet, if they wished, to withdraw from the whole enterprise and to cover the failure by the seizure of Alexandretta. We had lost fewer men killed and wounded than were often incurred in a trench raid on the West-

[1] Liman von Sanders: *Five Years in Turkey,* pp. 81–2.

ern Front, and no vessel of the slightest value had been sunk. I could not have complained of such a decision, however strongly I might have argued against it. But there was no necessity to argue. Lord Kitchener was always splendid when things went wrong. Confident, commanding, magnanimous, he made no reproaches. In a few brief sentences he assumed the burden and declared he would carry the operations through by military force. So here again there was no discussion: the agreement of the Admiral and the General on the spot, and the declaration of Lord Kitchener, carried all before them. No formal decision to make a land attack was even noted in the records of the Cabinet or the War Council. When we remember the prolonged discussions and study which had preceded the resolve to make the naval attack, with its limited risk and cost, the silent plunge into this vast military adventure must be regarded as an extraordinary episode. Three months before how safe, how sound, how sure would this decision have been. But now!

When Lord Kitchener undertook to storm the Gallipoli Peninsula with the Army, he was under the impression that a week would suffice to prepare and begin the operation. But when he had reversed the decision of February 16 to send the 29th Division, when he had countermanded and consequently dispersed its transports, when he had deliberately left the issue in suspense until March 10, when he had allowed the division to be embarked otherwise than in order for battle, he had tied his own hands inextricably. He had no choice now but to wait for weeks in the face of ever-accumulating dangers and difficulties, or to abandon the enterprise. This latter solution, however, he at no time entertained. On the contrary he braced himself resolutely for the effort, and events continued to drift steadily forward.

I still hoped that the continuance of the naval pressure, even within the limits now prescribed, would yield results which would encourage the Admiral to renew his attack, and thus perhaps spare the Army the dreaded ordeal.

However, he did not in the event pursue even limited operations. His energies and those of his staff soon became absorbed in the preparation of the comprehensive and complicated plans necessary for the landing of the army. The *Queen Elizabeth* never fired a gun, and all ships remained inactive against the enemy for another month. From this slough I was not able to lift the operations. All the negative forces began to band themselves together.

Henceforward the defences of the Dardanelles were to be reinforced by an insurmountable mental barrier. A wall of crystal, utterly immovable, began to tower up in the Narrows, and against this wall of inhibition no weapon could be employed. The "No" principle had become established in men's minds, and nothing could ever eradicate it. Never again could I marshal the Admiralty War Group and the War Council in favour of resolute action. Never again could I move the First Sea Lord. "No" had settled down for ever on our councils, crushing with its deadening weight what I shall ever believe was the hope of the world. Vain was it for Admiral de Robeck a month later, inspired by the ardent Keyes,[1] to offer to renew the naval attack. His hour had passed. I could never lift the "No" that had descended, and soon I was myself to succumb. Still vainer was it for Admiral Wemyss, when he succeeded de Robeck, to submit the Keyes plans and his own resolute convictions to the new Board of Admiralty. Vain was it for Keyes in October to resign his appointment as Chief of the Staff and hasten personally to London to plead with Lord Kitchener and my successor for permission to attack. "No" had won, with general assent and measureless ruin. Never again did the British Fleet renew the attack upon the Narrows which in pursuance of their orders they had begun on March 18, and which they then confidently expected to continue after a brief interval. Instead, they waited for nine months the spectators of the sufferings, the immense losses and imperishable glories of the Army, always hoping that their hour of intervention would come, always hoping for their turn to run every risk and make every sacrifice, until in the end they had the sorrow and mortification of taking the remains of the Army off and steaming away under the cloak of darkness from the scene of irretrievable failure.

And yet if the Navy had tried again they would have found that the door was open. Their improved sweeping forces could have concentrated upon clearing the few remaining mines out of the Eren Keui Bay. All their losses were made good. The battle of March 18 could have been resumed a month later in overwhelming favourable conditions; and had it been resumed it would, in a few hours, have become apparent that it could have only one ending. We knew at the time from secret sources, the credit of which was unquestionable, that the Turkish Army was short of ammunition.

We had only to resume a gradual naval advance and bombardment to discover the wonderful truth that they had, in fact, scarcely any more ammunition. We now know what we could have so easily found out then, that for the heavy guns which alone could injure the armoured ships, they had not twenty rounds apiece.

Not until Bulgaria joined the Central Powers could a single heavy shell be brought from Germany to Turkey. We know now what most certainly could have been ascertained through any attempt at sweeping that there were no more mines. Not a dozen mines, floating or moored, remained in Constantinople and, as with the shells, no mine could reach the scene for six long months.

---

[1] Commodore Keyes, afterwards Vice-Admiral Sir Roger Keyes, commander of the Dover Patrol and leader of the attack upon Zeebrugge, 1918.

The German official account written by the staff officer of Liman von Sanders, the German Commander-in-Chief of the Turks, says:

> Most of the Turkish ammunition had been expended. The medium howitzers and mine field batteries had fired half their supply. For the five 25.5 cm. (14-inch) guns there were only 271 rounds, say fifty each; for the eleven 23 cm. (9.2-inch) between thirty to fifty per gun. . . . Particularly serious was the fact that the long range H.E. shells, which alone were effective against armour, were nearly entirely used up. Fort Hamidieh had only seventeen of them; Kilid Bahr but ten. Also there was no reserve of mines. What, then, was to happen if the battle was resumed on the 19th and following days with undiminished violence?

The British Official Military Historian says:

> On the evening of March 18 the Turkish Command at the Dardanelles was weighed down by a premonition of fate. More than half the ammunition had been expended and it could not be replaced. . . . It is important to realize that had Constantinople been abandoned the Turks would have been unable to continue the war. Their only arms and ammunition factories were at the capital and would have been destroyed by the fleet, and the supply of material from Germany would have been impossible. . . . Their inadequate means of fire control had been seriously interrupted. The Turkish gun crews were demoralized, and even the German officers present had apparently little hope of successful resistance if the fleet attacked next day.

And again:

> Of the nine rows of mines many had been in position for six months, and a large proportion of these were believed either to have been carried away by the current or to have sunk to such a depth that ships would not have touched them. For the rest, many were of the old patterns and not at all trustworthy, and owing to the shortage of numbers they were at an average ninety yards apart, more than three times the beam of a ship.

Says the Turkish official account:

> In the attainment of such an important objective, disregarding comparatively small losses, the enemy should have repeated his attack with great force, and in all probability he would have succeeded in forcing the

Straits by sea. . . . In Fort Hamidieh there were but five to ten rounds left and the batteries on the European side were equally low.

With the knowledge we possessed at the time I had no doubt, as the Admiralty telegrams show, that the military risks far outweighed the naval risks, and that the military cost in soldiers' lives would far exceed the cost in sailors' lives. We suspected at the time the weakness and critical condition of the Turkish defence against the Fleet as now revealed. But no one estimated truly the tremendous strength of the Turkish resistance against the Army. Instead of 5,000 casualties, which was the War Office estimate of the cost of the landing and of a successful and decisive operation, more than 13,000 casualties were incurred to gain only a footing on one tiny indecisive tip of the Peninsula, and many more in efforts to enlarge the ground gained. And this takes no account of the heavy losses and wastage in the months before the Battle of Suvla Bay, of the 40,000 casualties sustained in that battle, and of the 20,000 others incurred before the final evacuation.

Could the pictures, on which we must presently look, of April 25 with its immortal heroism, of May with its staggering disappointment, of August with its tragedy, and of December with its world-ruining failure and defeat, have risen before the eyes of those in whose hands the power lay and upon whose heads the responsibility before history must descend, can we doubt that they would have thought it better to persevere resolutely and faithfully with the naval attack in accordance with the orders and undertakings which had been given and received?

CHAPTER XXVIII

THE FIRST DEFEAT OF THE U-BOATS

Chronology is the key to narrative. Yet where a throng of events are marching abreast, it is inevitable that their progress should be modified by selection and classification. Some must stand on one side until the main press is over; others, taking advantage of any interlude, may hasten forward to periods beyond the general account.

During all the operations at the Dardanelles which a series of chapters has described, the general naval war was proceeding unceasingly. The Grand Fleet still watched its antagonists with tireless vigilance. The Cabinet still laboured to perfect and maintain the Blockade against the enemy on the sea and the lawyers across the ocean. A stream of reinforcements and supplies flowed incessantly to France. And lastly, the Admiralty had been called upon to protect the merchant fleets of Britain from a novel and unprecedented form of attack. The first U-boat campaign had begun, and to narrate this episode in an intelligible form it is necessary to look back into the past and to advance somewhat before our time into the future.

When I went to the Admiralty in 1911 we had 57 submarines (11 A's already obsolete, 11 B's, 33 C's and 2 D's) compared to the German 15; but all our submarines, except the 2 D's, were of a class only capable of operating a short distance from their own coasts. They could not accompany the Fleet, nor make long independent voyages at sea; whereas 11 out of the German 15 were at least as good as our 2 D's. During the three years of preparation for which I was responsible, the submarine service was under Commodore Keyes. As early as 1912 we had begun to visualize in the over-sea submarine a new method of maintaining the close blockade of the German ports which was no longer possible by means of destroyers and surface craft. We therefore sought continually to build larger submarines of "over-sea" or even "ocean-going" capacity. We developed the E class and one or two other vessels of an even larger type. Great technical difficulties were encountered, and the delays of the contractors and of the Admiralty departments were vexatious in the extreme. The larger type was entirely experimental, and there were not wanting experts who doubted whether the technical difficulties of submerging vessels above a certain size could be surmounted. In addition, owing to the contracts which had been made, practically assigning the monopoly of submarine building to one particular firm, we were at first considerably hampered even in our experimental work. In 1912, on the recommendation of Commodore Keyes, we decided to break these fettering contracts and to place orders for submarines of different patterns on the Clyde and on the Tyne. We also purchased Italian and French submarines, in order to learn all that could be known of their design. Progress was, however, extremely slow, and beset by doubt at every stage.

At the outbreak of the war we had altogether 74 submarines built, 31 building, and 14 ordered or projected. The Germans had 33 built and 28 building. But of the British total of 74 built, only 18 (8 E's and 10 D's) were over-sea boats, whereas of the 33 German submarines built no fewer than 28 were "over-sea" vessels. The situation therefore was that we had a large force of submarines for the defence of our shores against invasion and for the protection of our harbours; but we had not enough "over-sea" boats to maintain a continuous complete Submarine Blockade of the Heligoland Bight; nor so many of this class as the Germans.

It would be affectation to pretend that we were contented with this state of affairs. On the other hand, it is probable that if we had launched out into an enormous scheme of submarine building before the war, we should have stimulated to an equal, or perhaps greater, extent a corresponding German programme. This would have exposed us to dangers which could never have been compensated by an increase in the number of British submarines. It may well be that all was for the best.

Neither the British nor the German Admiralty understood at the outbreak of hostilities all that submarines could do. It was not until these weapons began to be used under the stern conditions of war that their extraordinary sea-keeping capacity became apparent. It was immediately found on both sides that the larger class of submarines could remain at sea alone and unaided for eight or ten days at a time without breaking the endurance of their crews. These periods were rapidly doubled and trebled in both Navies. So far from having to return to port in bad weather, it appeared that submarines could ride out a gale better than any other class of vessel. Tried as they were forthwith to the extreme limit of human courage and fortitude, the skilled, highly trained, highly educated officers, sailors and engineers who manned them responded with incredible devotion.

Before the war what submarines could do was one mystery. What they would be ordered to do was another.

At the end of 1913, Lord Fisher, then unemployed, wrote his celebrated memorandum on the probable use by the Germans of submarines against commerce, and declared that they would certainly not hesitate to sink merchant vessels which they could not bring into port as required by the laws of war. The memorandum owed a great deal to the technical knowledge of Captain S. S. Hall, who was one of Lord Fisher's intimate followers; but the vision of the old Admiral governed and dominated the argument. I caused this memorandum to be immediately considered by the Sea Lords and by the technical departments.

Neither the First Sea Lord nor I shared Lord Fisher's belief that the Germans would use submarines for sinking unarmed merchantmen without challenge or any means of rescuing the crews. It was abhorrent to the immemorial law and practice of the sea. Prince Louis wrote to me that Lord Fisher's brilliant paper "was marred by this suggestion."

But if we did not believe that a civilized nation would ever resort to such a practice, we were sure that if they did, they would unite the world against them. In particular it seemed certain that a Power offending in this way would be unable to distinguish between enemy and neutral ships, and that mistakes would be made which, quite apart from moral indignation, would force powerful neutrals to declare war upon a pirate nation. In his diagnosis of the German character Lord Fisher was right and the Admiralty was wrong. But even if we had adopted his view it is not easy to see what particular action could have been taken before the war to guard against such an attack.

The submarine is the only vessel of war which does not fight its like. This is not to say that combats have not taken place between submarines, but these are exceptional and usually inconclusive. It follows therefore that the submarine fleet on one side ought not to be measured against the submarine fleet on the other. Its strength should be regulated not according to the number of enemy submarines, but according to your own war plan and the special circumstances of your country. If Germany had had four times as many submarines at the beginning of the war than was in fact the case, she would have gained a great advantage and placed us immediately in serious danger. It would have been no answer to this danger to have multiplied our submarines by four, nor should we have exposed Germany to an equal danger had we done so.

If I resist any impeachment of the Boards of Admiralty over whom I presided for their Submarine policy before the war, still less will I admit that the British Submarine Service was in any way inferior in skill or enterprise to that of Germany. On the contrary, I claim and will adduce proofs that their exploits proved them month by month incontestably superior. But they suffered from one overwhelming disadvantage which it was not in our power to remove, viz., a dearth of targets. Except for a few sudden dashes to sea by fast vessels, the occasional unexpected voyage of a single cruiser, or a carefully prepared, elaborately protected, swiftly executed parade of the High Sea Fleet, the German Navy remained locked in its torpedo-proof harbours; and outside of the Baltic all German commerce was at an end. On the other hand, every sea was crowded with British merchant craft—dozens of large vessels arriving and departing every day, while our fleets were repeatedly in the open sea and our patrolling cruisers and merchant cruisers maintained a constant and unbroken watch and distant blockade. If the positions had been reversed and had we permitted ourselves to attack defenceless merchantmen, far more formidable results would have been achieved. Nor is this a matter of assertion. It is capable of proof. As will be seen when the exploits of British submarines in the Sea of Marmora are recounted, one submarine alone—E11—three times passed and re-passed through the terrible dangers of the tenfold minefields, of the Nagara net, and of the long vigilantly guarded reaches of the Dardanelles, remained in the Marmora ninety-six days (forty-seven in one spell) and sunk single-handed 101 vessels, including a battleship, a modern destroyer and three gunboats. This prodigious feat of Commander Nasmith, V.C., though closely rivalled by that of Commander Boyle, V.C., in E14, remains unsurpassed in the history of submarine warfare.

On February 4, 1915, the German Admiralty issued the following declaration:

> All the waters surrounding Great Britain and Ireland, including the whole of the English Channel, are hereby declared to be a war zone. From February 18 onwards every enemy merchant vessel found within this war zone will be destroyed without its being always possible to avoid danger to the crews and passengers.
>
> Neutral ships will also be exposed to danger in the war zone, and in view of the misuse of neutral flags ordered on January 31 by the British Government,[1] and owing to unforeseen incidents to which naval warfare is liable, it is impossible to avoid attacks being made on neutral ships in mistake for those of the enemy.

We were now confronted with the situation which Lord Fisher had foreseen in his Memorandum of 1913. The event did not, however, cause the Admiralty serious alarm. Our information showed that the Germans could not possess more than twenty to twenty-five submarines capable of blockading the British Isles. As these could only work in three reliefs, not more than seven or eight were likely to be at work simultaneously: and having regard to the enormous volume of traffic moving in and out of the very numerous ports of the United Kingdom, it seemed certain that no appreciable effect would in fact be

---

[1] We had authorized recourse to this time-honoured naval stratagem, knowing well the embarrassment it would cause to the enemy submarines.

produced upon our trade, provided always that our ships continued boldly to put to sea. On the other hand, we were sure that the German declaration and the inevitable accidents to neutrals arising out of it would offend and perhaps embroil the United States: and that in any case our position for enforcing the blockade would be greatly strengthened. We looked forward to a sensible abatement of the pressure which the American Government was putting upon us to relax our system of blockade, and we received a whole armoury of practical arguments with which to reinforce our side of the contention. We consulted long and carefully together at the Admiralty on successive days, and thereafter I announced that we would publish every week the sinkings of merchant vessels effected by the German submarines, together with the numbers of ships entering and leaving British ports.

Meanwhile we made the most strenuous exertions to increase our resources for meeting the attack and to devise every method of countering it.

Regarding the cross-Channel communications as our first and vital care we netted in the Straits of Dover, and established thorough trawler and destroyer patrols. New Divisions were now passing almost every week to France, and their conduct and escort required ceaseless and intricate precautions. We also gave special attention to the North Channel (between Scotland and Ireland), the Southampton-Havre route, and bays and sheltered places where enemy submarines might be supposed to rest. Elaborate instructions for dealing with or avoiding submarine attacks were also given to the captains of British merchant ships, and many other measures were taken as recorded in the Official Naval History.[1]

Apart from arming and commissioning the enormous Mosquito Fleet on which we chiefly relied, our two principal devices for destroying the German submarines were the Bircham Indicator Nets and the Decoy Ships, afterwards called the Q-boats. The Indicator Net was a light flexible curtain of thin steel wire woven into 6 or 10-foot meshes and supplied in lengths of 200 yards. These were laid, clipped together, in long lines across particular channels, and their floats were watched continually by armed trawlers. We had tried them, not without some risk, on one of our own submarines with good results. The submergence of the glass buoys on which the net was hung or the automatic ignition of a calcium light betrayed immediately the presence of the submarine. The net trailing backward wrapped itself around the vessel with a good chance of entangling its propeller, while at the same time a tell-tale buoy attached to the net by a long line floated on the surface, and enabled the hunting vessels to follow their submarine enemy wherever he went. At least 1,000 miles of these

[1] Vol. II, pages 271-2-3.

nets were ordered during the first months of 1915; and by February 13 seventeen miles of the Straits of Dover were already obstructed by guarded nets. Such was the theory, but needless to say it encountered many difficulties and disappointments in practice.

The device of the Decoy Ships was also simple; the idea arose in the following manner. In the previous September a small steamer, plying between St. Malo and Southampton with fruit and vegetables, had been fired at by a German submarine. Admiral Sir Hedworth Meux, who commanded at Portsmouth, came to the Admiralty to see me on general business, and in conversation it was suggested that a gun might be concealed on this small ship under the fruit and vegetables. This was accordingly done. No opportunity of using it occurred, but the idea was revived under the renewed threat of extended submarine warfare. Early in February I gave directions for a number of vessels to be constructed or adapted for the purpose of trapping and ambushing German submarines. For the most part they were ordinary tramp steamers, but some were to be specially constructed of the build and type of Norwegian fishing vessels. These vessels carried concealed guns which by a pantomime trick of trap doors and shutters could suddenly come into action. Great ingenuity was shown by the Admiralty departments in developing this idea, and the use of these vessels afterwards afforded opportunity for some of the most brilliant and daring stratagems in the naval war.

In addition every form of scientific warfare against submarines was perseveringly studied. Already the microphone or hydrophone for detecting the beat of a submarine propeller in the distance had been discovered: but at this date it was only in an experimental condition. Bomb-lances, explosive sweeps, Actæon nets (or necklaces of explosives) were eagerly and simultaneously developed. A close and fruitful union between the scientist, the inventor, and the submarine officer was established, the best brains of the Navy were concentrated on the problem, and no idea, technical or tactical, was spurned by the Admiralty Staff.

The German U-boat campaign, or the so-called blockade of the British Isles, began as promised on February 18; and that same day a British merchant ship was torpedoed in the Channel. By the end of the first week eleven British ships had been attacked, of which seven had been sunk. In the same period no less than 1,381 merchant vessels had arrived in, or sailed from, British ports. The second week of the attack was completely ineffective: only three ships were assailed and all escaped. The arrivals and departures aggregated 1,474. By the end of February we were sure that the basis on which we were acting was sound: British trade was proceeding as usual, and the whole of our transportation across the Channel flowed on, division by division, uninterrupted. We continued to publish the weekly figures during the whole of March. In the four weeks of that month upwards of six thousand vessels reached or left British ports, out of which only twenty-one were sunk, and these together aggregated only 65,000 tons. April confirmed the conclusions of March: only twenty-three ships were sunk out of over six thousand arrivals and departures, and of these six were neutrals and only eleven, aggregating 22,000 tons, were British. The failure of the German submarine campaign was therefore patent to the whole world.

Meanwhile the Germans were themselves already paying heavily for their policy. At least four U-boats out of their small numbers available had been destroyed. On March 1 one became entangled in the Indicator Nets off Start Bay near Dartmouth, and was blown up under water the next day by an explosive sweep. On the 4th the Dover nets and destroyers detected, chased and sunk U8, her entire crew being rescued and made prisoners. On the 6th a hostile submarine, which proved finally to be U12, was sighted off Aberdeen, and after a four days' hunt of incredible perseverance and skill by our small craft, was destroyed and ten survivors taken prisoner. On the 16th a still more remarkable incident occurred: Commander Weddigen, who since his exploits in sinking the three cruisers off the Dutch coast in September, 1914, had become a German national hero, sank a merchant ship off the south coast of Ireland, after taking from it a small gun as a trophy. He was returning to Germany on the 18th when, near the Pentland Firth, he fell in with the Grand Fleet at exercise. The Fourth Battle Squadron was now commanded by Admiral Sturdee flying his flag in the *Dreadnought.* The luck which had brought about the Battle of the Falkland Islands had clearly not deserted Admiral Sturdee, for in ten minutes the *Dreadnought,* handled with great skill by its captain and navigating officer and aided by the *Temeraire,* rammed the submarine. Her bows reared out of the water revealing her number, U29, as she sank for ever to the bottom of the sea with every soul on board. So perished the destroyer of the *Cressy,* the *Aboukir* and the *Hogue.*

Most of the other U-boats returning to Germany had rough and grim experiences to report. One had been caught in the nets off Dover and only escaped after fearful adventures; another had been rammed by a well-handled merchant ship, the *Thordis,* and with difficulty managed to crawl home in a damaged condition; a third narrowly escaped at the end of a three hours' chase by the destroyer *Ghurka.* There were many other incidents of a similar character.

It was in the Straits of Dover that we had concentrated our greatest efforts. It was here that we achieved our most complete success. Early in April, U32 was entangled in the Dover nets, and preferred to return all round the North of Scotland rather than renew her experiences. The account which she gave to the German naval staff of the defences and barriers in the Straits of Dover was such that all U-boats were absolutely forbidden to attempt to pass the Straits; all must make a détour "north about" round Scotland on their way to our western approaches. This prohibition continued in force for more than a year. The eastern waters of the Channel thus became completely clear, and no sinkings within the Dover cordon occurred after the middle of April. We did not, however, know how well our measures and the exertions of Admiral Hood, who carried them out and constantly elaborated them, had succeeded. Injustice was done to this officer when, upon Lord Fisher's advice, I transferred him, about the middle of that month, to another command and appointed in his stead Admiral Bacon, whose mechanical aptitudes and scientific attainments seemed specially to be required on this critical station. It was not until the middle of May that I became aware, from constant study of our gathering information, how excellent had been Admiral Hood's work. Only a few more days were left me at the Admiralty. There was time, however, to repair the injustice, and almost my last official act was to appoint him to the command of the 3rd Battle-Cruiser Squadron. This great prize he accepted with the utmost delight. Alas, it led him to a glorious doom in the Battle of Jutland!

Surveying the situation in April, it was evident that not only had the Germans failed in the slightest degree to impede the movements of British trade, troops and supplies, but that they had themselves suffered heavy and disproportionate losses in the vital units on which their whole policy depended. By May their premature and feeble campaign had been completely broken, and for nearly eighteen months, in spite of tragic incidents, we suffered no appreciable inconvenience. All the measures which we had taken, and all the organizations which had been set on foot, to deal with this unprecedented form of attack, were, however, developed and perfected with the utmost energy. Our merchant skippers were made increasingly familiar with all the methods by which submarine attack should be encountered or avoided. The vigilance and ingenuity of our multiplying Mosquito Fleet was stimulated by a generous system of rewards. The Indicator Nets were improved, and produced in great quantities. Tireless scientific research pursued the secret of detecting the presence of a submerged submarine through the agency of the hydrophone. Lastly, the Decoy Ships were increased in numbers, and their ambuscades and stratagems raised to a fine art. To the providential warning of this impotent campaign and the exertions made in consequence of it, we were to owe our safety in the terrible days which were destined eventually to come upon us.

Results scarcely less to our advantage were experienced in our relations with the United States, on which the whole efficiency of our blockade of the Central Empires depended. This is not the place to discuss the grave and intricate questions of international law which had arisen since the beginning of the war between Great Britain and the United States and other neutral nations. The arguments on both sides were technical and interminable, and whole libraries can be filled with them. Underlying all the legal disputes and manœuvres, was that great fund of kinship and goodwill towards us, of sympathy for the cause of the Allies, of affection for France and of indignation against Germany, which always swayed, and in the end triumphantly dominated, American action. But in spite of this we might well at this time have been forced to give up the whole efficiency of our blockade to avoid a rupture with the United States.

There is nowadays a strong tendency to underestimate the real danger of an adverse decision in America at this period. The National tradition of the United States was not favourable to us. The Treaty with Prussia in 1793 in defence of "the freedom of the seas" constituted the first international relationship of the American Republic. The war of 1812, not forgotten in America, had arisen out of these very questions of neutrality. The established rules of international law did not cover the conditions which prevailed in the great struggle. The whole conception of conditional contraband was affected by the fact that the distinction between armies and nations had largely passed away. The old laws of blockade were, as has been shown, inapplicable in the presence of the submarine. It was not always possible to harmonize our action with the strict letter of the law. From this arose a series of delicate and deeply perplexing discussions in which rigid legalists across the Atlantic occupied a very strong position. There were in addition serious political dangers: Irish and German influences were powerful and active; a strong party in the Senate was definitely anti-British; the State Department was jealously and vigilantly watched, lest it should show partiality to Great Britain. The slightest mistake in dealing with the American situation might at this juncture have created a crisis of the first magnitude. It was the memorable achievement of Sir Edward Grey, seconded by our Ambassador at Washington, Sir Cecil Spring-Rice, that this peril was averted. British and American gratitude also illumines the memory of the United States Ambassador in London, Mr. Page, whose wisdom and generous nobility guarded the English-speaking world and its destiny from measureless injury.

It was in these issues that the first German U-boat campaign gave us our greatest assistance. The German announcement threatening neutral as well as British merchant ships had altered the whole position of our controversies with America. A great relief became immediately apparent. The torpedoing at the end of February of the Norwegian steamer *Belridge,* bound from America with oil for the Dutch Government, was another event which turned the current of American irritation from the British blockade to the German outrages. All the forces friendly to the Allies throughout the Union were animated and strengthened, and German influences proportionately cast down. The stringency of our measures against Germany could be increased without deranging the precarious equipoise of our relations with the great Republic. Sir Edward Grey, aided and guided by Mr. Page, was enabled by processes of patience, tact and conciliation to sustain our position without quarrelling through the whole of March and April: and in May an event occurred which was decisive.

CHAPTER XXIX

THE INCREASING TENSION

April was a month of painful and harassing suspense. Sir Ian Hamilton's Army was repacking at Alexandria; Admiral de Robeck's attention was absorbed in preparation for the landing. The Turks were concentrating, organizing and fortifying. Italy and the Balkans trembled in the balance. Our relations with the United States were most delicate. The position on and behind the Russian front caused profound anxiety. A complete breakdown in the methods of munition supply by the War Office plainly impended. The political situation grew tense.

After March 18 the attitude of the First Sea Lord had become one of quasi-detachment. He was greatly relieved that the burden had now been assumed by the Army. He approved every operational telegram which I or the Chief of the Staff drafted for him. In the end he assented to whatever steps were considered necessary for the proper support of the Army. But while he welcomed every sign of the dispatch of troops, he grudged every form of additional naval aid. He endeavoured repeatedly to turn my mind from the Dardanelles back to the Northern theatre, where, however, there could not be any serious naval operation on our initiative for many months. He evinced increasing concern about the situation in the North Sea.

Although I did not share Lord Fisher's anxiety, real or assumed, about the North Sea, I thought this month of April was a critical one. The Germans must know that we had a very considerable fleet, including some of our best modern ships, withdrawn from the main and for the Navy decisive theatre. We hoped that they would believe that the forces at the Dardanelles were even larger than they were. We had sent several of the dummy battleships to the Mediterranean, hoping thereby to tempt the enemy to battle in the North Sea.

The War Staff orders for the attack on the Dardanelles approved by Lord Fisher contained the following passage:

"A number of merchant vessels have been altered to represent 'Dreadnought' battleships and cruisers, and are indistinguishable from them at 3 or 4 miles distance. . . . They should be used with due precaution to prevent their character being discovered, and should be shown as part of the Fleet off the entrance to the Dardanelles, as if held in reserve. *They may mislead the Germans as to the margin of British strength in Home Waters.*" [1]

We now know that they completely deceived the Turks, who identified and reported one to Germany as the *Tiger*. When I saw the First Sea Lord cordially agree in such a policy of courting battle, I could not take very seriously his general attitude of apprehension. He knew perfectly well that we were strong enough to fight, and no one would have been better pleased had the battle begun.

I devised and carried through at this time the formation of the Battle Cruiser Fleet. This organization was to consist of three squadrons, each of three battle-cruisers, each attended by a light cruiser squadron of four of our latest and fastest vessels, together with the *M* flotilla of our swiftest destroyers. The central conception of this force was Speed. It presented a combination of Speed and Power far superior to any naval force at the disposal of the Germans. In the first instance, most of the light cruisers belonged to the Town class and could not steam more than 27 knots; but the Arethusas were now coming rapidly into commission, and would effectually improve the speed of the squadrons. In order to form this Fleet I telegraphed to the Commonwealth Government, asking them to place the *Australia* at our disposal. This they did with the utmost goodwill and characteristic loyalty to the general interest.

On April 7 the Second, Third and Fourth Sea Lords asked Lord Fisher by minute to reassure them on certain points connected with the conduct of the war. Was he satisfied that we were not putting in jeopardy the principle that the Grand Fleet should be always in such a position and of such strength that it could be at all times ready to meet the entire Fleet of the enemy with confident assurance as to the result? The attack on the Dardanelles, they said, was probably from the point of view of high policy quite correct, but could we afford the loss in ships and the expenditure on ammunition? In conclusion the Sea Lords asked Lord Fisher to assure them that the whole policy had his concurrence, and that he was satisfied with it.

Lord Fisher replied formally by minute the same day. He stated that he was entirely in agreement with the fundamental principle of the maintenance of the strength of the Grand Fleet.

> The Dardanelles operation [he continued] is undoubtedly one, the political result of which, if successful, will be worth some sacrifice in *matériel* and personnel; it will certainly shorten the period of the war by

[1] My italics.

bringing in fresh Allies in the Eastern theatre, and will break the back of the German-Turkish alliance, besides opening up the Black Sea.

It was with hesitation that I consented to this undertaking, in view of the necessarily limited force of ships which could be devoted to it, of the shortage of shell and cordite, and of the factor of uncertainty which must always obtain when ships attack land fortifications and mined areas under their protection.

But, as you state, these high points of policy must be decided by the Cabinet; and in this case the real advantages to be gained caused me eventually to consent to their view, subject to the strict limitation of the Naval Forces to be employed so that our position in the decisive theatre—the North Sea—should not be jeopardized in any one arm.

I am of opinion at the present time that our supremacy is secure in Home Waters and that the forces detached are not such as to prejudice a decisive result should the High Seas Fleet come out to battle. But at the same time I consider that we have reached the absolute limit, and that we must stand or fall by the issue, for we can send out no more help of any kind. I have expressed this view very clearly to the First Lord, and should there at a later period be any disposition on the part of the Cabinet to overrule me on this point, I shall request my Naval colleagues to give their support in upholding my view. . . .

The position of the First Sea Lord is thus very clearly defined. He is seen to be formally and deliberately identified with the enterprise. When notice was given of a Parliamentary question[1] asking whether the First Sea Lord had agreed to the attack of March 18, he wrote across the draft answer: "If Lord Fisher had not approved of this operation, he would not now be First Sea Lord." There is therefore no dispute upon the main issue. But it was not possible, having gone so far, to say, as he did in a letter to me of April 12, "I will not send another rope yarn." Great responsibilities had been incurred: a most serious operation impended; the Army was about to land. It was imperative that it should be properly supported. Subject to the paramount requirement of our safety in the North Sea, everything that was needed and could reasonably be spared, had to be given. Admiral de Robeck now telegraphed for a number of officers to assist in the landing. Lord Fisher was reluctant to accede to this request, and wished also to impose restrictions upon the employment not only of the *Queen Elizabeth,* but also of the *Agamemnon* and *Lord Nelson,* which would to a very large extent have deprived the Army of their support. I could not honourably agree to this, and my view was accepted. But every officer,

[1] Not eventually put.

every man, every ship, every round of ammunition required for the Dard-anelles, became a cause of friction and had to be fought for by me, not only with the First Sea Lord but to a certain extent with his naval colleagues. The labour of this was enormous, but although in the end I allowed no request which reached me from the Fleet to pass unheeded, the process was exhausting. I have no doubt that many requests perished before they reached me, or were not proffered because it was known they would not be welcome. All the time there were ample supplies of ammunition and many powerful naval reinforce-ments available which could have been sent without affecting our security in the North Sea. This is proved by the fact that they were subsequently sent on a far greater scale than was now in question, without evil consequences or undue risk and by a different Board of Admiralty.

On April 11 I wrote to Lord Fisher:

Seriously, my friend, are you not a little unfair in trying to spite this operation by side winds and small points when you have accepted it in principle? It is hard on me that you should keep on like this—every day something fresh: and it is not worthy of you or the great business we have in hand together.

You know how deeply anxious I am to work with you. Had the Dardanelles been excluded, our co-operation would have been impossible. It is not right now to make small difficulties or add to the burden which in these times we have to bear.

Excuse frankness—but friends have this right, and to colleagues it is a duty.

He replied the next day with equal frankness:

Never in all my whole life have I ever before so sacrificed my convic-tions as I have done to please you!—THAT'S A FACT! Off my own bat I sug-gested the immediate despatch of *Lord Nelson* and *Agamemnon* (hoping they would shield *Elizabeth* and *Inflexible!*). De Robeck will hoist his flag in the *Lord Nelson* you may be sure, instead of the *Vengeance,* his former Flagship. For the work in hand the *Vengeance* quite as good for close ac-tion. Nevertheless I say no more. The outside world is quite certain that I have pushed you, and not you me! So far as I know the Prime Minister is the solitary person who knows to the contrary. I have not said one word to a soul on the subject except to Crease[1] and Wilson and Oliver and Bartolomé, and you may be sure these four never open their mouths!

[1] Captain Crease, Naval Assistant to the First Sea Lord.

Indirectly I've worked up Kitchener from the very beginning *via* Fitzgerald.

I think it's going to be a success, but I want to lose the oldest ships and to be chary of our invaluable officers and men for use in the decisive theatre.

And again April 20:

I am quite sick about our submarines and mines and not shooting at Zeppelins (who never can go higher than 2,000 yards and light cruisers bound to bring them down). Really yesterday had it not been for the Dardanelles forcing me to stick to you through thick and thin I would have gone out of the Admiralty never to return, and sent you a postcard to get Sturdee up at once in my place. You would then be quite happy!!!

Since the beginning of the year the disquietude of several of the principal members of the War Council about the supply of munitions for the Army had been continually increasing. Mr. Lloyd George and Mr. Balfour, who with Lord Kitchener and me were members of a Cabinet Committee set up in January to investigate the position, were insistent that the measures of the War Office were in no way proportioned to our needs. Many hundreds of thousands of men had joined the colours and were now in training. The expansion of the British Army to 70 or even to 100 divisions had been designed, yet rifles had not been ordered to supply more than two-thirds of the men actually recruited. The orders placed for artillery were utterly inadequate. The new and special requirements of the war seemed still further neglected. No effective organization for the production of machine guns on the scale on which they were needed had been even planned. The supplies of shell of all kinds, particularly high explosive, and the provision of medium and heavy artillery were on a pitifully small scale. The manufacture of trench-mortars, bombs, and hand grenades was hardly begun.

When complaint was made to Lord Kitchener, the Secretary of State for War and his advisers replied that every factory and source of supply was working to its utmost power, and that the orders already given were far in excess of the capacity to produce, and that the deliveries even of the reduced amounts were enormously in arrear. This was true, but not exhaustive. It was urged that measures out of all proportion to anything previously conceived must be taken to broaden the sources of supply. The War Office replied that they had already done everything that was possible at the moment, and that the fruits of their exertions would not be apparent for many months. They adduced a great number of examples of their action and showed the orders they were placing abroad, principally in America and Japan. All this was still regarded as quite insufficient, and the argument on both sides became fierce.

The critics contended that the Ordnance and Contract branches of the War Office knew nothing whatever about the production of munitions on the gigantic scale required, and that they were far too small and weak a body to deal with these immense and complicated problems of manufacture and industry. To this the War Office rejoined that they could not take the responsibility of allowing these vital matters to pass out of the domain of the professional soldiers into the hands of civilians, politicians or business men, however well-meaning and enthusiastic. Thus on both sides the fires were banked up, and temperature and pressure rose together.

The stress increased with every week that passed. The demands of the Army grew incessantly. Each new division that took the field began to consume munitions of every kind on growing scales. Great numbers of troops at home were seen utterly unequipped. From the front flowed a torrent of complaints. Simultaneously the outputs fell hopelessly below the promises of the contractors. Lord Kitchener dreaded to send fresh divisions to the front even when they were equipped, for fear of revealing still further the inadequacy of the main plant by which they could be nourished. He made every conceivable personal exertion, but nothing in his training as a soldier or as an administrator had fitted him to organize this mighty and novel sphere. His assistants were few and rigid, and he himself took a strict view of the importance of military control.

From the indignation which was freely expressed to me by my colleagues during this month of April, I could not doubt that an explosion of a very violent kind was approaching. The Admiralty was in an easier position. We had maintained in peace incomparably the largest Navy in the world, and our sources of supply were upon the same scale. The British Army, on the other hand, was based on Arsenals narrowly measured by our tiny peace establishments. The Navy had expanded from a broad basis to perhaps double its size; the Army from its restricted basis had been called upon to expand to the equivalent of ten or fifteenfold. At the outbreak of the war we had placed very large orders for everything that the Navy needed with the great firms and dockyards which stood behind the Fleet. I had kept alive the Coventry Works by special measures in 1913, thus giving us a new additional source of heavy gun production. Even before Lord Fisher came to the Admiralty in November, 1914, we had set on foot, in accordance with maturely considered pre-war plans, a great volume of production. The old Admiral's impulse and inspiration supervened on this with cumulative effect. We were thus able, readily and easily, to cope with the developments which the course of the war and the progress of invention required. Already in January and February we were at full blast, and on the whole well ahead with our work in every department. Our task had not been comparable in difficulty with that of the War Office. In fact our very efficiency by absorbing much of the existing capacity for armament production aggravated their troubles. Still, the fact remained that the War Office were not solving their problems, and that there was no prospect of their doing so upon the existing lines.

Growing wrath and fear were not confined to the War Council. Lord Kitchener's embarrassments compelled him to restrict in the most drastic terms the demands of the Armies in the field in respect of all the supplies they needed most. He saw himself forced to give rulings upon the proportion of machine guns, high explosive shell and heavy artillery which seemed absurd and almost wicked to those who did not know his difficulties. Tension grew between the staff at General Headquarters and the War Office. The Army at the front carried its complaints through innumerable channels to Parliament and the Press; and though patriotism and the censorship prevented public expression, the tide of anxiety and anger rose day by day.

Well would it have been if in the solemn moment when we first drew the sword, a National Government resting on all parties had been formed. In those August days when our peaceful and, but for the Navy, almost unarmed people stood forth against the Aggressor, all hearts beat together. There was a unity and comradeship never after equalled. All were ardent for the Cause, and there had been no time to make mistakes in method. Then was the moment to have proclaimed National Government and National Service together. This was certainly my wish. But the moment was lost. The Conservative Party, its power magnified in the atmosphere of war, was left free from all responsibility to watch the inevitable mistakes, shortcomings, surprises and disappointments which the struggle had in store. Its leaders had held themselves hitherto under a public-spirited restraint, silent but passionate spectators. They could endure the strain no longer. Thus both from within and from without, at the War Office and in the Admiralty, in France and at the Dardanelles, tension grew into crisis, and crisis rose to climax.

CHAPTER XXX

THE BATTLE OF THE BEACHES

APRIL 25, 1915

The Gallipoli Peninsula stretches into the Ægean Sea for 52 miles and is at its broadest 12 miles across. But *its ankle,* the Isthmus which joins it to the Mainland, is only 3½ miles wide near the village of Bulair; and at *its neck* opposite Maidos at the south-western end the width is scarcely 6 miles. This very considerable area is mountainous, rugged, and broken by ravines. Four main hill features dominate the ground: the semi-circular chain of hills surrounding Suvla Bay rising to 600 or 700 feet; the Sari Bair Mountain just over a 1,000 feet high; the Kilid Bahr Plateau opposite the Narrows between 600 and 700 feet high; and about 6 miles from the south-western tip the peak of Achi Baba, also 700 feet high.

Outside the Straits the landing-places are comparatively few. The cliffs fall precipitously to the sea and are pierced only by occasional narrow gullies. The surface of the Peninsula is covered for the most part with scrub, interspersed with patches of cultivation. A considerable supply of water in springs and wells exists throughout the region, particularly in the neighbourhood of Suvla Bay. One other feature of practical significance requires to be noted. The tip of the Peninsula from Achi Baba to Cape Helles has the appearance from the sea of being a gradual slope, but in fact this all-important tip is spoon-shaped and thus to a very large extent protected by its rim from direct naval fire.

The operations which were now to take place presented to both sides the most incalculable and uncertain problems of War. To land a large army in the face of a long-warned and carefully prepared defence by brave troops and modern weapons was to attempt what had never yet been dared and what might well prove impossible. On the other hand, the mysterious mobility of amphibious power imposed equal perils and embarrassments upon the defenders. General Liman von Sanders knew, as we have seen, that an army estimated at between 80,000 and 90,000 men was being concentrated at Mudros, in Egypt or close at hand. Where and when would they strike? There were obviously three main alternatives, any one of which might lead to fatal consequences— the Asiatic shore, the Bulair Isthmus and the Southern end of the Peninsula. Of these the Asiatic shore gave the best prospects for the landing and manœuvring

432

of a large army. The Bulair Isthmus, if taken, cut the communications of all the troops on the Peninsula both by land and sea, and thus in von Sander's words, "afforded the prospect of a strategic decision." Thirdly, to quote von Sanders, 'The strip of coast on each side of Gaba Tepe was the landing-place best suited to obtaining a quick decision, as a broad depression interrupted by only one gentle rise led straight from it to Maidos.[1] There were also at the Southern end of the Peninsula the landing-places in the neighbourhood of Cape Helles giving access to the peak of Achi Baba whence the forts on the Narrows were directly commanded. The enemy had no means of knowing which of these widely separated and potentially decisive objectives would receive the impending attack. To meet this uncertain, unknown, unknowable and yet vital situation the German Commander was forced to divide the 5th Turkish Army into three equal parts, each containing about 20,000 men and 50 guns. Whichever part was first attacked must hold out for two or three days against superior numbers until help could come. To minimize this perilous interval the communications between the three parts had been, as we have seen, improved as far as possible. Roads had been made and boats and shipping accumulated at suitable points in the Straits. Nevertheless the fact remained that Liman von Sanders must resign himself to meet in the first instance the whole of the Allied Army with one-third of his own already equal forces, and nearly three days must elapse after battle was thus joined before any substantial Turkish reinforcements could arrive.

In fact, however, the British Commander had fewer alternatives open to him than those which Liman von Sanders was bound to take into account. Sir Ian Hamilton was under injunctions from Lord Kitchener not to involve his army in an extensive campaign in Asia, for which he had neither the numbers nor the land transport. The resources of the Navy in small craft were judged not to be sufficient at this time to maintain a large army landed at Enos, sixty or seventy miles from its base at Mudros, to assault Bulair. Thus there remained in practice only the Southern end of the Peninsula open to the Allied attack. But as von Sanders could not know this, he must still continue to provide against all three contingencies. The issue, therefore, on the eve of battle narrowed itself down to a three days' struggle between the whole Anglo-French forces available, or whatever more these Governments had chosen to make available, and the 20,000 Turks who with their 50 guns were occupying the Southern end of the Gallipoli Peninsula. To get ashore and crush or wear down these 20,000 men, and to seize the decisive positions they guarded near the Narrows, was the task of Sir Ian Hamilton; and for this purpose he had in his hand about 60,000 men and whatever support might be derived from the enor-

[1] Liman von Sanders: *Five Years in Turkey,* p. 80.

mous gun power of the Fleet. It was a grimly balanced trial of strength for life and death.

The first incalculable hazard was the landing under fire. This might well fail altogether. It was not inconceivable that most of the troops might be shot in the boats before they even reached the shore. No one could tell. But if the landing were successful, the next peril fell upon the Turks: they had for at least three days to try to hold out against superior forces. How superior no Turk could tell. It had rested entirely with Lord Kitchener how many men he would employ. If, however, the British and French forces were too few and the Turkish defence was maintained for three days, then the balance of advantage would turn against the Allies. After the third or fourth day the attackers would have expended their priceless treasure of surprise. Their choice would be disclosed and they would be committed almost irrevocably to it. Large reinforcements would reach the Turks; strong entrenchments would be completed; and ultimately the invaders would have to meet the main forces of Turkey which could gradually be brought against them from all parts of the Ottoman Empire. Rapidity and intensity of execution at the outset were therefore the essential of any sound plan.

At daybreak on April 25 Sir Ian Hamilton began his descent upon the Gallipoli Peninsula. The story of the Battle of the Beaches has been often told and will be often told again. From the sombre background of the Great War with its inexhaustible sacrifices and universal carnage this conflict stands forth in vivid outline. The unique character of the operations, the extraordinary amphibious spectacle, the degree of swiftly fatal hazard to which both armies were simultaneously exposed, the supreme issues at stake, the intensely fierce resolve of the soldiers—Christian and Moslem alike—to gain a victory the consequences of which were comprehended in every rank—all constitute an episode which history will long discern. It would not be fitting here to recount the feats of arms which signalized the day. To do them justice a whole volume would be required: each Beach deserves a chapter; each battalion, a page. Only the principal features and their consequences can here be traced.

Sir Ian Hamilton's plan comprised two main converging attacks on the Southern end of the Peninsula: the first by the 29th Division at five separate simultaneous landings in the vicinity of Cape Helles, the second by the Australian and New Zealand Army Corps near Gaba Tepe opposite Maidos. Both these attacks would have become related in the event of either making substantial progress, and both drew upon the resources of the two Turkish divisions which alone were available at this end of the Peninsula. In addition the French were to make a landing on the Asiatic shore near the ruins of Troy to effect a temporary diversion, and the Royal Naval Division in transports accompanied by warships pretended to be about to land at Bulair.

Liman von Sanders has described the emotions at the Turkish Headquarters in the town of Gallipoli when in the early morning the news of the invasion arrived.

> It was evident from the white faces of the reporting officers at this early hour that, although a hostile landing had been fully expected, its occurrence at so many places at once had surprised most of them and filled them with apprehension.

"My first feeling," he adds with some complacency (for he was completely deceived as to which were the true and which the feint attacks), "was that there was nothing to alter in our dispositions. The enemy had selected for landing those places which we ourselves had considered would be the most probable and had defended with especial care." He proceeded forthwith to where he considered the greatest danger lay. "Personally I had to remain for the present at Bulair, since it was of the utmost importance that the Peninsula should be kept open at that place." Thither he also ordered immediately the 7th Division encamped near the town of Gallipoli. All day long, in spite of the news that reached him of the desperate struggle proceeding at the other end of the Peninsula, he held this Division and the 5th intact close to the Bulair lines. It was only in the evening that he convinced himself that the ships and transports gathered in the Bay of Xeros were intended as a feint, and even then he dared only to dispatch by water five battalions from this vital spot to the aid of his hard-pressed forces beyond Maidos. Not until the morning of the 26th, twenty-four hours after the landings had begun, could he bring himself to order the remainder of the 5th and 7th Divisions to begin their voyage from Bulair to Maidos, where they could not arrive before the 27th. Thus in his own words, "the upper part of the Gulf of Xeros was almost completely denuded of Turkish troops," and finally only "a depot Pioneer Company and some Labour battalions" occupied empty tents along the ridge. "The removal of all the troops from the coast of the upper part of the Gulf of Xeros," he writes, "was a serious and responsible decision on my part in the circumstances, but it had to be risked in view of the great superiority of the enemy in the Southern part of the Peninsula. Had the British noted this weakness they might well have made great use of it."

Nothing more clearly reveals the vital character of the Turkish communications across the Isthmus of Bulair than the solicitude for them manifested at this juncture by this highly competent soldier. It is well to ponder in the light of this fact upon Lord Kitchener's observation, "Once the Fleet has passed the Straits the position on the Gallipoli Peninsula ceases to be of importance."

We must return to the Battle of the Beaches.[1] Of the five landings in the neighbourhood of Cape Helles that of the 88th Brigade on "V" Beach close to the ruined fort of Sedd-el-Bahr was intended to be the most important. Over two thousand men of the Dublin and Munster Fusiliers and of the Hampshire Regiment packed in the hold of the *River Clyde*, a steamer specially prepared for landing troops, were carried to within a few yards of the shore. It had been planned to bridge the intervening water space by two lighters or barges. Along this causeway the troops were to rush company by company on to the Beach. At the same time the rest of the Dublin Fusiliers approached the shore in boats. There were scarcely more than four or five hundred Turks to oppose this assault, but these were skilfully concealed in the cliffs and ruined buildings reinforced by a good many machine guns and protected by mines and wire both in the water and ashore. As the Irish troops rushed from the hold of the *River Clyde*, or as the boats reached the submerged barbed wire, an annihilating fire burst upon them from all parts of the small amphitheatre. The boats were checked by the wire or by the destruction of their rowers. The lighters, swayed by the current, were with difficulty placed and kept in position. In a few minutes more than half of those who had exposed themselves were shot down. The boats, the lighters, the gangways, the water, and the edge of the beach were heaped or crowded with dead and dying. Nevertheless the survivors struggled forward through the wire and through the sea, some few reaching the Beach, while successive platoons of Dublin and Munster Fusiliers continued to leap from the hold of the *River Clyde* into the shambles without the slightest hesitation until restrained by superior authority. Commander Unwin and the small naval staff responsible for fixing the lighters, and indeed for the plan of using the *River Clyde*, persevered in their endeavours to secure their lighters and lay down gangways unremittingly in the deadly storm, while others struggled with unsurpassed heroism to save the drowning and dying or to make their way armed to the shore. The scenes were enacted once again which Napier has immortalized in the breaches of Badajoz. Nothing availed. The whole landing encountered a bloody arrest. The survivors lay prone under the lip of the Beach, and but for the fire of the machine guns of Commander Wedgwood's armoured car squadron which had been mounted in the bows of the *River Clyde*, would probably have been exterminated. The Brigadier, Gen-

[1] The map on pp. 406–7 is revelant.

eral Napier, being killed, the whole attempt to land at this point was suspended until dark.

Fighting scarcely less terrible had taken place at "W" Beach. Here the Lancashire Fusiliers, after a heavy bombardment from the Fleet, were towed and rowed to the shore in thirty or forty cutters. Again the Turks reserved their fire till the moment when the leading boats touched the Beach. Again its effects were devastating. Undeterred by the most severe losses from rifle and machine-gun fire, from sea mines and land mines, this magnificent battalion waded through the water, struggled through the wire, and with marvellous discipline actually reformed their attenuated line along the Beach. From this position they were quite unable to advance, and this attack also would have been arrested, but for a fortunate accident. The boats containing the company on the left had veered away towards some rocks beneath the promontory of Cape Tekke. Here the soldiers landed with little loss, and climbing the cliffs fell upon the Turkish machine guns which were sweeping the Beach and bayonetted their gunners. Profiting by this relief, the remainder of the battalion already on the Beach managed to make their way to the shelter of the cliffs, and climbing them established themselves firmly on their summit. Here at about nine o'clock they were reinforced by the Worcesters, and gradually from this direction the foothold won was steadily extended during the day.

Still farther to the left the Royal Fusiliers had landed at "X" Beach, admirably supported at the closest ranges by the *Implacable* (Captain H. C. Lockyer). They were followed by the Inniskillings and the Border Regiment, and by fierce fighting and a resolute charge carried the high ground above Cape Tekke, thus establishing connection with the troops from "W" Beach.

A mile to the left of "X" Beach again, two battalions of Marines were landed without a single casualty at "Y." These were attacked at nightfall, and early the next morning signalled for boats and re-embarked. They, however, drew to their neighbourhood important Turkish forces, and thus for a time aided the other attacks. At the other end of the line, at "S" Beach, on the extreme right near the old fort called De Totts Battery, another battalion was easily landed and maintained an isolated position. When darkness fell, the remaining troops in the *River Clyde* managed to get ashore without further loss, and gradually secured possession of the edge of "V" Beach and some broken ground on either side of it. Thus when the day ended lodgments had been effected from all the five Beaches attacked, and about 9,000 men had been put on shore. Of these at least 3,000 were killed or wounded, and the remainder were clinging precariously to their dear-bought footholds and around the rim of the Peninsula. We must now turn to the second main attack.

• • •

It had been intended to land the Australian and New Zealand Army Corps near Gaba Tepe[1] with the purpose of striking across the neck of the Peninsula towards Maidos. In contrast to the landings of the 29th Division at Helles, this all-important descent was to take place before dawn and without artillery preparation. It was hoped that while the Turkish forces were involved at the end of Peninsula with the 29th Division, the Anzacs would make great headway in its most vulnerable part. The arrangements provided for successive landings from boats and launches, aided by destroyers, of 1,500 men at a time. A rugged and difficult spot half a mile north of Gaba Tepe, unlikely to be elaborately defended, was chosen for the landing. In the dark the long tows of boats missed their direction and actually reached the coast a mile farther to the north, entering a small bay steeply overhung by cliffs till then called Ari Burnu, but in future Anzac Cove. This accident led the attack to a point quite unexpected by the defenders. The actual landing was made with little loss, and the foot of the cliffs proved in practice well sheltered from artillery fire. On the other hand, it carried the Australian advance away from the broad depression from Gaba Tepe to Maidos into the tangled and confused underfeatures and deep ravines radiating in all directions from the mountain of Sari Bair. It also still further separated the Anzac attack from that of the 29th Division at Cape Helles.

As the flotilla approached the shore a scattered fire from the Turkish pickets rang out; but the Australians leaping from the boats into the water or on to the Beach scrambled up the cliffs and rocks, driving the Turks before them in the dim but growing light of dawn. The destroyers were close at hand with another 2,500 men, and in scarcely half an hour upwards of 4,000 men had been landed. The skirmish developing constantly into an action rolled inland towards the sunrise, and by daylight considerable progress had been made. By half-past seven, 8,000 men in all had been landed. In spite of rifle and artillery fire which steadily increased against the Beach, by two o'clock the whole infantry of the leading Australian Division, 12,000 strong, and two batteries of Indian mountain artillery, were ashore occupying a semi-circular position of considerable extent. The 2nd Division including a New Zealand brigade followed, and within a period of twenty-four hours in all 20,000 men and a small proportion of artillery were effectively landed.

The two Turkish divisions who were left without help of any sort to face the onslaught of the Allied Army were shrewdly disposed. Nine battalions of the 9th Division guarded the likely landing-places around the coast from Gaba Tepe to Morto Bay; the remaining three battalions of that Division and the nine battalions forming the 19th Division were all held concentrated in reserve

[1] See map of Anzac and Suvla Bay on p. 505.

near Maidos. At the head of the 19th Division there stood in this strange story a Man of Destiny. Mustapha Kemal Bey had on April 24 ordered his best regiment, the 57th, a field exercise for the next morning in the direction of the high mountain of Sari Bair (Hill 971) and, as Fate would have it, these three battalions stood drawn up on parade when at 5:30 a.m. the news of the first landings came in. A later message reported that about one British battalion had landed near Ari Burnu and were marching upon Sari Bair. Both Sami Pasha, who commanded at the Southern end of the Peninsula, and Sanders himself regarded the landing at Ari Burnu as a feint, and Mustapha Kemal was ordered merely to detach a single battalion to deal with it. But this General instantly divined the power and peril of the attack. On his own authority he at once ordered the whole 57th Regiment, accompanied by a Battery of Artillery, to march to meet it. He himself on foot, map in hand, set off across country at the head of the leading company. The distance was not great, and in an hour he met the Turkish covering forces falling back before the impetuous Australian advance. He at once ordered his leading battalion to deploy and attack, and himself personally planted his mountain Battery in position. Forthwith—again without seeking higher authority—he ordered his 77th Regiment to the scene. By ten o'clock, when the Turkish Commander-in-Chief galloped on to the field, practically the whole of the Reserves in the Southern part of the Peninsula had been drawn into the battle, and ten battalions and all the available artillery were in violent action against the Australians.[1]

Bitter and confused was the struggle which followed. The long-limbed athletic Anzacs thrust inland in all directions with fierce ardour as they had sprung pell-mell ashore from the boats, intent on seizing every inch of ground that they could. They now came in contact with extremely well-handled and bravely led troops and momentarily increasing artillery fire. In the deep gulleys, among the rocks and scrub, many small bloody fights were fought to the end. Quarter was neither asked nor given; parties of Australians cut off were killed to the last man; no prisoners wounded or unwounded were taken by the Turks.

Meanwhile on both sides reinforcements were being hurried into the swaying and irregular firing line. All through the day and all through the night the battle continued with increasing fury. In the actual fighting lines on both sides more than half the men engaged were killed or wounded. So critical did the position appear at midnight on the 25th, and so great was the confusion behind the firing line, that General Birdwood and the Australian Brigadiers advised immediate re-embarkation, observing that decision must be taken then or never. But at this juncture the Commander-in-Chief showed himself a truer judge of the spirit of the Australian troops than even their own most trusted leaders.

[1] This episode is well described in the Australian Official History.

Steady counsel being also given by Admiral Thursby, Sir Ian Hamilton wrote a definite order to "Dig in and stick it out." From that moment through all the months that followed the power did not exist in the Turkish Empire to shake from its soil the grip of the Antipodes.

All through the night of April 26 the position at "V" Beach continued critical. The landing-place was still exposed to Turkish rifle fire, and a further advance was imperative if any results were to be achieved. Accordingly at dawn on the 26th, preceded by a heavy bombardment from the Fleet, the remnants of the Dublin and Munster Fusiliers and of the Hampshire Regiment were ordered to assault the castle and village of Sedd-el-Bahr. Undaunted by their losses and experiences, unexhausted by twenty-four hours of continuous fighting, these heroic troops responded to the call. By nine o'clock they had stormed the castle, and after three hours' house-to-house fighting made themselves masters of the village. A Turkish redoubt strongly held by the enemy lay beyond. The wasted battalions paused before this new exertion, and the redoubt was subjected to a violent and prolonged bombardment by the battleship *Albion*. When the cannonade ceased the English and Irish soldiers mingled together, animated by a common resolve, issued forth from the shattered houses of Sedd-el-Bahr, and in broad daylight by main force and with cruel sacrifice stormed the redoubt and slew its stubborn defenders. The prolonged, renewed, and seemingly inexhaustible efforts of the survivors of these three battalions, their persistency, their will-power, their physical endurance, achieved a feat of arms certainly in these respects not often, if ever surpassed in the history of either island race. The reorganization of the troops at the water's edge, the preparation and inspiration of these successive assaults, are linked with the memory of a brave staff officer, Colonel Doughty-Wylie, who was killed like Wolfe in the moment of victory and whose name was given by the Army to the captured fort by which he lies.

As the result of these successes and of the continued pressure of the British attack from its various lodgments on the enemy, a continuous arc was established by the evening of the 26th along the whole coast from "V," "W" and "X" Beaches, and a junction was effected with the single battalion landed at "S." Profiting by the exhaustion, heavy losses and inferior numbers of the Turks, and reinforced by four French battalions, the Allies on the 27th converted this concave arc by a further advance into a line from a point about two miles north of Cape Tekke to De Totts Battery. The extreme tip of the Gallipoli Peninsula had thus been bitten off, all the Beaches were protected from rifle fire, and a substantial foothold had been established and consolidated upon land.

The rest of the 29th Division, the Royal Naval Division, and the French Division having landed during the 26th and 27th, Sir Ian Hamilton ordered on the 28th a general advance from the tip of the Peninsula towards Krithia Village. Although the Turks were beginning to receive reinforcements and had reorganized, they considered this a very critical day. The troops which had opposed the landing had lost heavily. Their battalions were reduced to about 500 strong. By midday the whole of the Turkish reserves were engaged. The British and French, however, were not strong enough to make headway against the Turkish rifle fire. Once inland in the spoon-shaped dip the ships' guns could not help them much, and they had not had time to develop their own artillery support. By the evening of the 28th, therefore, a complete equipoise was reached. If, during the 28th and 29th, two or three fresh divisions of French, British, or Indian troops could have been thrown in, the Turkish defence must have been broken and the decisive positions would have fallen into our hands. And all the time the lines of Bulair lay vacant, naked, unguarded—the spoil of any fresh force which could now be landed from the sea. Where was the extra Army Corps that was needed? It existed. It was destined for the struggle. It was doomed to suffer fearful losses in that struggle. But now when its presence would have given certain victory, it stood idle in Egypt or England.

The next move lay with the Turks. Reinforcements were steadily and rapidly approaching the hard-pressed two Divisions. The leading regiments of the Divisions from Bulair were already arriving at intervals. The 15th Division was coming by sea from Constantinople to Kilia Liman. The 11th Division was crossing from the Asiatic shore. In this situation the 29th and 30th passed away without event.

On the morning of the 27th we received at the Admiralty a telegram from Admiral de Robeck giving an account of the battle.

I took this across at once myself to Lord Kitchener. As soon as he saw that 29,000 men had been landed, he expressed the most lively satisfaction. He seemed to think that the critical moment had passed, and that once the troops had got ashore in large numbers the rest would follow swiftly. But the news of the heavy losses that came in on the 28th, and the further telegrams which were received, showed the great severity and critical nature of the fighting. On this day, therefore, Lord Fisher and I repaired together to the War Office and jointly appealed to Lord Kitchener to send Sir Ian Hamilton large reinforcements from the troops in Egypt and to place other troops in England under orders to sail. Fisher pleaded eloquently and fiercely and I did my best. Lord Kitchener was at first incredulous that more troops could be needed, but our evident anxiety and alarm shook him. That evening he telegraphed to Sir John Maxwell and to Sir Ian Hamilton assigning an Indian Brigade and the 42nd Territorial Division then in Egypt to the Dardanelles.

There was no reason whatever why these forces and others should not have been made available as a reserve to Sir Ian Hamilton before his attack was launched, in which case the preparations for bringing them to the Peninsula would have been perfected simultaneously with those of the attack and the transports could have carried them to the Peninsula the moment the Beaches were ready for their reception. These reinforcements aggregating 12,000 or 13,000 rifles could have fought in the battle of the 28th or enabled it to be renewed at dawn on the 29th. In fact, however, the Indian Infantry Brigade did not land until May 1, and the leading brigade of the 42nd Division did not disembark until May 5.

Meanwhile reinforcements from all quarters and artillery taken from the defences of the Straits were steadily reaching the Turks. By May 1 the local German Commander, Sodenstern, thought himself strong enough to begin a general counter-attack, and during the whole of the 1st, 2nd, and 3rd, he continued to thrust in his troops, wearied as they were either by march or battle, in a series of desperate and disconnected attempts to drive the Allies into the sea. But if Sir Ian Hamilton's army was not strong enough to advance itself, neither could it be shaken from its positions. By May 3 the Turkish attacks had broken down completely with very heavy loss. The first wave of Turkish reinforcements had spent itself, and it was again the turn of the Allies. The organization of the Beaches had been established; supplies, artillery, and ammunition had been landed in considerable quantities. There was nothing to prevent a renewed general advance on the 4th or 5th against the discouraged Turks, had additional troops proportionate to the new situation been available. As it was the attack could not be begun until the 6th, and so short of troops was Sir Ian Hamilton that he found it necessary to withdraw the 2nd Australian Brigade and the New Zealand Brigade from the Anzac area to Helles.

The new battle commenced on the morning of the 6th and was continued on the 7th and 8th. It was sustained by nearly 50,000 British and French troops with 72 guns, against which the Turks mustered approximately 30,000 men with 56 guns. The result was a great and bitter disappointment for the Allies. Only a few hundred yards were gained along the whole front. The losses both of the British and French had been very heavy. In all from the 25th to the cessation of the attack on the evening of the 8th, the British had lost nearly 15,000 killed and wounded and the French at least 4,000.

The situation disclosed on the morrow of this battle was grim. Sir Ian Hamilton's whole army was cramped and pinned down at two separate points on the Gallipoli Peninsula. His two main attacks, though joined by the sea, were now otherwise quite disconnected with each other. None of the decisive positions on the Peninsula were in our hands. A continuous line of Turkish entrenchments stood between the British and Achi Baba, and between the Australians and the mountain of Sari Bair or the town of Maidos. These entrenchments were growing and developing line upon line. The French having been withdrawn from Troy, the Turkish troops in Asia were free to reinforce the Peninsula. All the available British reserves, including the Indian Brigade and the 42nd Division, had been thrown in and largely consumed after their opportunity had passed. The casualties in every battalion had been serious, and there was no means at hand of filling the gaps. Not even the regular 10 per cent reserve which follows automatically every division sent on active service had been provided for the 29th Division. On the 9th Sir Ian Hamilton reported that it was impossible to break through the Turkish lines with the forces at his disposal, that conditions of trench warfare had supervened, and that reinforcements of at least an Army Corps were needed. At least a month must intervene before the drafts needed to restore the Divisions already engaged and the large new forces plainly required could be obtained from home. What would happen in this month of continued wastage in the Allied Army and of unceasing growth in the Turkish power? Initiative and Opportunity had passed to the enemy. A long, costly struggle lay before us and far greater efforts would now certainly be required.

CHAPTER XXXI

AFTER THE LANDING

In spite of the fact that the Army was brought to a standstill, the great event of the landing continued to produce its impression throughout Europe. Italy, Greece, Roumania, Bulgaria assumed that now that large allied forces were definitely ashore, they could and would be reinforced from the sea until the Turkish resistance was overcome. The Italian momentum towards war proceeded unchecked: and the Balkan states continued in an attitude of strained expectancy. At home the growing political crisis underwent a distinct set-back. The leaders of the Opposition had been advised by high authorities in France that the operation of landing would fail and that the troops would be repulsed at the Beaches with disastrous slaughter. They were of course greatly relieved when these predictions were falsified, and there was for the moment a corresponding easement of tension.

On May 5, while the battle on the Peninsula was still undecided, I had to go to Paris for a purpose of great importance. The negotiations with Italy which had been proceeding during March and April had in its last fortnight assumed a decisive character. On April 26 the Treaty of London, by which Italy agreed to come into the war, had been signed. On May 4 Italy denounced the Triple Alliance, and thereby made public her change of policy. Sir Edward Grey had on medical advice taken a brief spell of rest at the beginning of April, and the Prime Minister for ten days grasped the Italian business in his own hands with downright vigour. On the Foreign Secretary's return the advantage gained had been zealously pursued. The terms of the secret treaty which resulted in the entry of Italy into the war have long since been made public. They reveal with painful clearness the desperate need of the three Allies at this juncture. Locked in the deadly struggle, with the danger of the Russian collapse staring them in the face, and with their own very existence at stake, neither Britain nor France was inclined to be particular about the price they would pay or promise to pay for the accession to the alliance of a new first-class power. The Italian negotiators, deeply conscious of our anxiety, were determined to make the most advantageous bargain they could for their country.

The territorial gains which Italy was to receive on her frontiers, in the Adriatic, and from the Turkish Empire were tremendous. These political prizes were to be supplemented by Military and Naval conventions of the utmost importance. The British Fleet was actively to co-operate with the Italians in the Adriatic, and the Russians were to continue a vigorous offensive with at least 500,000 men against Austria in Galicia. Thus guaranteed both by sea and land, Italy seemed safe to advance and appropriate the enormous prizes for which she had stipulated. The hopes and calculations which inspired these arrangements were soon to be falsified. Those who launch out upon the stormy voyage of war can never tell beforehand what its length or fortunes will be, or in what port they will at last drop anchor. Within a fortnight of the signature of the Military Convention, Mackensen had fallen upon the Russians along the Dunajecs, the battle of Gorlice-Tarnau had been fought, and the Russian Armies were everywhere in retreat and recoil. The apparition of Yugo-Slavia as a strong new power at the end of the war rendered the conditions which Italy had exacted in the Adriatic obviously inapplicable. And lastly Turkey, beaten in the war, has risen resuscitated and virtually intact from the disasters of the peace. It was not to an easy war of limited liability and great material gains that Italian statesmen were to send their countrymen. Italy, like the other great combatants, was to be drenched with blood and tears. Year after year, her soil invaded, her manhood shorn away, her treasure spent, her life and honour in jeopardy, must she struggle on to a victory which was to bring no complete satisfaction to her ambitions. But though the calculations of statesmen had failed, the generous heart of the Italian nation proved not unequal to the long trials and disappointments of the struggle, nor unworthy to sustain amid its mocking fortunes the ancient fame of Rome.

As it seemed vital that no hitch nor delay should obstruct the signing of the Naval Convention, I proceeded to Paris armed on behalf of the Admiralty with plenary powers. The Italian apprehension was that if as the result of victory Russia established herself at Constantinople, and if Serbia also gained a great increase of territory, these combined Slavonic powers would develop a strong naval base on or off the Dalmatian coast. The prospect which had arisen from the Dardanelles operations, of Russia possessing Constantinople, forced Italy to make the greatest exertions to secure her own position in the Adriatic, which would have been irretrievably compromised by an allied victory in which Italy had taken no part. We therefore spent two days in intricate discussions between the French and the Italians about the naval bases which Italy was to secure on the Dalmatian coast in the treaties following a victorious war. Among these their most important claim was for what was called the Canal of Sabioncello. This strip of good anchorage for the largest vessels between two long islands, out of gunfire from the shore, and half-way down the Adriatic, presented indeed every ideal condition for an Italian Naval Base. But there were many other claims, and whenever the discussion seemed to prove discouraging to the Italians we threw the British trident into the scale, offering to agree to the request not only for cruisers and flotillas but for a squadron of battleships as well. Since it seemed that Admiral de Robeck had definitely abandoned the attempt to force the Dardanelles, his fleet had clearly ships to spare. In the end a complete agreement was reached between the naval authorities of the three countries. The Italians insisted on having British battleships, and the French without taking offence at this, agreed to replace a British Squadron taken from the Dardanelles by an equal number of their own vessels.

I left Paris early on the morning of the 7th, intending to pass a day at Sir John French's Headquarters on my way back to England. Arrived at St. Omer on the evening of the 7th, I learnt two things. Sir Ian Hamilton's telegrams showed that he was in full battle and that no decision was yet manifest on the Peninsula. Secondly, Sir John French intended to begin a general attack directed against the Aubers Ridge in conjunction with the French Army operating on his right against the Souchez position, and this momentous event was fixed for daybreak on the 9th. I therefore stayed to see one battle, glad to keep my mind off the other.

As the reader is aware, I was at this time convinced that the task set to the British and French troops was impossible. The Germans in their front were almost equal in strength, intensely fortified, and fully prepared. The preliminary wire-cutting by shrapnel bombardment had shown them exactly the gaps through which the assaulting troops were to be launched, and one could not doubt that every preparation had been made to mow them down. Moreover the British supplies of shell were extremely limited, and the high explosive needed to shatter the German trenches was practically non-existent. I made every effort in my power without incurring unjustifiable risks to view the battle. But neither far off from a lofty steeple nor close up on the fringe of the enemy's barrage was it possible to see anything except shells and smoke. Without actually taking part in the assault it was impossible to measure the real conditions. To see them you had to feel them, and feeling them might well feel nothing more. To stand outside was to see nothing, to plunge in was to be dominated by personal experiences of an absorbing kind. This was one of the cruellest features of the war. Many of the generals in the higher commands did not know the conditions with which their troops were ordered to contend, nor were they in a position to devise the remedies which could have helped them.

On the evening of this day I witnessed also the hideous spectacle of a large casualty clearing station in the height of a battle. More than 1,000 men suffering from every form of horrible injury, seared, torn, pierced, choking, dying, were being sorted according to their miseries into the different parts of the Convent at Merville. At the entrance the arrival and departure of the motor ambulances, each with its four or five shattered and tortured beings, was incessant: from the back door corpses were being carried out at brief intervals to a burying party constantly at work. One room was filled to overflowing with cases not worth sending any farther, cases whose hopelessness excluded them from priority in operations. Other rooms were filled with "walking wounded" all in much pain, but most in good spirits. For these a cup of tea, a cigarette, and another long motor journey were reserved. An unbroken file of urgent and critical cases were pressed towards the operating room, the door of which was wide open and revealed as I passed the terrible spectacle of a man being trepanned. Everywhere was blood and bloody rags. Outside in the quadrangle the drumming thunder of the cannonade proclaimed that the process of death and mutilation was still at its height.

In these days also came in the news of the sinking of the *Lusitania*. This gigantic liner had for some months definitely returned to passenger service, and had made several round trips across the Atlantic in that capacity. In the first week of May she was returning to Liverpool from New York, having on board nearly 2,000 persons all non-combatants, British and American. Included in her cargo was a small consignment of rifle ammunition and shrapnel shells weighing about 173 tons. Warnings that the vessel would be sunk, afterwards traced to the German Government, were circulated in New York before she sailed. On May 4 and 5 while she was approaching the British Isles, German U-boats were reported about the southern entrance to the Irish Channel and two merchant ships were sunk. Further reports of submarine activity in this area came in on the 6th. In consequence repeated and specific warnings and information were transmitted from the Admiralty wireless station at Valentia.

> May 6, 12:5 a.m. To all British ships.
> . . . Avoid headlands. Pass harbours at full speed. Steer midchannel course. Submarines off Fastnet.

> May 6, 7:50 p.m. To Lusitania.
> Submarines active off south coast of Ireland.

> May 7, 11:25 a.m. To all British ships.
> Submarines active in southern part of Irish Channel. Last heard of south of Coningbeg Lighthouse. Make certain *Lusitania* gets this.

> May 7, 12:40 p.m. To Lusitania.
> Submarines five miles south of Cape Clear proceeding west when sighted at 10 a.m.

All these messages were duly received.

The Admiralty confidential Memorandum of April 16, 1915, contained the following passage:

> War experience has shown that fast steamers can considerably reduce the chance of successful surprise submarine attack by zigzagging, that is to say, altering the course at short and irregular intervals, say in ten minutes to half an hour. This course is almost invariably adopted by warships when cruising in an area known to be infested with submarines. The underwater speed of a submarine is very low, and it is exceedingly difficult for her to get into position to deliver an attack unless she can preserve and predict the course of the ship attacked.

In spite of these warnings and instructions, for which the Admiralty Trade Division deserve credit, the *Lusitania* was proceeding along the usual trade route without zigzagging at little more than three-quarter speed when, at 2:10 p.m. on May 7, she was torpedoed eight miles off the Old Head of Kinsale by Commander Schweiger in the German submarine *U 20*. Two torpedoes were fired, the first striking her amidships with a tremendous explosion, and the second a few minutes later striking her aft. In twenty minutes she foundered by the head, carrying with her 1,195 persons, of whom 291 were women and 94 infants or small children. This crowning outrage of the U-boat war resounded through the world. The United States whose citizens had perished in large numbers, was convulsed with indignation, and in all parts of the great Republic the signal for armed intervention was awaited by the strongest elements of the American people. It was not given, and the war continued in its destructive equipoise. But henceforward the friends of the Allies in the United States were armed with a weapon against which German influence was powerless, and before which after a lamentable interval cold-hearted policy was destined to succumb.

Even in the first moments of realizing the tragedy and its horror, I understood the significance of the event. As the history of the Great War is pondered over, its stern lessons stand forth from the tumult and confusion of the times. On two supreme occasions the German Imperial Government, quenching compunction, outfacing conscience, deliberately, with calculation, with sinister resolve, severed the underlying bonds which sustained the civilization of the world and united even in their quarrels the human family. The invasion of Belgium and the unlimited U-boat war were both resorted to on expert dictation as the only means of victory. They proved the direct cause of ruin. They drew into the struggle against Germany mighty and intangible powers by which her strength was remorselessly borne down. Nothing could have deprived Germany of victory in the first year of war except the invasion of Belgium; nothing could have denied it to her in its last year except her unlimited submarine campaign. Not to the number of her enemies, nor to their resources or wisdom; not to the mistakes of her Admirals and Generals in open battle; not to the weakness of her allies; not assuredly to any fault in the valour or loyalty of her population or her armies; but only to these two grand crimes and blunders of history, were her undoing and our salvation due.

Meanwhile in the Flagship at the Dardanelles the most vehement discussion had been taking place.

Since March 18, two distinct currents of opinion had flowed in high naval circles. The forward school had been more than ever convinced that the quelling of the forts, the sweeping of the minefield, and ultimately the forcing of the Straits were practicable operations. They had no doubt whatever that the Fleet could make its way through into the Marmora. They had continually impressed upon the Admiral the duty of the Navy to attempt this task. Grieved beyond measure at the cruel losses that the Army had sustained, out of all proportion to anything expected, they felt it almost unendurable that the Navy should sit helpless and inactive after the orders they had received and the undertakings made on their behalf. They therefore pressed their Chief to propose to the Admiralty the renewal of the naval attack.

All these pressures and the spectacle of the Army's torment produced their effect upon a man of the courage and quality of Admiral de Robeck. He finally resolved to send a telegram to the Admiralty expressing his willingness to renew the naval attack. The telegram bears the imprint of several hands and of opposite opinions. But apparently, as we now know, all present at these conferences in the *Queen Elizabeth* believed that the telegram would be followed by immediate orders for battle from the Admiralty. Admiral Guépratte, the French Commander, telegraphed to the Minister of Marine showing that he fully expected to be launched in decisive attack and asking for an additional and stronger ship to reinforce the French Squadron. All the naval staff and commanders rested, therefore, under the impression of a great and sublime decision in pursuance of which they would readily face every risk and endure every loss.

VICE-ADMIRAL DE ROBECK TO ADMIRALTY.

May 10, 1915.

The position in the Gallipoli Peninsula.

General Hamilton informs me that the Army is checked, its advance on Achi Baba can only be carried out by a few yards at a time, and a condition of affairs approximate to that in Northern France is threatened.

The situation therefore arises, as indicated in my telegram 292:

If the Army is checked in its advance on Kilid Bahr, the question whether the Navy should not force the Narrows, leaving the forts intact, will depend entirely whether the Fleet could assist the Army in their advance to the Narrows best from below Chanak with communications intact or from above cut off from its base.

The help which the Navy has been able to give the Army in its advance has not been as great as was anticipated, though effective in keeping down the fire of the enemy's batteries; when it is a question of trenches and machine guns the Navy is of small assistance; it is these latter that have checked the Army.

From the vigour of the enemy's resistance it is improbable that the passage of the Fleet into the Marmora will be decisive and therefore it is equally probable that the Straits will be closed behind the Fleet. This will be of slight importance if the resistance of the enemy could be overcome in time to prevent the enforced withdrawal of the Fleet owing to lack of supplies.

The supporting of attack of Army, should the Fleet penetrate to the Sea of Marmora, will be entrusted to the cruisers and certain older battle-ships including some of the French, whose ships are not fitted for a serious bombardment of the Narrows, this support will obviously be much less than is now given by the whole of the Fleet.

The temper of the Turkish Army in the Peninsula indicates that the forcing of the Dardanelles and subsequent appearance of the Fleet off Constantinople will not, of itself, prove decisive.

The points for decision appear to be:

First—Can the Navy by forcing the Dardanelles ensure the success of the operations?

Second—If the Navy were to suffer a reverse, which of necessity could only be a severe one, would the position of the Army be so critical as to jeopardize the whole of the operations?

This message deserved very attentive study. It was clearly intended to raise the direct issue of the renewal of the naval attempt to force the Straits. In it Admiral de Robeck balanced the pros and cons, on the whole with an emphasis on the latter. But at the same time he intimated unmistakably his readiness to make the attempt if the Admiralty gave the order. His telegram caused me much perturbation. I was of course, as always, in favour of renewing the naval attack. But the situation at this moment was very different from what it had been in March and April, and in pursuance of Admiral de Robeck's decision of

March 22 we were now following another line of policy. Three important events had taken place.

First, the Army had been landed on the Gallipoli Peninsula with a loss of nearly 20,000 men. That army was, it is true, arrested, but Lord Kitchener had told me that he intended to reinforce it with the whole Army Corps for which Sir Ian Hamilton had asked. The landing under fire had always been the feature in the operation most to be dreaded. It had been accomplished, and it seemed that since the Turks had not been able to prevent the landing, they would certainly fail to stop the further advance of the Army, if the ample reinforcements which were available were rapidly poured in. There were, therefore, at this moment reasonable prospects of carrying the military operation through to success if adequate military reinforcements were sent with promptitude.

Secondly, Italy was about to enter the war. The Anglo-Italian Naval Convention which we had just signed obliged us to send four battleships and four light cruisers to join the Italian Fleet in the Adriatic. I had undertaken this on the basis which had ruled ever since March 22 that Admiral de Robeck had definitely abandoned the naval attack and that we were committed to fight the issue out by military force. The withdrawal of these ships from Admiral de Robeck's fleet, although mitigated by French reinforcements, was incompatible with a decision to make a determined or even desperate effort to force the Dardanelles by ships alone.

Thirdly, what we had so long dreaded had at last come to pass. The German submarines had arrived in the Ægean. One or perhaps two, or even three, were reported on different occasions in the neighbourhood of the Dardanelles. The position of the *Queen Elizabeth* became one of exceptional danger, and the security of the whole Fleet at the Dardanelles was affected to an extent which could not be readily measured. Moreover, if the Fleet succeeded in forcing the passage and arrived in the Marmora, it would be harassed in that sea by German submarines. Though this fact was not conclusive, the action of the Fleet would be impeded and, on the assumption that the Straits closed up behind it, its effective strategic life would be to a certain extent curtailed.

Furthermore, the responsibilities of the Fleet now that the Army was landed and heavily engaged were very greatly increased. As Admiral Oliver pithily put it—"On March 18 the Fleet was single, now it has a wife on shore."

All these considerations were present in my mind. Their cumulative effect was very great. Of course if Admiral de Robeck continued willing to make a decisive attack, it would be possible in a few weeks to recreate the conditions which would enable him to do so. Our naval resources were enormous and increasing almost daily. We could by the middle of June have raised his fleet to a greater strength than ever, and have perfected in every detail the preparations for the attempt. Moreover, by then we should have known where we stood with the German submarines in the Ægean and what that menace amounted to. For the moment, however, the arguments against decisive naval action were very weighty.

On the other hand, I was extremely anxious for a limited operation. I wished the Fleet to engage the forts at the Narrows and thus test the reports which we had received about the shortage of ammunition. Under cover of this engagement I wished the Kephez minefield to be swept and got out of the way. These were perfectly feasible operations now that the mine-sweeping force was thoroughly organized, and the Dardanelles fleet, although reduced, was ample for their purpose. The elimination of the Kephez minefield would in itself begin to imperil the communications of the army the Turks were building up on the Peninsula.

I could see, however, that Lord Fisher was under considerable strain. His seventy-four years lay heavy upon him. During my absence in Paris upon the negotiations for the Anglo-Italian Naval Convention he had shown great nervous exhaustion. He had evinced unconcealed distress and anxiety at being left alone in sole charge of the Admiralty. There is no doubt that the old Admiral was worried almost out of his wits by the immense pressure of the times and by the course events had taken. Admiral de Robeck's telegram distressed him extremely. He expected to be confronted with the demand he hated most and dreaded most, the renewal of the naval battle and fighting the matter out to a conclusion.

On the morning of the 11th we discussed the situation together. I endeavoured repeatedly to make it clear that all I wanted was the sweeping of the Kephez minefield under cover of a renewed engagement of the forts at the Narrows, and that I had no idea of pressing for a decisive effort to force the Straits and penetrate the Marmora. However, I failed to remove his anxieties. No doubt he felt that if the operation were successful, the case for the main thrust in a subsequent stage would be enormously strengthened; and no doubt this was true. The Kephez minefield was his as well as the Turks' first line of defence. After our conversation, Lord Fisher sent me on the same day "with much reluctance" a formal memorandum which presented a full and forceful restatement of his views of the Dardanelles operations, leading to the conclusion that he could not

> . . . under any circumstances be a party to any order to Admiral de Robeck to make an attempt to pass the Dardanelles until the shores have been effectively occupied . . . I therefore wish it to be clearly understood that I dissociate myself from any such project.

I replied on the same day that he would never receive from me any proposition to "rush" the Dardanelles, and that I agreed with his views on the subject. I returned to the possibility that Admiral de Robeck might be called upon to engage the forts and sweep the Kephez minefield as an aid to the military operations. Expressing again my hope that any real issue would always find us united, I appealed to him

> . . . We are now committed to one of the greatest amphibious enterprises in history. You are absolutely committed. Comradeship, resource, firmness, patience, all in the highest degree will be needed to carry the matter through to victory . . .

He wrote me next day that since my reply had not definitely repudiated the idea of a naval attack on the minefield before the Army had occupied the shores of the Narrows, he had sent the Prime Minister a copy of his memorandum to me.

> With reference to your remark that I am absolutely committed, I have only to say that you must know (as the Prime Minister also) that my unwilling acquiescence did not extend to such a further gamble as any repetition of March 18 until the Army had done their part.

Thus it will be seen that never after March 22 were the Admiralty and the Naval Commander-in-Chief able to come to a simultaneous resolve to attack. On the 21st all were united. Thereafter, when one was hot the other was cold. On March 23 and 24 the Admiralty without issuing actual orders pressed strongly for the attack, and the Admiral on the spot said "No." On May 10 the Admiral on the spot was willing, but the Admiralty said "No." On August 18, under the impression of the disaster at Suvla Bay, the Admiralty raised the question again and authorized the Admiral to use his old battleships to the fullest extent, and the Admiral met them by a reasoned but decisive refusal. Lastly, in the advent of the final evacuation Admiral Wemyss, who had succeeded to the command, armed with plans drawn up in the most complete detail by Commodore Keyes for forcing the Straits, made vehement appeals for sanction to execute them: and this time the Admiralty refused.

The bad news which came in from Russia from France and from the Dardanelles at this time, and the impression I had sustained while with the Army, led me to issue the following general minute to all Admiralty Departments:

SECRETARY AND MEMBERS OF THE BOARD.

May 11, 1915.

Please inform all heads of Departments in the Admiralty, that for the present it is to be assumed that the war will not end before December 31, 1916. All Admiralty arrangements and plans should be prepared on this basis, and any measures for the strengthening of our naval power, which will become effective before that date, may be considered. This applies to all questions of personnel, ships, armaments and stores, and to the organization and maintenance of the Fleet and Dockyards, which must be adapted to a long period of continually developing strength without undue strain. I await proposals from all departments for the development and expansion of their activities.

W. S. C.

On the night of May 12 the *Goliath* was torpedoed and sunk in the Dardanelles by a Turkish destroyer manned by a German crew. This event determined Lord Fisher to bring the *Queen Elizabeth* home, and he made upon me a most strenuous counter-demand to that effect. I did not myself object to this. The first two 14-inch gun Monitors (then named *Stonewall Jackson* and *Admiral Farragut*) were now ready; and I agreed with the First Sea Lord that the *Queen Elizabeth* should return, if they and other Monitors, two battleships of the "Duncan" class, and certain additional vessels, were sent to replace her. He was very much relieved at this and was grateful. The position into which we had got was most painful. He wished at all costs to cut the loss and come away from the hated scene. I was bound, not only by every conviction, but by every call of honour, to press the enterprise and sustain our struggling Army to the full.

I had now to break the news to Lord Kitchener. I invited him to come to a conference at the Admiralty on the evening of May 13. We sat round the octagonal table; Lord Kitchener on my left, Lord Fisher on my right, together with various other officers of high rank. As soon as Lord Kitchener realized that the Admiralty were going to withdraw the *Queen Elizabeth,* he became extremely angry. His habitual composure in trying ordeals left him. He protested vehemently against what he considered the desertion of the Army at its most critical moment. On the other side Lord Fisher flew into an even greater fury. "The *Queen Elizabeth* would come home; she would come home at once; she would come home that night, or he would walk out of the Admiralty then and there." Could we but have exchanged the positions of these two potentates at this juncture, have let Kitchener hold the Admiralty to its task, and sent Fisher to the War Office to slam in the reinforcements, both would have been happy and all would have been well. Such solutions were beyond us. I stood by my agreement with the First Sea Lord, and did my utmost to explain to Lord Kitchener that the Monitors would give equally good support with far less risk to naval strength. I recounted to him the vessels we were sending, and offered him the most solemn guarantees—in which I was supported by the Naval Staff—of our resolve to sustain the Army by the most effectual means. I thought he was to some extent reassured before he left.

I therefore agreed with Lord Fisher in a series of telegrams. We instructed Admiral de Robeck to send the *Queen Elizabeth* home with all dispatch and utmost secrecy. We informed him that *Exmouth* and *Venerable* would join his command at once, and before the end of the month he would have the first two monitors, the last word in bombarding vessels; their gain would more than compensate for the loss of the *Queen Elizabeth*. The first six monitors as delivered would be sent to him. As soon as the French Squadron under his command had been raised to a total of six battleships, he was to send the *Queen, London, Implacable* and *Prince of Wales* under Rear-Admiral Thursby—also with utmost secrecy—to Malta in readiness for service with the Italian Fleet in the Adriatic, in order to meet the provisions of the Anglo-Italian Naval Convention. We informed Admiral de Robeck that we thought the moment for an independent naval attempt to force the Narrows had passed, and would not arise again under existing conditions; accordingly, his rôle was to support the Army in its advance.

On these telegrams—the last we ever sent together—Lord Fisher and I parted for the night.

CHAPTER XXXII

THE FALL OF THE GOVERNMENT

The War Council of May 14 was sulphurous. We were in presence of the fact that Sir Ian Hamilton's army had been definitely brought to a standstill on the Gallipoli Peninsula, was suspended there in circumstances of peril, was difficult to reinforce, and still more difficult to withdraw. The Fleet had relapsed into passivity. Lord Fisher had insisted on the withdrawal of the *Queen Elizabeth:* German submarines were about to enter the Ægean, where our enormous concentrations of shipping necessary to support the Dardanelles operations lay in a very unprotected state. At the same time the failure of the British attacks in France on the Aubers Ridge was unmistakable. Sir John French's army had lost nearly 20,000 men without substantial results, and General Headquarters naturally demanded increased supplies of men and ammunition. The shell crisis had reached its explosion point—the shortage had been disclosed in *The Times* that morning—and behind it marched a political crisis of the first order. The weakness and failure of Russia were becoming every month more evident. Intense anxiety and extreme bad temper, all suppressed under formal demeanour, characterized the discussion.

Lord Kitchener began in a strain of solemn and formidable complaint. He had been induced to participate in the Dardanelles operations on the assurances of the Navy that they would force the passage. Now they had abandoned the attempt. Most particularly had his judgment been affected by the unique qualities of the *Queen Elizabeth.* Now she was to be withdrawn: she was to be withdrawn at the very moment when he had committed his army to a great operation on the Gallipoli Peninsula, and when that army was struggling for its life with its back to the sea. Lord Fisher at this point interjected that he had been against the Dardanelles operations from the beginning, and that the Prime Minister and Lord Kitchener knew this fact well. This remarkable interruption was received in silence. The Secretary of State for War then proceeded to survey other theatres of the war in an extremely pessimistic mood. The army in France was firing away shells at a rate which no military administration had ever been asked to sustain. The orders which had been placed for ammunition of every kind were all being completed late. The growing weakness of Russia might at any time enable the Germans to transfer troops to the West and resume the of-

456

fensive against us. Thirdly, he proceeded to dilate upon the dangers of invasion. How could he tell what would happen? Great Britain must be defended at all costs, all the more if other affairs miscarried. In these circumstances he could not send Sir John French the four new divisions he had promised him: they must be reserved for home defence.

When he had finished, the Council turned to me—almost on me. I thereupon spoke in the sense of the series of arguments with which the reader should now be familiar and which form the staple of this volume. If it had been known three months before that an army of from 80,000 to 100,000 men would be available in May for an attack on the Dardanelles, the attack by the Navy alone would never have been undertaken. Though matters had gone badly in many quarters and great disappointments had been experienced, there was no reason for despondency or alarm, still less to make things out worse than they were or to take unreasonable action. The naval operations at the Dardanelles did not depend and had never depended upon the *Queen Elizabeth*. They had been planned before it was known that she would go. She was now to be withdrawn because of the danger of submarines to so invaluable a ship. She would be replaced by monitors and other specially designed vessels better suited in many respects to bombarding operations and largely immune from submarine attack. The naval support of the army would in no way be affected. It was no good exaggerating the value of the *Queen Elizabeth,* or supposing that a great operation of this kind could turn on a single vessel. As for the shell shortage, that would remedy itself if we made the greatest exertions and did not meanwhile embark on premature offensives without adequate superiority in men, guns or ammunition. Lastly, what was this talk about invasion? The Admiralty did not believe that any landing in force could be effected; still less, if effected, that it could be sustained and nourished. What grounds were there for supposing that the enemy, now fully committed to the eastward effort against Russia, would spin round and bring troops back to invade England or attack the Western Front? And how many would they bring, and how long would it take? Stop these vain offensives on the Western Front until the new armies were ready and sufficient ammunition was accumulated. Concentrate the available reinforcements upon the Dardanelles and give them such ammunition as was necessary to reach a decision there at the earliest possible moment. Discard these alarms about the invasion of an island no longer denuded of troops as in 1914, but bristling with armed men and guarded by a fleet far stronger relatively than at the beginning of the war and possessed of sources of information never previously dreamed of. Let Sir John French have the new divisions for which he had asked, but otherwise remain on the defensive in France.

I am not quoting the actual words in either case, but their gist. The sense is fully sustained by the abbreviated records. These considerations appeared to produce a definite impression upon the Council. We separated without any decision. My arguments were, however, accepted almost in their entirety by the Coalition Administration which came into existence a few weeks later, and every one of the suppositions on which they rested was vindicated by events. The departure of the *Queen Elizabeth* did not prevent the naval support of the army at Gallipoli nor its supply by sea. The British and French offensives in France continued to fail for the next three years with ever-increasing bloody slaughter and the fruitless destruction of our new armies. The Germans did not and could not arrest their drive against Russia, which was in fact on the eve of its full intensity. They did not come back to the West, nor was it physically possible for them to do so for many months to come. They did not invade England: they never thought of invading England at this period, nor could they have done it had they tried.

However, events were now to supervene in the British political sphere which were destined fatally to destroy the hopes of a successful issue at the Dardanelles and preclude all possibility of a speedy termination of the war.

After the Council I wrote the following letter to the Prime Minister which I think shows exactly where I stood:

MR. CHURCHILL TO THE PRIME MINISTER.

May 14, 1915.

I must ask you to take note of Fisher's statement to-day that "he was against the Dardanelles and had been all along," or words to that effect. The First Sea Lord has agreed in writing to every executive telegram on which the operations have been conducted; and had they been immediately successful, the credit would have been his. But I make no complaint of that. I am attached to the old boy and it is a great pleasure to me to work with him. I think he reciprocates these feelings. My point is that a moment will probably arise in these operations when the Admiral and General on the spot will wish and require to run a risk with the Fleet for a great and decisive effort. If I agree with them, I shall sanction it, and I cannot undertake to be paralysed by the veto of a friend who whatever the result will certainly say, "I was always against the Dardanelles."

You will see that in a matter of this kind *someone* has to take the responsibility. I will do so—provided that my decision is the one that rules—and not otherwise.

It is also uncomfortable not to know what Kitchener will or won't do in the matter of reinforcements. We are absolutely in his hands, and I never saw him in a queerer mood—or more unreasonable. K. will punish the Admiralty by docking Hamilton of his divisions because we have withdrawn the *Queen Elizabeth;* and Fisher will have the *Queen Elizabeth* home if he is to stay.

Through all this with patience and determination we can make our way to one of the great events in the history of the world.

But I wish now to make it clear to you that a man who says, "I disclaim responsibility for failure," cannot be the final arbiter of the measures which may be found to be vital to success.

I spent the afternoon completing my proposals for the naval reinforcement of the Dardanelles and for the convoying of the two divisions with which I understood and trusted Sir Ian Hamilton was to be immediately reinforced.

Although there could be very little doubt about what naval reinforcements were needed, I did not want the demands to fall upon Lord Fisher with a shock. I therefore went into his room in the evening to talk over the whole position with him. Our conversation was quite friendly. He did not object to any of the particular measures proposed, but as usual he did not like the steady and increasing drain on our resources and the inflection given to our campaign by the growing demands of the Dardanelles. I then said to him that it was really not fair for him to obstruct the necessary steps at the Dardanelles and then, if there was a failure, to turn round and say, "I told you so, I was always against it." He looked at me in an odd way and said, "I think you are right—it isn't fair." However, he accepted the minutes and we parted amicably.

Into this extraordinary period, when intense situations succeeded each other with dazing rapidity, another event was now to break. Following the method which I had adopted since Lord Fisher came to the Admiralty, I resumed work in my room at about 10 o'clock that night. The Italian crisis was at its height. The Italian Government had resigned in consequence of the opposition to Italy entering the war, and this enormous and brilliant event which we had regarded as almost settled more than a fortnight before, now appeared once again to be thrown into the melting-pot. A little before midnight the Italian Naval Attaché, an officer ardently devoted to the cause of the Allies, asked to see me. He was accompanied by Admiral Oliver, who had a file of papers. The Naval Attaché said that the uncertainty and convulsions now prevailing in Rome made it vital that the arrangements for naval co-operation which had been conceived a week before in Paris should be brought into immediate effect. Under these arrangements we were to send *inter alia* four light cruisers to reinforce the Italian Fleet in the Adriatic. These cruisers were to reach Taranto by daybreak on the 18th. The Naval Attaché urged that their arrival should be accelerated. If they could arrive by the morning of the 16th, definite naval co-operation between Great Britain and Italy would be an accomplished fact, and this fact might well be decisive.

As I had myself negotiated the Naval Convention with Italy in Paris, I was of course fully acquainted with every detail. I had procured the First Sea Lord's agreement to all its terms, including the dispatch of the four cruisers. These cruisers had been detailed. Fisher's green initial directing their movement was prominent on the second page of the file. No question of principle was involved by accelerating their departure by forty-eight hours. It did not come within the limits of the working arrangement which Fisher and I had made with each other, viz., to take no important step except in consultation. It never occurred to me for a moment that it could be so viewed, nor did the Chief of the Staff suggest that we should wake up the First Sea Lord. He would begin his letters at about 4 o'clock in the morning and he would get the file then. I therefore approved the immediate dispatch of these cruisers and wrote, as I had done in similar cases before, "First Sea Lord to see after action."

For more than ten years I believed that this phrase was the spark that fired the train. We are assured however by Lord Fisher's biographers that he never saw the Italian paper until after he had resigned. Admiral Bacon in his *Life of Lord Fisher*, basing himself upon the first-hand evidence of Captain Crease, states explicitly that the fact that I had on this night proposed to the First Sea Lord the sending of two more submarines to the Dardanelles in addition to the reinforcements we had agreed upon in the evening, was "the last straw." If this be true the pretext is not the less scanty. But the cause behind the pretext was, as these pages may perhaps have shown, substantial. The old Admiral, waking in the early morning, saw himself confronted again with the minutes proposing the reinforcements for the Dardanelles which he knew he could not resist. He saw himself becoming ever more deeply involved in an enterprise which he distrusted and disliked. He saw that enterprise quivering on the verge of failure. He saw a civilian Minister, to whom indeed he was attached by many bonds of friendship, becoming every day a hard and stern taskmaster in all that was needed to sustain the hated operation. He saw the furious discontents of the Conservative Party at the shell shortage and the general conduct of the war. He saw a Field-Marshal in uniform at the head of the War Office, while he, whose name was a watchword throughout the country, was relegated to a secondary place, and in that place was compelled by arguments and pressures he had never been able to resist, but had never ceased to resent, to become responsible for operations to which he had taken an intense dislike. The hour had come.

When I awoke the next morning, Saturday, I received no morning letter from the First Sea Lord. This was unusual, for he nearly always wrote me his waking thoughts on the situation. I had to go over to the Foreign Office at about nine o'clock and was kept there some time. As I was returning across the Horse Guards' Parade, Masterton-Smith hurried up to me with an anxious face— "Fisher has resigned, and I think he means it this time." He gave me the following note from the First Sea Lord:

May 15, 1915.
First Lord.

After further anxious reflection I have come to the regretted conclusion I am unable to remain any longer as your colleague. It is undesirable in the public interests to go into details—Jowett said, "never explain"— but I find it increasingly difficult to adjust myself to the increasing daily requirements of the Dardanelles to meet your views—as you truly said yesterday I am in the position of continually veto-ing your proposals. This is not fair to you besides being extremely distasteful to me. I am off to Scotland at once so as to avoid all questionings.

Yours truly,
FISHER.

I did not, however, at first take a serious view. I remembered a similar letter couched in terms of the utmost formality earlier in the year on the air raids, and he had threatened or hinted resignation both in letters and in conversation on all sorts of matters, big and small, during the last four or five months. I was pretty sure that a good friendly talk would put matters right. However, when I got back to the Admiralty I found that he had entirely disappeared. He was not in the building; he was not in his house. None of his people knew where he was except that he was going to Scotland at once. He had sent a communication to the other Sea Lords which they were engaged in discussing at a meeting of their own.

I went over to the Prime Minister and reported the facts. Mr. Asquith immediately sent his Secretary with a written order commanding Lord Fisher in the name of the King to return to his duty. It was some hours before the First Sea Lord was discovered. He refused point-blank to re-enter the Admiralty or to discharge any function. He reiterated his determination to proceed at once to Scotland. He was, however, at length persuaded to come and see the Prime Minister. I was not present at the interview. After it was over Mr. Asquith told me that he thought he had shaken him in his intention, but that he was very much upset. He advised me to write to him, adding, "If you can get him back, well and good; but if not it will be a very difficult situation."

I tried my best. Again and again I had persuaded him by the written word. It was useless.

You, he replied, ARE BENT ON FORCING THE DARDANELLES AND NOTHING WILL TURN YOU FROM IT—NOTHING. I know you so well! I could give you no better proof of my desire to stand by you than my having remained by you in this Dardanelles business up to this last moment against the strongest conviction of my life as stated in the Dardanelles Defence Committee Memorandum.

You will remain and I SHALL GO—It is better so. Your splendid stand on my behalf I can never forget when you took your political life in your hands, and I really have worked very hard for you in return—*my utmost*—but here is a question beyond all personal obligations. I assure you it is only painful having further conversations. I have told the Prime Minister I will not remain. I have absolutely decided to stick to that decision. Nothing will turn me from it. You say with much feeling that *it will be a very great grief to you to part from me*—I am certain you know in your heart no one has ever been more faithful to you than I have since I joined you last October. *I have worked my very hardest.*

It was no use persisting, and I turned to consider new combinations. I was by no means sure that I should not be confronted with the resignation of the other three Sea Lords. On the Sunday morning, however, I learned that Sir Arthur Wilson had been consulted by the Sea Lords and that he had informed them that it was their duty to remain at their posts and that no case for resignation had arisen. I was led by this fact to ask Sir Arthur Wilson whether he would be willing himself to fill the vacancy of First Sea Lord. He asked for an hour to consider the matter, and then to my gratification, and I will add surprise, he informed me that he would do so. By Sunday at noon I was in a position to reconstitute the Board of Admiralty in all respects. I then motored down to the Prime Minister, who was in the country. I told him that Lord Fisher's resignation was final, and that my office was at his disposal if he required to make a change. He said, "No, I have thought of that. I do not wish it, but can you get a Board?" I then told him that all the other Members of the Board would remain, and that Sir Arthur Wilson would take Lord Fisher's place. I understood him to assent to this arrangement. Later his private secretary mentioned in conversation that the situation resulting from the shell shortage disclosure and the resignation of Lord Fisher was so serious that the Prime Minister thought the Unionist leaders would have to be consulted on the steps to be taken. I saw from this that the crisis would not be by any means confined to the Admiralty. Mr. Asquith asked me to stay and dine, and we had a pleasant evening amid all our troubles. I returned that night to London.

On Monday morning I asked Mr. Balfour to come to the Admiralty. I told him Lord Fisher had resigned, and that I understood from the Prime Minister that he would approve the reconstruction of the Board of Admiralty with Sir Arthur Wilson as First Sea Lord. I told him Sir Arthur Wilson was willing to accept office and that all the other Members of the Board would remain. I said if these arrangements were finally approved by the Prime Minister that afternoon, I would make an immediate announcement to the House of Commons and court a debate. Mr. Balfour was indignant at Lord Fisher's resignation. He said that it would greatly disturb his Unionist friends and that he would himself go and prepare them for it and steady their opinion. Nothing could exceed the kindness and firmness of his attitude. I spent the rest of the morning preparing my statement for Parliament, expecting a severe challenge but also to be successful. I still had no knowledge whatever of the violent political convulsions which were proceeding around me and beneath me.

I went down to the House with the list of my new Board complete, fully prepared to encounter the debate. Before seeing the Prime Minister I looked into the Chancellor of the Exchequer's room. Mr. Lloyd George then made to me the following disclosure. The leaders of the Opposition were in possession of all the facts about the shell shortage and had given notice that they intended to demand a debate. The resignation of Lord Fisher at this juncture created a political crisis. Mr. Lloyd George was convinced that this crisis could only be surmounted by the formation of a national Coalition Government. He had accordingly informed the Prime Minister that he would resign unless such a Government were formed at once. I said that he knew I had always been in favour of such a Government and had pressed it at every possible opportunity, but that I hoped now it might be deferred until my Board was reconstituted and in the saddle at the Admiralty. He said action must be immediate.

I then repaired, as had been arranged, to the Prime Minister. He received me with great consideration. I presented him with the list of the new Board. He said, "No, this will not do. I have decided to form a national Government by a coalition with the Unionists, and a very much larger reconstruction will be required." He told me that Lord Kitchener was to leave the War Office, and then added, after some complimentary remarks, "What are we to do for you?" I saw at once that it was decided I should leave the Admiralty, and I replied that Mr. Balfour could succeed me there with the least break in continuity; that for several months I had made him a party to all our secrets and to everything that was going forward; and that his appointment would be far the best that could be made. The Prime Minister seemed deeply gratified at this suggestion, and I saw that he already had it in his mind. He reverted to the personal question. "Would I take office in the new Government, or would I prefer a command in France?" At this moment the Chancellor of the Exchequer entered the room. The Prime Minister turned to him. Mr. Lloyd George replied, "Why do you not send him to the Colonial Office? There is great work to be done there." I did not accept this suggestion, and the discussion was about to continue when the door again opened and a secretary entered with the following message for me: "Masterton-Smith is on the telephone. Very important news of the kind that never fails has just come in. You must come back to the Admiralty at once." I repeated this information to my two colleagues and quitted them without another word.

It took only five minutes to get to the Admiralty. There I learned that the whole German Fleet was coming out. All its three Battle Squadrons, both Scouting Groups and 70 destroyers were involved. A message from the German Commander-in-Chief to the Fleet contained the phrase "Intend to attack by day." The political crisis and my own fate in it passed almost completely out of my mind. In the absence of the First Sea Lord, I sent for Admiral Oliver, the Chief of the Staff, and the Second Sea Lord. Sir Frederick Hamilton, and we together issued orders for the Grand Fleet and all other available forces to proceed to sea. I was determined that our whole power should be engaged if battle were joined, and that the enemy's retreat should be intercepted. At eight o'clock that evening when the complex business of co-ordination had been virtually completed, I telegraphed to Sir John Jellicoe:

> It is not impossible that to-morrow may be The Day. All good fortune attend you.

A detailed review of our available strength showed that the position at the moment was exceptionally good. Our margins were everywhere at their maximum. I requested Sir Arthur Wilson and the Second Sea Lord, Sir Frederick Hamilton, to sleep in the Admiralty at my house in order that we might be ready in concert to face the crisis which the dawn might bring. I did not return to the House of Commons but remained continuously in the Admiralty. Late that evening a red box came round from the Prime Minister enclosing a note stating that he had determined to form a Coalition Government and requesting all Ministers to place their resignations in his hands that same night. I complied with this request, adding:

> . . . I am strongly in favour of a National Government, and no personal claims or interests should stand in its way at the present crisis. I should be sorry to leave the Admiralty, where I have borne the brunt, but should always rely on you to vindicate my work here.

Having dispatched this, I went to bed. In the morning I had prepared for a Parliamentary ordeal of the most searching character; in the afternoon for a political crisis fatal to myself; in the evening for the supreme battle on the sea. For one day it was enough.

With the earliest daylight I went down to the War Room. From 3 a.m. onwards our directional stations had begun to pick up the Enemy Fleet. The German Fleet Flagship was found to have been in Lat. 53° 50′ N., Long. 4° 20′ E., at 2:9 a.m. She was thus some 126 miles westward of Heligoland and about 40 miles from Terschelling Island. All the Fleets were at sea. The Grand Fleet with its attendant squadrons and flotillas was hastening to the southward. Commodore Tyrwhitt with the Harwich flotillas, reinforced by the Dover destroyers and supported by eleven submarines, was off the Texel watching the narrow seas. It was only in southern waters that the enemy could strike an effective blow, such as attempting to block Calais or Boulogne. If this were their purpose the Harwich Force could either have attacked them by night, or drawn them into pursuit to the southward by day over a line of submarines. If by any means the German Fleet could be delayed in southern waters, the opportunity would be afforded to the Grand Fleet of blocking their return to German ports, either off Terschelling or by the eastern route into the Heligoland Bight. The situation after dawn was therefore for some time of the highest interest.

We got no further indication of the enemy's movements till 7 a.m. It then appeared that he had altered course and was steering southeast instead of west. All our faces fell together. Unless he turned again towards us, we should not be able to scoop him into our net. The morning wore on amid confusing indications. At 9 o'clock we learned that the German light cruiser *Danzig* had met with an accident—presumably from a mine—in 54° 40′ N., 7° 5′ E. Gloom settled on the War Room. This was much nearer the German coast. At last, at about half-past ten, it became certain that the German Fleet was on its way home. It had in fact—as far as we now know—been covering the laying of the minefields on the Dogger Bank which came into existence from this date. This operation being completed, the German Fleet re-entered the Heligoland Bight before our submarines could reach their intercepting position. The episode was over. All our fleets, squadrons and flotillas turned morosely away to resume their long-drawn, unrelenting watch, and I awoke again to the political crisis.

But my hour had passed, and during the afternoon, and still more the following day, I learned from a sure source that my position was being viewed with increasing disfavour by those into whose hands power had now fallen. I was not included in their conclaves, which proceeded with the utmost animation from hour to hour. The Unionist leaders on coming to the aid of the nation at this juncture made no conditions as to policy, but stipulated for half the places and patronage. Mr. Asquith had therefore to dispense with half his former colleagues. Those whose actions in the conduct of the war were held to have produced this disagreeable result were naturally the object of resentment in Liberal circles. Up till Monday night it had been determined that Lord Kitchener should be transferred from the War Office to some great position similar to that of Commander-in-Chief; but on Tuesday it was realized that his hold on the confidence of the nation was still too great for any Government to do without him. On Wednesday, Mr. Asquith issued the reassuring statement that both Lord Kitchener and Sir Edward Grey would remain in their respective posts.

On Friday the 21st, when Lord Northcliffe published an attack upon the War Minister of a vehement character, there was a spontaneous movement of public anger in many parts of the country, and the offending newspaper was burned upon the Stock Exchange. In the wake of these emotions it was natural that the vacant Garter should be bestowed upon Lord Kitchener, and he was at the same time awarded the Grand Cordon of the Belgian Order of Leopold. His rehabilitation was therefore complete. I alone was held to blame for all the upheaval and its discontents.

The more serious physical wounds are often surprisingly endurable at the moment they are received. There is an interval of uncertain length before sensation is renewed. The shock numbs but does not paralyse: the wound bleeds but does not smart. So it is also with the great reverses and losses of life. Before I had realized the intensity with which political irritation was being focused on me, I had resigned myself to leaving the Admiralty. But on the Wednesday evening an incident occurred which profoundly affected my feelings and judgment. One of the Sea Lords informed me that Sir Arthur Wilson, who had already provisionally assumed the duties of First Sea Lord, had written to the Prime Minister declining to serve under any First Lord except me.

SIR ARTHUR WILSON TO THE PRIME MINISTER.

May 19, 1915.

DEAR MR. ASQUITH,

In view of the reports in the papers this morning as to the probable reconstruction of the Government, I think I ought to tell you that although I agreed to undertake the office of First Sea Lord under Mr. Churchill because it appeared to me to be the best means of maintaining continuity of policy under the unfortunate circumstances that have arisen, I am not prepared to undertake the duties under any new First Lord, as the strain under such circumstances would be far beyond my strength.

Believe me,

Yours truly,

A. K. WILSON.

This utterly unexpected mark of confidence from the old Admiral astounded me. His reserve had been impenetrable. I had no idea how he viewed me and my work. Certainly I never counted on the slightest support or approbation from him.

I was greatly disturbed and now found it very hard indeed to leave the Admiralty. In the midst of general condemnation, violent newspaper censures, angry Lobbies, reproachful colleagues, here at any rate was a judge—competent, instructed, impartial—who pronounced by action stronger than words not merely an acquittal but a vindication. I knew well the profound impression which Sir Arthur Wilson's action, had it been made public, would have produced upon the Naval Service. It would instantly have restored the confidence which press attacks, impossible to answer, had undermined. In no other way could the persistent accusations of rash, ignorant interference by the civilian Minister in the naval conduct of the war be decisively repelled. I felt myself strong enough with this endorsement to carry forward to eventual success the great operations to which we were committed. I felt that working with Wilson and Oliver, the First Sea Lord and the Chief of the Staff linked together as they were, we should again have re-established that unity, comradeship and authority at the summit of the Admiralty with which alone the risks could be run and the exertions made which were indispensable to victory. The information which had reached me was confidential and could not then be disclosed to the public by me. It was not disclosed by the Prime Minister.

I am confident that had the Prime Minister, instead of submitting to the demand of the Chancellor of the Exchequer to form a Coalition Government, laid the broad outlines of his case, both naval and military, before both Houses of Parliament in Secret Session, he and the policy he was committed to would have been supported by large majorities. The impressive recital of all that the War Office had achieved under Lord Kitchener would greatly have mitigated the complaints on what had been neglected. I am sure I could have vindicated the Admiralty policy. Moreover on May 23, towering over domestic matters, came the Italian declaration of War against Austria. The Prime Minister's personal share in this event was a tremendous fact. I am certain that had he fought, he would have won; and had he won, he could then with dignity and with real authority have invited the Opposition to come not to his rescue but to his aid. On such a basis of confidence, comradeship and respect a true national coalition could have been formed to carry on the war, and Mr. Asquith would have been spared that interlude of distrustful colleagues, of divided or more often mutually paralysing counsels and of lost opportunities, which reached its end in December, 1916.

I wish here to record the opinion that Parliament is the foundation upon which Governments should rely, and that the House of Commons in particular has a right to be informed and consulted on all great occasions of political change. The only safe course is that men engaged as members of a Cabinet in an agreed and common policy should stand or fall by a vote of the House of Commons taken after full debate. Departure from these simple fundamental principles led to a disastrous breakdown, at a most critical moment, of the whole machinery for carrying on the war. It led to delay in taking urgent action, which delay, as will presently appear, was fatal in its consequences.

It was only when Mr. Asquith's *Memoirs* appeared in 1928 that Lord Fisher's ultimatum to the Government was made public. Nothing could more clearly, or more cruelly, expose the mental distress and wild excitement into which the strain of war had plunged the old Admiral. Nothing could portray more vividly the volcano upon which I had been living and upon which grave decisions of war and policy had been pursued.

Lord Fisher had written:

If the following six conditions are agreed to, I can guarantee the successful termination of the war, and the total abolition of the submarine menace.

I also wish to add that since Lord Ripon wished, in 1885, to make me a Lord of the Admiralty, but at my request made me Director of Naval Ordnance and Torpedoes instead, I have served under nine First Lords and seventeen years at the Admiralty, so I ought to know something about it.

(1) That Mr. Winston Churchill is not in the Cabinet to be always circumventing me. Nor will I serve under Mr. Balfour.

(2) That Sir A. K. Wilson leaves the Admiralty, and the Committee of Imperial Defence, and the War Council, as my time will be occupied in resisting the bombardment of Heligoland and other such wild projects. Also his policy is totally opposed to mine, and he accepted the position of First Sea Lord in succession to me, thereby adopting a policy diametrically opposed to my views.

(3) That there shall be an entire new Board of Admiralty as regards the Sea Lords and the Financial Secretary (who is utterly useless). New measures demand New Men.

(4) That I should have complete professional charge of the war at sea, together with the sole disposition of the Fleet and the appointment of all officers of all ranks whatsoever.

(5) That the First Lord of the Admiralty should be absolutely restricted to Policy and Parliamentary Procedure, and should occupy the

same position towards me as Mr. Tennant, M.P., does to Lord Kitchener (and very well he does it).

(6) That I should have the sole absolute authority for all new construction and all dockyard work of whatever sort whatsoever, and complete control over the whole of the Civil Establishments of the Navy.

(Initialled) F.

19.5.15

P.S.—The 60 per cent of my time and energy which I have exhausted on nine First Lords in the past I wish in the future to devote to the successful prosecution of the war. That is the sole reason for these six conditions. These six conditions must be published verbatim, so that the Fleet may know my position.

It is needless to say that this amazing document was answered only by the curt acceptance of Fisher's resignation.

The formation of the new Government proceeded haltingly. Although by what was naïvely called a "Self-Denying Ordnance" it was agreed between the party leaders that no Member of Parliament on either side who was serving at the Front should be included in the Administration, the adjustment of party and personal claims raised at numerous points obstinate difficulties. Though I was left alone at the Admiralty, I was fully informed of every phase in this intricate and by no means entirely edifying process. It is no part of my purpose to unfold these matters here: their chronicle may be safely left to the Grevilles and Crokers, of which posterity, and possibly even our own generation, are not likely to be destitute.

It was during this interval that I had the honour of receiving a visit of ceremony from Lord Kitchener. I was not at first aware of what it was about. We had differed strongly and on a broad front at the last meeting of the War Council. Moreover, no decision of any importance on naval and military affairs could be taken during the hiatus. We talked about the situation. After some general remarks he asked me whether it was settled that I should leave the Admiralty. I said it was. He asked what I was going to do. I said I had no idea; nothing was settled. He spoke very kindly about our work together. He evidently had no idea how narrowly he had escaped my fate. As he got up to go he turned and said, in the impressive and almost majestic manner which was natural to him, "Well, there is one thing at any rate they cannot take from you. The Fleet was ready." After that he was gone. During the months that we were still to serve together in the new Cabinet I was condemned often to differ from him, to oppose him and to criticize him. But I cannot forget the rugged kindness and warm-hearted courtesy which led him to pay me this visit.

By the 21st it was decided that Mr. Balfour was to come to the Admiralty. In accordance with what I knew were the Prime Minister's wishes, I endeavoured to persuade Sir Arthur Wilson to serve under him. He remained obdurate. No arguments would move him. He was at some pains to explain that his decision arose out of no personal consideration for me, but solely because he felt he could not undertake the burden without my aid. All the same, there seemed to be a quite unwonted element of friendliness in his demeanour, and this was proved a year later during the Parliamentry inquiry into the Dardanelles. Not only did he then give evidence which was of the greatest possible assistance to me, but he drew up in a single night a cogent paper on the technical gunnery aspects of the plan we had followed, and cast his ægis and authority over an enterprise which everybody was by then eager to condemn.

On the evening of the 21st I reported to the Prime Minister:

> I have tried very hard but without success to persuade Sir Arthur Wilson to hold himself at Mr. Balfour's disposition. In these circumstances I would advise Sir Henry Jackson.

This proposal was adopted, and meanwhile the process of Cabinet-making gradually completed itself. Mr. Asquith was good enough to offer me the Chancellorship of the Duchy of Lancaster. This office is a sinecure of much dignity. I should certainly not have felt able to accept it but for the fact that he coupled with it the promise that I should be a member of the War Council, or War Committee, of the Cabinet. I felt that thus situated I should be able to bring whatever knowledge I had acquired to the service of the Dardanelles expedition, and that it was my duty to aid and succour it by any effective means still left to me. I remained in the new Government so long as this condition was observed.

It was not till the 26th that the full list of the Government was announced and Ministers changed offices and kissed hands. The interval was full of anxiety. No councils were held on war matters and all questions of policy had necessarily to be reserved for the decision of the new Cabinet. No more troops were sent to the Dardanelles, and only day-to-day decisions could be taken. There was no First Sea Lord. In these circumstances I did the best I could.

Early on the morning of the 26th—my last at the Admiralty—arrived the sinister news that the *Triumph* had been torpedoed and sunk at the Dardanelles by a German submarine. However, my task was over, and before setting out for Buckingham Palace I wrote the following letter to the statesman on whom the burden of Admiralty affairs was now placed:

MR. CHURCHILL TO MR. BALFOUR

May 26, 1915.

I leave you one task of great difficulty which requires your immediate attention, viz., the protection of the Dardanelles fleet against submarine attack. Do not underrate the gravity of this danger. Unless it can be coped with, there are no limits to the evil consequences. For nearly a fortnight I have not had the authority to make important decisions. Your fresh mind and calm judgment will give the impulse which is necessary. I set out the following notes for what they are worth:

1. The military operations should proceed with all possible speed, so that the period of danger may be shortened. Whatever force is necessary, can be spared and can be used, should be sent at once, and all at once.

2. Until decisive operations on land can be resumed, the Fleet must remain in the safety of Mudros harbour—or the Suez Canal. Such ships as are required to cover the troops should, until the netted lighters arrive, be protected by colliers and empty transports lashed alongside.

3. As soon as possible ships must be provided which are immune from torpedo attack. As specified in my minute of the 13th instant to the First Sea Lord, the nine heavy monitors should go out as soon as each is ready; and the four "Edgars" which have been fitted with bulges, and which supply the medium battery for bombarding purposes, should be sent at once. Nearly a fortnight has been lost in regard to the "Edgars" by the interregnum here. Until these vessels arrive, and while no decisive land operations are in progress, the exposure of ships should be kept to the absolute minimum.

4. At least 100 trawlers and drifters, with 100 miles of indicator net, and eight more destroyers (which should on the way out escort transports) should be sent; in addition to all the other measures which have been taken, and of which you will be told.

5. The protection against submarines must take the form of developing a great netted area around the tip of the Gallipoli Peninsula, occupied by large numbers of armed trawlers and seaplanes always ready. I want to emphasize the fact that action must be drastic and on a large scale. Much has been done already.

6. The measures to watch and net the mouth of the Adriatic, and to search for submarine bases in Asia Minor, to mine-in likely bases, to develop a system of intelligence regardless of expense, all of which are now in progress, must be pressed forward.

7. Punishment must be doggedly borne.

From the bottom of my heart I wish you success in this and all other anxious business which has been thrust upon you, and which you have so loyally and courageously undertaken.

Thus ended my administration of the Admiralty. For thirty-four months of preparation and ten months of war I had borne the prime responsibility and had wielded the main executive power. The reader who has persevered thus far in this account will realize the difficulties that were coped with, the hazards that were encountered, the mistakes that were made, and the work that was done. Dubious years, many misfortunes, enormous toils, bitter disappointments, still lay before the Royal Navy. But I am entitled at this point in the story to place on record the situation and condition in which the mighty instrument of our sea power and of our salvation passed into the hands of my successors. At no moment during all the wars of Britain had our command of the seas been more complete, and in no previous war had that command been asserted more rapidly or with so little loss. Not only had the surface ships of the enemy been extirpated from the oceans of the world; not only in the North Sea had his fleets and squadrons been beaten, cowed and driven into port; but even the new and barbarous submarine warfare had been curbed and checked. For more than a year to come the German High Seas Fleet scarcely quitted its harbours, and even when they did so, it was with no intention of fighting a battle and in the unfounded hope that they could return unperceived or unmolested. For eighteen months their submarine campaign was virtually suspended. In spite of modern complications which have been explained, the economic blockade of Germany was established and maintained, so far as it rested with the Navy, with the utmost strictness: scarcely any ship that the Navy had authority to touch ever passed our far-spread cordons. The maintenance of the armies in France and in the East proceeded every month on a vaster scale, without the slightest substantial hindrance upon their communications becoming apparent to our commanders at the Front. The mercantile fleets of Britain and of her allies moved with freedom in all directions about the seas and oceans: and an insurance rate of 1 per cent left a substantial profit to the Government Fund. These conditions lasted during all the year 1915 and up to the last quarter of the year 1916. There never was in all the history of war such an unchallenged reign of sea power.

Meanwhile the British Navy was growing continually and rapidly in strength. The fruits of the exertions which had been made before and since the outbreak of the war were being reaped with each successive month. Battleships, battle cruisers, light cruisers in dozens, submarines in scores, destroyers in hundreds, small craft in thousands, were being armed and built, and were coming into commission in an unceasing and broadening tide. The manning arrangements to meet this enormous new construction were perfected for a year in advance. Every requirement known to the naval science of the day in guns, in torpedoes, in shells, in explosives, in propellant, in coal, in oil, and in auxiliary services had been foreseen and provided for in harmonious relation to the expansion of our naval power. At the Admiralty we were in hot pursuit of most of the great key inventions and ideas of the war; and this long in advance of every other nation, friend or foe. Tanks, smoke, torpedo-seaplanes, directional wireless, cryptography, mine fenders, monitors, torpedo-proof ships, paravanes—all were being actively driven forward or developed. Poison gas alone we had put aside—but not, as has been shown, from want of comprehension. Even for the new submarine campaign, not to burst upon us for nearly eighteen months, the principal safeguarding measures had already been devised: the multitudes of vessels were building; the decoy ships were at work.

Moreover the true war leaders of the Navy had already emerged from the ranks of peace-time merit; and in Beatty, Keyes, Tyrwhitt, Pakenham, and I must add Lewis Bayly—though under a temporary cloud—we had masters of the storm capable of rivalling upon the seas and against the enemy's coasts the exploits of the famous sailor figures of the past. There remained only to devise and perfect those schemes of naval offensive which in spite, and indeed by means of, modern science and invention would have liberated the pent-up skill and daring of our officers and men. There was also at hand that prolonged interlude of ease and tranquillity upon salt water in which every plan could be worked out with sure and deliberate study.

From all this reward and opportunity Fisher, by his own impulsive, fatal act, and I, through causes which these pages expose, were for ever disinherited. We lingered on, helpless spectators, until the period of halcyon weather came fearfully to an end and the very life of the State was plunged again into supreme hazard on the seas.

CHAPTER XXXIII

THE DARKENING SCENE

The new Administration met for the first time on May 26. From the very outset its defects as a war-making instrument were evident. The old Ministers had made an accommodation with their political opponents not on the merits but under duress. The new Ministers were deeply prejudiced against the work which their predecessors had done. Had they been responsible they would no doubt have made a somewhat different series of mistakes. The Unionists had little confidence in the Prime Minister. Indeed, one of the questions they had most anxiously debated was whether they would assent to his remaining at the head of the Government. Mr. Lloyd George, the powerful politician whose action had compelled the formation of the Coalition, found himself on the morrow of his success in a position of singular weakness. He had ceded the Exchequer to Mr. McKenna, and found in the new Cabinet, so largely his creation, an array of Conservative notables who regarded his political record with the utmost aversion. Mr. Bonar Law, the Leader of the Conservative Party in the House of Commons, might well have expected this dominant post, and although he was not himself affected by personal considerations, much soreness remained among his friends. Whereas practically all the important matters connected with the war had been dealt with in the late Government by four or five Ministers, at least a dozen powerful, capable, distinguished personalities who were in a position to assert themselves had now to be consulted.

The progress of business therefore became cumbrous and laborious in the last degree, and though all these evils were corrected by earnest patriotism and loyalty, the general result was bound to be disappointing. Those who had knowledge had pasts to defend; those free from war commitments were also free from war experience. At least five or six different opinions prevailed on every great topic, and every operative decision was obtained only by prolonged, discursive and exhausting discussions. Far more often we laboured through long delays to unsatisfactory compromises. Meanwhile the destroying war strode remorselessly on its course.

Although without executive power, I was treated with much consideration by the new Cabinet. I continued to sit in my old place on Lord Kitchener's left hand. I was nominated to serve on the committee of nine Ministers which, under the title of the Dardanelles Committee, was virtually the old War Council. I was invited to prepare statements on the situation, both naval and general, and every facility was placed at my disposal by the Admiralty for marshalling and checking the facts. Lord Kitchener was also desired to present to the new Cabinet similar statements from the War Office standpoint. These papers were prepared with the utmost dispatch. Meanwhile the education of the new Ministers in the inside and central point of view and their initiation in the secret and special information at the disposal of the Government continued. Opinion declared itself increasingly favourable to the prosecution of the enterprise at the Dardanelles and generally in the sense of the views which I had set forth on the military problem. It was not, however, until the afternoon of June 7 that the first meeting of the Dardanelles Committee was convened. It was composed of: The Prime Minister, Lord Kitchener, Lord Lansdowne, Mr. Bonar Law, Mr. Balfour, Lord Curzon, Lord Selborne, Lord Crewe, and myself.

Mr. Lloyd George, though a member, was not present on this occasion. Indeed from this time forward and for some months he immersed himself in the production of munitions, and concentrated his whole energies upon the task.

The Committee addressed itself to the requests for reinforcements contained in Sir Ian Hamilton's telegram of May 17. Lord Kitchener pronounced with the utmost decision in favour of prosecuting the campaign at the Dardanelles with the greatest vigour. He declared that he would reinforce Sir Ian Hamilton with three divisions of the New Army in addition to the Lowland Territorial Division, which had already been dispatched under orders issued before the interregnum. He stated that he could not consent to remain responsible for the conduct of the war if it were decided to abandon the attack upon the Gallipoli Peninsula. The Council accepted this clear guidance not merely with relief but with satisfaction. Opinion was unanimous. The following conclusions were recorded:

1. To reinforce Sir Ian Hamilton with the three remaining divisions of the First New Army with a view to an assault in the second week of July.

2. To send out the following naval units, which should be much less vulnerable to submarine attack than those under Admiral de Robeck's command:

Endymion and *Theseus* [light cruisers of the "Edgar" class just fitted with bulges].
Four monitors with 14-inch guns.
Six monitors with 9.2-inch guns.
Four monitors with 6-inch guns, and one of the latter to follow later.

Four sloops.
Two "E" Class submarines, now *en route.*
Four "H" Class submarines.

Thus the naval measures decided on by the new Board of Admiralty and the new War Council were in principle the same, slightly extended, as those which had been previously pressed by me upon Lord Fisher on the eve of his resignation. The military decisions were, however, on a far larger scale than any which Lord Kitchener had countenanced hitherto. Besides the two divisions which it was in contemplation to send on May 17 and May 30 respectively (one of which had already gone), two others were added; and of the four divisions so assigned to Sir Ian Hamilton, three were to be divisions of the New Army, which was considered, perhaps unjustly, superior to the Territorial divisions at this period.

The conclusions of the Dardanelles Committee of June 7 were brought before the Cabinet on the 9th; and a very hot discussion arose on the general principle of whether the Dardanelles enterprise should be persevered in, or whether we should "cut our loss" and come away. This was, in fact, going over the whole process by which the Dardanelles Committee had arrived at their conclusions. The sense of the Cabinet on the whole was however clearly with the Committee, and in the end it was agreed that the three divisions should go as reinforcements to Sir Ian Hamilton.

There was however from the outset to the end a duality of opinion in the Cabinet which, although it did not follow party lines, resembled a party cleavage, and at every stage in the rest of the Dardanelles operations caused serious embarrassment. Had the Prime Minister possessed or been able to acquire plenary authority, and had he been permitted to exercise it during May and June without distraction or interruption, it is my belief, based upon daily acquaintance with these transactions, that he would have taken the measures which even at this stage would have resulted in securing a decisive victory. But from the moment of the formation of the Coalition power was dispersed and counsels were divided, and every military decision had to be carried by the same sort of process of tact, temporizing, and exhaustion which occurs over a clause in a keenly contested Bill in the House of Commons in time of peace. These facts are stated not with a view of making reproaches where all were equally sincere and equally well-meaning, but to explain the melancholy turn of events.

We had now at length got on June 9 the kind of decisions which were necessary to carry the enterprise through to success. There was no *military* reason of any kind why the decisions which were reached on June 7 and June 9 should not have been taken within 48 hours of Sir Ian Hamilton's telegram of May 17. All the facts necessary to the decision were equally available on that date; all the troops were equally available; all the arguments were equally clamant. But from causes in which the enemy had no part, which arose solely from the confusion into which the governing instrument in this country had been thrown, from a fortnight to three weeks were lost for ever.

The consequences were momentous. Time was the dominating factor. The extraordinary mobility and unexpectedness of amphibious power can, as has been shown, only be exerted in strict relation to limited periods of time. The surprise, the rapidity, and the intensity of the attack are all dependent on the state of the enemy's preparations at a given moment. Every movement undertaken on one side can be matched by a counter-movement on the other. Force and time in this kind of operation amount to almost the same thing, and each can to a very large extent be expressed in terms of the other. A week lost was about the same as a division. Three divisions in February could have occupied the Gallipoli Peninsula with little fighting. Five could have captured it after March 18. Seven were insufficient at the end of April, but nine might just have done it. Eleven might have sufficed at the beginning of July. Fourteen were to prove insufficient on August 7. Moreover, one delay breeds another.

The date of the next great attack on the Gallipoli Peninsula was governed by two factors—the arrival of the new army, and to a lesser extent by the state of the moon. It was considered that a surprise landing at a fresh point could best be effected on a moonless night. If therefore the dark period of July was missed, the operation in the particular form adopted must stand over till the similar period in August. It will be seen by reference to the decisions of the Dardanelles Committee of June 7 that they contemplated an attack in the second week of July, and believed that the three new divisions would all have arrived by then. This would have been the most favourable moment. It could certainly have been achieved if the decision had been taken promptly on the receipt of Sir Ian Hamilton's telegram, or, if pending a general decision on policy, the dispatch of reinforcements by divisions could have proceeded while the Government were considering the matter. But as it was, the troops that it was now decided to send did not or could not arrive in time for a July attack. The three New Army divisions did not, in fact, finish arriving until July had ended. Thus the great battle at Anzac and Suvla Bay was fought in the second week of August, instead of, as would have been perfectly practicable, in the early part of July. During the month that was thus lost, i.e., from the beginning of July to the beginning of August, *ten new Turkish divisions,* or their equivalents, besides important drafts, according to our now certain knowledge, reached the defenders of the Peninsula, and thus our new divisions, which we had at last decided to send, and which if sent in time would have given us a good superiority, were equated and cancelled out before they got to the spot. Moreover, in the interval our land forces were greatly wasted and reduced by sickness and casualties, and the fleet was exposed to continuous danger from submarines. The Germans acquired an ever-increasing control of the Turkish Army, and the whole methods of defence were in consequence far better organized. The defeats of the Russians in Galicia during June and July produced a marked change in the fighting spirit of the Turks on the Peninsula. The removal from Batoum of General Istomine's army, which was thrown into the main Russian battlefields, liberated the considerable forces which the Turks had been forced to keep concentrated at or near Midia to guard against a landing there. Before June was half over it became clear that the reinforcements could not reach the Dardanelles in time for a July battle. The second week in August was the earliest date when the troops would be there, and the nights would be moonless.

All these considerations were present in my mind and filled me with intense anxiety about the issue of the next great effort. I therefore laboured by every means open to me to secure even larger reinforcements and above all their accelerated dispatch.

May and June saw the beginning of the great Russian retreat. Up till the end of March the strategy of Hindenburg and Ludendorff had aimed at the encirclement and capture of entire Russian armies. They had made their first cast towards Warsaw in November, 1914, but the German and Austrian forces were not strong enough to sustain so ambitious a conception, and the attempt was skilfully frustrated by the Grand Duke. They tried a second cast in January— this time Northward against the Russian armies in East Prussia. But although nearly 100,000 prisoners were captured in the fearful winter battle of the Masurian Lakes, the bulk of the Russian armies slipped away as the Germans closed round them, and no strategic result was attained. The plan was good and this time the forces employed were adequate, but the season was badly chosen and the difficulties of a winter campaign under-estimated.[1] By the beginning of March, 1915, the entire Eastern front had again subsided into trench warfare, and on March 22 Przemysl fell to the Russian Southern group of armies, setting free large Russian forces for the invasion of Hungary. The second Hindenburg-Ludendorff attempt to procure a supreme decision in the East had failed. But now a suggestion came from the Austrian Chief-of-the-Staff, Conrad von Hötzendorf, to force the Russians out of the trenches by a break through on a limited front. Hindenburg and Ludendorff, still intent upon repeating Tannenberg, opposed the Austrian plan, and wished in spite of their previous disappointments to achieve strategic results by undertaking another enveloping operation from the North on an even larger scale. For this the German Main Headquarters could find neither the men nor the munitions which were needed, and on April 4 Falkenhayn, who had succeeded Moltke as Chief of the

[1] General von François: a German authority.

German General Staff, decided to adopt the Austrian conception and to attempt a break through between Gorlice and Tarnow as Conrad von Hötzendorf had proposed. Tarnow lies in Galicia, near Cracow, at the junction of the Biala and the Dunajecs Rivers, and Gorlice, just north of the Carpathians, is about twenty-five miles south-east of Tarnow. The sector of attack lay on the south side of the Russian salient in Galicia, so that a considerable portion of the Russian front lay to the west of the German line of advance, under the menace of being cut off should it succeed. The blow was an upper-cut.

The German-Austrian attack began on May 2. It had been entrusted to Mackensen. Aided by poison gas and a tremendous artillery, the attack was immediately successful, both the first and second Russian positions being captured. The strategic instinct of Conrad von Hötzendorf was also to be vindicated, for the Grand Duke Nicholas, rather than allow the troops on either side of the gap to be taken in flank, withdrew the whole line in this part of the front. This process of attack on a limited front was repeated continuously by the Germans during the months that followed, and each time it induced large withdrawals of the Russian line, culminating in the clearance of the whole of Galicia and Poland, and the fall one after another of all the fortresses and towns on which the Russian armies had rested.

As this sombre development was recorded day after day during June and July on our maps, Lord Kitchener became increasingly anxious. He feared that Russia would collapse entirely, and that the Germans would then transfer immense forces from the Eastern to the Western front. He persuaded himself, on more than one occasion, that this transference was already in progress and that a hostile offensive in France was imminent. For reasons which have been abundantly explained, I could not share these apprehensions, and I endeavoured to combat them on every occasion. I believed that the Russians would succeed in retaining very large Austro-German armies on their front for an indefinite period. I did not believe that the Germans had any intention of abandoning their drive against Russia or of going back and re-opening an offensive in the West. Lastly, I pointed continuously to victory at the Dardanelles as the sole and supreme remedy open to us for the evils of our situation.

While Ministerial changes and Cabinet discussions had been taking place at home, the situation at the Dardanelles and on the Gallipoli Peninsula had passed through several critical phases. On May 19 the Turks, having received news of the arrival of German submarines, made a most determined and serious effort to drive the Anzacs into the sea. The attack, in which four divisions comprising 30,000 Turkish infantry took part, was maintained for many hours both in darkness and in daylight. It was completely and decisively repulsed at every point. When it ceased the Turks had lost at least 5,000 men, and 3,000 of their dead lay in front of the Anzac trenches. The British loss, on the other hand, did not exceed 600. On the morrow the Turkish Commander asked for an armistice to bury the dead and collect the wounded, and this was conceded by Sir Ian Hamilton.

"After May 19," said the Turkish War Office when the war was over, "it was realized that the British defence at Anzac was too strong to enable us to effect anything against it without heavy artillery with plenty of ammunition, and since our own position was also very strong in defence, two weak divisions were left in the trenches and the other two were withdrawn."

The position at Anzac was henceforward unchallenged.

On June 4 a general attack was delivered by the British and French along the whole front at Helles. In this action the 29th Division, the 42nd Division, the 2nd Naval Brigade and both French Divisions took part. The Allied forces numbered about 34,000 infantry and the Turks 25,000. Despite a woeful deficiency in artillery and ammunition, the British troops stormed the trenches of the Turkish centre. The French gained ground on the right; but were afterwards driven back by counter-attacks. This exposed the flank of the Naval and 42nd Divisions who were in succession compelled to yield up the greater part of their gains. In the end the general line of the Allies was advanced by no more than two or three hundred yards. The battle was costly for both sides. The Turkish losses amounted to 10,000, and those of the British alone to an equal number. As in all the battles on the Peninsula, the issue hung in a trembling balance. The Turks were thrown into such confusion that on only two kilometres of their front no less than twenty-five battalions (or parts of battalions) were mingled in the line without any higher organization. In these straits the Turkish Divisional Commander reported that no further British attack could be resisted. In a heated conference the Turkish Chief-of-the-Staff advised the withdrawal of the whole front to Achi Baba. It was only with the greatest difficulty and by the enemy's good luck that the intermingled troops were relieved by a fresh Turkish division on the night of June 7.

On June 21 another important action was fought by the French Corps, which attacked with great spirit on the right of the Helles Front, captured the Haricot Redoubt, and made a substantial advance. A portion of these gains were wrested from them the next day by a Turkish counter-attack.

A week later, June 28, the British being reinforced by the 52nd Division, made a general attack on the left of the Helles Front. Five lines of trenches were captured, and an advance of about 1,000 yards was secured. The Turkish force engaged comprised 38,000 infantry with 16 field and 7 heavy batteries. The fire of the ships was, on this occasion, found to be most effective, and the success of the attack again led to critical discussions at the Turkish Headquarters.

The German General, Weber, now commanding the Southern zone, wished to withdraw the whole front to the Kilid Bahr Plateau. Liman von Sanders, however, overruled him and demanded instead a speedy counter-attack. For this purpose, two fresh Turkish divisions were brought into the line, and a fierce surprise assault was delivered before dawn on July 5. The Turks were repulsed with a loss of 6,000 men.

"The affair of the 28th," said General Callwell in his cool and instructed account of the Campaign,[1] "following closely Gouraud's stroke on the opposite flank seemed to suggest that if there had been a plentiful reserve to throw into the scale at this juncture on the Helles Front, this might have proved the psychological moment for initiating a determined effort to secure Krithia, the high ground beyond that coveted village, and even possibly Achi Baba itself; no such reserves were, however, available." The paralysis of the British Executive during the formation of the Coalition Government and the education of its new ministers had effectually withheld this boon.

A third attack along the whole front was delivered with such ammunition and troops as could be found on July 12–13. The general line was advanced from 200 to 400 yards, but no important results were obtained. It had been evident from the beginning of July that considerable reinforcements were reaching the Turks. On the other hand, the British Army was woefully reduced by wastage and casualties. Already by the middle of May, after the first battles, the infantry of Sir Ian Hamilton's five divisions were 23,000 men, or 40 per cent below their war establishment. These deficiencies were never overtaken by the drafts supplied by the War Office. The 52nd Division and various minor reinforcements dribbled in during June, but did little more than keep pace with the wastage. While the new divisions were on the sea, the old divisions were dwindling. During the whole of May, June and July, the total of the British Forces on the Peninsula and at Anzac never exceeded 60,000 men.

Even more discouraging than depleted battalions was the scarcity of ammunition. "During the months of June and July," said Gen. Simpson-Baikie—who commanded the British Artillery[2]—"the total number of rounds of 18-pdr. ammunition at Cape Helles never reached 25,000. Before one of our attacks it used to reach its maximum, which was about 19,000 to 23,000. The total amount of 18-pdr. therefore was limited to about 12,000 rounds, as it was necessary to keep 6,000 to 10,000 rounds in reserve to guard against Turkish counter-attacks. As there was no high explosive shell for the 18-pdr. (except 640 rounds expended on June 4) only shrapnel could be used, and it is well-known

---

[1] Major-General Sir C. E. Callwell: *The Dardanelles*, p. 160.
[2] *Gallipoli Diary*, Appendix 1, 281; Statement of Major-General Simpson-Baikie.

that shrapnel is but little use for destroying hostile trenches." On July 13 only 5,000 rounds for the field artillery remained at Helles, and all active operations had, perforce, to be suspended.

The weight of field-gun ammunition available to prepare and support the British assaults in any of these battles on the Peninsula never exceeded 150 tons. For the purpose of judging the scale of the artillery preparation, this may be compared with over 1,300 tons fired in the first two days of the battle of Loos at the end of September in the same year; and with upwards of 25,000 tons often fired in two days during the August offensive of 1918. The rifle and machine-gun fire of the defence on each occasion remained a constant factor. Hard tasks were therefore set to the troops in Gallipoli, and the fact that the issue hung continually in the balance is the measure of their bravery and devotion.

The fact that during all this period the British Fleet neither attacked nor threatened the forts at the Narrows nor attempted to sweep the minefields enabled the German and Turkish Commanders to draw upon the medium and mobile artillery which defended the Straits for the purpose of succouring the Fifth Turkish Army in its desperate struggle. The first transferences began on April 27. On May 23 Admiral von Usedom, who on April 26 had assumed command of the Fortress of the Dardanelles and of all the Marine Defences of the Straits, reported to the Emperor that he had up to that date, under protest, already yielded to the Army the following artillery:

Six 8.2-inch mortars, eight 6-inch field howitzers, two 4.7-inch quick-firing field howitzers, nine 4.7-inch field howitzers, twelve 4.7-inch siege guns, and twelve field guns. In all forty-nine pieces.

During June and July the Fifth Turkish Army in its distress made ever-increasing inroads upon the artillery defence of the Straits. Admiral von Usedom's letters to the Emperor reveal his anxiety at this denudation of the marine artillery, and also the dire need of German ammunition, not only for the fortress system, but also for the Fifth Army. Without ammunition from Germany, he wrote, the Army could hold the enemy only a short time; Turkey must spare no effort to get German ammunition through the Balkan countries.

These efforts met with no success and on August 16 Admiral von Usedom reported to the Emperor that "the attempts of bringing ammunition ordered in Germany through Roumania have all failed." He was therefore forced to endure his precarious situation month after month. It must, however, be observed that whereas the Turkish shortage of ammunition arose from causes beyond their control, the British shortage sprang solely from lack of decision in the distribution of the available quantities between the various theatres of war.

•   •   •

The measures taken to cope with the German submarine attack upon our communications followed in the main the lines which have been indicated and proved, broadly speaking, completely successful. The Fleet was kept in the shelter of Mudros harbour; battleships were only exposed when required for some definite operation, and the ordinary support of the Army by fire from the sea was afforded during June by destroyers and light vessels.

This was found to be sufficient. The observation and direction of the ships' fire attained every week a higher efficiency. This process continued steadily until naval co-operation in land fighting on Gallipoli had become a factor of the utmost value. In July the monitors and "bulged" cruisers began to arrive. Thenceforward the fire of the Turkish guns from Asia was controlled and largely quelled. The four large monitors armed with 14-inch guns, four medium monitors armed with 9.2 or 6-inch guns, and four "bulged" cruisers (*Theseus, Endymion, Grafton* and *Edgar*) were all on the scene by the end of that month. Had action been taken when it was first proposed to Lord Fisher, the arrival of these vessels would have been antedated by more than three weeks. But the interval was passed without serious disadvantage to the Army: and when the whole Monitor Fleet had arrived, the Naval support of the troops was not only fully restored, but much enhanced.

Meanwhile the supply of the Army was maintained by the use of large numbers of small shallow-draft vessels and proceeded uninterruptedly, so that by the middle of July reserves of twenty-four days' rations had been accumulated for all troops ashore at Helles and Anzac. The reinforcements sent from home were conveyed to their destination, although several transports were torpedoed, and in one case a thousand lives were lost. It is remarkable that neither monitors, "bulged" cruisers, nor shallow-draught vessels were ever seriously attacked or threatened by submarines. Lastly, the great netted areas proved an effective deterrent against submarine attack. Although warships of every kind were continually moving about within them, they were in no case molested during the whole of the campaign. Thus, what had seemed to be a danger potentially mortal was entirely warded off by suitable measures perseveringly applied on a sufficient scale.

While the submarine attack upon the British sea communications was being frustrated, a far more effective pressure was being brought to bear upon the enemy. In December, 1914, Lieutenant-Commander Norman Holbrook had gained the Victoria Cross by diving his submarine B 11 under the minefields of the Dardanelles and sinking the Turkish cruiser *Messudieh*. On April 17 this desperate enterprise had been again attempted by submarine E 15 in conjunction with Sir Ian Hamilton's impending landing. The effort failed. The vessel ran aground in the Straits near Dardanos; her Captain, Lieutenant-

Commander T. S. Brodie, was killed; most of her crew were captured and her carcass, after being fiercely contended for, was finally shattered by a torpedo from a British picket boat. On April 25, while the landing was in progress, the Australian submarine AE 2, undeterred by the fate of her forerunner, most gallantly and skilfully dived through and under the minefields and succeeded in entering the Sea of Marmora. Here from the 25th to the 30th she attacked the Turkish shipping and sank a large gunboat. On April 30, however, being damaged and unable to dive properly, she was herself sunk, after a two hours' fight, by a Turkish torpedo boat. But the way had been re-opened. The passage, whatever its perils, was shown to be still not impossible. The losses of these two boats, which so greatly disturbed Lord Fisher, did not prevent a sublime perseverance. On April 27, E 14 under Lieutenant-Commander C. Boyle dived at 95 feet through the minefield, passed Kilid Bahr at 22 feet under the fire of all the Forts and torpedoed a Turkish gunboat near Gallipoli. From this time forward, till the end, one or more British submarines continuously operated in the Sea of Marmora, and their attacks upon the Turkish water communications, almost by themselves, achieved the ruin of the enemy.

E 14 remained in the Sea of Marmora from April 27 to May 18, continually hunted by torpedo boats and other patrol craft, and fired on so constantly that she could scarcely find breathing space to recharge her batteries and keep herself alive. Nevertheless she wrought decisive havoc on the Turkish transports. On the 29th she attacked two and sank one. On May 1 she sank a gunboat. On May 5 she attacked another transport and drove others back to Constantinople. On the 10th she attacked two transports convoyed by two Turkish destroyers, and fired at both. The second transport was a very large vessel, full of troops; a terrific explosion followed the impact of the torpedo, and the transport sank rapidly. An entire infantry brigade and several batteries of artillery, in all upwards of 6,000 Turkish soldiers, were drowned. This awful event practically arrested the movement of Turkish troops by sea. E 14 had now no torpedoes, and on May 17 she received wireless orders to return. On the 18th she again ran the gauntlet of the Forts at 22 feet, and dived, as she thought, under the minefields. She must, however, have passed right through the lines of mines in extreme danger.

Commander Nasmith in E 11 entered the Marmora on the following day. His vessel was newly equipped with a 6-pounder gun, and cruised for some days lashed alongside a sailing vessel, sinking a gunboat and several ships. On May 25 Commander Nasmith dived E 11 literally into Constantinople, and hit with a torpedo a large vessel alongside the arsenal. E 11 grounded several times and escaped with great difficulty from the enemy's harbour. She now established a reign of terror in the Marmora, attacking unsuccessfully the battleship *Barbarossa,* fighting with destroyers, sinking store-ships and steamers, with continued hair-breadth escapes from destruction. On June 7 she returned through the minefield, actually fouling a mine which she carried on her port hydroplane for a considerable distance while under heavy fire from the Forts. She had been in the Marmora for nineteen days, and had sunk 1 gunboat, 3 transports, 1 ammunition ship and 3 store-ships.

On June 10 Commander Boyle made his second entry into the Marmora where he remained for twenty-three days, sinking 1 large steamer and 13 sailing vessels. E 12 (Lieutenant-Commander Bruce) and E 7 (Lieutenant-Commander Cochrane) passed the Straits on the 20th and 30th June respectively, destroyed between them 7 steamers and 19 sailing vessels, and fired repeatedly on the roads and railways along the coast.

A new peril was now to be added to the passage. In the middle of July the Turks completed the Nagara anti-submarine net. This net was made in 10-foot meshes of 3-inch, strengthened with 5-inch wire, and except for a small gateway, completely closed the passage to a depth of over 220 feet. This barrier was guarded by five motor-gunboats armed with depth charges, and by numerous guns specially placed.

On July 21 Commander Boyle, for the third time, made the passage of the Straits in E 14. A mine scraped past her near the Narrows without exploding, and by good luck she passed through the gate of the net at Nagara. On July 22 she met E 7 in the Marmora, and both vessels together continued their depredations upon shipping. All hospital ships were spared, although their increase in numbers showed that they were being used for military transport. Commander Boyle's final return on August 12, i.e., his sixth passage of the minefield, was thus described by him:

> I missed the gate and hit the net. It is possible the net now extends nearly the whole way across. I was brought up from 80 feet to 45 feet in three seconds, but luckily only thrown 15 degrees off my course. There was a tremendous noise, scraping, banging, tearing and rumbling, and it sounded as if there were two distinct obstructions, as the noise nearly ceased and then came on again, and we were appreciably checked twice. It took about 20 seconds to get through. I was fired at on rounding Kilid Bahr, and a torpedo was fired at me from Chanak, breaking surface a few yards astern of me. A mile south-west of Chanak I scraped past a mine, but it did not check me—after I got out I found some twin electric wire round my propellers . . . and various parts of the boat were scraped and scored by wire.

On August 5, E 11 (Commander Nasmith) had made her second passage of the Straits. A mine bumped heavily along her side off Kephez point at a depth of 70 feet. To break the net at Nagara she dived to 110 feet and then charged. The net caught her bow and she was drawn violently upwards. Under the strain the wires of the net snapped with a crack, and the submarine was freed. An hour later she torpedoed a transport; all day she was harassed by patrol craft; at dawn the next morning she was attacked by the bombs of an aeroplane. Later in the day she torpedoed a gunboat. On the 7th she was in action with troops on the roads along the coast. On the 8th she torpedoed and sank the battleship *Barbarossa,* which, escorted by two destroyers, was hurrying to the Peninsula during the Battle of Suvla Bay. These adventures and exploits continued without cessation during twenty-nine days, at the end of which E 11 returned safely, having sunk or destroyed 1 battleship, 1 gunboat, 6 transports, 1 steamer and 23 sailing vessels.

The perilous duty was taken up successively by E 2, E 7, E 12, H 1 (Lieutenant Pirie) and E 20 (Lieutenant-Commander Clyfford Warren), as well as by the French submarine *Turquoise.* In all, the passage of Nagara was made twenty-seven times. Every one of these voyages is an epic in itself. Out of thirteen British and French submarines which made or attempted the passage into the Marmora, eight perished—four with all or nearly all hands. Besides E 15 and AE 11, Cochrane's E 7 was caught in the Nagara net on September 4. Bombed with depth charges for 16 hours, and having tried to fall through the bottom of the net by sinking to the excessive depth of 40 fathoms, Cochrane at last rose to the surface and finding himself inextricably enmeshed, ordered his crew to jump overboard, and sank his vessel with his own hands. His subsequent escapes from the Turks and adventures in captivity are an amazing tale of courage and pertinacity. Of the French submarines three were destroyed or captured at the entrance or in the net: *Saphir* in January; *Joule* in May; and *Mariotte* on July 26. The *Turquoise* was the only French submarine which achieved the passage, and she was disabled and captured after a brief career in the Marmora on October 30. In the captain's cabin of the *Turquoise* the enemy found his notebook, which he had forgotten to destroy. This notebook contained the rendezvous at which the *Turquoise* was to meet the British submarine E 20 on November 6. The German submarine U 14 was repairing at Constantinople. *She* kept the rendezvous, and E 20, expecting a friend, was blown to pieces by the torpedo of a foe.[1]

In all, the British submarines destroyed in the Marmora 1 battleship, 1 destroyer, 5 gunboats, 11 transports, 44 steamers and 148 sailing vessels. The effect of the virtual stoppage of the Turkish sea communication was most serious to the enemy; and towards the end of June the Turkish Army was reduced to the narrowest margin of food and ammunition. It was only by great exertions and

---

[1] *U-boote gegen U-boote,* by Lieutenant zur See von Heimburg (*Die Woche,* March 10, 1917).

in the nick of time that the land route was organized sufficiently to bear the strain. Henceforward the whole supply of the Peninsula was dependent upon 100 miles of bullock transport over a single road, itself vulnerable from the sea.

The Naval History of Britain contains no page more wonderful than that which records the prowess of her submarines at the Dardanelles. Their exploits constitute in daring, in skill, in endurance, in risk, the finest examples of submarine action in the whole of the Great War, and were, moreover, marked by a strict observance of the recognized rules of warfare. When one thinks of these officers and men, penned together amid the intricate machinery which crammed their steel, cigar-shaped vessels; groping, butting, charging far below the surface at unmeasured, unknown obstructions; surrounded by explosive engines, any one of which might destroy them at a touch; the target of guns and torpedoes if they rose for an instant to the light of day; harried by depth charges, hunted by gunboats and destroyers, stalked by the German U-boat; expecting every moment to be shattered, stifled, or hopelessly starved at the bottom of the sea; and yet in spite of all, enduring cheerfully such ordeals for weeks at a time; returning unflinchingly again and again through the Jaws of Death—it is bitter indeed to remember that their prowess and devotion were uncrowned by victory.

At the end of the first week in July, Lord Kitchener resolved to add the 53rd and 54th Territorial Divisions to the reinforcements that were going to the Dardanelles.

There is no principle of war better established than that everything should be massed for the battle. The lessons of military history, the practice of great commanders, the doctrines of the text-books, have in every age enjoined this rule. We see Napoleon before his battles grasping for every man he can reach, neglecting no resource however small, cheerfully accepting risks at other points, content with nothing less than the absolute maximum which human power can command.

This high prudence cannot be discerned in Lord Kitchener's preparations at this time. He did not decide to add the 53rd and 54th Divisions to the reinforcements that were going to the Dardanelles until it was impossible for the second of them to arrive before the battle had begun, thus having to go direct into action from a three weeks' voyage. The position of the troops in Egypt continued until the last moment undetermined. Including the Dardanelles details nearly 75,000 men were accumulated in Alexandria, Cairo and along the Canal. As long as we were threatening Constantinople there could be no danger of a serious Turkish invasion of Egypt. It should have been possible to organize from General Maxwell's troops at least 30,000 additional rifles as a reserve which could be thrown into the Gallipoli operations at the decisive moment and for a limited period. If General Maxwell had been ordered to organize such a force, and if Sir Ian Hamilton had been told that he could count it among the troops available for the battle, it would have been woven into the plans which were being prepared and would have sensibly improved the prospects. Lord Kitchener's treatment of the question was, however, most baffling. His telegraphic correspondence with Sir Ian Hamilton, which has been published, shows him at one moment counting large numbers of troops in Egypt as available if necessary for the Dardanelles, and at another chiding Sir Ian for attempting to draw on them. In consequence the British garrison of Egypt played no part in Sir Ian Hamilton's calculations and plans, and was only thrown in, like so much else, too late.

When on the eve of the battle, July 29, Lord Kitchener telegraphed to Sir Ian Hamilton informing him that he had "a total of about 205,000 men for the forthcoming operation," the General replied: "The grand total you mention does not take into account non-effectives or casualties; it includes reinforcements such as the 54th and part of the 53rd Divisions, etc., which cannot be here in time for my operation, and it also includes Yeomanry and Indian troops which, until this morning, I was unaware were at my unreserved disposal. For the coming operation the number of rifles available is about half the figure you quote, viz., 120,000." This figure was not effectively disputed by the War Office.

I was not able to discover the shortage of drafts, nor was I aware of the ambiguous conditions under which the garrison of Egypt was available as a reserve. But a young Staff Officer from the Dardanelles, who reached London in July, disclosed to me the shortage of ammunition and suggested that consignments sent by rail to Marseilles instead of by sea might still reach the Army in time for the battle. I therefore urged Lord Kitchener to send the whole of the latest weekly outputs by this route. Usually most kind and patient with my importunity, he took this request very much amiss. I declared I would demand a Cabinet decision, and we parted abruptly. I spent the afternoon and evening marshalling opinion, and informed the Prime Minister of my intention to raise the issue. However, when the decks were cleared for action and I was invited to state my case, Lord Kitchener ended the matter by stating that he had now found it possible to issue the necessary orders. Three train-loads of high explosive shell went accordingly.

Upon such preludes the event was now to supervene.

CHAPTER XXXIV

THE BATTLE OF SUVLA BAY

The long and varied annals of the British Army contain no more heart-breaking episode than the Battle of Suvla Bay. The greatness of the prize in view, the narrowness by which it was missed, the extremes of valiant skill and of incompetence, of effort and inertia, which were equally presented, the malevolent fortune which played about the field, are features not easily to be matched in our history. The tale has been often told, and no more than a general survey can here be attempted.[1]

Sir Ian Hamilton's plan had for its supreme object the capture of Hill 971 (Koja Chemen Tepe), the dominating point of the Sari Bair Ridge, and working from there, to grip the neck of the Peninsula from Gaba Tepe to Maidos. This conception was elaborated as follows:

(1) To break out with a rush from Anzac and cut off the bulk of the Turkish Army from land communication with Constantinople.

(2) To gain artillery positions which would cut off the bulk of the Turkish Army from sea traffic whether with Constantinople or with Asia.

(3) To secure Suvla Bay as a winter base for Anzac and all the troops operating in that neighbourhood.

For this purpose three separate attacks were prepared in extreme detail by the Army Staff during the month of July: first, a holding attack by two of the six divisions at Helles to prevent the Turks from removing any troops from this sector of the front; secondly, a great attack from Anzac on the main and dominating ridge of Sari Bair by the two Australasian divisions, reinforced by the 13th New Army Division and one British and one Indian brigade; and thirdly, a landing by two divisions (the 10th and 11th) forming the IXth Corps at Suvla Bay to secure the Anafarta Ridge and join their right hands to the Anzac attack and help it as it progressed.

The Helles sector was held by 35,000 men under General Davies. To the Anzac attack were assigned 37,000 under General Birdwood; and to the Suvla attack, 25,000 under General Stopford; the whole aggregating, with a reserve

---

[1] See Map on p. 505.

on the islands or approaching on the sea of 20,000 to 25,000, about 120,000 fighting men.

The Turks believed that the British had received reinforcements amounting perhaps to 100,000 men, and they expected a general attack, together with a landing, early in August. They realized that the Sari Bair Ridge was the key to the Narrows; they were apprehensive of landings near Kum Tepe or near Bulair, and in addition they had to guard the Asiatic shore. They knew that Suvla and Ejelmer Bays were possible landing-places, but they did not regard landings there as sufficiently probable to warrant further dissipation of their strength. On the evening of August 6 their dispositions were as follows: at Helles, 40,000 rifles with 94 guns; opposite Anzac and between Anzac and Helles, 30,000 rifles, supported by 76 guns; at Bulair, 20,000 rifles and 80 guns; on the Asiatic coast, 20,000 rifles with about 60 guns. In all, including detachments of troops guarding the coast at various points, the Turks had been able to marshal 20 divisions, comprising about 120,000 rifles with 330 guns, and of these 90,000 to 100,000 men and 270 guns were actually on the Gallipoli Peninsula.

The forces on both sides available for the battle are thus seen to be approximately equal. The British did not possess any of the preponderance necessary for an offensive. Once their attack was fully disclosed and battle was joined along the whole front, there was no reasonable expectation of their being able to defeat the Turkish Army. There was, however, a chance of seizing vital positions by surprise before the Turks could bring up all their forces. The situation, in fact, exactly reproduces that of April 25, but on a larger scale. Once again the advantages of sea power have been neutralized by delay and the enemy given time to gather forces equal to our own; once again a frightful and dubious ordeal has taken the place of a sound and reasonably sure operation; once again the only hope lies in the devotion of the troops and the skill of their leaders; once again all is at the mercy of time and chance.

On the afternoon of August 6 the great battle began with the attack of the Lancashire and Lowland Territorial Divisions on about 1,200 yards of the Turkish line at Helles. As it chanced, the Turks had just brought up two fresh divisions to this front. They were found in great strength, and their trench systems swarmed with men. Fierce fighting began at once and was maintained with increasing severity for a whole week. The conflict centred round a vineyard which was stormed at the outset by the British and held by them against repeated counter-attacks until the 12th, when it was recaptured by the enemy, who the next day were driven out by the British, with whom in the end it remained. It was not the only prize which had been purchased by costly valour. Of the seven Turkish divisions concentrated at the southern end of the Peninsula only one could be withdrawn to play its part in the real crisis of the battle.

Simultaneously with the British attack at Helles there began on the evening of the 6th an Australian attack on the Lone Pine Ridge to the right of the Anzac position. This attack was itself a subsidiary preliminary to the main Anzac operation. Its object was to deceive the enemy and draw him to the Anzac right, while all the time the decisive manœuvre was to proceed out on the Anzac left. Lone Pine Ridge and the fortifications surmounting it were stormed by the 1st Australian Brigade before sundown. The great beams which covered the Turkish trenches, converting them in the absence of adequate howitzer attack, into completely protected galleries, were torn asunder by main force. The Australians plunged through the apertures and slew or captured the defenders of the galleries. The Turks immediately counter-attacked with the utmost fury and in large numbers. Intense and bloody fighting continued at this point throughout the night. It was renewed on the 7th and again on a great scale on the 9th, but every hostile effort to retake Lone Pine failed, and it rested to the end in the strong hands of the 1st Australian Brigade. Other attacks akin and supplemental to the assault of Lone Pine were delivered by the Australians against various fortified points in the centre of their line, particularly upon a redoubt called the Chessboard. In spite of every sacrifice no ground was gained, and the attacking parties were in some cases almost completely destroyed.

While the roar of the cannonade at Helles and at Lone Pine resounded through the Peninsula, the great sortie from Anzac had begun. Each night for a week beforehand powerful reinforcements of troops had secretly and skilfully been crowded into Anzac Cove and lay concealed in gulleys and dugouts, until on August 6 General Birdwood's force comprised 37,000 men and 72 guns. Now in the darkness of a moonless night 16,000 men in two main columns crept out from the left of the Anzac position, toiled silently a mile along the beach, then wheeled to their right and proceeded to attack by three rugged, scrub-entangled, water-formed ravines which led up to the fateful summits of Sari Bair. The opening phase of this extraordinary enterprise involved the seizure of the fortified under-features to the left and right of the three ravines. The forces to whom these tasks had been assigned gained punctually and successfully both these strong points, and the main columns continued through the night to battle their way upward against darkness, boulders, scrub and the enemy's outposts. The hope of General Birdwood, of Sir Ian Hamilton, and of the staffs had been that dawn would see the heads of the Australian and British columns in possession of the decisive summits of Chunuk Bair and Koja Chemen Tepe. It would not have taken in daylight more than two hours to cover the distance unopposed. Six hours had been allowed under the actual conditions. But when dawn broke, the difficulties of the night and of the ground, and the stubborn and disconcerting resistance of the Turkish skirmishes, had prevented more than half the distance being covered. The troops were exhausted, and, after some vain efforts, it was determined to consolidate the position gained, to rest and reorganize the troops, and to renew the attack during the night of the 7th–8th.

Here was the cardinal fatality. Had it been possible to have leap-frogged the exhausted troops by a wave of fresh reinforcements, the whole crest of Sari Bair might well have fallen before noon into our possession. It had not been found possible to organize this in the face of the difficulties of the ground and of supplies, and meanwhile the direction and scale of the attack were now fully disclosed to the enemy.

It is at this point that we must move on to Suvla Bay. A number of the steel-plated motor-lighters which Lord Fisher had designed at the end of 1914 for the landing of troops upon hostile beaches had now been completed and sent to the Dardanelles. They were designed to carry five hundred infantry at a time at a speed of five knots, were bullet-proof and fitted with landing-bridges at their bows. Their appearance gained them throughout the ægean the nickname of "Beetles." In thirteen of these Beetles, with numerous destroyers lighters and transports, covered by a strong squadron of the Fleet, the 11th Division, followed by the 10th, had been moving through the blackest night towards Suvla Bay. Two hours before midnight the three brigades of the 11th Division reached the shore, the 34th Brigade landing at "A" Beach inside Suvla Bay, the 32nd and 33rd Brigades at "B" and "C" Beaches south of Nibrunesi Point. In spite of the rifle fire of the Turkish outposts guarding the coast, of the grounding of some of the Beetles before they reached the shore, and the disconcerting effect from land mines which exploded near Beach "A," the whole three brigades disembarked successfully without much loss in two or three hours. Their immediate duty was to occupy the two small eminences, Hill 10 and Lala Baba, on each side of the dried-up Salt Lake, and to take possession of the high ground to the northwards towards Kiretch Tepe Sirt. Thereafter as a second step a combined attack was to be made by the troops at Hill 10 and Lala Baba upon Chocolate Hill. If this was successful, the advance was to be continued against the rugged, scrub-covered and intricate under-feature known as Ismail Oglu Tepe. It was contemplated by the Staff that unless strong forces of the enemy were encountered, all these positions might well be in the hands of the troops by dawn. The event, however, turned very differently.[1]

It was 2 a.m. before the half battalion of Turks holding Lala Baba had been driven off and the hill occupied. Meanwhile the Brigadier commanding the 34th Brigade, having landed at Beach "A," perceived a sand-hill near the shore which he took to be Hill 10, and was content to occupy this until dawn. It was

---

[1] All these positions can be followed on the Map on p. 505.

broad daylight before Hill 10 was taken and its surviving defenders retired slowly into the scrub of the plain. Thus the morning of the 7th saw only the first part of the task of the 11th Division accomplished, and as the light grew stronger Turkish artillery from unseen positions in the hills began fitfully to shell the various Beaches and the landed troops. Darkness exercises so baffling and mysterious an effect upon the movements even of the most experienced troops that the time-table of the Staff may well be deemed too ambitious. But the performance fell far short of reasonable expectation. The British Intelligence believed that five Turkish battalions, aggregating 4,000 men with artillery, were guarding this part of the coast. In fact, however, only three battalions, two of which were gendarmerie, aggregating about 1,800 men and 20 guns, stood in the path of the 11th Division.

The 10th Division, under General Hill, now approached the shore near Lala Baba and began to disembark from dawn onwards under an occasional shell-fire. By 8 a.m. thirteen battalions of the 11th Division, two mountain batteries and the covering ships were all in action, and the 10th Division was rapidly growing behind them. This force, rising as the day passed to 20,000 men, had only to advance three miles from their landing-places to brush before them what was left of the 1,800 Turks and occupy positions where water was plentiful and which were of decisive importance in this part of the field. Instead of doing this all the troops that had landed either remained idle near Lala Baba for many hours or toiled along the sandy shore around the Salt Lake, a march of five miles in the heat of the day, before attacking Chocolate Hill. Thirst and exhaustion afflicted these young soldiers, and the evening was far advanced before by a spirited attack they made themselves masters of Chocolate Hill. Night closed with the troops much wearied, with their units intermingled, their water supply in confusion, and with only their earliest objectives obtained. About a thousand casualties had been sustained, and these were almost entirely confined to three or four battalions. Thus passed the first twenty-four hours at Suvla Bay.

On the evening of August 6 the field telephones had carried the news of the beginning of the battle to General Liman von Sanders in his headquarters at Gallipoli, almost as soon as he heard the opening of the cannonade. Heavy British and Australian attacks were beginning at Helles and at Lone Pine, while at the same time British feints in the Gulf of Xeros and opposite Mitylene were reported as actual or prospective landings. Precious as were the moments, it was impossible to take any measures before the intention of the assailants was fully disclosed. But before midnight news was received that large masses of troops were moving out from the left of the Anzac position along the coast northwards, and later, that numerous disembarkations were taking place at Suvla Bay. Two divisions in reserve at Maidos were ordered to reinforce the defenders of

Sari Bair. These could certainly come into action during the next day. Suvla Bay, however, was an inevitable surprise against which it would not have been reasonable to prepare on a great scale beforehand. Who could measure the strength of the attack? A division, two divisions, an entire corps, two corps—no one could tell. But whatever might be the strength of the invaders there stood between them and the vital positions of Kiretch Tepe Sirt, the Anafarta Ridge and Ismail Oglu Tepe, only the German Major Willmer with one battalion of Gallipoli gendarmes, one of Brussa gendarmes and one of the 31st regiment with 20 guns. No help could come from the south; all was becoming locked in general battle there. Liman von Sanders, repeating his procedure of April 26, ordered the 7th and 12th Divisions to march at once from Bulair to Suvla Bay, and all the troops on the Asiatic side to cross to Gallipoli. Once again, Asia and the vital Bulair lines must be left virtually unguarded, the easy spoil of any new disembarkation. "For the second time," says the German Commander, "the upper part of the Gulf of Xeros was completely denuded of troops and on the entire Asiatic side only three battalions and a few batteries had been left behind for coast defence." The 7th Turkish Division received orders to march at 3:40 a.m. and the 12th at 8:30 a.m. on August 7. Both divisions started from the neighbourhood of Bulair by the two roads running southward along the Peninsula. *The distance between them and Suvla Bay was more than thirty miles.*

It seemed to General von Sanders that no effective help could reach Major Willmer and his gendarmerie before the night of the 8th, and that no serious counter-attacks could be launched before the morning of the 9th. Daylight of the 7th revealed the extent of the British landings. The great Armada filled the Bay, its guns searched the hills, and swarms of troops were landing in successive waves upon the beach and gathering in the plain. Far away to the north the 7th and 12th Turkish Divisions, forming the XVIth Turkish Army Corps, had only just begun their march. However, during the afternoon Fezi Bey, the Turkish General commanding the Corps, reported, to Sanders's extreme surprise, that his two divisions had reached their destinations east of Anafarta, having covered a double march in the day. On this Sanders ordered a general attack at dawn on the 8th into the Anafarta Plain. Before daybreak on the 8th he mounted his horse and rode to the deployment area of this attack. He wandered about for some time looking vainly for his troops. He found at length a Staff Officer of the 7th Turkish Division, who reported that he was looking for an outpost position, that a large part of the 7th and 12th Divisions were still far behind, and that an attack that morning was out of the question. The Commander-in-Chief therefore ordered the attack to begin at sunset. He passed the day of the 8th in great anxiety, having still nothing between him and the immense forces of the invader but the exhausted and much reduced gendarmerie. Four hundred men, the remains of the Brussa gendarmes and of the 2nd/31st battalion, were at Ismail Oglu Tepe. Three hundred men, the remains of the Gallipoli gendarmes, were on Kiretch Tepe Sirt. There were no troops between these two points. Kavak and Tekke hills and all the low intervening ground was absolutely unoccupied. In these circumstances all the Turkish guns, except one, were withdrawn behind the Anafarta Ridge to avoid what seemed to be their otherwise inevitable capture. Towards evening General von Sanders learned from Major Willmer that the XVIth Turkish Corps had not yet arrived at its area of deployment. He summoned its commander to his presence and learned from him that the exhausted condition of the troops did not permit of any attack before the morning of the 9th. In his indignation at having been mocked by false hopes, he dismissed the General of the XVIth Corps and confided the vital fortunes of the whole of the Ottoman Empire to an officer of whom we have heard before—and since. "That same evening," he writes, "I transferred the command of all the troops in the Anafarta sector to Mustapha Kemal Bey, formerly commanding the 19th Division."

We must now return to the Anzacs and Sari Bair. The whole of the 7th was spent by General Birdwood's troops in reorganizing, resting and preparing for renewed battle at dawn. The line of Ghurkas, British and Anzacs lay across the mountain slopes, having gained about two-thirds of the distance to their summits. But those summits were now guarded by three times the defenders of the night before.

The advance from Anzac was resumed before dawn on the 8th. The right and centre columns, starting from Rhododendron Spur, assaulted Chunuk Bair. The left column starting from the head of the most northerly of the three ravines attacked Hill Q, a knoll upon the main ridge separated by a dip from Koja Chemen Tepe. This was a restriction of the original front of attack. An intense struggle now began and raged for three days without cessation. The right column of New Zealand troops soon after daybreak seized, conquered and held a substantial position on the south-western end of Chunuk Bair, and thus established themselves on the main ridge. The centre and left columns, unsupported by any help from Suvla Bay, were unable to make much progress. Night quenched for a while the bloody conflict. Meanwhile fresh Turkish troops continually reached the defence, and owing to the difficulties of water and ground no reinforcements could be employed in the attack.

The battle was renewed with undiminished fury on the 9th. The Anzac right maintained itself on Chunuk Bair; its left attacked Hill Q; its centre sought to join these two positions by occupying the saddle between them. These operations were preceded and sustained by an intense bombardment of every available gun of the Fleet and Army. The left attack, delayed by the darkness and the ground, was late in coming into action and failed to take Hill Q.

But in spite of this the 6th Ghurkas and two companies of the 6th South Lancashires, belonging to the centre, striving upwards, gained command of vital positions on the saddle between Chunuk Bair and Hill Q. The heroic officer, Colonel Cecil Allanson, in command of the 6th Ghurkas, who led the assault, has recorded his experiences in the tragedy which followed.[1] He passed the night of the 8th–9th in the firing line.

At an angle of about 35 degrees and about a hundred yards away were the Turks. . . . During the night a message came to me from the General Officer Commanding to try and get up on to 971 at 5:15 a.m., and that from 4:45 to 5:15 the Navy would bombard the top. I was to get all troops near me to co-operate. . . . As I could only get three companies of British troops, I had to be satisfied with this. . . . I had only 15 minutes left; the roar of the artillery preparation was enormous; the hill, which was almost perpendicular, seemed to leap underneath one. I recognized that if we flew up the hill the moment it stopped, we ought to get to the top. I put the three companies into the trenches among my men, and said that the moment they saw me go forward carrying a red flag, every one was to start. I had my watch out, 5:15. I never saw such artillery preparation; the trenches were being torn to pieces; the accuracy was marvellous, as we were only just below. At 5:18 it had not stopped, and I wondered if my watch was wrong. 5:20 silence; I waited three minutes to be certain, great as the risk was. Then off we dashed, all hand in hand, a most perfect advance, and a wonderful sight. . . . At the top we met the Turks; Le Marchand was down, a bayonet through the heart. I got one through the leg, and then for about what appeared 10 minutes, we fought hand to hand, we bit and fisted, and used rifles and pistols as clubs; and then the Turks turned and fled, and I felt a very proud man; the key of the whole Peninsula was ours, and our losses had not been so very great for such a result. Below I saw the Straits, motors and wheeled transport, on the roads leading to Achi Baba. As I looked round I saw we were not being supported, and thought I could help best by going after those [Turks] who had retreated in front of us. We dashed down towards Maidos, but had only got about 100 feet down when suddenly our own Navy put six 12-in. monitor shells into us, and all was terrible confusion.[2] It was a deplorable disaster; we were obviously mistaken for Turks, and we had to get back. It was an appalling sight: the first hit a Ghurka in the face; the place was a mass of

[1] Written forty-eight hours after the event.
[2] The size of these shells and who fired them has never been established.

THE BATTLE OF SUVLA BAY

blood and limbs and screams, and we all flew back to the summit and to our old position just below.[1] I remained on the crest with about 15 men; it was a wonderful view; below were the Straits, reinforcements coming over from the Asia Minor side, motor-cars flying. We commanded Kilid Bahr, and the rear of Achi Baba and the communications to all their Army there. . . . I was now left alone much crippled by the pain of my wound, which was stiffening, and loss of blood. I saw the advance at Suvla Bay had failed, though I could not detect more than one or two thousand against them, but I saw large Turkish reinforcements being pushed in that direction. My telephone lines were smashed. . . . I now dropped down into the trenches of the night before, and after getting my wound bound up, proceeded to try and find where all the regiment was; I got them all back in due course, and awaited support before moving up the hill again. Alas! it was never to come, and we were told to hold our position throughout the night of the 9th–10th. During the afternoon we were counter-attacked by large bodies of Turks five times between 5 and 7 p.m., but they never got to within 15 yards of our line. . . . Captain Tomes and Le Marchand are buried on the highest summit of the Chunuk Bair. . . . I was ordered back to make a report. I was very weak and faint. . . . I reported to the General, and told him that unless strong reinforcements were pushed up, and food and water could be sent us, we must come back, but that if we did we gave up the key of the Gallipoli Peninsula. The General then told me that nearly everywhere else the attack had failed, and the regiment would be withdrawn to the lower hills early next morning.

The morning of the 10th dawned on these vain prodigies of devotion. Twelve thousand men, at least half of those actually involved in the severity of the fighting, had fallen, and the terrible summits flamed unconquered as ever. Nevertheless the Anzac right held with relieved troops their important gain on the Chunuk Bair, and against this the Turkish reserves were darkly gathering.

We have seen how General Liman von Sanders spent May 8, awaiting with impatience in the hills behind Anafarta the arrival of reinforcements from Bulair. What meanwhile was happening at Suvla Bay? Our military annals, old and new, are not so lacking in achievement, that one need shrink from faithful record.

Lieutenant-General Sir Frederick Stopford, Commander of the 9th Corps,

---

[1] 150 men are said to have been killed by these shells.

had arrived with his staff in the sloop *Jonquil* at daylight on the 7th. He had remained on the *Jonquil* on account of the facilities of wireless and signal communication. During the afternoon of the 8th he had paid a visit to the shore. General Stopford was an agreeable and cultivated gentleman who fifteen years before had served in the South African War as Military Secretary to Sir Redvers Buller. After commanding the London District, he had left the Army in 1909, and had lived until the outbreak of the great struggle in a retirement unhappily marked by much ill-health. From this seclusion he had been drawn, like many others by the enormous expansion of our land forces. He had been entrusted by Lord Kitchener with the task of training an Army Corps in England, and he now found himself for the first time in his life in a position of high and direct responsibility and in actual command of troops in the presence of the enemy. In these circumstances we are certainly entitled to assume that he did his best.

The natural disquietudes with which he had contemplated the nocturnal landing on a hostile shore were no sooner relieved by success, than another set of serious considerations presented themselves. The enemy might be more numerous than the Staff believed; they might have more trenches than the aeroplane reconnaissance had reported. Moreover, they might at any time resume the desultory shelling of the Beaches which had died away on the evening of the 7th. In this situation the measures which he considered most necessary were the reorganization of the troops who had landed, the improvement of their supplies particularly in regard to water, the digging of trenches to secure the ground they had gained, and the landing of as much artillery as possible to support their further advance. In these occupations August 8, the second twenty-four hours since the landing, passed peacefully away, while his Chief-of-Staff, General Reed, who shared his Chief's outlook to the full, prepared the orders and arrangements for an advance at daybreak on the 9th. "The second day of the IXth Corps' stay at Suvla," writes General Callwell, at this time Director of Operations at the War Office, "was, from the fighting point of view, practically a day of rest." [1] We may pause to survey the scene on both sides of the front this sunny August afternoon. On the one hand, the placid, prudent, elderly English gentleman with his 20,000 men spread around the Beaches, the front lines sitting on the tops of shallow trenches, smoking and cooking, with here and there an occasional rifle shot, others bathing by hundreds in the bright blue bay where, disturbed hardly by a single shell, floated the great ships of war: on the other, the skilful German stamping with impatience for the arrival of his divisions, expecting with every hour to see his scanty covering forces brushed aside, while the furious Kemal animated his fanatic soldiers and hurled them forward towards the battle.

[1] *The Dardanelles Campaign*, p. 229.

• • •

Sir Ian Hamilton's General Staff Officer for Operations, Colonel Aspinall, had been ordered to report on the Suvla situation for the Commander-in-Chief. He arrived on the morning of the 8th. He has written a graphic account[1] of the peaceful scene that met his gaze. When his first incredulity had been confirmed by a tour of the shore, he proceeded on board the *Jonquil* where the Corps Commander still had his headquarters.

> General Stopford greeted me by "Well, Aspinall, the men have done splendidly and have been magnificent." "But they haven't reached the hills, Sir," I replied. "No," he answered, "but they are ashore!" I replied that I was sure the Commander-in-Chief would be disappointed that they had not yet reached the high ground covering the Bay, in accordance with the orders, and I impressed upon him the urgent importance of moving forward at the earliest possible moment, before the enemy's reinforcements forestalled him on the hills. General Stopford replied that he quite realized the importance of losing no time, but that it was impossible to advance until the men had rested. He intended to make a fresh advance on the following day.
>
> I then went on board the Admiral's flagship and sent the following telegram to General Headquarters:
>
> "Just been ashore where I found all quiet. No rifle fire, no artillery fire, and apparently no Turks. IX Corps resting. Feel confident that golden opportunities are being lost and look upon situation as serious."
>
> Shortly after sending this message I heard that the Commander-in-Chief was already on his way to Suvla, and a few minutes later he came in to harbour on the Admiral's yacht.

The harmony of Suvla Bay was marred late in the afternoon by the arrival of the Commander-in-Chief. Sir Ian Hamilton had been persuaded by his Staff that his proper place during this great triple battle was in his regular headquarters at Imbros. Here then he remained during the whole of the 7th and the morning of the 8th, digesting such information as the telegrams from the various sectors of the front contained. But at 11:30 on the morning of the 8th he became so disquieted with the want of news from Suvla that he could bear his isolation no longer, and determined to go there at once. A destroyer, the *Arno,* had been specially placed at his disposal by the Navy for the period of the oper-

---

[1] Colonel Aspinall has placed this statement at my disposal.

ations, and to the *Arno* accordingly signals for instant departure were made. It then appeared that the local Rear-Admiral had for reasons connected with the condition of the boilers, ordered the fires to be drawn from this vessel, and that she could not move for six or seven hours. Finding himself thus, in his own words, "marooned," the Commander-in-Chief became both distressed and indignant. His complaints induced the local Rear-Admiral to offer him a passage on the yacht *Triad*, which was leaving for Suvla at 4:15 p.m. On this accordingly the General embarked and reached Suvla Bay about 6 o'clock. Here he found the *Chatham* with Admiral de Robeck and Commodore Keyes on board. They expressed to him their profound uneasiness at the paralysis which seemed to have seized upon the troops. On the top of this came Colonel Aspinall. On hearing his report the Commander-in-Chief boarded the *Jonquil*, where he found General Stopford, tired from his walk on the shore, but otherwise happy. General Stopford said that "everything was quite all right and going well." He proceeded to explain that the men had been very tired, that he had not been able to get water up to them or land his guns as quickly as he hoped; he had therefore decided to postpone the occupation of the high ground which "might lead to a regular battle" until next morning; that meanwhile the Brigadiers had been told to gain what ground they could without serious fighting, but that actually they had not occupied any dominating tactical point.

The Commander-in-Chief did not accept this result. He knew that reinforcements were marching southward from Bulair. He believed that the Anafarta Ridge was still unoccupied by any appreciable enemy force. He apprehended, and rightly, that what might be gained on the evening of the 8th without fighting, would involve a bloody struggle in the dawn. He urged an immediate advance on Ismail Oglu and Tekke hills. General Stopford raised a number of objections, and the Commander-in-Chief determined to visit the Divisional Headquarters on shore and see for himself. General Stopford did not accompany him.

General Hammersley, the Divisional Commander, was not able to give a very clear account of the situation, and after a considerable discussion the Commander-in-Chief determined personally to intervene. General Hammersley had told him that the 32nd Brigade was available in the neighbourhood of Sulajik and was capable of moving forward. Sir Ian Hamilton thereupon told the Divisional Commander "in the most distinct terms that he wished this Brigade to advance and dig themselves in on the crest line." General Hammersley apparently concurred in this, and afterwards claimed that he had acted on his own responsibility, not as the result of a direct order, but of the expression of a wish personally made by the Commander-in-Chief. Accordingly after Sir Ian Hamilton had returned to the *Triad*, General Hammersley directed the

32nd Brigade to concentrate and endeavour to gain a foothold on the high ground north of Kuchuk Anafarta. He specially mentioned the 6th East York-shire Battalion as one that should be recalled from its existing position and con-centrated. On these decisions darkness fell.

The 32nd Brigade was not, however, disposed as its Divisional Commander imagined. On the contrary, with praiseworthy initiative two battalions had pushed forward far in advance of the rest of the 9th Corps, and finding no op-position, one had occupied a good position near Abrikjar and the other was ac-tually entrenching itself on Scimitar Hill. It is extraordinary that on such a quiet day this should not have been known at the Divisional Headquarters less than two miles away. Both these battalions were recalled from the positions which they had gained and were concentrated for the advance to Kuchuk Ana-farta. These movements deranged the general plan of attack which was fixed for dawn; they involved the evacuation of the valuable position of Scimitar Hill, never afterwards, in spite of all efforts, to be regained. Nor in the end was it possible for the 32nd Brigade to make its attack until daybreak.

At dawn on the morning of the 9th the British advance from Suvla was at last resumed. The attack was delivered by the 11th Division, the 31st Brigade of the 10th Division, and by some battalions of the 53rd Territorial Division which had been newly landed, and was directed against the high ground from Kuchuk Anafarta on the left to Ismail Oglu Hill. Simultaneously, however, the counter-attack ordered by Liman von Sanders also began. The leading reinforcements from the 7th and 12th Turkish Divisions had arrived overnight, and the enemy was perhaps three times as strong as on the previous day and constantly in-creasing. No sooner had the 6th East Yorkshire Battalion been withdrawn from Scimitar Hill than the Turks had reoccupied it. It was necessary that this hill should be taken before an effective advance could be made on its right against Ismail Oglu Hill. The 31st Brigade of the 10th Division therefore assaulted Scimitar Hill, but was unable to recapture it, and the whole of the right of the attack was prejudiced in consequence of the failure to regain this feature. The 32nd Brigade on the left of the line likewise failed to reach its goal, and in parts of the front the troops were driven back in disorder by the ardour with which the Turkish newcomers threw themselves into the fight.

The rest of the 53rd Division were landed during the 9th, and the battle was renewed on the morning of the 10th and maintained all day. Both Scimi-tar and Ismail Oglu Hills were partially captured, but were lost again under the pressure of violent counter-attacks. When night fell over the battlefield, lurid with the fiercely burning scrub, the IXth Corps occupied positions very little more advanced than those which it had gained on the first day of its land-ing, and ample Turkish forces stood entrenched and victorious upon all the decisive positions. The losses had not exceeded a thousand on the 7th, but nearly 8,000 officers and men were killed or wounded at Suvla Bay on the 9th and 10th.

The closing event of the battle has now to be recorded. When daylight broke on the morning of the 10th the British from Anzac still held their hard-won positions on Chunuk Bair. Two battalions of the 13th Division—the 6th North Lancashires and the 5th Wiltshires—had relieved the worn-out troops who had stormed the hill. They had barely settled down in their new position when they were exposed to a tremendous attack. After his successful action at Suvla Bay on the 9th, Mustapha Kemal passed the night in preparing a supreme effort to regain this priceless ridge. The whole of the Turkish 8th Division brought from the Asiatic shore with three additional battalions and aided by a powerful and converging artillery were led forward to the assault by Mustapha Kemal in person. The thousand British rifles—all for whom room could be found on the narrow summit—were engulfed and overwhelmed in this fierce flood. Very few of the Lancashire men escaped, and the Wiltshire battalion was literally annihilated. Flushed with victory the Turks pressed over the summit and poured down the steep face of the mountain in dense waves of men intent on driving the invaders into the sea. But here they encountered directly the whole blast of fire from the Fleet and from every gun and machine gun in the Anzac-British line. Under this storm the advancing Turkish masses were effectually crushed. Of three or four thousand men who descended the seaward slopes of the hill, only a few hundred regained the crest. But there they stayed—and stayed till the end of the story. Thus by the 10th the whole of the second great effort to win the Straits had ended at all points without decisive gains.

Two serious actions had still to be fought before the failure was accepted as final. The 54th Territorial Division had now landed at Suvla, and with its support on the 15th and 16th two brigades of the 10th Irish Division attacked along the high Kiretch Tepe Sirt Ridge which bounds Suvla Bay on the north. Well supported by fire from the sea, these troops under General Mahon at first made good progress. But in the end they were compelled by counter-attacks and bombing to give up most of the ground they had gained. This action does not bulk very largely in British accounts, and its critical character seems scarcely to have been appreciated. Liman von Sanders says of it:

> If during their attacks on August 15 and 16 the British had captured and held the Kiretch Tepe, the whole position of the 5th Army would have been outflanked. The British might have then achieved a decisive and final victory.

A further effort was made on August 21, directed this time to the capture of Ismail Oglu Hill. For this purpose the 29th Division was brought from Helles and the dismounted Yeomanry Division from Egypt to reinforce the 10th, 11th, 53rd and 54th Divisions now all landed at Suvla Bay. Strong forces of the Anzac left under General Cox also co-operated. But the Turks were now perfectly fortified and in great strength. Less than sixty guns, only sixteen of which were even of medium calibre, were available to support the attack, and for these the supply of ammunition was exiguous. The battle was fiercely fought in burning scrub and a sudden and unusual mist hampered the attacking artillery, and though the Anzac left gained and held some valuable ground, no general results were achieved. "The attacks," said Liman von Sanders, "were repulsed by the Turks after heavy loss and after putting in the last reserve, including the cavalry." The British losses, particularly of the Yeomanry and the 29th Division who assaulted with the utmost determination, were heavy and fruitless. On this dark battlefield of fog and flame Brigadier-General Lord Longford, Brigadier-General Kenna, V.C., Colonel Sir John Milbanke, V.C., and other paladins fell. This was the largest action fought upon the Peninsula, and it was destined to be the last. Since the new offensive had begun the British losses had exceeded 45,000, while those of the Turks were not less than 40,000. Already on the 16th Sir Ian Hamilton had telegraphed to Lord Kitchener stating that 50,000 additional rifles and drafts of 45,000 were required to enable offensive operations to be continued. These reinforcements, for reasons which the next chapter will explain, the British Government found themselves unable to supply, and a complete deadlock supervened along the fronts of both battered and exhausted armies.

At every phase in the battle, down even to the last action on the 21st, the issue between victory and defeat hung trembling in the balance. The slightest change in the fell sequence of events would have been sufficient to turn the scale. But for the forty-eight precious hours lost by the IXth Corps at Suvla, positions must have been won from which decisive operations were possible. "We all felt," wrote Sanders, "that the British leaders at the successive landings which began on August 6 stayed too long on the beach instead of pushing forward inland at all costs from each landing-place." Had the experienced 29th Division been employed at this point, had the Yeomanry from Egypt been made available from the beginning, success could hardly have been denied. When it was too late leaders of the highest quality—Byng, Fanshawe, Maude—were sent from France to replace those whose inertia or incapacity had produced such grievous results. These new Generals could be spared on the morrow of disaster, but not while their presence might have commanded success.

THE RELATIVE STRENGTHS

Date.	Turkish Divisions: Rifles.		Actual British and French Divisions: Rifles.		Available [1] British and French Divisions: Rifles.	
February 18 . . . (Opening of the Naval Attack)	nil	5,000	nil	2,000	4	36,000
March 20 . . . (End of the Naval Attack)	2	14,000	4	40,000 (but without the 29th Division)	5	60,000
April 25 . . . (The first Military Attack)	6	42,000	5	50,000	5	60,000
July 7 . . . (Earliest date for the second Military Attack)	10	70,000–75,000	8	52,000	14	150,000 [2]
August 7 . . . (The Battle of Suvla Bay)	20 [4]	120,000	14	120,000	14	120,000 [3]

(uncertain weather) — {between February 18 and March 20}

The three favourable occasions are shown in squares. It needed only a stroke of the pen in Whitehall to have produced any of them.

[1] 'Available' means ready, doing nothing, capable of being sent so as to be on the spot on the date mentioned, and actually sent within a month of that date.

[2] British { From home: 29th, 42nd, 52nd, 10th, 11th, 13th, 53rd, 54th and Royal Naval Divisions 9
From Egypt: Yeomanry Division, Indian Division, and various details 2
Australasian: The Australian and New Zealand Army Corps 2
The French Corps (1 Division with additional Units) 1
                                                                                                  ——
                                                                            Total 14

[3] The reduction of 10,000 from the July figures is accounted for by a month's net wastage among the divisions already on the Peninsula.

[4] The following are the Turkish Divisions on the spot: 1st, 2nd, 3rd, 4th, 5th, 6th, 7th, 8th, 9th, 10th, 11th, 12th, 13th, 14th, 15th, 16th, 19th, 20th, 26th and 27th.

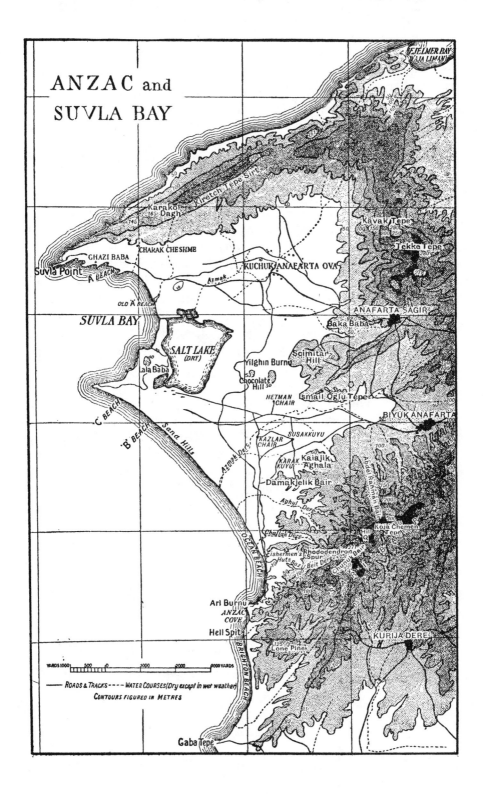

ANZAC and
SUVLA BAY

EJELMER BAY
ALA LIMANI

Kiretch Tepe Sirt

Karakol
Dagh

745

CHARAK CHESHME

GHAZI BABA

Suvla Point

A BEACH

KUCHUK ANAFARTA OVA

Azmak

OLD A BEACH

SUVLA BAY

Kavak Tepe

Tekke Tepe

ANAFARTA SAGIR

Baka Baba

SALT LAKE
(DRY)

Yilghin Burnu

Scimitar
Hill

Lala Baba

Chocolate
Hill

Ismail Oglu Tepe

HETMAN
CHAIR

C BEACH

BIYUK ANAFARTA

Sand Hills

B BEACH

KAZLAR
CHAIR

SUSAKKUYU

Azmak Dere

KARAK
KUYU

Kaiajik
Aghala

Abdel Rahman Bair

Damakjelik Bair

Aghyl Dere

Koja Chemen
Tepe

Chailak Dere

Hill

Fishermen's
Huts

Rhododendron
Spur
Beit Dere

Chunuk Bair

OCEAN BEACH

Ari Burnu

ANZAC
COVE

Hell Spit

KURIJA DERE

Lone Pine

BRIGHTON BEACH

YARDS 1000 500 0 1000 2000 3000 YARDS

—— ROADS & TRACKS ---- WATER COURSES (Dry except in wet weather)
CONTOURS FIGURED IN METRES

Gaba Tepe

Criticism severe and searching has been applied to many aspects of the Battle of Suvla Bay, but history will pronounce that it was not upon the Gallipoli Peninsula that it was lost. It is rarely that Opportunity returns. Yet in spite of the errors and misfortunes of the original operations, she had offered herself once more to our hand. But the golden moment was not in August. It was at the end of June or the beginning of July. And that moment was needlessly thrown away. "After the failure of the attacks which followed the first landing," say the Dardanelles Commissioners (Conclusion 5), "there was undue delay in deciding upon the course to be pursued in the future. Sir Ian Hamilton's appreciation was forwarded on May 17. It was not considered by the War Council or the Cabinet until June 7. The reconstruction of the Government which took place at this most critical period was the main cause of the delay. As a consequence the despatch of the reinforcements asked for by Sir Ian Hamilton in his appreciation was postponed for six weeks." This delay and the neglect to utilize the surplus forces in Egypt robbed us of the numerical superiority which it was in our power to command and which was essential to a victorious offensive. Had a reasonable action been taken even from May 17 onwards, as will be seen from the table on page 504, 15 allied divisions aggregating 150,000 rifles, could have attacked 10 Turkish divisions aggregating 70,000 to 75,000 rifles in the second week of July. Instead the mistakes which were committed in Downing Street and Whitehall condemned us gratuitously to a battle of equal numbers in August and to a hazard of the most critical kind, and from that hazard we emerged unsuccessful. The errors and miscarriages which took place upon the battlefield cannot be concealed, but they stand on a lower plane than these sovereign and irretrievable misdirections.

The cause of defeat is set forth in the cruel clarity of tabular statement on page 504.

CHAPTER XXXV

THE RUIN OF THE BALKANS[1]

The Christian States of the Balkans were the children of oppression and revolt. For four hundred years they had dwelt under the yoke of the Turkish
conqueror. They had recovered their freedom after cruel struggles only during
the last hundred years. Their national characteristics were marked by these hard
experiences. Their constitutions and dynasties resulted from them. Their populations were poor, fierce and proud. Their governments were divided from one
another by irreconcilable ambitions and jealousies. Every one of them at some
ancient period in its history had been the head of a considerable Empire in
these regions, and though Serbian and Bulgarian splendours had been of brief
duration compared to the glories of Greece, each looked back to this period
of greatness as marking the measure of its historic rights. All therefore simultaneously considered themselves entitled to the ownership of territories which
they had in bygone centuries possessed only in succession. All therefore were
plunged in convulsive quarrels and intrigues.

It is to this cause that their indescribable sufferings have been mainly and
primarily due. It was not easy for all or any of these small States to lift themselves out of this dismal and dangerous quagmire or find a firm foothold on
which to stand. Behind the national communities, themselves acting and reacting upon each other in confusion, there were in each country party and political divisions and feuds sufficient to shake a powerful Empire. Every Balkan
statesman had to thread his way to power in his own country through complications, dangers and surprising transformations, more violent, more intense than those which the domestic affairs of great nations revealed. He
arrived hampered by his past and pursued by foes and jealousies, and, thus harassed and weakened, had to cope with the ever-shifting combinations of
Balkan politics, as these in turn were influenced by the immense convulsions
of the Great War.

In addition to all this came the policy of the three great allied Powers.
France and Russia had each its own interests and outlook, its favourite Balkan
State and its favourite party in each State. Great Britain had a vague desire to

---

[1] See General Map of the Balkan Peninsula on p. 523.

507

see them all united, and a lofty impartiality and detachment scarcely less baffling. To this were super-added the distracting influences of the various Sovereigns and their Teutonic origins or relations. In consequence, the situation was
so chaotic and unstable, there were so many vehement points of view rising and
falling, that British, French and Russian statesmen never succeeded in devising
any firm, comprehensive policy. On the contrary, by their isolated, half-hearted
and often contradictory interventions, they contributed that culminating element of disorder which led every one of these small States successively to the
most hideous forms of ruin.

Yet all the time the main interests of the three great Allies and of the four
Balkan kingdoms were identical, and all could have been protected and advanced by a single and simple policy. The ambitions of every one of the Balkan
States could have been satisfied at the expense of the Turkish and Austrian Empires. There was enough for all, and more than enough. The interest of the
three great Allies was to range the Balkan States against these Empires. United
among themselves, the Balkan States were safe: joined to the three Allies, they
could not fail to gain the territories they coveted. The addition of the united
Balkan States to the forces of the *Entente* must have involved the downfall of
Austria and Turkey and the speedy, victorious termination of the war. For
everyone there was a definite prize. For Roumania, Transylvania; for Serbia,
Bosnia and Herzegovina, Croatia, Dalmatia and the Banat of Temesvar; for
Bulgaria, Adrianople and the Enos-Midia line; for Greece, Smyrna and its hin-
terland; and for all, safety, wealth and power.

To realize these advantages, certain concessions had to be made by the
Balkan States among themselves. Roumania could restore the Dobrudja to Bulgaria; Serbia could liberate the Bulgarian districts of Macedonia; Greece could
give Kavalla as a makeweight; and as an immediate solatium to Greece, there
was Cyprus which could have been thrown into the scale. As the final levers,
there were the financial resources of Great Britain and whatever military and
naval forces the *Entente* might decide to employ in this theatre.

It is astonishing that when all interests were the same, when so many powerful means of leverage and stimulus were at hand, everything should without
exception have gone amiss. If in February, 1915, or possibly after the Turkish
declaration of war in November, 1914, the British, French and Russian Governments could have agreed upon a common policy in the Balkans—and had sent
plenipotentiaries of the highest order to the Balkan Peninsula to negotiate on a
clear, firm basis with each and all of these States—a uniform, coherent action
could have been devised and enforced with measureless benefits to all concerned. Instead, the situation was dealt with by partial expedients suggested by
the rapid and baffling procession of events. Everything was vainly offered or

done by the Allies successively and tardily, which done all at once and in good time would have achieved the result.

The Balkan States offered by far the greatest possibility open to allied diplomacy at the beginning of 1915. This was never envisaged and planned as if it were the great battle which indeed it was. Fitful, sporadic, half-hearted, changeable, unrelated expedients were all that the statesmen of Russia, France and Britain were able to employ. Nor is it right for public opinion in these countries to condemn the Balkan States and Balkan politicians or sovereigns too sweepingly. The hesitations of the King of Roumania, the craft of King Ferdinand, the shifts and evasions of King Constantine, all arose from the baffling nature of the Balkan problem and the lack of policy of the Allies. Serbia, indeed, fought on desperately and blindly without consideration for any other interests but her own and with frightful consequences to herself, ultimately repaired only by the final victory. Roumania was throughout in peril of her life and perplexed to the foundations of her being. When at last, after infinite hesitations, bargainings and precautions, she entered the war, she was too late to decide or abridge the struggle but in good time to be torn in pieces. Bulgaria turned traitor alike to her past and to her future, and after many exertions was plunged in the woe of the vanquished. Greece, rescued in the nick of time by courage and genius, and emerging with little cost upon the side of the victors, survived incorrigible to squander all that she had gained. Yet in Roumania there was Také Jonesco always pointing clear and true; in Bulgaria, Stambulisky, braving the wrath of King Ferdinand and marching proudly to his long prison with the names of England and Russia on his lips; and in Greece, Venizelos, threading his way through indescribable embarrassments and triumphing over unimaginable difficulties, preserved his country for a time in spite of herself and might well have limited the miseries of Europe.

August, 1915, saw the culmination of the Russian disasters. By the end of June the German-Austrian offensive had driven the Russians out of nearly all the southern half of their huge Galician-Polish salient. This had been reduced to a semicircle 170 miles across, with Brest Litovsk at its centre and Warsaw almost on its outer circumference. Lemberg had been lost. Mackensen's front was now faced almost north and ahead of him lay the four railway lines which fed the salient. On July 13 he commenced, with a German and two Austrian Armies, an advance against the southernmost railway [the Kowel-Cholm-Lublin-Ivangorod line], with Field-Marshal Woyrsch on his left pressing eastward. By August 1 he was across the railway in the centre at Cholm and Lublin, and four days later Ivangorod and Warsaw were evacuated by the Russians. Novo-Georgievsk, where some eighty-five thousand second-class troops had been collected, made a show of defence, but capitulated on the 20th. But this was not the end of the disasters. In the north, in Lithuania, the German Eighth and Tenth Armies under Hindenburg, reinforced by German troops from the south where the line had been shortened, moved forward, and on August 10 had taken Kovno. All the Russian troops between Kovno and Riga were thus in danger of envelopment and fell back. Even Brest Litovsk, the long-vaunted model fortress, did not hold out long. Invested on August 11 on three sides, it was abandoned on the 26th after the forts on the south-west front had been stormed. Thus the last semblance of the great Salient had disappeared, and the Russian front, except for a forward bend covering Riga, had approximated to a north and south line. The Russians had evaded envelopment and capture, but all their gains in Galicia had gone, they had lost Poland, 325,000 prisoners and more than three thousand guns, besides rifles and equipment which it was impossible to replace. Worse than all, the Tsar was induced to remove the Grand Duke Nicholas from his command and send him to the Caucasus.

The Russian defeats from April onwards had reacted most unfortunately against Italy. In 1914 Austria could spare no more than local corps to watch the Italian frontier. By the date of the Italian declaration of war she had managed to collect 122 battalions, 10 squadrons and 216 guns against Italy, disposed in mixed groups behind carefully constructed entrenchments. But henceforward there was a constant flow of reinforcements from the Galician theatre. The Italian offensive towards Trieste, known as the first and second battles of the Isonzo, in June and July carried the Italians 6 miles into enemy territory, and thereafter left them as firmly rooted in trench warfare as the Armies on the Western Front. The Italian operations in the Tyrol led to no more than the occupation of five small separate salients of Austrian territory. Thus to the Russian disasters was added the Italian deadlock: and both exercised a fatal influence upon the Bulgarian mind.

Nevertheless all eyes in the Balkans were riveted on the Gallipoli Peninsula until the result of the Battle of Suvla Bay became known. Till it was lost the Bulgarians held their hand, and in the month of July there were still hopeful possibilities of bringing them in on the side of the Allies. The Austro-German attack upon Serbia which had seemed so imminent in February had not matured during all the months of the summer. The deep anxieties with which some members of the Cabinet viewed this great danger were happily not borne out as the months slipped away. I know of no cause for the delay of this attack other than the influence exercised upon the Balkan States and upon Bulgaria by the operations at the Dardanelles, and the belief so widely held throughout the Balkan States that England would never relinquish such an effort without achieving success. The continued fighting on the Gallipoli Peninsula, the knowledge that large reinforcements were pouring out, and that another great trial of strength in that theatre was impending, dominated the action of Bulgaria; and the action of Bulgaria was the fact which in turn governed the Austro-German attack on Serbia.

I was strongly of opinion during the month of July that we ought not to stake the whole Balkan policy solely on the result of a battle in Gallipoli, but that, while doing everything in our power to secure a victory there, we should also strive to win Bulgaria. This could be done only by territorial concessions forced upon Greece and Serbia, combined with the granting of loans and the expectation of success in the Dardanelles. The imminent peril in which Serbia stood, and the restricted conditions under which the Allies could afford her protection, made it indispensable that she should cede, and if necessary be made to surrender, the uncontested zone in Macedonia to the Bulgarians, to whom it belonged by race, by history, by treaty, and—until it was taken from them in the second Balkan War—by conquest. Serbia, even when at the last gasp during the first Austrian attack upon her in 1914, had found it necessary to keep large numbers of troops in the Bulgarian districts of Macedonia to hold down the native population. Right and reason, the claims of justice, and the most imperious calls of necessity, alike counselled the Serbians to surrender at least the uncontested zone. To the ordinary exhortations of diplomacy were added special appeals by the Sovereigns and the Rulers of the allied countries. The Prince Regent of Serbia was besought by the Tsar, by the President of the French Republic, and by King George V, to make a concession right in itself, necessary in the common cause, vital to the safety of Serbia. But to all these appeals the Serbian Government and Parliament proved obdurate. The allied diplomacy, moving ponderously forward—every telegram and measure having to be agreed to by all the other parties to the alliance—had just reached the point of refusing any further supplies of stores or money to Serbia unless she complied with their insistent demand, when the final invasion began.

The same sort of thing happened about Kavalla. M. Venizelos, with his almost unerring judgment of great issues, was prepared to imperil his whole personal popularity in Greece and place himself at a deadly disadvantage in his controversies with the King by intimating his readiness to acquiesce in the cession to Bulgaria of Kavalla in certain circumstances. Had the Allies been able to secure for Bulgaria the immediate cession of the uncontested zone in Macedonia and the port of Kavalla, it seems very probable that they might have been induced during the month of July to come to our aid and to march on Adrianople.

It seems certain that, even if this full result had not been obtained, the tangible cession of this territory to Bulgaria at the instance of the Allies would have made it impossible for King Ferdinand to carry his country into the hostile camp. Monsieur Radoslavoff gave in brutally frank language a perfectly truthful account of the Bulgarian position in these months. No effective measures were however taken, and all was left to the hazard of the battle on the Gallipoli Peninsula.

It would be unjust not to recognize at the same time the extraordinary difficulties with which Sir Edward Grey was confronted owing to the need of combining the diplomatic action of four separate great Powers in so delicate and painful a business as virtually coercing a then friendly Greece and an allied and suffering Serbia, specially shielded by Russia, to make territorial concessions deeply repugnant to them. Although a united diplomacy might have assisted, nothing less than a decisive victory at the Dardanelles could at this time have counteracted in the Balkans the terrible tide of Russian defeat.

By the end of the third week in August all prospects of an immediate victory at this vital point had vanished. When our failure was fully appreciated by the competent military personages at Sofia, the Bulgarian King and Government finally made up their minds to join Germany. From that moment the ruin of Serbia was certain and irremediable. The quaking dyke of the Dardanelles campaign that had so long held off the deluge had yielded at last. It was henceforth only a question of the time-tables of Austro-German troop movements. Serbia, however, though fully conscious of her danger, remained recalcitrant to all appeals to make effective concessions. Till the last moment she kept her heel on the conquered Bulgarian districts of Macedonia, and maintained a stubborn front to the overwhelming forces that were gathering against her.

A new tremendous event was now to strike across this darkening situation. At a Conference held at Calais early in July, the representatives of the Cabinet, viz., the Prime Minister, Lord Kitchener and Mr. Balfour, had, in accordance with the convictions of the overwhelming majority of their colleagues, argued against a further Anglo-French offensive in the West in 1915. They had proposed that the allied operations in France and Flanders should be confined to what was described as an "offensive defensive" or, to speak more accurately, an active defensive. The French had agreed; General Joffre had agreed. The agreement was open and formal. And it was on this basis that we had looked forward and prepared for the new battle on the Gallipoli Peninsula. No sooner, however, had General Joffre left the Conference than, notwithstanding these agreements, he had calmly resumed the development of his plans for his great attack in Champagne, in which he confidently expected to break the German lines and roll them back. It was not until after the Battle of Suvla Bay had been finally lost, and we were more deeply committed in the Peninsula than ever before, that we became aware of this.

To avoid unnecessary circulation of secret documents it had been arranged that members of the War Committee wishing to read the daily War Office telegrams could do so each morning at the War Office in Lord Kitchener's anteroom. It was my practice to read every word every day. On the morning of August 21 I was thus engaged when the private secretary informed me that Lord Kitchener, who had just returned from the French Headquarters, wished to see me. I entered his room and found him standing with his back to the light. He looked at me sideways with a very odd expression on his face. I saw he had some disclosure of importance to make, and waited. After appreciable hesitation he told me that he had agreed with the French to a great offensive in France. I said at once that there was no chance of success. He said the scale would be greater than anything ever before conceived; if it succeeded, it would restore everything, including of course the Dardanelles. He had an air of suppressed excitement, like a man who has taken a great decision of terrible uncertainty and is about to put it into execution. He was of course bracing himself for the announcement he had to make that morning to the War Committee and to the Cabinet. I continued unconvinced. It was then 11 o'clock, and he drove me across in his car to Downing Street.

The Committee assembled. Lord Kitchener had no doubt apprised the Prime Minister beforehand, and he was immediately invited to make his statement. He told us that owing to the situation in Russia he could not longer maintain the attitude which was agreed upon in conjunction with the French at Calais, i.e., that a real serious offensive on a large scale in the West should be postponed until the Allies were ready. As he put it to us, he had himself urged upon General Joffre the adoption of the offensive. In view of the fact that, as we now know, the French plans and preparations had long been in progress, had indeed never been interrupted, this must have been a work of supererogation. I immediately protested against departure from the decisions of the Cabinet maturely made and endorsed by the Calais Conference, and against an operation that could only lead to useless slaughter on a gigantic scale. I pointed out that we had neither the ammunition nor the superiority in men necessary to warrant such an assault on the enemy's fortified line; that it could not take place in time effectively to relieve Russia; that it would not prevent the Germans from pursuing their initiative in theatres other than the West; and that it would rupture fatally our plans for opening the Dardanelles. The following record has been preserved of these remarks:

> *Mr. Churchill* expressed his regret at such a course. The German forces on the Western Front had not been reduced and were some

2,000,000 against the Allies 2,500,000. This amounted to a superiority for the Allies of five to four, which was inadequate for the offensive. Since our last offensive effort our relative strength had not altered, while the German defences had been strengthened.

It seemed to him that in the hope of relieving Russia and to gratify our great and natural desire to do so, the Allies might throw away 200,000 or 300,000 lives[1] and [much] ammunition, and might possibly gain a little ground. The attack on May 9 (Festubert-Arras) had been a failure, and the line had not been altered by it. *After* an expenditure of lives and ammunition in this way by us, the Germans would have a chance worth seizing, and it would be worth their while to bring back great forces from the East. A superiority of two to one was laid down as necessary to attack, and we (the Allies) had not got it.

These views were not seriously disputed, but it was urged that the French would move in any case, and that if we did not march too, the alliance would be destroyed. Lord Kitchener was careful not to hold out any expectation of "a decisive success," and when pressed to define "a decisive success" he accepted my expression "a fundamental strategic alteration of the line." "There is," he said, "a great deal of truth in what Mr. Churchill has said, but unfortunately we have to make war as we must and not as we should like to."

I besought the Cabinet, which followed the War Council an hour later, not to yield to the French impatience without a further conference at which all the arguments could be stated and a final appeal made. I was strongly supported by others. I was forced to admit that if the French, after hearing what we had to say, still persisted in their intention, we should of course have to conform; but I urged that a last effort should be made to avert the vast, futile and disastrous slaughter that was now impending. Sir John French, who was in London, was interrogated by the Cabinet. He also declined to give any assurance of success, and was further extremely dissatisfied with the particular sector of attack in which he was required to operate. He had not ammunition for more than seven days' offensive battle. Nevertheless he was quite ready, if ordered, to throw himself into it with a good heart. I visited him privately at Lancaster Gate, where he was staying for the night, and urged my opinion. He used the usual arguments about the necessity of acting in harmony with the French, and then unfolded to me the fact that General Joffre intended to employ no fewer than forty divisions in the French sector of attack alone. Although I must admit that the tremendous scale of the operation seemed to carry the issue into the region of the unknown, I continued recalcitrant and quitted my friend in the deepest

---

[1] Obviously this should read "men," meaning men killed and wounded, i.e., casualties.

anxiety. I saw that we were confronted with the ruin of the campaign alike in the East and in the West.

The decision to make a general attack in France involved the immediate starvation, or at any rate malnutrition, in ammunition and in drafts, of the army on the Gallipoli Peninsula. Although large numbers of men had to be sent thither merely to keep Sir Ian Hamilton's units in the field, this number, while enough to be a heavy loss elsewhere, was not sufficient to produce any useful result. The operations on the Peninsula came to a standstill, and the Turks hastened to replace their heavy losses and reorganize their shaken and in some cases shattered formations. Meanwhile, disease and despondency were at work in our own army. The anguish of supreme success narrowly but fatally missed, the sense of being ill-supported from home, the uncertainty about the future intentions of the Government, the shortage of ammunition, the threatening advent of winter, the rigorous privations of officers and men, exposed the Dardanelles army to the most melancholy ordeal. The numerous and powerful opponents of the enterprise, the advocates of evacuation, the partisans of competing schemes, found themselves well supplied with all that they desired. In these depressing conditions only the patient endurance of the British troops and the unquenchable spirit of Anzac enabled a firm posture of the army and its consequent existence to be maintained.

But now a very curious incident occurred, which added greatly to the perplexities of the British Government. The political power and influence of General Sarrail rested upon foundations which it was not easy then precisely to define or explain. This officer, having been removed by General Joffre in July from the Verdun command in which he had distinguished himself, had obtained, through profound political influence, the command of the French troops in the Orient in succession to General Gouraud, who had been seriously wounded. Whatever dispute there might be about his military achievements, his irreligious convictions were above suspicion. There appeared to be an understanding in French governing circles that he was to be assigned an important independent rôle in the East, which would give him the opportunity of gathering the military laurels from which the French Radical-Socialist elements were determined anti-Clerical generals should not be debarred. Judge of our astonishment when, on September 1, in the midst of the preparations for a supreme battle in France, while our own army at the Dardanelles was cut to the barest minimum in drafts and ammunition, the Admiralty suddenly received, through the French naval attaché, the request to assist the French Ministry of Marine in dispatching from Marseilles four new French divisions to the Dardanelles! We were then informed that the French Government had decided to form a separate Army of the East, of six divisions, which, under the command of General

Sarrail, would during the month of October land on the Asiatic shore of the Dardanelles, and advance thence upon the forts of Chanak in conjunction with our renewed attacks upon the Gallipoli Peninsula. We were requested to arrange for the relief of the two French divisions at Helles, in order that, added to the four new French divisions from France, this separate army should be constituted for the new operation. It appeared for a space that what the most unanswerable arguments of reason, of daring, and of duty could not achieve, were to be easily secured by the interplay of French political forces. For once the gloomy embarrassments of our councils were broken by the sunlight of a happy hour. We made haste to accept the French proposal. Lord Kitchener instantly promised the two divisions to relieve the French at Helles. Mr. Balfour began at once to gather the necessary transport. Mr. Bonar Law joined with me in pressing the dispatch of still larger British forces, to "make a good job of it." Alas for the British Cabinet! They saw the truth quite clearly. They were sound and right in their general view. It was not through wrong judgment that they failed, but through want of will-power. In such times the Kingdom of Heaven can only be taken by storm.

But then the question arose, "Was it possible General Joffre could have agreed?" Inquiry showed that he had agreed upon conditions. His own position was not so secure as to leave him indifferent to the pressure from the political left flank. He had been forced to manœuvre. His conditions were that the reinforcing divisions for the Dardanelles were not to leave France before the main shock of his impending battle had occurred, nor until it could be seen whether its results would be decisive or not. Pressed on September 11, at Calais, by Lord Kitchener as to the time which it would take to ascertain this, he stated that he would know at the end of the first week's fighting one way or the other; that if it was clear by then that a general German retreat in the West—which would have to be followed up by every available man—was not going to be compelled, all the troops assigned to the Dardanelles would be released. October 10 was the date fixed for the embarkation of the leading divisions. It was noticed, however, that General Sarrail, instead of hurrying out to the Dardanelles to survey the situation on the spot and perfect his plans, as Lord Kitchener strongly pressed him to do, preferred to remain in Paris attending to matters which were doubtless of importance.

On September 20 the sinister news reached London that a Bulgarian mobilization was imminent and that Bulgaria was believed to have committed herself definitely to the Central Powers. On the next day the Bulgarian Prime Minister told a meeting of his followers that the cause of the Allies was lost; that Bulgaria must not attach herself to the losing side; that the Quadruple Alliance had only made vague proposals to Bulgaria about the occupation of the uncontested zone *after* the war; and that if Bulgaria went to war, she was assured of the neutrality of Roumania. At midnight on the 22nd, the Turks signed an agreement ceding the Dedeagatch Railway to Bulgaria; and that same day Serbia signalled with alarm the increasing movement of Austro-German forces towards her northern frontier. The long-dreaded southward thrust was about to begin.

It is significant that while Bulgaria had patiently awaited the result of the Battle of Suvla Bay before taking her ghastly plunge, her rulers did not hesitate to commit themselves on the eve of the far larger battle which was known to be impending in France. The Germans could not fail to note the massing of guns and troops in Artois and Champagne, and had in fact made all preparations to receive the shock. But their confidence in the result was shared by the Bulgarian General Staff.

At dawn on September 26 the great battle in the West began. It comprised a subsidiary attack by about thirty British and French divisions at Loos, and a main attack by forty French divisions in Champagne. Sir John French had been compelled, in order to combine with the French, to accept a sphere of attack against his better judgment; but, having agreed to conform to General Joffre's plans, he threw himself into their execution with his customary determination. The French attack in Champagne has since been described as "the unlimited method"—i.e., the armies were hurled on to advance as far as they could "into the blue," in the confident expectation that they would carry, not merely the front systems, which had been subjected to bombardment, but all intact positions and defences likely to be met with in rear. In the absurd misconceptions of the Staff, large masses of cavalry were brought up to press the victory to a decisive conclusion. At the fatal signal the brave armies marched into the firestorm. The ardour of the French infantry was not unmatched by their British comrades. The issue, however, was never in doubt. The German calculations of the strength of their front and of the numbers of troops needed to defend it were accurate and sound. Their drive against Russia, their project against the Balkans proceeded unchecked. In the first week the Anglo-French attack had secured slight advances of no strategic significance at various points, a few score of guns, and a few thousand prisoners, at the expense of more than 300,000 casualties.

The time had now come for General Joffre to release the troops for the East, but he was naturally reluctant to admit defeat. The downfall of his hopes was concealed by a continuance of the fighting, and the departure of the Dardanelles divisions receded week by week. Meanwhile, the winter season steadily approached the army on the Peninsula, and the catastrophe of the Balkans arrived.

On September 25 the general mobilization of the Bulgarian Army had

begun. Those who placed reliance on the optimistic accounts of the fighting in
France which were supplied by the military authorities here and in France
found it impossible to believe that the Germans, faced by such formidable assaults in the West, and extended in immense operations in the East, could spare
a new army to conquer Serbia, and they therefore continued incredulous to the
last. During the third and fourth weeks of September the concentration of considerable Austro-German forces north of the Danube became unmistakable.
On October 4 our Intelligence reported the presence of Mackensen at Temesvar. Belated and frantic efforts to deter the Bulgarians, exhausting the whole apparatus of promises and threats, were received with sullen impassivity, and the
mobilization of the Bulgarian armies proceeded regularly. King Ferdinand
pursued his profoundly considered and most perilous policy with mechanical
precision. An iron discipline gripped the peasant soldiers, and a ruthless suppression quelled the parliamentary forces. Serbia, unreasonable to the last, prepared to meet her doom with passionate appeals to her Allies and dauntless
heroism in the field.

The repercussion of these events must now be studied. The only power
which could come to the aid of Serbia before it was too late was Greece. Accordingly, at last, an earnest and united effort was made by all the Allies to procure the entry of Greece into the general war. Twice she had placed herself at
their disposal. Twice she had been rebuffed. Now it was the turn of the Allies to
ask. By treaty Greece was obliged to aid Serbia against a Bulgarian attack. King
Constantine and the Greece that followed him claimed that this treaty did not
apply to a war in which Serbia was attacked not only by Bulgaria but by a great
Power. Serbia invoked the treaty, demanded the support of Greece, and also appealed to the Allies for 150,000 men. M. Venizelos, again Prime Minister and at
the head of a parliamentary majority fresh from elections, urged the Allies to
send troops to Salonika to enable Greece to enter the war according to her honourable obligations. As a military measure to aid Serbia directly, the landing at
this juncture of allied forces at Salonika was absurd. The hostile armies concentrating on the eastern and northern frontiers of Serbia were certain to overwhelm and overrun that country before any effective aid, other than Greek aid,
could possibly arrive. As a political move to encourage and determine the action of Greece, the dispatch of allied troops to Salonika was justified. But the
question arose: Where were the troops to come from? Obviously from the
Dardanelles and only from the Dardanelles. A French and a British division,
all that could be spared and all that could get to Salonika in time, were accordingly taken from Sir Ian Hamilton's hard-pressed army in the closing days of
September.

The reader who has a true sense of the values in the problem will not be surprised to learn that this dispatch of troops from the Dardanelles produced the opposite effect to that intended or desired. King Constantine had been trained all his life as a soldier. He had studied very closely the strategic situation of his country and conceived himself to be an authority on the subject. The road to his heart was through some sound military plan, and this he was never offered by the Allies. When he learned that the allied help was to take the form of withdrawing two divisions from the Dardanelles, he naturally concluded that that enterprise was about to be abandoned. He saw himself, if he entered the war, confronted after a short interval not only with the Bulgarians but with the main body of the Turkish Army now chained to the Gallipoli Peninsula. He read in the British and French action a plain confession of impending failure in the main operation whose progress during the whole year had dominated the war situation in the East. It proved impossible to remove these anxieties from the Royal mind and added to his German sympathies they were decisive. "His Majesty," said Sir Francis Elliot [October 6], "was disturbed by the fact that troops had been brought from the Dardanelles to Salonika. He thought that it was the beginning of the abandonment of the expedition and would release the whole Turkish Army to reinforce the Bulgarians."

While the troops were already on the way and the British Navy were netting the harbour of Salonika against submarines, King Constantine dismissed M. Venizelos, on whose invitation they had come. The Allies therefore found themselves confronted with a pro-German Greece determined to repudiate its treaty obligations to Serbia. Thus the object of the expedition to Salonika had entirely disappeared. But those powerful persons in France and England who had advocated it were determined to persevere. The miseries of Serbia fighting desperately against superior forces, the shame and sorrow of watching a small ally trampled down, combined with dislike and weariness of the Dardanelles to form a tide of opinion impossible to resist. I continued to point to the Dardanelles as the master key to the problem, and to a naval attempt to force the Straits as the sole chance of changing the action of Bulgaria and averting the destruction of Serbia. Even up to the last moment the arrival of a British fleet in the Sea of Marmora might have transformed the situation. The Bulgarians, having mobilized against one side, might have marched against the other. Mr. Balfour, however, although perfectly ready to bear the supreme responsibility if Admiral de Robeck and the First Sea Lord, Sir Henry Jackson, had been willing to make the attempt, could not feel justified in overriding them or replacing them by others. It only remained, therefore, to await the catastrophe.

The Cabinet found the hopelessness of the situation unendurable, and apparently the French Government was similarly distressed. A vehement wish to rush troops to the aid of Serbia manifested itself. It was in vain that the impossibility of their arriving before it was too late was explained. On Friday, October 6, after heated and confused discussions, the Cabinet decided to refer the tangled situation to the considered judgment of the combined staffs of the Admiralty and the War Office. The great question—What to do? was accordingly remitted to the naval and military experts gathered together under the guidance of the Chief of the Imperial General Staff and the First Sea Lord. Through the whole of Saturday and Sunday these officers considered and prepared their report; and on Monday, October 9, this remarkable document was circulated to Ministers. The General Staff, in loyal accord with General Headquarters in France and with almost all orthodox military opinion, recommended that everything should be concentrated on the prolongation of the Battle of Loos, from which they considered decisive results might be obtained. In this they were proved wrong by the events not only of 1915, but of 1916 and of 1917. Although the British Army continued its operations with the fullest support and to the utmost limit of its ammunition, not only were they unable to break the German line but a very large proportion of their initial gains were wrested from them by the German counter-attacks. If Sir Douglas Haig with the enormous expenditure of munitions and life which characterized the battles on the Somme in 1916 or at Passchendaele in 1917 was unable to achieve any decisive results, what chance had Sir John French with the scanty offensive resources of 1915? The best and most orthodox military opinion was at this time so far out of touch with reality, that the General Staff still contemplated the irruption of a mass of cavalry through the German line. What the cavalry would have done if they had got through was not explained.

But passing from the general question of the offensive in France to the specific issues raised by the situation in the East, the General Staff of the Army and the Admiralty War Staff pronounced in no uncertain tones against the Salonika enterprise and in favour of a continuance of the operations at the Dardanelles. The advocates of Salonika had been those who had pressed most strongly for the remission of the disputed questions to the unbiased and undiluted judgment of the naval and military experts. They were completely indisposed to accept the pronouncement of the tribunal to which they had appealed.

When these matters came before the War Council (whose numbers had now been increased to include the prominent figures on both sides of the controversy) on the evening of October 9, it was evident that no agreement could be reached as between Salonika and the Dardanelles. On the other hand, it was common ground that large reinforcements should be sent to the Eastern theatre as soon as possible. As these troop movements would necessarily take several weeks, and it could be plausibly argued that the situation would develop in the meanwhile in such a way as to make ultimate concord possible, it was finally settled that six divisions should be withdrawn from France and sent to Egypt, and that what should happen to them after that should be settled later. The Prime Minister felt himself constrained to agree to this arrangement. He was, in my opinion, throughout unwavering in his intention to persevere at the Dardanelles, and he used every resource of patience and tact to guide and carry opinion in that direction and to secure the necessary decisions at the earliest possible moment. A more vigorous course would probably have broken up the Government. I was, and am, strongly of opinion that it would have been much better to break up the Cabinet, and let one section or the other carry out their view in its integrity, than to preserve what was called "the national unity" at the expense of vital executive action. But after that there would still have been the difficulty with the French.

The French Government had by this time made up their mind wholeheartedly in favour of Salonika. They declared their intention of sending General Sarrail's army thither instead of to the Dardanelles, and urged us to support them as strongly as possible. Another series of disputes therefore broke out in the Cabinet upon the proposal to divert to Salonika the troops now under orders for Egypt, and the consequent abandonment of any further great enterprise to open the Straits. Military authority was again appealed to; and the General Staff in a paper, every word of which was justified by subsequent events, showed that there was no possibility of saving the Serbians, and that the Salonika enterprise was a dangerous and futile dissipation and misdirection of forces. Fortified by the unequivocal recommendation of all the military and naval authorities, the Cabinet refused to agree to the French proposals, and insisted upon the reinforcing British divisions being sent according to the agreement to Egypt, where they were to be fitted out with their semi-tropical equipment, etc. On this General Joffre was sent by the French Government over to England. After his defeat in Champagne he was in no position to resist the strong tendencies of his Government, nor possibly particularly anxious to keep General Sarrail in Paris. He arrived, and in the absence of the Prime Minister, who was at this time temporarily incapacitated by illness, met the leading members of the Cabinet. I was excluded from this Conference, no doubt because it was known that I should certainly prove intractable. After the Conference was over the Cabinet was informed that General Joffre had pledged his military judgment in favour of the necessity and practicability of the Salonika expedition, and had threatened to resign the command of the French armies if the British did not effectively co-operate. In spite of the strenuous resistance of the British General Staff, and in the flattest defiance of their advice, the Cabinet yielded to this outrageous threat.

The final policy of the British Government, though erroneous in direction and too late in time, was not without its grandeur. On October 12 the following declaration was made both to Roumania and to Greece:

> The only effective manner in which help can be given to Serbia is by the immediate declaration of war by Roumania and Greece against the Austro-Germans and Bulgaria. The British Government in that event would be prepared to sign forthwith a Military Convention with Roumania, whereby Great Britain will guarantee to bring into action in the Balkan theatre, not including the forces already in Gallipoli, an army of at least 200,000 men. If the French send a force as they contemplate doing, that force would be part of this total; but if not, the British Government would undertake to provide the whole number themselves.
>
> This force would include a number of our best and most seasoned divisions, and we shall maintain them in the field waging war on behalf of our Allies until the objective is accomplished. A steady flow of troops will commence as soon as transport is available and will be continuously maintained. We estimate that 150,000 men will be available by the end of November, and the total 200,000 will be reached by the end of the year.
>
> The Military Convention will state precisely the dates at which the different portions of the army will arrive. We are repeating this offer to Greece, and if Roumania is prepared to act immediately, we shall call upon Greece imperatively to fulfil her treaty obligations to Serbia.

Such a spirit manifested three months earlier would have prevented the disasters by whose imminence it had been evoked. Such an army applied in August or September, either to the Gallipoli Peninsula or to the Asiatic shore, would have overpowered the Turks already extended at their fullest strain, and transformed defeat into victory throughout the East. But now these immense offers, not arising from foresight but extorted only by the pressure of events, fell upon deaf ears. Neither Roumania nor Greece would move an inch.

In these throes Sir Edward Carson resigned because of the failure to rescue Serbia, and M. Delcassé because of the attempt.

On October 9 the storm of ruin burst upon the Balkans, and Mackensen, crossing the Danube with nine German and Austrian divisions, entered Belgrade from the north. Two days later the Bulgarians invaded Serbia from the east. This double and converging attack was overwhelming. Uskub fell on October 22, and Nish on November 2. In another month Monastir was captured, and by the middle of December the Serbian Army was destroyed or driven completely from Serbian soil.

The relentless severity of the Bulgarian pursuit exposed the retreating Ser-

THE BALKAN
PENINSULA

bian forces and population to the worst horrors of war and winter. Scores of thousands of defenceless people perished, and the whole country was ravaged and reduced to complete subjugation. Meanwhile, large Anglo-French forces began to accumulate at Salonika as helpless spectators of these events, the Allied Army on the Gallipoli Peninsula was left to rot, and the British Fleet at the Dardanelles remained motionless.

CHAPTER XXXVI

THE ABANDONMENT OF
THE DARDANELLES

The events described in the last chapter led directly to the abandonment of the enterprise against the Dardanelles. In the first place, the impending opening of through communications between Germany and Turkey seemed to offer to the Turks the prospect of large supplies of all kinds and particularly of heavy guns and ammunition. Our troops on the Peninsula, whose positions did not allow of any local withdrawal, were threatened with a very great increase in the hostile bombardment. Secondly, the Salonika expedition must become a serious rival to the Dardanelles, drawing upon the existing strength of a harassed army and intercepting and diverting reinforcements and supplies. Apprehensions of approaching failure, if not indeed of final disaster, were rife. Only the fear of a massacre on the Beaches and of the loss of a large proportion of the Army delayed for a time the evacuation of Gallipoli and the abandonment of the enterprise. As a first step, on October 11, Lord Kitchener telegraphed to Sir Ian Hamilton:

> What is your estimate of the probable loss which would be entailed to our forces if the evacuation of the Gallipoli Peninsula was decided upon and carried out in the most careful manner?[1] . . .

Sir Ian Hamilton, who had already declared evacuation to be "unthinkable," replied on the 12th that

> It would not be wise to reckon on getting out of Gallipoli with less loss than that of half the total force, as well as guns which must be used to the last, stores, railway plant, horses. . . . We might be very lucky and lose considerably less than I have estimated.

On October 14 it was decided to recall Sir Ian Hamilton and to send out in his place General Monro, an officer who had already commanded an army in France and was deeply imbued with Western ideas. He belonged to that school

---

[1] *Gallipoli Diary,* p. 249.

whose supreme conception of Great War strategy was "killing Germans." Anything that killed Germans was right. Anything that did not kill Germans was useless, even if it made other people kill them, and kill more of them, or terminated their power to kill us. To such minds the capture of Constantinople was an idle trophy, and the destruction of Turkey as a military factor, or the rallying of the Balkan States to the Allies, mere politics, which every military man should hold in proper scorn. The special outlook of General Monro was not known to the Cabinet. His instructions were moreover exclusively military. He was to express an opinion whether the Gallipoli Peninsula should be evacuated, or another attempt made to carry it; and on the number of troops that would be required (1) to carry the Peninsula, (2) to keep the Straits open, and (3) to take Constantinople.[1] No reference was made to any part which might be played by the Fleet in this essentially amphibious operation. Very large masses of troops were now moving from France to the Eastern theatre, and the whole question of their employment was left open. In these circumstances General Monro's report was awaited with the utmost anxiety.

There was however no need for suspense. General Monro was an officer of swift decision. He came, he saw, he capitulated. He reached the Dardanelles on October 28; and already on the 29th he and his staff were discussing nothing but evacuation. On the 30th he landed on the Peninsula. Without going beyond the Beaches, he familiarized himself in the space of six hours with the conditions prevailing on the 15-mile front of Anzac, Suvla and Helles, and spoke a few discouraging words to the principal officers at each point. To the Divisional Commanders summoned to meet him at their respective Corps Headquarters, he put separately and in turn a question in the following sense: "On the supposition that you are going to get no more drafts can you maintain your position in spite of the arrival of strong reinforcements with heavy guns and limitless German ammunition?" He thus collected a number of dubious answers, armed with which he returned to Imbros. He never again set foot on the Peninsula during the tenure of his command. His Chief-of-the-Staff, also an enthusiast for evacuation, never visited it at all. On October 31 General Monro despatched his telegram recommending the total evacuation of the Gallipoli Peninsula and the final abandonment of the campaign. According to his own statements he contemplated, in addition to the ruin of the whole enterprise, a loss of from thirty to forty per cent, of the Army, i.e., about forty thousand officers and men. This he was prepared to accept. Two days later he left for Egypt, leaving the command of the Dardanelles Army temporarily in the hands of General Birdwood.

General Monro's telegram of "Evacuation" fell like a thunderbolt upon

---

[1] General Sir C. C. Monro's Despatch, *London Gazette*.

Lord Kitchener; and for the moment and under the shock he rose in all the strength which he commanded when he represented the indomitable core of our national character.

LORD KITCHENER TO GENERAL BIRDWOOD.

November 3, 1915.

Very secret.

You know the report sent in by Monro. I shall come out to you; am leaving to-morrow night. I have seen Captain Keyes, and I believe the Admiralty will agree to making naval attempt to force the passage of the Straits. We must do what we can to assist them, and I think as soon as our ships are in the Sea of Marmora we should seize the Bulair isthmus and hold it so as to supply the Navy if the Turks still hold out.

Examine very carefully the best position for landing near the marsh at the head of the Gulf of Xeros, so that we could get a line across the isthmus, with ships at both sides. In order to find the troops for this undertaking we should have to reduce the numbers in the trenches to the lowest possible, and perhaps evacuate positions at Suvla. All the best fighting men that could be spared, including your boys from Anzac and every one I can sweep up in Egypt, might be concentrated at Mudros ready for this enterprise.

There will probably be a change in the naval command, Wemyss being appointed in command to carry through the naval part of the work.

As regards the military command, you would have the whole force, and should carefully select your commanders and troops. I would suggest Maude, Fanshawe, Marshall, Peyton, Godley, Cox, leaving others to hold the lines. Please work out plans for this, or alternative plans as you may think best. We must do it right this time.

I absolutely refuse to sign orders for evacuation, which I think would be the gravest disaster and would condemn a large percentage of our men to death or imprisonment.

Monro will be appointed to the command of the Salonika force.

Here was the true Kitchener. Here in this flaming telegram—whether Bulair was the best place or not—was the Man the British Empire believed him to be, in whom millions set their faith—resolute, self-reliant, creative, lion-hearted.

Unhappily the next day:

LORD KITCHENER TO GENERAL BIRDWOOD.

November 4, 1915.

I am coming as arranged. . . . The more I look at the problem the less I see my way through, so you had better work out very quietly and secretly any scheme for getting the troops off the peninsula.

We may now once again exercise our privilege of crossing to the enemy's lines and of learning how the situation was viewed by the responsible German authorities. On the same October 31 that General Monro dispatched his telegram of evacuation to Lord Kitchener, Admiral von Usedom who, it will be remembered, commanded the fortress of the Dardanelles and all the marine defences of the Straits, completed a despatch to the Emperor dealing with the events of the past month.

"The great attack," he wrote, "which we have been expecting on the land front has not taken place since the advance inaugurated by the new landing on August 7 north of the Ariburnu front was brought to a standstill. At the end of September reports of moves of troops and vehicles increased. Information from Salonika confirms that troops are being drawn thither from the Dardanelles front. I do not, however, consider it probable that the enemy will evacuate his position without hard fighting. In order to drive him out a very thorough artillery preparation is necessary, and for this the munitions on the spot or which can be brought up are insufficient."

He proceeded to dwell upon the dangerous manner in which the fortress defences of the Straits had been weakened through the repeated withdrawals of the mobile artillery, particularly the howitzers, on which his whole system depended. In addition to the forty-nine howitzers and mobile guns with their supplies of ammunition withdrawn in May and June, he had during August and September been forced to cede another twenty-one of his most valuable howitzers and mobile guns. The whole of the vital Intermediate Defences of the forts contained at this time only twenty mobile howitzers and mortars.

Meanwhile Commodore Keyes, Chief of the Staff to Admiral de Robeck, could endure the position at the Dardanelles no longer. He had been throughout convinced that the Fleet could at any time with proper preparation force the Dardanelles and enter the Marmora in sufficient strength. During the summer detailed plans for this operation were prepared under his direction by the Naval Staff. These plans were now completed, and Commodore Keyes declared himself confident of their success. In this opinion he was most strongly supported by Rear-Admiral Wemyss. This officer was actually senior to Admiral de Robeck, but in circumstances which have already been explained[1] he had accepted the position of Second-in-Command upon the eve of the action of March 18. The qualities of character and judgment which he displayed during the war were destined to raise him from a Rear-Admiral to the position of First Sea Lord. In this supreme capacity he was eventually to sustain the burden of the last fourteen months of the struggle. His opinion therefore is retrospectively invested with very high authority. The joint representations of the Chief of Staff and of his Second-in-Command were not, however, acceptable to Admiral de Robeck. Commodore Keyes thereupon asked to be relieved of his appointment in order that he might return home and lay his plans before the Board of Admiralty. Admiral de Robeck, with a magnanimous gesture, asked him to retain his position and accorded him leave of absence, full liberty and "a fair field" to state his case, making it clear, however, that he could not himself in any circumstances become responsible for a further naval attempt. Commodore Keyes therefore repaired to London forthwith, where he arrived on October 28.

The Keyes plan was remarkable for its audacity. It discarded all the gradual methods around which it had alone been possible hitherto to rally naval opinion. The Fleet would be divided into four squadrons, three of which were to take part in the attack, while the fourth provided the support for the Army. The Second Squadron comprised about eight old battleships and cruisers, four very old battleships acting as supply ships, as many of the dummy battleships as possible, and a number of merchantmen carrying coal and ammunition. All these vessels were to be fitted with mine-bumpers. Preceded by four of the best sweepers and accompanied by eight destroyers and two scouts, this Second Squadron was to enter the Straits shortly before dawn, keeping below the illuminated area until dawn was about to break, when it would proceed to steam through the Narrows at its utmost speed. Commodore Keyes proposed to take command of this squadron himself. It was his firm conviction that with the improved sweepers and the mine-bumpers, and aided by smoke screens, darkness and surprise, certainly more than half of this squadron would arrive above Nagara. The battleships which survived were immediately to attack the forts of the Narrows from their rear, which would have been completely exposed.

Meanwhile at dawn the First Squadron, composed of the *Lord Nelson,* *Agamemnon, Exmouth,* two *King Edwards,* four French ships, the *Glory* and the *Canopus,* accompanied by eight sloops and ten destroyers for sweeping, would simultaneously attack the forts at the Narrows from below the Kephez minefield. The Third Squadron, consisting of two Monitors, the *Swiftsure,* and five cruisers or light cruisers, was to cover the Army and co-operate from across the

[1] See pp. 391–92.

Peninsula in the attack upon the forts at the Narrows. The bombardment of the forts at the Narrows by all three squadrons, and the sweeping of the minefields already deranged by the passage of the Second Squadron, were to be pursued continuously without slackening for a moment. An elaborate memorandum had been prepared by the staff, regulating every phase of this main attack which might well have been continued for two or even three days if necessary before the final advance of the First Squadron through the Narrows was ordered. In short, the Keyes plan was in principle the old plan of pinning down the forts in close and continuous action while the minefields were swept, but in addition it was to be preceded by a furious surprise rush of the oldest vessels to dislocate the defence, to sweep and break up the minefields and secure positions whence the forts could be taken in reverse. "The action recommended (in the staff memorandum)," wrote Commodore Keyes, "taken in conjunction with the preliminary rush and determined military offensive, generally represents the views of a number of experienced officers who strongly advocate a naval attack on the Straits and are confident of success. If success is achieved, the Turkish Army in Gallipoli will be entirely dependent on the Bulair Isthmus for supplies. This line of communication can be harassed day and night." Finally the plan comprised detailed arrangements for maintaining the successful ships in the Marmora while they were operating against the Turkish communications.

On November 2 the Prime Minister reconstituted the War Council or Dardanelles Committee as it had hitherto been styled. In its new form it was called the "War Committee" and was limited to the Prime Minister, Mr. Balfour, Lord Kitchener, Sir Edward Grey and Mr. Lloyd George. Mr. Bonar Law was added ten days later under Conservative pressure. I was excluded. It was announced that this Committee would be responsible to the Cabinet for the whole direction of the war. On November 3 the new Committee met to consider the question of evacuating the Dardanelles. Lord Kitchener's views have been fully exposed in his telegram to General Birdwood of that day. He had previously telegraphed to General Monro asking whether his opinions were shared by the Corps Commanders on the Peninsula. He had been answered that General Byng favoured evacuation and considered that Suvla could be evacuated without much loss, provided the attempt were made before German reinforcements arrived; that General Davies, commanding at Helles, concurred with General Monro; but that General Birdwood at Anzac was opposed to evacuation. General Maxwell, commanding in Egypt, had also independently telegraphed urging that a further effort should be made to hold on. Thus the military opinions were divided. The Committee had also before them the plans of Commodore Keyes, endorsed by Admiral Wemyss, in regard to which the Admiralty War Staff had pronounced no decided opinion. Keyes was still only a

Captain with the rank of Commodore. He was known as a daring and gifted officer, but he had no record of high command behind him, and he did not carry the authority necessary to override Admiral de Robeck's negative view. Could he at this juncture, with the fame of the leader of the Dover patrol, have laid upon the Council Table the credentials of Zeebrugge, the history of the Great War might have been much curtailed.

In the circumstances which existed the new War Committee found no difficulty in deciding to postpone the evil day of decision. Lord Kitchener proceeded to the Dardanelles to survey the situation on the spot and make further recommendations. The Secretary of State for War left London on November 4, apparently in great sympathy with Commodore Keyes's plan. He spoke on his way through Paris in an exceedingly resolute manner, and directed Commodore Keyes to explain the scheme to the French Minister of Marine, now Admiral Lacaze, and then follow him with all speed. Admiral Lacaze was wholly favourable to the plan, and immediately promised a reinforcement of six old French battleships to execute it.

Lord Kitchener arrived at the Dardanelles on November 9. His personal inspection of the troops and the defences convinced him that the troops could hold their positions unless confronted with very heavy German reinforcements of which there was no immediate prospect. His conferences with Admiral de Robeck led him however, in the absence of Commodore Keyes, to discard the idea of a renewed naval attempt. Instead he devised a plan for a new landing at Ayas in the Gulf of Alexandretta, with the double object of barring the path of a Turkish invasion of Egypt and of covering the effects of an impending withdrawal from Gallipoli. This plan did not commend itself either to the Admiralty or to the War Committee. With Salonika as well as the Dardanelles on their hands, they were naturally reluctant to commit themselves to another new and entirely separate enterprise which could at the best only achieve subsidiary objects. They therefore informed Lord Kitchener of their dissent from his views and announced that they had decided that the final decision about Gallipoli was to be relegated to a Conference to be held in Paris a few days later.

In accepting an office in the new Government after leaving the Admiralty at the end of May, I had been actuated by the feeling that it was my duty to sustain the Dardanelles enterprise to the best of my ability, and by the hope that with a seat on the War Council I should be able to do so. It was on this condition alone that I had found it possible to occupy a sinecure office. That condition had now disappeared. I was out of harmony with the views which were prevailing and to which the Prime Minister had at last submitted. I was also distressed at the methods of indecision arising from conflicting opinions which at this time pervaded and paralysed the conduct of the war. The rejection of the plans of Commodore Keyes and Admiral Wemyss filled me with despair. I was convinced that the evacuation of Gallipoli was intended and must follow as a consequence of what had taken place.

Awful as were the risks of this decision, it was inevitable unless further efforts on a great scale were to be made by sea or land. Even evacuation was better than leaving the Army to moulder piecemeal without support or purpose. If a British Cabinet or Admiralty were unable to face the responsibility of a naval attempt, there was still time for further military efforts. The important new armies gathering in the Near East, in Egypt and at Salonika, could have been landed at Besika Bay to advance along the Asiatic shore, or alternatively at some point in the Gulf of Xeros to cut the Isthmus of Bulair. Both these operations would have required a large number of additional small vessels—trawlers, lighters, beetles, etc.—but either could have been carried out before the position of the Allied Army holding the Gallipoli Peninsula became untenable through the arrival of great supplies of German artillery and ammunition. In neither case had the Turks sufficient reserves available to meet the new invasion. In both cases victory would have carried with it the destruction or capture of the whole Turkish Army of twenty divisions now concentrated on the Gallipoli Peninsula and the consequent liberation as a new factor of our own fourteen divisions. Bulgaria had joined our enemies; Serbia was overrun. But Greece and Roumania could still have been gained; Constantinople could still have been taken; communications could still have been reopened with Russia; and Turkey would have been driven out of Europe, if not indeed altogether out of the war.

But it would have been useless to advocate such a policy in the teeth of the opinions which were now prevailing, even had I been accorded a seat on the War Committee. It was better that other schemes of strategic and political thought now dominant should have their chance and be applied in their integrity by those who believed in them. I knew too much and felt too keenly to be able to accept Cabinet responsibility for what I believed to be a wholly erroneous conception of war. I therefore in the middle of November sought permission to retire from the Government.

It was impossible at that time to discuss in Parliament any of the grave and tormenting controversies which these pages expose. I had nothing but the friendliest personal feelings towards my colleagues and the Prime Minister, and I would not speak a word which might add to their difficulties or those of the State. I was content to base myself upon a desire to relinquish a well-paid sinecure office which I could not bear longer to hold at this sad juncture in our affairs.

I have tried to show what I believe to be the interplay of forces and se-

THE ABANDONMENT OF THE DARDANELLES

quence of events in this tragedy. Masses of documents can be produced which illustrate and elaborate all the phases of the story, and there are many minor episodes which it would have been only confusing to include. But from what has been written, the appalling difficulties and cruel embarrassments of those who, whatever their views, were endeavouring loyally and earnestly to discharge their great responsibilities can be readily understood. I have recorded my counsels at the time. The future was then unknown. No one possessed plenary power. The experts were frequently wrong. The politicians were frequently right. The wishes of foreign Governments, themselves convulsed internally by difficulties the counterpart of our own, were constantly thrusting themselves athwart our policy. Without the title deeds of positive achievement no one had the power to give clear brutal orders which would command unquestioning respect. Power was widely disseminated among the many important personages who in this period formed the governing instrument. Knowledge was very unequally shared. Innumerable arguments of a partial character could be quoted on every side of all these complicated questions. The situation itself was in constant and violent movement. We never at any time regained the initiative; we were always compelled to adapt ourselves to events. We could never overtake or forestall them. All the time, clear and simple solutions existed which would speedily have produced the precious element of victory.

I may perhaps close this chapter by reprinting some words of general import which I used in explaining my resignation to the House of Commons:

> There is no reason to be discouraged about the progress of the war. We are passing through a bad time now and it will probably be worse before it is better, but that it will be better, if we only endure and persevere, I have no doubt whatever. The old wars were decided by their episodes rather than by their tendencies. In this war the tendencies are far more important than the episodes. Without winning any sensational victories we may win this war. We may win it even during a continuance of extremely disappointing and vexatious events. It is not necessary for us in order to win the war to push the German lines back over all the territory they have absorbed, or to pierce them. While the German lines extend far beyond her frontiers, and while her flag flies over conquered capitals and subjugated provinces, while all the appearances of military success attend her arms, Germany may be defeated more fatally in the second or third year of the war than if the Allied Armies had entered Berlin in the first.
>
> . . . It is, no doubt, disconcerting for us to observe that the Government of a State like Bulgaria are convinced on an impartial survey of the chances that victory will rest with the Central Powers. All the small States

are hypnotized by German military pomp and precision. They see the glitter, the episode, but they do not see or realize the capacity of the ancient and mighty nations, against whom Germany is warring, to endure adversity, to put up with disappointments and mismanagement, to recreate and renew their strength, and to pass on with boundless obstinacy through boundless sufferings to the achievement of their cause.

CHAPTER XXXVII

THE CONSEQUENCES OF 1915

The closing scenes at the Dardanelles proceeded while I was serving with the 2nd Battalion of the Grenadier Guards near Laventie. I was not without information on the course of affairs from my friends both in the Cabinet and at General Headquarters. It was a comfort to be with these fine troops at such a time, to study their methods, unsurpassed in the Army, of discipline and trench warfare, and to share from day to day their life under the hard conditions of the winter and the fire of the enemy. The kindness with which I was received during my period of instruction with the Guards Division will ever be gratefully remembered by me. As in the shades of a November evening, I for the first time led a platoon of Grenadiers across the sopping fields which gave access to our trenches, while here and there the bright flashes of the guns or the occasional whistle of a random bullet accompanied our path, the conviction came into my mind with absolute assurance that the simple soldiers and their regimental officers, armed with their cause, would by their virtues in the end retrieve the mistakes and ignorances of Staffs and Cabinets, of Admirals, Generals and politicians—including, no doubt, many of my own. But, alas, at what a needless cost! To how many slaughters, through what endless months of fortitude and privation would these men, themselves already the survivors of many a bloody day, be made to plod before victory was won!

On November 22, Lord Kitchener, his Ayas bay project being vetoed, consented to the evacuation of Suvla and Anzac. He still hoped to save Helles, the retention of which was strongly advocated by Admiral de Robeck. The War Committee, however, decided that all three lodgments should be abandoned. With this decision Admiral de Robeck expressed himself in disaccord. He deprecated the evacuation of Suvla and Anzac, and when asked specifically on November 25 if he concurred in the evacuation of Helles, he observed bluntly that "he could not understand it." The situation cannot, however, be disentangled from his attitude towards the use of the Fleet. His health was now temporarily impaired by his long spell of hard work. He started immediately for home on a period of leave.

The command now devolved upon Admiral Wemyss. The new Naval

Commander-in-Chief, undeterred by past events, bent himself to a last effort to retrieve the situation. In a series of telegrams, he emphasized the dangers of a winter evacuation. He dwelt upon its difficulties; he endorsed the estimate of General Monro that 30 per cent of the force would be lost in evacuation; he urged that one more effort should be made to convert defeat into victory. In a spirit which cannot be censured in the Royal Navy, he asserted that the Fleet would do its part, and that even if the Army could not co-operate, he would carry out the Keyes plan and force the Dardanelles by naval power alone.

These stalwart counsels threw everything again into the melting pot. The Cabinet revolted against the decision of their new War Committee. It was resolved that no decision could be taken without a further conference with the French, and a meeting of the new Allied Standing Council was fixed for December 5 at Calais. Lord Kitchener again took heart. In common with the British General Staff he was strongly opposed to the whole Salonika expedition. On December 2 he telegraphed to General Monro:

> *Private and Secret.*
> The Cabinet has been considering the Gallipoli situation all day. Owing to the political consequences, there is a strong feeling against evacuation, even of a partial character. It is the general opinion we should retain Cape Helles.
> If the Salonika troops are placed at your disposal up to four divisions for an offensive operation to improve the position at Suvla, could such operations be carried out in time with a view to making Suvla retainable by obtaining higher position and greater depth? The Navy will also take the offensive in co-operation.

Meanwhile the activities of the British submarines in the Marmora had almost entirely severed the sea communications of the Turkish Army, and were also impeding their supply by the roads along the Marmora shore. To meet this peril, which had been approaching plainly, steadily and rapidly during the last two or three months, the German Staff had built a new branch railway from the main Turkish system to Kavak at the head of the Gulf of Xeros. This had been finished in the nick of time, and as the sea transport failed, it became the sole line of supply, relief or reinforcement for the twenty Turkish divisions on the Peninsula. From the new rail head at Kavak all transport was by bullock wagon or camel along roads across the Bulair Isthmus which were frequently disturbed by the fire of the Fleet. On December 2, Admiral Wemyss succeeded in destroying the three central spans of the Kavak Bridge by fire from the *Agamemnon, Endymion,* and a Monitor. The road was also so badly broken by the bombardment that wheeled traffic was completely interrupted. The Turkish 5th Army was now in serious straits. The British Intelligence reported growing demoralization of the enemy through losses, disease, stringency of supplies, the severe weather, and the increasingly searching character of the naval fire. We now know that these reports were correct. Food, clothes, boots, ammunition were frightfully scarce. The condition of the Turkish soldiers, often bare-footed, ragged, hungry, clinging to their trenches week after week, excited at this time the sympathy as well as the alarm of their German masters. Count Metternich, then German Ambassador at Constantinople, visited the Turkish lines on the Peninsula in December in company with Liman von Sanders. "If you had only known," he said, discussing these events after the war, "what the state of the Turkish Army was, it would have gone hard with us." It was not, however, knowledge that was lacking, but the collective will-power to turn it to account.

Admiral Wemyss and his staff were now confident that they had the power, even without forcing the Straits, not only to prevent the arrival of German artillery reinforcements on a large scale, but also gravely to compromise the existence of the whole Turkish Army on the Gallipoli Peninsula. Thus on the spot hope flared up again. It was at this moment, when for the first time a strong and competent naval command declared itself positive of success, that the improvident decision to evacuate was finally taken. On December 8 the Joint Staff Conference sitting at the French General Headquarters declared unanimously for the immediate organization of the defence of Salonika and for the immediate evacuation of Gallipoli. From this moment the perplexities of the British Government came to an end. Henceforward they remained steadfast in pusillanimous resolve. Admiral Wemyss, however, with Keyes at his side, did not readily yield; and the struggle of these two sailors against the now marshalled force of the Cabinet, the War Committee, the Joint Anglo-French Conference, the Admiralty and the War Office, constitutes an episode on which perhaps in future years British naval historians will be glad to dwell. His telegram of December 8 at least must in justice to the Royal Navy be quoted here:

> The navy is prepared to force the Straits and control them for an indefinite period, cutting off all Turkish supplies which now find their way to the Peninsula either by sea from the Marmora or across the Dardanelles from Asiatic to European shore. The only line of communications left would be the road along the Isthmus of Bulair, which can be controlled almost entirely from the Sea of Marmora and the Gulf of Xeros. What is offered the Army, therefore, is the practical, complete severance of all Turkish lines of communication, accompanied by the destruction of the large supply depots on the shore of the Dardanelles.
>
> In the first instance I strongly advocated that the naval attack should synchronize with an army offensive, and if the Army will be prepared to

attack in the event of a favourable opportunity presenting itself, nothing more need be required of them. The Navy here is prepared to undertake this operation with every assurance of success. If the units as described in your letter of November 24 can be provided, these hopes of success are greatly increased, and the possible losses greatly diminished.

The unanimous military opinion referred to in Admiralty telegram No. 422 has, I feel certain, been greatly influenced, and naturally so, by the military appreciations of Sir Charles Monro. These I have not seen, but their purport I have gathered in course of conversations. The Corps Commanders, I know, view the evacuation with the greatest misgiving. The forcing of the Dardanelles, as outlined in my telegrams, has never been put before them, and I am convinced that, after considering the certain results which would follow a naval success, they would favour an attack on the lines indicated, especially in view of the undoubted low morale of the Turkish Peninsular army, of which we have ample evidence.

The very extensive German propaganda being pursued all over the Near East, accompanied by the expenditure of vast sums of money, is not, I feel convinced, being undertaken merely as a side issue to the European war.

A position of stalemate on both fronts of the principal theatres of war appears the natural outcome of present situation. This opinion is freely expressed in the higher military circles in Greece, and would therefore appear to be fostered by the Germans—a significant point.

By surrendering our position here, when within sight of victory, we are aiding enemy to obtain markets the possession of which may enable her to outlast the Allies in the war of exhaustion now commencing.

A successful attack would once and for all disperse those clouds of doubt, a large amount of shipping would be released, and the question of Greece and Egypt settled.

I do not know what has been decided about Constantinople, but if the Turks could be told that we were in the Marmora to prevent its occupation by the Germans, such a course would inevitably lead to disruption, and therefore weakness amongst them.

I fear the effect on the Navy would be bad.

Although no word of attack has passed my lips except to my immediate staff and admirals, I feel sure that every officer and man would feel that the campaign had been abandoned without sufficient use having been made of our greatest force, viz., the Navy.

The position is so critical that there is no time for standing on ceremony, and I suggest that General Birdwood, the officer who would now have to carry out the attack or evacuation which is now ordered, be asked for his appreciation.

The logical conclusion, therefore, is the choice of evacuation or forcing the Straits. I consider the former disastrous tactically and strategically, and the latter feasible, and, so long as troops remain at Anzac, decisive.

I am convinced that the time is ripe for a vigorous offensive, and I am confident of success.

On August 18 the Admiralty had telegraphed to Admiral de Robeck authorizing and implicitly urging him to use the old battleships of the Fleet to force the Dardanelles, and Admiral de Robeck had declined. Now the conditions were reversed. On December 10 the same Board of Admiralty replied that they were not prepared to authorize the attempt by the Navy single-handed to force the Narrows. This sombre veto was final.

The risks that men are prepared to run in relation to circumstances present some of the strangest manifestations of psychology. One tithe of the hardihood they display to escape disaster, would often certainly achieve success. Contrast, for instance, the alternative hazards now presented to the British Government and Admiralty: on the one hand, the chance, even the probability according to all expert opinion, of losing 40,000 men in an evacuation, which if successful could only result in the total loss of the campaign; on the other, the chance of losing a squadron of old ships, and a small number of men in an operation which if successful would carry the campaign at a stroke from disaster to triumph. Yet we see Cabinet and Admiralty able to face the first alternative, and shrink from the second. While time is young, while prospects are favourable, while prizes inestimable may be gained, caution, hesitancy, half measures rule and fetter action. The grim afternoon of adverse struggle alone brings the hour of desperate resolve. The hopeful positive is rejected while all may be gained; the awful negative is embraced when nought but escape remains in view; and the energy and conviction which might have commanded victory are lavished upon the mere processes of flight.

The determination of the British Government to give in at all costs was now inflexible. The orders for the evacuation of Suvla and Anzac were reiterated by the Admiralty. On December 12, Admiral Wemyss bowed to these orders "with the greatest regret and misgiving." The plan for the evacuation, upon which a month's careful labour had been expended, was now completed, and the Admiral fixed the night of December 19 or 20 as the date of the operation.

Hope died hard. In ordering the evacuation of Suvla and Anzac the Government had consented to the retention for the time being of Helles which, while it was held, kept open the possibility of a renewed naval attack. In order to make Helles secure, the Admiral, in full accord with General Davies, commanding at Helles, elaborated plans for a combined attack by the Fleet and Army upon Achi Baba. The control and direction of the naval fire from the Monitors and the bulged "Edgars" had now been brought to a very high degree of efficiency. "Co-operation in an attack," wrote General Davies, "has now become a practical reality." Both the naval and military Commanders on the spot were therefore in complete agreement. It is not necessary to pronounce upon the prospects of such an operation, for at this moment General Monro returned from Salonika where after his one day's visit to the Peninsula and his sojourn in Egypt he had been residing. Already on December 1 he had forbidden General Birdwood and the Corps Commanders to confer with the Admiral without his permission. On the 10th he peremptorily forbade General Birdwood to discuss any military matter with the Admiral. On the 14th he telegraphed home dissociating himself from the Admiral's views and protesting against any expression of opinion by Admiral Wemyss upon military matters. He agreed, however, with the naval and local military view that Helles could not be held indefinitely without Achi Baba. Thus at last, since the capture of Achi Baba was deemed impossible, the decision was reached for the total evacuation of the Peninsula.

It was with melancholy but intense relief that I learned in France of the successful and bloodless execution of this critical operation which was accomplished on the night of December 19. The utmost credit belongs to the naval and military officers who perfected in exact detail the arrangements, and to the Admirals and Generals by whom they were so successfully carried out. The weather, on which all depended, was favourable for exactly the vital forty-eight hours, and the Turks were utterly unsuspecting. Indeed, when dawn broke on empty trenches and famous positions, bought at so terrible a cost, now silent as the graves with which they were surrounded, the haggard Turkish soldiers and their undaunted chiefs could hardly believe their eyes. Their position, and that of their country whose capital they had defended with soldierly tenacity, were now translated at a stroke from extreme jeopardy into renewed and resuscitated power. Conviction, determination and the will to win, steadfastly maintained by their High Command, had brought victory to the defence in spite of their inferiority in numbers and in resources of all kinds and of the inherent strategic perils of their position. The lack of these qualities on our side at the summit of power had defrauded the attackers of the reward, pregnant in its consequences to the whole world, to which their overwhelming potential strength and resources, their actual numbers and apparatus, their daring, their devotion and their fearful sacrifices had given them the right.

The evacuation of Helles was performed with equal skill and with equal good fortune on January 8, and the story of the Dardanelles came finally to an end. This consummation was acclaimed by the shallow and the uninstructed as if it had been a victory.

It is necessary however not only to relate the immediate sequel, but to outline the vast consequences which flowed from these events.

The campaign of the Dardanelles had been starved and crippled at every stage by the continued opposition of the French and British High Commands in France to the withdrawal of troops and munitions from the main theatre of the war. The abandonment of the Dardanelles led to the diversion of the Allied military forces on a scale far larger than its most ardent advocates had ever contemplated. Serbia had been destroyed; Bulgaria had joined our enemies; Roumania and Greece lay frozen in a terrorized neutrality. But still, as long as the British flag flew on the Peninsula and the British Fleet lay off the Straits, the main power of Turkey was gripped and paralysed. The evacuation set free twenty Turkish divisions on the Peninsula, and Turkey henceforth was able to form a common front with the Bulgarians in Thrace, to attack Russia, to aid Austria, to overawe Roumania. Turkey was also placed in a position simultaneously to threaten Egypt and to reinforce Mesopotamia. The thirteen evacuated British divisions,[1] having been rested and refitted, were required to guard against the last two of these new dangers. The whole of the new army sent by France and Britain from the French theatre, amounting to seven additional divisions, was assigned to the defence of Salonika. Apart from the Anzacs, scarcely any of these twenty divisions of Allied troops ever fought against the Germans during the rest of the war. Scarcely one came into any direct contact with any enemy for nearly six months, and during the same period thirteen out of the twenty liberated Turkish divisions were added to the hostile strength in other theatres. Eleven went to the Caucasus and two to Galicia, in both cases adding to the burden which Russia had to bear. Thus the first fruits of the evacuation of Gallipoli may be variously computed at a total loss of strength to the Allies of from thirty to forty divisions, half the Army of a first-class power. It was evident that a very grave prolongation of the war must arise from this cause alone.

From the moment when the grip on the heart of the Turkish Empire was relaxed, and breathing space was given, its widespread limbs under German stimulation regained and developed their power. The three campaigns which had either begun or were imminent from Salonika, from Egypt, or in Mesopotamia, all grew rapidly into very great undertakings, and all continued until the last day of the war to make enormous drains upon the British resources and, to a lesser degree, upon those of France. By 1918 seven British and

---

[1] The French Corps had already gone.

Indian divisions, composing an army of two hundred and seventy thousand men (exclusive of followers), were operating in Mesopotamia. The defence of the Suez Canal and subsequently the attack upon Turkey by the invasion of Palestine grew into a separate war which in any other period would have absorbed the attention of the world. Instead of thrusting at Constantinople, the heart of Turkey, or striking at her arm-pit at Alexandretta, or her elbow at Haifa, we began our attack from her finger-tips upwards. Slowly, painfully, with infinite exertion and expense, and by astonishing feats of arms and organization, we made our way across the deserts drawing artificial rivers with us through hundreds of miles of scorching sand. We toiled and fought our way mile by mile, and even yard by yard, from Gaza to Jerusalem, from Jerusalem to Damascus, never at any moment exacting from the enemy more than one-third of our own war effort. At the Armistice twelve British divisions, composing an army of nearly two hundred and eighty thousand men (exclusive of followers), were engaged in Palestine and Syria. The campaign from Salonika expanded not less formidably. At the end of 1917 twelve British and French divisions and two Italian divisions were in line against Turkish forces which perseverance at the Dardanelles might long ago have forced out of the war, and against the Bulgarian Army which a timely and prudent policy might have ranged upon our side. The sole addition gained by this great deployment of Allied force was six Serbian divisions brought by sea from the wreck of their country and four Greek divisions raised by Monsieur Venizelos after his revolt against King Constantine. In the end six hundred and thirty thousand Allied soldiers stood on the Salonika front.

The maintenance of these three great expeditions over long distances of sea threw a strain upon the maritime resources of Great Britain which, combined with the unlimited "U-boat" warfare, came near to compassing our complete ruin in the spring of 1917. Thus the Admirals who thought only of the Grand Fleet and the Generals who thought only of the Main Army may learn how cruel are the revenges which Fortune wreaks upon those who disdain her first and golden offerings.

Wasteful and roundabout as was the method, the strategic conceptions which inspired the Eastern policy were vindicated in the end; and the collapse of Bulgaria after three years' war was the signal for the general catastrophe of the Central Powers.

There ended with the Dardanelles all hope of forming direct and continuous contact with Russia. A railway 1,200 miles long might be built to Murmansk; Vladivostock might continue to pass supplies across a distance of 4,000 miles; but the intimate co-operation in men and munitions, the vast exportation of

South Russian wheat, the expansion of a vitalizing trade, which could alone spring from the opening of the Black Sea, was for ever denied us.

The abandonment of Gallipoli dispelled the Russian dream. In her darkest hours, under the flail of Ludendorff, driven out of Poland, driven out of Galicia, her armies enduring disaster and facing death often without arms, the cost of living rising continually throughout her vast, secluded Empire, Russia had cheered herself by dwelling on the great prize of Constantinople. A profound chill spread through all ranks of the Russian people, and with it came suspicion no less deep-seated. England had not really tried to force the Straits. From the moment when she had conceded the Russian claim to Constantinople, she had not been single-hearted, she had lost her interest in the enterprise. Her infirm action and divided counsels arose from secret motives hidden in the bosom of the State. And this while Russia was pouring out her blood as no race had ever done since men waged war. Such were the whispers which, winged by skilful German propaganda, spread far and wide through the Tsar's dominions, and in their wake every subversive influence gained in power. Lastly, the now inevitable prolongation of the struggle was destined to prove fatal to Russia. In the war of exhaustion to which we were finally condemned, which was indeed extolled as the last revelation of military wisdom, Russia was to be the first to fall, and in her fall to open upon herself a tide of ruin in which perhaps a score of millions of human beings have been engulfed. The consequences of these events abide with us to-day. They will darken the world for our children's children.

The failure of the Dardanelles Expedition was fatal to Lord Kitchener. During the whole of 1915 he had been in sole and plenary charge of the British military operations, and until November on every important point his will had been obeyed. The new Cabinet, like the leading members of the old, had now in their turn lost confidence in his war direction. The conduct of the Gallipoli campaign showed only too plainly the limitations of this great figure at this period of his life and in this tremendous situation both as an organiser and a man of action. His advocacy of the offensive in France which had failed so conspicuously at Loos and in Champagne was upon record. Under the agony of the Gallipoli evacuation his will power had plainly crumpled, and the long series of contradictory resolves which had marked his treatment of this terrible question was obvious to all who knew the facts.

Already, in November, had come direct rebuff. His plan for a fresh landing in the Gulf of Alexandretta, though devised by him in the actual theatre of operations, had been decisively vetoed by the new War Committee of the Cabinet and by the Allies in conference. In a series of telegrams the inclination of which could scarcely be obscure, he was encouraged to transform his definite mission at the Dardanelles into a general and extensive tour of inspection in the East. His prompt return to London showed that he was not himself unaware of the change in his position. The disposition of the British forces in the East which he made after the evacuation of Suvla and Anzac was certainly not such as to retrieve a waning prestige. It was natural that Egypt should loom disproportionately large in his mind. Almost his whole life had been spent and his fame won there. He now saw this beloved country menaced, as he believed, by an imminent Turkish invasion on a large scale. In an endeavour to ward off the imaginary peril he crowded division after division into Egypt, and evidently contemplated desperate struggles for the defence of the Suez Canal at no distant date. In the early days, at the end of 1914 and beginning of 1915, it had been worth while for a score of thousand Turks to threaten the Canal and create as much disturbance as possible in order to delay the movement of troops from India, Australia and New Zealand to the European battlefield. But both the usefulness and feasibility of such an operation were destroyed by the great increase in the scale of the war in the eastern Mediterranean theatre which had been in progress during the whole year. The German and Turkish staffs were well content to rely upon threats and boasting, and to make the proclamation of their intention a substitute for the diversion of armies. "Egypt," exclaimed Enver Pasha in December, "is our objective"; and following this simple deception the British concentration in Egypt was vehemently pursued.

On the top of this came the reverse in Mesopotamia, for which Lord Kitchener had no direct responsibility. General Townshend had marched on Baghdad, and the War Committee was led to believe that he was himself the mainspring of the enterprise. General Nixon, the Commander-in-Chief in Mesopotamia, had not informed them that his audacious and hitherto brilliantly successful subordinate had in writing recorded his misgivings about the operation. In the event Townshend's force of about 20,000 men was on November 25 forced to retreat after a well-contested action at Ctesiphon and only escaped by a swift and disastrous retreat to a temporary refuge at Kut.

On December 3 the War Committee determined to recreate the Imperial General Staff at the War Office in an effective form. The decision was drastic. The experiment of making a Field-Marshal Secretary of State for War had run its full course. Lord Kitchener might still hold the Seals of Office, but his power, hitherto so overwhelming that it had absorbed and embodied the authority alike of the ministerial and the professional Chief, was now to be confined within limits which few politicians would accept in a Secretaryship of State. Sir William Robertson, Chief of the General Staff in France, was brought to Whitehall, and an Order in Council was issued establishing his rights and responsibility in terms both strict and wide. Lord Kitchener acquiesced in the abrogation, not only of the exceptional personal powers which he had enjoyed, but of those which have always been inherent in the office which he retained.

The end of his great story is approaching: the long life full of action, lighted by hard-won achievement, crowned by power such as a British subject had rarely wielded and all the regard and honour that Britain and her Empire can bestow, was now declining through the shadows. The sudden onrush of the night, the deep waters of the North, were destined to preserve him and his renown from the shallows.

Better to sink beneath the shock,
Than moulder piecemeal on the rock.

The solemn days when he stood forth as Constable of Britain, beneath whose arm her untrained people braced themselves for war, were ended. His life of duty could only reach its consummation in a warrior's death. His record in the Great War as strategist, administrator and leader, will be judged by the eyes of other generations than our own. Let us hope they will also remember the comfort his character and personality gave to his countrymen in their hours of hardest trial.

It is impossible to assemble the long chain of fatal missed chances which prevented the forcing of the Dardanelles without experiencing a sense of awe. One sees in retrospect at least a dozen situations all beyond the control of the enemy, any one of which, decided differently, would have ensured success. If we had known when it was resolved to make the naval attack that an army would be available and would be given, a surprise combined naval and military attack upon the Gallipoli Peninsula would have been decided upon and backed with good-will. If an army had never been sent, the Navy with its mine-sweeping service well organized would have resumed its efforts after the check on March 18; and had it resumed, it would soon have exhausted the ammunition in the Turkish forts and swept the minefields. Had the dispatch of the 29th Division not been countermanded on February 20, or had it been packed in the transports in readiness to fight on disembarkation, Sir Ian Hamilton would have attacked the Gallipoli Peninsula almost immediately after March 18 and would, in that event, have found it ill-defended. The battles of June and July were all critical in the last degree. Any substantial addition to the attack would have been decisive. The paralysis of the Executive during the formation of the Coalition Government in May, delayed for six weeks the arrival of the British reinforcements, and enabled the Turks to double the strength of their Army. Thus the favourable moment at the beginning of July was thrown away. The Battle of Suvla Bay in August was marked by a combination of evil happenings extraordinary among the hazards of war. The story of the IXth British Corps and of the whole Suvla landing would be incredible if it were not true. The resignation of Lord Fisher, my dismissal from the Admiralty, and the unpopularity of the Dardanelles enterprise through ignorance, intimidated our successors on the Board of Admiralty from accepting responsibility for the risks that were necessary. The refusal of the Greek alliance and army when offered in 1914; the failure to obtain that alliance and army when sought in 1915; its mad rejection by Russia; the delicate balance on which the fateful decision of Bulgaria depended; the extraordinary circumstances in Paris which led in September, 1915, to the appointment of General Sarrail and to the proposal of the French Government to send a large expedition to take possession of the Asiatic shore of the Dardanelles, and the reversal of this policy which offered so many prospects of success; the diversion of all the forces that became available towards the end of 1915 from the vital objective of the Dardanelles and Constantinople to the prodigal, and for nearly three years indecisive, operations from Salonika; the final decision to evacuate Gallipoli, at the time when the position of the Turkish Army was most desperate and the British Navy most confident—all these are separate tragedies.

The end of the Dardanelles campaign closed the second great period of the struggle. There was nothing left on land now but the war of exhaustion—not only of armies but of nations. No more strategy, very little tactics; only the dull wearing down of the weaker combination by exchanging lives; only the multiplying of machinery on both sides to exchange them quicker. The continuous front now stretched not only from the Alps to the Seas, but across the Balkan Peninsula, across Palestine, across Mesopotamia. The Central Empires had successfully defended their southern flank in the Balkans and in Turkey. Their victory quelled simultaneously all likelihood of any attempt against their northern flank upon the Baltic. All such ideas had received their quietus. Good, plain, straightforward frontal attacks by valiant flesh and blood against wire and machine guns, "killing Germans" while Germans killed Allies twice as often, calling out the men of forty, of fifty, and even of fifty-five, and the youths of eighteen, sending the wounded soldiers back three or four times over into the shambles—such were the sole manifestations now reserved for the military art. And when at the end, three years later, the throng of uniformed functionaries who in the seclusion of their offices had complacently presided over this awful process, presented Victory to their exhausted nations, it proved only less ruinous to the victor than to the vanquished.

PART III

To All Who Endured

CHAPTER XXXVIII

THE BLOOD TEST

The New Year's light of 1916 rising upon a frantic and miserable world revealed in its full extent the immense battlefield to which Europe was reduced and on which the noblest nations of Christendom mingled in murderous confusion. It was now certain that the struggle would be prolonged to an annihilating conclusion. The enormous forces on either side were so well matched that the injuries they must suffer and inflict in their struggles were immeasurable. There was no escape. All the combatants in both combinations were gripped in a vice from which no single State could extricate itself.

The northern Provinces of France, invaded and in German occupation, inspired the French people with a commanding impulse to drive the enemy from their soil. The trench lines on which the armies were in deadlock ran—not along the frontiers, where perhaps parley would not have been impossible—but through the heart of France. The appeal to clear the national territory from foreign oppression went home to every cottage and steeled every heart. Germany on the other hand, while her armies stood almost everywhere on conquered territory, could not in the full flush of her strength yield what she had gained with so much blood, nor pay forfeit for her original miscalculations, nor make reparation for the wrong she had done. Any German Dynasty or Government which had proposed so wise and righteous a course would have been torn to pieces. The French losses and the German conquests of territory thus equally compelled a continuance of the struggle by both nations. A similar incentive operated upon Russia; and in addition the belief that defeat meant revolution hardened all governing resolves. In Britain obligations of honour to her suffering Allies, and particularly to Belgium, forbade the slightest suggestion of slackening or withdrawal. And behind this decisive claim of honour there welled up from the heart of the island race a fierce suppressed passion and resolve for victory at all costs and at all risks, latent since the downfall of Napoleon.

Not less peremptory were the forces dominating the other parties to the struggle. Italy had newly entered the war upon promises which offered her a dazzling reward. These promises were embodied in the Pact of London. They involved conditions to which Austria-Hungary could never submit without final ruin as a great Power. The acceptance by Britain and France of the Russian claim to Constantinople condemned Turkey to a similar fate. Failure meant therefore to both the Austrian and the Turkish Empires not only defeat but dissolution. As for Bulgaria, she could only expect from the victory of the Allies the dire measure she had meted to Serbia.

Thus in every quarter the stakes were desperate or even mortal; and each of the vast confederacies was riveted together within itself and each part chained to its respective foe by bonds which only the furnace of war could fuse or blast away.

It is necessary in this chapter to ask the reader, before the campaign of 1916 begins, to take a somewhat statistical view of the whole war in the West, and to examine its main episodes in their character, proportion and relation.

The events divide themselves naturally into three time-periods: the first, 1914; the second, 1915, 1916 and 1917; and the third, 1918: the First Shock; the Deadlock; and the Final Convulsion. The first period is at once the simplest and the most intense. The trained armies of Germany and France rushed upon each other, grappled furiously, broke apart for a brief space, endeavoured vainly to outflank each other, closed again in desperate conflict, broke apart once more, and then from the Alps to the sea lay gasping and glaring at each other not knowing what to do. Neither was strong enough to overcome the other, neither possessed the superior means or method required for the successful offensive. In this condition both sides continued for more than three years unable to fight a general battle, still less to make a strategic advance. It was not until 1918 that the main force of the armies on both sides was simultaneously engaged as in 1914 in a decisive struggle. In short, the war in the West resolved itself into two periods of supreme battle, divided from each other by a three-years' siege.

The scale and intensity of the First Shock in 1914 has not been fully realized even by the well-instructed French public, and is not at all understood in England. At the beginning all totals of casualties were suppressed in every combatant country by a vigorous censorship. Later on in the war when more was known, no one had time to look back in the midst of new perils to the early days; and since the war no true impression has ever reached the public. British eyes have been fixed upon the vivid pictures of Liège, Mons and Le Cateau, that part of the Battle of the Marne which occurred near Paris, and the desperate struggle round Ypres. The rest lies in a dark background, which it is now possible to illuminate.

In the first three months of actual fighting from the last week in August to the end of November, when the German drive against the Channel ports had come to an end and the first great invasion was definitely arrested, the French lost in killed, prisoners and wounded 854,000[1] men. In the same period the small British Army, about one-seventh of the French fighting strength, lost 85,000[2] men, making a total Allied loss of 939,000. Against this, in the same period, the Germans lost 677,000.[3] The fact that the Germans, although invading and presumably attacking, inflicted greater slaughter than they suffered, is due to the grave errors in doctrine, training and tactics of the French Army described in the previous chapter, and to the unsound strategic dispositions of General Joffre. But more than four-fifths of the French losses were sustained in the First Shock. In the fighting from August 21, when the main collision occurred, down to September 12, when the victory of the Marne was definitely accomplished (a period of scarcely three weeks), the French armies lost nearly 330,000 men killed or prisoners, or more than one-sixth of their total loss in killed or prisoners during the whole fifty-two months of the war. To these permanent losses should be added about 280,000 wounded, making a total for this brief period of over 600,000 casualties to the French armies alone; and of this terrific total three-fourths of the loss was inflicted from August 21 to 24, and from September 5 to 9, that is to say, in a period of less than eight days.

Nothing comparable to this concentrated slaughter was sustained by any combatant in so short a time, not even excluding the first Russian disasters, nor the final phase on the Western Front in 1918. That the French Army should have survived this frightful butchery, the glaring miscalculations which caused it, and the long and harassed retreats by which it was attended, and yet should have retained the fighting qualities which rendered a sublime recovery possible, is the greatest proof of their martial fortitude and devotion which History will record. Had this heroic army been handled in the First Shock with prudence, on a wise strategic scheme, and with practical knowledge of the effects of modern firearms and the use of barbed wire and entrenchments, there is no reason to doubt that the German invasion could have been brought to a standstill after suffering enormous losses within from thirty to fifty kilometres of the French frontiers. Instead, as events were cast, the French Army in the first few weeks of the war received wounds which were nearly fatal, and never curable.

Of these the gravest was the loss of regular regimental officers, who sacrificed themselves with unbounded devotion. In many battalions only two or three officers survived the opening battles. The cadres of the whole French Army were seriously injured by the wholesale destruction of the trained professional

[1] *Journal Officiel Documents Parlementaires.* Mars 29, 1920.
[2] *Military Effort of the British Empire.* Monthly Returns.
[3] German Federal Archives *(Reichsarchiv).*

element. The losses which the French suffered in the years which followed were undoubtedly aggravated by this impoverishment of military knowledge in the fighting units. Although the Germans are accustomed to bewail their own heavy losses of officers in the opening battles, their injury was not so deep, and until after the Ludendorff offensives they always possessed the necessary professional staff to teach and handle successive intakes of recruits.

After the situation was stabilized at the end of November, the long period of Siege warfare on the Western Front began. The Germans fortified themselves on French and Belgian soil, along a line chosen for its superior railway network, and the Allies for more than three years endeavoured, with unvarying failure, to break their front and force them to retreat.

In all, five great Allied assaults were made.

(i) By the French in Champagne and Artois, in the spring and early summer of 1915.

(ii) By the French in Champagne during the late autumn and winter of 1915, and by the British simultaneously at Loos.

(iii) By the British and French on the Somme from July to October, 1916.

(iv) By the British at Arras and by the French on the Aisne, from April to July, 1917, and

(v) By the British virtually alone at Paschendaele in the autumn and winter of 1917.

In these siege-offensives which occupied the years 1915, 1916 and 1917 the French and British Armies consumed themselves in vain, and suffered as will be seen nearly double the casualties inflicted on the Germans. In this same period the Germans made only one great counter-offensive stroke: Falkenhayn's prolonged attack on Verdun in the spring of 1916. The special features which this operation presented will be related in their place.

These sanguinary prodigious struggles, extending over many months, are often loosely described as "Battles." Judging by the number of men who took their turn in the fighting at different times, by the immense quantities of guns and shells employed, and by the hideous casualty totals, they certainly rank, taken each as a whole, among the largest events of military history. But we must not be misled by terminology. If to call them "battles" were merely a method of presenting a general view of an otherwise confusing picture, it might well pass unchallenged. But an attempt has been made by military Commanders and by a whole school of writers to represent these prolonged operations, as events comparable to the decisive battles of the past, only larger and more important. To yield to this specious argument is to be drawn into a wholly wrong impression, both of military science and of what actually took place in the Great War.

What is a battle? I wrote on March 5, 1918: "War between equals in power
. . . should be a succession of climaxes on which everything is staked, towards
which everything tends and from which permanent decisions are obtained.
These climaxes have usually been called battles. A battle means that the whole
of the resources on either side that can be brought to bear are, during the
course of a single episode, concentrated upon the enemy." The scale of a battle
must bear due proportion to the whole fighting strength of the armies. Five divisions engaged out of an army of seven may fight a battle. But the same operation in an army of seventy divisions, although the suffering and slaughter are
equal, sinks to the rank of a petty combat. A succession of such combats aug-
ments the losses without raising the scale of events.

Moreover a battle cannot, properly speaking, be considered apart from the
time factor. By overwhelming the enemy's right we place ourselves in a position
to attack the exposed flank or rear of his centre; or by piercing his centre we
gain the possibility of rolling up his flanks; or by capturing a certain hill we
command his lines of communication. But none of these consequential advantages will be gained, if the time taken in the preliminary operations is so long
that the enemy can make new dispositions—if, for instance, he can bend back
his lines on each side of the rupture and fortify them, or if he can withdraw his
army before the hill is taken which would command his communications. If he
has time to take such measures effectively, the first battle is over; and the second
stage involves a second battle. Now the amount of time required by the enemy
is not indefinite. One night is enough to enable a new position to be entrenched and organized. In forty-eight hours the railways can bring large
reinforcements of men and guns to any threatened point. The attacker is confronted with a new situation, a different problem, a separate battle. It is a
misnomer to describe the resumption of an attack in these different circumstances as a part of the original battle, or to describe a series of such disconnected efforts as one prolonged battle. Operations consisting of detached
episodes extending over months and divided by intervals during which a series
of entirely new situations are created, however great their scale, cannot be
compared—to take some modern instances—with Blenheim, Rossbach, Austerlitz, Waterloo, Gettysburg, Sedan, the Marne, or Tannenberg.

The real Battle crises of the Great War stand out from the long series of
partial, though costly, operations, not only by the casualties but by the number
of divisions simultaneously engaged on both sides. In 1914, during the four days
from August 21 to 24 inclusive, 80 German divisions were engaged with 62
French, 4 British and 6 Belgian divisions. The four decisive days of the Marne,
September 6 to 9 inclusive, involved approximately the same numbers. Practically all the reserves were thrown in on both sides, and the whole strength of

the armies utilized to the utmost. The operations in Artois in the spring of 1915, which lasted three months and cost the French 450,000 men,[1] never presented a single occasion where more than 15 divisions were simultaneously engaged on either side. The Battle of Loos-Champagne, beginning on September 25, 1915, comprised an attack by 44 French and 15 British divisions (total 59) upon approximately 30 German divisions. But within three days the decisive battle-period may be said to have passed, and the numbers engaged on the Anglo-French side were reduced rapidly. 1916 was occupied by Verdun and the Somme. In this year of almost continuous fighting, in which more than two and a half million British, French and German soldiers were killed or wounded, there is only one single day, July 1, on the Somme, where as many as 22 Allied divisions were engaged simultaneously. The rest of the Somme with all its slaughter contained no operations involving more than 18 Allied divisions, and in most cases the time was occupied by combats between 3 or 4 British or French divisions with less than half that number of the enemy. In the whole of the so-called "Battle of Verdun" there were never engaged on any single day more than 14 French and German divisions, and the really critical opening attack by which the fate of the Fortress was so nearly sealed was conducted by not more than 6 German divisions against 2 or 3 French. In 1917, with the accession of General Nivelle to the French command, an attempt was made to launch a decisive operation, and the French engaged in a single day, though with disastrous results, as many as 28 divisions. Thereafter the operations dwindled again into sanguinary insignificance. The autumn fighting in Flanders by the British Army produced a long succession of attacks delivered only by from 5 to 15 British divisions.

I wrote in October, 1917 (the reader will come to it in its proper place): "Success will only be achieved by the *scale and intensity* of our offensive effort within a limited period. We are seeking to conquer the enemy's army and not his position. . . . A policy of pure attrition between armies so evenly balanced cannot lead to a decision. It is not a question of wearing down the enemy's reserves, but of wearing them down so rapidly that recovery and replacement of shattered divisions is impossible. . . . Unless this problem can be solved satisfactorily, we shall simply be wearing each other out on a gigantic scale and with fearful sacrifices without ever reaping the reward."

It was not until March 21, 1918, when the third and final phase of the war

---

[1] This figure and other similar figures include the normal wastage of trench warfare on the quiet portions of the front. The official statistics do not enable me to distinguish between the actual battle front and the ordinary front. A uniform deduction of one-eighth would probably be sufficiently correct in all cases.

began, that Ludendorff reintroduced the great battle period. The mass of artillery, which the Germans had by then accumulated in the West, was sufficient to enable three or four great offensives to be mounted simultaneously against the Allies, and the power to release any one of these at will imparted the element of Surprise to Ludendorff's operations. The great reserves of which he disposed and which he used, after four years of carnage, with all the ruthlessness of the first invasion, carried the struggle leap by leap along the whole Western Front, until the entire structure of the opposing armies and all their organizations of attack and defence were strained to the utmost. The climax of the German effort was reached in July. Ludendorff had worn out his army in the grand manner, but thoroughly, and the Allied offensive, supported by an equally numerous artillery, then began. As this developed all the armies became involved in constantly moving battles, and nearly 90 Allied divisions were on numerous days simultaneously engaged with 70 or 80 German. Thus at last a decision was reached.

The fundamental proportion of events which the foregoing facts and figures reveal, is more apparent if weeks instead of days are taken as the test. Let us therefore multiply the number of divisions by the number of days in which they were actively engaged in any given week. The "Battle of the Frontiers" shows from August 21 to 28 about 600 division-battle days. The week of the Marne, September 5 to 12, shows a total of nearly 500. The week of Loos-Champagne in 1915, September 25 to October 2, produces a total of approximately 100. The continuous battle intensity of the first week of Verdun is only 72 divisions and never again attained that level. The opening week of the Somme, also the most important, is 46. General Nivelle's attack in April, 1917, engaged in a week 135. Paschendaele never rose above 85 division-battle days in a single week. With Ludendorff in 1918 we reach the figure of 328 between March 21 and 28. All through the summer of 1918 the weeks repeatedly show 300 entries by divisions of all the armies into battle: and finally, Foch's general advance, August, September and October, attained the maximum intensity of 554 divisional engagements a week and maintained an average weekly intensity in the fiercest month of over 400.

During the war it was the custom of the British and French staffs to declare that in their offensives they were inflicting far heavier losses on the Germans than they themselves suffered. Similar claims were advanced by the enemy. Ludendorff shared the professional outlook of the British and French High Commands. Even after the war was over, with all the facts in his mind or at his disposal had he cared to seek them, we find him writing "Of the two [policies] the offensive makes less demands on the men and gives no higher losses."[1] Let us subject these assertions and theories of the military schools of the three great belligerents to a blood test as pitiless as that to which they all in turn doomed their valiant soldiers.

Since the Armistice the facts are known; but before proceeding to detailed figures it will be well to take a general survey.

The Germans, out of a population of under 70 millions, mobilized during the war for military service 13¼ million persons. Of these; according to the latest German official figures for all fronts including the Russian, over 7 millions suffered death, wounds or captivity, of whom nearly 2 millions perished.[2] France, with a population of 38 millions, mobilized a little over 8 million persons. This however includes a substantial proportion of African troops outside the French population basis. Of these approximately 5 millions became casualties, of whom 1½ millions lost their lives. The British Empire, out of a white population of 60 millions, mobilized nearly 9½ million persons and sustained over 3 million casualties including nearly a million deaths.

The British totals are not directly comparable with those of France and Germany. The proportion of coloured troops is greater. The numbers who fell in theatres other than the Western, and those employed on naval service, are both much larger.

The French and German figures are however capable of very close comparison. Both the French and German armies fought with their whole strength from the beginning to the end of the war. Each nation made the utmost possible demand upon its population. In these circumstances it is not surprising that the official French and German figures tally with considerable exactness. The Germans mobilized 19 per cent. of their entire population, and the French, with their important African additions, 21 per cent. Making allowance for the African factor it would appear that in the life-and-death struggle both countries put an equal strain upon their manhood. If this basis is sound—and it certainly appears reasonable—the proportion of French and German casualties to persons mobilized displays an even more remarkable concordance. The proportion of German casualties to total mobilized is 10 out of every 19, and that of the French is 10 out of every 16. The ratios of deaths to woundings in Germany and France are almost exactly equal, viz., 2 to 5. Finally these figures yield a division of German losses between the Western and all other fronts of approximately 3 to 1 both in deaths and casualties. All the calculations which follow are upon the basis of the tables which yield these authoritative and harmonious general proportions.

---

[1] *My War Memories,* Ludendorff. Vol. II.

[2] *Zentral Nachweiseamt.* This figure is also given by the French military historian, Lieut.-Col. Corda, *La Guerre Mondiale,* p. 413.

The British War Office published in March 1922, its *Statistics of the Military Effort of the British Empire during the Great War.*[1] A section of this massive compilation records the comparative figures of British and German casualties on the British sector of the Western Front from February, 1915, to October, 1918, inclusive. The British figures are compiled from the official records of the War Office. The German figures have been obtained from the Federal Archives Office at Potsdam. The result of the calculation is summed up as follows: The total number of British 'Officer' casualties was 115,741 and of German 'Officer' casualties 47,256. The total number of British 'Other Ranks' casualties was 2,325,932 and of German 'Other Ranks' casualties 1,633,140. The casualties among British 'Officers' compared to German were therefore about 5 to 2, and of British 'Other Ranks' compared to German about 3 to 2.

Comparative tables are given in the same work which show the losses of both sides in the various offensive periods.[2]

BRITISH OFFENSIVES OF 1916 AND 1917

| | OFFICERS.[3] | | OTHER RANKS. | |
	BRITISH.	GERMAN.	BRITISH.	GERMAN.
1916 July–December THE SOMME	21,974	4,879	459,868	231,315
	over 4–1		about 2–1	
1917 January–June ARRAS and MESSINES	15,198	3,953	295,803	172,962
	about 4–1		about 5–3	
1917 July–December PASCHENDAELE and CAMBRAI	22,316	6,913	426,298	263,797
	about 3–1		about 5–3	
TOTALS	59,488	15,745	1,181,969	688,074
	about 4–1		nearly 2–1	

[1] Hereafter referred to as *The Military Effort.*
[2] *The Military Effort*, pp. 358 *et seq.*
[3] The German commissioned officers were less numerous per unit than in the British Service.

A. LOSSES ON THE WESTERN FRONT.

(Killed, died in hospital, missing, prisoners and wounded, including officers.)

Period.[1]	Description.	SUFFERED		
		by GERMANS.	FRENCH.	BRITISH.
Aug.–Nov., 1914	Battle of the Frontiers (Aug. 6–Sept. 5) and Battle of the Marne (Sept. 6–13). The race to the sea (1st battle of Artois, the Yser). *British:* 1st *Ypres*	677,440	854,000	84,575
Dec., 1914–Jan., 1915	Stabilization.	170,025	254,000	17,621
Feb.–Mar., 1915	1st offensive of 1915 (1st battle of Champagne)	114,492	240,000	33,678
Apr.–June, 1915	2nd battle of Artois. *British:* 2nd *Ypres*	233,506	449,000	119,557
July–Aug., 1915	Stabilization.	78,402	193,000	30,902
Sept.–Nov., 1915	2nd offensive of 1915 (2nd battle of Champagne, 3rd battle of Artois). *British: Loos* . .	186,188	410,000	94,787
Dec., 1915–Jan., 1916	Stabilization.	39,702	78,000	22,092
Feb.–June, 1916	Defensive battle of Verdun .	334,246	442,000	118,992
July–Oct., 1916	Battle of the Somme . . .	537,919	341,000	453,238
Nov.–Dec., 1916	1st offensive battle of Verdun.	92,273	93,000	60,041
Jan.–Mar., 1917	The German retreat . . .	65,381	108,000	67,217
Apr.–July, 1917	Offensive of the Aisne (Chemin-des-Dames, and battle of the Mounts). *British: Arras, Messines*	414,071	279,000	355,928
Aug.–Dec., 1917	Minor operations (Flanders, right bank of the Meuse, the Malmaison). *British: Paschendaele, Cambrai*	404,517	182,000	394,645
Jan.–Feb., 1918	Stabilization.	24,064	51,000	22,851
Mar.–June, 1918	Defensive campaign of 1918. *British: March 21, Lys* .	688,341	433,000	418,374
July–Nov., 1918	Offensive campaign of 1918 .	785,733	531,000	411,636
	TOTALS	4,846,000[2]	4,938,000[3]	2,706,000[4]
Four-fifths of 494,000 German casualties reported after Armistice : *and British additional* . . .		397,000		52,000
Casualties inflicted by Americans (say) . .		140,000	—	—
French officers killed (not included in periods) .		—	36,000	—
	FINAL TOTALS	5,383,000[6]	4,974,000	2,758,000[5]
Of which (*a*) **Deaths** (killed, died in hospital, permanently missing)		1,493,000[7]	1,432,000	684,000
(*b*) **Non-fatal casualties**		3,890,000	3,506,000	2,074,000
Ratios of (*a*) to (*b*)		*1 to 2·60*	*1 to 2·45*	*1 to 3·03*

[1] One-eighth may be deducted from all figures on both sides for casualties on parts of the front other than the battle-fronts in each period.

[2] Federal Archives (*Reichsarchiv*), Potsdam, Dec. 31, 1918.

[3] Official Returns to the Chamber, Resolution of Deputy Marin, March 29, 1922.

[4] Military Effort of the British Empire. Monthly Returns, pp, 253 to 271.

[5] A small percentage, probably less than 2 per cent., may be deducted from the British casualty totals in each period to allow for a more thorough recording than appears in the German figures of very slightly wounded men who remained at duty.

[6] Add German casualties suffered on Russian and other fronts, viz. 1,697,000, making German total loss 7,080,000, of which Deaths, 2,000,000.

[7] For method of estimating this figure see Appendix, Table III.

B. LOSSES ON THE WESTERN FRONT.[1]

(Killed, died in hospital, missing, prisoners and wounded, including officers.)

Period.	Description.	INFLICTED.		
		by GERMANS.	FRENCH.	BRITISH.
Aug.–Nov., 1914	Battle of the Frontiers (Aug. 6–Sept. 5) and Battle of the Marne (Sept. 6–13). The race to the sea (1st battle of Artois, the Yser). *British:* 1st Ypres	938,575 ⎫	747,465	say 100,000
Dec.–Jan., 1915	Stabilization.	271,621 ⎭		
Feb.–March	1st offensive of 1915 (1st battle of Champagne)	273,178	96,002	18,490
April–June	2nd battle of Artois. *British:* 2nd Ypres	568,557	190,420	43,086
July–August	Stabilization.	223,902	66,785	11,617
Sept.–Nov.	2nd offensive of 1915 (2nd battle of Champagne, 3rd battle of Artois). *British:* Loos	504,787	154,139	32,049
Dec.–Jan., 1916	Stabilization.	100,092	28,933	10,769
Feb.–June	Defensive battle of Verdun	560,992	278,739	55,507
July–Oct.	Battle of the Somme	794,238	338,011	199,908
Nov.–Dec.	1st offensive battle of Verdun.	153,041	56,037	36,236
Jan.–March, 1917	The German retreat	175,217	30,183	35,198
Apr.–July	Offensive of the Aisne (Chemin-des-Dames, and battle of the Mounts). *British: Arras, Messines*	634,928	238,310	175,771
Aug.–Dec.	Minor operations (Flanders, right bank of the Meuse, the Malmaison). *British: Paschendaele, Cambrai*	576,645	167,381	237,136
Jan.–Feb., 1918	Stabilization.	73,853	12,230	11,834
Mar.–June	Defensive campaign of 1918. *British: March 21, Lys*	851,374	253,204	435,137
July–Nov.	Offensive campaign of 1918	942,636	414,617	371,116
	TOTALS	7,644,000 [2]	3,072,000	1,774,000

Not included above.	by GERMANS.	
Additional British and German losses reported after Armistice and not classified by months or fronts	52,000	494,000
French officers killed (not distributed)	36,000	—
American losses	302,000	—
Belgian losses	93,000	—

[1] Authorities and deductions as on previous table.
[2] No figures are included for the enormous casualties inflicted by the Germans on the Russians; nor for those inflicted by the British on the Turks.

There is no reason to doubt the substantial accuracy of these authoritative and official calculations, nor the truth of the picture they present. But since 1918 supplementary casualty returns have been presented both in Germany and Britain which must be brought into the account. They do not materially alter the picture. The two tables printed on pages 558 and 559 show in their simplest form the respective total casualties suffered and inflicted according to the latest information by all the three main combatants on the Western Front. It would not be right to claim for any elaborate set of figures built up under such varying circumstances an exact and meticulous accuracy; nor is such exactness necessary for the use to which the figures are put in this account. The authority for every set of figures is given. All the modifications which are required have been made, and in the result I believe it to be a sound and correct presentation of fact.

Let us now proceed to draw the conclusions which emerge from the figures. They do not appear to have been at all appreciated even in the most expert circles. I state them in their simplest form.

During the whole war the Germans never lost in any phase of the fighting more than the French whom they fought, and frequently inflicted double casualties upon them. In no one of the periods into which the fighting has been divided by the French authorities, did the French come off best in killed, prisoners and wounded. Whether they were on the defensive or were the attackers the result was the same. Whether in the original rush of the invasion, or in the German offensive at Verdun, or in the great French assaults on the German line, or even in the long periods of wastage on the trench warfare front, it always took the blood of 1½ TO 2 Frenchmen to inflict a corresponding injury upon a German.

The second fact which presents itself from the tables is that *in all the British offensives the British casualties were never less than 3 to 2, and often nearly double the corresponding German losses.*

However, comparing the French and British efforts against the Germans on the Western Front, the French suffered in all the periods concerned irrespective of the kind of operation heavier losses than those they inflicted on the enemy: whereas while the British suffered heavier losses in all offensives, they exacted more than their own losses when attacked by the Germans.

In the series of great offensive pressures which Joffre delivered during the whole of the spring and autumn of 1915, the French suffered nearly 1,300,000 casualties. They inflicted upon the Germans in the same period and the same operations 506,000 casualties. They gained no territory worth mentioning, and no strategic advantages of any kind. This was the worst year of the Joffre régime. Gross as were the mistakes of the Battle of the Frontiers, glaring as had been the errors of the First Shock, they were eclipsed by the insensate obstinacy and lack of comprehension which, without any large numerical superiority, without adequate artillery or munitions, without any novel mechanical method, without any pretence of surprise or manœuvre, without any reasonable hope of victory, continued to hurl the heroic but limited manhood of France at the strongest entrenchments, at uncut wire and innumerable machine guns served with cold skill. The responsibilities of this lamentable phase must be shared in a subordinate degree by Foch, who under Joffre's orders, but as an ardent believer, conducted the prolonged Spring offensive in Artois, the most sterile and prodigal of all.

During the Somme in 1916, where the brunt of the slaughter was borne by the British, the French and German losses were much less unequal. But, on the other hand, their rigid method of defence at Verdun, which will be presently described, led the French to suffer in a far greater degree even than the attacking Germans.

In the face of the official figures now published and set out in the tables, what becomes of the argument of the "battle of attrition"? If we lose three or four times as many officers and nearly twice as many men in our attack as the enemy in his defence, how are we wearing him down? The result of every one of these offensives was to leave us relatively weaker—and in some cases terribly weaker—than the enemy. The aggregate result of all of them from 1915 to 1917 (after deducting the losses on both sides in the German attack on Verdun) was a French and British casualty list of 4,123,000 compared to a German total of 2,166,000. Not only is this true of numbers, but also of the quality of the troops. In the attack it is the bravest who fall. The loss is heaviest among the finest and most audacious fighters. In defence the casualties are spread evenly throughout the total number exposed to the fire. The process of attrition was at work; but it was on our own side that its ravages fell, and not on the German.

It may be contended that if one side is much more numerous than the other it may 'wear down' the enemy, as Grant sought vainly to wear down the Confederates before Richmond in 1864, even at a cost of two to one. But this argument cannot be applied to the struggle on the Western Front. First, the Allies never had the superiority to afford such an uneven sacrifice of life. Secondly, the German annual intake of recruits was large enough to repair the whole of their permanent loss in any year.

Let us here examine the total German losses on the Western Front.

CASUALTIES INFLICTED ON THE GERMANS [1]

		BY BRITISH.	FRENCH. [2]	TOTAL.
1914	(say)	100,000	748,000 [3]	848,000
1915		116,000	536,000	652,000
1916		291,000	673,000	964,000
1917		448,000	436,000	884,000
1918		818,000	680,000	1,498,000
Totals		1,773,000	3,073,000	4,846,000 [4]

From the tables of killed, missing, prisoners and wounded it is necessary to extract the permanent loss to the Army, i.e., men rendered incapable of taking any further part in the war. For this purpose we include all the killed, missing and prisoners and one-third only of the wounded. On this basis the total permanent German loss in the West during the three years of siege warfare was as follows:

1915	337,000
1916	549,000
1917	510,000
Total	1,396,000 [5]

Thus in the three years of siege conditions the losses of the Germans on the Western Front averaged 465,000 a year. Their annual intake of recruits through young men growing up was over 800,000. But, in their hard need, and often through the ardour of their young men, they heavily anticipated their annual harvests. From May, the normal conscription month, to the end of 1915, they drew 1,070,000 men to the Colours.[6] In the similar period of 1916 they overdrew no less than 1,443,000 men. Thus, in 1917 they could call up only 622,000. Nevertheless, the least of these figures far exceeded the attrition value of the Allied offensives. It was not until 1918 that the intake of available Germans fell to 405,000. It would probably, if the national resistance had not collapsed, have risen in 1919, for the ample crops of German youth were steadily

[1] See Table B.
[2] Including losses inflicted by the Belgians.
[3] 100,000 deducted for British share, no separate figures being available.
[4] These figures take no account of the supplementary German casualties not distributed into periods.
[5] No allowance is made in these figures for the supplementary German casualties, since these could at most vary the totals to the extent of 8 per cent.
[6] These figures include sick and wounded who had recovered and men combed from industries.

coming forward at 800,000 a year. The figures of German loss and intake for the three Siege years are therefore as follows:

	Loss in the West	Total Intake	Balance for all fronts
1915	337,000	1,070,000	733,000
1916	549,000	1,443,000	894,000
1917	510,000	622,000	112,000
Totals	1,396,000	3,135,000	1,739,000

Where then in mere attrition was the end to be discerned? On the terms of 1915, 1916, and 1917 the German man power was sufficient to last indefinitely. In fact in the three years of the Allied offensives on the Western Front they gained actually to the extent of 1,739,000 men more than their losses. We were in fact, as I wrote early in March, 1918, "merely exhanging lives upon a scale at once more frightful than anything that has been witnessed before in the world, and too modest to produce a decision."

It was not until 1918 that the change fatal for Germany occurred. There was one period in the warfare between the British and Germans in which the relative losses are strikingly reversed. That period is not, as the casual reader might expect, when our troops were gaining ground, storming trench lines, pulverizing fortified villages, gathering prisoners and the grisly spoils of battle, and when our propaganda, domestic and external, was eagerly proclaiming that the tide of victory flowed. It was during the period which probably in most people's minds represents the most agonizing and alarming phase of the war on the Western Front, the days of the greatest German victories and the most grievous British reverses. For the first time in Ludendorff's tremendous offensive of 1918, in the battles following the twenty-first of March and in the battles of the Lys, the German losses in men and officers in killed and wounded, especially killed, and above all in officers killed, towered up above those of the troops whom they thought they were defeating, and whom we knew they were driving back.

It was their own offensive, not ours, that consummated their ruin. They were worn down not by Joffre, Nivelle and Haig, but by Ludendorff. See again the remorseless figures from March 21, 1918, to the end of June.[1] In barely three months the Germans suffered against the British alone 16,000 officer casualties and 419,000 casualties among the other ranks. They lost in almost the same period[2] against the British alone, 3,860 officers killed compared with 3,878 officers killed by the British in the whole preceding two years. Against the French

[1] *Military Effort*, p. 62.
[2] Including the quiet month of July.

in the same three months, but mainly in the last five weeks, the Germans lost 253,000 officers and men. Their total casualties in only thirteen weeks amounted to 688,000, very few of whom in the short time that was left ever returned to the front. In this period their intake was reduced to 405,000 for the nine months of the year that the war lasted. Therefore they consumed nearly 700,000 men in a time when their corresponding intake did not exceed 150,000. Here then was the wearing down which, coming at the moment when the German national spirit was enfeebled by its exertions during four years and by the cumulative effects of the blockade, led to the German retreat on the Western Front; to the failure to make an effective withdrawal to the Antwerp-Meuse line with all the bargaining possibilities that this afforded, and to the sudden final collapse of German resistance in November, 1918.

But, it will be said, numerical attrition is not the only test, there is moral attrition which wears down the will power of an enemy who is constantly being attacked. He has to yield ground; he loses prisoners, guns, and trophies; he sees the strongest defences stormed; his battle line is constantly receding. It is this experience which wears him out in spite of the fact that he is killing two or often three assailants for each of his own men slain. It may be conceded that the ordeal of the defending troops in modern warfare is no less trying than that of the attacker. But after all there is no greater stimulus to the soldier in his agony than the knowledge of the loss he is inflicting on his foe. Crouched by his machine gun amid the awful bombardment he sees long lines mowed down, wave after wave, in hundreds and in thousands. He knows how few and far between are the defenders, he sees how many are their targets. With every attack repulsed he gains fresh confidence, and when at last he is overwhelmed there are others behind him who know what is happening and which side is suffering most.

But let us test the theory of moral attrition also by the facts. Can it be disputed that the confidence of the German armies was increased as well as their relative numerical strength by the repulse of the British and French at Loos and Champagne in 1915? Did these battles induce them to weaken in any way their pressure upon Russia? Was it not during these very battles that German divisions conquered Serbia and overran the Balkans? Was not the German High Command at the height of the Somme offensive able to withdraw more than a dozen divisions from the various fronts to strike down Roumania? Which army exulted over the great Nivelle offensive in 1917? Who emerged with the greatest confidence from the prolonged fighting which followed the Battle of Arras? What were the relative positions of the British and German Armies at the end of Paschendaele—the British exhausted, shot to pieces, every division having to be reduced from thirteen to ten battalions; the Germans training, resting, gathering their reinforcements from Russia for a greater effort than any they had yet made?

It is certain, surveying the war as a whole, that the Germans were strengthened relatively by every Allied offensive—British or French—launched against them, until the summer of 1918. Had they not squandered their strength in Ludendorff's supreme offensive in 1918, there was no reason why they should not have maintained their front in France practically unaltered during the whole of the year, and retreated at their leisure during the winter no farther than the Meuse.

But, it will be said, if the conditions over a prolonged period are such that all offensives are equally injurious to the attacker, how then is war to be waged? Are both sides to sit down with enormous armies year after year looking at each other, each convinced that whoever attacks will be the loser? Is this the sterile conclusion to which the argument tends? What positive courses should have been adopted? No one need go so far as to say that every Allied offensive could have been avoided. Indeed, there were at least five examples of short sudden 'set piece' attacks—the opening of the battle of Arras, the capture of the Messines Ridge, the French recaptures of Fort Douaumont and of Malmaison, and the first day's battle of Cambrai—which in themselves were brilliant events. All of these, if they had ended with the fruits of the initial surprise, would have been more costly in men as well as in repute to the Germans than to the Allies. It is indeed by such episodes that the prestige of an 'active defensive' might have been maintained. But the question is whether it was wise policy to seek and pursue prolonged offensives on the largest scale in order to wear down the enemy by attrition; whether instead of seeking the offensive ourselves in France, both British and French ought not consistently on all occasions to have endeavoured to compel the enemy to attack. If our whole strategy and tactics had been directed to that end, would not the final victory have been sooner won?

Once the enemy was committed to the attack we could have exacted a cruel forfeit. It would have been his part, not ours, to crunch the barbed wire and gorge machine guns with the noblest sacrifices of youth. And need the tale have ended there? The use of force for the waging of war is not to be regulated simply by firm character and text-book maxims. Craft, foresight, deep comprehension of the verities, not only local but general; strategems, devices, manœuvres, all of these on the grand scale are demanded from the chiefs of great armies.

Suppose we—both French and British—have trained our armies behind the trench line to a high standard of flexible manœuvring efficiency; suppose we have permanently fortified with concrete and every modern device those portions of the front where we cannot retreat; suppose we have long selected and shrewdly weakened those portions where we could afford to give 20 or 30 kilometres of ground; suppose we lure the enemy to attack there and make great pockets and bulges in a thin and yielding front, and then, just as he thinks himself pressing on to final victory, strike with independent counter-offensive on the largest scale and with deeply planned railways, not at his fortified trench line, but at the flanks of a moving, quivering line of battle! Are there not combinations here which at every stage would sell ground only subject to the full blood tax, and finally offer to brave, fresh, well-trained troops the opportunities of sudden and glorious victory?

And why should the view be limited to the theatre in which the best and largest armies happen to face each other? Sea power, railway communications, foreign policy, present the means of finding new flanks outside the area of deadlock. Mechanical science offers on the ground, in the air, on every coast, from the forge or from the laboratory, boundless possibilities of novelty and surprise. Suppose for instance the war power represented by the 450,000 French and British casualties in the Champagne-Loos battle of 1915 had been used to force the Dardanelles or to combine the Balkan States!

Let us, to cultivate a sense of proportion, digress for a moment from the Western Front to the "side-shows" of the war—many of them in themselves ill-judged—in order to measure the distribution of our total war power. A calculation has been made by the War Office and published in *The Military Effort*[1] on the basis, not of course of casualties, but of the men employed in any theatre multiplied by the number of days so employed. From this the following proportions are derived, taking the effort at the Dardanelles as the unit:

MAN-DAYS
(Officers Excluded)

Dardanelles	1.00
Salonica	6.40
North Russia	.08
Palestine	12.20
Mesopotamia	11.80
East Africa	8.20
France	73.00

And is there not also a virtue in "saving up"? We never gave ourselves the chance. We had to improvise our armies in face of the enemy. The flower of the nation, its manhood, its enterprise, its brains were all freely given. But there never was found the time to train and organize these elements before they were

---

[1] Pp. 742 *et seq.*

consumed. From the priceless metal successive half-sharpened half-tempered weapons were made, were used and broken as soon as they were fashioned, and then replaced by others similarly unperfected. The front had to be defended, the war had to be waged, but there was surely no policy in eagerly *seeking* offensives with immature formations or during periods when no answer to the machine gun existed. Suppose that the British Army sacrificed upon the Somme, the finest we ever had, had been preserved, trained and developed to its full strength till the summer of 1917, till perhaps 3,000 tanks were ready, till an overwhelming artillery was prepared, till a scientific method of continuous advance had been devised, till the apparatus was complete, might not a decisive result have been achieved at one supreme stroke?

It will be said—What of the Allies—what of Russia—what of Italy, would they have endured so long, while France and Britain perfected their plans and accumulated their power? But if direct aid had come to Russia through the destruction of Turkey, and to Italy through the marshalling of the Balkans against Austria, might not both these states have been spared the disasters to which they were in fact exposed? And is there any use in fighting a prolonged offensive in which the attacker suffers without strategic gain nearly double the loss of the defenders? How does the doing of an unwise, costly and weakening act help an Ally? Is not any temporary relief to him of pressure at the moment paid for by him with compound interest in the long run? What is the sense of attacking only to be defeated; or of 'wearing down the enemy' by being worn down more than twice as fast oneself? The uncontrollable momentum of war, the inadequacy of unity and leadership among Allies, the tides of national passion, nearly always *force* improvident action upon Governments or Commanders. Allowance must be made for the limits of their knowledge and power. The British commanders were throughout deeply influenced by the French mood and situation. But do not let us obscure the truth. Do not found conclusions upon error. Do not proclaim its melancholy consequences as the perfect model of the art of war or as the triumphant consummation of a great design.

CHAPTER XXXIX

FALKENHAYN'S CHOICE

The opening scene of the year 1916 lies in the Cabinet of the German Main Headquarters, and the principal figure is General von Falkenhayn, the virtual Commander-in-Chief of the Central Empires. On the evening of September 14, 1914, Falkenhayn, then Minister of War, had been appointed by the Emperor Chief of the German General Staff. From this post General von Moltke, who, when the decision of the Marne had become unmistakable, had said to the Emperor, "Your Majesty, we have lost the war," had retired, broken in health and heart. The new Director of the German Army also retained for a time his position as Minister of War; and when early in the New Year he ceded this latter post, it was to a nominee of his own. Falkenhayn was therefore armed with the fullest powers, and during a period of almost exactly two years he continued to wield them undisputed. He had succeeded to a stricken inheritance. The great stake had been played and lost by his predecessor. The rush on Paris, trampling down Belgium, and with it all hope of ending the war by one blow, had failed. It had cost Germany her good name before the world, it had brought into the field against her the sea power, the wealth and the ever-growing military strength of the British Empire. In the East the defeat of the Austrians in the Battle of Lemberg had balanced the victories of Hindenburg and Ludendorff, and the rulers of Germany, their armies at a standstill, their territories blockaded, their sea-borne commerce arrested, must prepare for a prolonged struggle against a combination of states of at least twice their population and wealth, commanding through sea power the resources of the whole world and possessed at this juncture of the choice where to strike the next blow.

The Truths of War are absolute, but the principles governing their application have to be deduced on each occasion from the circumstances, which are always different; and in consequence no rules are any guide to action. Study of the past is invaluable as a means of training and storing the mind, but it is no help without selective discernment of the particular facts and of their emphasis, relation and proportion.

German, like British military policy, oscillated throughout the Great War between two opposed conceptions of strategy. Reduced to the simplest terms the contrasted theories may be expressed as follows: To attack the strong, or to attack the weak. Once all attempts against the Dardanelles were finally excluded from consideration, little was left to Britain but to attack the strong. The Balkans were lost, and the scale of the armies required to produce decisive results in the Balkan Peninsula or in Turkey had by this time outrun the limits of available sea power. The prizes had disappeared or dwindled; the efforts required to gain them had been multiplied beyond all reason. But to Germany, with her central position and excellent railway system, both alternative policies were constantly open, and her leaders, in their torment of perplexity, were drawn now in one direction and now in the other.

To contend that either of these theories was wholly and invariably right and the other wrong would be to press argument beyond the bounds of common sense. Obviously if you can beat your strongest opponent in the hostile combination you should do so. But if you cannot beat your strongest opponent in the main theatre, nor he beat you; or if it is very unlikely that you can do so, and if the cost of failure will be very great, then surely it is time to consider whether the downfall of your strongest foe cannot be accomplished through the ruin of his weakest ally, or one of his weaker allies; and in this connection a host of political, economic and geographical advantages may arise and play their part in the argument. Every case must be judged upon its merits and in relation to the whole of the circumstances of the occasion. The issue is not one for rigid or absolute decision in general terms; but a strong inclination in theory, based upon profound reflection, is a good guide amid the conflict and confusion of facts.

This account will leave the reader in no doubt about the opinion of its author. From first to last it is contended that once the main armies were in deadlock in France the true strategy for both sides was to attack the weaker partners in the opposite combination with the utmost speed and ample force. According to this view, Germany was unwise to attack France in August, 1914, and especially unwise to invade Belgium for that purpose. She should instead have struck down Russia and left France to break her teeth against the German fortress and trench lines. Acting thus she would probably have avoided war with the British Empire, at any rate during the opening, and for her most important, phase of the struggle. The first German decision to attack the strongest led to her defeat at the Marne and the Yser, and left her baffled and arrested with the evergrowing might of an implacable British Empire on her hands. Thus 1914 ended.

But in 1915 Germany turned to the second alternative, and her decision was attended by great success. Leaving the British and French to shatter their armies against her trench lines in France, Germany marched and led her allies against Russia, with the result that by the autumn enormous territories had been conquered from Russia; all the Russian system of fortresses and strategic railways was in German hands, while the Russian armies were to a large extent destroyed and the Russian State grievously injured.

The only method by which the Allies could rescue Russia was by forcing the Dardanelles. This was the only counter-stroke that could be effective. If it had succeeded it would have established direct and permanent contact between Russia and her Western allies, it would have driven Turkey, or at the least Turkey in Europe, out of the war, and might well have united the whole of the Balkan States, Serbia, Greece, Bulgaria and Roumania, against Austria and Germany. Russia would thus have received direct succour, and in addition would have experienced an enormous relief through the pressure which the combined Balkan States would instantly have applied to Austria-Hungary. However, the narrow and local views of British Admirals and Generals and of the French Headquarters had obstructed this indispensable manœuvre. Instead of a clear strategic conception being clothed and armed with all that the science of staffs and the authority of Commanders could suggest, it had been resisted, hampered, starved and left to languish. The time gained by this mismanagement and the situation created by the Russian defeats enabled Germany in September to carry the policy of attacking the weaker a step farther. Falkenhayn organized an attack upon Serbia. Bulgaria was gained to the German side, Serbia was conquered, and direct contact was established between the Central Empires and Turkey. The failure and final abandonment of the Dardanelles campaign thus sealed the fate not only of the Balkan States but also of Russia. The defeat of the French and British armies in the disastrous battles of Champagne and Loos proved the German front unbreakable in the West. The direct contact between Germany and Turkey established through the accession of Bulgaria gripped Turkey and threw open the road to the East. The year 1915 was therefore one of great success for Germany, and Falkenhayn could claim with justice that by the mistakes of her enemies and by her own adoption of the policy of attacking the weaker she had retrieved in its course the disastrous situation in which she had been left at the end of 1914. Opportunity and initiative had returned to Germany: the next move lay with her, and 1916 dawned in breathless expectation of what it would be.

Nowhere was the choice of Germany awaited with more strained attention than in Roumania. The policy of a small State overshadowed by tremendous neighbouring Empires, at grips with one another, from both of whom she coveted important provinces, was necessarily one of calculation. In the years before the war Roumania conceived herself to have been defrauded of Bessarabia by Russia after the Russo-Turkish War of 1878. From Hungary her desires were at once natural and ambitious. Siebenburgen, Transylvania and to a lesser extent the

Bukovina were largely inhabited by men of Roumanian race, and in Transylvania particularly Roumanian sentiment was sternly repressed by the Hungarian Government. To be united to these unredeemed provinces, to join her outlying kinsfolk to the Motherland, to build in one form or another the integral, ethnological unit of a Great Roumania, was throughout the supreme and dominating motive at Bucharest. These aims had for generations been obvious both to Russia and to Austria-Hungary, who watched without illusion and fully armed every move in Roumanian affairs. On her other borders Roumania clashed with two Balkan States. She competed with Serbian ambitions for the eventual reversion of the Banat of Temesvar. She had profited by the crisis of the Balkan War of 1912 to take the Dobruja from Bulgaria. To her grave preoccupations about Russia and Austria-Hungary, Roumania must henceforward add a persisting fear of Bulgarian revenge.

These grim external relationships were aggravated by the complications of domestic and dynastic politics. The Roumanian Conservatives, headed by Majoresco, favoured Germany. The Liberals, headed by Bratiano, the new Prime Minister, favoured France. Outside official circles the most prominent politician on the side of the *Entente* was Také Jonescu, and on the side of Germany Carp. The King was not only pro-German but German, and a faithful son of the House of Hohenzollern to boot. The Heir Apparent was pro-French and his wife pro-English. Both the King and his successor had exceptional consorts. The poetry of "Carmen Sylva" is widely acclaimed; the courage of Queen Marie was to remain undaunted through every trial the tempest had in store. In short, Roumania, if war came, could move in either direction towards alternative prizes glittering across chasms, and in either case she would find a Party and a Royal Family apt and happy to execute her policy. To choose would be an awful hazard. Yet not to choose, to linger in futile neutrality, might cast away the supreme opportunity of Roumanian national history.

Upon the complicated politics of aspiring Roumania the Great War had thus supervened. Russia and Austria-Hungary sprang at each other in mortal conflict, while high above the European scene rose the flaming sword of Germany. Each side bid for Roumania's favours and offered bribes for Roumanian intervention. But the inducements of the Great Powers took the form, not of ceding portions of their own territory to Roumanian sovereignty, but rather of promising to cede portions of their rivals' territory to Roumania if with her assistance they won the war. The question which Roumania had to decide was, Who would win the War? It was very difficult to tell, yet on judging rightly depended Ruin or Empire. Long did Roumania hesitate before she gave her answer.

There was no doubt where at the outset her sympathies lay. Roumania saw like all neutral states, like all detached observers, how flagrantly the Central

Powers had put themselves in the wrong and how grossly they had blundered. On the balance far more was to be gained by Roumania from the downfall of Austria-Hungary than from that of Russia. The pro-French Bratiano ministry was in power. Také Jonescu, like Venizelos in Greece, never swerved from the conviction that England would always come out victorious. Sympathies, merits, interest, mood, all pointed towards Britain, France and Russia. On the other side was King Carol with the Treaty on his conscience—and the fear of national destruction at his heart.

Prudence enjoined delay, and in this atmosphere any proposal of honouring the alliance and joining Austria was out of the question. The Roumanian Government followed the Italian example of declaring that as there had not been an unprovoked attack upon Austria the *casus fœderis* had not arisen. Roumania declared neutrality, and King Carol had to be content with this. The policy of Roumania henceforward is sourly described by Czernin in the following terms, which cannot be considered just unless her difficulties are also comprehended: "The Roumanian Government consciously and deliberately placed itself between the two groups of Powers and allowed itself to be driven and pushed by each, got the largest amount of advantages from each, and watched for the moment when it could be seen which was the stronger, in order then to fall upon the weaker."

While the old King lived his influence was sufficient, in spite of the Battle of Lemberg and the Russian advance into Galicia, to prevent Roumania from declaring war upon Austria-Hungary. But on October 10, 1914, King Carol died. By this time it was evident that the war would be long, and its result was more than ever to Roumanian eyes incalculable. In the spring of 1915 the Germans began to shatter the Russian front, and the immense disasters and recoil of the Russian armies dominated the Roumanian mood and paralysed the disconnected British, French and Russian diplomacy. On the other hand, the attack upon the Dardanelles, the prospect of the fall of Constantinople and of the arrival of a British Fleet in the Black Sea was a counterpoise. All through 1915, while the Russian retreat was continual, the expectation of a British and French victory over Turkey kept Roumania true to her convictions and neutral in the war. She accepted money from both sides, she sold corn and oil to Germany, but she obstructed the passage of German munitions to the Dardanelles and closed no gate decisively upon the Allies. With the failure of the Dardanelles Expedition, with the accession of Bulgaria to the Teutonic cause, with the invasion and ruin of Serbia and the final evacuation of the Gallipoli Peninsula, all the military factors became adverse, and Roumania at the beginning of 1916 stood isolated and encompassed by the Central Empires.

• • •

There was however one factor of which Roumania took notice. An allied army based on Salonika faced the Bulgarians along their Southern frontier. We have seen the curious beginnings of this enterprise, and, so far as they are worth recording, the still more curious causes which led to its being entrusted to the command of General Sarrail.

Sarrail had arrived at Salonika in September, 1915, to find one British and two French divisions in or near the town. The Serbians were retreating in all the cruel severity of the winter before the German-Austro-Bulgarian invasion. Some small French detachments were sent northward up the Vardar valley; but of course it was already too late for Sarrail or the Allied Powers to give any effective help. Sarrail had neither the force nor the communications to enable him to act effectively. As the British General Staff had explained carefully to their Government in October, no sufficient force could be spared, or if spared, landed in Salonika in time, or if landed at Salonika, transported and maintained in Serbia. The roads and railways, the wagons and rolling stock which existed could not carry to the north any army large enough seriously to intervene in the tragedy of the Serbian overthrow. At the same time the attitude of King Constantine had become so openly pro-German that there was an obvious danger of Salonika being converted into a hostile town *behind* the French advanced detachments which were based upon it. In these circumstances, Sarrail had recalled his troops hastily to the town of Salonika, determined to keep a hold at any rate on his base: and the remnant of the Serbian Army managed in the end to make its escape to the shores of the Adriatic, whence French and Italian warships embarked the indomitable survivors and brought them round to Salonika by sea. Here then in November, 1915, had ended the first futile phase of the Salonika expedition.

But this as it had turned out was only to be the beginning of the story. Although Serbia was conquered, the remnants of her army rescued, Bulgaria committed to the side of the Central Powers, and although the effectual co-operation of Greece had become hopeless, the Salonika policy was to continue. At the beginning of 1915 both Lloyd George and Briand had had the same idea of sending a large army to Salonika to influence the Balkans. They had not then had the power to execute their plan while it had great prizes to offer; but when almost all the possible advantages had disappeared these two brilliant men, akin in many ways in temperament, found themselves advancing to controlling positions. They both adhered faithfully to their first conception, and neither seemed to realize how vastly its prospects had been curtailed. Such was their influence upon events that a numerous allied army was, at enormous cost, in defiance of military opinion, and after most of the original political objectives had disappeared, carried or being carried to Salonika. At the outset the oppositions to developing the Salonika expedition on a far larger scale seemed overwhelming; the majority of the British Government was against the plan; the General Staff were violently adverse; Lord Kitchener threatened several times to resign if it was pressed. Against this combination was Lloyd George. Similar conditions existed on the other side of the Channel; Joffre and the French Grand Quartier Général were adverse to the proposed diversion of forces from the main theatre. Clémenceau was violently hostile, but Briand, adroit, persuasive, and now Prime Minister, had many resources. Joffre's position had been weakened by his defeat in Champagne, and an accommodation was effected between him and the French Cabinet, of which the salient features were that Joffre should have the Salonika army as well as the armies in France under his general command, and that in return Joffre should wholeheartedly support the Salonika project in the councils of the Allies and also with the resources at his disposal. France thus united then threw her whole weight upon the British Cabinet and finally, aided by Lloyd George, induced their compliance.

The controversies which raged on both sides of the Channel upon the Salonika expedition were silenced by the remarkable fact that it was upon this much-abused front that the final collapse of the Central Empires first began. The falling away of Bulgaria, the weakest Ally, produced reactions in Germany as demoralizing as the heaviest blows they had sustained upon the Western Front. The Salonika policy, for all its burden upon our shipping and resources, its diversion of troops, its false beacon to Roumania, and its futile operations, was nevertheless largely vindicated by the extremely practical test of results. The consternation of Bulgaria at the defeats of the German armies in France was however at least as potent a factor in her collapse as the actual military pressures to which her own troops were subjected. The reactions were reciprocal: the German defeats undermined Bulgarian resistance; and the Bulgarian surrender pulled out the linchpin of the German combination.

Long and anxious were the reflections of the German High Command. They had been elaborately explained by the person chiefly responsible. During Christmas, 1915, Falkenhayn set himself to write a Memorandum for the eye of the Emperor. He has published it in his Memoirs. The document is not an impressive one and it bears evidence of being dressed to the taste of Falkenhayn's august master, but its argument and its conclusion were certainly clear. Falkenhayn deprecated but did not seek to veto the Austrian proposal for an attack on Italy. He disapproved of attacks on England in the East: "Victories at Salonika, the Suez Canal or in Mesopotamia can only help us in so far as they intensify the doubts about England's invulnerability which have already been aroused amongst the Mediterranean peoples and in the Mohammedan world. . . . We can in no case expect to do anything of decisive effect in the course of the war, as the advocates of an Alexander march to India or Egypt or an overwhelming blow at Salonika are always hoping. . . ." He rejected plans for continuing the offensive against Russia: "According to all reports the domestic difficulties of the 'Giant Empire' are multiplying rapidly. Even if we cannot perhaps expect a revolution in the grand style, we are entitled to believe that Russia's internal troubles will compel her to give in within a relatively short period. . . . Unless we are again prepared to put a strain on the troops which is altogether out of proportion—and this is prohibited by the state of our nerves—an offensive with a view to a decision in the East is out of the question for us until April, owing to the weather and the state of the ground. *The rich territory of the Ukraine is the only objective that can be considered.*[1] The communications towards that region are in no way sufficient. It is to be presumed that we should either secure the adhesion of Roumania or make up our minds to fight her; both are impracticable for the moment. A thrust at Petersburg, with its million inhabitants, whom we should have to feed from our own short stocks if the operations were successful, does not promise a decision. An advance on Moscow takes us nowhere. We have not the forces available for any of these undertakings. For all these reasons Russia as an object of our offensive must be considered as excluded. . . ." Falkenhayn then proceeds to examine the Western theatre. "In Flanders, as far as the Lorette Ridge, the state of the ground prevents any far-reaching operation until the middle of the spring. South of that point the local Commanders consider that about thirty divisions would be required. The offensive in the northern sector would need the same number. Yet it is impossible for us to concentrate those forces on one point of our front. . . . Moreover, the lessons to be deduced from the failure of our enemies' mass attacks are decisive against any imitation of their battle methods. An attempt at a mass break-through, even with an extreme accumulation of men and material, cannot be regarded as holding out prospects of success against a well-armed enemy whose morale is sound and who is not seriously inferior in number. The defender has usually succeeded in closing the gap. This is easy enough for him if he decides to withdraw voluntarily, and it is hardly possible to stop him doing so. The salients thus made, enormously exposed to the effect of flank fire, threaten to become a mere slaughter-house. The technical difficulties of directing and supplying the masses bottled up in them are so great as to seem practically insurmountable.

"We must equally discountenance any attempt to attack a British sector with comparatively inadequate means. We could only approve that course if we could give such an attack an objective within reasonable reach. There is no

[1] My italics.

such objective; our goal would have to be nothing less than to drive the English completely from the Continent and to force the French behind the Somme. If that object at least were not attained the attack would have been purposeless. . . ."

Having disposed of all these alternatives the General approaches the conclusion to which his reflections had led him: "There remains only France. . . . The strain in France has almost reached breaking-point. . . . The uncertain method of a mass break-through, in any case beyond our means, is unnecessary. Within our reach, behind the French sector of the Western Front, there are objectives for the retention of which the French General Staff would be compelled to throw in every man they have. If they do so, the forces of France will bleed to death—as there can be no question of a voluntary withdrawal—whether we reach our goal or not. If they do not do so, and we reach our objective, the moral effect on France will be enormous. For an operation limited to a narrow front, Germany will not be compelled to spend herself so completely, for all other fronts are practically drained. She can face with confidence the relief attacks to be expected on those fronts, and indeed hope to have sufficient troops in hand to reply to them with counter-attacks, for she is perfectly free to accelerate or draw out her offensive, to intensify or break it off from time to time as suits her purpose.

"The objectives of which I am speaking now are Belfort and Verdun. The considerations urged above apply to both; yet the preference must be given to Verdun. The French lines at that point are barely 12 miles distant from the German railway communication. Verdun is therefore the most powerful *point d'appui* for an attempt [by the French][1] with a relatively small expenditure of effort to make the whole German front in France and Belgium untenable. At Christmas," says Falkenhayn, "it was decided to give effect to the views which had crystallized out of this process of reasoning."

The execution of Falkenhayn's new policy required an almost complete relaxation of the pressure upon Russia. Hindenburg and Ludendorff were informed that no great enterprises against Russia could be set on foot in 1916, and that they could expect no reinforcements. All the German troops were withdrawn in the south from the Galician Front, and this theatre, so pregnant at once with menace and advantage, was confided entirely to Austrian hands. At the same time the Austrians were not dissuaded from preparing and developing an offensive against Italy in the Trentino, for which purpose they also withdrew a number of their best troops from their Eastern Front. And thus both north and south the Central Powers turned away from the eastern frontiers and their momentous problems, and leaving Russia to recover behind them and Rouma-

[1] W. S. C.

nia to brood over the scene with anxious eyes, plunged into desperate adventures in the West.

This was indeed a momentous decision. It involved the complete reversal of the policy by which General von Falkenhayn had in 1915 restored the German situation. Instead of pursuing his advantages against the weaker antagonists, he selected for the great German effort of 1916 the strongest enemy at that enemy's strongest point. That the decision was disastrous has been proved by the event. But it may be contended also that it was wrong. It was based first of all upon an erroneous appreciation of the offensive and defensive conditions on the great battle-fronts in France, and upon the mistaken belief that the general war could be brought to an end in 1916 by some strong effort there by one side or the other. Secondly, it took altogether too narrow and too purely military a view of the general position of Germany and her allies.

The vital need for Germany was to break the blockade. Unless she could secure to herself resources far greater than could be found within the frontiers of the Quadruple Alliance, the long war, to which the world was now condemned, must end inevitably in her exhaustion and defeat. She had no chance of breaking the blockade at sea. Its efficiency might be impaired by the devices of neutrals, but the vast process of starvation not only in food but in materials indispensable to modern armies was remorselessly and unceasingly at work. The British Fleet towered up in massive strength, and no one seriously doubted what the result of a fought-out battle on blue water would be. Sea Power and Land Power were arrayed against each other, and if Germany could not conquer Britain on the seas, where could she turn? Only in one direction lay salvation. If she could not break the blockade by sea, she must break it by land. If the oceans were closed, Asia was open. If the West was barred with triple steel, the East lay bare. Only in the East and South-East and in Asia could Germany find the feeding grounds and breathing room—nay, the man power—without which her military strength however impressive was but a wasting security. Only in spreading their frontiers over new enormous regions could the Central Empires make themselves a self-contained and self-sufficing organism, and only by becoming such an organism could they deprive their enemies of the supreme and deadly weapon—Time.

The true and indeed the only attainable political objectives open to Germany in 1916 were the final overthrow of Russia and the winning of Roumania to the side of the Central Empires. These were harmonious aims. Success in the first would go far to achieve the second. Roumania was essential to Germany. "As I now saw quite clearly," writes Ludendorff of the situation in October, 1916, "we should not have been able to exist, much less carry on the war, without Roumania's corn and oil. . . ." But if the battered corpse of an invaded and conquered Roumania was thus indispensable at the end of the year, how much more precious would have been Roumania with her resources and her armies as an Ally at the beginning. During 1915 a German convention with Roumania had secured to the Teutonic Powers the vital corn and oil supplies. But Germany in January, 1916, might reasonably look for a far more favourable development. Bulgaria had joined the Central Powers. The Dardanelles were safely shut. Russia was reeling. Roumania was therefore already almost surrounded, and any further collapse of Russia would isolate her completely. If she coveted Transylvania from Hungary, did she not also claim Bessarabia from Russia? A sagacious German policy at this juncture could have offered to Roumania in combination every inducement to join her neighbours, from high rewards to extreme duress.

Following upon this it would appear that the true strategic objectives of Germany in 1916 were the Black Sea and the Caspian. These lay within her grasp and required no effort beyond her strength. A continued advance against the south lands of Russia into the Ukraine and towards Odessa would have secured at comparatively little cost sufficient food for the Teutonic peoples. An upward thrust of Turkish armies sustained by German troops and organized by German generals would have conquered the Caucasus. Fleets and flotillas improvised by German science could easily dominate both the inland seas. The command of these waters would threaten simultaneously every point along their 5,000 miles of coast line, absorbing in negative defence ten Russians for every German employed, and multiplying in an almost unlimited degree the opportunities for further advance. Roumania completely encircled, cut from French and British aid by Bulgaria and Turkey, cut from the Russian armies by an Austro-German march from Lemberg to Odessa, could have had no choice but to join the Central Empires. The skilful employment of fifteen or twenty German divisions animating Austrian and Turkish armies would surely and easily have extended the territories which nourished Germany so as to include by the end of the summer of 1916 the whole of South-Eastern Europe, the Black Sea, the Caucasus and the Caspian. The Austro-German Front against Russia might have stretched from Riga to Astrakhan, with little more expenditure of force than was required to hold the existing Eastern line. At every moment and at every stage in these vast combinations the pressure upon Russia and upon her failing armies would have increased: and at every stage her troops and those of her allies would have been dissipated in vain attempts to wall in the ever-spreading flood in the East, or would have been mown down in frantic assaults upon the German trenches in France.

And this was itself only a stage in the process of land expansion and strategic menace open to the German military power. From the Caspian once navally commanded, Persia was a cheap and easy prey. There was no need to march large armies like Alexander to the East. Literally a few thousand Germans could have dominated Northern Persia, and eastward still beyond Persia lay Afghanistan and the threat to India. The consequences of such a German policy must have paralysed all British war effort from her Indian Empire. In Egypt, in Mesopotamia, and in India whole armies of British and Indian troops would have been forced to stand idle in apprehension of impending invasion or revolt, while the glory of the German eagles and the sense of approaching change swept far and wide through the peoples of Asia.

But from all the prospects so opened out to her in the East Germany was lured away. The final destruction of Russia, the overawing and conversion of Roumania, the conquest of granary after granary and oilfield after oilfield, the indefinite menace to the British Empire in Asia, with consequent diversion and dissipation of British forces, were all renounced by Falkenhayn in a few meagre sentences. Germany was made to concentrate her whole available offensive effort upon the cluster of wooded hills and permanent defences which constituted the strong fortress of Verdun. One-half the effort, one-quarter the sacrifice, lavished vainly in the attack on Verdun would have overcome the difficulty of the defective communications in "the rich lands of the Ukraine." The Russian armies in the south would have been routed long before they had gained their surprising victories under Brusiloff; and Roumania, her 500,000 men and her precious supplies of corn and oil, would have been brought into the war early not late and as an ally and not as a foe. But the school of formula had vanquished the school of fact, the professional bent of mind had overridden the practical; submission to theory had replaced the quest for reality. Attack the strongest at his strongest point, not the weakest at his weakest point, was once again proclaimed the guiding maxim of German military policy.

From the moment when he received the news of the total evacuation of the Gallipoli Peninsula, the opportunity of General von Falkenhayn, Chief of the German General Staff, was to pronounce the word *ROUMANIA*. He pronounced instead the word *VERDUN*.

CHAPTER XL

VERDUN

The drama of Verdun may perhaps be opened by the visit to the fortress in July, 1915, of a delegation from one of the Army Commissioners of the Chamber. The deputies had been disquieted by the rumours they had heard of the insecurity of the region before which lay the army of the German Crown Prince. The delegation were received by General Dubail, commanding the group of armies of the East, and by the Governor of Verdun, General Coutanceau. General Dubail explained that after the experiences of Liège and Namur permanent forts were no longer useful. They could be destroyed with certainly by heavy howitzers and were mere shell-traps for their garrisons. The only effective defence of Verdun lay in field troops holding an extended line around the fortress. Following these ideas, for which there was much to say, the forts had been dismantled and their coveted guns, garrisons and stores dispersed among the armies. The Governor, General Coutanceau, had the temerity to express a different opinion. He considered that the forts still had a high value and should play an important part in conjunction with the field defences. General Dubail was so irritated at this intervention of his subordinate and rebuked him in terms of such severity, that the Commission on their return to Paris thought it necessary to appeal to the Minister of War to shield the outspoken Governor from punishment and disgrace. In fact, however, after an interval of a few weeks General Coutanceau was removed from the Governorship of Verdun, and his place was taken by General Herr. At the beginning of February, 1916, on the very eve of the attack, the army of which the Verdun troops formed a part was transferred from the command of General Dubail to the centre group under General de Langle de Cary. Thus the responsibility for the neglect to develop to the full the defences of this area was divided and difficult to trace.

In a military sense, Verdun had no exceptional importance either to the French or to the Germans. Its forts were disarmed; it contained no substantial magazines; it guarded no significant strategic point. It was two hundred and twenty kilometres from Paris, and its capture would not have made any material difference to the safety either of the capital or of the general line. Falkenhayn and

Ludendorff both speak of it as a dangerous sally-port against their main railway communications, scarcely twelve miles away. But seeing that only two inferior lines of railway served Verdun, while the German occupied area in its front was fed by no less than fifteen, it should have been easy for the Germans to provide against such a sally. At its highest, the capture of Verdun would have been a military convenience to the Germans, and in a lesser degree an inconvenience to the French.

But then there was the sentiment which attached to Verdun. "It was," says a French historian,[1] "the great fortress proudly confronting its rival Metz, whose name had for centuries not ceased to haunt Germanic imaginations; it was the great advanced citadel of France; the principal bastion of her Eastern Frontier, whose fall resounding throughout Europe and the whole world would efface for ever the victories of the Marne and Yser."

This then was the foundation upon which Falkenhayn's conception of the German attack upon Verdun stood. It was not to be an attempt at a "break through." The assailants were not to be drawn into pockets from which they would be fired at from all sides. They were to fire at the French and assault them continually in positions which French pride would make it impossible to yield. The nineteen German divisions and the massed artillery assigned to the task were to wear out and "bleed white" the French Army. Verdun was to become an anvil upon which French military manhood was to be hammered to death by German cannon. The French were to be fastened to fixed positions by sentiment, and battered to pieces there by artillery. Of course this ingenious plan would be frustrated if the French did not lend themselves to it, and if they did not consider themselves bound to make disproportionate sacrifices to retain the particular hills on which stood the empty forts of Verdun.

It is not intended to press this argument too far. Verdun was a trophy. The German challenge had to be met by the whole resources of the French Army; but ground should have been sacrificed in the conflict as readily as men, with the sole object of exacting the highest price from the enemy at every stage. A greater manœuvring latitude accorded to the defence would have rendered the whole episode far less costly to the French Army, and would have robbed the plan of General von Falkenhayn of such reasons as it could muster. But the German commander, wrong in so much else, had rightly gauged the psychology of the French nation.

Writing in August, 1916. I tried to penetrate and analyse the probable motives which animated the Germans in their attack on Verdun.[2]

---

[1] Corda: *La Guerre Mondiale*. p. 187.
[2] The *London Magazine,* published in November, 1916.

". . . Suppose your gap is blasted—what then? Are you going to march to Paris through it? What is to happen, if you break the line of an otherwise unbeaten army? Will you really put your head into the hole?"

"No," say Main Headquarters; "we are not so foolish. We are not seeking Verdun. Nor are we seeking to blast a hole. Still less do we intend to march through such a hole. Our aim is quite different. We seek to wear down an army, not to make a gap; to break the heart of a nation, not to break a hole in a line. We have selected Verdun because we think the French will consider themselves bound to defend it at all costs; because we can so dispose our cannon around this apex of their front as to pound and batter the vital positions with superior range and superior metal, and force our enemy to expose division after division upon this anvil to our blows."

The strategic and psychological conceptions which had led Falkenhayn to select Verdun as the point of the German attack became mingled in the tactical sphere with his impressions derived from the success of the Gorlice-Tarnow attack on Russia in the previous year. There a punch followed by a scoop executed on a moderate front, but backed by a blasting concentration of artillery and gas, had led to a general withdrawal of the Russian line; and the process had been repeated again and again. His plan at Verdun was therefore by this intense punch on a narrow front with high-class troops and unprecedented cannon fire, to hammer the French on the anvil of fixed positions, and if successful, to rip their front as a purely subsidiary development to the right and left. In pursuance of this idea, he allocated to the Crown Prince nearly 2,000 extra guns, including all the latest types, and masses of shells, but added only four army corps to the forces of the Fifth German Army holding the line. He prescribed the exact frontage and scope of the attack and confined it strictly within the limits possible to these modest forces.

The French trench line ran in a half-moon salient five or six thousand yards around the permanent forts of Verdun. This position was cut in two unequal portions by the Meuse River, at this season nearly a kilometre wide. There were therefore the defences of the left bank (the West or the French left); the defences of the right bank (the East or French centre); and farther east (and to the French right) the plain of the Woeuvre and the fortified eastern heights of the Meuse. It was upon the French centre, between the Meuse and the Woeuvre plain, that the intense punch was to be directed. The German High Command believed that if this centre were pierced to a certain depth, the retreat of the two flanks would ensue automatically, or could easily be procured by further pressure. Their tactical studies of the ground before the war had led them to regard the positions of the left bank, unless and until compromised by the retreat of the French centre, as exceptionally strong and forbidding. All these conclusions

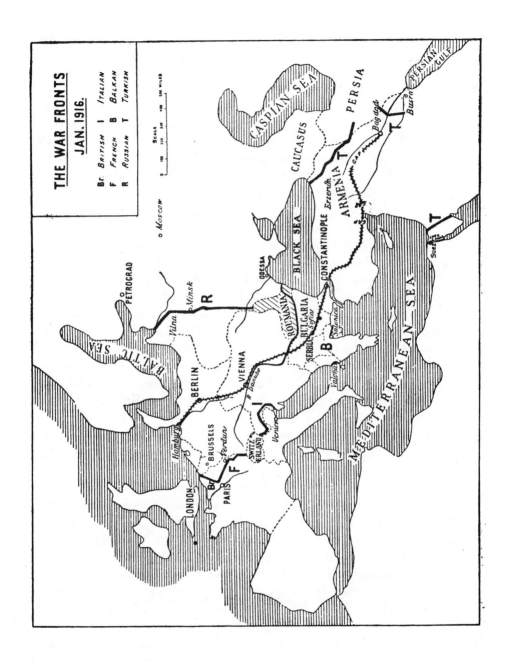

THE WAR FRONTS
JAN. 1916.

Br. BRITISH   I ITALIAN
F FRENCH   B BALKAN
R RUSSIAN   T TURKISH

SCALE
0   100   200   300   400   500 MILES

and decisions were duly imparted to the Crown Prince and the Fifth Army Staff of which General von Knobelsdorf was the chief.

The Crown Prince has been harshly judged in the passion and propaganda of the war. He has been represented at once as a fop and as a tyrant, as a callow youth and as a Moloch; as an irresponsible passenger and as a commander guilty of gross and disastrous military errors. None of these contradictory alternatives fit the truth. The German Imperial Princes in command of armies or groups of armies were held in strong control. The Headquarters Staff, main and local, decided and regulated everything, and the function of the ill-starred Heir Apparent was largely to bear the odium for their miscalculations and to receive, during the early years of the war, their ceremonious civilities. Even these civilities became attenuated as the long-drawn conflict deepened. Nevertheless, the Crown Prince had influence. He had with the All Highest the access of a son to a father. He had the right to express a view, to pose a question, to require an answer from any General, however august. He also had a share in the Emperor's unique point of view. He was a proprietor. Life, limb and fortune were risked by all the combatants in the Great War, but the inheritance to the Imperial throne, turning so nakedly on the general result, exercised from the first days of the war a sobering and concentrating effect upon a hitherto careless mind. It may also be said that no group of German armies was more consistently successful than his; and that there is evidence that his personal influence— whatever it may have been—was often thrown into the right side of the scales.

The Crown Prince did not feel comfortable about the attack at Verdun in 1916. He thought that it would be wiser to finish first with Russia in the East. He had of course a long-suppressed eagerness "to lead his tried and trusty troops once more to battle against the enemy, etc." But he was disquieted by Falkenhayn's repeated statements that the French Army was to be "bled white"at Verdun, and he felt no conviction that this would only happen to the French. It might even happen to the House of Hohenzollern. Moreover, on the tactical form of the attack his misgivings were supported or perhaps inspired by General von Knobelsdorf and his Staff. Their view was that the attack, if made at all, should be made on a broader front, comprising simultaneously both sides of the Meuse, and that large reserves should be at hand from the outset to exploit the advantages in the initial surprise. The Crown Prince sent Knobelsdorf to lay these claims before Falkenhayn. Falkenhayn insisted on his plan. He had framed it in relation to the whole situation as he saw it and he adhered to the smallest detail. There was to be an anvil. There was to be a punch on a narrow front. There was to be an unparalleled artillery, and only just enough infantry to exploit success. They were to proceed step by step, their way forward being blasted at each stage by cannon. Thus, whether Verdun was taken or not the

French Army would be ruined and the French nation sickened of war. It was a simple solution for world-wide problems, but it was Falkenhayn's solution, and he was in supreme control. By his determination and superior authority Knobelsdorf was soon overpersuaded, and the Crown Prince was thereafter overruled by the military hierarchy in mechanical unanimity. Such are the facts. While the newspapers of the time and in these days many of the histories have dwelt on the vanity and ruthless pride which prompted the heir to the Imperial throne to drive the manhood of Germany ceaselessly into the fires of Verdun, the truth is different. The Crown Prince, shocked and stricken by the butchery and opposed to the operation, continuously endeavoured to use such influence as he commanded to bring it to a close; and we have Ludendorff's testimony to his expressions of relief and pleasure when that decision was finally taken.

The first warning of the unprepared condition of the Verdun defences reached the French Government through an irregular channel. Colonel Driant, Deputy for Nancy, commanded a group of Chasseur battalions in the advanced lines of Verdun. At the end of November this officer and Member of Parliament came on leave to Paris and requested to be heard by the Army Commission of the Chamber, and on December 1 he exposed to his fellow-deputies the lack of organization and general inadequacy of the defences of the fortress. The Commission confirmed the account given by Colonel Driant, and their report was presented by the Commission to the Minister of War. The vigilant Galliéni was already possessed of similar statements from other quarters, and on December 16 he wrote to General Joffre. From different sources, he said, came accounts of the organization of the front which showed defects in the state of the defences at certain points, particularly and notably in the region of the Meurthe, and of Toul and Verdun. The network of trenches was not complete as it was on the greater part of the front. Such a situation, if it were true, ran the risk of presenting grave embarrassment. A rupture by the enemy in such circumstances would involve not only General Joffre's own responsibility but that of the whole Government. Recent experience of the war proved superabundantly that the first lines could be forced, but that the resistance of second lines could arrest even a successful attack. He asked for an assurance that on all the points of the front the organization at least of two lines should be designed and developed with all the necessary fortifications—barbed wire, inundations, abatis, etc.

The Commander-in-Chief hastened to reply on December 18 in a letter which holds its place in the records of ruffled officialdom. He asserted in categorical detail that nothing justified the misgivings of the Government. He concluded upon that peculiar professional note of which French military potentates have by no means the monopoly.

But since these apprehensions are founded upon reports which allege defects in the state of the defences, I request you to communicate these reports to me and to specify their authors. I cannot be party to soldiers placed under my command bringing before the Government, by channels other than the hierarchic channel, complaints or protests concerning the execution of my orders. Neither does it become me to defend myself against vague imputations, the source of which I do not know. The mere fact that the Government encourages communications of this kind, whether from mobilized Members of Parliament or directly or indirectly from officers serving on the front, is calculated to disturb profoundly the spirit of discipline in the Army. The soldiers who write know that the Government weighs their advice against that of their Chiefs. The authority of these Chiefs is prejudiced. The morale of all suffers from this discredit.

I could not lend myself to the continuation of this state of things. I require the whole-hearted confidence of the Government. If the Government trusts me, it can neither encourage nor tolerate practices which diminish that moral authority of my office, without which I cannot continue to bear the responsibility.

Evidently Colonel and Deputy Driant in his trenches before Verdun was in danger from more quarters than one.

It is asserted that General Galliéni had no mind to put up with this sort of thing, and that he framed a rejoinder both commanding and abrupt. But colleagues intervened with soothing processes. The Minister for War was marshalling with much assent the heads of a broad indictment of the Grand Quartier Général. He was persuaded to reduce this particular incident to modest proportions. At any rate, in the end he signed a soft reply. Joffre and G.Q.G. had vindicated their authority. The Ministry for War and the presumptuous and meddling deputies had been put in their places. But there were still the facts to be reckoned with—and the Germans.

Evidence continued to accumulate, and gradually a certain misgiving began to mingle with the assurance of Chantilly. Their own officers sent to examine the Verdun defences threw, in discreet terms, doubts upon the confident assertions with which the Commander-in-Chief had replied to the Minister of War. The troops on the spot and their Commanders were convinced they were soon to be attacked. The defences were still unsatisfactory. The Parliamentary Commissions buzzed incessantly. Finally, on January 20, General de Castelnau, the Major-General of the armies, and General Joffre's virtual Second-in-Command and potential successor, immediately on his return from Salonika, visited Verdun in person. He found much to complain of and gave various directions to remedy the neglects. A regiment of engineers was hurried to the scene; the necessary materials for fortification were provided; communications were improved and work begun. But time was now very short. The German masses were gathering fast. Their enormous magazines swelled each day. Their immense concentration of heavy artillery perfected itself.

Quite early in January the 2nd Bureau (Intelligence) began to indicate Verdun as the point at which a German attack would be delivered. A constant increase of batteries and troops in the regions north of Monfaucon and on both sides of the Meuse, the presence of "storm" divisions near Hattonchâtel, and the arrival of Austrian heavy howitzers were definitely reported. General Dupont, head of the 2nd Bureau, declared with conviction that Verdun was to be the object of a heavy and immediate attack.

The French Operations Staff, to judge by Pierrefeu's excellent account,[1] seemed to have abandoned their scepticism slowly. Certainly there seemed many parts of the French line more attractive to a hostile attack. But by the middle of February, those who doubted that a great German offensive was soon to break upon Verdun were few. The majority of the staff were at last convinced that the hour was near, and all—so we are told—were eager for the day and confident of its results. No one however had the least idea what the mechanical force of the onslaught would be.

At four o'clock in the morning of February 21 the explosion of a fourteen-inch shell in the Archbishop's Palace at Verdun gave signal of battle, and after a brief but most powerful bombardment three German Army Corps advanced upon the apex of the French front, their right hand on the Meuse. The troops in the forward positions attacked were, except towards the eastern flank, driven backwards towards the fortress line. The battle was continued on the 22nd and the 23rd. The brave Colonel Driant was killed in the woodlands covering the retreat of his Chasseurs. The line was reformed on the ridges near Douaumont: but the German six-inch artillery, dragged forward by tractors, hurled upon the new position so terrific a fire-storm that the French Division chiefly concerned collapsed entirely. During the afternoon of the 24th, both the General commanding the Verdun area and the Commander of the Group of Armies in which it lay (Langle de Cary), telegraphed to Chantilly, advising an immediate withdrawal to the left bank of the Meuse, and the consequent abandonment of the town and fortress of Verdun.

---

[1] "G.Q.G." by Jean de Pierrefeu. This officer was employed throughout the war to draft the official communiqués of the French Headquarters. He had the best opportunities of knowing exactly what took place. He is a writer of extraordinary force and distinction.

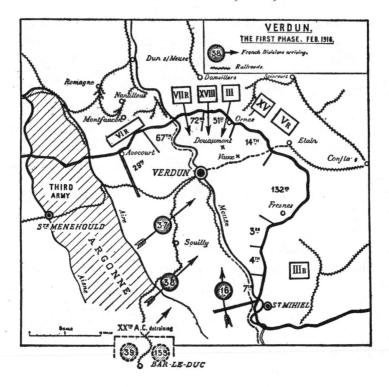

General Joffre was by no means disconcerted by these unexpected and un-toward events. He preserved throughout that admirable serenity for which he was noted, which no doubt would have equally distinguished him on the flaming crests of Douaumont. He assented on the 22nd to the movement of the 1st and XXth Corps, and to a request to Sir Douglas Haig to relieve in the line with British troops the Tenth French Army to reinforce Verdun. For the rest he remained in Olympian tranquillity, inspiring by his unaffected calm, regular meals and peaceful slumbers confidence in all about him. A less detached view was necessarily taken by Castelnau. The Second French Army had been relieved in the line some time before by the increasing British forces. This army was in the best order, rested and trained. Its staff had not been affected by the new French rule obliging every Staff Officer to do a spell of duty with the fighting troops. Its Commander, Pétain, had gained already in the war one of the highest reputations. On the evening of February 24, General de Castelnau presented himself to General Joffre and proposed to move the whole of the Second French Army to Verdun. The Commander-in-Chief assented to this. At eleven o'clock on the same night Castelnau, having received further reports of the most serious character, requested by telephone permission to proceed personally to Verdun with plenary powers. Pierrefeu has described the incident which followed. The Commander-in-Chief was already asleep. Following his almost invariable custom he had retired to rest at ten o'clock. The orderly officer on duty declared it impossible to disturb him. At first Castelnau submitted. But a few minutes later a further message from Verdun foreshadowing the immediate evacuation of the whole of the right bank of the Meuse arrived, and on this Castelnau would brook no further obstruction. He went in person to the villa Poiret in which the great soldier was reposing. Upon the express order of the Major-General an aide-de-camp took the responsibility of knocking at the formidable double-locked door. The supreme Chief, after perusing the telegrams, gave at once the authorization for General de Castelnau to proceed with full powers, declared there must be no retreat, and then returned to his rest.

Castelnau started forthwith a little after midnight. At Avize, Headquarters of Langle de Cary and the centre group of armies, he quelled the pessimism that existed, and from there telephoned to Verdun announcing his impending arrival and calling upon General Herr "on the order of the Commander-in-Chief not to yield ground but to defend it step by step," and warning him that if this order was not executed, "the consequences would be most grave for him (Herr)." By daylight of the 25th Castelnau reached Verdun and found himself confronted with the tragic scenes of confusion and disorder which haunt the immediate rear of a defeated battle-front. All accounts agree that the influence and authority of Castelnau on the 25th reanimated the defence and for the moment restored the situation. Wherever he went, decision and order followed him. He reiterated the command at all costs to hold the heights of the Meuse and to stop the enemy on the right bank. The XXth and 1st Army Corps now arriving on the scene were thrown into the battle with this intention. While taking these emergency measures, Castelnau had already telegraphed to Pétain ordering him to take command, not only of the Second French Army, which was now moving, but also of all the troops in the fortified region of Verdun.

On the morning of the 26th Pétain received from Castelnau the direction of the battle, which he continued to conduct, while at the same time mastering the local situation. The neglect of the field and permanent defences of a fortress which it was decided to defend to the death, now bequeathed a cruel legacy to the French troops. In advance of the permanent forts there were neither continuous lines of trenches nor the efficient organization of strong points. Telephone systems and communication trenches were scarce or non-existent. The forts themselves were all empty and dismantled. Even their machine guns and cupolas had been extracted and their flanking batteries disarmed. All these deficiencies had now to be repaired in full conflict and under tremendous fire. Besides the direction of the battle and the organization of his forces and rapidly growing artillery, Pétain took a number of general decisions. Four successive lines of defence were immediately set in hand. In full accord with the views of the much-chastised General Coutanceau, Pétain directed the immediate reoccupation and re-arming of all the forts. To each he assigned a garrison with fourteen days' food and water, and solemn orders never to capitulate. The immense value of the large subterranean galleries of these forts, in which a whole battalion could live in absolute security till the moment of counter-attack, was now to be proved. Lastly, the new commander instituted the marvellous system of motorlorries between Verdun and Bar le Duc. No less than three thousand of these passed up and down this road every twenty-four hours, and conveyed each week during seven months of conflict an average of 90,000 men and 50,000 tons of material. Along this "Sacred Way," as it was rightly called, no less than sixty-six divisions of the French Army were to pass on their journey to the anvil and the furnace fires.

By the end of February the first German onslaught had been stemmed. Large armies were on both sides grappling with each other round the fortress, ever-increasing streams of reinforcements and munitions flowed from all France and Germany towards the conflict, and ever-increasing trains of wounded ebbed swiftly from it. It had become a trial of strength and military honour between Germany and France. Blood was up and heads were down. Vain had it been for Falkenhayn to write at Christmas: Germany will be "perfectly free to accelerate or draw out her offensive; to intensify or break it off from time to time as suits her purpose." His own professional and official existence was now engaged. The wine had been drawn and the cup must be drained. The French and German armies continued accordingly to tear each other to pieces with the utmost fury, and the power of the German artillery inflicted grievous losses day by day on the now more numerous French.

When the Germans had attacked on February 21, they had, in accordance with Falkenhayn's plan, used only the three Army Corps of their centre, and three others had stood idle on the two flanks. It can scarcely be doubted that had the whole assaulting forces been thrown in at once, the position of the French, already so critical, could not at the outset have been maintained. However, on March 6 the three flanking Army Corps joined in the battle, and a new series of sanguinary engagements was fought during the whole of March and April for the possession mainly of the hill called "Le Mort Homme" on the left bank of the Meuse, and for the Côte du Poivre on the right. But the Germans achieved no success comparable to that of their opening. The conditions of the conflict had become more equal. Closely locked and battling in the huge crater-fields and under the same steel storm, German and French infantry fell together by scores of thousands. By the end of April nearly a quarter of a million French and Germans had been killed or wounded in the fatal area, though influencing in no decisive way the balance of the World War.

To the war of slaughter and battles was added that of propaganda and communiqués. In this the French had largely the advantage. They did not cease to proclaim day after day the enormous German losses which attended every assault. As the Germans were obviously storming entrenchments and forts, the world at large was prepared to believe that they must be making sacrifices far greater than those of the French. "Up till March," says Ludendorff, "the impression was that Verdun was a German victory," but thereafter opinion changed. Certainly during April and May Allies and neutrals were alike persuaded that Germany had experienced a profound disappointment in her attack on Verdun, and had squandered thereon the flower of her armies.

I myself shared the common impression that the German losses must be heavier than those of the French. All accounts however showed that the strain upon the French Army was enormous. They were compelled to defend all sorts of positions, good, bad and indifferent, and to fight every inch of the ground with constant counterattacks under a merciless artillery: and it was clear that they were conducting the defence in the most profuse manner. "The French." I wrote at the time, "suffered more than the defence need suffer by their valiant and obstinate retention of particular positions. Meeting an artillery attack is like catching a cricket ball. Shock is dissipated by drawing back the hands. A little 'give,' a little suppleness, and the violence of impact is vastly reduced. Yet, notwithstanding the obstinate ardour and glorious passion for mastery of the French, the German losses at Verdun greatly exceeded theirs." [1]

It is with surprise which will perhaps be shared by others that I have learned the true facts. During the defensive phase from February to June the French Army suffered at Verdun the loss of no fewer than 179,000 men (apart from officers) killed, missing or prisoners, and 263,000 wounded: a frightful total of 442,000; or with officers, probably 460,000. The Germans on the other hand, although the attackers, used their man-power so much less and their artillery so much more that their loss, including officers, did not exceed 72,000 killed, missing and prisoners, and 206,000 wounded; a total of 278,000. From the totals of both sides there should be deducted the usual one-eighth for casualties on other parts of the front where French and Germans faced each other. But this in no way alters the broad fact that the French sacrificed in defending Verdun more than three men to every two attacking Germans. To this extent therefore the tactical and psychological conceptions underlying Falkenhayn's scheme were vindicated.

Ever since the opening phase of the struggle of Verdun the personal position of General Joffre had deteriorated. The neglect to prepare the field defences of Verdun, the disarming of its forts, the proved want of information of

---

[1] *London Magazine.* Written August, published November, 1916.

the Commander-in-Chief and his Headquarters Staff upon this grave matter, the fact that it had been left to the Parliamentary Commission to raise the alarm, the obstinacy with which this alarm had been received and resented, were facts known throughout Government and Opposition circles in Paris. The respective parts played by Joffre and Castelnau in the first intense crisis of the Verdun situation were also widely comprehended. In the whole of this episode little credit could be discovered either for the Commander-in-Chief or for the gigantic organization of the Grand Quartier Général sourly described as "Chantilly." Consideration of all these facts led General Galliéni to a series of conclusions and resolves. First, he wished to bring Joffre to Paris, from which centre he would exercise that general command over all the French armies, whether in France or the Orient, which had been entrusted to him. Secondly, he wished to place General de Castelnau at the head of the armies in France. Thirdly, he proposed to diminish in certain respects the undue powers which Chantilly had engrossed to itself, and to restore to the Ministry of War the administrative functions of which it had to a large extent been deprived. Galliéni laid proposals in this sense, though without actually naming Castelnau, before the Council of Ministers on March 7, 1916. France now had the opportunity of securing for her armies and for her Allies military leadership in the field of the first order, without at the same time losing any advantage which could be derived from the world prestige of Joffre.

The Cabinet was greatly alarmed. They feared a political and ministerial crisis, as well as a crisis in the Supreme Command—all during the height of the great battles raging around Verdun. Briand intervened with dexterous argument, but General Galliéni was resolved. Stricken by an illness which compelled an early and grave operation, he had laid what he considered his testament and the last remaining service he could render France before his colleagues. When his advice was not accepted, he immediately resigned. For several days his resignation was kept a secret. Then it was explained on grounds of health, and the charge of the War Ministry was taken temporarily by the Minister of Marine. Finally, when his resolves were seen to be unshakable, a colourless but inoffensive successor was discovered in the person of General Roques, an intimate friend of Joffre and actually suggested by him. Thus did General Joffre receive a renewed lease of power sufficient to enable him to add to the dearly bought laurels of Verdun the still more costly trophies of the Somme.

Galliéni was now to quit the scene for ever. Within a fortnight of his resignation he withdrew to a private hospital for an operation—at his age of the greatest danger—but which, if successful, meant a swift restoration of activity and health. From the effects of this operation he expired on May 27. To his memory and record not only his countrymen, but also their Allies, who profited by his genius, sagacity and virtue, and might have profited far more, should not fail to do justice.

After the disasters of 1915 an earnest effort had been made by the British, French and Russian Governments to concert their action for 1916. No sooner had Briand attained the Premiership than he used a phrase which pithily expressed the first great and obvious need of the Allies—"Unity of front." Unity of front did not mean unity of command. That idea, although it had dawned on many minds, was not yet within the bounds of possibility. Unity of front, or "only one front," meant that the whole great circle of fire and steel within which the Allies were gripping the Central Powers should be treated and organized as if it were the line of a single army or a single nation; that everything planned on one part of the front should be related to everything planned on every other part of the front; that instead of a succession of disconnected offensives, a combined and simultaneous effort should be made by the three great Allies to overpower and beat down the barriers of hostile resistance. In these broad and sound conceptions Mr. Asquith, Mr. Lloyd George, Lord Kitchener, Monsieur Briand, General Joffre, General Cadorna, the Czar and General Alexeieff, all four Governments and all four General Staffs, were in full accord.

In pursuance and execution of this conception it had been decided to make a vast combined onslaught upon Germany and Austria, both in the east and in the west, during the summer months. The Russians could not be ready till June, nor the British till July. It was therefore agreed that a waiting policy should as far as possible be followed during the first six months of the year, while the Russians were re-equipping and increasing their armies, while the new British armies were perfecting their training, and while enormous masses of shells and guns were being accumulated. To these immense labours all four great nations thenceforth committed themselves.

It was further agreed that the Russians should endeavour to hold the Germans as far as possible on the northern part of the Eastern Front, and that the main Russian attack should be launched in Galicia in the southern theatre. At the same time, or in close relation to this, it was decided that a tremendous offensive, exceeding in scale anything ever previously conceived, should be delivered by the British and French, hand in hand, astride of the Somme *(à cheval sur la Somme)*. It was intended to attempt to break through on a front of seventy kilometres; the English to the north of the Somme on the twenty-five kilometres from Hébuterne to Maricourt; and the French astride the Somme, but mainly to the south of it, on a forty-five kilometre front from Maricourt right down to Lassigny. Two entire British armies, the Third and Fourth, under Allenby and Rawlinson, and comprising from twenty-five to thirty divisions, constituted the British attack; and three French armies, the Second, the Sixth and the Third, comprising thirty-nine divisions, were to be placed under the command of Foch for the French sector. The whole of these five armies, aggregating over one and a half million men and supported by four or five thousand guns, were thus to be hurled upon the Germans at a moment when it was hoped they and their Austrian allies would already be heavily and critically engaged on the Eastern Frontiers. The original scheme for this stupendous battle was outlined in December, 1915, at the first Conference of the Allied General Staffs at Chantilly, and its final shape was determined at a second conference on February 14.

The ink was hardly dry on these conventions when the cannon of Verdun began to thunder, and the Germans were seen advancing successfully upon the neglected defences of that fortress. It is certainly arguable that the French would have been wise to have played with the Germans around Verdun, economizing their forces as much as possible, selling ground at a high price in German blood wherever necessary, and endeavouring to lead their enemies into a pocket or other unfavourable position. In this way they might have inflicted upon the Germans very heavy losses without risking much themselves, and as we now know they would certainly have baffled Falkenhayn's plan of wearing out the French Army and beating it to pieces upon the anvil. By the end of June the Germans might thus have exhausted the greater part of their offensive effort, advancing perhaps a dozen miles over ground of no decisive strategic significance, while all the time the French would have been accumulating gigantic forces for an overwhelming blow upon the Somme.

However, other counsels—or shall we call them passions?—prevailed, and the whole French nation and army hurled itself into the struggle around Verdun. This decision not only wore out the French reserves and consumed the offensive strength of their army, but it greatly diminished the potential weight of the British attack which was in preparation. Already before the German attack opened, Sir Douglas Haig had taken over an additional sector of the French front, liberating, as we have seen, the Second French Army which was thus enabled to restore the situation at Verdun. As soon as the Battle of Verdun had begun, Joffre requested Haig to take over a fresh sector, and this was accordingly effected in the early days of March, thus liberating the whole of the Tenth French Army. Thus the number of British divisions resting and training for the great battle was at the outset sensibly diminished. As the Verdun conflict prolonged itself and deepened all through March, April and May, the inroads upon the fighting strength and disposable surplus of the French Army became increasingly grave. And as July approached the thirty-nine French divisions of the original scheme had shrunk to an available eighteen. This greatly diminished the front of the battle and the weight behind the blow. The numbers available were reduced by at least one-third, and the front to be attacked must be contracted from seventy to about forty-five kilometres. Whereas in the original conception the main onslaught would have been made by the French with the British co-operating in great strength as a smaller army, these rôles had now been reversed by the force of events. The main effort must be made by the British, and it was the French who would co-operate to the best of their ability in a secondary rôle.

While the eyes of the world were riveted on the soul-stirring frenzy of Verdun, and while the ponderous preparations for the Allied counterstroke on the Somme were being completed, great events were at explosion-point in the East. To those who knew that Russia was recovering her strength with every day, with every hour that passed, who knew of the marshalling of her inexhaustible manhood, and the ever-multiplying and broadening streams of munitions of war which were flowing towards her, the German attack on Verdun had come with a sense of indescribable relief. Russia had been brought very low in the preceding autumn, before the rearguards of the winter closed down on her torn and depleted line. But mortal injury had been warded off. Her armies had been extricated, her front was maintained, and now behind it, "the whole of Russia" was labouring to re-equip and reconstitute her power.

Few episodes of the Great War are more impressive than the resuscitation, re-equipment and renewed giant effort of Russia in 1916. It was the last glorious exertion of the Czar and the Russian people for victory before both were to sink into the abyss of ruin and horror. By the summer of 1916 Russia, who eighteen months before had been almost disarmed, who during 1915 had sustained an unbroken series of frightful defeats, had actually managed, by her own efforts and the resources of her Allies, to place in the field—organized, armed and equipped—sixty Army Corps in place of the thirty-five with which she had begun the war. The Trans-Siberian Railway had been doubled over a distance of 6,000 kilometres, as far east as Lake Baikal. A new railway 1,400 kilometres long, built through the depth of winter at the cost of unnumbered lives, linked Petrograd with the perennially ice-free waters of the Marman coast. And by both these channels munitions from the rising factories of Britain, France and Japan, or procured by British credit from the United States, were pouring into Russia in broadening streams. The domestic production of every form of war material had simultaneously been multiplied many fold.

It was however true that the new Russian armies, though more numerous and better supplied with munitions than ever before, suffered from one fatal deficiency which no Allied assistance could repair. The lack of educated men, men who at least could read and write, and of trained officers and sergeants, woefully diminished the effectiveness of her enormous masses. Numbers, brawn, cannon and shells, the skill of great commanders, the bravery of patriotic troops, were to lose two-thirds of their power for want, not of the higher military science, but of Board School education; for want of a hundred thousand human beings capable of thinking for themselves and acting with reasonable efficiency in all the minor and subordinate functions on which every vast organization—most of all the organization of modern war—depends. The mighty limbs of the giant were armed, the conceptions of his brain were clear, his heart was still true, but the nerves which could transform resolve and design into action were but partially developed or non-existent. This defect, irremediable at the time, fatal in its results, in no way detracts from the merit or the marvel of the Russian achievement, which will for ever stand as the supreme monument and memorial of the Empire founded by Peter the Great.

At the beginning of the summer the Russian front, stretching 1,200 kilometres from the Baltic to the Roumanian frontier, was held by three main groups of armies, the whole aggregating upwards of 134 divisions: the northern group under the veteran Kouropatkine; the centre group (between the Pinsk and the Pripet) under Evert; the southern group (to the south of the Pripet) under Brusiloff. Against this array the Central Empires marshalled the German armies of Hindenburg and Ludendorff in the north, of Prince Leopold of Bavaria and General von Linsingen opposite the centre and southern centre, and the three Austrian armies of the Archduke Frederick in the south. The drain of Verdun and the temptations of the Trentino had drawn or diverted from the Eastern Front both reserves and reinforcements, and practically all the heavy artillery. And in the whole of the sector south of the Pripet, comprising all Galicia and the Bukovina, not a German division remained to sustain the armies of the Austrian Archduke against the forces of Brusiloff.

The original scheme had contemplated July 1 as the date of the general Allied attack, both in the west and in the east. But the cries of Italy from the Trentino and the obvious strain under which the French were living at Verdun led to requests being made to the Czar to intervene if possible at an earlier date. Accordingly on June 4 Brusiloff, after a thirty-hours' bombardment, set his armies of over a million men in motion, and advanced in a general attack on the 350-kilometre front between the Pripet and the Roumanian frontier. The results were equally astounding to victors and vanquished, to friend and foe. It may well be that the very ante-dating of the attack imparted to it an element of surprise that a month later would have been lacking. Certainly the Austrians were entirely unprepared for the weight, vigour and enormous extent of the assault. The long loose lines in the east in no way reproduced the conditions of the Western Front. The great concentrations of artillery, the intricate systems of fortification, the continuous zones of machine-gun fire, the network of roads and railways feeding the front and enabling reserves to be thrown in thousands and tens of thousands in a few hours upon any threatened point, were entirely lacking in the east. Moreover, the Austrian armies contained large numbers of Czech troops fighting under duress for a cause they did not cherish and an Empire whose downfall they desired.

No one was more surprised than Falkenhayn.

> After the failure,[1] [he wrote] of the March offensive in Lithuania and Courland, the Russian front had remained absolutely inactive. . . . There was no reason whatever to doubt that the front was equal to any attack on it by the forces opposing it at the moment. . . . General Conrad von Hötzendorf . . . declared that a Russian attack in Galicia could not be undertaken with any prospect of success in less than from four to six weeks from the time when we should have learnt that it was coming. This period at least would be required for the concentration of the Russian forces, which must be a necessary preliminary thereto. . . . However, before any indication of a movement of this sort had been noticed, to say nothing of announced, a most urgent call for assistance from our ally reached the German G.H.Q. on the 5th of June.
>
> The Russians, under the command of General Brusiloff, had on the previous day attacked almost the entire front, from the Styr-Bend, near Kolki, below Lutsk, right to the Roumanian borders. After a relatively short artillery preparation they had got up from their trenches and simply marched forward. Only in a few places had they even taken the trouble to form attacking groups by concentrating their reserves. It was a matter not simply of an attack in the true sense of the word, but rather of a big scale reconnaissance. . . .
>
> A "reconnaissance" like Brusiloff's was only possible, of course, if the General had decisive reason for holding a low opinion of his enemy's power of resistance. And on this point he made no miscalculation. His attack met with splendid success, both in Volhynia and in the Bukovina. East of Lutsk the Austro-Hungarian front was clean broken through, and in less than two days a yawning gap fully thirty miles wide had been made in it. The part of the 4th Austro-Hungarian Army, which was in line here, melted away into miserable remnants.
>
> Things went no better with the 7th Austro-Hungarian Army in the Bukovina. It flowed back along its entire front, and it was impossible to judge at the moment whether and when it could be brought to a halt again. . . .
>
> We were therefore faced with a situation which had fundamentally

[1] *General Headquarters* 1914–1916 *and its Critical Decisions.* General von Falkenhayn, pp. 244–247.

changed. A wholesale failure of this kind had certainly not entered into the calculations of the Chief of the General Staff (himself). He had considered it impossible.

All along the front the Russian armies marched over the Austrian lines or through wide breaches in them. In the north the army of Kaledine advanced in three days on a 70-kilometre front no less than 50 kilometres, taking Lutsk. In the south the army of Letchitsky, forcing successively the lines of the Dniester and the Pruth, invested Czernovitch after an advance of 60 kilometres. The German front under Linsingen wherever attacked maintained itself unbroken or withdrew in good order in consequence of adjacent Austrian retirements. But within a week of the beginning of the offensive the Austrians had lost 100,000 prisoners, and before the end of the month their losses in killed, wounded, dispersed and prisoners amounted to nearly three-quarters of a million men. Czernovitch and practically the whole of the Bukovina had been reconquered, and the Russian troops again stood on the slopes of the Carpathians. The scale of the victory and the losses of the defeated in men, material and territory were the greatest which the war in the east had yet produced.

The Austrian offensive on the Trentino was instantly paralysed, and eight divisions were recalled and hurried to the shattered Eastern Front. Although the Battle of Verdun was at its height and Falkenhayn deeply committed to procuring at least a moral decision there, and while he could watch each week the storm clouds gathering denser and darker on the Somme, he found himself forced to withdraw eight German divisions from France to repair those dykes he had so improvidently neglected in the east, or at any rate to limit the deluge now pouring forward impetuously in so many directions. The Hindenburg-Ludendorff armies, which had successfully sustained the subsidiary attacks delivered by the Russians upon their front, were also called upon to contribute large reinforcements for the south; and an immense German effort was made to close the breaches and re-establish the Southern Front. By the end of June the failure of the Austro-German campaign of 1916, which had opened with such high prospects, was apparent. The Trentino offensive was hamstrung; Verdun was in Ludendorff's words "an open wasting sore";[1] and a disaster of the first magnitude had been suffered in that very portion of the Eastern Front which had offered the most fruitful prospects to Teutonic initiative. But this was not the end. The main struggle of the year was about to begin in the west, and Roumania, convulsed with excitement at the arrival of victorious Russian armies before her very gates, loomed up black with the menace of impending war.

[1] *War Memories,* Vol. 1, p. 267.

CHAPTER XLI

JUTLAND: THE PRELIMINARIES

There are profound differences between a battle where both sides wish for a full trial of strength and skill, and a battle where one side has no intention of fighting to a finish, and seeks only to retire without disadvantage or dishonour from an unequal and undesired combat. The problems before the Commanders, the conditions of the conflict itself, are widely different in a fleeting encounter—no matter how large its scale—from those of a main trial of strength. In an encounter between forces obviously unequal, the object of the weaker is to escape, and that of the stronger to catch and destroy them. Many of the tactical processes and manœuvres appropriate to a battle where both sides throw their whole might into the scale and continue at death-grips till the climax is reached and victory declares itself are not adapted to a situation in which keeping contact is the task of the stronger and evasion the duty of the weaker.

This is especially true of the preliminaries; the mode of approach, the deployment of the fleet, the development of the fire, the methods of meeting or parrying the attack of torpedo craft, would naturally be modified according to the view taken of the intentions of the enemy. If he were expected to seek a fight to a finish, there would be no need for hurry. There would be every reason to economize loss in the earlier stages and make every ship and gun play its maximum part in a supreme crisis. If on the other hand the enemy was certain to make off as soon as he saw himself in the presence of very superior forces, it would be necessary for the stronger fleet to run greater risks if it was determined to force a battle. Not only the light forces and the fast heavy ships would be thrown forward to attack, but the battle fleet itself would be driven at a speed which would leave the slowest squadrons and the slowest ships tailing away behind. Thus the pursuing squadrons would not come into action simultaneously but successively.

Moreover, modern inventions give new advantages to a retreating fleet. It may entice its enemy across mine-fields through which perhaps it alone knows the channels, or into a carefully prepared ambuscade of submarines. It can throw out mines behind it. It can fire torpedoes across the course of a pursuing fleet, and itself remain outside torpedo range. From these and other technical causes there can be no doubt that the task of forcing a battle against the enemy's desire involves a far higher degree of risk to the stronger fleet than would arise in a trial of strength willingly accepted or sought for by both sides. In studying the naval encounter of Jutland, the first question upon which it is necessary to form an opinion is what extra degree of risk beyond the risk of a pitched battle, the British Fleet was justified in incurring in the hopes of bringing the Germans to action and destroying them. This question cannot be decided without reference to the general strategic situation on the seas.

If the German Fleet had been decisively defeated on May 31, 1916, in battle off Jutland, very great reliefs and advantages would have been gained by the Allies. The psychological effect upon the German nation cannot be estimated, but might conceivably have been profound. The elimination of the German Battle Fleet would have been an important easement to Great Britain, enabling men and material required by the Admiralty for the Grand Fleet to be diverted for the support of the army. It would have brought the entry of the Baltic into immediate practical possibility. Whether the presence of the British squadrons in the Baltic during the winter of 1916 and the spring of 1917 would have prevented the Russian Revolution is a speculative question, but one which cannot be overlooked. The reactions of a great defeat at sea upon the U-boat attack of 1917, which the Germans were actively preparing, are diverse. On the one hand the disappearance of most of the German battleships might have led to a greater concentration of skilled men and resources upon the development of the U-boat campaign. On the other hand the liberation of the Grand Fleet flotillas and the increased sense of mastery at sea might well have led the Admiralty to more aggressive action against the German river mouths and to an earlier frustration of the U-boat attack. These important advantages must however be compared with the consequences to Britain and her Allies which would immediately have followed from a decisive British defeat. The trade and foodsupply of the British islands would have been paralysed. Our armies on the Continent would have been cut from their base by superior naval force. All the transportation of the Allies would have been jeopardized and hampered. The United States could not have intervened in the war. Starvation and invasion would have descended upon the British people. Ruin utter and final would have overwhelmed the Allied cause.

The great disparity of the results at stake in a battle between the British and German navies can never be excluded from our thoughts. In a pitched battle fought to a conclusion on British terms between the British and German navies our preponderance was always sufficient to make victory reasonably probable, and in the spring of 1916 so great as to have made it certain. No such assurance could be felt, in the earlier days at any rate, about the results of a piecemeal pursuing engagement against a retreating enemy. If that enemy succeeded in drawing part of our Fleet into a trap of mines or submarines, and eight or nine of the most powerful ships were blown up, the rest might have been defeated by the gunfire of the German Fleet before the whole strength of the British line of battle could have reached the scene. This as we know was always the German dream: but there would certainly be no excuse for a Commander to take risks of this character with the British Fleet at a time when the situation on sea was entirely favourable to us. Neither would there be any defence for a British Admiralty which endeavoured to put pressure upon their Admiral to try to achieve some spectacular result against his better judgment, and by overstraining risks when the prizes on either side were so unequal. To be able to carry on all business on salt water in every part of the world without appreciable let or hindrance, to move armies, to feed nations, to nourish commerce in the teeth of war, implies the possession of the command of the sea. If these are the tests, that priceless sovereignty was ours already. We had the upper hand; we had the advantage; time—so it then seemed, so in the end it proved—was on our side. We were under no compulsion to fight a naval battle except under conditions which made victory morally certain and serious defeat, as far as human vision goes, impossible. A British Admiralissimo cannot be blamed for making these grave and solid reasons the basis of his thought and the foundation from which all his decisions should spring.

In the tense naval controversy upon Jutland the keenest minds in the Navy have shifted every scrap of evidence. Every minute has been measured. The speed, the course, the position of every ship great or small, at every period in the operation, have been scrutinized. The information in the possession of every Admiral in each phase has been examined, weighed, canvassed. The dominant school of naval thought and policy are severe critics of Sir John Jellicoe. They disclaim all personal grounds or motives; they affirm that the tradition and future of the British Navy join in demanding that a different doctrine, other methods and above all another spirit must animate our captains at sea, if ever and whenever the Navy is once again at war. They declare that such an affirmation is more important to the public than the feelings of individuals, the decorous maintenance of appearances, the preservation of a superficial harmony, or the respect which may rightly be claimed by a Commander-in-Chief who, over the major portion of the war, discharged an immense and indeed inestimable responsibility.

Sir John Jellicoe was in experience and administrative capacity unquestionably superior to any British Admiral. He knew every aspect and detail of his profession. Afloat or at the Admiralty his intellect, energy, and efficiency won equal confidence from those he served and those he led. Moreover he was a fine sea officer, capable of handling in the most difficult circumstances of weather and navigation the immense Fleet with which he was entrusted. He had served on active service in more than one campaign with courage and distinction. Before the war he was marked out above all others for the supreme command. When at its outbreak he assumed this great duty, his appointment was acclaimed alike by the nation and the Navy. Nearly two years of the full strain of war had only enhanced the confidence and affection with which he was regarded by his officers and men. In judging his discharge of his task we must consider first his knowledge and point of view; secondly the special conditions of the war; and thirdly the spirit which should impel the Royal Navy.

The standpoint of the Commander-in-Chief of the British Grand Fleet was unique. His responsibilities were on a different scale from all others. It might fall to him as to no other man—Sovereign, Statesman, Admiral or General—to issue orders which in the space of *two or three hours* might nakedly decide who won the war. The destruction of the British Battle Fleet was final. Jellicoe was the only man on either side who could lose the war in an afternoon. First and foremost, last and dominating, in the mind of the Commander-in-Chief stood the determination not to hazard the Battle Fleet. The risk of under-water damage by torpedo and mine, and the consequent destruction of British battleship superiority, lay heavy upon him. It far outweighed all considerations of the results on either side of gunfire. It was the main preoccupation of Admiralty thought before the war. From the opening of hostilities the spectacle of great vessels vanishing in a few moments as the result of an under-water explosion constantly deepened the impression. Alone among naval authorities of the highest order Sir Reginald Custance had maintained the contrary view, and had ceaselessly laboured to correct what he conceived to be the exaggerated importance attached to the Whitehead torpedo. Again and again I have heard him contend that the torpedo would play only a very unimportant part in a great sea battle, and that the issue would be decided by a combination of gunfire and manœuvre. The results of Jutland seem to vindicate this unfashionable opinion. For twelve hours the main fleets of Britain and Germany were at sea in close contact with one another both by day and by night, amid torpedo flotillas of the highest strength and quality numbered by scores, and only three large ships out of over a hundred exposed to the menace were seriously damaged by the torpedo. The purely passive rôle enjoined upon the British destroyers during the night may partially explain this result. It was certainly at variance with the pre-war expectations of most of the leading naval authorities in England.

The safety and overwhelming strength of the Grand Fleet was Jellicoe's all-embracing aim. Its strength must be continually augmented. Every service ancillary to the Battle Fleet must be continually developed on the largest scale and to the highest efficiency. Every vessel that the northern harbours could contain must be placed at his disposal. With this object the Commander-in-Chief in his official letters to the Admiralty and by every other channel open to him continually dwelt upon the weakness and deficiencies of the force at his disposal, and at the same time magnified the power of the enemy. This habit of mind had been acquired during many years of struggle for money with peace-time Governments. It had now become ingrained in his nature.

The enemy, according to his view, would be more numerous than the Admiralty Intelligence Department admitted. Their best ships would be found re-armed with much heavier guns. The speed of these vessels would turn out to be greater than we knew. Almost certainly they had some astonishing surprises in store. "The Germans," he had written to Lord Fisher on December 4, 1914, "would have eight flotillas comprising eighty-eight torpedo boat destroyers, all of which would certainly be ready at the selected moment. They had five torpedoes each: total 440 torpedoes—*unless I can strike at them first.*" He then argued that he might fall as low as 32, or even 28, destroyers. "You know," he added, "the difficulty and objections to turning away from the enemy in a Fleet action: but with such a menace I am bound to do it, unless my own torpedo boat destroyers can stop or neutralize the movement." At the date which this story has now reached he was convinced that the 10,000 yards correctly assigned by the Admiralty Intelligence Department as the extreme range of the German torpedo was too little: 15,000 yards must be the margin of safety on which he should rely. Even at the very end of his command, when a large part of the American Navy was serving with our own and when the strength of the Allied Fleets was at least four times that of their antagonists, he is still found seriously disquieted at his relative strength in battle-cruisers. It is obvious that there are limits beyond which this outlook ceases to contribute to the gaining of victory in war. But this does not affect the main argument.

All Jellicoe's thought was rightly centred upon the naval battle which he would some day have to fight. On October 14, 1914, he addressed to the Admiralty a letter which reveals his deepest conviction and his consistent intentions. From this, extensive quotation is necessary.

> . . . The Germans have shown that they rely to a very great extent on submarines, mines and torpedoes, and there can be no doubt whatever that they will endeavour to make the fullest use of these weapons in a fleet action, especially since they possess an actual superiority over us in these particular directions. It therefore becomes necessary to consider our own tactical methods in relation to these forms of attack. . . .

The German submarines, if worked as is expected with the battle fleet, can be used in one of two ways:

(a) With the cruisers, or possibly with destroyers;

(b) With the battle fleet.

In the first case the submarines would probably be led by the cruisers to a position favourable for attacking our battle fleet as it advanced to deploy, and in the second case they might be kept in a position in rear, or to the flank, of the enemy's battle fleet, which would move in the direction required to draw our own Fleet into contact with the submarines.

The first move at *(a)* should be defeated by our own cruisers, provided we have a sufficient number present, as they should be able to force the enemy's cruisers to action at a speed which would interfere with submarine tactics. . . .

The second move at *(b)* can be countered by judicious handling of our battle fleet, but may, and probably will, involve a refusal to comply with the enemy's tactics by moving in the invited direction. If, for instance, the enemy battle fleet were to turn away from an advancing fleet, I should assume that the intention was to lead us over mines and submarines, and should decline to be so drawn.

I desire particularly to draw the attention of their Lordships to this point, since it may be deemed a refusal of battle, and, indeed, might possibly result in failure to bring the enemy to action as soon as is expected and hoped.

Such a result would be absolutely repugnant to the feelings of all British Naval Officers and men, but with new and untried methods of warfare new tactics must be devised to meet them.

I feel that such tactics, if not understood, may bring odium upon me, but so long as I have the confidence of their Lordships, I intend to pursue what is, in my considered opinion, the proper course to defeat and annihilate the enemy's battle fleet, without regard to uninstructed opinion or criticism.

The situation is a difficult one. It is quite within the bounds of possibility that half of our battle fleet might be disabled by underwater attack before the guns opened fire at all, if a false step is made, and I feel that I must constantly bear in mind the great probability of such attack and be prepared tactically to prevent its success.

The safeguard against submarines will consist in moving the battle fleet at very high speed to a flank before deployment takes place or the gun action commences.

This will take us off the ground on which the enemy desires to fight, but it may, of course, result in his refusal to follow me. . . .

The object of this letter is to place my views before their Lordships, and to direct their attention to the alterations in preconceived ideas of battle tactics which are forced upon us by the anticipated appearance in a fleet action of submarines and minelayers. . . .

Lord Fisher, Sir Arthur Wilson, and the Chief of the Naval Staff, then Admiral Sturdee, all considered fully this communication, which was of course only one of a regular stream of reports, despatches and private letters from the Commander-in-Chief. They had no doubt what answer should be sent. They advised me that Sir John Jellicoe's statement should receive the general approval of the Board of Admiralty. I agreed fully with their advice. An answer in the contrary sense was obviously impossible. To tell the Commander-in-Chief of the British Fleet, in the strategic situation which then existed, that even if he suspected the German Fleet were retiring to lead him into a trap of mines and submarines, he should nevertheless follow directly after them, and that if he failed to bring them to battle by manœuvring against his better judgment, no matter what the risk, he would be held blameworthy, would have been madness. The fullest possible latitude of manœuvre, the strongest assurances of personal confidence, were the indefeasible right of any officer in his great situation. Moreover, in October, 1914, our margins of superiority were at their minimum. A plurality of only six or seven Dreadnoughts could be counted on with certainty. We had never met the enemy's great ships in battle. No one could say with certainty to what degree of excellence their gunnery or torpedo practice had attained, or whether their projectiles or their tactics contained some utterly unexpected feature. There was certainly no reason in this first phase of the naval war for seeking a battle except on the best conditions.

I take the fullest responsibility for approving at this date the answer proposed to me by the First Sea Lord, Sir Arthur Wilson, and the Chief of the Staff. If I had not agreed with it, I should not have allowed it to pass unchallenged. But I was far from sharing the Commander-in-Chief's impressions upon the relative strength and quality of the British and German Fleets. I always believed that the British line of battle could fight the Germans ship for ship, and should never decline an encounter on those terms. I always regarded every addition to equality on our side as a precautionary advantage, not necessary to the gaining of victory, but justified by the far greater stake which a naval battle involved to Britain than to Germany. These views appeared to be vindicated three months later when on January 24, 1915, Admiral Beatty with five battle-cruisers met Admiral Hipper with four. On the morrow of that action, January 26, I wrote to Sir John Jellicoe as follows:

The action on Sunday bears out all I have thought of the relative British and German strength. It is clear that at five to four they have no thought but flight, and that a battle fought out on this margin could have only one ending. The immense power of the 13.5-inch gun is clearly decisive on the minds of the enemy, as well as on the progress of the action. I should not feel the slightest anxiety at the idea of your engaging with equality. Still I think it would be bad management on our part if your superiority was not much nearer six to four than five to four, even under the worst conditions.

And to the Prime Minister, January 24, 1915, 3:45 p.m.:

This action gives us a good line for judging the results of a general battle. It may be roughly said that we should probably fight six to four at the worst, whereas to-day was five to four.

In the great episode which has now to be described the British superiority was not five to four, nor six to four; it was at least two to one. Sir John Jellicoe is fully justified in pointing to his letter of October 14 as a proof that his conduct in the stress of action was in accord with what he had long purposed in cold blood, and with a general tactical policy which he had already laid before the Board of Admiralty. But I do not accept on behalf of the Board of Admiralty of 1914 any responsibility for the actual conduct by the Commander-in-Chief of an operation which took place eighteen months later in conditions of relative strength different from those which existed in October, 1914, and, as will be seen as this account proceeds, in tactical circumstances entirely different from those which were contemplated by him in his letter. A perception that a decisive battle is not a necessity in a particular situation, and ought not to be purchased at a heavy risk, should not engender a defensive habit of mind or scheme of tactics.

After these preliminary observations the story may be told in its simplest form, with pauses to examine the issues involved at the crucial moments.

Earlier in this account I recorded the events which secured for the Admiralty the incomparable advantage of reading the plans and orders of the enemy before they were executed. Without the cryptographers' department there would have been no Battle of Jutland. But for that department, the whole course of the naval war would have been different. The British Fleet could not have remained continuously at sea without speedily wearing down its men and machinery. Unless it had remained almost continuously at sea the Germans would have been able to bombard two or three times a month all our East Coast towns. The simplest measurements on the chart will show that their battle-cruisers and other fast vessels could have reached our shores, inflicted an injury, and returned each time safely, or at least without superior attack, to their own home bases. Such a state of affairs would not necessarily have altered the final course of the war. The nation would have been forced to realize that the ruin of its East Coast towns was as much their part of the trial and burden as the destruction of so many Provinces to France. After national resentment had expended itself in the removal of one or more Governments or Boards of Admiralty, a resolute people would have faced the facts with which they were confronted, would indeed have derived from them a new vigour of resistance.

But it so chanced that they were spared this particular ordeal. The secret signal-books of the German Navy fell into the hands of the Russians in the Baltic when the light cruiser *Magdeburg* was sunk in October, 1914, and were conveyed to London. These signal-books and the charts connected with them were subjected to a study in Whitehall in which self-effacing industry and imaginative genius reached their highest degree. By the aid of these books and the deductions drawn from their use, the Admiralty acquired the power of reading a proportion of the German wireless messages. Well as was the secret kept, the coincidence of events aroused suspicion in the German mind. They knew the British squadrons could not always be at sea; and yet often when a German raid was launched, there at the interception point, or very near it, were found important British naval forces. They therefore redoubled the precaution of their codes. Moreover they had themselves pierced to some extent the British codes, and had actually established at Neumünster a station for transmitting to their Fleet intercepted British messages. Nevertheless, during the central period of the war at any rate the Admiralty were capable of presenting to the Fleet a stream of valuable information.

The Naval Staff discovered in the last week of May, 1916, peculiar symptoms of impending activity in the German Fleet. The Intelligence had from other sources reported the appointment of Admiral Scheer to the chief command. This officer was reputed at the time to be the advocate of an aggressive war policy at sea. He had espoused an unlimited submarine campaign. He was the nominee of Tirpitz the Bold. The cautious and even timid tactics adopted by the German Navy under the direct orders of the Emperor ever since Beatty had broken into the Heligoland Bight at the end of August, 1914, were now to be abandoned. Admiral Scheer planned offensive action against the English coast for the purpose of drawing the British Fleet out over prepared ambuscades of submarines, and then if Fortune was favourable fighting that weakened Fleet, or better still a detached division of it, a decisive battle for the command of the seas. The imminence of an important operation was deduced by the Admiralty from the whole body of their intelligence.

At five o'clock on May 30 the Admiralty informed the Fleet that there were indications of the Germans putting to sea. The Fleet, which had been previously ordered to raise steam, was directed to concentrate "eastward of the Long Forties" (about 60 miles east of the Scottish coast) ready for eventualities.

The two Fleets that put to sea in the evening of May 30, 1916, constituted the culminating manifestation of naval force in the history of the world. But tremendous as was the power of the German Fleet, it could not compare with the British in numbers, speed or gun power. The British marshalled 28 Dreadnought battleships and 9 battle-cruisers against Admiral Scheer's 16 Dreadnoughts and 5 battle-cruisers. In addition the Germans had 6 pre-Dreadnought ships of the *Deutschland* class, whose slow speed and poor armament made them a source of anxiety to the German Commander. The speed of the British Fleet was decidedly superior. Its slowest battleship could steam 20 knots, while the 5th Battle Squadron, comprising four *Queen Elizabeths,* the strongest and swiftest battleships afloat, was capable of steaming 24 to 25 knots. The fastest German battleship could only steam 21 knots, while the 6 *Deutschlands* reduced the combined maximum speed of the Battle Fleet to 16 knots.

Still greater was the British superiority in gun fire. Sir John Jellicoe's battleships and battle-cruisers mounted 272 heavy guns against 200 German. But this superiority in number was magnified by an enormous superiority in size: 48 British 15-inch, 10 14-inch, 142 13.5-inch, and 144 12-inch guns were matched against 144 German 12-inch and 100 11-inch, making a total British broadside of 396,700 pounds against a German of 189,958.

The torpedo strength of the two Fleets, including vessels of every class, was numerically almost equal. The British mounted 382 21-inch and 75 18-inch torpedo tubes; the Germans 362 19.7-inch and 107 17.7-inch. The smaller short-ranged class of torpedoes on either side were hardly likely to be serviceable in a daylight action; and the British 21-inch were slightly superior to the German 19.7-inch in range and in speed. A clear advantage even in this arm therefore rested with the British.

The British preponderance in capital ships was fully maintained in cruisers and destroyers. The British had 31 cruisers at sea, of which eight were the most powerful armoured cruisers of the pre-Dreadnought era: the Germans had 11. On the long expected day of battle Sir John Jellicoe, although not provided with the cruisers and destroyers of the Harwich force, could muster 85 destroyers to the German 72. As in the case of the larger ships, the numerical superiorities alike in cruisers and in destroyers were enhanced by a great additional strength in gun power in every class, and a large advantage in the speed of the cruisers and in the size of the destroyers. Inferiority in any important arm or factor cannot be discerned at any point in the British array.

In consequence of the Admiralty orders, Sir John Jellicoe concentrated from Scapa Flow and Cromarty 24 Dreadnought battleships, 3 battle-cruisers, 3 cruiser-squadrons and 3 destroyer flotillas in the "Long Forties" on the morning of May 31. He had sent Admiral Beatty from the Forth about 65 miles ahead of him with 6 battle-cruisers, 2 light cruiser squadrons, 2 flotillas and—massive addition—4 *Queen Elizabeths*. In this formation both were to steam towards the Heligoland Bight till 2 p.m. when, if nothing was seen, Beatty was to come back into sight of the Battle Fleet, which would turn eastward for a further sweep towards the Horn Reef before returning home. The distance of 65 miles between the main Fleet and its powerful scouting forces has been criticized as excessive. It precluded visual contact between the two portions of the Fleet, and impeded their harmonious combination in the all-important preliminary phases of a great battle. If Beatty, arriving at his rendezvous, found the enemy there or thereabouts, Jellicoe would be out of tactical relation and too far off to force a battle. This disposition had however been used several times before; and Beatty with his fast powerful ships was quite capable of acting independently. Both Admirals had been out so often on these sweeps that though all precautions were observed neither, on the skeleton information available, had any particular expectation of encountering the enemy.

The day was bright and calm, and as the morning wore away such hopes as they had indulged gradually departed. The last gleam was finally extinguished by a signal from the Admiralty at 12:35 p.m. stating that directionals (i.e., directional wireless) placed the enemy flagship in the Jade at 11:10 a.m. Both Admirals tarried on their course to examine suspicious trawlers, and both were a few miles short of their prescribed positions and out of their reckoning when the hour for the battle-cruisers to turn northwards and close the Battle Fleet approached.[1] Admiral Beatty had already made the signal for an almost complete turn about, and at 2:15 p.m. all his heavy ships had obeyed it. His cruiser screen was in process of turning on to the new direction when the light cruiser *Galatea* saw a steamer about eight miles off apparently stopped and molested by two strange vessels. At 2:20 she signalled: "Enemy in sight. Two cruisers probably hostile bearing south-east, course unknown." The full situation is exposed in the plan on page 611. The strange vessels were two of the leading torpedo boats of the German Second Scouting Group. All the British light cruisers began spontaneously to draw towards the *Galatea,* and eight minutes later she opened fire. One after another German light cruisers and destroyers emerged and defined themselves from the dim-

---

[1] The main facts and times throughout this account are taken from the Official Admiralty Narrative of Jutland.

ness of the horizon, and behind them a long smoke cloud declared the presence of important hostile forces.

The *Galatea's* message at 2:20 and the sound of her guns at 2:28 were sufficient for Admiral Beatty. A hostile enterprise of some kind was in progress. German warships were at sea. At 2:32 the *Lion,* having already warned her consorts by signal of her intentions, turned about again, and increasing her speed to 22 knots set off in pursuit, steering for the Horn Reef Channel and meaning to cut whatever enemy might be abroad from their harbours. All the battle-cruisers followed the *Lion,* and executed the Vice-Admiral's order. But the 5th Battle Squadron, 4½ miles astern, continued to carry out the previous instructions, and for eight minutes steered in exactly the opposite direction along the left leg of a northward zigzag, as if oblivious to the vital change in the situation. During these eight minutes the 5th Battle Squadron was losing touch with the battle-cruisers at the rate of over forty miles an hour. When eventually they turned at 2:40, they were already 10 miles behind the van. This loss of distance and time their best efforts were not able fully to retrieve before action was joined.

One of the many controversies of Jutland centres around this delay in turning the 5th Battle Squadron. On the one hand, it is contended that Rear-Admiral Evan-Thomas, who commanded it, did not make out the signal flags until 2:40.[1] On the other, it is claimed that he knew at 2:20 that enemy ships were in sight; that the *Barham,* his flagship, received at 2:30 by wireless the course about to be steered by the *Lion,*[2] that his general and dominant orders were to keep supporting station 5 miles from the *Lion;* that whatever the difficulty in reading the signal flags, the movements of the battle-cruisers were obvious; that no one on the *Barham's* bridge could miss seeing all the six enormous British ships only 9,000 yards away suddenly turn about and steer eastward toward the enemy; and that no flag signals or wireless orders were needed to require Rear-Admiral Evan-Thomas's battle squadron to conform to the movements of the force and of the Commander his whole purpose and duty was to support. Such are the rival views, and decision upon them is scarcely difficult. It is common ground between all parties that Rear-Admiral Evan-Thomas, once he realized the situation, did all in his power to recover the lost distance, and that, profiting by the manœuvring deviations of the converging and fighting lines, he in fact recovered upwards of four miles of it. The result however of his eight minutes' delay in turning was inexorably to keep him and his tremendous guns out of the action for the first most critical and most fatal half-hour, and even thereafter to keep him at extreme range.

[1] Official Narrative: Lord Jellicoe's Remarks, Appendix G, p. 106.
[2] Admiralty footnote 2 to Lord Jellicoe's Remarks.

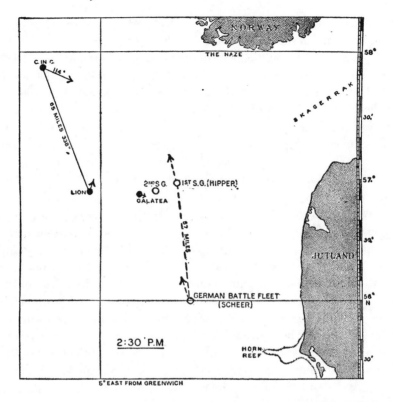

But the question has also been raised: was Admiral Beatty right to turn instantly in pursuit of the enemy? Ought he not first to have closed on the 5th Battle Squadron and turned his whole ten great ships together? To this question the answer also seems clear. It is the duty of a Commander, whenever possible, to concentrate a superior force for battle. But Beatty's six battle-cruisers were in themselves superior in numbers, speed, and gun power to the whole of the German battle-cruisers, even if, as was not at this moment certain, any or all of these were at sea. The issue for the British Admiral was not therefore whether to concentrate a superior force or not, but whether, having concentrated a superior force, to steam for six minutes away from the enemy in order to concentrate an overwhelming force. Six minutes' steaming away from the enemy might mean a loss of six thousand yards in pursuit. The last time Beatty had seen German ships was when Hipper's battle-cruisers faded out of sight of the crippled *Lion* sixteen months before at the Dogger Bank. The impression that every minute counted was dominant in his mind. Why should he wait to become stronger when by every test of paper and every memory of battle he was already strong enough? Had the 5th Battle Squadron turned when he turned, it would have been in close support if fighting occurred and took an adverse turn.

The doctrine that after sufficient force has been concentrated an Admiral should delay, and at the risk of losing the whole opportunity gather a still larger force, was one which could only be doubtfully applied even to the Battle Fleet, and would paralyse the action of fast scouting forces. It would however no doubt have been better if the original cruising formation of the battle-cruisers and the 5th Battle Squadron had been more compact. But the facts, when at 2:32 Beatty decided that the enemy was present in sufficient strength to justify turning the heavy ships about, made it his clear duty to steam at once and at the utmost speed in their direction. All that impulse, all that ardour give was no doubt present in the Admiral's mind; but these were joined by all that the coldest science of war and the longest view of naval history proclaimed.

It was unlikely that no stronger enemy forces should be behind the German scouting screen: but up till this moment nothing but light cruisers and destroyers had appeared. Now at about 3:20 the *New Zealand* sighted five enemy ships on her starboard bow; and from 3:31 onwards the *Lion* distinguished one after another the whole five German battle-cruisers. Admiral von Hipper had for an hour been passing through experiences similar to those of Admiral Beatty. His light cruisers had brushed into British scouting ships. He had hurried forward to their aid. Suddenly at 3:20 he was confronted with the apparition of Beatty's six battle-cruisers bearing down on him at full speed, accompanied by their flotillas and light cruisers and supported by the menace of dark smoke banks against the western sky. As on January 24, 1915, he acted with promptitude. He immediately turned about and ran apparently for home. But this time there were two new factors at work. Beatty knew for certain from their relative position in the sea that he could force his enemy to battle. Hipper knew that he was drawing Beatty into the jaws of the advancing High Sea Fleet. We see these splendid squadrons shearing through the waters that will soon be lashed by their cannonade, each Commander with the highest hopes—the British Admiral exulting because he had surely overtaken his foe; the German nursing the secret of his trap. So for a space both Fleets drove forward in a silence.

The combat of the battle-cruisers which preceded the encounter of the main Fleets off Jutland is a self-contained episode. Both Admirals, tactics apart, wished for a trial of strength and quality. Human beings have never wielded so resolutely such tremendous engines or such intense organizations of destruction. The most powerful guns ever used, the highest explosives ever devised, the fastest and the largest ships of war ever launched, the cream of the officers and men of the British and German nations, all that the martial science of either Navy could achieve—clashed against each other in this rigorous though intermittent duel. Each in turn faced an adverse superiority of numbers; each had behind him supporting forces which, could they be made available, would have involved the destruction of the other. Hipper counted on the High Sea Fleet, and Beatty could always fall back on his four *Queen Elizabeths.* Each in turn retired before superior forces and endeavoured to draw his opponent into overwhelming disadvantage. The officers and the men on both sides showed themselves completely unaffected in their decisions and conduct by the frightful apparatus which they used upon each other; and their conflict represents in its intensity the concentration and the consummation of the war effort of men. The battle-cruiser action would of course have been eclipsed by a general battle between the main Fleets. But since this never occurred to any serious extent, the two hours' fight between Beatty and Hipper constitutes the prodigy of modern war on sea.

The detailed story of the action has been told so often and told so well that it needs only brief repetition here. Both the German and French accounts are excellent, and the British Official Narrative is a model of exact and yet stirring professional description. The salient features can be recognized by anyone.

Both sides deliberately converged to effective striking distance. Fire was opened by the *Lützow* and answered by the *Lion* a little after a quarter to four. Each ship engaged its respective antagonist. As there were six British to five German battle-cruisers, the *Lion* and the *Princess Royal* were able to concentrate on the enemy's flagship *Lützow.* The chances of the battle on either side led to discrepancies in the selection of targets, and sometimes two British ships were firing at one German, while another was ignored, or *vice versa.* Two minutes after the great guns had opened fire at about 14,000 yards, the *Lion* was hit twice; and the third salvo of the *Princess Royal* struck the *Lützow.* On both sides four guns at a time were fired, and at every discharge four shells each weighing about half a ton smote target or water in a volley. In the first thirty-seven minutes of an action which lasted above two hours, one-third of the British force was destroyed. At four o'clock the *Indefatigable,* after twelve minutes at battery with the *Von der Tann,* hit by three simultaneous shells from a salvo of four, blew up and sank almost without survivors. Twenty-six minutes later the *Queen Mary,* smitten amidships by a plunging salvo from the *Derfflinger,* burst into flame, capsized, and after thirty seconds exploded into a pillar of smoke which rose 800 feet in the air, bearing with it for 200 feet such items as a 50-foot steamboat. The *Tiger* and the *New Zealand,* following her at the speed of an ordinary train, and with only 500 yards between them had barely time to sheer off port and starboard to avoid her wreck. The *Tiger* passed through the smoke cloud black as night, and her gunnery officer, unable to fire, took advantage of the pitch-darkness to reset to zero the director controls of his four turrets.[1]

[1] *Fighting at Jutland.*

Meanwhile the *Lion,* after being eight minutes in action, was hit on her midship turret (Q) by a shell which, but for a sublime act of personal devotion and comprehension, would have been fatal.

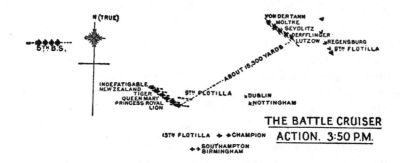

THE BATTLE CRUISER
ACTION. 3:50 P.M.

All the crew of the turret except its commanding officer, Major Hervey (Royal Marine Artillery), and his sergeant were instantly killed; and Major Hervey had both his legs shattered or torn off. Each turret in a capital ship is a self-contained organizm. It is seated in the hull of the vessel like a fort; it reaches from the armoured gunhouse visible to all, 50 feet downwards to the very keel. Its intricate hydraulic machinery, its ammunition trunk communicating with the shell-rooms and magazines—all turn together in whatever direction its twin guns may point. The shell of the *Lützow* wrecked the turret and set the wreckage on fire. The shock flung and jammed one of the guns upwards, and twenty minutes later the cartridge which was in its breech slid out. It caught fire and ignited the other charges in the gun-cages. The flash from these passed down the trunk to the charges at the bottom. None but dead and dying remained in the turret. All had been finished by the original shell burst. The men in the switch-board department and the handling parties of the shell-room were instantly killed by the flash of the cordite fire. The blast passed through and through the turret in all its passages and foundations, and rose 200 feet above its gaping roof. But the doors of the magazines were closed. Major Hervey, shattered, weltering, stifled, seared, had found it possible to give the order down the voice tube: "Close magazines doors and flood magazines." So the *Lion* drove on her course unconscious of her peril, or by what expiring breath it had been effectually averted. In the long, rough, glorious history of the Royal Marines there is no name and no deed which in its character and its consequences ranks above this.

Meanwhile the Vice-Admiral, pacing the bridge among the shell fragments rebounding from the water, and like Nelson of old in the brunt of the enemy's fire, has learned that the *Indefatigable* and the *Queen Mary* have been destroyed,

and that his own magazines are menaced by fire. It is difficult to compare sea
with land war. But each battle-cruiser was a unit comparable at least to a complete infantry division. Two divisions out of his six have been annihilated in the
twinkling of an eye. The enemy, whom he could not defeat with six ships to
five, are now five ships to four. Far away all five German battle-cruisers—grey
smudges changing momentarily into "rippling sheets of flame"—are still intact
and seemingly invulnerable. "Nevertheless," proceeds the official narrative, "the
squadron continued its course undismayed." But the movement of these blind,
inanimate castles of steel was governed at this moment entirely by the spirit of a
single man. Had he faltered, had he taken less than a conqueror's view of the
British fighting chances, all these great engines of sea power and war power
would have wobbled off in meaningless disarray. This is a moment on which
British naval historians will be glad to dwell; and the actual facts deserve to be
recorded. The *Indefatigable* had disappeared beneath the waves. The *Queen
Mary* had towered up to heaven in a pillar of fire. The *Lion* was in flames. A
tremendous salvo struck upon or about her following ship, the *Princess Royal,*
which vanished in a cloud of spray and smoke. A signalman sprang on to the
Lion's bridge with the words: "*Princess Royal* blown up, sir." On this the Vice-
Admiral said to his Flag Captain, "Chatfield, there seems to be something
wrong with our———ships to-day. Turn two points to port," i.e., two points
nearer the enemy.

Thus the crisis of the battle was surmounted. All the German damage was
done in the first half-hour. As the action proceeded the British battle-cruisers,
although reduced to an inferiority in numbers, began to assert an ascendancy
over the enemy. Their guns became increasingly effective, and they themselves
received no further serious injury. The deterioration in the accuracy and rate of
the German fire during the next hour and a half was obvious. Each side in turn
manœuvred nearer to or farther from the enemy in order to frustrate his aim.
And from ten minutes past four the 5th Battle Squadron had begun to fire, at
the long range of 17,000 yards, upon Admiral von Hipper's last two ships. The
influence of this intervention, tardy but timely, is somewhat lightly treated by
the British official narrators. It receives the fullest testimony in the German accounts. The four mighty ships of Admiral Evan-Thomas threw their 15-inch
shells with astonishing accuracy across the great distances which separated them
from the German rear. If only they had been 5,000 yards closer, the defeat, if
not the destruction, of Hipper's squadron was inevitable. That they were not
5,000 yards closer was due entirely to their slowness in grasping the situation
when the first contact was made with the enemy. However, they now came
thundering into battle; and their arrival within effective range would, in less
than an hour, have been decisive—if no other German forces had been at sea
that day. The battle-cruisers continued to fire at one another with the ut-

most rapidity at varying ranges. But from 4:30 onward the approaching and increasing fire of the 5th Battle Squadron, and the development by both sides of fierce destroyer attacks and counterattacks, sensibly abated the intensity of their action.

Admiral Scheer, advancing with the whole High Sea Fleet, had received the news of the first contact between the light cruisers at 2:28 p.m., almost immediately after it had occurred. At 3:25 he learned of the presence of the British battle-cruisers. A message received at 3:45 from the "Chief of Reconnaissance" showed that Admiral von Hipper was engaged with six enemy battle-cruisers on a south-easterly course. Scheer understood clearly that Hipper was falling back upon him in the hopes of drawing the British battle-cruisers under the guns of the main German Fleet. He accordingly steered at first so as to take the pursuing British if possible between two fires. But when he heard a few minutes later that the *Queen Elizabeth* had also appeared upon the scene, he conceived it his duty to hasten directly to the support of his now outnumbered battle-cruisers. Leaving his older battleships to follow at their best pace, he therefore steamed north in line at 17 knots shortly after four o'clock. The opposing forces were now approaching each other at 43 miles an hour.

The 2nd Light Cruiser Squadron, heralding Beatty's advance and guarding him from surprise, was the first to see the hostile fleet. At 4:33 the *Southampton*, carrying Commodore Goodenough's broad pennant, sighted the head of the long line of German battleships drawing out upon the horizon, and signalled the magic words "Battleships in sight." Almost as soon as the reports of the light cruisers had reached the *Lion*, Beatty himself sighted the High Sea Fleet. He grasped the situation instantly. Without losing a moment he led his remaining four ships round in a complete turn, and steamed directly back along his course towards Jellicoe. Hipper, now in touch with Scheer, turned immediately afterwards in the same direction. The situation of the two Admirals was thus exactly reversed: Beatty tried to lead Hipper and the German Battle Fleet up to Jellicoe; Hipper pursued his retreating foe without knowing that he was momentarily approaching the British Grand Fleet. In this phase of the action, which is called "The Run to the North," firing was continued by the battle-cruisers on both sides. The light was now far more favourable to the British, and the German battle-cruisers suffered severely from their fire.

On sighting the main German Fleet, Beatty had turned about so swiftly that his ships soon passed the 5th Battle Squadron coming up at full speed and still on their southerly course. As the two squadrons ran past each other on opposite courses, the *Lion* signalled to the *Barham* to turn about in succession. The *Lion's* signal of recall was flown at 4:48. She passed the *Barham* two miles away, with this signal flying, at 4:53; and Rear-Admiral Evan-Thomas responded to the signal three or four minutes later. Perhaps the Rear-Admiral,

ENEMY BATTLESHIPS IN SIGHT. 4:40 P.M

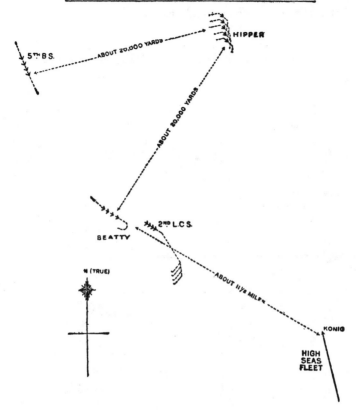

having been slow in coming into action, was inclined to be slow in coming out. Brief as was this interval, it was sufficient at the speed at which all the ships were moving to expose the 5th Battle Squadron to action with the van of the German Battle Fleet. The van was formed by the German 3rd Squadron, comprising the *Königs* and the *Kaisers,* the strongest and newest vessels in the German Navy. The four *Queen Elizabeths* were now subjected to tremendous fire concentrated particularly upon the point where each turned in succession. The two leading ships, the *Barham* and the *Valiant,* were engaged with the enemy's battle-cruisers; the rear ships, the *Warspite* and the *Malaya,* fought the whole of the finest squadron in the German Fleet. This apparently unequal conflict lasted for over half an hour. All the ships except the *Valiant* were struck repeatedly with the heaviest shells, the *Warspite* alone receiving thirteen hits and the *Malaya* seven. Such, however, was the strength of these vessels that none of their turrets were put out of action and their speed was wholly unaffected.

All the main forces were now fast drawing together, and all converged and arrived upon the scene in one great movement. Every ship was moving simultaneously, and after an almost unperceived interval, the duel of the battle-cruisers merged in the preliminaries of a general Fleet action.

THE TURN TO THE NORTH. 5:00 P.M.

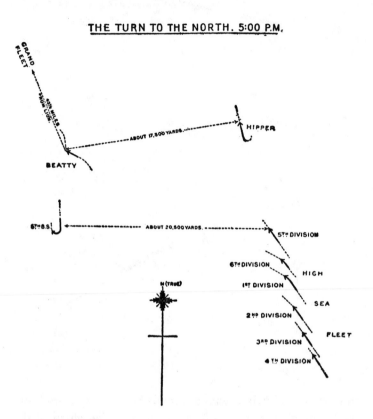

CHAPTER XLII

JUTLAND: THE ENCOUNTER

U p to this moment we have been moving through events which, although terrific, were nevertheless within the region of previous experience. The battle-cruisers had fought each other before, and their Admirals knew the character of the conflict, the power of the weapons, and what the ordeal was like. Moreover, as has been said, on neither side did the battle-cruiser force amount to a vital stake. But the battle fleets themselves are now approaching each other at a closing speed of over thirty-five miles an hour, and with every minute we enter the kingdom at once of the Decisive and of the Unknown.

The supreme moment on which all the thought and efforts of the British and German Admiralties had been for many years concentrated was now at hand. On both sides nearly the whole naval effort of the nation had been devoted to the battle fleets. In the British Navy, at any rate, the picture of the great sea-battle had dominated every other thought, and its needs had received precedence over every other requirement. Everything had been lavished upon the drawing out of a line of batteries of such a preponderance and in such an order that the German Battle Fleet would be blasted and shattered *for certain* in a very short space of time. Numbers, gun power, quality, training—all had been provided for the Commander-in-Chief to the utmost extent possible to British manhood and science. Unless some entirely unforeseen factor intervened or some incalculable accident occurred, there was no reason to doubt that thirty minutes' firing within ten thousand yards between two parallel lines of battle would achieve a complete victory.

Therefore for years Jellicoe's mind had been focussed upon the simplest form of naval battle: the single line and the parallel course; a long-range artillery conflict; and defensive action against torpedo attack. Everything beyond this opening phase was speculative and complicated. If the opening phase were satisfactory, everything else would probably follow from it. The Admiralty could not look beyond providing their Commander-in-Chief with an ample superiority in ships of every kind. The method and moment of joining battle and its tactical conduct could be ruled by him alone. It is now argued that it would have been better if, instead of riveting all attention and endeavour upon a long-range artillery duel by the two fleets in line on roughly parallel courses,

the much more flexible system of engaging by divisions, of using the fastest battleships apart from the slower, and of dealing with each situation according to
the needs of the moment, had been employed. It may well be so; and had there
been several battles or even encounters between the British and German fleets
in the war, there is no doubt that a far higher system of battle tactics would
have developed. But nothing like this particular event had ever happened before, and nothing like it was ever to happen again. The "Nelson touch" arose
from years of fighting between the strongest ships of the time. Nelson's genius
enabled him to measure truly the consequences of any decision. But that genius
worked upon precise practical data. He had seen the same sort of thing happen
on a less great scale many times over before the Battle of Trafalgar. Nelson did
not have to worry about underwater damage. He felt he knew what would happen in a Fleet action. Jellicoe did not know. Nobody knew. All he knew was
that a complete victory would not improve decisively an already favourable
naval situation, and that a total defeat would lose the war. He was prepared to
accept battle on his own terms; he was not prepared to force one at a serious
hazard. The battle was to be fought as he wished it or left unfought.

But while we may justify on broad grounds of national policy the general
attitude of the Commander-in-Chief towards the conditions upon which alone
a decisive battle should be fought, neither admiration nor agreement can adhere to the system of command and training which he had developed in the
Fleet. Everything was centralized in the Flagship, and all initiative except in
avoiding torpedo attack was denied to the leaders of squadrons and divisions. A
ceaseless stream of signals from the Flagship was therefore required to regulate
the movement of the Fleet and the distribution of the fire. These signals prescribed the course and speed of every ship, as well as every manœuvring turn.
In exercises such a centralization may have produced a better drill. But in the
smoke, confusion and uncertainty of battle the process was far too elaborate.
The Fleet was too large to fight as a single organization or to be minutely directed by the finger of a single man. The Germans, following the Army system
of command, had foreseen before the war that the intelligent co-operation of
subordinates, who knew thoroughly the general views and spirit of their Chief,
must be substituted in a Fleet action for a rigid and centralized control. At
this moment the line in which they were approaching was in fact three self-
contained independently manœuvring squadrons following one another. But
Jellicoe's system denied initiative not only to his battle squadrons, but even to
the flotillas. Throughout the battle he endeavoured personally to direct the
whole Fleet. He could, as his own account describes,[1] only see or know a small
part of what was taking place; and as no human mind can receive more than a

---

[1] The Grand Fleet.

limited number of impressions in any given period of time, his control disappeared as a guiding power, and only remained as a check on the enterprise of others.

Let us now take the position of Admiral Scheer. He had no intention of fighting a battle against the whole British Fleet. He was under no illusions about the relative strength of the rival batteries. Nothing could be more clownish than to draw up his fleet on parallel courses with an opponent firing twice his weight of metal and manned by a personnel whose science, seamanship and fortitude commanded his sincere respect. He had not come out with any idea of fighting a pitched battle. He had never intended to fight at a hopeless disadvantage. If he met weaker forces or equal forces, or any forces which gave a fair or sporting chance of victory, he would fight with all the martial skill and courage inseparable from the German name. But from the moment he knew that he was in the presence of the united Grand Fleet and saw the whole horizon bristling with its might, his only aim was to free himself as quickly as possible without dishonour from a fatal trap. In this he was entirely successful.

He had sedulously practised the turn-about movement by which under cover of torpedo attacks and smoke screens every ship in the line could circle about individually and steam in the opposite direction without fail even if the line was itself a curve or marred by the "kinks" and disorder of heavy action. To this manoeuvre and to its thorough comprehension by his captains the German Fleet was twice to owe its triumphant escape.

Having regard to the moods and intentions of the two Commanders, to their respective strategic problems, to their geographical position, to their relative speeds, and to the three hours' daylight that alone remained when they met, it will be seen that the chances of a general Fleet action being fought out on May 31 were remote.

The reader must now take his mental station on the bridge of the *Iron Duke* which all this time has been steaming forward leading the centre of the British Battle Fleet. Sir John Jellicoe has read every signal made by Admiral Beatty's light cruisers and battle-cruisers. He has therefore been able to follow on the chart the course of events from the first report of the suspicious vessels by the *Galatea* to the momentous announcement of Commodore Goodenough that the High Sea Fleet was in sight. The forces at his disposal are moving in a vast crescent. Its southern horn consists of Beatty's detached command, a fleet in itself. On the north or less-exposed flank is Admiral Hood with a force similar to, but smaller than Beatty's, and consisting of the 3rd Battle Cruiser Squadron with two light cruisers and destroyers. The immediate front of the Battle Fleet is screened by eight pre-Dreadnought armoured cruisers followed by four of the latest light cruisers *(Carolines)*.

The Commander-in-Chief knows that all his powerful advanced scouting forces of the southern flank are engaged, and that a heavy battle-cruiser action has been in progress for nearly two hours. From the first moment of the alarm he has been working his fleet up to its highest combined speed, and the whole of his twenty-four battleships[1] are now steaming at 20 knots. As soon as he heard that the German battle-cruisers were at sea, he had ordered Admiral Hood with the *Invincibles* and other vessels to reinforce Beatty. He finds time to telegraph to the Admiralty the solemn message "Fleet action imminent"; and far away around the indented coasts of Britain arsenals, dockyards, hospitals spring into a long-prepared intense activity.

The task is now the deployment of the Fleet. And here, while the armadas are closing, we must step aside for a few moments from the narrative to enable the lay reader to appreciate some of the technical issues involved.

The evolutions of cavalry in the days of shock tactics and those of a modern fleet resemble each other. Both approach in column and fight in line; and cavalry and fleet drill consist primarily in swift and well-executed changes from one formation to the other. The Grand Fleet was now advancing in a mass of six columns of four ships, each column a mile apart. The Fleet Flagship, the *Iron Duke,* led the fourth column from the right. Although the breadth of this array was over ten thousand yards, it was completely under the control of the Commander-in-Chief.[2] His ideal at the moment of contact would be to meet the enemy's fleet in front of him, and he could for this purpose use his power of changing direction within certain limits, exactly as a skilful rider sets his horse squarely at a fence. But though the mass formation is so handy for approach or manœuvre, it is, alike to a cavalry division or a great fleet, fatal to be caught in such order by an enemy who has already deployed into line.

Before the British Battle Fleet could fight, it must deploy into line. The nearer the Commander-in-Chief could bring his fleet to the enemy in mass, the more certain he would be of being able to lead it squarely in the right direction; but the longer he waited and the nearer he got before deploying, the greater his risk of being caught at a terrible disadvantage. It is a task, like the landing of an aeroplane, of choosing the right moment between two opposite sets of dangers. If the Commander-in-Chief has been skilful or lucky in guiding his mass of battleships in the true direction of the enemy's fleet and finds them exactly ahead of him, his deployment will be swift and easy. He has only to turn the leading ships of his columns to the right or to the left as the case may be, and the whole fleet in four minutes will draw up in one long line of battle, firing at

---

[1] These with the four *Queen Elizabeths* made up his twenty-eight.

[2] The diagrams on p. 624 will show some of the many evolutions which are possible from this formation.

its fullest strength. If, however, owing to facts beyond human control or judgment, he has not been able to point his mass in exactly the right direction, or if he is still uncertain as to the true position of the enemy, he has an alternative method of deployment. He can make either of his flank columns steam onwards and the others follow in succession until the long single file which constitutes the line of battle is fully formed. This second method has the advantage of being much more likely to fit an unexpected situation. The moment the enemy appears out of the horizon the leading ship of either flank division can be ordered to take up any course which is in good relation to the hostile line, and all the other ships will follow it in succession. But whereas to deploy into line by the first method would take the British Grand Fleet of that day only four minutes, the deployment in the wake of one of the flank columns, or as it is called "deployment on the wing," requires twenty-two minutes before its full fire can be developed. Meanwhile the whole of the enemy's fleet might be in action with only such a portion of ours as had drawn out into line of battle.

To deploy correctly, accurate and instantaneous information of the position of the hostile fleet is all-important. For this reason the Commander-in-Chief is protected by cruisers and light cruisers under his direct control, who strive to watch the enemy's fleet continuously and tell him every few minutes where it is going and how it is formed. In the quarter of an hour which precedes the moment of deployment these scouts, or several of them, ought to be both in sight of the enemy and of their own flagship. Out of intense complexities, intense simplicities emerge. Nothing ought to be trusted at such a crisis except direct visual signalling by searchlight flashes. This is almost like men speaking to each other. To trust in so cardinal a matter to the wireless reports of cruisers which are out of sight is to run a needless risk. Such reports are highly important and may sometimes disclose the exact situation. But if ever certainty is required, it is at the moment of fleet deployment; and certainty cannot be obtained from cruisers which are beyond the Commander-in-Chief's sight or not linked visually to vessels which he can see.

Both the Fleets and all the cruisers are moving fast and momentarily altering their whole relation to one another. The cruisers which are out of sight are very likely in heavy action, clinging on to the hostile fleet, zigzagging and turning suddenly to avoid gunfire or torpedo. They are sure to be out of their reckoning. Their reports have to be written, ciphered, dispatched, received, decoded before they reach the Commander-in-Chief. Ten minutes easily elapse in this process; and there are not ten minutes to spare. Moreover, the reports from different scouting ships may not agree. Three or four different versions may simultaneously reach the Commander-in-Chief, and not one of them will be absolutely accurate. Therefore the fateful act of deployment should invariably be founded upon the visual signal of a scout who is actually in sight of the

DEPLOYMENT DIAGRAMS.

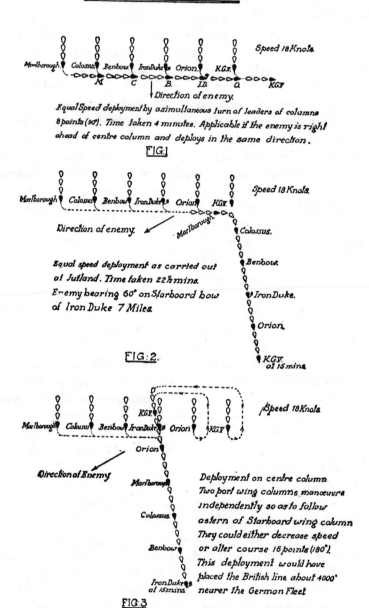

Speed 18 Knots.

Marlborough. Colossus. Benbow. IronDuke. Orion. K.G.V.

M. C. B. I.D. O. KGV

↓ Direction of enemy.

Equal Speed deployment by a simultaneous turn of leaders of columns
8 points (90°). Time taken 4 minutes. Applicable if the enemy is right
ahead of centre column and deploys in the same direction.

FIG. 1

Speed 18 Knots.

Marlborough. Colossus. Benbow. IronDuke. Orion. K.G.V.

Direction of enemy ← Marlborough.

Colossus.

Benbow.

IronDuke.

Equal speed deployment as carried out
at Jutland. Time taken 22½ mins.
Enemy bearing 60° on Starboard bow
of Iron Duke 7 Miles.

Orion.

K.G.V.
at 15 mins.

FIG. 2.

K.G.V.

Speed 18 Knots.

Marlborough. Colossus. Benbow. IronDuke. Orion. K.G.V.

Orion.

Direction of Enemy →

Marlborough.

Deployment on centre column.
Two port wing columns manœuvre
independently so as to follow
astern of Starboard wing column
They could either decrease speed
or alter course 16 points (180°).
This deployment would have
placed the British line about 4000°
nearer the German Fleet.

Colossus.

Benbow.

IronDuke
at 15 mins.

FIG. 3

enemy's fleet. The only sure method of knowing exactly where the hostile fleet is at the moment of deployment is the primitive plan of having light cruisers of your own which you can see and which can themselves see the enemy and each other. Such a network of lines of sight alone ensures exact knowledge of a vital matter.

The duty of clinging to the German High Sea Fleet and continually re-porting its whereabouts by wireless which could be read simultaneously by Beatty and by Jellicoe belonged in the first instance to the light cruisers of Beatty's scouting force; and admirably did Commodore Goodenough and his squadron discharge it. There is no ground for criticizing the *Lion* for not trans-mitting signals from the light cruisers while in heavy action herself. The *Iron Duke* read simultaneously everything that passed by wireless. But signals from light cruisers sixty, fifty, forty or even thirty miles away proved to be conflicting and erroneous. We now know that Goodenough was four miles out of his reck-oning, and the *Iron Duke* was more than six. Reports from any of Beatty's ves-sels, all of which were out of sight and beyond the horizon, were an invaluable means by which Jellicoe could learn the general course of events and approach of the enemy. But they were not, and ought never to have been relied on as, a substitute for the reports of scouting cruisers of his own.

Nor was the Commander-in-Chief unprovided with the necessary vessels. Apart from the fourteen light cruisers detached with Beatty's advance force, Jellicoe had reserved for his own special use four of the very latest *"Caroline"* class of light cruiser. He had besides the eight armoured cruisers of the pre-Dreadnought era (*Defence, Warrior,* etc.). At the first alarm he had ordered these old vessels to increase to full speed and cover his front; but as they could not steam more than twenty knots, and he was himself making eighteen and rising to twenty, they did not appreciably draw ahead of him in these important two hours. The *Carolines,* however, were designed for twenty-nine knots. Knowing that Beatty's force was committed to battle beyond the horizon, the Comman-der-in-Chief would have been prudent to use his four *Carolines* for the sole purpose of securing him early and exact information on which to base his de-ployment. His own battle orders declared that with less than twelve miles' visi-bility references to the enemy's latitude and longitude were quite useless, and emphasized the extreme importance of maintaining visual touch by means of linking cruisers.

In two hours the *Carolines* in a fan-shaped formation could have easily gained fifteen miles upon the *Iron Duke* in the general direction of the enemy. They would then have been in sight of the British armoured cruisers, which were themselves fully visible from the Grand Fleet. The *Carolines* themselves at this time could see at least seven miles. Thus the Commander-in-Chief could, had he so wished, have had more than twenty miles' accurate notice by visual signal of the position and line of advance of the German Fleet. This would have been an additional precaution to enable him to bring his fleet safely in mass formation to the exact position from which he could deploy on to the right course of battle by the four-minute method.

All the ships in both the Fleets were in the half-hour preceding the British deployment drawing together into a tremendous concourse. In that period the following principal events were taking place for the most part simultaneously. Beatty's battle-cruisers, with the 5th Battle Squadron behind them, were hurrying northward to make contact with, and draw the enemy on to the Grand Fleet. Hipper and Rear-Admiral Boedicker, with the German 1st and 2nd Scouting Groups, were also running north, covering the advance of the German High Sea Fleet. Beatty and Hipper were engaging each other on roughly parallel courses, and the 5th Battle Squadron was in heavy action with the leading German battleships as well as with Hipper's battle-cruisers. Meanwhile Admiral Hood in the *Invincible,* with the 3rd Battle-Cruiser Squadron, and preceded by the light cruisers *Chester* and *Canterbury,* was advancing on the northern flank of the British array. Thus at about 5:40 both German Scouting Groups were plunging into the centre of the British crescent (it had now become a horseshoe), of which the southern horn (Beatty) was rapidly retiring, and the northern horn (Hood) was rapidly advancing.

Hipper with the 1st Scouting Group was in renewed action to the southwest, when at 5:36 the *Chester,* reconnoitring for Admiral Hood, encountered the German 2nd Scouting Group. At 5:40 three of the four light cruisers of which it consisted emerged swiftly from the haze, and the *Chester* was "almost immediately smothered in a hail of fire."[1] Nearly all her guns were broken up, and her deck became a shambles. But the centre of the British crescent was also in rapid advance; and at 5:47 the *Defence* (Flagship of Rear-Admiral Sir Robert Arbuthnot) and the *Warrior,* the centre ships of the line of armoured cruisers directly covering the advance of the Grand Fleet, sighted the 2nd Scouting Group from the opposite direction, and opened a heavy fire upon them. Boedicker's light cruisers, glad to pursue the stricken *Chester,* turned away from the fire of these powerful though middle-aged vessels, only to meet a far more formidable antagonist.

Admiral Hood with his three battle-cruisers, swinging round towards the cannonade, came rushing out of the mist, and at 5:55 fell upon the German light cruisers with his 12-inch guns, crippling the *Wiesbaden* and badly damaging the *Pillau* and the *Frankfort* in a few minutes. The apparition of capital

[1] Official Narrative, p. 36.

ships to the northward "fell on Admiral Boedicker like a thunder-bolt."[1] From far in his rear came the reverberation of Beatty's cruiser action. This new antagonist must be the head of the main British Fleet. Boedicker instantly turned to escape from the closing jaws, leaving the wounded *Wiesbaden* to crawl out of danger as fast as she could. The explosion of Hood's guns carried—as will be seen—a similar warning to Hipper.

Meanwhile Arbuthnot in the *Defence*, followed by the *Warrior*, was pursuing the 2nd Scouting Group. He found the *Wiesbaden* dragging herself away. Determined to destroy her, he "came rushing down on her at full speed."[2] The *Lion*, heading the British battlecruisers again in action with Hipper, had also converged. Arbuthnot in impetuous ardour pressed across her bows, forcing her off her course, throwing out the fire of her squadron and blanketing their target with his funnel smoke. He was within 6,000 yards of the *Wiesbaden,* and had turned to starboard to bring his whole broadside to bear, when the again advancing Hipper swung his guns upon him, as did some of the German battleships now also coming into range. In a moment the *Defence,* struck by a succession of shells from the heaviest guns, blew up in a terrific explosion and at 6:19 p.m. vanished with nearly 800 men in a huge pillar of smoke. The *Warrior,* grievously smitten, seemed about to share her fate. But meanwhile greater events were happening. The Grand Fleet's deployment had begun at 6:15.

During these events the run to the north had come to an end. At 5:25 Beatty had resumed his action with Hipper. The light was now favourable to the British. The 15-inch guns of the *Barham* and the *Valiant* were also firing upon the German battle-cruisers, who began to suffer severely. In the midst of this, at 5:42, came the sound of the *Invincible's* guns attacking the 2nd Scouting Group to the north-eastward; and thereupon, having good reason to feel himself being surrounded by superior forces as well as being mastered in the actual fire-fight, Hipper turned his ships swiftly about and fell back on the High Sea Fleet. As his opponent turned away to starboard Beatty first conformed, then curled round him due east in the natural movement of the action, and also with the object of preventing Hipper, however he might turn, from discovering the British Battle Fleet. It was at this moment that the *Lion* came in sight of the *Iron Duke.* Her appearance was a surprise to Jellicoe. The reckoning from Beatty's wireless signals had led the *Iron Duke* to expect him a good deal farther to the eastward. The cumulative error of the two ships was no less than eleven miles. Fact now instantaneously superseded estimate. There was the *Lion*

---

[1] Official Narrative, p. 36.
[2] *Ibid.*

THE MEETING 5:30 P.M.

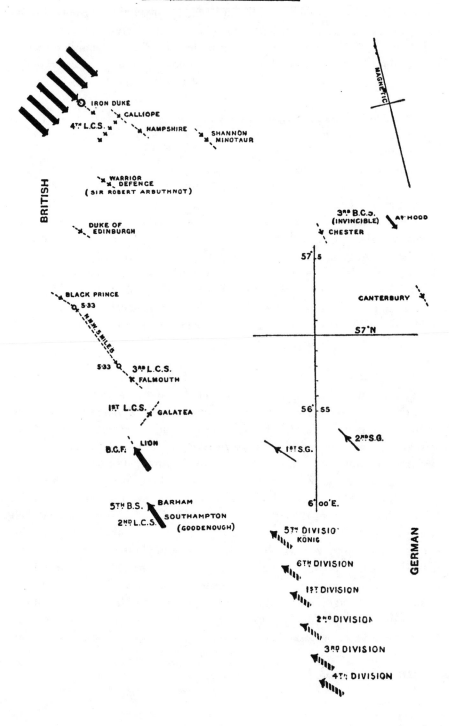

six miles away and nearly four points more to starboard of the *Iron Duke* than had been supposed. It was reasonable to assume that the enemy's Battle Fleet was also, and to an equal degree, more to the westward; and this meant that Jellicoe would not meet them ahead, or nearly ahead, but obliquely on the starboard bow.

The situation was critical, urgent and obscure. The Commander-in-Chief could feel the enemy's breath all round his right cheek and shoulder, and he now evidently wanted very much to point his fleet to the new direction. But this partial wheel[1] required fifteen minutes, and he had not got them. As soon as he saw Beatty steaming across his bows in action and at full speed, he flashed the question: "Where is the enemy's battle fleet?" (6:01). And a minute later, in consequence of Beatty's appearance and position, and not having time to wheel, he turned the leading ships of his divisions southward to improve his line of approach to the enemy by gaining ground in that direction. This movement lost no time and was absolutely right in conception, but it brought his fleet into an êchelon formation of divisions which was not at all convenient for deployment, and the German Fleet might be very near. At any minute it might emerge from the mist six or seven miles away, and forthwith open fire. And at 6:06 the Commander-in-Chief reverted to his previous formation, which though not pointing true still gave him the largest options for deployment.

Meanwhile Beatty, now only two miles ahead of the *Marlborough* (the right-hand corner vessel of the battleship mass), answered: "Enemy's battlecruisers bearing south-east."[2] On which the Commander-in-Chief repeated, "Where is the enemy's battle fleet?" To this the *Lion* could give no answer. Hipper had for the moment vanished, and the *Lion* had no enemy in sight.

Anxiously peering at the menacing curtains of the horizon or poring over the contradictions and obscurities of the chart, Jellicoe held on his course in tense uncertainty for another eight minutes. Then at last came illumination. At 6:10 the *Barham* had sighted Scheer's battleships to the S.S.E. and as her wireless had been shot away, the *Valiant* passed the news. Jellicoe received it at 6:14. Almost simultaneously the *Lion* reported the High Sea Fleet in sight S.S.W. These two reports placed the enemy four points on the starboard bow, or, in military parlance, half right. The direction was correct. But the leading German battleship *König* was placed three miles nearer than she actually was. On this view further delay seemed impossible. The moment of decision had come. "It became," says the Admiralty Narrative, "urgently necessary to deploy the Fleet."

The meeting having taken place at this unsatisfactory angle, a swift deployment of the Fleet by divisions to port or starboard was not open. It would have

---

[1] The sailors call it for short "altering the bearing of the guides by *(so many)* points."
[2] Their course was omitted.

brought the Fleet into a line out of proper relation to the enemy's potential bat-
tlefront. There remained only the twenty-two minutes' method of deployment
on the wing. Jellicoe conceived himself limited to two alternatives: either he
could let his right-hand column nearest the enemy go ahead and make the others follow it, or he could let his left-hand column farthest from the enemy take
the lead. If he chose the former, he ran the risk of the enemy concentrating
their fire on his leading ships while the rest of the Fleet could not reply. If he
chose the latter, he drew out his line of battle 10,000 yards farther away from
the enemy. Instead of deploying into action and opening fire at once, he would
deploy outside effective gun range; and his opening movement in the battle
would be a retirement.

Our present knowledge leads to the conclusion that he could have deployed on the starboard wing without misadventure. The 5th Battle Squadron,
with its unequalled guns, armour and speed was in fact about to take the van
ahead of the *Marlborough's* division of older Dreadnoughts. Beatty's battle-
cruisers were already ahead steaming upon the exact course. Still farther ahead
in front of all Hood in lively comprehension was about to wheel into the line.
The whole Fleet would have drawn out harmoniously into full battle at decisive
ranges, with all its fast heavy ships at the right end of the line for cutting the
enemy from his base. The Commander-in-Chief chose the safer course. No
one can say that on the facts as known to him at the moment it was a wrong
decision. There are ample arguments on either side, and anyhow he was the
man appointed to choose. If he had deployed on the wing towards the enemy,
and if the leading British squadrons had been overwhelmed by the fire of the
German Battle Fleet, or if a heavy torpedo attack had developed on the van
of the Fleet and if our whole line had thereby been checked and disordered
in its deployment, and four or five ships sunk (as might have happened in as
many minutes), there would have been no lack of criticism upon the imprudence of the Admiral's decision. And criticism would have been the least of the
consequences.

But there was surely a third course open to Sir John Jellicoe which had
none of the disadvantages of these hard alternatives.[1] Although it involved a
complicated evolution, it was in principle a very simple course. In fact it was
the simplest and most primitive of all courses. He could have deployed on his
centre and taken the lead himself. There is a very old and well-known signal in
the Royal Navy which would have enabled the Commander-in-Chief to lead
his own division out of the mass and make the others follow after him in any
sequence he might choose. It was only necessary to hoist the pennant "A" above
a succession of numerals indicating the order in which the various divisions

[1] See diagram on p. 634.

should follow. It involved every ship in the two port divisions either reducing speed or making a complete left-handed circle to avoid losing speed, while the starboard divisions were taking their places behind the Commander-in-Chief. But the Fleet was not under fire, and the manœuvre was practical. It meant in short, "Follow me." Out of a tangle of uncertainties and out of a cruel dilemma here was a sure, prudent and glorious middle course. By adopting it Sir John Jellicoe would have retained the greatest measure of control over his Fleet after deployment. He would have had three miles and ten minutes more to spare than if he had deployed on the wing towards the enemy. He would have avoided any retirement from the advancing foe. He would have led his Fleet, and they would have followed him.

It may seem strange that he should have never attempted to deal with this alternative in any of his accounts and explanations of his actions. It is perhaps easily explained. Sir John Jellicoe was working on a definite preconceived system. In the thunder and mystery of the preliminaries of what might be the greatest sea battle of the world, he held as long as he could rigidly to his rules. All his dispositions for battle had contemplated a deployment either on the port or starboard column of battleships. As a consequence the routine system of signals in the Grand Fleet battle orders did not contemplate any such deployment on the Admiral's flag. The old signal was well known. If hoisted, it would have been instantly comprehended. But it had fallen into desuetude, and it never seems to have occurred to the Commander-in-Chief at the time.

Equally it did not occur to him to take an obvious precaution against the escape of the enemy which could not have risked the safety of his Fleet. His cautious deployment on the outer wing made it the more imperative to make sure the enemy was brought to battle. To do this he had only to tell the four *Queen Elizabeths* of the 5th Battle Squadron, instead of falling tamely in at the tail of the line and thus wasting all their unique combination of speed and power, to attack separately the disengaged side of the enemy. These ships would not have been in any danger of being overwhelmed by the numbers of the enemy. They were eight or nine knots faster than Scheer's Fleet as long as it remained united. They could at any moment, if too hard pressed, break off the action. Thus assured, what could be easier than for them to swoop round upon the old *Deutschland* squadron and cripple or destroy two or three of these ships in a few minutes? It would have been almost obligatory for Scheer to stop and rescue them; and taken between two fires, he would have been irrevocably committed to battle. This was exactly the kind of situation for which the division of fast super-Dreadnoughts, combining speed, guns and armour in an equal degree, had been constructed at such huge expense and trouble as one of the main acts of my administration at the Admiralty. But neither the Commander-in-Chief nor their own Admiral could think of any better use for them than to let them steam uselessly along in rear of the Fleet at seventeen knots, their own speed being over twenty-four.

Therefore at 6:15 p.m. precisely the order was given by signal and wireless to deploy on the port wing. The fateful flags fluttered in the breeze, and were hauled down. The order became operative, and five-sixths of the immense line of British battleships turned away and began to increase their distance from the enemy. The first move of the Battle Fleet at Jutland had been made.

Both Beatty and the 5th Battle Squadron had been conveniently placed for a deployment on the starboard wing. The deployment to port forced Beatty to steam at full speed across the front of the line of battle in order to take his position in the van. Hood wheeled into the line ahead of Beatty. The smoke of the battle-cruisers obscured the vision of the battleships, and at 6:26 Jellicoe reduced the Fleet speed to fourteen knots in order to let the battle-cruisers draw ahead. The signal did not get through quickly, and bunching and overlapping began to occur, particularly at the turning-point. The 5th Battle Squadron, too far behind to cross the front of Jellicoe's deployment and receiving no orders to act independently, decided to take station in rear, and executed a left-handed turn under the concentrated fire both of the German battle-cruisers and the leading German battleships. Once more the 15-inch guns and 13-inch armour of the fast battleships came into heavy action against greatly-superior forces, and ponderous blows were given and received. The *Warspite*, with her helm temporarily jammed, fell out of the squadron and made a sweeping circle out of control and under intense fire. The circle carried her round the half-wrecked *Warrior*, who in the confusion, blessing her saviour's involuntary chivalry, struggled into safety.

At 6:25, while the deployment was proceeding, the Fleet began to fire, about one-third of the ships finding targets either on the unfortunate *Wiesbaden*, which lay between the lines a flaming wreck, or on the German 3rd Squadron *(Königs)* at the head of the hostile fleet. The range was fouled by smoke, and the visibility poor. But Jellicoe's manœuvre had procured the most favourable light for the British, and only the flashes of their guns could be seen by the enemy. When half the Fleet had turned the corner, Jellicoe seems to have thought of coming to closer quarters by altering course by sub-divisions towards the enemy. The L-shape in which the Fleet was then formed probably made him feel that this movement was impracticable, and the signal was cancelled before it was begun. Half the British Fleet was firing by the time the deployment was completed (6:47 p.m.); and the German 3rd Squadron was repeatedly hit, no British battleship being touched in return.

Meanwhile Hood with the 3rd Battle-Cruiser Squadron had been engaging

Hipper's battle-cruisers with good effect. But at 6:31 a salvo from the *Derfflinger* smote the *Invincible.* In the words of the Official Narrative,

> Several big explosions took place in rapid succession; masses of coal dust issued from the riven hull; great tongues of flame played over the ship; the masts collapsed; the ship broke in two, and an enormous pall of black smoke ascended to the sky. As it cleared away the bow and stern could be seen standing up out of the water as if to mark the place where an Admiral lay.[1]

Of her crew of 1,026 officers and men, six only survived.

We will now follow for a moment the German movements. Scheer found himself under fire from the British line of battle from 6:25 onwards. He mistook Hood's battle-cruisers for the van of the British line. He thus thought himself about to be enveloped. Instead of executing upon the British the manœuvre of "crossing the T," it seemed that they were about to do this to him. He therefore at 6:35, with the utmost promptitude, turned his whole Fleet about, every ship turning simultaneously, and made off to the westward, *towards England,* launching at the same time a flotilla to cover his retirement by a torpedo attack and smoke screens. This thoroughly practised evolution was performed with success and even precision, in spite of the pressure and disarray of battle. Jellicoe, threatened by the torpedo stream, turned away according to his long-resolved policy. The fleets fell rapidly apart, the Germans faded into a bank of mist, and Scheer found himself alone again.

But now ensued one of those astounding events utterly outside the bounds of reasonable expectation, which have often been the turning-points of history. No sooner did Scheer, after steaming for about twenty minutes to the westward, find himself free, than he turned each ship about right-handed and again steamed eastward. What was his purpose? After getting back to harbour he declared that it was to seek further conflict with the British Fleet. "When I noticed that the British pressure had quite ceased and that the fleet remained intact in my hands, I turned back under the impression that the action could not end in this way, and that I ought to seek contact with the enemy again."[2] This explanation is endorsed by the German official history. Nevertheless it seems more likely that he calculated that this movement would carry him across the British rear, and that he hoped to pass astern punishing the rear ships and getting again on the homeward side of the battle. We know that he was under the impression that the British battle-cruisers were the van of the British line of

---

[1] pp. 49–50.
[2] Official Narrative.

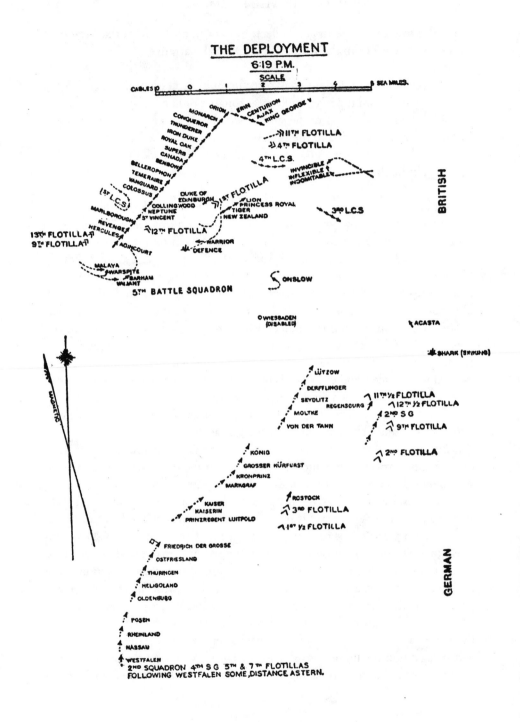

THE DEPLOYMENT
6:19 P.M.
SCALE

CABLES 0 | 0 | 1 | 2 | 3 | 4 | 5 SEA MILES.

BRITISH

ORION
ERIN
CENTURION
MONARCH
AJAX
KING GEORGE V
CONQUEROR
THUNDERER
IRON DUKE
ROYAL OAK
SUPERB
CANADA
BENBOW
BELLEROPHON
TEMERAIRE
VANGUARD
COLOSSUS

11TH FLOTILLA
4TH FLOTILLA
4TH L.C.S.
INVINCIBLE
INFLEXIBLE
INDOMITABLE

1ST L.C.S.

DUKE OF EDINBURGH
1ST FLOTILLA
LION
PRINCESS ROYAL
TIGER
NEW ZEALAND

COLLINGWOOD
NEPTUNE
ST VINCENT

3RD L.C.S.

MARLBOROUGH
REVENGE
HERCULES
AGINCOURT

13TH FLOTILLA
9TH FLOTILLA

12TH FLOTILLA

WARRIOR
DEFENCE

MALAYA
WARSPITE
BARHAM
VALIANT

5TH BATTLE SQUADRON

ONSLOW

WIESBADEN (DISABLED)

ACASTA

SHARK (SINKING)

MAGNETIC

LÜTZOW
DERFFLINGER
SEYDLITZ
REGENSBURG
MOLTKE
VON DER TANN

11TH ½ FLOTILLA
12TH ½ FLOTILLA
2ND S.G.
9TH FLOTILLA

2ND FLOTILLA

KÖNIG
GROSSER KÜRFÜRST
KRONPRINZ
MARKGRAF

KAISER
KAISERIN
PRINZREGENT LUITPOLD

ROSTOCK
3RD FLOTILLA
1ST ½ FLOTILLA

FRIEDRICH DER GROSSE
OSTFRIESLAND
THÜRINGEN
HELIGOLAND
OLDENBURG

POSEN
RHEINLAND
NASSAU
WESTFALEN

2ND SQUADRON 4TH S.G. 5TH & 7TH FLOTILLAS
FOLLOWING WESTFALEN SOME DISTANCE ASTERN.

GERMAN

battle. From this the conclusion inevitably presented to his mind would be that the British Battle Fleet was five miles ahead of its position. On these assumptions his movement would have carried him very nicely across the British tail. Instead of this he ran right into the centre of the whole British Fleet, which was certainly the last thing he sought. This mistake might well have been fatal to the Germans. It would have been impossible to have chosen a situation of greater peril. Jellicoe's fleet was also no doubt somewhat inconveniently arranged. He was steaming south with his divisions in échelon. In fact he now, at 7:12 p.m., was caught by the Germans while he was in the very posture he had so disliked before his original deployment. But nevertheless in practice no serious difficulty arose. As the German ships one after another emerged from the mist, all the British battleships whose range was clear opened a terrific fire upon them. The German van, the formidable *Königs,* saw the whole horizon as far as eye could reach alive with flashes. About six minutes' intense firing ensued. The concussion of the shell storm burst upon the German vessels. Hipper's long-battered but redoubtable scouting group once more bore the brunt. The *Seydlitz* burst into flames; the *Lützow* reeled out of the line. This was the heaviest cannonade ever fired at sea.

It did not last long. The moment Scheer realized what he had run into, he repeated—though less coolly—the manœuvre he had used at 6:35; and at 7:17 he again turned the Battle Fleet about to the westward, launched another series of flotilla attacks, threw up more smoke screens, ordered the gasping battle-cruisers to attack at all costs to cover his retreat (a "Death ride"), and sped again to the west. Once more Jellicoe, obedient to his method, turned away from the torpedo stream, first two points and then two points more. Here at any rate was a moment when, as a glance at the map will show, it would have been quite easy to divide the British Fleet with the 5th Battle Squadron leading the starboard division, and so take the enemy between two fires. But the British Commander-in-Chief was absorbed in avoiding the torpedo attack by turning away. The range opened, the Fleets separated, and Scheer vanished again from Jellicoe's view—this time for ever.

Between 6:0 and 7:30 the German flotillas had delivered no fewer than seven attacks upon the British Battle Fleet. The true answer to these attacks was the counter-attack of the British flotillas and Light Cruiser Squadrons, of which latter two were available and close at hand. These should have been ordered to advance and break up the enemy's torpedo craft, as they were fully capable of doing. Instead of using this aggressive parry, Jellicoe turned his battleships away on each occasion; and contact with the enemy ceased. The German flotillas in the whole of this phase lost only a single boat, but they effectively secured the safe withdrawal of their Fleet from the jaws of death.

Beatty however still sought to renew the action. It was above all things im-

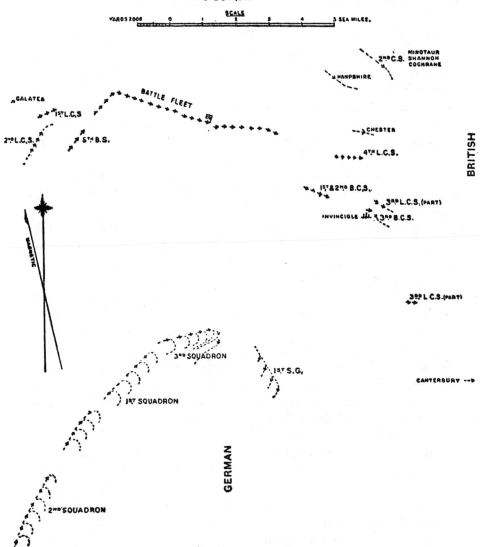

SCHEER'S FIRST TURN AWAY

6:35 P.M.

SCALE

YARDS 2000   0   1   2   3   4   5 SEA MILES.

MINOTAUR
2ND C.S.   SHANNON
COCHRANE

HAMPSHIRE

GALATEA

BATTLE FLEET

1ST L.C.S

2ND L.C.S.

5TH B.S.

CHESTER

4TH L.C.S.

1ST & 2ND B.C.S.

3RD L.C.S. (PART)

INVINCIBLE   3RD B.C.S.

BRITISH

3RD L.C.S. (PART)

MAGNETIC

3RD SQUADRON

1ST S.G.

CANTERBURY

1ST SQUADRON

GERMAN

2ND SQUADRON

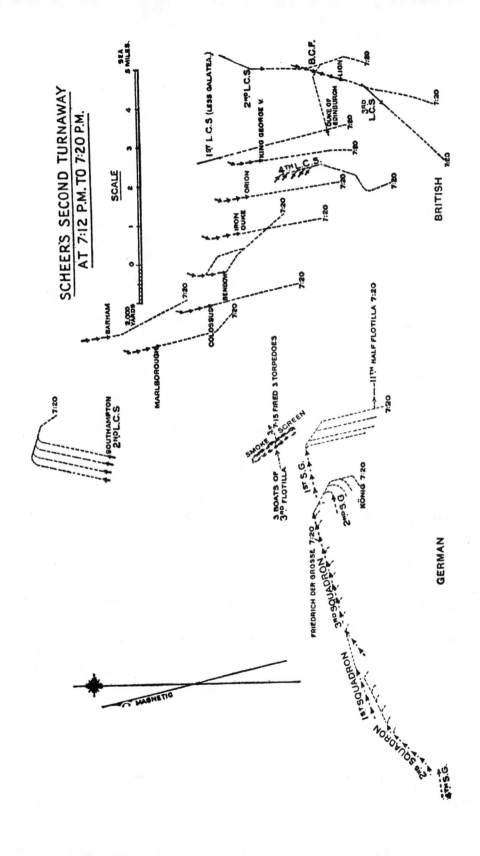

SCHEER'S SECOND TURNAWAY
AT 7:12 P.M. TO 7:20 P.M.

SCALE

0 1 2 3 4 5 SEA MILES.

2,000 YARDS

BARHAM 7:20

MARLBOROUGH

COLOSSUS 7:20 7:20

BENBOW 7:20

IRON DUKE 7:20 7:20

ORION 7:20

4TH L.C.S. 7:20 7:20

1ST L.C.S (LESS GALATEA.)

2ND L.C.S

KING GEORGE V. 7:20

DUKE OF EDINBURGH 7:20

3RD L.C.S

B.C.F. 7:20

LION 7:20

7:20

BRITISH

SOUTHAMPTON
2ND L.C.S 7:20

SMOKE 7:15 FIRED 3 TORPEDOES

3 BOATS OF
3RD FLOTILLA SCREEN

1ST S.G.

2ND S.G.

KÖNIG 7:20

11TH HALF FLOTILLA 7:20 7:20

FRIEDRICH DER GROSSE 7:20

3RD SQUADRON

1ST SQUADRON

2ND SQUADRON

4TH S.G.

GERMAN

MAGNETIC

portant to drive the Germans westward away from home. The *Lion* was in sight of the enemy; but the British Battle Fleet was drawing no nearer to her, and it was not possible for the battle-cruisers to engage Scheer single-handed. At 7:45 he signalled the bearing of the enemy through the *Minotaur* to the leading British battleship; and at 7:47 sent the much-discussed message to the Commander-in-Chief, "Submit that the van of the battleships follow me; we can then cut off the enemy's fleet." Almost immediately thereafter he altered course to close the enemy. Meanwhile Scheer homeward bent had gradually brought the High Sea Fleet from a westerly on to a southerly course. The fleets were once again converging. Light cruisers and destroyers on both sides began to fire. The British battle-cruisers would soon be engaged. Where was the van of our Battle Fleet? A quarter of an hour was allowed to pass after Jellicoe received Beatty's signal before he sent the necessary order—and that in no urgent terms—to the 2nd Battle Squadron. Vice-Admiral Jerram commanding that squadron did not increase his speed, did not draw ahead of the main fleet, and did not ask the *Minotaur* for the *Lion's* position. He merely held on his course, in much uncertainty of the general situation. Thus the *Lion* and her consorts were alone in the last as in the first encounter of great ships at Jutland and in the war. The German battle-cruisers, grievously wounded, were scarcely in a condition to fight, and the light was still favourable to the British. Firing began from the *Tiger* on different ships at ranges from 9,000 to 13,000 yards. One of the two remaining turrets of the *Derfflinger* was put out of action. The *Seydlitz* and *Lützow* could scarcely fire a shot. Suddenly the old *Deutschland* battleships came to the rescue of Hipper's gallant battered vessels; and the last salvoes of the big guns were exchanged with them in the twilight. After fifteen minutes the Germans turned off again to the westward and disappeared in the gathering gloom.

Night had now come on, and by nine o'clock darkness had fallen on the sea. Thereupon the conditions of naval warfare underwent profound changes. The rights of the stronger fleet faded into a grey equality. The far-ranging cruisers were blinded. The friendly destroyers became a danger to the ships they guarded. The great guns lost their range. Now, if ever, the reign of the torpedo would begin. The rival Navies, no more than six miles apart, steamed onwards through the darkness, silent and invisible, able to turn about in five minutes or less in any direction, no man knowing what the other would do or what might happen next.

But Admiral Scheer had made up his mind, and his course, though perilous, was plain. He was a man of resolution based on reasoned judgment. He knew that a superior hostile fleet lay between him and home. To be found in that position by the light of another day meant, in all probability, total destruc-

DARKNESS FALLS AT 9:00 P.M.

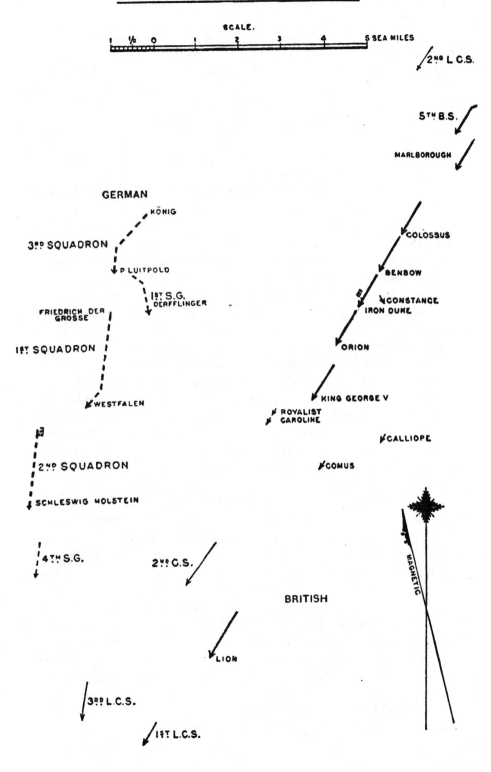

tion. The night was short. At half-past two dawn would be breaking. He must act without a moment's delay. His plan was simple: to go home as fast as possible by the shortest route, at all risks and at all costs. If he found the British Fleet in his path, he would crash through it. Many ships would be sunk on both sides, but the bulk of the German Navy would escape to harbour. Anything was better than being caught at sea by an overwhelming force with eighteen hours of battle light before it. At 9:14 he issued the following order by wireless: "Our own main body is to proceed in. Maintain course S.S.E. ¼ E; speed sixteen knots." Accordingly the High Seas Fleet turned from its southerly course, and preceded by its flotillas and light cruiser squadrons, steamed at its fastest united speed straight for the Horn Reef. No one can doubt that he acted rightly.

Sir John Jellicoe's problem was more complicated. He now had the enemy in a position which certainly was no part of any pre-arranged German plan. He rightly rejected the idea of a night action. Any battle brought on at daybreak would be free from all apprehensions of traps or elaborately prepared ambuscades. It would be a straightforward fight to a finish in blue water; and he was more than twice as strong. His obvious and supreme duty was to compel such a battle. But how?

Two minefields had been laid in the Heligoland Bight since the beginning of the war by the Germans to impede an attack by the British Fleet. The Germans had been aided in this task, for reasons requiring more explanation, by the British Admiralty; and in consequence of the exertions of both sides large parts of the Bight were closed by British and German mines. Through these the Germans had swept three broad channels: one to the north by the Horn Reef, one rather more in the centre by Heligoland, and one to the south by the Ems River. Both sides knew a great deal about each other's minefields. They were marked on their charts as clearly as rocks or shoals, and could be avoided with almost equal certainty. The British Admiralty knew not only the minefields, but all the three German channels through them. Sir John Jellicoe therefore had on his chart all the three passages open to Admiral Scheer marked out before him.

There was also a fourth alternative. Scheer might avoid the Heligoland Bight altogether, and turning northward as soon as darkness fell, steer homewards through the Kattegat and into the Baltic. Which of these four would he choose? No one in the position of the British Commander-in-Chief could expect to achieve certainty. Whatever decision Jellicoe had taken must have left a number of chances unguarded. All that could be expected of him was to act in accordance with reasonable probability, and leave the rest to Fate. The final question which this chapter must examine is whether he acted upon reasonable probability or not.

It was possible immediately to eliminate the least likely alternatives open to the enemy. Retreat into the Baltic by the Kattegat gave Scheer no security

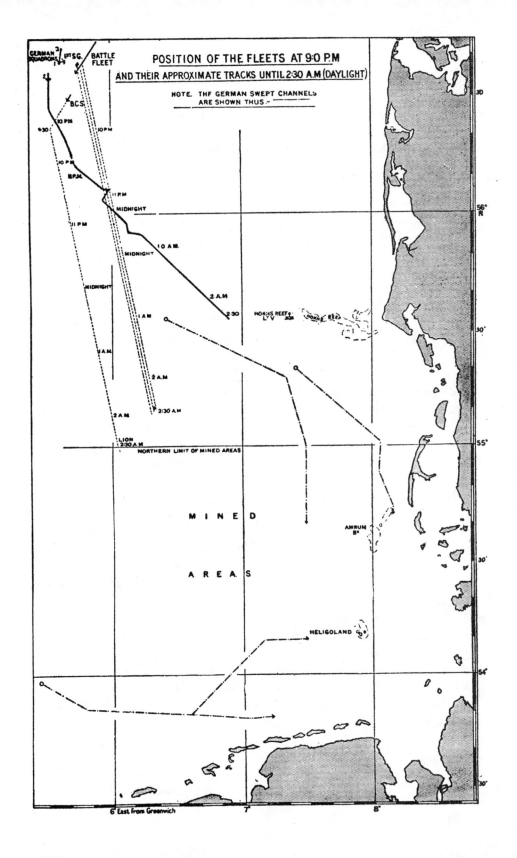

POSITION OF THE FLEETS AT 9·0 P.M
AND THEIR APPROXIMATE TRACKS UNTIL 2·30 A.M (DAYLIGHT)

NOTE. THE GERMAN SWEPT CHANNELS
ARE SHOWN THUS :-

GERMAN 3/
SQUADRONS 1ST S.G.
1 + 9
BATTLE
FLEET

B.C.S.

10 P.M
+·30
10 P.M
B.P.34.
11 P.M
MIDNIGHT
11 P.M
MIDNIGHT
MIDNIGHT
11 A.M.
2 A.M
1 A.M
2 A.M
2:30 AM
2 A M
LION
2:30 A.M

10 P.M
11 P.M
MIDNIGHT
10 A.M.
2 A.M
2:30
HORNS REEF
L.T.V
HORNS REEF

NORTHERN LIMIT OF MINED AREAS

M   I   N   E   D

A   R   E   A   S

AMRUN
B⁴

HELIGOLAND

56°
R

30'

55'

30'

54'

30'

6° East from Greenwich   7°   8°

against being brought to battle in daylight. It involved a voyage of nearly 350 miles, giving the faster British a long day to chase in the open sea. Jellicoe could have provided for this route by the simple process (which he did not however adopt) of sending a few light cruisers to watch the area, and thus ensure timely information at dawn. The Ems route, which was long and roundabout, might also have been dismissed as improbable. Thus the four alternatives could have been reduced to two, i.e., the Horn Reef channel and the Heligoland channel; and these two were not far apart. Sir John Jellicoe would have been justified in considering both the Horn Reef and Heligoland channels as open and likely. On this dual basis however a good movement presented itself. By steering for a point about ten miles to the south-westward of the Horn Reef light he would have been at daybreak in a favourable position to bring Scheer to battle whether he made for the Horn Reef or Heligoland channel. The British Fleet was at least three knots faster than the Germans and was nearer this point when darkness fell.

But Jellicoe seems to have formed the opinion that the alternative lay between the Heligoland channel and the Ems, and he nowhere mentions the possibility of the Horn Reef which was *prima facie* the most likely. "I was loth," he says,[1] "to forgo the advantage of position which would have resulted from an easterly or westerly course,[2] and I therefore decided to steer to the southward, where I should be in a position to renew the engagement at daylight, and should also be favourably placed to intercept the enemy should he make for his base by steering for Heligoland or towards the Ems and thence along the north German coast." This was hardly the most reasonable assumption, and did not gather, but on the contrary excluded, the major favourable chances. To continue on such a course until dawn broke at 2:30 a.m. would carry the British Fleet forty-three miles to the south-westward of Horn Reef and twenty-five miles to the westward of Scheer's direct course to Heligoland, thus failing to procure action in either case. Scheer was left free to retreat by the Horn Reef, Heligoland, or, if he chose, the Kattegat; and only the much less likely route by the Ems was barred.

At 9:1 p.m. the British Battle Fleet turned by divisions and proceeded almost due south at a speed of seventeen knots. At 9:17 p.m. it had assumed its night organization of three columns in close array, and at 9:27 p.m. the destroyer flotillas were told to take station five miles astern. This order served a double purpose. It freed the Battle Fleet during the darkness from the proximity of its own flotillas, and thus enabled it to treat all torpedo craft as foes and sink at sight any that appeared. It also prolonged the British line and thereby

---

[1] Commander-in-Chief's Despatches, Jutland Papers, p. 21.

[2] i.e., by his taking an easterly or westerly course.

increased the chances of intercepting the enemy. No orders to attack the enemy were however given to the flotillas, and they therefore steamed passively along their course without instructions or information. Jellicoe's signal to his flotillas was picked up by the German listening station at Neumünster, which reported to Scheer at 10:10 p.m. "Destroyers have taken up position five sea miles astern of enemy's main fleet." At about 10:50 p.m. the German 7th Flotilla reported that it had sighted British destroyers. Thus the German Admiral, if the Neumünster message reached him, had from this time forward a fairly clear idea of the relative positions of the two fleets.[1] Here ends the first phase of the night operations. The British Fleet is steaming southward at seventeen knots, and opening to the enemy every moment his two nearest and most likely lines of retreat. The Germans are making for the Horn Reef at sixteen knots, and are about to cut across Jellicoe's tail against which their destroyers have already brushed. There is still time to retrieve the situation.

At about 10:30 p.m. the 4th German Scouting Group came in contact with the British 2nd Light Cruiser Squadron which was following our Battle Fleet. There was a violent explosion of firing. The *Southampton* and the *Dublin* suffered heavy losses, and the old German cruiser *Frauenlob* was sunk by a torpedo. The gun flashes and searchlights of this encounter were noted in the log of nearly every vessel in the Grand Fleet. Firing in this quarter, though it was no proof, at least suggested that the enemy was seeking to pass astern of the British Fleet on the way to the Horn Reef. But confirmation of a decisive character was at hand.

Far away in Whitehall the Admiralty have been listening to the German wireless. They have heard and deciphered Admiral Scheer's order of 9:14 p.m. to the High Sea Fleet. At 10:41 the *Iron Duke,* and at about 11:30, after it had been decoded, Sir John Jellicoe, received the following electrifying message: "German battle fleet ordered home at 9:14 p.m. Battle cruisers in rear. Course S.S.E. ¾ east. Speed sixteen knots."[2] If this message was to be trusted, it meant, and could only mean, that the Germans were returning by the Horn Reef. Taken in conjunction first with the general probabilities and secondly with the firing heard astern, the Admiralty message, unless wholly erroneous, amounted almost to certainty. Had Jellicoe decided to act upon it, he had only to turn his fleet on to a course parallel to the Germans in order to make sure of bringing them to battle at daybreak. By so doing he would neither have risked a night action nor increased the existing dangers of torpedo attack.

But could the Admiralty message be trusted? Sir John Jellicoe thought not. He no doubt remembered that earlier in the day, a few minutes before the

[1] It is now said that he did not receive it till he got back to harbour.
[2] Official Narrative, p. 72.

enemy's battle-cruisers were sighted, the same authoritative information had told him that the German High Sea Fleet was probably not at sea as its flagship was speaking from harbour. When Scheer's course as given by the Admiralty was plotted on the *Iron Duke's* chart, it appeared, owing to a minor error, to bring the Germans into almost exactly the position occupied by his own flagship at that moment. This was absurd. Moreover, he had received a report from the *Southampton* timed 10:15 which suggested that the enemy was still to the westward. Generally he considered the position was not clear. He therefore rejected the Admiralty information and continued to steam southward at seventeen knots.

It is difficult to feel that this decision was not contrary to the main weight of the evidence. Certain it is that if Sir John Jellicoe had acted in accordance with the Admiralty message, he would have had—even if that message had proved erroneous—a justification for his action which could never have been impugned. He was leaving so many favourable chances behind him as he sped to the south, and guarding against so few, that it is difficult to penetrate his mind. Full weight must, however, be assigned to the elements of doubt and contradiction which have been described.

At 11:30 the High Sea Fleet, after some minor alterations in course, crashed into the 4th British Flotilla, and a fierce brief conflict followed. The destroyers *Tipperary* and *Broke* were disabled. The *Spitfire* collided with the battleship *Nassau*, and the *Sparrowhawk* collided with the injured *Broke*. The German cruiser *Elbing* was rammed and disabled by the *Posen*. The *Rostock* was torpedoed. The rest of the British flotilla made off into the night, and turning again on their course, ran a second time into the enemy, when the destroyers *Fortune* and *Ardent* were both sunk by gunfire. A little after midnight the armoured cruiser *Black Prince*, which had become detached from the Fleet and was endeavouring to rejoin, found herself within 1,600 yards of the German super-Dreadnought Squadron, and was instantly blown to pieces; and her crew of 750 men perished without survivors. At 12:25 the head of the German line, which was by now on the port quarter of the British Fleet, cut into the 9th, 10th and 13th British Flotillas and sank the destroyer *Turbulent*. In these unexpected clashes the British flotillas following dutifully in the wake of the Grand Fleet suffered as severely as if they had been launched in an actual attack. The last contact was at 2:10, when the 12th Flotilla sighting the enemy who had now worked right round to port, and led by Captain Stirling with an aggressive intention and definite plan of attack, destroyed the *Pommern* with her entire crew of 700 men, and sank the German destroyer V 4. This was the end of the fighting.

Up till half an hour after midnight there was still time for Jellicoe to reach the Horn Reef in time for a daylight battle. Even after that hour the German rear and stragglers could have been cut off. The repeated bursts of heavy firing, the flash of great explosions, the beams of searchlights—all taking place in succession from west to east—was not readily capable of more than one interpretation. But the Grand Fleet continued steadily on its course to the south; and when it turned northward at 2:30 a.m., the Germans were for ever beyond its reach. The Northern course also carried the British Fleet away from the retreating enemy; and it is clear that from this time onward the Commander-in-Chief had definitely abandoned all expectation of renewing the action. It remained only to collect all forces, to sweep the battle area on the chance of stragglers, and to return to harbour. This was accordingly done.

So ended the Battle of Jutland. The Germans loudly proclaimed a victory. There was no victory for anyone; but they had good reasons to be content with their young Navy. It had fought skilfully and well. It had made its escape from the grip of overwhelming forces, and in so doing had inflicted heavier loss in ships and men than it had itself received. The British Battle Fleet was never seriously in action. Only one ship, the *Colossus,* was struck by an enemy shell, and out of more than 20,000 men in the battleships only two were killed and five wounded. To this supreme instrument had been devoted the best of all that Britain could give for many years. It was vastly superior to its opponent in numbers, tonnage, speed, and above all gun power, and was at least its equal in discipline, individual skill and courage. The disappointment of all ranks was deep; and immediately there arose reproaches and recriminations, continued to this day, through which this account has sought to steer a faithful and impartial passage. All hoped that another opportunity would be granted them, and eagerly sought to profit by the lessons of the battle. The chance of an annihilating victory had been perhaps offered at the moment of deployment, had been offered again an hour later when Scheer made his great miscalculation, and for the third time when a little before midnight the Commander-in-Chief decided to reject the evidence of the Admiralty message. Three times is a lot.

Nevertheless one last chance of bringing the German Fleet to action was offered. Within six weeks of Jutland, on the evening of August 18, Admiral Scheer again put to sea. His object was to bombard Sunderland; and his hope, to draw the British Fleet, if it intervened, into his U-boat flotillas. His main flotilla of seventeen U-boats was disposed in two lines on the probable tracks of the British Fleet: one off Blyth and one off the Yorkshire coast; while twelve boats of the Flanders flotilla were stationed off the Dutch coast. Four Zeppelins patrolled between Peterhead and Norway: three off the British coast between Newcastle and Hull, and one in the Flanders Bight. The German 2nd Battle Squadron, composed of the slow *Deutschlands,* was on this occasion not allowed to accompany the Fleet. Thus protected by the airships, bristling with U-boats, and unencumbered by their older vessels, the Germans steamed boldly on their course.

The preliminary German movements had not passed unnoticed by the Admiralty; and during the forenoon of the 18th the Grand Fleet battle squadrons were ordered to rendezvous in the "Long Forties," the battle-cruisers to join farther south, and the Harwich force to rendezvous to the eastward of Yarmouth. Twenty-six British submarines—five in the Heligoland Bight, eight in the Flanders Bight, one off the Dutch coast and twelve off Yarmouth and the Tyne—were in their turn spread to intercept the enemy.

The movements of the two Fleets during the 19th are shown in broad outline on the chart. The day's operations were heralded by submarine attacks on both sides. At 5:5 a.m. the German battleship *Westfalen* was hit by a torpedo from the British submarine E.23, and she turned for home at 7:22. Admiral Scheer held steadily on his course with the remainder of the Fleet. About 6 a.m. the *Nottingham,* one of Beatty's advanced line of cruisers, was struck by two torpedoes from U-52, was hit again at 6:25, and sank at 7:10. At first there was some doubt whether she had been sunk by mine or torpedo. But at 6:48 a report from the *Southampton* was received by the Flagship, the *Iron Duke,* making it certain that the *Nottingham* had been sunk by a torpedo. About the same time a signal was received from the Admiralty, fixing the position of the German Fleet. Sir John Jellicoe however appears to have remained under the impression that the *Nottingham* had been destroyed by a mine. He consequently suspected a trap; and at 7 a.m. he turned the Grand Fleet about and steamed to the northward for over two hours, until 9:8 a.m.

It is not clear, even on the assumption that the *Nottingham* had been sunk by a mine, why this manœuvre was necessary. A comparatively slight alteration of course would have carried the Grand Fleet many miles clear of the area of the suspected minefields, and the possibility of getting between the German Fleet and home presented itself. U-52 had however struck harder than she knew. It took two hours after the Grand Fleet turned again towards the enemy to recover the lost ground. So that in all four hours were lost and the chance of cutting off the High Sea Fleet seriously reduced. It cannot however be said that this was the cause of preventing battle. An accident of a different character was to intervene. Admiral Tyrwhitt with the Harwich force was meanwhile cruising near the southern rendezvous. During the afternoon Scheer received five airship reports—one of the Grand Fleet and four of the Harwich force. He also received three submarine reports about the Grand Fleet. The British forces to the northward all seemed to be steaming away from him as if some concentration were taking place in that direction. At 12:35 p.m. however the German airship L13 reported strong British forces about seventy miles to the southward, and that these had been seen coming north at 11:30 a.m. This was of course the Harwich force. Admiral Scheer jumped to the conclusion that it was the Grand Fleet and that his retreat was compromised. He thereupon turned completely about at 3:15 and after waiting for his battle-cruisers to get ahead of him steamed for home. Meanwhile Sir John Jellicoe, having recovered his lost distance, and having received at 1:30 p.m. a signal from the Admiralty fixing the position of the German Flagship at 12:33, was now proceeding at nineteen knots towards the area which Scheer had just vacated. The chart on board the *Iron Duke* seemed to indicate that a Fleet action was imminent, and every preparation was made by Sir John Jellicoe to engage the enemy. After advancing for nearly two hours in full readiness for action, with the battle-cruisers on his starboard and the 5th Battle Squadron on his port bow, he still saw nothing of the enemy. At 3:57 all hope of meeting the Germans was abandoned and the Grand Fleet turned again homeward losing on the way another light cruiser, the *Falmouth*, by a U-boat torpedo. At about 6 o'clock the Harwich force sighted the German Fleet. But the Grand Fleet was too far off to offer them any support and at 7 p.m. Admiral Tyrwhitt turned for his base, and thus the operations of August 19 came to an end.

I feel it unfitting to end this chapter without drawing some conclusions from the events it has attempted to describe. First: Material. What was the cause of the swift destruction of the three British battle-cruisers? The side armour of the *Invincible* was only from 6 to 7 inches thick. She was in action at under 10,000 yards' range, and her magazines may well have been exploded by heavy shells which directly pierced her armour belt. But the *Queen Mary* was fighting at over 18,000 yards' range when the fatal salvo struck her. She was in her place in the line undamaged, steaming 25 knots and firing from all her guns, a minute or two before she blew up. The *Indefatigable* succumbed at the same extreme range as easily. There can be only two possible explanations. Either the magazines had been penetrated by a shell, or a shell bursting in the turret had ignited the ammunition there, and the flash and flame had roared down the 60-foot hoist into the magazines. There is no doubt that the magazines of British battle-cruisers were not sufficiently protected against long-range fire. The ranges at which the sea battles of the Great War were fought were vastly greater than any contemplated before the war. Our Naval Constructors had not therefore taken sufficient account of the plunging character of the fire to which the decks and turret roofs would be subjected. The German battle-cruiser armour was better distributed. Moreover the British battle-cruisers, as developed by Fisher and to a large extent by Jellicoe, though more heavily gunned were less strongly armoured than their German compeers. Casting a new eye on naval architecture in 1911, I had recoiled from the battle-cruiser type. To spend in those days two million pounds upon a vessel of the greatest power and speed which could not face a strong battleship seemed to me a fruitless proceeding. I therefore opposed the increase of the battle-cruiser class in which we already had superiority, and succeeded in persuading the Board of Admiralty to cancel the battle-cruiser projected for the programme of 1912, and to build instead of one battle-cruiser and four slow battleships, the five fast battleships of the *Queen Elizabeth* design. I also excluded the annual battle-cruiser from the programmes of 1913 and 1914. These matters have been fully set forth earlier in this account.

Nevertheless it is more likely that the *Queen Mary* and *Indefatigable* were destroyed by flash down the turret ammunition hoists than by penetration of their decks. The roofs of the gun-houses directly exposed to plunging fire were only 3 inches thick. From the working chambers of these turrets the ammunition tube led directly to the handing-room outside the magazine 60 feet below. The danger of the flash of an explosion passing down this tube had from the earliest days of modern ironclads always been recognized. Competition in gunnery practices between ships in peace time had however led to the omission of various precautions. The magazine doors at the bottom of the tube were not doubled. One of them could not therefore be kept always closed in action. Nor were they even shrouded by thick curtains of felt. The shutter which closed the hoist in which the charge was lifted had in some cases been removed for the sake of greater rapidity in loading. A free and easy habit of handling cordite in large quantities had grown up. The silk coverings of the British charges did not give the same security against fire as did the German brass cartridge cases, albeit that these had other disadvantages. All down the tube from the breech of the gun to the magazine, at least four double cordite charges made a complete train of explosive. The flash of a heavy shell exploding in the gun-house, or of a fire starting in the cordite charges there, might in these circumstances be carried almost simultaneously into the very magazine itself. Here is the most probable cause of the destruction both of the *Queen Mary* and the *Indefatigable,* and we know how nearly the *Lion* shared their fate.

Against this danger the Germans were forewarned and forearmed by an incident in the Dogger Bank action of January 1915. A 13.5-inch shell had penetrated the after turret of the *Seydlitz,* setting fire to the charges and to a small "ready magazine." A vast flame enveloped the turret and spread through the passages to the next, gutting both turrets completely and killing over two hundred men. This lesson led to drastic changes in the protection of the German ammunition supply and in drill, similar to those introduced into British ships after Jutland.

It was always argued by the Naval experts that although the later German battle-cruisers—about which we were not ill-informed—carried more armour than their British opposite numbers, this advantage was more than counter-

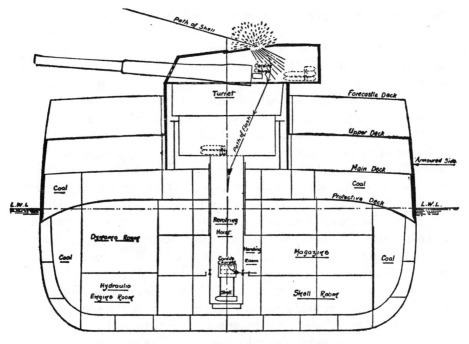

DIAGRAM SHEWING SECTION OF WARSHIP IN WAY OF TURRET
AND EFFECT OF SHELL STRIKING ROOF OF TURRET.

balanced by our having far heavier guns and shells. It was however proved by the test of battle that the British heavy armour-piercing shell was inferior to the German shell *of equal size* in carrying its explosion through the armour. Such a result should for ever banish complacency from the technical branches of our Naval Ordnance Department, and should lead successive Boards of Admiralty repeatedly to canvass and overhaul the scientific data with which they are presented and to compare them in an open-minded mood with foreign practices.

What bearing had these deficiencies upon the chances of a general fought-out Fleet battle? This question is at once fundamental and capable of decisive answer.

On no occasion either at the Dogger Bank or Jutland did even the heaviest German shell succeed in penetrating British armour over 7½ inches thick. All hits made on 9-inch armour were effectually resisted by the plate. The vitals of all British battleships engaged at Jutland were protected by 13-inch, 12-inch, 11-inch, or at the very least 9-inch armour. It follows that if the main British Battle Fleet had been seriously engaged at Jutland—apart from the ill-luck of an occasional flash carried down an ammunition hoist—it would not have suffered severely from German shell fire. We know that the main armaments and engines of the four *Queen Elizabeths* were undamaged after coming under a heavy fire from all the strongest vessels of the German Battle Fleet as well as from the German battle-cruisers. Out of five hits of 12-inch shell on their heavy armour, none penetrated. The roof of one of the *Malaya's* turrets (4½ inches) was hit by a heavy projectile without any damage being done. It may therefore be concluded that the armoured protection of the British Battle Fleet was ample to resist the 12-inch shell of the heaviest German guns afloat at Jutland.

On the other hand, at the Dogger Bank a British 13.5-inch shell pierced and burst inside the 9-inch armour of one of the *Seydlitz's* turrets; and at Jutland a British 15-inch shell penetrated the 10-inch armour on the front of the *Seydlitz's* "D" turret, and a 13.5-inch shell penetrated her 9-inch armour. In these two latter cases however the force of the explosion was expended outside. The *Lützow* at Jutland showed similar results. At least one 13.5-inch shell penetrated and burst inside 8-inch or 12-inch armour, while another drove in a 10-inch turret plate, causing a fire in the turret. At least one 15-inch shell penetrated and burst inside a 10-inch or 12-inch turret plate on the *Derfflinger,* causing a terrific fire which completely gutted the turret. Such were the results obtained in the two Fleets engaging at long range. It would be easy to add to these examples. Had the battle been fought to a conclusion at medium or shorter range, the penetration of the guns on both sides would have increased; but the superior relation of the heavier British shell would at every stage have been maintained.

It is upon this basis of ascertained fact that the numerical strength of the rival Fleets must be considered. The British superiority in the line of battle of 37 Dreadnought ships to 21 German similar units and the double weight of the British broadside were factors which may justly be described as overwhelming. The margin of safety both in numbers and in gun power was so large as to reduce the important defects mentioned to a minor scale, and to make full allowance against accidents.

In the sphere of tactics it is evident that the danger of underwater damage by mine or torpedo, the danger of "losing half the fleet before a shot is fired," dominated the mind of the British Commander-in-Chief. This danger, though less great than was supposed at the time, was nevertheless real and terrible. Coupled with a true measure of the disproportionate consequences of battle to the rival navies, it enforced a policy of extreme caution upon Sir John Jellicoe. This policy was deliberately adopted by him after prolonged thought, and inflexibly adhered to, not only before and during the encounter at Jutland but afterwards. The policy cannot be condemned on account of the unsatisfying episodes to which it led, without due and constant recognition of the fatal consequences which might have followed from the opposite course or from recklessness. Admitting this however to the full, it does not cover several of the crucial Jutland situations, nor that which arose in the German sortie of August 19. Tactical movements lay open on these occasions to the Grand Fleet for gripping the enemy without in any way increasing the risk of being led into an under-water trap. A more flexible system of fleet training and manœuvring would have enabled these movements to be made. The attempt to centralize in a single hand the whole conduct in action of so vast a fleet failed. The Commander-in-Chief, with the best will in the world, could not see or even know what was going on. No attempt was made to use the fast division of battleships *(Queen Elizabeths)* to engage the enemy on the opposite side and hold him up to the battle. The British light cruiser squadrons and flotillas were not used as they ought to have been to parry and rupture hostile torpedo attacks, but these were dealt with merely by the passive turn away of the whole Fleet. The sound and prudent reasoning of the Commander-in-Chief against being led into traps did not apply to situations where the enemy was obviously himself surprised, separated from his harbours, and dealing with utterly unforeseen and unforeseeable emergencies. Praiseworthy caution had induced a defensive habit of mind and scheme of tactics which hampered the Grand Fleet even when the special conditions enjoining the caution did not exist.

The ponderous, poignant responsibilities borne successfully, if not triumphantly, by Sir John Jellicoe during two years of faithful command, constitute unanswerable claims to the lasting respect of the nation. But the Royal Navy must find in other personalities and other episodes the golden links which carried forward through the Great War the audacious and conquering traditions of the past; and it is to Beatty and the battle-cruisers, to Keyes at Zeebrugge, to Tyrwhitt and his Harwich striking force, to the destroyer and submarine flotillas out in all weathers and against all foes, to the wild adventures of the Q-ships, to the steadfast resolution of the British Merchant Service, that the eyes of rising generations will turn.

CHAPTER XLIII

THE BATTLE OF THE SOMME

A sense of the inevitable broods over the battlefields of the Somme. The British armies were so ardent, their leaders so confident, the need and appeals of our Allies so clamant, and decisive results seemingly so near, that no human power could have prevented the attempt. All the spring the French had been battling and dying at Verdun, immolating their manhood upon that anvil-altar; and every chivalrous instinct in the new British armies called them to the succour of France, and inspired them with sacrifice and daring. Brusiloff's surprising successes redoubled, if that were possible, the confidence of the British Generals. They were quite sure they were going to break their enemy and rupture his invading lines in France. They trusted to the devotion of their troops, which they knew was boundless; they trusted to masses of artillery and shells never before accumulated in war; and they launched their attack in the highest sense of duty and the strongest conviction of success.

The end of the year had brought a change in the Command of the British armies in France. We have seen in what circumstances and with what misgivings Sir John French had allowed himself to be involved in the previous September at Loos in the unwisdom of the great French offensive in Champagne. He had conformed with loyalty and ultimately even with ardour to the wishes of Lord Kitchener and to the acquiescence of the British Cabinet. But all this stood him in no stead on the morrow of failure. Those who had not the conviction or resolution to arrest the forlorn attack became easily censorious of its conduct after the inevitable failure. During the course of December proceedings were set on foot by which, at the end of the year, Sir John French was transferred from the Command of the British Army in France to that of the forces at home, and succeeded in that high situation by the Commander of his First Army, Sir Douglas Haig.

Alike in personal efficiency and professional credentials, Sir Douglas Haig was the first officer of the British Army. He had obtained every qualification, gained every experience and served in every appointment requisite for the General Command. He was a Cavalry Officer of social distinction and independent means, whose whole life had been devoted to military study and practice. He had been Adjutant of his regiment; he had played in its polo team; he had passed through the Staff College; he had been Chief Staff Officer to the Cavalry Division in the South African war; he had earned a Brevet and decorations in the field; he had commanded a Column; he had held a command in India; he had served at the War Office; he had commanded at Aldershot the two divisions which formed the only organized British army corps, and from this position he had led the First British army corps to France. He had borne the principal fighting part in every battle during Sir John French's command. At the desperate crisis of the first Battle of Ypres, British battalions and batteries, wearied, out-numbered and retreating, had been inspirited by the spectacle of the Corps Commander riding slowly forward at the head of his whole staff along the shell-swept Menin Road into close contact with the actual fighting line.

It was impossible to assemble around any other officer a series of appointments and qualifications in any way comparable in their cumulative effects with these. He had fulfilled with exceptional credit every requirement to which the pre-war British military hierarchy attached importance. For many years, and at every stage in his career, he had been looked upon alike by superiors and equals as a man certain to rise, if he survived, to the summit of the British Army. Colonel Henderson, the biographer of Stonewall Jackson, Professor at the Staff College during Haig's graduation, had predicted this event. His conduct in the first year of the war had vindicated every hope. His appointment as Commander-in-Chief on the departure of Sir John French created no surprise, aroused no heart-burnings, excited no jealousy. The military profession reposed in him a confidence which the varied fortunes, disappointments and miscalculations attendant upon three years of war on the greatest scale left absolutely unshaken.

The esteem of his military colleagues found a healthy counterpart in his own self-confidence. He knew the place was his by merit and by right. He knew he had no rivals, and that he owed his place neither to favour nor usurpation. This attitude of mind was invaluable. Allied to a resolute and equable temperament it enabled him to sustain with composure, not only the shocks of defeat and disaster at the hands of the enemy, but those more complex and not less wearing anxieties arising from his relations with French allies and British Cabinets. He was as sure of himself at the head of the British Army as a country gentleman on the soil which his ancestors had trod for generations, and to whose cultivation he had devoted his life. But the Great War owned no Master; no one was equal to its vast and novel issues; no human hand controlled its hurricanes; no eye could pierce its whirlwind dust-clouds. In the course of this narrative it is necessary in the interests of the future to seek and set forth in all sincerity what are believed to be the true facts and values. But when this process is complete, the fact remains that no other subject of the King could have endured the ordeal which was his lot with the phlegm, the temper, and the fortitude of Sir Douglas Haig.

The military conceptions underlying the scheme of attack were characterized by simplicity. The policy of the French and British Commanders had selected as the point for their offensive what was undoubtedly the strongest and most perfectly defended position in the world.

> During nearly two years' preparation [1] [writes Sir Douglas Haig] he (the enemy) had spared no pains to render these defences impregnable. The first and second systems each consisted of several lines of deep trenches, well provided with bomb-proof shelters and with numerous communication trenches connecting them. The front of the trenches in each system was protected by wire entanglements, many of them in two belts forty yards broad, built of iron stakes interlaced with barbed wire, often almost as thick as a man's finger.
>
> The numerous woods and villages in and between these systems of defence had been turned into veritable fortresses. The deep cellars usually to be found in the villages, and the numerous pits and quarries common to a chalk country, were used to provide cover for machine guns and trench mortars. The existing cellars were supplemented by elaborate dugouts, sometimes in two storeys, and these were connected up by passages as much as thirty feet below the surface of the ground. The salients in the enemy's line, from which he could bring enfilade fire across his front, were made into self-contained forts and often protected by mine-fields; while strong redoubts and concrete machine-gun emplacements had been constructed in positions from which he could sweep his own trenches should these be taken. The ground lent itself to good artillery observation on the enemy's part, and he had skilfully arranged for cross-fire by his guns.
>
> These various systems of defense, with the fortified localities and other supporting points between them, were cunningly sited to afford each other mutual assistance and to admit of the utmost possible development of enfilade and flanking fire by machine guns and artillery. They formed, in short, not merely a series of successive lines, but one composite system of enormous depth and strength.
>
> Behind his second system of trenches, in addition to woods, villages and other strong points prepared for defence, the enemy had several other lines already completed; and we had learnt from aeroplane reconnaissance

---

[1] *Sir Douglas Haig's Despatches*, J. H. Boraston, pp. 22–3.

that he was hard at work improving and strengthening these and digging fresh ones between them, and still farther back.

All these conditions clearly indicated to the Staffs a suitable field for our offensive, and it was certain that if the enemy were defeated here, he would be more disheartened than by being overcome upon some easier battleground.

Sir Douglas also describes his own preparations, which were thorough and straightforward:[1]

> Vast stocks of ammunition and stores of all kinds had to be accumulated beforehand within a convenient distance of our front. To deal with these many miles of new railways—both standard and narrow gauge— and trench tramways were laid. All available roads were improved, many others were made, and long causeways were built over marshy valleys. . . . Scores of miles of deep communication trenches had to be dug, as well as trenches for telephone wires, assembly and assault trenches, and numerous gun-emplacements and observation posts.

Thus there was no chance of surprise. Nothing could be introduced to obscure the plain trial of strength between the armies, or diminish the opportunities for valour on the part of the assaulting troops. For months the Germans had observed the vast uncamouflaged preparations proceeding opposite the sector of attack. For a week a preliminary bombardment of varying but unexampled intensity had lashed their trenches with its scourge of steel and fire. Crouched in their deep chalk caves the stubborn German infantry, short often through the cannonade of food and water, awaited the signal to man their broken parapets. The lanes which the British shrapnel had laboriously cut through their barbed-wire entanglements were all carefully studied, and machine guns were accurately sited to sweep them or traverse the approaches with flanking fire. Even one machine gun in skilled resolute hands might lay five hundred men dead and dying on the ground; and along the assaulted front certainly a thousand such weapons scientifically related in several lines of defence awaited their prey. Afar the German gunners, unmolested by counter-battery, stood ready to release their defending barrages on the British front lines, on their communication trenches and places of assembly.

Colonel Boraston's account is studiously vague as to the objectives sought for by his Chief on July 1. The plan of the British and French was admittedly to pierce the whole German trench system on a front of many kilometres, and then by wheeling outwards—the British to the north-east and north and the

[1] *Sir Douglas Haig's Despatches*, p. 21.

French to the south-east—to roll up from the flanks the exposed portions of the German line; and British and French cavalry divisions were held ready to be pushed forward through the gap so made. The French objective was to gain the rising ground east of the Somme south of Péronne, while "the corresponding British objective" was "the semicircle of high ground running from the neighbourhood of Le Transloy through Bapaume to Achiet-le-Grand."[1] But these objectives, says Colonel Boraston, were not expected to be reached in the first assault. "These Somme positions were objectives for the armies concerned rather than for the troops from time to time engaged in the attack. They marked the stage at which it was thought that the penetration would be deep enough ... to enable the Allied armies to turn their attention to the second stage of the battle, this is to say, the rolling up of the German forces on the flank of the point of rupture."[2] It was certainly contemplated from the beginning that the battle would be long and hard fought; but it will be seen that the time factor is thus left altogether indefinite. One remains under the impression that it was comparatively immaterial whether this penetrating advance and outward movement were to be effected in a few days, a week, a fortnight, or even longer. But this argument cannot be sustained. The whole effectiveness of the plan depended on the speed of its execution. If for instance an interval of two or three days intervened between the penetration and the outward wheel, the enemy's line would be switched back on both sides of the gap and a whole new web of fortifications would obstruct a further advance. All prospect of a great rupture followed by rolling up the flanks was dependent upon a rate of progress so rapid as to preclude the construction and organization by the enemy of fresh defensive lines. If the Joffre-Haig plan was to achieve any success apart from mere attrition, progress must be continuous and rapid, and the objectives specified must be attained at the latest in two or three days. If this were not secured, the great attack would have failed. Other attacks might subsequently be planned and might be locally successful, but the scheme of a grand rupture was definitely at an end.

It is easy to prove that rapid progress was in fact contemplated and resolutely bid for. The use by Haig of his artillery clearly indicates the immediate ambitions which were in view. Instead of concentrating the fire on the first lines which were to be assaulted, the British artillery was dispersed in its action over the second and remoter lines and on many strong points far in the rear, the hope clearly being that all these would be reached in the course of the first day's or two-days' fighting. The position of the British and French cavalry in close

[1] *Sir Douglas Haig's Command*, p. 93.
[2] *Ibid.*

proximity to the battle front also reveals indisputably the hopes and expectations of the commanders.

At seven o'clock in the morning of July 1 the British and French armies rose from their trenches steel-helmeted, gas-masked, equipped with all the latest apparatus of war, bombs, mortars, machine guns light and heavy, and, supported by all their artillery, marched against the enemy on a front of 45 kilometres. Fourteen British divisions and five French divisions were almost immediately engaged.[1] South of the Somme on the French front the Germans were taken completely by surprise. They had not believed the French capable after their punishment at Verdun of any serious offensive effort. They expected at the most only demonstrations. They were not ready for the French, and the French attack, though unfortunately on a needlessly small scale, captured and overwhelmed the German troops throughout the whole of their first system of trenches.

Very different were the fortunes of the British. Everywhere they found the enemy fully prepared. The seven-days' bombardment had by no means accomplished what had been expected. Safely hidden in the deep dugouts, the defenders and their machine guns were practically intact. From these, they emerged with deadly effect at the moment of assault or even after the waves of attack had actually passed over and beyond them. Though the German front line was crossed at every point, the great advance into his position failed except on the right. The three British divisions on that flank captured Montauban and Mametz and an area 4½ miles wide by 1½ miles deep, thus isolating Fricourt on the south. The 21st Division north of this village also made progress and gained nearly a mile. But though the defenders of Fricourt were thus almost cut off, the attempt to storm the village failed. Northwards again the two divisions of the Third Army, though they advanced a thousand yards, failed in spite of repeated efforts to capture La Boiselle or Ovillers on the long spurs of the Pozières plateau. By nightfall the gain in this part of the field comprised only two pockets or bulges in the enemy's position. The attack of the X Corps with three divisions broke down before the immense defences of the Thiepval spur and plateau. Although two of its great supporting points, the Leipzig and Schwaben redoubts, were captured, all attacks on Thiepval failed, and the failure to take Thiepval entailed the evacuation of the Schwaben. Opposite Beaumont-Hamel, on the extreme left, the VIII Corps, after reaching the German front line, was driven back to its own trenches. The subsidiary attack made by the Third Army against Gommecourt completely failed, practically no damage to the German defences having been done in the long bombardment.

[1] See map on p. 663.

• • •

Let us descend from this general viewpoint into closer contact with a single Division. The 8th Division, with all its three brigades in line, was to assault the Ovillers spur: the centre brigade up the ridge; the others through the valleys on each side. Both the valleys were enfiladed from the German positions at La Boiselle and in front of Thiepval. Against these three brigades stood the German 180th Infantry Regiment with two battalions holding the front defences, and the third battalion in reserve north of Pozières. After allowing for battalion reserves, there were ten Companies comprising about 1,800 men to oppose the three brigades, together about 8,500 bayonets, of the 8th Division.

At 7:30 the British artillery barrage lifted. The trench mortars ceased fire, and the leading battalions of all three brigades rose and moved forward, each battalion extended on a frontage of 400 yards. A violent machine-gun and rifle fire opened immediately along the whole front of the German position, particularly from the machine-gun nests of La Boiselle and Ovillers; and almost simultaneously the German batteries behind Ovillers placed a barrage in No Man's Land and along the British front line and support trenches. Here let the German eyewitness speak.

> The intense bombardment was realized by all to be a prelude to the infantry assault at last. The men in the dugouts therefore waited ready, a belt full of hand grenades around them, gripping their rifles and listening for the bombardment to lift from the front defence zone on to the rear defences. It was of vital importance to lose not a second in taking up position in the open to meet the British infantry who would be advancing immediately behind the artillery barrage. Looking towards the British trenches through the long trench periscopes held up out of the dugout entrances, there could be seen a mass of steel helmets above their parapet showing that their storm-troops were ready for the assault. At 7:30 a.m. the hurricane of shells ceased as suddenly as it had begun. Our men at once clambered up the steep shafts leading from the dugouts to daylight and ran singly or in groups to the nearest shell craters. The machine guns were pulled out of the dugouts and hurriedly placed into position, their crews dragging the heavy ammunition boxes up the steps and out to the guns. A rough firing line was thus rapidly established. As soon as in position, a series of extended lines of British infantry were seen moving forward from the British trenches. The first line appeared to continue without end to right and left. It was quickly followed by a second line, then a third and fourth. They came on at a steady easy pace as if expecting to find nothing alive in our front trenches. . . . The front line, preceded

by a thin line of skirmishers and bombers, was now half-way across No Man's Land. "Get ready!" was passed along our front from crater to crater, and heads appeared over the crater edges as final positions were taken up for the best view and machine guns mounted firmly in place. A few minutes later, when the leading British line was within 100 yards, the rattle of machine gun and rifle fire broke out from along the whole line of craters. Some fired kneeling so as to get a better target over the broken ground, while others, in the excitement of the moment, stood up regardless of their own safety to fire into the crowd of men in front of them. Red rockets sped up into the blue sky as a signal to the artillery, and immediately afterwards a mass of shells from the German batteries in rear tore through the air and burst among the advancing lines. Whole sections seemed to fall, and the rear formations, moving in closer order, quickly scattered. The advance rapidly crumpled under this hail of shells and bullets. All along the line men could be seen throwing their arms into the air and collapsing never to move again. Badly wounded rolled about in their agony, and others less severely injured crawled to the nearest shell-hole for shelter. The British soldier, however, has no lack of courage, and once his hand is set to the plough he is not easily turned from his purpose. The extended lines, though badly shaken and with many gaps, now came on all the faster. Instead of a leisurely walk they covered the ground in short rushes at the double. Within a few minutes the leading troops had reached within a stone's throw of our front trench, and while some of us continued to fire at point-blank range, others threw hand grenades among them. The British bombers answered back, while the infantry rushed forward with fixed bayonets. The noise of battle became indescribable. The shouting of orders and the shrill British cheers as they charged forward could be heard above the violent and intense fusillade of machine guns and rifles and the bursting bombs, and above the deep thunderings of the artillery and the shell explosions. With all this were mingled the moans and groans of the wounded, the cries for help and the last screams of death. Again and again the extended lines of British infantry broke against the German defence like waves against a cliff, only to be beaten back.

It was an amazing spectacle of unexampled gallantry, courage and bull-dog determination on both sides.[1]

At several points the British who had survived the awful firestorm broke into the German trenches. They were nowhere strong enough to maintain their

[1] *Die Schwaben an der Ancre*, Gerster.

position; and by nine o'clock the whole of the troops who were still alive and unwounded were either back in their own front-line trenches, or sheltering in the shell-holes of No Man's Land, or cut off and desperately defending themselves in the captured German trenches. A renewed attack was immediately ordered by Divisional Headquarters. But the Brigadiers reported they had no longer the force to attempt it. A fresh brigade was sent from the III Corps Headquarters. But before it could share the fate of the others, all signs of fighting inside the German trenches by the British who had entered them had been extinguished; and the orders to renew the assault were cancelled.

In all, the Division lost in little more than two hours 218 out of 300 officers and 5,274 other ranks out of 8,500 who had gone into action. By the evening of July 1, the German 180th Infantry Regiment was again in possession of the whole of its trenches. Its losses during the day's fighting had been 8 officers and 273 soldiers killed, wounded and missing. Only two of its three battalions had been engaged. It had not been necessary to call the reserve battalion to their aid.

Night closed over the still-thundering battlefield. Nearly 60,000 British soldiers had fallen, killed or wounded, or were prisoners in the hands of the enemy. This was the greatest loss and slaughter sustained in a single day in the whole history of the British Army. Of the infantry who advanced to the attack, nearly half had been overtaken by death, wounds or capture. Against this, apart from territory, we had gained 4,000 prisoners and a score of cannon. It needs some hardihood for Colonel Boraston to write:[1]

> The events of July 1 . . . bore out the conclusions of the British higher command and amply justified the tactical methods employed.

The extent of the catastrophe was concealed by the Censorship, and its significance masked by a continuance of the fighting on a far smaller scale, four divisions alone being employed. The shattered divisions on the left were placed under General Gough, whose command, originally designated the "Reserve Corps" and intended to receive resting divisions, was renamed the "Reserve Army" and given orders to maintain "a slow and methodical pressure" on the enemy's front. Henceforward the battle degenerated into minor operations which proceeded continuously on a comparatively small front. The losses were however in this phase more evenly balanced, as the Germans delivered many vigorous counter-attacks.

[1] *Sir Douglas Haig's Command*, p. 103.

To sum up the results of the fighting of these five days' (says Haig with severe accuracy)[1] on a front of over six miles . . . our troops had swept over the whole of the enemy's first and strongest system of defence. . . . They had driven him back over a distance of more than a mile, and had carried four elaborately fortified villages.

These gains had however been purchased by the loss of nearly a hundred thousand of our best troops. The battle continued. The objectives were now pulverized villages and blasted woods, and the ground conquered was at each stage so limited both in width and depth as to exclude any strategic results. On July 14 a dawn attack towards Bazentin-le-Grand led to a local success, and the world was eagerly informed that a squadron of the 7th Dragoon Guards had actually ridden on their horses as far as High Wood, whence they were withdrawn the next day.

The enemy's second main system of defence (writes Sir Douglas)[2] had been captured on a front of over three miles. We had forced him back more than a mile. . . . Four more of his fortified villages and three woods had been wrested from him by determined fighting, and our advanced troops had penetrated as far as his third line of defence.

Unfortunately the enemy "had dug and wired many new trenches, both in front and behind his original front lines. He had also brought up fresh troops, and there was no possibility of taking him by surprise. The task before us was therefore a very difficult one. . . . At this juncture its difficulties were increased by unfavourable weather."[3]

As the divisions which had been specially prepared for the battle were successively shot to pieces and used up, their remnants were sent to hold the trenches in the quiet portions of the front, thus setting free other divisions, not previously engaged, for their turn in the furnace. It was not until July 20 that the battle again expanded to the proportions of a great operation. On this day and the two days following a general attack was organized by seventeen British and French divisions on the front Pozières-Foucaucourt. The losses were again very heavy, particularly to the British. Only a few hundred yards were gained upon the average along the front.

The conflict sank once more to the bloody but local struggles of two or

[1] *Sir Douglas Haig's Despatches*, p. 27.
[2] *Ibid.*, pp. 30–1.
[3] *Ibid.*, p. 33.

three divisions repeatedly renewed as fast as they were consumed, and consumed as fast as they were renewed. By the end of July an advance of about two and a half miles had been made on a front which at this depth did not exceed two miles. For these gains 171,000[1] British soldiers had fallen—killed or wounded. 11,400 German prisoners had been captured, but more than double that number of British prisoners and wounded had fallen into the hands of the enemy, of whom many had under the terrible conditions of the battle perished between the fighting lines beyond the aid of friend or foe.

The anatomy of the battles of Verdun and the Somme was the same. A battlefield had been selected. Around this battlefield walls were built—double, triple, quadruple—of enormous cannon. Behind these railways were constructed to feed them, and mountains of shells were built up. All this was the work of months. Thus the battlefield was completely encircled by thousands of guns of all sizes, and a wide oval space prepared in their midst. Through this awful arena all the divisions of each army, battered ceaselessly by the enveloping artillery, were made to pass in succession, as if they were the teeth of interlocking cog-wheels grinding each other.

For month after month the ceaseless cannonade continued at its utmost intensity, and month after month the gallant divisions of heroic human beings were torn to pieces in this terrible rotation. Then came the winter, pouring down rain from the sky to clog the feet of men, and drawing veils of mist before the hawk-eyes of their artillery. The arena, as used to happen in the Coliseum in those miniature Roman days, was flooded with water. A vast sea of ensanguined mud churned by thousands of vehicles, by hundred of thousands of men and millions of shells, replaced the blasted dust. Still the struggle continued. Still the remorseless wheels revolved. Still the auditorium of artillery roared. At last the legs of men could no longer move; they wallowed and floundered helplessly in the slime. Their food, their ammunition lagged behind them along the smashed and choked roadways.

As the battle progressed the conditions of offence and defence became more equal. Trenches were obliterated and barbed wire pulverized. The combats tended increasingly to become field actions in a wilderness of shell-holes. The enemy's losses grew as the weeks wore on. The battle flared up again into a great operation on September 25 and the following days; and November 13 saw large-scale attacks along the Ancre tributary and the brilliant storm of Beaumont-Hamel.

Although the Germans used and risked at almost every stage much smaller numbers of men than the attacking British, the experiences of defence for these

---

[1] *I.e.,* 196,000 minus 25,000 for the quiet sectors. *Military Effort,* Monthly Returns, p. 253 *et seq.*

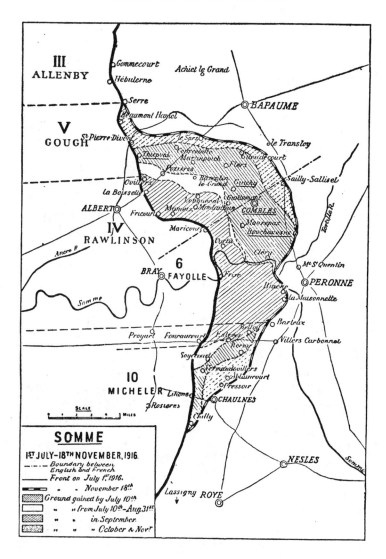

III
ALLENBY

Gommecourt
Achiet le Grand
Hébulerne
Serre
BAPAUME
Beaumont Hamel

V
GOUGH
St Pierre-Divon
le Sars
le Transloy
Thiepval
Courcelette
Martinpuich
Gueudecourt
Pozières
Flers
Ovillers
Bazentin le Grand
Guchy
Sailly-Sallisel
la Boisselle
Contalmaison
ALBERT
Fricourt
Mametz
Montauban
COMBLES
Maricourt
Maurepas
Bouchavesnes

IV
RAWLINSON
Ancre R.
Hardecourt
Cléry
Mt St Quentin
6
BRAY
FAYOLLE
Frise
PERONNE
Somme
Biaches
la Maisonnette
Barleux
Proyart
Fouraucourt
Estrées
Belloy
Villers Carbonnel
Herny
Soyécourt
10
MICHELER
Lihons
Armandovillers
Ablaincourt
Pressoir
Rosières
CHAULNES
SCALE
MILES
Chilly

SOMME
1ST JULY–18TH NOVEMBER, 1916.
————— Boundary between
English and French.
————— Front on July 1st 1916.
━━━━━━ " November 18th.
///// Ground gained by July 10th.
□ " " from July 10th–Aug. 31st.
▨ " " in September.
▨ " " October & Novr.

NESLES
Somme
Lassigny ROYE

smaller numbers were probably even more terrible than for the attack, and the moral effect upon the German Army of seeing position after position, trench after trench, captured and its defenders slaughtered or made prisoners, was undoubtedly deeply depressing. While the British, in spite of their far greater losses, felt themselves to be constantly advancing, and were cheered by captures of trophies and prisoners, the steadfast German soldiery could not escape the impression that they were being devoured piecemeal by the stronger foe. The effect was lasting. German shock troops and assault divisions were in later campaigns to show the highest qualities, and achieve wonderful feats of arms. But never again did the mass of German rank and file fight as they fought on the Somme.

The German 27th Division which defended Guillemont was one of the best divisions here engaged.

Its history says:

> Incontestably a culminating point was reached (at the Somme) that was never again approached. What we experienced surpassed all previous conception. The enemy's fire never ceased for an hour. It fell day and night on the front line and tore fearful gaps in the ranks of the defenders; it fell on the approaches to the front line and made all movement towards the front hell; it fell on the rearward trenches and the battery positions and smashed up men and material in a manner never seen before or since; it repeatedly reached even the resting battalions far behind the front and there occasioned exceptionally painful losses, and our artillery was power-less against it.

And again:

> *In the Somme fighting of 1916 there was a spirit of heroism which was never again found in the division,* however conspicuous it (the division) remained until the end of the war . . . *the men in 1918 had not the temper, the hard bitterness and spirit of sacrifice of their predecessors.*[1]

As the attackers became more experienced, the system of deep dugouts turned against the Germans. "The Entente troops," wrote Ludendorff,[2] "worked their way further and further into the German lines. We had heavy losses in men and material. At that time the front lines were still strongly held. The men took refuge in dugouts and cellars from the enemy's artillery fire. The enemy came up behind their barrage, got into the trenches and villages before our men could crawl out from their shelter. A continuous yield of prisoners to the enemy was the result. The strain on physical and moral strength was tremendous and divisions could only be kept in the line for a few days at a time. . . . The number of available divisions was shrinking . . . units were hope-lessly mixed up, the supply of ammunition was getting steadily shorter. . . . The situation on the Western front gave cause for greater anxiety than I had antici-pated. But at that time I did not realize its full significance. It was just as well, otherwise I could never have had the courage to take the important decision to

---

[1] *Die 27 Infanterie Division im Weltkrieg.*
[2] *My War Memories,* p. 244.

transfer still more divisions from the heavily engaged Western front to the Eastern in order to recover the initiative there and deal Roumania a decisive blow."

The increasing sense of dominating the enemy and the resolute desire for a decision at all costs led in September to a most improvident disclosure of the caterpillar vehicles. The first of these had early in January been manœuvred in Hatfield Park in the presence of the King, Lord Kitchener and several high authorities. Lord Kitchener was sceptical; but Mr. Lloyd George was keen, and the British Headquarters mildly interested. Fifty of these engines, developed with great secrecy under the purposely misleading name of "Tanks," had been completed. They arrived in France during the early stages of the Battle of the Somme for experimental purposes and the training of their crews. When it was seen how easily they crossed trenches and flattened out entanglements made for trial behind the British line, the force of the conception appealed to the directing minds of the Army. The Headquarters Staff, hitherto so lukewarm, now wished to use them at once in the battle. Mr. Lloyd George thought this employment of the new weapon in such small numbers premature. He informed me of the discussion which was proceeding. I was so shocked at the proposal to expose this tremendous secret to the enemy upon such a petty scale and as a mere make-weight to what I was sure could only be an indecisive operation, that I sought an interview with Mr. Asquith, of whom I was then a very definite opponent. The Prime Minister received me in the most friendly manner, and listened so patiently to my appeal that I thought I had succeeded in convincing him. But if this were so, he did not make his will effective; and on September 15 the first tanks, or "large armoured cars" as they were called in the Communiqué, went into action on the front of the Fourth Army attacking between the Combles ravine and Martin-puich.

In a memorandum drawn up by General Swinton several months before, when he was organizing the Tank Corps, it had been urged that the tanks should lead the attack, combined in as large numbers as possible, with large forces of infantry launched at once behind them. This advice was not accepted. The tanks—what there were—were dispersed in twos and threes against specified strong points or singly for special purposes. They were used as the merest make-weight. Of 59 tanks in France 49 reached the battlefield, and of these 35 reached their starting points, of which 31 crossed the German trenches. Although suffering from all the diseases of infancy, and with their crews largely untrained, it was immediately proved that a new factor had been introduced into the war. One single tank on this first occasion, finding the attacking infantry held up in front of Flers by wire and machine guns, climbed over the German trench, and travelling along behind it, immediately and without loss forced its occupants, 300 strong, to surrender. Only 9 tanks surmounted all the difficulties and pushed on ahead of the infantry. Wherever a tank reached its objective, the sight of it was enough, and the astounded Germans forthwith fled or yielded. Ten days later, on September 25, another tank, a female, followed by two companies of infantry, cleared 1,500 yards of the Gird Trench, and took 8 German Officers and 362 men prisoners, apart from numerous killed and wounded, with a total loss to the British of only 5 men. Let these episodes be contrasted with the massacre of the 8th Division already described.

Meanwhile, to achieve this miniature success, and to carry the education of the professional mind one stage further forward, a secret of war which well used would have procured a world-shaking victory in 1917 had been recklessly revealed to the enemy. Providentially however the scales of convention darkened also the vision of the German General Staff and clouded even the keen eye of Ludendorff. In the same way the Germans had exposed their secret plans of poison gas by its use on a small scale at Ypres in 1915, when they had no reserves ready to exploit the initial success. But their enemy did not in that instance neglect the knowledge they were given.

During the whole month of July, the public and the Cabinet were continually assured that the losses of the Germans in the Somme Battle far exceeded our own. The casualty tables in an earlier chapter, "The Blood Test," show the falsity of this impression. Sir Douglas Haig was not at this time well served by his advisers in the Intelligence Department of General Headquarters.[1] The temptation to tell a Chief in a great position the things he most likes to hear is one of the commonest explanations of mistaken policy. Thus the outlook of the leader on whose decision fateful events depend is usually far more sanguine than the brutal facts admit.

Yet when events are surveyed in retrospect, it does not seem just to throw the reproach of this battle upon Sir Douglas Haig. The esoteric Buddhists believe that at the end of each life a new being is created, heir to the faults or the virtues of his forerunner. The tragedies of 1916 had been decreed by the events of 1915. The failure of the Allied Governments in that year to effect the destruction of Turkey and the union of the Balkans against the Central Powers left open no favourable means of action. The French agony at Verdun compelled a British relieving counter-attack in France, before the new British armies, and

[1] The reader is here referred to my unabridged memoirs (*The World Crisis,* 1916–1918, Vol. 1) for the text of the memorandum exposing my conception of the true situation which I wrote while the Battle of the Somme was in progress and which was circulated to the Cabinet by Sir Frederick Smith, afterwards Lord Birkenhead. It is offered in support of my claim that I pass no important criticisms on the conduct of commanders in the light of after-knowledge unless there exists documentary proof that substantially the same criticisms were put on record before or during the event and while every point disputed was unknowable.

particularly their vastly expanded artillery, were sufficiently trained to save the assaulting troops the heaviest loss. The tanks, though already conceived, had yet to be born and reared. Resources did not exist sufficient to mount simultaneously several offensives along the battle front, thus leaving the enemy uncertain to the last moment of the true point of attack. Indispensable preparation destroyed equally indispensable surprise. Yet the call to attack was peremptory. Delay was impossible. Sir Douglas Haig, like all the Commanders on the Western Front, would no doubt, had he been responsible, have opposed the great turning movement in the south-east of Europe which was possible in 1915 and the consequences of which alone could have yielded decisive results in 1916. He was also confident and convinced of breaking the German front upon the Somme. But had he been as reluctant as he was ardent to attack the German positions, he could not have remained idle. Inexorable forces carried rulers and ruled along together as the wheels of Fate revolved.

Nevertheless the campaign of 1916 on the Western Front was from beginning to end a welter of slaughter, which after the issue was determined left the British and French armies weaker in relation to the Germans when it opened, while the actual battle fronts were not appreciably altered, and except for the relief of Verdun, which relieved the Germans no less than the French, no strategic advantage of any kind had been gained. The German unwisdom in attacking Verdun was more than cancelled in French casualties, and almost cancelled in the general strategic sphere by the heroic prodigality of the French defence. The loss in prestige which the Germans sustained through their failure to take Verdun was to be more than counterbalanced by their success in another theatre while all the time they kept their battle front unbroken on the Somme.

But this sombre verdict, which it seems probable posterity will endorse in still more searching terms, in no way diminishes the true glory of the British Army. A young army, but the finest we have ever marshalled; improvised at the sound of the cannonade, every man a volunteer, inspired not only by love of country but by a wide-spread conviction that human freedom was challenged by military and Imperial tyranny, they grudged no sacrifice however unfruitful and shrank from no ordeal however destructive. Struggling forward through the mire and filth of the trenches, across the corpse-strewn crater fields, amid the flaring, crashing, blasting barrages and murderous machine-gun fire, conscious of their race, proud of their cause, they seized the most formidable soldiery in Europe by the throat, slew them and hurled them unceasingly backward. If two lives or ten lives were required by their commanders to kill one German, no word of complaint ever rose from the fighting troops. No attack however forlorn, however fatal, found them without ardour. No slaughter however desolating prevented them from returning to the charge. No physical conditions however severe deprived their commanders of their obedience and loyalty. Martyrs not less than soldiers, they fulfilled the high purpose of duty with which they were imbued. The battlefields of the Somme were the graveyards of Kitchener's Army. The flower of that generous manhood which quitted peaceful civilian life in every kind of workaday occupation, which came at the call of Britain, and as we may still hope, at the call of humanity, and came from the most remote parts of her Empire, was shorn away for ever in 1916. Unconquerable except by death, which they had conquered, they have set up a monument of native virtue which will command the wonder, the reverence and the gratitude of our island people as long as we endure as a nation among men.

CHAPTER XLIV

THE ROUMANIAN DISASTER

We have seen how easily at the beginning of 1916 Roumania in her isolated position could have been induced or compelled to join the Teutonic Powers. We have seen how Falkenhayn, by turning to the west towards France and allowing Austria to do the same towards Italy, had relieved Roumania from adverse pressure and enabled her to preserve for another six months her attitude of ambiguous watchfulness. Events of a decided character were now to take place.

At the end of August the second of the two great catastrophes which Falkenhayn's unwisdom had prepared fell upon the Central Empires. Roumania declared war. Although this danger had been approaching since Brusiloff's victory at the beginning of June, and important precautionary measures taken to guard against it, the actual declaration came much sooner than the German Government had expected, and fell as a shock upon German public opinion. A spontaneous movement of anger and disgust swept across the German Empire. The position of Germany was indeed more critical at this juncture than at any other period of the war until the final collapse. The Battle of Verdun was still making enormous inroads upon German resources, and a most serious moral defeat impended there. The Battle of the Somme was in full blast. The British, undeterred by their losses, continued to throw fresh divisions into the struggle, and to launch their formidable attacks at brief intervals. The strain upon the Germans in the West was intense. The sense of failure at Verdun, and of being slowly overpowered and worn down by superior forces on the Somme, had affected the morale of their troops. Physical exhaustion and battle losses had reduced the German reserves to the slenderest proportions, and many more weeks of crisis and uncertainty lay between the hard-pressed front and the shield of winter. Meanwhile the failure of Austria was glaring. The whole Southern front in the East was still in a state of flux. The Russian tide rolled forward; no limits could yet be assigned to its advance. Scores of thousands of Czech troops had eagerly surrendered to the enemy, and were being enrolled bodily as a separate army corps in the Russian ranks. The Italian counter-offensive on the Isonzo was developing. The whole resisting power of the Austro-Hungarian Empire quivered on the verge of collapse. At this moment a fresh, brave and well-trained army of 500,000 Roumanians was thrown into the adverse scale, and entered the conflict in that very theatre where the Teutonic Powers were weakest and most vulnerable. The vital granaries and oil-fields of Roumania were lost, and even the great Hungarian Plain itself was in dire peril. All the time the pressure of the blockade sapped the vitality of the German masses, and hampered and complicated at a thousand points the manufacture of war material.

In this dark and almost desperate hour the Emperor, interpreting the mood of the German people, turned to the great twin captains of war who had defended the Eastern marches so long against heavy odds, and on whose brows still shone the lustre of Tannenberg. On August 28, the morrow of the Roumanian declaration, Falkenhayn was notified by Count von Lyncker, head of the Emperor's Military Cabinet, that His Majesty had decided to summon Hindenburg and Ludendorff to his presence. Rightly accepting this intimation as dismissal, Falkenhayn resigned forthwith; and that same evening Hindenburg as Chief of the Staff, and Ludendorff as First Quartermaster-General [1] with equal powers, assumed the supreme direction of the Central Empires in the war.

What are the relations between these two men? Hindenburg has described them as those of a happy marriage. "In such a relationship," he writes,[2] "how can a third party clearly distinguish the merits of the individuals? They are one in thought and action, and often what the one says is only the expression of the wishes and feelings of the other. After I had learnt the worth of General Ludendorff, and that was soon, I realized that one of my principal tasks was as far as possible to give free scope to the intellectual powers, the almost superhuman capacity for work and untiring resolution of my Chief of Staff, and if necessary clear the way for him, the way in which our common desires and our common goal pointed. . . . The harmony of our military and political convictions formed the basis for our joint views as to the proper use of our resources. Differences of opinion were easily reconciled, without our relations being disturbed by a feeling of forced submission on either side."

The old Field-Marshal was uplifted by his patriotism and character above jealousy. His great age and the vast changes which had taken place in warfare since he had passed his military prime led him willingly to leave the initiative, the preparation and the execution almost entirely to his volcanic colleague, while he himself in full agreement on the largest decisions came in with pon-

[1] In the German Army the deputies of the Chief of the General Staff bore the old title of Quartermaster-General.
[2] *Out of My Life,* Marshal von Hindenburg, p. 84.

derous weight to clear obstacles and opposition from the path. Throughout the struggle an absolute unity was presented.

But when we look beneath appearances to the facts, there can be no doubt that Ludendorff managed everything and that Hindenburg was chosen largely to enable him to manage everything. It was in Ludendorff's brain that the great decisions were taken. It was under his competent hand that the whole movement and control of the German armies, and of much more than the armies, proceeded. Ludendorff was the man of the German General Staff. This military priesthood was throughout the dominating and driving power of Germany, not only through the fifty-two months of the war, but to a very large extent in the situation that preceded it and brought it about. The representatives of the General Staff were bound together by the closest ties of professional comradeship and common doctrine. They were to the rest of the Army what the Jesuits in their greatest period had been to the Church of Rome. Their representatives at the side of every Commander and at Headquarters spoke a language and preserved confidences of their own. The German Generals of Corps, Armies, Army-Group Commanders, nay, Hindenburg himself, were treated by this confraternity, to an extent almost incredible, as figureheads, and frequently as nothing more. The staffs arranged everything without a word about the authority, opinions or desires of their generals. It is the General Staff which conducts the operations, gives decisions and notifies them to the subordinate formations. Ludendorff throughout appears as the uncontested master. In his numerous conversations with the Chief of the Staff of the Fourth Army, the name of Hindenburg is never mentioned to justify or to support a decision.

This in no way detracts from the fame of Hindenburg, who yielded himself with magnanimity to a process which he was sure was in the best interests of his King and Country. But it is necessary to state what is believed to be the truth.

The golden opportunity for which Roumania had so long watched had not only come. It had gone.

As soon as the extent of the Russian victory was plainly apparent, the Cabinet of Bratiano definitely decided to enter the war. The long period of perplexity, hesitation, and bargaining had reached its conclusion. Now or never was the moment for Roumania to strike with all her strength for her national ambition and for the unity and integrity of the Roumanian peoples. Once this decision was taken, not a day should have been lost in acting upon it. While Brusiloff's armies were rolling forward in Galicia, while the Bohemian troops of Austria were eagerly surrendering by scores of thousands, while the enormous booty in prisoners, arms and material was being collected by the astonished Russian soldiery, and before the German troops could be drawn from the north and the west to re-establish the shattered front—then was the hour for

Roumanian intervention. A general mobilization of the Roumanian Army, if ordered about June 10, would have enabled considerable Roumanian forces to have come into action before the end of that month and while the whole south-eastern front of the Central Powers was in complete disorder. The consequences of this must have been far-reaching and might perhaps have proved decisive.

The habit of bargaining, of waiting upon events, of trying to make hazard sure and wild adventure prudent, had become so deeply engrained in Bratiano's policy that nearly two months were wasted in negotiations. Before they would commit themselves, the Roumanian Government must have everything settled, must be promised the highest rewards and guaranteed a practically complete immunity. Military conventions regulating the contingent movements of Russian troops and of the Salonika armies, and the supply of arms and munitions, not less than the political, financial and territorial issues, were laboriously and meticulously debated by telegraph with the various Allied Cabinets. The British and French Governments—high in their hopes of impending victory on the Somme—were suddenly eager to secure Roumanian aid at almost any price. Russia, for reasons which will presently be understood, appeared less ardent. Yet it was with Russia that all the principal military arrangements had perforce to be settled. In these discussions the rest of June and the whole of July slipped rapidly away.

Meanwhile Falkenhayn was not idle. Everywhere in the east the German troops stood immovable against the Russians, and from all parts of the German lines reinforcements were scraped together and hurried to the scene of Brusiloff's incursion. By the end of June the Russian advance had slackened, and by the middle of July the Austro-German front was again continuous and more or less stabilized. The gravest apprehensions upon the attitude of Roumania were justly entertained in Vienna, Berlin and Sofia. And during June and July Austrian and Bulgarian forces were steadily and to the fullest extent possible brought into precautionary positions near the Roumanian frontiers.

It was not until August 27 that Roumania declared war on Austria-Hungary, ordered general mobilization and prepared to launch her armies into Transylvania. She had exacted the following military stipulations from the Allies: first, energetic action by the Russians against the Austrians, particularly in the Bukovina; secondly, two Russian divisions and a cavalry division to be sent on the first day of mobilization into the Dobruja; and thirdly, an offensive by the Allies from Salonika simultaneously with the Roumanian entry into the war.

Not all these measures and their political counterparts put together were worth the month or six weeks of precious time that had been lost in their discussion. Prudence had become imprudence, and safety had been jeopardized by care and forethought. The Teutonic Powers had escaped from the ruin with which the Brusiloff disaster had menaced them before they were called upon to bear the assault of a new antagonist. And this assault was no longer unexpected, but foreseen and, so far as their resources allowed, prepared against. Nevertheless the apparition in the field of Roumania with twenty-three organized divisions and with over 1,500,000 men capable of bearing arms, and the denial of the Roumanian supplies of corn and oil, seemed both to friend and foe to constitute at this moment one of the most terrible blows which Germany and her reeling partner had yet been called upon to encounter.

While the German and Bulgarian storm-clouds are gathering around Roumania, we must examine the situation on the Salonika front, from which Roumania had been led to expect timely and immediate succour.

The presence of the Allied Army based on Salonika was one of the determining factors in the decision of Roumania. Nearly 400,000 men of five nations—French, British and Serbian, an Italian division and a Russian Brigade—were now scattered along and behind the front established at the foot of the Bulgarian mountain wall. Roumania had stipulated that this army should begin a general offensive against the Bulgarians, if possible a fortnight before, and at the worst simultaneously with, her entry into the war. Both the British and French Governments had agreed to this. Accordingly on Joffre had fallen the duty of ordering General Sarrail who commanded the Allied Army to set his forces in motion not later than August 10. "At the moment which is judged opportune the Army of the Orient will attack, with all forces united, the Allied enemy along the Greek frontier, and in case of success will pursue them in the general direction of Sofia." This ambitious command did not correspond with the realities. The British Commander-in-Chief, General Milne, reported that an offensive against the Bulgarians would not succeed. He thought that determined troops could hold the Bulgarian position for ever. The extent of the front, the lack of adequate forces, the difficulties of co-operation between three nationalities, the doubtful quality of the Serbians on the exposed left flank, and the inadequate heavy artillery were among the adverse points on which he dwelt. Sir William Robertson recorded his opinion that the Bulgarians were fine fighters in their own country, that the Serbians had not recovered from their disaster, and that not a single British officer was in favour of the enterprise. The British Government had no confidence in General Sarrail, and friction was continuous between him and his British colleagues.

These pessimistic views were not entirely justified by the subsequent facts. The Serbians, after reorganization, training and feeding, showed themselves when the time came implacable troops. But it is remarkable that the British Cabinet, in the face of the reports submitted to them, should nevertheless have joined with the French in encouraging Roumania to count upon an effective

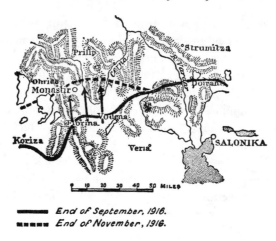

▬▬▬▬ *End of September, 1916.*
■■■■■ *End of November, 1916.*

offensive by the Salonika Army. There was indeed no means by which the Allied forces in the Balkans could prevent Bulgaria from throwing her main strength against Roumania. In the upshot it was arranged that General Milne with the British should guard Sarrail's right flank in an active defensive, while Sarrail himself was forced to reduce the general offensive ordered by Joffre to demonstrations and an enveloping attack by the Serbians. Even so he had to feed eight divisions along a single line of railway. On the whole front he could muster no more than 14 divisions against 23 Bulgarian and German divisions fortified on strong mountain lines. The date even of these limited operations was retarded until the end of September. Meanwhile the German-Bulgarians struck first, and though repulsed elsewhere reached the sea and captured a Greek Division at Kavala on September 18. In the circumstances it was remarkable that Sarrail should have succeeded to the extent of taking Monastir. On the actual front of attack the forces were almost equal; each mustered 190,000 men and 800 or 900 guns. But the achievement in no way influenced the struggle in which the fate of Roumania was decided. Had all the faults of temperament and character which are charged against General Sarrail been replaced by equally undisputed virtues, no better result could have been obtained.

The perilous position of Roumania became apparent from the moment of her declaration of war. The main portion of the Kingdom consisted of a tongue of land about three hundred miles long and a hundred wide between the wall of the Transylvanian Alps on the north and the broad Danube on the south. About the centre of this tongue lay the capital, Bucharest. Beyond the mountains gathered the Austrians and the Germans; behind the Danube the Bulgarians crouched. Four months sufficed to crack Roumania like a nut between these pincers.

A word may be said about each of the Roumanian frontiers. The Danube, which here flows for a great part of its course through a deep trough in the plain and is in many places nearly a mile wide, appeared a trusty barrier. The principal passages at Sistova, Turturkai and Silistria were guarded by fortresses reckoned formidable before the advent of the heavy howitzer. As the Danube descends to its mouth, it encloses between its waters and the Black Sea the province of the Dobruja which Roumania had at the end of the second Balkan war seized without fighting from prostrate Bulgaria. An advance into the Dobruja, left hand on the Danube, right hand on the seashore, stirred every Bulgarian ambition and cut at the very root of the Roumanian tongue.

The mountain range to the north was a more effective defence than the line of the Danube. The Transylvanian Alps rise to a height of six or seven thousand feet by three tiers of forest, of grassy upland and finally of rocky but rounded summits. This rampart is pierced from north to south by four major passes—sudden clefts two or three thousand feet deep and many miles in length, traversed by inferior roads of which the most westerly is the one which follows the Vulkan pass. The Transylvanian Alps turn at their eastern extremity through more than a right angle into the Carpathians, between which and the Russian frontier on the river Pruth lies Moldavia, the northern province of Roumania. Such was the theatre of the new war.

Roumania mobilized on August 27 twenty-three divisions, of which ten were well trained, five less well trained, and the remainder reserve formations aggregating over 500,000 men. The Roumanian Army was however weak in artillery and ill supplied with ammunition. Her principal arsenal had exploded mysteriously a few days before her entry into the war. She was ill equipped with field telephones, and possessed very few aeroplanes, no trench mortars and no poison gas. Her Statesmen seem at first to have cherished the hope—fantastic in view of the past—that Bulgaria would not declare war upon her. When this hope was dispelled on September 1, Roumania continued to trust to the intervention of General Sarrail to hold the Bulgarian strength on the Salonika front. She also hoped that the Germans would be too hard pressed to spare any substantial forces, and she relied upon definite promises of strong and prompt Russian aid. The Roumanian forces were divided into four armies, of which the Third guarded the Danube and the Dobruja, the First and Second held the passes through the Transylvanian Alps, and the Fourth, hoping later for co-operation from the Second, invaded Transylvania through the Carpathians. A central Reserve of 50,000 men guarded Bucharest.

At the outset there were in Transylvania only five tired Austrian divisions, but in the early part of September four German divisions were already approaching. Of these troops Falkenhayn was himself placed in command on September 6. Beyond the Danube and towards the Dobruja three Bulgarian divisions and a cavalry division and part of a German division from the Salonika front were assembled under the redoubtable Mackensen.

Although the Roumanians had a large numerical superiority, it was impossible to study the war map without anxiety. Mr. Lloyd George, then Secretary of State for War, explained to me fully the situation; and after we had mutually alarmed each other in a long talk at Walton Heath, he wrote a serious though belated warning to the Prime Minister. Sarrail and the Salonika Army could not be got into motion. There remained only the Russian aid, and here again fortune was perverse. The treaty which the old King of Roumania had made before the war with Austria-Hungary had led Russia to regard Roumania as a potential enemy. In consequence the south Russian railway system withered away towards the Roumanian frontier, and there was actually a gap of twenty miles between the Russian railhead at Reni and the nearest Roumanian line at Galatz. It was therefore impossible for Russia to come with any speed to the succour of her new Ally. Alexeieff and the very able Russian Staff understood the Roumanian problem far better than the impatient western Allies, and their misgivings had been apparent in the lukewarm attitude of Russia towards Roumanian intervention.

Jubilation at the accession of a new Ally was still resounding through the French and British Press when startling news arrived. On September 1 Mackensen invaded the Dobruja. On September 6, with the Bulgarian Army and German howitzers he smashed the Danubian fortress of Turturkai and captured 25,000 Roumanians and 100 guns. Swiftly advancing through the Dobruja, Mackensen had by the end of September come almost abreast of Constanza on the Black Sea, taking the abandoned fortress of Silistria on his way. By the third week in October he had taken Constanza. Leaving half his army to defend the conquered territory by an entrenched line from the Danube to the sea, he brought the remainder, strengthened by a Turkish division and an additional Bulgarian division, across the Danube opposite Bucharest, which he threatened at a distance of barely forty miles. This menace was not without its object. While the Bulgarian invasion of the Dobruja had been proceeding, Falkenhayn was probing the passes of the Transylvanian Alps and seeking incessantly—now here, now there—to force his way through. The First and Second Roumanian armies however maintained a stout resistance, while the Fourth, which had debouched from the Carpathians, continued to drive the Austrians westward. But the disaster at Turturkai, the invasion of the Dobruja, and finally Mackensen's menace to Bucharest, had already absorbed the Roumanian central reserve of 50,000 men. General Averescu, placed in command of the southern front, peremptorily demanded that the Roumanian Fourth Army should be recalled from Transylvania, that the Second and Third Armies should be reduced to the minimum compatible with holding the passes, and that the whole strength of

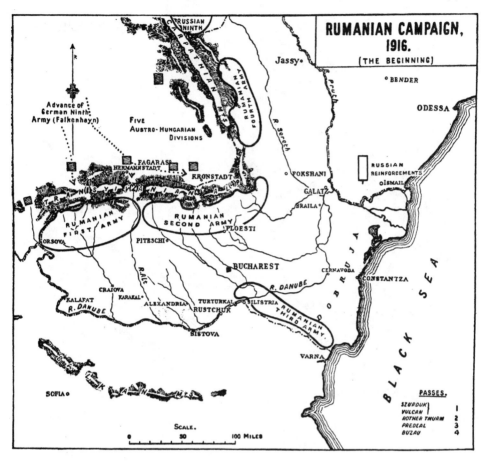

Roumania should be thrown against the Bulgarians. This at any rate was a military plan. It was resisted with equal vehemence by General Présan who commanded in the north. The controversy was acute, and the debate well balanced. In the end, as would be expected, a compromise was reached whereby General Présan continued to invade Transylvania with forces too weak to be effective; and General Averescu obtained enough troops from the armies holding the passes to endanger the defence, but not enough to overcome the Bulgarians.

Roumania had now been at war for two months, and by the beginning of November five additional German divisions and two cavalry divisions had

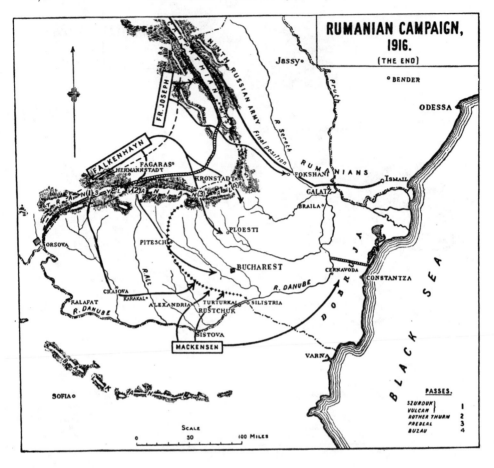

RUMANIAN CAMPAIGN,
1916.
(THE END)

joined Falkenhayn's army. Thus powerfully reinforced, he attacked the Vulkan pass in earnest. By November 26 he had forced his way through and entered the Roumanian plain, descending the valley of the Jiu and incidentally cutting off the Roumanian forces holding the tip of the tongue near Orsova. This movement compromised in succession the defence of the other passes. By the end of November, Falkenhayn had joined hands with Mackensen from across the Danube; and on December 6, after a well-contested three-days' battle between Falkenhayn's and Mackensen's armies, together amounting to fifteen divisions, and what was left of the Roumanian forces, he entered Bucharest in triumph. The Roumanians, defending themselves stubbornly, retreated eastward towards the considerable Russian Army which had now at last arrived. Notwithstanding torrential rains and winter conditions, Falkenhayn and Mackensen followed apace. The roads ceased to exist. The troops were short of food and every necessity. Ludendorff, according to Falkenhayn, sent "floods of telegrams, as superfluous as they were unpleasant," [1] but neither winter clothing nor supplies. Still the Germans persevered, and after a series of stern battles mainly against Russian forces, reached the Sereth River on January 7. Here their advance ended. The tongue of Roumania had been torn out by its roots. There remained of that unhappy Kingdom only the northern province. In this narrow region around the town of Jassy what remained of the armies which four months before had entered the war so full of hope endured for many months privation and even famine, from which not only thousands of soldiers but far larger numbers of refugees perished lamentably. Thus did Roumania share in the end the hideous miseries of all the Balkan peoples.

How unteachable, how blinded by their passions are the races of men! The Great War, bringing tribulation to so many, offered to the Christian peoples of the Balkans their supreme opportunity. Others had to toil and dare and suffer. They had only to forgive and to unite. By a single spontaneous realization of their common interests the Confederation of the Balkans would have become one of the great Powers of Europe, with Constantinople, under some international instrument, as its combined capital. A concerted armed neutrality followed by decisive intervention at the chosen moment against their common enemies, Turkey and Austria, could easily have given each individual State the major part of its legitimate ambitions, and would have given to all safety, prosperity and power. They chose instead to drink in company the corrosive cup of internecine vengeance. And the cup is not yet drained.

It is now necessary to return to those domains of British politics which we quitted after the formation of the Coalition Government at the end of May, 1915. It was then observed that the new Cabinet, although composed of a large number of eminent and upright men, was a cumbrous and unsatisfactory instrument for the waging of a great war. From the outset certain remarkable cleavages and personal currents were apparent. These cleavages and currents did not follow regular Party lines, but responded rather to the shades of temperament and opinion found in every Party. There was the old Liberal school gathered round the Prime Minister, which was reluctant to proceed to drastic domestic measures for the conduct of the war. They were not without their affinities among

---

[1] *Der Feldzug der 9 Armee*, 1916–17, Part II, pp. 93–100.

the Conservatives. This school was deeply impressed with the financial difficulties arising out of the enormous payments we were forced to make to the United States to equip ourselves and our Allies on the greatest scale. They were averse from proceeding to extremes in the industrial sphere in order to procure the greatest output in munitions. Above all they were opposed to the principle of compulsory service to maintain the armies in the field. It was upon this issue that the main division of opinion and feeling crystallized.

Up till the middle of 1915 the eager crowds of the volunteers had far exceeded our capacity to equip and organize them. Over three million men had already come forward freely. They represented all that was best and strongest in the patriotism of the British nation. But by the summer of 1915 the outflow was already greater than the intake. It was plain that British armies of 70 divisions and still less of 100 divisions could not be maintained in the field during 1916 without entirely new measures. The strict Liberal school, headed by the Prime Minister, favoured further efforts at voluntary recruiting. Most of the Conservative Ministers, supported by Mr. Lloyd George—and until I retired from the Government, by myself—were convinced that immediate compulsion was unavoidable. Lord Kitchener, however, rightly proud of the wonderful response which had assisted his successive appeals for volunteers, leaned to the side of Mr. Asquith and turned the balance against the adoption of compulsory service at this time. But the war ploughed mercilessly on and early in January, 1916, under the imperious force of events, the Cabinet crisis upon conscription renewed itself with violent intensity. And now the grim necessity of facts was reinforced by a movement of a moral character exciting the passions of enormous masses of people. Three and a half million men had volunteered. They were not enough. Were they in virtue of their voluntary engagement to be sent back to the front no matter how often they were wounded? Were elderly, weakly, shattered volunteers to be pressed into the conflict while hundreds of thousands of sturdy youths lived as far as possible their ordinary life? Were the citizens of the Territorial Force or soldiers of the Regular Army whose engagements had expired to be compelled to continue, while others who had made no sacrifice were not even to be compelled to begin? From three and a half million families whose beloved breadwinner, whose hero, was giving all freely to the country's cause—families representing the strongest elements on which the life of the nation depended—arose the demand that victory should not be delayed and slaughter prolonged because others refused to do their duty. At last, at the end of January, Lord Kitchener changed sides and Mr. Asquith gave way. In the end only one Minister, Sir John Simon, resigned from the administration. A Conscription Bill was presented to Parliament and swiftly passed by overwhelming majorities.

The new Act was however, as might be expected from the internal struggle which had produced it, an unsatisfying compromise. It neither secured the numbers of men that would be needed, nor did it meet the now fierce demand for equalization of sacrifice. In April a new crisis upon the extension of compulsion developed in the Cabinet. The previous struggle had left its marks on both sides, and differences of temperament of a profound character had been revealed between colleagues to all of whom the national cause was equally dear. This time it seemed certain that Mr. Lloyd George would resign and the Cabinet be broken up, and plans were elaborated to form a strong Opposition pledged to the enforcement of extreme war measures.

It was suggested that the Leaders of such an opposition in the House of Commons should be Mr. Lloyd George and Sir Edward Carson, and I was urged from many quarters to take my place at their side. The Scottish battalion I had been commanding for some months in Flanders having been disbanded through the lack of men, I was accorded leave to return to the Parliamentary sphere. In May Parliament appointed by Statute two Committees of Inquiry into the operations in Mesopotamia and at the Dardanelles, and I found myself immediately involved for nearly a year in a continued and harassing defence of my own responsibilities as set forth in this account. It is from the standpoint of a private member not without information upon secret matters that I record the events of the next twelve months.

The conscription crisis in April, 1916, was however averted by further concessions on the part of Mr. Asquith. A new National Service Bill was passed, and Mr. Lloyd George remained in the Government. During the summer and autumn the Coalition Government hung uneasily together racked by many stresses and strains. The reproaches which sprang from the ruin of Roumania and the downfall of all the hopes of 1916 renewed the struggle between the two sections of the Cabinet. The resignation of Mr. Lloyd George led immediately to the fall of the Government. The kaleidoscopic groupings and re-groupings of the Ministerial personages which accompanied this event, will some day form a profoundly instructive chapter in British constitutional history.

On December 5 Mr. Asquith tendered to the King his resignation and that of his Ministry. Mr. Bonar Law, summoned by the Sovereign, advised that Mr. Lloyd George was the only possible successor. Every effort to induce Mr. Asquith to associate himself with the new Administration was made without success. Followed by all his Liberal colleagues, with the exception of Mr. Lloyd George, he retired into patriotic opposition, and the new Triumvirate of Mr. Lloyd George, Mr. Bonar Law and Sir Edward Carson assumed, with what were in practice dictatorial powers, the direction of affairs. These decisions were not challenged by Parliament, were accepted by the nation, and were acclaimed by the Press.

The new Prime Minister wished to include me in his Government; but this idea was received with extreme disfavour by important personages whose influence during this crisis was decisive. Lord Northcliffe was animated at this time by a violent hostility to me. He made haste to announce in *The Times* and the *Daily Mail* that it had been firmly resolved to exclude from office those who had been responsible for the failures of the war, and that the public would "learn with relief and satisfaction that Mr. Churchill would not be offered any post in the new Administration." He also endeavoured—though happily without success—to veto the appointment of Mr. Balfour as Foreign Secretary. Four prominent Conservatives, judged indispensable to the new combination, signed or made a statement stipulating as a condition of taking office that neither I nor Lord Northcliffe should be Ministers. To this extent therefore—though perhaps in a manner scarcely complimentary to himself—Lord Northcliffe received a powerful reinforcement in his view. It could certainly be adduced with validity that my conduct while First Lord was *sub judice* until the Dardanelles Commission had presented its report. Mr. Lloyd George was in no position in these circumstances to resist this oddly combined but formidable cabal. He therefore sent me a message a few days later, through a common friend, Lord Riddell, that he was determined to achieve his purpose, but that the adverse forces were too strong for the moment. I replied through the same channel with a verbal declaration of political independence.

Nevertheless my relations with the new Prime Minister especially after a speech which I made in the Secret Session in May were such that although holding no office I became to a large extent his colleague. He repeatedly discussed with me every aspect of the war and many of his secret hopes and fears. He assured me of his determination to have me at his side. It was from this somewhat anomalous position that I watched for the next six months the crisis of the submarine war and the disastrous offensive in France to be described in Chapter XLVI.

Mr. Lloyd George possessed two characteristics which were in harmony with this period of convulsion. First, a power of living in the present, without taking short views. Every day for him was filled with the hope and the impulse of a fresh beginning. He surveyed the problems of each morning with an eye unobstructed by preconceived opinions, past utterances, or previous disappointments and defeats. In times of peace such a mood is not always admirable, nor often successful for long. But in the intense crisis when the world was a kaleidoscope, when every month all the values and relations were changed by some prodigious event and its measureless reactions, this inexhaustible mental agility, guided by the main purpose of Victory, was a rare advantage. His intuition fitted the crisis better than the logical reasoning of more rigid minds.

The quality of living in the present and starting afresh each day led directly to a second and invaluable aptitude. Mr. Lloyd George in this period seemed to have a peculiar power of drawing from misfortune itself the means of future success. From the U-boat depredations he obtained the convoy system: out of the disaster of Caporetto he extracted the Supreme War Council: from the catastrophe of the 21st of March he drew the Unified Command and the immense American reinforcement.

His ascendancy in the high circles of British Government and in the councils of the Allies grew in the teeth of calamities. He did not sit waiting upon events to give a wiseacre judgment. He grappled with the giant events and strove to compel them, undismayed by mistakes and their consequences. Tradition and convention troubled him little. He never sought to erect some military or naval figure into a fetish behind whose reputation he could take refuge. The military and naval hierarchies were roughly handled and forced to adjust themselves to the imperious need. Men of vigour and capacity from outside the Parliamentary sphere became the ministerial heads of great departments. He neglected nothing that he perceived. All parts of the task of Government claimed his attention and interest. He lived solely for his work and was never oppressed by it. He gave every decision when it was required. He scarcely ever seemed to bend under the burden. To his native adroitness in managing men and committees he now added a high sense of proportion in war policy and a power of delving to the root of unfamiliar things. Under his Administration both the Island and the Empire were effectually organized for war. He formed the Imperial War Cabinet which centred in a single executive the world-spread resources of the British Monarchy. The convoy system, which broke the U-boat attack at sea; the forward impulsion in Palestine, which overwhelmed the Turks, and the unified command which inaugurated the victories in France, belonged in their main stress and resolve as acts of policy to no one so much as to the First Minister of the Crown.

CHAPTER XLV

THE INTERVENTION OF THE UNITED STATES

Whereas the Imperial German Government have committed repeated acts of war against the Government and the people of the United States of America: Therefore be it resolved by the Senate and the House of Representatives of the United States of America in Congress assembled: That a state of war between the United States and the Imperial German Government which has been thrust upon the United States is hereby formally declared; and that the President be, and he is hereby authorized and directed to employ the entire naval and military forces of the United States and the resources of the Government to carry on war against the Imperial German Government; and to bring the conflict to a successful termination all the resources of the country are hereby pledged by the Congress of the United States.

[Congressional Resolution of April 6, 1917.]

The beginning of 1917 was marked by three stupendous events: the German declaration of unlimited U-boat war, the intervention of the United States, and the Russian revolution. Taken together these events constitute the second great climax of the war. The order in which they were placed was decisive. If the Russian revolution had occurred in January instead of in March, or if, alternatively, the Germans had waited to declare unlimited U-boat war until the summer, there would have been no unlimited U-boat war and consequently no intervention of the United States. If the Allies had been left to face the collapse of Russia without being sustained by the intervention of the United States, it seems certain that France could not have survived the year, and the war would have ended in a Peace by negotiation or, in other words, a German victory. Had Russia lasted two months less, had Germany refrained for two months more, the whole course of events would have been revolutionized. In this sequence we discern the footprints of Destiny. Either Russian endurance or German impatience was required to secure the entry of the United States, and both were forthcoming.

The total defeat of Germany was due to three cardinal mistakes: the decision to march through Belgium regardless of bringing Britain into the war; the decision to begin the unrestricted U-boat war regardless of bringing the United States into the war; and thirdly, the decision to use the German forces liberated from Russia in 1918 for a final onslaught in France. But for the first mistake they would have beaten France and Russia easily in a year; but for the second mistake they would have been able to make a satisfactory peace in 1917; but for the third mistake they would have been able to confront the Allies with an unbreakable front on the Meuse or on the Rhine, and to have made self-respecting terms as a price for abridging the slaughter. All these three errors were committed by the same forces, and by the very forces that made the military strength of the German Empire. The German General Staff, which sustained the German cause with such wonderful power, was responsible for all these three fatal decisions. Thus nations as well as individuals come to ruin through the over-exercise of those very qualities and faculties on which their dominion has been founded.

However long the controversy may last, there will never be any agreement between the belligerent nations on the rights or wrongs of U-boat warfare. The Germans never understood, and never will understand, the horror and indignation with which their opponents and the neutral world regarded their attack. They believed sincerely that the outcry was only hypocrisy and propaganda. The law and custom of the sea were very old. They had grown up in the course of centuries, and although frequently broken in the instance, had in the main stood the stress of many bitter conflicts between nations. To seize even an enemy merchant ship at sea was an act which imposed strict obligations on the captor. To make a neutral ship a prize of war stirred whole histories of international law. But between taking a ship and sinking a ship was a gulf. The captor of a neutral ship at sea had by long tradition been bound to bring his prize into harbour and judge her before the Prize Courts. To sink her incontinently was odious; to sink her without providing for the safety of the crew, to leave that crew to perish in open boats or drown amid the waves was in the eyes of all seafaring peoples a grisly act, which hitherto had never been practised deliberately except by pirates. Thus old seagoing nations, particularly Britain, France, Holland, Norway and the United States, saw in the U-boat war against merchant ships, and particularly neutral merchant ships, depth beyond depth of enormity. And indeed the spectacle of helpless merchant seamen, their barque shattered and foundering, left with hard intention by fellow-mariners to perish in the cruel sea, was hideous.

But the Germans were new-comers on salt water. They cared little for all these ancient traditions of seafaring folk. Death for them was the same in whatever form it came to men. It ended in a more or less painful manner their mortal span. Why was it more horrible to be choked with salt water than with poison gas, or to starve in an open boat than to rot wounded but alive in No

Man's Land? The British blockade treated the whole of Germany as if it were a beleaguered fortress, and avowedly sought to starve the whole population— men, women and children, old and young, wounded and sound—into submission. Suppose the issues had arisen on land instead of at sea; suppose large numbers of Americans and neutrals had carried food or shell into the zone of the armies under the fire of the German artillery; suppose their convoys were known to be traversing certain roads towards the front: who would have hesitated for a moment to overwhelm them with drum-fire and blast them from the face of the earth? Who ever hesitated to fire on towns and villages because helpless and inoffensive non-combatants were gathered there? If they came within reach of the guns, they had to take their chance, and why should not this apply to the torpedoes too? Why should it be legitimate to slay a neutral or a non-combatant on land by cannon if he got in the way, and a hideous atrocity to slay the same neutral or non-combatant by torpedo on the seas? Where was the sense in drawing distinctions between the two processes? Policy might spread its web of calculation, but in logic the path was clear. Yes, we will if necessary kill everyone of every condition who comes within our power and hinders us from winning the war, and we draw no distinction between land and sea. Thus the German Naval Staff. But the neutrals took a different view.

The original driving power behind the U-boat attack on merchant ships was the rasping and energetic personality of Admiral von Tirpitz. We have already seen the fate of his first efforts. On February 4, 1915, he had proclaimed that from February 18 onward "every Allied merchant vessel found within the waters surrounding the British Isles would be destroyed without its being always possible to avoid dangers to the crews and passengers," and that neutral ships would also be exposed to danger in the war zone. At that time Tirpitz had at his disposal no more than twenty to twenty-five suitable submarines, of which only one-third, say seven or eight, could be on duty at a time. Having regard to the enormous traffic and numerous harbours of the British Isles as well as to our defensive measures, we considered it certain that the effects of this attack would be comparatively unimportant to the volume of our trade. I therefore announced immediately that we would publish every week the sinkings of merchant vessels effected by the German submarines, together with the number of ships entering and leaving British ports. The result fully justified our confidence, and by May, 1915, Tirpitz's failure to impede sea traffic with such puny resources was apparent to all.

The anger of neutrals and the menacing attitude of the United States which the new form of sea warfare aroused, coupled with its feeble results in practice, convinced German Emperor, Chancellor and Foreign Office after the sinking of the *Lusitania* and *Arabic* that Tirpitz was wrong and must be restrained. The operations of the U-boats were accordingly restricted by successive orders and hampered by vacillations of policy, and by the autumn of 1915 they died away altogether. The premature exposure with inadequate forces of this method of warfare was of immense service to Great Britain. Counter-measures of every kind and on the largest scale were from the beginning of 1915 set on foot by the Admiralty under my direction. Armed small craft were multiplied to an enormous extent, both by building and conversion, the arming of merchantmen was pressed forward, the manœuvres of decoy ships—the "Q-boats," of which more hereafter—were perfected, and every scientific device, offensive and defensive against the submarines was made the object of ceaseless experiment and production. The first U-boat attack failed grotesquely, but the counter-measures which had been launched were continued at full speed by Mr. Balfour and his Board all through 1915 and 1916. To this perseverance after the danger had apparently passed away, we owe in great measure our ultimate salvation.

In the spring of 1916 Tirpitz renewed his pressure upon the German Chancellor to permit the resumption of the U-boat war. He marshalled all his forces for the assault on Bethmann-Hollweg. General von Falkenhayn was won over. Admiral von Holtzendorf was enthusiastic. Tirpitz himself in his memorandum of February, 1916, wrote:

> Immediate and relentless recourse to the submarine weapon is absolutely necessary. Any further delay in the introduction of unrestricted warfare will give England time for further naval and economic defensive measures and cause us greater losses in the end, and endanger quick success. The sooner the campaign be opened, the sooner will success be realized, and the more rapidly and energetically will England's hope of defeating us by a war of exhaustion be destroyed. If we defeat England, we break the backbone of the hostile coalition.[1]

Tirpitz accosted the Emperor aggressively on February 23, 1916, and demanded a decision. The Emperor, who no doubt realized that pressure was being brought to bear upon him and his Chancellor from many quarters, summoned a meeting on March 6, from which he deliberately excluded Tirpitz. As the result of this meeting, at which the Chancellor, Falkenhayn and Holtzendorf were present, it was decided to postpone the opening of unrestricted U-boat war indefinitely. Orders which had been actually issued for beginning it on April 1 were cancelled. Tirpitz immediately requested his dismissal, which was accorded to him on March 17. The conflict was however maintained by the Naval Staff, and by Admiral Scheer.

[1] *My Memoirs:* Von Tirpitz, Vol. II, p. 419.

There were available for a U-boat campaign in the spring of 1916 about fifty suitable vessels as against the twenty to twenty-five of the preceding year. Thus Tirpitz could have maintained less than twenty U-boats in constant action. Having regard to the progress of the British counter-measures, there is no reason to believe that this larger number would have imposed a serious strain upon our oversea supplies. But behind the fifty U-boats in commission no less than one hundred and fifty-seven were building within the German financial year 1916. When these were completed by the beginning of 1917, the issue would for the first time be of a grave character. The attack of twenty-five U-boats in February, 1915, was absurd; the attack by fifty U-boats in February, 1916, would easily have been defeated; but the attack of two hundred U-boats in February, 1917, raised possibilities of a different order. If Tirpitz, exercising almost superhuman foresight and self-control, had made no submarine attack on commerce until at least two hundred U-boats were ready, and had not provoked us to counter-preparations in the meanwhile, no one can say what the result would have been. Happily the remedy increased with the danger. The U-boat menace was taking vast and terrible dimensions, but

> *The young disease which shall destroy at length*
> *Grows with its growth and strengthens with its strength.*

Now however we are coming to the end of 1916, and in the breathing space which winter still affords to warring nations, the German Chiefs haggardly surveyed the deadly scene. In spite of the disasters which had followed Falkenhayn's decision to attack Verdun and to neglect the Eastern Fronts, Germany had survived. She had bled the French at Verdun; she had withstood the British upon the Somme; she had repaired the breach made by Brusiloff; she had even found strength to strike down Roumania, and had emerged from the year's welter with this trophy of victory. But the sense of frightful peril, of increasing pressure, of dwindling resources, of hard pressed fronts, of blockade-pinched populations, of red sand running out in the time-glass, lay heavily upon the leaders of Germany. In the West the Allies were preparing still more formidable blows for the spring; Russian resistance was unweakened; it was even reviving on a scale almost incredible. But for the first time two hundred U-boats were at hand. Would it be possible with these to starve Britain and so, even if war with the United States resulted, "break the backbone" of the Allies?

Had we been able, [writes Tirpitz] to foresee in Germany the Russian revolution, we should perhaps not have needed to regard the submarine campaign of 1917 as a last resource. But in January, 1917, there was no visible sign of the revolution.[1]

During November and December the German Chancellor and the Military and Naval leaders racked the Emperor with their contentions: Whether 200 U-boats in the hand were worth 120,000,000 Americans across the Atlantic: whether Britannia rules not only the waves but the waters underneath them too. Dire issue, exceeding in intensity the turning points in the struggles of Rome and Carthage!

There is no doubt that the responsibility for the decision rests upon Hindenburg and Ludendorff. Tirpitz was gone. He even argues that the moment for ruthless U-boat war had already passed, and records a somewhat hesitating comment of "Too late." But Main Headquarters had long been converted to the need of using the U-boat weapon at all costs to the full. In Ludendorff they had found a Chief who shrank from nothing, and upon whose mind supreme hazards exercised an evident fascination. The old Field-Marshal shared or adopted his resolve. He threw his whole weight against the Chancellor. The Admirals chimed in with promises of swift decisive success. The Civil Powers felt the balance turning against them. Their peace overtures had been unceremoniously rejected by the Allies. The stern interchange of telegrams between Hindenburg and Bethmann-Hollweg in the last week of the year marked the end of the Chancellor's resistance. His capitulation followed on January 9. It would have been better before history to have gone down with flag flying. No one can doubt what his convictions were, and we now know that they were right. Events forthwith began their new course.

Surely to no nation has Fate been more malignant than to Russia. Her ship went down in sight of port. She had actually weathered the storm when all was cast away. Every sacrifice had been made; the toil was achieved. Despair and Treachery usurped command at the very moment when the task was done.

The long retreats were ended; the munition famine was broken; arms were pouring in; stronger, larger, better equipped armies guarded the immense front; the depôts overflowed with sturdy men. Alexeieff directed the Army and Koltchak the Fleet. Moreover, no difficult action was now required: to remain in presence: to lean with heavy weight upon the far-stretched Teutonic line: to hold without exceptional activity the weakened hostile forces on her front: in a word to endure—that was all that stood between Russia and the fruits of general victory. Says Ludendorff, surveying the scene at the close of 1916:

[1] *My Memoirs:* Von Tirpitz, Vol. II, p. 442.

Russia, in particular, produced very strong new formations, divisions were reduced to twelve battalions, the batteries to six guns; new divisions were formed out of the surplus fourth battalions and the seventh and eighth guns of each battery. This reorganization made a great increase of strength.[1]

It meant in fact that the Russian Empire marshalled for the campaign of 1917 a far larger and better equipped army than that with which she had started the war. In March the Czar was on his throne; the Russian Empire and people stood, the front was safe, and victory certain.

It is the shallow fashion of these times to dismiss the Czarist régime as a purblind, corrupt, incompetent tyranny. But a survey of its thirty months' war with Germany and Austria should correct these loose impressions and expose the dominant facts. We may measure the strength of the Russian Empire by the battering it had endured, by the disasters it had survived, by the inexhaustible forces it had developed, and by the recovery it had made. In the Governments of States, when great events are afoot, the leader of the nation, whoever he be, is held accountable for failure and vindicated by success. No matter who wrought the toil, who planned the struggle, to the supreme responsible authority belongs the blame or credit for the result.

Why should this stern test be denied to Nicholas II? He had made many mistakes, what ruler had not? He was neither a great captain nor a great prince. He was only a true, simple man of average ability, of merciful disposition, upheld in all his daily life by his faith in God. But the brunt of supreme decisions centred upon him. At the summit where all problems are reduced to Yea or Nay, where events transcend the faculties of men and where all is inscrutable, he had to give the answers. His was the function of the compass-needle. War or no war? Advance or retreat? Right or left? Democratize or hold firm? Quit or persevere? These were the battlefields of Nicholas II. Why should he reap no honour from them? The devoted onset of the Russian armies which saved Paris in 1914; the mastered agony of the munitionless retreat; the slowly regathered forces; the victories of Brusiloff; the Russian entry upon the campaign of 1917, unconquered, stronger than ever; has he no share in these? In spite of errors vast and terrible, the régime he personified, over which he presided, to which his personal character gave the vital spark, had at this moment won the war for Russia.

He is about to be struck down. A dark hand, gloved at first in folly, now intervenes. Exit Czar. Deliver him and all he loved to wounds and death. Belittle his efforts, asperse his conduct, insult his memory; but pause then to

---

[1] Ludendorff, Vol. 1, p. 305.

tell us who else was found capable. Who or what could guide the Russian State? Men gifted and daring; men ambitious and fierce; spirits audacious and commanding—of these there was no lack. But none could answer the few plain questions on which the life and fame of Russia turned. With victory in her grasp she fell upon the earth, devoured alive, like Herod of old, by worms. But not in vain her valiant deeds. The giant mortally stricken had just time, with dying strength, to pass the torch eastward across the ocean to a new Titan long sunk in doubt who now arose and began ponderously to arm. The Russian Empire fell on March 16; on April 6 the United States entered the war.

Of all the grand miscalculations of the German High Command none is more remarkable than their inability to comprehend the meaning of war with the American Union. It is perhaps the crowning example of the unwisdom of basing a war policy upon the computation of material factors alone. The war effort of 120,000,000 educated people, equipped with science, and possessed of the resources of an unattackable Continent, nay, of a New World, could not be measured by the number of drilled soldiers, of trained officers, of forged cannon, of ships of war they happened to have at their disposal. It betokens ignorance of the elemental forces resident in such a community to suppose they could be permanently frustrated by a mechanical instrument called the U-boat. How rash to balance the hostile exertions of the largest, if not the leading, civilized nation in the world against the chance that they would not arrive in time upon the field of battle! How hard to condemn the war-worn, wearied, already outnumbered heroic German people to mortal conflict with this fresh, mighty, and, once aroused, implacable antagonist!

There is no need to exaggerate the material assistance given by the United States to the Allies. All that could be sent was given as fast and as freely as possible, whether in manhood, in ships or in money. But the war ended long before the material power of the United States could be brought to bear as a decisive or even as a principal factor. It ended with over 2,000,000 American soldiers on the soil of France. A campaign in 1919 would have seen very large American armies continually engaged, and these by 1920 might well have amounted to 5,000,000 of men. Compared to potentialities of this kind, what would have been the value of, let us say, the capture of Paris? As for the 200 U-boats, the mechanical hope, there was still the British Navy, which at this period, under the ægis of an overwhelming battle fleet, maintained upwards of 3,000 armed vessels on the seas.

But if the physical power of the United States was not in fact applied in any serious degree to the beating down of Germany; if for instance only a few score thousand Germans fell by American hands; the moral consequence of the United States joining the Allies was indeed the deciding cause in the conflict.

The war had lasted nearly three years; all the original combatants were at extreme tension; on both sides the dangers of the front were matched by other dangers far behind the throbbing lines of contact. Russia has succumbed to these new dangers; Austria is breaking up; Turkey and Bulgaria are wearing thin; Germany herself is forced even in full battle to concede far-reaching Constitutional rights and franchise to her people; France is desperate; Italy is about to pass within an ace of destruction; and even in stolid Britain there is a different light in the eyes of men. Suddenly a nation of one hundred and twenty millions unfurls her standard on what is already the stronger side; suddenly the most numerous democracy in the world, long posing as a judge, is hurled, nay, hurls itself into the conflict. The loss of Russia was forgotten in this new reinforcement. Defeatist movements were strangled on the one side and on the other inflamed. Far and wide through every warring nation spread these two opposite impressions—"The whole world is against us"—"The whole world is on our side."

American historians will perhaps be somewhat lengthy in explaining to posterity exactly why the United States entered the Great War on April 6, 1917, and why they did not enter at any earlier moment. American ships had been sunk before by German submarines; as many American lives were lost in the *Lusitania* as in all the five American ships whose sinking immediately preceded the declaration of war. As for the general cause of the Allies, if it was good in 1917 was it not equally good in 1914? There were plenty of reasons of high policy for staying out in 1917 after waiting so long.

It was natural that the Allies, burning with indignation against Germany, breathless and bleeding in the struggle, face to face with mortal dangers, should stand amazed at the cool, critical, detached attitude of the great Power across the Atlantic. In England particularly, where laws and language seemed to make a bridge of mutual comprehension between the two nations, the American abstention was hard to understand. But this was to do less than justice to important factors in the case. The United States did not feel in any immediate danger. Time and distance interposed their minimizing perspectives. The mass of the people engaged in peaceful industry, grappling with the undeveloped resources of the continent which was their inheritance, absorbed in domestic life and politics, taught by long constitutional tradition to shun foreign entanglements, had an entirely different field of mental interest from that of Europe. World Justice makes its appeal to all men. But what share, it was asked, had Americans taken in bringing about the situation which had raised the issue of World Justice? Was even this issue so simple as it appeared to the Allies? Was it not a frightful responsibility to launch a vast, unarmed, remote community into the raging centre of such a quarrel? That all this was overcome is the real wonder.

All honour to those who never doubted, and who from the first discerned the inevitable path.

The rigid Constitution of the United States, the gigantic scale and strength of its party machinery, the fixed terms for which public officers and representatives are chosen, invest the President with a greater measure of autocratic power than was possessed before the war by the Head of any great State. The vast size of the country, the diverse types, interests and environments of its enormous population, the safety-valve function of the legislatures of fifty Sovereign States, make the focussing of national public opinion difficult, and confer upon the Federal Government exceptional independence of it except at fixed election times. Few modern Governments need to concern themselves so little with the opinion of the party they have beaten at the polls; none secures to its supreme executive officer, at once the Sovereign and the Party Leader, such direct personal authority.

The accident of hereditary succession which brings a King or Emperor to the throne occurs on the average at intervals of a quarter of a century. During this long period, as well as in his whole life before accession, the qualities and disposition of the monarch can be studied by his subjects, and during this period parties and classes are often able to devise and create checks and counter-checks upon personal action. In limited monarchies where the responsibilities of power are borne by the Prime Minister, the choice of the nation usually falls upon Statesmen who have lived their lives in the public eye, who are moreover members of the Legislature and continuously accountable to it for their tenure. But the magnitude and the character of the electoral processes of the United States make it increasingly difficult, if not indeed already impossible, for any life-long politician to become a successful candidate for the Presidency. The choice of the party managers tends more and more to fall upon eminent citizens of high personal character and civic virtue who have not mingled profoundly in politics or administration, and who in consequence are free from the animosities and the errors which such combative and anxious experiences involve. More often than not the champion selected for the enthusiasms and ideals of tens of millions is unversed in State affairs, and raised suddenly to dazzling pre-eminence on the spur of the moment. The war-stained veterans of the party battle select, after many fierce internal convulsions, a blameless and honourable figure to bear aloft the party standard. They manufacture his programme and his policy, and if successful in the battle install him for four years at the summit of the State, clothed thenceforward with direct executive functions which in practical importance are not surpassed on the globe.

Like all brief generalizations upon great matters, the foregoing paragraph is subject to numerous and noteworthy exceptions. But President Wilson was not one of them. In all his strength and in all his weakness, in his nobility and in his foibles, he was, in spite of his long academic record and brief governorship, an unknown, an unmeasured quantity to the mighty people who made him their ruler in 1912. Still more was he a mystery to the world at large. Writing with every sense of respect, it seems no exaggeration to pronounce that the action of the United States with its repercussions on the history of the world depended, during the awful period of Armageddon, upon the workings of this man's mind and spirit to the exclusion of almost every other factor; and that he played a part in the fate of nations incomparably more direct and personal than any other man.

It is in this light that the Memoirs of Colonel House acquire their peculiar interest. In these pages we see a revelation of the President. Dwelling in the bosom of his domestic circle with the simplicity and frugality of Nicholas II, inaccessible except to friends and servitors—and very sparingly to them— towering above Congress, the Cabinet his mere implement, untempered and undinted in the smithy of public life, and guided by that "frequent recurrence to first principles" enjoined in the American Constitution, Woodrow Wilson, the inscrutable and undecided judge upon whose lips the lives of millions hung, stands forth a monument for human meditation.

First and foremost, all through and last, he was a Party man. His dominating loyalty was to the great political association which had raised him to the Presidency, and on whose continued prosperity he was sincerely convinced the best interests of mankind depended. We see him in the height of the American war effort, when all that the Union could give without distinction of class or party was lavished upon the Government of the day, using his natural position without scruple or apparent self-examination to procure the return to Congress of only those representatives whose names were on the Democratic ticket. Under his régime there were none of those temporary sacrifices of party rancour which were forced on European countries by their perils. The whole power and prestige of the American nation at war was politically impounded so far as possible by the office holders of the day and the party machine. This bred a hatred among political opponents whose sons were fighting, whose money was poured out, whose patriotism was ardent, which as soon as the fighting stopped, proved fatal to President Wilson and his hopes. Next he was a good American, an academic Liberal, and a sincere hater of war and violence. Upon these easily harmonized impulses there had fallen in intense interplay such of the stresses of the European war as rolled across the Atlantic, and all the internal pressures of American policy. He was confronted with four separate successive questions which searched his nature to its depths. How to keep the United States out of the war? How to win the Presidential election of 1916? How to help the Allies to win the war? and lastly, How to rule the world at its close?

He would have been greatly helped in his task if he had reached a definite conclusion where in the European struggle Right lay. Events like the German march through Belgium, or the sinking of the *Lusitania,* had a meaning which was apparent to friend and foe. They both proclaimed the intention to use force without any limit of forbearance to an absolute conclusion. Such a prospect directly affected the interests and indeed the safety of the United States. The victory of Germany and the concomitant disappearance of France and the British Empire as great Powers must, after an uncertain interval, have left the peaceful and unarmed population of the United States nakedly exposed to the triumph of the doctrine of Force without limit. The Teutonic Empires in the years following their victory would have been far stronger by land and sea than the United States. They could easily have placed themselves in a more favourable relationship to Japan than was open to the United States. In such a situation their views upon the destinies of South America could not have been effectively resisted. Immense developments of armed force would in any case have been required in the United States, and sooner or later a new conflict must have arisen in which the United States would have found herself alone.

President Wilson did not however during the first two and a half years of the war allow his mind to dwell upon the German use of force without restraint, and still less upon the ultimate consequences of its success. He did not therefore feel that American interests were involved from the outset in the European struggle. He distrusted and repressed those sentiments of indignation which the scenes in Belgium or the sinking of the *Lusitania* aroused in his breast. He did not truly divine the instinct of the American people. He underestimated the volume and undervalued the quality of the American feeling in favour of the Allies. Not until he was actually delivering his famous war message to Congress did he understand where, in the vast medley of American opinion, the dominant will-power of the nation lay and had always lain. Not until then did he move forward with confidence and conviction; not until then did he restate the cause of the Allies in terms unsurpassed by any of their own statesmen; not until then did he reveal to the American people where in his judgment world-right was founded, and how their own lives and material interests were at stake.

The desperate action of the German War-Leaders left him in the end no loophole of escape. On January 31 Germany informed the United States of her intention to begin the unrestricted submarine campaign. On February 3 the German Ambassador at Washington was given his passports, the United States representative at Berlin was recalled, and the severance of diplomatic relations with Germany was announced by the President to Congress. But Mr. Wilson had still another line of defence. He declined to believe that any "overt act" would follow the declaration of the German intention. On February 26 the virtual arrest of United States shipping through fear of German attack forced him to ask Congressional authority to arm American merchant ships. On February 26 an American ship was sunk and eight Americans drowned. Meanwhile the British Intelligence Service had ascertained that Herr Zimmermann, the German Foreign Secretary, had instructed the German Minister in Mexico to make an alliance with Mexico in the event of war between Germany and the United States, and to offer as an inducement to the Mexicans the United States territories of Texas, Arizona and New Mexico. This document, which dealt also with the possibilities of ranging Japan against the United States, was published by the American Government on March 1. During March four American vessels were sunk with the loss of twelve American lives. On April 1 the *Aztec* was sunk and twenty-eight Americans drowned. On the 2nd, President Wilson demanded from Congress a declaration that a state of war existed between the United States and Germany.

Step by step the President had been pursued and brought to bay. By slow merciless degrees, against his dearest hopes, against his gravest doubts, against his deepest inclinations, in stultification of all he had said and done and left undone in thirty months of carnage, he was forced to give the signal he dreaded and abhorred. Throughout he had been beneath the true dominant note of American sentiment. He had behind his policy a reasoned explanation and massive argument, and all must respect the motives of a statesman who seeks to spare his country the waste and horrors of war. But nothing can reconcile what he said after March, 1917, with the guidance he had given before. What he did in April, 1917, could have been done in May, 1915. And if done then what abridgment of the slaughter; what sparing of the agony; what ruin, what catastrophes would have been prevented; in how many million homes would an empty chair be occupied to-day; how different would be the shattered world in which victors and vanquished alike are condemned to live!

But anyhow all was settled now. "A drunken brawl," "Peace without victory," where were these festering phrases on April 2? Amid the clink and clatter of a cavalry escort the President has reached the Senate. He is reading his message to Congress and to mankind. Out roll the famous periods in which the righteousness of the Allied cause was finally proclaimed.

> Vessels of every kind, whatever their flag, their character, their cargo, their destination, their errand, have been ruthlessly sent to the bottom without warning and without thought of help or mercy for those on board, the vessels of friendly neutrals along with those of belligerents. Even hospital ships and ships carrying relief to the sorely bereaved and stricken people of Belgium, though the latter were provided with safe-conduct through the proscribed areas by the German Government itself,

and were distinguished by unmistakable marks of identity, have been
sunk with the same reckless lack of compassion or of principle. . . .
The peace of the world is involved and the freedom of its peoples, and
the menace to that peace and freedom lies in the existence of autocratic
governments backed by organized force which is controlled wholly by
their will, not by the will of their people. . . . The world must be made
safe for Democracy. . . . The right is more precious than peace, and we
shall fight for the things we have always carried nearest our hearts—
for Democracy, for the rights of those who submit to authority to have
a voice in their own governments, for the rights and liberties of small
nations, for a universal dominion of right by such a concert of free
people as shall bring peace and safety to all nations and make the world
itself at last free.

In response to all of this the House of Representatives on April 6 resolved
that a state of war was formally declared, and that "to bring the conflict to a
successful termination all the resources of the country are hereby pledged by the
Congress of the United States."

From the Atlantic to the Pacific the call was answered and obeyed. Iron
laws of compulsory service, reinforced by social pressures of mutual discipline
in which the great majority of the population took part, asserted an instantaneous unity of opinion. No one stood against the torrent. Pacifism, indifference, dissent, were swept from the path and fiercely pursued to extermination;
and with a roar of slowly gathered, pent-up wrath which overpowered in its din
every discordant yell, the American nation sprang to arms.

CHAPTER XLVI

GENERAL NIVELLE'S EXPERIMENT

Meanwhile on the heights of Verdun new figures destined powerfully to sway the course of events began to emerge under the blast of the cannonade. Pétain's most successful commander was a certain General Nivelle, an Artillery officer who by courage and address had won his way from a modest station to the head of an Army Corps. Nivelle's fighting arm was a certain General Mangin, of whom some brief description is required. Mangin belonged to the French Colonial Army, and had made his name in Morocco and Tunis. He had led Marchand's advanced guard to Fashoda in 1898. Engaged at the head of a brigade in the opening days of the war, he had won distinction at Dinant and Charleroi. In the widespread breaking of incompetent leaders which followed the opening defeats of the French Army, Mangin succeeded to the command of a dispirited division from whose control a discredited figure had been removed. "After having at our head," wrote a young Royalist who served as a clerk on the staff of this division, "a walking ruin, we actually possess one of the best generals of the French Army." [1] Mangin was not to belie this reputation. Bronzed and sombre, thick black hair bristling, an aquiline profile with gleaming eyes and teeth; alive and active, furious, luxurious, privileged, acquisitive—a dozen motor cars collected from all quarters, including the enemy, in his train as a simple Colonel of Brigade—reckless of all lives and of none more than his own, charging at the head of his troops, fighting rifle in hand when he could escape from his headquarters, thundering down the telephone implacable orders to his subordinates and when necessary defiance to his superiors, Mangin beaten or triumphant, Mangin the Hero or Mangin the Butcher as he was alternately regarded, became on the anvil of Verdun the fiercest warrior-figure of France.

During the spring Pétain entrusted the direction of the most important operations to Nivelle, and Nivelle confided their execution in the main to Mangin. When in April after three months of battle Pétain was promoted from Verdun to the command of a group of armies, Nivelle, Mangin still in hand, succeeded to the direction of the struggle.

One of the earliest decisions of the Hindenburg-Ludendorff régime had

---

[1] *De Sauret la Honte, à Mangin le Boucher.* Henry Dutheil, p. 88.

been to arrest the Verdun offensive; and from the end of August, to the intense relief of the Crown Prince, the German armies before the fortress adopted a purely defensive attitude. The decision, wise in the disastrous circumstances, presented nevertheless a fine opportunity to the French. The long months of battle had left the German line wedge-shaped. The fort of Douaumont, in actual contact at the very tip, was at once the greatest and the nearest trophy for France. Nothing would set the seal of defeat upon the German effort at Verdun more dramatically than the recapture of Douaumont, famous all over the world. It was on this that Nivelle and Mangin set their hearts.

The preparations were long and thorough. 530 heavy pieces, including a new 16-inch Creusot battery, in addition to the ordinary artillery of the Verdun army, were concentrated upon the German salient—or a gun to every fifteen yards of the front to be attacked. The three divisions which were to make the assault were brought to the highest point of strength and efficiency and trained for more than a month behind the line in the exact parts each was to play. The bombardment began in the middle of October, and fell with fury on all the German defences and organizations. The chief target was the German artillery. By the 20th nearly a third of the German batteries had been put out of action. On the 22nd, at 2 p.m., the French fire on the German front lines was suddenly lifted and the range lengthened. The stratagem was successful. Here then was the moment of assault. 158 German batteries, hitherto concealed, opened fire; betraying alike their own position and their system of defensive barrages. Of these 158 batteries only 90 remained in action when the true moment arrived.

Three fine days preceded the 24th of October, but on the day itself a dense fog overspread the ground. There was a moment of discussion at the French Headquarters whether the attack should be postponed. But Mangin rightly judged that the fog hampered the defence at least as much as the attack. His view prevailed. The French trench mortars, secretly massed on an unprecedented scale—a new feature—opened a terrific fire on the German front line crouching in the shell-holes to which their trenches were reduced; and after two hours the French infantry, in the cold passion of calculation and devotion, marched upon their ancient foe. In two hours more all was over. The German wedge was bitten off, the tricolour flew again upon Fort Douaumont, and 6,000 German prisoners were in Mangin's cages. The "corner-stone" of Verdun, as the Germans had precipitately called it, had been regained; and the name of Verdun was registered in history as one of the greatest misfortunes of the German arms.

In this brilliant local victory there lay, as will soon be seen, the seeds of a memorable disappointment.

•   •   •

General Joffre's plan for the campaign of 1917 was simple. It was to be a continuation of the Battle of the Somme, with only the shortest possible interlude during the extreme severity of the winter. The salient formed by the German line was to be crunched by convergent assaults of the British and the French. No time was to be lost in regrouping the armies; no delay was to be allowed for the arrival even of friendly reinforcements, or for the completion of the new artillery and munitions programmes of the Allies. February 1 was fixed for the opening of the new battle. All the British forces available for the offensive and the northern group of the French armies were to attack due east, the British from Vimy to Bapaume, the French between the Somme and the Oise; simultaneously another French Army of the centre group was to strike northward from the direction of Rheims. Then, after all these armies had been in full battle for a fortnight and the Germans if not broken were thoroughly gripped, the Fifth French Army, supported by the Reserve group to which it belonged, was to strike in to decide the struggle or exploit the victory. Taken in an enormous purse, or as between gigantic pincers, the German armies, if their front gave way on any considerable scale, were to see themselves confronted first with the capture of very large numbers of men and enormous masses of material, and secondly with a rupture of the front so wide as to be irreparable.

Such were the proposals which the French Generalissimo laid before the Allied Statesmen and Commanders at a Conference at Chantilly on November 16, 1916, and which he expounded with precision in his Instruction of November 27. "I have decided to seek the rupture of the enemy's forces by a general offensive executed between the Somme and the Oise at the same time as the British Armies carry out a similar operation between Bapaume and Vimy. This offensive will be in readiness for the 1st February, 1917, the exact date being fixed in accordance with the general military situation of the Allies."

As will be seen as the account progresses, the launching of these tremendous operations from the beginning and during the whole of February would have caught the Germans at a moment exceedingly unfavourable to them. Here perhaps at last, after so many regrettable misadventures and miscalculations, Joffre might have won unchallenged laurels. But these possibilities remain in the mists of the unknown; for at this very moment Joffre was removed from his command, and the supreme direction passed to another hand.

Although the fame of Verdun and the Somme had been valiantly trumpeted by Press and propaganda to the uttermost ends of the earth, instructed opinion in Paris was under no illusions about either battle. The glory of Verdun belonged to the French soldiers, who under Castelnau, Pétain, Nivelle and Mangin had sustained the honour of France. The neglect and inadequacy of its defences was clearly traceable to the Commander-in-Chief. His astonishing correspondence with Galliéni in December, 1915, had already been read in secret session to the Chamber in July; and although Briand had sustained the Commander-in-Chief, he had clearly intimated that his retention of the command must be reviewed at a more propitious season. To remove him while the Battle of Verdun was at its height, when the offensive he had concerted with the British on the Somme had just begun, and before that battle and the hopes involved in it had reached their conclusion, could not, he had urged, be in accordance with the interests of France. But the Battle of the Somme was now over. Its last engagement had been fought, and, for all the heroism and sacrifice of the soldiers, fought without decisive gains. The German line, sorely pressed, had nevertheless been maintained unbroken. Nay, some of the troops[1] to invade Roumania had actually been drawn from the Western Front. Roumania had been destroyed and the German prestige re-established as the year, so terrible in its slaughters, drew to a crimson close. Now was a time of reckoning.

Every great nation in times of crisis has its own way of doing things. The Germans looked to their Kaiser—the All-Highest—whose word was law—but they also looked after him. In some way or other the changing group of dominating personalities at the head of the German Empire worked the Imperial Oracle. We too in England have our own methods, more difficult to explain to foreigners perhaps than any others—and on the whole more inchoate, more crude, more clumsy. Still—they work. And there is also the French method. Studying French war-politics, one is struck first of all by their extreme complexity. The number of persons involved, the intricacy of their relations, the swiftness and yet the smoothness with which their whole arrangement is continually charged, all baffle the stranger during the event, and weary him afterwards in the tale. The prevailing impression is that of a swarm of bees—all buzzing together, and yet each bee—or nearly every bee—with a perfectly clear idea of what has got to be done in the practical interests of the hive.

Now also for the first time Briand considered himself to have discovered a fitting and suitable successor to Joffre. The three great Chiefs of the French Army, the war horses of the fighting front, Commanders of armies or groups of armies since the beginning of the war—Foch, Castelnau, Pétain—were all for reasons which seemed sufficient at the time ruled out. Of Castelnau it was said by the Socialist left that he was too religious. Of Pétain it was complained that he was not sufficiently gracious to members of the Parliamentary Commissions and other persons of distinction who visited his headquarters. And it was stated that General Sarrail, speaking to Clémenceau in August, 1915, had said of him, "Il n'est pas des notres" (He's not one of us), to which that grand old man had replied, "What do I care for that, if he can win us a victory?" But Clémenceau's day had not yet dawned, and the Sarrail suggestion festered wherever it had

---

[1] The Alpine Corps and the 187th Brigade.

reached. Of Foch a keen propaganda, widespread but untraceable, had said "His health is broken; his temper and his nerves have given way. He is finished." So much for Castelnau, Pétain and Foch.

But now a new figure had appeared. Nivelle had conducted the later battle of Verdun both with vigour and success, and under his orders Mangin had recovered the famous Fort of Douaumont. In the mood of the hour Joffre had already selected Nivelle to replace Foch. Forthwith a stream of celebrities took the road to Verdun and made for the first time the acquaintance of the new Army Commander. They found themselves in the presence of an officer whose modesty, whose personality, whose lucidity of expression, exercised an almost universal charm. A stream of glowing and delighted accounts flowed towards Paris. There can be no doubt of the attraction exercised by General Nivelle over the many experienced men of affairs with whom he came in contact. Briand, his Ministers, the delegations from the Chamber, were as swiftly impressed as Lloyd George and the British War Cabinet a few months later. Add to these pleasing impressions the glamour of unquestioned and newly won military achievement, and the elements of an alternative Commander-in-Chief were not in that weary moment lacking.

On December 27 Joffre was promoted Marshal of France and relieved of his command. A pleasing and pathetic personal light is thrown on the closing scene by Pierrefeu's skilful pen. No one has been a more stern or more instructed critic of General Joffre. His searching studies, made with the fullest knowledge of events and first-hand observation, have been more fatal to the Joffre legend than all the other attacks and exposures which have appeared in France. But Pierrefeu lights his severe pictures with many a deft and human touch. He has described the curious spectacle of Joffre's life at Chantilly during these two tremendous years. "This office without maps"; "this table without papers"; the long hours passed by the Commander-in-Chief in reading and in answering tributes of admiration received from all over the world; his comfortable and placid routine; his air of leisure and serenity; his excellent appetite and regular customs; his long full nights of unbroken repose far from the crash of the cruel cannonade, "cette vie de bon rentier au plus fort de la guerre." He tells us of Joffre's habit when in difficulties with the enemy or with his Government, of patting his massive head with his hand and ejaculating with a droll air, "Pauvre Joffre." He tells us of his little aide-de-camp Captain Thouzelier; so familiar a figure during all this period, flitting to and fro among the bureaus of the Grand Quartier Général, everywhere known as "Tou Tou." And how in moments of good humour and as a special compliment Joffre would address him as "Sacré Thouzelier." It is from such details that an impression is obtained of real historic value. But the picture is now to fade and vanish for ever.

The new Marshal assembled at the Villa Poiret his principal officers to bid them his adieux: the ceremony was sad. All these men were painfully affected at the idea of separation from the illustrious man who had directed them for so long. Each bore in his breast the anxiety for a future which seemed sombre. The Marshal, who by his rank had the right to three orderly officers, asked who among those present wished to accompany him in his retirement. Alone the Commandant Thouzelier lifted spontaneously his hand. As the Marshal seemed astonished, General Gamelin said to him softly, "Don't bear a grudge to those who have their career to make." And certainly Joffre never bore any such grudge. When all the company had gone, the Marshal cast a final glance at the house which had nursed so much glory. Then with a smile and giving a friendly tap to his faithful Thouzelier, passing his hand across his head, he uttered his favourite expression, "Pauvre Joffre—Sacré Thouzelier." [1]

The appointment of General Nivelle was clearly a very questionable proceeding. There are enormous dangers in selecting for the command of the National Army or Fleet some comparatively junior officer, however well supported by subordinate achievement. To supersede not only Joffre, but Foch, Castelnau, Pétain, by a General like Nivelle, who had only commanded a single army for five months, was a step which could only be vindicated by extraordinary results. Happier would it have been for General Nivelle had he been left to make his way step by step in the high circles of command to which his good conduct and substantial qualities had won him admission.

Meanwhile the French Staff in the dusk of Joffre had formed new conceptions on tactics. The principle that "the Artillery conquers the ground and the Infantry occupies it," which had played a comforting, if somewhat barren, part in 1915 and 1916, was to a large extent discarded in favour of greater audacity. The Nivelle-Mangin exploit on October 24 at Verdun had tended to become the model of the French Staff. It was the foundation, not only of General Nivelle's fame, but of his convictions. It comprised the whole of his message. He believed that he and his principal officers had found a sure, swift method of rupturing the German defence. He believed further that his method was capable of application on the largest possible scale. Multiply the scale of such an attack ten or fifteen times, and the resultant advantages would be multiplied in an even greater proportion. Just as Falkenhayn in his scheme of attack on Verdun had always in his mind the victory of Gorlice-Tarnow, so Nivelle a year later founded his hopes and reasoning upon his achievement at Douaumont.

[1] Pierrefeu: "G.Q.G.," Section 1.

No one will undervalue the tactics which gained success on October 24. They were hammered out by fighting Generals amidst the fiercest fires. However, it does not follow in war or in some other spheres that methods which work well on a small scale will work well on a great scale. As military operations become larger, they become more ponderous, and the time factor begins to set up complex reactions. Where days of preparation had sufficed, months may be required. Secrets that can be kept for days are apt to wear out in months. Surprise, the key to victory, becomes harder to secure with every additional man and gun. There were in the Nivelle-Mangin methods and in the spirit which animated them the elements of decisive success. But their authors had not learned to apply them on the gigantic scale with which they were now to be concerned: nor in the year 1917 did they possess the necessary superiority of force in its various forms. It was reserved for Ludendorff, on March 21, 1918, to execute what Nivelle had conceived, to combine audacity of action with a true sense of values, to make long preparations without prematurely losing secrecy, and to effect a strategic surprise on a front of fifty divisions. But this comparison cannot even be suggested without numerous reservations arising from the different circumstances.

Nivelle became Commander-in-Chief on December 12. He arrived at Chantilly on the 16th; and on that same date there issued from the French High Command a Memorandum on the new (Verdun) methods of the offensive which had no doubt been drawn up during the preceding month while Joffre still ruled, to greet the advent of the new Chief. General Nivelle lost no time in developing this theme in his own words. On December 21, in a letter to Sir Douglas Haig and in instructions to his own groups of armies, he wrote:

> The objective which the Franco-British armies should seek, is the destruction of the principal mass of the enemy. This result can only be attained as the consequence of a decisive battle. . . .

On the 24th, in a further Note to his Army Group Commanders, communicated to the British Staff, he affirmed:

> That the rupture of the front (penetration to the rear of the mass of the hostile batteries) is possible on condition it is made at a single stroke by a sudden attack in 24 or 48 hours.

And on January 29 to General Micheler whom he had placed in command of the three armies destined for the main attack, he emphasized "the character of violence, of brutality, and of rapidity which should clothe the offensive, and in particular its first phase, the break-through."

These quotations are typical of a continued flow of instructions and exhortations which General Nivelle, his Verdun Confraternity, and the French Headquarter Staff dutifully toiling behind them, lavished week after week upon their armies and their Allies.

The reader will remember Colonel de Grandmaison, the Director of Operations of the years before the war, the Apostle of the Offensive, immediately, every time—"à outrance, à la baïonnette," etc. War has claimed her Priest. The body of Colonel de Grandmaison lies mouldering in the grave—a grave, let no one fail to declare, guarded by the reputation of a brave gentleman eager to give his life for his country and his theories. He has fallen; but his theme has found a fleeting resting-place in the bosom of Colonel d'Alenson, Chief of the Staff of General Nivelle. Pierrefeu gives a vivid description of this officer who flitted so suddenly, so swiftly and so tragically across the scene. Immensely tall and thin, dark, sallow, cadaverous, silent, sombre, full of suppressed fire—a man absorbed in his convictions and ideas. The astonishing rocket rise of Nivelle had carried d'Alenson as an attendant star to the military zenith. But there is this fact about him which should be noted—he had but one year to live, and consequently but one coup to play. Gripped in the closing stages of consumption, he knew that his time was short. Still, short as it was, there was a deed to do which might win enduring honour. Such a personal situation is not favourable to the practical common sense and judgment peculiarly required in a Chief of Staff.

Fortune had no sooner hoisted General Nivelle to the topmost summit of power than she deserted him. From the moment of his assuming command of the French armies everything went against him. He was from the outset more successful in exciting the enthusiasm of the political than of the military leaders: and he was more successful with the British Government even than with his own. He proceeded immediately to extend the scope of the immense operations which had been contemplated by Joffre. In his general offensive against the German salient Joffre had been careful to avoid the formidable span of thirty kilometres from Soissons to Craonne along the Aisne so well known to the British in 1914. General Nivelle ordered an additional offensive to be mounted against this front, and another farther to the east at Moronvilliers. Joffre had planned to attack at the earliest moment, even if it involved the sacrifice of some degree of preparation. Not only must Nivelle's scale be larger, but his preparations must be more detailed and complete; and for all this he was willing to pay in terms of time. Whereas the French Staff under Joffre had defined his aim as "la recherche de la rupture du dispositif ennemi," Nivelle claimed nothing less than "la destruction de la masse principale des armées ennemies." Whereas Joffre had contemplated a revival of the Somme battle on a still larger scale and under more favourable conditions, with three or four tremendous attacks engaging successively over a period of weeks the front and resources of the Germans, Nivelle proclaimed the doctrine of the sudden general onslaught culminating in victory or defeat within twenty-four, or at the most forty-eight, hours. And whereas Joffre would have struck early in February, Nivelle's extensions involved delay till April. The effect of the Nivelle alterations upon the Joffre plan was to make it larger, more violent, more critical, and much later.

On December 20 Nivelle explained his ideas to Sir Douglas Haig and invited him to recast the previous plans and extend the British Right from Bouchavesnes to the road from Amiens to Roye. These discussions—not to say disputes—between the French and British Headquarters upon the share which each should assume upon the front were continuous throughout the war. All followed the same course; the French dwelt on the number of kilometres they guarded, the British on the number of German divisions by which they were confronted, and each reinforced these potent considerations by reminding their Ally that they were about to deliver or sustain a major offensive. On this occasion, however, Haig was not unwilling to meet the wishes of the French Command. He was in favour of renewing the offensive in France and was ready to fall in with Nivelle's views as to its direction and scope. Moreover when the French wished to assume the brunt of the new attack and asked for assistance for this purpose, it was hardly for the British to refuse. On December 25 therefore Haig wrote to Nivelle, "I agree in principle with your proposals and am desirous of doing all I can to help you on the lines you suggest." He also undertook to extend the British front from February 1 as far as the Amiens-St. Quentin Road. Both Haig and the British Headquarters were however extremely sceptical of the power of the French Army to carry out the part assigned to it in the ambitious programme of General Nivelle. They were further greatly preoccupied by the condition of the Nord railway which, as maintained by the French, was at this time quite inadequate to sustain the important operations expected of the British Army. They therefore pressed for the improvement of their communications and declared themselves unable to fix a date for the British offensive while this extremely practical point remained unsettled.

In the course of these discussions the first hint of the proposed renewal of the offensive and of its changed form was conveyed to the British War Cabinet on December 26. Monsieur Ribot who had come to London stated that the new French Commander had an idea of breaking through on a wide front, keeping in reserve an army of manœuvre to carry on the attack after the line had been broken. For this to be achieved the British Army must add 30 or 40 kilometres to their present line. Mr. Lloyd George was at first adverse to the renewal of the offensive in France and especially to the renewal of a long offensive like the Somme. In all our talks before he had become Prime Minister I had found him in sympathy with my general views on this subject. His first effort on obtaining power was to find some alternative. At the Rome Conference which he attended at the beginning of January he developed the proposal for a heavy attack on the Austrian front, mainly by Italian troops supported by an enormous concentration of Anglo-French batteries. The French, under the Nivelle influence, opposed this plan. Sir William Robertson gave it no support and it was merely remitted to the Staffs to study. As the train bringing the Prime Minister home from Italy waited at the Gare du Nord General Nivelle presented himself and unfolded his scheme in outline. The first impressions on both sides were favourable. Nivelle was invited to London and met the War Cabinet on January 15. His success was immediate. The British Ministers had never before met in Council a general who could express himself in forceful and continuous argument, and they had never before met a French general whom they could understand. Nivelle not only spoke lucidly, he spoke English. He had not only captured Fort Douaumont, but had an English mother. He explained that his method involved no resumption of the prolonged Somme battles but one short, sharp, decisive rupture. Mr. Lloyd George's resistance to the new offensive plan had been melting rapidly since the meeting at the Gare du Nord. It was soon to transform itself into ardent support. Haig was also in London; he and Robertson were summoned to the Council, and a Memorandum was drawn up and signed by all three Generals formally approving a renewed offensive on the Western Front to begin not later than April 1, with consequential preliminary extensions of the British Front.

So far all had been harmonious, but the Prime Minister in the process of being converted from his previous opposition to the offensive had evolved a further design. He was already set upon his great and simple conception of a united command. Like the War Cabinet he was attracted by the personality of General Nivelle and disposed to back him—if at all—whole-heartedly. It was believed that better war direction could be obtained from the French. It was also believed—and in this case with far more justification—that one single controlling hand ought to prevail on the whole of the Western Front. "It is not," as Lloyd George said when later in the war he had gained his point, "that one General is better than another, but that one General is better than two." So Nivelle returned to Chantilly carrying the virtual promise of the Prime Minister that Haig and the British Army should be subordinated to his directions. These important additional developments were not at this stage imparted by the Prime Minister or the War Cabinet to either Robertson or Haig.

During January the inadequacy of the rolling stock on the Nord railway became so marked that after strenuous British protests another conference was convened at Calais on February 26. The French then produced a detailed scheme or organization for an allied G.H.Q. in France. This provided for a French Generalissimo with a Headquarters Staff of French and British Officers under a British Chief of Staff. A British Commander-in-Chief was to be retained in name for Adjutant-General's work but without influence upon operations. The immediate resistance of the British Generals led to this proposal being put aside and instead an agreement was drawn up placing the control of the forthcoming operations solely in Nivelle's hands and the British Army under his orders for that period. To this Haig and Robertson—lest worse should befall—agreed.

The episode—in itself remarkable—had sensibly impaired the relations between the British and French Headquarters. It seemed to the British High Command that Nivelle had been concerned in an attempt with their own Government to procure their subordination to himself, if not indeed their supersession. From the outset they had viewed the appointment of the new Commander-in-Chief over the heads of all the best-known French soldiers with some surprise. Now mistrust and resentment were added. When on the strength of his new authority Nivelle sent instructions to Haig, couched in a tone of command, directing him to give up the long-planned British attack upon the Vimy Ridge in favour of the operations farther to the south of Arras, Haig refused to comply. He applied to the British Government and "requested to be told whether the War Cabinet wished the Commander-in-Chief of the British Expeditionary Force should be subject to such treatment by a junior foreign commander." The strain was sharp. A compromise was eventually reached, but the friendly and intimate co-operation which had existed for so long between the British and French Staffs had undergone a noticeable decline, and Nivelle was criticized in French high military circles for having provoked this unfavourable result.

At this moment an unexpected event occurred. Ludendorff intervened, and the Germans acted. The great military personality which Germany had discovered in her need, armed in the panoply and under the ægis of Hindenburg, by one sure stroke overturned all the strategy of General Nivelle. Towards the end of February the German evacuation of the whole sector from Arras to Noyon began. Leaving a screen of troops to occupy the abandoned positions and fire off their guns and rifles, the German Army withdrew fifty miles from the threatened area of the salient, and with unhurried deliberation assumed their new deeply considered positions on what was henceforward to be known as the Hindenburg line. The German General Staff called this long prepared operation by the code name *Alberich,* after the malicious dwarf of the Nibelungen legend. They left their opponents in the crater fields of the Somme, and with a severity barbarous because far in excess of any military requirements, laid waste with axe and fire the regions which they had surrendered.

The retrograde movement, rumoured for some days, was first detected on the front of the British Fifth Army. On February 24 suspicion was aroused by the German artillery shelling its own trench lines. British patrols found the hostile trenches empty. The Fifth Army Operations Order of that same night said "The enemy is believed to be withdrawing." Immense clouds of smoke and the glare of incendiary fires by night proclaimed the merciless departure of the enemy. On the 25th he was reported as much as 18,000 yards back in certain sectors, and on February 28 the British Intelligence spoke of a retirement to the Hindenburg line.

However absorbed a Commander may be in the elaboration of his own thoughts, it is necessary sometimes to take the enemy into consideration. Joffre's plan had been to bite the great German salient in February; and whether it would have succeeded or not, no man can tell. The Nivelle plan was to bite it with still larger forces in April. But by March the salient had ceased to exist. Three out of Nivelle's five armies, which were to have been employed in the assault, were now separated by a gulf of devastated territory from their objective. All their railroads, all their roads, all their magazines were so far removed from the enemy's positions that at least two months would be required to drag them forward into a new connection with the war. The remaining two armies were left with no other possibility before them than to deliver disconnected frontal attacks on the strongest parts of the old German line.

In these circumstances Nivelle's *Directive* to the British armies under his control is of great interest.

G.Q.G.,
March 6, 1917.

Direction for the Marshal.

The retirement of the enemy on the front of the Fifth British Army constitutes a new fact, the repercussion of which upon the joint offensive of the Franco-British Armies must be examined.

So far the retreat of the Germans has only been carried out on the front of the Fifth British Army. It will perhaps be extended to the region of the Somme and the Oise. But in any case there is no indication which would allow us to suppose that the enemy will act similarly on the front of attack of your Third and First Armies, any more than on that of the G.A.R. (Reserve Group). On the contrary, the so-called Hindenburg position is so disposed that the directions of our principal attacks, both in the British and the French zones, are such that they will outflank it and take it in reverse.

In this respect the German retirement may be entirely to our advantage, even if it becomes general; and on this assumption I base a first decision, which is *not to modify in any fundamental way the general plan of operations already settled,*[1] and in particular to stick to the date fixed for the launching of our attacks.

It must, however, be admitted that all our operations cannot be carried out in the way arranged, and I will therefore examine in succession the attitude to be adopted on the front of the British Armies and of the G.A.N. (Northern Group).

Distance, numbers, direction—all were changed. Yet it was decreed that the principle was unaffected and that the enterprise should proceed.

We have seen the tactical characteristics of the Joffre plan as developed by General Nivelle; the gigantic scale of the attack, its convergence upon the German salient; the minute study of detail and its comprehension by all ranks; and lastly, most precious and vital of all, the brutal, violent explosion of surprise. Of these four conditions, the Scale had been reduced by half, and the Convergence practically prevented by the German retreat. The other two—Detail and Surprise—were destined to destroy one another.

The progress of the immense preparations on those parts of the British and French fronts still in offensive relation to the enemy was continually visible from the air. From the south of Arras to the south of Soissons along a front of nearly 150 kilometres the Germans knew that since their retirement they could not be attacked. The 20-kilometres sector before Arras and perhaps a hundred kilometres in Champagne remained the only dangerous fronts. On these fronts they could watch each day the gathering of the storm. Good intelligence and aerial observation enabled the slight uncertainty as to where the main thrusts of the attack would take place to be reduced still further. But information of far greater precision and certainty was soon to be placed at their disposal.

In his desire that all ranks should comprehend the spirit of his plan, and that Battalion Commanders and even Company Commanders should know its whole scope, General Nivelle had caused various documents of high consequence to be circulated among the troops in the line. The first of these was the famous Staff memorandum on the new principles of the offensive dated December 16 which has already been quoted. The imprudence of allowing such a document to pass into the hands of troops holding the line often at even less than 100 yards from the enemy was swiftly punished. On March 3 a raid by a German division of the Crown Prince's army captured this fateful document. "This memorandum," writes the Crown Prince,[2] "contained matter of extraordinary value, it made clear that this time there was to be no question of a lim-

---

[1] My italics.
[2] *My War Experiences.*

ited attack but a breakthrough offensive on a grand scale was contemplated. . . . The memorandum also made disclosures above all as to the particular nature of the surprise which the attacker had in view. This was based on the fact alleged to have been observed on our side that our defensive artillery as a rule made only a weak reply to the artillery preparation which preceded the attack. The French therefore thought to avoid protracted digging of earthworks for the attacking troops, particularly for the artillery." . . . "Graf Von Schulenberg . . . at once formulated the logical reply for the defence, the artillery preparation not only to be powerfully returned, but even beforehand all recognized enemy preparations for attack to be overwhelmed by concentrated artillery fire. We ventured to hope that the surprise might in this way be most effectively met and the sting taken out of the first attack, which experience had shown to be the strongest and best prepared."

All through the month of March, General Nivelle's preparations for surprise continued to rivet the attention of the enemy. "By April," writes the Crown Prince, "a great deal of information already obtained led to the conclusion that the main attack was to be expected before long against the south front of the Seventh and Third Armies west of the Argonne. The Intelligence Service further confirmed the impression left by the French attack memorandum which had been captured. . . . Great depths of artillery, enormous supplies of ammunition, innumerable battery positions directly before the enemy's first line, no strong fortifications of battery positions, simply cover from the enemy's view, complete cessation of hostilities. . . ." Again, "On April 6 a clever attack by the 10th Reserve Division at Sapigneul brought us into possession of an order of attack of the French Fifth Army. In it the French attacking units were mentioned by name. The Fifth Army's objective was the line Prouvais-Proviseux-Aumenancourt. The Brimont [position] was to be taken by an enveloping movement from the north. Fresh information upon the anticipated French method of attack was given. The last veil concealing the intention of the French offensive was torn aside."

All this time the Germans, spurred and assisted by the most perfect information, were preparing their defences. The army commands were reorganized. In February, when Nivelle's preparations first began to be obvious, the Crown Prince's command was extended eastwards to include the Seventh Army (of Prince Rupprecht's group), thus unifying the control of the entire front to be attacked. In March a whole additional army—the First—was interpolated between the Seventh and the Third. The Crown Prince's Headquarters were moved from Stenay to Charleville. Throughout March the reinforcement of his group of armies was unceasing. Machine guns, artillery, battle-planes, intelligence service and labour battalions flowed in a broad stream to the threatened front. The relief gained by the Germans in the shortening of their line through their retirement from the salient enabled ever larger forces to be concentrated opposite the impending French attack. Night and day by ceaseless German toil the fortification of the whole area proceeded vehemently. Their position from Soissons to Rheims and beyond Rheims was by nature perhaps the strongest sector of the enemy's front. The Craonne plateau, the long hog's back of the Chemin des Dames, the wooded bluffs and ridges of the Argonne were all developed by ardent toil into one homogeneous labyrinth of trenches and tunnels, crowded with battalions and machine guns and swathed in tangles of barbed wire. At the beginning of the year eight or nine German divisions had stood upon this front; by the time Nivelle had perfected his plan of surprise forty, a number scarcely inferior to the attack, were waiting to receive him.

Other preoccupations began to gather round General Nivelle. He had been the choice of a French Government whose reputation and existence were largely bound up with his. In Briand, the Premier, and in Lyautey, the Minister of War, he had sponsors who could by no means separate themselves from him. No Government could afford to change their mind about a Commander they had violently elevated above all the recognized chiefs of the profession. But now suddenly this sure support was to fail. Early in March General Lyautey became entangled in the Parliamentary meshes. He precipitately resigned, and in his fall dragged down Briand and the whole Government. New rulers ascended the tribune of power, with whom Nivelle had no associations but those of hostility. Under a Ribot Administration Painlevé became Minister of War.

Paul Painlevé was a man of marked intellectual distinction, ardent in politics, great in mathematics, a faithful partisan of the Left, and ready to conform to all its formularies so far as a wide interpretation of the public interest allowed. In the original Briand Ministry Painlevé had been Minister of Education, charged with the study of inventions which might be serviceable to the armies. In this capacity he had constantly and freely toured the front, and discussed not only inventions but plans with most of the important Commanders. He knew them all, and most of them appreciated his keen intellect. Painlevé had discerned Pétain. This General was so cold and reserved to the Members of Parliamentary Commissions that he had incurred damaging unpopularity in influential circles. But Painlevé admired him for his independence, and perhaps Pétain had responded to such a recognition. Painlevé's nominee for the succession to Joffre had been Pétain. When Briand at the end of October, 1916, had reconstructed his Cabinet, he had done so on the basis of the dignified liquidation of Joffre and the enthronement of Nivelle. Painlevé, offered a renewal of his offices, had refused to continue on the specific ground that he did not agree with the appointment of Nivelle. His entrance into the Chamber after this decision—a serious one for any public man to take in time of war—had been marked by a salutation not only from the Left but almost of a general character.

Now he was Minister of War, and under the aged Prime Minister, the most important figure in the new French Administration. Instead of a Briand wedded to Nivelle's success, the new Commander-in-Chief now had a Painlevé who, however loyal to his subordinate, had publicly and in advance testified that he regarded his appointment as a mistake.

But Painlevé's objections to Nivelle were not limited to the personal aspect. Painlevé, and the political forces which at that time he embodied, were the declared opponents of the great offensives on the Western Front. He agreed with Pétain that France should not be bled to death, that the life of the French Army must be husbanded, that there was no chance of the break through *(la percée)* in that year in that theatre, that the gradual capture of limited objectives was the only prize within reach, and that moderation of aim and economy of the lives of French soldiers were the key-notes of the immediate military policy. Nivelle stood at the opposite pole: the offensive on the largest scale, the French in the van; the armies hurled on in absolute confidence of decisive victory; the rupture of the German line on an enormous front; the march through the gap of great armies of manœuvre; the re-establishment of open warfare; the expulsion of the invader from the soil of France. Nor were these differences of principle academic. Nivelle was actively planning the most ambitious offensive ever undertaken by the French; and Painlevé was the Minister who had to take responsibility before Parliament and before history for all that Nivelle might try to do. It is not easy to say which of the two men was in the more unpleasant position.

Had Painlevé acted upon his convictions, which in this case were proved right, he would have dismissed Nivelle and appointed to the Chief Command Pétain, in whom he had confidence and with whose general military outlook he and his party were in entire sympathy. But practical difficulties and many valid considerations dissuaded him from decisions which, if he had survived them, would have proved his title-deeds to fame. He temporized. He made the best of the situation as he found it. He bowed—who in great position has not had to do so?—before the day-to-day force and logic of circumstances, before the sullen drift of events. He acquiesced in Nivelle; he submitted to his plans—already so far advanced.

In the face of all the facts which marched upon him grimly and in spite of pressures of every kind, from every side, increasing constantly in severity, General Nivelle displayed an amazing persistence. In February he was aware of Pétain's scepticism, and of misgivings at the British Headquarters about his general plan. When the German retreat was apparent, General Micheler, his own man, chosen specially to command the main offensive, wrote to point out that everything was changed and to ask whether it was wise in the new circumstances to count on "an exploitation having the rapid character of a forward march." "The character of violence, of brutality and of rapidity," replied Nivelle on April 1, "must be maintained. It is in the speed and surprise caused by the rapid and sudden irruption of our Infantry upon the third and fourth positions that the success of the rupture will be found. No consideration should intervene of a nature to weaken the élan of the attack." Warned that the enemy were fully prepared; knowing as he did before the final signal was given that his detailed plan had fallen into their hands, he still extolled the virtue of Surprise. Behind him stood Colonel d'Alenson with fevered eye and a year to live. At his side was the redoubtable Mangin burning with the ardour of battle, confident that on the evening of the first day of the offensive his cavalry would be scampering in pursuit on the plains of Laon. But elsewhere in the high commands of the armies and in the Bureaux of the Headquarters Staff, doubt and distrust welled in chilling floods.

Painlevé became Minister of War on March 19. Everyone knew that the offensive was imminent. "On the 20th," wrote Painlevé, "before even being installed in the Ministry, I learned, I might say by public voice, that this was fixed for April 8, and that in consequence the British would attack at Arras on the 4th." These dates were eventually postponed from day to day by unsuitable weather until April 9 and 16 respectively. On March 22 the Minister had his first interview with the Commander-in-Chief. He told him that it was well known his choice for the Commander of the Army would have been different, but that was past, and he could count on his full support. Painlevé proceeded however to point out that the original plan of operations had been affected by a series of first-class events. The German retreat, the outbreak of the Russian revolution, the certain and imminent entry of the United States into the war against Germany—surely these had introduced some modification into the problem. In the name of the Government he urged the General to review the situation and reconsider his position freely, without feeling himself tied by any expectations he had previously formed himself or expressed to others. "A new situation ought to be considered with a new eye."

Nivelle's mind was not open to such argument. His confidence was unshakable. According to Painlevé,[1] he expressed himself as follows: The German retreat did not inconvenience him. It liberated more French than German divisions. He could not himself have prescribed movements of the enemy which would better have favoured his own decisions. The narrowing of the front of attack would be remedied by prolonging the French right and including a portion of the Army group under Pétain, opposite Moronvilliers. The enemy's front would be broken, it might almost be said, without loss. As for the Plateau of Craonne "he had it in his pocket," the only thing he feared was that the Germans would make off. The more they reinforced their front the more startling

---

[1] *"Comment j'ai nommé Foch et Pétain."*

would be the French victory, if only the intensity of the attack were continually increased. Perhaps the third day one might draw breath on the Serer after 30 kilometres of pursuit, but "it would be difficult to hold the troops back once they got started," and so on. Such was the mood of General Nivelle.

Upon the new Minister of War there flowed advices of a very different character. Staff Officers of the highest credentials wrote secretly, at the risk of their commissions, solemn, reasoned warnings of the impending disaster, if the orders which had been given were actually carried out. All the three Commanders of army groups, Franchet d'Espérey, Pétain, even Micheler, in respectful but decisive terms dissociated themselves from the idea that a sudden violent rupture of the front was practicable. All three however recognized the danger of allowing the initiative to pass to the enemy. Pétain alone suggested a pregnant alternative, namely to let the Germans attack the French, and then launch the prepared French offensive as a gigantic counterstroke.

Painlevé summoned a conference which met on the evening of April 3 at the War Ministry, at which the Prime Minister and the Commander-in-Chief, together with several other Ministers, were present. He drew General Nivelle's attention to the misgivings of his principal subordinates. To the last Nivelle was undaunted. Complete victory was certain. The first two positions of the enemy would be carried with insignificant loss. Did they think he was unaware that to take the third and fourth positions one must begin by taking the first and second? No one knew better than he that good weather was essential to his mode of attack. All would be decided in twenty-four hours, or forty-eight at the most. If within that time the rupture was not obtained it would be useless to persevere. "Under no pretext," he declared, "will I recommence a Somme battle." Finally, if he did not command their confidence, let them appoint a successor. The Ministers were overwhelmed by this extraordinary assurance, and General Nivelle left the conference convinced that the last word had been spoken.

Several times in this struggle the name of General Messimy occurs, and always finds itself associated with decided action for good or for ill. We see him in 1911 as War Minister arraigning Michel the Prophet before a Sanhedrin of Generals and dismissing him into the cool shades. We see him on August 25, 1914, again at the centre of power, serving General Joffre with the formal order to assign at least three Army Corps to the defence of Paris, which that General had proposed to declare an "open town" and to abandon as such. We see him a few days later removed from the War Office by one of the innumerable and to the foreigner baffling shufflings of French politics in the very height and climax of the war's opening convulsions, but not until he had ordered that Paris should be defended, had procured the necessary Army, and had appointed Galliéni, instead of his former victim, Michel, to the vital task. Thereafter at once he takes his place at the head of a Brigade and vanishes into the dust and confusion of the conflict, until now on April 5, 1917, two and a half years later, Messimy emerges quite suddenly with an extremely irregular letter which he presented to Monsieur Ribot. This letter marshalled all the arguments against the offensive. "Prisoners yes, guns yes, a narrow band of territory of perhaps 10 or 12 kilometres; but at an outrageous cost, and without strategic results. Urgent conclusion—give without losing an hour the order to delay the attack till the weather improves." These views he declared were written "almost under the dictation of Micheler," and represented the conviction of the "most famous Chiefs of the French Army."

But now the hour was imminent. The vast preparations were everywhere moving forward to explosion-point. The British Cabinet had been won over. The British Headquarters had been persuaded. The co-operation of England, the great Ally, had by a tremendous effort been obtained, and once obtained would be given with crude and downright force. To resist the plan, to dismiss the Commander, meant not only a Ministerial and a Parliamentary crisis— possibly fatal to the Government—but it also meant throwing the whole plan of campaign for the year into the melting-pot, and presumably, though not certainly, resigning the initiative to the Germans. So Nivelle and Painlevé, these two men whose highest ambitions had both been newly and almost simultaneously gratified, found themselves in the most unhappy positions which disillusioned mortals can occupy: the Commander having to dare the utmost risks with an utterly sceptical Chief behind him; the Minister having to become responsible for a frightful slaughter at the bidding of a General in whose capacity he did not believe, and upon a military policy of the folly of which he was justly convinced. Such is the pomp of power!

I shall not attempt to describe the course either of the French offensive which began on April 16 nor of the brilliant preliminary operation by which the British Army at the battle of Arras captured the whole of the Vimy Ridge. Numerous excellent accounts—French, English and German—are extant. It will here be sufficient to say that the French troops attacked in unfavourable weather with their customary gallantry. On a portion of the main front attacked they penetrated to a depth of 3 kilometres; they took between the 16th and the 20th, 21,000 prisoners and 183 guns, lost over 100,000 soldiers and failed to procure any strategic decision. It was only indeed on the fronts of Moronvilliers and Soissons-Craonne, added by Nivelle to the attack after the documents captured by the enemy had actually been written, that surprise and success were alike achieved. By the evening of the 16th Nivelle's high hopes and confidence had withered, and his orders for the resumption of battle on the 17th implied not merely tactical modifications but the substitution of far more moderate strategic aims.

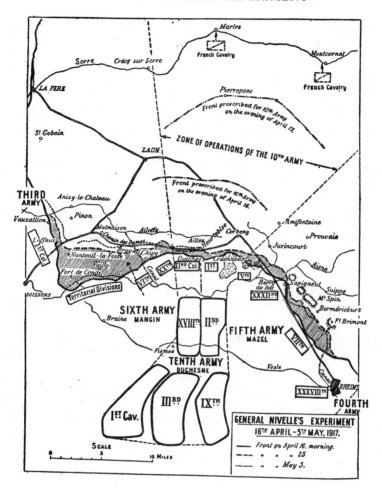

The later phases of the battle were in some respects more successful than its beginning; nor were the losses of the French so disproportionate to those of the Germans as in Joffre offensives. In fact the Nivelle offensive was the least costly both actually and relatively to the enemy's loss, of any ever undertaken by the French. But the General could never escape from the consequences of his sanguine declarations. Again and again he had affirmed that, unless the rupture was immediate and total "within twenty-four or forty-eight hours," it would be useless to continue the operation. He had predicted such a rupture with many circumstances of detail. Almost everyone had doubted before. Now all doubts were certainties. The slaughter, woeful to the shrunken manhood of France, was fiercely exaggerated. Disturbances broke out among the troops, and in the capital a storm of fury arose against the General. His wish to convert the great operation into a more modest enterprise was brushed aside. On April 29 Pétain became, as Chief of the General Staff, the adviser of the French Cabinet on the whole conduct of the military operations.

A peculiar situation followed the collapse of Nivelle's offensive. The British Army had, as we have seen, already entered with vigour and success upon their very important part in the general plan. The victory of Arras, with its capture of the Vimy Ridge, thirteen thousand prisoners and two hundred guns, had been achieved without undue sacrifice. Haig had originally intended to close these operations after the capture of Monchy-le-Preux and to begin as soon as possible the attempt to clear the coastal sector by the capture of the Messines and Paschendaele Ridges. But the conditions prevailing in the French Army and in Paris were such that it was thought dangerous to relax even for a few weeks the pressure upon the enemy. The continuance of the British attack was however very costly and unrewarded by any real success. At an early stage the Germans developed a new method of defence. Holding their front system of trenches with few men, they kept strong forces intact close at hand, and by heavy counter-attacks independently launched they robbed, in nearly every case, the British of their initial gains.

The Prime Minister was himself deeply committed by his facile acceptance of the Nivelle schemes to the offensive mood. He showed himself resolute to persevere. The British Army should be thrown ungrudgingly into the battle of attrition, and every effort must be made to induce the French to exert themselves unceasingly to the utmost. General Headquarters thus found in Mr. Lloyd George at this juncture a strong supporter. His action cannot be judged apart from the situation. The hour was tragic. The U-boat sinkings for April, surpassing all previous records, had reached the total of 800,000 tons. The fatal curve was still rising, and in British minds it dominated everything. "Let the armies fight while time remained." Or in Lord Fisher's challenging phrase, "Can the Army win the war before the Navy loses it?" Prime Minister, Commander-in-Chief and Sir William Robertson proceeded together to Paris, and in conference on May 4 and 5, Mr. Lloyd George addressed to Messieurs Ribot, Painlevé and General Pétain some of the most strenuous exhortations to continue the offensive that have ever passed between Allies. The whole proceedings of the conference have been published by Mermeix in one of his excellent books.[1] They form an astonishing chapter in Anglo-French relations and in the life of Mr. Lloyd George.

The undertakings extorted in full conference from the French Government by the imperious Welshman did not accord either with the final decision of the French Staff or the facts of the case. The battle was indeed continued, and dur-

---

[1] *Nivelle et Painlevé.*

ing the next fortnight both Craonne and the Chemin des Dames were captured. But upon the very day of the conference in Paris, there had occurred a deeply disquieting incident. A French division ordered into the line refused to march. The officers succeeded in recalling the soldiers to their duty, and the division took part in the fighting without discredit. It was the first drop before the downpour.

The demoralization of the French Army was proceeding apace. Want of confidence in their leader, cruel losses and an active defeatist propaganda had produced an intense spasm throughout its ranks. Mutinies—some of a very dangerous character—occurred in sixteen separate Army Corps. Some of the finest troops were involved. Divisions elected councils. Whole regiments set out for Paris to demand a peace by negotiation and more home leave. A Russian force of about 15,000 Infantry had before the Revolution been sent to be armed and equipped in France. These men were affected by the political developments in their own country. They had put it to the vote whether they should take part in the battle of April 16, and had decided by a majority to do so. They were used by the French in a ruthless manner, and nearly 6,000 had been killed or wounded. The survivors went into open revolt. One sentence in their Manifesto reveals the propaganda of a master hand. "We have been told," so the complaint begins, "that we have been sent to France to pay for munitions sold to Russia." It was not until prolonged artillery fire had been employed against these troops that they were reduced to submission and disbanded.

The spirit of the French nation was not unequal to this perilous trial. On May 15, Nivelle refusing to resign was dismissed, and Pétain became Commander-in-Chief. Loyal troops surrounded those who had fallen from their duty. Old Territorials, the fathers of families, pleaded with the infuriated linesmen. The disorders were pacified or suppressed. Over all a veil of secrecy was thrown so impenetrable that though scores of thousands of Frenchmen were concerned, no whisper ever reached the enemy, and whatever information was imparted to Sir Douglas Haig long remained buried in the bosom of his immediate staff. Pétain was of all others fitted to the healing task. In a period of several months he visited a hundred divisions of the Army, addressed the officers and men, heard grievances and complaints, mitigated the severities of the service, increased the leave of the soldiers, and diminished by every skilful shift the fighting on the French front. He thus restored by the end of the year the morale and discipline of that sorely tried, glorious Army upon whose sacrifices the liberties of Europe had through three fearful campaigns mainly depended.

CHAPTER XLVII

AT THE MINISTRY OF
MUNITIONS

On July 16, 1917, the Prime Minister invited me to join the new Government. He proposed to me either the Ministry of Munitions or the newly created Air Ministry, with the proviso that if I chose the latter, he must have till the afternoon to make certain personal rearrangements in the Administration. I said at once that I preferred Munitions; and the matter was settled in as many words as I here set down.

The appointment was announced the next morning. There was an outcry among those who at that time had accustomed themselves to regard me with hostility. An immediate protest was made by the Committee of the National Union of Conservative Associations, and an influential deputation of Unionist Members presented themselves to the leader of the Party in strong complaint. Mr. Lloyd George had however prepared the ground with his accustomed patience. Lord Northcliffe was on a mission to the United States, and appeased. Sir Edward Carson and General Smuts were warm advocates. The group of Ministers who had successfully prevented my entering the Government on its formation was no longer intact. Some had been previously placated: the remnant acquiesced. And Mr. Bonar Law, who had always been a friend, returned a very stiff answer to his deputation. I was re-elected for Dundee by a remarkable majority, and took up my duties without delay. Not allowed to make the plans, I was set to make the weapons.

The internal conditions of munitions supply, and indeed the whole structure of the British Executive, were vastly different from those I had quitted twenty months before, and still more from the days when I was First Lord of the Admiralty. In the first period of the war—indeed almost to the end of 1915—the resources of Britain far exceeded any organization which could employ them. Whatever was needed for the fleets and armies had only to be ordered in good time and on a large enough scale. The chief difficulty was to stretch the mind to a hitherto unimagined size of events. Megalomania was a positive virtue. Indeed, to add a nought, or a couple of noughts, to almost any requisition or plan for producing war supplies would have constituted an act of merit. Now all was changed. Three years of the struggle had engaged very nearly the whole might of the nation. Munition production of every kind was already upon a gigantic scale. The whole island was an arsenal. The enormous national factories which Mr. Lloyd George had planned were just beginning to function. The first difficulties with the Trade Unions about the dilution of labour had been overcome. Hundreds of thousands of women were making shells and fuses cheaper and better than the most skilled craftsmen had done before the war. The keenest spirits in British industry were gathered as State servants in the range of palatial hotels which housed the Ministry of Munitions. The former trickles and streamlets of war supplies now flowed in rivers rising continuously.

Nevertheless the demands of the fighting fronts eagerly and easily engulfed all that could be produced. We were in the presence of requirements at once imperative and apparently insatiable; and now at last our ultimate capacity began to come into view.

The principal limiting factors to munitions production with which I was confronted in the autumn of 1917 were four in number, viz., shipping (tonnage), steel, skilled labour and dollars. The last of these had been rendered less acute by the accession of the United States to the Allies. We had already sold a thousand millions sterling of American securities, and had borrowed heavily to feed and equip ourselves, and our Allies, before this decisive event. Our transatlantic credits were practically exhausted at the beginning of 1917. The dollar situation was now somewhat relieved. A door that would otherwise have closed altogether was now held partially open. None the less the limits of the power of purchase both in American and Canadian dollars imposed a restrictive finger on the lay-out of every programme.

The stringency in shipping was acute. The losses of the U-boat war, the requirements of the armies in every theatre, the food and what remained of the trade of Britain, the needs of the Allies, the increasing desires of the United States, and the importations of all the raw materials of war, had drawn out our Mercantile Marine to its most intense strain. Tonnage therefore was at this period the controlling factor in our production. Steel ranked next to tonnage, and was a more direct measure of war effort. The steel output of Great Britain had already nearly doubled. Mines which would not pay in peace had come into active production. But in the main we depended for iron ore upon the north coast of Spain, and all vessels which carried it ran perilous voyages amid frequent sinkings. In addition we bought finished steel to the utmost limit of our dollars from the United States and Canada, as well as shell castings of every intermediate form.

The growth of the Ministry of Munitions had far outstripped its organization. A year had passed since its creator, Mr. Lloyd George, had moved on to still more intense spheres. The two gifted Ministers who had succeeded him, Mr. Montagu and Dr. Addison, had dealt with the needs as they arose, shouldering one responsibility after another, adding department to department and branch to branch, without altering in essentials the central organization from the form it had assumed in the empirical and convulsive period of creation. All the main and numberless decisions still centred upon the Minister himself. I found a staff of 12,000 officials organized in no less than fifty principal departments each claiming direct access to the Chief, and requiring a swift flow of decisions upon most intricate and interrelated problems. I set to work at once to divide and distribute this dangerous concentration of power.

Under a new system the fifty departments of the Ministry were grouped into ten large units each in charge of a head who was directly responsible to the Minister. These ten heads of groups of departments were themselves formed into a Council like a Cabinet. The Members of the Council were charged with dual functions: first, to manage their group of departments; secondly, to take a general interest in the whole business of the Ministry. They were to develop a "Council sense," and not to regard themselves as confined to their own special sphere. Each group of departments was denoted by a letter. Thus D was design, G guns, F finance, P projectiles, X explosives, and so on. By ringing the changes upon these letters committees could be formed exactly adapted to handle any particular topic, while the general movement of business was held firmly together by means of a co-ordinating or 'Clamping' committee. The "big business men" who now formed the Council were assisted by a strong cadre of Civil Servants, and I obtained for this purpose from the Admiralty my old friends Sir William Graham Greene and Mr. Masterton-Smith. Thus we had at once the initiative, drive, force and practical experience of the open competitive world coupled with those high standards of experience, of official routine, and of method, which are the qualifications of the Civil Service.

The relief was instantaneous. I was no longer oppressed by heaps of bulky files. Every one of my ten Councillors was able to give important and final decisions in his own sphere. The daily Council meeting kept them in close relation with each other and with the general scheme; while the system of committees of councillors enabled special questions to be brought to speedy conclusion. Once the whole organization was in motion it never required change. Instead of struggling through the jungle on foot I rode comfortably on an elephant whose trunk could pick up a pin or uproot a tree with equal ease, and from whose back a wide scene lay open.

I confined myself to the assignment and regulation of work, to determining the emphasis and priority of particular supplies, to the comprehensive view of the war programmes, and to the initiation of special enterprises. After five months' experience of the new system I was able to say, "I practically always approve a Council Committee report exactly as it comes. I think I have hardly ever altered a word. I read each report through with great attention and see the decision on the question, which I know is ever so much better than I could have produced myself, if I had studied it for two whole days."

At the Ministry of Munitions I worked with incomparably the largest and most powerful staff in my experience. Here were gathered the finest business brains of the country working with might and main and with disinterested loyalty for the common cause. Many if not most of the leading men stood at the head of those industries which were most expanded by war needs. They therefore resigned altogether the immense fortunes which must inevitably have come to them, had they continued as private contractors. They served the State for honour alone. They were content to see men of lesser standing in their own industries amass great wealth and extend the scale of their business. In the service of the Crown there was a keen rivalry among them; and the position of Member of Council with its general outlook was deeply prized. According to the Statute constituting the office, the whole authority rested with the Minister; but in practice the Council had a true collective responsibility.

"As regards material," wrote Sir Douglas Haig in his final despatch in 1919, "it was not until midsummer, 1916, that the artillery situation became even approximately adequate to the conduct of major operations. Throughout the Somme battle the expenditure of artillery ammunition had to be watched with the greatest care. During the battles of 1917 ammunition was plentiful, but the gun situation was a source of constant anxiety. Only in 1918 was it possible to conduct artillery operations independently of any limiting consideration other than that of transport."

If in these pages I dwell with pride upon the extraordinary achievements of the Munitions Council in the field of supply, it is not to appropriate the credit. That belongs in the first instance to Mr. Lloyd George, who gathered together the great majority of these able men, and whose foresight in creating the national factories laid the foundations for subsequent production. It belongs also to the men who did the work, who quarried and shaped the stones, and to whose faithful, resourceful, untiring contrivance and exertion the Army and the nation owe a lasting debt.

At the time I rejoined the Government the British armies were on the eve of a new tremendous offensive. The long-prepared attack upon the Messines ridge had been executed with precision and success on June 7, and Sir Douglas Haig's further plan was to strike from the direction of Ypres towards Ostend. This was in fact a revival on a gigantic scale and by different methods of those ideas of clearing the sea flank by which Sir John French had been so much attracted in 1914. Forty divisions had been assembled between Kemmel Hill and the Belgian front. Mountains of ammunition had been accumulated, and the strongest concentration of artillery ever yet developed was to sustain the attack. The British Headquarters were as usual confident of a decisive success, and as usual they were stoutly supported by Sir William Robertson and the General Staff at the War Office. On the other hand, the positions to be assaulted were immensely strong. The enemy was fully prepared. The frowning undulations of the Paschendaele-Klercken ridge had been fortified with every resource of German science and ingenuity. The ground was studded with ferro-concrete blockhouses, "Pill Boxes" as they were soon called, crammed with machine guns, lapped in barbed wire, and impenetrable to the heaviest bombardment. The railway communications behind the enemy's front were at least as good as, if not indeed superior to, those which maintained the British offensive. A German army containing three times as many divisions as were required at any given moment to hold the ground had been assembled under Prince Rupprecht, and every facility for the relief and replacement of exhausted units had been carefully studied. The Dutch railways carried ceaseless supplies of gravel for the concrete, and the elaboration of the defences line behind line proceeded continually.

Apart from the hopes of decisive victory, which grew with every step away from the British front line and reached absolute conviction in the Intelligence Department, two reasons were adduced by General Headquarters to justify the renewed severe demand upon the troops. First, the alleged exhausted and quiescent condition of the French Army since the defeat of General Nivelle's April offensive; secondly, the importance of taking Ostend and Zeebrugge in order to paralyse or cripple the U-boat war. The first of these arguments was exaggerated. The French Army was no doubt saving its strength as much as possible; but the casualty tables show that during 1917 they inflicted nearly as many losses on the Germans as did our own troops. The U-boat argument was wholly fallacious. A grave responsibility rests upon the Admiralty for misleading Haig and his Staff about the value of Ostend and Zeebrugge to the submarine campaign. These two ports were convenient advanced bases for U-boats working in the English Channel, but they were in no way indispensable to the submarine war. Submarines able to go completely around the British Isles and to remain at sea a whole month at a time could work almost as easily from their own home bases in the Elbe, the Weser, and the Ems, as from the advanced and much-battered harbours of Belgium. The whole U-boat war was based on the main German naval harbours and was never dependent on anything else. In fact in May, 1918, the month after both Ostend and Zeebrugge had been sealed up by the Navy, the U-boat sinkings actually showed an increase over the preceding month in which they were open and in full activity. Whatever influence this erroneous argument may have had upon the Haig-Robertson decision to launch a new offensive, it certainly contributed to baffle the objections of the Prime Minister and the War Cabinet. It seemed to throw the army into the struggle against the submarines. It confused the issue, it darkened counsel, it numbed misgivings, overpowered the dictates of prudence, and cleared the way for a forlorn expenditure of valour and life without equal in futility.

In the war against Turkey in the south-eastern theatre the most costly and laborious policy was also pursued. The Turks, fortified between the desert and the sea at Gaza under Jemal Pasha, confronted successfully the British Army under Allenby, which had toiled forward by railway and water-pipe line from Egypt at extreme exertion and expense. This obstacle was surmounted or destroyed in the following year. Meanwhile however the obvious manœuvre of landing an army behind the Turks was dismissed by Sir William Robertson as venturesome and impracticable.

Even before I joined his Government the Prime Minister, as I have written, used to discuss the war situation with me freely. On my taking office he made me acquainted with everything. After his excursion with General Nivelle and its disillusionments, he had returned to those views against seeking offensives on the Western Front without the necessary superiority or method, with which the reader is familiar. The peak of the U-boat sinkings seemed to have been surmounted. If on land hopes had been dupes, fears at sea had also been liars. Mr. Lloyd George was now content to await in the main theatre the arrival of the American Armies. He wished Sir Douglas Haig to maintain an active defensive for the rest of the year and to nurse his strength. Meanwhile activity in Palestine and the reinforcement of Italy by British and French divisions might produce important results against Turkey and Austria, and would in any case not be unduly costly in life. At first the majority of the War Cabinet shared these general opinions. But between right thought and right action there was a gulf. Sir William Robertson, and under his direction the General Staff at the War Office, pressed unceasingly for further immediate exertions. Their insistence gained several adherents in the Cabinet. All through June the discussions were maintained. In the end the Prime Minister did not feel strong enough to face the Haig-Robertson combination. He submitted with resentful fatalism. The plan of sustaining Italy was dropped, and by the third week of July Robertson had extorted from the Cabinet and conveyed to Haig an assurance of "wholehearted" support[1] for the Paschendaele attack. When I had the opportunity of learning the facts it was too late. The decision had already been taken. My only hope was to limit the consequences. On July 22 I gave my counsel as follows:

MR. CHURCHILL TO THE PRIME MINISTER.

Many thanks for letting me see these most interesting papers which I return herewith. Broadly speaking I agree with Smuts. But I deplore with you the necessity for giving way to the military wish for a renewed offen-

---

[1] Robertson, *Soldiers and Statesmen,* Vol. II, p. 249.

sive in the West. The armies are equal. If anything, the Germans are the stronger. They have larger reserves and ample munitions. An endless series of fortified lines with all kinds of flooding possibilities and great natural difficulties of ground constitute insuperable obstacles. We already approach the end of July. Even if three or four battles as good as Messines are won, the situation in the West will not be appreciably altered by the end of the year.

It is clear however that no human power exists which can stop the attempt being made. The essential thing now is to arrive at a definition of success and "great results" which will enable a new decision to be taken after the first or second phases of this offensive have been fought. Such a definition must, it seems to me, involve three conditions, viz. objectives taken; casualties sustained; and thirdly (very important) the time taken or required between any one thrust and the next. Thus it should be possible, by reference to these forecasts, to settle definitely after (say) six weeks of fighting whether there really is any prospect of obtaining "great results" before winter sets in.

With regard to the East, the truth is staring us in the face. An army of six divisions, British or Franco-British, should be taken from [the] Salonica [front] and put in behind Jemal's army. This will force that army to surrender, and all the allied troops in Syria and Palestine, including Allenby's, would be free by the spring of next year for action in Italy or France.

The Prime Minister went so far as to offer the command of the British armies in Palestine to General Smuts. After deliberation Smuts replied that he was willing to accept the task on one condition, namely, that he should be allowed to land an adequate army to cut the Turkish communications. As this project was not considered open, he declined the command. But in his place was found a leader whose personality and skill were equal to the task of dislodging and ultimately of destroying the Turkish armies in Syria without the aid of a great amphibious operation. With the appointment of Allenby the whole situation in Palestine was rapidly transformed. Although he repeatedly demanded more reinforcements than could be spared, and prudently dwelt on the difficulties before him, Allenby by a series of masterly combinations succeeded with smaller forces both in out-manœuvring and in out-fighting the Turks under Jemal, advised by Falkenhayn. Feinting at Gaza in the last week of October, he stormed Beersheba by a surprise attack of two infantry divisions and a wide turning movement of cavalry and camelry. Having thus gained the enemy's desert flank, he rolled up from the eastward in a succession of fierce actions the strongly fortified Turkish lines. Gaza was taken on November 6: 10,000 Turks had been made prisoners, and at least as many killed and wounded: and a vigorous pursuit opened the port of Jaffa to the further supply of the British forces. Thus possessed of the coastal region, a new base, and an alternative short line of communication, Allenby advanced north-westward upon Jerusalem, continuing to drive the Seventh and Eighth Turkish Armies before him and compromising the eventual retreat of the Fourth. On December 8, 1917, the Turks abandoned Jerusalem after 400 years of blighting occupation, and the British Commander-in-Chief entered the city amid the acclamations of the inhabitants. Here he maintained himself in a situation of much delicacy throughout the winter, re-grouping his forces, wisely fostering the Arab revolt which grew around the astonishing personality of Lawrence, and preparing for even larger enterprises in the spring. With no more than 150,000 men he had expelled 170,000 German-led Turkish troops from fortified positions—Plevnas—on which years of labour had been spent, and had inflicted upon them most serious losses in men, guns and territory.

No praise is too high for these brilliant and frugal operations, which will long serve as a model in theatres of war in which manœuvre is possible. Nevertheless their results did not simplify the general problem. On the contrary, by opening up a competing interest which could not influence the main decision, they even complicated it. The very serious drain of men, munitions and transport which flowed unceasingly to the Palestine Expedition ought to have been arrested by action far swifter in character and far larger in scale. Brevity and finality, not less at this period than throughout the war, were the true tests of any diversion against Turkey. Prolonged and expanding operations in distant unrelated theatres, whether they languished as at Salonika, or crackled briskly and brightly forward under Allenby in Palestine, were not to be reconciled with a wise war policy. It would have been far safer and far cheaper in life and resources to run a greater risk for a shorter time. The advantage of the command of the sea should not have been neglected. If, while Allenby held the Turks at Gaza, a long-prepared descent had been made at Haifa or elsewhere on the sea coast behind them, and if the railway by which alone they could exist had been severed in September by a new army of six or eight divisions, the war in Syria would have been ended at a stroke. The Eastern drain on our resources would have been stopped from February onwards; all the British troops in Palestine would have been available to meet the supreme peril in France. But in Palestine as formerly at Gallipoli, the clash of the Western and Eastern schools of thought produced incoherence and half-measures. Enough was sent East to be a dangerous dispersion, and never at one time enough to compel a prompt conclusion. It will be incredible to future generations that the strategists of an island people then blessed with the unique and sovereign attribute of Sea Power should, throughout the whole of the Great War, have failed so utterly to turn it to offensive profit.

In the actual event, as will be seen, Ludendorff's offensive of 1918 dissipated in a day all Allenby's careful plans for the spring campaign. Not less than sixty battalions with many batteries were incontinently snatched from Palestine to plug the shot-hole of the twenty-first of March; and his depleted army remained till two Indian divisions arrived from Mesopotamia in August, in an extremely precarious position. That from such circumstances he should have contrived the captures of Deraa, Damascus and Aleppo, and the destruction of every vestige of Turkish power in Syria, military and civil before the armistice, is one of the most remarkable achievements of the war.

Meanwhile the British offensive against Paschendaele unrolled its sombre fate. The terrific artillery pulverized the ground, smashing simultaneously the German trenches and the ordinary drainage. By sublime devotion and frightful losses small indentations were made upon the German front. In six weeks at the farthest point we had advanced four miles. Soon the rain descended, and the vast crater fields became a sea of choking fetid mud in which men, animals and tanks floundered and perished hopelessly. The few tracks which alone could be preserved across this morass were swept with ceaseless shell fire, through which endless columns of transport marched with fortitude all night long. The impossibility of supplying the British field and medium batteries with ammunition at any distance from the only road maintained in being, led to their being massed in line by its side. Thus there could be no concealment, and the German counterfire caused very heavy losses in gunners and guns and killed nearly all the artillery horses.

The disappointing captures of ground were relieved by tales of prodigious German slaughter. The losses and anxieties inflicted upon the enemy must not be underrated. Ludendorff's admissions are upon record. These violent sustained thrusts shook the enemy to their foundations. But the German losses were always on a far smaller scale. They always had far fewer troops in the cauldron. They always took nearly two lives for one and sold every inch of ground with extortion.

Further efforts were made during October by the Prime Minister to bring the operations to an end. He went so far as to call Sir Henry Wilson and Lord French into counsel as "technical advisers" of the Cabinet, independent of the General Staff. We have the tale naïvely published by Robertson himself.[1] Lord French, we are told, after criticizing "in twenty pages out of twenty-six" the

---

[1] Robertson, *Soldiers and Statesmen,* Vol. II, pp. 256 *et seq.*

Haig-Robertson strategy and tactics, recommended that we should "stand everywhere on the defensive, only resorting to such offensive action as would make the defensive effective; await the development of the forces of the United States; and in the meantime rely upon a drastic economic war to weaken the enemy." In formally consulting outside advisers the Prime Minister obviously courted the resignation of the Chief of the Imperial General Staff. It was not forthcoming. The Cabinet were not prepared to demand it; and nothing but mutual mistrust resulted.

Accordingly in Flanders the struggle went on. New divisions continued to replace those that were shattered. The rain descended and the mud sea spread. Still the will-power of the Commander and the discipline of the Army remained invincible. By measureless sacrifices Paschendaele was won. But beyond, far beyond, still rose intact and unapproachable the fortifications of Klercken. August had passed away; September was gone; October was far spent. The full severity of a Flanders winter gripped the ghastly battlefield. Ceaselessly the Menin gate of Ypres disgorged its streams of manhood. Fast as the cannons fired, the ammunition behind them flowed in faster. Even in October the British Staff were planning and launching offensives and were confident of reaching the goal of decisive results. It was not until the end of November that final failure was accepted. *"Boche* is bad and *Boue* is bad," said Foch, then little more than an observer of events, "but *Boche* and *Boue* together . . . Ah!" He held up warning hands.

It cannot be said that "the soldiers," that is to say the Staff, did not have their way. They tried their sombre experiment to its conclusion. They took all they required from Britain. They wore down alike the manhood and the guns of the British Army almost to destruction. They did it in the face of the plainest warnings, and of arguments which they could not answer. Sir Douglas Haig acted from conviction; but Sir William Robertson drifted ponderously. He has accepted the main responsibility. He could not well avoid it. "I was more than a mere adviser. I was the professional head of all the British Armies, as Haig was of those in France. They looked to me, as did the whole Empire, to see that they were not asked to do impossible things, and were not in any way placed at a disadvantage unnecessarily." [1] And again (June 23), "My own responsibility . . . is not small in urging the continuance of a plan regarding which he [the Prime Minister] has grave misgivings . . ." [2] And lastly (Robertson to Haig, Sept. 27), "My own views are known to you. They have always been 'defensive' in all theatres but the West. But the difficulty is to *prove* the wisdom of this now that Russia is out. I confess I stick to it more because I see nothing better, and be-

[1] Robertson, *Soldiers and Statesmen,* Vol. I, p. 188.
[2] *Ibid.,* Vol. II, p. 247.

cause my instinct prompts me to stick to it, than because of any good argument by which I can support it."[1] These are terrible words when used to sustain the sacrifices of nearly four hundred thousand men.

Meanwhile the results of neglecting Italy for the sake of Paschendaele exploded with a violence which no one could have foreseen. On October 24 began the Italian disaster of Caporetto. Six German divisions were brought swiftly to the Isonzo by night marches and concealed in deep valleys behind the front. These and the presence of General von Below animated the large Austrian armies. A skilful attack by mountain roads gained a key position. A sudden bombardment by heavy artillery and gas shells, followed by a general assault along the whole front led at the decisive points by German troops, aided by the effects of defeatist propaganda within the Italian lines, produced in twelve hours a complete and decisive defeat of General Cadorna's army. By nightfall more than a million Italians were in full retreat. A large portion of the army passed into dissolution. In three days 200,000 men and 1,800 guns were captured, and before the long retreat was finished and the Italian front had been reconstituted 80 miles to the westward along the Piave, upwards of 800,000 soldiers through death, wounds, sickness, capture, desertion, and above all disappearance, had been torn from the Italian standards. This astounding disaster required immediate exertions by Britain and France.

I was resting at my house in Kent when authentic news arrived. The Prime Minister telephoned to me to motor at once to Walton Heath. He showed me the telegrams, which even in their guarded form revealed a defeat of the first magnitude. At this moment when our army had been bled white at Paschendaele and when the French were still recovering from the Nivelle offensive and its disquieting consequences, the prospect of having to make a large detachment of force for Italy was uninviting. The Prime Minister reacted with his accustomed resiliency. He set off in a few days to Rapallo, where he had proposed a meeting with the French and Italian political and military chiefs. Meanwhile five French and five British divisions under General Fayolle and Sir Herbert Plumer, two of the most successful and experienced Commanders on the Western Front, were moved with the utmost rapidity through the tunnels under the Alps, and began to appear from the 10th of November onwards upon the Italian front. Had they been sent a few months earlier, it is certain, even if the Ally-Italian offensive had not yielded important results, that events would have followed an entirely different course.

The greatness of the Italian nation shone forth in an hour which recalled the morrow of Cannae. "Defeatism" withered in the flame of national resolve. Immense as had been the Italian losses, the war effort of Italy was far greater

[1] *Ibid.,* Vol. II, p. 255.

from Caporetto onwards than in the earlier period of the war. Ruthless punishment restored the discipline of the armies: ardent reserves and volunteers refilled their ranks. But all this took time, and for several months the fate of Italy hung in the balance. It was necessary to contemplate a situation in which the North of Italy might be completely overrun by Teutonic armies; when Italy might be beaten out of the war, and when the development of a Swiss front might have been imposed upon France. Mercifully "the trees do not grow up to the sky," and offensives however successful lose their pristine force satiated with the ground they gain.

What would have happened had Germany prepared from the beginning to back her initial impulse with twelve or fourteen more divisions drawn from the vanished Russian front, is an inquiry which may well occupy and instruct the military student. But Ludendorff was nursing other plans, larger, more ambitious and as it turned out fatal to his country. Already the vast design of the German offensive in 1918 had gripped his mind. Italy was but a "side show," worth perhaps "the bones of a Pomeranian Grenadier," but never to obstruct a classical theory and the supreme trial of strength against the strongest foe. Yet the falling away of Italy, a people of 40 millions, a first-class power, from the cause of the Allies at this time would have been an event more pregnant with consequences than all the German triumphs of March 21, 1918. To overwhelm Italy and to sue for a general peace afforded still the surest hope for the Central Empires. It is a valid though inadequate claim on the part of the British High Command that the continuous pressure on Paschendaele played its part in influencing the German war mind. The almost inexhaustible resources of the British attack, its conquering of superhuman difficulties, its obstinate Commanders, its undaunted troops, the repeated destruction of the German front lines, the drain—the half of ours, but still frightful—on German resources, all riveted the eyes of Ludendorff on the Western Front. God forbid that such sacrifices, however needless, however disproportioned, should be vain!

From these deep matters I must recall the reader to the limited situation from which my tale is told.

It was imperative that Italy should be rearmed to the utmost possible extent by France and England. On November 18 I proceeded to Paris to meet in conclave with Loucheur and the Italian Minister of Armaments, General Dallolio. It was a cheerless experience; our margins were so small, our needs so exacting—and the Italian void gaped. In those hard days defeat was not leniently viewed by overstrained Allies. We all went through it in our turn—the politeness which veiled depreciation, the sympathy which scarcely surmounted resentment. And here I must pay my tribute to the dignity and quiet courage of the Italian Minister, and to the respect which in such circumstances he knew how to command from all.

• • •

The Paschendaele offensive had ended in mire and carnage, when suddenly there emerged from the British sector opposite Cambrai a battle totally different in character from any yet fought in the war. For the first time the mechanical method of securing Surprise was effectively used. Boraston's account points to this battle as a refutation of "the crude talk about the backward method of our leadership in France during 1916–17; its lack of genius or skill; its prodigious waste of life."[1] Here in his opinion was a superb example of scientific novelty and audacious tactics combined into a conception of military genius. But this conception, not only its underlying idea but its methods and even its instruments, had been pressed upon the British High Command for almost exactly two years. The plan of attack at Cambrai was inherent in the original conception of the tank. It was for this, and for this precisely, that tanks had been devised.

Tanks in considerable and growing numbers had been in action on the British front since their conception had been improvidently exposed to the enemy on the Somme in 1916. At the Headquarters of the Tank Corps the original tactical ideas inspiring their conception had been earnestly and thoroughly developed. The Tank Corps had never yet been allowed to put them into practice. These engines had been used in small numbers as mere ancillaries to infantry and artillery battles. They had been condemned to wallow in the crater fields under the full blast of massed German artillery, or to founder in the mud of Paschendaele. Never had they been allowed to have their own chance in a battle made for them, adapted to their special capacities, and in which they could render the inestimable service for which they had been specially designed.

The success of a few tanks in a minor operation at Paschendaele, where in the Army Corps of General Maxse they were correctly employed, was probably the means of rescuing the Tank Corps from the increasing disfavour into which their engines had fallen through being so long mishandled by the British Headquarters. Whatever may have been the reason, the fact remains that "a project which had been constantly in the mind of the General Staff of the Tank Corps for nearly three months and in anticipation of which preparations had already been undertaken, was approved, and its date fixed for November 20."[2] All the requisite conditions were at last accorded. The tanks were to operate on ground not yet ploughed up by artillery, against a front not yet prepared to meet an offensive. Above all, Surprise! The tanks were themselves to open the attack. With a daring acceptance of responsibility Sir Julian Byng, who commanded the Army, ordered that not a shot was to be fired by the British artillery, not even

[1] *Sir Douglas Haig's Command,* Vol. I, Ch. XV, p. 283.
[2] Colonel Fuller, *Tanks in the Great War,* Chapter XIX, p. 140.

for registration, until the tanks were actually launched. The Artillery schemes which for the first time rendered this feat practicable without mishap to the troops reflect the highest credit on their authors.

The minutely prepared scheme of the Tank Corps had the following aim: "To effect the penetration of four systems of trenches in a few hours without any type of artillery preparation."[1] Nearly 500 tanks were available. "To-morrow," wrote General Elles, Commander of the Tank Corps, in his Special Order to his men, "the Tank Corps will have the chance for which it has been waiting for many months—to operate on good going in the van of the battle."

"The attack," says the historian of the Tank Corps (Colonel Fuller), "was a stupendous success. As the tanks moved forward with the infantry following close behind, the enemy completely lost his balance, and those who did not fly panic-stricken from the field surrendered with little or no resistance. . . . By 4 p.m. on November 20 one of the most astonishing battles in all history had been won and, as far as the Tank Corps was concerned, tactically finished, for no reserves existing it was not possible to do more."[2] In the brief life of a November day the whole German trench system had been penetrated on a front of 6 miles, and 10,000 prisoners and 200 guns captured, without the loss of more than 1,500 British soldiers. "It is a question," declares the Staff Officer, "whether any stroke of the allied army on the Western Front was more fruitful ultimately of ground and result than this battle of Cambrai, despite its limited design."[3]

But if this was so, why not have done it before? Why not have done it on a far larger scale? If British and French war leaders had possessed—not more genius, for the possibilities had by this time been obvious to all who were studying the tank problem—but the vision and comprehension which is expected from the honoured chiefs of great armies, there was no reason why a battle like Cambrai could not have been fought a year before, or better still, why three or four concerted battles like Cambrai could not have been fought simultaneously in the spring of 1917. Then indeed the enemy's front line pierced at once in three or four places might have been completely overwhelmed on a front of 50 miles. Then indeed the roll forward of the whole army might have been achieved and the hideous deadlocks broken.

But, it will be said, such assertions take insufficient account of the practical difficulties, of the slowly gathered experience, of the immense refinements of study, discipline and organization required. Could, for instance, 3,000 tanks

---

[1] Colonel Fuller, *Tanks in the Great War,* Chapter XIX, p. 141.

[2] *Ibid.,* pp. 148, 150.

[3] *Sir Douglas Haig's Command,* p. 392.

have been manufactured by the spring of 1917? Could the men to handle them have been spared from the front? Could their tactical training have been perfected behind the line and out of contact with the enemy? Could the secret have been kept? Would not preparation on so large a scale, even behind the line, have become apparent to the enemy? To all these questions we will answer that one-tenth of the mental effort expended by the Headquarters Staff on preparing the old-fashioned offensives of which the war had consisted, one-twentieth of the influence they used to compel reluctant Governments to sanction these offensives, one-hundredth of the men lost in them, would have solved all the problems easily and overwhelmingly before the spring of 1917. As for the Germans getting to hear of it, learning, for instance, that the British were practising with Caterpillar armoured cars at dummy trenches behind their lines on a large scale—what use would they have made of their knowledge? What use did Ludendorff make of the awful disclosure, not as a mere rumour or questionable Intelligence report, but of the actual apparition of the tanks in September, 1916? There is a melancholy comfort in reflecting that if the British and French commands were short-sighted, the ablest soldier in Germany was blind. In truth, these high military experts all belong to the same school. Haig

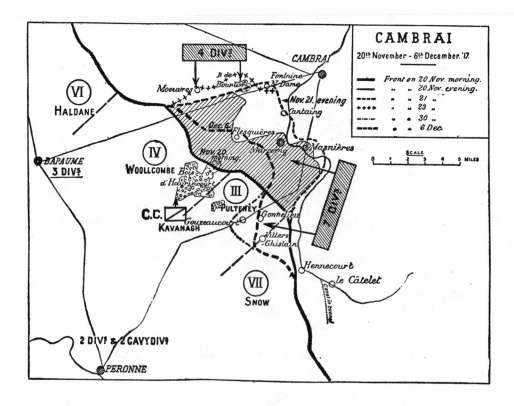

at least moved faster and farther along the new path, and in consequence, doubtingly and tardily, he reaped in the end a generous reward.

It has been necessary to the whole argument of this volume to dwell insistently upon these aspects of the Battle of Cambrai. Accusing as I do without exception all the great ally offensives of 1915, 1916, and 1917, as needless and wrongly conceived operations of infinite cost, I am bound to reply to the question. What else could be done? And I answer it, pointing to the Battle of Cambrai, *"This* could have been done." This in many variants, this in larger and better forms ought to have been done, and would have been done if only the Generals had not been content to fight machine-gun bullets with the breasts of gallant men, and think that that was waging war.

It remains only to be said of the Battle of Cambrai that the initial success so far exceeded the expectations of the Third Army Staff that no suitable preparations had been made to exploit it. The Cavalry who scampered forward were naturally soon held up by snipers and machine guns, and no important advance beyond the first day's gains was achieved. The railways at this part of the German front favoured a rapid hostile concentration, and ten days after the victory the Germans delivered a most powerful counter-stroke in which they recaptured a large portion of the conquered ground and took in their turn 10,000 prisoners and 200 guns. In this counter-attack the enemy used for the first time those tactics of "infiltration" by small highly competent parties of machine-gunners or trench-mortar men, which they were soon to employ on a larger scale. The bells which had been rung for Cambrai were therefore judged premature, and the year 1917 closed on the allied fronts, British, French, Italian, Russian and Balkan, in a gloom relieved only by Allenby's sword-flash at Jerusalem.

CHAPTER XLVIII

BRITAIN CONQUERS THE U-BOATS

It is commonly said that the German drive on Paris in 1914 and the unlimited U-boat warfare both "nearly succeeded." But this expression requires analysis, and also differentiation between the issues on land and sea. A partisan watching an evenly contested football match, an engineer watching a vehicle whose weight he does not know exactly, crossing a bridge whose strength he has never been able to measure, experience no doubt similar sensations of anxiety or excitement. The processes however are different. A football match like a great battle on land is in a continual state of flux and chance. But whether the vehicle will break down the bridge does not depend on chance. It depends on the weight of the vehicle and the strength of the bridge. When both these are unknown beforehand, anxiety is natural. But once it is known that the bridge will bear at least ten tons and the vehicle at the most weighs no more than eight, all misgivings are proved to have been unfounded. To say that the vehicle "nearly" broke down the bridge is untrue. There was never any chance of it. Whereas any one of a score of alternative accidents would have given the German Army Paris in 1914, the sea-faring resources of Great Britain were in fact and in the circumstances always superior to the U-boat attack. Moreover, that attack was inherently of a character so gradual that these superior resources could certainly obtain their full development.

Nevertheless, the struggle between the British sailormen, Royal and Mercantile—for both played an equally indispensable part—and the German U-boats stands among the most heart-shaking episodes of history, and its declared result will for generations be regarded as a turning point in the destiny of nations. It was in scale and in stake the greatest conflict ever decided at sea. It was almost entirely a duel between Britain and Germany. Austrian submarines assisted the Germans. Allied navies, United States and Japanese destroyers, helped Great Britain to the best of their power. But three-quarters of the tonnage sunk was British, and 175 U-boats out of a total German war loss of 182 were destroyed by British agency.

The shortcomings in the higher command of the British Navy, afloat and at home, which had led to Admiral de Robeck's failure to force the Dardanelles, to the abortive conclusion of Jutland, and to the neglect to carry the fighting into the German Bight, had given to the enemy during 1915 and 1916 the means of developing an entirely novel form of sea attack upon a scale the potential intensity of which no one could measure beforehand, and which if successful would be fatal. At first sight all seemed to favour the challengers. Two hundred U-boats each possessing between three and four weeks' radius of action, each capable of sinking with torpedo, gun fire or bomb four or five vessels in a single day, beset the approaches to an island along which there passed in and out every week several thousand merchant vessels. The submarine, with only a periscope showing momentarily like a broomstick above the waves, could discharge its torpedo unseen. It could rise to the surface and fire its gun to sink, burn or induce the surrender of a defenceless vessel, and disappear into the invisible depths of the vast waste of water without leaving a trace behind. Of all the tasks ever set to a Navy none could have appeared more baffling than that of sheltering this enormous traffic and groping deep below the surface of the sea for the deadly elusive foe. It was in fact a game of blind man's buff in an unlimited space of three dimensions.

Had the problem been surveyed in cold blood beforehand it might well have seemed insoluble. But in the event as the danger grew, so grew also the will-power of the threatened State and the courage, endurance and ingenuity of its servants. At the summit through the authority of the Prime Minister all misgivings were suppressed, all croakers silenced, and all doubters banished from executive responsibility. But strict inquiry was made into facts, and no official grimace passed long for argument. The qualities of audacity, initiative and seamanship inbred in the sailors and younger officers of the Navy found in this new warfare their highest opportunity. But without the unquenchable spirit of the Merchant Service nothing would have availed. The foundation of all defence lay in the fact that Merchant-seamen three or four times "submarined" returned unfalteringly to the perilous seas, and even in the awful month when one ship out of every four that left the United Kingdom never came home, no voyage was delayed for lack of resolute civilian volunteers.

To realize the issues of this strange form of warfare hitherto unknown to human experience, the reader must understand the general anatomy of the submarine. This delicate vessel is driven when on the surface by powerful oil engines which in those days yielded speeds up to sixteen or seventeen knots an hour. Submerged she depended upon electric accumulators which she could recharge by her oil engines when on the surface. These accumulators produced a maximum speed under water of about eight knots, and would last about one hour at full and twenty at economical speed. In order to dive, a submarine does not give herself negative buoyancy, i.e., make herself heavier than the water. She fills enough tanks to have about a ton of buoyancy in hand and then, by depressing her horizontal rudders and going ahead on her electric motors, swims down to the desired depth. A submarine is strong enough to resist the ever-increasing water pressures down to about two hundred and fifty feet below the surface. Beyond that depth there is increasing risk of leakage through the joints of her hull. Any serious penetration by salt water may liberate chlorine gas from the electric accumulators and choke the crew in tortures. Beyond a depth of three or four hundred feet a submarine would certainly be destroyed by the water pressure and would swiftly sink bilged to the ocean floor. In deep water therefore a submarine could only remain submerged while in motion, and could only keep in motion as long as her accumulators lasted. When these were exhausted, she must come to the surface and float defenceless during several hours while they were being recharged. On the other hand, where the sea was not more than two hundred and fifty feet deep, a submarine need not fear to give herself negative buoyancy. She could sink and sit on the bottom without using up her accumulators as long as the air and oxygen tubes she carried enabled the crew to breathe. This allowed her to remain below water for at least forty-eight hours, during which time she could also move perhaps sixty miles. The power to remain submerged for more than twenty hours was thus limited to the shallow seas. On the other hand, depths of less than fifty feet raised difficulties of another kind which prevented submerged attacks.

The prime weapon of all submarines was the torpedo; and as long as they fought warships, no other weapon was of any service. Thin-skinned submersible vessels could only engage in an artillery duel with armoured surface ships at a fatal disparity in risk. The penetration of a U-boat's hull by a single shot deprived her of the power of diving, even if it did not sink her outright. But when the Germans decided to use their U-boats to attack merchant ships, another set of arguments arose. The merchant ships were so numerous that the torpedo was an unsuitable weapon for procuring decisive results. It was expensive, difficult and lengthy to manufacture; the supply could only gradually be broadened out; and only from eight to twenty torpedoes could be carried in submarines according to their classes. As a large proportion of torpedoes missed their target for one fault or another, the destructive power of a U-boat against commerce during a single cruise was severely limited. Therefore the first move of the Germans was to arm their U-boats with guns to attack merchant ships on the surface of the water, sinking them either by gun fire or, after surrender, by bombs placed on board.

This method also enabled the U-boats to use their much superior surface speed, and allowed them to discriminate between different classes of merchant ships and between enemy and neutral ships; to observe their own Prize Law by visit and search; and finally to give time for the merchant crews, if they chose to surrender their vessel, to escape in open boats.

The first British counter-move, made on my responsibility in 1915, was to arm British merchantmen to the greatest possible extent with guns of sufficient power to deter the U-boat from surface attack. When this was achieved, the reduction of the assailant's speed and the limited torpedo supply increased the merchant ship's chance of escape proportionately. The argument was overwhelming. Unhappily there were at first hardly any guns either for merchant ships or for the coastal patrols. We searched every quarter of the globe and all the recesses of the Admiralty for guns, no matter how obsolete or various in pattern. A hundred coastal vessels by the spring of 1915 were provided with one 12-pounder gun apiece. The more important sea-going vessels were also armed. The scarcity was such that their guns had to be transferred from outward- to inward-bound vessels at ports outside the submarine zone, so as to make them go further. Despite every effort made by my successor, Mr. Balfour, the supply of guns expanded slowly; and it was not until the autumn of 1916 that he was in a position to undertake the arming of the whole of the Mercantile Marine. Good progress had however been made before the submarine danger renewed itself in its gravest form.

As the U-boats were forced by the progressive arming of the British Mercantile Marine to rely increasingly on under-water attacks, they encountered a new set of dangers. The submerged U-boat with its defective vision ran the greatest risk of mistaking neutral for British vessels and of drowning neutral crews, and thus of embroiling Germany with other great Powers. We also resorted to the well-known *ruse de guerre* of hoisting false colours in order further to baffle and confuse the enemy. Thus from a very early stage the U-boats were forced to choose between all the practical inconveniences and far-reaching diplomatic consequences of under-water attack with the torpedo, or on the other hand facing the disproportionate hazards of the gun duel on the surface. It was at this stage that we developed the stratagem of the Q-ship. A number of merchant vessels were specially equipped with torpedo tubes and with concealed guns firing from behind trap-door bulwarks, and sent along the trade routes to offer themselves to the hostile submarines. When the U-boat, wishing to economize torpedoes, attacked the Q-ship by gun fire on the surface, a portion of the British crew took to the boats and by every device endeavoured to entice the Germans to close quarters. Once the enemy was within decisive range, the White Ensign was hoisted, the trap-doors fell and a deadly fire by trained gunners was opened upon them. By these means in 1915 and 1916 eleven U-boats were destroyed and the rest, rendered far more nervous of attacking by gun fire, were thrown back more and more upon their torpedoes. By the end of 1917 this process was complete. The German submarine commanders would not face the unequal gun-fire combat. The stratagem of the Q-ship was thus exhausted, and its last victim, U.88, perished in September, 1917.

● ● ●

By all these manœuvres and pressures the Germans were confronted during 1916 with the dilemma either of losing a great many U-boats in gun duels or Q-ship ambuscades, or of resorting almost entirely to the torpedo with a vastly increased risk of offending neutrals. This complicated and nicely balanced discussion produced great stresses and cross-purposes between the German naval and civil authorities. The Naval Staff, headed by Tirpitz and Scheer, demanded that the authorities should sink at sight all vessels in the war zone. The Emperor and the Chancellor in their fear of offending neutrals insisted that the custom of visit and search should be complied with in the case of unarmed ships. But—protested the Naval Staff—which were the unarmed ships, and what would happen to the U-boat while she was making her inquiries? They declared moreover that unrestricted warfare would increase the sinkings to such an extent that Britain would be forced within six months to sue for peace.

The relative vulnerability of armed and unarmed ships can be judged from the following summary of U-boat attacks on British vessels between January 1, 1916, and January 25, 1917.

	DEFENSIVELY ARMED SHIPS.	UNARMED SHIPS.
Number attacked	310	302
Sunk by torpedoes without warning	62	30
Sunk by gun fire or bombs	12	205
Escaped	236	67
Percentage escaped	76	22

These figures are illuminating and conclusive. They show that the U-boat was scarcely ever willing to face the gun duel with an armed vessel; and in consequence that with equal numbers of ships attacked the armed ship had nearly four times the unarmed ship's chance of escape. So much for the first great measure of defence.

The principal means of *attacking* submarines under water was by dropping overboard charges which exploded at a certain depth. The shock of these explosions seriously jarred the submarine, and if near enough, deranged her mechanism or opened her joints. These depth charges were our earliest anti-submarine device. Gradually the methods of dropping them improved, and their size and number were multiplied many times. The arch-enemy of the submarine was the destroyer. She had the fastest speed, the greatest number of depth charges, and was herself cheaper than the quarry she hunted. When the periscope of a U-boat was seen in deep water all the available destroyers and motor launches and other fast small craft spread in an organized network over the surface so as to keep her down and force her to exhaust her accumulators; and alike in deep water or in shallow, the slightest indication of her whereabouts—an air bubble, an oil stain on the surface—drew the dreaded depth charges in a searching shower. As the struggle progressed the skill and methods of the hunting vessel perpetually improved. Wonderful instruments were devised for detecting the beat of a submarine propeller; and with this and other indications a U-boat was sometimes pursued to death after an intermittent but unrelenting chase of more than thirty-six hours, during which the U-boat had perhaps replenished her electric batteries on the surface unseen two or three times.

The second anti-submarine weapon was the thin wire net hung in long strips across straits or narrow channels. These nets, buoyed on the surface with glass balls, were intended to foul the propeller of the U-boat and to cling about the hull. A U-boat thus enveloped, even if her motive power was not affected, would unconsciously be trailing a fatal tell-tale buoy about upon the surface, thus guiding her pursuers. To these light nets there were added in particular channels elaborately devised necklaces of mines joined with nets and watched by large numbers of trawlers with destroyers at ready call. Collision was another danger for this slow-moving, half-blind creature; and the ram of battleship, cruiser, destroyer or merchant ship on frequent occasions exacted the final forfeit.

Lastly, submarines stalked one another, and a U-boat while attacking a merchant ship or recharging its batteries upon the surface was on more than one occasion blown to pieces by the torpedo of a submerged pursuer of whose approach she was unconscious. The brutal features inseparable from the submarine attack on merchant vessels, and the miserable fate which so often overtook the passengers and civilian crew, inspired this warfare with exceptional fierceness. The attack upon warships, however grievous in loss of life, was considered fair war by the Royal Navy. The sinking of merchant vessels or neutral ships or hospital ships seemed to be a barbarous, treacherous and piratical act deserving every conceivable means of extermination. When we consider that nearly thirteen thousand British lives were destroyed by the German U-boats and that many were civilians, and the cruel and shocking incidents—to some extent inevitable—which characterized this warfare, and when we remember further the awful character of the stakes, the fact that several hundred German officers and men were rescued from the sea or allowed to surrender after scuttling their vessels is a tribute to the restraint of the deeply injured conqueror.

The Germans had originally decided to begin unrestricted submarine war on April 1, 1916. The threat of the United States to break off relations after the attack on the *Sussex* led at the end of the month to the permission being withdrawn. When Admiral Scheer, an ardent advocate of unrestricted warfare, received this order he intemperately recalled the High Sea Fleet U-boats, refusing to permit them to work on the basis of visit and search. From May to October therefore the campaign was practically confined to the Mediterranean and to the mine-layers of the Flanders flotilla. The relief thus afforded to Great Britain in northern waters was however both fleeting and illusory. The Mediterranean U-boats, working in accordance with German prize procedure, succeeded in sinking a large number of ships, and the German Naval Staff on October 6 ordered Scheer to resume restricted warfare with the North Sea flotillas. In the interval the number of U-boats available for active service had risen from 47 in March to 93 in November. The sinkings consequently increased rapidly when operations were resumed. The average monthly loss for the period April to September had been 131,000 tons; that from November to February rose to 276,000 tons. By the end of 1916 it was evident that the development of anti-submarine measures had not kept pace with the increasing intensity of the attack. The defensive measures instituted during 1915 had increased the number of armed merchantmen and auxiliary patrol vessels, but the problem of actually attacking and destroying U-boats was still in a rudimentary stage.

On February 1 the unrestricted attack began in full vigour, and the numbers of the U-boats continually increased. The losses of British, Allied and neutral vessels increased from 181 in January to 259 in February, 325 in March, and 423 in April; the corresponding figures in gross tonnage being 298,000 in January, 468,000 in February, 500,000 in March, and 849,000 in April. We now know that the German Naval Staff estimated that British shipping could be reduced at a rate of 600,000 tons a month, and that in five months at this rate Britain would be forced to her knees. In April alone the total world tonnage lost reached the appalling figure of 849,000 tons. The average monthly loss of British shipping during April, May and June from U-boats amounted to 409,300 tons, corresponding to a rate of nearly five million tons a year. By the end of May, apart from vessels employed on naval and military services or essential trade in distant waters, and undergoing repairs, there was less than six million tons of shipping available for all the supplies and trade with the United Kingdom. If losses continued at this rate and were equally divided among the services exposed to attack, the tonnage available for trade at the beginning of 1918 would be reduced to under five million tons, that is to say, an amount almost exactly equal to the gross sinkings in 1917. It seemed that Time, hitherto counted as an incorruptible Ally, was about to change sides.

Nor did the entry of the United States into the war shed any beam of hope on these dark waters. The longed-for American resources required a vast array of British tonnage to transport them to the Front. The patrol system in the approaches to the English Channel and South of Ireland had completely broken down. Not only were the limited numbers of the patrol vessels unable to

COMPARISON BETWEEN NUMBERS OF GERMAN SUBMARINES DESTROYED BY DIFFERENT TYPES OF SHIPS.

AUXILIARY PATROL. (Trawlers, Drifters etc.) — 37

DESTROYERS. — 31

SUBMARINES. — 17

"Q" SHIPS. — 11

AIRCRAFT. — 7

MERCHANT SHIPS. — 5

CRUISERS. — 3

BATTLESHIPS. — 1

COMPARISON BETWEEN THE PRINCIPAL WEAPONS OF DESTRUCTION.

MINES. — 42

DEPTH CHARGES. — 31

GUNFIRE. — 30

RAM. — 19

TORPEDO. — 17

BLOWN UP BY GERMANS. (To avoid capture) — 14

WRECKS AND ACCIDENTS. — 10

MINE NETS. — 7

INTERNED. — 7

SWEEPS ETC. — 3

COMPARISON BETWEEN NUMBERS OF GERMAN SUBMARINES DESTROYED BY GREAT BRITAIN AND HER ALLIES.

TOTAL GERMAN SUBMARINE LOSSES _____ 199
TOTAL DESTROYED BY THE BRITISH NAVY _____ 175
(Including number blown up to avoid capture)
TOTAL DESTROYED BY THE FRENCH NAVY _____ 3
"   "   "   "   U.S.A.   " _____ 2
"   "   "   " RUSSIAN   " _____ 2

Data compiled from British and German sources

protect the shipping, but their mere presence assisted the submarines to find the traffic routes. In April the great approach route to the south-west of Ireland was becoming a veritable cemetery of British shipping, in which large vessels were sunk regularly day by day about 200 miles from land. During this month it was calculated that one in four merchant ships leaving the United Kingdom never returned. The U-boat was rapidly undermining not only the life of the British islands, but the foundations of the Allies' strength; and the danger of their collapse in 1918 began to loom black and imminent.

The stern pressure of events reacted upon Admiralty organization. In May the Naval Staff was given an appropriate position on the Board by the merging of the office of First Sea Lord and Chief of Staff, while the addition of a Deputy and Assistant who could each act with Board authority accelerated business and relieved the Chief of Staff of a mass of work. The Operations Division, hitherto troubled like Martha over many things, had not been able to think far enough ahead. In May a small planning section was instituted, charged with the study of policy and preparation of plans; and this was later in the year expanded into a separate Division. Younger officers were called to the Admiralty and more responsibility was given to them. Without this reorganization of the Staff, the measures that defeated the U-boat, even if conceived, could not have been executed. These measures took a threefold form: first, the preparation and launching of extensive mining plans; secondly, the further development of research and supply in the technical fields of mines, depth charges and hydrophones; and thirdly, the decisive step, the institution of a convoy system which involved the escort and control of all merchant shipping.

I had instituted the convoy system for troopships crossing the oceans at the beginning of the war. Then the attack by faster German light cruisers was the danger. The guns of an obsolete battleship or heavy cruiser could certainly drive away any hostile raiders then loose upon the surface of the seas. We had also from the beginning used destroyer escorts to convoy troopships in and out through the submarine zone. In no case did any mishap occur. It did not however seem reasonable to expect similar results from the convoy system in the case of attack by submarines upon merchant ships. On the contrary it seemed obvious that hostile submarines would work more damage in the midst of a crowd of merchantmen than against isolated vessels; and it was further evident that the escorting warships would themselves be among the targets of the enemy torpedoes. The U-boat attacks on trade in 1915 and the early part of 1916 seemed to have been confined within tolerable limits by the numbers of merchant vessels at sea, by the variety of their routes and ports, by the uncertainty of their times of arrival, and above all by the size of the sea. The system of watching and patrolling in the greatest strength possible the confluences of trade had worked well against the German raiding cruisers, and for the first two years of the war the Admiralty relied upon it against the U-boats without serious misadventure.

When under the pressure of ever-increasing losses the remedy of convoys was again advocated by the younger officers of the Admiralty War Staff, it encountered opposition from practically every quarter. Every squadron and every naval base was clamant for destroyers, and convoy meant taking from them even those that they had. There would be delays due to assembling. There must be reduction in speed of the faster vessels and congestion of ships in port. The scale and difficulties of the task were exaggerated, and it was argued that the larger the number of ships in company, the greater the risk from submarines. This convincing logic could only be refuted by the proof of facts. In January, 1917, the official Admiralty opinion was expressed as follows:

> A system of several ships sailing in company as a convoy is not recommended in any area where submarine attack is a possibility. It is evident that the larger the number of ships forming a convoy, the greater the chance of a submarine being able to attack successfully and the greater the difficulty of the escort in preventing such an attack.

The French and United States naval authorities were also opposed to the convoy system, and at a Conference held in February, 1917, representative Masters of merchant ships took the same view.

Now let us see what was overlooked in this high, keen and earnest consensus. The size of the sea is so vast that the difference between the size of a convoy and the size of a single ship shrinks in comparison almost to insignificance. There was in fact very nearly as good a chance of a convoy of forty ships in close order slipping unperceived between the patrolling U-boats as there was for a single ship; and each time this happened, forty ships escaped instead of one. Here then was the key to the success of the convoy system against U-boats. The concentration of ships greatly reduced the number of targets in a given area and thus made it more difficult for the submarines to locate their prey. Moreover, the convoys were easily controlled and could be quickly deflected by wireless from areas known to be dangerous at any given moment. Finally the destroyers, instead of being dissipated on patrol over wide areas, were concentrated at the point of the hostile attack, and opportunities of offensive action frequently arose. Thirteen U-boats were actually destroyed while endeavouring to molest convoys. This fear of instant retaliation from convoy escorts had a demoralizing effect upon the enemy, and consequently U-boat attacks were not always pressed home.

Most of this was still unproved in the early days of 1917. There stood only the fact that troopship convoys had always been escorted through the subma-

rine zones during 1915 and 1916, and had enjoyed complete immunity from attack. The highest professional opinion remained opposed to convoy as a defence against U-boats.

It fell to Sir Edward Carson's lot during his tenure as First Lord to face the
most anxious and trying period of the naval war. During those eight months
the U-boat sinkings of merchantmen reached their terrible climax. It was under
his administration that the peak was surmounted and most of the important
decisions of principle were taken by which the peril was ultimately overcome.
The trial of the convoy system was urged upon the naval authorities by the
Cabinet, and in this the Prime Minister took a decisive part.

At the end of April, 1917, the Director of the Anti-Submarine Division definitely advocated the introduction of convoys, and the first one left Gibraltar
on May 10. It was entirely successful, and regular convoys commenced from the
United States on June 4. Instructions were issued on June 22 to extend the system to Canadian ports, and on July 31 similar orders were issued for the South
Atlantic trade. The entry of the United States facilitated convoys by opening
her harbours as ports of assembly and by the precious aid of a number of her
destroyers for escort work. More than a quarter of the whole of the escorts
across the Atlantic were provided by American destroyers, and the comradeship
of this hard service forms an ineffaceable tradition for the two navies.

The convoy organization will for ever stand as a monument to the constancy and courage of the Royal Navy and Mercantile Marine. No credit is too
high for the officers and men who without previous training navigated these
fleets of forty or fifty ships in close formation through all the winds that blew.
No service ever carried out by the Navy was of greater value to the State than
that of the escort vessels. Those who have served in small ships will realize the
skill, faithfulness and hardihood required to carry out this duty day after day,
month after month, in wild weather and wintry seas without breakdown or
failure. The control and arrangements of the Admiralty and the Ministry of
Shipping became more thorough and perfect with every week that passed.

The convoy system was at first confined to homeward-bound vessels. The
percentage of sinkings in the outward sailings at once began to rise. In August,
1917, convoy was extended to outward-bound vessels. The triumph of convoy
was soon apparent. By the end of October, 1917, 99 homeward convoys, comprising over 1,500 steamers of a deadweight capacity of 10,656,000 tons, had
been brought in with the loss of only 10 ships torpedoed while actually in convoy, and of 14 which had become separated.

While convoy was vastly improving the protection of trade, all methods of
attacking the U-boats were progressively developed, and the rate of destruction
steadily rose. In April, 1917, British submarine flotillas were based upon Scapa
Flow, Lough Swilly on the North, and Killybegs on the West coast of Ireland,

and began to lie in wait for U-boats passing northabout to attack the great trade route. At the same time in the Southern part of the North Sea the small British "C" Class submarines were released from harbour defence for the same duties. This method by which submarine vessels preyed on each other yielded substantial results. Seven U-boats were destroyed by it in 1917 and six in 1918. The threat of submarine attack also forced the U-boats to submerge much more frequently and for longer periods on their passage, with consequent delays in reaching their beats.

The mine, however, proved to be the most effective killing weapon. The Admiralty, before the war, had not expected the mine to play an important part. In a war on the surface of the sea the weaker navy would no doubt use such a weapon to hamper the movements of its superior antagonist: but for the stronger fleet, the fewer mine-fields the better. These conclusions, which at the time were not ill-founded, were upset by the changes for which the prolongation of the war gave time. At the outset the British mines were few and inefficient. It was even stated in a German Order that "British mines generally do not explode." This was an exaggeration: but we were certainly at fault in the matter.

At the end of April, 1916, an attempt was made by the Dover Force, under Admiral Sir Reginald Bacon, to blockade the Flanders U-boats by a long and extensive barrage off the Belgian coast. This was completed by May 7. It consisted of 18 miles of moored mines and nets guarded from May to October by day patrols. U.B.13 was destroyed by one of its mines the day after the barrage was laid, and an immediate diminution of U-boat activity in the North Sea and the Channel followed. This was not unnaturally attributed to the new barrage and gave the Dover Command an exaggerated idea of its value. We now know that it was to Admiral Scheer's impulsive recall of the High Sea Fleet U-boat flotillas, and not to the Dover barrage that the marked improvement of these months was due, for only one U-boat was destroyed by its mines; nor did it seriously impede their movements in and out.

Efforts to improve the quality of the British mines had been unceasing since the beginning of the war. It was not until the autumn of 1917 that the new "horned" mines became available in large quantities. The improvement of the new type upon the old cannot be better measured than by the fact that out of forty-one U-boats destroyed by mines only five were prior to September, 1917. No less than 15,700 mines were laid in the Heligoland Bight during 1917 and 21,000 more in 1918, mainly by the 20th Destroyer Flotilla working from the Humber. This attempt to block in the U-boats developed into a protracted struggle between British mine-layers and German mine-sweepers. The enemy was forced to escort the U-boats both on their inward and outward journey with a whole array of mine-sweepers, of specially constructed ships with concrete-filled bows called "barrier-breakers," and torpedo boats. These escorts had to be protected, and from 1917 onwards the main occupation of the High Sea Fleet was the support of its sweeping forces working far afield on the submarine routes. As time went on the difficulties of egress and ingress increased. The "ways" or swept channels in the Bight were frequently closed, and in October, 1917, homeward-bound submarines began to be sent round by the Kattegat. Early in 1918 about 1,400 deep mines were laid in the Kattegat but could not be patrolled. The intensive mining of the Bight failed to achieve success because of the difficulties of attacking the German sweeping craft and the lack of destroyers for the patrol of the Kattegat. The effort however destroyed several U-boats, and increased their time on passage to and from the trade routes.

During 1917 the failure of the 1916 Barrage across the Dover Straits had been total. From February to November U-boats continued to pass through it at the rate of about twenty-four a month. The Dover passage saved a small Flanders U-boat nearly eight days on its fourteen-days' cruise, and a larger boat from the Bight six days out of twenty-five. It was decided to make a fresh attempt with all the improved appliances now at hand. On November 21 a new deep minefield was laid between the Varne and Gris Nez. When no fewer than twenty-one U-boats passed through this in the first fortnight, a sharp controversy arose at the Admiralty. Some authorities supported the contentions of the Dover Command that the barrage was largely successful and that additional patrolling was impracticable. Others held that an intensive patrol and the use of searchlights and flares at night to make the U-boats dive into the mines would achieve great results. About this time, and partly in connection with this discussion, Sir John Jellicoe was replaced as First Sea Lord by Admiral Wemyss, and Admiral Bacon was succeeded in the Dover Command by Admiral Keyes. Keyes revolutionized the situation. He redoubled the patrols, and by night the barrage from end to end became as bright as Piccadilly. The German destroyers from Ostend and Zeebrugge attempted to break down the patrols by sudden raids. They were repulsed in fierce night actions and the watch maintained with ever-increasing efficiency. Nine U-boats perished in the Dover area between January and May, 1918, and four more by September. As early as February the Bight boats ceased to use the Straits, and by April the Flanders boats had largely abandoned it. In September only two boats passed through, one of which was destroyed on its return.

The famous story of the blocking of Zeebrugge on St. George's Day by Admiral Keyes and the Dover Force cannot be repeated here. It may well rank as the finest feat of arms in the Great War, and certainly as an episode unsurpassed in the history of the Royal Navy. The harbour was completely blocked for about three weeks and was dangerous to U-boats for a period of two months. Although the Germans by strenuous efforts partially cleared the entrance after some weeks for U-boats, no operations of any importance were ever again carried out by the Flanders destroyers. The results of Admiral Keyes's command at Dover reduced the Allied losses in the English Channel from about twenty to six a month and the minefields laid by the Flanders boats fell from thirty-three a month in 1917 to six a month in 1918. These results, which constitute a recognizable part of the general victory, were achieved notwithstanding the fact that the numbers of U-boats in commission were maintained by new building at about two hundred.

The attempts to mine in the Heligoland Bight had been frustrated by the German sweeping operations, closely supported by the High Sea Fleet. It was thought that a more distant barrage, under the direct watch and ward of the Grand Fleet, might succeed. In 1918 an ambitious scheme for establishing a line of guarded minefields across the 180 miles of water between Norway and the Orkney Islands was developed by the British and American Navies. Enormous quantities of materials, regardless of cost or diversion of effort, were employed upon this supreme manifestation of defensive warfare. The large centre section was laid entirely by Americans, the Orkney section by the British, and the Norway section by the two Navies in combination. The Americans used a special type of mine with antennæ that exploded the charge on coming into contact with the metal hull. They laid no less than 57,000 mines, a large number of which exploded prematurely shortly after being laid. The British contribution was about 13,000 mines, but some of these were not laid deep enough for surface craft to pass over and had in consequence to be swept up. The efficiency of this enormous material effort cannot be judged, for the minefield was barely completed when the Armistice was signed. It is known however that two U-boats were damaged on the centre section, and four may possibly have been destroyed on the Orkney section.

The ever-increasing efficiency of the Anti-Submarine Organization during 1918 also mastered the mine-laying tactics of the U-boats. Closer co-operation between the British Intelligence and Mine Sweeping Divisions, the rapid distribution of news, the firmer control of shipping and the use of the "Otter" [1] all played their part. One hundred and twenty-three British merchant ships had been sunk by German mines in 1917. In 1918 this number was reduced to 10. All other anti-submarine devices were developed with ceaseless ingenuity. Aircraft, hydrophones and special types of mines levied an increasing toll upon the U-boats. During 1918 high hopes were based on systematic hunting tactics, and trawler flotillas equipped with ingenious listening devices were assembled in the

---

[1] A species of submerged wire-cutter towed on both bows for cutting the mooring ropes of mines.

northern area for this purpose. Several contacts were made, but the U-boats escaped by going dead slow so that their movements could not be detected by the instruments; and we could not provide enough destroyers over such wide areas to exhaust their accumulators.

The final phase of the U-boat war saw the rôles of the combatants reversed. It was the U-boat and not the merchant ship that was hunted. The experiences of U.B.110 on her first cruise may serve as an example. She sailed from Zeebrugge on July 5, 1918. Even before she had joined the Flanders Flotilla she had been attacked by two aeroplanes. Every day from July 7 onwards her log records the dropping of depth charges around her in ever-increasing numbers until the 18th, when twenty-six exploded close at hand. She was only able to fire two torpedoes during the cruise. The first one damaged an oil ship, but she could not see the result of the second owing to an immediate and violent counter-attack by destroyers. On the 19th, when attempting to attack a convoy, her diving rudders were damaged by a depth charge dropped from a motor launch; and while endeavouring to submerge she was rammed and sunk by a destroyer. In these latter days a Flanders U-boat could hope for only six voyages before meeting its dark doom. The unceasing presentiment of a sudden and frightful death beyond human sight or succour, the shuddering concussions of the depth charges, the continual attacks of escort vessels, the fear of annihilation at any moment from mines, the repeated hair-breadth escapes, produced a state of nervous tension in the U-boat crews. Their original high morale declined rapidly during 1918 under an intolerable strain. The surrender of more than one undamaged submarine and numerous cases of boats putting back for small repairs a few days after leaving harbour showed that even in this valiant age the limits of human endurance had been reached.

The various stages of the U-boat war and its strange conditions have now been examined. No sooner had the German war leaders taken their irrevocable decision to begin the unlimited attack on commerce than the Russian Revolution, by rendering their situation less desperate, removed the principal impulsion. No sooner had the unlimited U-boat warfare forced the United States into the field against Germany than the effectiveness of the U-boats began to decline. The month that saw President Wilson jingling among his Cavalrymen to the Senate to cast the life energy of a nation of a hundred and twenty millions into the adverse scales marked also the zenith of the U-boat attack. Never again did Germany equal the April sinkings. Many months of grievous losses and haunting anxiety lay before the Islanders and their Allies, and immense diversions—some needless—of straitened resources hampered their military effort. But with every month the sense of increasing mastery grew stronger. At one time the plotted curves of sinkings and replacements which our graphs revealed seemed a veritable "writing on the wall." But the awful characters faded

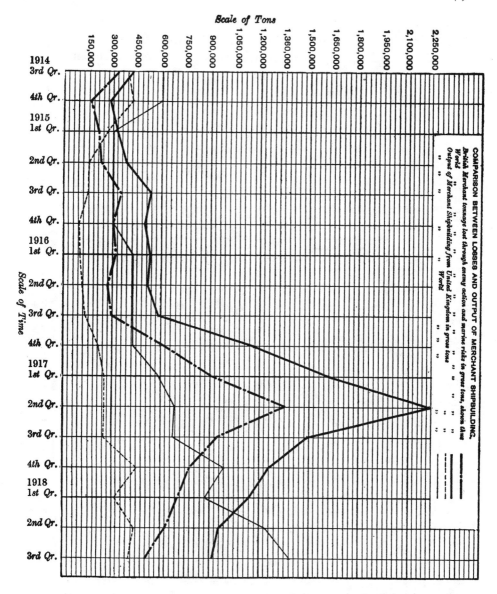

Scale of Tons

COMPARISON BETWEEN LOSSES AND OUTPUT OF MERCHANT SHIPBUILDING.

British Merchant tonnage lost through enemy action and marine risks in gross tons, above that
World
Output of Merchant Shipbuilding from United Kingdom in gross tons
World

steadily. The autumn of 1917, which was to have seen the fulfilment of German dreams, came, passed, and left us safer. By the end of the year it was certain we should not succumb. It was certain moreover that the war could be carried on until the power of the United States could if necessary be fully exerted on the battlefields of Europe. By the middle of 1918 the submarine campaign had been definitely defeated; and though new U-boats replaced those destroyed, every month added to their perils, to the restriction of their depredations and to the demoralization of their crews. The weapon purchased so dearly by the German war leaders had first been blunted and then broken in their hands. It remained for them only to pay the price, and meet the fury of the world in arms. But from this they did not shrink.

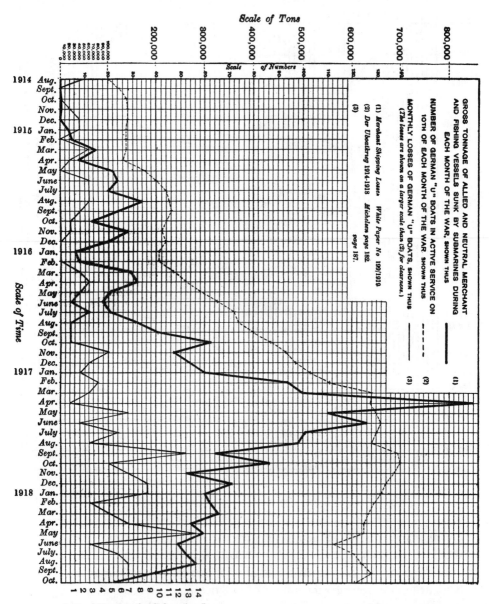

CHAPTER XLIX

THE GERMAN CONCENTRATION IN THE WEST

An acute crisis in Man-Power followed the prodigal campaign of 1917, and a prolonged and searching examination of our remaining resources was made by the War Cabinet. The British Infantry, on whom the brunt of the slaughter had fallen, were woefully depleted. The battalions were far below their proper strength, and even so, largely composed of new drafts. The losses of the artillery both in men and guns destroyed were also most severe. The loss in officers was out of all proportion even to the great losses of the rank and file. The task had throughout demanded an unprecedented degree of sacrifice from regimental officers. More than five thousand had been killed outright and over fifteen thousand had been wounded in the Paschendaele offensive. This loss was especially difficult to replace; could never in fact be fully replaced. We had every reason to expect that the main fighting of 1918 in France would fall upon Great Britain. The French, who had begun with the unequalled slaughter of 1914 and had ever since been engaged on a scale of nearly one hundred and twenty divisions, must necessarily and naturally be expected to reserve their remaining strength—grand it proved to be—for supreme emergencies. It was now certain that the United States, in spite of their utmost efforts and passionate desire to share the suffering, could not play more than a minor part in the actual battles. Only eight or nine American divisions were in fact due to enter the line before the summer was far spent. Substantial help had been sent perforce from the Western Front to Italy, and none could be expected in return. We had also almost the whole burden of the war against Turkey on our hands; and Allenby, so far from being able to release divisions, was continually pressing not only for drafts but for reinforcements. Additional forces, both British and Indian, were required for the army in Mesopotamia; and finally the Salonika Front, on which we bore our share, was a constant drain. It was in these grave circumstances that we had to anticipate a German onslaught far exceeding in power and fury anything that had yet been experienced.

The final collapse of Russia had liberated enormous masses of German and Austrian troops. During the whole of the winter the movement of divisions and guns from the Eastern to the Western Front, and to a lesser extent against Italy, was unceasing. How great this movement actually was we could not measure exactly, but the Intelligence reports, with which I endeavoured to saturate myself, revealed week after week an unending flow of men and material to the West. Surveying the forces on both sides in the main theatre, it could not be doubted that by the spring Germany would have for the first time in the war, not even excepting the original invasion, a large numerical preponderance on the Western Front. Moreover, the divisions coming from Russia would, by the opening of the new campaign, have had nearly a year without serious fighting in which to recuperate and train. All our fighting units, on the other hand, had been decimated fivefold in the last six months of 1917. Finally, in addition to the masses of German and Austrian artillery released from the Russian front, the enemy had captured at least four thousand guns from Russia and two thousand from Italy, together with immense supplies of war material of all kinds.

Sir Douglas Haig vehemently and naturally called for all the officers and men required to bring his divisions up to full strength at the earliest possible moment. Robertson supported him, and was evidently seriously alarmed. From my central position between the Army and the War Cabinet, with, I believe, the whole information available in my possession and with constant intimate access to the Prime Minister, I never ceased to press for the immediate reinforcement of Sir Douglas Haig. Mr. Lloyd George viewed with horror the task imposed on him of driving to the shambles by stern laws the remaining manhood of the nation. Lads of eighteen and nineteen, elderly men up to forty-five, the last surviving brother, the only son of his mother (and she a widow), the father the sole support of the family, the weak, the consumptive, the thrice wounded—all must now prepare themselves for the scythe. To meet the German onslaught when it came—if it came—everything must be thrown in: but the Prime Minister feared lest our last resources should be expended in another Paschendaele.

It was in December that the shadow fell darkly upon the military mind. Up till then the Cabinet had been assured that all was going well in the West, and that—granted the drafts—the New Year could be faced with confidence. At the Ministry of Munitions we had long been instructed to prepare for a renewed thirty weeks' offensive beginning in the earliest spring. With the end of Paschendaele came the end of illusions. A sudden sinister impression was sustained by the General Staff. The cry for a fresh offensive died away. The mood swung round to pure defence—and against heavy odds. It was a revolution at once silent and complete. I responded to it with instant relief. The War Cabinet however continued for some time to rest themselves upon the confident declarations of the Generals made in September in advocacy of perseverance at Paschendaele. They did not readily conform to the military *volte-face* and were sceptical of tales so utterly at variance with those of a few weeks before.

I urged that the Cabinet should send all the men that were needed to reconstitute the army, and should at the same time forbid absolutely any resumption of the offensive. The Prime Minister however did not feel that, if the troops were once in France, he would be strong enough to resist those military pressures for an offensive which had so often overborne the wiser judgment of Statesmen. He therefore held, with all his potent influence, to a different policy. He sanctioned only a moderate reinforcement of the army, while at the same time gathering in England the largest possible numbers of reserves. In this way he believed he would be able alike to prevent a British offensive and to feed the armies during the whole course of the fearful year which was approaching. This was in fact achieved. But I held, and hold still, that the War Cabinet should have been resolute, as I believe it would have been found strong enough, at once to support and to restrain the High Command in France.

My official or public arguments were reinforced by the strongest personal appeals. Nothing however had the slightest effect. The Prime Minister and his colleagues in the War Cabinet were adamant. Their policy was not decided without full deliberation. They were definitely opposed to any renewal of the British offensive in France. They wished the British and French armies to observe during 1918 a holding and defensive attitude. They wished to keep a tight control over their remaining man-power until the arrival of the American millions offered the prospect of decisive success. In the meanwhile action in Palestine, with forces almost inappreciable in the scale of the Western Front, might drive Turkey out of the war, and cheer the public mind during a long and grievous vigil. They were fully informed of the growing German concentration against Haig, and repeatedly discussed it. But they believed that the Germans if they attacked would encounter the same difficulties as had so long baffled us, and that our armies were amply strong enough for defence. Haig was accordingly left to face the spring with an army whose 56 infantry divisions were reduced from a thirteen to a ten-battalion basis,[1] and with three instead of five cavalry divisions,[2] which in the absence of alternate methods were at last to render valuable service.

But this was not the end of his trials. The French, also living in a world of illusions, now came forward with a vehement demand that the British should take over a larger part of the front. A cursory glance at the map shows that the French with 100 divisions comprising 700,000 rifles held 480 kilometres of front, whereas 56 British divisions comprising 504,000 rifles only held 200 kilometres. In other words, the British with more than two-thirds of the French rifle strength held less than one-third of the front. But this was a very superficial test. Large portions of the French front were in continual quiescence, and the

[1] Or from twelve to nine, if the Pioneer Battalion is excluded.
[2] Two Indian cavalry divisions were sent from France to Palestine.

weak railway communications opposite them excluded the possibility of a serious hostile offensive. The British, on the other hand, held nearly all the most
active front, and had opposite to them, even in January, a larger proportion
of German divisions than were marshalled against the French Army. Against
the long French front were arrayed 79 German divisions, while no fewer than
69 stood before the short British sector. Moreover, the German concentration
against the British front was growing week by week, and it was already extremely probable that the first and main thrust would be delivered upon them.
Further, the French had not fought a heavy battle since April and May, 1917,
while the British Army had maintained an almost continuous offensive, suffering, as we have seen, calamitous losses. Finally, the French soldier enjoyed
nearly three times as much leave to visit his home as his British comrade; that is
to say, there were in proportion three times as many French rifles absent from
the line at any given moment as there were British.

Under pressure both from the French and the British Governments, Haig
had agreed in December to extend his front by fourteen miles as far south
as Barisis; and this relief was effected in February. A further demand by the
French that the British front should be extended to Berry-au-Bac thirty miles
farther south-east, though backed with the threatened resignation of Monsieur
Clémenceau, was successfully resisted under a similar threat by the British
Commander-in-Chief.

The continued friction and want of confidence between Sir William
Robertson and Mr. Lloyd George came to a head at the beginning of February.
The Prime Minister was moving cautiously but tirelessly towards the conception of a unified command. He did not yet feel strong enough to disclose his
purpose. A proposal which obviously involved placing the British armies under
a French Commander was one which he judged as yet beyond his strength to
carry. It was a hazardous issue on which to challenge the joint resignations both
of Sir William Robertson and Sir Douglas Haig. It is probable that the War
Cabinet would not have been united in its support; and that the Liberal opposition would have been unanimous against it. The Prime Minister had therefore
so far suspended his wishes that speaking of an independent generalissimo he
told the House of Commons in December: "I am utterly opposed to that suggestion. It would not work. It would produce real friction, and might produce
not merely friction between the armies, but friction between the nations and
the Governments."

Nevertheless, Mr. Lloyd George continued by a series of extremely laborious and mystifying manœuvres to move steadily forward towards his solution.
On January 30, at the meeting of the Supreme War Council at Versailles, he secured a decision to create a general reserve of thirty divisions and to entrust it
to a Committee representing Britain, Italy, the United States and France, with

General Foch at its head. This proposal constitutes his answer and that of the War Cabinet to the charge of imprudently lowering the strength of the British Army in France in the face of the growing German concentration. There is no doubt that had this plan been put immediately into execution, and had Foch been armed with thirty divisions specifically assigned to the support of whatever part of the front was attacked, larger resources would have been secured to Haig in his approaching hour of supreme need. Haig did not however welcome the proposal. He declared that he had no divisions to spare for the general reserve, and that there were not even enough for the various army fronts. In such circumstances the earmarking of particular British divisions for service elsewhere could have been little more than a formality. None could have been taken from him unless the attack fell elsewhere.

The decision, like many others of the Supreme War Council, remained a dead letter; and events moved forward without the British Army receiving either the reinforcements for which Haig had pleaded or the reserves which Lloyd George had laboured to supply.

Although the thirty divisions were lacking, the Executive Committee to control them at Versailles was created. Sir William Robertson claimed that he, as Chief of the Imperial General Staff, should alone represent Great Britain upon it. This raised an issue upon which the Prime Minister felt himself strong enough to engage. He declared it a matter of fundamental principle that the two posts could not be held by one man. It was his undoubted intention to arm the Cabinet with an alternative set of military advisers whose opinions could be used to curb and correct the Robertson-Haig view, and so prevent a repetition of offensives like Paschendaele. No doubt he would also have used the new body to promote schemes of war outside the Western Front. The arrangement was indefensible in principle, but in the aftermath of Paschendaele its objects were worthy. Into the complications of the dispute and its manœuvres it is not necessary to enter here. On February 11, Robertson, returning to London, which he had somewhat imprudently quitted for a few days, was confronted by the Secretary of State for War with a note signed on February 9 by the Prime Minister. This reduced the functions of the C.I.G.S. to the limits which had existed before the Kitchener breakdown, and it prescribed the independent functions of the British Military Representative on the Versailles Committee. Thirdly, it nominated Sir William Robertson Military Representative, and Sir Henry Wilson Chief of the Imperial General Staff. Robertson, astonished at his supersession, declined the appointment to Versailles on the ground that the arrangement was unsound. The post of C.I.G.S., although originally designed for Wilson, was then incontinently offered to Sir Herbert Plumer, who with equal promptitude refused it. Finally, it was offered again to Robertson on the reduced basis of the Prime Minister's Note. On February 16 Robertson recorded his refusal to agree to the conditions prescribed, and that same evening the Official Press Bureau announced that the Government had "accepted his resignation." He had in fact been dismissed. Lord Derby, who did his best to compose the differences, also proffered his resignation, which was not accepted.

The principles of military duty on which Sir Douglas Haig invariably proceeded prevented him, even at this time of tension with the Government, from adding his own resignation to the dismissal of the Chief of the Imperial General Staff. On questions which in his view involved the safety of the British armies under his command, Sir Douglas Haig—right or wrong—was, whenever necessary, ready to resign. But these constituted the sole exceptions which he allowed himself to make in his obedience. Had any motive of personal intrigue been present in his mind, the crisis between the High Command and the Civil Power would have been gravely aggravated. The position of the Government at this time was strong and the issue one on which they could rely on public support. The Prime Minister did not flinch. Nevertheless Haig's retention, without comment, of his post was received with relief by the anxious War Cabinet; and Sir Henry Wilson was speedily appointed to the vacant chair in Whitehall.

It would certainly not be just to assume in these transactions that any of the parties were influenced otherwise than by public duty. But beneath the bald record of events the clash is plain. Both the Prime Minister and Sir William Robertson were in deadly earnest, both measured forces, and both knew the risks they ran. It was impossible for the two men to work together any longer. The situation at the centre of power had become intolerable. Action was long overdue. It was a pity it could not have taken a simpler form.

Sir William Robertson was an outstanding military personality. His vision as a strategist was not profound, but his outlook was clear, well-drilled and practical. During his tenure he had reintroduced orderly methods of dealing with War Office problems, and had revivified the General Staff system. He had no ideas of his own, but a sensible judgment negative in bias. He represented professional formalism expressed in the plainest terms. He held a conception of war policy wholly opposed to the views set out in these volumes, but honestly and consistently maintained. I was glad, as Secretary of State for War, when after the victory he eventually retired from the Army, to submit a recommendation to the King which enabled his long and honourable career from the rank of a private soldier to end with the baton of a Field-Marshal.

In the stresses of this internal disturbance I took no part. I was on the front during the whole week busily occupied, and it was only on my return that I learned the inner facts from various actors in the drama. The view which I took of my own work made it necessary for me to keep continually in touch with the actual conditions of the fighting line. The Commander-in-Chief accorded me the fullest liberty of movement in the British zone, and placed every facility at my disposal. I was most anxious to understand by personal observation the latest methods of holding the line which were involved in the preparations for a great defensive battle. I stayed with General Lipsett, commanding the 3rd Canadian Division, and under his deeply instructed guidance examined minutely from front to rear the whole of the sector which he occupied opposite to Lens.

Very different was the state of the line from what I had known it to be when serving with the Guards in 1915 or as a Battalion Commander in 1916. The system of continuous trenches with their barbed-wire networks, their parapets, firing-steps, traverses and dugouts, the first line of which was manned in great strength and often constituted the strongest line of resistance, had vanished. Contact with the enemy was maintained only by a fringe of outposts, some of which were fortified, while others trusted merely to concealment. Behind these over a distance of two or three thousand yards were sited intricate systems of machine-gun nests, nearly all operating by flank fire and mutually supporting each other. Slender communication trenches enabled these to be approached and relieved by night. The barbed-wire networks, instead of being drawn laterally in a continuous belt across the front, lay obliquely with intervals so as to draw the attacker into avenues mercilessly swept by machine-gun fire. Open spaces between important points were reserved for the full fury of the protecting barrages. This was the Battle Zone. Two thousand yards or so farther in the rear were the field battery positions. Strong works to which the long disused word "redoubt" was applied, and deep grids of trenches and deeper dugouts elaborately camouflaged, provided for the assembling and maintenance of the supporting troops. Behind these again in modest and obscure recesses lay the Brigade Headquarters; behind which again the groups of heavy and medium batteries were disposed in studied irregular array. Favoured by beautiful weather and a quiet day, we were able by taking care to make our way into the ruins of Avion village, in which in twos and threes the keen-eyed Canadian sharp-shooters maintained their ceaseless bickering against the German outposts fifty or a hundred yards away.

I must frankly admit that all that I saw, both in the line and of the minutely perfected organization far to the rear, inspired me with confidence in the strength of the defensive system which had gradually developed as the war proceeded. Holding the convictions which this volume describes of the relative power of offence and defence under modern conditions, I looked forward, at least so far as this sector was concerned, to the day when the Germans would taste a measure of that bitter draught our armies had been made to drink so long. Alas, the conditions here were by no means representative of the general state of the line.

• • •

It is no disparagement of the qualities of Sir William Robertson to record the very great pleasure with which I learned of the appointment of Sir Henry Wilson to be Chief of the Staff. We had known each other for many years. I had met him first by the banks of the Tugela in February, 1900, and my first picture of him is a haggard but jocular Major emerging from a bloody night's work in the Pieter's Hill fighting. It was in discussion with him from 1910 onwards that I had studied the problem of a war between France and Germany. Though I recorded at the time somewhat different conclusions about the opening phase from those on which he proceeded, my debt to him was very great. Never shall I forget the memorable forecast which in August, 1911, during the Agadir crisis, he had given to the Committee of Imperial Defence. At this period we were close confederates. The crisis passed away, and the Irish quarrel sundered our personal relations. A devoted son of Ulster, he resented with a passion which knew no bounds the Home Rule policy of the Liberal Government. During the intense days which preceded the British declaration of war upon Germany we were forced to meet on several occasions, but on a purely official basis. The mobilization of the Fleet and the final decision to join France, in which I had played my part, carried all before them in Wilson's heart. But this I did not know, and it was with surprise that one August morning I received at the Admiralty a visit of ceremony from him on the eve of his departure for France. He had come to say that all past differences were obliterated and that we were friends again. He was opposed later on to the Dardanelles expedition. At that time he saw the war only in the light of the struggle in France. Had he commanded the central point of view, he would perhaps have had a different opinion. At any rate his policy as Chief of the Staff was far wider in its scope than the Western Front. But these disagreements did not, so far as I am aware, impair our personal relations; and when later on I served in France as a Battalion Commander, he showed me every courtesy and often discussed the whole situation, military and political, with the freedom we had practised at Whitehall in days when my position was superior. His appointment as Chief of the Staff led immediately to the closest harmony between the spheres of Strategy and Material. The conceptions of war which I held, and which these pages record, received from him a keen and pregnant welcome. Almost his first act was to raise the War Office demand for the Tank Corps from 18,000 to 46,000 men.

In Sir Henry Wilson the War Cabinet found for the first time an expert adviser of superior intellect, who could explain lucidly and forcefully the whole situation and give reasons for the adoption or rejection of any course. Such gifts are, whether rightly or wrongly, the object of habitual distrust in England. But they are certainly a very great comfort in the transaction of public business. Sir Henry Wilson constantly corrected the clarity of his mind by whimsical mannerisms and modes of expression. He spoke in parables, used curious images and cryptic phrases. He had a vocabulary of his own. The politicians were "frocks"; Clémenceau, always the "Tiger." He even addressed him as Tiger. His faithful Aide-de-Camp, Duncannon, was "the Lord." He wantonly pronounced grotesquely the names of French towns and Generals. In discussing the gravest matters he used the modes of levity. "Prime Minister," he began one day to the War Cabinet, at a meeting which I attended, "to-day I am Boche." Then followed a penetrating description of the situation from the standpoint of the German Headquarters. On another day he would be France or Bulgaria, and always out of this affectation there emerged, to my mind, the root of the matter in hand. But some ministers were irritated. He did not go so far as Marshal Foch, who sometimes gave a military description in pantomime; but their methods of displaying a war proposition had much in common.

I can see him so clearly as I write, standing before the map in the Cabinet Room giving one of his terse telegraphese appreciations. "This morning, Sir, a new battle." (The reader will recognize it when it comes.) "This time it is we who have attacked. We have attacked with two armies—one British, one French. Sir Haig is in his train, Prime Minister, very uncomfortable, near the good city of Amiens. And Rawly[1] is in his left hand and Debeney in his right. Rawly is using five hundred tanks. It is a big battle, and we thought you would not like us to tell you about it beforehand." I cannot vouch for the actual words, but this was the sense and manner of it.

We should be thankful that the future is veiled. I was to be present at another scene in this room. There was no Henry Wilson. The Prime Minister and I faced each other, and on the table between us lay the pistols which an hour before had taken this loyal man's life.

I have strayed alike from narrative and chronology to make in deep respect this reference to the most comprehending military mind of our day in Britain and to a soldier who, although he commanded no armies, exerted on occasion a profound and fortunate influence over the greatest events.

With Sir Henry Wilson, as his deputy, came the brilliant Harington, who at Plumer's side had won for the Second Army its unequalled reputation. I think I may say that in all that concerned the making of the weapons for a campaign in 1919, with their inevitable profound reactions upon its plans, we thought as one. He supported me in all my principal projects for the supply of the armies, and used, under Sir Henry Wilson, the whole power of the General Staff to carry forward the plans for the great mechanical battle which we trusted, however late in the day, would bring finality.

I had also in the War Office at this time a friend in General Furse, the

---

[1] General Rawlinson.

Master-General of the Ordnance. He had commanded the Division in which I had served during the few months I was at the front, and we had many times argued out the kind of projects I was now in a position to put forward. To ensure the closest contact in the vast Artillery sphere I appointed him with Lord Milner's approval[1] to be an actual member of the Munitions Council. Thus all these far-reaching and, though subordinate, yet vital controls pulled together from this time forward, and we had to worry only about the enemy. In this favourable atmosphere at the beginning of March I completed a general survey of the war ostensibly from the Munitions standpoint, and unfolded the argument for the future mechanical battle.

But the fury of the storm was now about to break upon us, and arguments were soon to be illustrated and corrected by flaming events. Ludendorff, reintroducing the great Battle period and consuming the German strength in desperate offensives without the necessary mechanical weapons and vehicles, was destined to bring about the Allied "general battle on a 300 kilometre front" which ended the war; and to bring it about after periods of awful peril one year earlier than our best plans could have achieved.

[1] Lord Milner had now succeeded Lord Derby at the War Office.

CHAPTER L

THE TWENTY-FIRST OF MARCH

As the Paschendaele struggle died away in the storms and mud of winter, the military rulers of Germany addressed themselves to a new situation. The collapse of Russia had enabled them to transport 1,000,000 men and 3,000 guns from the Eastern to the Western Front. For the first time therefore since the invasion they found themselves possessed of a definite superiority over the Allies in France. But this superiority was fleeting. The United States had declared war and was arming, but had not yet arrived. Once the great masses of American manhood could be trained, equipped, transported and brought into the line of battle, all the numerical advantage Germany had gained from the destruction of Russia would be more than counterbalanced. At the same time the German Main Headquarters knew the grave losses the British Army had suffered at Paschendaele, and felt themselves entitled to count upon a marked decline in its strength and fighting quality. Lastly, the amazing character of the German-Austrian victory over the Italians at Caporetto glittered temptingly.

This was undoubtedly a favourable opportunity for peace negotiations. Russia down, Italy gasping, France exhausted, the British armies bled white, the U-boats not yet defeated, and the United States 3,000 miles away, constituted cumulatively a position where German statesmanship might well have intervened decisively. The immense conquests which Germany had made in Russia, and the hatred and scorn with which the Bolsheviks were regarded by the Allies, might well have made it possible for Germany to make important territorial concessions to France, and to offer Britain the complete restoration of Belgium. The desertion by Soviet Russia of the Allied cause, and the consequent elimination of all Russian claims, created a similar easement in negotiations for both Austria and Turkey. Such were the elements of this great opportunity. It was the last.

But Ludendorff cared for none of these things. We must regard him at this juncture as the dominating will. Since the fall of Bethmann-Hollweg, he and Hindenburg, at the head of the German General Staff machine, had usurped, or at least acquired, the main control over policy. The Emperor, inwardly appalled by the tide of events, suspected of being a pacifist at heart, failed increasingly to play his part. Thus on definite trials of strength the military power

proved repeatedly to be predominant. It stood on the specialized basis of military opinion, not capable of measuring justly many of the most important
forces which were at work internally and abroad. It was all the more dangerous
because it was not complete. Ludendorff and Hindenburg by threatening resignation could obtain the crucial decisions they desired. These decisions governed
the fate of Germany. But they were only acquainted with a portion of the problem, and they could only carry out such parts of the indispensable resultant
policy as fell within their own military sphere. There was altogether lacking that
supreme combination of the King-Warrior-Statesman which is apparent in the
persons of the great conquerors of history.

Ludendorff was bent on keeping Courland, Lithuania and Poland in the
east. Had his own fame not been gained in these regions? He was also determined to keep a part of Belgium, including Liege, where he had also distinguished himself. This he felt was imperative if the German armies were to
obtain a good strategic starting-point for a future war. So far from ceding any
portion of Alsace and Lorraine, he and the General Staff regarded the acquisition of a protective zone west of Metz, including the Briey Basin, as a bare measure of prudence. These postulates and the possession of the new armies
regathered from the Russian front settled the course of events.

On November 11, 1917, a day in the calendar afterwards celebrated for other
reasons, Ludendorff, von Kuhl and von der Schulenberg met at Mons. The
nominal masters of these great Staff Officers—Hindenburg, Prince Rupprecht
and the Crown Prince—were not troubled to attend. The basis of the conference was that there should be a supreme offensive in the West; that there would
only be enough troops for one such offensive without any diversion elsewhere;
that the offensive must be made in February or the beginning of March before
the Americans could develop their strength; and finally, that it was the British
Army which must be beaten. Various alternative schemes were discussed and
orders given for their detailed preparation. Each received its code name. Von
Kuhl's plan of an attack against the front La Bassée-Armentières was "St.
George I"; an attack on the Ypres salient, "St. George II"; one on Arras-Notre
Dame de Lorette, "Mars." Lastly, there were the "Michaels" I, II and III. It was
not until January 24, after profound detailed study, that the choice was finally
made in favour of the "Michaels."

The objective of this attack was to break through the Allied front and reach
the Somme from Ham to Péronne. The date originally fixed was March 20.
The battle was to be extended by the attack "Mars South" a few days later, and
a subsidiary attack, called "Archangel," by the Seventh Army south of the Oise
was to be used as a diversion. Preparations for both the "St. Georges" were also
to be completed by the beginning of April. Sixty-two divisions were available

for the three "Michaels" and "Mars South," viz., Seventeenth Army: fifteen attack divisions, two ordinary divisions; Second Army: fifteen attack divisions, three ordinary divisions; Eighteenth Army: nineteen attack divisions, five ordinary divisions; Reserve: three attack divisions. In spite of some differences of opinion with von der Schulenberg and with von Hutier as to the direction and emphasis of the offensive in its various stages, Ludendorff adhered to his own conception: "The British must be beaten." They could best be beaten by the attack on either side of St. Quentin biting off the Cambrai salient. The Eighteenth Army would thereafter form a defensive flank along the Somme to hold off the French, and all the rest of the available German forces, wheeling as they advanced, were to attack the British in a north-west direction and drive them toward the coast. The two "St. George" operations remained in hand as further and potentially final blows. On these foundations all the German armies concerned perfected their arrangements.

Finally on March 10 the Emperor approved the following order:

CHIEF OF THE GENERAL STAFF.
Great Headquarters 10.3, issued 12.3.

His Majesty commands:

(1) That the Michael Attack take place on 21st March. First penetration of the hostile position 9:40 a.m.

(2) The first great tactical objective of Crown Prince Rupprecht's Group of Armies will be to cut off the British in the Cambrai salient and, north of the river Omignon and as far as the junction of that river with the Somme, to capture the line Croisilles-Bapaume-Péronne . . . Should the progress of the attack by the right wing be very favourable it will push on beyond Croisilles. The subsequent task of the Group of Armies will be to push on towards Arras-Albert, left wing fixed on the Somme near Péronne, and with the main weight of the attack on the right flank to shake the English front opposite Sixth Army and to liberate further German forces from their stationary warfare for the advance. All divisions in rear of Fourth and Sixth Armies are to be brought forward forthwith in case of such an event.

(3) The German Crown Prince's Group of Armies is first of all to capture the Somme and Crozat Canal south of river Omignon. By advancing rapidly the Eighteenth Army must seize the crossings over the Somme and over the Canal. It must also be prepared to extend its right flank as far as Péronne. The Group of Armies will study the question of reinforcing the left wing of the Army by divisions from Seventh, First and Third Armies.

(4) O.H.L.[1] keeps control of 2nd Guard, 26th Württemberg and 12th Divisions.

(5) O.H.L. reserves its decision as regards Mars and Archangel, and will be guided by the course of events. Preparations for these are to be carried on uninterruptedly.

(6) The remaining Armies are to act in accordance with C.G.S. Operation Order 6925, dated 4th March. Rupprecht's Group of Armies will protect the right wing of the Mars-Michael operation against an English counter-attack. The German Crown Prince's Group of Armies will withdraw before any big attack by the French against Seventh (exclusive of Archangel front), Third and First Armies.

O.H.L. reserves its decision as regards the Groups of Armies of Gallwitz and Duke Albrecht concerning the strategic measures to be taken in the event of a big attack by the French or concerning the further withdrawal of divisions for the battle zone.

VON HINDENBURG.

Accompanied by the Master-General of the Ordnance, on March 19 I held a conference in the Armoury at Montreuil with the Chief of the Staff, the head of the Tank Corps, and a number of officers and experts, to settle the scheme of the tank programme for 1919, and to time and organize the deliveries of tanks in 1918. I stayed with the Commander-in-Chief. After luncheon Sir Douglas Haig took me into his private room and explained on his map the situation as he viewed it. The enormous German concentration on the British front, and particularly opposite the Fifth Army, was obvious. Though nothing was certain, the Commander-in-Chief was daily expecting an attack of the first magnitude. The enemy masses in the north made it possible that the British front from Ypres to Messines would be assaulted. But the main developments were clearly to be expected on the sectors of the front from Arras to Péronne and even farther south. All these possibilities had already been amplified to me the day before by General Birch, the Chief of Artillery. His map showed very clearly the areas which the Germans were infecting with mustard gas (presumably to forbid them as manœuvring ground to both sides for some days) and the wide gaps between these areas over which no doubt the hostile offensive would be launched. There were also heavy enemy concentrations, though less pronounced, against the French in the sector of the Aisne. Speaking generally, more than half the German divisions in the west were ranged against the front of the British armies; and over broad stretches, the estimated enemy rifle power, the most significant index, was four times what it was against the French.

---

[1] Main Headquarters.

The Commander-in-Chief viewed the coming shock with an anxious but resolute eye. He dwelt with insistence on the undue strain put upon his armies by the arrangement made by the War Cabinet with the French, in which he had reluctantly acquiesced, for the extension of the British front so far to the south as Barisis. He also complained of the pressure put upon him in such a situation to assign a large portion of his limited forces to the general reserve. His forces were inadequate for even sectional and G.H.Q. Reserves. How could he then find troops for a General Reserve? I suggested that if, as he believed, the enemy's main weight were to be thrown against the British, he would get the benefit of the whole of this reserve; and if not, *caderet quæstio.* To this he said he preferred the arrangements he had made with General Pétain, by which seven or eight British or French divisions were to be held ready to move laterally north or south according as the French or British should be found to be the object of the attack. From a general survey of the front it appeared that 110 German divisions faced 57 British, of which at least 40 German divisions faced our Fifth Army; that 85 German divisions faced 95 French; and that 4 German divisions faced the first 9 American divisions which had entered the line at various points, but particularly in the neighbourhood of St. Mihiel.

Our conversation ended about three o'clock. When I came out, the Master-General of the Ordnance suggested to me that as I had two days to spare before beginning the Chemical Warfare Conference at St. Omer, we should pay a flying visit to our old division, the 9th, which I had served in while it was in his charge, and which was now commanded by General Tudor, a friend of mine since subaltern days in India. We set off forthwith. General Tudor's headquarters were at Nurlu, in the devastated region ten miles to the north of Péronne, near the salient of the British line and in the centre of the threatened front. We received a hearty welcome when we arrived after dark upon a tranquil front lit rarely by a gun-flash.

General Tudor was in high expectation. Everything was in readiness. "When do you think it will come?" we asked. "Perhaps to-morrow morning. Perhaps the day after. Perhaps the week after." We spent the whole of the next day in the trenches. A deathly and suspicious silence brooded over the front. For hours not a cannon shot was fired. Yet the sunlit fields were instinct with foreboding. The 9th Division were holding what they called "The Disaster Front," i.e., where the line had been stabilized after the successful German counter-stroke following the Battle of Cambrai. We examined every part of the defences from Gauche Wood, held by the gallant South Africans, the "Springboks" as they were called, to the medium artillery positions on the slopes behind Havrincourt village. Certainly nothing that human thought and effort could accomplish had been neglected. For four miles in depth the front was a labyrinth of wire and scientifically sited machine-gun nests. The troops, though thin on the ground, were disposed so as to secure full value from every man. Rumours and reasonable expectations that the Germans would employ large numbers of tanks had led to the construction of broad minefields studded with buried shells with sensitive fuses amid wire-entanglements. Through the narrow paths across these areas we picked our way gingerly. The sun was setting as we left Gauche Wood and took our leave of the South Africans. I see them now, serene as the Spartans of Leonidas on the eve of Thermopylæ.

Before I went to my bed in the ruins of Nurlu, Tudor said to me: "It is certainly coming now. Trench raids this evening have identified no less than eight enemy battalions on a single half-mile of the front." The night was quiet except for a rumble of artillery fire, mostly distant, and the thudding explosions of occasional aeroplane raids. I woke up in a complete silence at a few minutes past four and lay musing. Suddenly, after what seemed about half an hour, the silence was broken by six or seven very loud and very heavy explosions several miles away. I thought they were our 12-inch guns, but they were probably mines. And then, exactly as a pianist runs his hands across the keyboard from treble to bass, there rose in less than one minute the most tremendous cannonade I shall ever hear. "At 4:30 a.m.," says Ludendorff in his account, "our barrage came down with a crash." Far away, both to the north and to the south, the intense roar and reverberation rolled upwards to us, while through the chinks in the carefully papered window the flame of the bombardment lit like flickering firelight my tiny cabin.

I dressed and went out. On the duckboards outside the Mess I met Tudor. "This is *it,*" he said. "I have ordered all our batteries to open. You will hear them in a minute." But the crash of the German shells bursting on our trench lines eight thousand yards away was so overpowering that the accession to the tumult of nearly two hundred guns firing from much nearer to us could not be even distinguished. From the Divisional Headquarters on the high ground of Nurlu one could see the front line for many miles. It swept around us in a wide curve of red leaping flame stretching to the north far along the front of the Third Army, as well as of the Fifth Army on the south, and quite unending in either direction. There were still two hours to daylight, and the enormous explosions of the shells upon our trenches seemed almost to touch each other, with hardly an interval in space or time. Among the bursting shells there rose at intervals, but almost continually, the much larger flames of exploding magazines. The weight and intensity of the bombardment surpassed anything which anyone had ever known before.

Only one gun was firing at the Headquarters. He belonged to the variety called "Percy," and all his shells fell harmlessly a hundred yards away. A quarter of a mile to the south along the Péronne road a much heavier gun was demolishing the divisional canteen. Daylight supervened on pandemonium, and the flame picture pulsated under a pall of smoke from which great fountains of the exploding "dumps" rose mushroom-headed. It was my duty to leave these scenes; and at ten o'clock, with mingled emotions, I bade my friends farewell and motored without misadventure along the road to Péronne. The impression I had of Tudor was of an iron peg hammered into the frozen ground, immovable. And so indeed it proved. The 9th Division held not only its Battle but its Forward Zone at the junction of the Third and Fifth Armies against every assault, and only retired when ordered to do so in consequence of the general movement of the line.

It is possible here to give only the barest outline of the battle. Many full and excellent accounts exist. Many more will be written. Taking its scale and intensity together, quantity and quality combined, "Michael" must be regarded without exception as the greatest onslaught in the history of the world. From the Sensée River to the Oise, on a front of forty miles, the Germans launched simultaneously thirty-seven divisions of infantry, covered by nearly 6,000 guns. They held in close support nearly thirty divisions more. On the same front the British line of battle was held by seventeen divisions and 2,500 guns, with five divisions in support. In all, the Germans had marshalled and set in motion rather more than three-quarters of a million men against 300,000 British. Over the two ten-mile sectors lying to the north and the south of the salient in which the 9th Division stood, the density of the enemy's formation provided an assaulting division for every thousand yards of ground, and attained the superiority of four to one.

The British troops involved constituted the whole of the Fifth and nearly half the Third Army under the command of General Gough and General Byng respectively. The system of defence comprised a Forward Zone intended to delay the enemy and to break his formations, and a Battle Zone in which the main struggle was to be fought. The average depth of the defensive system was about four miles; behind which again lay a Reserve Zone which there had not been time or labour to fortify, except for the defences of the medium and heavy batteries. Indeed, on the whole of the Fifth Army front, but especially in the newly-transferred sector from the Omignon to Barisis, many of the entrenched lines and points existed only in a rudimentary form. The rear zone, for instance, had a mere line a few inches deep cut in the turf, and communications in the shape of good roads and light railways were still lacking. The method of defence consisted in an intricate arrangement of small posts, machine-gun nests, and redoubts, mutually supporting each other, communicating with each other where necessary by trenches and tunnels, and covered or sustained by an exact organization of artillery barrages. Behind the front of the British lay the wilderness of the Somme battlefield. Their left hand rested in a strategic sense upon the massive buttress of the Vimy Ridge; their right was in touch with comparatively weak French forces.

There was no surprise about the time or general direction of the attack. The surprise consisted in its weight, scale and power.

After a bombardment of incredible fury for not more than two to four hours, accompanied at certain points by heavy discharges of poison gas, the German infantry began to advance. The whole of this region had been in their possession during 1915 and the greater part of 1916, and there was no lack in any unit of officers and men who knew every inch of the ground. The form of attack which they adopted was an extension of the method of "infiltration" first tried by them in their counter-stroke after the Battle of Cambrai. A low-lying fog, which was in some places dense, favoured their plan at any rate in the initial stages. The system of detached posts on which the British relied, and which their comparatively small numbers had made necessarily rather open in character, depended to a very large extent upon clear vision, both for the machine gunners themselves and to a lesser extent for their protecting artillery. Aided by the mist, the German infantry freely entered the Forward Zone in small parties of shock troops, carrying with them machine guns and trench mortars. They were followed by large bodies, and even by noon had at many points penetrated the Battle Zone. The British posts, blasted, stunned or stifled by the bombardment or the gas, mystified and baffled by the fog, isolated and often taken in the rear, defended themselves stubbornly and with varying fortunes. Over the whole of the battlefield, which comprised approximately 160 square miles, a vast number of bloody struggles ensued. But the Germans, guided by their excellent organization and their local knowledge, and backed by their immense superiority in numbers, continued during the day to make inroads upon the Battle Zone, and even to pierce it at several points. When darkness fell, nearly all the British divisions had been forced from their original fighting line, and were intermingled at many points with the enemy in the Battle Zone.

The devoted resistance of the isolated British posts levied a heavy toll upon the enemy and played a recognizable part in the final result. From the outset the Germans learned that they had to deal with troops who would fight as long as they had ammunition, irrespective of what happened in any other quarter of the field or whether any hope of success or escape remained.

The conflict was continuous. Fresh German troops poured ceaselessly into action. By the evening of the 22nd the British Fifth Army had been driven completely beyond its battle zone and half the Army was beyond its last prescribed defensive line. The British Third Army still fought in and around the Battle Zone. The German penetration south of the Oise had made serious progress. The British losses by death, wounds or capture exceeded 100,000

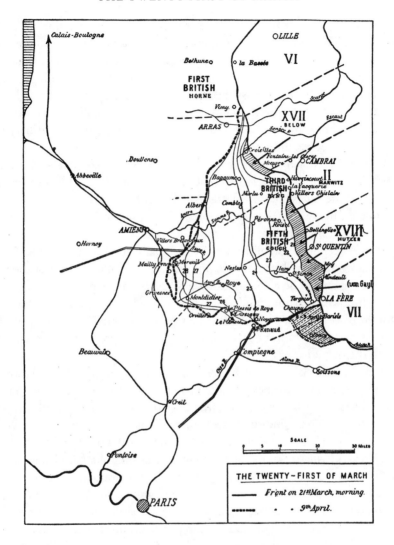

men; and nearly 500 guns were already lost. An immense slaughter was also wrought upon the German side. At every step they paid the price of the offensive, but their great numbers rendered their losses inappreciable during the crisis. Overwhelming reserves were close at hand. The British on the other hand had only eight divisions in general reserve, of which five were readily available; and the French were too slowly moved or too far away to give effective assistance for several days. Therefore on the night of the 22nd, Sir Hubert Gough ordered a general retreat of the Fifth Army behind the Somme. His orders had been "to protect at all costs the important centre of Péronne and the River Somme to the South" of it. He was fully justified in retiring in a general rear-guard action up to this line. But once the retreat of so thin a line on such a wide front had begun, it was very difficult to stop as long as the enemy pressure continued. The circumstances of each corps or division were so various that those who made a stand found their flanks exposed by others falling back. A great many of the bridges across the Somme were blown up; but enough were left—and among them the most important bridges, confided to the Railway authorities and not to the troops—to enable the Germans to pass artillery rapidly across. Moreover, the river was easily fordable at this time.

Backward then across the hideous desolation of the old crater-fields rolled the British front for five days in succession. The Cavalry Corps filled the gaps in the line, and the Air Force, concentrating all its strength upon the battle, flying low, inflicted heavy losses on the endless marching columns. Meanwhile reserves drawn from other parts of the line, and improvised forces from the schools and technical establishments, continually reached the scene. At the same time, with every day's advance, the strength and momentum of the German thrust abated. The actual fighting gave place to the painful toiling westward of two weary armies; and when the retreating British were sufficiently reinforced to come to a general halt, their pursuers found themselves not less exhausted, and far in front of their own artillery and supplies. By the evening of the 27th the first crisis of the great battle was over.

All the "Michaels" had struck their blow. But where was "Mars"? The Sixth Army and the right of the Seventeenth were to have entered the battle towards Arras and the Vimy Ridge on the 23rd. That they did not attack till the 28th was due to a deeply significant cause. General Byng had secretly withdrawn his troops from the line at Monchy, and already occupied a position four miles in the rear. The Germans bombarded the empty trenches of a false front. It took them four days and nights to bring their artillery forward and mount the assault against the new position. Thus the second great wave did not synchronize with the full surge of the first. The second great battle did not contribute to the intensity of the first, but came as a separate event after the climax of the first was over. Moreover, the progress made by the Second and the Seventeenth German Armies in the original attack had not fulfilled Ludendorff's expectations. At 9:30 on the morning of the 23rd he was led to abandon his prime strategic hope, namely the general defeat and driving to the coast of the British armies in France, and to content himself with the extremely valuable definite objective of dividing the British from the French through the capture of Amiens toward which the Eighteenth and Second Armies were progressing. His order given at noon was: "A considerable portion of the British Army has now been beaten. . . . The objective of the operation is now to separate the French and British by a rapid advance on both sides of the Somme." This was already a remarkable contraction of aim.

On the morning of the 28th the delayed attack against the Arras position (Mars) began. It was delivered on a twenty-mile front by twenty German divisions against eight British divisions. The methods of both sides were the same as on March 21. But the weather was clear, and the machine guns and artillery of the defence could reach their highest concert. Everywhere the attack was repulsed with tremendous slaughter. Even the Forward Zone was held at many points. Nowhere was the Battle Zone seriously affected. No outside reserves were required by the defending divisions. The Germans, who advanced with the utmost bravery, were mown down in heaps.[1] As the result of the eight days' struggle the British Army, virtually unaided by the French, had stemmed or broken the greatest offensive ever launched.

The French had been coming fitfully and feebly into action on the Southern portion of the battlefield from the morning of the 23rd. At dawn that day one division (the 125th) came into action. A French dismounted cavalry division entered the line in the evening. The 9th, 10th, 62nd and 22nd French Divisions were in line on the afternoon of the 24th, though two of them had no artillery and none of them had "cookers" or more than fifty rounds of rifle ammunition per man. On the morning of the 25th General Fayolle assumed responsibility for the whole of the Fifth Army front south of the Somme. But up till the 27th the main weight of the fighting, even in this area, still continued to be borne by the exhausted British troops. At no time up till the end of the 28th, when both the first and second crises of the battle were over, did the French have simultaneously in action more than six divisions, and none of these were seriously engaged. The struggle up till its turning point on the 28th was between the British and Germans alone.

Its last phase was now at hand, and in this the ever-gathering strength of the French on those portions of the front still involved played an equal part with the British. The Eighteenth German Army, brushing back weak French resistance, had actually taken Montdidier on the 27th. But this was the farthest point of the German advance. Says Ludendorff: "The enemy's line was now becoming denser, and in places they were even attacking themselves; while our armies were no longer strong enough to overcome them unaided. The ammunition was not sufficient, and supply became difficult. The repair of roads and railways was taking too long, in spite of all our preparations. After thoroughly replenishing ammunition, the Eighteenth Army attacked between Montdidier and Noyon on March 30. On April 4 the Second Army and the right wing of the Eighteenth attacked at Albert, south of the Somme towards Amiens. These

---

[1] "It would almost seem," says Sir Douglas Haig's Staff Officer, "as if the only difference numbers in the attack make to a properly located machine-gun defence, when there is light and time to see, is to provide a better target." No one can quarrel with such a conclusion.

actions were *indecisive*.[1] It was an established fact that the enemy's resistance was beyond our strength. . . . The battle was over by April."

Let us focus what had actually happened. With whom lay the victory? Contrary to the generally accepted verdict, I hold that the Germans, judged by the hard test of gains and losses, were decisively defeated. Ludendorff failed to achieve a single strategic object. By the morning of the 23rd he had been forced to resign his dream of overwhelming and crumpling back upon the sea the main strength of the British armies, and to content himself with the hope of capturing Amiens and perhaps dividing the British from the French. After April 4 he abandoned both these most important but to him secondary aims. "Strategically," he says, "we had not achieved what the events of the 23rd, 24th and 25th had encouraged us to hope for. That we had also failed to take Amiens . . . was specially disappointing." What then had been gained? The Germans had reoccupied their old battlefields and the regions they had so cruelly devastated and ruined a year before. Once again they entered into possession of those grisly trophies. No fertile province, no wealthy cities, no river or mountain barrier, no new untapped resources were their reward. Only the crater-fields extending abominably wherever the eye could turn. The old trenches, the vast graveyards, the skeletons, the blasted trees and the pulverized villages—these, from Arras to Montdidier and from St. Quentin to Villers-Bretonneux, were the Dead Sea fruits of the mightiest military conception and the most terrific onslaught which the annals of war record. The price they paid was heavy. They lost for the first time in the war, or at any rate since Ypres in 1914, two soldiers killed for every one British, and three officers killed for every two British. They made 60,000 prisoners and captured over a thousand guns, together with great stores of ammunition and material. But their advantage in prisoners was more than offset by their greater loss in wounded. Their consumption of material exceeded their captures. If the German loss of men was serious, the loss of time was fatal. The great effort had been made and had not succeeded. The German Army was no longer crouched, but sprawled. A great part of its reserves had been exposed and involved. The stress of peril on the other hand wrung from the Allies exertions and sacrifices which, as will be seen, far more than made good their losses.

The recriminations upon this battle left a lasting imprint on British political history. In April, General Maurice, the Director at the War Office of Military Operations, indignant at the failure to reinforce the Army in the winter, accused Mr. Lloyd George of incorrectly stating to the House of Commons the facts and figures of the case. Tension and uncertainty arose not only in the Opposition, but among the Government supporters, and even in its own ranks.

---

[1] My italics.

When a formal challenge in debate was made by Mr. Asquith, the Prime Minister convinced the House that his statement had been founded on information supplied in writing by General Maurice's Deputy. This was decisive on the issue, and the actual merits of the controversy were scarcely discussed. The division which followed was accepted by Mr. Lloyd George as marking the cleavage between his Liberal followers and those of Mr. Asquith. When, eight months later, in the hour of victory, the General Election took place, all who had voted against the Government on this occasion were opposed by the triumphant Coalition, and scarcely any escaped political exclusion. The reverberations of the quarrel continue to this day.

We may however attempt a provisional judgment. If Haig had not consumed his armies at Paschendaele, or if at least he had been content to stop that offensive in September, he would have commanded (without any addition to the drafts actually sent him from England in the winter) sufficient reserves on March 21 to enable him to sustain the threatened front. But for the horror which Paschendaele inspired in the minds of the Prime Minister and the War Cabinet, he would no doubt have been supplied with very much larger reinforcements. He would thus have gained both in economy of life and also in larger reinforcements. If, notwithstanding Paschendaele, the War Cabinet had reinforced him as they should have done, the front could still have been held on March 21. The responsibility for the causes which led to the British inadequacy of numbers is shared between General Headquarters and the War Cabinet. By constitutional doctrine the greatest responsibility unquestionably rests upon the War Cabinet, who failed to make their Commander conform to their convictions on a question which far transcended the military or technical sphere, and who also failed to do full justice to the Army because of their disagreement with the Commander-in-Chief. In view however of the preponderance of military influence in time of war, and the serious dangers of a collision between the "soldiers" and the politicians, a very considerable burden must be borne by the British Headquarters.

My work at the Chemical Warfare School near St. Omer occupied the whole of the 23rd, and I did not reach London till midday on the 24th. No information of any value about the progress of the battle had been available at the Chemical School. I therefore went immediately to the War Office to learn the news from France. Sir Henry Wilson, with the gravest face, showed me the telegrams and his own map. We both walked across to Downing Street, where the Prime Minister was expecting him. It was a bright crisp day, and Mr. Lloyd George was seated in the garden with Lord French. He seemed to think that I had news at first hand, and turned towards me. I explained that I knew nothing beyond what he had already read in his telegrams, and had seen nothing but the first few hours of the bombardment in a single sector. After some general conversation he took me aside and posed the following question: If we could not hold the line we had fortified so carefully, why should we be able to hold any positions farther back with troops already defeated? I answered that every offensive lost its force as it proceeded. It was like throwing a bucket of water over the floor. It first rushed forward, then soaked forward, and finally stopped altogether until another bucket could be brought. After thirty or forty miles there would certainly come a considerable breathing space, when the front could be reconstituted if every effort were made. It appeared that he had already dispatched Lord Milner to France, though I was not aware of this. The Chief of the Staff said that he himself intended to go over that night. We arranged to dine together at my house in Eccleston Square before he left. Only my wife was present. I never remember in the whole course of the war a more anxious evening. One of the great qualities in Mr. Lloyd George was his power of obliterating the past and concentrating his whole being upon meeting the new situation. There were 200,000 troops in England that could be swiftly sent. What about munitions and equipment? Wilson said, "We might well lose a thousand guns," and that mountains of ammunition and stores of every kind must have been abandoned. I was thankful to be in a position to say that about these at least there need be no worry. Everything could be replaced at once from our margins without affecting the regular supply. Presently the Chief of the General Staff went to catch his train, and we were left alone together. The resolution of the Prime Minister was unshaken under his truly awful responsibilities.

Meanwhile an event had occurred which, though it did not influence the course of the battle, was nevertheless of capital importance. On the night of the 24th, when the battle was at its worst, General Pétain, whose weak and tardy assistance was causing grave concern, met Haig and his Chief of Staff at Dury near Amiens. Although sixty-two German divisions had already been identified in the battle, of which forty-eight were fresh from the Reserve, Pétain asserted that the main blow was yet to fall, and that it would fall on the French in Champagne. He informed Haig that if the Germans continued to press on to Amiens, the French troops then concentrating about Montdidier would be withdrawn upon Beauvais to cover Paris in accordance with the orders of the French Government. He indicated that action in this sense had already been taken. Haig's original orders, given him personally by Lord Kitchener more than two years before, were in brief to "keep united with the French Army at all costs." But here at the crisis was a complete abandonment of the basic principle of unity.

On learning this fatal intention, Sir Douglas Haig telegraphed to the Secretary of State for War and the Chief of the Imperial General Staff to come over immediately. But both, as we have seen, had already started independently. Milner, acting with the necessary energy, after seeing Haig's Chief of the Staff at St. Omer, motored straight through to Paris and collected the President of the Republic, Clémenceau and Foch. Together they all proceeded to Compiègne on the 25th, examined Pétain as to his intentions, and finally, bringing Pétain with them, at noon on the 26th met Haig at Doullens, where Henry Wilson had already arrived. The magnitude of the danger had melted all prejudices and oppositions, personal and national alike. Only one name was in every mind. Foch, a week ago described as a "dotard," was the indispensable man. He alone possessed the size and the combative energy to prevent the severance of the French and British armies. Milner proposed that Foch should have control of the forces in front of Amiens. Haig declared that this was insufficient and that Foch must be given actual command of the French and British armies as a whole "from the Alps to the North Sea." At a conference in London a month before, the old "Tiger" had dealt abruptly with the outspoken misgivings of Foch. "Taisez-vous. I am the representative of France." Now it was Foch's turn to speak. "It is a hard task you offer me now: a compromised situation, a crumbling front, an adverse battle in full progress. Nevertheless I accept." Thus there was established for the first time on the Western Front that unity of command towards which Mr. Lloyd George had long directed his cautious, devious but persevering steps, and to which, whatever may be said to the contrary (and it is not little), history will ascribe an inestimable advantage for the cause of the Allies.

The emergency arrangements were confirmed and elaborated a few weeks later in the so-called "Beauvais Agreement" under which the Commander-in-Chief of a National Army was secured right of appeal to his own Government if he claimed that an order of the Generalissimo endangered the safety of his troops.

Hard measure was meted out to General Gough. The Fifth Army from the 28th onwards ceased to exist. Its shattered divisions were painfully reorganized behind the line. The gap was filled by the now rapidly arriving French, by the cavalry, by the improvised forces collected from the Schools, and by General Rawlinson who began, from scanty and diverse materials, to constitute a "Fourth Army" and to maintain the tottering and fluctuating line of battle.

Gough never received another fighting command. The Cabinet insisted on his removal on the ground, probably valid, that he had lost the confidence of his troops. This officer had fought his way upwards through the whole war from a Cavalry Brigade to the command of an Army. He was held to have greatly distinguished himself on the Ancre at the close of 1916. With Plumer he bore the brunt of Paschendaele while it continued, and its blame when it ended rested upon him. He was a typical cavalry officer, with a strong personality and a gay and boyish charm of manner. A man who never spared himself or his troops, the instrument of costly and forlorn attacks, he emerged from the

Paschendaele tragedy pursued by many fierce resentments among his high subordinates, rumours of which had even reached the rank and file. For over a year his reputation had been such that troops and leaders alike disliked inclusion in the Fifth Army. There was a conviction that in that Army supplies were awkward and attacks not sufficiently studied. In these circumstances Gough was not in a position to surmount the impression of a great disaster. The sternest critic has however been unable to find ground for censuring his general conduct of the battle of March 21. It appears that he took every measure, both before and during the battle, which experience and energy could devise and of which his utterly inadequate resources admitted; that his composure never faltered, that his activity was inexhaustible, that his main decisions were prudent and resolute, and that no episode in his career was more honourable than the disaster which entailed his fall.

It was my responsibility to make good the assurance I had given that all losses in material would be immediately replaced; and for this the Munitions Council, its seventy departments and its two and a half million workers, men and women, toiled with a cold passion that knew no rest. Everywhere the long-strained factories rejected the Easter breathing space which health required. One thought dominated the whole gigantic organization—to make everything good within a month. Guns, shells, rifles, ammunition, Maxim guns, Lewis guns, tanks, aeroplanes and a thousand ancillaries were all gathered from our jealously hoarded reserves. Risks are relative, and I decided, without subsequent misadventure, to secure an earlier month's supply of guns by omitting the usual firing tests.

Before the end of March I was able to assure the War Cabinet and General Headquarters that nearly two thousand new guns of every nature, with their complete equipments, could be supplied by April 6 as fast as they could be handled by the receiving department of the Army. In fact, however, twelve hundred met the need.

CHAPTER LI

THE CLIMAX

On Tuesday, April 9, the third great battle effort of the Germans against the British began. In order to stem the German advance upon Amiens, Sir Douglas Haig had been forced to thin his line elsewhere. Instead of doing this evenly, he had exercised a wise process of selection. He held in strength the great central bastion from Arras to the La Bassée Canal at Givenchy. This comprised the highly defensible and important area of the Lens coalfields, as well as the mass of commanding ground which included the key positions of the Vimy and Lorette Heights. To the north of this it was inevitable that the line should be dangerously weak. Out of fifty-eight British infantry divisions, forty-six had already been engaged on the Somme. The Fifth Army divisions were reorganizing and unfit to enter the line. To hold the front of 40,000 yards between the La Bassée Canal and the Ypres Canal, Haig could only provide six divisions. Each of these divisions must be stretched to cover over 7,000 yards—stretched wider, that is to say, than the Fifth Army divisions before March 21; and almost all the troops had fought with most severe losses in the preceding fortnight on the Somme. Since even these precarious dispositions could not be completed in the pressure of events before the German blow fell, nearly 10,000 yards of front by Neuve Chapelle were at the moment held by a Portuguese division of four brigades.

It was upon this denuded front, the day before the Portuguese were to have been relieved by two British divisions, that Ludendorff struck. By April 3, seventeen divisions had been added to the German Sixth and four to the German Fourth Army. The Sixth Army was to attack towards Hazebrouck and the heights beyond Kemmel, and the Fourth was to support it and exploit success. The town of Armentières, having been smothered with gas shells by a bombardment beginning on the evening of the 7th, constituted an impassable area; and with their northern flank thus protected, ten German divisions in an eleven-miles line marched against the 2nd Portuguese Division and the 40th and 55th British Divisions on each side of it. No less than seven German divisions fell upon the four Portuguese brigades, and immediately swept them out of existence as a military force. The 40th Division, its flank opened by the Portuguese disaster, was also speedily overwhelmed. A thick mist blanketed the

British machine-gun nests arranged in depth behind the line. Within two hours of the advance of the German infantry a gap of over 15,000 yards had been opened in the front, through which the German masses were pouring. The 50th and 51st Divisions, who formed the British reserves, moved to their appointed stations in the second line of defence at the crossings of the Lys and the Lawe Rivers as soon as the battle began; but the unexampled suddenness of the break-through, the vehemence of the German advance, the streams of retreating Portuguese, and the general confusion prevented them from fully occupying their prepared positions. They were rapidly absorbed in a moving battle against vastly superior numbers. After a day of violent fighting the Germans had reached the outskirts of Estaires, five kilometres behind the original line, and around this pocket of assault the remains of five British divisions struggled to create and maintain a front against sixteen German divisions all fully engaged.

At daylight on the morning of the 10th a second wave of German assault was launched by the German Fourth Army to the north of Armentières on a four-mile front. This phase of the offensive had been timed to begin twenty-four hours after the main attack, in the well-founded expectation that the British reserves in this sector would by then have been drawn into the first battle. Four brigades had in fact been diverted, and the whole weight of five German divisions fell upon five brigades of the 19th and 25th Divisions, who had behind them in reserve only the remaining brigade of the 29th Division. The assault was successful. The front was broken. "Plugstreet" village, the greater part of Messines and the crest of the Wytschaete Ridge fell into the hands of the enemy by noon. The 34th Division was in the greatest danger of being cut off around Armentières, and by the evening of the 10th the Germans were actual or potential masters of the whole British defensive system from Wytschaete to Givenchy. During the day both Lestrem and Estaires had been taken, and night found the survivors of eight British divisions holding an improvised front of thirty miles at death grips with twenty-seven German divisions, of which twenty-one had actually been involved in the battle. The 34th Division extricated itself from Armentières during the night, and only by skill escaped the fast-closing pincers.

But while this formidable inroad had been made upon the greater part of the front assailed, the line on either flank held firm. A Lancashire division, the 55th, perfectly fortified and organized in Givenchy and Festubert, continued to repulse for seven successive days every attack, losing 3,000 men and taking 900 prisoners. On the northern flank of the offensive lay the 9th Scottish Division whom we left unshakable at Nurlu on the morning of March 21. After fighting with the utmost distinction and success in that great battle and losing over 5,000 officers and men, it had been hastily filled with drafts and brought to rest

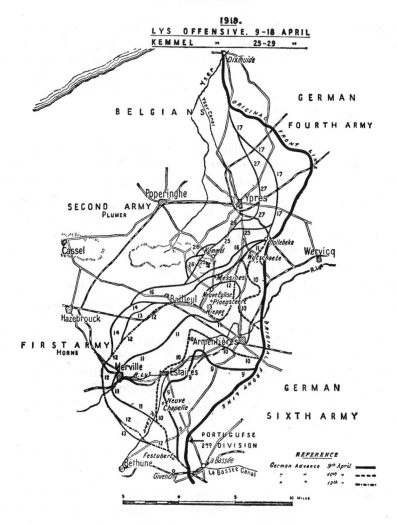

and recuperate in what was believed to be a quiet station. The whole front to the southward having been beaten in, its right flank was turned back, and the resurrected South African brigade, at four in the afternoon of the 10th, drove the Germans from the Messines crest. All efforts to oust this division from the position into which it had clawed itself failed. Thus the buttresses stood immovable, although the wall between them was completely battered in. Upon this fact the safety of the whole front and the final result of the battle unquestionably depended.

On the 11th the enemy, his Sixth and Fourth Army fronts united, extended his inroads in every direction except the flanks which he could not widen. Villages and townships, which had for more than three years been the home of the

British armies or whose names were associated with hard-won victories, fell into his hands. Merville, Nieppe and the rest of Messines were lost. As his front extended the enemy was able to deploy additional divisions and simultaneously to increase the weight of the attack and stretch the thin-drawn fluctuating line of the defence. The 50th and 51st Divisions maintained during the whole of April 10 and 11 a desperate struggle with seven or more German divisions along an oscillating but receding front of 20,000 yards.

By the end of this day the German line formed a salient or bulge fifteen kilometres deep and sixty-four wide in the original British positions. Meanwhile reinforcements were hurrying to the scene by march, bus and train. The rest of the 29th Division began to arrive on the northern front of attack, and the 4th, 5th, 31st (including the 4th Guards Brigade), 33rd, 61st and 1st Australian Divisions were all moving to the southern sector. Every yard of the ground was disputed, and in the close fierce fighting which never ceased night or day the German losses, like their numbers, were at least double those of the British. Here at last, though perilous, agonizing and unrecognized, was the real battle of attrition.

The initial success of the German thrust had exceeded Ludendorff's expectations, and during the first forty-eight hours of the battle he formed the resolve to extend the scale of the attack and strike with all his strength for the Channel ports. From April 12 onwards the German reserves were thrown profusely into the conflict, and both the German Army Commanders, Quast and Sixt von Arnim, were encouraged to draw freely from the main concentrations in the north. Begun as a diversion to draw Allied reserves from the Amiens front, the Battle of the Lys had now become a primary operation.

From the general not less than from the British point of view, April 12 is probably, after the Marne, the climax of the war. It looked as if the Germans had resolved to stake their fate and their regathered superiority on battering the life out of the British Army. During twenty days they had hurled nearly ninety divisions in three great battles upon an Army which counted no more than fifty-eight, and of these nearly half were fastened to fronts not under attack. With a superiority of numbers in the areas of assault of three and often four to one, with their brilliantly trained shock troops, with their extraordinary skill and enterprise in manœuvring with machine guns and trench mortars, with their new infiltration scheme, with their corroding mustard gas, with their terrific artillery and great science of war, they might well succeed. The French seemed to the British Headquarters sunk in stupor and passivity. Since the Nivelle disaster they had been grappling with mutiny and nursing their remaining resources. With the exception of the "set piece" battle of Malmaison in the winter, and the stinted and tardy divisions which had been involved south of the Somme in the later stages of March 21, they had only fought in ordinary trench warfare for nearly nine months. During that time the much smaller British Army had fought almost unceasingly, and wisely or unwisely had sacrificed in the common cause, apart from the prolonged Arras-Messines offensive of 1917, more than 400,000 men in the Paschendaele tragedy, and had now lost nearly 300,000 more under Ludendorff's terrible hammer. It was upon an Army bled white by frightful losses, its regimental officers shorn away by scores of thousands, its batteries and battalions filled and refilled with young soldiers plunged into battle before they knew their officers or each other, that the massed might of the desperate German Empire now fell.

Moreover, the shock could not be deadened nor breathing space gained by ceding ground. No large retirement like the *"Alberich"* manœuvre was open to Sir Douglas Haig. A few kilometres might be yielded here and there. The dearly bought ground of Paschendaele could be given up and some relief obtained thereby. Ypres could in the last resource be let go. But in front of Amiens, in front of Arras, in front of Béthune, in front of Hazebrouck he must stand or fall. Therefore on the morning of the 12th the Commander, usually so restrained and, as it had seemed, unresponsive, published to his troops the order of the day which is printed in facsimile on page 785: "There is no other course open to us but to fight it out. Every position must be held to the last man. There must be no retirement. With our backs to the wall and believing in the justice of our cause, each one of us must fight on to the end." All units and all ranks of the British Expeditionary Force therefore prepared themselves to conquer or die.

The convulsion continued. The reinforcements closed the gaps that were hourly torn in the struggling line. Companies, battalions, even whole brigades were obliterated where they stood. Ludendorff, resolute, ruthless, hazard-loving, raised his stakes. More and more of the German reserves were committed to the onset. The roar of the cannonade resounded through Flanders and reverberated across the Channel. But nothing could move the 55th Division on the right nor the 9th on the left. The Australians were coming, and the 4th Guards Brigade all through the 12th and 13th may be discerned, where all was valour, barring the path to Hazebrouck. So intermingled were the units and formations in the fighting line, that across the Bailleul-Armentières road, Freyberg, V.C., four years before a Sub-Lieutenant, found himself holding a front of 4,000 yards with elements of four different divisions, and covered by the remnants of two divisional artilleries that had drifted back with the line. Neuve Eglise was lost, and Bailleul and Méteren; and under the intense pressure the front bent backwards. But it did not break. When on the 17th eight German divisions—seven of them fresh—were violently repulsed in their attack on the famous hill of Kemmel, the crisis of the Battle of the Lys was over. The orders of the Commander had been strictly and faithfully fulfilled.

Even before the beginning of the Battle of the Lys, Sir Douglas Haig had convinced himself that Ludendorff meant to make a dead-set at the British Army. He accordingly appealed to Foch for aid.

He asked the Generalissimo to take without delay one of the three following courses, viz.:

(1) To open an offensive in the next five or six days with the French armies on a scale sufficient to attract the enemy's reserves, or

(2) To relieve the British troops south of the Somme (a total of four divisions), or

(3) To place a group of four French divisions in the neighbourhood of St. Pol as a reserve to the British front.

He wrote again on the 10th after the battle had begun that the—

enemy would without a doubt continue to strike against his troops until they were exhausted. It was vital that the French Army should take immediate steps to relieve some part of the British front and take an active share in the battle.

He renewed his solicitations on the 11th and on the 14th. Finally on the 15th he recorded his—

opinion that the arrangements made by the Generalissimo were insufficient to meet the military situation.

In order to press his demands with greater insistency, and withal to maintain good relations with the Supreme Commander, Haig, as early as April 10, had taken General Du Cane, who was actually commanding the XVth British Corps in full battle on the Lys, and sent him to reside at Foch's headquarters as a High "Go-between" or Liaison Officer.

These requests were intensely painful to Foch. His primary endeavour was to gather and husband his reserves. The control exercised over the reserves was, he considered, the main function of a Commander on the defensive. Ten British divisions had already on account of their losses had to be reduced to cadre, and their survivors used as reinforcements for the rest. When could these divisions, he asked, be reconstituted? Could not the British when the crisis of

To / All ranks of the British Forces in France

Three weeks ago today the enemy began his terrific attacks against us on a 50 mile front. His objects are to separate us from the French, to take the Channel ports and destroy the British army.

Inspite of throwing already 106 Divisions into the battle and ~~suffering~~ enduring the most reckless sacrifice of human life, he has as yet made little progress towards his goals.

We owe this to the determined fighting & self sacrifice of our troops. Words fail me to express the admiration which I feel for the splendid resistance offered by all ranks of our army under the most trying circumstances.

Many amongst us now are ~~tired~~ ~~very~~ tired. To those I would say that Victory will belong to the side which holds out the longest. The French army is moving rapidly & in great force to our support . . . . . .

There is no other course open to us but to fight it out! Every position must be held to the last man: there must be no retirement . . With our backs to the wall, and believing in the justice of our cause each one of us must fight on to the end. The safety of our Homes and the Freedom of mankind alike depend upon the conduct of each one of us at this critical moment . ~~But~~ ~~every good cheer,~~ ~~the British Empire~~ ~~must win in the end~~ . —

Thursday
11 April 1918 }

D. Haig. F.M.

the battle was over start a "roulement" of tired British divisions to quiet parts of the French front? These counter-requests ill accorded with the desperate struggle in which the British were involved. Painful differences developed at a conference held at Abbeville on April 14 between Foch and Haig, at which Lord Milner was present. Foch took the view that "la bataille du Nord," as he called it, was dying down, and that his reserves were suitably placed to intervene either in the Flanders battle or in the battle of Arras-Amiens-Montdidier, which he expected would be renewed at any moment. His attitude excited the resentment of the British representatives, and no agreement was reached. He had seen the 1st British Army Corps fight at Ypres in 1914; and the impression that British troops would stand any test if resolutely called upon was indelible.

It was no doubt the duty of Foch to hoard his reserves and to extort the fullest effort from every part of the Allied armies; but he was at least premature in his judgment that "the battle in the North was dying down," nor had he any right to count upon the intense resistance which was in the event forthcoming from the desperately pressed British troops. Foch's doctrine of never relieving troops during a battle may apply to a battle of two or three days; but struggles prolonged over weeks do not admit of such rules. Divisions after a certain point, if not relieved, simply disappear through slaughter and intermingling with the reinforcements who are sent to sustain them; and the individual survivors of many days of ceaseless peril, horror and concussion become numb and lifeless, even though unscathed by steel.

The British, Government and Headquarters alike, upon whose initiative Foch had just been raised to the supreme control, were already distrustful of the use he would make of his power. It must be conceded however that Foch was vindicated by the event, for the British Armies weathered the storm practically unaided and the German impulsion gradually died away.

Slowly and reluctantly Foch was compelled to part with a small portion of his reserves, and on April 18 a detachment from the French Army of the North (D.A.N.) consisting of five infantry and three cavalry divisions was formed to take over the front Bailleul-Wytschaete. These troops however, even after they had arrived on the scene, only gradually came into the line. In the end this French force was raised to nine infantry divisions. But before then the crisis had passed.

But the continuance of the battle, the power of the enemy and the obvious jeopardy in which our Army stood forced most grave reflections. Suppose the Germans continued tearing at our throats with all their might, suppose they shook the life out of our Army, suppose the straining front broke or was swept back by an inexorable tide! There were at any rate "the water lines." The advanced line ran from Dunkirk back to the second or main line. This ran along the stream of the Aa from Gravelines through St. Omer to St. Venant. A vast amount of work had been done upon it. It was called "the water line" on account of the great part which inundations could be made to play in its defence. This line would shorten the front and be a substantial relief, but it meant the loss of Dunkirk and the continuous bombardment of Calais. Both these ports played a notable part in the reception of our supplies, and far-reaching checks and complications would follow on their loss.

Even darker possibilities were afoot. Suppose we had to choose between giving up the Channel ports or being separated from the mass of the French armies! In the former case all our best and closest communications would be destroyed. We should have to rely entirely on Havre till other bases could be developed. All our programmes would vanish at a stroke. I was deeply concerned that this issue should be calmly probed before it actually came upon us.

This issue was put to Foch at the meeting of the Supreme War Council which met at Abbeville on May 1 and 2. Both Wilson and Haig felt that decision from the Supreme Commander was necessary in order that precautionary preparations could be made. The Chief of the Imperial General Staff persuaded the representatives of the British Government to press insistently for an answer. The utmost that Foch could be induced to admit was that it was more important to retain touch between the two armies than to retain possession of the Channel Ports. But he returned resolutely to his main contention: "I mean to fight for both. The question, therefore, cannot arise until I am beaten. I will never give up either. Ni l'un ni l'autre. Cramponnez partout." He hazarded a great deal upon the endurance of the British Army. But he was not disappointed.

On the 25th an unlucky event occurred. The French divisions which from the 18th onwards had deployed behind our front, had taken over a portion of the line, which they held in strength with divisional fronts of no more than 3,000 yards. Included in this sector, the French 28th Division held the invaluable height of Scherpenberg and Kemmel, the latter defended by one battalion of the 99th Regiment. At dawn the Germans concentrated upon the hill and the trenches round its foot a most astonishing storm of high explosive and gas shells from cannon and *minenwerfer*. It is said that the French masks were only partially proof against the gas. Whatever the cause, the French troops on either side of the hill, after repulsing three infantry attacks, and sustaining heavy losses, gave way and were streaming back by seven o'clock in the morning. Their retirement left the troops on the summit, including some of our own trench-mortar batteries, to be cut off. A similar fate overwhelmed the British brigade who were holding the trenches on the French left. They were rolled up from the flank, and none escaped death or captivity. The disaster might have taken a still worse turn but for the promptitude with which the Highland Brigade next in succession threw back its right and formed a defensive flank.

There is no doubt that the relations between the French and British commands during the battle period which began on March 21 were not remarkable for a high appreciation of each other's military qualities. The French staff considered that the British had failed and caused a great disaster on the common front, and they openly expressed the opinion that the quality of the British troops at this time was mediocre. The British, on the other hand, felt that the help given under a terrific strain had been both thin and slow, and that the entry of French relieving divisions into the battle was nearly always followed by further retirements. Instances are given by Colonel Boraston of joint attacks which miscarried through the French divisions not being set in motion, although their British comrades were already committed.

He also records a curious incident of which I was myself a witness. At about ten o'clock on April 29 I was breakfasting with Sir Douglas Haig. Sir Herbert Lawrence, his Chief of the Staff, and two or three Aides-de-Camp were present. The Commander-in-Chief had just sat down to his coffee when the following message was put in his hand: "G.O.C. 39th French Division reports that there is no doubt but that the enemy holds Mont Rouge and Mont Vidaigne. Troops on right of Scherpenberg badly cut up. . . . Enemy reported to be pushing between the Scherpenberg and Mont Rouge." Simultaneously there arrived from Plumer a confirmatory message requesting the Chief of the Staff to come at once to the Headquarters of the Second Army. No Reserves of any kind were available and the news if true involved the grim issue discussed in my Memorandum of the 18th. The room was rapidly emptied. Haig disappeared into his office observing, "The situation is never so bad or so good as first reports indicate": and Lawrence vanished in a motor car.

I thought I would go and see for myself what was happening, and accordingly I motored to the area of Sir Alexander Godley's Corps, which was the nearest to the reported break-through. A violent cannonade loaded the air; but at the Corps Headquarters faces were beaming. The French Commander had telephoned that it was all a mistake and that nothing of importance was occurring. Such accidents from time to time are inevitable. But this is an illustration of the tension under which both the French and British leaders were living in these very hard times.

However, the worst was over for the British Headquarters though they did not know it, and the rest of the war with all its slaughters and exertions contained for them only hopes and triumphs. The capture of Mount Kemmel was the last effort of the Germans in this battle. It is astounding that after having gained so great a prize at so high a cost they did not use it. The decision was

Ludendorff's. The war diaries and archives of the German Fourth Army for the period April 9–30, captured by the French, show that so far from urging the Army Staff to press on to victory, it was Ludendorff who suggested that they stand fast and prepare to meet a British counter-stroke. "In view of the solidarity of the defence," he wrote, "it should be considered whether the attack should be interrupted or continued." To this General von Lossberg, Chief of the Fourth Army Staff, replied that "our troops encountered everywhere in the field of attack a very solid defence, well distributed in depth and particularly difficult to overcome on account of the numerous machine-gun nests. . . . With the forces at present at our disposal the operation offers no chance of success. Better interrupt it." And Ludendorff approved. The stubborn defence had succeeded at the moment when it had sustained its most dangerous wound.

So ended the most fierce and intense grapple of the British and Germans. For forty days, from March 21 to the end of April, the main strength of Germany had been ceaselessly devoted to the battery and destruction of the British Army. One hundred and twenty German divisions had repeatedly assaulted 58 British, piercing the front, gaining great successes and capturing more than a thousand cannon, and seventy or eighty thousand prisoners. During these forty days the British Army had lost in officers 2,161 killed, 8,619 wounded, and 4,023 missing or prisoners: and of other ranks 25,967 killed, 172,719 wounded, and 89,380 missing or prisoners: a total loss of 14,803 officers and 288,066 men.[1] This was more than one-quarter of the whole number of British fighting troops under Sir Douglas Haig's command on March 21. But these terrible losses concentrated in so short a period on a relatively small military organism had not quenched its life-force. No vital position had been wrested from its grip. No despondency had overwhelmed the troops or their leaders. The machine continued to function, and the men continued to fight. Doggedly and dauntlessly they fought without a doubt that whatever their own fate, Britain would come victoriously through as she had always done before. By their stubborn and skilful resistance at every point, by numberless small parties fighting unchronicled till they were blotted out, the British inflicted upon the Germans losses even greater than those they themselves endured, losses irreparable at this period in the war, losses which broke the supreme German effort for victory at the outset, and rang the knell of doom in the ears of the overwrought German people. There fell of the Germans against the British in these same forty days, 3,075 officers killed, 9,305 wounded, and 427 missing or prisoners; and 53,564 other ranks killed, 242,881 wounded, and 39,517 missing or prisoners; a total of 12,807 officers and 335,962 men. An advancing army always gathers the prisoners and missing on a scale far exceeding its retreating opponent. These cut off

[1] *Military Effort*, p. 362.

units are the heavy price of retirement, and they are a permanent loss to the defenders. But if—under these reserves—the missing and prisoners are deducted from each side, the fact emerges that the British shot 308,825 Germans during these battles at a cost of 209,466; or briefly three Germans shot for every two British.

It was now to be the turn of our Ally. The flail under which we had suffered was soon to be uplifted against the French. If we had known beforehand what their ordeal was to be, we should have been thankful they had nursed and guarded their remaining strength to face it.

CHAPTER LII

THE SURPRISE OF THE CHEMIN DES DAMES

At the end of April when the battle in the north died down Ludendorff, finding too many troops in front of him, looked elsewhere. "The most favourable operation in itself," he writes,[1] "was to continue the attack on the English Army at Ypres and Bailleul. . . . Before we could attack here again, the enemy must become weaker and our communications must be improved." He had thus resigned all the decisive strategic objects for which the German armies had been fighting since March 21. He had first abandoned the great roll-up of the British line from Arras northwards and the general destruction of the British armies, in favour of the more definite but still vital aim of taking Amiens and dividing the British from the French armies. Arrested in this, he had struck in the north to draw British reserves from the Amiens battlefield. But the Battle of the Lys, began as a diversion, had offered the lesser yet still enormous prize of the northern Channel ports. Now he must abandon that; and his strategic ambition, already thrice contracted, must henceforward sink to an altogether lower plane. The fourth German offensive battle of 1918 was to a large extent a mere bid for a local victory, and apart from its usefulness in diverting Allied troops from the fateful fronts, offered no direct deadly strategic possibilities.

Marshall Foch saw with unerring eye the grand and simple proportion of events. Not deceived by the vast mass of frightfully important but irrelevant considerations which obscured the primary issues, he ranged the strategic necessities of the Allied armies in their true order. Of these the first beyond compare was the union of the French and British armies; second, the preservation of the Channel ports; and third, though in a less decisive sphere, the defence of Paris. Pétain on the other hand showed on more than one occasion that his valuations were different. His attitude on the night of March 24, which precipitated the Doullens Conference, proves that he would have rated the loss of Paris as a greater misfortune than the severing of the connection between the French and British armies. We shall see later a still more glaring example of this error, which in so accomplished a soldier can only be attributed to the intrusion of

[1] *My War Memories,* p. 615.

sentiment. Paris could have been occupied by the Germans in June, 1918, without preventing the collapse of the Central Empires in November. But the loss of the Channel ports and the consequent halving of the British military effort would have meant another year of war; and the severance of the British and French armies might easily have led to their total and final defeat. Mercifully the good sense of Foch pierced through the fog of false appearances. From the moment when he obtained the supreme command, he steadily massed the reserves, in full harmony with the British view, to safeguard the junction of the British and French armies. And behind him, with equal comprehension, Clémenceau when the need came declared: "I shall fight in front of Paris. I shall fight in Paris. I shall fight behind Paris." Thus these great men were able to exalt their minds above the dearest temptations of their hearts, and thus we found the path to safety by discerning the beacons of truth.

It followed from Foch's decision to gather the reserves in Flanders and between Compiègne and Amiens that dangerous denudations must be accepted on other important parts of the front. The movement northwards of so many French divisions was viewed with deep anxiety by Pétain and the French Army Headquarters. Pétain indeed made a strenuous effort to retain the last instalment. But Foch insisted. Thus Ludendorff found, when the Battle of the Lys ended in deadlock, that it was not open to him to renew the battle of Amiens. He was already committed to two great bulges which he had conquered at the cost of heavy drafts upon the superior reserves he had gathered for the campaign. In neither could he advance in face of the strength against him, and from both he was unwilling to retire lest he should shatter the glittering but, as he knew well, already brittle confidence of Germany. Each of these bulges had its special disadvantages for the German troops. In the Somme region they were condemned to dwell amid their own devastations, and with communications which, although improved, made the mounting of a first-class offensive impossible. In the Bailleul salient the conditions were far worse. The scale was smaller, but for this very reason the discomfort was more intense. The whole of the conquered ground was commanded by the encircling British artillery. And this artillery, fed with unlimited ammunition and fresh guns, raked and swept the German salient night and day from three quarters of the compass. In this cauldron nearly twenty German divisions must be constantly maintained at a cost which melted the reserves apace.

It must have been with darkening misgivings that Ludendorff selected the point of his next attack. Outwardly all seemed to be going well. Actually all had miscarried. But the consolation of spectacular vengeance yet remained. Immense resources were still in hand. A dazzling victory could yet be won which, though barren in consequences, would still preserve the illusion of increasing success. As early as April 17 the Crown Prince's Army group was ordered urgently to prepare an offensive on the Chemin des Dames, with the object of breaking through between Soissons and Rheims. The arrangements were made with the customary thoroughness and science and with unexampled secrecy. The Seventh and First German Armies assembled twenty-nine divisions for the battle. No less than 1,158 batteries were deployed, and the moment was fixed for 2 a.m. on May 27.

Foch knew as well as Pétain the forfeits to which his wise dispositions exposed the French armies, and both Generals were during the whole of May unable to divine where the blow would fall. Blame has been attributed to the staff of the French Sixth Army. The choleric temperament of its Commander General Duchêne had discouraged and estranged his subordinates, and the machine worked with friction.[1] At this time above all others efforts should have been made, without regard to losses, to pierce the enemy's screen by sudden raids, now here now there, and gain the indispensable information. But nothing of this kind was done successfully either by the Sixth Army or elsewhere along the French front. Four French divisions were in line on the Chemin des Dames, with four more in reserve behind the Aisne. On their right was the Ninth British Army Corps under Sir Alexander Hamilton Gordon, comprising three divisions in the line (the 21st, 8th and 50th), also the 25th Division in reserve, all shockingly mutilated in the northern battle, and sent at Foch's earnest desire to what was stated by the French to be the quietest sector of the front in order to refit and train their recruits. In reply to formal warnings from the British General Headquarters that an attack had been mounted against the Aisne front, the French Sixth Army Staff stated on the morning of May 25: "In our opinion there are no indications that the enemy has made preparations that would enable him to attack to-morrow."

What followed is exciting. At daybreak on the 26th two German prisoners were taken by the French. One was a private and the other an *officer-aspirant,* belonging to different regiments of Jäger. On the way to Divisional Headquarters their captors entered into conversation with them. The private said there was going to be an attack; the officer contradicted him. Arrived at the Army Corps Intelligence centre the prisoners were examined separately. The officer, questioned first, was voluble, and declared that the Germans had no intention of making an offensive on this front. The interrogation of the private followed. He said that the soldiers believed that they would attack that night or the following night. He was not sure of the date. Pressed, he said that cartridges and grenades had already been distributed, but not the field rations. He had seen

---

[1] Une humeur de dogue, un grondement perpétuel, un orage de rebuffades, tout de suite les gros mots à la bouche, sans raison.—Pierrefeu, *G.Q.G.,* Secteur I, Vol. II, p. 178.

the previous day near his billets soldiers belonging to Guards regiments. He knew no more. The officer was then recalled. He was told that the laws of war had in no way forced him to speak, but that he had volunteered statements for which he would be held responsible. To give false information was the act of a spy. On this he became visibly perturbed, and under pressure gave in the end the most complete details of the attack which impended the next day. It was already three o'clock in the afternoon of the 26th. The alarm was given, and the troops available took up their battle positions.

Pierrefeu has described the terrible hours which Pétain and the French Headquarters Staff now endured far away at Provins.[1] They knew that an immense disaster was certain. They knew that no reinforcements could reach the scene for several days, and thereafter for a still longer period only at the rate of two divisions a day. Meanwhile there was nothing in human power that could be done. All through the night they sat in their silent offices, bowed under the blow about to fall and suffering another form of the tortures to which the troops were doomed. At one o'clock next morning the German barrage descended on a thirty-kilometre front, and three hours later eighteen divisions advanced upon the four French and three refitting British divisions. Although the troops on the ground were alert, the strategic surprise was complete and overwhelming.

> "After three-and-a-half hours' artillery and trench-mortar preparation," says the Crown Prince,[2] "the divisions surged forward against the Chemin des Dames. . . . The small enemy force holding the position, six French and three English trench divisions, were overrun and the Chemin des Dames and the Aisne-Marne Canal reached in one swoop. As early as the afternoon our leading units were over the Aisne. By the evening the centre of the Third Army had already reached the Vesle on both sides of Fismes. A break-through with a depth of twenty kilometres had been attained in one day. The Aisne-Marne Canal was also crossed by the left wing of the Seventh Army."

A most stubborn defence was made by the three British divisions which were in the line, and by the 25th Division almost immediately involved. On their right stood the 45th French-Algerian Division which, not being itself attacked, gave energetic assistance. Hinging on this, the British line swung back under immense pressure on its front and with its left continually compromised. The retiring British found behind them fortunately the hilly and wooded coun-

---

[1] *G.Q.G.*, Section I, Vol. II, p. 187.
[2] *My War Experiences*, p. 318.

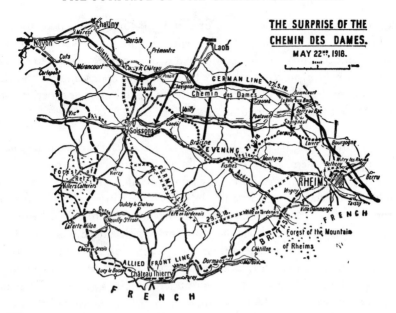

try to the west of Rheims, which helped the defence in a receding battle. The 19th British Division had also luckily arrived at Chalons for rest and recuperation, and on the fourth day they sustained the British line. The 21st Division was by then practically destroyed, and by June 1 the whole five British divisions were hardly equal to the full strength of one. All the troops bore themselves as on the Lys a month earlier. Battalions were completely exterminated, and a large portion of the artillery perished with their guns upon the field. The French villagers in their ignorance and terror assailed the retreating troops with hostile demonstrations.

Meanwhile upon the British left the German punch had smashed right through. General Duchêne's staff delayed too long the destruction of the bridges across the Aisne, and most of them fell intact into the hands of the invaders. By June 2 Soissons had fallen and the Germans had reached the Marne at Château-Thierry.

Pierrefeu has described in a moving passage the next event. Now suddenly the roads between Provins and the front towards Meaux and towards Coulommiers began to be filled with endless streams of Americans. The impression made upon the hard-pressed French by this seemingly inexhaustible flood of gleaming youth in its first maturity of health and vigour was prodigious. None were under twenty, and few were over thirty. As crammed in their lorries they clattered along the roads, singing the songs of a new world at the tops of their voices, burning to reach the bloody field, the French Headquarters were thrilled with the impulse of new life. "All felt," he says, "that they were present at the

magical operation of the transfusion of blood. Life arrived in floods to reani-
mate the mangled body of a France bled white by the innumerable wounds of
four years." Indeed the reflection conformed with singular exactness to the fact.
Half trained, half organized, with only their courage, their numbers and their
magnificent youth behind their weapons, they were to buy their experience at a
bitter price. But this they were quite ready to do.

The misfortunes of the Battle of the Chemin des Dames had the remarkable effect of improving the relations between the British and French armies. After a
surprise so glaring and retreat of twenty kilometres in a single day—the record
for all battles on the Western Front—the French were in no position to maintain the airs of superiority which they had been unable to conceal from the
Italians after Caporetto or altogether from the British after the 21st of March.
Up till the moment when they in their turn felt the force of a Ludendorff offensive, they had complacently assumed that the French Army contained the
only troops who could really hold a front under modern conditions. These illusions had been swept away by the German scythe. The intensity of their common tribulations united the Allies more closely than ever. Moreover, the French
command were deeply grieved at the destructive losses suffered by the five
British divisions committed to their care for a period of recuperation. They
paid their tribute in generous and soldierly terms to the fighting achievements
of these troops. The words of General Maistre, the Commander of the Group
of Armies concerned, may be here transcribed: "With a doggedness, permit me
to say thoroughly English, submerged by the hostile flood, you have reconstituted without failing new units to carry on the struggle which have at last enabled us to form the dyke by which this deluge has been mastered. That
achievement no Frenchman who was a witness will forget."[1] The 2nd Devons
and the 5th Battery of the Forty-fifth British Field Artillery Brigade were
awarded the Croix de Guerre in consequence of their having fought until only
the memory remained.

The advance of the Germans to Château-Thierry, barely a hundred kilometres
from Paris, confronted me with problems almost as serious and quite as imminent as those which had glared at us during the Battle of the Lys. I was responsible among other things for the whole supply of aeroplanes and aviation
material of all kinds. The Ministry of Munitions was a gigantic shop from
which the Air Ministry ordered all they wanted. Under the incredible activities
of Sir William Weir, then Secretary of State, the Air Force demands became
staggering. We discovered that the French had a large surplus manufacturing

---

[1] *Sir Douglas Haig's Command,* Vol. II.

capacity. I had therefore, in agreement with Loucheur, directed Sir Arthur Duckham to place enormous orders with them. The French factories on which we depended for an essential part of our programme were mostly grouped around Paris. The danger to the capital required elaborate plans for moving these establishments southwards in case of need, and at the same time a very nice decision whether and when to put them into operation. If we moved without cause, we interrupted production. If we tarried too long, we should not be able to get our machinery away. Paris was calm and even pleasant in these days of uncertainty. The long-range German cannon, which threw its shells about every half-hour, had effectually cleared away nearly all those who were not too busy nor too poor. The city was empty and agreeable by day, while by night there was nearly always the diversion of an air raid. The spirit of Clémenceau reigned throughout the capital. "We are now giving ground, but we shall never surrender. We shall be victorious if the Public Authorities are equal to their task."

Ludendorff had now made a third bulge in the Allied front. In all three the German troops were uncomfortable, their communications extremely inferior, and their general strategic position delicate. It seemed probable that they would try to bite off or beat in the French salient which jutted out between Montdidier and Château-Thierry as far as Noyon. The deep forest region about Villers-Cotterets and the fact that there was only a single line of railway for all the Germans in the Château-Thierry bulge, made an attack from an eastern direction unlikely. The front before Compiègne from Montdidier to Noyon was clearly the most interesting. M. Clémenceau had authorized and even urged me to go everywhere, see everything, and "tell Lloyd George what we are doing." Accordingly as the work of the Inter-Allied Munitions Conference which was then proceeding permitted, I visited the armies of Generals Humbert and Debeny, who awaited the expected shock. I knew both these Generals personally, and was still better acquainted with General Fayolle who commanded the Army Group. One could reach the front line from Paris in less than three hours, and I followed with the closest attention the improved methods of defence which the French were adopting. Nothing of consequence was now offered to the German opening bombardment. A strong picquet line of detached machine-gun nests, carefully concealed, was alone in contact with the enemy. Behind these devoted troops, for whom an assault could only mean destruction, was a zone three or four thousand yards deep, in which only strong points were held by comparatively small forces. It was not until at least 7,000 yards separated them from the hostile batteries that the real resistance of the French Infantry and Artillery was prepared. When one saw all the fortifications and devices, the masses of batteries and machine-guns, with which the main line of defence bristled, and knew that this could not be subjected to heavy bombard-

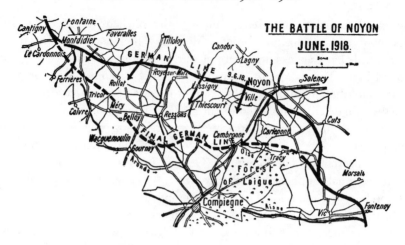

ment until the stubborn picquets far in front had been exterminated, it seemed difficult to believe that any troops in the world could carry the whole position from front to rear in a single day.

On the evening of June 8 I walked over the centre of the French line in front of Compiègne. The presage of battle was in the air. All the warnings had been given, and everyone was at his post. The day had been quiet, and the sweetness of the summer evening was undisturbed even by a cannon shot. Very calm and gallant, and even gay, were the French soldiers who awaited the new stroke of fate. By the next evening all the ground over which they had led me was in German hands, and most of those with whom I had talked were dead or prisoners.

Early on the morning of the 9th the Eighteenth German Army began what they have called the Battle of Noyon, and at the same time the Seventh German Army attacked south-west of Soissons. The whole of the threatened front was thus on fire. The severity of this onslaught lasted for two days only. The Germans penetrated to a depth of fifteen kilometres, and set their feet on the heights before Compiègne. But the methods of defence exacted a heavy toll, and a wise elasticity in the use of ground enabled the French to economize losses. From the 11th onwards Fayolle began to launch carefully prepared counter-attacks in great force, particularly in the direction of Méry. These continued throughout the 12th and 13th; but already on the 11th Ludendorff had felt the task beyond his power. "In consequence," he says,[1] "of the great accumulation of enemy troops G.H.Q. directed the Eighteenth Army to break off the attack on the 11th, in order to avoid casualties. It was quite evident that the attack commenced in the meantime by the Seventh Army south-west of Sois-

---

[1] *My War Memories*, p. 634.

sons would not get through. The action of the Eighteenth Army had not altered the strategical situation . . . nor had it provided any fresh tactical data."

So far in all this year the Allies had experienced nothing but recoil. The
martial might of Germany lay heavy on all. The sense of grappling with a monster of seemingly unfathomable resources and tireless strength, invulnerable—
since slaughter even on the greatest scale was no deterrent—could not be
excluded from the mind. No one hoped for a swift result. But the idea that the
war could reach any end other than the total defeat of Germany was strictly excluded even from private conversation. All the dominant personalities were resolved to fight on to victory, and the soldiers with simple faith took this for
granted. Says Ludendorff,[1] "It was certainly discouraging that our two great attacks had not forced a decision. That they had been victorious was obvious. . . .
The evil effect of disillusionment was doubled by the fact that we could not
overcome it in our then state of mind." But they were not victories: they were
only placards. Of the five great battles which had been fought, the first three
against the British had failed to achieve any one of the progressively diminishing strategic results at which they had aimed. The fourth against the French was
a local victory, very spectacular but without strategic consequence; and the
last, the Battle of Noyon, was a very decided arrest. The Supreme offensive was
in slack water. The 11th of June on the French front had marked just such a
milestone in the war as had the 12th of April with the British Army. On the
German side, in spite of sensational triumphs, all was "disillusionment." Behind the Allied front, with all their bitter experiences, the foundation of confidence was solid.

These three months of ceaseless battle had indeed witnessed a profound alteration of the strategic balance. The main forces of Germany were now deeply
committed. The sovereign element of surprise, without which no great offensive was possible, depended upon the power to have simultaneously in readiness
on different parts of the front four or five attacks of the first magnitude. This
had been the baffling factor to the Allies before the 21st of March. But most of
these had now already been let off. The remaining possibilities open to Ludendorff were restricted and to a large extent defined. His reservoirs were low; ours
were filling full.

The balance of numbers had turned heavily. The British had actually killed
and wounded or captured nearly four hundred thousand Germans in the five
weeks' grapple, while all their own losses in men and material had by the activities of their Government been more than replaced. Indeed our Army at the
end of June was somewhat stronger than on the eve of the 21st of March. Divisions had been drawn from Italy, from Salonika and from Egypt. Masses of

[1] *Ibid.*, p. 642.

troops had been released from home by the War Office rising superior at long last to the absurd fear of invasion. Sedentary divisions of older men had been formed to hold the trench lines. When the time came they proved they could march as well as stand. Sir Douglas Haig was conscious of a continued accretion of strength; and as the event was to prove, he was able to measure it better than anyone else.

The resources of France, so prodigally spent at the beginning, so jealously husbanded in the later years, were sufficient for a final effort. And behind them the Americans gathered in tens of thousands day by day. By this date the British Marine alone, military and merchant, had carried and convoyed to France nearly three-quarters of a million American troops. All these facts justified confidence in the successful termination of the year's campaign, and that the next year would be decisive.

The personal position of Marshal Foch after the 27th of May was not however entirely unshaken. On him France fixed the prime responsibility of having diverted the French reserves to cover the juncture of the British and French armies. The appointment of a Generalissimo had only been carried in the face of serious and natural oppositions. The first fruits of "unity of command" and of Foch's personal direction of the front had been a blazing disaster. Strong undercurrents ran of complaint and reproach. The British did not think they had been well treated in their intense trial. Moreover, there were reasonable grounds for misgiving. Unlike Haig or Pétain, Marshal Foch had not at his disposal the great machinery of a General Staff. He acted only through what he has pleasingly described as "ma famille militaire,"—a small band of devoted officers who had throughout the war shared his varied fortunes. At their head stood a certain young General Weygand, alert, discreet and silent in manner, afterwards to become better known. Whether this extremely restricted circle would be able to inform their Chief upon the vast and innumerable masses of technical detail which must be mastered before the operations of great modern armies can be weighed and selected from among alternatives, was a question at that time without an answer. On this account also many doubts were entertained. Nevertheless Marshal Foch, building his house on the rock of strategic truth, possessed his soul in patience.

CHAPTER LIII

THE TURN OF THE TIDE

A drear panorama confronted the rulers of Germany in the month that followed the Battle of Noyon, and a growing sense of the inevitable began to chill all hearts. No rift, no crack, no crevice appeared in the mighty concourse of States, almost the world in arms, which glared stonily across the lines of battle at Germany and her Allies. France under Clémenceau was flint. The British Army was known to be rapidly recovering, and under Lloyd George's leadership the whole Empire resounded with the clang of redoubled exertion. The Americans were pouring in across the open seas. Italy, so nearly extinguished in the preceding winter, renewed her strength. Meanwhile from every quarter dark tidings flowed in upon Great Headquarters. Turkey was desperate. A sinister silence brooded in Bulgaria. The Austro-Hungarian Empire was upon the verge of dissolution. A mutinous outbreak had occurred in the German Navy. And now the valiant German Army itself, the foundation and life of the whole Teutonic Powers, showed disquieting symptoms. The German nation had begun to despair, and the soldiers became conscious of their mood. Ugly incidents occurred. Desertion increased, and the leave men were reluctant to return. The German prisoners liberated from Russia by the Treaty of Brest-Litovsk returned infected with the Lenin virus. In large numbers they refused to go again to the front. A campaign of unmerited reproach was set on foot against the German officer class. Their painstaking and thorough routine, which had enabled them on all the fronts to exact two Ally lives for every German, was no protection from the charge that they did not share the privations of the troops. The British fire had bitten deep in March and April, and for the first time since the earliest days of the war Germany felt the swift blood-drain she was accustomed to exact from others. Still the majestic war machine obeyed the levers of authority, and the teeth of its thousand wheels, in spite of occasional jars and tremors, kept grinding on remorselessly.

And in Ludendorff was found a hardy gambler incapable of withdrawing from the game while he still had heavy stakes to play. Who shall say whether at this moment he was right or wrong? He could not tell whether the adoption of a defensive policy, of great strategic retirements, of gaining at all costs the winter for negotiation, might not have been the signal for the collapse he dreaded.

No, it was better to brazen it out to the bitter end. He had gathered the strength for one more plunge. Was there not still one more good chance? A crashing victory against the French, the advance to Paris, and then, when all Allied reserves had been interposed to shield the Capital, a sudden right-handed drive against the British and the Channel ports. Such at least was his resolve.

The ordeal of the German Emperor during the great Battle of Rheims has been the subject of an imaginative but profoundly instructive study by a German writer of distinction.[1] The story is confined to the hour-to-hour doings and experiences of the Emperor during the period of less than ten days in which the battle was launched and decided. And with German thoroughness more than five hundred closely printed pages are devoted to this theme. The arrival of the Imperial train at a wayside station; the supreme War Lord's meeting with his Generals, Hindenburg solemn, deferential, vague; Ludendorff preoccupied, terse, reserved, the man at the wheel—such is the opening picture. The Imperial trappings are becoming threadbare. These men are grappling with doom. They do not seek to add a third to their confidence. The Emperor is ceremoniously relegated to a tall wooden tower specially constructed in a wood from whose platform above the level of the tree-tops the All Highest would be in the most favourable position to witness what might happen. And here with his immediate retinue he must dwell perched for six whole days, eyes glued to telescopes that show nothing but distant fumes and blurs and smudges; while his throne totters and his people's fortune is decided, utterly helpless and useless, a prey to the worst anxieties, but at any rate out of the way.

Ludendorff's plan for the battle of Rheims followed the usual German pincer model, and was in itself almost on the scale of the 21st of March. Two separate simultaneous attacks, with a silent gap of 20 kilometres between them, were launched on each side of Rheims with the object of biting off that city and the difficult hilly region around it. The Seventh German Army attacked across the Marne to the west of Rheims, and the First and Third German Armies to the east. Fifteen divisions were assigned to the first wave of each attack. The total width of the offensive, including the gap, was nearly 70 kilometres. Its general convergence was upon Chalons. If this battle prospered, the growing threat to Paris would draw the Allied reserves southward to defend the capital. Whereupon, when the situation was ripe, the Crown Prince Rupprecht with thirty-one divisions would fall on the British in Flanders and resume the battle of the Lys and the drive at the Channel ports. The conception was vast, and the forces employed in the whole combination the most widespread used since the original invasion.

[1] *Der König,* by Carl Rosner.

The secret of these designs was not hidden from the Allies. The concentrations of the enemy were correctly defined. Information from deserters and from prisoners taken in organized raids supplied the French and British Headquarters with full confirmatory details, while time for the necessary preparations yet remained. Haig braced himself to meet Rupprecht, and Pétain organized the Rheims front with minute and studious care. The French line was held to the west of Rheims by the army of Berthelot and to the east by that of Gouraud, both comprised in the army group of Maistre. These measures taken, the general concert of the gigantic battle rested with Foch.

The intervention of the supreme control was decisive. Neither Haig nor Pétain, with their own intense preoccupations, could have achieved the general view. Nor is it likely that from a discussion between two equally threatened equals, each with vital objectives to guard, the right arrangements would have emerged. Between co-operation, however loyal, and united action, there is a gap wide enough to turn victory into defeat. Foch, trusting to the information to hand in spite of all its uncertainty, resolved to allow the Rheims battle to develop, and then at its height to strike at the right flank of the advancing Germans with a heavy counter-stroke. For this purpose he massed with all possible secrecy in the forests around Villers-Cotterets an army of more than twenty divisions and 350 small French tanks. He drew these forces from the reserves which Pétain wished to keep to guard Paris. He also on the 12th asked that four British divisions should be moved into the French zone, two south of the Somme and two astride of that river to ensure the connection between the French and British armies about Amiens, and to enable him to move four French divisions farther to the east and nearer to the impending battle. This was agreed to by the British Headquarters and orders were given accordingly. On the 13th Foch demanded that these four divisions should be immediately placed unreservedly at his disposal for the battle, and further that four more British divisions should be dispatched to take their places.

These were serious requests. Opposite the Hazebrouck sector, perilously near the coast, Rupprecht was known to have eight divisions in the line, and twenty-three, of which twenty-one were fresh, divisions in reserve. Against this already mounted attack the British could muster only fifteen divisions, including reserves, and of these two were half-trained and one of second line personnel. Sir Douglas Haig moved immediately the two additional divisions which were to replace those astride of the Somme, but he then dwelt upon the accumulating preparations of the Germans to attack the British front and the uncertainty as to where the next blow would fall, and declared himself against dispatching any troops to Champagne at the moment. He asked that at least decision should be deferred on this last point till he could meet Foch at Mouchy as had been arranged for the 15th.

Meanwhile the British Government were alarmed by the substantial weakening of the British Reserves when unquestionably a series of enormous attacks could be launched at any moment upon our much tried troops. They were also deeply offended by the diversion from the British zone of almost all the American troops who had arrived. The Prime Minister called a meeting of the War Cabinet on the evening of the 13th at Hassocks, and as the result General Smuts was sent to Haig to say that if he considered it desirable to invoke the "Beauvais agreement" the Government would support him. Matters were in this position when the battle began.

As the curtain rises on the new scene we may take a sweeping glance at the principal characters. The Emperor before the dawn of July 15 is on his leafy perch among the tree-tops. Ludendorff is at Avesnes on tenterhooks. Pétain's attention is riveted upon his front, and the capital city which lies only 90 kilometres behind it, on which the storm is about to break. Haig and his Chief of Staff think on the whole that the second, rather than the first blow, is reserved for them; but that it will be terrible they have no doubt. The French line, they believe, will hold after bending; but the possibility of a French counter-stroke is too good to be true. East of Rheims behind a false front elaborately maintained lies Gouraud, a fiery spirit in a war-shattered frame, skilful, knightly, accurately informed. He knows even the German zero; and three hours before the German bombardment begins, all his artillery open counter-preparation fire on the crowded batteries and assembly trenches of the assault. In the forests of Villers-Cotterets crouches the army of Foch's counter-stroke—two strong American divisions, and eighteen of bitter Frenchmen. At its head we see again the impetuous Mangin. Dark days have come to him since Douaumont was recaptured: the Nivelle disaster of which he was the scapegoat, dismissal from his command, indeed from all commands, a Ministerial order not to reside within 50 kilometres of Paris, afterwards petty employment while Armageddon rages—horrible to endure. Suddenly Clémenceau, above scapegoat-making, reaches down a strong hand. Foch, then only an adviser, proposes "To Mangin a Corps." Opposition and prejudice are swept aside. After six months' probation in command of the IXth Corps, "Mangin the Butcher" is placed once again at the head of an army. And now, like a hungry leopard on a branch, sees Incomparable Opportunity approaching and about to pass below. And last of all in the beautiful Château of Bombon, where the sunrise bathes the lawns and the ripple of waters joins the accompaniment of summer, sits Marshal Foch with Weygand at his side and his "military family" around him. He has battles to fight behind the line as well as in front of it.

Down from beyond the German parapets leaped the cataracts of fire and steel. Forward the indomitable veterans of the Fatherland! It is the Marne that must be crossed. Thousands of cannon and machine guns lash its waters into foam. But the shock troops go forward, war-worn, war-hardened, and once again *"Nach Paris"* is on their lips. Launching frail pontoons and rafts in a whistling, screaming, crashing hell they cross the river, mount the farther bank, grapple with the French; grapple also with the Americans—numerous, fresh and coolly handled. After heavy losses they drive them back, and make good their lodgments. They throw their bridges, drag across guns and shells, and when night falls upon the bloody field, 50,000 Germans have dug themselves in on a broad front 4 miles beyond the Marne. Here they stop to gather further strength after performing all that soldiers have ever done.

But it was otherwise to the east of Rheims. Gouraud's counter-preparation smote the First and Third German Armies even before the signal to advance was due. The general had unmasked all his batteries on the hazard of his information. Would he be justified by the event? His Chief of Staff entered his room at Chalons watch in hand. "They have not begun. It is past zero. We have been betrayed by the prisoners." "There are still two minutes," answered Gouraud, also watch in hand: and thus the two men stood waiting breathlessly for a new cannonade to supervene upon the muffled thunder of the French bombardment. Punctually as Gouraud's watch pointed to the hour, a roar like a railway train passed overhead, and with deafening detonation a gigantic German shell shattered the neighbouring lighting plant and plunged the Headquarters in total darkness. The two French officers received this unmistakable message with feelings of profound thankfulness and relief. Their batteries had not been exposed in vain.

Very heavy losses were inflicted upon the assembled Germans by the forestalling fire. The advance began under heavy disadvantages. The false French front resisted ruggedly and must be laboriously exterminated. And then, beyond the range of their own artillery, the Germans collided with the real front, flaming, impenetrable, alive with counter-attacks. All along the line from end to end without exception, the advance of the First and Third Armies withered before the French defence; and after a day of frightful slaughter, nothing of consequence had been gained. The check was decisive. "By noon of the 16th," says Ludendorff, "G.H.Q. had given orders for the suspension of the offensive to the First and Third Armies and for their organization for defence by withdrawing certain divisions for this purpose. . . . Once the difficult decision to suspend the offensive of these armies had been taken, it was useless to attempt to advance further across the Marne or to leave our troops on the Southern bank. We had to make arrangements for crossing before the retreat could even begin." The retreat was fixed for the night between the 20th and 21st. He still hoped however to make progress up the valley of the Ardre towards Rheims.

These decisions of Ludendorff were not of course known to Foch or Pétain, and the 15th was a day of great stress for General Foch. The first reports of the battle on the morning of the 15th from Gouraud's army were so satisfactory that Foch set off for his rendezvous with Haig at Mouchy. There can be little doubt that Grand Quartier Général was lukewarm about the Mangin counter-stroke. It is at least certain that they strove to delay it. In later years it has been said that Pétain argued: "It is too soon. Let the Germans advance further. Let them engage their reserves fully in the main battle, and your counter-stroke will be all the more effective." Whether this was the real motive or an after explanation to cover undue sensitiveness about Paris, will long be disputed. But there can be no dispute about the action of General Foch. On his way to Mouchy he stopped at General Fayolle's headquarters at Noailles. There he heard that Grand Quartier Général had issued instructions for all available French reserves to be held in readiness to go to Rheims. He immediately cancelled these orders and said that the preparations for Mangin's attack should be pressed on with all speed and that the attack should take place as soon as possible. He wanted it to take place on the 17th, but acquiesced reluctantly in the date being finally fixed for the 18th.

Further protests were raised by the French Headquarters. Whether they emanated directly from Pétain is not certain; but at 12:25 Foch telephoned to Pétain from Mouchy—"There can be no question of any slowing down, still less of stopping the Mangin preparations. In case of urgent, extreme need you may take troops absolutely indispensable, informing me at once." This done he opened his discussion with Haig. The British Headquarters believed that the defeat of the 27th of May had grievously affected the morale of the French Army. They were extremely sceptical of the ability and resolve of the French to deliver a heavy offensive punch. They feared lest their own reserves should be reduced, not for the purpose of a decisive counter-stroke at the proper moment, but merely to add to the mass of troops between Paris and the enemy. The British and French High Commands were in close touch with each other, and the defensive views of Pétain were well known to Haig. The Generalissimo had nothing to his record but the disaster of the 27th of May, and no machine at his disposal beyond his group of personal staff officers in the Château of Bombon. Haig might sympathize with Foch's conception. But would it be translated into action? In the crisis of the battle on the Rheims front, with Paris perhaps in the balance, would not the known views of Pétain and the power of the French staff organization prevail? Nevertheless Haig agreed to move the whole of the second four British divisions to the aid of the French, and the first two of them were actually ordered to complete the XXIInd Corps south of the Somme.

Late that same night General Smuts, member and envoy of the War Cabinet, arrived upon the scene. He explained his mission to the Commander-in-

Chief, and offered him the support of the British Government, if he thought he was being unduly pressed. Haig replied "that he would take the risk, that he accepted the responsibility, and that he had acted in the main interest of the Allied cause." He even gave Smuts a written note that he "took the risk and fully realized that if the dispositions (of Foch) proved to be wrong, the blame will rest on me. On the other hand, if they prove right, the credit will lie with Foch. With this," he added pointedly, "the Government should be well satisfied!"

Meanwhile a tense discussion was in progress at Provins. After the dismissal of General Anthoine in the aftermath of the 27th of May a new figure had appeared at the French Headquarters. The young and audacious Buat, chosen by Foch and Clémenceau, had been appointed the Major-General of the Armies and, independently of Pétain's wishes, had become his right-hand man. Buat, as he was no doubt expected to do by those who had selected him, hurled his weight upon the side of the immediate counter-stroke; and in the end Pétain and the French staff consented to obey the orders of the Supreme Commander-in-Chief.

The battle on the Marne raged during the whole of the 16th with heavy French counter-attacks. On the morning of the 17th Foch sent General Du Cane with a letter to Haig on the subject of the attack threatening on the British front, and the precautionary disposal of the British reserves to meet it. As Du Cane was stepping into his car, Weygand, who had followed him through the doorway, said: "General Foch authorizes you to tell Sir Douglas Haig that Mangin's army will attack to-morrow morning, at 8 a.m. with twenty divisions."

The British Headquarters Staff were filled with the deepest misgivings upon the dispersal of their Reserves. Fortified by the Smuts visit they had made the strongest representation to the Commander-in-Chief during the 16th. General Du Cane was confronted on arrival with the draft of a letter which awaited Haig's signature, demanding the immediate return to the north of the Somme of all the four divisions of the XXIInd Corps. His personal interview with the Commander-in-Chief did not prevent the signing and sending of this letter. But Haig, convinced that the great counter-attack was now certain, added a verbal message that "if the British troops were wanted to exploit a success, they should of course be used." This in the event was all that was needed.

I have described these transactions in some detail, because they mark the crucial moment in Foch's career as Supreme Commander of the Allied Armies, and show, as it is right to do, alike his difficulties and the dominating personal part he played in victories which all henceforward were to share. They show also the important aid which in a crisis of terrible uncertainty was given him by Sir Douglas Haig and the British Army.

• • •

Let us now for a moment cross the lines.

> "In the night of the 17th–18th," writes Ludendorff,[1] "I myself went to
> the Headquarters of the Army Group of Crown Prince Rupprecht, to re-
> view once more the state of their preparations. The attack was intended as
> a continuation of that which had been suspended at the end of April. It
> was to be made by the Fourth and Sixth Armies north of the Lys, its ob-
> jectives being the possession of the commanding heights between Poper-
> inghe and Bailleul, as well as the high ground round Hazebrouck. During
> the discussion with the Army Group of Crown Prince Rupprecht on the
> morning of the 18th I received the first news that, by means of an unex-
> pected tank attack, the French had pierced the line south-west of Sois-
> sons. . . . I concluded the conference at the Army Group of Crown Prince
> Rupprecht (naturally in a state of the greatest nervous tension) and then
> returned to Avesnes."

At the appointed hour Mangin's army had sprung. His battle followed the
Cambrai model. There was no artillery preparation. Three hundred and thirty
small Renault tanks came out of the woods and ground their way through the
German line. Behind them the French infantry rolled forward in immense superiority. Upon a wide front the enemy were overwhelmed. Behind the front
the German troops were placidly harvesting the abundant crops. They cast
down their sickles and fought where they stood. The high corn hampered their
machine-guns except where occasionally provided with special tripods, and the
small tanks continued murderously to break up the defence. By nightfall
Mangin's army had advanced an average of 5 kilometres on a front of 45. The
decisive blow on the Western Front had not yet been struck; but from this moment onwards to the end of the war, without exception, the Allies continued to
advance and the Germans to retreat.

During these tremendous days the British, French, American and Italian Munitions authorities had been in continuous conference in Paris. The distant rumble of the cannonade and the dull crash of the half-hourly Bertha shells
reminded us that the campaign of 1918 was going on. But all our work was concerned with 1919. The provision and division of steel, of coal, of nitrates; the
manufacture of artillery, shells, machine-guns, tanks, aeroplanes, poison gas,
upon the greatest possible scale and under the most harmonious arrangements,

---

[1] *My War Memories,* pp. 667–8.

kept us, and the enormous technical staffs we directed, at the Conference table every day and all day. And of course while the battle hung in the balance I waited ready to set in motion, if it must be so, the far-reaching, elaborate scheme for evacuation and reconstituting the Paris munition factories in which we were concerned. In the last week of July we were invited to take a day off and visit the scene of the victory. Passing through Château-Thierry and along the pulverized front, we repaired to Mangin's headquarters at Versigny. We approached the General's house through a long avenue of captured German cannon and trench mortars. Mangin received us with cordiality. His modest bearing did not conceal his joy. After luncheon I found myself alone with him, and knowing the ups and downs which he had survived, I offered some few words of admiration upon his signal victory. I record his reply exactly as he gave it: "Le Maréchal Foch l'a conçue. Le Général Gouraud l'a rendue possible. Moi, je l'ai faite." Some years afterwards when I repeated these words to General Gouraud, he considered them for an appreciable moment and then said: "That is quite true." And indeed I think they may well serve as an epitome of this memorable event.

Unseen upon the surface, the turn of the tide had now begun. Nevertheless Ludendorff persevered, and the Crown Prince and his staff were found capable of stemming the French inroad on their flank. The divisions which would have backed the drive on Paris rapidly formed a front to the French counter-stroke; and after the first surprise very few more kilometres were taken away from the stubborn enemy. In a fortnight of hard fighting the Germans skilfully extricated their masses of men and material from the perilous Marne salient. But Rupprecht, whose hammer was actually uplifted in Flanders, was frozen where he stood. At first it was a mere postponement: a week or two while the German position in the Marne salient was reorganized. And then a few divisions were taken from his army to help in the reorganization; and then a few more; and then another week's delay. Thus Rupprecht remained for twenty days, waiting for the signal. But the signal never came. The scale in which the struggling armies and the nations behind them were weighed had tilted. The inclination was imperceptible to the public eye, but the controlling minds of the German Headquarters registered a definite sensation.

But now an event was to occur which would resolve all doubts. "August 8," writes Ludendorff, "was the black day of the German Army in the history of this war. . . . The 8th of August opened the eyes of the staff on both sides; mine were certainly opened. . . . The Emperor told me later on, after the failure of the July offensive and after August 8, he knew the war could be no longer won."

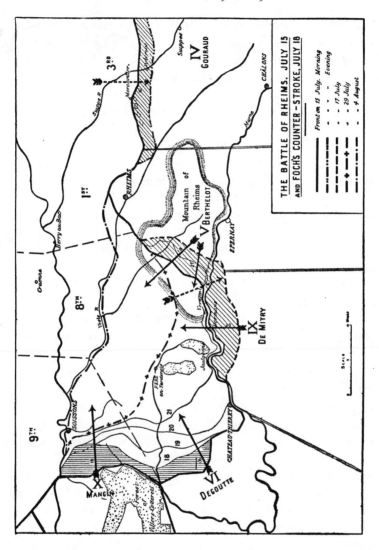

On July 24 the only conference ever held between the Allied Commanders took place at Bombon. Foch presented to Haig, Pershire and Pétain a document setting forth in outline his policy for the rest of the year. His plans may be shortly described as follows: First, to reduce the three principal salients on the enemy's front—Amiens, Château-Thierry and St. Mihiel, with a view to improving for the campaign of 1919 the lateral railway communications along the whole front from the Vosges Mountains to the sea, and by a subsidiary action to free the Bruay coalfield, and certain other minor enterprises. Secondly, if successful in these operations, to carry out a general offensive with all the troops available. It is said that he had among his intimates already begun to dwell on the hope of obtaining final victory in 1918. His favourite expression at this time was, "L'édifice commence à craquer. Tout le monde à la bataille!" On the other hand his memorandum stated that it would depend on the measure of success gained in these various operations whether that success could be more fully exploited "before the winter sets in." All his plans aimed at the summer of 1919. In August, when asked when the war would end, his official answer was "about next autumn—in twelve months"; and as late as the middle of October his Staff made the answer "in the spring."

The British Headquarters had been agreeably surprised by the success of Mangin's counter-stroke. Their scepticism was however fortified by the failure of the French, in spite of the initial surprise of July 18, to make effective progress against the Germans in the Château-Thierry salient or to prevent the Crown Prince from extricating his troops from their dangerous position. Nevertheless Haig was resolute for the attack, and entirely agreed with the Generalissimo upon the immediate practical steps. He had as early as July 13 directed Rawlinson to prepare an offensive by the Fourth Army against the German salient before Amiens. Rawlinson's plans were in consequence well advanced. He had accepted with logic and conviction the whole model of a Tank battle. There were available in all nearly 600 tanks, of which, apart from spare machines, 96 were supply tanks, 22 gun carriers and 420 fighting tanks. Of the fighting tanks 324 were of the new Mark 5 pattern of superior speed and manœuvring power, and weighed over thirty tons apiece. Everything was subordinated to the surprise of the tank attack. One hundred and twenty brigades of British artillery of all natures were assembled, but all preliminary bombardment was prohibited. Not a shot was to be fired even for registration. The tanks were to advance, unfettered and unprejudiced, simultaneously with the infantry and about 200 yards behind the creeping barrage. Their approach was assisted by special noise barrages, by the morning mist, and by artificial fog. The British heavy and medium artillery was mainly to be directed upon the enemy's similar guns. The infantry, closely accompanied by numerous field batteries and with large bodies of cavalry at hand, were to exploit the success of the tanks. The essence of the whole plan was surprise. Rawlinson's army had a restricted position of assembly, and German counter-preparation, if it caught our troops in the act of assembling, would have serious results. For these reasons Rawlinson did not wish to fight hand in hand with the French on his right. He feared lest secrecy should be endangered by a joint operation. Moreover, Debeney's French army had few tanks and could not attack without artillery preparation. To ensure complete co-operation Foch placed all the troops, British and French, under Sir Douglas Haig. The danger lest the French preliminary bombardment should spoil the surprise was overcome by timing the French infantry attack three-quarters of an hour later than the British. Thus not a shot would be fired before zero. On the second and third days of the battle the rest of Debeney's army and Humbert's army were in succession to intervene.

At 4:20 a.m. on August 8, in the half light of a misty dawn, the British tanks rolled forward into No Man's Land, and simultaneously the Allied artillery opened fire. Four Canadian, four Australian and two British divisions, followed by three more in reserve and the Cavalry Corps, advanced on the British front. Eight French divisions cooperated later in *échelon* on their right. All along the line, but especially in the centre where the Canadians and Australians fought, victory declared itself forthwith. Ludendorff had taken special measures to strengthen the German line. "In this storm-centre," he writes, "the divisional fronts were narrow, artillery was plentiful, and the trench system was organized in depth. All experience gained on the 18th July had been acted upon." It was of no avail. The Germans were unable to resist the tanks. "Six battle-worthy divisions"[1] collapsed almost immediately before forces scarcely superior in numbers. In less than two hours 16,000 prisoners and more than 200 guns were taken by the British, and by noon tanks and armoured motor cars, followed by cavalry, were scouring the country 14 kilometres behind the German front. The French, who attacked without tanks, advanced about half as far. But the British advance enabled Chaulnes junction to be brought under close fire and consequently destroyed the German communications on which their whole front from Montdidier to Lassigny depended. This was decisive. Two days later, when Humbert's army joined the battle, the high ground near Lassigny was found abandoned; and the advance of the Allies was general along a front of 120 kilometres.

I spent the 9th and 10th on the battlefield. I had been at the War Cabinet the day before when Sir Henry Wilson had announced the opening of the attack, and when in the afternoon the first reports of a great Tank victory began to come through, I decided to get into my aeroplane and take a couple of days' holiday. Rawlinson's Headquarters were at Flixicourt, near Amiens. I was much delayed in reaching them by enormous columns of German prisoners which endlessly streamed along the dusty roads. No one who has been a prisoner of war himself can be indifferent to the lot of the soldier whom the fortunes of war condemn to this plight. The woe-begone expression of the Officers contrasted sharply with the almost cheerful countenances of the rank and file. All had passed through a severe experience, the crashing bombardment, the irresistible on-rush of the tanks spurting machine-gun bullets from every unexpected quarter, the catastrophe of surrender, the long march from the battlefield

[1] Ludendorff.

with many claims to consideration in front of theirs, night in the advanced cages—now another long march since dawn. "A la guerre, comme à la guerre!"

The General received me with his customary good humour, and at luncheon, while the tramp of new columns of prisoners proclaimed his victory, explained how it had been achieved. It was, truly, *his* victory, and that of the Fourth Army which he directed. He had put aside old-fashioned ideas, he had used new weapons as they should be used, he had reaped swift and rich reward.

This is perhaps the place where I may give the reader some slight impression of Sir Henry Rawlinson. I had known him since Omdurman, where he was one of Kitchener's leading Staff Officers. In the Great War we had met in every variety of fortune. First on the Aisne in September, 1914, before he had any command at all, when we lay on an unfinished haystack watching the shells play on the Soissons road: next at Antwerp, where he arrived to take over the command at the moment when further defence had become extremely questionable: next in my room at the Admiralty, after the Seventh Division under his command had been virtually destroyed in the first battle of Ypres and when many were ready to lay blame on his tactics. In April, 1918, I had been with him at Dury in the last extremes of the 21st March, when with a few cavalry and machine-guns and details from the training establishments, he was covering and enduring the dissolution of the Fifth Army. Now we met at the zenith of his career, when he had largely by his personal contribution gained a battle which we now know ranks among the decisive episodes of war.

During these vicissitudes he was always the same. In the best of fortunes or the worst, in the most dangerous and hopeless position or on the crest of the wave, he was always the same tough, cheery gentleman and sportsman. He had always the same welcome for a friend, be he highly or lowly placed, and the same keen, practical, resolute outlook on facts however they might be marshalled. The readers of Rawlinson's "History of Assyria" and another Rawlinson's "Herodotus" will trace with confidence the hereditary source of his strongly-marked capacity.

The battle was still in full blast and I asked how best to see it. There is a road well known to the Royal Air Force which runs straight as a die for 50 kilometres due East from Amiens to Vermand. "It is being shelled, but there is no congestion, you can go ahead along it as far as you care." So off we went along this famous road, through deserted, battered, ghostly Amiens; through Villers-Bretonneux, a heap of smouldering wreckage, threading our way through the intervals of an endless convoy which moved slowly forward from one shell-hammered point to another. The battlefield had all its tales to tell. The German dead lay everywhere, but scattered in twos and threes and half-dozens over a very wide area. Rigid in their machine-gun nests, white flaccid corpses, lay those faithful legionaries of the Kaiser who had tried to stem the rout of "six battle-worthy German divisions." A British war balloon overhead burst into a sheet of fire, from which tiny black figures fell in parachutes. Cavalry cantered as gaily over the reconquered territory as if they were themselves the cause of victory. By a small wood seven or eight Tanks with scattered German dead around them lay where a concealed battery had pierced them, twisted and scorched by the fierce petrol fires in which they had perished. "Crews nearly all burned to death," said the Officer of the burying party. "Those still alive are the worst off."

Finally where bullets began to cut the leafage and freshly wounded men streamed back from an advancing fighting line, an Australian soldier said: "It's the best we've ever had. We went hard all day yesterday, but this morning we have been relieved, and *an Imperial brigade*" (note the phrasing) "is now attacking."

CHAPTER LIV

THE TEUTONIC COLLAPSE

Before the war it had seemed incredible that such terrors and slaughters, even if they began, could last more than a few months. After the first two years it was difficult to believe that they would ever end. We seemed separated from the old life by a measureless gulf. The adaptive genius of man had almost habituated him to the horrors of his new environment. Far away shone a pale star of home and peace; but all around the storm roared with unabated and indeed increasing fury. Year after year every optimist had been discredited, every sober hope cast down, and the British nation had doggedly resigned itself to pursue its task without inquiry when the end would come. In the circles of Government, where so many plans had to be made for more than a year ahead, this mood formed the subconscious foundation of our thoughts. Ultimate victory seemed certain. But how it would come, and whether it would come in 1919 or in 1920, or later, were inquiries too speculative to pursue amid the imperious needs of each day. Still less would anyone dare to hope for peace in 1918. Nevertheless, when from time to time the mental eye fell upon these puzzles, this question immediately presented itself: Would Germany collapse all of a sudden as she had done after Jena, or would she fight it out to the bitter end like the French under Napoleon or the Confederates under Lee? The Great War came when both sides were confident of victory. Would it continue after one side was sure it had no hope? Was it in the German nature, so valiant yet at the same time so logical, to fight on in revengeful despair? Should we have a year of battle on the Rhine, the march to Berlin, the breaking up of the armies in the open field, the subjugation of the inhabitants; or would there be some intense nervous spasm, some overwhelming and almost universal acceptance of defeat and all that defeat involved? We had always fancied it would be Jena. But all our plans were for a long-drawn alternative.

Certainly the highest interests of Germany, once all hope of victory was closed, required the orderly retreat of the greater part of her armies to the Antwerp-Meuse line, and thence to the German frontier. To secure this at all costs became, after the battle of August 8, and the conclusions drawn from it by the rulers of Germany, the paramount duty of soldiers and statesmen, and of all parties and classes. Moreover, such a retreat could assuredly have been accomplished, provided the decision was immediate. Apart from all the methods of delaying a pursuit which tactics and strategy suggest, the Germans possessed at this time a simple mechanical device, the full use of which would with certainty have gained them a breathing space until the spring of 1919. They had developed time fuses for exploding mines or shells, which could be regulated to retard the explosion, not merely for days or weeks, but actually for many months. It would therefore have been possible for the retreating invaders to have sown the roads and railways behind them with mines and buried shells so that they would be continually destroyed day after day by a fresh and inexhaustible series of explosions at points and moments which their pursuers could never foresee. The only method of dealing with a railway thus mined would be to build an entirely new line out of such material as could be salved alongside the original. It would therefore not have been possible for the Allied armies to advance to the German frontiers until they had reconstructed the whole intervening railway system. This could certainly not have been completed before the end of the year. Not till then could the process of dragging forward the ponderous mass of material necessary to mount a grand offensive have ever been begun.

There might therefore have been gained for Germany a period of perhaps six months before the full strength of the Allied armies could have been brought to bear upon her frontiers and before she was exposed to actual invasion. The time was sufficient for strong positions to be selected and prepared, and for the whole remaining resources of the nation to be marshalled in defence of its territory. But far more important than any military advantage was the effect which Germany, by admitting defeat and withdrawing completely from France and Belgium, would have produced upon the cohesion and driving power of the Allies. The liberation of the soil of France was the dominating impulse which held the French people to the war. The rescue of Belgium was still the main rallying point of the British war resolve. Had Germany therefore removed both these motives, had she stood with arms in her hands on the threshold of her own land ready to make a defeated peace, to cede territory, to make reparation; ready also if all negotiation were refused to defend herself to the utmost, and capable of inflicting two million casualties upon the invader, it seemed, and seems, almost certain that she would not have been put to the test. The passion for revenge ran high, and stern was the temper of the Allies; but retribution, however justified, would not in the face of real peace offers have been in itself a sufficient incentive to lead the great war-wearied nations into another year of frightful waste and slaughter. In the lull and chill of the winter with the proud foe suing for terms and with all his conquests already abandoned, a peace by negotiation was inevitable. Even in this last phase Germany need not have placed herself in the appalling position of yielding to the discretion of those upon whom she had inflicted the utmost injuries of hate.

Many factors and influences were no doubt simultaneously at work upon those who still ruled Germany. But it is probable that the last chance was lost for a very inadequate reason. The German Headquarters could not make up its mind to face the consequences of a swift and immediate retreat. Foch is reported to have said at the end of August, pointing to the war map: "This man (the German) could still escape if he did not mind leaving his luggage behind him." The immense masses of munitions and war stores of all kinds which the Germans had in four years accumulated in France and Belgium became a fatal encumbrance. The German Staff could not bear to sacrifice them. Their railways soon became congested with mountainous impedimenta. Meanwhile the supreme policy of the State was paralysed, and the hard-strained fighting front began to quiver and rock and crack.

It is possible in these pages to do little more than mention the series of great and bloody battles and other events by which the German armies were now to be driven out of France and Belgium and the German Empire into collapse, unconditional surrender and internal revolution. The victory of August 8 was no sooner ended, than both Foch and Haig sought to renew the attack. But some divergence arose upon the method and direction. Foch's Directive of August 10 prescribed the immediate advance of Rawlinson's Fourth British and Debeney's First French Armies towards the Somme in the general direction of Ham. The Third French Army was ordered to prolong the attack and profit by the advance of the First; and Haig was directed to launch at the earliest moment the British Third Army (Byng, lying northward of the Fourth) in an offensive towards Bapaume and Péronne. Haig had other ideas. He did not consider a further immediate advance towards the Somme by Rawlinson and Debeney practicable. The hostile artillery fire, he said, had greatly increased. The enemy had established themselves in their old front line of 1914–15, which was still in good order and well wired. The ground was broken and unsuitable for tanks. At least sixteen German divisions were holding this sector of the front. In these circumstances and after personal inspection, Haig directed that the attack should be postponed until the heavy guns could be brought forward and a full artillery battle mounted. He was however in complete accord with the attack of the British Third Army, and had in fact upon his own initiative given orders to General Byng before the issue of Foch's directive of the 10th. He now planned to use the right of the British First Army (Horne) as well.

Foch reiterated his instructions on August 14. He saw no need to delay the Rawlinson-Debeney frontal attack till Byng could participate. He had not considered the possibility of using Horne. Haig continued to refuse to attack until his artillery preparation was complete. "Nothing," he said, "had happened to cause him to alter his opinion. . . . He declined to change his orders to either of the armies in question." Meanwhile he was rapidly and secretly transferring his reserves to Byng, and reinforcing Horne with the fresh and powerful Canadian Corps. In short, Foch called for a continuance of the frontal attack south of the Somme, and Haig insisted on opening a new and wider battle to the north (on the front Monchy-le-Preux-Miraumont). The difference between the two plans was fundamental. A conference was held at Sarcus on the 15th. Haig adhered to his intentions, and though "observing a most friendly tone," emphasized his "sole responsibility to his Government and fellow-citizens for the handling of the British forces." Foch saw no headway could be made, and submitted. In his Directive issued after the conference he accepted the British plan and its argument. But he withdrew forthwith the First French Army from Sir Douglas Haig, and from noon on August 16 it reverted to the command of General Pétain.

Haig may have exaggerated the resisting powers of the Germans south of the Somme (on the front Roye-Chaulnes); but his reasons were as solid as his refusal, and the event proved most fortunate. On August 21 the Third British Army began the important battle of Bapaume.[1] Reinforced by 100 tanks and striking south-south-eastward over country not unsuited—as would have been the crater fields of the Somme—to the operations of these sovereign weapons, General Byng pressed back the German line. The German Seventeenth Army, on whom the onset fell, was disposed three miles behind a false front on the Gouraud model. This Army counter-attacked along the whole line on the 22nd. But the British having themselves warily engaged at first only a part of their forces, strongly reinforced their assault, beat off the counter-attack and maintained their forward movement. Albert was recovered on the 22nd, and on the 23rd Haig was able to order a general advance on a 33-miles front. The battle was unrelentingly contested, but the British progress was continuous. On the 26th the right of the British First Army from Arras intervened and added another 7 miles to the breadth of the attack, which thus became the longest unbroken front of any offensive battle yet fought in the West. The Fourth Army was also by now in motion again.

That same day, yielding to the pressure from the north, the Germans retired from Roye and fell back to the line of the Somme. Thus the immediate objective which Marshal Foch demanded, and would have sought through a frontal attack of the Fourth British Army, was gained automatically by the attack of the Third. The ruins of Bapaume were retrieved on the 29th. From Péronne to Noyon the Germans stood fast; but on the night of August 30–31 the 2nd Australian Division by a remarkable feat of arms captured Mont St. Quentin, the key of Péronne, and thus compromised the whole of the river

[1] See general map, pp. 826–27.

line. Péronne changed hands again on September 1. On the 2nd, the left of the British First Army came into the battle, and with the Canadian Corps and the British 4th Division, after a bloody conflict, broke through in the north the strong system of trenchments known as the "Drocourt-Quéant switch." Whereupon the Germans abandoned the whole line of the Somme, and from the Oise River to the Sensée retreated towards the Hindenburg Line.

This great British drive may be said to have ended on September 3, by which date the three British armies and particularly the Third Army had advanced on their wide fronts an average of 20 miles, and had captured 53,000 German prisoners and 470 German guns. The German movements, not only during this battle, but till the end of the war, resembled those of a squad of soldiers trying to align themselves by their right, and kept in a continual shuffle by the fact that their right-hand man was himself thrust violently backward by British pressure, every time they tried to take up their correct position.

Mangin's Tenth Army had meanwhile pressed with increasing force northeast through Soissons; and although neither the scale nor the results of his operations were so large as those of the British, the double movement was followed by the general retreat of the German centre. Thus the rest of the Fourth British Army and the First and Third French armies on its right moved forward abreast without heavy losses, and by September 3 the Allied front stood along a line running almost north and south from below Douai to the gates of La Fère. The success of the British attacks exceeded Foch's imperious expectations, and with a magnanimity not always exhibited by great Commanders he was unrestrained in his approval. He sent General Du Cane to tell Sir Douglas Haig that "the operations of the British Army in August and the early part of September would serve as a model for all time." But these operations were by no means at an end.

It was galling to the British Headquarters, justly conscious of the predominant part which our armies were beginning to play in these great successes, to find the credit ascribed by their own Cabinet and public opinion to Marshal Foch. The part the Prime Minister had played in establishing unity of command led him unconsciously to dwell upon the brilliant conceptions of the Generalissimo, and to view only in a half light the potent forward heave of the British Army without which the results would have been mediocre. The Press and public at home followed the lead thus given, and the prevailing impression during these months—and never since effectually corrected—was that after many disasters and much mismanagement, an extraordinary genius had obtained the supreme command and had almost instantaneously converted defeat into victory. Care has been taken in this account to describe some of the splendid decisions on which the fame of Marshal Foch is founded; but this in no way diminishes the services in this campaign of the British Commander-in-Chief. His armies bore the lion's share in the victorious advance, as they had already borne the brunt of the German assault. Foch took a wider survey because he had a higher sphere. It was Haig's duty to take a more restricted view.

Act well thy part; there all the honour lies.

But nevertheless, as has been and will be shown, on more than one cardinal occasion Haig by strenuous insistence deflected the plans of the Supreme Commander with results which were glorious. And ever his shot-pierced divisions, five times decimated within the year, strode forward with discipline, with devotion and with gathering momentum.

Reaction from the mode in fashion at home led the British Headquarters into some disparagement of the French contribution to the final advance. In this they were as far from the truth in one direction as their own Government in the other. In the victorious period from July to November 11, the French suffered no less than 531,000 casualties themselves, and inflicted 414,000 upon the enemy. That an army and a nation engaged at their full strength from the beginning of the war, which had sustained 700,000 casualties in the first few weeks and nearly 3 millions in the first three years, should have been capable of so noble an effort at the end will ever command the admiration and gratitude of their Ally.

None of the British Authorities, military or civilian, at home or in France, was induced by these remarkable victories to predict an early end of the war. General Headquarters, Sir Henry Wilson, the Imperial War Cabinet, the Prime Minister, all proceeded rigorously upon the belief that another most severe campaign would be necessary in 1919. For this every preparation continued to be made on the largest scale by the Ministry of Munitions. The War Cabinet were concerned lest Haig should be drawn by the successes of his army into enterprises beyond the strength of troops who had suffered so much. The Hindenburg Line might well, they feared, not without excuse, become the scene of another Paschendaele. The state of our Man Power, with men of fifty already summoned to the colours and the standards of physical fitness lowered to a harsh point, made the maintenance of the armies in 1919, on a scale of sixty Divisions, a problem of extreme difficulty. Another three or four hundred thousand men shorn away would compel a melancholy contraction in the number of British Divisions available for 1919, which it now seemed not unreasonable to hope would be the final and decisive year. The Cabinet therefore at the end of August sent their Commander-in-Chief a message warning him of the grave consequences which would result from a further heavy blood drain. The "Staff Officer" writes some unpleasantly turned sentences about this improper interference with the prerogatives of the High Command, and the pitiful inability of politicians to face casualties with a hearty spirit.

The Cabinet acted only in accord with prudence and duty in their intervention. Nevertheless, Haig at this time held a truer view both of the deterioration of the Germans and of the resilience of his own army. He shared the military doctrines of Foch. Both these illustrious soldiers had year after year conducted with obstinacy and serene confidence offensives which we now know to have been as hopeless as they were disastrous. But the conditions had now changed. Both were now provided with offensive weapons, which the military science of neither would have conceived. The German losses in Ludendorff's attacks had affected alike the number and quality of the enemy. The swift and ceaseless inflow of the Americans turned the balance of Man Power heavily in favour of the Allies; there was at last enough artillery for formidable attacks to be delivered against almost any part of the hostile line. The Goddess of Surprise had at last returned to the Western Front. Thus both Haig and Foch were vindicated in the end. They were throughout consistently true to their professional theories, and when in the fifth campaign of the war the facts began for the first time to fit the theories, they reaped their just reward.

I was at this time so often at the Front and in such agreeable relations with the Headquarters, British and French, that I was able to appreciate to some extent the new conditions. Sir Douglas Haig's conviction that the British armies would continue to drive the Germans from their successive lines was intense. In his train at Frévant in the closing stages of the Battle of Bapaume, he showed me the order he had just given for three British armies to attack simultaneously; and pointing to the German lines, Siegfried, Wotan, Brunhilde, Hindenburg, etc., with which the map was scored, he said: "Now you will see what all these fortifications are worth when troops are no longer resolved to defend them."

At the end of September General Birch, Chief of the Artillery, showed me a captured German document which greatly affected my outlook. I drew the attention of the Cabinet to it on September 26 in a note on Ammunition from which the following is an extract:

> There is no foundation for the view that the conditions of semi-open warfare which have now supervened in France and the abandonment of the prolonged artillery bombardment previous to assaults will afford us any relief in shell consumption. On the contrary, since this matter was last discussed in Cabinet, the heaviest firings yet recorded have taken place in France during a period of open warfare. For fifteen successive days the expenditure exceeded 10,000 tons a day. These very wide battles, fought on the fronts of two or three British armies simultaneously, in which almost all the guns in France are employed, use more and not less ammunition than

was required for the intense local fighting of Messines, Paschendaele, etc. On the other hand, this great consumption of ammunition is being attended by remarkable results. A recent order of General Ludendorff's which has been captured states that in a single month more than 13 per cent of the German artillery in the West has been completely destroyed by counter-battery fire. As this method is comparatively little used by the French, the main credit of this astonishing achievement falls to the British Artillery. A superior Artillery supplied with ample ammunition and working in combination with a superior and highly-trained Air Force is thus producing an immense effect, not only in destroying the enemy's power of resistance but in saving our own men. If the destruction of German artillery could be maintained at the rate stated by General Ludendorff, it would become practically necessary to replace the whole of the German artillery in the West, apart altogether from the wear of guns, twice in the course of a year. This would be quite impossible. We are therefore in this field also perhaps within measurable distance of decisive and final results. It would be disastrous if, for any reason, we were compelled to stint our gunners in ammunition at the very time when the result of all the immense efforts which have been made to increase the power and perfect the combination of our Artillery and Air Services is coming to hand. Rather than do that we ought to be ready to make very great sacrifices indeed in every direction.

I do not burden the reader with the further arguments about steel and tonnage to which this extract was the prelude. It carried to my mind the first sure sign that the end was approaching, and faster than we had dared to hope.

CHAPTER LV

VICTORY

The war was now entered upon its final phase. During the year 1918, the effort of Britain and of the British Empire reached its highest pitch. The Imperial forces in the field against the enemy in all theatres amounted to four and a half million men, and those under arms to nearly six millions. The strength of the Grand Fleet in vessels of every kind reached its maximum, and the Germans were no longer in a condition even to put to sea. The U-boat warfare was defeated and kept down by the operations of nearly 4,000 armed vessels flying the White Ensign. Under the protection of these agencies upwards of two million United States troops were transported across the Atlantic, of which more than half were carried in British ships, and landed in France during the year. The British Mercantile Marine of 20,000 vessels maintained the supply of all the British armies and carried without appreciable hindrance all the food and materials needed for the life of the British islands, for their war industries and for any commerce not required for war production. The control of the seas against the enemy in every quarter of the globe was absolute, and this result was obtained by the employment in the fighting fleets and flotillas, in the Mercantile Marine, in the Naval arsenals and dockyards, and in the shipbuilding yards of over 1,200,000 men. The British munition plants absorbing the labours of nearly two and a half million persons produced all the shell and artillery that the British armies could use, together with every other requisite in increasing abundance. In addition Britain furnished steel, coal, and other war materials in immense quantities to France and Italy, and was preparing, without prejudice to any other obligation, to supply the United States with the whole of the medium artillery required for an Army of eighty divisions for a campaign in 1919. All the preparations had been made, and the process was far advanced of fitting the British armies with technical equipment of every kind for 1919 on a scale in quality and in novelty far superior to any outputs yet achieved. In all there were actually employed under the Crown in the armies, in the fleets and in the war factories, excluding those engaged in the production of food, coal and civil necessaries, nearly eight million men and three-quarters of a million women. The financial measures needed to develop and sustain this prodigious manifestation had required in 1918 alone over three thousand million pounds sterling, of which one thousand millions were raised by the taxation of forty-five million persons in the British Isles and sixteen hundred millions were borrowed at home from the same persons and four hundred millions borrowed abroad mainly from the United States on the credit of the British Government.

But it is with the final effort of the British Army that this chapter is chiefly concerned. From the opening of the campaign of 1918 on March 21 down to the Armistice on November 11 the British armies in France suffered 830,000 casualties, and inflicted on the Germans in killed, wounded and prisoners a comparable loss of 805,000 men. During the same period the French (and Belgians) sustained 964,000 casualties and inflicted 666,000 upon the enemy. Up to July when the tide began definitely to turn, the British armies had already lost during the year chiefly in bearing the brunt of the German attack over 400,000 men. In spite of this loss they were almost continuously engaged in full battle and took from that time onwards at least as many prisoners and guns from the Germans as all the other Allied forces on the Western Front put together.[1] At the same time Great Britain provided the second largest Allied army in the Balkans and terminated the enemy's resistance in German East Africa. Finally, Great Britain and India bore unaided the whole burden of the war against the Turkish Empire, and with an army of over 400,000 men in Mesopotamia and nearly 300,000 men in Palestine, shattered or destroyed three-quarters of the whole remaining Turkish forces and conquered all the regions and provinces in which the operations took place. Such was the culminating war effort of a State which, before the campaign of 1918 began, had already been at war for three and a half years, suffered more than a million and three-quarters casualties, sustained a loss of over six and a half million tons of shipping and expended six thousand millions sterling. These facts and figures will excite the wonder of future generations.

The first stage of the Great Advance may be said to have closed on September 3. But once the general success of the Battle of Bapaume was assured, new and even wider combinations were open to Marshal Foch. Of the original projects of biting off the three German salients—Amiens, Château-Thierry, St. Mihiel, and freeing the important lateral railways behind them, the two first and greatest were already accomplished, and the American enterprise against the third—St. Mihiel—was mounted and imminent. These great local operations which at one time had seemed sufficient for the year, could now be followed by a delib-

---

[1] The above figures do not include the supplementary German casualties set forth in the tables of the chapter entitled "The Blood Test."

erately-conceived combined attempt, involving all the Allied forces, to break up the German front and drive their armies out of France before the winter.

It is now necessary to take a parting glance at the structure of railways on which the German armies in France had depended during the four years of the war. The tap root of their supplies was the main trunk railway (**A**) from the munition factories of Westphalia through Cologne, Liège, Namur and Maubeuge. Through Maubeuge ran in a crescent shaped **T** (lying thus ⌐____A) the great lateral line (**B**) on which the invading front was built, ⌐B viz., the railway from Germany through Metz, Mezières, Hirson, Maubeuge, Mons, Ghent and Bruges. From this railway there branched southward and westward all the lines which with various subsidiary laterals fed the German armies spread fanwise towards Calais, Amiens and Paris. Behind the southern portion lay the rugged forest region of the Ardennes, comparatively roadless and railless, and an impassable barrier to the organized retreat of huge modern armies. The German Army in France was therefore strategically to a large extent "formed to a flank" along their main lateral communications. If these were broken or they were driven beyond them, the bulk would never get away.

Further, nearly three-quarters of the whole German strength radiated from the lateral arc Mezières-Hirson-Aulnoye-Mons. The railway junctions of Mezières and Aulnoye (near the lost French fortress and railway centre of Maubeuge) were therefore vital organs of the enemy. If these junctions could be captured or paralysed, the immense mass of invaders depending on them, or on the lateral line between them, would be cut off. Hitherto the Germans had not been in any strategic anxiety. The front with its successive systems of defence stood, except before Verdun, 50 miles ahead of the lateral line. But now the front was bending and recoiling fast, and the margin of safety space narrowed day by day.

Lastly it must be remembered that all the traffic from the Flanders front, from the Arras front, from the Somme and the Aisne fronts, as well as the bulk of that from the Argonne, passed in the end through Liège. This bottle neck was too small to cope with the deluge of retreating stores and munitions, and at the same time to supply the imperative to-and-fro needs of the armies when all were continually in heavy battle.

These considerations dictated the movements of the Allies. It was obvious that apart from Verdun, barred by its inferior communications, the nearest point at which the most deadly blow could be delivered upon the enemy was the junction of Aulnoye near Maubeuge. A British advance against the enemy's front, Cambrai-St. Quentin, in the direction of Maubeuge would if successful compromise and compel the early retreat of all the hostile armies deployed with

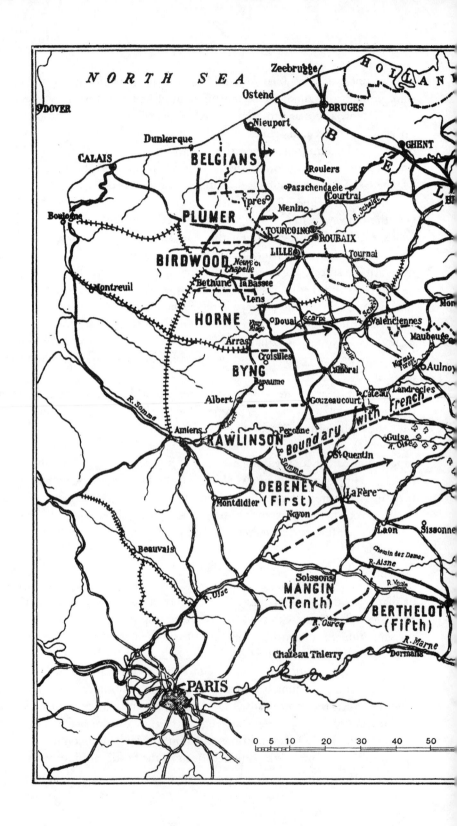

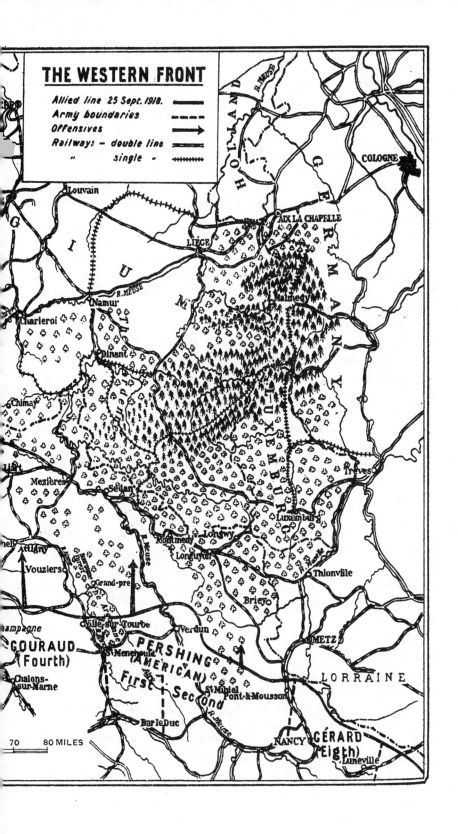

THE WESTERN FRONT

Allied line 25 Sept. 1918. ━━━━
Army boundaries ━ ━ ━ ━
Offensives ━━━▶
Railways - double line ━━━
  "   single   " ╼┼┼┼┼┼┼╾

HOLLAND

R. MEUSE

COLOGNE

G   E   R   M   A   N   Y

Louvain

BELGIUM

AIX LA CHAPELLE

LIÈGE

Namur

R. MEUSE

Charleroi

Dinant

Malmedy

LUXEMBURG

Chimay

Mezières

Sedan

Treves

Luxemburg

Liart

Longwy

Attigny

Montmedy

Longuyon

Vouziers

R. Meuse

R. Meuse

Thionville

Grand-pré

Brieyo

Ville-sur-Tourbe

Verdun

METZ

ampagne

GOURAUD
(Fourth)

PERSHING
(AMERICAN)

St. Menehould

LORRAINE

Châlons-
sur-Marne

First

Second

St. Mihiel
Pont-à-Mousson

Bar-le-Duc

R. Meuse

70   80 MILES

NANCY   GÉRARD
(Eigth)

Luneville

the Ardennes at their back between Maubeuge and Verdun. This, from the moment when these possibilities came into the practical sphere, was the goal of Sir Douglas Haig. Marshal Foch independently from his higher standpoint held of course the same view; and it fell to him to concert the whole immense operation. He had however at General Pershing's desire lent himself reluctantly to an American advance upon Metz and into the Saar Valley, if the St. Mihiel attack succeeded. This was an irrelevant and divergent feature. If the British Army was to undertake the tremendous task of smashing through the Hindenburg Line and advancing upon Maubeuge, it was imperative that all other operations should aim at the vital point and contribute to the supreme result. Haig therefore at the end of August urged Foch to alter the American offensive from a divergent to a convergent direction, i.e., from east to north-west, and towards Mezières instead of towards Metz. Foch entirely agreed, and after further conferences with Pershing obtained his assent to the change of plan.

On September 3, Marshal Foch's "Directive" prescribed that while (1) the British armies supported by the left of the French armies continue to attack in the general direction Cambrai-St. Quentin, and (2) the centre of the French armies continues its action to drive the enemy beyond the Aisne and the Ailette, (3) the American Army after delivering at the latest by September 10 their attack on the St. Mihiel salient should prepare "as strong and violent an offensive as possible in the general direction of Mezières, covered on the East by the Meuse and supported on the left by the attack of the Fourth French Army (Gouraud)."

In addition to this, by a Note of September 8, Foch prescribed a third offensive in Belgium in the general direction of Ghent. A new army group was to be formed comprising the British Second Army (now again under Plumer), the Belgian Army and a French contingent, in all sixteen infantry and seven cavalry divisions. These forces were placed under the command of the King of the Belgians with the French General Dégouttes as Chief of the Staff. The attack was in principle a left-handed scoop pivoting on the British troops holding the Lys near Armentières.

Such was the gigantic triple offensive of the Allies: towards Mezières by the French and Americans; towards Maubeuge by the British; and towards Ghent by the Belgians and British with a French contingent. The time was fixed for the end of September. The interval was filled by the forward movement of the Allied armies towards the new main fronts of assault. This involved important preliminary battles. Of these the first and most famous was the attack by the First American Army on the St. Mihiel salient. On the morning of September 11, nine United States divisions (each equal in infantry numbers to two and a half French or British divisions) and three French divisions

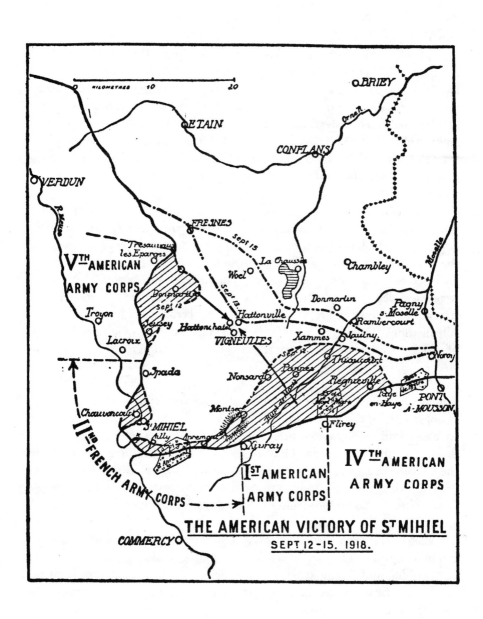

THE AMERICAN VICTORY OF S.ͭ MIHIEL
SEPT 12-15. 1918.

broke into the St. Mihiel salient. The German and Austrian defenders who had already been ordered to evacuate were caught in the early stages of that operation. The Americans attacking with the utmost ardour penetrated at the first shock of their Eastern attack nearly 6 miles upon a front of 11. On the 12th they joined hands across the salient with their western attack, and by the 14th when the operation was completed had captured 16,000 prisoners and 450 guns. On September 18 the Fourth and Third British armies attacked on a 17-mile front centring on Epéhy, with the object of bringing the main forces into striking distance of the Hindenburg Line. This preparatory battle was most severe. The British advanced about 3 miles and captured 12,000 prisoners and 100 guns, but with heavy loss. Meanwhile the French armies slanting back from the British right had on the night of the 8th surprised the crossing of the Crozat Canal, and by continual fighting emphasized and exploited the German retreat.

The map on pages 832–33, which was given to me by Sir Douglas Haig, shows the position of all the troops on the Western Front on the eve of its largest battle. Colonel Boraston discharges a necessary task when he sets forth the respective forces on the three fronts of the assault. The facts which follow are based on his account, independently checked. For the southern battle there were assembled 31 French and 13 United States divisions, the latter equal in rifle strength to at least 30 French divisions; a total comparable mass of above 60 Ally divisions. To this the enemy opposed 1 Austrian and 19 German divisions, of which 6 were first-class troops. For the northern battle the Allies had gathered 8 Belgian, 5 British and 3 French Infantry divisions, with 1 Belgian, 3 British and 3 French cavalry divisions. Against this army stood 12 German divisions, 4 of good quality. But in the central battle the Germans were actually superior in numbers to the British. No less than 57 German divisions, 18 of which were assault divisions, were concentrated in the battle area behind the far-famed defences of the Hindenburg Line. To storm these fortifications and to defeat the German masses upon its front, Sir Douglas Haig could marshal no more than 40 British divisions and the IInd American Corps. Moreover, the interposition of the Canal du Nord and the Scheldt Canal deprived the British attack almost entirely of the aid of tanks.

Each of these episodes would make a thrilling monograph, but these pages can only record in a few sentences the outstanding results.

Pershing and Gouraud fell on shoulder to shoulder at daybreak on the 26th, the Americans engaging on a 20-, the French on a 24-mile front. The Americans, undaunted by severe losses, stormed the German first system of defences and almost the whole front of attack and penetrated at some points nearly 6¾ miles. Gouraud's army also advanced from 1¼ to 2¼ miles, but thereafter neither attack made much progress. The American supply arrangements broke down, the roads became hopelessly blocked for tens of miles with stationary vehicles. The nourishment of the American fighting line with food, ammunition and reinforcements was only achieved partially and with extreme difficulty. The German counter-attacks retrieved some of the lost ground, and in places cut off or destroyed the American units which had advanced the farthest. The ground was difficult in the extreme, and a weltering deadlock supervened for several weeks. During this time however the French and Americans captured 39,000 prisoners and 300 guns, and held the outnumbered German forces stoutly in their grip.

The northern battle was victorious. The Germans over-matched fell back before the assault, the British and Belgian divisions fought their way forward through the awful desolation of the Ypres-Paschendaele battlefield, and in three days stood on the Menin-Roulers road 10 miles from their starting point, having captured with small losses nearly 11,000 prisoners and 300 guns. The French contingent was not at this stage engaged.

The centre battle had begun on the 27th, on which day the extraordinary obstacle of the Canal du Nord, with its cutting often 60 feet deep, was stormed by the right of the First Army (Horne) and the left of the Third (Byng). Upon a 13-mile front, a four-mile advance was achieved with a capture of 10,000 prisoners and 200 guns. This enabled the rest of the Third Army and the Fourth Army (Rawlinson) to come into action to the southward. Rawlinson's artillery in the absence of tanks in large numbers had on this occasion subjected the Hindenburg positions to 48 hours' intense bombardment in the old style. Nevertheless when his army attacked on the 29th it encountered a most severe resistance. The American Corps led the centre of the assault. They were supported and were to be leap-frogged by the Australians. A noble rivalry—carried by the Americans to an utter disregard of losses—prevailed between these proud soldiers, sprung from the same stock, speaking the same language, yet drawn from far distant quarters of the globe and by different paths of history. Several strong posts in advance of the German front had not as was intended been reduced on the previous day, and moreover both American divisions started 1,000 yards behind their barrage. Over a part of the attack their dead lay "in orderly lines" mowed down by machine-gun fire. Elsewhere their extraordinary ardour carried them deep into the German defences. The great tunnel through which the canal passed and the deep dugouts of the long prepared fortifications disgorged strong German forces who took the ambitious assailants in rear, and cut off and slew large numbers. But all fought desperately without thought of retirement. The war-experienced Australians advanced in succour, and after further close and bloody fighting all the ground was gripped and held.

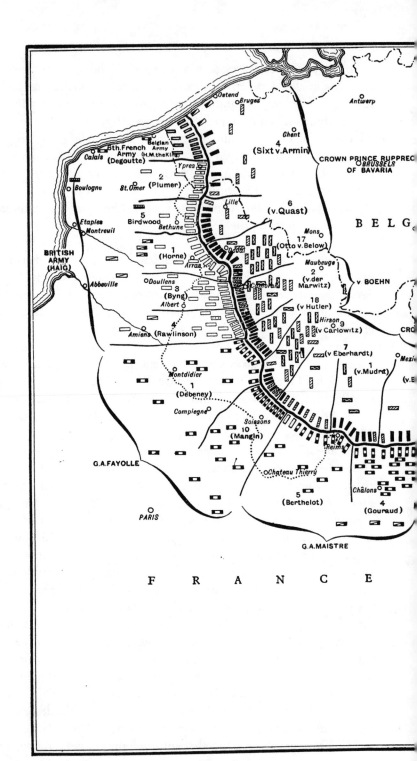

Antwerp

Ostend
Bruges

Ghent

4
(Sixt v.Armin)

CROWN PRINCE RUPPREC
BRUSSELS
OF BAVARIA

Belgian
Army
(H.M.the King)
5th.French
Army
(Degoutte)
Calais

Ypres

2
(Plumer)
St.Omer

Lille

6
(v.Quast)

B E L G

5
Birdwood
Bethune

Mons
17
(Otto v.Below)

Boulogne

Etaples
Montreuil

1
(Horne)

Arras

Maubeuge
2
(v.der
Marwitz)

v.BOEHN

BRITISH
ARMY
(HAIG)

Abbeville

Doullens
3
(Byng)
Albert

Cambrai

18
(v Hutler)

Hirson
9
(v Carlowitz)

CR

Amiens (Rawlinson)

(v Eberhardt)

7
(v Mudra)

Mezi

(v.E

Montdidier

1
(Débeney)

Compiegne

Soissons
10
(Mangin)

Reims

G.A.FAYOLLE

Chateau Thierry

Chalons

5
(Berthelot)

4
(Gouraud)

PARIS

G.A.MAISTRE

F R A N C E

HOLLAND

Cologne

Liege

M

GERMANY

SITUATION ON SEPT. 25ᵀᴴ 1918.

ALLIED DIVISIONS   GERMAN DIVISIONS

BRIT. Inf. ☐ Cav. ▱   ASSAULT   ▱
FR.   Inf. ▰ Cav. ▱   ORDINARY   ▬
AM.   ▦   LANDWEHR   ◣
BEL.   ▬   CAVALRY   ◿
ITL.   ▬   AUST. HUNG. ▤
PORT.   ▥

German Divisions in Reserve
FRESH   ∿
TIRED   ⧖

FRONT LINE 17ᵀᴴ JULY ·············

CE

LUXEMBOURG

v.GALLWITZ

5
(v.Francois ?)

C Det.
(Fuchs)

19
(v Bothmer)

Metz

2

St. Mihiel

Verdun

1

Nancy

8
(Gèrard)

"A" Det.
(?)

Strassbourg

DUKE ALBRECHT
OF
WURTTEMBURG

AMERICAN ARMY
(PERSHING)

Epinal

7
(Boissoudy)

G.A. de CASTELNAU

'B' Det.
v Gundell

SWITZERLAND

This tragic glorious episode was only a part of the Fourth Army's battle, and all three British armies were fully and continuously engaged. By the night of the 30th the Hindenburg Line on a front of 25 miles was blasted and pierced to an average depth of seven miles, and 36,500 prisoners and 380 guns were reported to Sir Douglas Haig. The total British casualties in France from the beginning of September to October 9 were over 200,000, of which 6,500 officers and 135,700 men fell in the series of battles for the Hindenburg Line, otherwise called Cambrai-St. Quentin. To these must be added 6,000 Americans, or a fifth of the infantry of the United States IInd Army Corps. The battle and advance were continued from the 8th to the 10th October, 20 kilometres being gained by the latter date on the whole Cambrai-St. Quentin front and 12,000 more prisoners and 230 guns being captured. Under the impulsion of this tremendous central thrust and of the northern and southern battles, the Germans withdrew their forces in all the intervening sectors of the front. They were followed in the closest contact by all the opposing Allied troops.

Yet it was only indirectly from the tremendous collisions in the West that the final blow to German resisting power came. The theatre where the war had languished in a costly and futile fashion since the summer of 1915, the theatre in which exertions were universally condemned by all the highest military authorities of the Allies, was destined to produce the culminating decision. The strength of a chain, however ponderous, is that of its weakest link. The Bulgarian link was about to snap, and with it the remaining cohesion of the whole hostile coalition. This event was not however induced by local circumstances. It resulted from the consternation which followed the defeat of the German armies in France. On September 15, agreeably with the general forward movement of the Allies on all the fronts, the so-called Salonika Army developed an offensive against Bulgaria, having for its central objective the important town and railway junction of Uskub. It was indeed a heterogeneous army that advanced under the orders of Franchet d'Esperey, the ultimate successor of Sarrail. Eight French, seven British, six Greek (Venizelist), six Serbian, and four Italian Divisions—all under strength, wasted with fever, and modestly equipped with artillery, set themselves in motion against the mountainous frontiers of Bulgaria. Seventeen Bulgarian and two Turkish divisions, gripped and guided by a few German battalions and batteries and the prestige of Mackensen, constituted a force ample for a successful defence of such difficult country. But the Bulgarians would fight no more. Bulgaria quitted the field as sullenly, as callously, and as decidedly as she had entered it. The accession of the tepid Malinoff Ministry to power in the last week of June had caused anxiety in Berlin, and

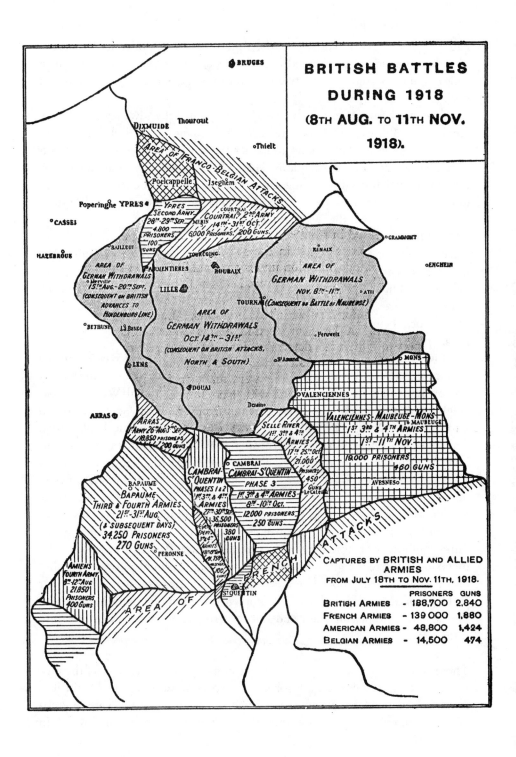

BRITISH BATTLES
DURING 1918
(8TH AUG. TO 11TH NOV.
1918).

ᴼ BRUGES

Thourout

ᴼ Thielt

DIXMUIDE

AREA OF FRANCO-BELGIAN ATTACKS

Poelcappelle   Iseghem

Poperinghe YPRES ᴼ

ᴼ CASSEL

HAZEBROUK ᴼ

YPRES
SECOND ARMY
28ᵀᴴ-29ᵀᴴ SEP.
4,800
PRISONERS
100
GUNS

COURTRAI
MENIN

COURTRAI, 2ᴺᴰ ARMY
14ᵀᴴ-31ˢᵀ OCT.
6,000 PRISONERS, 200 GUNS.

ᴼ GRAMMONT

ᴼ BAILLEUL

AREA OF
GERMAN WITHDRAWALS
15ᵀᴴ AUG.-20ᵀᴴ SEPT.
ᴼ Merville
(CONSEQUENT ON BRITISH
ADVANCES TO
HINDENBURG LINE)

ARMENTIÈRES

TOURCOING

ROUBAIX

RENAIX
ᴼ

AREA OF
GERMAN WITHDRAWALS
NOV. 8ᵀᴴ-11ᵀᴴ
(CONSEQUENT ON BATTLE OF MAUBEUSE)

ᴼ ENGHEIN

LILLE ᴼ

ᴼ ATH

ᴼ BETHUNE

La Basse

AREA OF
GERMAN WITHDRAWALS
OCT. 14ᵀᴴ-31ˢᵀ
(CONSEQUENT ON BRITISH ATTACKS,
NORTH & SOUTH)

TOURNAI ᴼ

ᴼ Peruwelz

ᴼ LENS

ᴼ DOUAI

St Amand ᴼ

ᴼ MONS

ᴼ VALENCIENNES

ARRAS ᴼ

Denaine

ARRAS
1ˢᵀ ARMY 26 AUG.-3 SEP.
18,850 PRISONERS
200 GUNS

SELLE RIVER
1ˢᵀ 3ᴿᴰ & 4ᵀᴴ
ARMIES
17ᵀᴴ 25ᵀᴴ OCT.
21,000
GUNS
450

VALENCIENNES-MAUBEUGE-MONS
TO MAUBEUGE
1ˢᵀ 3ᴿᴰ & 4ᵀᴴ ARMIES
1ˢᵀ-11ᵀᴴ NOV.
19,000 PRISONERS
460 GUNS

AVESNES ᴼ

BAPAUME
ᴼ

CAMBRAI ᴼ

CAMBRAI-St QUENTIN
PHASES 1 & 2
1ˢᵀ 3ᴿᴰ & 4ᵀᴴ
ARMIES
27ᵀᴴ-30ᵀᴴ SEP.
36,500
PRISONERS
380
GUNS

CAMBRAI-St QUENTIN
PHASE 3
1ˢᵀ, 3ᴿᴰ & 4ᵀᴴ ARMIES
8ᵀᴴ-10ᵀᴴ OCT.
12,000 PRISONERS
250 GUNS

PRISONERS
Le Cateau ᴼ

BAPAUME
THIRD & FOURTH ARMIES
21ˢᵀ-31ˢᵀ AUG.
(& SUBSEQUENT DAYS)
34,250 PRISONERS
270 GUNS
ᴼ PERONNE

3ᴿᴰ & 4ᵀᴴ
ARMIES
18ᵀᴴ-26ᵀᴴ

100
GUNS

FRENCH ATTACKS

AMIENS
FOURTH ARMY
8ᵀᴴ-12ᵀᴴ AUG.
21,850
PRISONERS
400 GUNS

St QUENTIN

AREA OF

CAPTURES BY BRITISH AND ALLIED
ARMIES
FROM JULY 18TH TO NOV. 11TH, 1918.

	PRISONERS	GUNS
BRITISH ARMIES -	188,700	2,840
FRENCH ARMIES -	139,000	1,880
AMERICAN ARMIES -	48,800	1,424
BELGIAN ARMIES -	14,500	474

had afforded to the diplomacy of the Allies a fertile opportunity. In particular the influence of the United States, who had never declared war against Bulgaria and whose representative was still in Sofia, was exerted with potent skill.

After weak resistance, which nevertheless revealed the advantages of the defenders, the Bulgarian soldiers retreated, ceased to fight, and declared their intention of going to their homes to gather the harvest. These sturdy peasants were deaf to German expostulations. They were quite friendly to the small German forces which steadily advanced to sustain the front. The retreating battalions even spared the time to help the German cannon out of the ruts. But turn, or stand, or fight—all that was over for ever!

On the night of September 26, a Bulgarian Staff Officer carried a flag of truce to General Milne's Headquarters, and in the name of his Commander-in-Chief sought a 48-hours' suspension of hostilities, to be followed by a peace delegation. On the 28th, Bulgaria agreed unconditionally to demobilize her army, to restore all conquered territory, to surrender all means of transport, to cease to be a belligerent, and to place her railways and her territory at the disposal of the Allies for their further operations.

I was in Paris with Loucheur when the news arrived, and it was recognized at once that the end had come. On September 29 a Conference convened at Spa on Ludendorff's initiative decided to approach President Wilson, whose "high ideals" fostered hope, with proposals on behalf of Germany for an armistice. On October 1 Hindenburg, under the pressure of the Triple battle, demanded that the request for an armistice should be made by the next morning. On October 4 King Ferdinand abdicated the Bulgarian crown and fled to Vienna. This extraordinary figure, who combined the extremes of craft, fierceness, resolution, and miscalculation, now vanished from view. It had been twice in his power to achieve a large part of those overweening ambitions of his country which he so ardently championed. Alike after the first Balkan war (against Turkey) in 1912, or before Bulgaria joined the Central Powers in 1915, he could, by taking a different and easier course, have raised his country to the headship of a Balkan confederation: but the erroneous valuations on which the power and logic of his mind based itself in complete exclusion of moral factors, forced him at immense personal risk and toil to thrust his country twice over into utter disaster.

Those who choose the moment for beginning wars do not always fix the moment for ending them. To ask for an armistice is one thing, to obtain it is another. The new Chancellor—Prince Max of Baden—sent his Note to President Wilson on the 5th. He based himself on the "Fourteen Points," which in the name of Germany he accepted. The President replied on the 8th, asking questions and demanding a German withdrawal from invaded territory as a guarantee of good faith. On the 12th Germany and Austria declared themselves willing to evacuate all invaded territory as a preliminary to an armistice. On the 14th the President indicated that there could be no negotiation with the Emperor. As for an armistice, the conditions must be left to the Commanders in the field, but absolute safeguards must be provided for the maintenance of "the present military supremacy of the armies of the United States and of the Allies in the field." During this correspondence, which Mr. Wilson was peculiarly fitted to conduct, and which promised to be lengthy, the Allied armies rolled forward all along the line in France maintaining a ceaseless battle and at an ever more powerful crescendo of attack. The vital German lateral railway still worked in front of the Ardennes. Pershing and Gouraud were steadily approaching it in the south, and Haig's heavy artillery already held Aulnoye Junction under continual fire. On the northern flank King Albert's army advanced upon Courtrai. The German troops in the wide intervals between these main thrusts fell back continually in conformity with battle results. Ludendorff's reserves were exhausted. A large proportion of his Divisions could not be relied upon to fight with determination; all were reduced to a third or a fifth of their fighting strength. The Siegfried Line collapsed at many points. Feverish exertions were made to fortify the Antwerp-Meuse positions, and Ludendorff with true instinct but tardy decision began to survey a line along the German frontier. Desperate agitated councils were held between the military leaders and the new political figures who had appeared. On the 20th the German Government renounced the submarine campaign. Meanwhile in Italy the whole of the Italian Army with their Allies—Lord Cavan's British Army in the van—hurled themselves across the Piave upon the forces of the liquefying Austro-Hungarian Empire, and in the last week of October completely shattered their military value. The Vatican stretched out an appealing hand. On November 4 an armistice which deprived the Empire of the Hapsburgs of every means of resistance, and placed her territories at the disposal of the Allies for further operations, brought hostilities in this theatre to an end.

The British armies had now passed the Selle River, taking in the process 21,000 prisoners and 450 guns, and were marching swiftly forward on Valenciennes, Mons and Maubeuge, driving the enemy before them. The ardour of the troops knew no bounds. The conviction that the terrible enemy they had fought so long was breaking up under their hammer blows, and the rapture and joy of the liberated populations, made them more ready to sacrifice their lives in these last days than even in the darkest periods of the war. Every soldier felt himself at once a Conqueror and a Deliverer. The same impulses inflamed the Americans. As for the French, who shall describe the emotions with which haggard and torn, but regardless of a loss which in these last months (July to November) exceeded half a million men, they day by day battered down their ancient foe, and redeemed the sacred soil of France?

The armistice for which Hindenburg and Ludendorff had argued wore by now the aspect of an unconditional surrender. Ludendorff thereupon wished to fight on, declaring with truth that nothing could worsen the terms which Germany would receive. On the 27th the German Government, being resolved on total submission, moved the Emperor to dismiss him from his post. Hindenburg remained "greatly falling with a falling State." To him and to the German machine gunners belong the honours of the final agony.

When the great organizations of this world are strained beyond breaking point, their structure often collapses at all points simultaneously. There is nothing on which policy, however wise, can build; no foothold can be found for virtue or valour, no authority or impetus for a rescuing genius. The mighty framework of German Imperial Power, which a few days before had overshadowed the nations, shivered suddenly into a thousand individually disintegrating fragments. All her Allies whom she had so long sustained, fell down broken and ruined, begging separately for peace. The faithful armies were beaten at the front and demoralized from the rear. The proud, efficient Navy mutinied. Revolution exploded in the most disciplined and docile of States. The Supreme War Lord fled.

Such a spectacle appals mankind; and a knell rang in the ear of the victors, even in their hour of triumph.

Parliament was disposed to be suspicious of the Armistice terms until they heard them. But when the document was read overwhelming thankfulness filled all hearts. No one could think of any further stipulation. Immediate evacuation of invaded countries; repatriation of all inhabitants; surrender in good condition of 5,000 guns, 30,000 machine guns, 3,000 minenwerfers, 2,000 aeroplanes; evacuation of the left bank of the Rhine; surrender of three bridgeheads on the Rhine; surrender of 5,000 locomotives, 150,000 waggons, 5,000 motor lorries in good working order (and with spare parts); disclosure of all mines, of delay-action fuses, and assistance in their discovery and destruction; immediate repatriation without reciprocity of all prisoners of war; abandonment of the Treaties of Bucharest and Brest-Litovsk; surrender of 6 battle-cruisers, the best 10 battleships, 8 light cruisers, 50 of the best destroyers; surrender of all submarines; the right of the Allies on failure of execution of any condition to denounce the Armistice within 48 hours. Such were the covenanted clauses. And thus did Germany hand herself over powerless and defenceless to the discretion of her long tortured and now victorious foes!

It was a few minutes before the eleventh hour of the eleventh day of the eleventh month. I stood at the window of my room looking up Northumberland Avenue towards Trafalgar Square, waiting for Big Ben to tell that the war was over. My mind strayed back across the scarring years to the scene and emotions of the night at the Admiralty when I listened for these same chimes in order to give the signal of war against Germany to our Fleets and squadrons across the world. And now all was over! The unarmed and untrained island nation, who with no defence but its Navy had faced unquestioningly the strongest manifestation of military power in human record, had completed its task. Our country had emerged from the ordeal alive and safe, its vast possessions intact, its war effort still waxing, its institutions unshaken, its people and Empire united as never before. Victory had come after all the hazards and heartbreaks in an absolute and unlimited form. All the Kings and Emperors with whom we had warred were in flight or exile. All their Armies and Fleets were destroyed or subdued. In this Britain had borne a notable part, and done her best from first to last.

The minutes passed. I was conscious of reaction rather than elation. The material purposes on which one's work had been centred, every process of thought on which one had lived, crumbled into nothing. The whole vast business of supply, the growing outputs, the careful hoards, the secret future plans—but yesterday the whole duty of life—all at a stroke vanished like a nightmare dream, leaving a void behind. My mind mechanically persisted in exploring the problems of demobilization. What was to happen to our three million Munition workers? What would they make now? How would the roaring factories be converted? How in fact are swords beaten into plough-shares? How long would it take to bring the Armies home? What would they do when they got home? We had of course a demobilization plan for the Ministry of Munitions. It had been carefully worked out, but it had played no part in our thoughts. Now it must be put into operation. The levers must be pulled—*Full Steam Astern.* The Munitions Council must meet without delay.

And then suddenly the first stroke of the chime. I looked again at the broad street beneath me. It was deserted. From the portals of one of the large hotels absorbed by Government Departments darted the slight figure of a girl clerk, distractedly gesticulating while another stroke resounded. Then from all sides men and women came scurrying into the street. Streams of people poured out of all the buildings. The bells of London began to clash. Northumberland Avenue was now crowded with people in hundreds, nay, thousands, rushing hither and thither in a frantic manner, shouting and screaming with joy. I could see that Trafalgar Square was already swarming. Around me in our very head-quarters, in the Hotel Metropole, disorder had broken out. Doors banged. Feet clattered down corridors. Everyone rose from the desk and cast aside pen and paper. All bounds were broken. The tumult grew. It grew like a gale, but from all sides simultaneously. The street was now a seething mass of humanity. Flags appeared as if by magic. Streams of men and women flowed from the Embank-ment. They mingled with torrents pouring down the Strand on their way to ac-claim the King. Almost before the last stroke of the clock had died away, the strict, war-straitened, regulated streets of London had become a triumphant pandemonium. At any rate it was clear that no more work would be done that day. Yes, the chains which had held the world were broken. Links of impera-tive need, links of discipline, links of brute-force, links of self-sacrifice, links of terror, links of honour which had held our nation, nay, the greater part of mankind, to grinding toil, to a compulsive cause—every one had snapped upon a few strokes of the clock. Safety, freedom, peace, home, the dear one back at the fireside—all after fifty-two months of gaunt distortion. After fifty-two months of making burdens grievous to be borne and binding them on men's backs, at last, all at once, suddenly and everywhere the burdens were cast down. At least so for the moment it seemed.

My wife arrived, and we decided to go and offer our congratulations to the Prime Minister, on whom the central impact of the home struggle had fallen, in his hour of recompense. But no sooner had we entered our car than twenty people mounted upon it, and in the midst of a wildly cheer-ing multitude we were impelled slowly forward through Whitehall. We had driven together the opposite way along the same road on the afternoon of the ultimatum. There had been the same crowd and almost the same enthusi-asm. It was with feelings which do not lend themselves to words that I heard the cheers of the brave people who had borne so much and given all, who had never wavered, who had never lost faith in their country or its destiny, and who could be indulgent to the faults of their servants when the hour of deliverance had come.

It will certainly not fall to this generation to pronounce the final verdict upon the Great War. The German people are worthy of better explanations than the shallow tale that they were undermined by enemy propaganda. If the propaganda was effective, it was because it awoke an echo in German hearts, and stirred misgivings which from the beginning had dwelt there. Thus when four years of blockade and battle against superior numbers and resources had sapped the vitality of the German people, the rebellious whispers of conscience became the proclaimed opinion of millions.

Yet in the sphere of force, human records contain no manifestation like the eruption of the German volcano. For four years Germany fought and defied the five continents of the world by land and sea and air. The German armies upheld her tottering confederates, intervened in every theatre with success, stood everywhere on conquered territory, and inflicted on their enemies more than twice the bloodshed they suffered themselves. To break their strength and science and curb their fury, it was necessary to bring all the greatest nations of mankind into the field against them. Overwhelming populations, unlimited resources, measureless sacrifice, the Sea Blockade, could not prevail for fifty months. Small states were trampled down in the struggle; a mighty Empire was battered into unrecognizable fragments; and nearly twenty million men perished or shed their blood before the sword was wrested from that terrible hand. Surely, Germans, for history it is enough!

The curtain falls upon the long front in France and Flanders. The soothing hands of Time and Nature, the swift repair of peaceful industry, have already almost effaced the crater-fields and the battle lines which in a broad belt from the Vosges to the sea lately blackened the smiling fields of France. The ruins are rebuilt, the riven trees are replaced by new plantations. Only the cemeteries, the monuments and stunted steeples, with here and there a mouldering trench or huge mine-crater lake, assail the traveller with the fact that twenty-five millions of soldiers fought here and twelve millions shed their blood or perished in the greatest of all human contentions less than twenty years ago. Merciful oblivion draws its veils; the crippled limp away; the mourners fall back into the sad twilight of memory. New youth is here to claim its rights, and the perennial stream flows forward even in the battle zone, as if the tale were all a dream.

Is this the end? Is it to be merely a chapter in a cruel and senseless story? Will a new generation in their turn be immolated to square the black accounts of Teuton and Gaul? Will our children bleed and gasp again in devastated lands? Or will there spring from the very fires of conflict that reconciliation of the three giant combatants, which would unite their genius and secure to each in safety and freedom a share in rebuilding the glory of Europe?

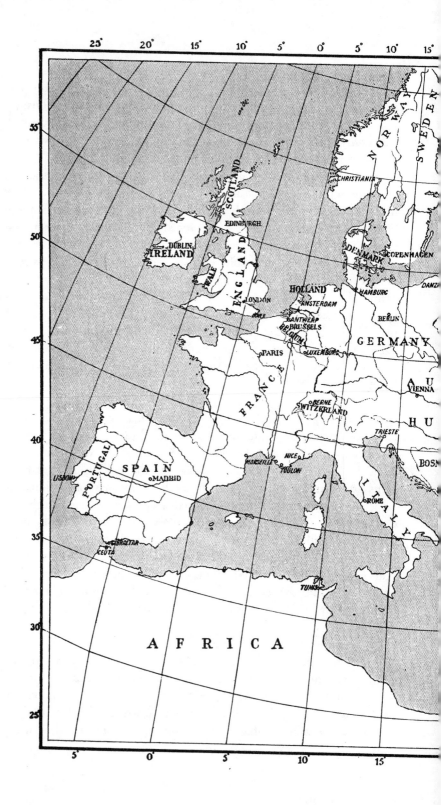

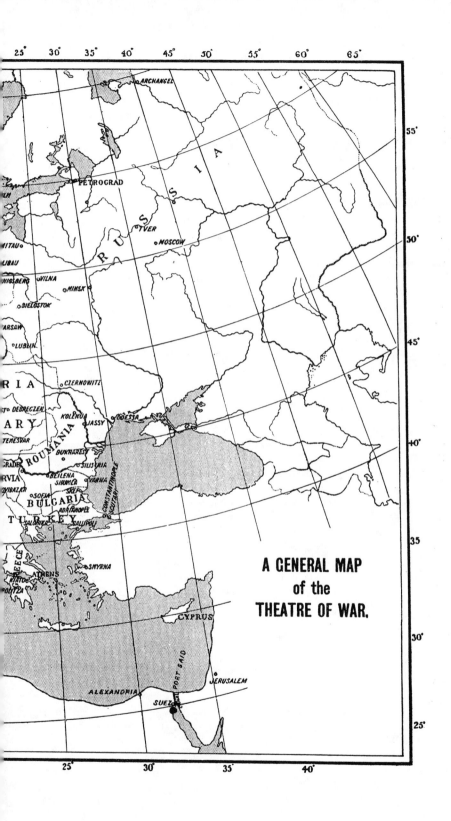

A GENERAL MAP
of the
THEATRE OF WAR.

APPENDIX

TOTAL BRITISH CASUALTIES ON THE WESTERN FRONT MONTH BY MONTH

Taken from 'The Military Effort,' page 253 et seq.

Year	Month	Casualties		Year	Month	Casualties
1914.	August	14,409			November	46,238
	September	15,189			December	13,803
	October	30,192		1917.	January	15,289
	November	24,785			February	26,140
	December	11,079			March	25,788
1915.	January	6,542			April	120,070
	February	9,195			May	76,040
	March	24,483			June	75,123
	April	31,264			July	84,695
	May	65,730			August	81,080
	June	22,563			September	81,249
	July	16,315			October	119,808
	August	14,587			November	73,888
	September	59,615			December	38,620
	October	25,909		1918.	January	13,042
	November	9,263			February	9,809
	December	11,117			March	173,721
1916.	January	10,975			April	143,168
	February	13,014			May	69,049
	March	18,949			June	32,436
	April	22,409			July	32,562
	May	24,661			August	122,272
	June	39,959			September	114,831
	July	196,081			October	121,046
	August	75,249			November	20,925
	September	115,056				
	October	66,852			Total	2,706,154

PERTES DES ARMEES FRANÇAISES (NORD-EST ET ORIENT) REPARTIES PAR PERIODES

Journal Officiel, Documents parlementaires, Session Extraordinaire 1920, Annexe 633, Séance du 29 Mars, 1920, proposition de résolution Marin.

(Ces chiffres ne comprennent pas les officiers.)

Dates.	Designation.	Morts sur le Terrain disparus et prisonniers.	Mort dans le formations sanitaires et hôpitaux de la zone des armées.	Morts dans les hôpitaux de la zone l'intérieur.	Evacués sur l'intérieur
Août-Septembre, 1914	Bataille des frontières (Août 6-Septembre 5) et Bataille de la Marne (Septembre 6-13)	313,000	7,000	9,000	400,000
Octobre-Novembre, 1914	La course à la mer, la Bataille d'Artois, l'Yser	104,000	11,000	10,000	
Décembre, 1914-Janvier, 1915	Stabilisation	62,000	5,000	7,000	180,000
Février-Mars, 1915	1 Offensive de 1915 (1 Bataille de Champagne)	55,000	7,000	7,000	171,000
Avril-Mai-Juin, 1915	2 Bataille d'Artois	121,000	13,000	9,000	306,000
Juillet-Août, 1915	Stabilisation	39,000	6,000	3,000	145,000
Septembre-Novembre, 1915	2 Offensive 1915 (2 Bataille Champagne, 2 Bataille d'Artois)	115,000	10,000	9,000	279,000
Décembre, 1915-Janvier, 1916	Stabilisation	15,000	5,000	2,000	56,000
Février-Juin, 1916	Bataille défensive de Verdun	156,000	15,000	8,000	263,000
Juillet-Octobre, 1916	Bataille de la Somme	114,000	16,000	6,000	205,000
Novembre-Décembre, 1916	1 Bataille offensive de Verdun	30,000	5,000	3,000	55,000
Janvier-Mars, 1917	Repli Allemand	20,000	4,000	6,000	78,000
Avril-Juillet, 1917	Offensive de l'Aisne (Chemin des Dames et Bataille des Monts)	87,000	15,000	8,000	169,000
Août-Décembre, 1917	Opérations à objectifs limités (Flandres, rive droite de la Meuse, la Malmaison)	38,000	9,000	7,000	128,000
Janvier-Février, 1918	Stabilisation	4,000	3,000	3,000	41,000
Mars-Juin, 1918	Campagne défensive de 1918	145,000	13,000	9,000	266,000
Juillet-Novembre, 1918	Campagne offensive de 1918	110,000	35,000	18,000	368,000
		1,528,000[1]	179,000	121,000	3,110,000

Total, 4,938,000[2]

[1] Dont: 477,800 prisonniers vivants en pays ennemi ou en Suisse, au Novembre 11, 1918, et 30,000 prisonniers rapatriés ou evadés depuis Juillet, 1916.
[2] Add Officers killed 36,000.

GERMAN LOSSES ON THE WESTERN FRONT BY MAIN OPERATION PERIODS

(From the Statistics of the Reichsarchiv.)

THE GERMAN LOSSES OPPOSITE THE FRANCO-BELGIAN AND BRITISH FRONTS.

Period.	Opposite the Franco-Belgian Front.[1]			Opposite the British Front.[1]			Opposite the Combined Franco-Belgian-British Fronts.[2]		
	Dead.[3]	Missing and Prisoner.[4]	Wounded.	Dead.[3]	Missing and Prisoner.[4]	Wounded.	Dead.[3]	Missing and Prisoner.[4]	Wounded.
August–November, 1914	—[5]	—[5]	—[5]	—[5]	—[5]	—[5]	116,750[5]	107,640[5]	453,050[5]
December, 1914–January, 1915	—[5]	—[5]	—[5]	—[5]	—[5]	—[5]	54,825[5]	11,100[5]	104,100[5]
February–March, 1915	20,446	9,457	66,079	2,927	4,394	11,169	23,373	13,851	77,248
April–June, 1915	37,020	23,283	130,117	8,233	4,937	29,916	45,253	28,220	160,033
July–August, 1915	13,427	4,805	48,553	2,225	708	8,684	15,652	5,513	57,237
September–November, 1915	24,551	31,164	98,424	6,165	5,363	20,521	30,716	36,527	118,945
December, 1915–January, 1916	5,623	2,312	20,998	2,279	82	8,408	7,902	2,394	29,406
February–June, 1916	46,973	25,316	206,450	10,845	2,531	42,131	57,818	27,847	248,581
July–October, 1916	49,510	72,935	215,566	32,338	36,288	131,332	81,848	109,223	346,898
November–December, 1916	8,455	14,395	33,187	6,135	7,207	22,894	14,590	21,602	56,081
January–March, 1917	5,826	1,241	23,116	6,878	5,226	23,094	12,704	6,467	46,210
April–July, 1917	38,122	48,285	151,903	29,642	40,806	105,323	67,764	89,091	257,226
August–December, 1917	25,728	33,548	108,105	37,630	51,848	147,658	63,358	85,396	255,763
January–February, 1918	2,049	1,441	8,740	2,351	545	8,938	4,400	1,986	17,678
March–June, 1918	41,121	26,424	185,659	73,130	47,049	314,958	114,251	73,473	500,617
July–November, 1918 [6]	45,169	154,313	215,135	33,027	193,554	144,535	78,196	347,867	359,670
							789,400[7]	968,197	3,088,743

[1] Including the German losses opposite the Portuguese troops, for a time interpolated in the British line.

[2] The losses opposite the American front are estimated at about 25,000; there are no data available on which to base an exact figure.[8]

[3] 'Dead' here only means fallen on the field of battle, and does not include those who died in hospital, etc., from wounds or sickness.

[4] Taken from the figures reported every ten days to the Supreme Command by the troops. The totals of missing include both men only temporarily absent from their units, and those first reported dead or wounded later.

[5] For the losses from August, 1914, to January, 1915 (inclusive), only general totals are available, which are partly based on estimates.

[6] The figures for October, 1918, are not quite complete; and those for November, 1918, are entirely lacking.

[7] The total of German War Deaths on the Western Front in Table A, viz., 1,493,000, is obtained from these tables as follows : Killed 789,000 (*Reichsarchiv*) + died in hospital 300,000 (i.e., the same proportion as the French) + missing now believed dead in *Reichsarchiv* return 94,000 + ⅘ths additional dead in *Nachweiseamt*'s final return 170,000 + estimate of Germans killed by Americans, 40,000 = 1,493,000.

[8] This figure is now stated by the German Reichsarchiv to be incorrect. An unofficial German estimate places the total between 100,000 and 140,000. I have adopted the higher total.—W. S. C.

LOSSES OF MEN IN THE GERMAN LAND FORCES

(From Information supplied by the Central Enquiry Office (Zentral Nachweiseamt) for War Casualties and War Graves.)

On the Authority of the Official Casualty List.	Dead (Killed in Action and Died of Wounds or Sickness).			Number of Woundings[1] so far as they were not mortal (not number of wounded men).			Prisoner and Missing, not including those known to have died in captivity (included in col. 2).[3]		
	Officers.	Other Ranks.	Total.	Officers.	Other Ranks.	Total.	Officers.	Other Ranks.	Total.
Up to 31.12.14	5,847	136,655	142,502	11,519	529,199	540,718	908	153,682	154,590
,, 31.12.15	16,921	611,524	628,445	29,030	1,566,376	1,595,406	3,191	316,963	320,154
,, 31.12.16	24,910	938,591	963,501	45,587	2,425,568	2,471,155	6,245	495,012	501,257
,, 31.12.17	33,272	1,238,301	1,271,573	61,093	3,117,743	3,178,836	9,659	656,745	666,404
,, 31.12.18	46,946	1,574,088	1,621,034	88,888	4,014,931	4,103,819	14,698	846,692	861,390
,, 31.12.19	50,555	1,668,053	1,718,608	92,310	4,123,285	4,215,595	18,607	1,061,648	1,080,255
,, 31.12.20	52,024	1,711,955	1,763,979	92,358	4,122,221	4,214,579[2]	18,143	1,047,089	1,065,232
,, 30. 9.21	52,673	1,740,160	1,792,833	92,384	4,122,435	4,214,819	17,985	1,031,436	1,049,421
,, 31.10.22	53,229	1,768,693	1,821,922	92,441	4,123,057	4,215,498	18,103	1,019,809	1,037,912
,, 30. 6.23	53,386	1,781,138	1,834,524[4]	92,458	4,123,315	4,215,773	18,042	1,012,032	1,030,074[4]

[1] The number of individuals wounded and the number of wound cases cannot be given separately.

[2] The number of wound cases is smaller than before because the number of individuals who were reported as died of wounds was greater than the fresh cases of wounds in the period.

[3] The total of those who died in captivity has not been finally settled. Up to the present, 55,066 deaths of German prisoners have been reported by the States with which we were at war. Of these 40,300 are included in the casualty lists, the rest are still left in the total of Prisoner and Missing.

[4] It must be assumed that the greater number of the German nationals still missing (170,000) are dead. The total of dead will therefore be increased to approximately 2,000,000.

INDEX

(Names of warships omitted)